Cutoff Points for the Student's Distribution

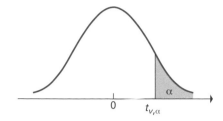

For selected probabilities, α, the table shows the values $t_{v,\alpha}$ such that $P(t_v > t_{v,\alpha}) = \alpha$, where t_v is a Student's t random variable with v degrees of freedom. For example, the probability is .10 that a Student's t random variable with 10 degrees of freedom exceeds 1.372.

v	α				
	0.100	0.050	0.025	0.010	0.005
1	3.078	6.314	12.706	31.821	63.657
2	1.886	2.920	4.303	6.965	9.925
3	1.638	2.353	3.182	4.541	5.841
4	1.533	2.132	2.776	3.747	4.604
5	1.476	2.015	2.571	3.365	4.032
6	1.440	1.943	2.447	3.143	3.707
7	1.415	1.895	2.365	2.998	3.499
8	1.397	1.860	2.306	2.896	3.355
9	1.383	1.833	2.262	2.821	3.250
10	1.372	1.812	2.228	2.764	3.169
11	1.363	1.796	2.201	2.718	3.106
12	1.356	1.782	2.179	2.681	3.055
13	1.350	1.771	2.160	2.650	3.012
14	1.345	1.761	2.145	2.624	2.977
15	1.341	1.753	2.131	2.602	2.947
16	1.337	1.746	2.120	2.583	2.921
17	1.333	1.740	2.110	2.567	2.898
18	1.330	1.734	2.101	2.552	2.878
19	1.328	1.729	2.093	2.539	2.861
20	1.325	1.725	2.086	2.528	2.845
21	1.323	1.721	2.080	2.518	2.831
22	1.321	1.717	2.074	2.508	2.819
23	1.319	1.714	2.069	2.500	2.807
24	1.318	1.711	2.064	2.492	2.797
25	1.316	1.708	2.060	2.485	2.787
26	1.315	1.706	2.056	2.479	2.779
27	1.314	1.703	2.052	2.473	2.771
28	1.313	1.701	2.048	2.467	2.763
29	1.311	1.699	2.045	2.462	2.756
30	1.310	1.697	2.042	2.457	2.750
40	1.303	1.684	2.021	2.423	2.704
60	1.296	1.671	2.000	2.390	2.660
∞	1.282	1.645	1.960	2.326	2.576

Statistics for Business and Economics

Statistics for Business and Economics

SEVENTH EDITION

Paul Newbold
University of Nottingham

William L. Carlson
St. Olaf College

Betty M. Thorne
Stetson University

Prentice Hall
Boston Columbus Indianapolis New York San Francisco Upper Saddle River
Amsterdam Cape Town Dubai London Madrid Milan Munich Paris Montreal Toronto
Delhi Mexico City Sao Paulo Sydney Hong Kong Seoul Singapore Taipei Tokyo

Editorial Director: Sally Yagan
Editor in Chief: Eric Svendsen
Editorial Project Manager: Susan Abraham
Editorial Assistant: Valerie Patruno
Director of Marketing: Patrice Lumumba Jones
Marketing Manager: Anne Fahlgren
Senior Managing Editor: Judy Leale
Project Manager: Ana Jankowski
Senior Operations Supervisor: Arnold Vila
Design Director: Christy Mahon

Senior Art Director: Janet Slowik
Art Director: Mike Fruhbeis
Text and Cover Design: Frubilicious Design Group
Cover Art: VEER Brian Fraunfelter
Lead Media Project Manager: Allison Longley
Full-Service Project Management/Composition: GEX
Publishing Services
Printer/Binder: Edwards Brothers
Cover Printer: Coral Graphics
Text Font: Palatino 10/12

Credits and acknowledgments borrowed from other sources and reproduced, with permission, in this textbook appear on appropriate page within text.

Microsoft® and Windows® are registered trademarks of the Microsoft Corporation in the U.S.A. and other countries. Screen shots and icons reprinted with permission from the Microsoft Corporation. This book is not sponsored or endorsed by or affiliated with the Microsoft Corporation.

Library of Congress Cataloging-in-Publication information is on file.

10 9 8 7 6 5 4 3

Prentice Hall
is an imprint of

www.pearsonhighered.com

ISBN 10: 0-13-608536-9
ISBN 13: 978-0-13-608536-2

I dedicate this book to Sgt Lawrence Martin Carlson who gave his life in service to his country on November 19, 2006 and to his mother Charlotte Carlson, his brother and sister Andrea and Douglas, to his wife and children Karlyn, Savannah, and Ezra, and to his nieces Helana, Anna, Eva Rose, and Emily.

William L. Carlson

I dedicate this book to my husband, Jim, and to our family Jennie, Ann, Renee, Jon, Chris, Jon, Hannah, Leah, Marius, Mihaela, Cezara, Anda, Mara Iulia, and Silvia.

Betty M. Thorne

Bill Carlson is professor emeritus of economics at St. Olaf College where he taught for 31 years serving several times as department chair and in various administrative functions including director of academic computing. He has also held leave assignments with the United States government and the University of Minnesota, in addition to lecturing at many different universities. He was elected an honorary member of Phi Beta Kappa. In addition, he spent 10 years in private industry and contract research prior to beginning his career at St. Olaf. His education includes engineering degrees from the Michigan Technological University (BS) and from the Illinois Institute of Technology (MS) and a PhD in quantitative management from the Rackham Graduate School at the University of Michigan. Numerous research projects related to management, highway safety, and statistical education have produced over 50 publications. He received the Metropolitan Insurance Award of Merit for Safety Research. He has previously published two statistics textbooks. Professor Carlson led a number of study abroad programs, ranging from 1 to 5 months, for study in various countries around the world. His present assignments include executive director of the Cannon Valley Elder Collegium and memberships in both the Methodist and Lutheran disaster relief teams. He enjoys his grandchildren, woodworking, travel, reading, and being on assignment on the North Shore of Lake Superior.

Dr. Betty M. Thorne, author, researcher, and award-winning teacher, is a professor of decision sciences and director of undergraduate studies in the School of Business Administration at Stetson University in DeLand, Florida. Winner of Stetson University's McEniry Award for Excellence in Teaching, the highest honor given to a Stetson University faculty member. Dr. Thorne is also the recipient of the Outstanding Teacher of the Year Award and Professor of the Year Award in the School of Business Administration at Stetson. Dr. Thorne also teaches in Stetson University's summer program in Innsbruck, Austria; Stetson University's College of Law; Stetson University's Executive MBA program; and Stetson University's Executive Passport program. Dr. Thorne was selected in 2004 and 2005 as the best professor in the JD/MBA program at Stetson's College of Law. She received her bachelor of science degree from Geneva College and the master of arts and PhD degrees from Indiana University. Dr. Thorne co-authored *Applied Statistical Methods for Business, Economics and the Social Sciences* (with William Carlson; Prentice-Hall, 1997), and *Statistics for Business and Economics*, fifth edition and sixth edition (with Paul Newbold and William Carlson; Prentice-Hall, 2003 and 2007). Dr. Thorne is a member of the Academy of International Business, Beta Alpha Psi, and Beta Gamma Sigma. She and her husband, Jim, have four children. They travel extensively, attend theological seminars, participate in international organizations dedicated to helping disadvantaged children, and do missionary work in Romania.

BRIEF CONTENTS

CONTENTS

PREFACE

INTENDED AUDIENCE

Statistics for Business & Economics, 7th edition was written to meet the need for an introductory text that provides a strong introduction to business statistics that develops understanding of concepts and emphasizes problem solving using realistic examples from business and economics.

- MBA or undergraduate business programs that teach business statistics
- Graduate and undergraduate economics programs
- Executive MBA programs
- Graduate courses for business statistics

SUBSTANCE

This book was written to provide a strong introductory understanding of applied statistical procedures so that individuals could do solid statistical analysis in many business and economic situations. We have emphasized an understanding of the assumptions that are necessary for professional analysis. With modern computers it is easy to compute, from data, the output needed for many statistical procedures. Thus it is tempting to merely apply simple "rules" using these outputs—an approach used in many textbooks. Our approach is to combine understanding with many examples and student exercises that show how understanding of methods and their assumptions lead to useful understanding of business and economic problems.

NEW TO THIS EDITION

The seventh edition of this book has been revised and updated to provide students with improved problem contexts for learning how statistical methods can improve their analysis and understanding of business and economics. A number of significant changes and additions have been made to this edition. These include the following:

1. Increased number of real-world examples derived from current businesses and current events.
2. Expanded discussion of variance, shape of a distribution, and the Interquartile Range.
3. Improved readability based on real and relevant business concerns.
4. Revised and improved discussion of probability, including further emphasis on Conditional Probability and Bayes Theorem, which are important for management decision making.

5. Expanded Portfolio analysis using new monthly stock price and stock return data for the post 2,000 time period.
6. Portfolio methodology extending beyond two securities, which indicates the complexity and procedures for developing portfolio means and variances.
7. Very strong and in-depth development of linear regression. This includes extensions to non-linear models including dummy variables and exponential models.
8. Extended discussion of multicollinearity with guidelines for adjustment.
9. Estimation of Financial Beta coefficients and their interpretation.
10. Application of dummy variable models to public sector policy analysis.
11. Improved discussion of finite population sampling and confidence intervals.
12. Increased applications in finance, accounting, and marketing.
13. Expanded discussion of categorical data analysis with marketing applications.

SUPPLEMENT PACKAGE

The supplement package that accompanies this text includes the following for students:

Student Solutions Manual—This manual provides detailed solutions to even-numbered exercises and applications from the book.

Instructor resources are available for download at *www.pearsonhighered.com/newbold*. A Pearson Educator access code is required to register online to use the following resources:

Instructor Solutions Manual—This manual includes worked out solutions for end-of-section and end-of-chapter exercises and applications. These are available in Word and PDF formats.

PowerPoint Lecture Slides—A set of chapter-by-chapter PowerPoint slides are available to use as a guide and organizational tool for classroom presentations.

Test Item File—The test item file contains true/false, multiple choice, and short answer questions based on concepts and ideas developed in each chapter of the text.

TestGen software—This computerized package allows instructors to create and customize their own tests and quizzes based on the test item file questions. The test program permits instructors to edit, add, or delete questions from the test bank, analyze test results, and organize a database of tests and student results.

COURSE AND HOMEWORK MANAGEMENT TOOLS

MyStatLab—This robust on-line homework and assessment tool is designed to help students practice statistics problems, improve their understanding of course concepts, and give instructors feedback on their performance. Students can use a "Study Plan" of algorithmically-generated assignments based on textbook content with step-by-step tutorial help. Additionally, instructors can use this on-line platform to assign and manage homework, quizzes, and tests for their course.

ACKNOWLEDGMENTS

We appreciate the following colleagues who provided feedback to us on the book to guide our thoughts on this revision: Jannet Chang, Northwestern University; Aureo de Paula, University of Pennsylvania; David Hudgins, University of Oklahoma; Carlos Lamarche, University of Oklahoma; Robert J. Lemke, Lake Forest College; Hui Li, Eastern Illinois University; Richard Stern, University of California at Los Angeles.

The authors would like to especially acknowledge the help of Liliana Pinkasovych, Executive Editor ISReview, International Statistical Institute, the Netherlands and Karen Chapman-Novakofski, RD, LDN, PhD, Professor, Nutrition, University of Illinois, Editor-in-Chief, Journal of Nutrition Education and Behavior for special assistance in obtaining publication permission for key material in the book.

We recognize the support of Professor Steve Soderlind, Associate Dean for Social and Applied Sciences, St. Olaf College, in the preparation of various copies of intermediate materials during the writing.

From Stetson University, we extend appreciation to Jim Scheiner, Dean of the School of Business Administration, and to Richard Gaughran, Stetson University's Director of Technology Services, Information Technology. In addition, special thanks is given to Clemens Pirker, Consumer Science Manager with Groupe Danone, Paris, France. A special note of appreciation is extended to Micah Petillo, Project Manager, GEX Publishing Services, for his outstanding leadership with the production of this book.

In addition, we express special thanks for continuing support from our families. Bill Carlson especially acknowledges his best friend and wife Charlotte, their adult children Andrea and Doug, and grandchildren, Ezra, Savannah, Helena, Anna, Eva Rose, and Emily. Betty Thorne extends special thanks to her best friend and husband Jim, and to their daughters Jennie (and her husband Chris), Ann, Renee (and her husband Jon), to their son Jon, to their grandchildren Hannah and Leah, and to their Romanian family Marius, Mihaela, Cezara, Anda, Mara Iulia, and Silvia (Ps 30.12). In addition, Betty acknowledges (in memory) the support of her parents, Westley and Jennie Moore.

The authors acknowledge the strong foundation and tradition created by the original author, Paul Newbold. Paul understood the importance of rigorous statistical analysis and its foundations. He realized that there are some complex ideas that need to be developed and he worked to provide clear explanations of difficult ideas. In addition, these ideas only become useful when used in realistic problem-solving situations. Thus, many examples and many applied student exercises were included in the early editions. We have worked to continue and expand this tradition in preparing a book that meets the needs of future business leaders in the information age.

Chapter 1

Describing Data: Graphical

Introduction

What are the projected sales of a new product such as Apple's new iPhone? Will the cost of Google shares continue to increase? Who will win the next presidential election? How do the European Soccer Championship games affect sales of Adidas products? What will be the best jobs available when you graduate from college? How satisfied were you with your last purchase at Starbucks, Best Buy, or Sports Authority? Answers to questions like these come from an understanding of numbers, fluctuations in the market, consumer preferences, trends, and so on.

Numbers are used to predict or forecast sales of a new product, constructions costs, customer satisfaction levels, the weather, election results, university enrollment figures, grade point averages, interest rates, currency exchange rates, and many other variables that affect our daily lives. We need to absorb and interpret substantial amounts of data. Governments, businesses, and scientific researchers spend billions of dollars collecting data. But once the data are collected, what do we do with them? How does data impact decision making?

Statistics is a tool to help us process, summarize, analyze, and interpret data for the purpose of making better decisions in an uncertain environment. Basically, an understanding of statistics will permit us to make sense of all the data.

In this chapter we introduce tables and graphs that help us gain a better understanding of data and that provide visual support for improved decision making. Reports are enhanced by the inclusion of appropriate tables and graphs, such as frequency distributions, bar charts, pie charts, Pareto diagrams, line charts, histograms, stem-and-leaf displays, or ogives. Visualization of data is important. We should always ask the following questions: What does the graph suggest about the data? What is it that we see?

1.1 DECISION MAKING IN AN UNCERTAIN ENVIRONMENT

Decisions are often made based on limited information. Accountants may need to select a portion of records for auditing purposes. Financial investors need to understand the market's fluctuations and they need to choose between various portfolio investments. Managers may use surveys to find out if customers are satisfied with their company's products or services. Perhaps a marketing executive wants information concerning customers' taste preferences, their shopping habits, or the demographics of Internet shoppers. An investor does not know with certainty whether financial markets will be buoyant, steady, or depressed. Nevertheless, the investor must decide how to balance a portfolio among stocks, bonds, and money market instruments while future market movements are unknown.

For each of these situations, we must carefully define the problem, determine what data are needed, collect the data, and use statistics to summarize the data and make inferences and decisions based on the data obtained. Statistical thinking is essential from initial problem definition to final decision, which may lead to reduced costs, increased profits, improved processes, and increased customer satisfaction.

Before bringing a new product to market, a manufacturer wants to arrive at some assessment of the likely level of demand and may undertake a market research survey. The manufacturer is, in fact, interested in *all* potential buyers (the population). However, populations are often so large that they are unwieldy to analyze; collecting complete information for a population could be impossible or prohibitively expensive. Even in circumstances where sufficient resources seem to be available, time constraints make the examination of a subset (sample) necessary.

Population and Sample
A **population** is the complete set of all items that interest an investigator. Population size, N, can be very large or even infinite. A **sample** is an observed subset (or portion) of a population with sample size given by n.

Examples of populations include the following:

- All potential buyers of Apple's new 3G iPhones
- All stocks traded on the NYSE Euronext
- All registered voters in a particular city or country
- All accounts receivable for a corporation

Our eventual aim is to make statements based on sample data that have some validity about the population at large. We need a sample, then, that is representative of the population. How can we achieve that? One important principle that we must follow in the sample selection process is randomness.

Random Sampling

Simple random sampling is a procedure used to select a sample of *n* objects from a population in such a way that each member of the population is chosen strictly by chance, the selection of one member does not influence the selection of any other member, each member of the population is equally likely to be chosen, and every possible sample of a given size, *n*, has the same chance of selection. This method is so common that the adjective *simple* is generally dropped, and the resulting sample is called a **random sample**.

Other sampling procedures in addition to simple random sampling include systematic sampling (see the chapter appendix), stratified, and cluster sampling (see Chapter 17).

Suppose that we want to know the average age of registered voters in the United States. Clearly, the population size is so large that we might take only a random sample, perhaps 500 registered voters, and calculate their average age. Because this average is based on sample data, it is called a *statistic*. If we were able to calculate the average age of the entire population, then the resulting average would be called a *parameter*.

Parameter and Statistic

A **parameter** is a numerical measure that describes a specific characteristic of a population. A **statistic** is a numerical measure that describes a specific characteristic of a sample.

Throughout this book we will study ways to make decisions about a population parameter, based on a sample statistic. We must realize that some element of uncertainty will always remain, as the exact value of the parameter is not known. That is, when a sample is taken from a population, the value of any population parameter will not be able to be known *precisely*. One source of error, called **sampling error**, results from the fact that information is available on only a subset of all the population members. In Chapters 6, 7, and 8 we will develop statistical theory that allows us to characterize the nature of the sampling error and to make certain statements about population parameters.

In practical analyses there is the possibility of an error unconnected with the kind of sampling procedure used. Indeed, such errors could just as well arise if a complete census of the population was taken. These are referred to as **nonsampling errors**. This type of error could results from the following: 1) the population actually sampled is not the relevant one; 2) survey subjects may give inaccurate or dishonest answers; or 3) nonresponse to survey questions (see the chapter appendix).

There is no general procedure for identifying and analyzing nonsampling errors. But nonsampling errors could be important. The investigator must take care in such matters as identifying the relevant population, designing the questionnaire, and dealing with nonresponse in order to minimize the significance of nonsampling errors. In the remainder of this book it is assumed that such care has been taken, and our discussion centers on the treatment of sampling errors.

To think statistically begins with problem definition: 1) What information is required? 2) What is the relevant population? 3) How should sample members be selected? 4) How should information be obtained from the sample members? Next we will want to know how to use sample information to make decisions about our population of interest. Finally, we will want to know what conclusions can be drawn about the population.

After we identify and define a problem, we collect data produced by various processes according to a design, and then we analyze that data using one or more statistical procedures. From this analysis, we obtain information. Information is in turn converted into knowledge, using understanding based on specific experience, theory, literature, and additional statistical procedures. Both descriptive and inferential statistics are used to change data into knowledge that leads to better decision making. To do this, we will use descriptive statistics and inferential statistics.

Descriptive and Inferential Statistics

Descriptive statistics focus on graphical and numerical procedures that are used to summarize and process data. **Inferential statistics** focus on using the data to make predictions, forecasts, and estimates to make better decisions.

1.2 CLASSIFICATION OF VARIABLES

A variable is a specific characteristic (like age or weight) of an individual or object. Variables can be classified in several ways. One method of classification refers to the type and amount of information contained in the data. Data are either categorical or numerical. Another method, introduced in 1946 by an American psychologist Stanley Smith Stevens (Reference 9), is to classify data by levels of measurement, giving either qualitative or quantitative variables. Correctly classifying data is an important first step to selecting the correct statistical procedures needed to analyze and interpret data.

Categorical or Numerical

Categorical variables produce responses that belong to groups or categories. For example, responses to yes/no questions are categorical. "Are you a business major?" and "Do you own an iPhone?" are limited to yes or no answers. A health care insurance company may classify incorrect claims according to the type of errors, such as procedural and diagnostic errors, patient information errors, and contractual errors. Other examples of categorical variables include questions on gender or marital status. Sometimes categorical variables include a range of choices, such as "strongly disagree" to "strongly agree." For example, consider a faculty evaluation form where students are to respond to statements such as the following: "The instructor in this course was an effective teacher" (1: strongly disagree; 2: slightly disagree; 3: neither agree nor disagree; 4: slightly agree; 5: strongly agree).

Numerical variables include both discrete and continuous variables. A **discrete numerical variable** may (but does not necessarily) have a finite number of values. However, the most common type of discrete numerical variable produces a response that comes from a counting process. Examples of discrete numerical variables include the number of students enrolled in a class, the number of university credits earned by a student at the end of a particular semester, and the number of Microsoft stocks in an investor's portfolio.

A **continuous numerical variable** may take on any value within a given range of real numbers and usually arises from a measurement (not a counting) process. Someone might say that he is 6 feet (or 72 inches) tall, but his height could actually be 72.1 inches, 71.8 inches, or some other similar number, depending on the accuracy of the instrument used to measure height. Other examples of continuous numerical variables include the weight of cereal boxes, the time to run a race, the distance between two cities, or the temperature. In each case the value could deviate within a certain amount, depending on the precision of the measurement instrument used. We tend to truncate continuous variables in daily conversation and treat them as though they were the same as discrete variables without even giving it a second thought.

Measurement Levels

We can also describe data as either **qualitative** or **quantitative**. With qualitative data there is no measurable meaning to the "difference" in numbers. For example, one basketball player is assigned the number "20" and another player has the number "10." We cannot conclude that the first player plays twice as well as the second player. However, with quantitative data there is a measurable meaning to the difference in numbers. When one student scores 90 on an exam and another student scores 45, the difference is measurable and meaningful.

Qualitative data include nominal and ordinal levels of measurement. Quantitative data include interval and ratio levels of measurement.

Nominal and ordinal levels of measurement refer to data obtained from categorical questions. Responses to questions on gender, country of citizenship, political affiliation, and ownership of a mobile phone are nominal. **Nominal** data are considered the lowest or weakest type of data, since numerical identification is chosen strictly for convenience and does not imply ranking of responses.

The values of nominal variables are words that describe the categories or classes of responses. The values of the gender variable are male and female; the values of "Do you own an iPhone?" are "yes" and "no." We arbitrarily assign a code or number to each response. However, this number has no meaning other than for categorizing. For example, we could code gender responses or yes/no responses as follows:

1 = Male; 2 = Female
1 = Yes; 2 = No

Ordinal data indicate the rank ordering of items, and similar to nominal data the values are words that describe responses. Some examples of ordinal data and possible codes are as follows:

1. Product quality rating (1: poor; 2: average; 3: good)
2. Satisfaction rating with university food service (1: very dissatisfied; 2: moderately dissatisfied; 3: no opinion; 4: moderately satisfied; 5: very satisfied)

3. Consumer preference among three different types of soft drink (1: most preferred; 2: second choice; 3: third choice)

In these examples the responses are ordinal, or put into a rank order, but there is no measurable meaning to the "difference" between responses. That is, the difference between your first and second choices may not be the same as the difference between your second and third choices.

Interval and ratio levels of measurement refer to data obtained from numerical variables and meaning is given to the *difference* between measurements. An interval scale indicates rank and distance from an arbitrary zero measured in unit intervals. That is, data are provided relative to an arbitrarily determined benchmark. Temperature is a classic example of this level of measurement, with arbitrarily determined benchmarks generally based on either Fahrenheit or Celsius degrees. Suppose that it is 80 degrees Fahrenheit in Orlando, Florida, and only 20 degrees Fahrenheit in St. Paul, Minnesota. We can conclude that the difference in temperature is 60 degrees, but we cannot say that it is four times as warm in Orlando as it is in St. Paul. The year is another example of an interval level of measurement, with benchmarks based most commonly on the Gregorian calendar.

Ratio data indicate both rank and distance from a natural zero, with ratios of two measures having meaning. A person who weighs 200 pounds is twice the weight of a person who weighs 100 pounds; a person who is 40 years old is twice the age of someone who is 20 years old.

After collecting data, we first need to classify responses as categorical or numerical or by measurement scale. Next, we assign an arbitrary number to each response. Some graphs are appropriate for categorical variables, and others are used for numerical variables.

Note that data files usually contain "missing values." For example, respondents to a questionnaire may choose not to answer certain questions about gender, age, income, or some other sensitive topic. Missing values require a special code in the data entry stage. Unless missing values are properly handled, it is possible to obtain erroneous output. Statistical software packages handle missing values in different ways.

EXERCISES

Basic Exercises

1.1 State whether each of the following variables is categorical or numerical. If categorical, give the level of measurement. If numerical, is it discrete or continuous?

a. Number of e-mail messages sent daily by a financial planner
b. Actual cost (in dollars, euros, etc.) of a student's textbooks for a given semester
c. The actual cost (in dollars, euros, etc.) of your electricity bill last month
d. Faculty ranks (professor, associate professor, assistant professor, or instructor)

1.2 A new Starbucks store recently opened in Cluj-Napoca, Romania. Upon visiting the store, suppose that customers were given a brief survey. Is the answer to each of the following questions categorical or numerical? If categorical, give the level of measurement. If numerical, is it discrete or continuous?

a. Is this your first visit to this Starbucks store?
b. On a scale from 1 (very dissatisfied) to 5 (very satisfied), rate your level of satisfaction with today's purchase?
c. What was the actual cost (in RON) of your purchase today?

1.3 A questionnaire was distributed at a large university to find out the level of student satisfaction with various activities and services. For example, concerning parking availability, students were asked to indicate their level of satisfaction on a scale from 1 (very dissatisfied) to 5 (very satisfied). Is a student's response to this question numerical or categorical? If numerical, is it discrete or continuous? If categorical, give the level of measurement.

1.4 Faculty at one university were asked a series of questions in a recent survey. State the type of data for each question.

   a. Indicate your level of satisfaction with your teaching load (very satisfied, moderately satisfied, neutral, moderately dissatisfied, or very dissatisfied).

   b. How many of your research articles were published in refereed journals during the last five years?

   c. Did you attend the last university faculty meeting?

   d. Do you think that the teaching evaluation process needs to be revised?

1.5 A random sample of Florida tourists was asked a series of questions. Identify the type of data for each question.

   a. What is your favorite tourist destination in Florida?

   b. How many days do you expect to be in Florida?

   c. Do you have children under the age of 10 traveling with you on this visit to Florida?

   d. Rank the following Florida attractions in order with 1: most favorite; to 5: least favorite.

      Aquatica
      Busch Gardens
      Disney World
      Kennedy Space Center
      SeaWorld

1.6 Residents in one housing development were asked a series of questions by their homeowners' association. Identify the type of data for each question.

   a. Did you play golf during the last month on the development's new golf course?

   b. How many times have you eaten at the country club restaurant during the last month?

   c. Do you own a camper?

   d. Rate the new security system for the development (very good, good, poor, or very poor).

Application Exercises

1.7   A survey of students at one college was conducted to provide information to address various concerns about the college's library. The data are stored in the data file **Library**.

   a. Give an example of a categorical variable with ordinal responses.

   b. Give an example of a categorical variable with nominal responses.

   c. Give an example of a numerical variable with discrete responses.

1.8   A group of business students conducted a survey on their campus to determine student demand for a particular product: a protein supplement for Smoothies. They randomly sampled 113 students and obtained data that could be helpful in developing their marketing strategy. The responses to this survey are contained in the data file **Smoothies**.

   a. Give an example of a categorical variable with ordinal responses.

   b. Give an example of a categorical variable with nominal responses.

1.3 GRAPHS TO DESCRIBE CATEGORICAL VARIABLES

We can describe categorical variables using frequency distribution tables and graphs such as bar charts, pie charts, and Pareto diagrams. These graphs are commonly used by managers and marketing researchers to describe data collected from surveys and questionnaires.

Frequency Distribution

A **frequency distribution** is a table used to organize data. The left column (called classes or groups) includes all possible responses on a variable being studied. The right column is a list of the frequencies, or number of observations, for each class.

Tables

The classes that we use to construct frequency distribution tables of a categorical variable are simply the possible responses to the categorical variable.

Example 1.1   Health Awareness Levels Among University Students (Bar Charts)

A team of business students is considering opening a café on its campus that would specialize in smoothies and other nutritional drinks. The survey data are contained in the data file **Smoothies**. Set up a frequency distribution of students' health awareness levels.

Solution   Table 1.1 is a frequency distribution of students' level of health awareness.

Table 1.1   How health conscious are you?

CATEGORY	NUMBER OF STUDENTS
Very Health Conscious	29
Moderately Health Conscious	55
Slightly Health Conscious	20
Not Very Health Conscious	9

Bar Charts and Pie Charts

Bar charts and pie charts are commonly used to describe categorical data. If our intent is to draw attention to the *frequency* of each category, then we will most likely draw a **bar chart**. In a bar chart the height of a rectangle represents this frequency. There is no need for the bars to touch. Figure 1.1 is a bar chart of the health conscious level responses from Table 1.1.

An interesting and useful extension to the simple bar chart can be used when components of individual categories are also of interest. For example, Table 1.2 shows the number of males and females for each health conscious category. Figure 1.2 shows this information in a *component* or *stacked bar* and Figure 1.3 shows the data in a *cluster* or *side-by-side* bar chart. Both graphs allow us to make visual comparisons of totals and individual components.

Figure 1.1
Health Awareness
Levels (Bar Chart)

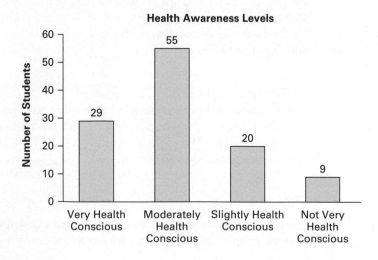

Table 1.2 Health Conscious Level by Gender

	MALES	FEMALES
Very Health Conscious	16	13
Moderately Health Conscious	26	29
Slightly Health Conscious	12	8
Not Very Health Conscious	7	2

Figure 1.2
Health Awareness
Levels
(Component Bar
Chart)

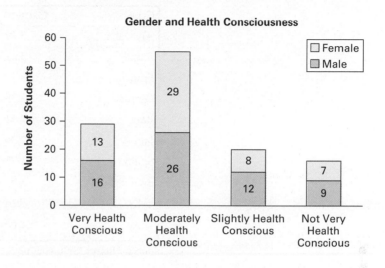

Figure 1.3
Health Awareness
Levels by Gender
(Cluster Bar Chart)

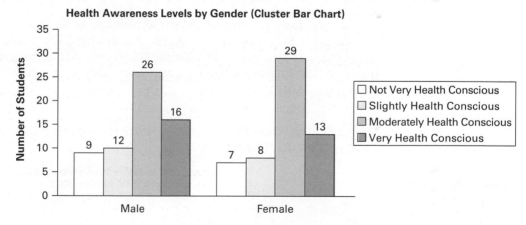

Example 1.2 Growth in Active Home Internet Users by Country, April 2008 to May 2008 (Nielsen Online)

In 2007 the Nielsen Company, a global information and media company, purchased NetRatings and BuzzMetrics forming Nielsen Online. The Nielson Company is active in more than 100 countries with headquarters in the Netherlands and in New York. Nielsen Online currently operates in the United States, and 16 countries from

Europe to Latin America to Asia Pacific (see www.nielsen.com). According to Nielsen Online the growth (%) of active Internet home users worldwide from April 2008 to May 2008 is given in Table 1.3 (Reference 17). Graph this data.

Solution

Table 1.3 Growth (%) in Active Home Internet Users by Country, April 2008 to May 2008

COUNTRY	GROWTH (%)
Australia	5.79
Brazil	3.22
France	8.23
Germany	2.38
Italy	7.64
Japan	2.36
Spain	1.79
Switzerland	−1.5
U.K.	0.14
U.S.	1.53

SOURCE: Nielsen Online, 2008

From this data, we can see that the number of active home Internet users decreased in Switzerland from April 2008 to May 2008. There was a very slight increase (only 0.14%) in the United Kingdom, while the greatest increase in active home Internet users was in France with a growth of 8.23%. Figure 1.4 shows this data.

Figure 1.4 Growth (%) in Active Home Internet Users by Country: April 2008 to May 2008 (Bar Chart)

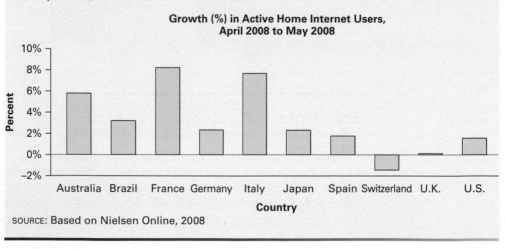

SOURCE: Based on Nielsen Online, 2008

If we want to draw attention to the *proportion* of frequencies in each category, then we will probably use a **pie chart** to depict the division of a whole into its constituent parts. The circle (or "pie") represents the total, and the segments (or "pieces of the pie") cut from its center depict shares of that total. The pie chart is constructed so that the area of each segment is proportional to the corresponding frequency.

Example 1.3 Global 500: World's Largest Revenue Corporations by Industry Type (Pie Chart)

Annually *Fortune* magazine provides data about the world's largest 500 corporations in terms of revenues, profits, assets, stockholders' equity, number of employees, type of industry, and country. Graph the data in Table 1.4, which is based on *Fortune*'s global top 20 highest revenue corporations by industry type for 2007 (Reference 16).

Table 1.4   Global Top Twenty Revenue Corporations by Industry Type

INDUSTRY CLASSIFICATION	NUMBER OF CORPORATIONS
Petroleum Refining	7
Motor Vehicles and Parts	5
Banks: Commercial and Savings	5
General Merchandisers	1
Diversified Financials	1
Insurance: Life, Health (Stock)	1

Solution   Figure 1.5 is a pie chart of the data in Table 1.4.

Figure 1.5   Global Top 20 Highest Revenue Corporations by Industry Type (Pie Chart)

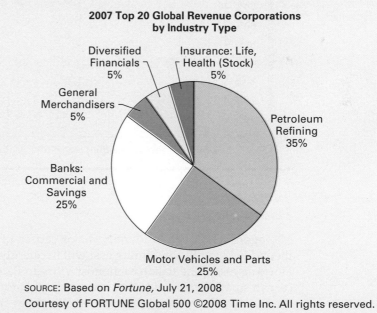

2007 Top 20 Global Revenue Corporations by Industry Type

SOURCE: Based on *Fortune*, July 21, 2008

Courtesy of FORTUNE Global 500 ©2008 Time Inc. All rights reserved.

Example 1.4 Sarbanes-Oxley Act of 2002

Regulatory Agencies and the U.S. Congress are recognizing both the values and emerging issues for small firms as the Sarbanes-Oxley Act of 2002 (SOX) is implemented. On April 23, 2006 the Advisory Committee on Smaller Public Companies issued a final report to the Security and Exchange Commission assessing the impact of Sarbanes-Oxley Act of 2002 on smaller public companies (Final Report of the Advisory Committee on Smaller Public Companies to the U.S. Securities and Exchange Commission, April 23, 2006). What is the overall impact of SOX on small, medium, and large firms (defined by annual revenue)?

Solution Michelson, Stryker, and Thorne (Reference 5) recently surveyed a random sample of CEOs, CFOs, and board members of small, medium, and large firms and obtained the data in Table 1.5 concerning their opinion of the overall impact of SOX on their firm. We illustrate this finding in Figure 1.6.

Table 1.5 Impact of Sarbanes-Oxley Verses Size of the Firm

IMPACT OF SOX	SMALL FIRMS	MEDIUM SIZE FIRMS	LARGE FIRMS
Little or No Impact	17	13	6
Moderate to Very Major Impact	13	41	22

Figure 1.6 Impact of Sarbanes-Oxley Act of 2002 by Revenue Size of the Firm (Cluster Bar Chart)

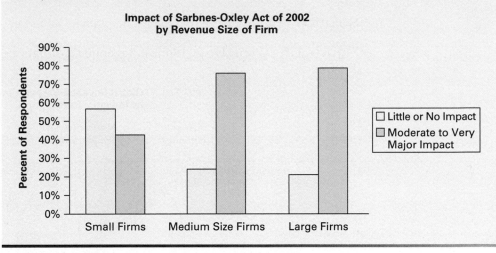

Pareto Diagrams

Managers who need to identify major causes of problems and attempt to correct them quickly with a minimum cost will frequently use a special bar chart known as a *Pareto diagram*. The Italian economist Vilfredo Pareto (1848–1923) noted that in most cases a small number of factors are responsible for most of the problems. We arrange the bars in a Pareto diagram from left to right to emphasize the most frequent causes of defects.

Pareto Diagram

A **Pareto diagram** is a bar chart that displays the frequency of defect causes. The bar at the left indicates the most frequent cause and bars to the right indicate causes with decreasing frequencies. A Pareto diagram is used to separate the "vital few" from the "trivial many."

Pareto's result is applied to a wide variety of behavior over many systems. It is sometimes referred to as the "80–20 Rule." A cereal manufacturer may find that most of the packaging errors are due to only a few causes. A student might think that 80% of the work on a group project was done by only 20% of the team members. The use of a Pareto diagram can also improve communication with employees or management and within production teams. Example 1.5 illustrates the Pareto principle applied to a problem in a health insurance company.

Example 1.5 Insurance Claims Processing Errors (Pareto Diagram)

Analysis and payment of health care insurance claims is a complex process that can result in a number of incorrectly processed claims leading to an increase in staff time to obtain the correct information, an increase in costs, or a negative effect on customer relationships. A major health insurance company set a goal to reduce errors by 50%. Show how we would use Pareto analysis to help the company determine the most significant factors contributing to processing errors. The data are stored in the data file **Insurance**.

Solution   The health insurance company conducted an intensive investigation of the entire claims submission and payment process. A team of key company personnel was selected from the claims processing, provider relations and marketing, internal auditing, data processing, and medical review departments. Based on their experience and a review of the process, the team members finally agreed on a list of possible errors. Three of these errors (procedural and diagnostic, provider information, and patient information) are related to the submission process and must be checked by reviewing patient medical records in clinics and hospitals. Three possible errors (pricing schedules, contractual applications, and provider adjustments) are related to the processing of claims for payment within the insurance company office. Program and system errors are included in the category "Others."

A complete audit of a random sample of 1,000 claims began with checking each claim against medical records in clinics and hospitals and then proceeded through the final payment stage. Claims with errors were separated, and the total number of errors of each type was recorded. If a claim had multiple errors, then each error was recorded. In this process many decisions were made concerning error definition. If a child was coded for a procedure typically used for adults and the computer processing system did not detect this, then this error would be recorded as error 7 (Program and System Errors) and also as error 3 (Patient Information). If treatment for a sprain was coded as a fracture, this would be recorded as error 1 (Procedural and Diagnostic Codes). Table 1.6 is a frequency distribution of the categories and the number of errors in each category.

Next, the team constructed the Pareto diagram in Figure 1.7.

Table 1.6 Errors in Health Care Claims Processing

Category	Error Type	Frequency
1	Procedural and diagnostic codes	40
2	Provider information	9
3	Patient information	6
4	Pricing schedules	17
5	Contractual applications	37
6	Provider adjustments	7
7	Others	4

Figure 1.7 Errors in Health Care Claims Processing (Pareto Diagram)

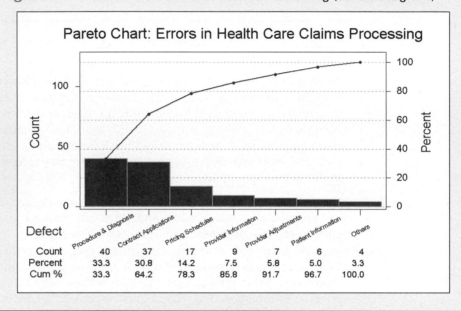

We can see in Figure 1.7 that, as the defect percentages for the types of error are added (from left to right), the increase in the cumulative frequency line indicates the relative improvement that would result from correcting each of the most frequent problems. From the Pareto diagram the analysts saw that error 1 (Procedural and Diagnostic Codes) and error 5 (Contractual Applications) were the major causes of error. The combination of errors 1, 5, and 4 (Pricing Schedules) resulted in nearly 80% of the errors. By examining the Pareto diagram in Figure 1.7, the analysts can quickly determine which causes should receive most of the problem correction effort. Pareto analysis separated the "vital few" causes from the "trivial many."

Armed with this information, the team made a number of recommendations to reduce errors and bring the process under control.

Basic Exercises

1.9 A university administrator requested a breakdown of travel expenses for faculty to attend various professional meetings. It was found that 31% of the travel expenses were spent for transportation costs, 25% for lodging, 17% for food, 20% for conference registration fees, and the remainder was spent for miscellaneous costs.

a. Construct a pie chart.

b. Construct a bar chart.

1.10 A company has determined that there are seven possible defects for one of its product lines. Construct a Pareto diagram for the following defect frequencies:

Defect Code	Frequency
A	10
B	70
C	15
D	90
E	8
F	4
G	3

1.11 Bank clients were asked to indicate their level of satisfaction with the service provided by the bank's tellers. Responses from a random sample of customers were as follows: 69 were very satisfied, 55 were moderately satisfied, 5 had no opinion, 3 were moderately dissatisfied, and 2 were very dissatisfied.

a. Draw a bar chart.

b. Draw a pie chart.

1.12 The supervisor of a plant obtained a random sample of employee experience (in months) and times to complete a task (in minutes). Graph the data with a component bar chart.

Experience/ Time	Less Than 5 Minutes	5 Minutes to Less Than 10 Minutes	10 Minutes to Less Than 15 Minutes
Less than 3 months	10	13	25
3 < 6 months	10	13	12
6 < 9 months	9	22	8
9 < 12 months	5	18	19

Application Exercises

1.13 Suppose that an estimate of U.S. federal spending showed that 46% was for entitlements, 18% was for defense, 15% was for grants to states and localities, 14% was for interest on debt, 6% was for other federal

operations, and 1% was for deposit insurance. Construct a pie chart to show this information.

1.14 The *Statistical Abstract of the United States* provides a reliable and complete summary of statistics on the political, social, and economic organization of the United States. The following table gives a partial list of the number of endangered wildlife species both inside and outside the United States as of April 2007 (Reference 6):

Item	Endangered Wildlife Species in United States	Endangered Wildlife Species Outside the United States
Mammals	70	255
Birds	76	175
Reptiles	13	65
Amphibians	13	8
Fishes	74	11

SOURCE: U.S. Fish and Wildlife Service. http://www.census.gov/prod/2007pubs/08abstract/geo.pdf (Accessed December 19, 2008).

a. Construct a bar chart of the number of endangered wildlife species in the United States.

b. Construct a bar chart of the number of endangered wildlife species outside the United States.

c. Construct a bar chart to compare the number of endangered species in the United States to the number of endangered species outside the United States.

1.15 Jon Payne, tennis coach, kept a record of the most serious type of errors made by each of his players during a 1-week training camp. The data are stored in the data file **Tennis**.

a. Construct a Pareto diagram of total errors committed by all players.

b. Construct a Pareto diagram of total errors committed by male players.

c. Construct a Pareto diagram of total errors committed by female players.

d. Construct a component bar chart showing type of error and gender of the player.

1.16 On what type of Internet activity do you spend the most time? The responses from a random sample of 700 Internet users were banking on-line, 40; buying a product, 60; getting news, 150; sending or reading e-mail, 200; buying or making a reservation for travel, 75; checking sports scores or information, 50; and searching for an answer to a question, 125. Describe the data graphically.

1.17 A random sample of 100 business majors was asked a series of demographic questions including gender, age, year in school, and current grade point average (GPA). Other questions were also asked for their levels of satisfaction with campus parking, campus housing, and campus dining. Responses to these satisfaction questions were measured on a scale from 1 to 5 with 5 being the highest level of satisfaction. Finally, these students were asked if they planned to attend graduate school within 5 years of their college graduation (0: no; 1: yes). These data are contained in the data file **Finstad and Lie Study**.

a. Draw a cluster bar chart of the respondents' major and gender.
b. Draw a pie chart of their majors.

1.18 The Dean of the Business School obtained the following enrollment information comparing the number of Finance, Marketing, and Accounting majors in 2004 with the numbers in 2009.

Major	2004	2009
Finance	160	250
Marketing	140	200
Accounting	100	150

a. Construct a component bar chart of this data.
b. Construct a cluster bar chart of this data.

1.19 Data on U.S. Exports, Imports, and Merchandise Trade Balance by Country are found in the *Statistical Abstract of the United States* (Reference 8). The top five purchasers of U.S. exports (data in million dollars) for 2006 are given in the following table:

Canada	230,656
Mexico	133,979
Japan	59,613
China	55,186
United Kingdom	45,410

SOURCE: U.S. Census Bureau.

a. Graph the top five purchasers of U.S. exports using a bar chart.
b. Graph the top five purchasers of U.S. exports for the most recent year. Data can be obtained at http://www.census.gov/compendia/statab.

1.4 GRAPHS TO DESCRIBE TIME-SERIES DATA

Suppose that we take a random sample of 100 boxes of a new variety of cereal. If we collect our sample at one point in time and weigh each box, then the measurements obtained are known as *cross-sectional* data. However, we could collect and measure a random sample of 5 boxes every 15 minutes or 10 boxes every 20 minutes. Data measured at successive points in time are called *time-series* data. A graph of time-series data is called a *line chart* or *time-series plot*.

Line Chart (Time-Series Plot)
A **line chart**, also called a **time-series plot**, is a series of data plotted at various time intervals. Measuring time along the horizontal axis and the numerical quantity of interest along the vertical axis yields a point on the graph for each observation. Joining points adjacent in time by straight lines produces a time-series plot.

Examples of time-series data include monthly product sales and interest rates, quarterly corporate earnings, daily closing prices for shares of common stock, annual university enrollments, and daily exchange rates between various world currencies.

Example 1.6 U.S. Dollars (USD) to 1 Euro (EUR)(Time-Series Plot)

Investors, business travelers, tourists, and students studying abroad are all aware of the fluctuations in the exchange rates between various world currencies. A group of U.S. university students who plan to study in Innsbruck, Austria, during a special summer program obtained the exchange rates for U.S. Dollars (USD) to 1 Euro (EUR) for a period of one month prior to their departure (actual dates of the exchange rates are May 20, 2008 to June 19, 2008, Reference 14). These data are contained in the data file **USD Exchange Rates**. Graph the data with a time-series plot.

Solution Although the data in Figure 1.8 seem to fluctuate significantly, we notice that the exchange rates vary only from 1.54 to 1.58.

Figure 1.8 Currency Exchange Rates: USD to EUR (Time-Series Plot)

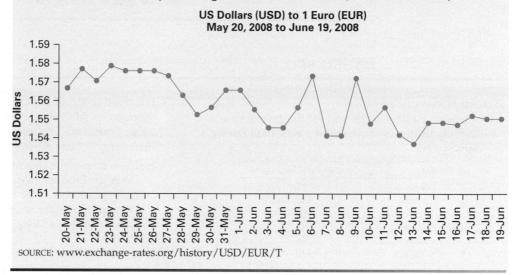

SOURCE: www.exchange-rates.org/history/USD/EUR/T

Example 1.7 Daily Closing Prices of Shares of Microsoft (MSFT) Stock

You are considering a stock investment and obtain the opening, high, low, and closing prices of shares of Microsoft stock for the last month. Graph the closing costs over the last 23 days (actual data are for the time period from May 20, 2008, through June 20, 2008). These data are contained in the data file **MSFT Stock Prices**.

Solution Although many other factors will affect your investment decision and you may need the help of a financial advisor, you can begin your search with a look at the time-series plot for closing prices as illustrated in Figure 1.9.

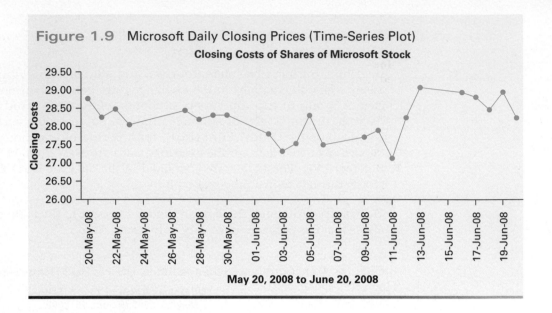

Figure 1.9 Microsoft Daily Closing Prices (Time-Series Plot)

EXERCISES

Basic Exercises

1.20 Construct a time-series plot for the following number of customers shopping at a new mall during a given week.

Day	Number of Customers
Monday	525
Tuesday	540
Wednesday	469
Thursday	500
Friday	586
Saturday	640

1.21 What percent of undergraduate alumni made donations to their alma mater? The Institutional Research Office at one university reported the following percentages for the last 5 years. Draw a time-series plot of the data. What action could the school take?

Year	Percent
5 years ago	26.72
4 years ago	27.48
3 years ago	24.89
2 years ago	25.83
1 year ago	30.22

Application Exercises

1.22 🌐 Degrees awarded by degree type at a private 4-year university are stored in the data file **Degrees 1998–2005**.

   a. Graph the data with a time-series plot.

   b. What possible conclusions or actions might the university consider?

1.23 Information about the Gross Domestic Product in the area of Manufacturing can be found in the 2008 *Statistical Abstract of the United States* (Reference 7). Data is in billion dollars.

   a. Use a time-series plot to graph the Gross Domestic Product in Manufacturing in current dollars by industry for durable goods (such as wood products, furniture and related products, motor vehicles, and equipment) from 1998 to 2006.

   b. Use a time-series plot to graph the Gross Domestic Product in manufacturing in chained dollars (2000) by industry for nondurable goods (such as food, apparel, and leather products) from 1998 to 2006.

1.24 🌐 In Example 1.6 we plotted the U.S. Dollar (USD) to 1 Euro (EUR) for a 30-day time period relevant for U.S. students studying abroad.

   a. Compare the Euro (EUR) to 1 U.S. Dollar (USD) for the data contained in the data file **USD Exchange Rates**.

   b. Compare your currency with an appropriate world currency for a time period relevant to you.

1.25 🌐 The inventory-sales ratio for manufacturing and trade in the United States over a period of 12 years is stored in the data file **Inventory Sales**. Plot the data with a time-series plot.

1.26 Select annual returns on a stock market index over 14 years from the Internet. Graph the data with a time-series plot.

1.27 ⬤ The data file **Gold Price** shows the year-end price of gold (in dollars) over 14 consecutive years. Graph the data with a time-series plot.

1.28 ⬤ The data file **Housing Starts** shows private housing units started per thousand persons in the U.S. population over a period of 24 years. Describe the data with a graph.

1.29 ⬤ Earnings per share of a corporation over a period of 28 years are stored in the data file **Earnings per Share**. Graph the series and comment on the plot.

1.5 GRAPHS TO DESCRIBE NUMERICAL VARIABLES

In this section we briefly present histograms, ogives, and stem-and-leaf displays that summarize and describe numerical data. First, we consider a frequency distribution for numerical data.

Frequency Distributions

Similar to a frequency distribution for categorical data (Section 1.3), a frequency distribution for numerical data is a table that summarizes data by listing the classes in the left column and the number of observations in each class in the right column. However, the classes or intervals for a frequency distribution of numerical data are not as easily identifiable.

To determine the intervals of a frequency distribution for numerical data requires answers to certain questions: How many intervals should be used? How wide should each interval be? There are some general rules (such as Equation 1.1) for preparing frequency distributions that make it easier for us to answer these types of questions, to summarize data, and to communicate results.

Construction of a Frequency Distribution

Rule 1: Determine k, the number of intervals (classes).

Rule 2: Intervals (classes) should be the same width, w; the width is determined by the following:

$$w = Interval\ Width = \frac{(Largest\ Data\ Value - Smallest\ DataValue)}{Number\ of\ Intervals} \tag{1.1}$$

Both k and w should be rounded upward, possibly to the next largest integer.

Rule 3: Intervals (classes) must be inclusive and nonoverlapping.

Rule 1. Number of Intervals

The number of intervals (classes) used in a frequency distribution is decided in a somewhat arbitrary manner.

Quick Guide to Approximate Number of Intervals for a Frequency Distribution

SAMPLE SIZE	NUMBER OF INTERVALS
Fewer than 50	5–7
50 to 100	7–8
101 to 500	8–10
501 to 1,000	10–11
1,001 to 5,000	11–14
More than 5,000	14–20

Practice and experience provide the best guidelines. Larger data sets require more intervals; smaller data sets require fewer intervals. If we select too few classes, the patterns and various characteristics of the data may be hidden. If we select too many classes, we will discover that some of our intervals may contain no observations or have a very small frequency.

Rule 2. Interval Width

After choosing the number of intervals, the next step is to choose the interval width:

$$w = Interval\ Width = \frac{(Largest\ Number\ -\ Smallest\ Number)}{Number\ of\ Intervals}$$

The interval width is often rounded to a convenient whole number to provide for easy interpretation.

Rule 3. Inclusive and Nonoverlapping Intervals

Intervals must be inclusive and nonoverlapping. Each observation must belong to one and only one interval. Consider a frequency distribution for the ages (rounded to the nearest year) of a particular group of people. If the frequency distribution contains the intervals "age 20 to age 30" and "age 30 to age 40," to which of these two classes would a person age 30 belong?

The *boundaries*, or endpoints, of each class must be clearly defined. To avoid overlapping, age intervals could be defined as "age 20 *but less than* age 30," followed by "age 30 *but less than* age 40" and so on. Another possibility is to define the age intervals as "20–29," "30–39," and so forth. Since age is an integer, no overlapping occurs. Boundary selection is subjective. Simply be sure to define interval boundaries that promote a clear understanding and interpretation of the data.

Two special frequency distributions are the *cumulative frequency distribution* and the *relative cumulative frequency distribution*.

Relative, Cumulative, and Relative Cumulative Frequency Distributions

A **relative frequency distribution** is obtained by dividing each frequency by the number of observations and multiplying the resulting proportion by 100%. A **cumulative frequency distribution** contains the total number of observations whose values are less than the upper limit for each interval. We construct a cumulative frequency distribution by adding the frequencies of all frequency distribution intervals up to and including the present interval. In a **relative cumulative frequency distribution**, cumulative frequencies can be expressed as cumulative proportions or percents.

Example 1.8   Employee Completion Times (Statistical Thinking)

The supervisor of a very large plant obtained the time (in seconds) for a random sample of 110 employees to complete a particular task. The goal is to complete this task in less than 4.5 minutes. Table 1.7 contains these times (in seconds).

Table 1.7 Completion Times (Seconds)

271	236	294	252	254	263	266	222	262	278	288
262	237	247	282	224	263	267	254	271	278	263
262	288	247	252	264	263	247	225	281	279	238
252	242	248	263	255	294	268	255	272	271	291
263	242	288	252	226	263	269	227	273	281	267
263	244	249	252	256	263	252	261	245	252	294
288	245	251	269	256	264	252	232	275	284	252
263	274	252	252	256	254	269	234	285	275	263
263	246	294	252	231	265	269	235	275	288	294
263	247	252	269	261	266	269	236	276	248	299

The data are stored in the data file **Employee Completion Times**. What do the data indicate?

Solution   Table 1.7 by itself offers little guidance to the supervisor. We can find some information in Table 1.7 such as, the quickest time that the task was completed by an employee was 222 seconds, and the maximum time used was 299 seconds. However, we will need more information than this before submitting any report to senior-level executives. To better understand what the data in Table 1.7 indicate, we first develop a frequency distribution.

From the Quick Guide we develop a frequency distribution with eight classes for the data in Table 1.7. From Equation 1.1, the width of each class is

$$w = \frac{299 - 222}{8} = 10 \text{ (rounded up)}$$

Since the smallest value is 222, one choice for the first interval is "220 but less than 230." Subsequent intervals of equal width are added to the frequency distribution, as well as the number of seconds that belong to each class. Table 1.8 is a frequency distribution for the mobile phone data in Table 1.7.

Table 1.8 Frequency and Relative Frequency Distributions for Employee Completion Times

Completion Times (in Seconds)	Frequency	Percent
220 less than 230	5	4.5
230 less than 240	8	7.3
240 less than 250	13	11.8
250 less than 260	22	20.0
260 less than 270	32	29.1
270 less than 280	13	11.8
280 less than 290	10	9.1
290 less than 300	7	6.4

Table 1.9 is a cumulative frequency distribution and a cumulative percent distribution.

The frequency distributions in Table 1.8 and Table 1.9 are an improvement over the original list of data in Table 1.7. We have at least summarized 110 observations into eight categories and are able to tell the supervisor that less than three-fourths (72.7%) of the employees sampled used completed the task within the desired goal. The supervisor may initiate an extra training session for the employees who failed to meet the time constraint.

Table 1.9 Cumulative Frequency and Relative Cumulative Frequency Distributions for Completion Times

COMPLETION TIMES (IN SECONDS)	CUMULATIVE FREQUENCY	CUMULATIVE PERCENT
Less than 230	5	4.5
Less than 240	13	11.8
Less than 250	26	23.6
Less than 260	48	43.6
Less than 270	80	72.7
Less than 280	93	84.5
Less than 290	103	93.6
Less than 300	110	100.0

Histograms and Ogives

Once we develop frequency distributions, we are ready to graph this information. We will briefly discuss *histograms* and *ogives*.

Histogram
A **histogram** is a graph that consists of vertical bars constructed on a horizontal line that is marked off with intervals for the variable being displayed. The intervals correspond to those in a frequency distribution table. The height of each bar is proportional to the number of observations in that interval. The number of observations can be displayed above the bars.

Ogive
An **ogive**, sometimes called a *cumulative line graph*, is a line that connects points that are the cumulative percent of observations below the upper limit of each interval in a cumulative frequency distribution.

Figure 1.10 is a histogram of the completion times in Table 1.8. Figure 1.11 is an ogive that describes the cumulative relative frequencies in Table 1.9.

Although histograms may provide us with insight as to the shape of the distribution, it is important to remember that histograms may not be "mathematically correct," because they often cannot be scaled on the vertical axis. In Section 1.7 we provide some warnings about histograms that distort the truth.

Figure 1.10
Employee
Completion Times
(Histogram)

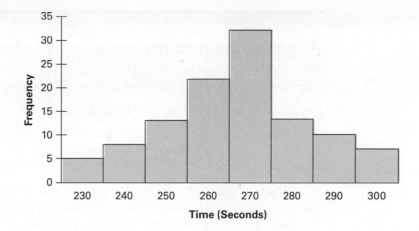

Figure 1.11
Employee
Completion Times
(Ogive)

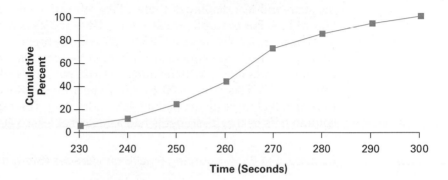

Stem-and-Leaf Displays

Exploratory data analysis (EDA) consists of procedures used to describe data in simple arithmetic terms with easy-to-draw pencil-and-paper pictures (Reference 13). One such procedure is the *stem-and-leaf display*. Before computers, this procedure was a quick way to identify possible patterns in small data sets. We include here only a brief discussion of this procedure.

Stem-and-Leaf Display

A **stem-and-leaf display** is an EDA graph that is an alternative to the histogram. Data are grouped according to their leading digits (called the stem), while listing the final digits (called leaves) separately for each member of a class. The leaves are displayed individually in ascending order after each of the stems.

The number of digits in each class indicates the class frequency. The individual digits indicate the pattern of values within each class. Except for extreme *outliers* (data values that are much larger or smaller than other values in the data set), all stems are included even if there are no observations in the corresponding subset. We illustrate stem-and-leaf displays for both a small random sample of 10 students and a larger random sample of 112 students in Example 1.9.

Example 1.9 Accounting Grades and Grade Point Averages (Stem-and-Leaf Display)

An accounting professor obtained two random samples of data. The first data set is for a small random sample of 10 final exam grades for an introductory accounting class.

| 88 | 51 | 63 | 85 | 79 | 65 | 79 | 70 | 73 | 77 |

The second set of data is a list of grade point averages (GPAs) of a random sample of 112 accounting majors. Both sets of data are contained in the data file **Accounting Grades and GPAs**. Describe both data sets with stem-and-leaf displays.

Solution Figure 1.12 shows that most of the students earned a grade of C on the accounting final exam. In Chapter 2 we will discuss other observations from this data. In another study, the professor obtained GPAs (recorded to the nearest hundredth) for a random sample of graduating accounting majors. Figure 1.13 is the stem-and-leaf display of these GPAs. We can make several observations from Figure 1.13. For example, we see that a GPA of 3.25 is recorded as a stem of "32" and a leaf of "5." The lowest GPA is 2.12 and the highest GPA is 3.87. The leftmost column of the output contains cumulative frequencies, separated by a number in parentheses. In Figure 1.13 the number 10 (in parentheses) tells us that the data are centered at GPAs from 3.00 to 3.09. The number 40 in the leftmost column indicates that 40 students had a GPA under 2.90. The number 27 in the leftmost column tells us that 27 students had a GPA of at least 3.40.

Figure 1.12 Accounting Final Exam Grades (Stem-and-Leaf)

```
Stem-and-leaf of Grade  N = 10
Leaf Unit = 1.0

  1    5   1
  3    6   35
 (5)   7   03799
  2    8   58
```

Figure 1.13 Grade Point Averages (Stem-and-Leaf)

Cumulative Frequency	Stem	Leaf
1	21	2
3	22	2 9
7	23	3 4 5 9
13	24	0 1 3 4 7 9
19	25	1 2 3 5 5 7
24	26	1 1 1 2 6
30	27	1 2 3 5 6 8
40	28	0 2 3 4 4 4 5 6 9 9
51	29	0 1 2 2 4 4 4 5 7 7 7
(10)	30	1 1 1 2 6 7 8 8 8 9
51	31	0 1 1 1 2 4 5 6 8
42	32	1 1 4 5 6 8 9
35	33	1 2 3 5 7 8 8 9
27	34	0 0 1 1 1 3 3 3 4 6
17	35	1 6 7 7
13	36	0 1 2 5 5 6 6 8 8
4	37	2 3
2	38	0 7

Basic Exercises

1.30 Use the Quick Guide to find an approximate number of classes for a frequency distribution if the sample size is as follows:

a. $n = 47$
b. $n = 80$
c. $n = 150$
d. $n = 400$
e. $n = 650$

1.31 Determine an appropriate interval width for a random sample of 110 observations that fall between and include the following:

a. 20 to 85
b. 30 to 190
c. 40 to 230
d. 140 to 500

1.32 Consider the following data:

17	62	15	65
28	51	24	65
39	41	35	15
39	32	36	37
40	21	44	37
59	13	44	56
12	54	64	59

a. Construct a frequency distribution.
b. Draw a histogram.
c. Draw an ogive.
d. Draw a stem-and-leaf display.

1.33 Construct a stem-and-leaf display for the hours that 20 students spent studying for a marketing test.

3.5	2.8	4.5	6.2	4.8	2.3	2.6	3.9	4.4	5.5
5.2	6.7	3.0	2.4	5.0	3.6	2.9	1.0	2.8	3.6

1.34 Consider the following frequency distribution:

Class	Frequency
0 < 10	8
10 < 20	10
20 < 30	13
30 < 40	12
40 < 50	6

a. Construct a relative frequency distribution.
b. Construct a cumulative frequency distribution.
c. Construct a cumulative relative frequency distribution.

Application Exercises

1.35 The following table shows the ages of Internet visitors to a travel agency Web site:

Age	Percent
18–24	11.30
25–34	19.11
35–44	23.64
45–54	23.48
55+	22.48

a. Construct a relative cumulative frequency distribution.
b. What percent of the Internet visitors were under 45 years of age?
c. What percent of the Internet visitors were at least 35 years of age?

1.36 The demand for bottled water increases during the hurricane season in Florida. The manager at a plant that bottles drinking water wants to be sure that the process to fill 1-gallon bottles (approximately 3.785 liters) is operating properly. Currently, the company is testing the volumes of 1-gallon bottles. A random sample of 75 bottles is tested. Study the filling process for this product and submit a report of your findings to the operations manager. Construct a frequency distribution, cumulative frequency distribution, histogram, ogive, and stem-and-leaf display. Incorporate these graphs into a well-written summary. How could we apply statistical thinking in this situation? The data are stored in the data file **Water**.

1.37 The test scores of 40 students are stored in the data file **Scores**.

a. Construct a frequency distribution of the data.
b. Construct a cumulative frequency distribution of the data.
c. Based on your answer to part (a), construct an appropriate histogram of the data.
d. Construct a stem-and-leaf display of the data.

1.38 Percentage returns for the 25 largest U.S. common stock mutual funds for a particular day are stored in the data file **Returns**.

a. Construct a histogram to describe the data.
b. Draw a stem-and-leaf display to describe the data.
c. Construct an ogive to describe the data.

1.39 Ann Thorne, the operations manager at a suntan lotion manufacturing plant, wants to be sure that the filling process for 8 oz (237 mL) bottles of SunProtector is operating properly. Suppose that a random sample of 100 bottles of this lotion is selected, the contents are measured, and the volumes (in mL) are stored in the data file **Sun**. Describe the data graphically.

1.6 TABLES AND GRAPHS TO DESCRIBE RELATIONSHIPS BETWEEN VARIABLES

In the preceding sections we developed graphs to describe a single variable. These "pictures" helped us to better analyze information contained in a large data set. In this section we extend graphical measures to describe relationships between two variables. First, we present a *scatter plot* to study possible relationships between two quantitative variables. Next, we look at two-way *cross tables* to consider possible relationships between qualitative variables.

Business and economic analyses are often concerned about relationships between variables. Do higher SAT mathematics scores predict higher college GPAs? What is the change in quantity sold as the result of a change in price? How are total sales influenced by total disposable income in a geographic region? Does advertising increase sales? What is the change in infant mortality in developing countries as per capita income increases?

In these examples we notice that one variable may depend to a certain extent on the other variable. For example, a student's GPA may depend on the student's SAT math score. We then call GPA the *dependent variable* and label it Y. We call the SAT math score the *independent variable* and label it X. Similarly, we would label the quantity sold as Y and the price of a commodity as X.

To answer these questions, we gather and analyze random samples of data collected from relevant populations. Our analysis begins with constructing a graph called a scatter plot (or scatter diagram).

Scatter Plots

A picture often provides insight as to the relationship that may exist between two variables.

> ### Scatter Plot
> We can prepare a **scatter plot** by locating one point for each pair of two variables that represent an observation in the data set. The scatter plot provides a picture of the data, including the following:
>
> 1. The range of each variable
> 2. The pattern of values over the range
> 3. A suggestion as to a possible relationship between the two variables
> 4. An indication of outliers (extreme points)

We could prepare scatter plots by plotting individual points on graph paper. However, all modern statistical packages contain routines for preparing scatter plots directly from an electronic data file. Preparation of such a plot–as shown in Example 1.10—is a common task in any initial data analysis that occurs at the beginning of an economic or business study. In Example 1.10 we illustrate a scatter plot of two quantitative variables.

Example 1.10 Entrance Scores and College GPA (Scatter Plots)

Are SAT mathematics scores a good indicator of college success? All of us have taken one or more academic aptitude tests as part of a college admission procedure. The admissions staff at your college used the results of these tests to determine your admission status. Table 1.10 gives the SAT math scores from a test given before admission to college and the GPAs at college graduation for a random sample of 11 students at one small private university in the Midwest. Draw a scatter plot and determine what information it provides.

Solution   Using Excel, we obtain Figure 1.14, a scatter plot of the dependent variable, college GPA, and the independent variable, SAT math score.

We can make several observations from examining the scatter plot in Figure 1.14. GPAs range from around 2.5 to 4, and SAT math scores range from 450 to 700. An interesting pattern is the positive upward trend—GPA scores tend to increase directly with increases in SAT math scores. Note also that the relationship does not provide an exact prediction. Some students with low SAT math scores have higher GPA scores than do students with higher SAT math scores. We see that the basic pattern appears to indicate that higher entrance scores predict higher grade point averages, but the results are not perfect.

Table 1.10   SAT Math Versus GPA

SAT Math	GPA
450	3.25
480	2.60
500	2.88
520	2.85
560	3.30
580	3.10
590	3.35
600	3.20
620	3.50
650	3.59
700	3.95

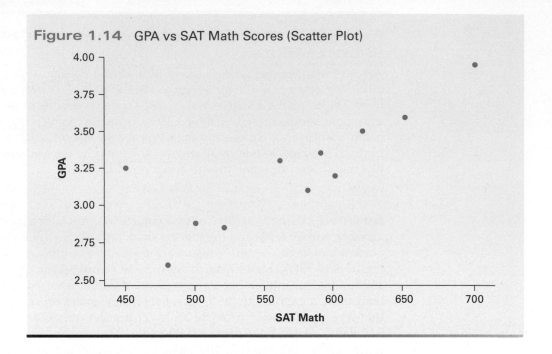

Figure 1.14   GPA vs SAT Math Scores (Scatter Plot)

Cross Tables

There are situations in which we need to describe relationships between categorical or ordinal variables. Market research organizations describe attitudes toward products, measured on an ordinal scale, as a function of educational levels, social status measures, geographic areas, and other ordinal or categorical variables. Personnel departments study employee evaluation levels versus job classifications, educational levels, and other employee variables. Production analysts study relationships between departments or production lines and performance measures to determine reasons for product change, reasons for interruption of production, and quality of output. These situations are usually described by cross tables and pictured by bar charts.

Cross Tables

A **cross table**, sometimes called a contingency table, lists the number of observations for every combination of values for two categorical or ordinal variables. The combination of all possible intervals for the two variables defines the cells in a table. A cross table with r rows and c columns is referred to as an $r \times c$ cross table.

Example 1.11   Product Demand by Residential Area (Cross Table)

A building products retailer has been working on a plan for new store locations as part of a regional expansion. In one city proposed for expansion there are three possible locations: north, east, and west. From past experience the retailer knows that the three major profit centers in his stores are tools, lumber, and paint. In selecting a location, the demand patterns in the different parts of the city are important. Thus, the retailer has requested help from the market research department to obtain and analyze relevant data. This retailer believes that he has a comparative advantage in selling tools.

Solution　Table 1.11 is a 3 × 4 contingency table for the variables "residential location" and "product purchased." This table has been prepared by market research personnel using data obtained from a random sample of households in three major residential areas of the city. Each residential area had a separate phone number prefix, and the last four digits were chosen using a computer random number generator. If the number was not a residence, another phone number was generated randomly. If the phone number was not answered, the number was called again up to a maximum of five times to ensure a high participation rate.

In each residential area 250 households were contacted by telephone and asked to indicate which of three categories of products they had purchased during their last trip to a building supply store. The survey was conducted to determine the demand for tools, lumber, and paint. The three residential areas contain the same number of households, and, thus, the random sample of 750 represents the population of households in the entire city.

Every cell in Table 1.11 shows the number of sampled households in each of the residential areas that had purchased tools, lumber, or paint in the past month. If they had purchased from more than one category, they indicated the category with the largest sales value. For example, 100 sampled households in the east area had purchased tools, and 75 sampled households in the west area had purchased paint. At the right side of each row we see the total number of sampled households (250) in that row. Similarly, the number of sampled households that had purchased from each product category is displayed at the bottom of each column. The displays at the right-hand side of the rows and the bottom of the columns are referred to as marginal distributions. These numbers are the frequency distributions for each of the two variables presented in the cross table.

Table 1.11　Cross Table of Household Demand for Products by Residential Area

AREA	TOOLS	LUMBER	PAINT	NONE	TOTAL
East	100	50	50	50	250
North	50	95	45	60	250
West	65	70	75	40	250
TOTAL	215	215	170	150	750

Table 1.11 provides a summary of the purchase patterns for households in the three neighborhoods. Figure 1.15 is a cluster bar chart of Table 1.11. If geographic region and products purchased were unrelated, we would expect similarities in the bar charts.

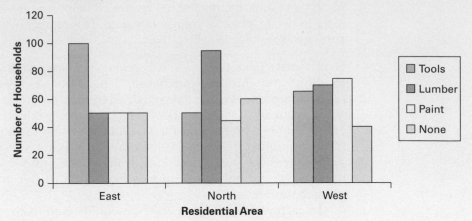

Figure 1.15 Household Demand for Products by Residential Area (Cluster Bar Chart)

However, we see that the bar charts do differ, suggesting a relationship between these two variables. Based on this research the marketing staff now knows that people in the east area are more frequent purchasers of tools, whereas households in the north purchase more lumber. Demand for paint is highest in the west. Based on these patterns the retailer decides to locate in the east because of the greater potential for tool sales.

Example 1.12   Blood Alcohol Concentration (Cross Table)

A research team was assigned the task of determining the alcohol consumption sources of motor vehicle drivers with various blood alcohol levels.

Solution   A random sample of drivers was obtained, and the resulting data were used to prepare Table 1.12. This table displays the relationship between blood alcohol concentration (BAC) and the location of the first drinking episode for night drivers who had been drinking. The data for this table were obtained from a random sample of drivers in Washtenaw County, Michigan, during the hours of 7 P.M. to 3 A.M. The columns indicate the blood alcohol concentration of the driver, obtained from a breath test. Common interpretations of these concentrations are ≤ 0.02%, essentially no blood alcohol and no driving impairment; 0.03% to 0.04%, social drinking with no impairment for most drivers; 0.05% to 0.09%, almost all drivers will have noticeable impairment and could be convicted by a court; ≥ 0.10%, all drivers are seriously impaired and represent a threat to other vehicles and pedestrians. Table 1.12 also includes the percentage of drivers in each intoxication category for each row. This makes it possible to compare the various sources of drinking drivers easily, even though the number of drivers from each drinking source is different.

Table 1.12 Cross Table of Driver BAC by Location of First Drinking Episode

LOCATION	BAC				TOTAL
	≤ 0.02%	0.03%–0.04%	0.05%–0.09%	≥ 0.10%	
Bar					
Number	22	25	17	14	78
Percent	28.2	32.1	21.8	17.9	100.0
Restaurant					
Number	11	3	9	1	24
Percent	45.8	12.5	37.5	4.2	100.0
Own home					
Number	45	16	11	10	82
Percent	54.9	19.5	13.4	12.2	100.0
Another home					
Number	42	10	6	0	58
Percent	72.5	17.2	10.3	0	100.0
Total					
Number	120	54	43	25	242
Percent	49.6	22.3	17.8	10.3	100.0

From Table 1.12 it was possible to obtain some important indications concerning drinking and driving behavior. The sample contained only drivers who had consumed at least one alcoholic beverage during the day. From the bottom row, which summarizes the entire set, over 70% did not have BACs that would seriously reduce their driving ability (e.g., ≤ 0.02% and 0.03%−0.04%). The most likely source of seriously impaired drivers was bars. For the 78 people who drank first in a bar, 17.9% had BACs at or above 0.10%. For the 82 drivers who began drinking at home, 12.2% were at the highest BAC level. However, in this group of home drinkers almost 75% were in the lowest two BAC categories and thus not seriously impaired. Those people who had their first drink in another home were least likely to have high BAC levels. One important outcome of this analysis is that efforts to reduce the number of seriously impaired drivers should consider bars as a major source (Reference 2).

Graphs have a stronger visual impact than cross tables. The cluster bar chart in Figure 1.16 is certainly a stronger visual presentation of the blood alcohol content than the cross table in Table 1.12.

Statistical computer programs can prepare most of these tables. In Chapter 14 we will present more powerful statistical procedures for analyzing cross tables.

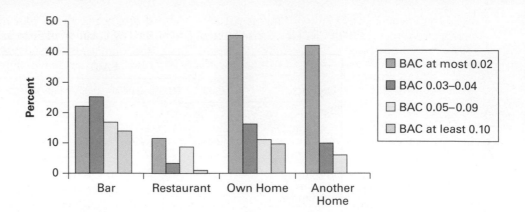

Figure 1.16
Blood Alcohol Concentration (BAC) by Location of First Drinking Episode (Cluster Bar Chart)

Legend:
- BAC at most 0.02
- BAC 0.03–0.04
- BAC 0.05–0.09
- BAC at least 0.10

EXERCISES

Basic Exercises

1.40 Prepare a scatter plot of the following data:

(5, 53) (21, 65) (14, 48) (11,66) (9, 46) (4, 56)
(7, 53) (21, 57) (17, 49) (14, 66) (9, 54) (7, 56)
(9, 53) (21, 52) (13, 49) (14, 56) (9, 59) (4, 56)

1.41 Refer to Example 1.11. Suppose that the market survey data had resulted in the following table instead of the data in Table 1.11. Explain the conclusions from this survey in terms of the product strategy.

Revised Cross Table of Household Demand for Products by Residential Area

Area	Tools	Lumber	Paint	None	Total
East	100	40	60	50	250
North	70	45	95	40	250
West	75	70	65	40	250
Total	245	155	220	130	750

1.42 Three subcontractors, A, B, and C, supplied 58, 70, and 72 parts, respectively, to a plant during the last week. Of the parts supplied by subcontractor A, only four were defective. From the parts supplied by subcontractor B, 60 were good parts; from those supplied by subcontractor C, only six were defective.

a. Set up a cross table for the data.
b. Draw a bar chart.

Applications Exercises

1.43 🌐 Bishop's supermarket records the actual price for consumer food products and the weekly quantities sold. Use the data file **Bishop** to obtain the scatter plot for the actual price of a gallon of orange juice and the weekly quantities sold at that price.

Does the scatter plot follow the pattern from economic theory?

1.44 Acme Delivery offers three different shipping rates for packages under 5 pounds delivered from Maine to the West Coast: regular, $3; fast, $5; and lightning, $10. To test the quality of these services, a major mail-order retailer shipped 15 packages at randomly selected times from Maine to Tacoma, Washington. The packages were shipped in groups of three by the three services at the same time to reduce variation resulting from the shipping day. The following data show the shipping cost, x, and the number of days, y, in (x, y) pairs:

(3, 7) (5, 5) (10, 2) (3, 9) (5, 6) (10, 5) (3, 6) (5, 6) (10, 1)
(3, 10) (5, 7) (10, 4) (3, 5) (5, 6) (10, 4)

Prepare a scatter plot of the points and comment on the relationship between shipping cost and observed delivery time.

1.45 🌐 Sales revenue totals (in dollars) by day of the week are contained in the **Stordata** data file. Prepare a cross table that contains the days of the week as rows and the four sales quartile intervals as columns.

a. Compute the row percentages.
b. What are the major differences in sales level by day of the week as indicated by the row percentages?
c. Describe the expected sales volume patterns over the week based on this table.

1.46 🌐 Many small cities make significant efforts to attract commercial operations such as shopping centers and large retail stores. One of the arguments is that these facilities will contribute to the property that can be taxed and thus provide additional funds for local government needs. The data stored in the data file **Citydat** come from a study of municipal revenue generation capability. Prepare a scatter plot of "taxbase"—the assessed value of all city property in millions of dollars—versus "comper"—the percent of assessed property value that is commercial property. What information does this scatter plot provide about the assessable tax base and percent of commercial property in the city?

1.7 DATA PRESENTATION ERRORS

Poorly designed graphs can easily distort the truth. Used sensibly and carefully, graphs can be excellent tools for extracting the essential information from what would otherwise be a mere mass of numbers. Unfortunately, it is not invariably the case that an attempt at data summarization is carried out either sensibly or carefully. In such circumstances one can easily be misled by the manner in which the summary is presented. We must draw from data as clear and accurate a picture as possible. Improper graphs can produce a distorted picture, yielding a false impression. It is possible to convey the wrong message without being deliberately dishonest.

Gerald Everett Jones (Reference 4) provides numerous examples of distorted and unreliable graphs, and he presents principles to help you make graphs that are persuasive, clear, and truthful. He discusses the importance of graphic design in today's global markets and emphasizes various cultural biases that influence the way people view charts. For example, in Western cultures people read from left to right, and will automatically do so when reading bar charts or time-series plots. In this situation, you should aim for your most important information on the right-hand side of the chart. According to Jones,

> "If you are using PowerPoint or Excel or any other computer application to make charts for an audience – it is almost certain that you are lying to them in some way. . . But the problem is more serious than that. You don't know you're doing it. So you're getting away with it until a manager or an investor or a sales prospect makes a bad decision based on the information that you were so helpful to provide." (Reference 4)

In this section we present some examples of misleading graphs, the intent being not to encourage their use but to caution against their dangers. Example 1.13 shows that distortions in histograms can lead to incorrect conclusions. Example 1.14 illustrates that different choices for the vertical axis in time-series plots can lead to different conclusions. There are many other possibilities for misleading graphs, and for further study we recommend Edward Tufte (Reference 12) and Howard Wainer (Reference 15), who are leaders in the area of data presentation. They have studied the proper design of graphs, as well as the causes and dangers of making inferences from graphs that are poorly drawn.

Misleading Histograms

We know that the width of all intervals should be the same. Suppose a data set contains many observations that fall into a relatively narrow part of the range, while others are widely dispersed. We might be tempted to construct a frequency distribution with narrow intervals where the bulk of the observations are and broader ones elsewhere. Even if we remember that it is the areas, rather than the heights, of the rectangles of the histogram that must be proportional to the frequencies, it is still never a desirable option to construct such a histogram with different widths, as it may easily deceive or distort the findings. We include this section simply to point out potential errors that we might find in histograms. In Example 1.13 we illustrate the construction of a histogram when interval widths are not all the same.

Example 1.13 Grocery Receipts (Unequal Interval Widths)

The dollar amounts of a random sample of 692 grocery receipts are summarized in the frequency distribution given in Table 1.13.

One possible error in constructing a histogram is to make the *heights* of the rectangles, and not the *areas* of the rectangles, proportional to the frequencies. We see this misleading histogram in Figure 1.17. Inspection of this incorrect histogram gives us the mistaken impression of a very large proportion of observations in the highest class. *Under no circumstance should we ever construct a histogram with this error. We illustrate this mistake only as a warning against deceptive graphs.*

With continuous upgrades in software packages has come an increase in the use and misuse of computer-generated graphs. Figure 1.18 illustrates a computer-generated histogram with equal interval widths, even though three of the classes vary in width. Again, *under no circumstance should we ever construct a histogram with this error. We illustrate this mistake only as a warning against deceptive graphs.*

Table 1.13 Grocery Receipts (Dollar Amounts)

DOLLAR AMOUNT	NUMBER OF RECEIPTS	PROPORTIONS
$ 0 < $10	84	84/692
$10 < $20	113	113/692
$20 < $30	112	112/692
$30 < $40	85	85/692
$40 < $50	77	77/692
$50 < $60	58	58/692
$60 < $80	75	75/692
$80 < $100	48	48/692
$100 < $200	40	40/692

To construct a histogram, we should observe that the quantities in Table 1.13 are interpreted in the usual way. Thus, of all these receipts, 113/692, or 16.3%, were in the range from $10 to under $20. We need to draw a histogram with the areas of the rectangles drawn over the intervals proportional to their frequencies. Since each of the first six intervals has a width of 10, we can draw rectangles of heights 84, 113, 112, 85, 77, and 58 over these intervals. The next two intervals have a width of 20, that is, twice the width of each of the first six. Thus, in order for their areas to be proportional to the frequencies, the rectangles drawn over these intervals should have heights that are one-half of the corresponding frequencies—that is 37.5 and 24.

Finally, the last interval has a width of 100, ten times the width of each of the first six. It follows that the height of the rectangle drawn over this last interval should be one-tenth of the frequency. That is, the height of the last rectangle should be 4. The reason that we make the areas of these rectangles proportional to the frequencies is that visually we associate area with size. We see in Figure 1.19 a histogram that avoids the errors illustrated in Figure 1.17 and Figure 1.18.

Figure 1.17   Misleading Histogram of Grocery Receipts (Error: Heights Proportional to Frequencies)

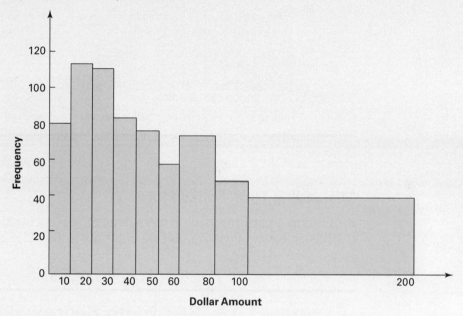

Figure 1.18   Misleading Histogram of Grocery Receipts (Error: Unequal Interval Widths)

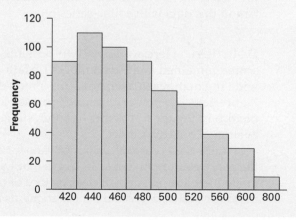

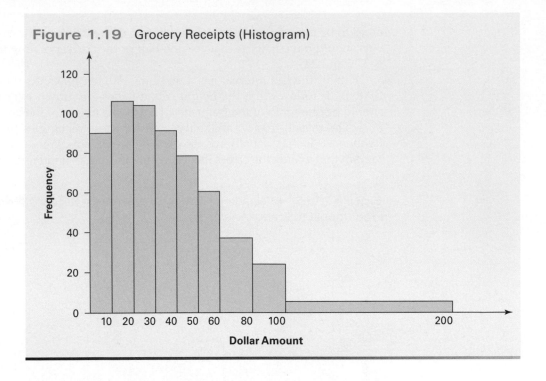

Figure 1.19 Grocery Receipts (Histogram)

Misleading Time-Series Plots

By selecting a particular scale of measurement, we can, in a time-series plot, create an impression either of relative stability or of substantial fluctuation over time.

Example 1.14 SAT Math Scores 1989–2009 (Choice of Scale for Time-Series Plot)

The average SAT mathematics scores for the incoming first-year students at one university from 1989 to 2009 are contained in the data file **SAT Math 1989–2009**. Graph this data with a time-series plot.

Solution Here we show two possible time-series plots for the SAT math scores contained in the data file **SAT Math 1989–2009**. Figure 1.20 suggests quite wide fluctuations in average scores. Precisely the same information is graphed in Figure 1.21, but now with a much coarser scale on the vertical axis. The resulting picture in Figure 1.21 is much flatter, suggesting considerably less variability in average scores over time.

There is no "correct" choice of scale for any particular time series plot. Rather, the conclusion from Example 1.14 is that looking at the shape of the plot alone is inadequate for obtaining a clear picture of the data. It is also necessary to keep in mind the scale on which the measurements are made.

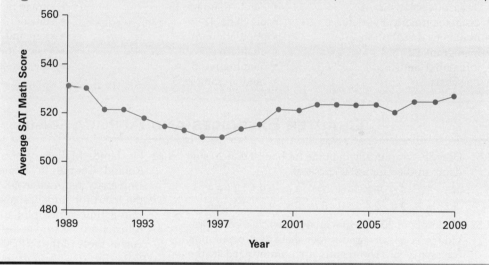

Figure 1.20 SAT Math Scores: First-Year Students (Time-Series Plot)

Figure 1.21 SAT Math Scores: First-Year Students (Revised Time-Series Plot)

EXERCISES

Basic Exercises

1.47 A supervisor of a plant kept records of the time (in seconds) that employees needed to complete a particular task. The data are summarized as follows:

Time	30 < 40	40 < 50	50 < 60	60 < 80	80 < 100	100 < 150
Number	10	15	20	30	24	20

a. Graph the data with a histogram.
b. Discuss possible errors.

1.48 The following table lists the number of daily visitors to the Web site of a new business during its first year.

Month	Number	Month	Number
1	5,400	7	5,600
2	5,372	8	5,520
3	5,265	9	5,280
4	5,250	10	5,400
5	5,289	11	5,448
6	5,350	12	5,500

a. Graph the data with a time-series plot using a vertical scale from 5,000 to 5,700.
b. Graph the data with a time-series plot using a vertical scale from 4,000 to 7,000.
c. Comment on the difference between these two time-series plots.

Application Exercises
1.49 ● The data file **Exchange Rate** shows an index of the value of the U.S. dollar against trading partners' currencies over 12 consecutive months.

a. Draw a time-series plot of this data using a vertical axis that ranges from 92 to 106.
b. Draw a time-series plot of this data using a vertical axis that ranges from 75 to 120.
c. Comment on these two time-series plots.

1.50 ● The data file **Inventory Sales** shows the inventory-sales ratio for manufacturing and trade in the United States over a period of 12 years. Draw two time-series plots for this series with different vertical ranges. Comment on your findings.

KEY WORDS

- bar chart, 8
- categorical variable, 4
- continuous numerical variable, 5
- cross table, 28
- cumulative frequency distribution, 20
- descriptive statistics, 4
- discrete numerical variable, 5
- frequency distribution, 7
- histogram, 22
- inferential statistics, 4
- line chart, 16

- nominal, 5
- nonsampling errors, 3
- numerical variables, 5
- ogive, 22
- ordinal, 5
- parameter, 3
- Pareto diagram, 13
- pie chart, 11
- population, 2
- qualitative, 5
- quantitative, 5
- random sample, 3

- relative frequency distribution, 20
- relative cumulative frequency distribution, 20
- sample, 2
- sampling error, 3
- scatter plot, 26
- simple random sampling, 3
- statistic, 3
- stem-and-leaf display, 23
- systematic sampling, 40
- time-series plot, 16

CHAPTER EXERCISES AND APPLICATIONS

1.51 Describe graphically the time (in hours) that 20 students studied for a statistics test.

| 6.5 | 5.8 | 4.5 | 6.2 | 4.8 | 7.3 | 4.6 | 3.9 | 4.4 | 5.5 |
| 5.2 | 6.7 | 3.0 | 2.4 | 5.0 | 3.6 | 2.9 | 4.0 | 2.8 | 3.6 |

1.52 A sample of 20 financial analysts was asked to provide forecasts of earnings per share of a corporation for next year. The results are summarized in the following table:

Forecast	9.95	10.45	10.95	11.45	11.95
($ per share)	<10.45	<10.95	<11.45	<11.95	<12.45
Number of Analysts	2	8	6	3	1

a. Draw the histogram.
b. Find the relative frequencies.
c. Find the cumulative frequencies.
d. Find and interpret the relative cumulative frequencies.

1.53 In one region it was found that 28% of people with incomes less than $50,000 use the Internet; 48% of those with incomes between $50,000 to $74,999 use the Internet; and 70% of those with incomes of at least $75,000 use the Internet. Use a pie chart or a bar chart to plot this data.

1.54 Dr. James Mallett, professor and director of the Roland George Investment Institute at Stetson University, reported in *USA Today* (Reference 3) that the trend for student-managed funds is increasing. Use a time-series plot to describe the quarterly returns of one university MBA Investment Fund versus those of the S&P 500:

	Nov. 1998	Feb. 1999	May 1999	Aug. 1999	Nov. 1999
MBA Investment Fund	16.1%	12.5%	2.5%	3.6%	7.0%
S&P 500	21.6%	6.4%	5.1%	1.4%	5.2%

1.55 Are Americans familiar with the new tax laws? One survey (Reference 1) found the following percentages of respondents who were familiar with tax law changes: 70% were familiar with the child tax credit, 52% with the marriage penalty, 51% with capital gains, 44% with dividends, 41% with marginal tax rates, and 25% were unaware of any changes. Describe the data graphically.

1.56 A team of undergraduate business students was asked to recommend improvement to the data entry process at the county appraiser's office. The team identified several types of errors, such as posting an incorrect name or entering an incorrect parcel number. The deed abstractors were asked to keep a record of the errors in data entry that were sent to them. The following table is a frequency distribution of errors:

Defect	Total
Posting error in name	23
Posting error in parcel	21
Property sold after tax bills were mailed	5
Inappropriate call transfer (not part of deeds/mapping)	18
Posting error in legal description/incomplete legal description	4
Deeds received after tax bills printed	6
Correspondence errors	2
Miscellaneous errors	1

    a. Construct a Pareto diagram of these defects in data entry.

    b. What recommendations would you suggest to the county appraiser?

1.57 The top five on-line retailers as listed by Nielsen Online for December 2007 are given in the following table (Reference 11). Graphically display the data.

Rank	Retailer	Dec 07 Unique Audience
1	eBay	124,132,042
2	Amazon	99,863,339
3	Target	37,717,553
4	Wal-Mart Stores	36,994,959
5	Best Buy	24,089,267

1.58 The top five on-line apparel/beauty retailers as listed by Nielsen Online for December 2007 are given in the following table (Reference 10). Graphically display the data.

Rank	Apparel/Beauty Retailer	Dec 07 Unique Audience
1	eBay Clothing, Shoes, & Accessories	22,865,384
2	eBay Jewelry and Watches	8,561,389
3	L.L. Bean	5,886,068
4	Victoria's Secret	5,789,312
5	Zappos.com	5,747,256

1.59 What is the relationship between the price of paint and the demand for this paint? A random sample of (price, quantity) data for 7 days of operation was obtained. Prepare a plot and describe the relationship between quantity and price, with emphasis on any unusual observations.

(10, 100) (8, 120) (5, 200) (4, 200) (10, 90) (7, 110) (6, 150)

1.60 A consumer goods company has been studying the effect of advertising on total profits. As part of this study, data on advertising expenditures (1,000s) and total sales (1,000s) were collected for a 5-month period and are as follows:

(10, 100)　(15, 200)　(7, 80)　(12, 120)　(14, 150)

The first number is advertising expenditures and the second is total sales. Plot the data.

1.61 The president of Floor Coverings Unlimited wants information concerning the relationship between retail experience (years) and weekly sales (in hundreds of dollars). He obtained the following random sample of experience and weekly sales:

(2, 5) (4, 10) (3, 8) (6, 18) (3, 6) (5, 15) (6, 20) (2, 4)

The first number for each observation is years of experience and the second is weekly sales. Plot the data.

1.62 A random sample of 12 college baseball players participated in a special weight-training program in an attempt to improve their batting averages. The program lasted for 20 weeks immediately prior to the start of the baseball season. The average number of hours per week and the change in their batting averages from the preceding season are as follows:

(8.0, 10)　(20.0, 100)　(5.4, −10)　(12.4, 79)　(9.2, 50)
(15.0, 89)　(6.0, 34)　(8.0, 30)　(18.0, 68)　(25.0, 110)
(10.0, 34)　(5.0, 10)

Plot the data. Does it appear that the weight-training program was successful?

1.63 Four types of checking accounts are offered by one bank. Suppose that recently a random sample of 300 bank customers was surveyed and asked several questions. It was found that 60% of the respondents preferred Easy Checking, 12% Intelligent Checking, 18% Super Checking, and the remainder preferred Ultimate Checking. Of those who selected Easy Checking, 100 were females; one-third of the respondents who selected Intelligent Checking were males; half of the respondents who selected Super Checking were males; and 80% of respondents who selected Ultimate Checking were males.

    a. Describe the data with a cross table.

    b. Describe the data graphically.

1.64 How did people first learn about a new product? A random sample of 200 shoppers at a particular store was asked their age and whether they heard about the product from a friend or through a local newspaper advertisement. The results indicated that 50 respondents were under 21 years of age, 90 people were in the age group between 21 and 35, and 60 respondents were older than 35 years of age. Of those under

21 years old, 30 heard about the product from a friend, and the remainder learned about the product through an advertisement in the local paper. One-third of the people in the age category from 21 to 35 first learned about the product from the same newspaper advertisement; the remainder of this age group learned about the product from a friend. A friend informed 30% of the people in the over-35 age category about the product; the remainder learned about it from the local newspaper advertisement.

   a. Describe the data with a cross table.
   b. Describe the data graphically.

1.65 A random sample of customers was asked to select their favorite soft drink from a list of five brands. The results showed that 30 preferred Brand A, 50 preferred Brand B, 46 preferred Brand C, 100 preferred Brand D, and 14 preferred Brand E.

   a. Construct a pie chart.
   b. Construct a bar chart.

1.66 ⬤ The president of a small private 4-year university requested data on the number of first-year students and the number of transfer students who entered the university this year and for the last 10 years. The data are stored in the data file **University Enrollments 1995–2005**.

   a. Construct a time-series plot of first-year enrolments.
   b. Construct a time-series plot of transfer enrolments.

1.67 Construct a time-series plot of population growth for the state of New York from 1997 to the present. (*Hint*: check www.census.gov)

1.68 ⬤ Florin, owner of Florin' Flower Mart, randomly sampled 124 customers in order to obtain data such as a customer's method of payment (Visa, MasterCard, American Express, cash, or some other method) and the day of the week that the customer made the purchase (except for when the store is closed on Sundays). The data is contained in the data file **Florin**. Construct the following:

   a. A cross table of the variables "method of payment" and "day of purchase"
   b. A pie chart of day of purchase

1.69 A supermarket developer has conducted a large study to determine alcohol preferences based on the type of vehicle typically driven to a shopping center. A random sample of 100 car drivers and a second random sample of 100 pickup truck drivers were interviewed and asked to indicate their preference for beer or wine. The results indicated that 68% of car drivers preferred wine, while 71% of pickup truck drivers preferred beer. Construct a cross table and bar chart of this information.

1.70 ⬤ The closing costs of shares of Microsoft (MSFT) from May 20, 2008, through June 20, 2008, are contained in the data file **MSFT Stock Prices**. Construct a time-series plot of the closing costs.

Appendix

1   SYSTEMATIC SAMPLING

Systematic sampling is a statistical sampling procedure often used as an alternative to random sampling.

> ### Systematic Sampling
> Suppose that the population list is arranged in some fashion unconnected with the subject of interest. **Systematic sampling** involves the selection of every jth item in the population, where j is the ratio of the population size N to the desired sample size, n; that is, $j = N/n$. Randomly select a number from 1 to j to obtain the first item to be included in your systematic sample.

Suppose that a sample size of 100 is desired and that the population consists of 5,000 names in alphabetical order. Then $j = 50$. Randomly select a number from 1 to 50. If your number is 20, select it and every 50th number, giving the systematic sample of elements numbered 20, 70, 120,

170, and so forth until all 100 items are selected. A systematic sample is analyzed in the same fashion as a simple random sample on the grounds that, relative to the subject of inquiry, the population listing is already in random order. The danger is that there could be some subtle, unsuspected link between the ordering of the population and the subject under study. If this was so, bias would be induced if systematic sampling was employed. Systematic samples provide a good representation of the population if there is no cyclical variation in the population.

2   NONSAMPLING ERRORS

Examples of nonsampling errors include the following:

1. *The population actually sampled is not the relevant one.*   A celebrated instance of this sort occurred in 1936, when *Literary Digest* magazine confidently predicted that Alfred Landon would win the presidential election over Franklin Roosevelt. However, Roosevelt won by a very comfortable margin. This erroneous forecast resulted from the fact that the members of the *Digest*'s sample had been taken from telephone directories and other listings, such as magazine subscription lists and automobile registrations. These sources considerably underrepresented the poor, who were predominantly Democrats. To make an inference about a population (in this case the U.S. electorate), it is important to sample that population and not some subgroup of it, however convenient the latter course might appear.

2. *Survey subjects may give inaccurate or dishonest answers.*   This could happen because questions are phrased in a manner that is difficult to understand or in a way that appears to make a particular answer seem more palatable or more desirable. Also, many questions that one might want to ask are so sensitive that it would be foolhardy to expect uniformly honest responses. Suppose, for example, that a plant manager wants to assess the annual losses to the company caused by employee thefts. In principle, a random sample of employees could be selected and sample members asked, "What have you stolen from this plant in the past 12 months?" This is clearly not the most reliable means of obtaining the required information!

3. *Nonresponse to survey questions.*   Survey subjects may not respond at all, or they may not respond to certain questions. If this is substantial, it can induce additional sampling and nonsampling errors. The sampling error arises because the achieved sample size will be smaller than that intended. Nonsampling error possibly occurs because, in effect, the population being sampled is not the population of interest. The results obtained can be regarded as a random sample *from the population that is willing to respond*. These people may differ in important ways from the larger population. If this is so, a bias will be induced in the resulting estimates.

REFERENCES

1. Block, Sandra. Source: H&R Block November 2003 survey. Reprinted in "The Trouble with Taxes: They're Too Hard, They Don't Make Sense, and There's No Easy Fix." *USA Today*, April 9, 2004, p. B1.

2. Carlson, William L. 1972. Alcohol Usage of the Nighttime Driver. *Journal of Safety Research* 4 (March): 12.

3. Fogarty, Thomas A. 1999. Student-Run Funds Teach Real Skills with Real Cash. *USA Today* (December): 12B.

4. Jones, Gerald Everett Jones. 2007. *How to Lie with Charts*. Santa Monica, CA: La Puerta Productions.

5. Michelson, Stuart, J. Stryker and B. Thorne. 2008. The Sarbanes-Oxley Act of 2002: What Impact Has It Had on Small Business Firms? Submitted for publication.

6. "No. 373. Threatened and Endangered Wildlife and Plant Species— Number: 2007." Source: U.S. Fish and Wildlife Service, *Endangered Species Bulletin*. Reprinted in the 2008 *Statistical Abstract of the United States*, Geography and Environment. See http://www.census.gov/prod/2007pubs/08abstract/geo.pdf (Accessed 19 December 2008). Information for the current year is available at http://www.census.gov/compendia/statab/

7. "No. 969. Gross Domestic Product in Manufacturing in Current and Real (2000) Dollars by Industry: 2000-2006." Source: U.S. Bureau of Economic Analysis, *Survey of Current Business*, May 2007. Reprinted in the 2008 *Statistical Abstract of the United States*, Manufacturers. See http://www.census.gov/compendia/statab/tables/08s0969.xls. Information for the current year is available at http://www.census.gov/compendia/statab/.

8. "No. 1278. U.S. Exports, Imports, and Merchandise Trade Balance by Country: 1990–2006." Source: U.S. Census Bureau. Reprinted in the 2008 *Statistical Abstract of the United States*, Foreign Commerce and Aid. See http://www.census.gov/compendia/statab/tables/08s1278.xls. Information for the current year is available at http://www.census.gov/compendia/statab/

9. Stevens, Stanley Smith. 1946. On the theory of scales of measurement. *Science* 103:677–680.

10. "Top Ten Apparel/Beauty Retailers – December 07 Unique Audience." Source: Nielsen Online, December, 2007. Reprinted in "Nielsen Reports 875 Million Consumers Have Shopped Online." Nielsen Media Research, January 28, 2008. See http://www.nielsenmedia.com. Viewed July 27, 2008.

11. "Top Ten Online Retailers – December 07 Unique Audience." Source: Nielsen Online, December 2007. Reprinted in "Nielsen Reports 875 Million Consumers Have Shopped Online." Nielsen Media Research, January 28, 2008. See http://www.nielsenmedia.com. Viewed July 27, 2008.

12. Tufte, E. R. 1983. *The Visual Display of Quantitative Information*. Cheshire, CT: Graphics Press.

13. Tukey, J. 1977. *Exploratory Data Analysis*. Reading, MA: Addison-Wesley.

14. US Dollars (USD) to 1 Euro (EUR). http://www.exchange-rates.org/history/USD/EUR/T.

15. Wainer, H. 1997. *Visual Revelations: Graphical Tales of Fate and Deception from Napoleon Bonaparte to Ross Perot*. New York: Copernicus/Springer-Verlag.

16. "World's Largest Corporations." July 21, 2008. *Fortune*, F-1.

17. "Worldwide Active Internet Home Users, May 2008." Source: Nielsen Online, 2008. Reprinted in "Active Home Internet Users by Country, May 2008" by Enid Burns, The ClickZ Network, July 11, 2008. See http://www.clickz.com/showPage.html?page=3630197.

Chapter 2

Describing Data: *Numerical*

Introduction

In Chapter 1 we described data graphically. In this chapter we describe data numerically with measures of central tendency, measures of variability, measures for grouped data, and measures of the direction and strength of relationships between two variables.

2.1 MEASURES OF CENTRAL TENDENCY

We are often able to determine if data tend to center or cluster around some value by constructing a histogram. Measures of central tendency provide numerical information about a "typical" observation in the data. In this section we discuss the mean, median, mode, and the geometric mean.

Mean, Median, Mode

In Chapter 1 we introduced the terms *parameter* and *statistic*. A parameter refers to a specific population characteristic; a statistic refers to a specific sample characteristic. Measures of central tendency are usually computed from sample data, rather than from population data. One measure of central tendency that quickly comes to mind is the *arithmetic mean*, usually just called the *mean*.

43

Arithmetic Mean

The **arithmetic mean** (or simply *mean*) of a set of data is the sum of the data values divided by the number of observations. If the data set is the entire population of data, then the *population mean*, μ, is a *parameter* given by

$$\mu = \frac{\sum_{i=1}^{N} x_i}{N} = \frac{x_1 + x_2 + \cdots + x_N}{N} \qquad (2.1)$$

where N = population size and Σ means "the sum of."

If the data set is from a sample, then the *sample mean*, $\bar{x}$, is a *statistic* given by

$$\bar{x} = \frac{\sum_{i=1}^{n} x_i}{n} \qquad (2.2)$$

where n = sample size and Σ means "the sum of."

To locate the *median*, we must arrange the data in either increasing or decreasing order.

Median

The **median** is the middle observation of a set of observations that are arranged in increasing (or decreasing) order. If the sample size, n, is an odd number, the median is the middle observation. If the sample size, n, is an even number, the median is the average of the two middle observations. The median will be the number located in the

$$0.50(n+1)\text{th ordered position.} \qquad (2.3)$$

Mode

The **mode**, if one exists, is the most frequently occurring value.

Example 2.1 Accounting Final Exam Grades (Measures of Central Tendency)

The 10 accounting final exam grades given in Example 1.9 are as follows:

88	51	63	85	79	65	79	70	73	77

Find the mean, median, and mode.

Solution The sample mean grade is as follows:

$$\bar{x} = \frac{\sum_{i=1}^{n} x_i}{n} = \frac{88 + 51 + 63 + \cdots + 77}{10} = 73$$

Next, we arrange the data from lowest to highest grade.

51   63   65   70   73   77   79   79   85   88

The median grade is 75, which is located in the 0.5(10+1) = 5.5th ordered position; that is, the median grade is midway between the 5th and 6th ordered data points: (73 + 77)/2 = 75. The mode is 79 since it appears twice and all the other grades appeared only once. Some data sets have no mode; other data sets may be bimodal with two modes.

The decision as to whether the mean, median, or mode is the appropriate measure to describe the central tendency of data is context-specific. One factor that influences our choice is the type of data, categorical or numerical, as discussed in Chapter 1.

Categorical data are best described by the median or the mode, not the mean. If one person strongly agrees (coded 5) with a particular statement and another person strongly disagrees (coded 1), is the mean "no opinion"? An obvious use of median and mode is by clothing retailers considering inventory of shoes, shirts, and other such items that are available in various sizes. The size of items sold most often, the mode, is then the one in heaviest demand. Knowing that the mean shirt size of European men is 41.13 or that the average shoe size of American women is 8.24 is useless, but knowing that the modal shirt size is 40 or the modal shoe size is 7 is valuable for inventory decisions. However, the mode may not represent the true center of numerical data. For this reason, the mode is used less frequently than either the mean or the median in business applications.

Example 2.2   Percentage Change in Earnings per Share (Measures of Central Tendency)

Find the mean, median, and mode for a random sample of eight U.S. corporations with the following percentage changes in earnings per share in the current year compared with the previous year:

0%   0%   8.1%   13.6%   19.4%   20.7%   10.0%   14.2%

Solution   The mean percentage change in earnings per share for this sample is

$$\bar{x} = \frac{\sum\limits_{i=1}^{n} x_i}{n} = \frac{0 + 0 + 8.1 + 13.6 + \cdots + 14.2}{8} = 10.75 \text{ or } 10.75\%$$

and the median percentage change in earnings per share is 11.8%. The mode is 0%, since it occurs twice and the other percentages occur only once. But this modal percentage rate does not represent the center of this sample data.

Numerical data are usually best described by the mean. However, in addition to the type of data, another factor to consider is the presence of outliers. The median is not affected by outliers, but the mean is. Whenever there are outliers in the data, we first need to look for possible causes. Check to see if simply an error in data entry occurred. The mean will be greater if large outliers are present, and it will be less when the data contain small outliers. The relationship between the mean and the median leads to an understanding of the shape of the distribution.

Shape of a Distribution

The shape of a distribution reveals whether data are evenly spread from its middle or center. Sometimes the center of the data divides a graph of the distribution into two "mirror images," so that the portion on one side of the middle is nearly identical to the portion on the other side. Graphs that have this shape are *symmetric*; those without this shape are asymmetric or *skewed*.

Symmetry
The shape of a distribution is said to be **symmetric** if the observations are balanced, or approximately evenly distributed, about its middle.

Skewness
A distribution is **skewed**, or asymmetric, if the observations are not symmetrically distributed on either side of the middle. A *positively skewed* distribution has a tail that extends to the right, in the direction of positive values. A *negatively skewed* distribution has a tail that extends to the left, in the direction of negative values.

A comparison of the mean to the median generally reveals information about the shape of the distribution. Figure 2.1A is negatively skewed, with the lowest observations extending over a wide range to the left. In this type of distribution the mean is less than the median. Figure 2.1B is symmetric and here the mean is equal to the median. Figure 2.1C has a long tail to the right, with a far more abrupt cut-off to the left. This distribution is *skewed to the right*, or *positively skewed* and the mean is greater than the median.

Figure 2.1A
Negatively
Skewed
Distribution
(*mean<median*)

Figure 2.1B
Symmetric
Distribution
(*mean=median*)

Figure 2.1C
Positively Skewed
Distribution
(*mean>median*)

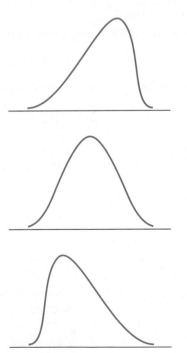

Manual computation of skewness is presented in the chapter appendix. In business and economics we most often identify skewness by the comparison of the mean and the median as illustrated in Figure 2.1A and Figure 2.1C.

Example 2.3   Grade Point Averages (Negatively Skewed)

Describe the distribution of grade point averages contained in the data file **GPAs**.

Solution   The data file **GPAs** contains a random sample of 155 grade point averages for students at one university. Figure 2.2 is a histogram of the data. Notice the long tail to the left. Figure 2.3 gives the descriptive measures of the data using SPSS. The mean of 3.14 is less than the median of 3.31. Also the median is less than the mode of 3.42. The graph and the comparison of the mean to the median suggest that this distribution is negatively skewed (a more formal computation of skewness appears in the chapter appendix).

Figure 2.2   Grade Point Averages (Negatively Skewed)

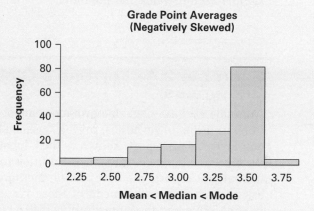

Figure 2.3   Grade Point Averages (SPSS)

Grade Point Averages

N	Valid	155
	Missing	0
Mean		3.1366
Median		3.3100
Mode		3.42
Std. Deviation		.36066
Variance		.130
Skewness		−1.221
Std. Error of Skewness		.195
Range		1.60
Minimum		2.12
Maximum		3.72
Percentiles	25	2.9800
	50	3.3100
	75	3.3700

The median is the preferred measure to describe the distribution of incomes in a city, state, or country. Distribution of incomes is often positively skewed since incomes tend to contain a relatively small proportion of high values. A large proportion of the population has relatively modest incomes, but the incomes of say, the highest 10% of all earners extend over a considerable range. As a result, the mean of such distributions is typically quite a bit higher than the median. The mean, which is inflated by the very wealthy, gives too optimistic a view of the economic well-being of the community. The median is then preferred to the mean.

We do *not* intend to imply that the median should *always* be preferred to the mean when the population or sample is skewed. There are times when the mean would still be the preferred measure even if the distribution were skewed. Consider an insurance company that most likely faces a right-skewed distribution of claim sizes. If the company wants to know the most typical claim size, the median is preferred. But suppose the company wants to know how much money needs to be budgeted to cover claims. Then the mean is preferred.

Distribution of profits may contain the presence of outliers. Unusually large observations tend to increase the mean, possibly resulting in positive skewness. Example 2.4 illustrates this situation.

Example 2.4 Fortune's Global 500 (Positive Skewness)

Annually *Fortune* magazine provides data about the world's largest 500 corporations in terms of revenues, profits, assets, stockholders' equity, and number of employees. This report, known as the Global 500, ranks corporations in terms of the aforementioned categories. In addition to individual company data, *Fortune*'s Global 500 reports median profits, median revenues, and median returns on assets, rather than the mean of these values due to extreme outliers. In 2007 ExxonMobile had the largest profits ($40.6 billion) making it the first company to ever exceed $40 billion in profits. Although General Motors was ranked 9th in revenues, it had a loss of $38.7 billion, making its rank 500 in terms of profits. Due to outliers like these, the Global 500 reports the median profit for 2007 ($2,029.2 billion) rather than the mean profit. Based on *Fortune*'s Global 500 listing for the year 2007 (Reference 14), we know that Telefónica is ranked 25th with a $12,190.2 billion profit and the Santander Group is ranked 26th with profits of $12,401.3 billion. We calculated the mean profit for these 50 companies as $13,709.7 billion as shown in Figure 2.4. Describe the shape of the distribution of profits for the top 50 highest profit companies.

Solution By Equation 2.3 with $n = 50$, the median profit will be found in the 25.5th ordered position. Since Telefónica is ranked 25th with a $12,190.2 billion profit and the Santander Group is ranked 26th with profits of $12,401.3 billion, the median is found as follows:

$$\text{Median} = \$12,190.2 + 0.50(\$12,401.3 - \$12,190.2) = \$12,295.75 \text{ billion}$$

Thus, the mean profit for these 50 companies ($13,709.7 billion) exceeds the median profit of $12,295.75 billion. The shape of the distribution of profits for the top 50 of the world's largest companies appears to be positively skewed.

Figure 2.4 World's Top 50 Highest Profit Corporations (Positively Skewed)

2007 Profits ($millions)

Mean	**13709.68**
Standard Error	812.874
Median	**12295.75**
Mode	#N/A
Standard Deviation	5747.887
Sample Variance	33038207
Range	32183.9
Minimum	8426.1
Maximum	40610
Sum	685483.9
Count	50

In spite of its advantage in discounting extreme observations, the median is used less frequently than the mean. In Chapter 7 we discuss certain properties of the mean that make it more attractive than the median in many situations. The reason is that the theoretical development of inferential procedures based on the mean, and measures related to it, is considerably more straightforward than the development of procedures based on the median.

Geometric Mean

Another measure of central tendency that is important in business and economics, but often overlooked, is the *geometric mean*.

Geometric Mean

The **Geometric Mean**, $\bar{x}_g$, is the nth root of the product of n numbers:

$$\bar{x}_g = \sqrt[n]{(x_1 \times x_2 \times \cdots \times x_n)} = (x_1 \times x_2 \times \cdots \times x_n)^{\frac{1}{n}} \qquad (2.4)$$

The **Geometric Mean Rate of Return**, $\bar{r}_g$,

$$\bar{r}_g = (x_1 \times x_2 \times \cdots \times x_n)^{\frac{1}{n}} - 1 \qquad (2.5)$$

gives the mean percentage return of an investment over time.

Consider the two numbers 20 and 5. The arithmetic mean is 12.5. But the geometric mean of the numbers 20 and 5 is $\sqrt{100} = 10$.

Business analysts and economists who are interested in growth over a number of time periods use the geometric mean. Applications of the geometric mean in finance include compound interest over several years, total sales growth, and population growth. An important question concerns the average growth each year that will result in a certain total growth over several years.

Example 2.5   Annual Growth Rate (Geometric Mean)

Find the annual growth rate if sales have grown 25% over 5 years.

Solution   The intuitive but naive temptation is simply to divide total growth, 25%, by the number of time periods, 5, and conclude that the average annual growth rate is 5%. This result is incorrect because it ignores the compound effect of growth.

Suppose that the annual growth rate is actually 5%; then the total growth over 5 years will be

$$(1.05)\,(1.05)\,(1.05)\,(1.05)\,(1.05) = 1.2763$$

or 27.63%. However, the annual growth rate, r, that would yield 25% over 5 years must satisfy this equation:

$$(1 + r)^5 = 1.25$$

First, solve for the geometric mean:

$$\overline{X}_g = 1 + r = (1.25)^{1/5} = 1.046$$

The geometric mean growth rate is $\overline{r}_g = 0.046$, or 4.6%.

EXERCISES

Basic Exercises

2.1   A random sample of 5 weeks showed that a cruise agency received the following number of weekly specials to the Caribbean:

20   73   75   80   82

   a. Compute the mean, median, and mode.
   b. Which measure of central tendency best describes the data?

2.2   A department store manager is interested in the number of complaints received by the customer service department about the quality of electrical products sold by the store. Records over a 5-week period show the following number of complaints for each week:

13   15   8   16   8

   a. Compute the mean number of weekly complaints.
   b. Calculate the median number of weekly complaints.
   c. Find the mode.

2.3   Ten economists were asked to predict the percentage growth in the Consumer Price Index over the next year. Their forecasts were as follows:

3.6   3.1   3.9   3.7   3.5
3.7   3.4   3.0   3.7   3.4

   a. Compute the sample mean.
   b. Compute the sample median.
   c. Find the mode.

2.4   A department store chain randomly sampled 10 stores in a state. After a review of sales records, it was found that, compared with the same period last year, the following percentage increases in dollar sales had been achieved over the Christmas period this year:

10.2   3.1   5.9   7.0   3.7
2.9   6.8   7.3   8.2   4.3

   a. Calculate the mean percentage increase in dollar sales.
   b. Calculate the median.
   c. Comment on symmetry.

2.5   A sample of 12 senior executives found the following results for percentage of total compensation derived from bonus payments:

15.8   17.3   28.4   18.2   15.0   24.7
13.1   10.2   29.3   34.7   16.9   25.3

   a. Compute the sample median.
   b. Compute the sample mean.

2.6   The demand for bottled water increases during the hurricane season in Florida. A random sample of

7 hours showed that the following numbers of 1-gallon bottles were sold in one store:

40 55 62 43 50 60 65

a. Describe the central tendency of the data.
b. Comment on symmetry or skewness.

2.7 A manufacturer of portable radios obtained a sample of 50 radios from a week's output. The radios were thoroughly checked, and the number of defects was recorded as follows:

Number of defects	0	1	2	3
Number of radios	12	15	17	6

Find the measures of central tendency.

2.8 The ages of a sample of 12 students enrolled in an on-line macroeconomics course are as follows:

21 22 27 36 18 19

22 23 22 28 36 33

a. What is the mean age for this sample?
b. Find the median age.
c. What is the value of the modal age?

Application Exercises

2.9 The assessment rates (in percentages) assigned to a random sample of 40 commercially zoned parcels of land in the year 2008 are contained in the data file **Rates**.

a. Compute the mean, median, and modal percentage assessment rates.
b. Describe the symmetry or skewness of the data.

2.10 A sample of 33 accounting students recorded the number of hours spent studying the course material during the week before the final exam. The data are stored in the data file **Study**.

a. Compute the sample mean.
b. Compute the sample median.
c. Comment on symmetry or skewness.

2.11 The data file **Sun** contains the volumes for a random sample of 100 bottles (237 mL) of a new suntan lotion.

a. Find and interpret the mean volume.
b. Determine the median volume.
c. Are the data symmetric or skewed? Explain.

2.2 MEASURES OF VARIABILITY

The mean alone does not provide a complete or sufficient description of data. In this section we present descriptive numbers that measure the variability or spread of the observations from the mean. In particular, we include the range, quartiles, interquartile range, variance, standard deviation, and coefficient of variation. We will also describe data numerically by the five-number summary, with a brief discussion of basic rules to help us determine the percentage of observations within varying distances of the mean. We will conclude this section with a brief discussion of variability and shapes of histograms.

No two things are exactly alike. Variation exists in all areas. In sports, the star basketball player might score five 3-pointers in one game and none in the next or play 40 minutes in one game and only 24 minutes in the next game. The weather varies greatly from day to day, and even from hour to hour; grades on a test differ for students taking the same course with the same instructor; a person's blood pressure, pulse, cholesterol level, and caloric intake will vary daily. In business, variation is seen in sales, advertising costs, the percentage of product complaints, the number of new customers, and so forth.

While two data sets could have the same mean, the individual observations in one set could vary more from the mean than do the observations in the second set. Consider the following two sets of sample data:

Sample A:	1	2	1	36
Sample B:	8	9	10	13

Although the mean is 10 for both samples, clearly, the data in sample A are further from 10 than are the data in sample B. We need descriptive numbers to measure this spread.

Range and Interquartile Range

Range
Range is the difference between the largest and smallest observations.

The greater the spread of the data from the center of the distribution, the larger the range will be. Since the range takes into account only the largest and smallest observations, it is susceptible to considerable distortion if there is an unusual extreme observation. Although the range measures the *total* spread of the data, the range may be an unsatisfactory measure of variability (spread) because outliers, either very high or very low observations, influence it. One way to avoid this difficulty is to arrange the data in ascending or descending order, discard a few of the highest and a few of the lowest numbers, and find the range of those remaining. Sometimes the lowest 25% of the data and the highest 25% of the data will be removed. To do this, we define quartiles and the *interquartile range*, which measures the spread of the middle 50% of the data.

Quartiles
The **first quartile**, Q_1, (or 25th *percentile*) separates the smallest 25% of the data from the remainder of the data. The **second quartile**, Q_2, (or 50th percentile) is the median (see Equation 2.3).

The **third quartile**, Q_3, (or 75th **percentile**), separates the smallest 75% of the data from the remaining largest 25% of the data.

$$Q_1 = \text{the value in the } 0.25\ (n + 1)\text{th ordered position} \qquad (2.6)$$

$$Q_2 = \text{the value in the } 0.50\ (n + 1)\text{th ordered position}$$

$$Q_3 = \text{the value in the } 0.75\ (n + 1)\text{th ordered position} \qquad (2.7)$$

Example 2.6 Accounting Final Exam Grades (Quartiles)
Find the first and third quartiles of the ten accounting final exam grades (Example 1.9 and Example 2.1) listed here from lowest to highest grade:

51	63	65	70	73	77	79	79	85	88

Solution The first quartile, Q_1, is the value in the 0.25(10+1)th ordered position—that is, the value in the 2.75th ordered position. Some statisticians suggest that we round 2.75 to 3 and call the third ordered number, which is 65, the first quartile. However, we prefer to interpolate. First find the value in the 2nd ordered position. This grade is 63. Now add to it 75% of the distance between 63 and 65, which are the values in the 2nd and 3rd ordered positions. This gives the following:

$$Q_1 = 63 + 0.75(65 - 63) = 63 + 1.5 = 64.5$$

Do the same for the third quartile. $Q_3 =$ the value in the 0.75(10+1)th ordered position—that is, the value in the 8.25th ordered position. Again, some statisticians would simplify and reduce this to the 8th ordered position, or the value 79. Again, we interpolate. Find the value in the 8th ordered position, which is 79, and add to it 25% of the distance between the 8th and 9th ordered positions.

$$Q_3 = 79 + 0.25(85 - 79) = 79 + 1.5 = 80.5$$

Statisticians do not agree on one best method to calculate quartiles and have proposed different ways to find Q_1 and Q_3 (References 6, 7, 9, and 10). Langford (Reference 10) discusses 12 different methods to calculate quartiles that are used by statisticians and computer/calculator packages (such as SAS, MINITAB, JMP, TI-83 Plus, and Excel). Equation 2.6 and Equation 2.7, which rely on linear interpolation between ranked values, are used in this book.

Interquartile Range

The **Interquartile range (*IQR*)** measures the spread in the *middle 50%* of the data; it is the difference between the observation at Q_3, the **third quartile** (or 75th **percentile**), and the observation at Q_1, the **first quartile** (or 25th *percentile*). Thus,

$$IQR = Q_3 - Q_1 \qquad (2.8)$$

For the 10 accounting final exam scores, the interquartile range would be as follows:

$$IQR = Q_3 - Q_1 = 80.5 - 64.5 = 16$$

Five-Number Summary

The **five-number summary** refers to the five descriptive measures: minimum, first quartile, median, third quartile, and maximum. Clearly,

$$\text{Minimum} < Q_1 < \text{Median} < Q_3 < \text{Maximum}$$

For the accounting final exam data in Example 2.6, the five number summary is as follows:

$$51 < 64.5 < 75 < 80.5 < 88$$

Example 2.7 Self-Checkout Times at Gilotti's (Five-Number Summary)

Gilotti's, a neighborhood grocery, advertises that customers take less than 1 minute to pay if they use the self checkout system. Figure 2.5 is a stem-and-leaf display for a random sample of 25 self-checkout times (in seconds). Compute the five-number summary. The data is contained in the data file **Gilotti**.

Solution   From the stem-and-leaf display we see that the minimum time is 11 seconds and the maximum time is 42 seconds. The first quartile, Q_1, is located in the 0.25(25 + 1)th ordered position, which is the 6.5th ordered

Figure 2.5 Self-Checkout Times at Gilotti's Grocery

```
Stem-and-leaf
Minutes    N  = 25
Leaf Unit = 1.0

  9    1  1  2  4  6  7  8  8  9  9
 (9)   2  1  2  2  2  4  6  8  9  9
  7    3  0  1  2  3  4
  2    4  0  2
```

position. The value is 18 seconds. The third quartile, Q_3, is located in the 0.75(25 + 1)th ordered position, which is the 19.5th ordered position. The value is 30.5 seconds. The median time is 22 seconds. The range is calculated as 42 − 11 = 31 seconds; interquartile range = 30.5 − 18 = 12.5 seconds; that is, the *middle 50%* of the data have a spread of only 12.5 seconds. The five number summary is as follows:

$$\text{Minimum} = 11 < Q_1 = 18 < \text{Median} = 22 < Q_3 = 30.5 < \text{Maximum} = 42$$

Variance and Standard Deviation

Although range and interquartile range measure the spread of data, both measures take into account only two of the data values. We need a measure that would *average* the total (Σ) distance between each of the data values and the mean. But for *all* data sets, this sum will *always equal zero* since the mean is the center of the data. If the data value is less than the mean, the difference between the data value and the mean would be negative (and distance is not negative). If each of these differences is squared, then each observation (both above and below the mean) contributes to the sum of the squared terms. The average of the sum of squared terms is called the *variance*.

Variance

With respect to **variance**, the *population variance*, σ^2, is the sum of the squared differences between each observation and the population mean divided by the population size, N:

$$\sigma^2 = \frac{\sum_{i=1}^{N}(x_i - \mu)^2}{N} \tag{2.9}$$

The *sample variance*, s^2, is the sum of the squared differences between each observation and the sample mean divided by the sample size, n, minus 1:

$$s^2 = \frac{\sum_{i=1}^{n}(x_i - \bar{x})^2}{n - 1} \tag{2.10}$$

Notice that, for sample data, variance in Equation 2.10 is found by dividing the numerator by $(n-1)$ and not n. Since our goal is to find an average of squared deviations about the mean, one would expect division by n. So why is the denominator of sample variance given as $(n-1)$ in Equation 2.10? If we were to take a very large number of samples, each of size n, from the population and compute the sample variance, as given in Equation 2.10 for each of these samples, then the average of all of these sample variances would be the population variance, σ^2. In Chapter 6 we will see that this property indicates that the sample variance is an "unbiased estimator" of the population variance, σ^2. For now, we rely on mathematical statisticians who have shown that, if the population variance is unknown, a sample variance is a better estimator of the population variance if the denominator in the sample variance is $(n-1)$, rather than n.

To compute the variance requires squaring the distances, which then changes the unit of measurement to square units. The *standard deviation*, which is the square root of variance, restores the data to their original measurement unit. If the original measurements were in feet, the variance would be in feet squared, but the standard deviation would be in feet. The standard deviation measures the *average* spread around the mean.

Standard Deviation

With respect to **standard deviation**, the population *standard deviation*, σ, is the (positive) square root of the population variance and is defined as follows:

$$\sigma = \sqrt{\sigma^2} = \sqrt{\frac{\sum\limits_{i=1}^{N}(x_i - \mu)^2}{N}} \qquad (2.11)$$

The *sample standard deviation*, s, is as follows:

$$s = \sqrt{s^2} = \sqrt{\frac{\sum\limits_{i=1}^{n}(x_i - \bar{x})^2}{n-1}} \qquad (2.12)$$

Example 2.8 Corporate Executive Exercise Time (Variance and Standard Deviation)

How much time do corporate executives exercise daily? In the *Atlanta-Journal Constitution*'s on-line article "Stick to exercise time as if it were an appointment" the writer states that a study by Tufts Medical School of *Fortune* 500 Executives found that these executives had "elevated levels of cholesterol and blood pressure, typically worked up to 70 hours a week while devoting little time to exercise" (Reference 8). Training programs exist to help executives improve their health so that they can think more clearly and make better business decisions (Reference 1). Suppose that we randomly sample ten executives and obtain the following daily exercise times (in minutes):

20   35   28   22   10   40   23   32   28   30

Compute the variance and standard deviation.

Solution To calculate the standard deviation manually, follow these three steps:
Step 1: Calculate the sample mean, $\bar{x}$, by Equation 2.2. It is equal to 26.8 minutes.
Step 2: Find the difference between each of the daily times and the mean of 26.8.
Step 3: Square each difference. The result is Table 2.1.

Table 2.1 Executive Exercise Time

TIMES (MINUTES) X_I	DEVIATION ABOUT THE MEAN $(x_i - \bar{x})$	SQUARED DEVIATION ABOUT THE MEAN $(x_i - \bar{x})^2$
20	−6.8	46.24
35	8.2	67.24
28	1.2	1.44
22	−4.8	23.04
10	−16.8	282.24
40	13.2	174.24
23	−3.8	14.44
32	5.2	27.04
28	1.2	1.44
30	3.2	10.24

$$\sum_{i=1}^{10} x_i = 268 \qquad \sum_{i=1}^{10} (x_i - \bar{x}) = 0 \qquad \sum_{i=1}^{10} (x_i - \bar{x})^2 = 647.6$$

$$\bar{x} = 26.8$$

$$s = \sqrt{s^2} = \sqrt{\frac{\sum_{i=1}^{n} (x_i - \bar{x})^2}{n - 1}}$$

$$= \sqrt{\frac{647.6}{9}} \approx 8.5$$

There are numerous applications of standard deviation in business. Investors may want to compare the risk of different assets. If two assets have the same mean rates of return, then the asset with the smaller standard deviation has less risk than the asset with the larger standard deviation.

Example 2.9 Risk of a Single Asset (Standard Deviation)

Wes and Jennie Moore, owners of Moore's Foto Shop in western Pennsylvania, are considering two investment alternatives, asset A and asset B. They are not sure which of these two single assets is better, and they ask Sheila Newton, a financial planner, for some assistance.

Solution Sheila knows that the standard deviation, s, is the most common single indicator of the risk or variability of a single asset. In financial situations the fluctuation around a stock's actual rate of return and its expected rate of return is called the *risk* of the stock. The standard deviation measures the variation of returns around an asset's mean. Sheila obtains the rates of return on each asset for the last 5 years and calculates the means and standard deviations of each asset. The results for asset A are shown in Table 2.2.

Table 2.2 Rates of Return: Assets A

x_i	$(x_i - \bar{x})$	$(x_i - \bar{x})^2$
11.3	−0.9	0.81
12.5	0.3	0.09
13.0	0.8	0.64
12.0	−0.2	0.04
12.2	0	0

$$\sum_{i=1}^{5} x_i = 61.0 \qquad \sum_{i=1}^{5}(x_i - \bar{x}) = 0 \qquad \sum_{i=1}^{5}(x_i - \bar{x})^2 = 1.58$$

$$\bar{x} = \frac{\sum x_i}{n} = \frac{61.0}{5} = 12.2\% \qquad s = \sqrt{s^2} = \sqrt{\frac{\sum_{i=1}^{n}(x_i - \bar{x})^2}{n-1}}$$

$$= \sqrt{\frac{1.58}{4}} \approx 0.63$$

Similar computations would show that the mean of asset B is also 12.2% but the standard deviation of asset B is equal to 3.12. Since each asset has the same average rate of return of 12.2%, Sheila compares the standard deviations and determines that asset B is a more risky investment.

If the mean rates of return differ for the two assets, then the asset with the smaller coefficient of variation (Equation 2.14) will be less risky.

Coefficient of Variation

The *coefficient of variation* expresses the standard deviation as a percentage of the mean.

Coefficient of Variation
The **coefficient of variation, CV**, is a measure of relative dispersion that expresses the standard deviation as a percentage of the mean (provided the mean is positive).

The *population coefficient of variation* is

$$CV = \frac{\sigma}{\mu} \times 100\% \qquad \text{if } \mu > 0 \qquad (2.13)$$

The *sample coefficient of variation* is

$$CV = \frac{s}{\bar{x}} \times 100\% \qquad \text{if } \bar{x} > 0 \qquad (2.14)$$

If the standard deviations in sales for large and small stores selling similar goods are compared, the standard deviation for large stores will almost always be greater. A simple explanation is that a large store could be modeled as a number of small stores. Comparing variation using the standard deviation would be misleading. The coefficient of variation overcomes this problem by adjusting for the scale of units in the population.

Example 2.10 Stock Purchase Comparison (Coefficient of Variation)

In Example 2.9 two different investments with the same mean rate of return were considered. Now, the owners are considering purchasing shares of stock A or shares of stock B, both listed on the New York Stock Exchange. From the closing prices of both stocks over the last several months the standard deviations were found to be considerably different, with $s_A = \$2.00$ and $s_B = \$8.00$. Should stock A be purchased, since the standard deviation of stock B is larger?

Solution We might think that stock B is more volatile than stock A. However, the mean closing price for stock A is $4.00 and the mean closing price for stock B is $80.00. Next, the coefficients of variation are computed to measure and compare the risk of these competing investment opportunities:

$$CV_A = \frac{\$2.00}{\$4.00} \times 100\% = 50\% \quad \text{and} \quad CV_B = \frac{\$8.00}{\$80.00} \times 100\% = 10\%$$

Notice that the market value of stock A fluctuates more from period to period than does that of stock B.

Example 2.11 Employee Completion Times (Descriptive Measures)

In Example 1.8, we constructed a histogram for the time 110 employees took to complete a task. Provide the supervisor with numerical descriptive measures of the data contained in the data file **Employee Completion Times**.

Solution For larger data sets, it is much easier to obtain numerical measures with Excel or some statistical software. In Figure 2.6 (Excel output) we see that the mean completion time of 261 seconds is slightly less than the median completion time of 263 seconds. The most frequent time (mode) is 252 seconds, and the data ranges from a high of 299 seconds to a low of 222 seconds. The standard deviation is 17.5 seconds. Figure 2.7 (Minitab output) also includes the coefficient of variation, five-number summary, and interquartile range.

Figure 2.6   Employee Completion Times (Excel)

Time(seconds)	
Mean	261.0636
Standard Error	1.669741
Median	263
Mode	252
Standard Deviation	17.5124
Sample Variance	306.684
Kurtosis	−0.33805
Minimum	222
Maximum	299
Sum	28717
Count	110

Figure 2.7   Employee Completion Times (Minitab)

Descriptive Statistics: Time/Seconds

Variable	N	N*	Mean	SE Mean	StDev	Variance	CoefVar	Minimum
Minutes	110	0	261.06	1.67	17.51	306.68	6.71	222.00

Variable	Q1	Median	Q3	Maximum	Range	IQR	Skewness
Minutes	251.75	263.00	271.25	299.00	77.00	19.50	0.00

Chebychev's Theorem and the Empirical Rule

A Russian mathematician, Pafnuty Lvovich Chebychev (1821–1894), established data intervals for any data set, *regardless* of the shape of the distribution.

Chebychev's Theorem
For any population with mean μ, standard deviation σ, and k > 1, the percent of observations that lie within the interval $[\mu \pm k\sigma]$ is

$$\textit{at least } 100[1 - (1/k^2)]\% \tag{2.15}$$

where *k* is the number of standard deviations.

To see how Chebychev's theorem works in practice, we construct Table 2.3 for selected values of *k*.

Suppose that the mean grade on an exam is 72, with a standard deviation of 4. According to Chebychev's theorem, at least 75% of the scores are in the interval between 64 and 80, and at least 88.9% of the scores are in the interval between 60 and 84. Or suppose that the mean salary for a sample of employees is $33,500 and the standard

Table 2.3 Chebychev's Theorem for Selected Values of *k*

Selected Values of k > 1	1.5	2	2.5	3
[1 − (1/k²)]%	55.56%	75%	84%	88.89%

deviation is $1,554. By Chebychev's theorem at least 55.6% of the salaries must fall within (1.5) ($1,554) = $2,331 around the mean—that is, within the range $31,169–$35,831. Similarly, at least 75% of the salaries in this population must fall within $3,108 around the mean—that is, within the range $30,392 –$36,608.

The advantage of Chebychev's theorem is that its applicability extends to any population. However, it is within this guarantee that its major drawback lies. For many populations the percentage of values falling in any specified range is much higher than the *minimum* assured by Chebychev's theorem. In the real world many large populations provide mounded data that is at least approximately symmetric, with many of the data points clustered around the mean. We often think of this as the bell-shaped distribution. In Chapter 5 we will give a much more detailed explanation as the Empirical Rule and its more exact formula are one of the main focus points of statistics.

Empirical Rule (68%, 95%, or Almost All)

For many large populations (mounded, bell-shaped) the **empirical rule** provides an estimate of the approximate percentage of observations that are contained within one, two, or three standard deviations of the mean:

- Approximately **68%** of the observations are in the interval $\mu \pm 1\sigma$.
- Approximately **95%** of the observations are in the interval $\mu \pm 2\sigma$.
- Almost all of the observations are in the interval $\mu \pm 3\sigma$.

Consider a very large number of students taking a college entrance exam such as the SAT. And suppose the mean score on the mathematics section of the SAT is 550 with a standard deviation of 50.

Then by the empirical rule we estimate that roughly 68% of the scores are between 500 and 600 and that approximately 95% fall within the range 450 to 650. There is only a relatively small chance that an observation will differ from the mean by more than $\pm 2\sigma$; any observation that differs from the mean by more than $\pm 3\sigma$ is an outlier.

Example 2.12 Lifetimes of Light Bulbs (Chebychev's Theorem and Empirical Rule)

A company produces light bulbs with a mean lifetime of 1,200 hours and a standard deviation of 50 hours.

a. Describe the distribution of lifetimes if the shape of the population is unknown.
b. Describe the distribution of lifetimes if the shape of the distribution is known to be bell-shaped.

Solution   Using the mean of 1,200 and the standard deviation of 50, we find the following intervals:

$$\mu \pm 1\sigma = 1{,}200 \pm 50 = (1150, 1250)$$

$$\mu \pm 2\sigma = 1{,}200 \pm 2(50) = (1100, 1300)$$

$$\mu \pm 3\sigma = 1{,}200 \pm 3(50) = (1050, 1350)$$

a. Assuming that the shape of the distribution is unknown, we apply Chebychev's theorem. But be aware that $k > 1$. Therefore we cannot make any conclusions about the percentage of bulbs that last between 1,150 hours and 1,250 hours. We can conclude that at least 75% of the light bulbs will last between 1,100 hours and 1,300 hours and that at least 88.89% of the light bulbs will last between 1,050 hours and 1,350 hours.

b. If the shape of the distribution is bell-shaped, then we can conclude that approximately 68% of the light bulbs will last between 1,150 hours and 1,250 hours; that approximately 95% of the light bulbs will last between 1,100 hours and 1,300 hours; and that almost all of the bulbs will last between 1,050 hours and 1,350 hours. It would be very unusual for a light bulb to burn out in say 600 hours or 1,600 hours. Such values are possible, but not very likely. These lifetimes would definitely be outliers.

EXERCISES

Basic Exercises

2.12 Compute the variance and standard deviation of the following sample data:

6 8 7 10 3 5 9 8

2.13 Compute the variance and standard deviation of the following sample data:

3 0 −2 −1 5 10

2.14 Calculate the coefficient of variation for the following sample data:

10 8 11 7 9

2.15 The time (in seconds) that a random sample of employees took to complete a task is as follows:

23 35 14 37 28 45
12 40 27 13 26 25
37 20 29 49 40 13
27 16 40 20 13 66

a. Find the mean time.
b. Find the standard deviation.
c. Find the five-number summary.
d. Find the coefficient of variation.

2.16 The following stem-and-leaf display contains sample data:

Stem	Leaves
3	0 1
4	5 8 8
5	0 3 4 5 7 8 9
6	1 4 7 9
7	3 6 9
8	0 3 7

a. Calculate IQR.
b. Find the 8th decile.
c. Find the 92nd percentile.

2.17 A random sample of data has a mean of 75 and a variance of 25.

a. Use Chebychev's theorem to determine the percent of observations between 65 and 85.
b. If the data are mounded, use the empirical rule to find the approximate percent of observations between 65 and 85.

2.18 If the mean of a population is 250 and its standard deviation is 20, approximately what proportion of observations is in the interval between

    a. 190 and 310?
    b. 210 and 290?

2.19 A set of data is mounded with a mean of 450 and a variance of 625. Approximately what proportion of the observations is

    a. greater than 425?
    b. less than 500?
    c. greater than 525?

Application Exercises

2.20 The annual percentage returns on common stocks over a 7-year period were as follows:

    4.0% 14.3% 19.0% −14.7% −26.5% 37.2% 23.8%

    Over the same period the annual percentage returns on U.S. Treasury bills were as follows:

    6.5% 4.4% 3.8% 6.9% 8.0% 5.8% 5.1%

    a. Compare the means of these two population distributions.
    b. Compare the standard deviations of these two population distributions.

2.21 A sample of eight U.S. corporations showed the following percentage changes in earnings per share in the current year compared with the previous year:

    13.6% 25.5% 43.6% −19.8%
    12.0% 36.3% 14.3% −13.8%

Find the sample mean percentage change in earnings per share.

2.22 🔵 The operations manager at a plant that bottles natural spring water wants to be sure that the filling process for 1-gallon bottles (1 gallon is approximately 3.785 liters) is operating properly. A random sample of 75 bottles is selected and the contents are measured. The volume of each bottle is contained in the data file **Water**.

    a. Find the range, variance, and standard deviation of the volumes.
    b. Find the five-number summary of the volumes.
    c. Find and interpret the interquartile range for the data.
    d. Find the value of the coefficient of variation.

2.23 🔵 The test scores of 40 students are stored in the data file **Scores**.

    a. Find the mean grade on this test.
    b. Find the standard deviation in test scores.
    c. Find the coefficient of variation.
    d. Find and interpret the interquartile range.

2.24 🔵 The assessment rates (in percentages) assigned to a random sample of 40 commercially zoned parcels of land in the year 2008 are stored in the data file **Rates**.

    a. What is the standard deviation in the assessment rates?
    b. Approximately what proportion of the rates will be within ± 2 standard deviations of the mean?

2.25 🔵 Calculate the mean dollar amount and the standard deviation for the dollar amounts charged to a Visa account at Florin's Flower Shop. Data are stored in the data file **Florin**.

2.3 WEIGHTED MEAN AND MEASURES OF GROUPED DATA

Some situations require a special type of mean called a *weighted mean*. Applications of weighted means include, but are not limited to, calculating GPA, determining average stock recommendation, and approximating the mean of grouped data.

Weighted Mean
The **weighted mean** of a set of data is

$$\bar{x} = \frac{\sum\limits_{i=1}^{n} w_i x_i}{n} = \frac{w_1 x_1 + w_2 x_2 + \cdots + w_n x_n}{n} \tag{2.16}$$

where w_i = weight of ith observation and $n = \sum w_i$.

One important situation that requires the use of a weighted mean is the calculation of grade point average (GPA).

Example 2.13 Grade Point Average (Weighted Mean)

Suppose that a student who completed 15 credit hours during his first semester of college received one A, one B, one C, and one D. Suppose that a value of 4 is used for an A, 3 for a B, 2 for a C, 1 for a D, and 0 for an F. Calculate the student's semester GPA.

Solution If each course were given the same number of credit hours, the student's semester GPA would equal the following:

$$\bar{x} = \frac{\sum_{i=1}^{n} x_i}{n} = \frac{x_1 + x_2 + \cdots + x_n}{n} = \frac{4 + 3 + 2 + 1}{4} = 2.5$$

However, each course is not worth the same number of credit hours. The A was earned in a *three*-credit-hour English course, and the B was earned in a *three*-credit-hour math course, but the C was earned in a *four*-credit-hour biology lab course, and the D grade, unfortunately, was earned in a *five*-credit-hour Spanish class. Computation of the mean is

$$\bar{x} = \frac{(4 + 4 + 4) + (3 + 3 + 3) + (2 + 2 + 2 + 2) + (1 + 1 + 1 + 1 + 1)}{15} = \frac{34}{15} = 2.267$$

where the numerator is the sum of (4 + 4 + 4) representing the three English credits, plus (3 + 3 + 3) for the three math credits, plus (2 + 2 + 2 + 2) for the four biology lab credits, plus (1 + 1 + 1 + 1 + 1) for the five Spanish credits. Using Equation 2.16 the computation of the GPA is given in Table 2.4.

$$\bar{x} = \frac{\sum_{i=1}^{n} w_i x_i}{n} = \frac{w_1 x_1 + w_2 x_2 + \cdots + w_n x_n}{n} = \frac{12 + 9 + 8 + 5}{15} = \frac{34}{15} = 2.267$$

Table 2.4 Semester Academic Record

COURSE	GRADE	CREDIT HOURS w_i	VALUE x_i	CREDIT HOURS × (VALUE) $w_i x_i$
English	A	3	4	12
Math	B	3	3	9
Biology lab	C	4	2	8
Spanish	D	5	1	5
Total		15		34

Example 2.14 Microsoft Corp.: Zack's Recommendation (Weighted Mean)

Zack's Investment Research is a leading investment research firm. Zack's will make one of the following recommendations with corresponding weights for a given stock: Strong Buy (1), Moderate Buy (2), Hold (3), Moderate Sell (4), or

Strong Sell (5). On a particular day 10 analysts recommend Strong Buy, 3 analysts recommend Moderate Buy, and 6 analysts recommend Hold for Microsoft Stock (Reference 11)? Find Zack's mean recommendation.

Solution Zack's computes the weighted mean. Table 2.5 shows the weights for each recommendation and the computation leading to Zack's Investment Research's recommendation. Zack's Investment Research's decision is based on the following weighted mean recommendation conversion values: if the weighted mean is 1, Strong Buy; 1.1 through 2.0, Moderate Buy; 2.1 through 3.0, Hold; 3.1 through 4.0, Moderate Sell; 4.1 through 5, Strong Sell (Reference 11).

Table 2.5 Computation of Zack's Investment Research's Average Brokerage Recommendation

COURSE	NUMBER OF ANALYSTS w_i	VALUE x_i	CREDIT HOURS × (VALUE) $w_i x_i$
Strong Buy	10	1	10
Moderate Buy	3	2	6
Hold	6	3	18
Moderate Sell	0	4	0
Strong Sell	0	5	0

$$\bar{x} = \frac{\sum_{i=1}^{n} w_i x_i}{n} = \frac{10 + 6 + 18 + 0 + 0}{19} = 1.79$$

The weighted mean of 1.79 yielded a Moderate Buy recommendation.

A survey may ask respondents to select an age category such as "20–29," rather than giving their specific age. Or respondents may be asked to select a cost category such as "$4.00 to under $6.00" for a purchase at a local coffee shop. In these situations *exact* values of the mean and variance are not possible. However, we are able to approximate the mean and the variance.

Approximate Mean and Variance for Grouped Data
Suppose that data are grouped into K classes, with frequencies f_1, f_2, ..., f_K. If the midpoints of these classes are m_1, m_2, ..., m_K, then the sample mean and sample standard deviation of grouped data are approximated in the following manner:
The mean is

$$\bar{x} = \frac{\sum_{i=1}^{K} f_i m_i}{n} \tag{2.17}$$

where $n = \sum_{i=1}^{K} f_i$ and the variance is

$$s^2 = \frac{\sum_{i=1}^{K} f_i (m_i - \bar{x})^2}{n - 1} \tag{2.18}$$

Example 2.15 Cost of Coffee Shop Purchase (Mean and Variance for Grouped Values)

Coffee shop customers were randomly surveyed and asked to select a category that described the cost of their recent purchase. The results were as follows:

Cost (in USD)	$0 < 2$	$2 < 4$	$4 < 6$	$6 < 8$	$8 < 10$
Number of Customers	2	3	6	5	4

Find the sample mean and standard deviation of these costs.

Solution The frequencies are the number of customers for each cost category. The computations for the mean and the standard deviation are set out in Table 2.6.

Table 2.6 Cost of Purchase (Grouped Data Computation)

COSTS (USD)	FREQUENCY f_i	MIDPOINT m_i	$f_i m_i$	$(m_i - \bar{x})$	$(m_i -)^2$	$f_i(m_i -)^2$
$0 < 2$	2	1	2	−4.6	21.16	42.32
$2 < 4$	3	3	9	−2.6	6.76	20.28
$4 < 6$	6	5	30	−0.6	0.36	2.16
$6 < 8$	5	7	35	1.4	1.96	9.8
$8 < 10$	4	9	36	3.4	11.56	46.24
	20	Sums	112			120.8

From Table 2.6,

$$n = \sum_{i=1}^{K} f_i = 20 \qquad \text{and} \qquad \sum_{i=1}^{K} f_i m_i = 112$$

The sample mean is estimated by

$$\bar{x} = \frac{\sum_{i=1}^{K} f_i m_i}{n} = \frac{112}{20} = 5.6$$

Since these are sample data, the variance is estimated by

$$s^2 = \frac{\sum_{i=1}^{K} f_i(m_i - \bar{x})^2}{n - 1} = \frac{120.8}{19} = 6.3579$$

Hence, the sample standard deviation is estimated as

$$s = \sqrt{s^2} = \sqrt{6.3579} = 2.52$$

Therefore, the mean coffee shop purchase price is estimated as $5.60 and the sample standard deviation is estimated to be $2.52.

Basic Exercises

2.26 Consider the following sample of five values and corresponding weights:

x_i	w_i
4.6	8
3.2	3
5.4	6
2.6	2
5.2	5

a. Calculate the arithmetic mean of the x_i values without weights.
b. Calculate the weighted mean of the x_i values.

2.27 Consider the following frequency distribution for a sample of 40 observations:

Class	Frequency
0–4	5
5–9	8
10–14	11
15–19	9
20–24	7

a. Calculate the sample mean.
b. Calculate the sample variance and sample standard deviation.

Application Exercises

2.28 Find the weighted mean per capita personal income for the following random sample of seven states for 2007 (References 3, 4):

State	Population	Per Capita Personal Income
Alabama	4,627,851	38,564
Georgia	9,544,750	33,416
Illinois	12,852,548	40,919
Indiana	6,345,289	33,152
New York	19,297,729	46,664
Pennsylvania	12,432,792	38,740
Tennessee	6,156,719	33,373

2.29 A manufacturer of portable radios obtained a sample of 50 radios from a week's output. The radios were checked and the number of defects was recorded as follows:

Number of defects	0	1	2	3
Number of radios	12	15	17	6

Calculate the standard deviation.

2.30 A random sample of 50 personal property insurance policies showed the following number of claims over the past two years.

Number of claims	0	1	2	3	4	5	6
Number of policies	21	13	5	4	2	3	2

a. Find the mean number of claims per day.
b. Find the sample variance and standard deviation.

2.31 For a random sample of 25 students from a very large university, the accompanying table shows the amount of time (in hours) spent studying for final exams.

Study time	$0 < 4$	$4 < 8$	$8 < 12$	$12 < 16$	$16 < 20$
Number of students	3	7	8	5	2

a. Estimate the sample mean study time.
b. Estimate the sample standard deviation.

2.32 A sample of 20 financial analysts was asked to provide forecasts of earnings per share of a corporation for next year. The results are summarized in the following table:

Forecast ($ per share)	Number of Analysts
$9.95 to under $10.45	2
$10.45 to under $10.95	8
$10.95 to under $11.45	6
$11.45 to under $11.95	3
$11.95 to under $12.45	1

a. Estimate the sample mean forecast.
b. Estimate the sample standard deviation.

2.33 A publisher receives from a printer a copy of a 500-page textbook. The page proofs are carefully read and the number of errors on each page is recorded, producing the data in the following table:

Number of errors	0	1	2	3	4	5
Number of pages	102	138	140	79	33	8

Find the mean and standard deviation in number of errors per page.

2.34 The mean and standard deviation of completion times for a random sample of employees were calculated in Example 2.11. Now calculate and compare the mean and standard deviation based only on the frequency distribution given in Table 1.8.

2.4 MEASURES OF RELATIONSHIPS BETWEEN VARIABLES

We introduced scatter plots in Chapter 1 as a graphical way to describe a relationship between two variables. In this section we introduce *covariance* and *correlation*, numerical ways to describe a linear relationship, giving more attention to these concepts in Chapters 11 to 13. Covariance is a measure of the *direction* of a linear relationship between two variables.

Covariance
Covariance (***Cov***) is a measure of the linear relationship between two variables. A positive value indicates a direct or increasing linear relationship, and a negative value indicates a decreasing linear relationship.

A *population covariance* is

$$Cov(x, y) = \sigma_{xy} = \frac{\sum_{i=1}^{N}(x_i - \mu_x)(y_i - \mu_y)}{N} \tag{2.19}$$

where x_i and y_i are the observed values, μ_x and μ_y are the population means, and N is the populations size.

A *sample covariance* is

$$Cov(x, y) = s_{xy} = \frac{\sum_{i=1}^{n}(x_i - \bar{x})(y_i - \bar{y})}{n - 1} \tag{2.20}$$

where x_i and y_i are the observed values, $\bar{x}$ and $\bar{y}$ are the sample means, and n is the sample size.

The value of the covariance varies if a variable such as height is measured in feet or inches, or weight is measured in pounds, ounces, or kilograms. Also, covariance does not provide a measure of the strength of the relationship between two variables. The most common measure to overcome these shortcomings is called Pearson's product-moment correlation coefficient, Pearson's *r*, or simply the correlation coefficient. Although this measure is named after Karl Pearson, it was Sir Francis Galton who first introduced the concept in the late 1800s (Reference 13). This correlation coefficient will give us a standardized measure of the linear relationship between two variables. It is generally a more useful measure, as it provides both the *direction* and the *strength* of a relationship. The covariance and corresponding correlation coefficient have the same sign (both are positive or both are negative). There are other measures of correlation such as Spearman's rank correlation coefficient which we will discuss in Chapter 14.

Correlation Coefficient

The **correlation coefficient** is computed by dividing the covariance by the product of the standard deviations of the two variables.

A *population correlation coefficient*, ρ, is

$$\rho = \frac{Cov(x, y)}{\sigma_x \sigma_y} \tag{2.21}$$

where σ_x and σ_y are the population standard deviations of the two variables, and $Cov(x, y)$ is the population covariance.

A *sample correlation coefficient*, r, is

$$r = \frac{Cov(x, y)}{s_x s_y} \tag{2.22}$$

where s_x and s_y are the sample standard deviations of the two variables, and $\hat{Cov}(x, y)$ is the sample covariance.

A useful rule to remember is that a relationship exists if

$$|r| \geq \frac{2}{\sqrt{n}} \tag{2.23}$$

It can be shown that the correlation coefficient ranges from -1 to +1. The closer r is to +1, the closer the data points are to an increasing straight line indicating a *positive* linear relationship. The closer r is to –1, the closer the data points are to a decreasing straight line indicating a *negative* linear relationship. When $r = 0$, there is no *linear* relationship between x and y, but not necessarily a lack of relationship. In Chapter 1 we presented scatter plots as a graphical measure to determine relationship. Figure 2.8 presents some examples of scatter plots and their corresponding correlation coefficients. Figure 2.9 is a plot of quarterly sales for a major retail company.

Note that sales vary by quarter of the year, reflecting consumers' purchasing patterns. The correlation coefficient between the time variable and quarterly sales is zero. However, we can see a very definite seasonal relationship, but the relationship is not linear.

Figure 2.8
Scatter Plots and
Correlation

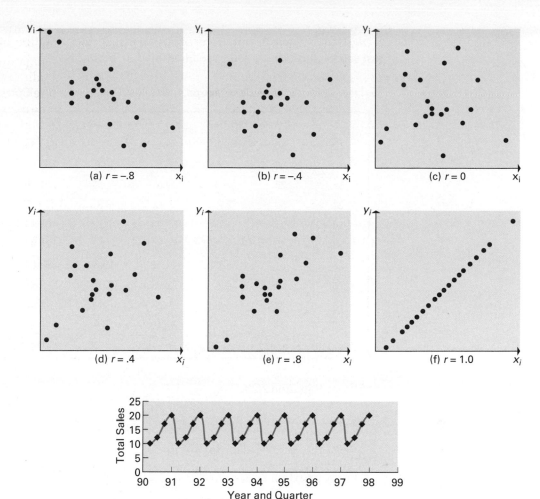

Figure 2.9
Retail Sales by
Quarter

Example 2.16 Aptitude Test Scores and Sales (Covariance and Correlation Coefficient)

A corporation administers an aptitude test to all new sales representatives. Management is interested in the extent to which this test is able to predict weekly sales of new representatives. Table 2.7 records aptitude test scores (of a 30-point test) and average weekly sales (in hundreds of dollars) for a random sample of eight representatives. The data is contained in the data file **Aptitude Test Score**.

Table 2.7 Aptitude Test Scores and Sales

Test Score, x	12	30	15	24	14	18	28	26	19	27
Weekly Sales, y	20	60	27	50	21	30	61	54	32	57

Solution The computations of covariance and correlation between aptitude test scores and weekly sales are illustrated in Table 2.8.

Table 2.8 Aptitude Test Scores and Sales (Covariance and Correlation)

x	y	$(x_i - \bar{x})$	$(x_i - \bar{x})^2$	$(y_i - \bar{y})$	$(y_i - \bar{y})^2$	$(x_i - \bar{x})(y_i - \bar{y})$
12	20	−9.3	86.49	−21.2	449.44	197.16
30	60	8.7	75.69	18.8	353.44	163.56
15	27	−6.3	39.69	−14.2	201.64	89.46
24	50	2.7	7.29	8.8	77.44	23.76
14	21	−7.3	53.29	−20.2	408.04	147.46
18	30	−3.3	10.89	−11.2	125.44	36.96
28	61	6.7	44.89	19.8	392.04	132.66
26	54	4.7	22.09	12.8	163.84	60.16
19	32	−2.3	5.29	−9.2	84.64	21.16
27	57	5.7	32.49	15.8	249.64	90.06
$\Sigma = 213$	**$\Sigma = 412$**		**$\Sigma = 378.1$**		**$\Sigma = 2505.6$**	**$\Sigma = 962.4$**

From Equation 2.20,

$$Cov(x, y) = s_{xy} = \frac{\sum_{i=1}^{n}(x_i - \bar{x})(y_i - \bar{y})}{n - 1} = \frac{962.4}{9} = 106.93$$

From Equation 2.22,

$$r = \frac{Cov(x, y)}{s_x s_y} = \frac{106.93}{\sqrt{42.01}\sqrt{278.4}} = 0.989$$

From Equation 2.23,

$$|0.989| > \frac{2}{\sqrt{10}} = 0.63$$

We conclude that there is a strong positive linear relationship between aptitude test scores and weekly sales. More formal procedures to determine if two variables are linearly related will be discussed in Chapters 11 and 12.

Example 2.17 Analysis of Stock Portfolios (Correlation Coefficient Analysis)

Jim Busse, financial analyst for Integrated Securities, is considering a number of different stocks for a new mutual fund he is developing. One of his questions concerns the correlation coefficients between prices of different stocks. To determine the patterns of stock prices, he prepared a series of scatter plots and computed the sample correlation coefficient for each plot. What information does Figure 2.10 provide?

Figure 2.10 Relationships Between Various Stock Prices

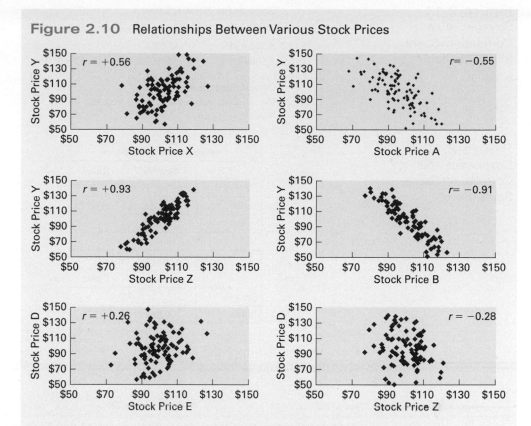

Solution Jim sees that it is possible to control the variation in the average mutual fund price by combining various stocks into a portfolio. The portfolio variation is increased if stocks with positive correlation coefficients are included because the prices tend to increase together. In contrast, the portfolio variation is decreased if stocks with negative correlation coefficients are included. When the price of one stock increases, the price of the other decreases, and the combined price is more stable. Experienced observers of stock prices might question the possibility of very large negative correlation coefficients. Our objective here is to illustrate graphically the correlation coefficients for certain patterns of observed data and not to accurately describe a particular market. After examining these correlation coefficients, Jim is ready to begin constructing his portfolio. Correlation coefficients between stock prices affect the variation of the entire portfolio.

Minitab, Excel, SPSS, SAS, and many other statistical packages can be used to compute descriptive measures such as the sample covariance and the sample correlation coefficient. Figure 2.11 shows the Minitab output for computing covariance, and Figure 2.12 shows the Excel output for the same data.

Special care must be taken if we use Excel to compute covariance. In Example 2.16 the covariance between aptitude test scores and weekly sales was found to be 106.93 (the same value in the Minitab output in Figure 2.11). But the covariance of 96.24 given in the Excel output is the population covariance, not the sample covariance. That is, Excel automatically calculates the population covariance. To obtain the sample covariance, we must multiply the population covariance by a factor of $n/(n-1)$.

Figure 2.11
Covariance and
Correlation: Score,
Sales (Minitab)

Covariances: Scores, Sales

	Scores	Sales
X, Scores	42.0111	
Y, Sales	106.9333	278.4000

Correlations: Scores, Sales
Pearson correlation of x and y = 0.989
P-Value = 0.000

Figure 2.12
Covariance and
Correlation: Score,
Sales (Excel)

Covariance: Scores, Sales		
	Scores	Sales
Scores	37.81	
Sales	**96.24**	250.56

Correlation: Scores, Tables		
	Scores	Sales
Scores	1	
Sales	**0.988773**	1

From the Excel output the sample covariance between aptitude test scores and weekly sales is found as follows:

$$Cov(x, y) = 96.24 \times \frac{10}{9} = 106.9333$$

It is important to understand that correlation does not imply causation (References 12, 13). It is possible for two variables to be highly correlated, but that does not mean that one variable causes the other variable. We need to be careful about jumping to conclusions based on television news reports, newspaper articles, on-line Web sites, or even medical studies that claim that A causes B.

A Canadian medical study (May 16, 2008) found that three-fourths of the "women in the study who had breast cancer also had a vitamin D deficiency" (Reference 2). Headlines such as "Study links vitamin D deficiency, aggressive breast cancer" (Reference 2) and "Study finds breast cancer linked to Vitamin D deficiency" (Reference 5) quickly appeared on the news and Internet. "While 'link' does not mean one thing causes the other, the Canadian study has American women taking notice" (Reference 2). It may well be that there is a cause-and-effect between Vitamin D deficiency and breast cancer, but correlation does not prove it; it points to the need for further study and research. Statisticians will understand this difference; but women (especially breast cancer survivors) may view this situation with more urgency.

EXERCISES

Basic Exercises

2.35 Following is a random sample of seven (x, y) pairs of data points:

(1, 5)　(3, 7)　(4, 6)　(5, 8)　(7, 9)　(3, 6)　(5, 7)

a. Compute the covariance.
b. Compute the correlation coefficient.

2.36 Following is a random sample of five (x, y) pairs of data points:

(12, 200)　(30, 600)　(15, 270)　(24, 500)　(14, 210)

a. Compute the covariance.
b. Compute the correlation coefficient.

2.37 Following is a random sample of price per piece of plywood, X, and quantity sold, Y (in thousands):

Price per Piece (X)	Thousands of Pieces Sold (Y)
$6	80
7	60
8	70
9	40
10	0

   a. Compute the covariance.
   b. Compute the correlation coefficient.

Application Exercises

2.38 River Hills Hospital is interested in determining the effectiveness of a new drug for reducing the time required for complete recovery from knee surgery. Complete recovery is measured by a series of strength tests that compare the treated knee with the untreated knee. The drug was given in varying amounts to 18 patients over a 6-month period. For each patient the number of drug units, X, and the days for complete recovery, Y, are given by the following (x, y) data:

(5, 53) (21, 65) (14, 48) (11, 66) (9, 46) (4, 56)
(7, 53) (21, 57) (17, 49) (14, 66) (9, 54) (7, 56)
(9, 53) (21, 52) (13, 49) (14, 56) (9, 59) (4, 56)

   a. Compute covariance.
   b. Compute the correlation coefficient.
   c. Briefly discuss the relationship between the number of drug units and the recovery time. What dosage might we recommend based on this initial analysis?

2.39 Acme Delivery offers three different shipping rates for packages fewer than 5 pounds delivered from Maine to the West Coast: regular, $3; fast, $5; and lightning, $10. To test the quality of these services, a major mail-order retailer shipped 15 packages at randomly selected times from Maine to Tacoma, Washington. The packages were shipped in groups of three by the three services at the same time to reduce variation resulting from the shipping day. The following data show the shipping cost, X, and the number of days, Y, in (x, y) pairs:

(3, 7) (5, 5) (10, 2) (3, 9) (5, 6) (10, 5) (3, 6) (5, 6)
(10, 1) (3, 10) (5, 7) (10, 4) (3, 5) (5, 6) (10, 4)

   a. Describe the data numerically (covariance and correlation).
   b. Discuss the value of the higher-priced services in terms of quicker delivery.

2.40 The following data give X, the price charged for a particular item, and Y, the quantity of that item sold (in thousands):

Price per Piece (X)	Hundreds of Pieces Sold (Y)
$5	55
6	53
7	45
8	40
9	20

   a. Compute the covariance.
   b. Compute the correlation coefficient.

2.41 A random sample for five exam scores produced the following (hours of study, grade) data values:

Hours Studied (X)	Test Grade (Y)
3.5	88
2.4	76
4	92
5	85
1.1	60

   a. Compute the covariance.
   b. Compute the correlation coefficient.

2.42 A consumer goods company has been studying the effect of advertising on total profits. As part of this study, data on advertising expenditures (in thousands of dollars) and total sales (in thousands of dollars) were collected for a five-month period and are as follows:

(10, 100) (15, 200) (7, 80) (12, 120) (14, 150)

The first number is advertising expenditures and the second is total sales. Plot the data and compute the correlation coefficient.

2.43 The president of Floor Coverings Unlimited wants information concerning the relationship between retail experience (years) and weekly sales (in hundreds of dollars). He obtained the following random sample on experience and weekly sales:

(2, 5) (4, 10) (3, 8) (6, 18) (3, 6) (5, 15) (6, 20) (2, 4)

The first number for each observation is years of experience, and the second number is weekly sales. Compute the covariance and the correlation coefficient.

KEY WORDS

- arithmetic mean, 44
- coefficient of variation, CV, 57
- correlation coefficient, 68
- covariance (Cov), 67
- empirical rule, 60
- first quartile, 52
- five-number summary, 53
- geometric mean, 49
- geometric mean rate of return, 49
- interquartile range (IQR), 53
- median, 44
- mode, 44
- range, 52
- skewed, 46
- standard deviation, 55
- symmetry, 46
- third quartile, 52
- variance, 54

CHAPTER EXERCISES AND APPLICATIONS

2.44 A major airport recently hired consultant John Cadariu to study the problem of air traffic delays. He recorded the number of minutes planes were late for a sample of flights in the following table:

Minutes late	0 < 10	10 < 20	20 < 30	30 < 40	40 < 50	50 < 60
Number of flights	30	25	13	6	5	4

   a. Estimate the mean number of minutes late.
   b. Estimate the sample variance and standard deviation.

2.45 ◉ Snappy Lawn Inc. keeps records of charges for its professional lawn care services. A random sample of charges is stored in the data file **Snappy**. Describe the data numerically.

2.46 Find the variance and standard deviation of the 10 accounting exams in Example 2.1.

2.47 Describe the following data numerically:

   (4, 53) (10, 65) (15, 48) (10, 66) (8, 46) (5, 56)
   (7, 60) (11, 57) (12, 49) (14, 70) (10, 54) (7, 56)
   (9, 50) (8, 52) (11, 59) (10, 66) (8, 49) (5, 50)

2.48 ◉ Graduation GPAs versus entering SAT verbal scores are contained in the data file **Student GPA** for a random sample of 67 students.

   a. Describe the data graphically.
   b. Describe the data numerically.

2.49 Consider the following four populations:

   - 1, 2, 3, 4, 5, 6, 7, 8
   - 1, 1, 1, 1, 8, 8, 8, 8
   - 1, 1, 4, 4, 5, 5, 8, 8,
   - −6, −3, 0, 3, 6, 9, 12, 15

All of these populations have the same mean. *Without doing the calculations*, arrange the populations according to the magnitudes of their variances, from smallest to largest. Then calculate each of the variances manually.

2.50 An auditor finds that the values of a corporation's accounts receivable have a mean of $295 and a standard deviation of $63.

   a. It can be guaranteed that 60% of these values will be in what interval?
   b. It can be guaranteed that 84% of these values will be in what interval?

2.51 In one year, earnings growth of the 500 largest U.S. corporations averaged 9.2%; the standard deviation was 3.5%.

   a. It can be guaranteed that 84% of these earnings growth figures will be in what interval?
   b. Using the empirical rule, it can be estimated that approximately 68% of these earnings growth figures will be in what interval?

2.52 Tires of a particular brand have a lifetime mean of 29,000 miles and a standard deviation of 3,000 miles.

   a. It can be guaranteed that 75% of the lifetimes of tires of this brand will be in what interval?
   b. Using the empirical rule, it can be estimated that approximately 95% of the lifetimes of tires of this brand will be in what interval?

Appendix

Skewness

In nearly all situations, we would compute skewness with a statistical software package or Excel. If skewness is zero or close to zero, then the distribution is symmetric or approximately symmetric. A negative value of skewness tells us that the distribution is skewed to the left. Similarly, a positive value of skewness tells us that the distribution is skewed to the right.

Skewness
Skewness is as follows:

$$\text{skewness} = \frac{1}{n} \frac{\sum_{i=1}^{n} (x_i - \bar{x})^3}{s^3} \tag{2.24}$$

The important part of this expression is the numerator; the denominator serves the purpose of standardization, making units of measurement irrelevant. Positive skewness will result if a distribution is skewed to the right, since average cubed discrepancies about the mean are positive. Skewness will be negative for distributions skewed to the left and 0 for distributions, such as the bell-shaped distribution that is mounded and symmetric about its mean.

In Example 2.3 we found that the mean grade point average for a random sample of 155 students was 3.14 and the median grade point average was 3.42, thus, indicating negative skewness. From the SPSS output in Figure 2.3 the measure of skewness is -1.22, again indicating negative skewness. The same value is obtained using Equation 2.24.

References

1. Banda Performance. http://www.bandaperformance.com/executives/index.html (accessed June 24, 2008).
2. Barrett, Katherine. 2008. Study links vitamin D deficiency, aggressive breast cancer. http://www.wvec.com/news/health/stories/wvec_medical_051608_cancer_vitamin_d.1089cb712.html (accessed June 26, 2008).
3. Bureau of Economic Analysis. Table SA1-3—Per Capita Personal Income, 2007. http://www.bea.gov/bea/regional/spi/drill.cfm (accessed November 1, 2008).
4. Bureau of Economic Analysis. Table SA1-3—Population, 2007. http://www.bea.gov/bea/regional/spi/drill.cfm (accessed November 1, 2008).
5. Campbell, Carol Ann. 2008. *Study finds breast cacner linked to Vitamin D deficiency.* http://www.nj.com/news/index.ssf/2008/05/study_breast_cancer_linked_to.html (accessed November 1, 2008).

6. Freund, J. and Perles, B. 1987. A New Look at Quartiles of Ungrouped Data. *American Stat.* 41:200–203.

7. Hoaglin, D.; Mosteller, F.; and Tukey, J. (Ed.) 1983. *Understanding Robust and Exploratory Data Analysis.* New York: Wiley, 39, 54, 62, 223.

8. Kalajian, Douglas. Stick to exercise time as if it were an appointment. Cox News Service. *Atlanta Journal Constitution*'s http://www.ajc.com/health/content/shared/health/weightloss/diet_january.html (accessed June 24, 2008).

9. Kenney, J. F. and Keeping, E. S. 1962. Quartiles. §3.3 in *Mathematics of Statistics, Pt. 1, 3rd ed.* Princeton, NJ: Van Nostrand, 35–37.

10. Langford, Eric. 2006. Quartiles in Elementary Statistics. *Journal of Statistics Education* 14, (3): www.amstat.org/publications/jse/v14n3/langford.html (accessed July 26, 2008).

11. Microsoft Corp.: Analyst Ratings. http://moneycentral.msn.com/investor/invsub/analyst/recomnd.asp?Symbol=MSFT (accessed June 26, 2008).

12. Pearl, Judea. 2000. *Causality: Models, Reasoning, and Inference.* Cambridge University Press.

13. Salsburg, David. 2002. *The Lady Tasting Tea: How Statistics Revolutionized Science in the Twentieth Century.* New York: Henry Holt and Company.

14. 2008. The Corporations, by Performance: How the Companies Stack Up. *Fortune* F-17.

Chapter 3

Probability

Introduction

In this chapter we develop probability models that can be used to study business and economic problems for which future outcomes are unknown.

Consider the problem faced by George Smith, president of Advanced Systems Development Inc. (ASD). The company has submitted five separate project proposals for the next year. George knows that the company will have to complete up to five projects over the next year. At present the company staff can handle up to two projects, and personnel could be hired to staff a third project. But if four or five projects are awarded to ASD, there will be a need for subcontracting or major staff expansion. In this chapter we develop probability concepts that George can use to determine the likely occurrence of the possible events—0, 1, 2, 3, 4, or 5 projects awarded. The probability of each event is a number from 0 to 1, such that the probabilities of all six events sum to exactly 1.0. The larger the probability of an event, the more likely it will occur, compared to the others. If the probability of exactly two contracts being awarded is 0.80, then George will be more confident of that event, compared to the case where the probability is 0.20. But in either case George cannot be certain that the event will occur.

We will show how probability models are used to study the variation in observed data so that inferences about the underlying process can be developed. Our objective, both in this chapter and in the next two chapters, is to understand probabilities, how they can be determined, and how they can be used.

3.1 RANDOM EXPERIMENT, OUTCOMES, AND EVENTS

For the manager the probability of a future event presents a level of knowledge. The manager could know with certainty that the event will occur—e.g., a legal contract will exist. Or the manager may have no idea if the event will occur—e.g., the event could occur or not occur as part of a new business opportunity. In most business situations we cannot be certain about the occurrence of a future event, but if the probability of the event is known, then we have a better chance of making the best possible decision, compared to having no idea about the likely occurrence of the event. Business decisions and policies are often based on an implicit or assumed set of probabilities.

To help you develop a clear and rigorous understanding of probability we will first develop definitions and concepts that provide a structure for constructing probability models.

These definitions and concepts—such as sample space, outcomes, and events—are the basic building blocks for defining and computing probabilities.

For our study of probability we will be concerned with processes that can have two or more outcomes, with uncertainty about which outcome will occur.

Random Experiment
A **random experiment** is a process leading to two or more possible outcomes, without knowing exactly which outcome will occur.

Examples of random experiments include the following:

1. A coin is tossed and the outcome is either a head or a tail.
2. In the ASD example, the company has the possibility of receiving 0–5 contract awards.
3. The number of persons admitted to a hospital emergency room during any hour is recorded.
4. A customer enters a store and either purchases a shirt or does not.
5. The daily change in an index of stock market prices is observed.
6. A bag of cereal is selected from a packaging line and weighed to determine if the weight is above or below the stated package weight.
7. A baseball hitter has a number of different outcomes—such as a hit, walk, strikeout, flyout, and more—each time he is at bat.

In each of the random experiments listed we can specify the possible outcomes, defined as *basic outcomes*. For example, a customer either purchases a shirt or does not.

We must define the basic outcomes in such a way that no two outcomes can occur simultaneously. In addition, the random experiment must necessarily lead to the occurrence of one of the basic outcomes.

Example 3.1 Professional Baseball Hitter (Sample Space)

What is the Sample Space for a professional baseball hitter? A high quality professional baseball player could have the following outcomes occur when at bat, and the sample space is shown in Table 3.1. The sample space consists of six basic outcomes. No two outcomes can occur together, and one of the seven must occur. The probabilities were obtained by examining baseball batter data.

Table 3.1 Outcomes for a Baseball Hitter

	SAMPLE SPACE S	PROBABILITY
O_1	Safe Hit	0.30
O_2	Walk or Hit by pitcher	0.10
O_3	Strike Out	0.10
O_4	Ground Ball Out	0.30
O_5	Fly Ball Out	0.18
O_6	Reach Base on Error	0.02

Example 3.2 Investment Outcomes (Sample Space)

An investor follows the Dow Jones Industrial index. What are the possible basic outcomes at the close of the trading day?

Solution The sample space for this experiment is as follows:

$$S = [\{1. \text{ The index will be higher than at yesterday's close}\}, \\ \{2. \text{ The index will not be higher than at yesterday's close}\}]$$

One of these two outcomes must occur. They cannot occur simultaneously. Thus, these two outcomes constitute a sample space.

In many cases we are interested in some subset of the basic outcomes and not the individual outcomes. For example, we might be interested in whether the batter reached the base safely—that is, Safe Hit, Walk, or Reach Base on Error. This subset of outcomes is defined as an event.

Event

An **event**, E, is any subset of basic outcomes from the sample space. An event occurs if the random experiment results in one of its constituent basic outcomes. The null event represents the absence of a basic outcome and is denoted by $\emptyset$.

In some applications we are interested in the simultaneous occurrence of two or more events. In the hitter example we might be interested in two events: "The batter reaches base safely" (Event A [O_1, O_2, O_6]) and "The batter hits the ball" (Event B [O_1, O_4, O_5, O_6]). One possibility is that specific outcomes in both events occur simultaneously. This will happen for outcomes that are contained in both events—that is, Safe Hit, O_1, or Reach Base on Error O_6. This later set of outcomes is the intersection $A \cap B$. Thus in the batter example the outcomes, Safe Hit, O_1, or Reach Base on Error, O_6, belong to the two events: "The batter reaches base safely" (Event A [O_1, O_2, O_6]) and "The batter hits the ball" (Event B [O_1, O_4, O_5, O_6]). Note that the probability of this intersection is 0.32 (0.30 + 0.02).

Intersection of Events

Let A and B be two events in the sample space S. Their **intersection**, denoted by $A \cap B$, is the set of all basic outcomes in S that belong to both A and B. Hence, the intersection $A \cap B$ occurs if and only if both A and B occur. We will use the term **joint probability** of A and B to denote the probability of the intersection of A and B.

More generally, given K events E_1, E_2, . . ., E_K, their intersection, $E_1 \cap E_2 \cap \cdots \cap E_K$, is the set of all basic outcomes that belong to every $E_i(i = 1, 2 . . ., K)$.

It is possible that the intersection of two events is the empty set. In the hitter example if we had defined an event C "Batter is out" then the intersection of events A and C would be an empty set.

Mutually Exclusive

If the events A and B have no common basic outcomes, they are called **mutually exclusive**, and their intersection, $A \cap B$, is said to be the empty set indicating that $A \cap B$ cannot occur.

More generally, the K events E_1, E_2, . . ., E_K are said to be mutually exclusive if every pair (E_i, E_j) is a pair of mutually exclusive events.

In the batter example Events A and C from above are mutually exclusive.

Figure 3.1 illustrates intersections using a Venn diagram. In part (a) of Figure 3.1 the rectangle S represents the sample space, and the two closed figures represent the events A and B. Basic outcomes belonging to A are within the circle labeled A, and

Figure 3.1
Venn Diagrams for the Intersection of Events *A* and *B*: (a) $A \cap B$ is the Shaded Area; (b) *A* and *B* are Mutually Exclusive

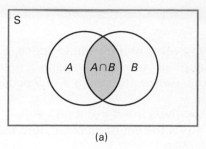
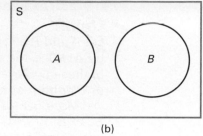

(a)   (b)

basic outcomes belonging to *B* are in the corresponding *B* circle. The intersection of *A* and *B*, $A \cap B$, is indicated by the shaded area where the figures intersect. We see that a basic outcome is in $A \cap B$ if and only if it is in both *A* and *B*. Thus, in the hitter example outcomes, Safe Hit, O_1, or Reach Base on Error, O_6, belong to the two events: "The batter reaches base safely" (Event A $[O_1, O_2, O_6]$) and "The batter hits the ball" (Event B $[O_1, O_4, O_5, O_6]$). In Figure 3.1(b) the figures do not intersect, indicating that events *A* and *B* are mutually exclusive. For example, if a set of accounts is audited, the events "Less than 5% contain material errors" and "More than 10% contain material errors" are mutually exclusive.

Tables 3.2a and 3.2b can also be used to demonstrate the same conditions. The entire table represents S the sample space. Basic outcomes belonging to *A* are in the first row labeled *A*, and basic outcomes belonging to *B* are in the first column labeled *B*. The intersection of *A* and *B*, $A \cap B$, is indicated by the upper left table cell. A basic outcome is in $A \cap B$ if and only if it is in both *A* and *B*. Thus, in the hitter example outcomes, Safe Hit, O_1, or Reach Base on Error, O_6, belong to the two events: "The batter reaches base safely" (Event A $[O_1, O_2, O_6]$) and "The batter hits the ball" (Event B $[O_1, O_4, O_5, O_6]$). In Table 3.2b the figures do not intersect, indicating that events *A* and *B* are mutually exclusive. For example, if a set of accounts is audited, the events "Less than 5% contain material errors" and "More than 10% contain material errors" are mutually exclusive and the upper-left-hand cell is empty.

When we consider jointly several events, another possibility of interest is that at least one of them will occur. This will happen if the basic outcome of the random experiment belongs to at least one of the events. The set of basic outcomes belonging to at least one of the events is called their *union*. For the hitter example the two events, "The batter reaches base safely" (Event A $[O_1, O_2, O_6]$) and "The batter hits the ball" (Event B $[O_1, O_4, O_5, O_6]$), the events $[O_1, O_2, O_4, O_5, O_6]$ are included in at least one of the Events. This is an example of the union of two events.

Table 3.2a Intersection

	B	$\overline{B}$
A	$A \cap B$	$A - (A \cap B)$
$\overline{A}$	$B - (\overline{A} \cap B)$	$\overline{A} \cap \overline{B}$

Table 3.2b Mutually Exclusive

	B	$\overline{B}$
A	$\varnothing$	A
$\overline{A}$	B	$\overline{A} \cap \overline{B}$

The Venn diagram in Figure 3.2 shows the union, from which it is clear that a basic outcome will be in $A \cup B$ if and only if it is in either A or B or both.

Figure 3.2
Venn Diagram for the Union of Events A and B

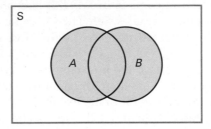

If the union of several events covers the entire sample space, S, we say that these events are *collectively exhaustive*. Since every basic outcome is in S, it follows that every outcome of the random experiment will be in at least one of these events. In the baseball example, the events, the hitter gets on base and hitter makes an out are collectively exhaustive.

We can see that the set of all basic outcomes contained in a sample space is both mutually exclusive and collectively exhaustive. We have already noted that these outcomes are such that one must occur, but no more than one can simultaneously occur.

Next, let A be an event. Suppose that our interest is all of the basic outcomes not included in A.

Clearly, events A and $\overline{A}$ are mutually exclusive—no basic outcome can belong to both—and collectively exhaustive—every basic outcome must belong to one or the

Figure 3.3
Venn Diagram for
the Complement
of Event *A*

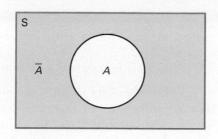

other. Figure 3.3 shows the complement of *A* using a Venn diagram. We have now defined three important concepts—the intersection, the union, and the complement—that will be important in our development of probability.

Example 3.3 Batter Performance Showing Unions, Intersections, and Complements

The following examples help to illustrate these concepts. When a batter is up two events of Interest are "The batter reaches base safely"(Event $[O_1, O_2, O_6]$) and "The batter hits the ball"(Event $[O_1, O_4, O_5, O_6]$), using the definitions from Example 3.1.

1. The complements of these events are respectively

$$\overline{A} = [O_3, O_4, O_5] \qquad \overline{B} = [O_2, O_3]$$

2. The intersection of *A* and *B* is the event "Batter reaches base safely as the result of hitting the ball" and so,

$$A \cap B = [O_2, O_3]$$

3. The union is the event "The batter reaches base safely or the batter hits the ball" and so,

$$A \cup B = [O_1, O_2, O_4, O_5, O_6]$$

4. Note that the events $A[O_1, O_2, O_6]$ and $\overline{A}[O_3, O_4, O_5]$ are mutually exclusive since their intersection is the empty set, and collectively exhaustive since their union is the sample space—*S* that is,

$$A \cup \overline{A} = [O_1, O_2, O_3, O_4, O_5, O_6]$$

The same statements apply for $B[O_1, O_4, O_5, O_6]$ and $\overline{B}[O_2, O_3]$.

Consider also the intersection of events $\overline{A}\left[O_3, O_4, O_5\right]$ and $B\left[O_1, O_4, O_5, O_6\right]$. The events O_4, ground ball out, and O_5, fly ball out, represent the condition where the batter hits the ball but makes an out.

Example 3.4 Dow Jones Industrial Average (Unions, Intersections, and Complements)

We will designate four basic outcomes for the Dow Jones Industrial average over 2 consecutive days:

O_1: The Dow Jones average rises on both days.
O_2: The Dow Jones average rises on the first day but does not rise on the second day.

O_3: The Dow Jones average does not rise on the first day but rises on the second day.

O_4: The Dow Jones average does not rise on either day.

Clearly, one of these outcomes must occur, but more than one cannot occur at the same time. We can, therefore, write the sample space as $S = [O_1, O_2, O_3, O_4]$. Now, we will consider these two events:

A: The Dow Jones average rises on the first day.

B: The Dow Jones average rises on the second day.

Find the intersection, union, and complement of A and B.

Solution We see that A occurs if either O_1 or O_2 occurs, and, B occurs if either O_1 or O_3 occurs and thus,

$$A = [O_1, O_2] \quad \text{and} \quad B = [O_1, O_3]$$

The intersection of A and B is the event "The Dow Jones average rises on the first day and rises on the second day." This is the set of all basic outcomes belonging to both A and B, $A \cap B = [O_1]$.

The union of A and B is the event "The Dow Jones average rises on at least one of the two days." This is the set of all outcomes belonging to either A or B, or both. Thus,

$$A \cup B = [O_1, O_2, O_3]$$

Finally, the complement of A is the event "The Dow Jones average does not rise on the first day." This is the set of all basic outcomes in the sample space, S, that do not belong to A. Hence,

$$\overline{A}[O_3, O_4] \text{ and similarly } \overline{B}[O_2, O_4]$$

Figure 3.4 shows the intersection of events $\overline{A}$ and B. This intersection contains all outcomes that belong in both $\overline{A}$ and B. Clearly, $\overline{A} \cap B = [O_3]$.

Figure 3.4 Venn Diagram for the Intersection of $\overline{A}$ and B

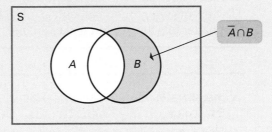

Additional results are shown in the chapter appendix.

Basic Exercises

For exercises 3.1–3.4 use the sample space S defined as follows:

$$S = [E_1, E_2, E_3, E_4, E_5, E_6, E_7, E_8, E_9, E_{10}]$$

3.1 Given $A = [E_1, E_3, E_6, E_9]$, define $\overline{A}$.

3.2 Given $A = [E_1, E_3, E_7, E_9]$ and $B = [E_2, E_3, E_8, E_9]$,

    a. what is A intersection B?
    b. what is the union of A and B?
    c. is the union of A and B collectively exhaustive?

3.3 Given $\overline{A} = [E_1, E_3, E_7, E_9]$ and $\overline{B} = [E_2, E_3, E_8, E_9]$,

    a. what is A intersection B?
    b. what is the union of A and B?
    c. is the union of A and B collectively exhaustive?

3.4 Given $A = [E_3, E_5, E_6, E_{10}]$ and $B = [E_3, E_4, E_6, E_9]$,

    a. what is A intersection B?
    b. what is the union of A and B?
    c. is the union of A and B collectively exhaustive?

Application Exercises

3.5 A corporation takes delivery of some new machinery that must be installed and checked before it becomes available to use. The corporation is sure that it will take no more than 7 days for this installation and check to take place. Let A be the event "It will be more than 4 days before the machinery becomes available" and B be the event "It will be less than 6 days before the machinery becomes available."

    a. Describe the event that is the complement of event A.
    b. Describe the event that is the intersection of events A and B.
    c. Describe the event that is the union of events A and B.

    d. Are events A and B mutually exclusive?
    e. Are events A and B collectively exhaustive?
    f. Show that $(A \cap B) \cup (\overline{A} \cap B) = B$.
    g. Show that $A \cup (\overline{A} \cap B) = A \cup B$.

3.6 Consider Example 3.4, with the following four basic outcomes for the Dow Jones Industrial Average over 2 consecutive days:

    O_1: The Dow Jones average rises on both days.
    O_2: The Dow Jones average rises on the first day but does not rise on the second day.
    O_3: The Dow Jones average does not rise on the first day but rises on the second day.
    O_4: The Dow Jones average does not rise on either day.

Let events A and B be the following:

    A: The Dow Jones average rises on the first day.
    B: The Dow Jones average rises on the second day.

    a. Show that $(A \cap B) \cup (\overline{A} \cap B) = B$.
    b. Show that $A \cup (\overline{A} \cap B) = A \cup B$.

3.7 Florin Frenti operates a small used car lot that has three Mercedes (M_1, M_2, M_3) and two Toyotas (T_1, T_2). Two customers, Cezara and Anda, come to his lot, and each selects a car. The customers do not know each other, and there is no communication between them. Let the events A and B be defined as follows:

    A: The customers select at least one Toyota.
    B: The customers select two cars of the same model.

    a. Identify all pairs of cars in the sample space.
    b. Describe event A.
    c. Describe event B.
    d. Describe the complement of A.
    e. Show that $(A \cap B) \cup (\overline{A} \cap B) = B$.
    f. Show that $A \cup (\overline{A} \cap B) = A \cup B$.

3.2 PROBABILITY AND ITS POSTULATES

Now, we are ready to use the language and concepts developed in the previous section to determine how to obtain an actual probability for a process of interest. Suppose that a random experiment is to be carried out and we want to determine the probability that a particular event will occur. Probability is measured over the range from 0 to 1. A probability of 0 indicates that the event will not occur, and a probability of 1 indicates that the event is certain to occur. Neither of these extremes is typical in applied problems. Thus, we are interested in assigning probabilities between 0 and 1 to uncertain events. To do this, we need to utilize any information that might be available. For example, if incomes are high, then sales of luxury automobiles will occur more often. An experienced sales manager may be able to establish a probability that future sales will exceed the company's profitability goal. In this section we consider three definitions of probability:

1. Classical probability
2. Relative frequency probability
3. Subjective probability

Classical Probability

Classical Probability

Classical probability is the proportion of times that an event will occur, assuming that all outcomes in a sample space are equally likely to occur. Dividing the number of outcomes in the sample space that satisfy the event by the total number of outcomes in the sample space determines the probability of an event. The probability of an event A is

$$P(A) = \frac{N_A}{N} \tag{3.4}$$

where N_A is the number of outcomes that satisfy the condition of event A, and N is the total number of outcomes in the sample space. The important idea here is that one can develop a probability from fundamental reasoning about the process.

The classical statement of probability requires that we count outcomes in the sample space. Then we use the counts to determine the required probability. The following example indicates how classical probability can be used in a relatively simple problem.

Example 3.5 Computer Purchase Selection (Classical Probability)

Karlyn Akimoto operates a small computer store. On a particular day she has three Gateway and two Compaq computers in stock. Suppose that Susan Spencer comes into the store to purchase two computers. Susan is not concerned about which brand she purchases—they all have the same operating specifications—so Susan selects the computers purely by chance: Any computer on the shelf is equally likely to be selected. What is the probability that Susan will purchase one Gateway and one Compaq computer?

Solution   The answer can be obtained using classical probability. To begin, the sample space is defined as all possible pairs of two computers that can be selected from the store. The number of pairs is then counted, as is the number of outcomes that meet the condition—one Gateway and one Compaq. Define the three Gateway computers as, G_1, G_2, and G_3 and the two Compaq computers as C_1 and C_2. The sample space, S, contains the following pairs of computers:

$$S = \{G_1C_1, G_1C_2, G_2C_1, G_2C_2, G_3C_1, G_3C_2, G_1G_2, G_1G_3, G_2G_3, C_1C_2\}$$

The number of outcomes in the sample space is 10. If A is the event "One Gateway and one Compaq computer are chosen," then the number, N_A, of outcomes that have one Gateway and one Compaq computer is six. Therefore, the required probability of event A—one Gateway and one Compaq—is

$$P(A) = \frac{N_A}{N} = \frac{6}{10} = 0.6$$

Counting all of the outcomes would be very time-consuming if we first had to identify every possible outcome. However, from previous courses many of you may have learned the basic formula to compute *the number of combinations* of n items taken k at a time.

Formula for Determining the Number of Combinations

The counting process can be generalized by using the following equation to compute the **number of combinations** of n items taken k at a time:

$$C_k^n = \frac{n!}{k!(n-k)!} \qquad 0! = 1 \tag{3.5}$$

The following section develops combinations, and you should study this section if you need to learn about or review your understanding of combinations.

Permutations and Combinations

A practical difficulty that sometimes arises in computing the probability of an event is counting the numbers of basic outcomes in the sample space and the event of interest. For some problems the use of *permutations* or *combinations* can be helpful.

1. Number of Orderings

We begin with the problem of ordering. Suppose that we have some number x of objects that are to be placed in order. Each object may be used only once. How many different sequences are possible? We can view this problem as a requirement to place one of the objects in each of x boxes arranged in a row.

Beginning with the left box in Figure 3.5, there are x different ways to fill it. Once an object is put in that box, there are $(x - 1)$ objects remaining, and so $(x - 1)$ ways to fill the second box. That is, for each of the x ways to place an object in the first box, there are $(x - 1)$ possible ways to fill the second box, so the first two boxes can be filled in a total of $x \times (x - 1)$ ways. Given that the first two boxes are filled, there are now $(x - 2)$ ways of filling the third box, so the first three boxes can be filled in a

Figure 3.5
The Orderings of x Objects

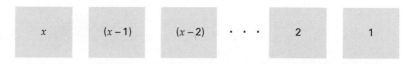

total of $x \times (x - 1) \times (x - 2)$ ways. When we arrive at the last box, there is only one object left to put in it. Finally, we arrive at the number of possible orderings.

Number of Possible Orderings

The total number of possible ways of arranging x objects in order is given by

$$x(x - 1)(x - 2) \cdots (2)(1) = x!$$

where $x!$ is read "x factorial."

2. Permutations

Suppose that now we have a number n of objects with which the x *ordered* boxes could be filled (with $n > x$). Each object may be used only once. The number of possible orderings is called the number of *permutations* of x objects chosen from n and is denoted by the symbol P_x^n.

Now, we can argue precisely as before, except that there will be n ways to fill the first box, $(n - 1)$ ways to fill the second box, and so on, until we come to the final box. At this point there will be $(n - x + 1)$ objects left, each of which could be placed in that box, as illustrated in Figure 3.6.

Permutations

The total number of **permutations** of x objects chosen from n, P_x^n, is the number of possible arrangements when x objects are to be selected from a total of n and arranged in order.

$$P_x^n = n(n - 1)(n - 2) \cdots (n - x + 1)$$

Multiplying and dividing by

$$(n - x)(n - x - 1) \cdots (2)(1) = (n - x)!$$

gives

$$P_x^n = \frac{n(n - 1)(n - 2) \cdots (n - x + 1)(n - x)(n - x - 1) \cdots (2)(1)}{(n - x)(n - x - 1) \cdots (2)(1)}$$

or

$$P_x^n = \frac{n!}{(n - x)!}$$

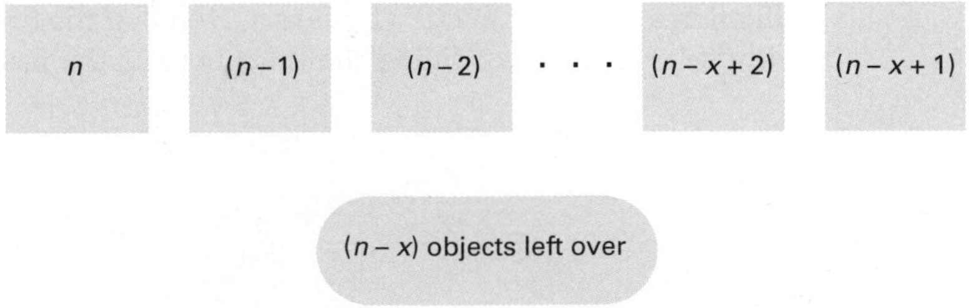

Figure 3.6
The Permutations of x Objects Chosen From n Objects

| n | $(n-1)$ | $(n-2)$ | $\cdots$ | $(n-x+2)$ | $(n-x+1)$ |

$(n - x)$ objects left over

Example 3.6 Five Letters (Permutations)

Suppose that two letters are to be selected from A, B, C, D, and E and arranged in order. How many permutations are possible?

Solution The number of permutations, with $n = 5$ and $x = 2$, is as follows:

$$P_2^5 = \frac{5!}{3!} = 20$$

These are

AB	AC	AD	AE	BC
BA	CA	DA	EA	CB
BD	BE	CD	CE	DE
DB	EB	DC	EC	ED

3. Combinations

Finally, suppose that we are interested in the number of different ways that x objects can be selected from n (where no object may be chosen more than once) but are *not concerned about the order*. Notice in Example 3.6 that the entries in the second and fourth rows are just rearrangements of those directly above them and may, therefore, be ignored. Thus, there are only 10 possibilities for selecting two objects from a group of five if order is not important. The number of possible selections is called the number of *combinations* and is denoted by C_x^n; here x objects are to be chosen from n. To find this number, note first that the number of possible permutations is P_x^n. However, many of these will be rearrangements of the same x objects and, therefore, are irrelevant. In fact, since x objects can be ordered in $x!$ ways, we are concerned with only a proportion $1/x!$ of the permutations. This leads us to a previously stated outcome—namely, Equation 3.5.

Number of Combinations

The **number of combinations**, C_x^n, of x objects chosen from n is the number of possible selections that can be made. This number is

$$C_x^n = \frac{P_x^n}{x!}$$

or simply

$$C_x^n = \frac{n!}{x!(n - x)!} \tag{3.5}$$

In some applications the notation

$$\binom{n}{x} = C_x^n = \frac{n!}{x!(n-x)!}$$

is used.

We illustrate the combination equation, Equation 3.5, by noting that in Example 3.5 the number of combinations of the five computers taken two at a time is the number of elements in the sample space:

$$C_2^5 = \frac{5!}{2!(5-2)!} = \frac{5 \cdot 4 \cdot 3 \cdot 2 \cdot 1}{2 \cdot 1(3 \cdot 2 \cdot 1)} = 10$$

Example 3.7 Probability of Employee Selection (Combinations)

A personnel officer has eight candidates to fill four similar positions. Five candidates are men, and three are women. If, in fact, every combination of candidates is equally likely to be chosen, what is the probability that no women will be hired?

Solution   First, the total number of possible combinations of four candidates chosen from eight is as follows:

$$C_4^8 = \frac{8!}{4!4!} = 70$$

Now, in order for no women to be hired, it follows that the four successful candidates must come from the available five men. The number of such combinations is as follows:

$$C_4^5 = \frac{5!}{4!1!} = 5$$

Therefore, if at the outset each of the 70 possible combinations was equally likely to be chosen, the probability that one of the five all-male combinations would be selected is $5/70 = 1/14$.

Example 3.8 Computer Selection Revised (Classical Probability)

Suppose that Karlyn's store now contains 10 Gateway Computers, 5 Compaq Computers, and 5 Acer computers. Susan enters the store and wants to purchase 3 computers. The computers are selected purely by chance from the shelf. Now what is the probability that 2 Gateway computers and 1 Compaq computer are selected?

Solution   The classical definition of probability will be used. But in this example the combinations formula will be used to determine the number of outcomes in the sample space and the number of outcomes that satisfy the condition A: [2 Gateways and 1 Compaq].

The total number of outcomes in the sample space is as follows:

$$N = C_3^{20} = \frac{20!}{3!(20-3)!} = 1140$$

The number of ways that we can select 2 Gateway computers from the 10 available is computed by the following:

$$C_2^{10} = \frac{10!}{2!(10-2)!} = 45$$

Similarly, the number of ways that we can select 1 Compaq computer from the 5 available is 5 and therefore, the number of outcomes that satisfy event A is as follows:

$$N_A = C_2^{10} \times C_1^5 = 45 \times 5 = 225$$

Finally, the probability of $A = [2$ Gateways and 1 Compaq$]$ is as follows:

$$P_A = \frac{N_A}{N} = \frac{C_2^{10} \times C_1^5}{C_3^{20}} = \frac{45 \times 5}{1140} = 0.197$$

Relative Frequency

We often use relative frequency to determine probabilities for a particular population. The *relative frequency probability* is the number of events in the population that meet the condition divided by the total number in the population. These probabilities indicate how often an event will occur compared to other events. For example, if event A has a probability of 0.40, we know that it will occur 40% of the time. This is more often than event B if event B has only a 0.30 probability of occurrence. But we do not know which event, A or B, will occur next.

Relative Frequency Probability
The **relative frequency probability** is the limit of the proportion of times that event A occurs in a large number of trials, n,

$$P(A) = \frac{n_A}{n} \tag{3.6}$$

where n_A is the number of A outcomes and n is the total number of trials or outcomes. The probability is the limit as n becomes large (or approaches infinity).

The probabilities for the baseball hitter in Example 3.1 were computed from baseball statistical files using the Relative Frequency definition.

Example 3.9 Probability of Incomes Above $75,000 (Relative Probability)

Sally Anderson is considering an opportunity to establish a new car dealership in Great Rivers County, which has a population of 150,000 people. Experience from many other dealerships indicates that in similar areas a dealership will be successful if at least 40% of the households have annual incomes over $75,000. She has asked Aysha Toprak, a marketing consultant, to estimate the proportion of family incomes above $75,000, or the probability of such incomes.

Solution   After considering the problem, Aysha decides that the probability should be based on the relative frequency. She first examines the most recent census data and finds that there were 54,345 households in Great Rivers County and that 31,496 had incomes above \$75,000. Aysha computed the probability for event A, "Family income greater than \$75,000," as follows:

$$P(A) = \frac{n_A}{n} = \frac{31{,}496}{54{,}345} = 0.580$$

Since Aysha knows that there are various errors in census data, she also consulted a recent population data source on the web to which her company subscribes. From this source she found 55,100 households, with 32,047 having incomes above \$75,000. Aysha computed the probability of event A from this source as follows:

$$P(A) = \frac{n_A}{n} = \frac{32{,}047}{55{,}100} = 0.582$$

Since these numbers are close, she could report either. Aysha chose to report the probability as 0.58.

This example shows that probabilities based on the relative frequency approach often can be obtained using existing data sources. It also indicates that different results can and do occur, and that experienced analysts and managers will seek to verify their results by using more than one source. Experience and good judgment are needed to decide if confirming data is close enough.

Subjective Probability

Subjective Probability
Subjective probability expresses an individual's degree of belief about the chance that an event will occur. These subjective probabilities are used in certain management decision procedures.

We can understand the subjective probability concept by using the concept of fair bets. For example, if I assert that the probability of a stock price rising in the next week is 0.5, then I believe that the stock price is just as likely to increase as it is to decrease. In assessing this subjective probability I am not necessarily thinking in terms of repeated experimentation, but instead I am thinking about a stock price over the next week. My subjective probability assessment implies that I would view as fair a bet in which I paid \$1 if the price decreased and I would be paid \$1 if the price increased. If I would receive more than \$1 for a price increase, then I would regard the bet as being in my favor. Similarly, if I believe that the probability of a horse winning a particular race is 0.4, then I am asserting the personal view that there is a 40-to-60 chance of it winning. Given this belief, I would regard as fair a bet in which I would gain \$3 if the horse won and lose \$2 if the horse lost.

We emphasize that subjective probabilities are personal. There is no requirement that different individuals arrive at the same probabilities for the same event. In the stock price example most people would conclude that the appropriate probability of a stock increase is 0.50. However, an individual with more information about the stock might believe otherwise. In the horse race example it is likely that two bettors will reach different subjective probabilities. They may not have the same information, and, even if they do, they may interpret the information differently. We know that individual investors do not all hold the same views on the future behavior of the stock market. Their subjective probabilities depend on their knowledge and experience and the way they interpret it. Managers of different firms have different subjective probabilities about the potential sales opportunities in a given regional market, and, thus, they make different decisions.

Probability Postulates

We need to develop a framework for assessing and manipulating probabilities. To do this, we will first set down three rules (or postulates) that probabilities will be required to obey and show that these requirements are "reasonable."

Probability Postulates

Let S denote the sample space of a random experiment, O_i the basic outcomes, and A an event. For each event A of the sample space, S, we assume that $P(A)$ is defined and we have the following **probability postulates**:

1. If A is any event in the sample space, S,

$$0 \leq P(A) \leq 1$$

2. Let A be an event in S, and let O_i denote the basic outcomes. Then

$$P(A) = \sum_A P(O_i)$$

where the notation implies that the summation extends over all the basic outcomes in A.

3. $P(S) = 1$

The first postulate requires that the probability lie between 0 and 1. The second postulate can be understood in terms of relative frequencies. Suppose that a random experiment is repeated N times. Let N_i be the number of times the basic outcome O_i occurs, and let N_A be the number of times event A occurs. Then, since the basic outcomes are mutually exclusive, N_A is just the sum of N_i for all basic outcomes in A; that is,

$$N_A = \sum_A N_i$$

and, on dividing by the number of trials, N, we obtain

$$\frac{N_A}{N} = \sum_A \frac{N_i}{N}$$

But under the relative frequency concept of probability, N_A/N tends to $P(A)$, and each N_i/N tends to $P(O_i)$ as N becomes infinitely large. Thus, the second postulate can be seen as a logical requirement when probability is viewed in this way.

The third postulate can be paraphrased as "When a random experiment is carried out, something has to happen." Replacing A by the sample space, S, in the second postulate gives

$$P(S) = \sum_S P(O_i)$$

where the summation extends over all the basic outcomes in the sample space. But since $P(S) = 1$ by the third postulate, it follows that

$$\sum_S P(O_i) = 1$$

That is, the sum of the probabilities for all basic outcomes in the sample space is 1.

Consequences of the Postulates

We now list and illustrate some immediate consequences of the three postulates.

1. If the sample space, S, consists of n equally likely basic outcomes, $E_1, E_2, \ldots, E_n$, then

$$P(O_i) = \frac{1}{n} \quad i = 1, 2, \cdots, n$$

This follows because the n outcomes cover the sample space and are equally likely. For example, if a fair die is rolled, the probability for each of the six basic outcomes is $1/6$.

2. If the sample space, S, consists of n equally likely basic outcomes and event A consists of n_A of these outcomes, then

$$P(A) = \frac{n_A}{n}$$

This follows from consequence 1 and postulate 2. Every basic outcome has the probability $1/n$, and, by postulate 2, $P(A)$ is just the sum of the probabilities of the n_A basic outcomes in A. For example, if a fair die is rolled and A is the event "Even number results," there are $n = 6$ basic outcomes, and $n_A = 3$ of these are in A. Thus, $P(A) = 3/6 = 1/2$.

3. Let A and B be mutually exclusive events. Then the probability of their union is the sum of their individual probabilities—that is,

$$P(A \cup B) = P(A) + P(B)$$

In general, if $E_1, E_2, \ldots, E_K$ are mutually exclusive events,

$$P(E_1 \cup E_2 \cup \cdots \cup E_K) = P(E_1) + P(E_2) + \cdots P(E_K)$$

This result is a consequence of postulate 2. The probability of the union of A and B is

$$P(A \cup B) = \sum_{A \cup B} P(O_i)$$

where the summation extends over all basic outcomes in $A \cup B$. But since A and B are mutually exclusive, no basic outcome belongs to both, so

$$\sum_{A \cup B} P(O_i) = \sum_A P(O_i) + \sum_B P(O_i) = P(A) + P(B)$$

4. If $E_1, E_2, \ldots, E_K$ are collectively exhaustive events, the probability of their union is

$$P(E_1 \cup E_2 \cup \cdots \cup E_K) = 1$$

Since the events are collectively exhaustive, their union is the whole sample space, S, and the result follows from postulate 3.

Example 3.10   Web Advertising (Probability)

The Web site for a specialty clothing retailer receives 1,000 hits on a particular day. From past experience it has been determined that every 1,000 hits results in 10 large sales of $500 and 100 small sales less than $500. Assuming that all hits have the same probability of a sale what is the probability of a large sale from a particular hit? What is the probability of a small sale? What is the probability of any sale?

Solution   Over many days with 1,000 hits there will be 10 large sales, 100 small sales, and 890 will result in no sales. Our single hit is selected from the 1,000 total hits. Let A be the event "Selected hit results in a large sale" and let B be the event "Selected hit results in a small sale." The probabilities are as follows:

$$P(A) = \frac{10}{1,000} = 0.01$$
$$P(B) = \frac{100}{1,000} = 0.10$$

The event "Hit results in a sale" is the union of events A and B. Since these events are mutually exclusive,

$$P(A \cup B) = P(A) + P(B) = 0.01 + 0.10 = 0.11$$

Example 3.11   Dow Jones Revisited (Probability)

In Example 3.4 we considered the course of the Dow Jones Industrial Average over 2 days and defined four basic outcomes:

O_1: The Dow Jones average rises on both days.
O_2: The Dow Jones average rises on the first day but does not rise on the second day.
O_3: The Dow Jones average does not rise on the first day but rises on the second day.
O_4: The Dow Jones average does not rise on either day.

Suppose that we assume these four basic outcomes are equally likely. In that case what is the probability that the market will rise on at least 1 of the 2 days?

Solution   The event of interest, "Market rises on at least 1 of the 2 days," contains three of the four basic outcomes—O_1, O_2, and O_3. Since the basic outcomes are all equally likely, it follows that the probability of this event is 3/4, or 0.75.

Example 3.12   Oil Well Drilling (Probability)

In the early stages of the development of the Hibernia oil site in the Atlantic Ocean, the Petroleum Directorate of Newfoundland estimated the probability to be 0.1 that economically recoverable reserves would exceed 2 billion barrels. The probability for reserves in excess of 1 billion barrels was estimated to be 0.5. Given this information, what is the estimated probability of reserves between 1 and 2 billion barrels?

Solution Let A be the event "Reserves exceed 2 billion barrels" and B the event "Reserves between 1 and 2 billion barrels." These are mutually exclusive, and their union, $A \cup B$, is the event "Reserves exceed 1 billion barrels." We therefore have the following:

$$P(A) = 0.1 \quad P(A \cup B) = 0.5$$

Then, since A and B are mutually exclusive,

$$P(B) = P(A \cup B) - P(A) = 0.5 - 0.1 = 0.4$$

EXERCISES

Basic Exercises

3.8 The sample space contains 5 As and 7 Bs. What is the probability that a randomly selected set of 2 will include 1 A and 1 B?

3.9 The sample space contains 6 As and 4 Bs. What is the probability that a randomly selected set of 3 will include 1 A and 2 Bs?

3.10 The sample space contains 10 As and 6 Bs. What is the probability that a randomly selected set of 4 will include 2 As and 2 Bs?

3.11 In a city of 120,000 people there are 20,000 Norwegians. What is the probability that a randomly selected person from the city will be Norwegian?

3.12 In a city of 180,000 people there are 20,000 legal immigrants from Latin America. What is the probability that a random sample of two people from the city will contain two legal immigrants from Latin America?

Application Exercises

3.13 A corporation has just received new machinery that must be installed and checked before it becomes operational. The accompanying table shows a manager's probability assessment for the number of days required before the machinery becomes operational.

Number of days	3	4	5	6	7
Probability	0.08	0.24	0.41	0.20	0.07

Let A be the event "It will be more than 4 days before the machinery becomes operational," and let B be the event "It will be less than 6 days before the machinery becomes available."

a. Find the probability of event A.
b. Find the probability of event B.
c. Find the probability of the complement of event A.
d. Find the probability of the intersection of events A and B.
e. Find the probability of the union of events A and B.

3.14 A fund manager is considering investing in a new software firm based in India. The manager's assessment of probabilities for rates of return on this stock over the next year is summarized in the accompanying table. Let A be the event "Rate of return will be more than 10%" and B be the event "Rate of return will be negative."

Rate of Return	Less than −10%	−10% to 0%	0% to 10%	10% to 20%	More than 20%
Probability	0.04	0.14	0.28	0.33	0.21

a. Find the probability of event A.
b. Find the probability of event B.
c. Describe the event that is the complement of A.
d. Find the probability of the complement of A.
e. Describe the event that is the intersection of A and B.
f. Find the probability of the intersection of A and B.
g. Describe the event that is the union of A and B.
h. Find the probability of the union of A and B.
i. Are A and B mutually exclusive?
j. Are A and B collectively exhaustive?

3.15 A manager has available a pool of eight employees who could be assigned to a project-monitoring task. Four of the employees are women and four are men. Two of the men are brothers. The manager is to make the assignment at random so that each of the eight employees is equally likely to be chosen. Let A be the event "Chosen employee is a man" and B the event "Chosen employee is one of the brothers."

a. Find the probability of A.
b. Find the probability of B.
c. Find the probability of the intersection of A and B.

3.16 If two events are mutually exclusive, we know that the probability of their union is the sum of their individual probabilities. However, this is *not* the case for events that are not mutually exclusive. Verify this assertion by considering the events A and B of Exercise 3.2.

3.17 A department store manager has monitored the number of complaints received per week about poor service. The probabilities for numbers of complaints in a week, established by this review, are shown in the following table. Let A be the event "There will be at least 1 complaint in a week" and B the event "There will be fewer than 10 complaints in a week."

Number of Complaints	0	1 to 3	4 to 6	7 to 9	10 to 12	More than 12
Probability	0.14	0.39	0.23	0.15	0.06	0.03

a. Find the probability of A.
b. Find the probability of B.
c. Find the probability of the complement of A.
d. Find the probability of the union of A and B.
e. Find the probability of the intersection of A and B.
f. Are A and B mutually exclusive?
g. Are A and B collectively exhaustive?

3.18 A corporation receives a particular part in shipments of 100. Research indicated the probabilities shown in the accompanying table for numbers of defective parts in a shipment.

Number Defective	0	1	2	3	More than 3
Probability	0.29	0.36	0.22	0.10	0.03

a. What is the probability that there will be fewer than 3 defective parts in a shipment?
b. What is the probability that there will be more than 1 defective part in a shipment?
c. The five probabilities in the table sum to 1. Why must this be so?

3.3 PROBABILITY RULES

We now develop some important rules for computing probabilities for compound events. The development begins by defining A as an event in the sample space, S, with A and its complement, $\overline{A}$, being mutually exclusive and collectively exhaustive.

$$P(A \cup \overline{A}) = P(A) + P(\overline{A}) = 1$$

This is the *complement rule*.

Complement Rule
Let A be an event and $\overline{A}$ its complement. Then the **complement rule** is as follows:

$$P(\overline{A}) = 1 - P(A) \tag{3.7}$$

For example, when a die is rolled, the probability of obtaining a 1 is 1/6, and, thus, by the complement rule the probability of not getting a 1 is 5/6. This result is important because in some problems it may be easier to find $P(\overline{A})$ and then obtain $P(A)$, as seen in Example 3.13.

Example 3.13 Personnel Selection (Complement Rule)

Wipro Ltd., an Indian-owned software firm, is hiring candidates for four key positions in the management of its new office in Denver. The candidates are five from India and three from the United States. Assuming that every combination of Indian and American is equally likely to be chosen, what is the probability that at least one American will be selected?

Solution   We will solve this problem by first computing the probability of the complement $\overline{A}$ "No American is selected," and then using the complement rule to compute the probability of A "At least one American is selected." This will be easier than computing the probabilities of one through three Americans being selected. Using the method of Classical Probability

$$P(\overline{A}) = \frac{C_4^5}{C_4^8} = \frac{1}{14}$$

and therefore the required probability is

$$P(A) = 1 - P(\overline{A}) = 1 - \frac{1}{14} = \frac{13}{14}$$

Previously, we showed that if two events are mutually exclusive, then the probability of their union is the sum of the probabilities of each event:

$$P(A \cup B) = P(A) + P(B)$$

Next, we want to determine the result when events A and B are not mutually exclusive. In Section 3.1 we noted that events A and $\overline{A} \cap B$ are mutually exclusive and, thus,

$$P(A \cup B) = P(A) + P(\overline{A} \cap B)$$

In addition, events $A \cap B$ and $\overline{A} \cap B$ are mutually exclusive, and their union is B:

$$P(B) = P(A \cap B) \cup P(\overline{A} \cap B)$$

From this we can derive the following result:

$$P(\overline{A} \cap B) = P(B) - P(A \cap B)$$

Combining these two results, we obtain the *addition rule of probabilities* as shown in Figure 3.7.

Figure 3.7   Venn Diagram for Addition Rule $P(A \cup B) = P(A) + P(B) - P(A \cap B)$

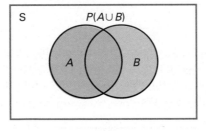

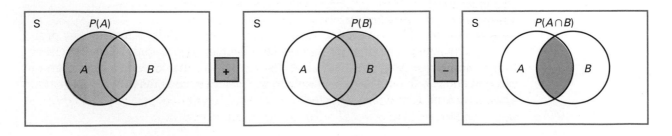

The Addition Rule of Probabilities

Let A and B be two events. Using the **addition rule of probabilities**, the probability of their union is as follows:

$$P(A \cup B) = P(A) + P(B) - P(A \cap B) \qquad (3.8)$$

The Venn diagram in Figure 3.7 provides an intuitive understanding of the addition rule. The larger rectangle, S, represents the entire sample space. The smaller circles, A and B, represent events A and B. We can see that the area where A and B overlap represents the intersection of the two probabilities, $P(A \cap B)$. To compute the probability of the union of events A and B, we first add the events' probabilities, $P(A) + P(B)$. However, notice that the probability of the intersection, $P(A \cap B)$, is counted twice and thus must be subtracted once.

Example 3.14 Product Selection (Addition Rule)

A cell phone company found that 75% of all customers want text messaging on their phones, 80% want photo capability, and 65% want both. What is the probability that a customer will want at least one of these?

Solution Let A be the event "Customer wants text messaging," and B be the event "Customer wants photo capability." Thus,

$$P(A) = 0.75 \qquad P(B) = 0.80 \quad \text{and} \quad P(A \cap B) = 0.65$$

The required probability is as follows:

$$P(A \cup B) = P(A) + P(B) - P(A \cap B) = 0.75 + 0.80 - 0.65 = 0.90$$

Conditional Probability

Consider a pair of events, A and B. Suppose that we are concerned about the probability of A, given that B has occurred. This problem can be approached using the concept of *conditional probability*. The basic idea is that the probability of any event occurring often depends on whether or not other events have occurred. For example, a manufacturer planning to introduce a new brand may test-market the product in a few selected stores. This manufacturer will be much more confident about the brand's success in the wider market if it is well accepted in the test market than if it is not. The firm's assessment of the probability of high sales will, therefore, be conditioned by the test-market outcome.

If I knew that interest rates would fall over the next year, I would be far more bullish about the stock market than if I believed they would rise. What I know, or believe, about interest rates conditions my probability assessment of the course of stock prices. Next, we give a formal statement of conditional probability that can be used to determine the effect of prior results on a probability.

Conditional Probability

Let A and B be two events. The **conditional probability** of event A, given that event B has occurred, is denoted by the symbol $P(A|B)$ and is found to be as follows:

$$P(A \mid B) = \frac{P(A \cap B)}{P(B)} \text{ provided } P(B) > 0 \qquad (3.9)$$

Similarly,

$$P(B \mid A) = \frac{P(A \cap B)}{P(A)} \text{ provided that } P(A) > 0$$

We can better understand these results and those that follow by considering Table 3.3. The conditional probability, $P(A|B)$, is the ratio of the joint probability, $P(A \cap B)$, divided by the probability of the conditional variable, $P(B)$. This conditional probability could be thought of as using only the first row of the table that deals only with condition B. A similar analysis could be made for the conditional probability $P(B|A)$.

Relative frequencies can also help us understand conditional probability. Suppose that we repeat a random experiment n times, with n_B occurrences of event B and $n_{A \cap B}$ occurrences of A and B together. Then the proportion of times that A occurs, when B has occurred, is $n_{A \cap B}/n_B$, and one can think of the conditional probability of A, given B, as the limit of this proportion as the number of replications of the experiment becomes infinitely large:

$$\frac{n_{A \cap B}}{n_B} = \frac{n_{A \cap B}/n}{n_B/n}$$

As n becomes large, the numerator and denominator of the right-hand side of this expression approach $P(A \cap B)$ and $P(B)$, respectively.

Table 3.3
Joint Probability
of A and B

	A	$\overline{A}$	
B	$P(A \cap B)$	$P(\overline{A} \cap B)$	$P(B)$
$\overline{B}$	$P(A \cap \overline{B})$	$P(\overline{A} \cap \overline{B})$	$P(\overline{B})$
	$P(A)$	$P(\overline{A})$	1.0

Example 3.15   Product Choice: Cell Phone Features (Conditional Probability)

In Example 3.14 we noted that 75% of the customers want text messaging, 80% want photo capability, and 65% want both. What are the probabilities that a person who wants text messaging also wants photo capability and that a person who wants photo capability also wants text messaging?

Solution   Designating A as text messaging and B as photo capability we know that $P(A) = 0.75$, $P(B) = 0.80$, and $P(A \cap B) = 0.65$. The probability that a person who wants photo capability also wants text messaging is the conditional probability of event A, given event B:

$$P(A \mid B) = \frac{P(A \cap B)}{P(B)} = \frac{0.65}{0.80} = 0.8125$$

In the same way, the probability that a person who wants text messaging also wants photo capability is as follows:

$$P(B \mid A) = \frac{P(A \cap B)}{P(A)} = \frac{0.65}{0.75} = 0.8667$$

These calculations can also be developed using Table 3.4.

Note that the conditional probability that a person wanting photo capability also wants text messaging is the joint probability 0.65 divided by the probability of a person wanting photo capability, 0.80. A similar calculation can be made for the other conditional probability. We have found that some people believe that using a table such as Table 3.4 provides better motivation and success for solving conditional probability and related problems that follow. Using the table correctly will provide exactly the same results as using the equations. So if this helps you with these problems you can feel perfectly comfortable with using tables to solve the problems.

Table 3.4
Joint Probability
for Example 3.15

	TEXT MESSAGING	NO TEXT MESSAGING	
Photo	0.65	0.15	0.80
No Photo	0.10	0.10	0.20
	0.75	0.25	1.0

The Multiplication Rule of Probabilities

Let A and B be two events. Using the **multiplication rule of probabilities**, the probability of their intersection can be derived from conditional probability as

$$P(A \cap B) = P(A \mid B) \, P(B) \qquad \text{(3.10)}$$

and also as

$$P(A \cap B) = P(B \mid A) \, P(A)$$

Example 3.16 Cell Phone Features (Multiplication Rule)

When the conditional probability of text messaging, given photo capability,

$$P(A \mid B) = \frac{0.65}{0.80} = 0.8125$$

is multiplied by the probability of photo capability, then we have the joint probability of both messaging and photo capability:

$$P(A \cap B) = (0.8125)(0.80) = 0.65$$

In the following example we see an interesting application of the multiplication rule of probabilities. We also tie together some ideas introduced previously.

Example 3.17 Sensitive Questions (Multiplication Rule)

Suppose that a survey was carried out in New York, and each respondent was faced with the following two questions:

   a. Is the last digit of your Social Security number odd?
   b. Have you ever lied on an employment application?

The second question is, of course, quite sensitive, and for various reasons we might expect that a number of people would not answer the question honestly, especially if their response was yes. To overcome this potential bias, respondents were asked to flip a coin and then to answer question (a) if the result was "head" and (b) otherwise. A "yes" response was given by 37% of all respondents. What is the probability that a respondent who was answering the sensitive question, (b), replied "yes"?

Solution We define the following events:

   A: Respondent answers "yes."
   E_1: Respondent answers question (a).
   E_2: Respondent answers question (b).

From the problem discussion we know that $P(A) = 0.37$. We also know that the choice of question was determined by a flip of a coin and that $P(E_1) = 0.50$ and $P(E_2) = 0.50$. In addition, we know the answers to question (a). Since half of all Social Security numbers have an odd last digit, it must be that the probability of a "yes" answer, given that question (a) has been answered, is 0.50—that is, $P(A \mid E_1) = 0.50$.

However, we require $P(A \mid E_2)$, the conditional probability of a "yes" response, given that question (b) was answered. We can obtain this probability by using two results from previous sections. We know that E_1 and E_2 are mutually exclusive and collectively exhaustive. We also know that intersections $E_1 \cap A$ and $E_2 \cap A$ are mutually exclusive and that their union is A. It therefore follows that the sum of the probabilities of these two intersections is the probability of A, so

$$P(A) = P(E_1 \cap A) + P(E_2 \cap A)$$

Next, we use the multiplication rule to obtain

$$P(E_1 \cap A) = P(A \mid E_1) \, P(E_1) = (0.50) \, (0.50) = 0.25$$

and

$$P(E_2 \cap A) = P(A) - P(E_1 \cap A) = 0.37 - 0.25 = 0.12$$

Then we can solve for the conditional probability:

$$P(A \mid E_2) = \frac{P(E_2 \cap A)}{P(E_2)} = \frac{0.12}{0.50} = 0.24$$

From this result, we estimate that 24% of the surveyed population has lied on some employment application.

Statistical Independence

Statistical independence is a special case for which the conditional probability of A, given B, is the same as the unconditional probability of A—that is, $P(A \mid B) = P(A)$. In general, this result is not true, but when it is, we see that knowing that event B has occurred does not change the probability of event A.

> ### Statistical Independence
> Let A and B be two events. These events are said to be **statistically independent** if and only if
>
> $$P(A \cap B) = P(A) P(B) \qquad (3.10)$$
>
> From the multiplication rule it also follows that
>
> $$P(A \mid B) = P(A) \quad \text{(if } P(B) > 0)$$
>
> $$P(B \mid A) = P(B) \quad \text{(if } P(A) > 0)$$
>
> More generally, the events $E_1, E_2, \ldots, E_K$ are mutually statistically independent if and only if
>
> $$P(E_1 \cap E_2 \cap \cdots \cap E_K) = P(E_1) P(E_2) \cdots P(E_K)$$

The logical basis for the definition of statistical independence is best seen in terms of conditional probabilities and is most appealing from a subjective view of probability. Suppose that I believe the probability that event A will occur is $P(A)$. Then I am given the information that event B has occurred. If this new information does not change my view of the probability of A, then $P(A) = P(A \mid B)$, and the information about the occurrence of B is of no value in determining $P(A)$. This definition of statistical independence agrees with a commonsense notion of "independence." To help understand independence, we present in Table 3.5 a revised version of our photo and messaging problem. In this case the marginal probabilities of messaging and photo capabilities are the same, but their usage is independent. Note how the above definitions for independence yield a conclusion of independence for Table 3.5, but not for Table 3.4.

In our following discussions we will refer to events being "independent." For example, the events "Dow Jones will rise" and "Neckties are wider" are independent. Whatever I believe about the likelihood of the latter will not influence my judgment of the chances of the former. Example 3.18 illustrates a test for independence.

Table 3.5
Joint Probability for Photo and Messaging When They Are Independent

	MESSAGING	NO MESSAGING	
Photo	0.60	0.20	0.80
No Photo	0.15	0.05	0.20
	0.75	0.25	1.0

Example 3.18 Probability of College Degrees (Statistical Independence)

Suppose that women obtain 54% of all bachelor degrees in a particular country and that 20% of all bachelor degrees are in business. Also, 8% of all bachelor degrees go to women majoring in business. Are the events "The bachelor degree holder is a woman" and "The bachelor degree is in business" statistically independent?

Solution   Let A denote the event "The bachelor degree holder is a woman" and B denote the event "The bachelor degree is in business." We then have the following:

$$P(A) = 0.54 \quad P(B) = 0.20 \quad P(A \cap B) = 0.08$$

Since

$$P(A)\,P(B) = (0.54)\,(0.20) = 0.108 \neq 0.08 = P(A \cap B)$$

these events are not independent. The dependence can be seen from the conditional probability:

$$P(A \mid B) = \frac{P(A \cap B)}{P(B)} = \frac{0.08}{0.20} = 0.40 \neq 0.54 = P(A)$$

Thus, in the country of interest only 40% of business degrees go to women, whereas women constitute 54% of all degree recipients.

It is also important to distinguish between the terms *mutually exclusive* and *independent*. Two events are mutually exclusive if they cannot occur jointly; that is, the probability of their intersection is 0. For independent events the probability of their intersection is the product of their individual probabilities, and, in general, that probability is not 0 (unless the probability of one of the events is 0, and that result is not very interesting). Also note that if we know two events are mutually exclusive, then if one occurs, the other cannot, and the events are not independent.

In some circumstances independence can be deduced, or at least reasonably inferred, from the nature of a random experiment. For example, if we toss a fair coin two or more times, the probability of a "head" is the same for each toss and is not influenced by the outcome of the previous toss. Then the probability of the intersection can be computed from the product of individual probabilities. This is particularly useful in the case of repeated trials that are logically independent.

Example 3.19 Computer Repair (Independence)

The experience for a particular computer model is that 90% of the computers will operate for at least 1 year before repair is required. A manager purchases three of these computers. What is the probability that all three will work for 1 year without requiring any repair?

Solution   In this case it is reasonable to assume that computer failures are independent for the three computers. They were all produced on the same production line, and their use in the company is likely to be similar. Given the assumption of independence, let E_i be "The ith computer works for 1 year without needing repair." The assumption of independence then leads to the following:

$$P(E_1 \cap E_2 \cap E_3) = P(E_1)\, P(E_2)\, P(E_3) = 0.90^3 = 0.729$$

We must emphasize that events are not always independent. In Example 3.19 the computers might have their power supply from the same electrical circuit, and that circuit may not be protected against electrical surges. In that case a power surge that increases the probability of failure for one computer would result in an increase for all computers. Therefore, the events are not independent. The condition that the events are independent is an assumption and should be used only after careful analysis of the process that is being analyzed.

The following two examples illustrate how we can often simplify the determination of the probability of an event by first computing the probability of the complement and then using the probability of the complement to obtain the probability of the event of interest.

Example 3.20   The Birthday Problem (Complement Rule)

A great question for a party is "What is the probability that at least two people in this room have the same birthday?" Unfortunately, it will be difficult for you to share the solution procedure at the party.

To make the problem manageable, we assign all those born on February 29 to March 1 and assume that all 365 possible birthdays are equally likely in the population at large. We also assume that the people in the room are a random sample, with respect to birthdays, of the larger population. (These simplifications have only very small effects on the numerical results.)

Solution   Let M be the number in the group and A the event "At least one pair has a common birthday." Now, to find the probability of A directly would be very tedious, since we would have to take into account the possibility of more than one pair of matching birthdays. It is easier to find the probability that "All M people have different birthdays"; this is $\overline{A}$.

Since there are 365 possible birthdays for each person, and each can be associated with every possible birthday of other individuals, the total number of equally likely distinct arrangements for M people is 365^M. Next, we ask how many of these outcomes are contained in the event $\overline{A}$, that is, how many that involve the M individuals all having different birthdays. This is precisely the same as asking in how many ways M birthdays can be selected from 365 possible birthdays and arranged in order. The first person's birthday can occur on any of 365 days, the second on any of 364 days, the third on any of 363 days, and so forth. Thus, for M people the number of different birthdays is as follows:

$$(365)\,(364)\,(363) \cdots (365 - M + 1)$$

The number of possible birthdays for M people is 365^M. Hence, the probability that all M birthdays will be different is as follows:

$$P(\overline{A}) = \frac{(365)(364)\cdots(365 - M+1)}{365^M}$$

The required probability of at least two persons is the complement:

$$P(A) = 1 - P(\overline{A}) = 1 - \frac{(365)(364)\cdots(365-M+1)}{365^M}$$

Probabilities for selected numbers of people, M, are

M	10	20	22	23	30	40	60
$P(A)$	0.117	0.411	0.476	0.507	0.706	0.891	0.994

If at least 23 people are in the group, the probability of at least one pair with the same birthday exceeds 0.50. This probability rises sharply as the group size increases until, with 60 people in the group, we are almost certain to find at least one pair. This result is surprising to most people. The probability that any given pair of people will have the same birthday is 1/365. But as the group size increases, the number of possible matches increases until the probability of at least one match becomes quite large. Here, we have the union of events that are individually unlikely, but when the events are considered together, the probability is quite large. Careful analysis using the rather simple probability rules sometimes leads to surprising results.

Example 3.21   Winning Airline Tickets (Complement Rule)

In a promotion for a particular airline, customers and potential customers were given vouchers. A 1/325 proportion of these were worth a free round-trip ticket anywhere this airline flies. How many vouchers would an individual need to collect in order to have a 50% chance of winning at least one free trip?

Solution   The event of interest, A, is "At least one free trip is won from M vouchers." Again, it is easier to find first the probability of the complement, $\overline{A}$ where $\overline{A}$ is the event "No free trips are won with M vouchers." The probability of a win with one voucher is 1/325, and, thus, the probability of not winning is 324/325. If the individual has M vouchers, the event that none of these wins is just the intersection of the "No win" events for each of the vouchers. Moreover, these events are independent, and, thus,

$$P(\overline{A}) = \left(\frac{324}{325}\right)^M$$

and the probability of at least one win is

$$P(A) = 1 - P(\overline{A}) = 1 - \left(\frac{324}{325}\right)^M$$

In order for $P(A)$ to be at least 0.5, the individual needs at least $M = 225$ vouchers.

Again, this result is surprising. One might guess that, if the probability of a win for a single voucher was $1/325$, then 163 vouchers would be enough to ensure a 50% chance of a win. However, in that case one would be implicitly assuming that the probability of a union is the sum of the individual probabilities, neglecting to subtract for double counting in the intersections (which in this case would involve more than one win from M vouchers).

EXERCISES

Basic Exercises

3.19 The probability of A is 0.60, the probability of B is 0.45, and the probability of either is 0.80. What is the probability of both A and B?

3.20 The probability of A is 0.40, the probability of B is 0.45, and the probability of either is 0.85. What is the probability of both A and B?

3.21 The probability of A is 0.60, the probability of B is 0.40, and the probability of either is 0.76. What is the probability of both A and B?

3.22 The probability of A is 0.60, the probability of B is 0.45, and the probability of both is 0.30. What is the probability of either A and B?

3.23 The probability of A is 0.60, the probability of B is 0.45, and the probability of both is 0.30. What is the conditional probability of A, given B? Are A and B independent in a probability sense?

3.24 The probability of A is 0.80, the probability of B is 0.10, and the probability of both is 0.08. What is the conditional probability of A, given B? Are A and B independent in a probability sense?

3.25 The probability of A is 0.30, the probability of B is 0.40 and the probability of both is 0.30. What is the conditional probability of A given B? Are A and B independent in a probability sense?

3.26 The probability of A is 0.70, the probability of B is 0.80, and the probability of both is 0.50. What is the conditional probability of A, given B? Are A and B independent in a probability sense?

Application Exercises

3.27 A company knows that a rival is about to bring out a competing product. It believes that this rival has three possible packaging plans (superior, normal, and cheap) in mind and that all are equally likely. Also, there are three equally likely possible marketing strategies (intense media advertising, price discounts, and the use of a coupon to reduce the price of future purchases). What is the probability that the rival will employ superior packaging in conjunction with an intense media advertising campaign? Assume that packaging plans and marketing strategies are determined independently.

3.28 A financial analyst was asked to evaluate earnings prospects for seven corporations over the next year and to rank them in order of predicted earnings growth rates.
   a. How many different rankings are possible?
   b. If, in fact, a specific ordering is the result of a guess, what is the probability that this guess will turn out to be correct?

3.29 A company has 50 sales representatives. It decides that the most successful representative during the previous year will be awarded a January vacation in Hawaii, while the second most successful will win a vacation in Las Vegas. The other representatives will be required to attend a conference on modern sales methods in Buffalo. How many outcomes are possible?

3.30 A securities analyst claims that, given a specific list of six common stocks, it is possible to predict, in the correct order, the three that will perform best during the coming year. What is the probability of making the correct selection by chance?

3.31 A student committee has six members—four undergraduate and two graduate students. A subcommittee of three members is to be chosen randomly so that each possible combination of three of the six students is equally likely to be selected. What is the probability that there will be no graduate students on the subcommittee?

3.32 The soccer league in one community has five teams. You are required to predict, in order, the top three teams at the end of the season. Ignoring the possibility of ties, calculate the number of different predictions you could make. What is the probability of making the correct prediction by chance?

3.33 A manager has four assistants—Mohamed, Hosea, Mary, and Xun—to assign to four tasks. Each assistant will be assigned to one of the tasks with one assistant for each task.

a. How many different arrangements of assignments are possible?
b. If assignments are made at random, what is the probability that Mary will be assigned to a specific task?

3.34 The senior management of a corporation has decided that in the future it wishes to divide its consulting budget between two firms. Eight firms are currently being considered for this work. How many different choices of two firms are possible?

3.35 You are one of seven female candidates auditioning for two parts—the heroine and her best friend—in a play. Before the auditions you know nothing of the other candidates, and you assume all candidates have equal chances for the parts.

a. How many distinct choices are possible for casting the two parts?
b. In how many of the possibilities in part (a) would you be chosen to play the heroine?
c. In how many of the possibilities in part (a) would you be chosen to play the best friend?
d. Use the results in parts (a) and (b) to find the probability that you will be chosen to play the heroine. Indicate a more direct way of finding this probability.
e. Use the results in parts (a), (b), and (c) to find the probability that you will be chosen to play one of the two parts. Indicate a more direct way of finding this probability.

3.36 A work crew for a building project is to be made up of two craftsmen and four laborers selected from a total of five craftsmen and six laborers.

a. How many different combinations are possible?
b. The brother of one of the craftsmen is a laborer. If the crew is selected at random, what is the probability that both brothers will be selected?
c. What is the probability that neither brother will be selected?

3.37 A mutual fund company has six funds that invest in the U.S. market and four that invest in international markets. A customer wants to invest in two U.S. funds and two international funds.

a. How many different sets of funds from this company could the investor choose?
b. Unknown to this investor, one of the U.S. funds and one of the international funds will seriously underperform next year. If the investor selects funds for purchase at random, what is the probability that at least one of the chosen funds will seriously underperform next year?

3.38 It was estimated that 30% of all seniors on a campus were seriously concerned about employment prospects, 25% were seriously concerned about grades, and 20% were seriously concerned about both. What is the probability that a randomly chosen senior from this campus is seriously concerned about at least one of these two things?

3.39 A video movie store owner finds that 30% of the customers entering the store ask an assistant for help and that 20% of the customers make a purchase before leaving. It is also found that 15% of all customers both ask for assistance and make a purchase. What is the probability that a customer does at least one of these two things?

3.40 Refer to the information in Exercise 3.39, and consider the two events "Customer asks for assistance" and "Customer makes purchase." In answering the following questions, provide reasons expressed in terms of probabilities of relevant events.

a. Are the two events mutually exclusive?
b. Are the two events collectively exhaustive?
c. Are the two events statistically independent?

3.41 A local public-action group solicits donations by telephone. For a particular list of prospects it was estimated that for any individual the probability was 0.05 of an immediate donation by credit card, 0.25 of no immediate donation but a request for further information through the mail, and 0.7 of no expression of interest. Information is mailed to all people requesting it, and it is estimated that 20% of these people will eventually donate. An operator makes a sequence of calls, the outcomes of which can be assumed to be independent.

a. What is the probability that no immediate credit card donation will be received until at least four unsuccessful calls have been made?
b. What is the probability that the first call leading to any donation (either immediately or eventually after a mailing) is preceded by at least four unsuccessful calls?

3.42 A mail-order firm considers three possible events in filling an order:

A: The wrong item is sent.
B: The item is lost in transit.
C: The item is damaged in transit.

Assume that A is independent of both B and C and that B and C are mutually exclusive. The individual event probabilities are $P(A) = 0.02$, $P(B) = 0.01$, and $P(C) = 0.04$. Find the probability that at least one of these foul-ups occurs for a randomly chosen order.

3.43 A coach recruits for a college team a star player who is currently a high school senior. In order to play next year the senior must both complete high school with adequate grades and pass a standardized test. The coach estimates that the probability the athlete will fail to obtain adequate high school grades is 0.02, that the probability the athlete will not pass the standardized test is 0.15, and that these are independent events. According to these estimates, what is the probability that this recruit will be eligible to play in college next year?

3.44 Market research in a particular city indicated that during a week 18% of all adults watch a television program oriented to business and financial issues, 12% read a publication oriented to these issues, and 10% do both.

a. What is the probability that an adult in this city who watches a television program oriented to business and financial issues reads a publication oriented to these issues?

b. What is the probability that an adult in this city who reads a publication oriented to business and financial issues watches a television program oriented to these issues?

3.45 An inspector examines items coming from an assembly line. A review of his record reveals that he accepts only 8% of all defective items. It was also found that 1% of all items from the assembly line are both defective and accepted by the inspector. What is the probability that a randomly chosen item from this assembly line is defective?

3.46 An analyst is presented with lists of four stocks and five bonds. He is asked to predict, in order, the two stocks that will yield the highest return over the next year and the two bonds that will have the highest return over the next year. Suppose that these predictions are made randomly and independently of each other. What is the probability that the analyst will be successful in at least one of the two tasks?

3.47 A bank classifies borrowers as high-risk or low-risk. Only 15% of its loans are made to those in the high-risk category. Of all its loans, 5% are in default, and 40% of those in default were made to high-risk borrowers. What is the probability that a high-risk borrower will default?

3.48 A conference began at noon with two parallel sessions. The session on portfolio management was attended by 40% of the delegates, while the session on chartism was attended by 50%. The evening session consisted of a talk titled "Is the Random Walk Dead?" This was attended by 80% of all delegates.

a. If attendance at the portfolio management session and attendance at the chartism session are mutually exclusive, what is the probability that a randomly chosen delegate attended at least one of these sessions?

b. If attendance at the portfolio management session and attendance at the evening session are statistically independent, what is the probability that a randomly chosen delegate attended at least one of these sessions?

c. Of those attending the chartism session, 75% also attended the evening session. What is the probability that a randomly chosen delegate attended at least one of these two sessions?

3.49 A stock market analyst claims expertise in picking stocks that will outperform the corresponding industry norms. This analyst is presented with a list of five high-technology stocks and a list of five airline stocks, and he is invited to nominate, in order, the three stocks that will do best on each of these two lists over the next year. The analyst claims that success in just one of these two tasks would be a substantial accomplishment. If, in fact, the choices are made randomly and independently, what is the probability of success in at least one of the two tasks merely by chance? Given this result, what do you think of the analyst's claim?

3.50 A quality control manager found that 30% of work-related problems occurred on Mondays and that 20% occurred in the last hour of a day's shift. It was also found that 4% of worker-related problems occurred in the last hour of Monday's shift.

a. What is the probability that a worker-related problem that occurs on a Monday does not occur in the last hour of the day's shift?

b. Are the events "Problem occurs on Monday" and "Problem occurs in the last hour of the day's shift" statistically independent?

3.51 A corporation was concerned with the basic educational skills of its workers and decided to offer a selected group of them separate classes in reading and practical mathematics. Of these workers 40% signed up for the reading classes and 50% for the practical mathematics classes. Of those signing up for the reading classes 30% signed up for the mathematics classes.

a. What is the probability that a randomly selected worker signed up for both classes?

b. What is the probability that a randomly selected worker who signed up for the mathematics classes also signed up for the reading classes?

c. What is the probability that a randomly chosen worker signed up for at least one of these two classes?

d. Are the events "Signs up for the reading classes" and "Signs up for the mathematics classes" statistically independent?

3.52 A lawn-care service makes telephone solicitations, seeking customers for the coming season. A review of the records indicates that 15% of these solicitations produce new customers and that, of these new customers, 80% had used some rival service in the previous year. It is also estimated that, of all solicitation calls made, 60% are to people who had used a rival service the previous year. What is the probability that a call to a person who had used a rival service the previous year will produce a new customer for the lawn-care service?

3.53 An editor may use all, some, or none of three possible strategies to enhance the sales of a book:

   a. An expensive prepublication promotion
   b. An expensive cover design
   c. A bonus for sales representatives who meet predetermined sales levels

In the past, these three strategies have been applied simultaneously to only 2% of the company's books. Twenty percent of the books have had expensive cover designs, and, of these, 80% have had expensive prepublication promotion. A rival editor learns that a new book is to have both an expensive prepublication promotion and an expensive cover design and now wants to know how likely it is that a bonus scheme for sales representatives will be introduced. Compute the probability of interest to the rival editor.

3.4 BIVARIATE PROBABILITIES

In this section we introduce a class of problems that involve two distinct sets of events, which we label $A_1, A_2, \ldots, A_h$ and $B_1, B_2, \ldots, B_k$. These problems have broad application in business and economics. They can be studied by constructing two-way tables that develop intuition for problem solutions. The events A_i and B_j are mutually exclusive and collectively exhaustive within their sets, but intersections $(A_i \cap B_j)$ can occur between all events from the two sets. These intersections can be regarded as basic outcomes of a random experiment. Two sets of events, considered jointly in this way, are called *bivariate*, and the probabilities are called *bivariate probabilities*.

We also consider situations where it is difficult to obtain desired conditional probabilities, but where alternative conditional probabilities are available. It may be difficult to obtain probabilities because the costs of enumeration are high or because some critical, ethical, or legal restriction prevents direct collection of probabilities.

Table 3.6 illustrates the outcomes of bivariate events labeled $A_1, A_2, \ldots, A_h$ and $B_1, B_2, \ldots, B_k$. If probabilities can be attached to all intersections $(A_i \cap B_j)$, then the whole probability structure of the random experiment is known, and other probabilities of interest can be calculated.

As a discussion example, consider a potential advertiser who wants to know both income and other relevant characteristics of the audience for a particular television show. Families may be categorized, using A_i, as to whether they regularly, occasionally, or never watch a particular series. In addition, they can be categorized, using B_j, according to low-, middle-, and high-income subgroups. Then the nine possible cross-classifications can be set out in the form of Table 3.7, with $h = 3$ and $k = 3$. The sub-setting of the population can also be displayed using a

Table 3.6
Outcomes for Bivariate Events

	B_1	B_2	$\ldots$	B_K
A_1	$P(A_1 \cap B_1)$	$P(A_1 \cap B_1)$	$\ldots$	$P(A_1 \cap B_k)$
A_2	$P(A_2 \cap B_1)$	$P(A_2 \cap B_2)$	$\ldots$	$P(A_2 \cap B_k)$
.	.	.	.	.
.	.	.	.	.
.	.	.	.	.
A_h	$P(A_h \cap B_1)$	$P(A_h \cap B_2)$	$\ldots$	$P(A_h \cap B_k)$

Table 3.7
Probabilities for
Television
Viewing and
Income Example

VIEWING FREQUENCY	HIGH INCOME	MIDDLE INCOME	LOW INCOME	TOTALS
Regular	0.04	0.13	0.04	0.21
Occasional	0.10	0.11	0.06	0.27
Never	0.13	0.17	0.22	0.52
Totals	0.27	0.41	0.32	1.00

tree diagram, as shown in Figure 3.8. Beginning at the left, we have the entire population of families. This population is separated into three branches, depending on their television viewing frequency. In turn, each of these branches is separated into three sub-branches, according to the family income level. As a result, there are nine sub-branches corresponding to all combinations of viewing frequency and income level.

Now it is necessary to obtain the probabilities for each of the event intersections. These probabilities, as obtained from viewer surveys, are all presented in Table 3.7. For example, 10% of the families have high incomes and occasionally watch series. These probabilities are developed using the relative frequency concept of probability, assuming that the survey is sufficiently large so that proportions can be approximated as probabilities. On this basis, the probability that a family chosen at random from the population has a high income and occasionally watches the show is 0.10.

Joint and Marginal Probabilities

In the context of bivariate probabilities the intersection probabilities, $P(A_i \cap B_j)$, are called joint probabilities. The probabilities for individual events, $P(A_i)$ or $P(B_j)$, are called **marginal probabilities**. Marginal probabilities are at the margin of a table such as Table 3.5 and can be computed by summing the corresponding row or column.

Figure 3.8
Tree Diagram for
Television Viewing
and Income
Example

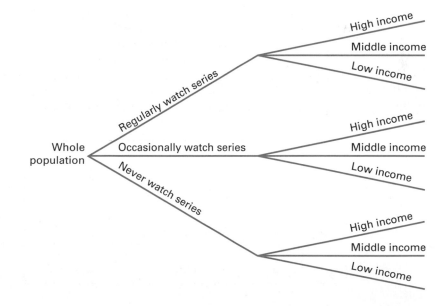

To obtain the marginal probabilities for an event, we merely sum the corresponding mutually exclusive joint probabilities:

$$P(A_i) = P(A_i \cap B_1) + P(A_i \cap B_2) + \ldots + P(A_i \cap B_k)$$

Note that this would be equivalent to summing the probabilities for a particular row in Table 3.7. An analogous argument shows that the probabilities for B_j are the column totals.

Continuing with the example, define the television watching subgroups as A_1, "Regular"; A_2, "Occasional"; and A_3, "Never." Similarly define the income subgroups as B_1, "High"; B_2, "Middle"; and B_3, "Low." Then the probability that a family is an occasional viewer is as follows:

$$P(A_2) = P(A_2 \cap B_1) + P(A_2 \cap B_2) + P(A_2 \cap B_3) = 0.10 + 0.11 + 0.06 = 0.27$$

Similarly, we can add the other rows in Table 3.7 to obtain $P(A_1) = 0.21$ and $P(A_3) = 0.52$. We can also add the columns in Table 3.7 to obtain

$$P(B_1) = 0.27 \quad P(B_2) = 0.41 \quad \text{and} \quad P(B_3) = 0.32$$

Marginal probabilities can also be obtained from tree diagrams like Figure 3.9, which has the same branches as Figure 3.8. The right-hand side contains all of the joint probabilities, and the marginal probabilities for the three viewing frequency events are entered on the main branches by adding the probabilities on the corresponding sub-branches. The tree-branch model is particularly useful when there are more than two events of interest. In this case, for example, the advertiser might also be interested in the age of head of household or the number of children. The marginal probabilities for the various events sum to 1 because those events are mutually exclusive and mutually exhaustive.

In many applications we find that the conditional probabilities are of more interest than the marginal probabilities. An advertiser may be more concerned about the probability that a high-income family is watching than the probability of any family watching. The conditional probability can be obtained easily from the table because we have all of the joint probabilities and the marginal probabilities.

Figure 3.9
Tree Diagram for the Television Viewing—Income Example, Showing Joint and Marginal Probabilities

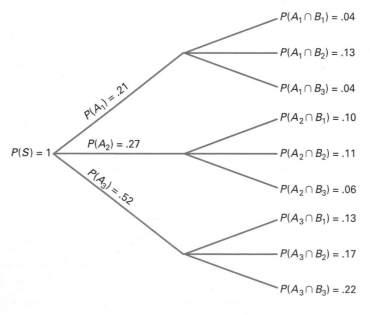

A_1: Regularly watch
A_2: Occasionally watch
A_3: Never watch
B_1: High income
B_2: Middle income
B_3: Low income
S : Sample space

For example, the probability of a high-income family regularly watching the show is as follows:

$$P(A_1 \mid B_1) = \frac{P(A_1 \cap B_1)}{P(B_1)} = \frac{0.04}{0.27} = 0.15$$

Table 3.8 shows the probability of the viewer groups conditional on income levels. Note that the conditional probabilities with respect to a particular income group always add up to 1, as seen for the three columns in Table 3.8. This will always be the case, as seen by the following:

$$\sum_{i=1}^{h} P(A_i \mid B_j) = \sum_{i=1}^{h} \frac{P(A_i \cap B_j)}{P(B_j)} = \frac{P(B_j)}{P(B_j)} = 1$$

The conditional probabilities for the income groups, given viewing frequencies, can also be computed, as shown in Table 3.9, using the definition for conditional probability and the joint and marginal probabilities.

To obtain the conditional probabilities with respect to income groups in Table 3.7 we divide each of the joint probabilities in a row by the marginal probability in the right-hand column. For example,

$$P(\text{LowIncome} \mid \text{OccasionalViewer}) = \frac{0.06}{0.27} = 0.22$$

We can also check, by using a two-way table, whether or not paired events are statistically independent. Recall that events A_i and B_j are independent if and only if their joint probability is the product of their marginal probabilities—that is, if

$$P(A_i \cap B_j) = P(A_i)\, P(B_j)$$

In Table 3.7 joint events A_2 ("Occasionally watch") and B_1 ("High income") have a probability of

$$P(A_2 \cap B_1) = 0.10$$

and

$$P(A_2) = 0.27 \quad P(B_1) = 0.27$$

The product of these marginal probabilities is 0.0729 and, thus, not equal to the joint probability of 0.10. Hence, events A_2 and B_1 are not statistically independent.

Table 3.8
Conditional Probabilities of Viewing Frequencies, Given Income Levels

VIEWING FREQUENCY	HIGH INCOME	MIDDLE INCOME	LOW INCOME
Regular	0.15	0.32	0.12
Occasional	0.37	0.27	0.19
Never	0.48	0.41	0.69

Table 3.9
Conditional Probabilities of Income Levels, Given Viewing Frequencies

VIEWING FREQUENCY	HIGH INCOME	MIDDLE INCOME	LOW INCOME
Regular	0.19	0.62	0.19
Occasional	0.37	0.41	0.22
Never	0.25	0.33	0.42

> **Independent Events**
> Let A and B be a pair of events, each broken into mutually exclusive and collectively exhaustive event categories denoted by labels $A_1, A_2, \ldots, A_h$ and $B_1, B_2, \ldots, B_k$. If every event A_i is statistically independent of every event B_j, then A and B are **independent events**.

Since A_2 and B_1 are not statistically independent, it follows that the events "Viewing frequency" and "Income" are not independent.

In many practical applications the joint probabilities will not be known precisely. A sample from a population is obtained, and estimates of the joint probabilities are made from the sample data. We want to know, based on this sample evidence, if these events are independent of one another. We will develop a procedure for conducting such a test later in the book.

Odds

Odds are used to communicate probability information in some situations. For example, a sports analyst might report that the odds in favor of team A winning over team B are 2 to 1. Odds can be converted directly to probabilities, and probabilities can be converted to odds using the following equations.

> **Odds**
> The **odds** in favor of a particular event are given by the ratio of the probability of the event divided by the probability of its complement. The odds in favor of A are as follows:
>
> $$\text{Odds} = \frac{P(A)}{1 - P(A)} = \frac{P(A)}{P(\overline{A})} \qquad (3.11)$$

Therefore, the odds of 2 to 1 can be converted to the probability of A winning,

$$\frac{2}{1} = \frac{P(A)}{1 - P(A)}$$

and by basic algebra

$$2 \times (1 - P(A)) = P(A)$$

giving

$$P(A) = 0.67$$

Similarly, if the odds in favor of winning are 3 to 2, then the probability of winning is 0.60. Note that $0.60/0.40$ is equal to $3/2$.

Overinvolvement Ratios

There are a number of situations where it is difficult to obtain desired conditional probabilities, but alternative conditional probabilities are available. It may be difficult to obtain probabilities because the costs of enumeration are high or because some critical, ethical, or legal restriction prevents direct collection of probabilities. In some of those cases it may be possible to use basic probability relationships to derive desired probabilities from available probabilities. In this section we develop one such approach based on the use of overinvolvement ratios (Reference 3).

We will start by considering a simple example. Suppose that we know 60% of the purchasers of our product have seen our advertisement, but only 30% of the nonpurchasers have seen the advertisement. The ratio of 60% to 30% is the overinvolvement of the event "Seen our advertisement" in the purchasers group, compared to the nonpurchasers group. In the analysis to follow we show how an overinvolvement ratio greater than 1.0 provides evidence that, for example, advertising influences purchase behavior.

An overinvolvement ratio, presented in Equation 3.12, is the ratio of the probability of an event—such as viewing an advertisement—that occurs under two mutually exclusive and complementary outcome conditions, such as a product sale or not a product sale. If the ratio of the conditional probabilities is not equal to 1.0, then the event has an influence on the outcome condition. These ratios have applications in a number of business situations, including marketing, production, and accounting. In this section we develop the theory and application of *overinvolvement ratios*.

Overinvolvement Ratios

The probability of event A_1, conditional on event B_1, divided by the probability of A_1, conditional on event B_2, is defined as the **overinvolvement ratio**:

$$\frac{P(A_1 \mid B_1)}{P(A_1 \mid B_2)} \tag{3.12}$$

An overinvolvement ratio greater than 1,

$$\frac{P(A_1 \mid B_1)}{P(A_1 \mid B_2)} > 1.0$$

implies that event A_1 increases the conditional odds ratio in favor of B_1:

$$\frac{P(B_1 \mid A_1)}{P(B_2 \mid A_1)} > \frac{P(B_1)}{P(B_2)}$$

Consider a company that wishes to determine the effectiveness of a new advertisement. An experiment is conducted in which the advertisement is shown to one customer group and not to another, followed by observation of the purchase behavior of both groups. Studies of this type have a high probability of error; they can be biased because people who are watched closely often behave differently than they do when not being observed. It is possible, however, to measure the percentage of buyers who have seen an ad and to measure the percentage of nonbuyers who have seen the ad. Let us consider how those study data can be analyzed to determine the effectiveness of the new advertisement.

Advertising effectiveness is determined using the following analysis. The population is divided into the following categories:

B_1: Buyers
B_2: Nonbuyers

And

A_1: Those who have seen the advertisement
A_2: Those who have not seen the advertisement

The odds in favor of the buyer in this problem are as follows:

$$\frac{P(B_1)}{P(B_2)}$$

Similarly, we can define the conditional odds, in which we use the ratio of the probabilities that are both conditional on the same event. For this problem the odds of a buyer being conditional on the event "Have seen an advertisement" are as follows:

$$\frac{P(B_1 \mid A_1)}{P(B_2 \mid A_1)}$$

If the conditional odds are greater than the unconditional odds, the conditioning event is said to have an influence on the event of interest. Thus, advertising would be considered effective if

$$\frac{P(B_1 \mid A_1)}{P(B_2 \mid A_1)} > \frac{P(B_1)}{P(B_2)}$$

The left-hand terms are equal to the following:

$$P(B_1 \mid A_1) = \frac{P(A_1 \mid B_1)P(B_1)}{P(A_1)}$$

$$P(B_2 \mid A_1) = \frac{P(A_1 \mid B_2)P(B_2)}{P(A_1)}$$

By substituting these later terms, the first equation becomes the following:

$$\frac{P(A_1 \mid B_1)P(B_1)}{P(A_1 \mid B_2)P(B_2)} > \frac{P(B_1)}{P(B_2)}$$

Dividing both sides by the right-hand ratio, we obtain the following:

$$\frac{P(A_1 \mid B_1)}{P(A_1 \mid B_2)} > 1.0$$

This result shows that, if a larger percent of buyers have seen the advertisement, compared to nonbuyers, then the odds in favor of purchasing being conditional on having seen the advertisement are greater than the unconditional odds. Therefore, we have evidence that the advertising is associated with an increased probability of purchase.

From the original problem, 60% of the purchasers and 30% of the nonpurchasers had seen the advertisement. The overinvolvement ratio is 2.0 (60/30), and, thus, we conclude that the advertisement increases the probability of purchase. Market researchers use this result to evaluate the effectiveness of advertising and other sales promotion activities. Purchasers of products are asked whether they have seen certain advertisements. This is combined with random sample surveys of households from which the percentage of nonpurchasers who have seen an advertisement is determined.

Consider another situation in which it is difficult, illegal, or unethical to obtain probability results.

Example 3.22 Alcohol and Highway Crashes (Overinvolvement Ratios)

Researchers at the National Highway Traffic Safety Administration in the U.S. Department of Transportation wished to determine the effect of alcohol on highway crashes. Clearly, it would be unethical to provide one group of drivers with alcohol and then compare their crash involvement with that of a group that did not have alcohol. However, researchers did find that 10.3% of the nighttime drivers in a specific county had been drinking and that 32.4% of the single-vehicle-accident drivers during the same time and in the same county had been drinking. Single-vehicle accidents were chosen to ensure that any driving error could be assigned to only one driver, whose alcohol usage had been measured. Based on these results they wanted to know if there was evidence to conclude that accidents increased at night when drivers had been drinking. Use the data to determine if alcohol usage leads to an increased probability of crashes (Reference 2).

Solution Using the overinvolvement ratios can help solve this problem. First, the events in the sample space need to be defined:

A_1: The driver had been drinking.
A_2: The driver had not been drinking.
C_1: The driver was involved in a crash.
C_2: The driver was not involved in a crash.

We know that alcohol, A_1, increases the probability of a crash if

$$\frac{P(A_1 \mid C_1)}{P(A_1 \mid C_2)} > 1.0$$

From the research the conditional probabilities are as follows:

$$P(A_1 \mid C_1) = 0.324$$

$$P(A_1 \mid C_2) = 0.103$$

Using these results, the overinvolvement ratio is as follows:

$$\frac{P(A_1 \mid C_1)}{P(A_1 \mid C_2)} = \frac{0.324}{0.103} = 3.15$$

Based on this analysis there is evidence to conclude that alcohol increases the probability of automobile crashes.

The overinvolvement ratio is a good example of how mathematical manipulations of probabilities can be used to obtain results that are useful for business decisions. The wide usage of automated methods of data collection, including bar code scanners, audience segmentation, and census data on tapes and disks, provides the possibility to compute many different probabilities, conditional probabilities, and overinvolvement ratios. As a result, analyses similar to those presented in this chapter have become part of the daily routine for marketing analysts and product managers.

EXERCISES

Basic Exercises

Basic exercises 3.54–3.60 refer to Table 3.10.

3.54 What is the joint probability of "High income" and "Never"?

3.55 What is the joint probability of "Low income" and "Regular"?

3.56 What is the joint probability of "Middle income" and "Never"?

3.57 What is the joint probability of "Middle income" and "Occasional"?

3.58 What is the conditional probability of "High income," given "Never"?

3.59 What is the conditional probability of "Low income," given "Occasional"?

3.60 What is the conditional probability of "Regular," given "High income"?

3.61 The probability of a sale is 0.80. What are the odds in favor of a sale?

3.62 The probability of a sale is 0.50. What are the odds in favor of a sale?

3.63 Consider two groups of students: B_1, are students who received high scores on tests; and B_2, are students who received low scores on tests. In group B_1, 80% study more than 25 hours per week, and in group B_2, 40% study more than 25 hours per week. What is the overinvolvement ratio for high study levels in high test scores over low test scores?

3.64 Consider two groups of students: B_1, are students who received high scores on tests; and B_2, are students who received low scores on tests. In group B_1, 40% study more than 25 hours per week, and in group B_2, 20% study more than 25 hours per week. What is the overinvolvement ratio for high study levels in high test scores over low test scores?

3.65 Consider two groups of students: B_1, are students who received high scores on tests; and B_2, are students who received low scores on tests. In group B_1, 20% study more than 25 hours per week, and in group B_2, 40% study more than 25 hours per week. What is the overinvolvement ratio for high study levels in high test scores over low test scores?

Application Exercises

3.66 A survey carried out for a supermarket classified customers according to whether their visits to the store are frequent or infrequent and whether they often, sometimes, or never purchase generic products. The accompanying table gives the proportions of people surveyed in each of the six joint classifications.

Frequency of Visit	Purchase of Generic Products		
	Often	Sometimes	Never
Frequent	0.12	0.48	0.19
Infrequent	0.07	0.06	0.08

a. What is the probability that a customer both is a frequent shopper and often purchases generic products?

b. What is the probability that a customer who never buys generic products visits the store frequently?

c. Are the events "Never buys generic products" and "Visits the store frequently" independent?

d. What is the probability that a customer who infrequently visits the store often buys generic products?

e. Are the events "Often buys generic products" and "Visits the store infrequently" independent?

f. What is the probability that a customer frequently visits the store?

g. What is the probability that a customer never buys generic products?

h. What is the probability that a customer either frequently visits the store or never buys generic products or both?

3.67 A consulting organization predicts whether corporations' earnings for the coming year will be unusually low, unusually high, or normal. Before deciding whether to continue purchasing these forecasts, a stockbroker compares past predictions with actual outcomes. The accompanying table shows proportions in the nine joint classifications.

Table 3.10 Probabilities for Television Viewing and Income

VIEWING FREQUENCY	HIGH INCOME	MIDDLE INCOME	LOW INCOME	TOTALS
Regular	0.10	0.15	0.05	0.30
Occasional	0.10	0.20	0.10	0.40
Never	0.05	0.05	0.20	0.30
Totals	0.25	0.40	0.35	1.00

	Prediction		
	Unusually	Normal	Unusually
Outcome	High		Low
Unusually high	0.23	0.12	0.03
Normal	0.06	0.22	0.08
Unusually low	0.01	0.06	0.19

a. What proportion of predictions have been for unusually high earnings?

b. What proportion of outcomes have been for unusually high earnings?

c. If a firm were to have unusually high earnings, what is the probability that the consulting organization would correctly predict this event?

d. If the organization predicted unusually high earnings for a corporation, what is the probability that these would materialize?

e. What is the probability that a corporation for which unusually high earnings had been predicted will have unusually low earnings?

3.68 Subscribers to a local newspaper were asked whether they regularly, occasionally, or never read the business section and also whether they had traded common stocks (or shares in a mutual fund) over the last year. The table shown here indicates the proportions of subscribers in six joint classifications.

Traded	Read Business Section		
Stocks	Regularly	Occasionally	Never
Yes	0.18	0.10	0.04
No	0.16	0.31	0.21

a. What is the probability that a randomly chosen subscriber never reads the business section?

b. What is the probability that a randomly chosen subscriber has traded stocks over the last year?

c. What is the probability that a subscriber who never reads the business section has traded stocks over the last year?

d. What is the probability that a subscriber who traded stocks over the last year never reads the business section?

e. What is the probability that a subscriber who does not regularly read the business section traded stocks over the last year?

3.69 A corporation regularly takes deliveries of a particular sensitive part from three subcontractors. It found that the proportion of parts that are good or defective from the total received were as shown in the following table:

	Subcontractor		
Part	A	B	C
Good	0.27	0.30	0.33
Defective	0.02	0.05	0.03

a. If a part is chosen randomly from all those received, what is the probability that it is defective?

b. If a part is chosen randomly from all those received, what is the probability it is from subcontractor B?

c. What is the probability that a part from subcontractor B is defective?

d. What is the probability that a randomly chosen defective part is from subcontractor B?

e. Is the quality of a part independent of the source of supply?

f. In terms of quality, which of the three subcontractors is most reliable?

3.70 Students in a business statistics class were asked what grade they expected in the course and whether they worked on additional problems beyond those assigned by the instructor. The following table gives proportions of students in each of eight joint classifications.

Worked	Expected Grade			
Problems	A	B	C	Below C
Yes	0.12	0.06	0.12	0.02
No	0.13	0.21	0.26	0.08

a. Find the probability that a randomly chosen student from this class worked on additional problems.

b. Find the probability that a randomly chosen student from this class expects an A.

c. Find the probability that a randomly chosen student who worked on additional problems expects an A.

d. Find the probability that a randomly chosen student who expects an A worked on additional problems.

e. Find the probability that a randomly chosen student who worked on additional problems expects a grade below B.

f. Are "Worked additional problems" and "Expected grade" statistically independent?

3.71 The accompanying table shows proportions of computer salespeople classified according to marital status and whether they left their jobs or stayed over a period of 1 year.

Marital Status	Stayed 1 Year	Left
Married	0.64	0.13
Single	0.17	0.06

a. What is the probability that a randomly chosen salesperson was married?

b. What is the probability that a randomly chosen salesperson left the job within the year?

c. What is the probability that a randomly chosen single salesperson left the job within the year?

d. What is the probability that a randomly chosen salesperson who stayed in the job over the year was married?

3.72 The accompanying table shows proportions of adults in metropolitan areas, categorized as to whether they are public radio contributors and whether or not they voted in the last election.

Voted	Contributors	Non-Contributors
Yes	0.63	0.13
No	0.14	0.10

a. What is the probability that a randomly chosen adult from this population voted?

b. What is the probability that a randomly chosen adult from this population contributes to public radio?

c. What is the probability that a randomly chosen adult from this population did not contribute and did not vote?

3.73 A campus student club distributed material about membership to new students attending an orientation meeting. Of those receiving this material 40% were men and 60% were women. Subsequently, it was found that 7% of the men and 9% of the women who received this material joined the club.

a. Find the probability that a randomly chosen new student who receives the membership material will join the club.

b. Find the probability that a randomly chosen new student who joins the club after receiving the membership material is a woman.

3.74 An analyst attempting to predict a corporation's earnings next year believes that the corporation's business is quite sensitive to the level of interest rates. He believes that, if average rates in the next year are more than 1% higher than this year, the probability of significant earnings growth is 0.1. If average rates next year are more than 1% lower than this year, the probability of significant earnings growth is estimated to be 0.8. Finally, if average interest rates next year are within 1% of this year's rates, the probability for significant earnings growth is put at 0.5. The analyst estimates that the probability is 0.25 that rates next year will be more than 1% higher than this year and 0.15 that they will be more than 1% lower than this year.

a. What is the estimated probability that both interest rates will be 1% higher and significant earnings growth will result?

b. What is the probability that this corporation will experience significant earnings growth?

c. If the corporation exhibits significant earnings growth, what is the probability that interest rates will have been more than 1% lower than in the current year?

3.75 Forty-two percent of a corporation's blue-collar employees were in favor of a modified health care plan, and 22% of its blue-collar employees favored a proposal to change the work schedule. Thirty-four percent of those favoring the health care plan modification favored the work schedule change.

a. What is the probability that a randomly selected blue-collar employee is in favor of both the modified health care plan and the changed work schedule?

b. What is the probability that a randomly chosen blue-collar employee is in favor of at least one of the two changes?

c. What is the probability that a blue-collar employee favoring the work schedule change also favors the modified health care plan?

3.76 The grades of a freshman college class, obtained after the first year of college, were analyzed. Seventy percent of the students in the top quarter of the college class had graduated in the upper 10% of their high school class, as had 50% of the students in the middle half of the college class and 20% of the students in the bottom quarter of the college class.

a. *What is the probability that a randomly chosen freshman graduated in the upper 10% of his high school class?*

b. What is the probability that a randomly chosen freshman who graduated in the upper 10% of his high school class will be in the top quarter of the college class?

c. What is the probability that a randomly chosen freshman who did not graduate in the upper 10% of his high school class will not be in the top quarter of the college class?

3.77 Before books aimed at preschool children are marketed, reactions are obtained from a panel of preschool children. These reactions are categorized as "favorable," "neutral," or "unfavorable." Subsequently, book sales are categorized as "high," "moderate," or "low," according to the norms of this market. Similar panels have evaluated 1,000 books in the past. The accompanying table shows their reactions and the resulting market performance of the books.

Sales	Panel Reaction		
	Favorable	Neutral	Unfavorable
High	173	101	61
Moderate	88	211	70
Low	42	113	141

a. If the panel reaction is favorable, what is the probability that sales will be high?

b. If the panel reaction is unfavorable, what is the probability that sales will be low?

c. If the panel reaction is neutral or better, what is the probability that sales will be low?

d. If sales are low, what is the probability that the panel reaction was neutral or better?

3.78 A manufacturer produces boxes of candy, each containing 10 pieces. Two machines are used for this purpose. After a large batch has been produced, it is discovered that one of the machines, which produces 40% of the total output, has a fault that has led to the introduction of an impurity into 10% of the pieces of candy it makes. From a single box of candy, one piece is selected at random and tested. If that piece contains no impurity, what is the probability that the faulty machine produced the box from which it came?

3.79 A student feels that 70% of his college courses have been enjoyable and the remainder have been boring. This student has access to student evaluations of professors and finds out that professors who had previously received strong positive evaluations from their students have taught 60% of his enjoyable courses and 25% of his boring courses. Next semester the student decides to take three courses, all from professors who have received strongly positive student evaluations. Assume that this student's reactions to the three courses are independent of one another.

a. What is the probability that this student will find all three courses enjoyable?

b. What is the probability that this student will find at least one of the courses enjoyable?

3.5 BAYES' THEOREM

In this section we introduce an important result that has many applications to management decision making. Bayes' theorem provides a way of revising conditional probabilities by using available information. It also provides a procedure for determining how probability statements should be adjusted, given additional information.

Reverend Thomas Bayes (1702–1761) developed Bayes' theorem, originally published in 1763 after his death and again in 1958 (Reference 1). Because games of chance and hence probability were considered to be works of the devil, the results were not widely publicized. Since World War II a major area of statistics and a major area of management decision theory have developed based on the original works of Thomas Bayes. We begin our development with an example problem followed by a more formal development.

Example 3.23 Drug Screening (Bayes' Theorem)

A number of amateur and professional sports organizations use routine screening tests to determine if athletes are using performance enhancing drugs. Jennifer Smith, president of an amateur athletic union, has requested an analysis to determine the feasibility of screening athletes to determine if they are using performance enhancing drugs. Sanctions against professional athletes using these drugs have increased substantially. Amateur athletes are increasingly denied participation or deprived of victories if they are found to be users. Suppose that 10% of the athletes seeking participation in the athletic union have used performance enhancing drugs. In addition, suppose that a test is available that correctly identifies an athlete's drug usage 90% of the time. If an athlete is a drug user, the probability is 0.90 that the athlete is correctly identified by the test as a drug user. Similarly, if the athlete is not a drug user, the probability is 0.90 that the athlete is correctly identified as not using performance enhancing drugs.

We should note that there are potential ethical and possible legal questions concerning the use of these tests. Here, we are concerned about the feasibility of using such a test if one has decided that such a test is proper, given the legal and value systems.

Solution The first step in the analysis is to identify the events in the sample space:

D_1: The athlete is a user of performance enhancing drugs.
D_2: The athlete is not a user of performance enhancing drugs.

The proposed test indicates positive or negative results:

T_1: Test says that the athlete is a user of performance enhancing drugs.
T_2: Test says that the athlete is not a user of performance enhancing drugs.

From the information provided the following probabilities can be defined:

$$P(D_1) = 0.10 \qquad P(D_2) = 0.90$$
$$P(T_1 \mid D_1) = 0.90 \qquad P(T_2 \mid D_1) = 0.10$$
$$P(T_1 \mid D_2) = 0.10 \qquad P(T_2 \mid D_2) = 0.90$$

Using these probabilities, a two-way table containing the joint probabilities can be constructed:

$$P(D_1 \cap T_1) = P(T_1 \mid D_1)P(D_1) = 0.90 \times 0.10 = 0.90$$

$$P(D_1 \cap T_2) = P(T_2 \mid D_1)P(D_1) = 0.10 \times 0.10 = 0.01$$

$$P(D_2 \cap T_1) = P(T_1 \mid D_2)P(D_2) = 0.10 \times 0.90 = 0.90$$

$$P(D_2 \cap T_2) = P(T_2 \mid D_2)P(D_2) = 0.90 \times 0.90 = 0.81$$

From Table 3.11 we can easily determine the conditional probability of a drug user, given that the test says drug user, by dividing the joint probability of D_1 and T_1 (0.09) by the marginal probability of T_1 (0.18):

$$P(D_1 \mid T_1) = \frac{P(D_1 \cap T_1)}{P(T_1)} = \frac{0.90}{0.18} = 0.50$$

Similarly, the probability of not a drug user, given that the test says not a drug user, can be obtained from the second column of Table 3.11:

$$P(D_2 \mid T_2) = \frac{P(D_2 \cap T_2)}{P(T_2)} = \frac{0.81}{0.82} = 0.988$$

From these results we see that, if the test says an athlete is not a drug user, the probability is very high that the test result is correct. However, if the test says that the athlete is a drug user, the probability is only 0.50 that the athlete is a drug user. This is a large increase over a probability of 0.10 for a randomly selected athlete. However, it is clear that the athletic association would not want to reject athletes merely on the results of this screening test. The potential for unethical actions and

Table 3.11 Drug Test Subgroups

	T_1 (TEST SAYS DRUG USER)	T_2 (TEST SAYS NOT A DRUG USER)	TOTAL
D_1 (Drug User)	0.09	0.01	0.10
D_2 (Not a Drug User)	0.09	0.81	0.90
Total	0.18	0.82	1.0

serious legal action would be too great. The best strategy would be to use a second independent test to further screen the athlete identified as a drug user by the first test. We stress again that there may be serious ethical and medical concerns if athletes are rejected because they are drug users.

Given this background, we will now provide a more formal development of Bayes' theorem. To begin, we first review the multiplication rule, Equation 3.10:

$$P(A \cap B) = P(A \mid B)P(B) = P(B \mid A)P(A)$$

Bayes' theorem follows from this rule.

Bayes' Theorem

Let *A* and *B* be two events. Then **Bayes' theorem** states that

$$P(B \mid A) = \frac{P(A \mid B)P(B)}{P(A)} \tag{3.13}$$

and

$$P(A \mid B) = \frac{P(B \mid A)P(A)}{P(B)}$$

Solution Steps for Bayes' Theorem

1. Define the subset events from the problem.
2. Define the probabilities for the events defined in Step 1.
3. Compute the complements of the probabilities.
4. Apply Bayes' theorem to compute the probability for the problem solution.

Here, we apply these solution steps to a problem that requires careful analysis. We consider Example 3.23 again. The first task is to identify the events in the sample space. The sample space in Example 3.23 consists of athletes separated into D_1, users of performance enhancing drugs, and D_2, not users of the drugs. This required an independent judgment of which athletes were actually drug users and which were not. These events cover the sample space. Events were also identified by their test classification. Events are T_1, the test indicates drug user, and T_2, the test indicates not a drug user. These events also cover the sample space. Note that a test result T_1, which indicates drug user, does not guarantee that the person is a drug user.

After the events have been defined, we need to determine the capability of the procedure to predict, using the data. Thus, in Example 3.23 the test was given to a group of known users of performance enhancing drugs and to a group of known non-drug users. These test results provided the conditional probabilities of the test results, given either drug user or not. The data were converted to information concerning the quality of the screening test predictions by using Bayes' theorem. The final task is to express one or more questions in the form of Bayes' theorem. In Example 3.23 we were interested in the probability that an athlete was a drug user, given that the athlete obtained a positive result on the test. We also realized that it was important to know the probability that an athlete was not a drug user, given a positive test result.

An interesting interpretation of Bayes' theorem has been developed in the context of subjective probabilities. Suppose that an individual is interested in event B and forms a subjective view of the probability that B will occur; in this context the probability $P(B)$ is called a *prior* probability. If the individual then acquires an additional piece of information—namely, that event A has occurred—this may cause a modification of the initial judgment as to the likelihood of the occurrence of B. Since A is known to have happened, the relevant probability for B is now the conditional probability of B, given A, and is termed the *posterior* probability. Viewed in this way, Bayes' theorem can be thought of as a mechanism for updating a prior probability to a posterior probability when the information that A has occurred becomes available. The theorem then states that the updating is accomplished through the multiplication of the prior probability by $P(A \mid B)/P(A)$.

We know that people commonly form and subsequently modify subjective probability assessments. For example, an important part of an auditor's work is to determine whether or not the account balances are correct. Before examining a particular account, the auditor will have formed an opinion, based on previous audits, of the probability that there is an error. However, if the balance is found to be substantially different from what might be expected on the basis of the last few years' figures, the auditor will believe that the probability of an error is higher and, therefore, give the account particularly close attention. Here, the prior probability has been updated in the light of additional information.

Example 3.24 Auditing Business Records (Bayes' Theorem)

Based on an examination of past records of a corporation's account balances, an auditor finds that 15% have contained errors. Of those balances in error 60% were regarded as unusual values based on historical figures. Of all the account balances 20% were unusual values. If the figure for a particular balance appears unusual on this basis, what is the probability that it is in error?

Solution Solution Let A be "Error in account balance" and B be "Unusual value based on historical figures." Then from the available information,

$$P(A) = 0.15 \qquad P(B) = 0.20 \qquad P(B \mid A) = 0.60$$

Using Bayes' theorem,

$$P(A \mid B) = \frac{P(B \mid A)P(A)}{P(B)} = \frac{(0.60)(0.15)}{0.20} = 0.45$$

Thus, given the information that the account balance appears unusual, the probability that it is in error is modified from the prior 0.15 to the posterior 0.45.

Bayes' theorem is often expressed in a different, but equivalent, form that uses more detailed information. Let $E_1, E_2, \ldots, E_K$ be K mutually exclusive and collectively exhaustive events, and let A be some other event. We can find the probability of E_i, given A, by using Bayes' theorem:

$$P(E_i \mid A) = \frac{P(A \mid E_i)P(E_i)}{P(A)}$$

The denominator can be expressed in terms of the probabilities of A, given the various E_is, by using the intersections and the multiplication rule:

$$P(A) = P(A \cap E_1) + P(A \cap E_2) + \cdots + P(A \cap E_K)$$

$$= P(A \mid E_1) P(E_1) + P(A \mid E_2) P(E_2) + \cdots + P(A \mid E_K) P(E_K)$$

These results can be combined to provide a second form of Bayes' theorem.

Bayes' Theorem (Alternative Statement)

Let $E_1, E_2, \ldots, E_K$ be K mutually exclusive and collectively exhaustive events, and let A be some other event. The conditional probability of E_i, given A, can be expressed as Bayes' theorem:

$$P(E_i \mid A) = \frac{P(A \mid E_i)P(E_i)}{P(A)}$$

$$P(E_i \mid A) = \frac{P(A \mid E_i)P(E_i)}{P(A \mid E_1)P(E_1) + P(A \mid E_2)P(E_2) + \cdots + P(A \mid E_K)P(E_K)} \tag{3.14}$$

Where,

$$P(A) = P(A \cap E_1) + P(A \cap E_2) + \ldots + P(A \cap E_K)$$

$$= P(A \mid E_1) \ P(E_1) \ + \ P(A \mid E_2) \ P(E_2) \ + \ \ldots + \ P(A \mid E_K) \ P(E_K)$$

The advantage of this restatement of the theorem lies in the fact that the probabilities it involves are often precisely those that are directly available.

This process for solving conditional probability and/or Bayes' problems can be summarized as follows.

Example 3.25 Automobile Sales Incentive (Bayes' Theorem)

A car dealership knows from past experience that 10% of the people who come into the showroom and talk to a salesperson will eventually purchase a car. To increase the chances of success, you propose to offer a free dinner with a salesperson for all people who agree to listen to a complete sales presentation. You know that some people will do anything for a free dinner even if they do not intend to purchase a car. However, some people would rather not spend a dinner with a car salesperson. Thus, you wish to test the effectiveness of this sales promotion incentive. The project is conducted for six months, and 40% of the people who purchased cars had a free dinner. In addition, 10% of the people who did not purchase cars had a free dinner.

The specific questions to be answered are the following:

a. Do people who accept the dinner have a higher probability of purchasing a new car?

b. What is the probability that a person who does not accept a free dinner will purchase a car?

Solution

Step 1. Define the subset events from the problem:

D_1: The customer has dinner with the salesperson.
D_2: The customer does not have dinner with the salesperson.
P_1: The customer purchases a car.
P_2: The customer does not purchase a car.

Step 2. Define the probabilities for the events defined in Step 1:

$$P(P_1) = 0.10 \quad P(D_1 | P_1) = 0.40 \quad P(D_1 | P_2) = 0.10$$

Step 3. Compute the complements of the probabilities:

$$P(P_2) = 0.90 \quad P(D_2 | P_1) = 0.60 \quad P(D_2 | P_2) = 0.90$$

Step 4. Apply Bayes' theorem to compute the probability for the problem solution.

a. We know that the sales promotion plan has increased the probability of a car purchase if more than 10% of those that had dinner purchased a car. Specifically, we ask if

$$P(P_1 | D_1) > P(P_1) P(P_1 | D_1) > 0.10$$

Using Bayes' theorem, we find that

$$P(P_1 | D_1) = \frac{P(D_1 | P_1) P(P_1)}{P(D_1 | P_1) P(P_1) + P(D_1 | P_2) P(P_2)}$$

$$= \frac{0.40 \times 0.10}{0.40 \times 0.10 + 0.10 \times 0.90}$$

$$= 0.308$$

Therefore, the probability of purchase is higher, given the dinner with the salesperson.

b. This question asks that we compute the probability of purchase, P_1, given that the customer does not have dinner with the salesperson, D_2. We again apply Bayes' theorem to compute the following:

$$P(P_1 | D_2) = \frac{P(D_2 | P_1) P(P_1)}{P(D_2 | P_1) P(P_1) + P(D_2 | P_2) P(P_2)}$$

$$= \frac{0.60 \times 0.10}{0.60 \times 0.10 + 0.90 \times 0.90}$$

$$= 0.069$$

We see that those who refuse the dinner have a lower probability of purchase. To provide additional evaluation of the sales program, we might also wish to compare the 6-month sales experience with that of other dealers and with previous sales experience, given similar economic conditions.

We have presented a logical step-by-step or linear procedure for solving Bayes' problems. This procedure works very well for persons experienced in solving this type of problem. The procedure can also help you to organize Bayes' problems. However, most real problem solving in new situations does not follow a step-by-step or linear procedure. Thus, you are likely to move back to previous steps and revise your initial definitions. In some cases you may find it useful to write out Bayes' theorem before you define the probabilities. The mathematical form defines the probabilities that must be obtained from the problem description. Alternatively, you may want to construct a two-way table, as we did in Example 3.23. As you are learning to solve these problems, use the structure, but learn to be creative and willing to go back to previous steps.

Example 3.26 Market Research (Bayes' Throrem)

Blue Star United, a major electronics distributor, has hired Southwest Forecastors, a market research firm, to predict the level of demand for its new product that combines cell phone and complete internet capabilities at a price substantially below its major competitors. As part of its deliverables Southwest provides a rating of "poor," "fair," or "good," on the basis of its research. Prior to engaging Southwest Blue Star management concluded the following probabilities for the market demand levels:

$$P(low) = P(s_1) = 0.1 \quad P(moderate) = P(s_2) = 0.5 \quad P(high) = P(s_3) = 0.4$$

Southwest completes its study and concludes that the market potential for this product is poor. What conclusion should Blue Star reach based on the market study results?

Solution A review of the market research company's records reveals the quality of its past predictions in this field. Table 3.12 shows, for each level of demand outcome, the proportion of poor, fair, and good assessments that were made prior to introducing the product to the market.

Table 3.12 Proportion of Assessments Provided by a Market Research Organization Prior to Various Levels of Market Demand

| | MARKET DEMAND THAT ACTUALLY OCCURRED AFTER ASSESSMENT WAS PROVIDED | | |
Assessment	Low Demand (s_1)	Moderate Demand (s_2)	High Demand (s_3)
POOR	0.6	0.3	0.1
FAIR	0.2	0.4	0.2
GOOD	0.2	0.3	0.7

For example, on 10% of occasions that demand was high, the assessment prior to market introduction was "poor." Thus, in the notation of conditional probability, denoting *low*, *moderate*, and *high* demand levels by s_1, s_2, and s_3, respectively, it follows that

$$P(\text{Poor} \mid s_1) = 0.6 \quad P(\text{Poor} \mid s_2) = 0.3 \quad P(\text{Poor} \mid s_3) = 0.1$$

Given this new information, the prior probabilities

$$P(s_1) = 0.1 \quad P(s_2) = 0.5 \quad P(s_3) = 0.4$$

for the three demand levels can be modified using Bayes' theorem. For a low level of demand, the posterior probability is as follows:

$$P(s_1 \mid \text{Poor}) = \frac{P(\text{Poor} \mid s_1)P(s_1)}{P(\text{Poor} \mid s_1)P(s_1) + P(\text{Poor} \mid s_2)P(s_2) + P(\text{Poor} \mid s_3)P(s_3)}$$

$$= \frac{(0.6)(0.1)}{(0.6)(0.1) + (0.3)(0.5) + (0.1)(0.4)} = \frac{0.06}{0.25} = 0.24$$

Similarly, for the other two demand levels, the posterior probabilities are as follows:

$$P(s_2 \mid \text{Poor}) = \frac{(0.3)(0.5)}{0.25} = 0.6 \quad P(s_3 \mid \text{Poor}) = \frac{(0.1)(0.4)}{0.25} = 0.16$$

Based on this analysis we see that the probability for high demand is now reduced to 0.16 and the most likely outcome is moderate demand with a posterior probability of 0.6.

EXERCISES

Basic Exercises

The following basic exercises use a sample space defined by events A_1, A_2, B_1, and B_2.

3.80 Given $P(A_1) = 0.40$, $P(B_1 \mid A_1) = 0.60$, and $P(B_1 \mid A_2) = 0.70$, what is the probability of $P(A_1 \mid B_1)$?

3.81 Given $P(A_1) = 0.80$, $P(B_1 \mid A_1) = 0.60$, and $P(B_1 \mid A_2) = 0.20$, what is the probability of $P(A_1 \mid B_1)$?

3.82 Given $P(A_1) = 0.50$, $P(B_1 \mid A_1) = 0.40$, and $P(B_1 \mid A_2) = 0.70$, what is the probability of $P(A_1 \mid B_2)$?

3.83 Given $P(A_1) = 0.40$, $P(B_1 \mid A_1) = 0.60$, and $P(B_1 \mid A_2) = 0.70$, what is the probability of $P(A_2 \mid B_2)$?

3.84 Given $P(A_1) = 0.60$, $P(B_1 \mid A_1) = 0.60$, and $P(B_1 \mid A_2) = 0.40$, what is the probability of $P(A_1 \mid B_1)$?

Application Exercises

3.85 A publisher sends advertising materials for an accounting text to 80% of all professors teaching the appropriate accounting course. Thirty percent of the professors who received this material adopted the book, as did 10% of the professors who did not receive the material. What is the probability that a professor who adopts the book has received the advertising material?

3.86 A stock market analyst examined the prospects of the shares of a large number of corporations. When the performance of these stocks was investigated one year later, it turned out that 25% performed much better than the market average, 25% much worse, and the remaining 50% about the same as the average. Forty percent of the stocks that turned out to do much better than the market were rated "good buys" by the analyst, as were 20% of those that did about as well as the market and 10% of those that did much worse. What is the probability that a stock rated a "good buy" by the analyst performed much better than the average?

3.87 The Watts New Lightbulb Corporation ships large consignments of light bulbs to big industrial users. When the production process is functioning correctly, which is 90% of the time, 10% of all bulbs produced are defective. However, the process is susceptible to an occasional malfunction, leading to a defective rate of 50%. If a defective bulb is found what is the probability that the process is functioning correctly? If a non-defective bulb is found that is the probability that the process is operating correctly?

KEY WORDS

- addition rule of probabilities, 99
- basic outcomes, 79
- Bayes' theorem, 123
- Bayes' theorem (alternative statement), 125
- classical probability, 86
- collectively exhaustive, 82
- combinations, 87
- complement, 82
- complement rule, 97
- conditional probability, 100
- event, 80
- independent events, 114
- intersection, 80
- joint probability, 80
- marginal probabilities, 111
- multiplication rule of probabilities, 101
- mutually exclusive, 80
- number of combinations, 87
- odds, 114
- overinvolvement ratios, 115
- permutations, 88
- probability postulates, 93

CHAPTER EXERCISES AND APPLICATIONS

3.88 Suppose that you have an intelligent friend who has not studied probability. How would you explain to your friend the distinction between mutually exclusive events and independent events? Illustrate your answer with suitable examples.

3.89 State, with evidence, whether each of the following statements is true or false:

   a. The complement of the union of two events is the intersection of their complements.

   b. The sum of the probabilities of collectively exhaustive events must equal 1.

   c. The number of combinations of x objects chosen from n is equal to the number of combinations of $(n - x)$ objects chosen from n, where $1 \leq x \leq (n - 1)$.

   d. If A and B are two events, the probability of A, given B, is the same as the probability of B, given A, if the probability of A is the same as the probability of B.

   e. If an event and its complement are equally likely to occur, the probability of that event must be 0.5.

   f. If A and B are independent, then $\overline{A}$ and $\overline{B}$ must be independent.

   g. If A and B are mutually exclusive, then $\overline{A}$ and $\overline{B}$ must be mutually exclusive.

3.90 Explain carefully the meaning of conditional probability. Why is this concept important in discussing the chance of an event's occurrence?

3.91 "Bayes' theorem is important, as it provides a rule for moving from a prior probability to a posterior probability." Elaborate on this statement so that it would be well understood by a fellow student who has not yet studied probability.

3.92 State, with evidence, whether each of the following statements is true or false:

   a. The probability of the union of two events cannot be less than the probability of their intersection.

   b. The probability of the union of two events cannot be more than the sum of their individual probabilities.

   c. The probability of the intersection of two events cannot be greater than either of their individual probabilities.

   d. An event and its complement are mutually exclusive.

   e. The individual probabilities of a pair of events cannot sum to more than 1.

   f. If two events are mutually exclusive, they must also be collectively exhaustive.

   g. If two events are collectively exhaustive, they must also be mutually exclusive.

3.93 Distinguish among joint probability, marginal probability, and conditional probability. Provide some examples to make the distinctions clear.

3.94 State, with evidence, whether each of the following claims is true or false:

   a. The conditional probability of A, given B, must be at least as large as the probability of A.

   b. An event must be independent of its complement.

   c. The probability of A, given B, must be at least as large as the probability of the intersection of A and B.

   d. The probability of the intersection of two events cannot exceed the product of their individual probabilities.

   e. The posterior probability of any event must be at least as large as its prior probability.

3.95 Show that the probability of the union of events A and B can be written as follows:

$$P(A \cup B) = P(A) + P(B)\,[1 - P(A\,|\,B)]$$

3.96 An insurance company estimated that 30% of all automobile accidents were partly caused by weather conditions and that 20% of all automobile accidents involved bodily injury. Further, of those accidents that involved bodily injury, 40% were partly caused by weather conditions.

   a. What is the probability that a randomly chosen accident both was partly caused by weather conditions and involved bodily injury?

   b. Are the events "Partly caused by weather conditions" and "Involved bodily injury" independent?

   c. If a randomly chosen accident was partly caused by weather conditions, what is the probability that it involved bodily injury?

   d. What is the probability that a randomly chosen accident both was not partly caused by weather conditions and did not involve bodily injury?

3.97 A company places a rush order for wire of two thicknesses. Consignments of each thickness are to be sent immediately when they are available. Previous experience suggests that the probability is 0.8 that at least one of these consignments will arrive within a week. It is also estimated that, if the thinner wire arrives within a week, the probability is 0.4 that the thicker wire will also arrive within a week. Further, it is estimated that, if the thicker wire arrives within a week, the probability is 0.6 that the thinner wire will also arrive within a week.

   a. What is the probability that the thicker wire will arrive within a week?
   b. What is the probability that the thinner wire will arrive within a week?
   c. What is the probability that both consignments will arrive within a week?

3.98 Staff Inc., a management consulting company, is surveying the personnel of Acme Ltd. It determined that 35% of the analysts have an MBA and that 40% of all analysts are over age 35. Further, of those who have an MBA, 30% are over age 35.

   a. What is the probability that a randomly chosen analyst both has an MBA and also is over age 35?
   b. What is the probability that a randomly chosen analyst who is over age 35 has an MBA?
   c. What is the probability that a randomly chosen analyst has an MBA or is over age 35?
   d. What is the probability that a randomly chosen analyst who is over age 35 does not have an MBA?
   e. Are the events MBA and over age 35 independent?
   f. Are the events MBA and over age 35 mutually exclusive?
   g. Are the events MBA and over age 35 collectively exhaustive?

3.99 In a campus restaurant it was found that 35% of all customers order vegetarian meals and that 50% of all customers are students. Further, 25% of all customers who are students order vegetarian meals.

   a. What is the probability that a randomly chosen customer both is a student and orders a vegetarian meal?
   b. If a randomly chosen customer orders a vegetarian meal, what is the probability that the customer is a student?
   c. What is the probability that a randomly chosen customer both does not order a vegetarian meal and is not a student?
   d. Are the events "Customer orders a vegetarian meal" and "Customer is a student" independent?
   e. Are the events "Customer orders a vegetarian meal" and "Customer is a student" mutually exclusive?
   f. Are the events "Customer orders a vegetarian meal" and "Customer is a student" collectively exhaustive?

3.100 It is known that 20% of all farms in a state exceed 160 acres and that 60% of all farms in that state are owned by persons over 50 years old. Of all farms in the state exceeding 160 acres, 55% are owned by persons over 50 years old.

   a. What is the probability that a randomly chosen farm in this state both exceeds 160 acres and is owned by a person over 50 years old?
   b. What is the probability that a farm in this state either is bigger than 160 acres or is owned by a person over 50 years old (or both)?
   c. What is the probability that a farm in this state, owned by a person over 50 years old, exceeds 160 acres?
   d. Are size of farm and age of owner in this state statistically independent?

3.101 In a large corporation 80% of the employees are men and 20% are women. The highest levels of education obtained by the employees are graduate training for 10% of the men, undergraduate training for 30% of the men, and high school training for 60% of the men. The highest levels of education obtained are also graduate training for 15% of the women, undergraduate training for 40% of the women, and high school training for 45% of the women.

   a. What is the probability that a randomly chosen employee will be a man with only a high school education?
   b. What is the probability that a randomly chosen employee will have graduate training?
   c. What is the probability that a randomly chosen employee who has graduate training is a man?
   d. Are gender and level of education of employees in this corporation statistically independent?
   e. What is the probability that a randomly chosen employee who has not had graduate training is a woman?

3.102 A large corporation organized a ballot for all its workers on a new bonus plan. It was found that 65% of all night-shift workers favored the plan and that 40% of all female workers favored the plan. Also, 50% of all employees are night-shift workers and 30% of all employees are women. Finally, 20% of all night-shift workers are women.

   a. What is the probability that a randomly chosen employee is a woman in favor of the plan?
   b. What is the probability that a randomly chosen employee is either a woman or a night-shift worker (or both)?
   c. Is employee gender independent of whether the night shift is worked?
   d. What is the probability that a female employee is a night-shift worker?

e. If 50% of all male employees favor the plan, what is the probability that a randomly chosen employee both does not work the night shift and does not favor the plan?

3.103 A jury of 12 members is to be selected from a panel consisting of 8 men and 8 women.

a. How many different jury selections are possible?
b. If the choice is made randomly, what is the probability that a majority of the jury members will be men?

3.104 A consignment of 12 electronic components contains 1 component that is faulty. Two components are chosen randomly from this consignment for testing.

a. How many different combinations of 2 components could be chosen?
b. What is the probability that the faulty component will be chosen for testing?

3.105 Of 100 patients with a certain disease 10 were chosen at random to undergo a drug treatment that increases the cure rate from 50% for those not given the treatment to 75% for those given the drug treatment.

a. What is the probability that a randomly chosen patient both was cured and was given the drug treatment?
b. What is the probability that a patient who was cured had been given the drug treatment?
c. What is the probability that a specific group of 10 patients was chosen to undergo the drug treatment? (Leave your answer in terms of factorials.)

3.106 Subscriptions to a particular magazine are classified as gift, previous renewal, direct mail, and subscription service. In January 8% of expiring subscriptions were gift; 41%, previous renewal; 6%, direct mail; and 45%, subscription service. The percentages of renewals in these four categories were 81%, 79%, 60%, and 21%, respectively. In February of the same year 10% of expiring subscriptions were gift; 57%, previous renewal; 24%, direct mail; and 9%, subscription service. The percentages of renewals were 80%, 76%, 51%, and 14%, respectively.

a. Find the probability that a randomly chosen subscription expiring in January was renewed.
b. Find the probability that a randomly chosen subscription expiring in February was renewed.
c. Verify that the probability in part (b) that is higher than that in part (a). Do you believe that the editors of this magazine should view the change from January to February as a positive or negative development?

3.107 In a large city 8% of the inhabitants have contracted a particular disease. A test for this disease is positive in 80% of people who have the disease and is negative in 80% of people who do not have the disease. What is the probability that a person for whom the test result is positive has the disease?

3.108 A life insurance salesman finds that, of all the sales he makes, 70% are to people who already own policies. He also finds that, of all contacts for which no sale is made, 50% already own life insurance policies. Furthermore, 40% of all contacts result in sales. What is the probability that a sale will be made to a contact who already owns a policy?

3.109 A professor finds that he awards a final grade of A to 20% of his students. Of those who obtain a final grade of A, 70% obtained an A on the midterm examination. Also, 10% of the students who failed to obtain a final grade of A earned an A on the midterm exam. What is the probability that a student with an A on the midterm examination will obtain a final grade of A?

3.110 The accompanying table shows, for 1,000 forecasts of earnings per share made by financial analysts, the numbers of forecasts and outcomes in particular categories (compared with the previous year).

| | Forecast | | |
| | | About the | |
Outcome	Improvement	Same	Worse
Improvement	210	82	66
About the Same	106	153	75
Worse	75	84	149

a. Find the probability that, if the forecast is for a worse performance in earnings, this outcome will result.
b. If the forecast is for an improvement in earnings, find the probability that this outcome fails to result.

3.111 A dean has found that 62% of entering freshmen and 78% of community college transfers eventually graduate. Of all entering students, 73% are freshmen and the remainder are community college transfers.

a. What is the probability that a randomly chosen entering student is a freshman who will eventually graduate?
b. Find the probability that a randomly chosen entering student will eventually graduate.
c. What is the probability that a randomly chosen entering student either is a freshmen or will eventually graduate (or both)?
d. Are the events "Eventually graduates" and "Enters as community college transfer" statistically independent?

3.112 A market research group specializes in providing assessments of the prospects of sites for new children toy stores in shopping centers. The group assesses prospects as good, fair, or poor. The records of assessments made by this group were examined, and it was found that, for all stores that had annual sales over $1,000,000, the assessments were good for 70%, fair for 20%, and poor for 10%. For all stores that turned out to be unsuccessful, the assessments were good for 20%, fair for 30%, and poor for 50%. It is known that 60% of new clothing stores are successful and 40% are unsuccessful.

a. For a randomly chosen store, what is the probability that prospects will be assessed as good?
b. If prospects for a store are assessed as good, what is the probability that it will be successful?
c. Are the events "Prospects assessed as good" and "Store is successful" statistically independent?
d. Suppose that five stores are chosen at random. What is the probability that at least one of them will be successful?

3.113 A restaurant manager classifies customers as regular, occasional, or new, and finds that of all customers 50%, 40%, and 10%, respectively, fall into these categories. The manager found that wine was ordered by 70% of the regular customers, by 50% of the occasional, and by 30% of the new customers.

a. What is the probability that a randomly chosen customer orders wine?
b. If wine is ordered, what is the probability that the person ordering is a regular customer?
c. If wine is ordered, what is the probability that the person ordering is an occasional customer?

3.114 A record store owner assesses customers entering the store as high school age, college age, or older, and finds that of all customers 30%, 50%, and 20%, respectively, fall into these categories. The owner also found that purchases were made by 20% of high school age customers, by 60% of college age customers, and by 80% of older customers.

a. What is the probability that a randomly chosen customer entering the store will make a purchase?
b. If a randomly chosen customer makes a purchase, what is the probability that this customer is high school age?

3.115 Note that this exercise represents a completely imaginary situation. Suppose that a statistics class contained exactly eight men and eight women. You have discovered that the teacher decided to assign five Fs on an exam by randomly selecting names from a hat. He concluded that this would be easier than actually grading all those papers and that his students are all equally skilled in statistics—but

someone has to get an F. What is the probability that all 5 Fs were given to male students?

3.116 A robbery has been committed and McGuff, the crime-fighting dog, has been called in to investigate. He discovers that Sally Coldhands was seen wearing gloves in the neighborhood shortly after the crime, and, thus, he concludes that she should be arrested. From past experience you know that 50% of the people that McGuff says should be arrested for robbery are actually guilty. Before making the arrest, you order some additional investigation. From a large population of convicted robbers you find that 60% wore gloves at the time of the crime and continued to wear them for an interval after the crime. Further investigation reveals that 80% of the people in the neighborhood of the crime were wearing gloves around the time of the crime.

a. Based on the fact that Sally was wearing gloves, what is the probability that Sally actually committed the crime?
b. If you charged her with the crime, do you think a jury would convict her based on the glove evidence? Explain why or why not.

3.117 You are responsible for detecting the source of the error when the computer system fails. From your analysis you know that the source of error is the disk drive, the computer memory, or the operating system. You know that 50% of the errors are disk drive errors, 30% are computer memory errors, and the remainder are operating system errors. From the component performance standards you know that, when a disk drive error occurs, the probability of failure is 0.60; when a computer memory error occurs, the probability of failure is 0.7; and when an operating system error occurs, the probability of failure is 0.3. Given the information from the component performance standards, what is the probability of a disk drive error, given that a failure occurred?

3.118 After meeting with the regional sales managers, Lauretta Anderson, president of Cowpie Computers Inc., you find that she believes that the probability that sales will grow by 10% in the next year is 0.70. After coming to this conclusion, she receives a report that John Cadariu of Minihard Software Inc. has just announced a new operating system that will be available for customers in 8 months. From past history she knows that, in situations where growth has eventually occurred, new operating systems have been announced 30% of the time. However, in situations where growth has not eventually occurred, new operating systems have been announced 10% of the time. Based on all of these facts, what is the probability that sales will grow by 10%?

Appendix: Unions and Intersections of Events

The Venn diagrams in Figures 3.8, 3.9, and 3.10 illustrate three results involving unions and intersections of events.

Result 1

Let A and B be two events. Then the events $A \cap B$ and $\overline{A} \cap B$ are mutually exclusive, and their union is B, as illustrated in the Venn diagram in Figure 3.8. Clearly,

$$(A \cap B) \cup (\overline{A} \cap B) = B \tag{3.27}$$

Result 2

Let A and B be two events. The events A and $\overline{A} \cap B$ are mutually exclusive, and their union is $A \cup B$, is illustrated in the Venn diagram in Figure 3.9—that is,

$$A \cup (\overline{A} \cap B) = A \cup B \tag{3.28}$$

Result 3

Let $E_1, E_2, \ldots, E_K$ be K mutually exclusive and collectively exhaustive events, and let A be some other event. Then the K events $E_1 \cap A, E_2 \cap A, \ldots, \ldots, E_K \cap A$ are mutually exclusive, and their union is A—that is,

$$(E_1 \cap A) \cup (E_2 \cap A) \cup \ldots \cup (E_K \cap A) = A \tag{3.29}$$

We can better understand the third statement by examining the Venn diagram in Figure 3.10. The large rectangle indicates the entire sample space and is divided into smaller rectangles depicting K mutually exclusive and collectively exhaustive events, $E_1, E_2, \ldots, E_K$. The event A is represented by the closed figure. We see that the events composed of the intersection of A and each of the E events are indeed exclusive and that their union is simply the event A. We can therefore write the following:

$$(E_1 \cap A) \cup (E_2 \cap A) \cup \ldots \cup (E_K \cap A) = A$$

Figure 3.10 Venn Diagram for Result 1: $(A \cap B) \cup (\overline{A} \cap B) = [4, 5, 6] = B$

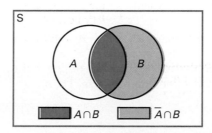

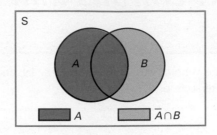

Figure 3.12
Venn Diagram for
Result 3

	E_1	E_2	E_3	E_4	E_5	....	E_K
A	$E_1 \cap A$	$E_2 \cap A$	$E_3 \cap A$	$E_4 \cap A$	$E_5 \cap A$	....	$E_K \cap A$
$\overline{A}$							

Example 3.27   Single Die (Results 1 and 2)

Consider a die-rolling experiment with $A = [2, 4, 6]$ and $B = [4, 5, 6]$. Show the following:

a. $(A \cap B) \cup (\overline{A} \cap B) = B$
b. $A \cup (\overline{A} \cap B) = A \cup B$

Solution   We know that

$$\overline{A} = [1, 3, 5]$$

It follows that

$$A \cap B = [4, 6] \quad \text{and} \quad \overline{A} \cap B = [5]$$

Then $A \cap B$ and $\overline{A} \cap B$ are mutually exclusive, and their union is $B = [4, 5, 6]$—that is,

$$(A \cap B) \cup (\overline{A} \cap B) = [4, 5, 6] = B \qquad \text{(Result 1)}$$

Also, A and $\overline{A} \cap B$ are mutually exclusive, and their union is

$$A \cup (\overline{A} \cap B) = [2, 4, 5, 6] = A \cup B \qquad \text{(Result 2)}$$

Example 3.28   Single Die (Result 3)

Consider a die-rolling experiment with events $A, E_1, E_2,$ and E_3 given by the following:

$$A = [2, 4, 6] \quad E_1 = [1, 2] \quad E_2 = [3, 4] \quad E_3 = [5, 6]$$

Show that $E_1 \cap A, E_2 \cap A,$ and $E_3 \cap A$ are mutually exclusive and that their union is A.

Solution   First, we notice that $E_1, E_2,$ and E_3 are mutually exclusive and collectively exhaustive. Then,

$$E_1 \cap A = [2] \quad E_2 \cap A = [4] \quad E_3 \cap A = [6]$$

Clearly, these three events are mutually exclusive, and their union is as follows:

$$(E_1 \cap A) \cup (E_2 \cap A) \cup (E_3 \cap A) = [2, 4, 6] = A$$

REFERENCES

1. Bayes, Thomas. 1958. Essay Towards Solving a Problem in the Doctrine of Chance. *Biometrika* 45:293–315 (reproduction of 1763 paper).
2. Carlson, William L. 1972. Alcohol Usage of the Night Driver. *Journal of Safety Research* 4 (1): 12–29.
3. Carlson, William L., and Betty Thorne. 1997. *Applied Statistical Methods for Business and Economics*. Upper Saddle River, NJ: Prentice Hall.

Chapter 4

Discrete Random Variables and Probability Distributions

Introduction

In Chapter 3 we began our development of probability to represent situations with uncertain outcomes. In this chapter we use those ideas to develop probability models with an emphasis on discrete random variables. In Chapter 5 we will develop probability models for continuous random variables.

Probability models have extensive application to a number of business problems, and some of these applications will be developed here. Suppose that you have a business that rents a variety of equipment. From past experience—relative frequency—you know that 30% of the people who enter your store want to rent a trailer. Today you have three trailers available. Five completely unrelated people enter your store (the probability of one of them renting a trailer is independent of that of the others). What is the probability that these five people are seeking to rent a total of four or five trailers? If that happens, rental opportunities will be missed and customers will be disappointed. The probability of the events (number of trailers desired) can be computed using the binomial model that is developed in this chapter.

4.1 RANDOM VARIABLES

When the outcomes are numerical values, these probabilities can be conveniently summarized through the notion of a *random variable*.

> ### Random Variable
> A **random variable** is a variable that takes on numerical values determined by the outcome of a random experiment.

It is important to distinguish between a random variable and the possible values that it can take. Using notation, this is done with capital letters, such as X, to denote the random variable and the corresponding lowercase letter, x, to denote a possible value. For example, a store has five computers on the shelf. From past experience we know that the probabilities of selling one through five computers are equal and at least one computer will be sold. We can use the random variable X to denote the outcome. This random variable can take the specific values $x = 1$, $x = 2$, ..., $x = 5$, each with probability 0.2 and the random variable X as a discrete random variable.

> ### Discrete Random Variable
> A random variable is a **discrete random variable** if it can take on no more than a countable number of values.

It follows from the definition that any random variable that can take on only a finite number of values is discrete. For example, the number of sales resulting from 10 customer contacts is a discrete random variable. Even if the number of possible outcomes is infinite but countable, the random variable is discrete. An example is the number of customer contacts needed before the first sale occurs. The possible outcomes are 1, 2, 3, . . ., and a probability can be attached to each. (A discrete random variable that can take a countably infinite number of values will be discussed in Section 4.6.) Some other examples of discrete random variables are as follows:

1. The number of defective items in a sample of 20 items from a large shipment
2. The number of customers arriving at a checkout counter in an hour
3. The number of errors detected in a corporation's accounts
4. The number of claims on a medical insurance policy in a particular year

By contrast, suppose that we are interested in the day's high temperature. The random variable, temperature, is measured on a continuum and so is said to be *continuous*.

> ## Continuous Random Variable
> A random variable is a **continuous random variable** if it can take any value in an interval.

For continuous random variables we can only assign probabilities to a range of values. The probabilities can be determined for ranges, using a mathematical function, so that one could compute the probability for the event "Today's high temperature will be between 75 and 76°." Some other examples of continuous random variables include the following:

1. The yearly income for a family
2. The amount of oil imported into the United States in a particular month
3. The change in the price of a share of IBM common stock in a month
4. The time that elapses between the installation of a new component and its failure
5. The percentage of impurity in a batch of chemicals

The distinction that we have made between discrete and continuous random variables may appear rather artificial. After all, rarely is anything actually measured on a continuum. For example, we cannot report today's high temperature more precisely than the measuring instrument allows. Moreover, a family's income in a year will be some integer number of cents. However, we will find that it is convenient to act as if measurements had truly been made on a continuum when the differences between adjacent values are of no significance. The difference between family's incomes of $35,276.21 and $35,276.22 is of very little significance, and the attachment of probabilities to each would be a tedious and worthless exercise.

For practical purposes we treat random variables as discrete when probability statements about the individual possible outcomes have worthwhile meaning; all other random variables are regarded as continuous. We treat these two types separately and useful models have been developed for each type. Discrete random variables are developed in this chapter and continuous random variables will be developed in Chapter 5.

EXERCISES

Basic Exercises

4.1 A store sells from 0 to 12 computers per day. Is the daily computer sales a discrete or continuous random variable?

4.2 A factory production process produces a small number of defective parts in its daily production. Is the number of defective parts a discrete or continuous random variable?

4.3 For each of the following indicate if a discrete or a continuous random variable provides the best definition:
   a. The number of cars that arrive each day for repair in a two-person repair shop
   b. The number of cars produced annually by General Motors
   c. Total daily e-commerce sales in dollars
   d. The number of passengers that are bumped from a specific airline flight 3 days before Christmas

4.4 An equity actor auditions 100 times a year. Is her work schedule (number of plays) a discrete or random variable?

Application Exercises
4.5 List four examples of discrete random variables that could be observed in a new consulting business.

4.6 Define three continuous random variables that a marketing vice president should regularly examine.

4.7 A presidential election poll contacts 2,000 randomly selected people. Should the number of people that support candidate A be analyzed using discrete or continuous probability models?

4.8 A salesperson contacts 20 people each day and requests that they purchase a specific product. Should the number of daily purchases be analyzed using discrete or continuous probability models?

4.2 PROBABILITY DISTRIBUTIONS FOR DISCRETE RANDOM VARIABLES

Suppose that X is a discrete random variable and that x is one of its possible values. The probability that random variable X takes specific value x is denoted $P(X = x)$. The *probability distribution function* of a random variable is a representation of the probabilities for all the possible outcomes. This representation might be algebraic, graphical, or tabular. For discrete random variables one simple procedure is to list the probabilities of all possible outcomes according to the values of x.

> ## Probability Distribution Function
> The **probability distribution function**, $P(x)$, of a discrete random variable X expresses the probability that X takes the value x, as a function of x. That is,
>
> $$P(x) = P(X = x), \text{ for all values of } x \qquad (4.1)$$
>
> We will use the term *probability distribution* to represent probability distribution functions in this book, following the common practice.

Because the probability function takes nonzero values only at discrete points x, it is sometimes called a *probability mass function*. Once the probabilities have been calculated, the function can be graphed.

Example 4.1 Number of Product Sales (Probability Function Graph)

Define and graph the probability distribution function for the number of sales experience for a sandwich shop. This shop offers sandwiches that have a price of $3.00 each.

Solution Let the random variable X denote the number of sales during a single hour of business from 3 to 5 p.m. The probability distribution of sales is given by Table 4.1, and Figure 4.1 is a graphical picture of the distribution.

Table 4.1 Probability Distribution for Example 4.1

x	P(x)
0	0.10
1	0.20
2	0.40
3	0.30

Figure 4.1 Graph of Probability Distribution for Example 4.1

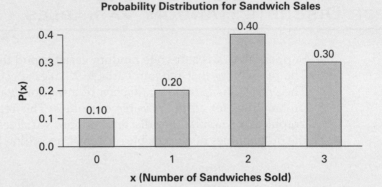

From the probability distribution function we see that for example the probability of selling one sandwich is 0.20 and the probability of selling two or more is 0.70 (0.40 + 0.30).

The probability distribution function of a discrete random variable must satisfy the following two properties.

Required Properties of Probability Distribution Functions of Discrete Random Variables

Let X be a discrete random variable with probability distribution function $P(x)$. Then,

1. $0 \leq P(x) \leq 1$ for any value x, and
2. the individual probabilities sum to 1—that is,

$$\sum_{x} P(x) = 1$$

where the notation indicates summation over all possible values of x.

Property 1 merely states that probabilities cannot be negative or exceed 1. Property 2 follows from the fact that the events "$X = x$," for all possible values of x, are mutually exclusive and collectively exhaustive. The probabilities for these events must, therefore, sum to 1. It is simply a way of saying that when a random experiment is to be carried out, something must happen.

Another representation of discrete probability distributions is also useful.

Example 4.2   Automobile Sales (Probabilities)

Olaf Motors Inc. is a car dealer in a small southern town. Based on an analysis of its sales history, the managers know that on any single day the number of Prius cars sold can vary from 0 to 4. How can the probability distribution function shown in Table 4.2 be used for inventory planning?

Table 4.2   Probability Distribution Function for Automobile Sales

x	$P(x)$	$F(x)$
0	0.15	0.15
1	0.30	0.45
2	0.20	0.65
3	0.20	0.85
4	0.10	0.95
5	0.05	1.00

Solution   The random variable, X, takes on the values of x indicated in the first column, and the probability function, $P(x)$, is defined in the second column. The third column contains the cumulative distribution, $F(x)$. This model could be used for planning the inventory of cars. For example, if there are only four cars in stock, Olaf Motors could satisfy customers' needs for a car 95% of the time. But if only two cars are in stock, then 35% [$(1 - 0.65) \times 100$] of the customers would not have their needs satisfied.

For discrete random variables the cumulative probability function is sometimes called the *cumulative mass function*. It can be seen from the definition that, as x_0 increases, the cumulative probability function will change values only at those points x_0 that can be taken by the random variable with positive probability. Its evaluation at these points can be carried out in terms of the probability function.

where the notation implies that summation is over all possible values of x that are less than or equal to x_0.

The result in Equation 4.3 follows, since the event "$X \leq x_0$" is the union of the mutually exclusive events "$X = x$," for all possible values of x less than or equal to x_0. The probability of the union is then the sum of these individual event probabilities.

> **Derived Properties of Cumulative Probability Functions for Discrete Random Variables**
> Let X be a discrete random variable with cumulative probability function $F(x_0)$. Then we can show that
>
> 1. $0 \leq F(x_0) \leq 1$ for every number x_0; and
> 2. if x_0 and x_1 are two numbers with $x_0 < x_1$, then $F(x_0) \leq F(x_1)$.

Property 1 simply states that a probability cannot be less than 0 or greater than 1. For example, note the probabilities for automobile sales in Table 4.2. Property 2 implies that the probability that a random variable does not exceed some number cannot be more than the probability that it does not exceed any larger number.

EXERCISES

Basic Exercises

4.9 What is the probability distribution function of the number of heads when a fair coin is tossed?

4.10 Show the probability distribution function of the face values of a single die when a fair coin is tossed.

4.11 Show the probability distribution function of the number of heads when three fair coins are tossed independently.

4.12 Let the random variable represent the number of times that you will miss class this semester. Prepare a table that shows the probability function and the cumulative probability function.

Application Exercises

4.13 The number of computers sold per day at Dan's Computer Works is defined by the following probability distribution:

X	0	1	2	③	4	⑤	6
$P(x)$	0.05	0.10	0.20	0.20	0.20	0.15	0.10

a. $P(3 \leq x < 6) = ?$
b. $P(x > 3) = ?$
c. $P(x \leq 4) = ?$
d. $P(2 < x \leq 5) = ?$

4.14 American Travel Air has asked you to study flight delays during the week before Christmas at Midway Airport. The random variable X is the number of flights delayed per hour.

X	0	1	2	3	4	5	6	7	8	9
$P(x)$	0.10	0.08	0.07	0.15	0.12	0.08	0.10	0.12	0.08	0.10

a. What is the cumulative probability distribution?
b. What is the probability of five or more delayed flights?
c. What is the probability of three through seven (inclusive) delayed flights?

4.3 PROPERTIES OF DISCRETE RANDOM VARIABLES

The probability distribution contains all the information about the probability properties of a random variable, and graphical inspection of this distribution can certainly be valuable. However, it is frequently desirable to have some summary measures of the distribution's characteristics.

Expected Value of a Discrete Random Variable

In order to obtain a measure of the center of a probability distribution, we introduce the notion of the *expectation* of a random variable. In Chapter 2 we computed the sample mean as a measure of central location for sample data. The *expected value* is the corresponding measure of central location for a random variable. Before introducing its definition, we show the fallacy of a superficially attractive alternative measure.

Consider the following example: A review of textbooks in a segment of the business area found that 81% of all pages of texts were error-free, 17% of all pages contained one error, and the remaining 2% contained two errors. We use the random variable X to denote the number of errors on a page chosen at random from one of these books, with possible values of 0, 1, and 2, and the probability distribution function

$$P(0) = 0.81 \quad P(1) = 0.17 \quad P(2) = 0.02$$

We could consider using the simple average of the values as the central location of a random variable. In this example the possible numbers of errors on a page are 0, 1, and 2. Their average is, then, one error. However, a moment's reflection will convince the reader that this is an absurd measure of central location. In calculating this average, we paid no attention to the fact that 81% of all pages contain no errors, while only 2% contain two errors. In order to obtain a sensible measure of central location, we *weight* the various possible outcomes by the probabilities of their occurrence.

Expected Value

The **expected value**, $E(X)$, of a discrete random variable X is defined as

$$E(X) = \mu = \sum_{x} xP(x) \tag{4.4}$$

where the notation indicates that the summation extends over all possible values of x.

The expected value of a random variable is also called its **mean** and is denoted μ.

We can express expected value in terms of long-run relative frequencies. Suppose that a random experiment is repeated N times and that the event "$X = x$" occurs in N_x of these trials. The average of the values taken by the random variable over all N trials will then be the sum of xN_x/N over all possible values of x. Now, as the number of replications, N, becomes infinitely large, the ratio N_x/N tends to the probability of the occurrence of the event "$X = x$"—that is, to $P(x)$. Hence, the quantity xN_x/N tends to $xP(x)$. Thus, we can view the expected value as the long-run average value that a random variable takes over a large number of trials. Recall that in Chapter 2 we used the *mean* for the average of a set of numerical observations. We use the same term for the expectation of a random variable.

Example 4.3   Errors in Textbooks (Expected Value)

Suppose that the probability function for the number of errors, X, on pages from business textbooks is as follows:

$$P(0) = 0.81 \quad P(1) = 0.17 \quad P(2) = 0.02$$

Find the mean number of errors per page.

Figure 4.2 Probability Function for Number of Errors per Page in Business Textbooks for Example 4.3

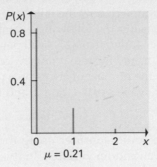

$\mu = 0.21$

Solution   We have

$$\mu_x = E(X) = \sum_x xP(x) = (0)(0.81) + (1)(0.17) + (2)(0.02) = 0.21$$

From this result it is concluded that over a large number of pages, the expectation would be to find an average of 0.21 error per page. Figure 4.1 shows the probability function, with the location of the mean indicated.

Variance of a Discrete Random Variable

In Chapter 2 we found that the sample variance was one useful measure of the spread of a set of numerical observations. The sample variance is the average of the squared discrepancies of the observations from their mean. We will use this same idea to measure dispersion in the probability distribution of a random variable. We define the *variance* of a random variable as the weighted average of the squares of its possible deviations, $(x - \mu)$, from the mean; the weight associated with $(x - \mu)^2$ is the probability that the random variable takes the value x. The variance can then be viewed as the average value that will be taken by the function $(X - \mu)^2$ over a very large number of repeated trials, as defined by Equation 4.5.

Variance and Standard Deviation of a Discrete Random Variable

Let X be a discrete random variable. The expectation of the squared discrepancies about the mean, $(X - \mu)^2$, is called the **variance**, denoted as σ^2 and given by

$$\sigma^2 = E[(X - \mu)^2] = \sum_x (x - \mu)^2 P(x) \tag{4.5}$$

The variance of a discrete random variable X can also be expressed as

$$\sigma^2 = E(X^2) - \mu^2 = \sum_x x^2 P(x) - \mu^2 \tag{4.6}$$

The **standard deviation**, σ_x, is the positive square root of the variance.

In some practical applications the alternative, but equivalent, formula for the variance is preferable for computational purposes. That alternative formula is defined by Equation 4.6, which can be verified algebraically (see the chapter appendix).

The concept of variance can be very useful in comparing the dispersions of probability distributions. Consider, for example, viewing as a random variable the daily return over a year on an investment. Two investments may have the same expected returns but will still differ in an important way if the variances of these returns are substantially different. A higher variance indicates that returns substantially different from the mean are more likely than if the variance of returns amount is small. In this context, then, variance of the return can be associated with the concept of the risk of an investment—the higher the variance, the greater the risk.

Taking the square root of the variance to obtain the standard deviation yields a quantity in the original units of measurement, as noted in Chapter 2.

Example 4.4 Expected Value and Variance of Automobile Sales (Expected Value and Variance)

In Example 4.2 Olaf Motors Inc. determined that the number of Prius cars sold daily could vary from 0 to 5, with the probabilities given in Table 4.1. Find the expected value and variance for this probability distribution.

Solution Using Equation 4.4, the expected value is as follows:

$$\mu_X = E(X) = \sum_x xP(x) = 0(0.15) + 1(0.30) + \cdots + 5(0.05) = 1.95$$

Using Equation 4.5, the variance is as follows:

$$\sigma_X^2 = (0 - 1.95)^2(0.15) + (1 - 1.95)^2(0.3) + \cdots + (5 - 1.95)^2(0.05) = 1.9475$$

For more complex probability distributions Excel, Minitab, SPSS or another statistical Package can be used for these computations. Table 4.3 contains an alternative probability distribution function for car sales. We will examine the effect of this alternative probability distribution on the mean and variance. Note the higher probabilities for 0 and 5 cars sold and smaller probabilities for intermediate daily sales. In Table 4.3 we see the detailed calculations that are used to compute the mean and variance of sales. These detailed calculations are presented to indicate the calculation details.

Table 4.3 Probability Distribution Function for Olaf Motors Automobile Sales

x	$P(x)$	Mean	Variance
0	0.30	$(0.30)(0)$	$(0.30)(0 - 1.95)^2$
1	0.20	$(0.20)(1)$	$(0.20)(1 - 1.95)^2$
2	0.10	$(0.10)(2)$	$(0.10)(2 - 1.95)^2$
3	0.05	$(0.05)(3)$	$(0.05)(3 - 1.95)^2$
4	0.15	$(0.15)(4)$	$(0.15)(4 - 1.95)^2$
5	0.20	$(0.20)(5)$	$(0.20)(5 - 1.95)^2$
	1.0	2.15	3.83

Mean and Variance of Linear Functions of a Random Variable

The notion of expectation is not restricted to the random variable itself but can be applied to any function of the random variable. For example, a contractor may be uncertain of the time required to complete a contract. This uncertainty could be represented by a random variable whose possible values are the number of days elapsing from the beginning to the completion of work on the contract. However, the contractor's primary concern is not with the time taken but rather with the cost of fulfilling the contract. This cost will be a function of the time taken, so in determining expected value of the random variable "Cost," we need to find the expectation of a function of the random variable "Time to completion."

Expected Value of Functions of Random Variables

Let X be a discrete random variable with probability function $P(x)$, and let g(X) be some function of X. Then the expected value, $E[g(X)]$, of that function is defined as follows:

$$E[g(X)] = \sum_x g(x)P(x) \tag{4.7}$$

We define the expectation of a function of a random variable X by Equation 4.7. That is, the expectation can be thought of as the average value that $g(X)$ would take over a very large number of repeated trials. In general

$$E[g(x)] \neq g(\mu_x) \tag{4.8}$$

as shown in the chapter appendix. However, if $g(x)$ is a linear function of x there are some simple results for the mean and variance. These results are very useful for business and economics because many applications can be approximated by a linear function.

We now consider the expected value and variance for linear functions of a random variable using the linear function $a + bX$, where a and b are constant fixed numbers. Let X be a random variable that takes the value x with probability $P(x)$, and consider a new random variable Y, defined by the following:

$$Y = a + Bx$$

When random variable X takes the specific value x, Y must take the value $a + bx$. The mean and variance of such variables are frequently required. The mean, variance, and standard deviation for a linear function of a random variable are derived in the chapter appendix. The results are summarized in Equations 4.9 and 4.10.

Summary of Properties for Linear Functions of a Random Variable

Let X be a random variable with mean μ_X and variance σ_X^2, and let a and b be any constant fixed numbers. Define the random variable Y as $a + bX$. Then, the **mean and variance of Y** are

$$\mu_Y = E(a + bX) = a + b\mu_X \qquad (4.9)$$

and

$$\sigma_Y^2 = \text{var}(a + bX) = b^2\sigma_X^2 \qquad (4.10)$$

so that the standard deviation of Y is

$$\sigma_y = |b|\sigma_x$$

Example 4.5 Total Project Cost (Computations for Functions of Random Variables)

A contractor is interested in the total cost of a project on which she intends to bid. She estimates that materials will cost \$25,000 and that her labor will be \$900 per day. If the project takes X days to complete, the total labor cost will be $900X$ dollars, and the total cost of the project (in dollars) will be as follows:

$$C = 25,000 + 900X$$

The contractor forms subjective probabilities (Table 4.4) of likely completion times for the project.

a. Find the mean and variance for completion time X.
b. Find the mean, variance, and standard deviation for total cost C.

Table 4.4 Probability Distribution for Completion Times

Completion time X (days)	10	11	12	13	14
Probability	0.1	0.3	0.3	0.2	0.1

Solution

a. The mean and variance for completion time X can be found using Equations 4.4 and 4.5.

$$\mu_X = E(X) = \sum_x xP(x)$$

$$= (10)(0.1) + (11)(0.3) + (12)(0.3) + (13)(0.2) + (14)(0.1) = 11.9 \quad \text{days}$$

And

$$\sigma_x^2 = E[(X - \mu_x)^2] = \sum_x (x - \mu_x)^2 P(x)$$

$$= (10 - 11.9)^2(0.1) + (11 - 11.9)^2(0.3) + \cdots + (14 - 11.9)^2(0.1) = 1.29$$

b. The mean, variance, and standard deviation of total cost, C, are obtained using Equations 4.8, 4.9, and 4.10.

The mean is as follows:

$$\mu_C = E(25{,}000 + 900X) = (25{,}000 + 900\mu_X) = 25{,}000 + (900)(11.9) = \$35{,}710$$

The variance is as follows:

$$\sigma_C^2 = \mathrm{Var}(25{,}000 + 900X) = (900)^2\,\sigma_X^2 = (810{,}000)(1.29) = 1{,}044{,}900$$

The standard deviation is as follows:

$$\sigma_C = \sqrt{\sigma_C^2} = \$1{,}022.20$$

Three special examples of the linear function $W = a + bX$ are important. The first example considers a constant function, $W = a$, for any constant a. In this situation the coefficient $b = 0$. In the second example $a = 0$, giving $W = bX$. The expected value and the variance for these functions are defined by Equations 4.11 and 4.12. The third example is significant in later chapters. The mean and variance of this special linear function are defined by Equations 4.13 and 4.14. Thus, subtracting its mean from a random variable and dividing by its standard deviation yields a random variable with mean 0 and standard deviation 1.

Summary Results for the Mean and Variance of Special Linear Functions

a. Let $b = 0$ in the linear function $W = a + bX$. Then let $W = a$ (for any constant a).

$$E(a) = a \quad \text{and} \quad Var(a) = 0 \tag{4.11}$$

If a random variable always takes the value a, it will have a mean a and a variance 0.

b. Let $a = 0$ in the linear function $W = a + bX$. Then let $W = bX$.

$$E(bX) = b\mu_X \quad \text{and} \quad var(bX) = b^2\sigma_X^2 \tag{4.12}$$

c. The Mean and Variance of

$$Z = \frac{X - \mu_X}{\sigma_X}$$

Let $a = -\mu_X/\sigma_X$ and $b = 1/\sigma_X$ in the linear function $Z = a + bX$. Then

$$Z = a + bX = \frac{X - \mu_X}{\sigma_X} = \frac{X}{\sigma_X} - \frac{\mu_X}{\sigma_X}$$

so that

$$E\!\left(\frac{X - \mu_X}{\sigma_X}\right) = -\frac{\mu_X}{\sigma_X} + \frac{1}{\sigma_X}\mu_x = 0 \tag{4.13}$$

and

$$\mathrm{Var}\!\left(\frac{X - \mu_X}{\sigma_X}\right) = \frac{1}{\sigma_X^2}\sigma_X^2 = 1 \tag{4.14}$$

Basic Exercises

4.15 Consider the probability distribution function.

x	0	1
Probability	0.40	0.60

   a. Draw the probability distribution function.
   b. Calculate and draw the cumulative probability function.
   c. Find the mean of the random variable X.
   d. Find the variance of X.

4.16 Given the probability distribution function consider the following:

x	0	1	2
Probability	0.25	0.50	0.25

   a. Draw the probability distribution function.
   b. Calculate and draw the cumulative probability function.
   c. Find the mean of the random variable X.
   d. Find the variance of X.

4.17 Consider the probability distribution function

x	0	1
Probability	0.50	0.50

   a. Draw the probability distribution function.
   b. Calculate and draw the cumulative probability function.
   c. Find the mean of the random variable X.
   d. Find the variance of X.

4.18 An automobile dealer calculates the proportion of new cars sold that have been returned a various numbers of times for the correction of defects during the warranty period. The results are shown in the following table.

Number of returns	0	1	2	3	4
Proportion	0.28	0.36	0.23	0.09	0.04

   a. Draw the probability distribution function.
   b. Calculate and draw the cumulative probability function.
   c. Find the mean of the number of returns of an automobile for corrections for defects during the warranty period.
   d. Find the variance of the number of returns of an automobile for corrections for defects during the warranty period.

4.19 A company specializes in installing and servicing central heating furnaces. In the pre-winter period service calls may result in an order for a new furnace. The following table shows estimated probabilities for the numbers of new furnace orders generated in this way in the last 2 weeks of September.

Number of orders	0	1	2	3	4	5
Probability	0.10	0.14	0.26	0.28	0.15	0.07

   a. Draw the probability distribution function.
   b. Calculate and draw the cumulative probability function.
   c. Find the probability that at least three orders will be generated in this period.
   d. Find the mean of the number of orders for new furnaces in this 2-week period.
   e. Find the standard deviation of the number of orders for new furnaces in this 2-week period.

Application Exercises

4.20 Forest Green Inc. produces bags of cypress mulch. The weight in pounds per bag varies, as indicated in the accompanying table.

Weight in Pounds	44	45	46	47	48	49	50
Proportion of bags	0.04	0.13	0.21	0.29	0.20	0.10	0.03

   a. Draw the probability function.
   b. Calculate and draw the cumulative probability function.
   c. What is the probability that a randomly chosen bag will contain between 46 and 48 pounds of mulch (inclusive)?
   d. Two packages are chosen at random. What is the probability that at least one of them contains at least 47 pounds?
   e. Compute—using a computer—the mean and standard deviation of the weight per bag.
   f. The cost (in cents) of producing a bag of mulch is $75 + 2X$, where X is the number of pounds per bag. The revenue from selling the bag, regardless of weight, is $2.50. If profit is defined as the difference between revenue and cost, find the mean and standard deviation of profit per bag.

4.21 A municipal bus company has started operations in a new subdivision. Records were kept on the numbers of riders from this subdivision during the early-morning service. The accompanying table shows proportions over all weekdays.

Number of riders	20	21	22	23	24	25	26	27
Proportion	0.02	0.12	0.23	0.31	0.19	0.08	0.03	0.02

   a. Draw the probability function.

b. Calculate and draw the cumulative probability function.

c. What is the probability that on a randomly chosen weekday there will be at least 24 riders from the subdivision on this service?

d. Two weekdays are chosen at random. What is the probability that on both of these days there will be fewer than 23 riders from the subdivision on this service?

e. Find the mean and standard deviation of the number of riders from this subdivision on this service on a weekday.

f. If the cost of a ride is $1.50, find the mean and standard deviation of the total payments of riders from this subdivision on this service on a weekday.

4.22 a. A very large shipment of parts contains 10% defectives. Two parts are chosen at random from the shipment and checked. Let the random variable X denote the number of defectives found. Find the probability function of this random variable.

b. A shipment of 20 parts contains two defectives. Two parts are chosen at random from the shipment and checked. Let the random variable Y denote the number of defectives found. Find the probability function of this random variable. Explain why your answer is different from that for part (a).

c. Find the mean and variance of the random variable X in part (a).

d. Find the mean and variance of the random variable Y in part (b).

4.23 A student needs to know details of a class assignment that is due the next day and decides to call fellow class members for this information. She believes that for any particular call the probability of obtaining the necessary information is 0.40. She decides to continue calling class members until the information is obtained. Let the random variable X denote the number of calls needed to obtain the information.

a. Find the probability function of X.

b. Find the cumulative probability function of X.

c. Find the probability that at least three calls are required.

4.24 A college basketball player who sinks 75% of her free throws comes to the line to shoot a "one and one" (if the first shot is successful, she is allowed a second shot, but no second shot is taken if the first is missed; one point is scored for each successful shot). Assume that the outcome of the second shot, if any, is independent of that of the first. Find the expected number of points resulting from the "one and one." Compare this with the expected number of points from a "two-shot foul," where a second shot is allowed, irrespective of the outcome of the first.

4.25 A professor teaches a large class and has scheduled an examination for 7:00 p.m. in a different classroom. She estimates the probabilities in the table for the number of students who will call her at home in the hour before the examination asking where the exam will be held.

Number of calls	0	1	2	3	4	5
Probability	0.10	0.15	0.19	0.26	0.19	0.11

Find the mean and standard deviation of the number of calls.

4.26 Students in a large accounting class were asked to rate the course by assigning a score of 1, 2, 3, 4, or 5 to the course. A higher score indicates that the students received greater value from the course. The accompanying table shows proportions of students rating the course in each category.

Rating	1	2	3	4	5
Proportion	0.07	0.19	0.28	0.30	0.16

Find the mean and standard deviation of the ratings.

4.27 A store owner stocks an out-of-town newspaper that is sometimes requested by a small number of customers. Each copy of this newspaper costs her 70 cents, and she sells them for 90 cents each. Any copies left over at the end of the day have no value and are destroyed. Any requests for copies that cannot be met because stocks have been exhausted are considered by the store owner as a loss of 5 cents in goodwill. The probability distribution of the number of requests for the newspaper in a day is shown in the accompanying table. If the store owner defines total daily profit as total revenue from newspaper sales, less total cost of newspapers ordered, less goodwill loss from unsatisfied demand, how many copies per day should she order to maximize expected profit?

Number of requests	0	1	2	3	4	5
Probability	0.12	0.16	0.18	0.32	0.14	0.08

4.28 A factory manager is considering whether to replace a temperamental machine. A review of past records indicates the following probability distribution for the number of breakdowns of this machine in a week.

Number of breakdowns	0	1	2	3	4
Probability	0.10	0.26	0.42	0.16	0.06

a. Find the mean and standard deviation of the number of weekly breakdowns.

b. It is estimated that each breakdown costs the company $1,500 in lost output. Find the mean and standard deviation of the weekly cost to the company from breakdowns of this machine.

4.29 An investor is considering three strategies for a $1,000 investment. The probable returns are estimated as follows:

- *Strategy 1:* A profit of $10,000 with probability 0.15 and a loss of $1,000 with probability 0.85

- *Strategy 2:* A profit of $1,000 with probability 0.50, a profit of $500 with probability 0.30, and a loss of $500 with probability 0.20
- *Strategy 3:* A certain profit of $400

Which strategy has the highest expected profit? Would you necessarily advise the investor to adopt this strategy?

4.4 BINOMIAL DISTRIBUTION

We now develop the binomial probability distribution that is used extensively in many applied business and economic problems. Our approach begins by first developing the Bernoulli model, which is a building block for the binomial. We consider a random experiment that can give rise to just two possible mutually exclusive and collectively exhaustive outcomes, which for convenience we will label "success" and "failure." Let P denote the probability of success, so that the probability of failure is $(1 - P)$. Now, define the random variable X so that X takes the value 1 if the outcome of the experiment is success and 0 otherwise. The probability function of this random variable is then

$$P(0) = (1 - P) \quad \text{and} \quad P(1) = P$$

This distribution is known as the *Bernoulli distribution*. Its mean and variance can be found by direct application of the equations in Section 4.3.

Derivation of the Mean and Variance of a Bernoulli Random Variable

The **mean** is

$$\mu_X = E(X) = \sum_x xP(x) = (0)(1 - P) + (1)P = P \tag{4.15}$$

and the **variance** is

$$\sigma_X^2 = E[(X - \mu_X)^2] = \sum_X (x - \mu_X)^2 P(x)$$

$$= (0 - P)^2(1 - P) + (1 - P)^2 P = P(1 - P) \tag{4.16}$$

Example 4.6 Contract Sale (Compute Bernoulli Mean and Variance)

Shirley Ferguson, an insurance broker, believes that for a particular contact the probability of making a sale is 0.4. If the random variable X is defined to take the value 1 if a sale is made and 0 otherwise, then X has a Bernoulli distribution with probability of success P equal to 0.4. Find the mean and the variance of the distribution.

Solution The probability function of X is $P(0) = 0.6$ and $P(1) = 0.4$. The mean of the distribution is $P = 0.40$, and the variance is $\sigma^2 = P(1 - P) = (0.4)(0.6) = 0.24$.

An important generalization of the Bernoulli distribution concerns the case where a random experiment with two possible outcomes is repeated several times and the repetitions are independent. We can determine the probabilities here by using the binomial probability distribution. Suppose again that the probability of a success in a single trial is P and that n independent trials are carried out, so that the result of any one trial has no influence on the outcome of any other. The number of successes X resulting from these n trials could be any whole number from 0 to n, and we are interested in the probability of obtaining exactly $X = x$ successes in n trials.

Suppose that Shirley in Example 4.6 seeks a total of three sales and to do this she contacts four potential customers. She would like to know the probability of exactly three sales out of the four contacts. If we label a sale as (S) and a non-sale as (F), one possible sequence that results in three sales would be [S, S, S, F]. Given that each customer contact is independent the probability of this particular event is as follows:

$$(0.40 \times 0.40 \times 0.40 \times 0.60) = 0.40^3 0.60^1 = 0.0384$$

The sequences of S and F can be arranged in combinations of four outcomes taken three at a time as developed in Chapter 3 and thus there are

$$C_3^4 = \frac{4!}{3!(4-3)!} = 4$$

possible ways that she can obtain 3 sales and thus the probability of exactly three sales would be four times 0.0384 equal to 0.1536 or, as expressed in equation form,

$$C_3^4 0.40^3 0.60^1 = 4 \times 0.0384 = 0.1536$$

Continuing from this specific example we develop the result in two stages. First, observe that the n trials will result in a sequence of n outcomes, each of which must be either success (S) or failure (F). One sequence with x successes and $(n - x)$ failures is as follows:

$$\begin{array}{cc} S, S, \ldots, S & F, F, \ldots, F \\ (x \text{ times}) & (n - x \text{ times}) \end{array}$$

In other words, the first x trials result in success, while the remainder result in failure. Now, the probability of success in a single trial is P, and the probability of failure is $(1 - P)$. Since the n trials are independent of one another, the probability of any particular sequence of outcomes is, by the multiplication rule of probabilities (Chapter 3), equal to the product of the probabilities for the individual outcomes. Thus, the probability of observing the specific sequence of outcomes just described is as follows:

$$\underset{(x \text{ times})}{[P \times P \times \ldots \times P]} \times \underset{(n - x \text{ times})}{[(1 - P) \times (1 - P) \times \ldots \times (1 - P)]} = P^x (1 - P)^{(n-x)}$$

This line of argument establishes that the probability of observing *any specific sequence* involving x successes and $(n - x)$ failures is $P^x(1 - P)^{n-x}$. For example, suppose that there are five independent trials, each with probability of success $P = 0.60$, and the probability of exactly three successes is required. Using + to designate a success and 0 to indicate a nonsuccess, the desired outcomes could be designated as follows:

$$+++00 \quad \text{or} \quad +0+0+$$

The probability of either of these specific outcomes is $(0.6)^3(0.4)^2 = 0.03456$.

The original problem concerned the determination not of the probability of occurrence of a particular sequence but of the probability of precisely x successes, regardless of the order of the outcomes. There are several sequences in which x successes could be arranged among $(n - x)$ failures. In fact, the number of such possibilities is just the number of combinations of x objects chosen from n, since any x locations can be selected from a total of n in which to place the successes and the total number of successes can be computed using Equation 4.17. Returning to the example of three successes in five trials $(P = 0.60)$, the number of different sequences with three successes would be as follows:

$$C_3^5 = \frac{5!}{3!(5 - 3)!} = 10$$

The probability of three successes in five independent Bernoulli trials is, thus, 10 times the probability of each of the sequences that has three successes, and, thus,

$$P(X = 3) = (10)(0.03456) = 0.3456$$

Next, this result will be generalized for any combination of n and x.

Number of Sequences with x Successes in n Trials
The number of sequences with x successes in n independent trials is

$$C_x^n = \frac{n!}{x!(n - x)!} \tag{4.17}$$

where $n! = n \times (n - 1) \times (n - 2) \times \ldots \times 1$ and $0! = 1$.

These C_x^n sequences are mutually exclusive, since no two of them can occur at the same time. This result was developed in Chapter 3.

The event "x successes resulting from n trials" can occur in C_x^n mutually exclusive ways, each with probability $P^x(1 - P)^{n-x}$. Therefore, by the addition rule of probabilities (Chapter 3) the probability required is the sum of these $C^n{}_x$ individual probabilities. The result is given by Equation 4.18.

The Binomial Distribution
Suppose that a random experiment can result in two possible mutually exclusive and collectively exhaustive outcomes, "success" and "failure," and that P is the probability of a success in a single trial. If n independent trials are carried out, the distribution of the number of resulting successes, x, is called the **binomial distribution**. Its probability distribution function for the binomial random variable $X = x$ is as follows:

$P(x \text{ successes in } n \text{ independent trials})$

$$= P(x) = \frac{n!}{x!(n - x)!} P^x (1 - P)^{(n-x)} \text{ for } x = 0, 1, 2, \cdots, n \tag{4.18}$$

The mean and variance are derived in the chapter appendix, and the results are given by Equations 4.19 and 4.20.

Derived Mean and Variance of a Binomial Probability Distribution

Let X be the number of successes in n independent trials, each with probability of success P. Then X follows a binomial distribution with **mean**

$$\mu = E(X) = nP \tag{4.19}$$

and **variance**

$$\sigma_X^2 = E[(X - \mu_X)^2] = nP(1 - P) \tag{4.20}$$

The binomial distribution is widely used in business and economic applications involving the probability of discrete occurrences. Before using the binomial, the specific situation must be analyzed to determine if

1. the application involves several trials, each of which has only two outcomes: yes or no, on or off, success or failure.
2. the probability of the outcome is the same for each trial.
3. the probability of the outcome on one trial does not affect the probability on other trials.

In the following examples typical applications will be provided.
Binomial distribution probabilities can be obtained using the following:

1. Equation 4.18 (good for small values of n); see Example 4.7
2. Tables in the appendix (good for selected value of n and P); see Example 4.8
3. Computer-generated probabilities; see Example 4.9

Example 4.7 Multiple Contract Sales

Suppose that the Real Estate Agent, Jeanette Nelson, has five contacts, and she believes that for each contact the probability of making a sale is 0.40. Using Equation 4.18 do the following:

a. Find the probability that she makes at most one sale.
b. Find the probability that she makes between two and four sales (inclusive).
c. Graph the probability distribution function.

Solution

a. $P(\text{At Most 1 Sale}) = P(X \leq 1) = P(X = 0) + P(X = 1) = 0.078 + 0.259 = 0.337$, since

$$P(\text{no sales}) = P(0) = \frac{5!}{0!5!}(0.4)^0 (0.6)^5 = (0.6)^5 = 0.078$$

$$P(\text{1 sale}) = P(1) = \frac{5!}{1!4!}(0.4)^1(0.6)^4 = 5(0.4)(0.6)^4 = 0.259$$

b. $P(2 \leq X \leq 4) = P(2) + P(3) + P(4) = 0.346 + 0.230 + 0.077 = 0.653$, since

$$P(2) = \frac{5!}{2!3!}(0.4)^2 (0.6)^3 = 10(0.4)^2 (0.6)^3 = 0.346$$

$$P(3) = \frac{5!}{3!2!}(0.4)^3 (0.6)^2 = 10(0.4)^3 (0.6)^2 = 0.230$$

$$P(4) = \frac{5!}{4!1!}(0.4)^4 (0.6)^1 = 5(0.4)^4 (0.6)^1 = 0.077$$

c. The probability distribution function is shown in Figure 4.3.

Figure 4.3 Graph of Binomial Probability Function for Example 4.7

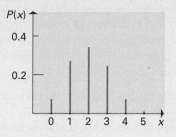

Comments
• This shape is typical for binomial probabilities when P is neither very large nor very small.
• At the extremes (0 or 5 sales), the probabilities are quite small.

Unless the number of trials n is very small, the calculation of binomial probabilities is likely to be extremely cumbersome. Binomial probabilities can also be obtained from tables in the appendix.

Example 4.8   College Admissions

Early in August an undergraduate college discovers that it can accommodate a few extra students. Enrolling those additional students would provide a substantial increase in revenue without increasing the operating costs of the college; that is, no new classes would have to be added. From past experience the college knows that the frequency of enrollment given admission for all students is 40%.

a. What is the probability that at most 6 students will enroll if the college offers admission to 10 more students?
b. What is the probability that more than 12 will actually enroll if admission is offered to 20 students?
c. If the frequency of enrollment given admission for all students was 70%, what is the probability that at least 12 out of 15 students will actually enroll?

Solution

a. This probability can be obtained using the cumulative binomial probability distribution from Table 3 in the appendix. The probability of at most 6 students enrolling if $n = 10$ and $P = 0.40$ is as follows:

$$P(X \leq 6 \mid n = 10, P = 0.40) = 0.945$$

b. $P(X > 12 \mid n = 20, P = 0.40) = 1 - P(X \leq 12) = 1 - 0.979 = 0.021$

c. The probability that at least 12 out of 15 students enroll is the same as the probability that at most 3 out of 15 students do not enroll (the probability of a student not enrolling is $1 - 0.70 = 0.30$).

$$P(X \geq 12 \mid n = 15, P = 0.70) = P(X \leq 3 \mid n = 15, P = 0.30) = 0.297$$

Most good computer packages have the capability to compute binomial and other probabilities for various probability distribution functions. Example 4.9 presents a probability table computed using Minitab, but other packages have similar capabilities.

Example 4.9 Sales of Airline Seats

Have you ever agreed to give up your airplane ticket in return for a free ticket? Have you ever searched for the cheapest flight so that you could visit a special friend? The following example provides some of the analysis that leads to results such as overbooked flights and reduced fares on certain flights.

Suppose that you are in charge of marketing airline seats for a major carrier. Four days before the flight date you have 16 seats remaining on the plane. You know from past experience data that 80% of the people that purchase tickets in this time period will actually show up for the flight.

    a. If you sell 20 extra tickets, what is the probability that you will overbook the flight or have at least one empty seat?
    b. If you sell 18 extra tickets, what is the probability that you will overbook the flight or have at least one empty seat?

Solution

    a. To find $P(X > 16)$, given $n = 20$ and $P = 0.80$, use the cumulative probability distribution in Table 4.5 that was computed using Minitab.

Table 4.5 Cumulative Binomial Probabilities Obtained from Minitab for $n = 20$, $P = 0.80$

x	$P(X <= x)$
10	0.0026
11	0.0100
12	0.0321
13	0.0867
14	0.1958
15	0.3704
16	0.5886
17	0.7939
18	0.9308
19	0.9885
20	1.0000

The probability of overbooking is

$$P(X > 16) = 1 - P(X <= 16) = 1 - 0.589 = 0.411$$

and we see that the probability of overbooking when 20 seats are sold is 41.1%. If 20 tickets are sold, this also means that the probability that 15 or fewer people will arrive is

$$P(X <= 15) = 0.37.$$

and so, there is a 37% chance that selling 20 tickets results in at least one empty seat!

b. To find the chance that you overbook the flight by selling 18 tickets, compute the cumulative probability distribution using n = 18. The chance that you overbook the flight will be only 10%, but the probability of at least one empty seat will increase to 72.9%!

The airline management then must evaluate the cost of overbooking (providing free tickets) versus the cost of empty seats that generate no revenue. Airlines analyze data to determine the number of seats that should be sold at reduced rates to maximize the ticket revenue from each flight. This analysis is complex, but it has its starting point in analyses such as the example presented here.

EXERCISES

Basic Exercises

4.30 For a Bernoulli random variable with probability of success $P = 0.5$, compute the mean and variance.

4.31 For a binomial probability function with $P = 0.5$ and $n = 12$, find the probability that the number of successes is equal to 7 and the probability that the number of successes is fewer than 6.

4.32 For a binomial probability function with $P = 0.3$ and $n = 14$, find the probability that the number of successes is equal to 7 and the probability that the number of successes is fewer than 6.

4.33 For a binomial probability function with $P = 0.4$ and $n = 20$, find the probability that the number of successes is equal to 9 and the probability that the number of successes is fewer than 7.

4.34 For a binomial probability function with $P = 0.7$ and $n = 18$, find the probability that the number of successes is equal to 12 and the probability that the number of successes is fewer than 6.

Application Exercises

4.35 A production manager knows that 5% of components produced by a particular manufacturing process have some defect. Six of these components, whose characteristics can be assumed to be independent of each other, are examined.

a. What is the probability that none of these components has a defect?

b. What is the probability that one of these components has a defect?

c. What is the probability that at least two of these components have a defect?

4.36 A state senator believes that 25% of all senators on the Finance Committee will strongly support the tax proposal she wishes to advance. Suppose that this belief is correct and that five senators are approached at random.

a. What is the probability that at least one of the five will strongly support the proposal?

b. What is the probability that a majority of the five will strongly support the proposal?

4.37 A public interest group hires students to solicit donations by telephone. After a brief training period students make calls to potential donors and are paid on a commission basis. Experience indicates that early on these students tend to have only modest success and that 70% of them give up their jobs in their first 2 weeks of employment. The group hires six students, which can be viewed as a random sample.

a. What is the probability that at least two of the six will give up in the first 2 weeks?

b. What is the probability that at least two of the six will not give up in the first 2 weeks?

4.38 Suppose that the probability is 0.2 that the value of the U.S. dollar will rise against the Chinese yuan over any given week and that the outcome in one week is independent of that in any other week. What is the probability that the value of the U.S. dollar will rise against the Chinese yuan at least twice over a period of 7 weeks?

4.39 A company installs new central heating furnaces and has found that for 15% of all installations a return visit is needed to make some modifications. Six installations were made in a particular week. Assume independence of outcomes for these installations.

a. What is the probability that a return visit will be needed in all of these cases?

b. What is the probability that a return visit will be needed in none of these cases?

c. What is the probability that a return visit will be needed in more than one of these cases?

4.40 The Minnesota Twins are to play a series of five games in Boston against the Red Sox. For any one game it is estimated that the probability of a Twins win is 0.5. The outcomes of the five games are independent of one another.

a. What is the probability that the Twins will win all five games?
b. What is the probability that the Twins will win a majority of the five games?
c. If the Twins win the first game, what is the probability that they will win a majority of the five games?
d. Before the series begins, what is the expected number of Twins wins in these five games?
e. If the Twins win the first game, what is the expected number of Twins wins in the five-game series?

4.41 A small commuter airline flies planes that can seat up to eight passengers. The airline has determined that the probability that a ticketed passenger will not show up for a flight is 0.2. For each flight the airline sells tickets to the first 10 people placing orders. The probability distribution for the number of tickets sold per flight is shown in the accompanying table. For what proportion of the airline's flights does the number of ticketed passengers showing up exceed the number of available seats? (Assume independence between the number of tickets sold and the probability that a ticketed passenger will show up.)

Number of tickets	6	7	8	9	10
Probability	0.25	0.35	0.25	0.10	0.05

4.42 Following a touchdown, a college football coach has the option to elect to attempt a "2-point conversion"; that is, 2 additional points are scored if the attempt is successful and none if it is unsuccessful. The coach believes that the probability is 0.35 that his team will be successful in any attempt and that outcomes of different attempts are independent of each other. In a particular game the team scores four touchdowns and 2-point conversion attempts were made each time.

a. What is the probability that at least two of these attempts will be successful?
b. Find the mean and standard deviation of the total number of points resulting from these four attempts.
c. What is the required success rate for completing one point conversions so that the same mean number of points are obtained.

4.43 An notebook dealer mounts a new promotional campaign. Purchasers of new computers may, if dissatisfied for any reason, return them within 2 days of purchase and receive a full refund. The cost to the dealer of such a refund is $100. The dealer estimates that 15% of all purchasers will indeed return computers and obtain refunds. Suppose that 50 computers are purchased during the campaign period.

a. Find the mean and standard deviation of the number of these computers that will be returned for refunds.
b. Find the mean and standard deviation of the total refund costs that will accrue as a result of these 50 purchases.

4.44 A family of mutual funds maintains a service that allows clients to switch money among accounts through a telephone call. It was estimated that 3.2% of callers either get a busy signal or are kept on hold so long that they may hang up. Fund management assesses any failure of this sort as a $10 goodwill loss. Suppose that 2,000 calls are attempted over a particular period.

a. Find the mean and standard deviation of the number of callers who will either get a busy signal or may hang up after being kept on hold.
b. Find the mean and standard deviation of the total goodwill loss to the mutual fund company from these 2,000 calls.

4.45 We have seen that, for a binomial distribution with n trials, each with probability of success P, the mean is as follows:

$$\mu_X = E(X) = nP$$

Verify this result for the data of Example 4.7 by calculating the mean directly from

$$\mu_X = \sum xP(x)$$

showing that for the binomial distribution the two formulas produce the same answer.

4.46 A campus finance officer finds that, for all parking tickets issued, fines are paid for 78% of the tickets. The fine is $2. In the most recent week 620 parking tickets have been issued.

a. Find the mean and standard deviation of the number of these tickets for which the fines will be paid.
b. Find the mean and standard deviation of the amount of money that will be obtained from the payment of these fines.

4.47 A company receives a very large shipment of components. A random sample of 16 of these components will be checked, and the shipment will be accepted if fewer than 2 of these components are defective. What is the probability of accepting a shipment containing

a. 5% defectives?
b. 15% defectives?
c. 25% defectives?

4.48 The following two acceptance rules are being considered for determining whether to take delivery of a large shipment of components:

- A random sample of 10 components is checked, and the shipment is accepted only if none of them is defective.
- A random sample of 20 components is checked, and the shipment is accepted only if no more than 1 of them is defective.

Which of these acceptance rules has the smaller probability of accepting a shipment containing 20% defectives?

4.49 A company receives large shipments of parts from two sources. Seventy percent of the shipments come from a supplier whose shipments typically contain 10% defectives, while the remainder are from a supplier whose shipments typically contain 20% defectives. A manager receives a shipment but does not know the source. A random sample of 20 items from this shipment is tested, and 1 of the parts is found to be defective. What is the probability that this shipment came from the more reliable supplier? [*Hint:* Use Bayes' theorem.]

4.5 HYPERGEOMETRIC DISTRIBUTION

The binomial distribution presented in Section 4.4 assumes that the items are drawn independently, with the probability of selecting an item being constant. In many applied problems these assumptions can be met if a small sample is drawn from a large population. But here we consider, for example, a situation where it is necessary to select 5 employees from a group of 15 equally qualified applicants—a small population. In the group of 15 there are 9 women and 6 men. Suppose that, in the group of 5 selected employees, 3 are men and 2 are women. What is the probability of selecting that particular group if the selections are made randomly without bias. In the initial group of 15 the probability of selecting a woman is 9/15. If a woman is not selected in the first drawing, then the probability of selecting a woman in the second drawing is 9/14. Thus, the probabilities change with each selection. Because the assumptions for the binomial are not met, a different probability model must be selected. This probability distribution is the *hypergeometric probability distribution*. The hypergeometric probability model is given in Equation 4.21.

The example above describes a situation of "sampling without replacement" since an item drawn from the small population is not replaced before the second item is selected. Thus the probability of selection changes after each succeeding selection. This change is particularly important when the population is small relative to the size of the sample.

We can use the binomial distribution in situations that are defined as "sampling with replacement." If the selected item is replaced in the population, then the probability of selecting that type of item remains the same and the binomial assumptions are met. In contrast, if the items are not replaced—"sampling without replacement"—the probabilities change with each selection, and, thus, the appropriate probability model is the hypergeometric distribution. If the population is large ($N > 10,000$) and the sample size is small ($< 1\%$), then the change in probability after each draw is very small. In those situations the binomial is a very good approximation and is typically used.

Hypergeometric Distribution
Suppose that a random sample of n objects is chosen from a group of N objects, S of which are successes. The distribution of the number of

successes, X, in the sample is called the **hypergeometric distribution**. Its probability function is

$$P(x) = \frac{C_x^S C_{n-x}^{N-S}}{C_n^N} = \frac{\dfrac{S!}{x!(S-x)!} \times \dfrac{(N-S)!}{(n-x)!(N-S-n+x)!}}{\dfrac{N!}{n!(N-n)!}} \qquad (4.21)$$

where x can take integer values ranging from the larger of 0 and $[n - (N - S)]$ to the smaller of n and S.

The logic for the hypergeometric distribution was developed in Section 3.3 using the classic definition of probability and the counting formulas for combinations. In Equation 4.21 the individual components are as follows:

1. The number of possible ways that x successes can be selected for the sample out of S successes contained in the population:

$$C_x^s = \frac{S!}{x!(S-x)!}$$

2. The number of possible ways that $n - x$ nonsuccesses can be selected from the population that contains $N - S$ nonsuccesses:

$$C_{n=x}^{N-S} = \frac{(N-S)!}{(n-x)!(N-S-n+x)!}$$

3. And, finally, the total number of different samples of size n that can be obtained from a population of size N:

$$C_n^N = \frac{N!}{n!(N-n)!}$$

When these components are combined using the classical definition of probability, the hypergeometric probability distribution is obtained.

Example 4.10 Shipment of Items (Compute Hypergeometric Probability)

A company receives a shipment of 20 items. Because inspection of each individual item is expensive, it has a policy of checking a random sample of 6 items from such a shipment, and if no more than 1 sampled item is defective, the remainder will not be checked. What is the probability that a shipment of 5 defective items will not be subjected to additional checking?

Solution If "defective" is identified with "success" in this example, the shipment contains $N = 20$ items and $S = 5$ of the 20 that are successes. A sample of $n = 6$ items is selected. Then the number of successes, X, in the sample has a hypergeometric distribution with the probability function

$$P(x) = \frac{C_x^S C_{n-x}^{N-S}}{C_n^N} = \frac{C_x^5 C_{6-x}^{15}}{C_6^{20}} = \frac{\dfrac{5!}{x!(5-x)!} \times \dfrac{15!}{(6-x)!(9+x)!}}{\dfrac{20!}{6!14!}}$$

The shipment is not checked further if the sample contains either zero or one success (defective), so that the probability of its acceptance is as follows:

$$P(\text{Shipment Accepted}) = P(0) + P(1)$$

The probability of no defectives in the sample is as follows:

$$P(0) = \frac{\dfrac{5!}{0!5!} \times \dfrac{15!}{6!9!}}{\dfrac{20!}{6!14!}} = 0.129$$

The probability of 1 defective item in the sample is as follows:

$$P(1) = \frac{\dfrac{5!}{1!4!} \times \dfrac{15!}{5!10!}}{\dfrac{20!}{6!14!}} = 0.387$$

Therefore, we find that the probability that the shipment of 20 items containing 5 defectives is not checked further is $P(\text{Shipment Accepted}) = P(0) + P(1) = 0.129 + 0.387 = 0.516$. This is a high error rate, which indicates a need for a new acceptance rule that requires total inspection if one or more defectives are found. With this new rule only 12.9% of these shipments would be missed.

Hypergeometric probabilities can also be computed using computer packages following a procedure similar to the procedure in Example 4.9 for the binomial.

EXERCISES

Basic Exercises

4.50 Compute the probability of 5 successes in a random sample of size $n = 12$ obtained from a population of size $N = 50$ that contains 25 successes.

4.51 Compute the probability of 7 successes in a random sample of size $n = 14$ obtained from a population of size $N = 60$ that contains 25 successes.

4.52 Compute the probability of 9 successes in a random sample of size $n = 20$ obtained from a population of size $N = 80$ that contains 42 successes.

4.53 Compute the probability of 3 successes in a random sample of size $n = 5$ obtained from a population of size $N = 40$ that contains 25 successes.

4.54 Compute the probability of 8 successes in a random sample of size $n = 15$ obtained from a population of size $N = 400$ that contains 200 successes.

Application Exercises

4.55 A company receives a shipment of 16 items. A random sample of 4 items is selected, and the shipment is rejected if any of these items proves to be defective.

   a. What is the probability of accepting a shipment containing 4 defective items?

   b. What is the probability of accepting a shipment containing 1 defective item?

   c. What is the probability of rejecting a shipment containing 1 defective item?

4.56 A committee of eight members is to be formed from a group of eight men and eight women. If the choice of committee members is made randomly, what is the probability that precisely half of these members will be women?

4.57 A bond analyst was given a list of 12 corporate bonds. From that list she selected 3 whose ratings she felt were in danger of being downgraded in the next year. In actuality, a total of 4 of the 12 bonds on the list had their ratings downgraded in the next year. Suppose that the analyst had simply chosen 3 bonds randomly from this list. What is the probability that at least 2 of the chosen bonds would be among those whose ratings were to be downgraded in the next year?

4.58 A bank executive is presented with loan applications from 10 people. The profiles of the applicants are similar, except that 5 are minorities and 5 are not minorities. In the end the executive approves 6 of the applications. If these 6 approvals are chosen at random from the 10 applications, what is the probability that less than half the approvals will be of applications involving minorities?

The *Poisson probability distribution* was first proposed by Simeon Poisson (1781–1840) in a book published in 1837. The number of applications began to increase early in the twentieth century, and the availability of the computer has brought about further applications in the twenty-first century. The Poisson probability distribution is an important discrete probability distribution for a number of applications, including the following:

1. The number of failures in a large computer system during a given day
2. The number of replacement orders for a part received by a firm in a given month
3. The number of ships arriving at a loading facility during a 6-hour loading period
4. The number of delivery trucks to arrive at a central warehouse in an hour
5. The number of dents, scratches, or other defects in a large roll of sheet metal used to manufacture washers
6. The number of customers to arrive for flights during each 15-minute time interval from 3:00 p.m. to 6:00 p.m. on weekdays
7. The number of customers to arrive at a checkout aisle in your local grocery store during a particular time interval

We can use the Poisson probability distribution to determine the probability of each of these random variables, which are characterized as the number of occurrences or successes of a certain event in a given continuous interval (such as time, surface area, or length).

A Poisson probability distribution is modeled according to certain assumptions.

Assumptions of the Poisson Probability Distribution

Assume that an interval is divided into a very large number of subintervals so that the probability of the occurrence of an event in any subinterval is very small. The **assumptions of a Poisson probability distribution** are as follows:

1. The probability of the occurrence of an event is constant for all subintervals.
2. There can be no more than one occurrence in each subinterval.
3. Occurrences are independent; that is, the occurrences in nonoverlapping intervals are independent of one another.

We can derive the equation for computing Poisson probabilities directly from the binomial probability distribution by taking the mathematical limits as $P \rightarrow 0$ and $n \rightarrow \infty$. With these limits the parameter $\lambda = nP$ is a constant that specifies the average number of occurrences (successes) for a particular time and/or space. We can see intuitively that the Poisson is a special case of the binomial obtained by extending these limits. However, the mathematical derivation is beyond the scope of this book. The interested reader is referred to page 244 of Hogg and Craig (1995). The Poisson probability distribution function is given in Equation 4.22.

The Poisson Probability Distribution Function, Mean, and Variance

The random variable X is said to follow the **Poisson probability distribution** if it has the probability function

$$P(x) = \frac{e^{-\lambda}\lambda^x}{x!}, \text{ for } x = 0,1,2\ldots \qquad (4.22)$$

where

$P(x)$ = the probability of x sucesses over a given time or space, given λ

λ = the expected number of successes per time or space unit; $\lambda > 0$

$e \cong 2.71828$ (the base for natural logarithms)

The **mean and variance of the Poisson probability distribution** are

$$\mu_x = E(X) = \lambda \quad \text{and} \quad \sigma_x^2 = E[(X - \mu_x)^2] = \lambda$$

The sum of Poisson random variables is also a Poisson random variable. Thus, the sum of K Poisson random variables, each with mean λ, is a Poisson random variable with mean $K\lambda$.

An important application of the Poisson probability distribution in the modern global economy concerns the probability of failures in complex systems and the probability of defective products in large production runs of several hundred thousand to a million units. A large world wide shipping company such as Federal Express has a complex and extensive pickup, classification, shipping, and delivery system for millions of packages each day. There is a very small probability of handling failure at each step for each of the millions of packages handled every day. The company is interested in the probability of various numbers of failed deliveries each day when the system is operating properly. If the number of actual failed deliveries observed on a particular day has a small probability given proper operations then the management begins a systematic checking process to identify and correct the reason for excessive failures.

Example 4.11 System Component Failure (Poisson Probabilities)

Andrew Whittaker, computer center manager, reports that his computer system experienced three component failures during the past 100 days.

- a. What is the probability of no failures in a given day?
- b. What is the probability of one or more component failures in a given day?
- c. What is the probability of at least two failures in a 3-day period?

Solution   A modern computer system has a very large number of components, each of which could fail and thus result in a computer system failure. To compute the probability of failures using the Poisson distribution, assume that each of the millions of components has the same very small probability of failure. Also assume that the first failure does not affect the probability of a second failure (in some cases, these assumptions may not hold, and more complex distributions would be used).

From past experience the expected number of failures per day is 3/100, or $\lambda = 0.03$.

    a. P(no failures in a given day) $= P(X = 0 \mid \lambda = 0.03) = \dfrac{e^{-0.03}\lambda^0}{0!} = 0.970446$

    b. The probability of at least one failure is the complement of the probability of 0 failures:

$$P(X \geq 1) = 1 - P(X = 0) = 1 - \left[\frac{e^{-\lambda}\lambda^x}{x!}\right] = 1 - \left[\frac{e^{-0.03}\lambda^0}{0!}\right]$$

$$= 1 - e^{-0.03} = 1 - 0.970446 = 0.029554$$

    c. P(At Least Two Failures in a 3-Day Period) $= P(X \geq 2 \mid \lambda = 0.09)$, where the average over a 3-day period is $\lambda = 3(0.03) = 0.09$:

$$P(X \geq 2 \mid \lambda = 0.09) = 1 - P(X \leq 1) = 1 - [P(X = 0) + P(X = 1)] =$$

$$1 - [0.913931 + 0.082254]$$

and, thus,

$$P(X \geq 2 \mid \lambda = 0.09) = 1 - 0.996185 = 0.003815$$

The Poisson distribution has been found to be particularly useful in *waiting line*, or *queuing*, problems. These important applications include the probability of various numbers of customers waiting for a phone line or waiting to check out of a large retail store. These queuing problems are an important management issue for firms that draw customers from large populations. If the queue becomes too long customers might quit the line or might not return for a future shopping visit. If a store has too many checkout lines then there will be personnel idle waiting for customers resulting in lower productivity. By knowing the probability of various numbers of customers in the line management can balance the trade-off between long lines and idle customer service associates. In this way the firm can implement its strategy for the desired customer service level—shorter wait times imply higher customer service levels but have a cost of more idle time for checkout workers.

Example 4.12   Customers at a Photocopying Machine (Poisson Probability)

Customers arrive at a photocopying machine at an average rate of two every 5 minutes. Assume that these arrivals are independent, with a constant arrival rate, and that this problem follows a Poisson model, with X denoting the number of arriving customers in a 5-minute period and mean $\lambda = 2$. Find the probability that more than two customers arrive in a 5-minute period.

Solution   Since the mean number of arrivals in 5 minutes is two, then $\lambda = 2$. To find the probability that more than two customers arrive, first compute the probability of at most two arrivals in a 5-minute period, and then use the complement rule.

    These probabilities can be found in Table 5 in the appendix or by using a computer:

$$P(X = 0) = \frac{e^{-2}2^0}{0!} = e^{-2} = 0.135335$$

$$P(X = 1) = \frac{e^{-2}2^1}{1!} = 2e^{-2} = 0.27067$$

$$P(X = 2) = \frac{e^{-2}2^2}{2!} = 2e^{-2} = 0.27067$$

Thus, the probability of more than two arrivals in a 5-minute period is as follows:

$$P(X > 2) = 1 - P(X \le 2) = 1 - [0.135335 + 0.27067 + 0.27067] = 0.323325$$

Example 4.13   Ship Arrivals at a Dock

The Canadian government has built a large grain shipping port at Churchill, Manitoba, on the Hudson Bay. Grain grown in southern Manitoba is carried by rail to Churchill during the open water shipping season. Unfortunately the port is open only 50 days per year during July and August. This leads to some critical crew staffing decisions by management. The port has the capacity load up to seven ships simultaneously provided that each loading bay has an assigned crew. The remote location and short shipping season results in a very high labor cost for each crew assigned and management would like to minimize the number of crews. Ships arrive in a random pattern that can be modeled using the Poisson probability model. If a ship arrives and all available loading bays are filled the ship will be delayed resulting in a large cost that must be paid to the owner of the ship. This penalty was negotiated to encourage ship owners to send their ships to Churchill.

Results of an initial analysis indicates that each ship requires six hours for loading by a single crew. The port can remain open only 50 days per year and 500 ships must be loaded during this time. Each additional crew costs $200,000 and each boat delay costs $10,000. How many crews should be scheduled?

Solution   The final decision is based on the probability of ship arrivals during a 6-hour period and the cost of additional crews versus the penalty cost for delayed ships. The first step is to compute the probabilities of various numbers of ships arriving during a 6-hour period and then the cost of ship delays. Then we compute the cost of crews and the cost of ship delays for various levels of crew assignment.

Ship arrivals can be modeled by assuming that there are thousands of ships in the world and each has a small probability of arriving during a 6-hour loading period. An alternative model assumption is that during 6 hours there are a large number of small time intervals—say 0.1 second—in this case 216,000 such intervals. We also need to assume that ships do not travel in convoys. With 500 ships arriving over 50 days we have a mean of ten ships per day or $\lambda = 2.5$ ship arrivals during a 6-hour period. The probability of, x, arrivals during a 6-hour period is computed using the following:

$$P(X = x \mid \lambda = 2.5) = \frac{2.5^x e^{-2.5}}{x!}$$

If four crews are scheduled the probabilities of delaying ships are as follows:

$$P(Delay\ 1\ ship) = P(5\ ships\ arrive) = \frac{2.5^5 e^{-2.5}}{5!} = 0.0668$$

$$P(\textit{Delay 2 ships}) = P(6 \textit{ ships arrive}) = \frac{2.5^6 e^{-2.5}}{6!} = 0.0278$$

$$P(\textit{Delay 3 ships}) = P(7 \textit{ ships arrive}) = \frac{2.5^7 e^{-2.5}}{7!} = 0.0099$$

The probabilities of idle crews are as follows:

$$P(1 \textit{ crew idle}) = P(3 \textit{ ships arrive}) = \frac{2.5^3 e^{-2.5}}{3!} = 0.2138$$

$$P(2 \textit{ crews idle}) = P(2 \textit{ ships arrive}) = \frac{2.5^3 e^{-2.5}}{3!} = 0.2565$$

$$P(3 \textit{ crews idle}) = P(1 \textit{ ship arrives}) = \frac{2.5^1 e^{-2.5}}{1!} = 0.2052$$

$$P(4 \textit{ crews idle}) = P(0 \textit{ ships arrive}) = \frac{2.5^0 e^{-2.5}}{0!} = 0.0821$$

With four crews scheduled the expected number of boats delayed during a 6-hour period would be as follows:

$$(1 \times 0.0668 + 2 \times 0.0278 + 3 \times 0.0099) = 0.1521$$

With a 50-day shipping season there are 200 six-hour periods and thus the delay cost is as follows:

$$(0.1521)(200)(10,000) = \$304,200$$

Following the same computational form we would find that with 5 crews scheduled the expected cost of delays would be $95,200 and, thus, the extra crew would save $209,200. Since the cost of an extra crew is $200,000 the scheduling of 5 crews would be the correct decision.

We note that scheduling an additional crew would also lead to increased crew idle time. However, the higher service level makes it economically sensible to have crews idle in order to reduce ship delays.

Poisson Approximation to the Binomial Distribution

Previously, we noted that the Poisson probability distribution is obtained by starting with the binomial probability distribution with P approaching 0 and n becoming very large. Thus, it follows that the Poisson distribution can be used to approximate the binomial probabilities when the number of trials, n, is large and at the same time the probability, P, is small (generally such that $\lambda = nP \leq 7$). Examples of situations that would satisfy these conditions include the following:

- An insurance company will hold a large number of life policies on individuals of any particular age, and the probability that a single policy will result in a claim during the year is very low. Here, we have a binomial distribution with large n and small P.
- A company may have a large number of machines working on a process simultaneously. If the probability that any one of them will break down in a single day is small, the distribution of the number of daily breakdowns is binomial with large n and small P.

Example 4.14   Probability of Bankruptcy (Poisson Probability)

An analyst predicted that 3.5% of all small corporations would file for bankruptcy
in the coming year. For a random sample of 100 small corporations, estimate the
probability that at least 3 will file for bankruptcy in the next year, assuming that
the analyst's prediction is correct.

Solution   The distribution of X, the number of filings for bankruptcy, is
binomial with $n = 100$ and $P = 0.035$, so that the mean of the distribution is
$\mu_x = nP = 3.4$. Using the Poisson distribution to approximate the probability of at
least 3 bankruptcies, we find the following:

$$P(X \geq 3) = 1 - P(X \leq 2)$$

$$P(0) = \frac{e^{-3.5}(3.5)^0}{0!} = e^{-3.5} = 0.030197$$

$$P(1) = \frac{e^{-3.5}(3.5)^1}{1!} = (3.5)(0.030197) = 0.1056895$$

$$P(2) = \frac{e^{-3.5}(3.5)^2}{2!} = (6.125)(0.030197) = 0.1849566$$

Thus, $P(X \leq 2) = P(0) + P(1) + P(2) = 0.030197 + 0.1056895 + 0.1849566 = 0.3208431$

$$P(X \geq 3) = 1 - 0.3208431 = 0.6791569$$

The binomial probability of $X \geq 3$ is as follows:

$$P(X \geq 3) = 0.684093$$

Thus the Poisson probability is a close estimate of the actual binomial probability.

Comparison of the Poisson and Binomial Probability Distributions

We should indicate at this point that confusion may exist about the choice of the binomial or the Poisson probability distribution for particular applications. The choice in
many cases can be made easier by carefully reviewing the assumptions for the two
probability distributions. For example, if the problem uses a small sample of observations, then it is not possible to find a limiting probability with n large, and, thus, the

binomial is the correct probability distribution. Further, if we have a small sample and the probability of a success for a single trial is between 0.05 and 0.95, then there is further support for choosing the binomial. If we knew or could assume that each of 10 randomly selected customers in an automobile showroom had the same probability of purchase (assume $0.05 \leq P \leq 0.95$), then the number of purchases from this group would follow a binomial probability distribution. However, if the set of cases that could be affected is very large—say, several thousand—and the mean number of "successes" over that large set of cases is small—say, fewer than 30—then there is strong support for choosing the Poisson probability distribution. If we wanted to compute the probability of a certain number of defective parts in a set of 100,000 parts when the mean number of 15 defectives per 100,000 parts represented a typical production cycle, then we would use the Poisson probability distribution.

In the previous discussion it was noted that, when P is less than 0.05 and n is large, we can approximate the binomial probability distribution by using the Poisson probability distribution. It can also be shown that, when $n \geq 20$, $P \leq 0.05$, and the population mean is the same, we will find that both the binomial and the Poisson probability distributions generate approximately the same probability values. This result is shown in Exercise 4.72.

EXERCISES

Basic Exercises

4.59 Determine the probability of exactly 7 successes for a random variable with a Poisson distribution with parameter $\lambda = 3.4$.

4.60 Determine the probability of exactly 4 successes for a random variable with a Poisson distribution with parameter $\lambda = 2.4$.

4.61 Determine the probability of more than 7 successes for a random variable with a Poisson distribution with parameter $\lambda = 4.4$.

4.62 Determine the probability of fewer than 6 successes for a random variable with a Poisson distribution with parameter $\lambda = 3.4$.

4.63 Determine the probability of fewer than or equal to 9 successes for a random variable with a Poisson distribution with parameter $\lambda = 8.0$.

Application Exercises

4.64 Customers arrive at a busy checkout counter at an average rate of three per minute. If the distribution of arrivals is Poisson, find the probability that in any given minute there will be two or fewer arrivals.

4.65 The number of accidents in a production facility has a Poisson distribution with a mean of 2.6 per month.

   a. For a given month what is the probability there will be fewer than two accidents?

   b. For a given month what is the probability there will be more than three accidents?

4.66 A customer service center in India receives, on average, 4.2 telephone calls per minute. If the distribution of calls is Poisson, what is the probability of receiving at least three calls during a particular minute?

4.67 Records indicate that, on average, 3.2 breakdowns per day occur on an urban highway during the morning rush hour. Assume that the distribution is Poisson.

   a. Find the probability that on any given day there will be fewer than two breakdowns on this highway during the morning rush hour.

   b. Find the probability that on any given day there will be more than four breakdowns on this highway during the morning rush hour.

4.68 Blue Cross Health Insurance reported that 4.5% of claims forms submitted for payment after a complex surgical procedure contain errors. If 100 of these forms are chosen at random, what is the probability that fewer than 3 of them contain errors? Use the Poisson approximation to the binomial distribution.

4.69 A corporation has 250 personal computers. The probability that any 1 of them will require repair in a given week is 0.01. Find the probability that fewer than 4 of the personal computers will require repair in a particular week. Use the Poisson approximation to the binomial distribution.

4.70 An insurance company holds fraud insurance policies on 6,000 firms. In any given year the probability that any single policy will result in a claim is 0.001. Find the probability that at least three claims are made in a given year. Use the Poisson approximation to the binomial distribution.

4.71 A state has a law requiring motorists to carry insurance. It was estimated that, despite this law, 7.5% of all motorists in the state are uninsured. A random sample of 60 motorists was taken. Use the Poisson approximation to the binomial distribution to estimate the probability that at least 3 of the motorists in this sample are uninsured. Also indicate what calculations would be needed to find this probability exactly if the Poisson approximation was not used.

4.72 A new warehouse is being designed and a decision concerning the number of loading docks is required. There are two models for the use of this warehouse, given that loading a truck requires 1 hour. The warehouse could be serviced by one of the many thousands of independent truckers who arrive randomly to obtain a load for delivery. It is known that, on average, one of these trucks would arrive each hour. Alternatively, the company might hire a fleet of 10 trucks that are assigned full-time to shipments from this warehouse. Under that assumption the trucks would arrive randomly, but the probability of any truck arriving during a given hour is 0.1. Obtain the appropriate probability distribution for each of these assumptions and compare the results.

4.7 JOINTLY DISTRIBUTED DISCRETE RANDOM VARIABLES

Business and economic applications of statistics are often concerned about the relationships between variables. Products at different quality levels are priced at different prices. Age groups have different preferences for clothing, for automobiles, and for music. The percent returns on two different stocks may tend to be related, and the returns for both may increase when the market is growing. Alternatively, when the return on one stock is growing, the return on the other might be decreasing. When we work with probability models for problems involving relationships between variables, it is important that the effect of these relationships is included in the probability model. For example, assume that a car dealer is selling the following automobiles: (1) a red two-door compact, (2) a blue minivan, and (3) a silver full-size sedan; the probability distribution for purchasing would not be the same for women in their 20s, 30s, and 50s. Thus, it is important that probability models reflect the joint effect of variables on probabilities.

In Section 3.4 we discussed joint probabilities. We now consider the case where two or more, possibly related, discrete random variables are examined. With a single random variable, the probabilities for all possible outcomes can be summarized in a probability function, where as now we need to define the probabilities that the random variables of interest simultaneously take specific values. Consider the following example involving the use of jointly distributed discrete random variables.

Example 4.15   Market Research (Joint Probabilities)

Sally Peterson, a marketing analyst, has been asked to develop a probability model for the relationship between the sale of luxury cookware and age group. This model will be important for developing a marketing campaign for a new line of chef-grade cookware. She believes that purchasing patterns for luxury cookware are different for different age groups.

Solution   To represent the market, Sally proposes to use three age groups—16 to 25, 26 to 45, and 46 to 65—and two purchasing patterns—"buy" and "not buy." Next, she collects a random sample of persons for the age range 16 to 65 and records their age group and desire to purchase. The result of this data collection is the joint probability distribution contained in Table 4.6. Table 4.6, therefore, provides a summary of the probability of purchase and age group that will be a valuable resource for marketing analysis.

Table 4.6 Joint Probability Distribution of Age Group (X) versus Purchase Decision (Y)

PURCHASE DECISION (Y)	AGE GROUP (X)			
	1 (16 TO 25)	2 (26 TO 45)	3 (46 TO 65)	$P(y)$
1 (buy)	0.10	0.20	0.10	0.40
2 (not buy)	0.25	0.25	0.10	0.60
$P(x)$	0.35	0.45	0.20	1.00

Joint Probability Function

Let X and Y be a pair of discrete random variables. Their **joint probability function** expresses the probability that simultaneously X takes the specific value x, and Y takes the value y, as a function of x and y. We note that the discussion here is a direct extension of the material in Section 4.4, where we presented the probability of the intersection of two events, $P(A_i \cap B_j)$. Here, we will use random variables. The notation used is $P(x, y)$, so

$$P(x, y) = P(X = x \cap Y = y)$$

The probability functions for the individual random variables are frequently desired when dealing with jointly distributed random variables.

Derivation of the Marginal Probability Function

Let X and Y be a pair of jointly distributed random variables. In this context the probability function of the random variable X is called its **marginal probability function** and is obtained by summing the joint probabilities over all possible values—that is,

$$P(x) = \sum_y P(x, y) \tag{4.24}$$

Similarly, the marginal probability function of the random variable Y is as follows:

$$P(y) = \sum_x P(x, y) \tag{4.25}$$

An example of these marginal probability functions is shown in the lower row and the right column in Table 4.5.

Joint probability functions must have the following properties.

Properties of Joint Probability Functions of Discrete Random Variables

Let X and Y be discrete random variables with joint probability function $P(x, y)$. Then,

1. $0 < P(x, y) < 1$ for any pair of values x and y; and
2. the sum of the joint probabilities $P(x, y)$ over all possible pairs of values must be 1.

The *conditional probability function* of one random variable, given specified values of another, is the collection of conditional probabilities.

Conditional Probability Function

Let X and Y be a pair of jointly distributed discrete random variables. The **conditional probability function** of the random variable Y, given that the random variable X takes the value x, expresses the probability that Y takes the value y, as a function of y, when the value x is fixed for X. This is denoted $P(y \mid x)$, and so by the definition of conditional probability is as follows:

$$P(y \mid x) = \frac{P(x, y)}{P(x)} \qquad (4.26)$$

Similarly, the conditional probability function of X, given $Y = y$, is as follows:

$$P(x \mid y) = \frac{P(x, y)}{P(y)} \qquad (4.27)$$

For example, using the probabilities in Table 4.6, we can compute the conditional probability of purchase ($y = 1$), given age group 26 to 45 ($x = 2$), as

$$P(1 \mid 2) = \frac{P(2, 1)}{P(2)} = \frac{0.20}{0.45} = 0.44$$

In Chapter 3 we discussed independence of events. This concept extends directly to random variables.

Independence of Jointly Distributed Random Variables

The jointly distributed random variables X and Y are said to be **independent** if and only if their joint probability function is the product of their marginal probability functions; that is, if and only if

$$P(x, y) = P(x)P(y)$$

for all possible pairs of values x and y. And k random variables are independent if and only if

$$P(X_1, X_2, \ldots, X_k) = P(X_1) \, P(X_2) \ldots P(X_K) \qquad \text{(4.28)}$$

From the definition of conditional probability functions it follows that, if the random variables X and Y are independent, then the conditional probability function of Y, given X, is the same as the marginal probability function of Y—that is,

$$P(y \mid x) = P(y)$$

Similarly, it follows that

$$P(x \mid y) = P(x)$$

Example 4.16 considers the possible percent returns for two stocks, A and B, illustrates the computation of marginal probabilities and tests for independence, and finds the means and variances of two jointly distributed random variables.

Example 4.16 Stock Returns, Marginal Probability, Mean, and Variance (Joint Probabilities)

Suppose that Charlotte King has two stocks, A and B. Let X and Y be random variables of possible percent returns (0%, 5%, 10%, and 15%) for each of these two stocks, with the joint probability distribution given in Table 4.7.

a. Find the marginal probabilities.
b. Determine if X and Y are independent.
c. Find the means and variances of both X and Y.

Table 4.7   Joint Probability Distribution for Random Variables X and Y

X RETURN	Y RETURN 0%	5%	10%	15%
0%	0.0625	0.0625	0.0625	0.0625
5%	0.0625	0.0625	0.0625	0.0625
10%	0.0625	0.0625	0.0625	0.0625
15%	0.0625	0.0625	0.0625	0.0625

Solution

a. This problem is solved using the definitions developed in this chapter. Note that for every combination of values for X and Y, $P(x, y) = 0.0625$. That is, there is a 6.25% probability for each possible combination of x and y returns. To find the marginal probability that X has a 0% return consider the following:

$$P(X = 0) = \sum_y P(0, y) = 0.0625 + 0.0625 + 0.0625 + 0.0625 = 0.25$$

Here all the marginal probabilities of X are 25%. Notice that the sum of the marginal probabilities is 1. Similar results can be found for the marginal probabilities of Y.

b. To test for independence, we need to check if $P(x, y) = P(x)P(y)$ for all possible pairs of values x and y.

$P(x, y) = 0.0625$ for all possible pairs of values x and y

$P(x) = 0.25$ and $P(y) = 0.25$ for all possible pairs of values x and y

$P(x, y) = 0.0625 = (0.25)(0.25) = P(x)P(y)$

Therefore, X and Y are independent.

c. The mean of X is as follows:

$$\mu_X = E(X) = \sum_X xP(x) = 0(0.25) + 0.05(0.25) + 0.10(0.25) + 0.15(0.25) = 0.075$$

Similarly, the mean of Y is $\mu_Y = E(y) = 0.075$.

The variance of X is

$$\sigma_X^2 = \sum_X (x - \mu_X)^2 P(x) = P(x) \sum_X (x - \mu_X)^2 = (0.25) \sum_x (x - \mu_X)^2$$

$$= (0.25)[(0 - 0.075)^2 + (0.05 - 0.075)^2 (0.10 - 0.075)^2 + (0.15 - 0.075)^2$$

$$= 0.003125$$

and the standard deviation of X is

$$\sigma_X = \sqrt{0.003125} = 0.0559016, \text{ or } 5.59\%.$$

Follow similar steps to find the variance and standard deviation of Y.

Conditional Mean and Variance

The conditional mean is computed using the following:

$$\mu_{Y|X} = E[Y|X] = \sum_Y (y|x)P(y|x)$$

Using the joint probability distribution in Table 4.6 we can compute the expected value of Y given that $x = 2$:

$$E[Y|x = 2] = \sum_Y (y|x = 2)P(y|x = 2) = (1)\frac{0.20}{0.45} + (2)\frac{0.25}{0.45} = \frac{0.7}{0.45} = 1.56$$

Similarly the conditional variance is computed using the following:

$$\sigma^2{}_{Y|X} = E[(Y - \mu_{Y|X})^2 |X] = \sum_Y (y - \mu_{Y|X})^2|x)P(y|x)$$

Using the joint probability distribution in Table 4.6 we can compute the variance of Y given that $x = 2$:

$$\sigma^2 (Y|x = 2) = \sum_Y ((y - 1.56)^2)|x = 2)P(y|x = 2)$$

$$= (1 - 1.56)^2 \frac{0.20}{0.45} + (2 - 1.56)^2 \frac{0.25}{0.45} = \frac{0.111}{0.45} = 0.247$$

Computer Applications

Computation of marginal probabilities, means, and variances for jointly distributed random variables can be developed in Excel or other computer packages. For example, we can compute marginal probabilities, means, and variances for

Figure 4.4
Marginal
Probabilities,
Means, and
Variances for
X and Y

X Return	Y Return 0%	5%	10%	15%	P(x)	Mean of	Var of X	StDev of
0%	0.0625	0.0625	0.0625	0.0625	0.25	0	0.0014063	
5%	0.0625	0.0625	0.0625	0.0625	0.25	0.0125	0.0001563	
10%	0.0625	0.0625	0.0625	0.0625	0.25	0.025	0.0001563	
15%	0.0625	0.0625	0.0625	0.0625	0.25	0.0375	0.0014063	
P(y)	0.25	0.25	0.25	0.25		0.075	0.003125	0.055902
Mean of Y	0	0.0125	0.025	0.0375	0.075			
Var of Y	0.00140625	0.00015625	0.00015625	0.00140625	0.003125			
StDev of Y					0.055902			

jointly distributed random variables X and Y using the format shown in Figure 4.4.

Linear Functions of Random Variables

Previously, the expectation of a function of a single random variable was defined. This definition can now be extended to functions of several random variables.

Expected Values of Functions of Jointly Distributed Random Variables

Let X and Y be a pair of discrete random variables with joint probability function $P(x, y)$. The expectation of any function $g(X, Y)$ of these random variables is defined as follows:

$$E[g(X, Y)] = \sum_x \sum_y g(x, y) P(x, y) \tag{4.29}$$

Of particular interest are numerous applications involving linear combinations of random variables that have the general form

$$W = aX + bY$$

An important application is the total revenue random variable, W, resulting from monthly sales of two products where X and Y are random variables representing the sales of each product with the selling prices fixed as a and b. The mean and variance, as developed in the chapter appendix, are as follows:

$$\mu_W = E[W] = a\mu_X + b\mu_Y$$

$$\sigma_w^2 = a^2\sigma_X^2 + b^2\sigma_Y^2 + 2ab\,Cov\,(X, Y)$$

These results can be extended to the linear combination of many random variables

$$W = a_1X_1 + a_2X_2 + \cdots + a_kX_k = \sum a_iX_i$$

$$\mu_W = E[W] = \sum_{i=1}^{k} a_i\mu_i$$

$$\sigma_w^2 = \sum_{i=1}^{k} a_i^2\sigma_i^2 + 2\sum_{i=1}^{k-1}\sum_{j>i}^{k} a_ia_j Cov\,(X_i, Y_j)$$

The term, $Cov\,(X, Y)$ is the covariance between the two random variables, which will be developed next.

Covariance

The *covariance* is a measure of the joint variability for two random variables. The covariance can be used to compute the variance of linear combinations of random variables—such as the variance for the total value for the combination of two stocks in a portfolio. In addition, the covariance is used to compute a standardized measure of joint variability called the correlation. We first develop the definition of the covariance and then present some important applications.

Suppose that X and Y are a pair of random variables that are not statistically independent. We would like some measure of the nature and strength of the relationship between them. This is rather difficult to achieve, since the random variables could conceivably be related in any number of ways. To simplify matters, attention is restricted to the possibility of linear association. For example, a high value of X might be associated, on average, with a high value of Y, and a low value of X with a low value of Y, in such a way that, to a good approximation, a straight line might be drawn through the associated values when plotted on a graph.

Suppose that the random variable X has mean μ_X and Y has mean μ_Y, and consider the product $(X - \mu_X)(Y - \mu_Y)$. If high values of X tend to be associated with high values of Y and low values of X with low values of Y, we would expect this product to be positive, and the stronger the association, the larger the expectation of $(X - \mu_X)(Y - \mu_Y)$, to be defined as $E[(X - \mu_X)(Y - \mu_Y)]$. By contrast, if high values of X are associated with low values of Y and low X with high Y, the expected value for this product, $E[(X - \mu_X)(Y - \mu_Y)]$, would be negative. An expectation that $E[(X - \mu_X)(Y - \mu_Y)]$ equals 0 would imply an absence of linear association between X and Y. Thus, the expected value, $E[(X - \mu_X)(Y - \mu_Y)]$, will be used as a measure of linear association in the population.

> ### Covariance
>
> Let X be a random variable with mean μ_X, and let Y be a random variable with mean μ_Y. The expected value of $(X - \mu_X)(Y - \mu_Y)$ is called the **covariance** between X and Y, denoted as Cov(X,Y). For discrete random variables
>
> $$\text{Cov}(X,Y) = E[(X - \mu_X)(Y - \mu_Y)] = \sum_x \sum_y (x - \mu_X)(y - \mu_Y)P(x,y) \qquad (4.30)$$
>
> An equivalent expression is as follows:
>
> $$\text{Cov}(X,Y) = E[XY] - \mu_X\mu_Y = \sum_x \sum_y xyP(x,y) - \mu_X\mu_Y$$

Correlation

Although the covariance provides an indication of the direction of the relationship between random variables, the covariance does not have an upper or lower bound, and its size is greatly influenced by the scaling of the numbers. A strong linear relationship is defined as a condition where the individual observation points are close to a straight line. It is difficult to use the covariance to provide a measure of the strength of a linear relationship because it is unbounded. A related measure, the correlation coefficient, provides a measure of the strength of the linear relationship between two random variables, with the measure being limited to the range from –1 to +1.

Correlation

Let X and Y be jointly distributed random variables. The **correlation** between X and Y is as follows:

$$\rho = \text{Corr}(X, Y) = \frac{\text{Cov}(X,Y)}{\sigma_X \sigma_Y} \qquad (4.31)$$

The correlation is the covariance divided by the standard deviations of the two random variables. This results in a standardized measure of relationship that varies from -1 to $+1$. The following interpretations are important:

1. A correlation of 0 indicates that there is no linear relationship between the two random variables. If the two random variables are independent, the correlation is equal to 0.
2. A positive correlation indicates that if one random variable is high (low), then the other random variable has a higher probability of being high (low), and we say that the variables are positively dependent. Perfect positive linear dependency is indicated by a correlation of $+1.0$.
3. A negative correlation indicates that if one random variable is high (low), then the other random variable has a higher probability of being low (high), and we say that the variables are negatively dependent. Perfect negative linear dependency is indicated by a correlation of -1.0.

The correlation is more useful for describing relationships than the covariance. With a correlation of $+1$ the two random variables have a perfect positive linear relationship, and, therefore, a specific value of one variable, X, predicts the other variable, Y, exactly. A correlation of -1 indicates a perfect negative linear relationship between two variables, with one variable, X, predicting the negative of the other variable, Y. A correlation of 0 indicates no linear relationship between the two variables. Intermediate values indicate that variables tend to be related, with stronger relationships occurring as the absolute value of the correlation approaches 1.

We also know that correlation is a term that has moved into common usage. In many cases correlation is used to indicate that a relationship exists. However, variables that have nonlinear relationships will not have a correlation coefficient close to 1.0. This distinction is important for us in order to avoid confusion between correlated random variables and those with nonlinear relationships.

Example 4.17 Joint Distribution of Stock Prices (Compute Covariance and Correlation)

Find the covariance and correlation for the stocks A and B from Example 4.16 with the joint probability distribution in Table 4.6.

Solution The computation of covariance is tedious for even a problem such as this, which is simplified so that all of the joint probabilities, $P(x, y)$, are 0.0625 for all pairs of values x and y. By definition, you need to find the following:

$$\text{Cov}(X,Y) = \sum_x \sum_y xy P(x,y) - \mu_X \mu_Y$$

$$= 0[(0)(0.0625) + (0.05)(0.0625) + (0.10)(0.0625) + (0.15)(0.0625)]$$
$$+ \& + (0.15)[(0)(0.0625) + (0.05)(0.0625) + (0.10)(0.0625)$$
$$+ (0.15)(0.0625)] - (0.075)(0.075)$$
$$= 0.005625 - 0.005625 = 0$$

Thus,

$$\rho = \text{Corr}(X,Y) = \frac{\text{Cov}(X,Y)}{\sigma_X \sigma_Y} = 0$$

Microsoft Excel can be used for these computations by carefully following the example in Figure 4.5.

Figure 4.5 Covariance and Correlation Using Microsoft Excel

X Return	Y Return 0%	5%	10%	15%	P(x)	Mean of	Var of X	StDev of
0%	0.0625	0.0625	0.0625	0.0625	0.25	0	0.0014063	
5%	0.0625	0.0625	0.0625	0.0625	0.25	0.0125	0.0001563	
10%	0.0625	0.0625	0.0625	0.0625	0.25	0.025	0.0001563	
15%	0.0625	0.0625	0.0625	0.0625	0.25	0.0375	0.0014063	
P(y)	0.25	0.25	0.25	0.25		0.075	0.003125	0.055902
Mean of Y	0	0.0125	0.025	0.0375	0.075			
Var of Y	0.00140625	0.00015625	0.00015625	0.00140625	0.003125			
StDev of Y					0.055902			
xyP(x)	0.0000000	0.0009375	0.0018750	0.0028125	0.0056250			
ΣΣ xyP(x)	0.0000000							

Covariance and Statistical Independence
If two random variables are **statistically independent**, the **covariance** between them is 0. However, the converse is not necessarily true.

The reason a covariance of 0 does not necessarily imply statistical independence is that covariance is designed to measure linear association, and it is possible that this quantity may not detect other types of dependency. Suppose that the random variable X has probability function

$$P(-1) = 1/4 \quad P(0) = 1/2 \quad P(1) = 1/4$$

Let the random variable Y be defined as follows:

$$Y = X^2$$

Thus, knowledge of the value taken by X implies knowledge of the value taken by Y, and, therefore, these two random variables are certainly not independent. Whenever $X = 0$, then $Y = 0$, and if X is either –1 or 1, then $Y = 1$. The joint probability function of X and Y is

$$P(-1, 1) = 1/4 \quad P(0, 0) = 1/2 \quad P(1, 1) = 1/4$$

with the probability of any other combination of values being equal to 0. It is then straightforward to verify that

$$E(X) = 0 \quad E(Y) = 1/2 \quad E(XY) = 0$$

The covariance between X and Y is 0.

To conclude the discussion of joint distributions, consider the mean and variance of a random variable that can be written as the sum or difference of other random variables. These results are summarized below and can be derived using Equation 4.29.

Summary Results for Linear Sums and Differences of Random Variables

Let X and Y be a pair of random variables with means μ_X and μ_Y and variances $\sigma^2{}_X$ and $\sigma^2{}_Y$. The following properties hold:

1. The **expected value of their sum** is the sum of their expected values:

$$E(X + Y) = \mu_X + \mu_Y \tag{4.32}$$

2. The **expected value of their difference** is the difference between their expected values:

$$E(X - Y) = \mu_X - \mu_Y \tag{4.33}$$

3. If the covariance between X and Y is 0, the **variance of their sum** is the sum of their variances:

$$\text{Var}(X + Y) = \sigma_X^2 + \sigma_Y^2 \tag{4.34}$$

But if the covariance is not 0, then

$$\text{Var}(X + Y) = \sigma_X^2 + \sigma_Y^2 + 2\,\text{cov}\,(X,Y)$$

4. If the covariance between X and Y is 0, the **variance of their difference** is the *sum* of their variances:

$$\text{Var}(X - Y) = \sigma_X^2 + \sigma_Y^2 \tag{4.35}$$

But if the covariance is not 0, then

$$\text{Var}(X + Y) = \sigma_X^2 + \sigma_Y^2 - 2\,\text{cov}(X,Y)$$

Let $X_1, X_2, \ldots, X_K$ be K random variables with means $\mu_1, \mu_2, \ldots, \mu_k$ and variances $\sigma_1^2, \sigma_2^2, \ldots, \sigma$. The following properties hold:

5. The expected value of their sum is as follows:

$$E(X_1 + X_2 + \ldots + X_K) = \mu_1 + \mu_2 + \ldots + \mu_K \tag{4.36}$$

6. If the covariance between every pair of these random variables is 0; the variance of their sum is as follows:

$$\text{Var}(X_1 + X_2 + \cdots + X_K) = \sigma_1^2 + \sigma_2^2 + \cdots + \sigma_K^2 \tag{4.37}$$

Example 4.18 Simple Investment Portfolio (Means and Variances, Functions of Random Variables)

An investor has $1,000 to invest and two investment opportunities, each requiring a minimum of $500. The profit per $100 from the first can be represented by a random variable X, having the following probability functions:

$$P(X = -5) = 0.4 \quad \text{and} \quad P(X = 20) = 0.6$$

The profit per $100 from the second is given by the random variable Y, whose probability functions are as follows:

$$P(Y = 0) = 0.6 \quad \text{and} \quad P(Y = 25) = 0.4$$

Random variables X and Y are independent. The investor has the following possible strategies:

a. $1,000 in the first investment
b. $1,000 in the second investment
c. $500 in each investment

Find the mean and variance of the profit from each strategy.

Solution   Random variable X has mean

$$\mu_X = E(X) = \sum_x xP(x) = (-5)(0.4) + (20)(0.6) = \$10$$

and variance

$$\sigma_X^2 = E[(X - \mu_x)^2] = \sum_x (x - \mu_x)^2 P(x) = (-5 - 10)^2 (0.4) + (20 - 10)^2 (0.6) = 150$$

Strategy (a) has mean profit of $E(10X) = 10E(X) = \$100$ and variance of

$$\text{Var}(10X) = 100\text{Var}(X) = 15,000$$

Random variable Y has mean

$$\mu_Y = E(Y) = \sum_y yP(y) = (0)(0.6) + (25)(0.4) = \$10$$

and variance

$$\sigma_Y^2 = E[(Y - \mu_Y)^2] = \sum_y (y - \mu_Y)^2 P(y) = (0 - 10)^2 (0.6) + (25 - 10)^2 (0.4) = 150$$

Strategy (b) has mean profit $E(10Y) = 10E(Y) = \$100$ and variance of

$$\text{Var}(10Y) = 100\text{Var}(Y) = 15,000$$

Now consider strategy (c): $500 in each investment. The return from strategy (c) is $5X + 5Y$, which has mean

$$E(5X + 5Y) = E(5X) + E(5Y) = 5E(X) + 5E(Y) = \$100$$

Thus, all three strategies have the same expected profit. However, since X and Y are independent and the covariance is 0, the variance of the return from strategy (c) is as follows:

$$\text{Var}(5X + 5Y) = \text{Var}(5X) + \text{Var}(5Y) = 25\text{Var}(X) + 25\text{Var}(Y) = 7,500$$

This is smaller than the variances of the other strategies, reflecting the decrease in risk that follows from diversification in an investment portfolio. This investor should certainly prefer strategy (c), since it yields the same expected return as the other two, but with lower risk.

Portfolio Analysis

Investment managers spend considerable effort developing investment portfolios that consist of a set of financial instruments that each have returns defined by a probability distribution model. Portfolios are used to obtain a combined investment that has a given expected return and risk. Stock portfolios with a high risk can be constructed by combining several individual stocks whose values tend to increase or decrease together. With such a portfolio an investor will have either large gains or large losses. Stocks whose values move in opposite directions could be combined to create a portfolio with a more stable value, implying less risk. Decreases in one stock price would be balanced by increases in another stock price.

This process of **portfolio analysis** and construction is conducted using probability models defined by random variables and probability distribution functions. The mean value of the portfolio is the linear combination of the mean values of the two stocks in the portfolio. The variance of the portfolio value is computed using the sum of the variances and the covariance of the joint distribution of the stock values. We will develop the method using an example with a portfolio consisting of two stocks.

Consider a portfolio that consists of a shares of stock A, and b shares of stock B. It is important to be able to find the mean and variance for the market value, W, of a portfolio, where W is the linear function $W = aX + bY$. The mean and variance are derived in the chapter appendix.

The Mean and Variance for the Market Value of a Portfolio

The random variable X is the price for stock A, and the random variable Y is the price for stock B. The **portfolio market value**, W, is given by the linear function

$$W = aX + bY$$

where a is the number of shares of stock A, and b is the number of shares of stock B.

The **mean value for W** is as follows:

$$\mu_w = E[W] = E[aX + bY] = a\mu_X + b\mu_Y \qquad (4.38)$$

The **variance for W** is

$$\sigma_W^2 = a^2\sigma_X^2 + b^2\sigma_Y^2 + 2ab\text{Cov}(X, Y) \qquad (4.39)$$

or, using the correlation, is

$$\sigma_W^2 = a^2\sigma_X^2 + b^2\sigma_Y^2 + 2ab\text{Corr}(X,Y)\sigma_X\sigma_Y$$

Portfolio analysis developed using discrete random variables will be expanded in Chapter 5 using continuous random variables. The development here using discrete random variables is more intuitive compared to using continuous random variables. However, the results for means, variances, covariances and linear combinations of random variables also apply directly to continuous random variables. Since portfolios involve prices that are continuous random variables and thus the development in Chapter 5 will be more realistic. In addition the normal distribution developed in Chapter 5 provides important analysis tools.

Example 4.19 Analysis of Stock Portfolios (Means and Variances, Functions of Random Variables)

George Tiao has 5 shares of stock A and 10 shares of stock B, whose price variations are modeled by the probability distribution in Table 4.8. Find the mean and variance of the portfolio.

Table 4.8 Stock A and Stock B Prices

Stock A Price	Stock B Price			
	$40	$50	$60	$70
$45	0.24	0.003333	0.003333	0.003333
$50	0.003333	0.24	0.003333	0.003333
$55	0.003333	0.003333	0.24	0.003333
$60	0.003333	0.003333	0.003333	0.24

Solution   The value, W, of the portfolio can be represented by the linear combination

$$W = 5X + 10Y$$

The mean and variance for stock A are $53 and 31.3, respectively, while for stock B they are $55 and 125. The covariance is 59.17 and the correlation is 0.947.

The mean value for the portfolio is as follows:

$$\mu_W = E[W] = E[5X + 10Y] = 5(53) + (10)(55) = 815$$

The variance for the portfolio value is as follows:

$$\sigma_W^2 = 5^2\sigma_X^2 + 10^2\sigma_Y^2 + 2 \times 5 \times 10 \times \text{Cov}(X,Y)$$
$$= 5^2 \times 31.3 + 10^2 \times 125 + 2 \times 5 \times 10 \times 59.17 = 19{,}199.5$$

George knows that high variance implies high risk. He believes that the risk for this portfolio is too high. Thus, he asks you to prepare a portfolio that has lower risk. After some investigation you discover a different pair of stocks whose prices follow the probability model in Table 4.9.

The mean for stock C is $53, the same as for stock A. Similarly, the mean for stock D is $55, the same as for stock B. Thus, the mean value of the portfolio is not changed.

The variance for each stock is also the same, but the covariance is now −59.17. Thus, the variance for the new portfolio includes a *negative covariance* term and is as follows:

$$\sigma_W^2 = 5^2\sigma_X^2 + 10^2\sigma_Y^2 + 2 \times 5 \times 10 \times \text{Cov}(X,Y)$$
$$= 5^2 \times 31.3 + 10^2 \times 125 + 2 \times 5 \times 10 \times (-59.17) = 7{,}365.5$$

We see that the effect of the negative covariance is to reduce the variance and hence to reduce the risk of the portfolio.

Table 4.9 New Portfolio of Stock C and Stock D

STOCK C PRICE	STOCK D PRICE			
	$40	$50	$60	$70
$45	0.003333	0.003333	0.003333	0.24
$50	0.003333	0.003333	0.24	0.003333
$55	0.003333	0.24	0.003333	0.003333
$60	0.24	0.003333	0.003333	0.003333

Figure 4.6 shows how portfolio variance, and hence risk, changes with different correlations between stock prices. Note that the portfolio variance is linearly related to the correlation. To help control risk, designers of stock portfolios select stocks based on the correlation between prices.

Figure 4.6 Portfolio Variance Versus Correlation of Stock Prices

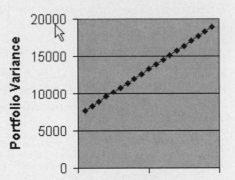

Portfolio Variance vs Correlation of Stock Prices

As seen in Example 4.19, the correlation between stock prices, or between any two random variables, has important effects on the portfolio value random variable. A positive correlation indicates that both prices, X and Y, increase or decrease together. Thus, large or small values of the portfolio are magnified, resulting in greater range and variance compared to a zero correlation. Conversely, a negative correlation leads to price increases for X matched by price decreases for Y. As a result, the range and variance of the portfolio are decreased compared to a zero correlation. By selecting stocks with particular combinations of correlations, fund managers can control the variance and the risk for portfolios.

Basic Exercises

4.73 Consider the joint probability distribution:

		X	
		1	2
Y	0	0.25	0.25
	1	0.25	0.25

a. Compute the marginal probability distributions for X and Y.
b. Compute the covariance and correlation for X and Y.

4.74 Consider the joint probability distribution:

		X	
		1	2
Y	0	0.20	0.25
	1	0.30	0.25

a. Compute the marginal probability distributions for X and Y.
b. Compute the covariance and correlation for X and Y.

4.75 Consider the joint probability distribution:

		X	
		1	2
Y	0	0.25	0.25
	1	0.25	0.25

a. Compute the marginal probability distributions for X and Y.
b. Compute the covariance and correlation for X and Y.
c. Compute the mean and variance for the linear function $W = X + Y$.

4.76 Consider the joint probability distribution:

		X	
		0	1
Y	0	0.30	0.20
	1	0.25	0.25

a. Compute the marginal probability distributions for X and Y.
b. Compute the covariance and correlation for X and Y.
c. Compute the mean and variance for the linear function $W = 2X + Y$.

4.77 Consider the joint probability distribution:

		X	
		1	2
Y	0	0.70	0.0
	1	0.0	0.30

a. Compute the marginal probability distributions for X and Y.
b. Compute the covariance and correlation for X and Y.
c. Compute the mean and variance for the linear function $W = 3X + 4Y$.

4.78 Consider the joint probability distribution:

		X	
		1	2
Y	0	0.25	0.25
	1	0.25	0.25

a. Compute the marginal probability distributions for X and Y.
b. Compute the covariance and correlation for X and Y.
c. Compute the mean and variance for the linear function $W = X + Y$.

4.79 Consider the joint probability distribution:

		X	
		1	2
Y	0	0.30	0.20
	1	0.25	0.25

a. Compute the marginal probability distributions for X and Y.
b. Compute the covariance and correlation for X and Y.
c. Compute the mean and variance for the linear function $W = 2X + Y$.

4.80 Consider the joint probability distribution:

		X	
		1	2
Y	0	0.0	0.60
	1	0.40	0.0

a. Compute the marginal probability distributions for X and Y.

b. Compute the covariance and correlation for X and Y.
c. Compute the mean and variance for the linear function $W = 2X - 4Y$.

4.81 Consider the joint probability distribution:

		X	
		1	2
Y	0	0.70	0.0
	1	0.0	0.30

a. Compute the marginal probability distributions for X and Y.
b. Compute the covariance and correlation for X and Y.
c. Compute the mean and variance for the linear function $W = 10X - 8Y$.

Application Exercises

4.82 A researcher suspected that the number of between-meal snacks eaten by students in a day during final examinations might depend on the number of tests a student had to take on that day. The accompanying table shows joint probabilities, estimated from a survey.

Number of Snacks (Y)	Number of Tests (X)			
	0	1	2	3
0	0.07	0.09	0.06	0.01
1	0.07	0.06	0.07	0.01
2	0.06	0.07	0.14	0.03
3	0.02	0.04	0.16	0.04

a. Find the probability function of X and, hence, the mean number of tests taken by students on that day.
b. Find the probability function of Y and, hence, the mean number of snacks eaten by students on that day.
c. Find and interpret the conditional probability function of Y, given that $X = 3$.
d. Find the covariance between X and Y.
e. Are number of snacks and number of tests independent of each other?

4.83 A real estate agent is interested in the relationship between the number of lines in a newspaper advertisement for an apartment and the volume of inquiries from potential renters. Let volume of inquiries be denoted by the random variable X, with the value 0 for little interest, 1 for moderate interest, and 2 for strong interest. The real estate agent used historical records to compute the joint probability function shown in the accompanying table.

Number of Lines (Y)	Number of Enquiries (X)		
	0	1	2
3	0.09	0.14	0.07
4	0.07	0.23	0.16
5	0.03	0.10	0.11

a. Find the joint cumulative probability function at $X = 1$, $Y = 4$, and interpret your result.
b. Find and interpret the conditional probability function for Y, given $X = 0$.
c. Find and interpret the conditional probability function for X, given $Y = 4$.
d. Find and interpret the covariance between X and Y.
e. Are number of lines in the advertisement and volume of inquiries independent of one another?

4.84 The accompanying table shows, for credit card holders with one to three cards, the joint probabilities for number of cards owned (X) and number of credit purchases made in a week (Y).

Number of Cards (X)	Number of Purchases in Week (Y)				
	0	1	2	3	4
1	0.08	0.13	0.09	0.06	0.03
2	0.03	0.08	0.08	0.09	0.07
3	0.01	0.03	0.06	0.08	0.08

a. For a randomly chosen person from this group, what is the probability function for number of purchases made in a week?
b. For a person in this group who has three cards, what is the probability function for number of purchases made in the week?
c. Are number of cards owned and number of purchases made statistically independent?

4.85 A market researcher wants to determine whether a new model of a personal computer that had been advertised on a late-night talk show had achieved more brand-name recognition among people who watched the show regularly than among people who did not. After conducting a survey, it was found that 15% of all people both watched the show regularly and could correctly identify the product. Also, 16% of all people regularly watched the show and 45% of all people could correctly identify the product. Define a pair of random variables as follows:

| | | X = 1 | if regularly watch the show | X = 0 | otherwise |

$X = 1$ if regularly watch the show $X = 0$ otherwise

$Y = 1$ if product correctly identified $Y = 0$ otherwise

   a. Find the joint probability function of X and Y.
   b. Find the conditional probability function of Y, given $X = 1$.
   c. Find and interpret the covariance between X and Y.

4.86 A college bookseller makes calls at the offices of professors and forms the impression that professors are more likely to be away from their offices on Friday than any other working day. A review of the records of calls, 1/5 of which are on Fridays, indicates that for 16% of Friday calls, the professor is away from the office, while this occurs for only 12% of calls on every other working day. Define the random variables as follows:

$X = 1$ if call is made on a Friday $X = 0$ otherwise

$Y = 1$ if professor is away from the office $Y = 0$ otherwise

   a. Find the joint probability function of X and Y.
   b. Find the conditional probability function of Y, given $X = 0$.
   c. Find the marginal probability functions of X and Y.
   d. Find and interpret the covariance between X and Y.

4.87 A restaurant manager receives occasional complaints about the quality of both the food and the service. The marginal probability functions for the number of weekly complaints in each category are shown in the accompanying table. If complaints about food and service are independent of each other, find the joint probability function.

Number of Food Complaints	Probability	Number of Service Complaints	Probability
0	0.12	0	0.18
1	0.29	1	0.38
2	0.42	2	0.34
3	0.17	3	0.10

4.88 Refer to the information in Exercise 4.87. Find the mean and standard deviation of the total number of complaints received in a week. Having reached this point, you are concerned that the numbers of food and service complaints may not be independent of each other. However, you have no information about the nature of their dependence. What can you now say about the mean and standard deviation of the total number of complaints received in a week?

4.89 A company has 5 representatives covering large territories and 10 representatives covering smaller territories. The probability distributions for the numbers of orders received by each of these types of representatives in a day are shown in the accompanying table. Assuming that the number of orders received by any representative is independent of the number received by any other, find the mean and standard deviation of the total number of orders received by the company in a day.

Numbers of Orders (Large Territory)	Probability	Numbers of Orders (Smaller Territory)	Probability
0	0.08	0	0.18
1	0.16	1	0.26
2	0.28	2	0.36
3	0.32	3	0.13
4	0.10	4	0.07
5	0.06		

KEY WORDS

- Bernoulli random variable, 151
- binomial distribution, 153
- conditional probability function, 171
- continuous random variable, 138
- correlation, 176
- covariance, 175
- cumulative probability function, 141

- marginal probability function, 170
- differences between random variables, 178
- discrete random variable, 137
- expected value, 143
- expected value for functions of random variables, 178
- hypergeometric distribution, 160

- independence of jointly distributed random variables, 171
- joint probability function, 170
- marginal probability function, 170
- mean, 143
- mean of binomial distribution, 154
- mean of functions of random variables, 151

CHAPTER EXERCISES AND APPLICATIONS

4.90 As an investment advisor, you tell a client that an investment in a mutual fund has (over the next year) a higher expected return than an investment in the money market. The client then asks the following questions:

a. Does that imply that the mutual fund will certainly yield a higher return than the money market?

b. Does it follow that I should invest in the mutual fund rather than in the money market?

How would you reply?

4.91 A contractor estimates the probabilities for the number of days required to complete a certain type of construction project as follows:

Time (days)	1	2	3	4	5
Probability	0.05	0.20	0.35	0.30	0.10

a. What is the probability that a randomly chosen project will take less than 3 days to complete?

b. Find the expected time to complete a project.

c. Find the standard deviation of time required to complete a project.

d. The contractor's project cost is made up of two parts—a fixed cost of $20,000, plus $2,000 for each day taken to complete the project. Find the mean and standard deviation of total project cost.

e. If three projects are undertaken, what is the probability that at least two of them will take at least 4 days to complete, assuming independence of individual project completion times?

4.92 A car salesman estimates the following probabilities for the number of cars that she will sell in the next week:

Number of cars	0	1	2	3	4	5
Probability	0.10	0.20	0.35	0.16	0.12	0.07

a. Find the expected number of cars that will be sold in the week.

b. Find the standard deviation of the number of cars that will be sold in the week.

c. The salesman receives for the week a salary of $250, plus an additional $300 for each car sold. Find the mean and standard deviation of her total salary for the week.

d. What is the probability that the salesman's salary for the week will be more than $1,000?

4.93 A multiple-choice test has nine questions. For each question there are four possible answers from which to select. One point is awarded for each correct answer, and points are not subtracted for incorrect answers. The instructor awards a bonus point if the students spells their name correctly. A student who has not studied for this test decides to choose at random an answer for each question.

a. Find the expected number of correct answers for the student on these nine questions.

b. Find the standard deviation of the number of correct answers for the student on these nine questions.

c. The student spells her name correctly:
   i. Find the expected total score on the test for this student.
   ii. Find the standard deviation of her total score on the test.

4.94 Develop realistic examples of pairs of random variables for which you would expect to find the following:

a. Positive covariance

b. Negative covariance

c. Zero covariance

4.95 A long-distance taxi service owns four vehicles. These are of different ages and have different repair records. The probabilities that, on any given day, each vehicle will be available for use are 0.95, 0.90, 0.90, and 0.80. Whether one vehicle is available is independent of whether any other vehicle is available.

a. Find the probability function for the number of vehicles available for use on a given day.
b. Find the expected number of vehicles available for use on a given day.
c. Find the standard deviation of the number of vehicles available for use on a given day.

4.96 Students in a college were classified according to years in school (X) and number of visits to a museum in the last year ($Y = 0$ for no visits, 1 for one visit, 2 for more than one visit). The joint probabilities in the accompanying table were estimated for these random variables.

Number of Visits (Y)	Years in School (X)			
	1	2	3	4
0	0.07	0.05	0.03	0.02
1	0.13	0.11	0.17	0.15
2	0.04	0.04	0.09	0.10

a. Find the probability that a randomly chosen student has not visited a museum in the last year.
b. Find the means of the random variables X and Y.
c. Find and interpret the covariance between the random variables X and Y.

4.97 A basketball team's star 3-point shooter takes six 3-point shots in a game. Historically, she makes 40% of all 3-point shots taken in a game. State at the outset what assumptions you have made.

a. Find the probability that at least two shots will be made.
b. Find the probability that exactly three shots will be made.
c. Find the mean and standard deviation of the number of shots made.
d. Find the mean and standard deviation of the total number of points scored as a result of these shots.

4.98 It is estimated that 55% of the freshmen entering a particular college will graduate from that college in four years.

a. For a random sample of five entering freshmen, what is the probability that exactly three will graduate in four years?
b. For a random sample of five entering freshmen, what is the probability that a majority will graduate in four years?
c. Eighty entering freshmen are chosen at random. Find the mean and standard deviation of the proportion of these 80 that will graduate in four years.

4.99 The World Series of baseball is to be played by team A and team B. The first team to win four games wins the series. Suppose that team A is the better team, in the sense that the probability is 0.6 that team A will win any specific game. Assume also that the result of any game is independent of that of any other.

a. What is the probability that team A will win the series?
b. What is the probability that a seventh game will be needed to determine the winner?
c. Suppose that, in fact, each team wins two of the first four games.
   i. What is the probability that team A will win the series?
   ii. What is the probability that a seventh game will be needed to determine the winner?

4.100 Using detailed cash flow information, a financial analyst claims to be able to spot companies that are likely candidates for bankruptcy. The analyst is presented with information on the past records of 15 companies and told that, in fact, 5 of these have failed. He selects as candidates for failure 5 companies from the group of 14. In fact, 3 of the 5 companies selected by the analyst were among those that failed. Evaluate the financial analyst's performance on this test of his ability to detect failed companies.

4.101 A team of five analysts is about to examine the earnings prospects of 20 corporations. Each of the five analysts will study 4 of the corporations. These analysts are not equally competent. In fact, one of them is a star, having an excellent record of anticipating changing trends. Ideally, management would like to allocate to this analyst the 4 corporations whose earnings will deviate most from past trends. However, lacking this information, management allocates corporations to analysts randomly. What is the probability that at least 2 of the 4 corporations whose earnings will deviate most from past trends are allocated to the star analyst?

4.102 On average, 2.4 customers per minute arrive at an airline check-in desk during the peak period. Assume that the distribution of arrivals is Poisson.

a. What is the probability that there will be no arrivals in a minute?
b. What is the probability that there will be more than three arrivals in a minute?

4.103 A recent estimate suggested that, of all individuals and couples reporting income in excess of $200,000, 6.5% either paid no federal tax or paid tax at an effective rate of less than 15%. A random sample of 100 of those reporting income in excess of $200,000 was taken. What is the probability that more than 2 of the sample members either paid no federal tax or paid tax at an effective rate of less than 15%.

4.104 A company has two assembly lines, each of which stalls an average of 2.4 times per week according to a Poisson distribution. Assume that the performances of these assembly lines are independent of one another. What is the probability that at least one line stalls at least once in any given week?

4.105 George Allen has asked you to analyze his stock portfolio, which contains 10 shares of stock D and 5 shares of stock C. The joint probability distribution of the stock prices is shown in Table 4.10. Compute the mean and variance for the total value of his stock portfolio.

Table 4.10 Joint Probability Distribution for Stock Prices

STOCK C PRICE	STOCK D PRICE			
	$40	$50	$60	$70
$45	0.00	0.00	0.05	0.20
$50	0.05	0.00	0.05	0.10
$55	0.10	0.05	0.00	0.05
$60	0.20	0.10	0.05	0.00

4.106 Consider a country that imports steel and exports automobiles. The value per unit of cars exported is measured in units of thousands of dollars per car by the random variable X. The value per unit of steel imported is measured in units of thousands of dollars per ton of steel by the random variable Y. Suppose that the country annually exports 10 cars and imports 5 tons of steel. Compute the mean and variance of the trade balance where the trade balance is the total dollars received for all cars exported minus the total dollars spent for all steel imported. The joint probability distribution for the prices of cars and steel is shown in Table 4.11.

Table 4.11 Joint Distribution of Automobile and Steel Prices

PRICE OF STEEL (Y)	PRICE OF AUTOMOBILES (X)		
	$3	$4	$5
$4	0.10	0.15	0.05
$6	0.10	0.20	0.10
$8	0.05	0.15	0.10

4.107 Delta International delivers approximately one million packages a day between East Asia and the United States. A random sample of the daily number of package delivery failures over the past six months provided the following results 15, 10, 8, 16, 12,11, 9, 8, 12, 9, 10, 8, 7, 16, 14, 12, 10, 9, 8, 11. There was nothing unusual about the operations during these days and, thus, the results can be considered typical. Using this data and your understanding of the delivery process answer the following:

a. What probability model should be used and why?

b. What is the probability of 10 or more failed deliveries on a typical future day?

c. What is the probability of less than six failed deliveries?

d. Find the number of failures such that the probability of exceeding this number is 10% or less.

4.108 Bright Star Financial Advisers receives a mean of 19.5 applications per week for a personal financial review. Each review requires one day of an analyst's time to prepare a review. Assume that requests received during any week are assigned to an analyst for completion during the following week. If the analysis is not completed during the second week the customer will cancel.

a. How many analysts should be hired so that the company can claim that 90% of the reviews will be completed during the second week?

b. What is the probability that two of the analysts hired for part a would have no clients for an entire week?

c. Suppose that they decided to hire one less analyst than determined in part a. What is the probability that customers would cancel given this staffing level?

d. Given the number of analysts hired in, part c, what is the probability that two analysts would be idle for an entire week?

Appendix: Verifications

1   VERIFICATION OF AN ALTERNATIVE FORMULA FOR THE VARIANCE OF A DISCRETE RANDOM VARIABLE (EQUATION 4.6)

Begin with the original definition of variance:

$$\sigma_X^2 = \sum_x (x - \mu_X)^2 P(x) = \sum_x (x^2 - 2\mu_X x + \mu_X^2)P(x)$$

$$= \sum_x x^2 P(x) - 2\mu_X \sum_x xP(x) + \mu_X^2 \sum_x P(x)$$

But we have seen that

$$\sum_x xP(x) = \mu_X \quad \text{and} \quad \sum_x P(x) = 1$$

Thus,

$$\sigma_X^2 = \sum_x x^2 P(x) - 2\mu_X^2 + \mu_X^2$$

and, finally,

$$\sigma_X^2 = \sum_x x^2 P(x) - \mu_X^2$$

2   VERIFICATION OF THE MEAN AND VARIANCE OF A LINEAR FUNCTION OF A RANDOM VARIABLE (EQUATIONS 4.8 AND 4.9)

It follows from the definition of expectation that if Y takes the values $a + bx$ with probabilities $P_X(x)$, its mean is as follows:

$$E(W) = \mu_W = \sum_x (a + bx)P(x) = a\sum_x P(x) + b\sum_x xP(x)$$

Then, since the first summation on the right-hand side of this equation is 1 and the second summation is the mean of X, we have

$$E(Y) = a + b\mu_X \text{ as in Equation 4.8.}$$

Further, the variance of Y is, by definition,

$$\sigma_Y^2 = E[(W - \mu_Y)^2] = \sum_X [(a + bx) - \mu_Y]^2 P(x)$$

Substituting $a + b\mu_X$ for μ_Y then gives

$$\sigma_Y^2 = \sum_X (bx - b\mu_X)^2 P(x) = b^2 \sum_X (x - \mu_X)^2 P(x)$$

Since the summation on the right-hand side of this equation is, by definition, the variance of X, the result in Equation 4.9 follows:

$$\sigma_W^2 = \text{Var}(a + bX) = b^2 \sigma_X^2$$

3   Example to demonstrate Equation 4.8

Show that in general

$$E[g(x)] \neq g(\mu_x)$$

Using the results in Table 4.12 we will show this result for the nonlinear function

$$g(x) = bx^2$$

Where b is a constant and we see that

$$E[bX^2] = 1.2b \neq b(E[X])^2 = b0.8^2 = 0.64b$$

And, therefore,

$$E[g(x)] \neq g(\mu_x)$$

Table 4.12

x	bx^2	$P(x)$	$E[X]$	$E[bX^2]$
0	0	0.40	0	0
1	b	0.40	0.40	$0.4b$
2	$4b$	0.20	0.40	$0.8b$
			0.80	$1.2b$

4   Verification of the Mean and Variance of the Binomial Distribution (Equations 4.19 and 4.20)

To find the mean and variance of the binomial distribution, it is convenient to return to the Bernoulli distribution. Consider n independent trials, each with probability of success P, and let $X_i = 1$ if the ith trial results in success and 0 otherwise. The random variables $X_1, X_2, \ldots,$ X_n are, therefore, n independent Bernoulli variables, each with probability of success P. Moreover, the total number of successes X is as follows:

$$X = X_1 + X_2 + \ldots + X_n$$

Thus, the binomial random variable can be expressed as the sum of independent Bernoulli random variables.

The mean and the variance for Bernoulli random variables can be used to find the mean and variance of the binomial distribution. Using Equation 4.15, we know that

$$E(X_i) = P \quad \text{and that} \quad \sigma^2 X_i = P(1 - P) \quad \text{for all } i = 1, 2, \cdots, n$$

Then, for the binomial distribution

$$E(X) = E(X_1 + X_2 + \ldots + X_n) = E(X_1) + E(X_2) + \ldots + E(X_n) = Np$$

Since the Bernoulli random variables are independent, the covariance between any pair of them is zero, and

$$\sigma_X^2 = \sigma^2 (X_1 + X_2 + \cdots X_n)$$

5 VERIFICATION OF THE MEAN AND VARIANCE OF THE MARKET VALUE, W, OF A PORTFOLIO (EQUATIONS 4.38 AND 4.39)

You are given a linear combination, W, of random variables X and Y, where $W = aX + bY$ and a and b are constants. The mean of W is

$$\mu_W = E[W] = E[aX + bY] = a\mu_X + b\mu_Y$$

and the variance of W is

$$\sigma_W^2 = E[(W - \mu_W)^2]$$
$$= E[(aX + bY - (a\mu_X + b\mu_Y)^2]$$
$$= E[(a(X - \mu_X) + b(Y - \mu_Y)^2]$$
$$= E[a^2(X - \mu_X)^2 + b^2(Y - \mu_Y)^2 + 2ab(X - \mu_X)(Y - \mu_Y)]$$
$$= a^2E[(X - \mu_X)^2] + b^2E[(Y - \mu_Y)^2] + 2abE[(X - \mu_X)(Y - \mu_Y)]$$
$$= a^2\sigma_x^2 + b^2\sigma_Y^2 + 2ab\text{Cov}(X, Y)$$

REFERENCES

1. Hogg, R, & Craig. 1995. *Mathematical Statistics*, 5th Ed. Prentice Hall.

Chapter 5

Continuous Random Variables and Probability Distributions

Introduction

In Chapter 4 we developed discrete random variables and probability distributions. Here, we extend the probability concepts to continuous random variables and probability distributions. The concepts and insights for discrete random variables also apply to continuous random variables, so we are building directly on the previous chapter. Many economic and business measures such as sales, investment, consumption, costs, and revenues can be represented by continuous random variables. In addition, measures of time, distance, temperature, and weight fit into this category. Probability statements for continuous random variables are specified over ranges. The probability that sales are between 140 and 190 or greater than 200 is a typical example. Mathematical theory leads us to conclude that, in reality, random variables for all applied problems are discrete because measurements are rounded to some value. But for us the important fact is that continuous random variables and probability distributions provide good approximations for many applied problems. Thus, these models are very important and provide excellent tools for business and economic applications.

Here, we again define X as a random variable and x as a specific value of the random variable. We begin by defining the *cumulative distribution function*. Then we will define the probability density function, which is analogous to the probability distribution function used for discrete random variables.

Cumulative Distribution Function

The **cumulative distribution function**, $F(x)$, for a continuous random variable X expresses the probability that X does not exceed the value of x, as a function of x:

$$F(x) = P(X \leq x) \tag{5.1}$$

We illustrate the cumulative distribution function by using a simple probability structure. Consider a gasoline station that has a 1,000-gallon storage tank that is filled each morning at the start of the business day. Analysis of past history indicates that it is not possible to predict the amount of gasoline sold on any particular day, but the lower limit is 0 and the upper limit is, of course, 1,000 gallons, the size of the tank. In addition, past history indicates that any demand in the interval from 1 to 1,000 gallons is equally likely. The random variable X indicates the gasoline sales in gallons for a particular day. We are concerned with the probability of various levels of daily gasoline sales, where the probability of a specific number of gallons sold is the same over the range from 0 to 1,000 gallons. The distribution of X is said to follow a **uniform probability distribution**, and the cumulative distribution is as follows:

$$F(x) = \begin{cases} 0 \rightarrow \text{if} \cdots x < 0 \\ 0.001x \rightarrow \text{if} \cdots 0 \leq x \leq 1{,}000 \\ 1 \rightarrow \text{if} \cdots x > 1{,}000 \end{cases}$$

This function is graphed as a straight line between 0 and 1,000, as shown in Figure 5.1. From this we see that the probability of sales between 0 and 400 gallons is as follows:

$$P(X \leq 400) = F(400) = (0.001)(400) = 0.40$$

To obtain the probability that a continuous random variable X falls in a specified range, we find the difference between the cumulative probability at the upper end of the range and the cumulative probability at the lower end of the range.

Probability of a Range Using a Cumulative Distribution Function

Let X be a continuous random variable with a cumulative distribution function $F(x)$, and let a and b be two possible values of X, with $a < b$. The **probability that X lies between a and b** is as follows:

$$P(a < X < b) = F(b) - F(a) \tag{5.2}$$

For continuous random variables, it does not matter whether we write "less than" or "less than or equal to" because the probability that X is precisely equal to b is 0.

Figure 5.1
Cumulative
Distribution
Function for a
Random Variable
Over 0 to 1,000

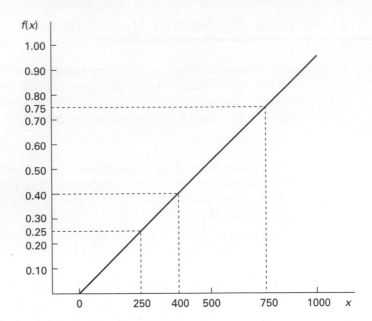

For the random variable that is distributed uniformly in the range 0 to 1,000, the cumulative distribution function in that range is $F(x) = 0.001x$. Therefore, if a and b are two numbers between 0 and 1,000 with $a < b$,

$$P(a < X < b) = F(b) - F(a) = 0.001(b - a)$$

For example, the probability of sales between 250 and 750 gallons is

$$P(250 < X < 750) = (0.001)(750) - (0.001)(250) = 0.75 - 0.25 = 0.50$$

as shown in Figure 5.1.

We have seen that the probability that a continuous random variable lies between any two values can be expressed in terms of its cumulative distribution function. This function, therefore, contains all the information about the probability structure of the random variable. However, for many purposes a different function is more useful. In Chapter 4 we discussed the probability function for discrete random variables, which expresses the probability that a discrete random variable takes any specific value. Since the probability of a specific value is 0 for continuous random variables, that concept is not directly relevant here. However, a related function, called the *probability density function*, can be constructed for continuous random variables, allowing for graphical interpretation of their probability structure.

Probability Density Function

Let X be a continuous random variable, and let x be any number lying in the range of values this random variable can take. The **probability density function**, $f(x)$, of the random variable is a function with the following properties:

1. $f(x) > 0$ for all values of x.
2. The area under the probability density function, $f(x)$, over all values of the random variable, X, is equal to 1.0.
3. Suppose that this density function is graphed. Let a and b be two possible values of random variable X, with $a < b$. Then the probability

that X lies between a and b is the area under the density function between these points.

$$P(a \leq X \leq b) = \int_a^b f(x)dx$$

4. The cumulative distribution function, $F(x_0)$, is the area under the probability density function, $f(x)$, up to x_0,

$$F(x_0) = \int_{x_m}^{x_0} f(x)dx$$

where x_m is the minimum value of the random variable X.

The probability density function can be approximated by a discrete probability distribution with many discrete values close together, as seen in Figure 5.2.

Figure 5.3 shows the plot of an arbitrary probability density function for some continuous random variable. Two possible values, a and b, are shown, and the shaded area under the curve between these points is the probability that the random variable lies in the interval between them as shown in the chapter appendix.

Areas Under Continuous Probability Density Functions

Let X be a continuous random variable with probability density function $f(x)$ and cumulative distribution function $F(x)$. Then, consider the following properties:

1. The total area under the curve $f(x)$ is 1.
2. The area under the curve $f(x)$ to the left of x_0 is $F(x_0)$, where x_0 is any value that the random variable can take.

Figure 5.2
Approximation of a Probability Density Function by a Discrete Probability Distribution

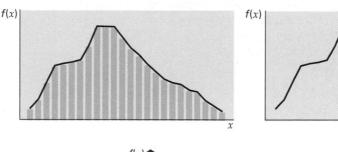
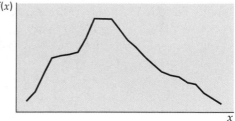

Figure 5.3
Shaded Area Is the Probability That X is Between a and b

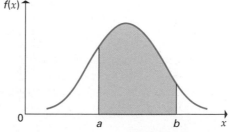

These results are shown in Figure 5.4, with Figure 5.4(a) showing that the entire area under the probability density function is equal to 1, and Figure 5.4(b) indicating the area to the left of x_0.

The Uniform Distribution

Now, we consider a probability density function that represents a probability distribution over the range of 0 to 1. Figure 5.5 is a graph of the uniform probability density function. This is the probability density function for the gasoline sales example. Since the probability is the same for any interval of the sales range from 0 to 1, we deduce that the probability density function is constant over the range from 0 to 1,000 and can be defined as the uniform probability density function, which can be written as follows:

$$f(x) = \begin{cases} 0.001 \rightarrow 0 \leq x \leq 1,000 \\ 0 \rightarrow \text{else} \end{cases}$$

For any uniform random variable defined over the range from a to b, the probability density function is as follows:

$$f(x) = \begin{cases} \dfrac{1}{b-a} \rightarrow a \leq x \leq b \\ 0 \rightarrow \text{else} \end{cases}$$

This probability density function can be used to find the probability that the random variable falls within a specific range. For example, the probability that sales are between 250 gallons and 750 gallons is shown in Figure 5.6. Since the height of the density function is $f(x) = 0.001$, the area under the curve between 250 and 750 is equal to 0.50, which is the required probability. Note that this is the same result obtained previously using the cumulative probability function.

We have seen that the probability that a random variable lies between a pair of values is the area under the probability density function between these two values. There are two important results worth noting. The area under the entire probability

Figure 5.4
Properties of the Probability Density Function

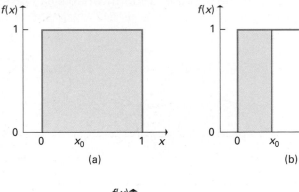

(a)   (b)

Figure 5.5
Probability Density Function for a Uniform 0 to 1 Random Variable

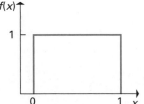

Figure 5.6
Density Function
Showing the
Probability That *X*
is Between 250
and 750

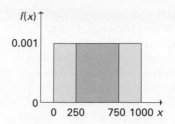

density function is 1, and the cumulative probability, $F(x_0)$, is the area under the density function to the left of x_0.

Example 5.1 Probability of Pipeline Failure (Cumulative Distribution Function)

A repair team is responsible for a stretch of oil pipeline 2 miles long. The distance (in miles) at which any fracture occurs can be represented by a uniformly distributed random variable, with probability density function

$$f(x) = 0.5$$

Find the cumulative distribution function and the probability that any given fracture occurs between 0.5 mile and 1.5 miles along this stretch of pipeline.

Solution Figure 5.7 shows a plot of the probability density function, with the shaded area indicating $F(x_0)$, the cumulative distribution function evaluated at x_0. Thus, we see that

$$F(x_0) = 0.5x_0 \quad \text{for } 0 < x_0 \leq 2$$

The probability that a fracture occurs between 0.5 mile and 1.5 miles along the pipe is as follows:

$$P(0.5 < X < 1.5) = F(1.5) - F(0.5) = (0.5)(1.5) - (0.5)(0.5) = 0.5$$

This is the area under the probability density function from $x = 0.5$ to $x = 1.5$.

Figure 5.7 Probability Density Function for Example 5.1

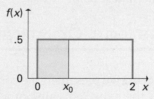

EXERCISES

Basic Exercises

5.1 Using the uniform probability density function shown in Figure 5.7, find the probability that the random variable *X* is between 1.4 and 1.8.

5.2 Using the uniform probability density function shown in Figure 5.7, find the probability that the random variable *X* is between 1.0 and 1.9.

5.3 Using the uniform probability density function shown in Figure 5.7, find the probability that the random variable *X* is less than 1.4.

5.4 Using the uniform probability density function shown in Figure 5.7, find the probability that the random variable *X* is greater than 1.3.

Application Exercises

5.5 An analyst has available two forecasts, F_1 and F_2, of earnings per share of a corporation next year. He intends to form a compromise forecast as a weighted average of the two individual forecasts. In forming the compromise forecast, weight X will be given to the first forecast and weight $(1 - X)$ to the second, so that the compromise forecast is $XF_1 + (1 - X)F_2$. The analyst wants to choose a value between 0 and 1 for the weight X, but he is quite uncertain of what will be the best choice. Suppose that what eventually emerges as the best possible choice of the weight X can be viewed as a random variable uniformly distributed between 0 and 1, having the probability density function

$$f(x) = \begin{cases} 1 & \text{for } 0 \leq x \leq 1 \\ 0 & \text{for all other values of } x \end{cases}$$

a. Draw the probability density function.
b. Find and draw the cumulative distribution function.
c. Find the probability that the best choice of the weight X is less than 0.25.
d. Find the probability that the best choice of the weight X is more than 0.75.
e. Find the probability that the best choice of the weight X is between 0.2 and 0.8.

5.6 The jurisdiction of a rescue team includes emergencies occurring on a stretch of river that is 4 miles long. Experience has shown that the distance along this stretch, measured in miles from its northernmost point, at which an emergency occurs can be represented by a uniformly distributed random variable over the range 0 to 4 miles. Then, if X denotes the distance (in miles) of an emergency from the northernmost point of this stretch of river, its probability density function is as follows:

$$f(x) = \begin{cases} .25 & \text{for } 0 < x < 4 \\ 0 & \text{for all other } x \end{cases}$$

a. Draw the probability density function.
b. Find and draw the cumulative distribution function.
c. Find the probability that a given emergency arises within 1 mile of the northernmost point of this stretch of river.
d. The rescue team's base is at the midpoint of this stretch of river. Find the probability that a given emergency arises more than 1.5 miles from this base.

5.7 The incomes of all families in a particular suburb can be represented by a continuous random variable. It is known that the median income for all families in this suburb is $60,000 and that 40% of all families in the suburb have incomes above $72,000.

a. For a randomly chosen family, what is the probability that its income will be between $60,000 and $72,000?
b. Given no further information, what can be said about the probability that a randomly chosen family has an income below $65,000?

5.8 At the beginning of winter, a homeowner estimates that the probability is 0.4 that his total heating bill for the three winter months will be less than $380. He also estimates that the probability is 0.6 that the total bill will be less than $460.

a. What is the probability that the total bill will be between $380 and $460?
b. Given no further information, what can be said about the probability that the total bill will be less than $400?

5.2 EXPECTATIONS FOR CONTINUOUS RANDOM VARIABLES

In Section 4.2 we presented the concepts of expected value of a discrete random variable and the expected value of a function of that random variable. Here, we will extend those ideas to continuous random variables. Because the probability of any specific value is 0 for a continuous random variable, we need to use Equation 5.3.

Rationale for Expectations of Continuous Random Variables
Suppose that a random experiment leads to an outcome that can be represented by a continuous random variable. If N independent replications of this experiment are carried out, then the **expected value** of the random variable is the average of the values taken, as the number of replications becomes infinitely large. The expected value of a random variable is denoted by $E(X)$.

Similarly, if $g(X)$ is any function of the random variable X, then the expected value of this function is the average value taken by the function over repeated independent trials, as the number of trials becomes infinitely large. This expectation is denoted $E[g(X)]$.

By using calculus we can define expected values for continuous random variables similar to those used for discrete random variables:

$$E[g(x)] = \int_x g(x)f(x)dx \tag{5.3}$$

These concepts can be clearly presented if one understands integral calculus, as shown in the chapter appendix. Using Equation 5.3, we can obtain the mean and variance for continuous random variables. Equations 5.4 and 5.5 present the mean and variance for continuous random variables.

Mean, Variance, and Standard Deviation for Continuous Random Variables

Let X be a continuous random variable. There are two important expected values that are used routinely to define continuous probability distributions.

1. The **mean of X**, denoted by μ_X, is defined as the expected value of X:

$$\mu_X = E(X) \tag{5.4}$$

2. The **variance of X**, denoted by σ_X^2 is defined as the expectation of the squared deviation, $(X - \mu_X)^2$, of the random variable from its mean:

$$\sigma_X^2 = E[(X - \mu_X)^2] \tag{5.5}$$

or an alternative expression can be derived:

$$\sigma_X^2 = E(X^2) - \mu_X^2 \tag{5.6}$$

The **standard deviation of X**, σ_X, is the square root of the variance.

The mean and variance provide two important pieces of summary information about a probability distribution. The mean provides a measure of the center of the distribution. Consider a physical interpretation as follows: Cut out the graph of a probability density function. The point along the x-axis at which the figure exactly balances on one's finger is the mean of the distribution. For example, in Figure 5.4 the uniform distribution is symmetric at about $x = 0.5$, and, thus, $\mu_X = 0.5$ is the mean of the random variable.

The variance—or its square root, the standard deviation—provides a measure of the dispersion or spread of a distribution. Thus, if we compare two uniform distributions with the same mean, $\mu_X = 1$—one over the range 0.5 to 1.5 and the other over the range 0 to 2—we will find that the latter has a larger variance because it is spread over a greater range.

For a *uniform distribution* defined over the range from a to b, we have the following results:

$$f(x) = \frac{1}{b - a}$$
$$a \leq X \leq b$$

$$\mu_X = E[X] = \frac{a+b}{2}$$

$$\sigma_X^2 = E\big[(X-\mu_X)^2\big] = \frac{(b-a)^2}{12}$$

The mean and the variance are also called the first and second moments.

In Section 5.3 we showed how to obtain the means and variances of linear functions of discrete random variables. The results are the same for continuous random variables because the derivations make use of the expected value operator. The summary results from Chapter 4 are repeated here.

Linear Functions of Random Variables

Let X be a continuous random variable with mean μ_X and variance σ_X^2 and let a and b be any constant fixed numbers. Define the random variable W as follows:

$$W = a + bX$$

Then the mean and variance of W are

$$\mu_W = E(a + bX) = a + b\mu_X \tag{5.7}$$

and

$$\sigma_W^2 = \text{Var}(a + bX) = b^2\sigma_X^2 \tag{5.8}$$

and the standard deviation of W is

$$\sigma_W = |b|\sigma_X \tag{5.9}$$

An important special case of these results is the standardized random variable

$$Z = \frac{X - \mu_X}{\sigma_X} \tag{5.10}$$

which has mean 0 and variance 1.

Linear functions of random variables have many applications in business and economics. Suppose that the number of units sold during a week are a random variable and the selling price is fixed. Thus, the total revenue is a random variable that is a function of the random variable units sold. Quantity demanded is a linear function of price that can be a random variable. Thus, quantity demanded is a random variable. The total number of cars sold per month in a dealership is a linear function of the random variable number of cars sold per sales person multiplied by the number of sales persons. Thus, total sales is a random variable.

Example 5.2   Home Heating Costs (Mean and Standard Deviation)

A homeowner estimates that within the range of likely temperatures his January heating bill, Y, in dollars, will be

$$Y = 290 - 5T$$

where T is the average temperature for the month, in degrees Fahrenheit. If the average January temperature can be represented by a random variable with a mean of 24 and a standard deviation of 4, find the mean and standard deviation of this homeowner's January heating bill.

Solution   The random variable T has mean $\mu_T = 24$ and standard deviation $\sigma_T = 4$. Therefore, the expected heating bill is

$$\mu_Y = 290 - 5\,\mu_T$$
$$= 290 - (5)(24) = \$170$$

and the standard deviation is

$$\sigma_Y = |{-5}|\,\sigma_T = (5)(4) = \$20$$

EXERCISES

Basic Exercises

5.9   The total cost for a production process is equal to $1,000 plus two times the number of units produced. The mean and variance for the number of units produced are 500 and 900, respectively. Find the mean and variance of the total cost.

5.10   The profit for a production process is equal to $1,000 minus two times the number of units produced. The mean and variance for the number of units produced are 50 and 90, respectively. Find the mean and variance of the profit.

5.11   The profit for a production process is equal to $2,000 minus two times the number of units produced. The mean and variance for the number of units produced are 500 and 900, respectively. Find the mean and variance of the profit.

5.12   The profit for a production process is equal to $6,000 minus three times the number of units produced. The mean and variance for the number of units produced are 1,000 and 900, respectively. Find the mean and variance of the profit.

Application Exercises

5.13   An author receives a contract from a publisher, according to which he is to be paid a fixed sum of $10,000 plus $1.50 for each copy of his book sold. His uncertainty about total sales of the book can be represented by a random variable with a mean of 30,000 and a standard deviation of 8,000. Find the mean and standard deviation of the total payments he will receive.

5.14   A contractor submits a bid on a project for which more research and development work needs to be done. It is estimated that the total cost of satisfying the project specifications will be $20 million plus the cost of the further research and development work. The contractor views the cost of this work as a random variable with a mean of $4 million and a standard deviation of $1 million. The contractor wishes to submit a bid such that his expected profit will be 10% of his expected costs. What should be the bid? If this bid is accepted, what will be the standard deviation of the profit made by the project?

5.15   A charitable organization solicits donations by telephone. Employees are paid $60 plus 20% of the money their calls generate each week. The amount of money generated in a week can be viewed as a random variable with a mean of $700 and a standard deviation of $130. Find the mean and standard deviation of an employee's total pay in a week.

5.16   A salesman receives an annual salary of $6,000 plus 8% of the value of the orders he takes. The annual value of these orders can be represented by a random variable with a mean of $600,000 and a standard deviation of $180,000. Find the mean and standard deviation of the salesman's annual income.

5.3 THE NORMAL DISTRIBUTION

In this section we present the normal probability distribution, which is the continuous random variable probability distribution used most often for economics and business applications. An example of the normal probability density function is shown in Figure 5.8.

Figure 5.8
Probability
Density Function
for a Normal
Distribution

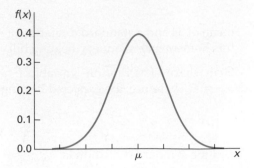

There are many reasons for its wide application.

1. The normal distribution closely approximates the probability distributions of a wide range of random variables. For example, the dimensions of parts and the weights of food packages often follow a normal distribution. This leads to quality control applications. Total sales or production often follows a normal distribution, which leads us to a large family of applications in marketing and production management. The patterns of stock and bond prices are often modeled using the normal distribution in large computer-based financial trading models. Economic models use the normal distribution for a number of economic measures.
2. Distributions of sample means approach a normal distribution, given a "large" sample size.
3. Computation of probabilities is direct and elegant.
4. The most important reason is that the normal probability distribution has led to good business decisions for a number of applications.

A formal definition of the normal probability density function is given by Equation 5.11.

Probability Density Function of the Normal Distribution

The **probability density function for a normally distributed random variable X is**

$$f(x) = \frac{1}{\sqrt{2\pi\sigma^2}} e^{-(x-\mu)^2/2\sigma^2} \qquad \text{for} \qquad -\infty < x < \infty \qquad (5.11)$$

where μ and σ^2 are any numbers such that $-\infty < \mu < \infty$ and $0 < \sigma^2 < \infty$, and where e and π are physical constants, $e = 2.71828$ ...and $\pi = 3.14159$....

The normal probability distribution represents a large family of distributions, each with a unique specification for the parameters μ and σ^2. These parameters have a very convenient interpretation.

For our applied statistical analyses the normal distribution has a number of important characteristics. It is symmetric. Different central tendencies are indicated by differences in μ. In contrast, differences in σ^2 result in density functions of different widths. By selecting values for μ and σ^2 we can define a large family of normal probability density functions. Differences in the mean result in shifts of entire distributions. In contrast, differences in the variance result in distributions with different widths.

The distribution mean provides a measure of central location, and the variance gives a measure of dispersion about the mean. Thus, the parameters μ and σ^2 have different effects on the probability density function of a normal random variable. Figure 5.9(a) shows probability density functions for two normal distributions with a common variance and different means. We see that increases in the mean shift the distribution without changing its shape. In Figure 5.9(b) the two density functions have the same mean but different variances. Each is symmetric about the common mean, but the larger variance results in a wider distribution.

Our next task is to learn how to obtain probabilities for a specified normal distribution. First, we introduce the *cumulative distribution function*.

Figure 5.9
Effects of μ and σ^2 on the Probability Density Function of a Normal Random Variable

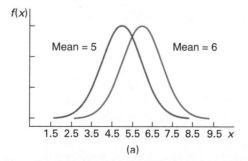

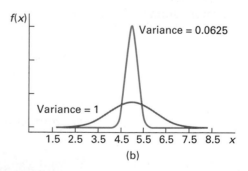

a. Two Normal Distributions with Different Means
b. Two Normal Distributions with Different Variances and Mean = 5

Cumulative Distribution Function of the Normal Distribution

Suppose that X is a normal random variable with mean μ and variance σ^2—that is, $X \sim N(\mu,\sigma^2)$. Then the cumulative distribution function is as follows:

$$F(x_0) = P(X \leq x_0)$$

This is the area under the normal probability density function to the left of x_0, as illustrated in Figure 5.10. As for any proper density function, the total area under the curve is 1—that is,

$$F(\infty) = 1$$

Figure 5.10   The Shaded Area is the Probability That X Does Not Exceed x_0 for a Normal Random Variable

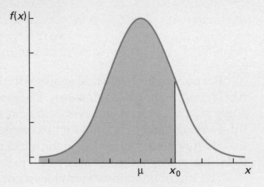

We do not have a simple algebraic expression for calculating the cumulative distribution function for a normally distributed random variable (see the chapter appendix). The general shape of the cumulative distribution function is shown in Figure 5.11. Equation 5.12 is used to compute normal probabilities using the cumulative distribution function.

Figure 5.11
Cumulative
Distribution for a
Normal Random
Variable

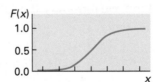

Range Probabilities for Normal Random Variables

Let X be a normal random variable with cumulative distribution function $F(x)$, and let a and b be two possible values of X, with $a < b$. Then,

$$P(a < X < b) = F(b) - F(a) \tag{5.12}$$

The probability is the area under the corresponding probability density function between a and b, as shown in Figure 5.12.

Figure 5.12 Normal Density Function with the Shaded Area Indicating the Probability That *X* Is Between *a* and *b*

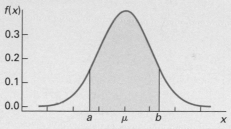

Any probability can be obtained from the cumulative distribution function. However, we do not have a convenient way to directly compute the probability for any normal distribution with a specific mean and variance. We could use numerical integration procedures with a computer, but that approach would be tedious and cumbersome. Fortunately, we can convert any normal distribution to a *standard normal distribution* with mean 0 and variance 1.

The Standard Normal Distribution

Let *Z* be a normal random variable with mean 0 and variance 1—that is,

$$Z \sim N(0,1)$$

We say that *Z* follows the **standard normal distribution**.

Denote the cumulative distribution function as *F*(*z*) and *a* and *b* as two possible values of *Z* with *a* < *b*; then,

$$P(a < Z < b) = F(b) - F(a) \tag{5.13}$$

We can obtain probabilities for any normally distributed random variable by first converting the random variable to the standard normally distributed random variable, Z. There is always a direct relationship between any normally distributed random variable and Z. That relationship uses the transformation

$$Z = \frac{X - \mu}{\sigma}$$

where *X* is a normally distributed random variable:

$$X \sim N(\mu, \sigma^2)$$

This important result allows us to use the standard normal table to compute probabilities associated with any normally distributed random variable. Now let us see how probabilities can be computed for the standard normal Z.

The cumulative distribution function of the standard normal distribution is tabulated in Table 1 in the appendix. This table gives values of

$$F(z) = P(Z \le z)$$

for non-negative values of *z*. For example, the cumulative probability for a *Z* value of 1.25 from Table 1 is as follows:

$$F(1.25) = 0.8944$$

Figure 5.13 Standard Normal
Distribution with Probability for $z = 1.25$

Figure 5.14 Standard Normal
Distribution for Negative z Equal to –1

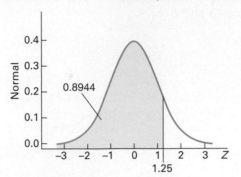

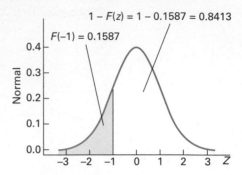

This is the area, designated in Figure 5.13, for Z less than 1.25. Because of the symmetry of the normal distribution, the probability that $Z > -1.25$ is also equal to 0.8944. In general, values of the cumulative distribution function for negative values of Z can be inferred using the symmetry of the probability density function.

To find the cumulative probability for a negative Z (for example, $z = -1.0$) defined as

$$F(-Z_0) = P(Z \leq -z_0) = F(-1.0)$$

we use the complement of the probability for $z = +1$, as shown in Figure 5.14.

From the symmetry we can state that

$$F(-Z) = 1 - P(Z \leq +Z) = 1 - F(Z)$$
$$F(-1) = 1 - P(Z \leq +1) = 1 - F(1)$$

Figure 5.15 indicates the symmetry for the corresponding positive values of Z.

In Figure 5.16 we can see that the area under the curve to the left of $z = -1$ is equal to the area to the right of $z = +1$ because of the symmetry of the normal distribution. The area substantially below $-Z$ is often called the "lower tail," and the area substantially above $+Z$ is called the "upper tail."

We can also use normal tables that provide probabilities for just the upper half, or positive Z, values from the normal distribution. An example of this type of table is shown inside the front cover of this textbook. This form of the normal table is used to

Figure 5.15 Normal Distribution for
Positive $z = +1$

Figure 5.16 Normal Density Function with
Symmetric Upper and Lower Values

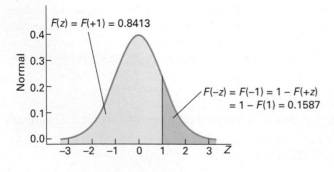

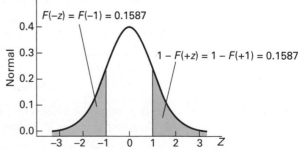

find probabilities, the same as those previously shown. With positive Z values we add 0.50 to the values given in the table inside the front cover of the textbook. With negative values of Z we utilize the symmetry of the normal to obtain the desired probabilities.

Example 5.3 Investment Portfolio Value Probabilities (Normal Probabilities)

A client has an investment portfolio whose mean value is equal to $1,000,000 with a standard deviation of $30,000. He has asked you to determine the probability that the value of his portfolio is between $970,000 and $1,060,000.

Solution   The problem is illustrated in Figure 5.17. To solve the problem, we must first determine the corresponding Z values for the portfolio limits. For $970,000 the corresponding Z value is as follows:

$$Z_{970,000} = \frac{970,000 - 1,000,000}{30,000} = -1.0$$

And for the upper value, $1,060,000, the Z value is as follows:

$$Z_{1,060,000} = \frac{1,060,000 - 1,000,000}{30,000} = +2.0$$

As shown in Figure 5.17, the probability that the portfolio value, X, is between $970,000 and $1,060,000, is equal to the probability that Z is between −1 and +2. To obtain the probability, we first compute the probabilities for the lower and the upper tails and subtract these probabilities from 1. Algebraically, the result is as follows:

$$P(970,000 \leq X \leq 1,060,000) = P(-1 \leq Z \leq +2) = 1 - P(Z \leq -1) - P(Z \geq +2)$$

$$= 1 - 0.1587 - 0.0228 = 0.8185$$

The probability for the indicated range is, thus, 0.8185.

Figure 5.17   Normal Distribution for Example 5.3

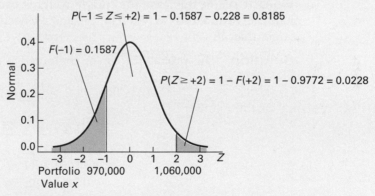

Recall from Chapter 1 that we presented the empirical rule, which states as a rough guide that $\mu \pm \sigma$ covers about 68% of the range, while $\mu \pm 2\sigma$ covers about 95% of the range. For all practical purposes almost none of the range is outside $\mu \pm 3\sigma$. This useful approximation tool for interpretations based on descriptive statistics is based on the normal distribution.

Probabilities can also be computed by using Equation 5.14.

Finding Probabilities for Normally Distributed Random Variables

Let X be a normally distributed random variable with mean μ and variance σ^2. Then random variable $Z = (X-\mu)/\sigma$ has a standard normal distribution of $Z \sim N(0,1)$.

It follows that, if a and b are any possible values of X with $a < b$, then,

$$P(a < X < b) = P\left(\frac{a-\mu}{\sigma} < Z < \frac{b-\mu}{\sigma}\right)$$

$$= F\left(\frac{b-\mu}{\sigma}\right) - F\left(\frac{a-\mu}{\sigma}\right) \tag{5.14}$$

where Z is the standard normal random variable and F denotes its cumulative distribution function.

Example 5.4 Analysis of Turkey Weights (Normal Probabilities)

Whole Life Organic Inc. produces high quality organic frozen turkeys for distribution in organic food markets in the upper Midwest. The company has developed a range feeding program with organic grain supplements to produce their product. The mean weight of one of its frozen turkeys is 15 pounds with a variance of 16. Historical experience indicates that weights can be approximated by the normal probability distribution. Market research indicates that sales for frozen turkeys over 18 pounds are limited. What percentage of the company's turkey units will be over 18 pounds?

Solution In this case the turkey weights can be represented by a random variable, X, and, thus, $X \sim N(15, 16)$, and we need to find the probability that X is larger than 18.

Solution This probability can be computed as follows:

$$P(x > 18) = P\left(Z > \frac{18-\mu}{\sigma}\right)$$

$$= P\left(Z > \frac{18 - 15}{4}\right)$$

$$= P(Z > 0.75)$$

$$= 1 - P(Z < 0.75)$$

$$= 1 - F(0.75)$$

From Table 1 in the appendix, $F(0.75)$ is 0.7734, and, therefore,

$$P(X > 18) = 1 - 0.7734 = 0.2266$$

Thus, Whole Life can expect that 22.7% of its turkeys will weigh more than 18 pounds.

Example 5.5 Lightbulb Life (Normal Probabilities)

A company produces lightbulbs whose life follows a normal distribution, with a mean of 1,200 hours and a standard deviation of 250 hours. If we choose a lightbulb at random, what is the probability that its lifetime will be between 900 and 1,300 hours?

Solution Let X represent lifetime in hours. Then,

$$P\left(900 < X < 1,300\right) = P\left(\frac{900-1,200}{250} < Z < \frac{1,300-1,200}{250}\right)$$

$$= P\left(-1.2 < Z < 0.4\right)$$

$$= F(0.4) - F(-1.2)$$

$$= 0.6554 - (1-0.8849) = 0.5403$$

Hence, the probability is approximately 0.54 that a lightbulb will last between 900 and 1,300 hours.

Example 5.6 Sales of Cell Phones (Normal Probabilities)

Silver Star Inc. has a number of stores in major metropolitan shopping centers. The company's sales experience indicates that daily cell phone sales in its stores follow a normal distribution with a mean of 60 and a standard deviation of 15. The marketing department conducts a number of routine analysis of sales data to monitor sales performance. What proportion of store sales days will have sales between 85 and 95 given that sales are following the historical experience?

Solution Let X denote the daily cell phone sales. Then, the probability can be computed as follows:

$$P\left(85 < X < 95\right) = P\left(\frac{85-60}{15} < Z < \frac{95-60}{15}\right)$$

$$= P\left(1.67 < Z < 2.33\right)$$

$$= F(2.33) - F(1.67)$$

$$= 0.9901 - 0.9525 = 0.0376$$

That is, 3.76% of the daily sales will be in the range 85 to 95 based on historical sales patterns. Note that if actually reported sales in this range for a group of stores were above 10% we would have evidence for higher than historical sales.

Example 5.7 Cutoff Points for Daily Cell Phone Sales (Normal Random Variables)

For the daily cell phone sales of Example 5.6 find the cutoff point for the top 10% of all daily sales.

Solution Define b as the cutoff point. To determine the numerical value of the cutoff point, we first note that the probability of exceeding b is 0.10, and, thus, the probability of being less than b is 0.90. The upper tail value of 0.10 is shown in

Figure 5.18. We can now state the probability from the cumulative distribution as follows:

$$0.90 = P\left(Z < \frac{b - 60}{15}\right)$$

$$= F\left(\frac{b - 60}{15}\right)$$

From Table 1 of the appendix, we find that $Z = 1.28$ when $F(Z) = 0.90$. Therefore, solving for b, we have the following:

$$\frac{b-60}{15} = 1.28$$
$$b = 79.2$$

Thus, we conclude that 10% of the daily cell phone sales will be above 79.2 as shown in Figure 5.18.

Figure 5.18 Normal Distribution with Mean 60 and Standard Deviation 15 Showing Upper Tail Probability Equal To 0.10

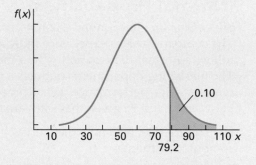

We note that daily sales, such as those in Examples 5.6 and 5.7, are typically given as integer values, and, thus, their distribution is discrete. However, because of the large number of possible outcomes, the normal distribution provides a very good approximation for the discrete distribution. In most applied business and economic problems we are, in fact, using the normal distribution to approximate a discrete distribution that has many different outcomes.

Normal Probability Plots

The normal probability model is the most used probability model for the reasons previously noted. In applied problems we would like to know if the data have come from a distribution that approximates a normal distribution closely enough to ensure a valid result. Thus, we are seeking evidence to support the assumption that the normal distribution is a close approximation to the actual unknown distribution. Normal probability plots provide a good way to test this assumption and determine if the normal model can be used. Usage is simple. If the data follow a normal distribution, the plot will be a straight line. More rigorous tests are also possible as shown in Chapter 14.

Figure 5.19 is a normal probability plot for a random sample of $n = 1,000$ observations from a normal distribution with $\mu = 100$ and $\sigma = 25$. The plot was generated

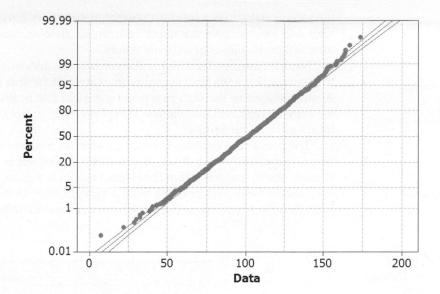

Figure 5.19
Normal
Probability Plot for
a Normal
Distribution
(Minitab Output)

using Minitab. The horizontal axis indicates the data points ranked in order from the smallest to the largest. The vertical axis indicates the cumulative normal probabilities of the ranked data values if the sample data were obtained from a population whose random variables follow a normal distribution. We see that the vertical axis has a transformed normal scale. The data plots in Figure 5.19 are close to a straight line even at the upper and lower limits, and that result provides solid evidence that the data have a normal distribution. The dotted lines provide an interval within which data points from a normally distributed random variable would occur in most cases. Thus, if the plotted points are within the boundaries established by the dotted lines, we can conclude that the data points represent a normally distributed random variable.

Next, consider a random sample of $n = 1,000$ observations drawn from a *uniform distribution* with limits 25 to 175. Figure 5.20 shows the normal probability plot. In this case the data plot has an S shape that clearly deviates from a straight line, and

Figure 5.20
Normal
Probability Plot for
a Uniform
Distribution
(Minitab Output)

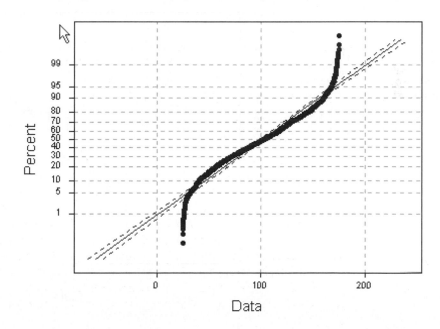

the sample data do not follow a normal distribution. Large deviations at the extreme high and low values are a major concern because statistical inference is often based on small probabilities of extreme values.

Next, let us consider a highly skewed discrete distribution, as shown in Figure 5.21. In Figure 5.22 we see the normal probability plot for this highly skewed distribution. Again, we see that the data plot is not a straight line but has considerable deviation at the extreme high and low values. This plot clearly indicates that the data do not come from a normal distribution.

The previous examples provide us with an indication of possible results from a normal probability plot. If the plot from your problem is similar to Figure 5.19, then you are safe in assuming that the normal model is a good approximation. Note, however, that if your plot deviates from a straight line, as do those in Figures 5.20 and 5.22, then the sample data does not have a normal distribution.

Figure 5.21
Skewed Discrete Probability Distribution Function

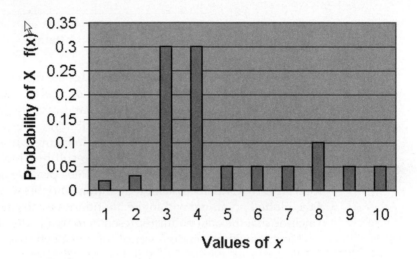

Figure 5.22
Normal Probability Plot for a Highly Skewed Distribution (Minitab Output)

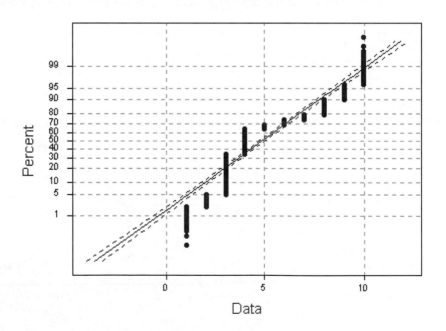

Basic Exercises

5.17 Let the random variable Z follow a standard normal distribution.

  a. Find $P(Z < 1.20)$.
  b. Find $P(Z > 1.33)$.
  c. Find $P(Z < -1.70)$.
  d. Find $P(Z > -1.00)$.
  e. Find $P(1.20 < Z < 1.33)$.
  f. Find $P(-1.70 < Z < 1.20)$.
  g. Find $P(-1.70 < Z < -1.00)$.

5.18 Let the random variable Z follow a standard normal distribution.

  a. The probability is 0.70 that Z is less than what number?
  b. The probability is 0.25 that Z is less than what number?
  c. The probability is 0.2 that Z is greater than what number?
  d. The probability is 0.6 that Z is greater than what number?

5.19 Let the random variable X follow a normal distribution with $\mu = 50$ and $\sigma^2 = 64$.

  a. Find the probability that X is greater than 60.
  b. Find the probability that X is greater than 35 and less than 62.
  c. Find the probability that X is less than 55.
  d. The probability is 0.2 that X is greater than what number?
  e. The probability is 0.05 that X is in the symmetric interval about the mean between which two numbers?

5.20 Let the random variable X follow a normal distribution with $\mu = 80$ and $\sigma^2 = 100$.

  a. Find the probability that X is greater than 60.
  b. Find the probability that X is greater than 72 and less than 82.
  c. Find the probability that X is less than 55.
  d. The probability is 0.1 that X is greater than what number?
  e. The probability is 0.08 that X is in the symmetric interval about the mean between which two numbers?

5.21 Let the random variable X follow a normal distribution with $\mu = 0.2$ and $\sigma^2 = .0025$.

  a. Find the probability that X is greater than 0.4.
  b. Find the probability that X is greater than 0.15 and less than 0.28.
  c. Find the probability that X is less than 0.10.
  d. The probability is 0.2 that X is greater than what number?

  e. The probability is 0.05 that X is in the symmetric interval about the mean between which two numbers?

Application Exercises

5.22 It is known that amounts of money spent on clothing in a year by students on a particular campus follow a normal distribution with a mean of $380 and a standard deviation of $50.

  a. What is the probability that a randomly chosen student will spend less than $400 on clothing in a year?
  b. What is the probability that a randomly chosen student will spend more than $360 on clothing in a year?
  c. Draw a graph to illustrate why the answers to parts (a) and (b) are the same.
  d. What is the probability that a randomly chosen student will spend between $300 and $400 on clothing in a year?
  e. Compute a range of yearly clothing expenditures—measured in dollars—that includes 80% of all students on this campus? Explain why any number of such ranges could be found, and find the shortest one.

5.23 Anticipated consumer demand in a restaurant for free range steaks next month can be modeled by a normal random variable with mean 1,200 pounds and standard deviation 100 pounds.

  a. What is the probability that demand will exceed 1,000 pounds?
  b. What is the probability that demand will be between 1,100 and 1,300 pounds?
  c. The probability is 0.10 that demand will be more than how many pounds?

5.24 The tread life of Road Stone tires has a normal distribution with a mean of 35,000 miles and a standard deviation of 4,000 miles.

  a. What proportion of these tires has a tread life of more than 38,000 miles?
  b. What proportion of these tires has a tread life of less than 32,000 miles?
  c. What proportion of these tires has a tread life of between 32,000 and 38,000 miles?
  d. Draw a graph of the probability density function of tread lives, illustrating why the answers to parts (a) and (b) are the same and why the answers to parts (a), (b), and (c) sum to 1.

5.25 An investment portfolio contains stocks of a large number of corporations. Over the last year the rates of return on these corporate stocks followed a normal distribution with mean 12.2% and standard deviation 7.2%.

   a. For what proportion of these corporations was the rate of return higher than 20%?

   b. For what proportion of these corporations was the rate of return negative?

   c. For what proportion of these corporations was the rate of return between 5% and 15%?

5.26 Southwest Co-op produces bags of fertilizer, and it is concerned about impurity content. It is believed that the weights of impurities per bag are normally distributed with a mean of 12.2 grams and a standard deviation of 2.8 grams. A bag is chosen at random.

   a. What is the probability that it contains less than 10 grams of impurities?

   b. What is the probability that it contains more than 15 grams of impurities?

   c. What is the probability that it contains between 12 and 15 grams of impurities?

   d. It is possible, without doing the detailed calculations, to deduce which of the answers to parts (a) and (b) will be the larger. How would you do this?

5.27 A contractor has concluded from his experience that the cost of building a luxury home is a normally distributed random variable with a mean of $500,000 and a standard deviation of $50,000.

   a. What is the probability that the cost of building a home will be between $460,000 and $540,000?

   b. The probability is 0.2 that the cost of building will be less than what amount?

   c. Find the shortest range such that the probability is 0.95 that the cost of a luxury home will fall in this range.

5.28 Scores on an economics test follow a normal distribution. What is the probability that a randomly selected student will achieve a score that exceeds the mean score by more than 1.5 standard deviations?

5.29 A new television series is to be shown. A broadcasting executive feels that his uncertainty about the rating that the show will receive in its first month can be represented by a normal distribution with a mean of 18.2 and a standard deviation of 1.5. According to this executive, the probability is 0.1 that the rating will be less than what number?

5.30 A broadcasting executive is reviewing the prospects for a new television series. According to his judgment, the probability is 0.25 that the show will achieve a rating higher than 17.8, and the probability is 0.15 that it will achieve a rating higher than 19.2. If the executive's uncertainty about the rating can be represented by a normal distribution, what are the mean and variance of that distribution?

5.31 The number of hits per day on the Web site of Professional Tool Inc. is normally distributed with a mean of 700 and a standard deviation of 120.

   a. What proportion of days have more than 820 hits per day?

   b. What proportion of days have between 730 and 820 hits?

   c. Find the number of hits such that only 5% of the days will have the number of hits below this number.

5.32 I am considering two alternative investments. In both cases I am unsure about the percentage return but believe that my uncertainty can be represented by normal distributions with the means and standard deviations shown in the accompanying table. I want to make the investment that is more likely to produce a return of at least 10%. Which investment should I choose?

	Mean	Standard Deviation
Investment A	10.4	1.2
Investment B	11.0	4.0

5.33 Tata Motors Ltd. purchases computer process chips from two suppliers and the company is concerned about the percentage of defective chips. A review of the records for each supplier indicates that the percentage defectives in consignments of chips follow normal distributions with the means and standard deviations given in the following table. The company is particularly anxious that the percentage of defectives in a consignment not exceed 5% and wants to purchase from the supplier that's more likely to meet that specification. Which supplier should be chosen?

	Mean	Standard Deviation
Supplier A	4.4	0.4
Supplier B	4.2	0.6

5.34 A furniture manufacturer has found that the time spent by workers assembling a particular table follows a normal distribution with a mean of 150 minutes and a standard deviation of 40 minutes.

   a. The probability is 0.9 that a randomly chosen table requires more than how many minutes to assemble?

   b. The probability is 0.8 that a randomly chosen table can be assembled in fewer than how many minutes?

   c. Two tables are chosen at random. What is the probability that at least one of them requires at least 2 hours to assemble?

5.35 A company services copiers. A review of its records shows that the time taken for a service call can be represented by a normal random variable with a mean of 75 minutes and a standard deviation of 20 minutes.

a. What proportion of service calls takes less than 1 hour?
b. What proportion of service calls takes more than 90 minutes?
c. Sketch a graph to show why the answers to parts (a) and (b) are the same.
d. The probability is 0.1 that a service call takes more than how many minutes?

5.36 Scores on an achievement test are known to be normally distributed with a mean of 420 and a standard deviation of 80.

a. For a randomly chosen person taking this test, what is the probability of a score between 400 and 480?
b. What is the minimum test score needed in order to be in the top 10% of all people taking the test?
c. For a randomly chosen individual, state, without doing the calculations, in which of the following ranges his score is most likely to be: 400–439, 440–479, 480–519, or 520–559.
d. In which of the ranges listed in part (c) is the individual's score least likely to be?
e. Two people taking the test are chosen at random. What is the probability that at least one of them scores more than 500 points?

5.37 It is estimated that the time that a well-known rock band, the Living Ingrates, spends on stage at its concerts follows a normal distribution with a mean of 200 minutes and a standard deviation of 20 minutes.

a. What proportion of concerts played by this band lasts between 180 and 200 minutes?
b. An audience member smuggles a tape recorder into a Living Ingrates concert. The reel-to-reel tapes have a capacity of 245 minutes. What is the probability that this capacity will be insufficient to record the entire concert?
c. If the standard deviation of concert time was only 15 minutes, state, without doing the calculations, whether the probability that a concert would last more than 245 minutes would be larger than, smaller than, or the same as that found in part (b). Sketch a graph to illustrate your answer.
d. The probability is 0.1 that a Living Ingrates concert will last less than how many minutes? (Assume, as originally, that the population standard deviation is 20 minutes.)

5.38 The daily selling price per 100 pounds of buffalo meat is normally distributed with a mean of $70, and the probability that the daily price is less than $85 is 0.9332. Four days are chosen at random. What is the probability that at least one of the days has a price that exceeds $80?

5.4 NORMAL DISTRIBUTION APPROXIMATION FOR BINOMIAL DISTRIBUTION

In this section we show how the normal distribution can be used to approximate the discrete binomial and proportion random variables that are used extensively in business and economics. This approximation can be used to compute probabilities for larger sample sizes when tables are not readily available. The normal distribution approximation of the binomial distribution also provides a benefit for applied problem solving. We learn that procedures based on the normal distribution can also be applied in problems involving binomial and proportion random variables. Thus, you can reduce the number of different statistical procedures that you need to know to solve business problems.

Let us consider a problem with n independent trials, each with the probability of success P. In Section 4.4 we saw that the binomial random variable X could be written as the sum of n independent Bernoulli random variables,

$$X = X_1 + X_2 + \cdots + X_n$$

where the random variable X_i takes the value 1 if the outcome of the ith trial is "success" and 0 otherwise, with respective probabilities P and $1-P$. The number X of successes that result have a binomial distribution with a mean and variance:

$$E(X) = \mu = nP$$
$$Var(X) = \sigma^2 = nP(1 - P)$$

The plot of a binomial distribution with $P = 0.5$ and $n = 100$, in Figure 5.23, shows us that this binomial distribution has the same shape as the normal distribution. This visual evidence that the binomial can be approximated by a normal distribution with the same mean and variance is also established in work done by mathematical statisticians. This close approximation of the binomial distribution by the normal distribution is an example of the Central Limit Theorem that will be developed in Chapter 6. A good rule for us is that the normal distribution provides a good approximation for the binomial distribution when $nP(1-P) > 5$. If this value is less than 5 then use the binomial distribution to determine the probabilities.

In order to better understand the normal distribution approximation for the binomial distribution, consider Figure 5.24(a) and (b). In both (a) and (b) we have shown points from a normal probability density function compared to the corresponding probabilities from a binomial distribution using graphs prepared using Minitab. In part (a) we note that the approximation rule value is

$$nP(1-P) = 100(0.5)(1-0.5) = 25 > 5$$

and that the normal distribution provides a very close approximation to the binomial distribution. In contrast, the example in part (b) has an approximation rule value of

$$nP(1-P) = 25(0.2)(1-0.2) = 4 < 5$$

and the normal distribution does not provide a good approximation for the binomial distribution. Evidence such as that contained in Figure 5.24 has provided the rationale for widespread application of the normal approximation for the binomial. We will now proceed to develop the procedure for its application.

By using the mean and the variance from the binomial distribution, we find that, if the number of trials n is large—such that $nP(1-P) > 5$—then the distribution of the random variable

$$Z = \frac{X - E(X)}{\sqrt{\mathrm{Var}(X)}} = \frac{X - nP}{\sqrt{nP(1 - P)}}$$

is approximately standard normal distribution.

Figure 5.23
Binomial
Distribution with
$n = 100$ and
$P = 0.50$.

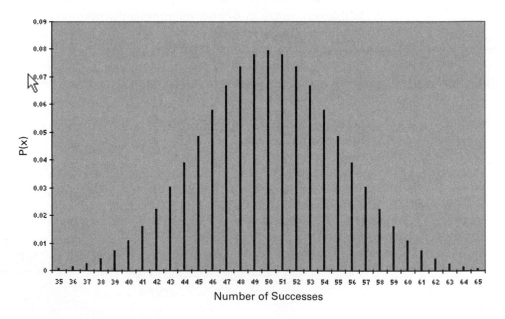

Figure 5.24 Comparison of Binomial and Normal Approximation

a. Binomial with P = 0.50 and *n* = 100, and Normal with μ = 50 and σ = 5

b. Binomial with P = 0.20 and *n* = 25, and Normal with μ = 5 and σ = 2

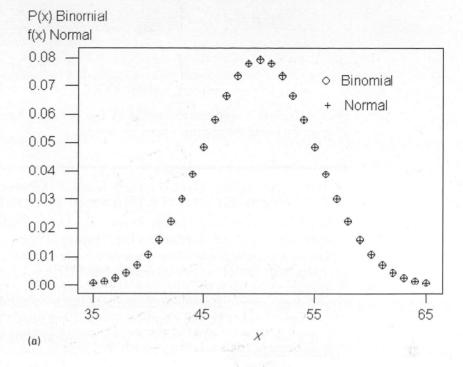

(a)

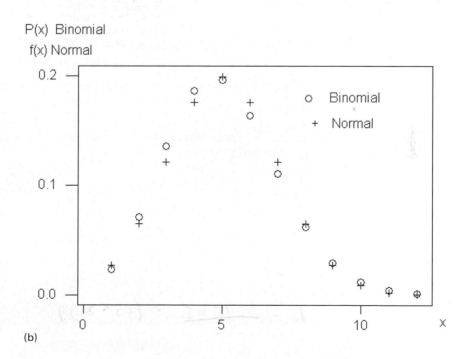

(b)

This result is very important because it allows us to find, for large n, the probability that the number of successes lies in a given range. If we want to determine the probability that the number of successes will be between a and b, inclusive, we have

$$P(a \le X \le b) = P\left(\frac{a - nP}{\sqrt{nP(1 - P)}} \le \frac{X - nP}{\sqrt{nP(1 - P)}} \le \frac{b - nP}{\sqrt{nP(1 - P)}} \right)$$

$$= P\left(\frac{a - nP}{\sqrt{nP(1 - P)}} \le Z \le \frac{b - nP}{\sqrt{nP(1 - P)}} \right)$$

With n large, Z is well approximated by the standard normal, and we can find the probability using the methods from Section 5.3.

Example 5.8   Customer Visits Generated From Web Page Contacts (Normal Probabilities)

Mary David makes the initial telephone contact with customers who have responded to an advertisement on her company's Web page in an effort to assess whether a follow-up visit to their homes is likely to be worthwhile. Her experience suggests that 40% of the initial contacts lead to follow-up visits. If she has 100 Web page contacts, what is the probability that between 45 and 50 home visits will result?

Solution   Let X be the number of follow-up visits. Then X has a binomial distribution with $n = 100$ and $P = 0.40$. Approximating the required probability gives the following:

$$P\left(45 \le X \le 50\right) \cong P\left(\frac{45 - (100)(0.4)}{\sqrt{(100)(0.4)(0.6)}} \le Z \le \frac{50 - (100)(0.4)}{\sqrt{(100)(0.4)(0.6)}} \right)$$
$$= P\left(1.02 \le Z \le 2.04\right)$$
$$= F(2.04) - F(1.02)$$
$$= 0.9793 - 0.8461 = 0.1332$$

This probability is shown as an area under the standard normal curve in Figure 5.25.

Figure 5.25   Probability of 45 to 50 Successes for a Binomial Distribution with $n = 100$ and P $= 0.4$

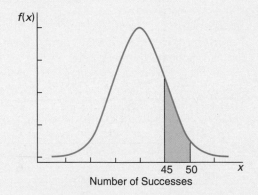

Proportion Random Variable

In a number of applied problems we have a need to compute probabilities for proportion or percentage intervals. We can do this by using a direct extension of the normal distribution approximation for the binomial distribution. A proportion random variable, P, can be computed by dividing the number of successes, X, by the sample size, n:

$$P = \frac{X}{n}$$

Then, using the linear transformation of random variables, the mean and the variance of P can be computed as follows:

$$\mu = P$$
$$\sigma^2 = \frac{P(1-P)}{n}$$

We can use the resulting mean and variance with the normal distribution to compute the desired probability.

Example 5.9   Election Forecasting (Proportion Probabilities)

We have often observed the success of television networks in forecasting elections. This is a good example of the successful use of probability methods in applied problems. Consider how elections can be predicted by using relatively small samples in a simplified example. An election forecaster has obtained a random sample of 900 voters, in which 500 indicate that they will vote for Susan Chung. Should Susan anticipate winning the election?

Solution   In this problem we assume only two candidates, and, thus, if more than 50% of the population supports Susan, she will win the election. We compute the probability that 500 or more voters out of a sample of 900 support Susan under the assumption that exactly 50%, $P = 0.50$, of the entire population supports Susan.

$$P(X \geq 500)\,|\,n = 900, P = 0.50) \approx P(X \geq 500\,|\,\mu = 450, \sigma^2 = 225)$$

$$= P\left(Z \geq \frac{500-450}{\sqrt{225}}\right)$$

$$= P(Z \geq 3.33)$$

$$= 0.0004$$

The probability of 500 successes out of 900 trials if $P = 0.50$ is very small, and, therefore, we conclude that P must be greater than 0.50. Hence, we predict that Susan Chung will win the election.

We could also compute the probability that more than 55.6% (500/900) of the sample indicates support for Susan if the population proportion is $P = 0.50$. Using the mean and variance for proportion random variables,

$$\mu = P = 0.50$$

$$\sigma^2 = \frac{P(1-P)}{n} = \frac{.50(1-.50)}{900}$$

$$\sigma = 0.0167$$

$$P(P \geq 0.556 \mid n = 900, P = 0.50) \approx P(P \geq 0.556 \mid \mu = 0.50, \sigma = 0.0167)$$

$$= P\left(Z \geq \frac{0.556 - 0.50}{0.0167}\right)$$

$$= P(Z \geq 3.33)$$

$$= 0.0004$$

Note that the probability is exactly the same as that for the corresponding binomial random variable. This is always the case because each proportion or percentage value is directly related to a specific number of successes. Because percent is a more common term than proportion in business and economic language, we will tend to use percent more often than proportion in exercises and discussion in this textbook.

EXERCISES

Basic Exercises

5.39 Given a random sample size of $n = 900$ from a binomial probability distribution with $P = 0.50$ do the following:

a. Find the probability that the number of successes is greater than 500.

b. Find the probability that the number of successes is fewer than 430.

c. Find the probability that the number of successes is between 440 and 480.

d. With probability 0.10 the number of successes is fewer than how many?

e. With probability 0.08 the number of successes is greater than how many?

5.40 Given a random sample size of $n = 1,600$ from a binomial probability distribution with $P = 0.40$, do the following:

a. Find the probability that the number of successes is greater than 1,650.

b. Find the probability that the number of successes is fewer than 1,530.

c. Find the probability that the number of successes is between 1,550 and 1,650.

d. With probability 0.09 the number of successes is fewer than how many?

e. With probability 0.20 the number of successes is greater than how many?

5.41 Given a random sample size of $n = 900$ from a binomial probability distribution with $P = 0.10$ do the following:

a. Find the probability that the number of successes is greater than 110.

b. Find the probability that the number of successes is fewer than 53.

c. Find the probability that the number of successes is between 55 and 120.

d. With probability 0.10 the number of successes is fewer than how many?

e. With probability 0.08 the number of successes is greater than how many?

5.42 Given a random sample size of $n = 1,600$ from a binomial probability distribution with $P = 0.40$ do the following:

a. Find the probability that the percentage of successes is greater than 0.45.

b. Find the probability that the percentage of successes is less than 0.35.

c. Find the probability that the percentage of successes is between 0.37 and 0.44.

d. With probability 0.20 the percentage of successes is less than what percent?

e. With probability 0.09 the percentage of successes is greater than what percent?

5.43 Given a random sample size of $n = 400$ from a binomial probability distribution with $P = 0.20$ do the following:

a. Find the probability that the percentage of successes is greater than 0.25.

b. Find the probability that the percentage of successes is less than 0.15.

c. Find the probability that the percentage of successes is between 0.17 and 0.24.

d. With probability 0.15 the percentage of successes is less than what percent?

e. With probability 0.11 the percentage of successes is greater than what percent?

Application Exercises

5.44 A car rental company has determined that the probability a car will need service work in any given month is 0.2. The company has 900 cars.

  a. What is the probability that more than 200 cars will require service work in a particular month?

  b. What is the probability that fewer than 175 cars will need service work in a given month?

5.45 It is known that 10% of all the items produced by a particular manufacturing process are defective. From the very large output of a single day, 400 items are selected at random.

  a. What is the probability that at least 35 of the selected items are defective?

  b. What is the probability that between 40 and 50 of the selected items are defective?

  c. What is the probability that between 34 and 48 of the selected items are defective?

  d. Without doing the calculations, state which of the following ranges of defectives has the highest probability: 38–39, 40–41, 42–43, 44–45, or 46–47.

5.46 A random sample of 100 blue-collar employees at a large corporation are surveyed to assess their attitudes toward a proposed new work schedule. If 60% of all blue-collar employees at this corporation favor the new schedule, what is the probability that fewer than 50 in the random sample will be in favor?

5.47 A hospital finds that 25% of its accounts are at least 1 month in arrears. A random sample of 450 accounts was taken.

  a. What is the probability that fewer than 100 accounts in the sample were at least 1 month in arrears?

  b. What is the probability that the number of accounts in the sample at least 1 month in arrears was between 120 and 150 (inclusive)?

5.48 The tread life of Stone Soup tires can be modeled by a normal distribution with a mean of 35,000 miles and a standard deviation of 4,000 miles. A sample of 100 of these tires is taken. What is the probability that more than 25 of them have tread lives of more than 38,000 miles?

5.49 Bags of a chemical produced by a company have impurity weights that can be represented by a normal distribution with a mean of 12.2 grams and a standard deviation of 2.8 grams. A random sample of 400 of these bags is taken. What is the probability that at least 100 of them contain fewer than 10 grams of impurities?

5.5 THE EXPONENTIAL DISTRIBUTION

We now introduce a continuous distribution, the *exponential distribution*, that has been found to be particularly useful for waiting-line, or queuing, problems. In many service-time problems the service times can be modeled using the exponential distribution. We should note that the exponential distribution differs from the normal in two important ways: It is restricted to random variables with positive values, and its distribution is not symmetric.

The Exponential Distribution

The exponential random variable $T(t > 0)$ has a probability density function

$$f(t) = \lambda e^{-\lambda t} \text{ for } t > 0 \tag{5.15}$$

where λ is the mean number of independent arrivals per time unit, t is the number of time units until the next arrival, and $e = 2.71828....$ Then T is said to follow an **exponential probability distribution**. Arrivals are independent if an arrival does not effect the probability of waiting time t until the next arrival. It can be shown that λ is the same parameter used for the Poisson distribution in Section 5.6 and that the mean time between occurrences is $1/\lambda$.

The cumulative distribution function is as follows:

$$F(t) = 1 - e^{-\lambda t} \text{ for } t > 0 \tag{5.16}$$

The distribution has a mean of $1/\lambda$ and a variance of $1/\lambda^2$.

The probability that the time between arrivals is t_a or less is as follows:

$$P\left(T \le t_a\right) = \left(1 - e^{-\lambda t_a}\right)$$

The probability that the time between arrivals is between t_b and t_a is as follows:

$$P\left(t_b \le T \le t_a\right) = \left(1 - e^{-\lambda t_a}\right) - \left(1 - e^{-\lambda t_b}\right)$$

$$= e^{-\lambda t_b} - e^{-\lambda t_a}$$

The random variable T can be used to represent the length of time until the end of a service time or until the next arrival to a queuing process, beginning at an arbitrary time 0. The model assumptions are the same as those for the Poisson distribution. Note that the Poisson distribution provides the probability of X successes or arrivals during a time unit. In contrast, the exponential distribution provides the probability that a success or arrival will occur during an interval of time t. Figure 5.26 shows the probability density function for an exponential distribution with $\lambda = 0.2$. The area to the left of 10 gives the probability that a task will be completed before time 10. This area can be obtained by evaluating the function $1 - e^{-\lambda t}$ for the given value of $t = 10$. The function can be computed by using your electronic calculator. The probability that an arrival occurs between time 10 and 20 can be computed as follows:

$$P\left(t_{10} \le T \le t_{20}\right) = \left(1 - e^{-0.2 t_{20}}\right) - \left(1 - e^{-0.2 t_{10}}\right)$$

$$= e^{-0.2 t_{10}} - e^{-0.2 t_{20}}$$

$$= 0.1353 - 0.0183$$

$$= 0.1170$$

Now let us consider an example problem to demonstrate the application of the exponential distribution.

Figure 5.26
Probability Density Function for an Exponential Distribution with $\lambda = 0.2$.

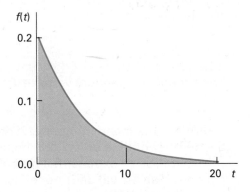

Example 5.10   Service Time at Library Information Desk (Exponential Probabilities)

Service times for customers at a library information desk can be modeled by an exponential distribution with a mean service time of 5 minutes. What is the probability that a customer service time will take longer than 10 minutes?

Solution Let t denote the service time in minutes. The service rate is $\lambda = 1/5 = 0.2$ per minute, and the probability density function is

$$f(t) = \lambda e^{-\lambda t}$$

which is shown in Figure 5.26. The required probability can be computed as follows:

$$P(T > 10) = 1 - P(T < 10)$$
$$= 1 - F(10)$$
$$= 1 - (1 - e^{-(0.20)(10)})$$
$$= e^{-2.0} = 0.1353$$

Thus, the probability that a service time exceeds 10 minutes is 0.1353.

Example 5.11 Time Between Accidents in Typical British Industrial Plants (Exponential Probabilities)

An industrial plant in Britain with 2,000 employees has a mean number of lost-time accidents per week equal to $\lambda = 0.4$, and the number of accidents follows a Poisson distribution. What is the probability that the time between accidents is less than 2 weeks?

Solution In this problem we note that the time interval is measured in weeks and our rate is $\lambda = 0.4$ per week, giving a mean time between accidents of $\mu = 1/(0.4) = 2.5$ weeks. Then the probability that the time between accidents is less than 2 weeks is as follows:

$$P(T < 2) = F(2) = 1 - e^{-(0.4)(2)}$$
$$= 1 - e^{-0.8}$$
$$= 1 - 0.4493 = 0.5507$$

Thus, the probability of less than 2 weeks between accidents is about 55%.

Example 5.12 Time Between Boat Arrivals at a Grain Shipping Dock

In Example 4.13 we showed how to compute the probability of the number of boats arriving at a grain shipping dock in Churchill Manitoba using the Poisson probability distribution. In this example we will compute the probability of a particular time interval between boat arrivals using the exponential probability distribution. In the previous problem we found that the mean number of arrivals was $\lambda = 2.5$ per 6-hour period. Now we want to compute the probability that a boat will arrive within 3 hours of the last boat arrival and also to compute the probability that a boat will arrive between 2 and 4 hours of the last arrival.

Solution To compute both of these probabilities we need to adjust the time scale to the same form as the arrival rate. The arrival rate is given as 2.5 arrivals per 6-hour period. Thus in terms of a 6-hour time unit, 3 hours is 3/6 time units,

2 hours is 2/6 time units, and 4 hours is 4/6 time units. Thus, the probability of an arrival within 3 hours is computed as follows:

$$P\left(T \le \frac{3}{6} \mid \lambda = 2.5\right) = (1 - e^{(-2.5)(0.5)})$$

$$= 0.713$$

And the probability that an arrival will occur between 2 and 4 hours is computed as follows:

$$P\left(\frac{2}{6} \le T \le \frac{4}{6}\right) = (1 - e^{(-2.5)(0.67)}) - (1 - e^{(-2.5)(0.33)})$$

$$= e^{(-2.5)(0.33)} - e^{(-2.5)(0.67)}$$

$$= 0.4382 - 0.1873$$

$$= 0.2509$$

EXERCISES

Basic Exercises

5.50 Given an arrival process with $\lambda = 1.0$, what is the probability that an arrival occurs in the first $t = 2$ time units?

5.51 Given an arrival process with $\lambda = 8.0$, what is the probability that an arrival occurs in the first $t = 7$ time units?

5.52 Given an arrival process with $\lambda = 5.0$, what is the probability that an arrival occurs after $t = 7$ time units?

5.53 Given an arrival process with $\lambda = 5.0$, what is the probability that an arrival occurs after $t = 5$ time units?

5.54 Given an arrival process with $\lambda = 3.0$, what is the probability that an arrival occurs in the first $t = 2$ time units?

Application Exercises

5.55 A professor sees students during regular office hours. Time spent with students follows an exponential distribution with a mean of 10 minutes.

  a. Find the probability that a given student spends fewer than 20 minutes with the professor.
  b. Find the probability that a given student spends more than 5 minutes with the professor.
  c. Find the probability that a given student spends between 10 and 15 minutes with the professor.

5.56 Times to gather preliminary information from arrivals at an outpatient clinic follow an exponential distribution with mean 15 minutes. Find the probability, for a randomly chosen arrival, that more than 18 minutes will be required.

5.57 It is known that for a laboratory computing system the number of system failures during a month has a Poisson distribution with a mean of 0.8. The system

has just failed. Find the probability that at least 2 months will elapse before a further failure.

5.58 Suppose that the time between successive occurrences of an event follows an exponential distribution with a mean of $1/\lambda$ minutes. Assume that an event occurs.

  a. Show that the probability that more than 3 minutes elapses before the occurrence of the next event is $e^{-3\lambda}$.
  b. Show that the probability that more than 6 minutes elapses before the occurrence of the next event is $e^{-6\lambda}$.
  c. Using the results of parts (a) and (b), show that, if 3 minutes have already elapsed, the probability that a further 3 minutes will elapse before the next occurrence is $e^{-3\lambda}$. Explain your answer in words.

5.59 Swapna David is a customer assistant consultant for Acme Information Systems, who provides assistance for computer users. The mean number of calls per hour is 40 from across the United States and calls are independent. She has just finished a call and is scheduled to take the next call. What is the probability that she will have a least 3 minutes to obtain her cup of tea?

5.60 Delivery trucks arrive independently at the Floorstore Regional distribution center with various consumer items from the company's suppliers. The mean number of trucks arriving per hour is 20. Given that a truck has just arrived answer the following:

  a. What is the probability that the next truck will not arrive for at least 5 minutes?
  b. What is the probability that the next truck will arrive within the next 2 minutes?
  c. What is the probability that the next truck will arrive between 4 and 10 minutes?

5.6 JOINTLY DISTRIBUTED CONTINUOUS RANDOM VARIABLES

In Section 4.7 we introduced jointly distributed discrete random variables. Here, we show that many of the concepts and results from discrete random variables also apply for continuous random variables. Many continuous random variables can be modeled using jointly distributed random variables. The market values of various stock prices are regularly modeled as joint random variables. Studies of the production and sales patterns for various companies and industries use jointly distributed continuous random variables. The number of units sold by a large retail store during a particular week and the price per unit can be modeled by joint random variables. Studies of import and export behavior for various countries regularly use joint random variables as part of the analysis.

After we have developed some basic concepts, we present a number of application examples to show the importance of the procedures and how to analyze jointly distributed continuous random variables.

Joint Cumulative Distribution Function
Let X_1, X_2, ..., X_k be continuous random variables.

1. Their **joint cumulative distribution function**, $F(x_1, x_2, ..., x_k)$, defines the probability that simultaneously X_1 is less than x_1, X_2 is less than x_2, and so on—that is,

$$F(x_1, x_2, ..., x_k) = P(X_1 < x_1 \cap X_2 < x_2 \cap \cdots \cap X_k < x_k) \qquad (5.17)$$

2. The cumulative distribution functions—$F(x_1)$, $F(x_2)$, ..., $F(x_k)$—of the individual random variables are called their **marginal distribution functions**. For any i, is $F(x_i)$ the probability that the random variable X_i does not exceed the specific value x_i.

3. The random variables are *independent* if and only if

$$F(x_1, x_2, ..., x_k) = F(x_1)F(x_2)\cdots F(x_k) \qquad (5.18)$$

We note that the notion of independence here is precisely the same as in the discrete case. Independence of a set of random variables implies that the probability distribution of any one of them is unaffected by the values taken by the others. Thus, for example, the assertion that consecutive daily changes in the price of a share of common stock are independent of one another implies that information about the past price changes is of no value in assessing what is likely to happen tomorrow.

The notion of expectation extends to functions of jointly distributed continuous random variables. As in the case of discrete random variables, we have the concept of *covariance*, which is used in assessing linear relationships between pairs of random variables.

Covariance
Let X and Y be a pair of continuous random variables with respective means μ_x and μ_y. The expected value of $(X - \mu_x)(Y - \mu_y)$, is called the **covariance** (Cov), between X and Y,

$$\text{Cov}(X,Y) = E[(X-\mu_X)(Y-\mu_Y)] \qquad (5.19)$$

An alternative, but equivalent, expression can be derived as

$$\text{Cov}(X, Y) = E(XY) - \mu_X \mu_Y \tag{5.20}$$

If the random variables X and Y are independent, then the covariance between them is 0. However, the converse is not necessarily true.

In Section 4.7 we also presented the *correlation* as a standardized measure of the relationship between two discrete random variables. The same results hold for continuous random variables.

Correlation

Let X and Y be jointly distributed random variables. The **correlation** (Corr) between X and Y is as follows:

$$\rho = \text{Corr}(X,Y) = \frac{\text{Cov}(X,Y)}{\sigma_X \sigma_Y} \tag{5.21}$$

In Section 5.7 we presented the means and variances for sums and differences of discrete random variables. The same results apply for continuous random variables because the results are established using expectations and, thus, are not affected by the condition of discrete or continuous random variables.

Sums of Random Variables

Let $X_1, X_2, ..., X_K$ be K random variables with means $\mu_1, \mu_2, ..., \mu_K$ and variances $\sigma_1^2, \sigma_2^2, ..., \sigma_K^2$. Consider the following properties:

1. The mean of their sum is the sum of their means—that is,

$$E(X_1 + X_2 + \cdots + X_K) = \mu_1 + \mu_2 + \cdots + \mu_K \tag{5.22}$$

2. If the covariance between every pair of these random variables is 0, then the variance of their sum is the sum of their variances—that is,

$$\text{Var}(X_1 + X_2 + \cdots X_K) = \sigma_1^2 + \sigma_2^2 + \cdots + \sigma_K^2 \tag{5.23}$$

However, if the covariances between pairs of random variables are not 0, the variance of their sum is as follows:

$$\text{Var}(X_1 + X_2 + \cdots + X_K) = \sigma_1^2 + \sigma_2^2 + \cdots + \sigma_K^2 + 2\sum_{i=1}^{K-1} \sum_{j=i+1}^{K} \text{Cov}(X_i, X_j) \tag{5.24}$$

Differences Between a Pair of Random Variables

Let X and Y be a pair of random variables with means μ_X and μ_Y and variances σ_x^2 and σ_y^2. Consider the following properties:

1. The mean of their difference is the difference of their means—that is,

$$E(X-Y) = \mu_X - \mu_Y \tag{5.25}$$

2. If the covariance between X and Y is 0, then the variance of their difference is as follows:

$$\text{Var}(X-Y) = \sigma_X^2 + \sigma_Y^2 \qquad (5.26)$$

3. If the covariance between X and Y is not 0, then the variance of their difference is as follows:

$$\text{Var}(X-Y) = \sigma_X^2 + \sigma_Y^2, 2\,\text{Cov}(X-Y) \qquad (5.27)$$

Example 5.13 Total Project Costs (Mean and Standard Deviation)

A contractor is uncertain of the precise total costs for either materials or labor for a project. In addition, the total line of credit for financing the project is $260,000, and the contractor wants to know the probability that total costs exceed $260,000. It is believed that material costs can be represented by a normally distributed random variable with mean $100,000 and standard deviation $10,000. Labor costs are $1,500 a day, and the number of days needed to complete the project can be represented by a normally distributed random variable with mean 80 and standard deviation 12. Assuming that material and labor costs are independent, what are the mean and standard deviation of the total project cost (materials plus labor)? In addition, what is the probability that the total project cost is greater than $260,000?

Solution   Let the random variables X_1 and X_2 denote, respectively, materials and labor costs. Then X_1 has mean $\mu_1 = 100{,}000$ and standard deviation $\sigma_1 = 10{,}000$. For the random variable X_2

$$\mu_2 = (1{,}500)(80) = 120{,}000 \quad \text{and} \quad \sigma_2 = (1{,}500)(12) = 18{,}000$$

The total project cost is $W = X_1 + X_2$, and we have mean cost

$$\mu_W = \mu_1 + \mu_2 = 100{,}000 + 120{,}000 = \$220{,}000$$

and since X_1 and X_2 are independent, the variance of their sum is as follows:

$$\sigma_W^2 = \sigma_1^2 + \sigma_2^2 = (10{,}000)^2 + (18{,}000)^2 = 424{,}000{,}000$$

Taking the square root, we find that the standard deviation is $20,591.

Since X_1 and X_2 are normally distributed, it can be shown that their sum, W, is also normally distributed. The probability that W is greater than $260,000 can be determined by computing a standard normal random variable Z, using the mean and variance of W as follows:

$$Z = \frac{(260{,}000 - 220{,}000)}{20{,}591} = 1.94$$

Using the cumulative normal probability table, we find that the probability that the total cost exceeds $260,000 is 0.0262. Since this probability is small, the contractor has some confidence that the project can be completed within the available line of credit.

Example 5.14 Investment Portfolio Risk (Linear Function Mean and Variance)

Henry Chang has asked for your assistance in establishing a portfolio containing two stocks. Henry has $1,000, which can be allocated in any proportion to two alternative stocks. The returns per dollar from these investments will be designated as random variables X and Y. Both of these random variables are independent and have the same mean and variance. Henry wishes to know the risk for various allocation options. You point out that risk is directly related to variance and, thus, that his question would be answered if he knew the variance of various allocation options.

Solution The amount of money allocated to the first investment will be designated as α, and, hence, the remaining $1,000 - \alpha$ will be allocated to the second investment. The total return on the investment is as follows:

$$R = \alpha X + (1,000 - \alpha)Y$$

This random variable has the expected value

$$E(R) = \alpha E(X) + (1,000 - \alpha)E(Y) = \alpha \mu + (1,000 - \alpha)\mu = \$1,000\mu$$

Thus, we see that the expected return is the same for any allocation.
    However, the risk or variance is a different story.

$$\begin{aligned}
\text{Var}(R) &= \alpha^2 \text{Var}(X) + (1,000 - \alpha)^2 \text{Var}(Y) \\
&= \alpha^2 \sigma^2 + (1,000 - \alpha)^2 \sigma^2 \\
&= (2\alpha^2 - 2,000\,\alpha + 1,000,000)\sigma^2
\end{aligned}$$

If α is equal to either 0 or 1,000, so that the entire portfolio is allocated to just one of the stocks, the variance of the total return is $1,000,000\,\sigma^2$. However, if $500 is allocated to each investment, the variance of the total return is $500,000\,\sigma^2$, which is the smallest possible variance. By spreading his investment over two stocks, Henry is able to mitigate the effect of either high or low returns from one of the shares. Thus, it is possible to obtain the same expected return with a variety of risk levels.

Linear Combinations of Random Variables

In Chapter 4 we developed the mean and variance for linear combinations of discrete random variables. These results also apply for continuous random variables because their development is based on operations with expected values and does not depend on the particular probability distributions. Equations 5.28 through 5.31 indicate the important properties of linear combinations.

Linear Combinations of Random Variables
The linear combination of two random variables, X and Y, is

$$W = aX + bY \tag{5.28}$$

where a and b are constant numbers.

The mean value for W is

$$\mu_W = E[W] = E[aX + bY] = a\mu_X + b\mu_Y \qquad (5.29)$$

The variance for W is

$$\sigma_W^2 = a^2\sigma_X^2 + b^2\sigma_Y^2 + 2ab\,\text{Cov}\,(X,Y) \qquad (5.30)$$

or, using the correlation,

$$\sigma_W^2 = a^2\sigma_X^2 + b^2\sigma_Y^2 + 2ab\,\text{Corr}(X,Y)\sigma_X\sigma_Y \qquad (5.31)$$

If the linear combination in Equation 5.28 is a difference. That is, if

$$W = aX - bY \qquad (5.32)$$

then the mean and the variance are

$$\mu_W = E[W] = E[aX - bY] = a\mu_X - b\mu_Y \qquad (5.33)$$

$$\sigma_W^2 = a^2\sigma_X^2 - b^2\sigma_Y^2 - 2ab\,\text{Cov}\,(X,Y) \qquad (5.34)$$

or using the correlation

$$\sigma_W^2 = a^2\sigma_X^2 - b^2\sigma_Y^2 - 2ab\,\text{Corr}(X,Y)\sigma_X\sigma_Y \qquad (5.35)$$

These results come directly from Equations 5.28 through 5.31 by merely substituting a negative value for the coefficient b in the equations.

If both X and Y are joint normally distributed random variables, then the resulting random variable, W, is also normally distributed with mean and variance derived as shown. This result enables us to determine the probability that the linear combination, W, is within a specific interval.

Financial Investment Portfolios

Example 5.15 Portfolio Analysis (Probability of a Portfolio)

Judy Chang, the account manager for Northern Securities, has a portfolio that includes 20 shares of Allied Information Systems and 30 shares of Bangalore Analytics. Both firms provide Web access devices that compete in the consumer market. The price of Allied stock is normally distributed with mean $\mu_X = 25$ and variance $\sigma_X^2 = 81$. The price of Bangalore stock is also normally distributed with the mean $\mu_Y = 40$ and the variance $\sigma_Y^2 = 121$. The stock prices have a negative correlation, $\rho_{XY} = -0.40$. Judy has asked you to determine the probability that the portfolio value exceeds 2,000.

Solution   The value of Judy's portfolio, W, is defined by the linear combination

$$W = 20X + 30Y$$

and W is normally distributed. The mean value for her stock portfolio is as follows:

$$\mu_W = 20\mu_X + 30\mu_Y$$
$$= 20 \times 25 + 30 \times 40 = 1,700$$

The variance for the portfolio value is

$$\sigma_W^2 = 20^2 \sigma_X^2 + 30^2 \sigma_Y^2 + 2 \times 20 \times 30 \, \text{Corr}(X,Y)\sigma_X\sigma_Y$$

$$= 20^2 \times 81 + 30^2 \times 121 + 2 \times 20 \times 30 \times (-0.40) \times 9 \times 11 = 93{,}780$$

and the standard deviation of the portfolio value is

$$\sigma_W = 306.24$$

The standard normal Z for 2,000 is as follows:

$$Z_W = \frac{2{,}000 - 1{,}700}{306.24} = 0.980$$

And the probability that the portfolio value exceeds 2,000 is 0.1635. From the symmetry of the normal distribution, it follows that the probability that the portfolio value is less than 1,400 is also 0.1635.

If the two stock prices had a positive correlation, $\rho = +0.40$, the mean would be the same, but the variance and standard deviation would be as follows:

$$\sigma_W^2 = 20^2 \sigma_X^2 + 30^2 \sigma_Y^2 + 2 \times 20 \times 30 \, \text{Corr}(X,Y)\sigma_X\sigma_Y$$

$$= 20^2 \times 81 + 30^2 \times 121 + 2 \times 20 \times 30 \times (+0.40) \times 9 \times 11 = 188{,}820$$

$$\sigma_W = 434.53$$

The standard normal Z for 2,000 is as follows:

$$Z_W = \frac{2{,}000 - 1{,}700}{434.53} = 0.690$$

The probability that her portfolio value exceeds 2,000 is 0.2451, and the probability that it is less than 1,400 is also 0.2451.

Thus, we see that a positive correlation between stock prices leads to a higher variance and higher risk. The risk in this example increases the probability that the portfolio exceeds 2,000, from 0.1635 to 0.2451. This also implies a similar change in the probability that the portfolio value is less than 1,400. The higher risk implies that there is a higher probability that the portfolio has higher or lower values compared to the lower risk option.

The previous example illustrates a very important fundamental principle in the design of investment portfolios. Recall that the risk of an investment is directly related to the variance of the investment value. In the previous example it was shown that, if the values of the two stock prices are positively correlated, then the resulting portfolio will have a larger variance and hence a higher risk. And if the two stock prices are negatively correlated, then the resulting portfolio will have a smaller variance and hence a lower risk. The term *hedging* is often used by fund managers to describe this phenomenon. This important principle for a two-stock portfolio extends directly to a portfolio with a large number of different stocks, but in that case the algebra is more complex and is typically computed using a sophisticated computer program.

The use of linear combinations of random variables also applies directly to the estimation of portfolio return given the returns on individual stocks.

$$
\begin{pmatrix} Return \\ on \\ Portfolio \end{pmatrix} = \begin{pmatrix} Proportion \\ of\ Portfolio \\ Value \\ Stock\ 1 \end{pmatrix} \times \begin{pmatrix} Stock\ 1 \\ Return \end{pmatrix} + \begin{pmatrix} Proportion \\ of\ Portfolio \\ Value \\ Stock\ 2 \end{pmatrix} \times \begin{pmatrix} Stock\ 2 \\ Return \end{pmatrix} +
$$

$$
\cdots + \begin{pmatrix} Proportion \\ of\ Portfolio \\ Value \\ Stock\ N \end{pmatrix} \times \begin{pmatrix} Stock\ N \\ Return \end{pmatrix}
$$

Investment fund managers use this principle to select combinations of many different stocks in order to obtain the desired portfolio return with the risk characteristics that are the objectives for a particular investment fund. Example 5.16 will develop the computations for determining portfolio return and risk.

Example 5.16 General Portfolio Analysis

In actual practice portfolios such as mutual funds there may be 100 to 300 or more different stocks. This leads to extensive computations that could not be reasonably done without powerful computers and large databases. In this discussion we will indicate how the computations can be made and illustrate this with a reduced example. A large portfolio can be modeled with the *"return on stock price"* for each of k stock prices represented as k random variables, X_i, with means, μ_i, with variances, σ_i^2, and with covariances between stock prices, $Cov\ (X_i, Y_t)$. The dollar value proportion of the portfolio for each stock is a_i. The total value of the portfolio can be expressed as follows:

$$
W = \sum_{i=1}^{k} a_i X_i
$$

The mean value for W is as follows:

$$
\mu_W = E[W] = E[\sum_{i=1}^{k} a_i X_i]
$$

$$
= \sum_{i=1}^{k} a_i \mu_i \tag{5.36}
$$

The variance for W is as follows:

$$
\sigma_w^2 = \sum_{i=1}^{k} a_i^2 \sigma_i^2 + 2 \sum_{i=1}^{k-1} \sum_{j=i+1}^{k} a_i a_j\ Cov(X_i, X_j) \tag{5.37}
$$

These equations can be used to develop computer-based computations that can be used with a large data base of stock prices or other measures of performance.

Example 5.17 Returns on Financial Portfolios

Susan Chang, Fund Manager at Northlake Financial Growth has asked you to analyze a portfolio consisting of **Infosys Technologies, Alcoa Inc., and Pearson PLC** as part of a larger project to develop a new growth fund. In particular she wishes to know the monthly growth rate and the variance of this growth.

Solution   You decide to use the monthly *"return on stock price"* percent growth over the 5-year period from May 2003 through April 2008. The stock price data was obtained from Stock Investor Professional. The *"return on stock price"* was computed by dividing the change in month-end closing by the most recent month-end closing. Figure 5.27 contains the mean, variance, and covariance of the return on stock price for three firms, **Infosys Technologies, Alcoa Inc., Pearson Plc** for the 60 months from May 2003 through April 2008. Return on stock price is expressed as a proportion change for one month. This data is contained in the file **"Return on Stock Price 60 month."** After a discussion with Susan you decide to consider a portfolio whose dollar value includes 40% of Infosys, 30% of Alcoa, and 30% of Pearson. The mean value is computed using Equation 5.36 as follows:

$$\mu_W = E[W] = (0.40)(0.0196)+(0.30)(0.00439)+(0.30)(0.00621)$$
$$= 0.01102$$

Note that this portfolio mean is 1.101% per month or 13.2% growth per year. The variance is computed using Equation 5.37 as follows:

$$\sigma_W^2 = \left(0.40^2\right)(0.0086) + \left(0.30^2\right)(0.00506) + \left(0.30^2\right)(0.00217)$$
$$+ 2[(0.40)(0.30)(0.00168845) + (0.40)(0.30)(0.00086330) + (0.30)(0.30)(0.00150291)]$$
$$= 0.00291$$

The standard deviation for the portfolio value is as follows:

$$\sigma_W = 0.05394$$

These computations can also be made by computing the value of the portfolio each month and then computing the mean and variance of the monthly portfolio values. The results are of course the same as shown for the variable, portfolio 1, in Figure 5.27. We have also included the mean and variance for the Standard and Poors (S & P) index for the same time period for perspective. Note that the mean growth ratio is higher for portfolio 1 compared to the S & P.

Assuming that stock price growth is normally distributed we can also compute the probabilities that the total value of the portfolio is above or below particular values. For example the probability that the portfolio value is above 0.10 for one month can be determined by computing the standard normal Z:

$$Z = \frac{(0.10 - 0.01101)}{0.0539} = 1.651$$

And the probability that the portfolio exceeds 0.10 is 0.049. We can also compute the probability that the portfolio value is less than 0.0 by first computing the standard normal Z:

$$Z = \frac{(0.0 - 0.01101)}{0.0539} = -0.204$$

And the probability that the portfolio value is less than 0.0 is 0.081.

Figure 5.27 Portfolio Statistics for Example 5.17 (Minitab Output)

Descriptive Statistics: Infosys Tech, Alcoa Inc., Pearson PLC (ADR)

Variable	N	Mean	StDev	Variance	Min	Median	Max
Infosys Tech	60	0.0196	0.0926	0.0086	−0.2456	0.0254	0.1945
Alcoa Inc.	60	0.00439	0.07113	0.00506	−0.12813	0.01134	0.17137
Pearson PLC	60	0.00621	0.04655	0.00217	−0.09474	0.00391	0.10108

Covariances: Infosys Tech, Alcoa Inc., Pearson DLC (ADR)

	Infosys Tech	Alcoa Inc.	Pearson PLC
Infosys Tech	0.00857204		
Alcoa Inc.	0.00168845	0.00505950	
Pearson PLC	0.00086330	0.00150291	0.00216704

Descriptive Statistics: Portfolio 1

Variable	N	Mean	StDev	Variance	Min	Median	Max
Portfolio 1	60	0.01101	0.05390	0.00290	−0.13783	0.01950	0.15579

Descriptive Statistics: S & P 500

Variable	N	Mean	StDev	Variance	Min	Median	Max
SP 500	60	0.00655	0.02512	0.00063	−0.06515	0.01157	0.05210

EXERCISES

Basic Exercises

5.61 A random variable X is normally distributed with a mean of 100 and a variance of 100, and a random variable Y is normally distributed with a mean of 200 and a variance of 400. The random variables have a correlation coefficient equal to 0.5. Find the mean and variance of the random variable:

$$W = 5X + 4Y$$

5.62 A random variable X is normally distributed with a mean of 100 and a variance of 100, and a random variable Y is normally distributed with a mean of 200 and a variance of 400. The random variables have a correlation coefficient equal to −0.5. Find the mean and variance of the random variable:

$$W = 5X + 4Y$$

5.63 A random variable X is normally distributed with a mean of 100 and a variance of 100, and a random variable Y is normally distributed with a mean of 200 and a variance of 400. The random variables have a correlation coefficient equal to 0.5. Find the mean and variance of the random variable:

$$W = 5X - 4Y$$

5.64 A random variable X is normally distributed with a mean of 500 and a variance of 100, and a random variable Y is normally distributed with a mean of 200 and a variance of 400. The random variables have a correlation coefficient equal to 0.5. Find the mean and variance of the random variable:

$$W = 5X - 4Y$$

5.65 A random variable X is normally distributed with a mean of 100 and a variance of 500, and a random variable Y is normally distributed with a mean of 200 and a variance of 400. The random variables have a correlation coefficient equal to −0.5. Find the mean and variance of the random variable:

$$W = 5X - 4Y$$

Application Exercises

5.66 An investor plans to divide $200,000 between two investments. The first yields a certain profit of 10%, while the second yields a profit with expected value 18% and standard deviation 6%. If the investor divides the money equally between these two investments, find the mean and standard deviation of the total profit.

5.67 A homeowner has installed a new energy-efficient furnace. It is estimated that over a year the new furnace will reduce energy costs by an amount that can be regarded as a random variable with a mean of

$200 and a standard deviation of $60. Stating any assumptions you need to make, find the mean and standard deviation of the total energy cost reductions over a period of 5 years.

5.68 A consultant is beginning work on three projects. The expected profits from these projects are $50,000, $72,000, and $40,000. The associated standard deviations are $10,000, $12,000, and $9,000. Assuming independence of outcomes, find the mean and standard deviation of the consultant's total profit from these three projects.

5.69 A consultant has three sources of income—from teaching short courses, from selling computer software, and from advising on projects. His expected annual incomes from these sources are $20,000, $25,000, and $15,000, and the respective standard deviations are $2,000, $5,000, and $4,000. Assuming independence, find the mean and standard deviation of his total annual income.

5.70 Five inspectors are employed to check the quality of components produced on an assembly line. For each inspector the number of components that can be checked in a shift can be represented by a random variable with mean 120 and standard deviation 15. Let X represent the number of components checked by an inspector in a shift. Then the total number checked is $5X$, which has a mean of 600 and a standard deviation of 80. What is wrong with this argument? Assuming that inspectors' performances are independent of one another, find the mean and standard deviation of the total number of components checked in a shift.

5.71 It is estimated that in normal highway driving the number of miles that can be covered by automobiles of a particular model on 1 gallon of gasoline can be represented by a random variable with mean 28 and standard deviation 2.4. Sixteen of these cars, each with 1 gallon of gasoline, are driven independently under highway conditions. Find the mean and standard deviation of the average number of miles that will be achieved by these cars.

5.72 Shirley Johnson, portfolio manager, has asked you to analyze a newly acquired portfolio to determine its mean value and variability. The portfolio consists of 50 shares of Xylophone Music and 40 shares of Yankee Workshop. Analysis of past history indicates that the share price of Xylophone Music has a mean of 25 and a variance of 121. A similar analysis indicates that Yankee has a mean share price of 40 with a variance of 225. Your best evidence indicates that the share prices have a correlation of +0.5.

a. Compute the mean and variance of the portfolio.
b. Suppose that the correlation between share prices was actually –0.5. Now what are the mean and variance of the portfolio?

5.73 Prairie Flower Cereal has an annual sales revenue of $400,000,000. George Severn, a 58-year-old senior vice president, is responsible for production and sales of Nougy 93 Fruity cereal. Daily production in cases is normally distributed with a mean of 100 and a variance of 625. Daily sales in cases are also normally distributed with a mean of 100 and a standard deviation of 8. Sales and production have a correlation of 0.60. The selling price per case is $10. The variable production cost per case is $7. The fixed production costs per day are $250.

a. What is the probability that total revenue is greater than total costs on any day?
b. Construct a 95% acceptance interval for total sales revenue minus total costs.

5.74 The nation of Olecarl, located in the South Pacific, has asked you to analyze international trade patterns. You first discover that each year it exports 10 units and imports 10 units of wonderful stuff. The price of exports is a random variable with a mean of 100 and a variance of 100. The price of imports is a random variable with a mean of 90 and a variance of 400. In addition, you discover that the prices of imports and exports have a correlation of $\rho = -0.40$. The prices of both exports and imports follow a normal probability density function. Define the balance of trade as the difference between the total revenue from exports and the total cost of imports.

a. What are the mean and variance of the balance of trade?
b. What is the probability that the balance of trade is negative?

5.75 You have been asked to determine the probability that the contribution margin for a particular product line exceeds the fixed cost of $2,000. The total number of units sold is a normally distributed random variable with a mean of 400 and a variance of 900 $X \sim N(400, 900)$. The selling price per unit is $10. The total number of units produced is a normally distributed random variable with a mean of 400 and a variance of 1,600 $Y \sim N(400, 1,600)$. The variable production cost is $4 per unit. Production and sales have a positive correlation of 0.50.

5.76 The nation of Waipo has recently created an economic development plan that includes expanded exports and imports. It has completed a series of extensive studies of the world economy and Waipo's economic capability, following Waipo's extensive 10-year educational enhancement program. The resulting model indicates that in the next year exports will be normally distributed with a mean of 100 and a variance of 900 (in billions of Waipo yuan). In addition, imports are expected to be normally distributed with a mean of 105 and a variance of 625 in the same units. The correlation between exports and imports is expected to be +0.70. Define the trade balance as exports minus imports.

a. Determine the mean and variance of the trade balance (exports minus imports) if the model parameters given above are true.
b. What is the probability that the trade balance will be positive?

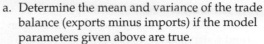

KEY WORDS

CHAPTER EXERCISES AND APPLICATIONS

5.77 A consultant knows that it will cost him $10,000 to fulfill a particular contract. The contract is to be put out for bids, and he believes that the lowest bid, excluding his own, can be represented by a distribution that is uniform between $8,000 and $20,000. Therefore, if the random variable X denotes the lowest of all other bids (in thousands of dollars), its probability density function is as follows:

$$f(x) = \begin{cases} 1/12 & \text{for } 8 < x < 20 \\ 0 & \text{for all other values of } x \end{cases}$$

a. What is the probability that the lowest of the other bids will be less than the consultant's cost estimate of $10,000?
b. If the consultant submits a bid of $12,000, what is the probability that he will secure the contract?
c. The consultant decides to submit a bid of $12,000. What is his expected profit from this strategy?
d. If the consultant wants to submit a bid so that his expected profit is as high as possible, discuss how he should go about making this choice.

5.78 The ages of a group of executives attending a convention are uniformly distributed between 35 and 65 years. If the random variable X denotes ages in years, the probability density function is as follows:

$$f(x) = \begin{cases} 1/30 & \text{for } 35 < x < 65 \\ 0 & \text{for all other values of } x \end{cases}$$

a. Draw the probability density function for X.
b. Find and draw the cumulative distribution function for X.
c. Find the probability that the age of a randomly chosen executive in this group is between 40 and 50 years.
d. Find the mean age of the executives in the group.

5.79 The random variable X has probability density function as follows:

$$f(x) = \begin{cases} x & \text{for } 0 < x < 1 \\ 2-x & \text{for } 1 < x < 2 \\ 0 & \text{for all other values of } x \end{cases}$$

a. Draw the probability density function for X.
b. Show that the density has the properties of a proper probability density function.
c. Find the probability that X takes a value between 0.5 and 1.5.

5.80 An investor puts $2,000 into a deposit account with a fixed rate of return of 10% per year. A second sum of $1,000 is invested in a fund with an expected rate of return of 16% and a standard deviation of 8% per year.

a. Find the expected value of the total amount of money this investor will have after a year.
b. Find the standard deviation of the total amount after a year.

5.81 A hamburger stand sells burgers for \$1.45 each. Daily sales have a distribution with a mean of 530 and a standard deviation of 69.

a. Find the mean daily total revenues from the sale of hamburgers.
b. Find the standard deviation of total revenues from the sale of hamburgers.
c. Daily costs (in dollars) are given by

$$C = 100 + 0.95X$$

where X is the number of hamburgers sold. Find the mean and standard deviation of daily profits from sales.

5.82 An analyst forecasts corporate earnings, and his record is evaluated by comparing actual earnings with predicted earnings. Define the following:

Actual Earnings = Predicted Earnings +

Forecast Error

If the predicted earnings and forecast error are independent of each other, show that the variance of predicted earnings is less than the variance of actual earnings.

5.83 Let X_1 and X_2 be a pair of random variables. Show that the covariance between the random variables $(X_1 + X_2)$ and $(X_1 - X_2)$ is 0 if and only if X_1 and X_2 have the same variance.

5.84 Grade point averages of students on a large campus follow a normal distribution with a mean of 2.6 and a standard deviation of 0.5.

a. One student is chosen at random from this campus. What is the probability that this student has a grade point average higher than 3.0?
b. One student is chosen at random from this campus. What is the probability that this student has a grade point average between 2.25 and 2.75?
c. What is the minimum grade point average needed for a student's grade point average to be among the highest 10% on this campus?
d. A random sample of 400 students is chosen from this campus. What is the probability that at least 80 of these students have grade point averages higher than 3.0?
e. Two students are chosen at random from this campus. What is the probability that at least one of them has a grade point average higher than 3.0?

5.85 A company services home air conditioners. It is known that times for service calls follow a normal distribution with a mean of 60 minutes and a standard deviation of 10 minutes.

a. What is the probability that a single service call takes more than 65 minutes?
b. What is the probability that a single service call takes between 50 and 70 minutes?

c. The probability is 0.025 that a single service call takes more than how many minutes?
d. Find the shortest range of times that includes 50% of all service calls.
e. A random sample of four service calls is taken. What is the probability that exactly two of them take more than 65 minutes?

5.86 It has been found that times taken by people to complete a particular tax form follow a normal distribution with a mean of 100 minutes and a standard deviation of 30 minutes.

a. What is the probability that a randomly chosen person takes less than 85 minutes to complete this form?
b. What is the probability that a randomly chosen person takes between 70 and 130 minutes to complete this form?
c. Five percent of all people take more than how many minutes to complete this form?
d. Two people are chosen at random. What is the probability that at least one of them takes more than an hour to complete this form?
e. Four people are chosen at random. What is the probability that exactly two of them take longer than an hour to complete this form?
f. For a randomly chosen person, state in which of the following ranges (expressed in minutes) the time to complete the form is most likely to lie. 70−89, 90−109, 100−129, 130−149
g. For a randomly chosen person, state in which of the following ranges (expressed in minutes) the time to complete the form is least likely to lie. 70−89, 90−109, 110−129, 130−149

5.87 A pizza delivery service delivers to a campus dormitory. Delivery times follow a normal distribution with a mean of 20 minutes and a standard deviation of 4 minutes.

a. What is the probability that a delivery will take between 15 and 25 minutes?
b. The service does not charge for the pizza if delivery takes more than 30 minutes. What is the probability of getting a free pizza from a single order?
c. During final exams, a student plans to order pizza five consecutive evenings. Assume that these delivery times are independent of each other. What is the probability that the student will get at least one free pizza?
d. Find the shortest range of times that includes 40% of all deliveries from this service.
e. For a single delivery, state in which of the following ranges (expressed in minutes) the delivery time is most likely to lie. 18−20, 19−21, 20−22, 21−23

f. For a single delivery, state in which of the following ranges (expressed in minutes) the delivery time is least likely to lie.
18−20, 19−21, 20−22, 21−23

5.88 A video rental chain estimates that annual expenditures of members on rentals follow a normal distribution with a mean of $100. It was also found that 10% of all members spend more than $130 in a year. What percentage of members spend more than $140 in a year?

5.89 It is estimated that amounts of money spent on gasoline by customers at a gas station follow a normal distribution with a standard deviation of $2.50. It is also found that 10% of all customers spent more than $25. What percentage of customers spent less than $20?

5.90 A market research organization has found that 40% of all supermarket shoppers refuse to cooperate when questioned by its pollsters. If 1,000 shoppers are approached, what is the probability that fewer than 500 will refuse to cooperate?

5.91 An organization that gives regular seminars on sales motivation methods determines that 60% of its clients have attended previous seminars. From a sample of 400 clients what is the probability that more than half have attended previous seminars?

5.92 An ambulance service receives an average of 15 calls per day during the time period 6 p.m. to 6 a.m. for assistance. For any given day what is the probability that fewer than 10 calls will be received during the 12-hour period? What is the probability that more than 17 calls during the 12-hour period will be received?

5.93 In a large department store a customer complaints office handles an average of six complaints per hour about the quality of service. The distribution is Poisson.

a. What is the probability that in any hour exactly six complaints will be received?
b. What is the probability that more than 20 minutes will elapse between successive complaints?
c. What is the probability that fewer than 5 minutes will elapse between successive complaints?
d. The store manager observes the complaints office for a 30-minute period, during which no complaints are received. He concludes that a talk he gave to his staff on the theme "The Customer Is Always Right" has obviously had a beneficial effect. Suppose that, in fact, the talk had no effect. What is the probability of the manager observing the office for a period of 30 minutes or longer with no complaints?

5.94 A Chicago radio station believes that 40% of its listeners are younger than 25 years of age. Six hundred listeners are chosen at random.

a. If the station's belief is correct, what is the probability that more than 260 of these listeners are younger than 25?
b. If the station's belief is correct, the probability is 0.6 that more than how many of these 600 listeners are younger than 25?

5.95 It is estimated that major league baseball games' times-to-completion follow a normal distribution with a mean of 132 minutes and a standard deviation of 12 minutes.

a. What proportion of all games last between 120 minutes and 150 minutes?
b. Thirty-three percent of all games last longer than how many minutes?
c. What proportion of games last less than 120 minutes?
d. If 100 games are chosen at random, what is the probability that at least 25 of these games last less than 120 minutes?

5.96 A management consultant found that the amount of time per day spent by executives performing tasks that could be done equally well by subordinates followed a normal distribution with a mean of 2.4 hours. It was also found that 10% of executives spent over 3.5 hours per day on tasks of this type. For a random sample of 400 executives find the probability that more than 80 spend more than 3 hours per day on tasks of this type.

5.97 Financial Managers Inc. buys and sells a large number of stocks routinely for the various accounts that it manages. Portfolio manager Andrea Colson has asked for your assistance in the analysis of the Johnson Fund. A portion of this portfolio consists of 10 shares of stock A and 8 shares of stock B. The price of A has a mean of 10 and a variance of 16, while the price of B has a mean of 12 and a variance of 9. The correlation between prices is 0.3.

a. What are the mean and variance of the portfolio value?
b. Andrea has been asked to reduce the variance (risk) of the portfolio. She offers to trade the 10 shares of stock A and receives two offers from which she can select one: 10 shares of stock 1 with a mean price of 10, a variance of 25, and a correlation with the price of stock B equal to −0.2; or 10 shares of stock 2 with a mean price of 10, a variance of 9, and a correlation with the price of stock B equal to +0.5. Which offer should she select?

5.98 Financial Managers Inc. buys and sells a large number of stocks routinely for the various accounts that it manages. Portfolio manager Sarah Bloom has asked for your assistance in the analysis of the Burde Fund. A portion of this portfolio consists of

10 shares of stock A and 8 shares of stock B. The price of A has a mean of 12 and a variance of 14, while the price of B has a mean of 10 and a variance of 12. The correlation between prices is 0.5.

a. What are the mean and variance of the portfolio value?

b. Sarah has been asked to reduce the variance (risk) of the portfolio. She offers to trade the 10 shares of stock A and receives two offers from which she can select one: 10 shares of stock 1 with a mean price of 12, a variance of 25, and a correlation with the price of stock B equal to −0.2; or 10 shares of stock 2 with a mean price of 10, a variance of 9, and a correlation with the price of stock B, equal to +0.5. Which offer should she select?

5.99 Big Nail Construction Inc. is building a large new student center for a famous midwestern liberal arts college. During the project Christine Buildumbig, the project manager, requests that a pile of sand weighing between 138,000 pounds and 141,000 pounds be placed on the newly constructed driveway. You have been asked to determine the probability that the delivered sand satisfies Christine's request. You have ordered that one big truck and one small truck be used to deliver the sand. Sand loads in the big truck are normally distributed with a mean of 80,000 and a variance of 1,000,000, and sand loads in the small truck are also normally distributed with a mean weight of 60,000 pounds and a variance of 810,000. From past experience with the sand-loading facility, you know that the weight of sand in the two trucks has a correlation of 0.40. What is the probability that the resulting pile of sand has a weight that is between 138,000 and 141,000 pounds?

5.100 Flybynite Airlines has a regularly scheduled flight from Minneapolis to Frankfurt every weekday evening at 6:30. Based on a complex relationship between Flybynite and Bigrain Airlines, a local line that flys to a number of small towns, 100 seats are reserved for passengers from two of Bigrain's flights that arrive at 5:00 p.m. each weekday. The number of passengers on the flight from Tri-mountain, Montana, has a normal distribution with a mean of 40 passengers and a variance of 100. The number of passengers on the other flight, from Bighog, Iowa, is also normally distributed with a mean of 35 passengers and a variance of 144. The numbers of passengers on these two flights have a correlation of 0.5.

a. What is the probability that all 100 seats on the Frankfurt flight will be filled?

b. What is the probability that between 75 and 90 seats will be filled?

5.101 Shirley Johnson is developing a new mutual fund portfolio and in the process has asked you to develop the mean and variance for the stock price that consists of 10 shares of stocks from each of the following firms: Alcoa Inc., Reliant Energy, and Sea Container. Using the data file **Stock Price File Edition 7** compute the mean and variance for this portfolio. Prepare the analysis by using means, variances, and covariances for individual stocks following the methods used in Example 5.16 and then confirm your results by obtaining the portfolio price for each year using the computer. Assuming that the portfolio price is normally distributed determine the narrowest interval that contains 95% of the distribution of portfolio value.

5.102 Zafer Toprak is a developing a new mutual fund portfolio and in the process has asked you to develop the mean and variance for the stock price that consists of 10 shares of stocks from Alcoa Inc., 20 shares from AB Volvo, 10 shares from TCF Financial, and 20 shares from Pentair Inc. Using the data file **Stock Price File Edition 7** compute the mean and variance for this portfolio. Prepare the analysis by using means, variances, and covariances for individual stocks following the methods used in Example 5.16, and then confirm your results by obtaining the portfolio price for each year using the computer. Assuming that the portfolio price is normally distributed determine the narrowest interval that contains 95% of the distribution of portfolio value.

5.103 Charles Thorson has asked you to determine the mean and variance for a portfolio that consists of 100 shares of stock from each of the following firms: 3M Company, Alcoa Inc., Intel Corporation, Potlatch Corp., General Motors, and Sea Containers. Using the data file **Stock Price File Edition 7** compute the mean and variance for this portfolio. Assuming that the portfolio price is normally distributed determine the narrowest interval that contains 95% of the distribution of portfolio value.

5.104 You have been asked to evaluate the monthly stock price growth for a portfolio which contains the following firms: 3M Company, Alcoa Inc., Intel Corporation, Potlatch Corp., General Motors, and Sea Containers. The fraction of the portfolio dollar value for each firm will be the same. Data for this problem is contained in the data file **Return on Stock Price 60 month**. Compute the mean and variance for the stock price growth and the covariance between them. Then determine the mean and variance for the entire portfolio.

5.105 Deep Water Financial of Duluth, MN has asked you to evaluate the stock price growth for a portfolio containing the following firms: General Motors,

International Business Machines, Potlatch Inc., Sea Containers Ltd., and Tata Communications. Compute the means, variances, and covariances for the stocks. Then compute the mean and variance for a portfolio that represents the five stocks equally. Second modify the portfolio by removing Potlatch and Sea Containers and including in the portfolio 40% General Motors, 30% International Business Machines, and 30% Tata Communications. Determine the mean and variance for the second portfolio and compare it with the first.

5.106 ● Consider a portfolio that contains stocks from the following firms: AB Volvo, Pentair Inc., Reliant Energy Inc., TCF Financial, 3M Company, and Restoration Hardware. Data for these stocks for a 60 month period (May 2003–April 2008) is contained in the data file **Return on Stock Price 60 month**, which is contained on your data disk. Compute the means, variances, and covariances for the monthly stock price growth rate. Determine the mean and variance for a portfolio that contains equal fractions of the six stocks. Construct a second portfolio by removing TCF Financial and Restoration Hardware. Determine the mean and variance of this second portfolio that includes 20% AB Volvo, 30% Pentair, 30% Reliant Energy, and 20% 3M Company. Compare this portfolio with the first and recommend a choice between them.

Appendix

1. Readers with a knowledge of calculus will recognize that the probability that a random variable lies in a given range is the integral of the probability density function between the endpoints of the range—that is,

$$P(a < X < b) = \int_a^b f(x)\, dx$$

2. Formally, in integral calculus notation

$$\int_{-\infty}^{\infty} f(x)dx = 1$$

The cumulative distribution function is thus the integral

$$F(x_0) = \int_{-\infty}^{x_0} f(x)\, dx$$

It, therefore, follows that the probability density function is the derivative of the cumulative distribution function—that is,

$$f(x) = \frac{dF(x)}{dx}$$

3. Formally using integral calculus we express the expected value of the random variable X by

$$E(X) = \int_{-\infty}^{\infty} x\, f(x)dx$$

and the expected value of the function $g(X)$ by

$$E[g(X)] = \int_{-\infty}^{\infty} g(x)\, f(x)dx$$

As was shown for discrete random variables

$$E[g(X)] \neq g(E[X])$$

unless $g(X)$ is a linear function of X as developed in Section 6.6.

Notice that in forming these expectations the integral plays the same role as the summation operator in the discrete case.

4. The integral

$$F(x_0) = \int_{-\infty}^{x_0} \frac{1}{\sqrt{2\pi\sigma^2}} e^{-(x-\mu)^2/2\sigma^2} dx$$

does not have a simple algebraic form.

5. Using integral calculus we see that

$$P(t \leq T) = \int_0^T \lambda e^{-\lambda t} dt$$
$$= 1 - e^{-\lambda T}$$

REFERENCES

1. Stock Investor Pro, American Association of Individual Investors, 2007.

Chapter 6

Sampling and Sampling Distributions

Introduction

In Chapters 3, 4, and 5 we developed probability models that can be used to represent the underlying variability of various business and economic processes. Chapter 1 introduced and developed the important methods and concepts that are used in actually collecting data samples for business and economics studies. In Chapter 2 we presented descriptive statistics that can be used to summarize samples of data obtained from these various processes. In this chapter we link these concepts. This combination enables us to construct probability models for various statistics computed from sample data. These probability models are called *sampling distributions* and will be used to develop various procedures for statistical inference throughout the remainder of this book.

Statistical procedures focus on drawing inferences about large populations of items by using a small sample of the items. Typical examples of populations include the following:

1. *All* families living in the city of Chicago
2. *All* stocks traded on the New York Stock Exchange
3. The set of *all* claims for automobile accident insurance coverage received during a year
4. *All* cars of a particular model
5. *All* accounts receivable for a large automobile parts supplier

We might be interested in learning about specifically measured characteristics for individuals in these populations. For example, we might want to make an inference about the mean and variance of the population distribution of family incomes in Chicago, or about the proportion of all families in the city with annual incomes below $30,000.

6.1 SAMPLING FROM A POPULATION

We often use samples instead of the entire population because the cost and time of measuring every item in the population would be prohibitive. Also, in some cases measurement requires destruction of individual items. In general, we achieve greater accuracy by carefully obtaining a random sample of the population instead of spending the resources to measure every item. There are three important reasons for this result. First, it is often very difficult to obtain and measure every item in a population, and even if possible, the cost would be very high for a large population. For example, it is well known among statistical professionals that the census conducted every 10 years produces an undercount in which certain groups are seriously underrepresented (Reference 2). Second, as we learn in this chapter, properly selected samples can be used to obtain measured estimates of population characteristics that are quite close to the actual population values. The ideal sample for this purpose is a *simple random sample*. Finally by measuring a smaller number of items we can spend more effort to improve the precision of our measurement.

Simple Random Sample
Suppose that we want to select a sample of *n* objects from a population of *N* objects. A **simple random sample** is selected such that every object has an equal probability of being selected and the objects are selected independently—the selection of one object does not change the probability of selecting any other objects.

Simple random samples are the ideal. In a number of real-world sampling studies analysts develop alternative sampling procedures to lower the costs of sampling. But the basis for determining if these alternative sampling strategies are acceptable is how closely the results approximate those of a simple random sample.

It is important that a sample represent the population as a whole. If a marketing manager wants to assess reactions to a new food product, she does not sample only her friends and neighbors. Those groups are unlikely to have views that represent those of the entire population and are likely to be concentrated over a narrower range. To avoid these problems, we select a simple random sample. Random sampling is our insurance policy against allowing personal biases to influence the selection.

Simple random sampling can be implemented in many ways. We can place the *N* *population* items—for example, the numbered balls used in a bingo or lottery event—in a large barrel and mix them thoroughly. Then from this well-mixed barrel we can select individual balls from different parts of the barrel. In practice, we often use random numbers to select objects that can be assigned some numerical value. For example, market research groups may use random numbers to select telephone numbers to call and ask about preferences for a product. Various statistical computer packages and spreadsheets have routines for obtaining random numbers, and these are generally used for most sampling studies. These computer-generated random numbers have the required properties to develop random samples. Organizations that require random samples from large human populations—for example, political candidates seeking to determine voter preference—will use professional sampling firms, which are organized to select and manage the sampling process. Sampling that accurately represents the population requires considerable work and has a high cost.

We focus here on methods for analyzing results from simple random samples to gain information about the population. This process, our coverage of which will extend over the next seven chapters, is known as classical inference. These methods generally assume that simple random samples are being used. However, there are other sampling procedures and in some applied circumstances alternative sampling schemes may be preferred.

Random samples provide protection against the sample's being unrepresentative of the population. If a population is repeatedly sampled using random sampling procedures, no particular subgroup is overrepresented or underrepresented in the samples. Moreover, the concept of a sampling distribution allows us to determine the probability of obtaining a particular sample.

We use sample information to make inferences about the parent population. The distribution of all values of interest in this population can be represented by a random variable. It would be too ambitious to attempt to describe the entire population distribution based on a small random sample of observations. However, we may well be able to make quite firm inferences about important characteristics of the population distribution, such as the population mean and variance. For example, given a random sample of the fuel consumption for 25 cars of a particular model, we can use the sample mean and variance to make inferential statements about the population mean and variance of fuel consumption. This inference will be based on the sample information. We can ask questions such as this: "If the fuel consumption, in miles per gallon, of the population of all cars of a particular model has a mean of 30 and a standard deviation of 2, what is the probability that for a random sample of 25 such cars the sample mean fuel consumption will be less than 29 miles per gallon?" We can then use the sampling distribution of the sample mean to answer that question.

We need to distinguish between the population attributes and the random sample attributes. In the preceding paragraph the population of fuel consumption measurements for all automobiles of a particular model has a distribution with a specific mean. This mean, an attribute of the population, is a fixed (but unknown) number. We make inferences about this attribute by drawing a random sample from the population and computing the sample mean. For each sample we draw, there will be a different sample mean, and the sample mean can be regarded as a random variable with a probability distribution. The distribution of possible sample means provides a basis for inferential statements about the sample. In this chapter we examine the properties of *sampling distributions*.

Sampling Distributions

Consider a random sample selected from a population that is used to make an inference about some population characteristic, such as the population mean, μ, using a sample statistic, such as the sample mean, $\bar{x}$.

The inference is based on the realization that every random sample has a different number for $\bar{x}$, and, thus, $\bar{x}$ is a random variable. The **sampling distribution** of the sample mean is the probability distribution of the sample means obtained from all possible samples of the same number of observations drawn from the population.

We illustrate the concept of a sampling distribution by considering the position of a supervisor with six employees, each of whose years of experience are

$$2 \quad 4 \quad 6 \quad 6 \quad 7 \quad 8$$

The mean of the years of experience for this population of six employees is

$$\mu = \frac{2 + 4 + 6 + 6 + 7 + 8}{6} = 5.5$$

Two of these employees are to be chosen randomly for a particular work group. In this example we are sampling without replacement in a small population and thus the first observation has a probability of 1/6 of being selected, while the second observation has a probability of 1/5 of being selected. For most applied problems when sampling from large populations this is not an issue to worry about. If we were selecting from a population of several thousand or more employees then the change in probability from the first to the second observation would be trivial and is ignored. Thus we assume that we are sampling with replacement of the first observation in essentially all real world sampling studies.

Now, let us consider the mean number of years of experience of the two employees chosen randomly from the population of six. Fifteen possible different random samples could be selected. Table 6.1 shows all of the possible samples and associated sample means. Note that some samples (such as 2, 6) occur twice because there are two employees with six years of experience in the population.

Each of the 15 samples in Table 6.1 has the same probability, 1/15, of being selected. Note that there are several occurrences of the same sample mean. For example, the sample mean 5.0 occurs three times, and, thus, the probability of obtaining a sample mean of 5.0 is 3/15. Table 6.2 presents the sampling distribution for the various sample means from the population, and the probability function is graphed in Figure 6.1.

Table 6.1 Samples and Sample Means from the Worker Population Sample Size $n = 2$

Sample	Sample Mean	Sample	Sample Mean
2, 4	3.0	4, 8	6.0
2, 6	4.0	6, 6	6.0
2, 6	4.0	6, 7	6.5
2, 7	4.5	6, 8	7.0
2, 8	5.0	6, 7	6.5
4, 6	5.0	6, 8	7.0
4, 6	5.0	7, 8	7.5
4, 7	5.5		

Table 6.2 Sampling Distribution of the Sample Means from the Worker Population Sample Size $n = 2$

SAMPLE MEAN $\bar{x}$	PROBABILITY OF $\bar{x}$
3.0	1/15
4.0	2/15
4.5	1/15
5.0	3/15
5.5	1/15
6.0	2/15
6.5	2/15
7.0	2/15
7.5	1/15

We see that, while the number of years of experience for the six workers ranges from 2 to 8, the possible values of the sample mean have a range from only 3.0 to 7.5. In addition, more of the values lie in the central portion of the range.

Table 6.3 presents similar results for a sample size of $n = 5$, and Figure 6.2 presents the graph for the sampling distribution. Notice that the means are concentrated over a narrower range. These sample means are all closer to the population mean, $\mu = 5.5$. We will always find this to be true—the sampling distribution becomes concentrated closer to the population mean as the sample size increases. This important result provides an important foundation for statistical inference. In the following sections and chapters we will build a set of rigorous analysis tools on this foundation.

In this section we have developed the basic concept of sampling distributions. Here, the examples have come from a simple discrete distribution where it is possible to define all possible samples of a given sample size. From each possible sample the sample mean was computed, and the probability distribution of all possible sample means was constructed. From this simple process we discovered that, as the sample size increases, the distribution of the sample means—the sampling distribution—becomes more concentrated around the population mean. In most applied statistical

Figure 6.1 Probability Function for the Sampling Distribution of Sample Means: Sample Size $n = 2$

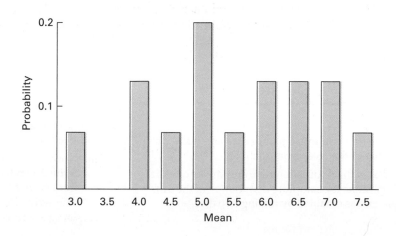

Figure 6.2
Probability
Function for the
Sampling
Distribution of
Sample Means:
Sample Size *n* = 5

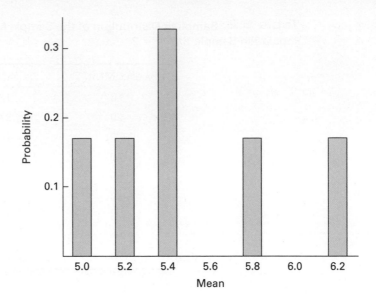

Table 6.3 Sampling Distribution of the Sample Means from the Worker Population Sample Size *n* = 5

SAMPLE	$\bar{x}$	PROBABILITY
2, 4, 6, 6, 7	5.0	1/6
2, 4, 6, 6, 8	5.2	1/6
2, 4, 6, 7, 8	5.4	1/3
2, 6, 6, 7, 8	5.8	1/6
4, 6, 6, 7, 8	6.2	1/6

work the populations are very large, and it is not practical or rational to construct the distribution of all possible samples of a given sample size. But by using what we have learned about random variables, we will be able to show that the sampling distributions for samples from all populations have the same characteristics as those shown for our simple discrete population. That result provides the basis for the many useful applications that will be developed in subsequent chapters.

EXERCISES

Basic Exercises

6.1 Suppose that you toss a pair of dice and write down the value of the faces from each die.

    a. What is the population distribution for one die?

    b. Determine the sampling distribution of the sample means obtained by tossing two dice.

6.2 Suppose that you have a fair coin and you label the head side as 1 and the tail side as 0.

    a. Now, you are asked to flip the coin 2 times and write down the numerical value that results from each toss. Without actually flipping the coin write down the sampling distribution of the sample means.

b. Repeat part (a) with the coin flipped 4 times.

c. Repeat part (a) with the coin flipped 10 times.

Application Exercises

6.3 A population contains six million 0s and four million 1s. What is the approximate sampling distribution of the sample mean when

a. the sample size is $n = 5$.

b. the sample size is $n = 100$.

Note: There is a hard way and an easy way to answer this question. We recommend the latter.

6.4 Suppose that a mathematician said that it is impossible to obtain a simple random sample from a real-world population. Therefore, the whole basis for applying statistical procedures to real problems is useless. How would you respond?

6.2 SAMPLING DISTRIBUTIONS OF SAMPLE MEANS

We now develop important properties of the sampling distribution of the sample means. Our analysis begins with a random sample of n observations from a very large population with mean μ and variance σ^2; the sample observations are denoted by $X_1, X_2, ..., X_n$. Before the sample is observed, there is uncertainty about the outcomes. This uncertainty is modeled by viewing the individual observations as random variables from a population with mean μ and variance σ^2. Our primary interest is in making inferences about the population mean μ. An obvious starting point is the *sample mean*.

> ### Sample Mean
> Let the random variables $X_1, X_2, ..., X_n$ denote a random sample from a population. The **sample mean** value of these random variables is defined as follows:
>
> $$\overline{X} = \frac{1}{n} \sum_{i=1}^{n} X_i$$

Consider the sampling distribution of the random variable $\overline{X}$. At this point we cannot determine the shape of the sampling distribution, but we can determine the mean and variance of the sampling distribution from basic definitions we have learned in Chapters 4 and 5. First, determine the mean of the distribution. In Chapters 4 and 5 we saw that the expectation of a linear combination of random variables is the linear combination of the expectations:

$$E(\overline{X}) = E\left(\frac{1}{n}(X_1 + X_2 + \cdots + X_n)\right) = \frac{n\mu}{n} = \mu$$

Thus, the mean of the sampling distribution of the sample means is the population mean. If samples of n random and independent observations are repeatedly and independently drawn from a population, then as the number of samples becomes very large, the mean of the sample means approaches the true population mean. This is an important result of random sampling and indicates the protection that random samples provide against unrepresentative samples. A single sample mean could be larger or smaller than the population mean. However, on average, there is no reason for us to expect a sample mean that is either higher or lower than the population mean. Later in this section this result is demonstrated using computer-generated random samples.

Example 6.1   Expected Value of the Sample Mean (Expected Value)

Compute the expected value of the sample mean for the employee group example previously discussed.

Solution   The sampling distribution of the sample means is shown in Table 6.2 and Figure 6.1. From this distribution we can compute the expected value of the sample mean as

$$E(\overline{X}) = \sum \overline{x}P(\overline{x}) = (3.0)\left(\frac{1}{15}\right)+(4.0)\left(\frac{2}{15}\right)+\cdots+(7.5)\left(\frac{1}{15}\right)=5.5$$

which is the population mean, μ. A similar calculation can be made to obtain the same result using the sampling distribution in Table 6.3.

Now that we have established that the distribution of sample means is centered about the population mean, we need to determine the variance of the distribution of sample means. Suppose that a random sample of 25 cars yields an average fuel consumption of 31 miles per gallon. The sample mean can be used as an estimate of the population mean. But we also wish to know how good $\overline{x} = 31$ is as the approximation of the population mean. We use the variance of the sampling distribution of the sample means to provide the answer.

If the population is very large compared to the sample size, then the distributions of the individual independent sample members from random samples are the same. In Chapters 4 and 5 we saw that the variance of a linear combination of independent random variables is the sum of the linear coefficients squared times the variance of the random variables. It follows that

$$\text{Var}(\overline{X})=\text{Var}\left(\frac{1}{n}X_1 + \frac{1}{n}X_2 + \cdots + \frac{1}{n}X_n\right)=\sum_{i=1}^{n}\left(\frac{1}{n}\right)^2\sigma_i^2 = \frac{n\sigma^2}{n^2} = \frac{\sigma^2}{n}$$

The variance of the sampling distribution of $\overline{X}$ decreases as the sample size n increases. In effect, this says that larger sample sizes result in more concentrated sampling distributions. The simple example in the previous section demonstrated this result. Thus, larger samples result in greater certainty about our inference of the population mean. This is to be expected. As we obtain more information from a population—from a larger sample—we are able to learn more about population characteristics such as the population mean. The variance of the sample mean is denoted as $\sigma_{\overline{x}}^2$ and the corresponding standard deviation, called the standard error of $\overline{X}$, is given by the following:

$$\sigma_{\overline{x}} = \frac{\sigma}{\sqrt{n}}$$

If the sample size, n, is not a small fraction of the population size, N, then the individual sample members are not distributed independently of one another as noted in Section 6.1. Thus, the observations are not selected independently. It can be shown in this case that the variance of the sample mean is as follows:

$$\text{Var}(\overline{X})=\frac{\sigma^2}{n}\cdot\frac{N-n}{N-1}$$

The term $(N-n)/(N-1)$ is often called a **finite population correction factor**. This result is included for completeness since almost all of the real sampling studies use large populations. However, there are some examples in business applications, such as auditing, that involve finite populations. We will see examples using the finite population correction factor in Chapters 7 and 9. Careful evaluation of this expression would also dispel the notion that it is important that the sample be a substantial fraction of the population in order to provide useful information. As we will establish in this chapter it is the sample size—not the fraction of the population in the sample—that determines the quality of results from a random sample.

We have now developed expressions for the mean and variance of the sampling distribution of $\overline{X}$. For most applications the mean and variance will define the sampling distribution. These results for the mean and variance of the sampling distribution apply for any probability distribution that defines the pattern of the values in the population. If it were impossible to extend these results any further, then these results might be interesting theoretically but would have little value for applied applications. Fortunately, we will see that with some additional analysis these results can become very powerful for many practical applications. First, we examine these results under the assumption that the underlying population has a normal probability distribution. Next, we explore the sampling distributions of the sample mean when the underlying population does not have a normal distribution. This second case will provide some very powerful results for many practical applications in business and economics.

First, we consider the results if the parent population has a normal distribution. The parent population is the population of interest from which the random sample is obtained. If the parent population has a normal distribution, then the sampling distribution of the sample means also has a normal distribution. This intuitive conclusion comes from the well-established result that linear functions of normally distributed random variables are also normally distributed. We saw applications of this in the portfolio problems in Chapter 5. With the sampling distribution as a normal probability distribution, we can compute the standard normal Z for the sample mean. In Chapter 5 we saw that we can use the standard normal Z to compute probabilities for any normally distributed random variable. That result also applies for the sample mean.

Standard Normal Distribution for the Sample Means
Whenever the sampling distribution of the sample means is a normal distribution, we can compute a **standardized normal random variable, Z**, that has a mean of 0 and a variance of 1:

$$Z = \frac{\overline{X}-\mu}{\sigma_{\overline{X}}} = \frac{\overline{X}-\mu}{\dfrac{\sigma}{\sqrt{n}}} \qquad (6.1)$$

Finally, the results of this section are summarized in the following section.

Results for the Sampling Distribution of the Sample Means
Let $\overline{X}$ denote the sample mean of a random sample of n observations from a population with mean μ_x and variance σ^2. Then,

1. the sampling distribution of $\overline{X}$ has mean

$$E(\overline{X}) = \mu \qquad (6.2)$$

2. and the sampling distribution of $\overline{X}$ has standard deviation

$$\sigma_{\overline{X}} = \frac{\sigma}{\sqrt{n}} \qquad (6.3)$$

This is called the standard error of $\overline{X}$.

3. If the sample size, n, is not small compared to the population size, N, then the standard error of $\overline{X}$ is as follows:

$$\sigma_{\overline{X}} = \frac{\sigma}{\sqrt{n}} \cdot \sqrt{\frac{N-n}{N-1}} \qquad (6.4)$$

4. If the parent population distribution is normal and, thus, the sampling distribution of the sample means is normal, then the random variable

$$Z = \frac{\overline{X} - \mu}{\sigma_{\overline{X}}} \qquad (6.5)$$

has a standard normal distribution with a mean of 0 and a variance of 1.

Figure 6.3 shows the sampling distribution of the sample means for sample sizes $n = 25$ and $n = 100$ from a normal distribution. Each distribution is centered on the mean, but as the sample size increases, the distribution becomes concentrated more closely around the population mean because the standard error of the sample mean decreases as the sample size increases. Thus, the probability that a sample mean is a fixed distance from the population mean decreases with increased sample size.

Figure 6.3
Probability
Density Functions
for Sample Means
from a Population
with $\mu = 100$ and
$\sigma = 5$

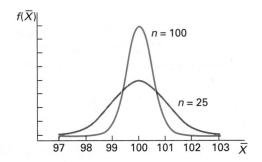

Example 6.2 Executive Salary Distributions (Normal Probability)

Suppose that based on historical data we believe that the annual percentage salary increases for the chief executive officers of all midsize corporations are normally distributed with a mean of 12.2% and a standard deviation of 3.6%. A random sample of nine observations is obtained from this population and the sample mean computed. What is the probability that the sample mean will be greater than 14.4%?

Solution We know that

$$\mu = 12.2 \quad \sigma = 3.6 \quad n = 9$$

Let $\bar{x}$ denote the sample mean, and compute the standard error of the sample mean:

$$\sigma_{\bar{x}} = \frac{\sigma}{\sqrt{n}} = \frac{3.6}{\sqrt{9}} = 1.2$$

Then we can compute

$$P(\bar{x} > 14.4) = P\left(\frac{\bar{x}-\mu}{\sigma_{\bar{x}}} > \frac{14.4-12.2}{1.2}\right) = P(z > 1.83) = 0.0336$$

where Z has a standard normal distribution and the resulting probability is obtained from Table 1 of the appendix using the procedures developed in Chapter 5.

From this analysis we conclude that the probability that the sample mean will be greater than 14.4% is only 0.0336. If a sample mean greater than 14.4% actually occurred, we might begin to suspect that the population mean is greater than 12.2%.

Example 6.3 Spark Plug Life (Normal Probability)

A spark plug manufacturer claims that the lives of its plugs are normally distributed with a mean of 60,000 miles and a standard deviation of 4,000 miles. A random sample of 16 plugs had an average life of 58,500 miles. If the manufacturer's claim is correct, what is the probability of finding a sample mean of 58,500 or less?

Solution To compute the probability, we need to first obtain the standard error of the sample mean:

$$\sigma_{\bar{x}} = \frac{\sigma}{\sqrt{n}} = \frac{4,000}{\sqrt{16}} = 1,000$$

The desired probability is as follows:

$$P(\bar{x} < 58,500) = P\left(\frac{\bar{x}-\mu}{\sigma_{\bar{x}}} < \frac{58,500-60,000}{1,000}\right) = P(z < -1.50) = 0.0668$$

Figure 6.4a shows the probability density function of $\overline{X}$, with the shaded portion indicating the probability that the sample mean is less than 58,500. In Figure 6.4b we see the standard normal density function, and the shaded area indicates the probability that Z is less than –1.5. Note that in comparing these figures we see that every value of $\overline{X}$ has a corresponding value of Z and that the comparable probability statements provide the same result.

Using the standard normal Z, the normal probability values from Table 1 of the appendix, and the procedures from Chapter 5, we find that the probability that $\overline{X}$ is less than 58,500 is 0.0668. This probability suggests that, if the manufacturer's claims—$\mu = 60,000$ and $\sigma = 4,000$—are true, then a sample mean of 58,500 or less has a small probability. As a result if we obtained a sample mean less than

58,500 we would be skeptical about the manufacturer's claims. This important concept—using the probability of sample statistics to question the original assumption—will be developed more fully in Chapter 9.

Figure 6.4 a. Probability That Sample Mean Is Less than 58,500 b. Probability That a Standard Normal Random Variable Is Less than −1.5

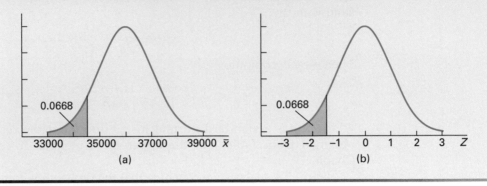

Central Limit Theorem

In the previous section we learned that the sample mean, $\bar{x}$ for a random sample of size n drawn from a population with a normal distribution with mean μ and variance σ^2, is also normally distributed with mean μ and variance σ^2/n. In this section we present the *central limit theorem*, which shows that the mean of a random sample, drawn from a population with any probability distribution, will be approximately normally distributed with mean μ and variance σ^2/n, given a large enough sample size. The central limit theorem shows that the sum of n random variables from any probability distribution will be approximately normally distributed if n is large. This result is developed in the chapter appendix. Since the mean is the sum divided by n, the mean is also approximately normally distributed and that is the result that is important for our statistical applications in business and economics.

   This important result enables us to use the normal distribution to compute probabilities for sample means obtained from many different populations. In applied statistics the probability distribution for the population being sampled is often not known, and in particular there is no way to be certain that the underlying distribution is normal.

Statement of the Central Limit Theorem
Let $X_1, X_2, ..., X_n$ be a set of n independent random variables having identical distributions with mean μ, variance σ^2, and $\bar{X}$ as the mean of these random variables. As n becomes large, the **central limit theorem** states that the distribution of

$$Z = \frac{\bar{X} - \mu_{\bar{X}}}{\sigma_{\bar{X}}}$$ (6.6)

approaches the standard normal distribution.

The central limit theorem provides the basis for considerable work in applied statistical analysis. As indicated, many random variables can be modeled as sums or means of independent random variables and the normal distribution very often provides a good approximation of the true distribution. Thus, the standard normal distribution can be used to obtain probability values for many observed sample means.

The central limit theorem can be applied to both discrete and continuous random variables. In Section 6.3 we use this theorem with discrete random variables to develop probabilities for proportion random variables by treating proportions as a special case of sample means.

A related and important result is the **law of large numbers**, which concludes that given a random sample of size n from a population, the sample mean will approach the population mean as the sample size n becomes large regardless of the underlying probability distribution. One obvious result is of course a sample that contains the entire population. However, we can also see that as the sample size n becomes large the variance becomes small until eventually the distribution approaches a constant which is the sample mean. This result combined with the central limit theorem provides the basis for statistical inference about populations by using random samples.

The central limit theorem has a formal mathematical proof that is beyond the scope of this book. Results from random sample simulations can also be used to demonstrate the central limit theorem. In addition, there are homework problems that enable you to conduct further experimental analysis.

We now present some results using Monte Carlo sample simulations to obtain sampling distributions. To obtain each of these results, we selected 1,000 random samples of size n generated from computer simulations produced using Minitab 15 and displayed the sampling distributions of the sample means in histograms. This process constructs empirical sampling distributions of the sample means. Histograms showing the results of these simulations are shown in Figures 6.5, 6.6, and 6.7, and these results are discussed below. The chapter appendix presents the procedure for obtaining sampling distributions for the sample means from any probability distribution. In this appendix and on the data disk we include a Minitab Computer Macro for easily obtaining your own sampling distributions.

First for Figure 6.5 we constructed a population of 100 randomly selected values using the normal distribution. The actual histogram of the population used is shown. Next we obtained 1,000 random samples—sampling with replacement—from this distribution using sample sizes $n = 10$, $n = 25$, and $n = 50$. In this example the histograms of the sample means for all three sample sizes follow a normal distribution as shown by the normal curve drawn over the histogram. Note also that the distributions are narrower with increasing sample size because the standard deviation of the sample means become smaller with larger sample sizes. The normal distribution used to obtain the observations had a mean of 5 and a standard deviation of 2. Thus, about 95% of the observations for the histogram should be between 5 plus or minus 2 standard deviations, or between 1 and 9. For the histogram with sample size 50 the interval for 95% of the sample means would be as follows:

$$5 \pm (1.96)\frac{2}{\sqrt{50}}$$

$$5 \pm 0.55$$

$$4.45 \rightarrow 5.55$$

Figure 6.5

Sampling
Distributions from
a Distribution of
100 Normally
Distributed
Random Values
with Various
Sample Sizes:
Demonstration of
Central Limit
Theorem

Distribution of Random Variable

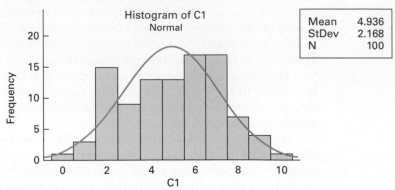

Sample Size n = 10

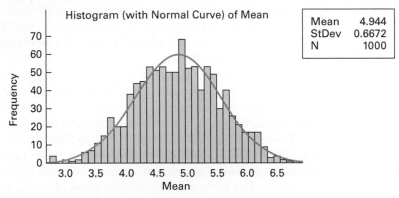

Sample Size n = 25

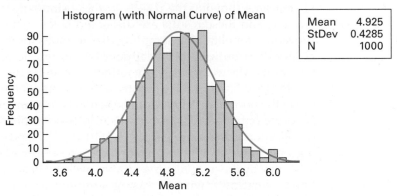

Sample Size n = 50

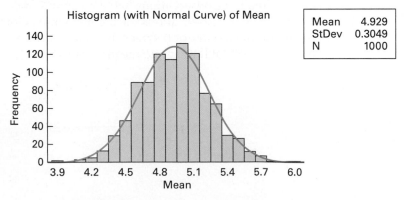

When random samples of various sizes are obtained from a population with known mean and variance we see that the range for various percentages of the sample means follow the results obtained using the normal distribution.

Next we considered a uniform probability distribution over the range 1 to 10. The probability distribution is shown in Figure 6.6. Clearly, the values of the random variable are not normally distributed, since the values are uniform over the range from 1 to 10. The distributions of sample means for sample sizes 10, 25, and 50 are shown in Figure 6.6. A normal probability density function with the same mean and variance is sketched over each histogram to provide a comparison. Generally, the distribution of sample means from uniform or symmetric distributions can be closely approximated by the normal distribution, with samples of size 25 or more. The mean for the uniform distribution is 5.5 and the standard deviation is 2.886. From a normal distribution of sample means, with $n = 50$, we would expect to find 95% of the sample means in the following interval:

$$5.5 \pm (1.96)\frac{2.887}{\sqrt{50}}$$

$$5.5 \pm 0.80$$

$$4.70 \rightarrow 6.30$$

An examination of Figure 6.6 would indicate that the normal interval applies here.

Next, let us consider a population with a probability distribution that is skewed to the right as shown in Figure 6.7. Distributions of observations for many business and economic processes are skewed. For example, family incomes and housing prices in a city, state, or country are often skewed to the right. There is typically a small percentage of families with very high incomes, and these families tend to live in expensive houses. Consider the discrete probability distribution shown in Figure 6.7. This could be a distribution of family incomes for a developing country. Suppose that you wanted to compare the mean income for that country with the means for a larger set of countries with similar educational levels.

The sampling distributions of mean incomes are compared using random samples of size 10, 25, and 50 from the probability distribution. If you use a random sample of size $n = 10$ and assume that the sample mean is normally distributed, the chances for estimating incorrect probabilities are great. These mistakes in probability estimates are particularly large for sample means in the upper tail of the distribution. Note that the histogram is different from one that would be obtained from a normal distribution. But if you use a random sample of size $n = 25$, your results are much better. Note that the second histogram—$n = 25$—is much closer to a normal distribution. The results are even better when the sample size is 50. Thus, even when the distribution of individual observations is highly skewed, the sampling distribution of sample means closely approximates a normal distribution when $n \geq 25$. The mean and standard deviation for the skewed distribution is 3.3 and 4.247. Thus, the interval from the normal distribution for 95% of the sample means would be as follows:

$$3.3 \pm (1.96)\frac{4.247}{\sqrt{50}}$$

$$3.3 \pm 1.18$$

$$2.12 \rightarrow 4.48$$

The distribution of sample means for $n = 50$ appears to fit this interval.

Figure 6.6
Sampling
Distributions from
a Uniform
Distribution with
Various Sample
Sizes:
Demonstration of
Central Limit
Theorem

Distribution of Random Variable

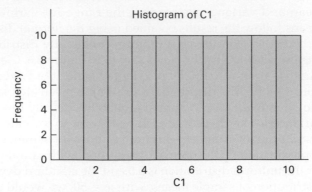

Sample Size n = 10

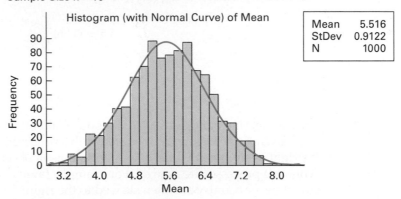

Mean	5.516
StDev	0.9122
N	1000

Sample Size n = 25

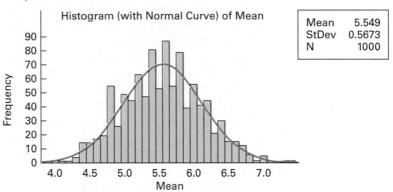

Mean	5.549
StDev	0.5673
N	1000

Sample Size n = 50

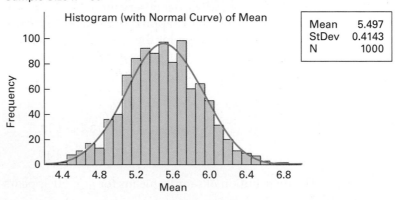

Mean	5.497
StDev	0.4143
N	1000

Figure 6.7

Sampling Distributions from a Skewed Distribution with Various Sample Sizes: Demonstration of Central Limit Theorem

Distribution of Random Variable

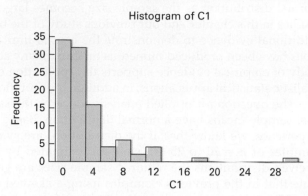

Distribution of Sample means with n = 10

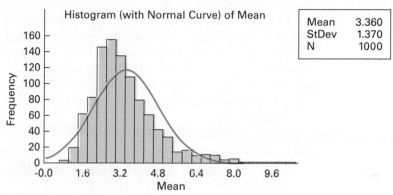

Mean	3.360
StDev	1.370
N	1000

Distribution of Sample Means with n = 25

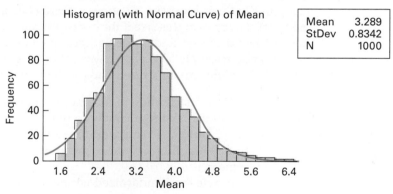

Mean	3.289
StDev	0.8342
N	1000

Distribution of Sample Means with n = 50

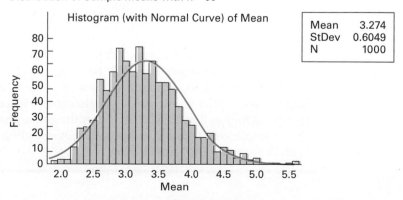

Mean	3.274
StDev	0.6049
N	1000

In Chapter 5 we learned that the binomial random variable has an approximate normal distribution as the sample size becomes large. From the random sampling studies in this chapter and our previous study of the binomial distribution, we have additional evidence to demonstrate the central limit theorem. Similar demonstrations have been produced numerous times by many statisticians. As a result, a large body of empirical evidence supports the application of the central limit theorem to realistic statistical applications, in addition to theoretical results.

The question for applied analysis concerns the sample size required to ensure that sample means have a normal distribution. Based on considerable research and experience, we know that, if the distributions are symmetric, then the means from samples of $n = 20$ to 25 are well approximated by the normal distribution. For skewed distributions the required sample sizes are generally somewhat larger. But note that in the previous examples using a skewed distribution a sample size of $n = 25$ produced a sampling distribution of sample means that closely followed a normal distribution.

In this chapter we have begun our discussion of the important statistical problem of making inferences about a population based on results from a sample. The sample mean or sample proportion is often computed to make inferences about population means or proportions. By using the central limit theorem we have a rationale for applying the techniques we will develop in future chapters to a wide range of problems. The following examples show important applications of the central limit theorem.

Example 6.4 Marketing Study for Antelope Coffee (Normal Probability)

Antelope Coffee Inc. is considering the possibility of opening a gourmet coffee shop in Big Rock, Montana. Previous research has indicated that its shops will be successful in cities of this size if the per capita annual income is above $70,000. It is also known that the standard deviation of income is $5,000.

A random sample of 36 people was obtained and the mean income was $72,300. Does this sample provide evidence to conclude that a shop should be opened?

Solution   The distribution of incomes is known to be skewed, but the central limit theorem enables us to conclude that the sample mean is approximately normally distributed. To answer the question, we need to determine the probability of obtaining a sample mean at least as high as $\bar{x} = 72,300$ if the population mean is $\mu = 70,000$.

First, compute the standardized normal Z statistic:

$$z = \frac{\bar{x} - \mu}{\sigma/\sqrt{n}} = \frac{72,300 - 70,000}{5,000/\sqrt{36}} = 2.76$$

From the standard normal table we find that the probability of obtaining a Z value of 2.76 or larger is 0.0029. Because this probability is very small, we can conclude that it is likely that the population mean income is not 70,000, but is a larger value. This result provides strong evidence that the population mean income is higher than $70,000 and that the coffee shop is likely to be a success. In this example we can see the importance of sampling distributions and the central limit theorem for problem solving.

Acceptance Intervals

In many statistical applications we would like to determine the range within which sample means are likely to occur. Determining such ranges is a direct application of the sampling distribution concepts we have developed. An **acceptance interval** is an interval within which a sample mean has a high probability of occurring, given that we know the population mean and variance. If the sample mean is within that interval, then we can accept the conclusion that the random sample came from the population with the known population mean and variance. The probability that the sample mean is within a particular interval can be computed if the sample means have a distribution that is close to normal.

Acceptance intervals find wide application for monitoring manufacturing processes to determine if product standards are continuing to be achieved. In addition these intervals are also used for monitoring various business activities that involve customer service. For example in a manufacturing process the manufacturing engineer carefully sets and tests a new process so that it will produce products that all meet the guaranteed specifications for size, weight, or other measured properties. Thus, the mean and standard deviation for the units produced are specified so that the desired product quality will be obtained.

However, it is possible that the process could come out of adjustment and produce defective product items. Therefore, the process is monitored regularly by obtaining random samples and measuring the important properties, such as the sample mean and variance. If the measured values are within the "Acceptance Interval" then the process is allowed to continue. If the values are not then the process is stopped and necessary adjustments are made.

Acceptance intervals based on the normal distribution are defined by the distribution mean and variance. From the central limit theorem we know that the sampling distribution of sample means is often approximately normal, and, thus, acceptance intervals based on the normal distribution have wide applications. Assuming that we know the population mean μ, and variance σ^2, then we can construct a symmetric acceptance interval

$$\mu \pm z_{\alpha/2}\, \sigma_{\bar{x}}$$

provided that $\bar{x}$ has a normal distribution and $z_{\alpha/2}$ is the standard normal when the upper tail probability is $\alpha/2$. The probability that the sample mean $\bar{x}$ is included in the interval is $1 - \alpha$.

As noted, acceptance intervals are widely used for quality control monitoring of various production and service processes. The interval

$$\mu \pm z_{\alpha/2}\, \sigma_{\bar{x}}$$

is plotted over time (the result is called an X-bar chart) and provides limits for the sample mean $\bar{x}$, given that the population mean is μ. Typically, α is very small ($\alpha < .01$), and standard practice in U.S. industries is to use $z = 3$. If the sample mean is outside the acceptance interval, then we suspect that the population mean is not μ. In a typical example engineers will take various steps to achieve a small variance for important product measurements that are directly related to product quality. Once the process has been adjusted so that the variance is small, an acceptance interval for a sample mean—called a *control interval*—is established in the form of a control chart. Then periodic random samples are obtained and compared to the control interval. If the sample mean is within the control interval, it is concluded that the process is operating properly and no action is taken. But if the sample mean is outside of the control interval, it is concluded that the process is not operating properly and steps are taken to correct the process.

Example 6.5 Monitoring Health Insurance Claims (Acceptance Interval)

Charlotte King, vice president of financial underwriting for a large health insurance company, wishes to monitor daily insurance claim payments to determine if the average dollar value of subscriber claims is stable, increasing, or decreasing. The value of individual claims varies up and down from one day to the next, and it would be naive to draw conclusions or change operations based on these daily variations. But at some point the changes become substantial and should be noted. She has asked you to develop a procedure for monitoring the dollar value of individual claims.

Solution Your initial investigation indicates that health insurance claims are highly skewed, with a small number of very large claims for major medical procedures. To determine changes, you first need to determine the historical mean and variance for individual claims. After some investigation you also find that the mean for random samples of $n = 100$ claims is normally distributed. Based on past history the mean, μ, level for individual claims is \$6,000 with a standard deviation of $\sigma = 2,000$.

Using this information you proceed to develop a claims monitoring system that obtains a random sample of 100 claims each day and computes the sample mean. The company has established a 95% acceptance interval for monitoring claims. An interval defined for the standard normal using $Z=\pm1.96$ includes 95% of the values. From this you compute the 95% acceptance interval for insurance claims as follows:

$$6,000\pm1.96\frac{2,000}{\sqrt{100}}$$

$$6,000\pm392$$

Each day the sample mean for 100 randomly selected claims is computed and compared to the acceptance interval. If the sample mean is outside the interval 5,608 to 6,392, Ms. King can conclude that claims are deviating from the historical standard. You explain to her that this conclusion will be correct 95% of the time. The sample mean could be outside the interval even if the population mean is 6,000 with probability 0.05. In those cases Ms. King's conclusion that the mean claim level has changed from the historical standard would be wrong. To simplify the analysis, you instruct the analysts to plot the daily claims mean on a control chart, shown in Figure 6.8. Using this control chart Charlotte King and her staff can study the patterns of the sample means and determine if there are trends and if means are outside of the boundaries that indicate standard claims behavior.

Figure 6.8 Ninety-Five Percent Acceptance Interval for Health Insurance Claims

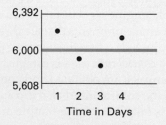

Example 6.6 Prairie View Cereal Package Weights (Acceptance Intervals)

Prairie View Cereals Inc. is concerned about maintaining correct package weights at its cereal packaging facility. The package label weight is 440 grams, and company officials are interested in monitoring the process to ensure that package weights are stable.

Solution A random sample of five packages is collected every 30 minutes and each package is weighed electronically. The mean weight is then plotted on an X-bar control chart such as the one in Figure 6.9. When an X-bar chart is used for monitoring limits on product quality—this usage is practiced by numerous highly successful firms—the central limit theorem provides the rationale for using the normal distribution to establish limits for the small sample means. Thus, a fundamentally important statistical theory drives a key management process.

In this chart SL is the standard deviation for the sample mean. The upper and lower limits are set at $\pm 3\sigma_{\overline{X}}$ instead of $\pm 1.96\sigma_{\overline{X}}$, or 95%, the acceptance interval used in the previous example. The interval $\overline{X} \pm 3\sigma_{\overline{X}}$ (Minitab labels the mean for the entire population as $\overline{\overline{X}}$) includes almost all of the sample means under the normal distribution, given a stable mean and variance. Thus, a sample mean outside of the control limits indicates that something has changed and that corrections should be made. Given the number of points outside the acceptance interval, we recommend that the process be stopped and adjusted.

Figure 6.9 X-Bar Chart For Cereal Package Weight

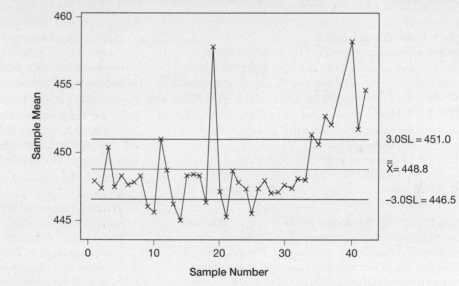

EXERCISES

Basic Exercises

6.5 Given a population with a mean of $\mu = 100$ and a variance of $\sigma^2 = 81$, the central limit applies when the sample size $n \geq 25$. A random sample of size $n = 25$ is obtained.

a. What are the mean and variance of the sampling distribution for the sample means?
b. What is the probability that $\overline{x} > 102$?
c. What is the probability that $98 \leq \overline{x} \leq 101$?
d. What is the probability that $\overline{x} \leq 101.5$?

6.6 Given a population with a mean of $\mu = 100$ and a variance of $\sigma^2 = 900$, the central limit applies when the sample size $n \geq 25$. A random sample of size $n = 30$ is obtained.

   a. What are the mean and variance of the sampling distribution for the sample means?

   b. What is the probability that $\bar{x} > 109$?

   c. What is the probability that $96 \leq \bar{x} \leq 110$?

   d. What is the probability that $\bar{x} \leq 107$?

6.7 Given a population with a mean of $\mu = 200$ and a variance of $\sigma^2 = 625$, the central limit applies when the sample size $n \geq 25$. A random sample of size $n = 25$ is obtained.

   a. What are the mean and variance of the sampling distribution for the sample mean?

   b. What is the probability that $\bar{x} > 209$?

   c. What is the probability that $198 \leq \bar{x} \leq 211$?

   d. What is the probability that $\bar{x} \leq 202$?

6.8 Given a population with mean $\mu = 400$ and variance $\sigma^2 = 1,600$, the central limit applies when the sample size $n \geq 25$. A random sample of size $n = 35$ is obtained.

   a. What are the mean and variance of the sampling distribution for the sample means?

   b. What is the probability that $\bar{x} > 412$?

   c. What is the probability that $393 \leq \bar{x} \leq 407$?

   d. What is the probability that $\bar{x} \leq 389$?

Application Exercises

6.9 When a production process is operating correctly, the number of units produced per hour has a normal distribution with a mean of 92.0 and a standard deviation of 3.6. A random sample of 4 different hours was taken.

   a. Find the mean of the sampling distribution of the sample means.

   b. Find the variance of the sample mean.

   c. Find the standard error of the sample mean.

   d. What is the probability that the sample mean exceeds 93.0 units?

6.10 The lifetimes of lightbulbs produced by a particular manufacturer have a mean of 1,200 hours and a standard deviation of 400 hours. The population distribution is normal. Suppose that you purchase nine bulbs, which can be regarded as a random sample from the manufacturer's output.

   a. What is the mean of the sample mean lifetime?

   b. What is the variance of the sample mean?

   c. What is the standard error of the sample mean?

   d. What is the probability that, on average, those nine lightbulbs have lives of fewer than 1,050 hours?

6.11 The fuel consumption, in miles per gallon, of all cars of a particular model has a mean of 25 and a standard deviation of 2. The population distribution can be assumed to be normal. A random sample of these cars is taken.

   a. Find the probability that sample mean fuel consumption will be fewer than 24 miles per gallon if

      i. a sample of 1 observation is taken.

      ii. a sample of 4 observations is taken.

      iii. a sample of 16 observations is taken.

   b. Explain why the three answers in part (a) differ in the way they do. Draw a graph to illustrate your reasoning.

6.12 The mean selling price of senior condominiums in Green Valley over a year was $215,000. The population standard deviation was $25,000. A random sample of 100 new unit sales from was taken.

   a. What is the probability that the sample mean selling price was more than $210,000?

   b. What is the probability that the sample mean selling price was between $213,000 and $217,000?

   c. What is the probability that the sample mean selling price was between $214,000 and $216,000?

   d. Without doing the calculations, state in which of the following ranges the sample mean selling price is most likely to lie:
$213,000 to $215,000; $214,000 to $216,000; $215,000 to $217,000; $216,000 to $218,000

   e. Suppose that, after you had done these calculations, a friend asserted that the population distribution of selling prices of senior condominiums in Green Valley was almost certainly not normal. How would you respond?

6.13 Candidates for employment at a city fire department are required to take a written aptitude test. Scores on this test are normally distributed with a mean of 280 and a standard deviation of 60. A random sample of nine test scores was taken.

   a. What is the standard error of the sample mean score?

   b. What is the probability that the sample mean score is less than 270?

   c. What is the probability that the sample mean score is more than 250?

   d. Suppose that the population standard deviation is, in fact, 40, rather than 60. Without doing the calculations, state how this would change your answers to parts (a), (b), and (c). Illustrate your conclusions with the appropriate graphs.

6.14 A random sample of 16 junior managers in the offices of corporations in a large city center was taken to estimate average daily commuting time for all such managers. Suppose that the population times have a normal distribution with a mean of 87 minutes and a standard deviation of 22 minutes.

a. What is the standard error of the sample mean commuting time?
b. What is the probability that the sample mean is fewer than 100 minutes?
c. What is the probability that the sample mean is more than 80 minutes?
d. What is the probability that the sample mean is outside the range 85 to 95 minutes?
e. Suppose that a second (independent) random sample of 50 junior managers is taken. Without doing the calculations, state whether the probabilities in parts (b), (c), and (d) would be higher, lower, or the same for the second sample. Sketch graphs to illustrate your answers.

6.15 A company produces breakfast cereal. The true mean weight of the contents of its cereal boxes is 20 ounces, and the standard deviation is 0.6 ounce. The population distribution of weights is normal. Suppose that you purchase four boxes, which can be regarded as a random sample of all those produced.

a. What is the standard error of the sample mean weight?
b. What is the probability that, on average, the contents of these four boxes will weigh fewer than 19.7 ounces?
c. What is the probability that, on average, the contents of these four boxes will weigh more than 20.6 ounces?
d. What is the probability that, on average, the contents of these four boxes will weigh between 19.5 and 20.5 ounces?
e. Two of the four boxes are chosen at random. What is the probability that the average contents of these two boxes will weigh between 19.5 and 20.5 ounces?

6.16 Assume that the standard deviation of monthly rents paid by students in a particular town is $40. A random sample of 100 students was taken to estimate the mean monthly rent paid by the whole student population.

a. What is the standard error of the sample mean monthly rent?
b. What is the probability that the sample mean exceeds the population mean by more than $5?
c. What is the probability that the sample mean is more than $4 below the population mean?
d. What is the probability that the sample mean differs from the population mean by more than $3?

6.17 The times spent studying by students in the week before final exams follows a normal distribution with standard deviation 8 hours. A random sample of four students was taken in order to estimate the mean study time for the population of all students.

a. What is the probability that the sample mean exceeds the population mean by more than 2 hours?
b. What is the probability that the sample mean is more than 3 hours below the population mean?
c. What is the probability that the sample mean differs from the population mean by more than 4 hours?
d. Suppose that a second (independent) random sample of 10 students was taken. Without doing the calculations, state whether the probabilities in parts (a), (b), and (c) would be higher, lower, or the same for the second sample.

6.18 An industrial process produces batches of a chemical whose impurity levels follow a normal distribution with standard deviation 1.6 grams per 100 grams of chemical. A random sample of 100 batches is selected in order to estimate the population mean impurity level.

a. The probability is 0.05 that the sample mean impurity level exceeds the population mean by how much?
b. The probability is 0.10 that the sample mean impurity level is below the population mean by how much?
c. The probability is 0.15 that the sample mean impurity level differs from the population mean by how much?

6.19 The price-earnings ratios for all companies whose shares are traded on the New York Stock Exchange follow a normal distribution with a standard deviation 3.8. A random sample of these companies is selected in order to estimate the population mean price-earnings ratio.

a. How large a sample is necessary in order to ensure that the probability that the sample mean differs from the population mean by more than 1.0 is less than 0.10?
b. Without doing the calculations, state whether a larger or smaller sample size compared to the sample size in part (a) would be required to guarantee that the probability of the sample mean differing from the population mean by more than 1.0 is less than 0.05.
c. Without doing the calculations, state whether a larger or smaller sample size compared to the sample size in part (a) would be required to

guarantee that the probability of the sample mean differing from the population mean by more than 1.5 hours is less than 0.05.

6.20 The number of hours spent studying by students on a large campus in the week before final exams follows a normal distribution with a standard deviation of 8.4 hours. A random sample of these students is taken to estimate the population mean number of hours studying.

a. How large of a sample is needed to ensure that the probability that the sample mean differs from the population mean by more than 2.0 hours is less than 0.05?

b. Without doing the calculations, state whether a larger or smaller sample size compared to the sample size in part (a) would be required to guarantee that the probability of the sample mean differing from the population mean by more than 2.0 hours is less than 0.10.

c. Without doing the calculations, state whether a larger or smaller sample size compared to the sample size in part (a) would be required to guarantee that the probability of the sample mean differing from the population mean by more than 1.5 hours is less than 0.05.

6.21 Greenstone Coffee is experiencing financial pressures due to increased competition for its numerous urban coffee shops. Total sales revenue has dropped by 15% and the company wishes to establish a sales monitoring process to identify shops that are underperforming. Historically the daily mean sales for a shop has been $11,500 with a variance of 4,000,000. Their monitoring plan will take a random sample of 5 days sales per month and use the sample mean sales to identify shops that are underperforming. Establish the lower limit sales such that only 5% of the shops would have a sample sales mean below this value.

6.22 In taking a sample of n observations from a population of N members, the variance of the sampling distribution of the sample means is as follows:

$$\sigma_{\bar{x}}^2 = \frac{\sigma_x^2}{n} \cdot \frac{N-n}{N-1}$$

The quantity $\frac{(N-n)}{(N-1)}$ is called the *finite population correction factor*.

a. To get some feeling for possible magnitudes of the finite population correction factor, calculate it for samples of $n = 20$ observations from populations of members.

b. Explain why the result for , found in part (a), is precisely what one should expect on intuitive grounds.

c. Given the results in part (a), discuss the practical significance of using the finite population correction factor for samples of 20 observations from populations of different sizes.

6.23 A town has 500 real estate agents. The mean value of the properties sold in a year by these agents is $800,000, and the standard deviation is $300,000. A random sample of 100 agents is selected, and the value of the properties they sold in a year is recorded.

a. What is the standard error of the sample mean?

b. What is the probability that the sample mean exceeds $825,000?

c. What is the probability that the sample mean exceeds $780,000?

d. What is the probability that the sample mean is between $790,000 and $820,000?

6.24 An English literature course was taken by 250 students. Each member of a random sample of 50 of these students was asked to estimate the amount of time she spent on the previous week's assignment. Suppose that the population standard deviation is 30 minutes.

a. What is the probability that the sample mean exceeds the population mean by more than 2.5 minutes?

b. What is the probability that the sample mean is more than 5 minutes below the population mean?

c. What is the probability that the sample mean differs from the population mean by more than 10 minutes?

6.25 For an audience of 600 people attending a concert, the average time on the journey to the concert was 32 minutes, and the standard deviation was 10 minutes. A random sample of 150 audience members was taken.

a. What is the probability that the sample mean journey time was more than 31 minutes?

b. What is the probability that the sample mean journey time was less than 33 minutes?

c. Draw a graph to illustrate why the answers to parts (a) and (b) are the same.

d. What is the probability that the sample mean journey time was not between 31 and 33 minutes?

6.3 SAMPLING DISTRIBUTIONS OF SAMPLE PROPORTIONS

In Section 4.4 we developed the binomial distribution as the sum of n independent Bernoulli random variables, each with probability of success P. To characterize the distribution, we need a value for P. Here, we indicate how we can use the sample proportion to obtain inferences about the population proportion. The proportion random variable has many applications, including percent market share, percent successful business investments, and outcomes of elections.

Sample Proportion

Let X be the number of successes in a binomial sample of n observations with the parameter P. The parameter is the proportion of the population members that have a characteristic of interest. We define the **sample proportion** as follows:

$$\hat{p} = \frac{X}{n} \tag{6.7}$$

X is the sum of a set of n independent Bernoulli random variables, each with probability of success P. As a result, $\hat{p}$ is the mean of a set of independent random variables, and the results we developed in the previous sections for sample means apply. In addition, the central limit theorem can be used to argue that the probability distribution for $\hat{p}$ can be modeled as a normally distributed random variable.

There is also a variation of the Law of Large Numbers that applies when sampling to determine the percent successes in a large population that has a known proportion P of success. If random samples are obtained from the population and the success or failure is determined for each observation then the sample proportion of success approaches P as the sample size increases. Thus we can make inferences about the population proportion using the sample proportion and the sample proportion will get closer as our sample size increases. However the difference between the expected number of sample successes—the sample size multiplied by P—and the number of successes in the sample is likely to grow.

In Section 5.4 it was shown that the number of successes in a binomial distribution and the proportion of successes have a distribution that is closely approximated by a normal distribution (see Figures 5.23 and 5.24). This provides a very close approximation when $nP(1 - P) > 5$.

The mean and variance of the sampling distribution of the sample proportion $\hat{p}$ can be obtained from the mean and variance of the number of successes, X:

$$E(X) = nP \quad \text{Var}(X) = nP(1-P)$$

And, thus,

$$E(\hat{p}) = E\left(\frac{X}{n}\right) = \frac{1}{n}E(X) = P$$

We see that the mean of the distribution of $\hat{p}$ is the population proportion, P.

The variance of $\hat{p}$ is the variance of the population distribution of the Bernoulli random variables divided by n:

$$\sigma_{\hat{p}}^2 = \text{Var}\left(\frac{X}{n}\right) = \frac{1}{n^2}\,\text{Var}(X) = \frac{P(1-P)}{n}$$

The standard deviation of $\hat{p}$, which is the square root of the variance, is called its standard error.

Since the distribution of the sample proportion is approximately normal for large sample sizes, we can obtain a standard normal random variable by subtracting P from $\hat{p}$ and dividing by the standard error.

Sampling Distribution of the Sample Proportion

Let $\hat{p}$ be the sample proportion of successes in a random sample from a population with proportion of success P. Then,

1. the sampling distribution of $\hat{p}$ has mean P:

$$E(\hat{p}) = P \tag{6.8}$$

2. the sampling distribution of p has standard deviation

$$\sigma_{\hat{p}} = \sqrt{\frac{P(1-P)}{n}} \tag{6.9}$$

3. and, if the sample size is large, the random variable

$$Z = \frac{\hat{p} - P}{\sigma_{\hat{p}}} \tag{6.10}$$

is approximately distributed as a standard normal. This approximation is good if

$$nP(1-P) > 5$$

Similar to the results from the previous section, we see that the standard error of the sample proportion, $\hat{p}$, decreases as the sample size increases and the distribution becomes more concentrated, as seen in Figure 6.10. This is expected because the sample proportion is a sample mean. With larger sample sizes our inferences about the

Figure 6.10
Probability
Density Functions
for the Sample
Proportions

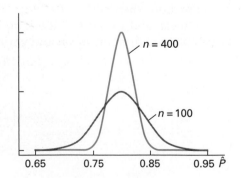

population proportion improve. From the central limit theorem we know that the binomial distribution can be approximated by the normal distribution with corresponding mean and variance. We see this result in the following examples.

Example 6.7 Evaluation of Home Electric Wiring (Probability of Sample Proportion)

A random sample of 270 homes was taken from a large population of older homes to estimate the proportion of homes with unsafe wiring. If, in fact, 20% of the homes have unsafe wiring, what is the probability that the sample proportion will be between 16% and 24% of homes with unsafe wiring?

Solution   For this problem we have the following:

$$P = 0.20 \quad n = 270$$

We can compute the standard deviation of the sample proportion, $\hat{p}$, as follows:

$$\sigma_{\hat{p}} = \sqrt{\frac{P(1-P)}{n}} = \sqrt{\frac{0.20(1-0.20)}{270}} = 0.024$$

The required probability is

$$P(0.16 < \hat{p} < 0.24) = P\left(\frac{0.16-P}{\sigma_{\hat{p}}} < \frac{\hat{p}-P}{\sigma_{\hat{p}}} < \frac{0.24-P}{\sigma_{\hat{p}}}\right)$$

$$= P\left(\frac{0.16-0.20}{0.024} < Z < \frac{0.24-0.20}{0.024}\right)$$

$$= P(-1.67 < Z < 1.67)$$

$$= 0.9050$$

where the probability for the Z interval is obtained using Table 1 in the appendix.

Thus, we see that the probability is 0.9050 that the sample proportion is within the interval 0.16 to 0.24, given $P = 0.20$, and a sample size of $n = 270$. This interval can be called a 90.50% acceptance interval. We can also note that, if the sample proportion was actually outside this interval, we might begin to suspect that the population proportion, P, is not 0.20.

Example 6.8 Business Course Selection (Probability of Sample Proportion)

It has been estimated that 43% of business graduates believe that a course in business ethics is very important for imparting ethical values to students (Reference 1). Find the probability that more than one-half of a random sample of 80 business graduates have this belief.

Solution   We are given that

$$P = 0.43 \quad n = 80$$

We will first compute the standard deviation of the sample proportion:

$$\sigma_{\hat{p}} = \sqrt{\frac{P(1-P)}{n}} = \sqrt{\frac{0.43(1-0.43)}{80}} = 0.055$$

Then the required probability can be computed as follows:

$$P(\hat{p} > 0.50) = P\left(\frac{\hat{p} - P}{\sigma_{\hat{p}}} > \frac{0.50 - P}{\sigma_{\hat{p}}}\right)$$

$$= P\left(Z > \frac{0.50 - 0.43}{0.055}\right)$$

$$= P(Z > 1.27)$$

$$= 0.1020$$

This probability, as shown in Figure 6.11, was obtained from Table 1 in the appendix. The probability of having one-half of the sample believing in the value of business ethics courses is approximately 0.1.

Figure 6.11 The Probability that a Standard Normal Random Variable Exceeds 1.27

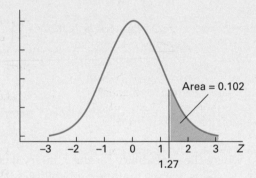

EXERCISES

Basic Exercises

6.26 Suppose that we have a population with proportion $P = 0.40$ and a random sample of size $n = 100$ drawn from the population.

  a. What is the probability that the sample proportion is greater than 0.45?
  b. What is the probability that the sample proportion is less than 0.29?
  c. What is the probability that the sample proportion is between 0.35 and 0.51?

6.27 Suppose that we have a population with proportion $P = 0.25$ and a random sample of size $n = 200$ drawn from the population.

  a. What is the probability that the sample proportion is greater than 0.31?
  b. What is the probability that the sample proportion is less than 0.14?
  c. What is the probability that the sample proportion is between 0.24 and 0.40?

6.28 Suppose that we have a population with proportion $P = 0.60$ and a random sample of size $n = 100$ drawn from the population.

  a. What is the probability that the sample proportion is greater than 0.66?
  b. What is the probability that the sample proportion is less than 0.48?

c. What is the probability that the sample proportion is between 0.52 and 0.66?

6.29 Suppose that we have a population with proportion $P = 0.50$ and a random sample of size $n = 900$ drawn from the population.

   a. What is the probability that the sample proportion is greater than 0.52?

   b. What is the probability that the sample proportion is less than 0.46?

   c. What is the probability that the sample proportion is between 0.47 and 0.53?

Application Exercises

6.30 In 1992, Canadians voted in a referendum on a new constitution. In the province of Quebec, 42.4% of those who voted were in favor of the new constitution. A random sample of 100 voters from the province was taken.

   a. What is the mean of the distribution of the sample proportion in favor of a new constitution?

   b. What is the variance of the sample proportion?

   c. What is the standard error of the sample proportion?

   d. What is the probability that the sample proportion is bigger than 0.5?

6.31 According to the Internal Revenue Service, 75% of all tax returns lead to a refund. A random sample of 100 tax returns is taken.

   a. What is the mean of the distribution of the sample proportion of returns leading to refunds?

   b. What is the variance of the sample proportion?

   c. What is the standard error of the sample proportion?

   d. What is the probability that the sample proportion exceeds 0.8?

6.32 A record store owner finds that 20% of customers entering her store make a purchase. One morning 180 people, who can be regarded as a random sample of all customers, enter the store.

   a. What is the mean of the distribution of the sample proportion of customers making a purchase?

   b. What is the variance of the sample proportion?

   c. What is the standard error of the sample proportion?

   d. What is the probability that the sample proportion is less than 0.15?

6.33 An administrator for a large group of hospitals believes that of all patients 30% will generate bills that become at least 2 months overdue. A random sample of 200 patients is taken.

   a. What is the standard error of the sample proportion that will generate bills that become at least 2 months overdue?

   b. What is the probability that the sample proportion is less than 0.25?

c. What is the probability that the sample proportion is more than 0.33?

d. What is the probability that the sample proportion is between 0.27 and 0.33?

6.34 A corporation receives 120 applications for positions from recent college graduates in business. Assuming that these applicants can be viewed as a random sample of all such graduates, what is the probability that between 35% and 45% of them are women if 40% of all recent college graduates in business are women?

6.35 A charity has found that 42% of all donors from last year will donate again this year. A random sample of 300 donors from last year was taken.

   a. What is the standard error of the sample proportion who will donate again this year?

   b. What is the probability that more than half of these sample members will donate again this year?

   c. What is the probability that the sample proportion is between 0.40 and 0.45?

   d. Without doing the calculations, state in which of the following ranges the sample proportion is more likely to lie: 0.39 to 0.41, 0.41 to 0.43, 0.43 to 0.45, or 0.45 to 0.46.

6.36 A corporation is considering a new issue of convertible bonds. Management believes that the offer terms will be found attractive by 20% of all its current stockholders. Suppose that this belief is correct. A random sample of 130 current stockholders is taken.

   a. What is the standard error of the sample proportion who find this offer attractive?

   b. What is the probability that the sample proportion is more than 0.15?

   c. What is the probability that the sample proportion is between 0.18 and 0.22?

   d. Suppose that a sample of 500 current stockholders had been taken. Without doing the calculations, state whether the probabilities in parts (b) and (c) would have been higher, lower, or the same as those found.

6.37 A store has determined that 30% of all lawn mower purchasers will also purchase a service agreement. In 1 month 280 lawn mowers are sold to customers who can be regarded as a random sample of all purchasers.

   a. What is the standard error of the sample proportion of those who will purchase a service agreement?

   b. What is the probability that the sample proportion will be less than 0.32?

   c. Without doing the calculations, state in which of the following ranges the sample proportion is most likely to be: 0.29 to 0.31, 0.30 to 0.32, 0.31 to 0.33, or 0.32 to 0.34.

6.38 A random sample of 100 voters is taken to estimate the proportion of a state's electorate in favor of increasing the gasoline tax to provide additional revenue for highway repairs. What is the largest value that the standard error of the sample proportion in favor of this measure can take?

6.39 In Exercise 6.38, suppose that it is decided that a sample of 100 voters is too small to provide a sufficiently reliable estimate of the population proportion. It is required instead that the probability that the sample proportion differs from the population proportion (whatever its value) by more than 0.03 should not exceed 0.05. How large a sample is needed to guarantee that this requirement is met?

6.40 A company wants to estimate the proportion of people who are likely to purchase electric shavers and who watch the nationally telecast baseball playoffs. A random sample obtained information from 120 people who were identified as likely to purchase electric shavers. Suppose that the proportion of those likely to purchase electric shavers in the population who watch the telecast is 0.25.

   a. The probability is 0.10 that the sample proportion watching the telecast exceeds the population proportion by how much?

   b. The probability is 0.05 that the sample proportion is lower than the population proportion by how much?

   c. The probability is 0.30 that the sample proportion differs from the population proportion by how much?

6.41 Suppose that 50% of all adult Americans believe that a major overhaul of the nation's health care delivery system is essential. What is the probability that more than 56% of a random sample of 150 adult Americans would hold this belief?

6.42 Suppose that 50% of all adult Americans believe that federal budget deficits at recent levels cause long-term harm to the nation's economy. What is the probability that more than 58% of a random sample of 250 adult Americans would hold this belief.

6.43 A journalist wanted to learn the views of the chief executive officers of the 500 largest U.S. corporations on program trading of stocks. In the time available, it was only possible to contact a random sample of 81 of these chief executive officers. If 55% of all the population members believe that program trading should be banned, what is the probability that less than half the sample members hold this view?

6.44 Forty percent of students at small colleges have brought their own personal computers to campus. A random sample of 120 entering freshmen was taken.

   a. What is the standard error of the sample proportion bringing their own personal computers to campus?

   b. What is the probability that the sample proportion is less than 0.33?

   c. What is the probability that the sample proportion is between 0.38 and 0.46?

6.45 An employee survey conducted two years ago Packard Motors Inc. found that 53% of its employees were concerned about future health care benefits. A random sample of 80 of these employees were asked if they were now concerned about future health care benefits. Answer the following assuming that there has been no change in the level of concern about health care benefits compared to the survey two years ago.

   a. What is the standard error of the sample proportion who are concerned?

   b. What is the probability that the sample proportion is less than 0.5?

   c. What is the upper limit of the sample proportion such that only 3% of the time the sample proportion would exceed this value?

6.46 The annual percentage salary increases for the chief executive officers of all midsize corporations are normally distributed with mean 12.2% and standard deviation 3.6%. A random sample of 81 of these chief executive officers was taken. What is the probability that more than half the sample members had salary increases of less than 10%?

6.4 SAMPLING DISTRIBUTIONS OF SAMPLE VARIANCES

Now that sampling distributions for sample means and proportions have been developed, we will consider sampling distributions of sample variances. As business and industry increase their emphasis on producing products that satisfy customer quality standards, there is an increased need to measure and reduce population variance. High variance for a process implies a wider range of possible values for important product characteristics. This wider range of outcomes will result in more individual products that perform below an acceptable standard. After all, a customer does not care if a product performs well "on average." She is concerned that the particular item that she purchased works. High-quality products can be obtained from a manufacturing process if the process has a low population variance, so that fewer units are below the desired quality standard. By understanding the sampling distribution of sample variances, we can make inferences about the population variance. Thus, processes that have high variance can be identified and corrected. In addition, a smaller population variance improves our ability to make inferences about population means using sample means.

We begin by considering a random sample of n observations drawn from a population with unknown mean μ and unknown variance σ^2. Denote the sample members as $x_1, x_2, ..., x_n$. The population variance is the expectation

$$\sigma^2 = E[(X-\mu)^2]$$

which suggests that we consider the mean of $(x_i - \bar{x})^2$ over n observations. Since μ is unknown, we will use the sample mean $\bar{x}$ to compute a sample variance.

Sample Variance
Let $x_1, x_2, ..., x_n$ be a random sample of observations from a population. The quantity

$$s^2 = \frac{1}{n-1}\sum_{i=1}^{n}(x_i - \bar{x})^2$$

is called the **sample variance**, and its square root, s, is called the *sample standard deviation*. Given a specific random sample, we could compute the sample variance, and the sample variance would be different for each random sample because of differences in sample observations.

We might be initially surprised by the use of $(n - 1)$ as the divisor in the above definition. One simple explanation is that in a random sample of n observations we have n different independent values or degrees of freedom. But after we know the computed sample mean, there are only $n - 1$ different values that can be uniquely defined. In addition, it can be shown that the expected value of the sample variance computed in this way is the population variance. This result is established in the chapter appendix and holds when the actual sample size, n, is a small proportion of the population size N:

$$E(s^2) = \sigma^2$$

The conclusion that the expected value of the sample variance is the population variance is quite general. But for statistical inference we would like to know more about the sampling distribution. If we can assume that the underlying population distribution is normal, then it can be shown that the sample variance and the population variance are related through a probability distribution known as the *chi-square distribution*.

The chi-square family of distributions is used in applied statistical analysis because it provides a link between t he sample and the population variances. The chi-square distribution with $n - 1$ degrees of freedom is the distribution of the sum of squares of $n - 1$ independent standard normal random variables. The above chi-square distribution and the resulting computed probabilities for various values of s^2 require that the population distribution be normal. Thus, the assumption of an underlying normal distribution is more important for determining probabilities of sample variances than it is for determining probabilities of sample means.

The distribution is defined for only positive values, since variances are all positive values. An example of the probability density function is shown in Figure 6.12. The density function is asymmetric with a long positive tail. We can characterize a particular member of the family of chi-square distributions by a single parameter referred to as the degrees of freedom, denoted as v. A χ^2 distribution with v degrees of freedom will be denoted as χ_v^2. The mean and variance of this distribution are equal to the number of degrees of freedom and twice the number of degrees of freedom:

$$E\left(\chi_v^2\right) = v \quad \text{and} \quad \text{Var}\left(\chi_v^2\right) = 2v$$

Using these results for the mean and variance of the chi-square distribution, we find that

$$E\left[\frac{(n-1)s^2}{\sigma^2}\right] = (n-1)$$
$$\frac{(n-1)}{\sigma^2}E(s^2) = (n-1)$$
$$E(s^2) = \sigma^2$$

Figure 6.12
Probability
Density Functions
for the Chi-Square
Distribution 4, 6,
and 8 Degrees of
Freedom

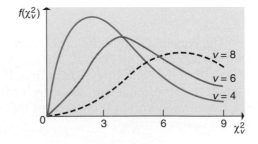

To obtain the variance of s^2, we have

$$\text{Var}\left[\frac{(n-1)s^2}{\sigma^2}\right] = 2(n-1)$$

$$\frac{(n-1)^2}{\sigma^4}\text{Var}(s^2) = 2(n-1)$$

$$\text{Var}(s^2) = \frac{2\sigma^4}{(n-1)}$$

We can use the properties of the χ^2 distribution to find the variance of the sampling distribution of the sample variance when the parent population is normal.

The parameter v of the χ^2 distribution is called the *degrees of freedom*. To help understand the degrees of freedom concept, consider first that the sample variance is the sum of squares for n values of the form $(x_i - \bar{x})$. These n values are not independent because their sum is zero (as we can show using the definition of the mean). Thus, if we know any $n - 1$ of the values $(x_i - \bar{x})$,

$$\sum_{i=1}^{n}(x_i - \bar{x}) = 0$$

$$x_n - \bar{x} = \sum_{i=1}^{n-1}(x_i - \bar{x})$$

Since we can determine the nth quantity if we know the remaining $n - 1$ quantities, we say that there are $n - 1$ degrees of freedom—independent values—for computing s^2. In contrast, if μ were known, we could compute an estimate of σ^2 by using the quantities

$$(x_1 - \mu), (x_2 - \mu), ..., (x_n - \mu)$$

each of which is independent. In that case we would have n degrees of freedom from the n independent sample observations, x_i. However, μ is not known, and we must use its estimate $\bar{x}$ to compute the estimate of σ^2. As a result, one degree of freedom is lost in computing the sample mean, and we have $n - 1$ degrees of freedom for s^2.

For many applications involving the population variance we need to find values for the cumulative distribution of χ^2, especially the upper and lower tails of the distribution—for example,

$$P(\chi_{10}^2 < K) = 0.05$$

$$P(\chi_{10}^2 > K) = 0.05$$

For this purpose we have the distribution of the chi-square random variable tabulated in Table 7 in the appendix. In Table 7 the degrees of freedom are noted in the left column and the critical values of K for various probability levels are indicated in the other columns. Thus, for 10 degrees of freedom the value of K for the lower interval is 3.94. This result is found by going to the row with 10 degrees of freedom in the left column and then reading over to the column headed by the probability 0.950 to the right of these column entries. The chi-square value is 3.94. Similarly, for the upper 0.05 interval the value of K is 18.31. This result is found by going to the row with 10 degrees of freedom in the left column and then reading over to the column headed by the probability 0.050 to the right of these column entries. The chi-square value is 18.31. These probabilities are shown schematically in Figure 6.13.

$$P(\chi^2_{10} < 3.94) = 0.05$$

$$P(\chi^2_{10} > 18.31) = 0.05$$

The sampling distribution results are summarized next.

Sampling Distribution of the Sample Variances

Let s^2 denote the sample variance for a random sample of n observations from a population with a variance σ^2.

1. The sampling distribution of s^2 has mean σ^2:

$$E(s^2) = \sigma^2 \tag{6.11}$$

2. The variance of the sampling distribution of s^2 depends on the underlying population distribution. If that distribution is normal, then

$$Var(s^2) = \frac{2\sigma^4}{n-1} \tag{6.12}$$

3. If the population distribution is normal, then $\dfrac{(n-1)s^2}{\sigma^2}$ is distributed as $\chi^2_{(n-1)}$.

Thus, if we have a random sample from a population with a normal distribution, we can make inferences about the sample variance σ^2 by using s^2 and the chi-square distribution. This process is illustrated in the following examples.

Figure 6.13
Upper and Lower χ^2_{10} Probabilities with 10 Degrees of Freedom

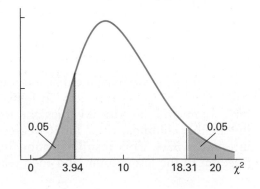

Example 6.9 Process Monitoring for Integrated Electronics (Probability of Sample Variance)

George Samson is responsible for quality assurance at Integrated Electronics. Integrated Electronics has just signed a contract with a company in China to manufacture a control device that is a component of its manufacturing robotics products. Integrated Electronics wants to be sure that these new lower cost components meet its high quality standards. George has asked you to establish a quality monitoring process for checking shipments of control device A. The variability of the electrical resistance, measured in ohms, is critical for this device. Manufacturing standards specify a standard deviation of 3.6, and the population distribution of resistance measurements is normal when the components meet the quality specification. The monitoring process requires that a random sample of $n = 6$ observations be obtained from each shipment of devices and the sample variance be computed. Determine an upper limit for the sample variance such that the probability of exceeding this limit, given a population standard deviation of 3.6, is less than 0.05.

Solution For this problem we have $n = 6$ and $\sigma^2 = (3.6)^2 = 12.96$. Using the chi-square distribution, we can state that

$$P(s^2 > K) = P\left(\frac{(n-1)s^2}{12.96} > 11.07\right) = 0.05$$

where K is the desired upper limit and $\chi_5^2 = 11.07$ is the upper 0.05 critical value of the chi-square distribution with 5 degrees of freedom, from row 5 of the chi-square distribution from Table 7 in the appendix. The required upper limit for s^2—labeled as K—can be obtained by solving

$$\frac{(n-1)K}{12.96} = 11.07$$

$$K = \frac{(11.07)(12.96)}{(6-1)} = 28.69$$

If the sample variance, s^2, from a random sample of size $n = 6$ exceeds 28.69, there is strong evidence to suspect that the population variance exceeds 12.96 and that the supplier should be contacted and appropriate action taken. This action could include returning the entire shipment or checking each item in the shipment at the suppliers expense.

Example 6.10 Process Analysis for Green Valley Foods (Probability of Sample Variance)

Shirley Mendez is the manager of quality assurance for Green Valley Foods Inc., a packer of frozen vegetable products. Shirley wants to be sure that the variation of package weights is small so that the company does not produce a large proportion of packages that are under the stated package weight. She has asked you to obtain upper and lower limits for the ratio of the sample variance divided by the population variance for a random sample of $n = 20$ observations. The limits are such that the probability that the ratio is below the lower limit is 0.025 and the probability that the ratio is above the upper limit is 0.025. Thus, 95% of the ratios will be between these limits. The population distribution can be assumed to be normal.

Solution   We are asked to obtain values K_L and K_U such that

$$P\left(\frac{s^2}{\sigma^2} < K_L\right) = 0.025 \quad \text{and} \quad P\left(\frac{s^2}{\sigma^2} > K_U\right) = 0.025$$

given that a random sample of size $n = 20$ is used to compute the sample variance. For the lower limit we can state the following:

$$0.025 = P\left[\frac{(n-1)s^2}{\sigma^2} < (n-1)K_L\right] = P\left[\chi_{19}^2 < (n-1)K_L\right]$$

For the upper limit we can state the following:

$$0.975 = P\left[\frac{(n-1)s^2}{\sigma^2} > (n-1)K_U\right] = P\left[\chi_{19}^2 > (n-1)K_U\right]$$

These upper and lower limits of chi-square define an interval such that, if the sample computed chi-square is within that interval, we accept the assumption that the process variance is at the assumed value. This interval is defined as an *acceptance interval*.

Using the lower and upper bounds for the chi-square acceptance interval, we can compute the acceptance interval limits, K_L and K_U, for the ratio of sample variance to population variance. The upper and lower values for the chi-square distribution can be found in Table 7 as

$$\chi_{19L}^2 = 8.91$$

$$\chi_{19U}^2 = 32.85$$

$$0.025 = P\left[\chi_{19L}^2 < (n-1)K_L\right] = P\left[8.91 < (19)K_L\right]$$

and, thus,

$$K_L = 0.469$$

For the upper limit we have

$$0.975 = P\left[\chi_{19U}^2 > (n-1)K_U\right] = P\left[32.85 > (19)K_U\right]$$

and, thus,

$$K_U = 1.729$$

The 95% acceptance interval for the ratio of sample variance divided by population variance is as follows:

$$P\left(0.469 \leq \frac{s^2}{\sigma^2} \leq 1.729\right) = 0.95$$

Thus, the sample variance is between 46.9% and 172.9% of the population variance with probability 0.95.

At this point it is important that we emphasize that the procedures used to make inferences about the population variance are substantially influenced by the assumption of a normal population distribution. Inferences concerning the population mean based on the sample mean are not substantially affected by departures from a normal distribution. In addition, inferences based on the sample mean can make use of the central limit theorem, which states that sample means will typically be normally distributed if the sample size is reasonably large. Thus, we state that inferences based on the sample mean are robust with respect to the assumption of normality. Unfortunately, inferences based on sample variances are not robust with respect to the assumption of normality.

We know that in many applications the population variance is of direct interest to an investigator. But when using the procedures we have demonstrated, we must keep in mind that if only a moderate number of sample observations are available, serious departures from normality in the parent population can severely invalidate the conclusions of analyses. The cautious analyst will therefore be rather tentative in making inferences in these circumstances.

EXERCISES

Basic Exercises

6.47 A random sample of size $n = 16$ is obtained from a normally distributed population with a population mean of $\mu = 100$ and a variance of $\sigma^2 = 25$.

 a. What is the probability that $\bar{x} > 101$?
 b. What is the probability that the sample variance is greater than 45?
 c. What is the probability that the sample variance is greater than 60?

6.48 A random sample of size $n = 25$ is obtained from a normally distributed population with a population mean of $\mu = 198$ and a variance of $\sigma^2 = 100$.

 a. What is the probability that the sample mean is greater than 200?
 b. What is the value of the sample variance such that 5% of the sample variances would be less than this value?
 c. What is the value of the sample variance such that 5% of the sample variances would be greater than this value?

6.49 A random sample of size $n = 18$ is obtained from a normally distributed population with a population mean of $\mu = 46$ and a variance of $\sigma^2 = 50$.

 a. What is the probability that the sample mean is greater than 50?
 b. What is the value of the sample variance such that 5% of the sample variances would be less than this value?
 c. What is the value of the sample variance such that 5% of the sample variances would be greater than this value?

6.50 A process produces batches of a chemical whose impurity concentrations follow a normal distribution with a variance of 1.75. A random sample of 20 of these batches is chosen. Find the probability that the sample variance exceeds 3.10.

6.51 Monthly rates of return on the shares of a particular common stock are independent of one another and normally distributed with a standard deviation of 1.6. A sample of 12 months is taken.

 a. Find the probability that the sample standard deviation is less than 2.5.
 b. Find the probability that the sample standard deviation is more than 1.0.

6.52 It is believed that first-year salaries for newly qualified accountants follow a normal distribution with a standard deviation of $2,500. A random sample of 16 observations was taken.

 a. Find the probability that the sample standard deviation is more than $3,000.
 b. Find the probability that the sample standard deviation is less than $1,500.

Application Exercises

6.53 A mathematics test of 100 multiple-choice questions is to be given to all freshmen entering a large university. Initially, in a pilot study the test was given to a random sample of 20 freshmen. Suppose that, for the population of all entering freshmen, the distribution of the number of correct answers would be normal with a variance of 250.

a. What is the probability that the sample variance would be less than 100?

b. What is the probability that the sample variance would be more than 500?

6.54 In a large city it was found that summer electricity bills for single-family homes followed a normal distribution with a standard deviation of $100. A random sample of 25 bills was taken.

a. Find the probability that the sample standard deviation is less than $75.

b. Find the probability that the sample standard deviation is more than $150.

6.55 The number of hours spent watching television by students in the week before final exams has a normal distribution with a standard deviation of 4.5 hours. A random sample of 30 students was taken.

a. Is the probability more than 0.95 that the sample standard deviation exceeds 3.5 hours?

b. Is the probability more than 0.95 that the sample standard deviation is less than 6 hours?

6.56 In Table 6.1 we considered the 15 possible samples of two observations from a population of $N = 6$ values of years on the job for employees. The population variance for these six values is as follows:

$$\sigma = \frac{47}{12}$$

For each of the 15 possible samples, calculate the sample variance. Find the average of these 15 sample variances, thus confirming that the expected value of the sample variance is not equal to the population variance when the number of sample members is not a small proportion of the number of population members. (In fact, as you can verify here, $E(s^2) = N\sigma^2/(N-1)$.)

6.57 A production process manufactures electronic components with timing signals whose duration follows a normal distribution. A random sample of six components was taken, and the durations of their timing signals were measured.

a. The probability is 0.05 that the sample variance is bigger than what percentage of the population variance?

b. The probability is 0.10 that the sample variance is less than what percentage of the population variance?

6.58 A random sample of 10 stock market mutual funds was taken. Suppose that rates of returns on the population of all stock market mutual funds follow a normal distribution.

a. The probability is 0.10 that sample variance is bigger than what percentage of the population variance?

b. Find any pair of numbers, a and b, to complete the following sentence: The probability is 0.95 that the sample variance is between a% and b% of the population variance.

c. Suppose that a sample of 20 mutual funds had been taken. Without doing the calculations, indicate how this would change your answer to part (b).

6.59 Each member of a random sample of 15 business economists was asked to predict the rate of inflation for the coming year. Assume that the predictions for the whole population of business economists follow a normal distribution with standard deviation 1.8%.

a. The probability is 0.01 that the sample standard deviation is bigger than what number?

b. The probability is 0.025 that the sample standard deviation is smaller than what number?

c. Find any pair of numbers such that the probability that the sample standard deviation that lies between these numbers is 0.90.

6.60 A precision instrument is checked by making 12 readings on the same quantity. The population distribution of readings is normal.

a. The probability is 0.95 that the sample variance is more than what percentage of the population variance?

b. The probability is 0.90 that the sample variance is more than what percentage of the population variance?

c. Determine any pair of appropriate numbers, a and b, to complete the following sentence: The probability is 0.95 that the sample variance is between a% and b% of the population variance.

6.61 A drug company produces pills containing an active ingredient. The company is concerned about the mean weight of this ingredient per pill, but it also requires that the variance (in squared milligrams) be no more than 1.5. A random sample of 20 pills is selected, and the sample variance is found to be 2.05. How likely is it that a sample variance this high or higher would be found if the population variance is, in fact, 1.5? Assume that the population distribution is normal.

6.62 A manufacturer has been purchasing raw materials from a supplier whose consignments have a variance of 15.4 (in squared pounds) in impurity levels. A rival supplier claims that she can supply consignments of this raw material with the same mean impurity level but with lower variance. For a random sample of 25 consignments from the second supplier, the variance in impurity levels was found to be 12.2. What is the probability of observing a value this low or lower for the sample variance if, in fact, the true population variance is 15.4? Assume that the population distribution is normal.

CHAPTER EXERCISES AND APPLICATIONS

6.63 What is meant by the statement that the sample mean has a sampling distribution?

6.64 An investor is considering six different money market funds. The average number of days to maturity for each of these funds is as follows:

$$41, \quad 39, \quad 35, \quad 35, \quad 33, \quad 38$$

Two of these funds are to be chosen at random.

a. How many possible samples of two funds are there?
b. List all possible samples.
c. Find the probability function of the sampling distribution of the sample means.
d. Verify directly that the mean of the sampling distribution of the sample means is equal to the population mean.

6.65 Of what relevance is the central limit theorem to the sampling distribution of the sample means?

6.66 The scores of all applicants taking an aptitude test required by a law school have a normal distribution with a mean of 420 and a standard deviation of 100. A random sample of 25 scores is taken.

a. Find the probability that the sample mean score is higher than 450.
b. Find the probability that the sample mean score is between 400 and 450.
c. The probability is 0.10 that the sample mean score is higher than what number?
d. The probability is 0.10 that the sample mean score is lower than what number?
e. The probability is 0.05 that the sample standard deviation of the scores is higher than what number?
f. The probability is 0.05 that the sample standard deviation of the scores is lower than what number?
g. If a sample of 50 test scores had been taken, would the probability of a sample mean score higher than 450 be smaller than, larger than, or

the same as the correct answer to part (a)? It is not necessary to do the detailed calculations here. Sketch a graph to illustrate your reasoning.

6.67 A company services home air conditioners. It has been found that times for service calls follow a Normal distribution with a mean of 60 minutes and a standard deviation of 10 minutes. A random sample of four service calls was taken.

a. What is the probability that the sample mean service time is more than 65 minutes?
b. The probability is 0.10 that the sample mean service time is less than how many minutes?
c. The probability is 0.10 that the sample standard deviation of service times is more than how many minutes?
d. The probability is 0.10 that the sample standard deviation of service times is less than how many minutes?
e. What is the probability that more than two of these calls take more than 65 minutes?

6.68 In a particular year, the percentage rates of return of U.S. common stock mutual funds had a normal distribution with a mean of 14.8 and a standard deviation of 6.3. A random sample of nine of these mutual funds was taken.

a. What is the probability that the sample mean percentage rate of return is more than 19.0?
b. What is the probability that the sample mean percentage rate of return is between 10.6 and 19.0?
c. The probability is 0.25 that the sample mean percentage return is less than what number?
d. The probability is 0.10 that the sample standard deviation of percentage return is more than what number?
e. If a sample of 20 of these funds was taken, state whether the probability of a sample mean percentage rate of return of more than 19.0 would be smaller than, larger than, or the same as the correct answer to part (a). Sketch a graph to illustrate your reasoning.

6.69 The lifetimes of a certain electronic component are known to be normally distributed with a mean of 1,600 hours and a standard deviation of 400 hours.

    a. For a random sample of 16 components find the probability that the sample mean is more than 1,500 hours.

    b. For a random sample of 16 components the probability is 0.15 that the sample mean lifetime is more than how many hours?

    c. For a random sample of 16 components the probability is 0.10 that the sample standard deviation lifetime is more than how many hours?

6.70 Refer to the chapter appendix in order to derive the mean of the sampling distribution of the sample variances for a sample of n observations from a population of N members when the population variance is σ^2. By appropriately modifying the argument regarding variances in the chapter appendix, show that

$$E(s^2) = N\sigma^2/(N-1)$$

Note the intuitive plausibility of this result when $n = N$.

6.71 It has been found that times taken by people to complete a particular tax form follow a normal distribution with a mean of 100 minutes and a standard deviation of 30 minutes. A random sample of nine people who have completed this tax form was taken.

    a. What is the probability that the sample mean time taken is more than 120 minutes?

    b. The probability is 0.20 that the sample mean time taken is less than how many minutes?

    c. The probability is 0.05 that the sample standard deviation of time taken is less than how many minutes?

6.72 It was found that 80% of seniors at a particular college had accepted a job offer before graduation. For those accepting offers, salary distribution was normal with a mean of $37,000 and a standard deviation of $4,000.

    a. For a random sample of 60 seniors what is the probability that less than 70% have accepted job offers?

    b. For a random sample of 6 seniors what is the probability that less than 70% have accepted job offers?

    c. For a random sample of 6 seniors who have accepted job offers what is the probability that the average salary is more than $38,000?

    d. A senior is chosen at random. What is the probability that she has accepted a job offer with a salary of more than $38,000?

6.73 Plastic bags used for packaging produce are manufactured so that the breaking strengths of the bags are normally distributed with a standard deviation of 1.8 pounds per square inch. A random sample of 16 bags is selected.

    a. The probability is 0.01 that the sample standard deviation of breaking strengths exceeds what number?

    b. The probability is 0.15 that the sample mean exceeds the population mean by how much?

    c. The probability is 0.05 that the sample mean differs from the population mean by how much?

6.74 A quality control manager was concerned about variability in the amount of an active ingredient in pills produced by a particular process. A random sample of 21 pills was taken. What is the probability that the sample variance of the amount of an active ingredient was more than twice the population variance?

6.75 A sample of 100 students is to be taken to determine which of two brands of beer is preferred in a blind taste test. Suppose that, in the whole population of students, 50% would prefer brand A.

    a. What is the probability that more than 60% of the sample members prefer brand A?

    b. What is the probability that between 45% and 55% of the sample members prefer brand A?

    c. Suppose that a sample of only 10 students was available. Indicate how the method of calculation of probabilities would differ, compared with your solutions to parts (a) and (b)?

6.76 Scores on a particular test, taken by a large group of students, follow a normal distribution with a standard deviation of 40 points. A random sample of 16 scores was taken to estimate the population mean score. Let $\overline{X}$ denote the sample mean. What is the probability that the interval $(\overline{X} - 10)$ to $(\overline{X} + 10)$ contains the true population mean?

6.77 A manufacturer of liquid detergent claims that the mean weight of liquid in containers sold is at least 30 ounces. It is known that the population distribution of weights is normal with a standard deviation of 1.3 ounces. In order to check the manufacturer's claim, a random sample of 16 containers of detergent is examined. The claim will be questioned if the sample mean weight is fewer than 29.5 ounces. What is the probability that the claim will be questioned if, in fact, the population mean weight is 30 ounces?

6.78 In a particular year 40% of home sales were partially financed by the seller. A random sample of 250 sales is examined.

    a. The probability is 0.8 that the sample proportion is bigger than what amount?

b. The probability is 0.9 that the sample proportion is smaller than what amount?

c. The probability is 0.7 that the sample proportion differs from the population proportion by how much?

6.79 A candidate for office intends to campaign in a state if her initial support level exceeds 30% of the voters. A random sample of 300 voters is taken, and it is decided to campaign if the sample proportion supporting the candidate exceeds 0.28.

a. What is the probability of a decision not to campaign if, in fact, the initial support level is 20%?

b. What is the probability of a decision not to campaign if, in fact, the initial support level is 40%?

6.80 It is known that the incomes of subscribers to a particular magazine have a normal distribution with a standard deviation of $6,600. A random sample of 25 subscribers is taken.

a. What is the probability that the sample standard deviation of their incomes is bigger than $4,000?

b. What is the probability that the sample standard deviation of their incomes is less than $8,000?

6.81 Batches of chemical are manufactured by a production process. Samples of 20 batches from a production run are selected for testing. If the standard deviation of the percentage of impurity contents in the sample batches exceeds 2.5%, the production process is thoroughly checked. Assume that the population distribution of percentage impurity concentrations is normal. What is the probability that the production process will be thoroughly checked if the population standard deviation of percentage impurity concentrations is 2%?

6.82 🌐 A consumer product that has flourished in the last few years is bottled natural spring water. Jon Thorne is the CEO of a company that sells natural spring water. He has requested a report of the filling process of the 24 oz (710 mL) bottles to be sure that they are being properly filled. To check if the process needs to be adjusted, Emma Astrom, who monitors the process, randomly samples and weighs five bottles every 15 minutes for a 5-hour period. The data are contained in the data file **Bottles**.

a. Compute the sample mean, sample standard deviations for individual bottles, and the standard deviation of the sample mean for each sample.

b. Determine the probability that the sample means are below 685 mL if the population mean is 710.

c. Determine the probability that the sample means are above 720 mL.

6.83 🌐 Prairie Flower Cereal Inc. is a small but growing producer of hot and ready-to-eat breakfast cereals. The company was started in 1910 by Gordon Thorson, a successful grain farmer. You have been asked to test the cereal-packing process of 18 oz (510-gram) boxes of sugar-coated wheat cereal. Two machines are used for the packaging process. Twenty samples of five boxes each are randomly sampled and weighed. The data are contained in the file **Sugar Coated Wheat**.

a. Compute the overall sample mean, sample variance, and variance of the sample means for each sample.

b. Determine the probability that a single sample mean is below 500 if the process is operating properly for each machine.

c. Determine the probability that a single sample mean is above 508 if the process is operating properly for each machine.

6.84 🌐 Another product packaged by Prairie Flower Cereal Inc. is an apple cinnamon cereal. To test the packaging process of 40 oz (1,134-gram) boxes of this cereal, 23 samples of six boxes each are randomly sampled and weighed. The lower and upper acceptance limits have been set at 1,120 grams and 1,150 grams respectively. The data are contained in the data file **Granola**.

a. Compute the overall sample mean, sample variance, and variance of the sample means for each sample.

b. Compute the probability that the sample means will be within the acceptance limits.

Appendix

1. CENTRAL LIMIT THEOREM FROM LINEAR SUM OF RANDOM VARIABLES

In applied statistical analysis many of the random variables used can be characterized as the sum or mean of a large number of random variables. For example, total daily sales in a store are the result of a number of sales to individual customers—each of whom can be modeled as a random variable. Total national investment spending in a month is the sum of many individual investment decisions by specific firms. Thus, if $X_1, X_2, ..., X_n$ represents the result of individual random events, the observed random variable

$$X = X_1 + X_2 + \cdots + X_n$$

and from Chapter 5

$$E(X) = n\mu \qquad \text{Var}(X) = n\sigma^2$$

The central limit theorem states that the resulting sum, X, is normally distributed and can be used to compute a random variable, Z, with a mean of 0 and a variance of 1:

$$Z = \frac{X - E(X)}{\sqrt{\text{Var}(X)}} = \frac{X - n\mu}{\sqrt{n\sigma^2}}$$

In addition, if X is divided by n to obtain a mean of $\overline{X}$, then a corresponding Z with a mean of 0 and a variance of 1 can also be computed:

$$Z = \frac{\overline{X} - \mu_X}{\sigma_{\overline{X}}} = \frac{\overline{X} - \mu_X}{\dfrac{\sigma_X}{\sqrt{n}}}$$

Using these results, we have the central limit theorem.

2. MONTE CARLO SAMPLE SIMULATIONS USING MINITAB

In Section 6.2 we presented results from Monte Carlo sampling simulations to demonstrate the central limit theorem. In this appendix we will indicate how you can construct similar simulations for a probability distribution. The simulation can be performed using a Minitab macro named **Centlimit.mac**, which is contained on the disk supplied with the textbook. To use this macro, copy it to the directory

```
MTBWIN\MACROS\
```

using the Windows Explorer. This macro will then be stored with other macros supplied with the Minitab package. When the macro is stored in this directory, it can be run directly in Minitab. Alternatively, the macro can be stored in another directory, and the entire path is supplied to run the macro. To run the sampling simulation, use the following steps:

1. In column one store a set of values that have the frequency indicated by the probability distribution that you are interested in simulating. Typically, we store 100 values, but any number could be stored. For example, to store a binomial distribution with $P = 0.40$, you would store forty 1s and sixty 0s in column one. You could also store an empirical distribution of numbers from a population being studied. Another procedure for obtaining the sample values is to use the following command:

```
CALC>RANDOM DATA>"SELECT PROBABILITY DISTRIBUTION"
```

This would provide you with a random sample from one of a number of common probability distributions.

2. In the Minitab Session Window type the command

```
MTB>%CENTLIMIT N1 N2 C1-C3
```

where N1 is the sample size for the individual samples being simulated, and N2 is the number of samples whose means are to be obtained from the simulation. Generally, 500 to

1,000 samples will provide a good sampling distribution, but you can select any reasonable value. Recognize that the greater the number of samples, the longer it will take to run the simulation. C1 to C3 are the columns used by Minitab for the simulation with your probability distribution of interest in column one. You could use any columns as long as your probability distribution is in column one.

Figure 6.14 shows a run of the sampling simulation.

The simulation will generate samples in column two and compute the sample mean. The mean for each sample will be stored in column three, titled "Mean." Descriptive statistics and histograms will be computed for the "random variable" values in column one and for the sample means in column three. By clicking on the menu command

```
WINDOWS>TILE
```

you can obtain the screen in Figure 6.15, which is useful for comparing the original distribution and the sampling distribution with a comparable normal.

In Figure 6.15 we see that the distribution of the random variable is definitely not normal; rather, it is highly skewed to the right. In contrast, the sampling distribution of the means closely approximates a normal distribution. Figure 6.16 presents a copy of the Centlimit.mac Minitab macro, which is also stored on the data disk for the textbook. Users familiar with Minitab macros could modify this macro to obtain different outputs.

Figure 6.14
Monte Carlo Sampling Simulation in Minitab

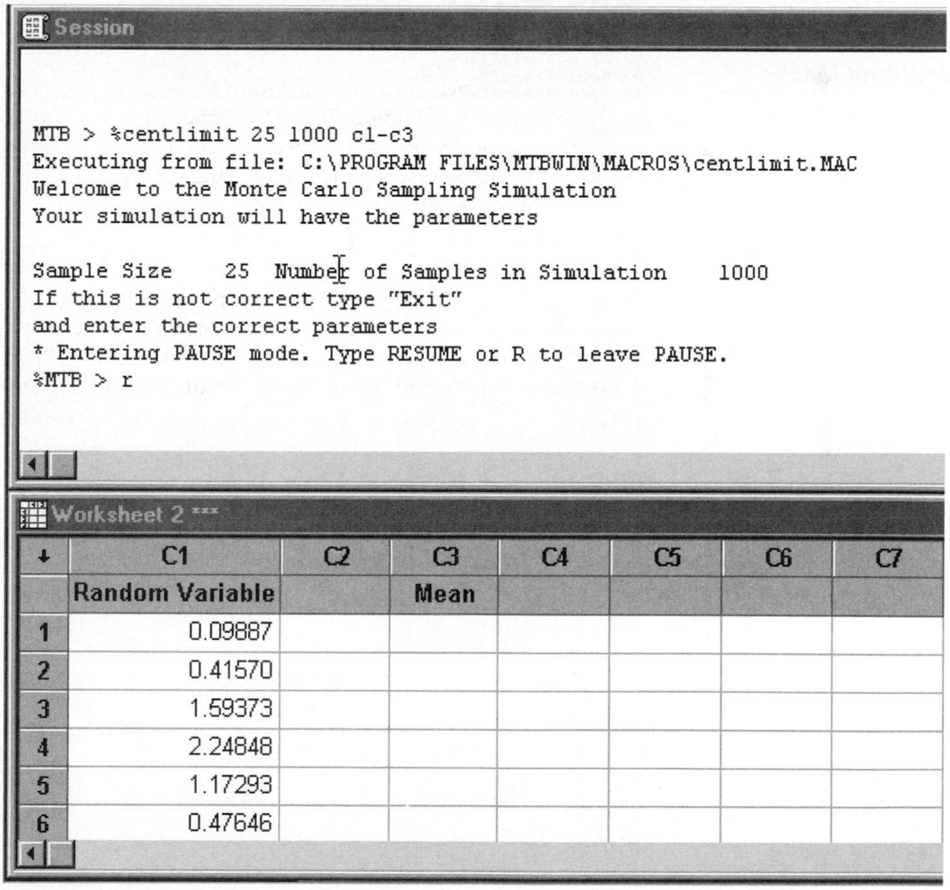

Figure 6.15
Results of the
Monte Carlo
Sampling
Simulation

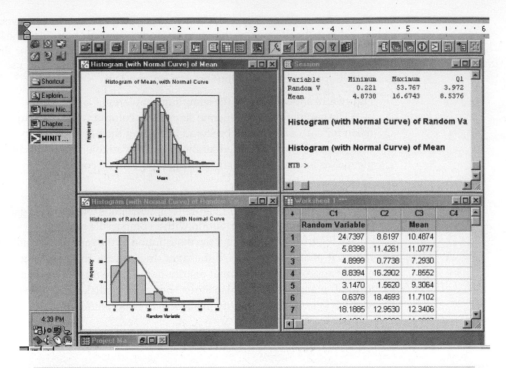

Figure 6.16
Copy of the
Minitab Macro
"Centlimit.Mac"

```
Macro
Centlimit n1,n2,Dist,Samp,Xbar
#  Dr.William L. Carlson
#  Professor of Economics
#  St Olaf College
#  Northfield MN   55057
#  Carlson@Stolaf.edu
#  To Execute this Macro in Minitab  Type
#  %Centlimit "sample size"  "Number of Samples"  C1 C2 C3
#
#The output includes a histogram and a normal probability plot for the
original #distribution and a histogram and normal probability plot for the
sampling #distribution of sample means
#Macro is Stored as a text file in C:\program
files\mtbwin\macros\centlimit.mac
#
#Definition of Variables
#
# n1  Sample size obtained from probability distribution
# n2  Number of samples of size n1 obtained in this simulation
# Dist       Column that contains an empirical distribution from which the
random #          sample is obtained.
# Xbar       Column that contains the sample means from each of the n2 samples
#            obtained in the simulation
# Samp       Column that will be used to generate each of the samples.
#
#
Mconstant  n1 n2 k1 k2
Mcolumn Dist Xbar Samp c11 c12 c13 c14
Name Dist 'Random Variable' Xbar 'Mean'
Let c11="Sample Size"
Let c12= n1
Let c13="Number of Samples in Simulation"
Let c14=n2
Note Welcome to the Monte Carlo Sampling Simulation
Note Your simulation will have the parameters
Write 'Terminal' c11-c14
Note If this is not correct type "exit"
Note and enter the correct parameters
Pause
Brief 0
Do k1=1:n2
Sample n1 Dist Samp;
Replace.
Mean Samp k2
Let xbar(k1)=k2
Enddo
Brief
Describe Dist Xbar;
GNHist.
Endmacro
```

3. Mean of the Sampling Distribution of the Sample Variances

In this appendix, we show that the mean of the sampling distribution of the sample variances is the population variance. We begin by finding the expectation of the sum of squares of the sample members about their mean—that is, the expectation of

$$\sum_{i=1}^{n}(X_i - \overline{X})^2 = \sum_{i=1}^{n}\left[(X_i - \mu)-(\overline{X} - \mu)\right]^2$$

$$= \sum_{i=1}^{n}\left[(X_i - \mu)^2 - 2(\overline{X} - \mu)(X_i - \mu)+(\overline{X} - \mu)^2\right]$$

$$= \sum_{i=1}^{n}(X_i - \mu)^2 - 2(\overline{X} - \mu)\sum_{i=1}^{n}(X_i - \mu)+\sum_{i=1}^{n}(\overline{X} - \mu)^2$$

$$= \sum_{i=1}^{n}(X_i - \mu)^2 - 2n(\overline{X} - \mu)^2+n(\overline{X} - \mu)^2$$

$$= \sum_{i=1}^{n}(X_i - \mu)^2 - n(\overline{X} - \mu)^2$$

Taking expectations then gives

$$E\left[\sum_{i=1}^{n}(X_i - \overline{X})^2\right] = E\left[\sum_{i=1}^{n}(X_i - \mu)^2\right] - nE\left[(\overline{X} - \mu)^2\right]$$

$$= \sum_{i=1}^{n}E\left[(X_i - \mu)^2\right] - nE\left[(\overline{X} - \mu)^2\right]$$

Now, the expectation of each $(X_i - \mu)^2$ is the population variance, σ^2, and the expectation of $(\overline{X} - \mu)^2$ is the variance of the sample mean, σ^2/n. Hence, we have the following:

$$E\left[\sum_{i=1}^{n}(X_i - \overline{X})^2\right] = n\sigma^2 - \frac{n\sigma^2}{n} = (n - 1)\sigma^2$$

Finally, for the expected value of the sample variance we have the following:

$$E(s^2) = E\left[\frac{1}{n - 1}\sum_{i=1}^{n}(X_i - \overline{X})^2\right]$$

$$= \frac{1}{n - 1}E\left[\sum_{i=1}^{n}(X_i - \overline{X})^2\right]$$

$$= \frac{1}{n - 1}(n - 1)\sigma^2 = \sigma^2$$

This is the result we set out to establish.

REFERENCES

1. David, F. R., L. M. Anderson, and K. W. Lawrimore. 1990. Perspectives on Business Ethics in Management Education. *S. A. M. Advanced Management Journal* 55 (4): 26–32.
2. Hogan, H. 1992. The 1990 Post-enumeration Survey: An Overview. *American Statistician* 46: 261–269.

Chapter 7

Estimation: Single Population

Chapter Outline

Introduction

This chapter emphasizes inferential statements concerning estimation of a single population parameter, based on information contained in a random sample. We focus on procedures to estimate a population mean or a proportion of population members that possess some specific characteristic. For example, we may want an estimate of average weekly demand for a particular brand of orange juice or an estimate of the proportion of a corporation's employees favoring the introduction of a modified bonus plan.

We present two estimation procedures in this chapter. First, we estimate an unknown population parameter by a single number called a point estimate. Properties of this point estimate are considered in Section 7.1. For most practical problems a point estimate alone is not adequate. A more complete understanding of the process that generated the population also requires a measure of variability. Next we discuss a procedure that takes into account this variation by establishing an interval of values, known as a confidence interval, which is likely to include the quantity. Initially we consider populations that are infinite or very large compared to the sample size where sampling is with replacement.

Other topics included in this chapter are the use of the finite population correction factor (Section 7.5), sample size determination (Section 7.6), and estimation of the population variance (Section 7.7).

Estimation of the difference between the means or proportions of two populations will be considered in Chapter 8.

7.1 PROPERTIES OF POINT ESTIMATORS

Any inference drawn about the population will be based on sample statistics. The choice of appropriate statistics will depend on which population parameter is of interest. The value of the population parameter will be unknown, and one objective of sampling is to estimate its value. A distinction must be made between the terms *estimator* and *estimate*.

> ### Estimator and Estimate
> An **estimator** of a population parameter is a random variable that depends on the sample information; its value provides approximations of this unknown parameter. A specific value of that random variable is called an **estimate**.

Hildebrand and Ott (Reference 4) point out that there is "a technical distinction between an *estimator* as a function of random variables and an *estimate* as a single number. It is the distinction between a process (the *estimator*) and the result of that process (the estimate)." To clarify this distinction between estimator and estimate, consider the estimation of the mean weekly sales of a particular brand of orange juice. One possible *estimator* of the population mean is the sample mean. If the mean of a random sample of weekly sales is found to be 3,280 gallons, then 3,280 is an *estimate* of the population mean weekly sales. Another possible *estimator* of the mean weekly sales could be the sample median.

In Chapter 2 we studied other descriptive statistics, such as sample variance, s^2, and sample correlation coefficient, r. If the value of the sample variance for the weekly demand of orange juice is 300 gallons, then s^2 is the estimator and 300 is the estimate.

In discussing the estimation of an unknown parameter, two possibilities must be considered. First, a *single number* could be computed from the sample as most representative of the unknown population parameter. This is called a *point estimate*. The estimate of 3,280 gallons of orange juice is an example of a point estimate. Alternatively, it might be possible to find an interval or range that most likely contains the value of the population parameter. For example, the mean weekly demand in this store for this particular brand of orange juice is, with some specified degree of confidence, between 2,500 and 3,500 gallons. This interval estimate is an example of one type of *confidence interval* that we will discuss in this chapter.

Point Estimator and Point Estimate

Consider a population parameter such as the population mean μ or the population proportion P. A **point estimator** of a population parameter is a function of the sample information that produces a single number called a **point estimate**. For example, the sample mean $\overline{X}$ is a point estimator of the population mean, μ, and the value that $\overline{X}$ assumes for a given set of data is called the point estimate, $\bar{x}$.

At the outset it must be pointed out that no single mechanism exists for the determination of a uniquely "best" point estimator in all circumstances. What is available instead is a set of criteria under which particular estimators can be evaluated. The sample median also gives a point estimate of the population mean, μ. However, we show later in this chapter that the median is not the best estimator for the mean of some distributions.

We will evaluate estimators based on two important properties: unbiasedness and efficiency. (See the chapter appendix for the property of consistency.)

Unbiased Estimator

In searching for an estimator of a population parameter, the first property an estimator should possess is *unbiasedness*.

Unbiased Estimator

A point estimator $\hat{\theta}$ is said to be an **unbiased estimator** of a population parameter θ if its expected value is equal to that parameter; that is, if

$$E(\hat{\theta}) = \theta$$

then $\hat{\theta}$ is an unbiased estimator of θ.

Notice that unbiasedness does not mean that a *particular* value of $\hat{\theta}$ must be exactly the correct value of θ. Rather, an unbiased estimator has "the capability of estimating the population parameter correctly on the average.... An unbiased estimator is correct on the average. We can think of the expected value of $\hat{\theta}$ as the average of $\hat{\theta}$ values for all possible samples, or alternatively, as the long-run average of $\hat{\theta}$ values for repeated samples. The condition that the estimator $\hat{\theta}$ should be unbiased says that the *average* $\hat{\theta}$ value is exactly correct. It does not state that a particular $\hat{\theta}$ value is exactly correct" (Reference 4).

Sometimes $\hat{\theta}$ will overestimate and other times underestimate the parameter, but it follows from the notion of expectation that, if the sampling procedure is repeated many times, then, on the average, the value obtained for an unbiased estimator will be equal to the population parameter. It seems reasonable to assert that, all other things being equal, unbiasedness is a desirable property in a point estimator. Figure 7.1 illustrates the probability density functions for two estimators, $\hat{\theta}_1$ and $\hat{\theta}_2$, of the parameter θ. It should be obvious that $\hat{\theta}_1$ is an unbiased estimator of θ and $\hat{\theta}_2$ is not an unbiased estimator of θ.

In Chapter 6 we showed the following:

1. The sample mean is an unbiased estimator of μ, $[E(\overline{X}) = \mu]$.
2. The sample variance is an unbiased estimator of σ^2, $[E(s^2) = \sigma^2]$.
3. The sample proportion is an unbiased estimator of P, $[E(\hat{p}) = P]$.

Figure 7.1
Probability
Density Functions
for Estimators $\hat{\theta}_1$
(Unbiased) and $\hat{\theta}_2$
(Biased)

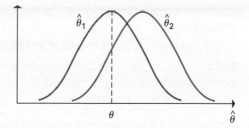

It follows then that the sample mean, sample variance, and sample proportion are unbiased estimators of their corresponding population parameters.

An estimator that is not unbiased is *biased*. The extent of the bias is the difference between the mean of the estimator and the true parameter.

Bias

Let $\hat{\theta}$ be an estimator of θ. The **bias** in $\hat{\theta}$ is defined as the difference between its mean and θ:

$$\text{Bias}(\hat{\theta}) = E(\hat{\theta}) - \theta$$

It follows that the bias of an unbiased estimator is 0.

Unbiasedness alone is not the only desirable characteristic of an estimator. There may be several unbiased estimators for a population parameter. For example, if the population is normally distributed, both the sample mean and the median are unbiased estimators of the population mean.

Efficient Estimator

In many practical problems, different unbiased estimators can be obtained, and some method of choosing among them needs to be found. In this situation it is natural to prefer the estimator whose distribution is most closely concentrated about the population parameter being estimated. Values of such an estimator are less likely to differ, by any fixed amount, from the parameter being estimated than are those of its competitors. Using variance as a measure of concentration, the *efficiency* of an estimator as a criterion for preferring one estimator to another estimator is introduced.

Most Efficient Estimator and Relative Efficiency

If there are several unbiased estimators of a parameter, then the unbiased estimator with the smallest variance is called the **most efficient estimator** or the **minimum variance unbiased estimator**. Let $\hat{\theta}_1$ and $\hat{\theta}_2$ be two unbiased estimators of θ, based on the same number of sample observations. Then

1. $\hat{\theta}_1$ is said to be more efficient than $\hat{\theta}_2$ if $\text{Var}(\hat{\theta}_1) < \text{Var}(\hat{\theta}_2)$ and

2. the **relative efficiency** of $\hat{\theta}_1$ with respect to $\hat{\theta}_2$ is the ratio of their variances.

$$\text{Relative Efficiency} = \frac{\text{Var}(\hat{\theta}_2)}{\text{Var}(\hat{\theta}_1)}$$

Example 7.1 Selection from Competing Unbiased Estimators (Relative Efficiency)

Let $x_1, x_2, ..., x_n$ be a random sample from a normally distributed population with mean μ and variance σ^2. Should the sample mean or the sample median be used to estimate the population mean?

Solution Assuming a population that is normally distributed with a very large population size compared to the sample size, the sample mean, $\overline{X}$, is an unbiased estimator of the population mean, μ, with variance (Chapter 6):

$$\text{Var}(\overline{X}) = \frac{\sigma^2}{n}$$

As an alternative estimator, the median of the sample observations could be used. It can be shown that this estimator is also unbiased for μ, and that when n is large, its variance is as follows:

$$\text{Var}(\text{Median}) = \frac{\pi}{2} \times \frac{\sigma^2}{n} = \frac{1.57\sigma^2}{n}$$

The sample mean is more efficient than the median, the relative efficiency of the mean with respect to the median being as follows:

$$\text{Relative Efficiency} = \frac{\text{Var}(\text{Median})}{\text{Var}(\overline{X})} = 1.57$$

The variance of the sample median is 57% higher than that of the sample mean. Here, in order for the sample median to have as small a variance as the sample mean, it would have to be based on 57% more observations. One advantage of the median over the mean is that it gives less weight to extreme observations. A potential disadvantage of using the sample median as a measure of central location lies in its relative efficiency.

We emphasize the importance of using a normal probability plot to determine if there is any evidence of non-normality. If the population is not normally distributed, the sample mean may not be the most efficient estimator of the population mean. In particular, if outliers heavily affect the population distribution, the sample mean is less efficient than other estimators (such as the median). Table 7.1 is a summary of some properties for selected point estimators. It is neither an exhaustive list of estimators nor an exhaustive list of properties that an estimator possesses.

Table 7.1 Properties of Selected Point Estimators

POPULATION PARAMETER	POINT ESTIMATOR	PROPERTIES
Mean, μ	$\overline{X}$	Unbiased, most efficient (assuming normality)
Mean, μ	Median	Unbiased (assuming normality), but not most efficient
Proportion, P	$\hat{p}$	Unbiased, most efficient
Variance, σ^2	s^2	Unbiased, most efficient (assuming normality)

Example 7.2 Price-Earnings Ratios (Estimators)

Suppose that we randomly sampled stocks traded on the New York Stock Exchange on a particular day and found the price-earnings ratios of these stocks to be as follows:

10	16	13	11	12	14	12
15	14	14	13	13	13	

Does the normal probability plot suggest non-normality? Find point estimates of the mean and variance. Discuss the properties of these estimators.

Solution From the normal probability plot in Figure 7.2 there appears to be no evidence of non-normality. Assuming a normal distribution, an estimate of the mean price-earnings ratios is the sample mean, 13.1, and an estimate of the variance is $s^2 = 2.58$. Both $\overline{X}$, and s^2 are unbiased and efficient point estimators of μ and σ^2, respectively.

Figure 7.2 Price-Earnings Ratios (Normality)

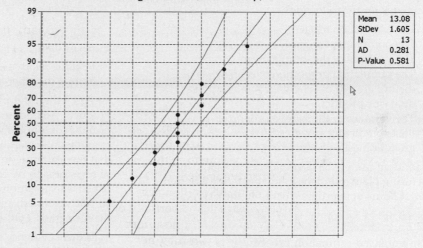

A problem that often arises in practice is how to choose an appropriate point estimator for a population parameter. An attractive possibility is to choose the most efficient of all unbiased estimators. However, sometimes there are estimation problems for which no unbiased estimator is very satisfactory, or there may be situations in which it is not always possible to find a minimum variance unbiased estimator. It is also possible that data may not be normally distributed. In these situations selecting the best point estimator is not straightforward and involves considerable mathematical intricacy beyond the scope of this book.

EXERCISES

Basic Exercises

7.1 The following data is from a random sample:

6   8   7   10   3   5   9   8

a. Check for evidence of non-normality.

b. Find a point estimate of the population mean that is unbiased and efficient.

c. Use an unbiased estimation procedure to find a point estimate of the variance of the sample mean.

7.2 A random sample of eight homes in a particular suburb had the following selling prices (in thousands of dollars):

192 183 312 227 309 396 402 390

a. Check for evidence of non-normality.
b. Find a point estimate of the population mean that is unbiased and efficient.
c. Use an unbiased estimation procedure to find a point estimate of the variance of the sample mean.
d. Use an unbiased estimator to estimate the proportion of homes in this suburb selling for less than $250,000.

7.3 A random sample of 10 economists produced the following forecasts for percentage growth in real gross domestic product in the next year:

2.2 2.8 3.0 2.5 2.4 2.6 2.5 2.4 2.7 2.6

Use unbiased estimation procedures to find point estimates for the following:

a. The population mean
b. The population variance
c. The variance of the sample mean
d. The population proportion of economists predicting growth of at least 2.5% in real gross domestic product
e. The variance of the sample proportion of economists predicting growth of at least 2.5% in real gross domestic product

7.4 A random sample of 12 employees in a large manufacturing plant found the following figures for number of hours of overtime worked in the last month:

22 16 28 12 18 36 23 11 41 29 26 31

Use unbiased estimation procedures to find point estimates for the following:

a. The population mean
b. The population variance
c. The variance of the sample mean
d. The population proportion of employees working more than 30 hours of overtime in this plant in the last month
e. The variance of the sample proportion of employees working more than 30 hours of overtime in this plant in the last month

Application Exercises

7.5 🌐 Project Romanian Rescue (PRR) is a registered Romanian foundation ministering to the needs of the tragically disadvantaged children in Constanta, Romania (Reference 7). As an interdenominational Christian mission, PRR's services include street outreach, a day center, a boys' group home (Casa Charis), a girls' group home (Casa Chara), and individualized educational assistance for children from poor families. PRR intends to open a village center in nearby Kogalniceanu to house additional street children. Suppose that Daniel Mercado, the project founder, and Camelia Vilcoci, the managing director of the project, maintain records such as the number of meals delivered daily to street children, the number of children who attend the day center, and the ages of the children, and suppose that a random sample of such records is contained in the data file **PRR**.

a. Check each variable to determine if the data are normally distributed.
b. Find unbiased estimates of the population mean and population variance.

7.6 Suppose that x_1 and x_2 are random samples of observations from a population with mean μ and variance s^2. Consider the following three point estimators, X, Y, Z, of μ:

$$X = \frac{1}{2}x_1 + \frac{1}{2}x_2 \qquad Y = \frac{1}{4}x_1 + \frac{3}{4}x_2 \qquad Z = \frac{1}{3}x_1 + \frac{2}{3}x_2$$

a. Show that all three estimators are unbiased.
b. Which of the estimators is the most efficient?
c. Find the relative efficiency of X with respect to each of the other two estimators.

7.7 🌐 Al Fiedler, the plant manager at LDS Vacuum Products, Altamonte Springs, Florida, applies statistical thinking in his workplace. As a major supplier to automobile manufacturers, LDS wants to be sure that the leak rate (in cubic centimeters per second) of transmission oil coolers (TOCs) meets the established specification limits. A random sample of 50 TOCs is tested, and the leak rates are recorded in the file named **TOC** (Reference 3).

a. Is there evidence that the data are not normally distributed?
b. Find a minimum variance unbiased point estimate of the population mean.
c. Use an unbiased estimation procedure to find a point estimate of the variance of the sample mean.

7.8 🌐 The demand for bottled water increases during the hurricane season in Florida. The operations manager at a plant that bottles drinking water wants to be sure that the filling process for 1-gallon bottles (1 gallon is approximately 3.785 liters) is operating properly. Currently, the company is testing the volumes of 1-gallon bottles. Suppose that a random sample of 75 bottles is tested, and the measurements are recorded in the data file **Water**.

a. Is there evidence that the data are not normally distributed?
b. Find a minimum variance unbiased point estimate of the population mean.
c. Find a minimum variance unbiased point estimate of the population variance.

7.2 CONFIDENCE INTERVAL ESTIMATION FOR THE MEAN OF A NORMAL DISTRIBUTION: POPULATION VARIANCE KNOWN

We first assume that a random sample is taken from a population that is normally distributed with an unknown mean and a *known* variance. Our objective is to find a range of values, rather than a single number, to estimate a population mean. *This problem is somewhat unrealistic, since rarely will a population variance be precisely known and yet the mean be unknown*. It does sometimes happen, however, that similar populations have been sampled so often in the past that the variance of the population of interest can be assumed known to a very close approximation on the basis of past experience. When the sample size n is large enough, the procedures developed for the case where the population variance is known can be used even if that variance has to be estimated from the sample. Nevertheless, the chief virtue in beginning with this problem is that it allows a fairly straightforward exposition of the procedures involved in finding confidence intervals.

The average number of cars produced per day in a factory is an important measure. Wide variation above and below the mean might result in excessive inventory costs or lost sales. An estimator and an estimate that take into account this variation are needed, giving a range of values in which the quantity to be estimated appears likely to lie. In this section the general format for such estimators is established.

In sampling from a population, with all other things being equal, a more secure *knowledge* about that population is obtained with a relatively large sample than would be obtained from a smaller sample. However, this factor is not reflected in point estimates. For example, a point estimate of the proportion of defective parts in a shipment would be the same if 1 defective part in a sample of 10 parts is observed or if 100 defective parts in a sample of 1,000 parts are observed. Increased precision in our information about population parameters is reflected in *confidence interval estimates*; specifically, all other things being equal, the larger the sample size, the narrower the interval estimates that reflect our uncertainty about a parameter's true value.

> ### Confidence Interval Estimator
> A **confidence interval estimator** for a population parameter is a rule for determining (based on sample information) an interval that is likely to include the parameter. The corresponding estimate is called a **confidence interval estimate**.

So far, interval estimators have been described as being "likely" or "very likely" to include the true, but unknown value of the population parameter. To make our discussion more precise, it is necessary to phrase such terms as probability statements. Suppose that a random sample has been taken and that, based on the sample information, it is possible to find two random variables, A and B, with A less than B. If the specific sample values of the random variables A and B are a and b, then the interval extending from a to b either includes the parameter or it doesn't. We really don't know for sure.

However, suppose that random samples are repeatedly taken from the population and in the same fashion similar intervals are found. In the long run a certain percentage of these intervals (say, 95% or 98%) will contain the unknown value.

According to the relative frequency concept of probability, an interpretation of such intervals follows: *If the population is repeatedly sampled and intervals are calculated in this fashion, then in the long run 95% (or some other percentage) of the intervals would contain the true value of the unknown parameter.* The interval from A to B is then said to be a 95% confidence interval estimator for the population proportion. The general case follows.

Confidence Interval and Confidence Level

Let θ be an unknown parameter. Suppose that on the basis of sample information, random variables A and B are found such that $P(A < \theta < B) = 1 - \alpha$, where α is any number between 0 and 1. If the specific sample values of A and B are a and b, then the interval from a to b is called a $100(1 - \alpha)\%$ **confidence interval** of θ. The quantity $100(1 - \alpha)\%$ is called the **confidence level** of the interval.

If the population is repeatedly sampled a very large number of times, the true value of the parameter θ will be covered by $100(1 - \alpha)\%$ of intervals calculated this way. The confidence interval calculated in this manner is written as $a < \theta < b$ with $100(1 - \alpha)\%$ confidence.

Keep in mind that any time sampling occurs, one expects the possibility of a difference between the particular value of an estimator and the parameter's true value. The true value of an unknown parameter might be somewhat greater or somewhat less than the value determined by even the best point estimator. It is not surprising that for many estimation problems a confidence interval estimate of the unknown parameter takes on this form: best point estimate ± an error factor.

Intervals Based on the Normal Distribution

Let $x_1, x_2, ..., x_n$ be a random sample of n observations from a normally distributed population with unknown mean μ and known variance σ^2. Suppose that we want a $100(1-\alpha)\%$ confidence interval of the population mean. In Chapter 6 we saw that

$$Z = \frac{\bar{x} - \mu}{\sigma/\sqrt{n}}$$

has a standard normal distribution and $z_{\alpha/2}$ is the value from the standard normal distribution such that the upper tail probability is $\alpha/2$. We use basic algebra to find the following:

$$1 - \alpha = P(-z_{\alpha/2} < Z < z_{\alpha/2})$$

$$= P\left(-z_{\alpha/2} < \frac{\bar{x} - \mu}{\sigma/\sqrt{n}} < z_{\alpha/2}\right)$$

$$= P\left(-z_{\alpha/2}\frac{\sigma}{\sqrt{n}} < \bar{x} - \mu < z_{\alpha/2}\frac{\sigma}{\sqrt{n}}\right)$$

$$= P\left(\bar{x} - z_{\alpha/2}\frac{\sigma}{\sqrt{n}} < \mu < \bar{x} + z_{\alpha/2}\frac{\sigma}{\sqrt{n}}\right)$$

For a 95% confidence level it follows that

$$P\left(\bar{x} - 1.96\frac{\sigma}{\sqrt{n}} < \mu < \bar{x} + 1.96\frac{\sigma}{\sqrt{n}}\right) = 0.95$$

Figure 7.3 shows that the probability is 0.95 and that a standard normal random variable falls between the numbers –1.96 and 1.96.

Confidence Interval Estimation for the Mean of a Population that is Normally Distributed: Population Variance Known

Consider a random sample of n observations from a normal distribution with mean μ and variance σ^2. If the sample mean is $\bar{x}$, then a $100(1-\alpha)\%$ **confidence interval for the population mean with known variance** is given by

$$\bar{x} - z_{\alpha/2}\frac{\sigma}{\sqrt{n}} < \mu < \bar{x} + z_{\alpha/2}\frac{\sigma}{\sqrt{n}} \tag{7.1}$$

or equivalently

$$\bar{x} \pm ME$$

where ME, the **margin of error** (also called the **sampling error**), is given by

$$ME = z_{\alpha/2}\frac{\sigma}{\sqrt{n}} \tag{7.2}$$

The **width**, w, is equal to twice the margin of error:

$$w = 2(ME) \tag{7.3}$$

The **upper confidence limit, UCL**, is given by

$$UCL = \bar{x} + z_{\alpha/2}\frac{\sigma}{\sqrt{n}} \tag{7.4}$$

The **lower confidence limit, LCL**, is given by

$$LCL = \bar{x} - z_{\alpha/2}\frac{\sigma}{\sqrt{n}} \tag{7.5}$$

We need to interpret accurately confidence intervals. If random samples of n observations are drawn repeatedly and independently from the population and $100(1 - \alpha)\%$ confidence intervals are calculated by Equation 7.1, then over a very large number of repeated trials, $100(1 - \alpha)\%$ of these intervals will contain the true value of the population mean.

Figure 7.3
$P(–1.96 < Z < 1.96)$ $= 0.95$, Where Z Is a Standard Normal Random Variable

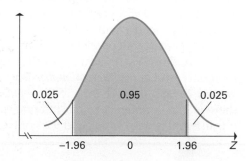

Table 7.2 Selected Confidence Levels and Corresponding Values of $z_{\alpha/2}$

CONFIDENCE LEVEL	90%	95%	98%	99%
α	0.100	0.05	0.02	0.01
$z_{\alpha/2}$	1.645	1.96	2.33	2.58

For selected confidence levels, Table 7.2 lists corresponding values of $z_{\alpha/2}$, sometimes called the **reliability factor**. For a 90% confidence interval Equation 7.1 becomes the following:

$$\bar{x} - 1.645\frac{\sigma}{\sqrt{n}} < \mu < \bar{x} + 1.645\frac{\sigma}{\sqrt{n}}$$

For a 95% confidence interval Equation 7.1 becomes the following:

$$\bar{x} - 1.96\frac{\sigma}{\sqrt{n}} < \mu < \bar{x} + 1.96\frac{\sigma}{\sqrt{n}}$$

Example 7.3 Time at the Grocery Store (Confidence Interval)

Suppose that shopping times for customers at a local grocery store are normally distributed. A random sample of 16 shoppers in the local grocery store had a mean time of 25 minutes. Assume $\sigma = 6$ minutes. Find the standard error, margin of error, and width for a 95% confidence interval for the population mean, μ.

Solution The standard error and the margin of error are as follows:

$$\frac{\sigma}{\sqrt{n}} = \frac{6}{\sqrt{16}} = 1.5$$

$$ME = z_{\alpha/2}\frac{\sigma}{\sqrt{n}} = 1.96(1.5) = 2.94$$

It follows that the width = 2(2.94) = 5.88 and the 95% confidence interval is 22.06 < μ < 27.94.

How should such a confidence interval be interpreted? Based on a sample of 16 observations, a 95% confidence interval for the unknown population mean extends from approximately 22 minutes to approximately 28 minutes. Now, this particular sample is just one of many that might have been drawn from the population. If we start over again and take a second sample of 16 shoppers, it is virtually certain that the mean of the second sample will differ from that of the first. Accordingly, if a 95% confidence interval is calculated from the results of the second sample, it probably will differ from the interval just found. Imagine taking a very large number of independent random samples of 16 observations from this population and, from each sample result, calculating a 95% confidence interval. *The confidence level of the interval implies that in the long run 95% of intervals found in this manner contain the true value of the population mean.* It is in this sense reported that there is 95% confidence in our interval estimate. However, it is not known whether our interval is one of the good 95% or bad 5% without knowing μ.

Figure 7.4 shows the sampling distribution of the sample mean of n observations from a population that is normally distributed with mean μ and standard deviation σ. This sampling distribution is normally distributed with mean μ and standard deviation $\sigma/\sqrt{n}$. A confidence interval for the population mean will be based on the observed value of the sample mean—that is, on an observation drawn from our sampling distribution.

Figure 7.5 shows a schematic description of a sequence of 95% confidence intervals, obtained from independent samples taken from the population. The centers of these intervals, which are just the observed sample means, will often be quite close to the population mean, μ. However, some may differ quite substantially from μ. It follows that 95% of a large number of these intervals will contain the population mean.

Example 7.4 Refined Sugar (Confidence Interval)

A process produces bags of refined sugar. The weights of the contents of these bags are normally distributed with standard deviation 1.2 ounces. The contents of a random sample of 25 bags had a mean weight of 19.8 ounces. Find the upper and lower confidence limits of a 99% confidence interval for the true mean weight for all bags of sugar produced by the process.

Solution   For a 99% confidence interval the reliability factor is

$$z_{0.005} = 2.58$$

and with a sample mean of 19.8, $n = 25$, and a standard deviation of 1.2, the confidence limits are as follows:

$$UCL = \bar{x} + z_{\alpha/2}\frac{\sigma}{\sqrt{n}} = 19.8 + 2.58\frac{1.2}{\sqrt{25}} = 20.42$$

$$LCL = \bar{x} - z_{\alpha/2}\frac{\sigma}{\sqrt{n}} = 19.8 - 2.58\frac{1.2}{\sqrt{25}} = 19.18$$

Reducing Margin of Error

Can the margin of error (and, consequently, the width) of a confidence interval be reduced? Consider the factors that affect the margin of error: the population standard deviation, the sample size n, and the confidence level.

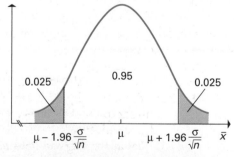

Figure 7.4 Sampling Distribution of Sample Mean of n Observations from a Normal Distribution with Mean μ, Variance σ^2, and 95% Confidence Level

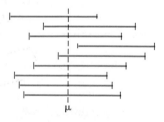

Figure 7.5 Schematic Description of 95% Confidence Intervals

Figure 7.6
Effects of Sample
Size, Population
Standard
Deviation, and
Confidence Level
on Confidence
Intervals

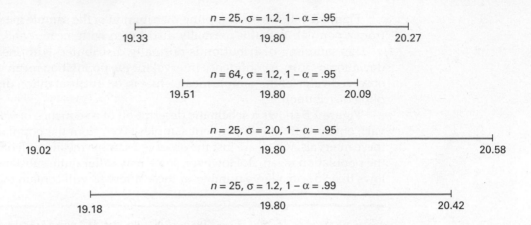

Keeping all other factors constant, the more that the population standard deviation, σ, can be reduced, the smaller the margin of error. Corporations strive to reduce variability in product measurements. When possible, this should be the first step to decrease width. However, sometimes the population standard deviation cannot be reduced.

Another way to reduce the margin of error is to increase the sample size. This will reduce the standard deviation of the sampling distribution of the sample mean and hence the margin of error. That is, keeping all other factors constant, an increase in the sample size n will decrease the margin of error. The more information obtained from a population, the more precise our inference about its mean. When looking at Equation 7.2 for the margin of error, notice that the interval width is directly proportional to $1/\sqrt{n}$. For example, if the sample size is increased by a factor of 4, the interval width will be reduced by half. If the original sample size were 100, an increase to a sample size of 400 would lead to an interval half the width of the original confidence interval (keeping all other factors constant). The disadvantage to an increased sample size is increased costs.

Finally, keeping all other factors constant, if the confidence level $(1 - \alpha)$ is decreased, the margin of error will be reduced. For example, a 95% confidence interval will be shorter than a 99% confidence interval based on the same information. *Caution:* The reduction of the confidence level reduces the probability that the interval includes the value of the true population parameter. Figure 7.6 illustrates some of the effects of sample size n, population standard deviation σ, and confidence level $(1 - \alpha)$ on confidence intervals for the mean of a population that has a normal distribution; in each case the sample mean is 19.80.

EXERCISES

Basic Exercises

7.9 Find the reliability factor, $z_{\alpha/2}$, for each of the following:

   a. 96% confidence level
   b. 88% confidence level
   c. 85% confidence level
   d. $\alpha = 0.07$
   e. $\alpha/2 = 0.07$

7.10 Calculate the margin of error to estimate the population mean, μ, for the following:

   a. 98% confidence level; $n = 64$; $\sigma^2 = 144$
   b. 99% confidence level; $n = 120$; $\sigma = 100$

7.11 Calculate the width to estimate the population mean, μ, for the following:

   a. 90% confidence level; $n = 100$; $\sigma^2 = 169$
   b. 95% confidence level; $n = 120$; $\sigma = 25$

7.12 Calculate the *LCL* and *UCL* for each of the following:

a. $\bar{x} = 50$; $n = 64$; $\sigma = 40$; $\alpha = 0.05$
b. $\bar{x} = 85$; $n = 225$; $\sigma^2 = 400$; $\alpha = 0.01$
c. $\bar{x} = 510$; $n = 485$; $\sigma = 50$; $\alpha = 0.10$

Application Exercises

7.13 A personnel manager has found that historically the scores on aptitude tests given to applicants for entry-level positions follow a normal distribution with a standard deviation of 32.4 points. A random sample of nine test scores from the current group of applicants had a mean score of 187.9 points.

a. Find an 80% confidence interval for the population mean score of the current group of applicants.
b. Based on these sample results, a statistician found for the population mean a confidence interval extending from 165.8 to 210.0 points. Find the confidence level of this interval.

7.14 It is known that the standard deviation in the volumes of 24-ounce (710-mL) bottles of natural spring water bottled by a particular company is 6 mL. Ninety bottles are randomly sampled and measured.

a. Find the reliability factor for a 92% confidence interval for the population mean volume.
b. Calculate the standard error of the mean.
c. Calculate the width for a 92% confidence interval for the population mean volume.

7.15 A college admissions officer for an MBA program has determined that historically applicants have undergraduate grade point averages that are normally distributed with standard deviation 0.45. From a random sample of 25 applications from the current year, the sample mean grade point average is 2.90.

a. Find a 95% confidence interval for the population mean.
b. Based on these sample results, a statistician computes for the population mean a confidence interval extending from 2.81 to 2.99. Find the confidence level associated with this interval.

7.16 A process producing bricks is known to give output whose weights are normally distributed with standard deviation of 0.12 lb. A random sample of 16 bricks from today's output had a mean weight of 4.07 lb.

a. Find a 99% confidence interval for the mean weight of all bricks produced this day.
b. Without doing the calculations, explain whether a 95% confidence interval for the population mean would be wider than, narrower than, or the same width as that found in part (a).
c. It is decided that tomorrow a sample of 20 bricks will be taken. Without doing the calculations, explain whether a correctly calculated 99% confidence interval for the mean weight of tomorrow's output would be wider than, narrower than, or the same width as that found in part (a).
d. Suppose that the population standard deviation for today's output is 0.15 pound (not 0.12 pound). Without doing the calculations, explain whether a correctly calculated 99% confidence interval for the mean weight of today's output would be wider than, narrower than, or the same width as that found in part (a).

7.3 CONFIDENCE INTERVAL ESTIMATION FOR THE MEAN OF A NORMAL DISTRIBUTION: POPULATION VARIANCE UNKNOWN

In the preceding section confidence intervals for the mean of a normal population when the population variance was known were derived. Now, we study the case of considerable practical importance where the value of the population variance is unknown. For example, consider the following:

1. Corporate executives employed by retail distributors may want to estimate mean daily sales for their retail stores.
2. Manufacturers may want to estimate the average productivity, in units per hour, for workers using a particular manufacturing process.
3. Automobile/truck manufacturers may want to estimate the average fuel consumption, measured in miles per gallon, for a particular vehicle model.

In these types of situations, there probably is no historical information concerning either the population mean or the population variance. To proceed further, it is necessary to introduce a new class of probability distributions that were developed by William Sealy Gosset, an Irish statistician, who was employed by the Guinness Brewery in Dublin in the early 1900s (Reference 5, 8).

Student's *t* Distribution

Gosset sought to develop a probability distribution, when the population variance σ^2 is not known, for a normally distributed random variable. At this time laboratory tests and the scientific method were beginning to be applied to the brewing industry. Gosset, whose works appeared under the pseudonym "Student," was influential in the development of modern statistical thinking and process variation: "The circumstances of brewing work, with its variable materials and susceptibility to temperature change ... emphasize the necessity for a correct method of treating small samples. It was thus no accident, but the circumstances of his work, that directed Student's attention to this problem, and led to his discovery of the distribution of the sample standard deviation..." (Reference 6). Gosset showed the connection between statistical research and practical problems. The distribution is still known as the "Student's *t* distribution." The Student-*t* distribution developed by Gosset is the ratio of the distributions, the standard normal distribution, and the square root of the chi-square distribution divided by its degrees of freedom, v (see the chapter appendix).

The development of Section 7.2 was based on the fact that the random variable, Z, given by

$$Z = \frac{\bar{x} - \mu}{\sigma / \sqrt{n}}$$

has a standard normal distribution. In the case where the population standard deviation is unknown, this result cannot be used directly. It is natural in such circumstances to consider the random variable obtained by replacing the unknown σ by the sample standard deviation, s, giving

$$t = \frac{\bar{x} - \mu}{s / \sqrt{n}}$$

This random variable does not follow a standard normal distribution. However, its distribution is known and is, in fact, a member of a family of distributions called Student's *t*.

Student's *t* Distribution

Given a random sample of n observations, with mean $\bar{x}$ and standard deviation s, from a normally distributed population with mean μ, the random variable t follows the **Student's *t* distribution** with $(n-1)$ degrees of freedom and is given by

$$t = \frac{\bar{x} - \mu}{s / \sqrt{n}}$$

A specific member of the family of Student's t distributions is characterized by the number of degrees of freedom associated with the computation of the standard error. We will use the parameter v to represent the degrees of freedom and a Student's t random variable with v degrees of freedom will be denoted t_v. The shape of the Student's t distribution is rather similar to that of the standard normal distribution. Both distributions have mean 0, and the probability density functions of both are symmetric about their means. However, the density function of the Student's t distribution has a wider dispersion (reflected in a larger variance) than the standard normal distribution. This can be seen in Figure 7.7, which shows density functions for the standard normal distribution and the Student's t distribution with 3 degrees of freedom.

The additional dispersion in the Student's t distribution arises as a result of the extra uncertainty caused by replacing the known population standard deviation with its sample estimator. As the number of degrees of freedom increases, the Student's t distribution becomes increasingly similar to the standard normal distribution. For large degrees of freedom the two distributions are virtually identical. That is, the Student's t distribution converges to $N(0,1)$, which is quite close to the t as long as n is large. This is intuitively reasonable and follows from the fact that for a large sample the sample standard deviation is a very precise estimator of the population standard deviation.

In order to base inferences about a population mean on the Student's t distribution, critical values analogous to $z_{\alpha/2}$ are needed. Just as $z_{\alpha/2}$ is the value from the standard normal distribution such that the upper tail probability is $\alpha/2$, so $t_{v,\alpha/2}$ is the value from the Student's t distribution for v (degrees of freedom) such that the upper tail probability is $\alpha/2$ as shown in Figure 7.8.

Notation

A random variable having the Student's t distribution with v degrees of freedom will be denoted t_v. Then $t_{v,\alpha/2}$ is the reliability factor, defined as the number for which

$$P(t_v > t_{v,\alpha/2}) = \alpha/2$$

Figure 7.7
Probability Density Functions of the Standard Normal and the Student's t Distribution with 3 Degrees of Freedom

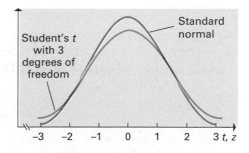

Figure 7.8
$P(t_v > t_{v,\alpha/2}) = \alpha/2$,
Where t_v is a
Student's t
Random Variable
with v Degrees of
Freedom

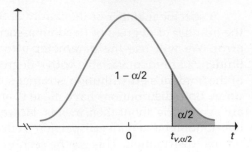

Suppose that the number that is exceeded with probability 0.05 by a Student's t random variable with 15 degrees of freedom is required:

$$P(t_{15} > t_{15,0.05}) = 0.05$$

Reading directly from the Student's t distribution table,

$$t_{15,0.05} = 1.753$$

Many computer programs can be used to obtain these values as well.

Intervals Based on the Student's t Distribution

We will encounter many situations in which the population variance is not known. Finding the $100(1 - \alpha)\%$ confidence interval for this type of problem follows precisely the same line of reasoning as in Section 7.2. Terminology is analogous.

Confidence Intervals for the Mean of a Normal Population: Population Variance Unknown

Suppose there is a random sample of n observations from a *normal distribution* with mean μ and unknown variance. If the sample mean and standard deviation are, respectively, $\bar{x}$ and s, then the degrees of freedom $v = n{-}1$ and a $100(1{-}\alpha)\%$ **confidence interval for the population mean, variance unknown**, is given by

$$\bar{x} - t_{n-1,\alpha/2}\frac{s}{\sqrt{n}} < \mu < \bar{x} + t_{n-1,\alpha/2}\frac{s}{\sqrt{n}} \tag{7.6}$$

or equivalently

$$\bar{x} \pm ME$$

where *ME*, the **margin of error**, is given by

$$ME = t_{n-1,\alpha/2}\frac{s}{\sqrt{n}} \tag{7.7}$$

Assume that a random sample of n observations is available from a normal population with mean μ and unknown variance and that confidence intervals for the population mean are required. The normal probability plot is one method to test if the data are not normally distributed. We assume normality throughout this chapter. In applications to business, government, and medical or other research, we should check first to determine if the data indicate non-normality. Confidence interval terminology for a population mean with unknown variance is similar to the situation with variance known.

Example 7.5 Trucks: Gasoline Consumption (Confidence Interval)

Gasoline prices rose drastically during the early years of this century. Suppose that a recent study was conducted using truck drivers with equivalent years of experience to test run 24 trucks of a particular model over the same highway. Estimate the population mean fuel consumption for this truck model with 90% confidence if the fuel consumption, in miles per gallon, for these 24 trucks was as follows:

15.5	21.0	18.5	19.3	19.7	16.9	20.2	14.5
16.5	19.2	18.7	18.2	18.0	17.5	18.5	20.5
18.6	19.1	19.8	18.0	19.8	18.2	20.3	21.8

The data is stored in the data file **Trucks**.

Solution   The normal probability plot in Figure 7.9 does not provide evidence of non-normality.

Calculating the mean and standard deviation, we find the following:

$$\bar{x} = 18.68 \quad s = 1.69526 \quad t_{n-1,\alpha/2} = t_{23,0.05} = 1.714$$

Figure 7.9   Normal Probability Plot

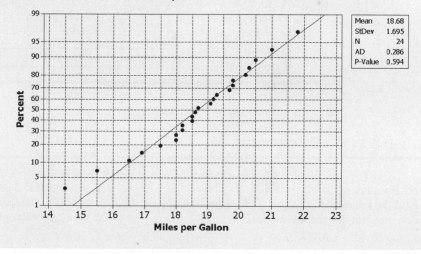

By Equation 7.6 the 90% confidence interval is as follows:

$$\bar{x} \pm t_{n-1,\alpha/2}\frac{s}{\sqrt{n}} = 18.68 \pm t_{23,0.05}\frac{1.69526}{\sqrt{24}} = 18.68 \pm (1.714) \times (0.3460)$$

$$= 18.68 \pm 0.5930$$

The confidence interval then is $18.1 < \mu < 19.3$. For larger data sets we will want to use the computer. Figure 7.10 is the Minitab output and Figure 7.11 is the Excel output generated for Example 7.5.

The interpretation of the confidence interval is important. If independent random samples of 24 trucks are repeatedly selected from the population and confidence intervals for each of these samples are determined, then over a very large number of repeated trials 90% of these intervals will contain the value of the true mean fuel consumption for this model truck. In practice, however, one does not repeatedly draw such independent samples.

Figure 7.10 Output for Data File **Trucks** (Minitab)

Variable	N	Mean	StDev	SE Mean	90% cr
MPG	24	18.6792	1.6953	0.3460	(18.0861, 19.2722)

Figure 7.11 Output for Data File **Trucks** (Excel)

Mean	**18.67917**
Standard Error	0.346043
Median	18.65
Mode	18.5
Standard Deviation	1.695257
Sample Variance	2.873895
Kurtosis	0.624798
Skewness	−0.60902
Range	7.3
Minimum	14.5
Maximum	21.8
Sum	448.3
Count	24
Confidence Level (90.0%)	**0.593073**

EXERCISES

Basic Exercises

7.17 Find the reliability factor, $t_{v,\alpha/2}$, to estimate population mean, μ, for the following:

a. $n = 20$; 90% confidence level

b. $n = 7$; 98% confidence level
c. $n = 16$; 95% confidence level
d. $n = 23$; 99% confidence level

7.18 Find the margin of error for each of the following:
   a. $n = 20$; 90% confidence level; $s = 36$
   b. $n = 7$; 98% confidence level; $s = 16$
   c. $n = 16$; 95% confidence level; $s^2 = 43$
   d. 99% confidence level; $x_1 = 15$; $x_2 = 17$; $x_3 = 13$; $x_4 = 11$

7.19 Times (in minutes) that a random sample of five people spend driving to work are as follows:

   30   42   35   40   45

   a. Calculate the standard error.
   b. Find $t_{v,\alpha/2}$ for a 95% confidence interval for the true population mean.
   c. Calculate the width for a 95% confidence interval for the population mean time spent driving to work.

7.20 Find the *LCL* and *UCL* for each of the following:
   a. $\alpha = 0.05$; $n = 25$; $\bar{x} = 560$; $s = 45$
   b. $\alpha/2 = 0.05$; $n = 9$; $\bar{x} = 160$; $s^2 = 36$
   c. $1 - \alpha = 0.98$; $n = 22$; $\bar{x} = 58$; $s = 15$

7.21 Calculate the margin of error to estimate the population mean, μ, for each of the following:
   a. 98% confidence level; $n = 64$; $s^2 = 144$
   b. 99% confidence level; $n = 120$; $s = 100$
   c. 95% confidence level; $n = 200$; $s = 40$

7.22 Calculate the width for each of the following:
   a. $n = 6$; $s = 40$; $\alpha = 0.05$
   b. $n = 22$; $s^2 = 400$; $\alpha = 0.01$
   c. $n = 25$; $s = 50$; $\alpha = 0.10$

Application Exercises

7.23 ● Al Fiedler, plant manager at LDS Vacuum Products, Altamonte Springs, Florida, applies statistical thinking in his workplace. As a major supplier to automobile manufacturers, LDS wants to be sure that the leak rate (in cubic centimeters per second) of transmission oil coolers (TOCs) meets the established specification limits. A random sample of 50 TOCs is tested, and the leak rates are recorded in the data file named **TOC** (Reference 3).

   a. Estimate with 95% confidence the mean leak rate for this particular product.
   b. Estimate with 98% confidence the mean leak rate for this particular product.

7.24 ● A machine that packages 18-ounce (510-gram) boxes of sugar-coated wheat cereal is being studied. The weights for a random sample of 100 boxes of cereal packaged by this machine are contained in the data file **Sugar**.

   a. Find a 90% confidence interval for the population mean cereal weight.
   b. Without doing the calculations, state whether an 80% confidence interval for the population mean would be wider than, narrower than, or the same as the answer to part (a).

7.25 A clothing store is interested in how much college students spend on clothing during the first month of the school year. For a random sample of nine students the mean expenditure was $157.82, and the sample standard deviation was $37.89. Assuming that the population is normally distributed, find the margin of error of a 95% confidence interval for the population mean.

7.26 There is concern about the speed of automobiles traveling over a particular stretch of highway. For a random sample of seven automobiles radar indicated the following speeds, in miles per hour:

   79   73   68   77   86   71   69

   Assuming a normal population distribution, find the margin of error of a 95% confidence interval for the mean speed of all automobiles traveling over this stretch of highway.

7.27 A clinic offers a weight-loss program. A review of its records found the following amounts of weight loss, in pounds, for a random sample of 10 of its clients at the conclusion of the program:

   18   25   6   11   15   20   16   19   12   17

   a. Find a 99% confidence interval for the population mean.
   b. Without doing the calculations, explain whether a 90% confidence interval for the population mean would be wider than, narrower than, or the same as that found in part (a).

7.28 A business school placement director wants to estimate the mean annual salaries five years after students graduate. A random sample of 25 such graduates found a sample mean of $42,740 and a sample standard deviation of $4,780. Find a 90% confidence interval for the population mean, assuming that the population distribution is normal.

7.29 A car rental company is interested in the amount of time its vehicles are out of operation for repair work. State all assumptions and find a 90% confidence interval for the mean number of days in a year that all vehicles in the company's fleet are out of operation if a random sample of nine cars showed the following number of days that each had been inoperative:

   16   10   21   22   8   17   19   14   19

7.4 CONFIDENCE INTERVAL ESTIMATION FOR POPULATION PROPORTION (LARGE SAMPLES)

What percent of European students expect to pursue doctoral degrees? What percent of college admission personnel think that SAT scores are a good indicator of academic success in college? What proportion of the students at a particular university would like classes to be offered on Saturdays? What proportion of local residents will attend the Innsbruck Promenade Concerts? In each of these scenarios the proportion of population members possessing some specific characteristic is of interest. If a random sample is taken from the population, the sample proportion provides a natural point estimator of the population proportion. In this section confidence intervals for the population proportion are established.

Using the binomial setup, let $\hat{p}$ denote the proportion of "successes" in n independent trials, each with probability of success P. It was seen earlier in this book that, if the number n of sample members is large, then the random variable

$$Z = \frac{\hat{p} - P}{\sqrt{\dfrac{P(1 - P)}{n}}}$$

has, to a close approximation, a standard normal distribution. If the sample size is large enough that $(n)(P)(1 - P) > 5$, then a good approximation is obtained if P is replaced by the point estimator $\hat{p}$ in the denominator:

$$\sqrt{\frac{P(1 - P)}{n}} \approx \sqrt{\frac{\hat{p}(1 - \hat{p})}{n}}$$

Hence, for large sample sizes the distribution of the random variable

$$Z = \frac{\hat{p} - P}{\sqrt{\hat{p}(1 - \hat{p})/n}}$$

is approximately standard normal. This result can now be used to obtain confidence intervals for the population proportion. The derivation is similar to the preceding examples.

$$1 - \alpha = P(-z_{\alpha/2} < Z < z_{\alpha/2})$$

$$= P\left(-z_{\alpha/2} < \frac{\hat{p} - P}{\sqrt{\dfrac{\hat{p}(1 - \hat{p})}{n}}} < z_{\alpha/2} \right)$$

$$= P\left(-z_{\alpha/2}\sqrt{\frac{\hat{p}(1 - \hat{p})}{n}} < \hat{p} - P < z_{\alpha/2}\sqrt{\frac{\hat{p}(1 - \hat{p})}{n}} \right)$$

$$= P\left(\hat{p} - z_{\alpha/2}\sqrt{\frac{\hat{p}(1 - \hat{p})}{n}} < p < \hat{p} + z_{\alpha/2}\sqrt{\frac{\hat{p}(1 - \hat{p})}{n}} \right)$$

Therefore, if the observed sample proportion is $\hat{p}$, an approximate $100(1 - \alpha)\%$ confidence interval for the population proportion is given, as seen in Equation 7.8, which follows.

Confidence Intervals for Population Proportion (Large Samples)

Let $\hat{p}$ denote the observed proportion of "successes" in a random sample of n observations from a population with a proportion of successes P. Then, if n is large enough that $(n)(P)(1-P) > 5$, a $100(1-\alpha)\%$ **confidence interval for the population proportion** is given by

$$\hat{p} - z_{\alpha/2}\sqrt{\frac{\hat{p}(1-\hat{p})}{n}} < P < \hat{p} + z_{\alpha/2}\sqrt{\frac{\hat{p}(1-\hat{p})}{n}} \tag{7.8}$$

or equivalently

$$\hat{p} \pm ME$$

where ME, **the margin of error**, is given by

$$ME = z_{\alpha/2}\sqrt{\frac{\hat{p}(1-\hat{p})}{n}} \tag{7.9}$$

Recent research suggests the possibility of other intervals as alternatives to the confidence interval stated in Equation 7.8. Such adjusted intervals are useful with both large and small samples (References 1 and 2). These readings are recommended for more advanced studies.

Confidence intervals for the population proportion are centered on the sample proportion. Also, it can be seen that, all other things being equal, the larger the sample size, n, the narrower the confidence interval. This reflects the increasing precision of the information about the population proportion obtained as the sample size becomes larger.

Example 7.6 Modified Bonus Plan (Confidence Interval)

Management wants an estimate of the proportion of the corporation's employees who favor a modified bonus plan. From a random sample of 344 employees it was found that 261 were in favor of this particular plan. Find a 90% confidence interval estimate of the true population proportion that favors this modified bonus plan.

Solution If P denotes the true population proportion and $\hat{p}$ the sample proportion, then confidence intervals for the population proportion are obtained from Equation 7.8 as

$$\hat{p} - z_{\alpha/2}\sqrt{\frac{\hat{p}(1-\hat{p})}{n}} < P < \hat{p} + z_{\alpha/2}\sqrt{\frac{\hat{p}(1-\hat{p})}{n}}$$

where, for a 90% confidence interval, $\alpha = 0.10$, so that from the standard normal distribution

$$\alpha/2 = 0.05 \quad \text{and} \quad z_{\alpha/2} = z_{0.05} = 1.645$$

It follows that

$$n = 344 \quad \hat{p} = 261/344 = 0.759$$

and

$$z_{\alpha/2} = 1.645$$

Therefore, a 90% confidence interval for the population proportion is

$$0.759 - 1.645\sqrt{\frac{(0.759)(0.241)}{344}} < P < 0.759 + 1.645\sqrt{\frac{(0.759)(0.241)}{344}}$$

or $0.721 < P < 0.797$. Strictly speaking, what do these numbers imply? We could say that, in the long run, approximately 76% (with a 4% margin of error at the 90% confidence level) of the population of all employees in this corporation favor a modified bonus plan.

We compare the 90% and the 99% confidence intervals in Figures 7.12 and 7.13, respectively.

We see that, by increasing the confidence level from 90% to 99%, the margin of error (and the width) also increased. For the 90% confidence interval the range was from approximately 72.1% to 79.7%, giving a 3.8% margin of error, whereas for the 99% confidence interval the range was from approximately 69.9% to 81.8%, giving a 5.95% margin of error. Wide intervals for a given α reflect imprecision in our knowledge about the population proportion. Narrower confidence intervals can be obtained by taking larger samples.

Figure 7.12   Modified Bonus Plan (90% Confidence Interval)

Confidence Interval for Proportion

Sample	X	N	Sample p	90.0% CI	Z-Value	P-Value
1	261	344	0.758721	(0.720776, 0.796665)	9.60	0.000

Figure 7.13   Modified Bonus Plan (99% Confidence Interval)

Confidence Interval for Proportion

Sample	X	N	Sample p	99% CI	Z-Value	P-Value
1	261	344	0.758721	(0.699300, 0.818142)	9.60	0.000

EXERCISES

Basic Exercises

7.30 Find the standard error of the proportion for the following:

a. $n = 250; \hat{p} = 0.30$

b. $n = 175; \hat{p} = 0.45$

c. $n = 400; \hat{p} = 0.05$

7.31 Find the margin of error for the following:

  a. $n = 250; \hat{p} = 0.30; \alpha = 0.05$
  b. $n = 175; \hat{p} = 0.45; \alpha = 0.08$
  c. $n = 400; \hat{p} = 0.05; \alpha = 0.04$

7.32 Find the confidence interval for estimating the population proportion for the following:

  a. 92.5% confidence level; $n = 650; \hat{p} = 0.10$
  b. 99% confidence level; $n = 140; \hat{p} = 0.01$
  c. $\alpha = 0.09; n = 365; \hat{p} = 0.50$

Application Exercises

7.33 Suppose that a random sample of 142 graduate admissions personnel was asked what role scores on standardized tests (such as the GMAT or GRE) play in the consideration of a candidate for graduate school. Of these sample members 87 answered "very important." Find a 95% confidence interval for the population proportion of graduate admissions personnel with this view.

7.34 In a random sample of 95 manufacturing firms 67 indicated that their company attained ISO certification within the last two years. Find a 99% confidence interval for the population proportion of companies that have been certified within the last two years.

7.35 ⊙ In a recent study of a university library, students were asked if they thought that the school's library had an adequate collection of books. The survey results are stored in a data file called **Library**.

  a. Find an unbiased point estimate of the proportion of students who think that the collection is adequate (coded as 1-yes, 2-no).
  b. Find a 90% confidence interval for the proportion of students who think that the school's library collection is adequate.

7.36 The University of Michigan School of Business publishes the American Customer Satisfaction Index (ACSI) four times a year (Reference 1). Started in 1994 and based on thousands of customer interviews, customer satisfaction ratings based on a scale from 0 to 100 are gathered for retailers, supermarkets, financial services, parcel-delivery services, airlines, and so forth. "Understaffed stores, clueless sales clerks, automated phone lines that lead you in circles" are a few reasons why the scores for most companies declined between 1995 and 2000 (Reference 9). Concerned about this report, the manager of a national retail store in one community surveyed a random sample of 320 customers. The survey indicated that 80 customers thought that customer service in this store was also on the decline. What conclusions can we draw from this data? State the level of confidence.

7.37 From a random sample of 400 registered voters in one city, 320 indicated that they would vote in favor of a proposed policy in an upcoming election.

  a. Calculate the LCL for a 98% confidence interval estimate for the population proportion in favor of this policy.
  b. Calculate the width of a 90% confidence interval estimate for the population proportion in favor of this policy.

7.38 Of a random sample of 198 marketing students 98 rated a case of résumé inflation as unethical. Based on this information (Reference 2), a statistician computed for the population proportion a confidence interval extending from 0.445 to 0.545. What is the confidence level of this interval?

7.39 In a presidential election year, candidates want to know how voters in various parts of the country will vote. Suppose that 420 registered voters in the Northeast are asked if they would vote for a particular candidate if the election were held today. From this sample 223 indicated that they would vote for this particular candidate. What is the margin of error? Determine the 95% confidence interval estimate of this candidate's support in the Northeast.

7.40 Suppose that the U.S. Centers for Disease Control and Prevention (CDC) believe that influenza activity will be lower than the same period last year. Residents in the Atlanta metropolitan area were asked if this news by the CDC would persuade them to not take the flu vaccine. If only 40 people from a random sample of 246 stated that they now would not take the flu vaccine, estimate with 98% confidence the proportion of all residents in the Atlanta metro area who now consider the flu vaccine unnecessary.

7.41 It is important for airlines to follow the published scheduled departure times of flights. Suppose that one airline that recently sampled the records of 246 flights originating in Orlando found that 10 flights were delayed for severe weather, 4 flights were delayed for maintenance concerns, and all the other flights were on time.

  a. Estimate the percentage of on-time departures using a 98% confidence level.
  b. Estimate the percentage of flights delayed for severe weather using a 98% confidence level.

7.5 CONFIDENCE INTERVAL ESTIMATION FOR THE VARIANCE OF A NORMAL DISTRIBUTION

On occasion, interval estimates are required for the variance of a population. As might be expected, such estimates are based on the sample variance.

Suppose a random sample of n observations from a normally distributed population with variance σ^2 and sample variance s^2 is taken. The random variable

$$\chi^2_{n-1} = \frac{(n-1)s^2}{\sigma^2}$$

follows a chi-square distribution with $(n-1)$ degrees of freedom. This result forms the basis for the derivation of confidence intervals for the population variance when sampling from a normal distribution.

In order to develop the formula for calculating confidence intervals for the variance, an additional notation is needed. We illustrate this notation in Figure 7.14.

> **Notation**
> A random variable having the chi-square distribution with $v = n - 1$ degrees of freedom will be denoted by χ^2_v or simply χ^2_{n-1}. Define as $\chi^2_{n-1,\alpha}$ the number for which
>
> $$P(\chi^2_{n-1} > \chi^2_{n-1,\alpha}) = \alpha$$

For a specified probability α, a chi-square number for $n-1$ degrees of freedom is needed—that is, $\chi^2_{n-1,\alpha}$. This can be found from values of the cumulative distribution function of a chi-square random variable. For instance, suppose the number that is exceeded with probability 0.05 by a chi-square random variable with 6 degrees of freedom is needed:

$$P(\chi^2_6 > \chi^2_{6,0.05}) = 0.05$$

From Table 7 in the appendix, $\chi^2_{6,0.05} = 12.59$. Similarly,

$$P(\chi^2_{n-1} > \chi^2_{n-1,\alpha/2}) = \frac{\alpha}{2}$$

Figure 7.14
Chi-Square
Distribution

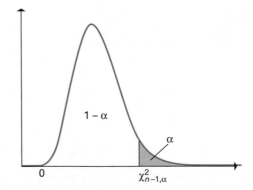

It follows that $\chi^2_{n-1,1-\alpha/2}$ is given by

$$P(\chi^2_{n-1} > \chi^2_{n-1,1-\alpha/2}) = 1 - \frac{\alpha}{2}$$

and hence

$$P(\chi^2_{n-1} < \chi^2_{n-1,1-\alpha/2}) = \frac{\alpha}{2}$$

Finally,

$$P(\chi^2_{n-1,1-\alpha/2} < \chi^2_{n-1} < \chi^2_{n-1,\alpha/2}) = 1 - \frac{\alpha}{2} - \frac{\alpha}{2} = 1 - \alpha$$

This probability is illustrated in Figure 7.15.

Suppose a pair of numbers is needed such that the probability that a chi-square random variable with 6 degrees of freedom lying between these numbers is 0.90. Then $\alpha = 0.10$ and

$$P(\chi^2_{6,0.95} < \chi^2_6 < \chi^2_{6,0.05}) = 0.90$$

Previously, it was found that $\chi^2_{6,0.05} = 12.59$. From Table 7 in the appendix we find that $\chi^2_{6,0.95} = 1.64$.

The probability is 0.90 that this chi-square random variable falls between 1.64 and 12.59.

To find confidence intervals for the population variance,

$$1 - \alpha = P(\chi^2_{n-1,1-\alpha/2} < \chi^2_{n-1} < \chi^2_{n-1,\alpha/2})$$

$$= P\left(\chi^2_{n-1,1-\alpha/2} < \frac{(n-1)s^2}{\sigma^2} < \chi^2_{n-1,\alpha/2}\right)$$

$$= P\left(\frac{(n-1)s^2}{\chi^2_{n-1,\alpha/2}} < \sigma^2 < \frac{(n-1)s^2}{\chi^2_{n-1,1-\alpha/2}}\right)$$

Figure 7.15
Chi-Square
Distribution for
$n - 1$ Degrees
of Freedom
and $(1 - \alpha)\%$
Confidence Level

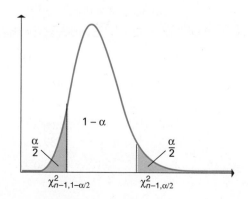

$1 - \alpha$

$\dfrac{\alpha}{2}$ $\dfrac{\alpha}{2}$

$\chi^2_{n-1,1-\alpha/2}$ $\chi^2_{n-1,\alpha/2}$

Confidence Intervals for the Variance of a Normal Population

Suppose that there is a random sample of n observations from a normally distributed population with variance σ^2. If the observed sample variance is s^2, then a $100(1-\alpha)\%$ **confidence interval for the population variance** is given by

$$\frac{(n-1)s^2}{\chi^2_{n-1,\alpha/2}} < \sigma^2 < \frac{(n-1)s^2}{\chi^2_{n-1,1-\alpha/2}} \qquad (7.10)$$

where $\chi^2_{n-1,\alpha/2}$ is the number for which

$$P(\chi^2_{n-1} > \chi^2_{n-1,\alpha/2}) = \frac{\alpha}{2}$$

and $\chi^2_{n-1,1-\alpha/2}$ is the number for which

$$P(\chi^2_{n-1} < \chi^2_{n-1,1-\alpha/2}) = \frac{\alpha}{2}$$

and the random variable χ^2_{n-1} follows a chi-square distribution with $(n-1)$ degrees of freedom.

Although it is assumed throughout this section that the population is normally distributed, we should always check for any evidence that this assumption fails. Notice that the confidence interval in Equation 7.10 is not the usual form, sample point estimator ± margin of error.

Example 7.7 Comparing Temperature Variances (Confidence Interval)

The manager of Northern Steel Inc. wants to assess the temperature variation in the firm's new electric furnace. A random sample of 25 temperatures over a one-week period is obtained, and the sample variance is found to be $s^2 = 100$. Find a 95% confidence interval for the population variance temperature.

Solution Here, $n = 25$ and $s^2 = 100$, and for a 95% confidence interval, $\alpha = 0.05$. It follows from the chi-square distribution in Table 7 in the appendix (see Figure 7.16) that

$$\chi^2_{n-1,1-\alpha/2} = \chi^2_{24,0.975} = 12.401 \qquad and \qquad \chi^2_{n-1,\alpha/2} = \chi^2_{24,0.025} = 39.364$$

The 95% confidence interval for the population variance is given by

$$\frac{(n-1)s^2}{\chi^2_{n-1,\alpha/2}} < \sigma^2 < \frac{(n-1)s^2}{\chi^2_{n-1,1-\alpha/2}}$$

Substitution yields

$$\frac{(24)(100)}{39.364} < \sigma^2 < \frac{(24)(100)}{12.401}$$

$$60.97 < \sigma^2 < 193.53$$

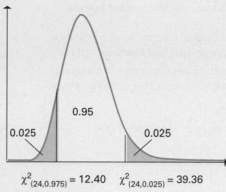

Figure 7.16 Chi-Square Distribution for $n = 25$ and 95% Confidence Level

0.95

0.025   0.025

$\chi^2_{(24, 0.975)} = 12.40$ $\chi^2_{(24, 0.025)} = 39.36$

It is dangerous to follow the procedure just demonstrated when the population distribution is not normal. The validity of the interval estimator for the variance depends far more critically on the assumption of normality than does that of the interval estimator for the population mean.

EXERCISES

Basic Exercises

7.42 Find the lower confidence limit for each of the following normal populations:

a. $n = 21$; $\alpha = 0.025$; $s^2 = 16$
b. $n = 16$; $\alpha = 0.05$; $s = 8$
c. $n = 28$; $\alpha = 0.01$; $s = 15$

7.43 Find the upper confidence limit for parts (a) through (c) of Exercise 7.42.

7.44 Consider the following random sample from a normal population:

12   16   8   10   9

a. Find the 90% confidence interval for population variance.
b. Find the 95% confidence interval for the population variance.

Application Exercises

7.45 ⬤LDS wants to be sure that the leak rate (in cubic centimeters per second) of transmission oil coolers (TOCs) meets the established specification limits. A random sample 50 TOCs is tested, and the leak rates are recorded in the data file **TOC** (Reference 4). Estimate the variance in leak rate with a 95% confidence level (check normality).

7.46 A clinic offers a weight-loss program. A review of its records found the following amounts of weight loss, in pounds, for a random sample of 10 clients at the conclusion of the program:

18.2 25.9 6.3 11.8 15.4 20.3 16.8 18.5 12.3 17.2

Find a 90% confidence interval for the population variance of weight loss for clients of this weight-loss program.

7.47 The quality control manager of a chemical company randomly sampled twenty 100-pound bags of fertilizer to estimate the variance in the pounds of impurities. The sample variance was found to be 6.62. Find a 95% confidence interval for the population variance in the pounds of impurities.

7.48 A psychologist wants to estimate the variance of employee test scores. A random sample of 18 scores had a sample standard deviation of 10.4. Find a 90% confidence interval for the population variance. What are the assumptions, if any, to calculate this interval estimate?

7.49 A manufacturer is concerned about the variability of the levels of impurity contained in consignments of raw material from a supplier. A random sample of 15 consignments showed a standard deviation of

2.36 in the concentration of impurity levels. Assume normality.

a. Find a 95% confidence interval for the population variance.

b. Would a 99% confidence interval for this variance be wider or narrower than that found in part (a)?

7.50 A manufacturer bonds a plastic coating to a metal surface. A random sample of nine observations on the thickness of this coating is taken from a week's output, and the thicknesses (in millimeters) of these observations are as follows:

19.8 21.2 18.6 20.4 21.6 19.8 19.9 20.3 20.8

Assuming normality, find a 90% confidence interval for the population variance.

7.6 CONFIDENCE INTERVAL ESTIMATION: FINITE POPULATIONS

In this section we consider confidence intervals where the number of sample members is not a negligible proportion of the number of population members. Generally, the sample size is considered to be relatively large compared to the population size if it is more than 5% of the population size, that is if $n > 0.05N$. It will be assumed that the sample is sufficiently large and that recourse to the central limit theorem (Chapter 6) is appropriate. As a result, the **finite population correction (fpc) factor**, $(N - n)/(N - 1)$, which was introduced in Chapter 6, will be used. In these situations the individual members are not distributed independently of one another and sampling is without replacement.

Population Mean and Population Total

Here, we consider problems where a sample of n individuals or objects is to be drawn from a population containing N members. We develop confidence intervals for the population mean and the population total when the sample size is more than 5% of the population size.

Estimation of the Population Mean, Simple Random Sample, Finite Population

Let $x_1, x_2, ..., x_n$ denote the values observed from a simple random sample of size n, taken from a population of N members with mean μ.

1. The sample mean is an unbiased estimator of the population mean, μ. The point estimate is

$$\bar{x} = \frac{1}{n}\sum_{i=1}^{n} x_i$$

2. An unbiased estimation procedure for the variance of the sample mean yields the point estimate

$$\hat{\sigma}_{\bar{x}}^2 = \frac{s^2}{n}\left(\frac{N - n}{N - 1}\right) \tag{7.11}$$

3. A 100(1−α)% confidence interval for the population mean is given by

$$\bar{x} - t_{n-1,\alpha/2}\hat{\sigma}_{\bar{x}} < \mu < \bar{x} + t_{n-1,\alpha/2}\hat{\sigma}_{\bar{x}} \tag{7.12}$$

Example 7.8 Mortgages (Confidence Interval)

In a particular city 1,118 mortgages were financed last year. A random sample of 60 of these had a mean amount $87,300 and a standard deviation $19,200. Estimate the mean amount of all mortgages financed in this city last year, and find a 95% confidence interval.

Solution Denote the population mean by μ. It is known that

$$N = 1{,}118 \quad n = 60 \quad \bar{x} = \$87{,}300 \quad s = 19{,}200$$

To obtain interval estimates, use Equation 7.11

$$\hat{\sigma}_{\bar{x}}^2 = \frac{s^2(N - n)}{n(N - 1)} = \frac{(19{,}200)^2}{60} \frac{1{,}058}{1{,}117} = 5{,}819{,}474$$

and take the square root to obtain the estimated standard error,

$$\hat{\sigma}_{\bar{x}} = 2{,}412$$

With $t_{59,0.025} \cong 2.00$ (Table 8 in the appendix) the 95% confidence interval for the mean amount of all mortgages financed in this city last year is

$$\$87{,}300 - (2.00)(2{,}412) < \mu < \$87{,}300 + (2.00)(2{,}412)$$

or

$$\$82{,}476 < \mu < \$92{,}124$$

That is, the interval runs from $82,476 to $92,124.

Auditors may be asked to conduct a sampling audit of a firm's accounts receivable to estimate the mean value of the accounts receivable.

Example 7.9 Confirmation Audit of Receivables (Confidence Interval)

Toivo Steendahl Associates, a major auditing firm, has been engaged to audit Big Woods Furniture, an upper Midwest furniture retailer, in order to determine the value of the firm's assets preceding a take over by National Distributor. As part of this audit we have been asked to conduct a sampling audit of the accounts receivable to estimate mean value of the accounts receivable. The company presently has 1,420 accounts receivable on the ledger.

Solution Based on our experience from past audits we decide to conduct a customer confirmation audit by contacting a random sample of 100 accounts receivable customers and asking them to either verify the value of the receivable in the company transaction file or to indicate the correct value of the receivable. From this sample of 100 customers we have a value for the receivable. From the data the sample, the mean and variance are as follows:

$$\bar{x} = 784$$

$$s^2 = 2{,}300$$

Thus we can report that the point estimate for the mean value of the receivables is $784. However, in addition we wish to report a confidence interval for our estimate. Since we are working with a finite population it is necessary to obtain an estimate for the population variance as

$$\hat{\sigma}_{\bar{x}}^2 = \frac{s^2}{n}\left(\frac{N-n}{N-1}\right) = \frac{2,300}{100}\left(\frac{1,320}{1,419}\right) = 21.395$$

and take the square root to obtain the estimated standard error,

$$\hat{\sigma}_{\bar{x}} = 4.626$$

Using Equation 7.12 and $t_{99,0.025} \simeq 1.96$, a 95% confidence interval estimation of the mean accounts receivable is

$$\bar{x} - t_{n-1,\alpha/2}\hat{\sigma}_{\bar{x}} < \mu < \bar{x} + t_{n-1,\alpha/2}\hat{\sigma}_{\bar{x}}$$

$$784 - 1.96(4.626) < \mu < 784 + 1.96(4.626)$$

We report the 95% confidence interval estimate for the accounts receivable as $775 to $793.

Frequently, interest centers on the population total rather than the mean. For example, the publisher of a business statistics text will want an estimate of the total number of students taking business statistics courses in all U.S. colleges. Inference about the population total is straightforward. The relevant results follow from the fact that, in our notation, population total = $N\mu$.

Estimation of the Population Total, Simple Random Sample, Finite Population

Suppose a simple random sample of size n from a population of size N is selected and that the quantity to be estimated is the population total $N\mu$.

1. An unbiased estimation procedure for the population total $N\mu$ yields the point estimate $N\bar{x}$.
2. An unbiased estimation procedure for the variance of our estimator of the population total yields the point estimate

$$N^2\hat{\sigma}_{\bar{x}}^2 = N^2\frac{s^2}{n}\frac{(N-n)}{(N-1)} \tag{7.13}$$

It follows that,

$$N\hat{\sigma}_{\bar{x}} = \frac{Ns}{\sqrt{n}}\sqrt{\frac{(N-n)}{(N-1)}} \tag{7.14}$$

3. A $100(1-\alpha)$% confidence interval for the population total is obtained from

$$N\bar{x} - t_{n-1,\alpha/2}N\hat{\sigma}_{\bar{x}} < N\mu < N\bar{x} + t_{n-1,\alpha/2}N\hat{\sigma}_{\bar{x}} \tag{7.15}$$

Example 7.10 Enrollment in Business Statistics Courses (Confidence Interval)

Suppose that there are 1,395 colleges in the United States. From a simple random sample of 400 of these schools, it was found that the sample mean enrollment during the past year in business statistics courses was 320.8 students, and the sample standard deviation was found to be 149.7 students. Estimate the total number of students enrolled in business statistics courses in the previous year, and find a 99% confidence interval.

Solution If the population mean is μ, an estimate of $N\mu$ includes the following:

$$N = 1,395 \quad n = 400 \quad \bar{x} = 320.8 \quad s = 149.7$$

Our point estimate for the total is

$$N\bar{x} = (1,395)(320.8) = 447,516$$

It is estimated that a total of 447,516 students are enrolled in business statistics courses. To obtain interval estimates, Equation 7.14 is used to obtain

$$N\hat{\sigma}_{\bar{x}} = \frac{Ns}{\sqrt{n}}\sqrt{\frac{N-n}{N-1}} = \frac{(1,395)(149.7)}{\sqrt{400}}\sqrt{\frac{995}{1,394}} = 8,821.6$$

Since the sample size is large, the 99% confidence interval for the population total is found by Equation 7.15 and the Central Limit Theorem with $z_{\alpha/2} = 2.58$:

$$N\bar{x} - Z_{\alpha/2}N\hat{\sigma}_{\bar{x}} < N\mu < N\bar{x} + Z_{\alpha/2}N\hat{\sigma}_{\bar{x}}$$

or

$$447,516 - (2.58)(8,821.6) < N\mu < 447,516 + (2.58)(8,821.6)$$

or

$$447,516 \pm 22,760$$

$$424,756 < N\mu < 470,276$$

Thus, our interval runs from 424,756 to 470,276 students.

Population Proportion

Finally, consider the case where it is required to estimate the proportion P of individuals in the population possessing some specific characteristic. Inference about this proportion should be based on the hypergeometric distribution when the number of sample members is not very small compared to the number of population members. Again, assume that the sample size is large enough to allow the central limit theorem to be invoked.

Estimation of the Population Proportion, Simple Random Sample, Finite Population

Let $\hat{p}$ be the proportion possessing a particular characteristic in a random sample of n observations from a population with a proportion, P, of whose members possess that characteristic.

1. The sample proportion, $\hat{p}$, is an unbiased estimator of the population proportion, P.
2. An unbiased estimation procedure for the variance of our estimator of the population proportion yields the point estimate

$$\sigma_{\hat{p}}^2 = \frac{\hat{p}(1 - \hat{p})}{n - 1} \times \frac{(N - n)}{(N - 1)} \tag{7.16}$$

3. Provided the sample size is large, $100(1 - \alpha)\%$ confidence intervals for the population proportion are given by

$$\hat{p} - z_{\alpha/2}\hat{\sigma}_{\hat{p}} < P < \hat{p} + z_{\alpha/2}\hat{\sigma}_{\hat{p}} \tag{7.17}$$

Example 7.11 Two Semesters of Business Statistics (Confidence Interval)

From a simple random sample of 400 of the 1,395 colleges in our population, it was found that business statistics was a two-semester course in 141 of the sampled colleges. Estimate the proportion of all colleges for which the course is two semesters long, and find a 90% confidence interval.

Solution   Given

$$N = 1,395 \qquad n = 400 \qquad \hat{p} = \frac{141}{400} = 0.3525$$

our point estimate of the population proportion, P, is simply $\hat{p} = 0.3525$. That is, the course is two semesters long in approximately 35.25% of all colleges. To calculate interval estimates, the variance of our estimate is found by Equation 7.16:

$$\hat{\sigma}_{\hat{p}}^2 = \frac{\hat{p}(1 - \hat{p})}{n} \times \frac{(N - n)}{(N - 1)} = \frac{(0.3525)(0.6475)}{400} \times \frac{995}{1,394} = 0.0004073$$

so

$$\hat{\sigma}_{\hat{p}} = 0.0202$$

For a 90% confidence interval, $z_{\alpha/2} = z_{0.05} = 1.645$. The 90% confidence interval is found by Equation 7.17:

$$\hat{p} - z_{\alpha/2}\hat{\sigma}_p < P < \hat{p} + z_{\alpha/2}\hat{\sigma}_{\hat{p}}$$

or

$$0.3525 - (1.645)(0.0202) < P < 0.3525 + (1.645)(0.0202)$$

or

$$0.3193 < P < 0.3857$$

Thus, the 90% confidence interval for the percentage of all colleges in which business statistics is a two-semester course runs from 31.93% to 38.57%.

EXERCISES

Basic Exercises

7.51 Assume simple random sampling. Calculate the variance of the sample mean, $\sigma_{\bar{x}}^2$ for each of the following:

   a. $N = 1200$; $n = 80$; $s = 10$
   b. $N = 1425$; $n = 90$; $s^2 = 64$
   c. $N = 3200$; $n = 200$; $s^2 = 129$

7.52 Assume simple random sampling. Calculate the confidence interval estimate for the population mean for each of the following:

   a. $N = 1200$; $n = 80$; $s = 10$; $\bar{x} = 142$
   b. $N = 1425$; $n = 90$; $s^2 = 64$; $\bar{x} = 232.4$
   c. $N = 3200$; $n = 200$; $s^2 = 129$; $\bar{x} = 59.3$

7.53 Assume simple random sampling. Calculate the confidence interval for the population total for each of the following:

   a. $N = 1325$; $n = 121$; $s = 20$; $\bar{x} = 182$; 95% confidence level
   b. $N = 2100$; $n = 144$; $s = 50$; $\bar{x} = 1,325$; 98% confidence level

7.54 Assume simple random sampling. Calculate the confidence interval for the population proportion, P, for each of the following:

   a. $N = 1058$; $n = 160$; $x = 40$; 95% confidence level
   b. $N = 854$; $n = 81$; $x = 50$; 99% confidence level

Application Exercises

7.55 Take a random sample of 50 pages from this book and estimate the proportion of all pages that contain figures.

7.56 A firm employs 189 junior accountants. In a random sample of 50 of these, the mean number of hours overtime billed in a particular week was 9.7, and the sample standard deviation was 6.2 hours.

   a. Find a 95% confidence interval for the mean number of hours overtime billed per junior accountant in this firm that week.

   b. Find a 99% confidence interval for the total number of hours overtime billed by junior accountants in the firm during the week of interest.

7.57 An auditor, examining a total of 820 accounts receivable of a corporation, took a random sample of 60 of them. The sample mean was $127.43, and the sample standard deviation was $43.27.

   a. Using an unbiased estimation procedure, find an estimate of the population mean.

   b. Using an unbiased estimation procedure, find an estimate of the variance of the sample mean.

   c. Find a 90% confidence interval for the population mean.

   d. A statistician found, for the population mean, a confidence interval running from $117.43 to $137.43. What is the probability content of this interval?

   e. Find a 95% confidence interval for the total amount of these 820 accounts.

7.58 On a particular day a consumer advice bureau received 125 calls. For a random sample of 40 of these calls, it was found that mean time taken in providing the requested advice was 7.28 minutes, and the sample standard deviation was 5.32 minutes.

   a. Find a 99% confidence interval for the mean time taken per call.

   b. Find a 90% confidence interval for the total amount of time taken in answering these 125 calls.

7.59 State whether each of the following statements is true or false:

   a. For a given number of population members and a given sample variance, the larger the number of sample members, the wider the 95% confidence interval for the population mean.

   b. For a given number of population members and a given number of sample members, the larger the sample variance, the wider the 95% confidence interval for the population mean.

c. For a given number of sample members and a given sample variance, the larger the number of population members, the wider the 95% confidence interval for the population mean. Justify your answer.

d. For a given number of population members, a given number of sample members, and a given sample variance, a 95% confidence interval for the population mean is wider than a 90% confidence interval for the population mean.

7.60 A senior manager, responsible for a group of 120 junior executives, is interested in the total amount of time per week spent by these people in internal meetings. A random sample of 35 of these executives was asked to keep diary records during the next week. When the results were analyzed, it was found that these sample members spent a total of 143 hours in internal meetings. The sample standard deviation was 3.1 hours. Find a 90% confidence interval for the total number of hours spent in internal meetings by all 120 junior executives in the week.

7.61 A simple random sample of 400 from a total 1,395 colleges in the United States maintained that 39 colleges use the text *Statistics Made Difficult and Boring*. Find a 95% confidence interval for the proportion of all colleges using this text.

7.62 A business school dean is contemplating proposing a change in the requirements for graduation. At present, business majors are required to take one science course, chosen from a list of possible courses. The proposal is that this be replaced by the requirement that a course in ecology be taken. The business school has 420 students. In a random sample of 100 of these students, 56 expressed opposition to this proposal. Find a 90% confidence interval for the proportion of all the school's students opposed to the proposed change in requirements.

7.63 In a college dormitory 257 of the residents are first-year students. Of a random sample of 120 of them, 37 indicated strong interest in living in the dormitory next year. Find a 95% confidence interval for the proportion of first-year students in this dormitory with a strong interest in living there next year.

7.64 A class has 420 students. The final examination is optional—taking it can raise, but cannot lower, a student's grade. Of a random sample of 80 students, 31 indicated that they would take the final examination. Find a 90% confidence interval for the total number of students in this class intending to take the final examination.

KEY WORDS

- bias, 289
- confidence interval, 294
  - estimate, 293
  - estimator, 293
  - mean, with known variance, 295
  - mean, with unknown variance, 302
  - mean, fpc, 314
  - population total, fpc, 316
  - proportion, 307
  - proportion, fpc, 318
- confidence level, 294
- consistent estimator, 323
- efficient estimator, 289
- estimate, 287
- estimator, 287
- finite population correction factor, 314
- lower confidence limit, *LCL*, 295
- margin of error, 295
- minimum variance unbiased estimator, 289
- most efficient estimator, 289
- point estimate, 288
- point estimator, 288
- relative efficiency, 289
- reliability factor, 296
- sampling error, 295
- Student's *t* distribution, 300
- unbiased estimator, 288
- upper confidence limit, *UCL*, 295
- width, 295

CHAPTER EXERCISES AND APPLICATIONS

7.65 Several drugs are used to treat diabetes. A sales specialist for a leading pharmaceutical company needs an estimate of the number of new prescriptions that were written during a particular month for his company's new diabetes drug. The numbers of new prescriptions in a sample of 10 sales districts are as follows:

| 210 | 240 | 190 | 275 | 290 |
| 265 | 312 | 284 | 261 | 243 |

a. Find a 90% confidence interval for the average number of new prescriptions written for this new drug among all the sales districts. State the assumptions.

b. Calculate the widths for 95% and 98% confidence intervals.

7.66 Suppose that Brent Matthews, manager of a Sam's Club in Chattanooga, Tennessee, wants to estimate the mean number of gallons of milk that are sold during a typical weekday. Brent checked the sales records for a random sample of 16 days and found the mean number of gallons sold is 150 gallons per day; the sample standard deviation is 12 gallons. With 95% confidence, estimate the number of gallons that Brent should stock daily.

7.67 Everyone knows that exercise is important. Recently, residents in one community were surveyed and asked, "How many minutes do you spend daily on some form of rigorous exercise?" From a random sample of 50 residents the mean time spent on vigorous daily exercise was half an hour. The standard deviation was found to be 4.2 minutes. Find a 90% interval estimate of the time spent daily on rigorous exercise by these residents.

7.68 The following data represent the number of passengers per flight for a random sample of 50 flights from Jacksonville, Florida, to Baltimore, Maryland, on one particular airline:

163 165 094 137 123 095 170 096 117 129

152 138 147 119 166 125 148 180 152 149

167 120 129 159 150 119 113 147 169 151

116 150 110 110 143 090 134 145 156 165

174 133 128 100 086 148 139 150 145 100

Estimate the average number of passengers per flight with a 95% interval estimate.

7.69 ● The supervisor of a bottle-filling plant randomly sampled bottles to determine if any of the following defects were present: dents, missing labels, incorrect labels, and a wrong color. The types of defects are in the data file **Defects**.

a. Estimate the proportion of defects due to an incorrect label. Use a 5% risk.
b. Estimate the percentage of defects due to a missing label. Use a 90% confidence level.

7.70 Eight randomly selected batches of a chemical were tested for impurity concentration. The percentage impurity levels found in this sample were as follows:

3.2 4.3 2.1 2.8 3.2 3.6 4.0 3.8

a. Find the most efficient estimates of the population mean and variance.
b. Estimate the proportion of batches with impurity levels greater than 3.75%.

7.71 A marketing research assistant for a veterinary hospital surveyed a random sample of 457 pet owners. Respondents were asked to indicate the number of times that they visit their veterinarian each year. The sample mean response was 3.59 and the sample standard deviation was 1.045. Based on these

results a confidence interval from 3.49 to 3.69 was calculated for the population mean. Find the probability content for this interval.

7.72 A random sample of 174 college students was asked to indicate the number of hours per week that they surf the Internet for either personal information or material for a class assignment. The sample mean response was 6.06 hours and the sample standard deviation was 1.43 hours. Based on these results, a confidence interval extending from 5.96 to 6.16 was calculated for the population mean. Find the confidence level of this interval.

7.73 ● A sample of 33 accounting students recorded the number of hours that they spent studying for a final exam. The data are stored in the data file **Study**.

a. Give an example of an unbiased, consistent, and efficient estimator of the population mean.
b. Find the sampling error for a 95% confidence interval estimate of the mean number of hours students studied for this exam.

7.74 Dr. Mihaela Sabou wants to estimate the average length of a hospital stay (number of days) for patients with a certain infectious disease. From a random sample of 25 patient records she finds that the average number of days in the hospital for such patients is 6 days with a standard deviation of 1.8 days.

a. Find the reliability factor for a 95% confidence interval estimate of the population mean length of stay.
b. Find the *LCL* for a 99% confidence interval estimate of the population mean length of stay.

7.75 Suppose that a survey of race fans at this week's Daytona 500 NASCAR race were asked, "Is this your first time attending the Daytona 500?" From a random sample of 250 race fans 100 answered in the affirmative.

a. Find the standard error to estimate the population proportion of first timers.
b. Find the sampling error to estimate the population proportion of first timers.
c. Estimate the proportion of repeat fans with 92% confidence level.

7.76 The following data represent the number of passengers per flight in a random sample of 20 flights from Vienna, Austria, to Cluj-Napoca, Romania, with a new airline:

63 65 94 37 83 95 70 96 47 29

52 38 47 79 66 25 48 80 52 49

a. What is the reliability factor for a 90% confidence interval estimate of the mean number of passengers per flight?

b. Find the LCL for a 99% confidence interval estimate of the mean number of passengers per flight?

7.77 🌐 A group of business students conducted a survey on their university campus to determine student demand for a particular product, a protein supplement for smoothies. As part of their initial steps they randomly sampled 113 students and obtained data that could be helpful in developing their marketing strategy. The responses to this survey are contained in the data file **Smoothies**.

a. Find a 95% confidence interval estimate for the population proportion of students who would like supplements such as protein, creatine, or energy boosters in their smoothies.
b. Estimate the population proportion of students who consider that they are very health conscious with a 98% confidence level.
c. Of the 113 respondents 77 indicated that they drank smoothies in the afternoon. Determine with 90% confidence an estimate of the population proportion who drink smoothies in the afternoon.

7.78 🌐 A random sample of 100 students at a small university were asked a series of questions such as their status as an American or international student, major, gender, age, year in school, and current GPA. Other questions were asked about levels of satisfaction with campus parking, campus housing, and campus dining. Finally, students were asked if they planned to attend graduate school within five years of their college graduation. These data are contained in the data file **Finstad and Lie Study**.

a. Estimate the population grade point average with 95% confidence level.
b. Estimate the population proportion of students who were very dissatisfied (code 1) or moderately dissatisfied (code 2) with parking facilities on campus. Use a 90% confidence level.
c. Estimate the population proportion of students who were at least moderately satisfied (codes 4 and 5) with on-campus food service.

7.79 🌐 The manager of Florin's Flower Mart obtained customer information that is stored in the data file **Florin**.

a. Estimate the mean age of the store's customers.
b. Estimate the population proportion of customers that are dissatisfied with the store's delivery system.
c. Estimate the population mean amount charged to a Visa credit card.

7.80 What is the most common method to renew vehicle registration? In checking a random sample of 500 motor vehicle renewal registrations in one county, the finance department found that 200 were mailed, 160 were paid in person at the county finance department office, and the remainder were paid on-line at the county's Web site. Phone registration renewals were not available.

a. Estimate the population proportion to pay for vehicle registration renewals in person at the county finance department office. Use a 90% confidence level.
b. Estimate the population proportion of on-line renewals. Use a 95% confidence level.

7.81 Consider the data in Exercise 7.80. Suppose that we computed for the population proportion who pay for vehicle registration by mail a confidence interval extending from 0.34 to 0.46. What is the confidence level of this interval?

7.82 Consider the data in Exercise 7.80. It was reported in the local paper that less than one-third (from 23.7% to 32.3%) of the population prefers the on-line renewal process. What is the confidence level of this interval estimate?

7.83 The county finance department also wants information about renewals of disabled parking placards. Suppose that in a sample of 350 transactions for disabled parking placards it was found that 250 were paid electronically.

a. What is the margin of error for a 99% confidence interval estimate of the population proportion of disabled renewal transactions paid electronically?
b. Without calculating, is the margin of error for a 95% confidence interval estimate of the population proportion of disabled renewal transactions paid electronically larger, smaller, or the same as that found in part (a) for a 99% confidence interval?

7.84 What is the typical age of a person who renews his driver's license on-line? From a random sample of 460 driver's license renewal transactions the mean age was 42.6 and the standard deviation was 5.4. Compute the 98% confidence interval estimate of the mean age of on-line renewal users in this county.

7.85 A test was taken by 90 students. A random sample of 10 scores found the following results:

93 71 62 75 81 63 87 59 84 72

a. Find a 90% confidence interval for the population mean score.
b. Without doing the calculations, state whether a 95% confidence interval for the population mean would be wider or narrower than the interval found in part (a).

7.86 A corporation has 272 accounts receivable in a particular category. A random sample of 50 of them was taken. The sample mean was $492.36 and the sample standard deviation was $149.92.

a. Find a 99% confidence interval for the population mean value of these accounts receivable.
b. Find a 95% confidence interval for the total value of these accounts receivable.
c. Without doing the calculations, state whether a 90% confidence interval for the population total would be wider or narrower than the interval found in part (b).

7.87 A corporation employs 148 sales representatives. A random sample of 60 of them was taken, and it was found that, for 36 of the sample members, the volume of orders taken this month was higher than for the same month last year. Find a 95% confidence interval for the population proportion of sales representatives with a higher volume of orders.

Appendix

CONSISTENT ESTIMATOR

Consistency is another property that some estimators possess.

CONSISTENT ESTIMATOR

A point estimator $\hat{\theta}$ is said to be a **consistent estimator** of the parameter θ if the difference between the expected value of the estimator and the parameter decreases as the sample size increases. In other words the bias becomes smaller with increased sample size.

Consistent estimators are used in cases where it is difficult or impossible to obtain unbiased estimators, which occurs in some advanced econometric work. Not all unbiased estimators are consistent, and by no means are all consistent estimators unbiased. If the sample variance were calculated as

$$s^2 = \frac{\sum_{i=1}^{n}(x_i - \overline{x})^2}{n}$$

then it would be a biased estimator of the population variance. However, it is consistent, since it approaches the unbiased estimator

$$s^2 = \frac{\sum_{i=1}^{n}(x_i - \overline{x})^2}{n - 1}$$

as the sample size increases.

Loosely speaking, the use of a consistent estimator with an infinite amount of sample information gives the correct result. Conversely, the use of an inconsistent estimator does not yield the correct result even with an infinite amount of sample information. For this reason, inconsistency in a point estimator is regarded as undesirable.

STUDENT'S *t* DISTRIBUTION

Gosset sought to develop a probability distribution for normally distributed random variables that did not include the population variance σ^2. As a result, he took the ratio of Z, a standard normal random variable, and the square root of $\chi 2$ divided by its degrees of freedom, v. In mathematical notation

$$t = \frac{Z}{\sqrt{\chi^2/v}}$$

$$t = \frac{(x - \mu)/\sigma}{\sqrt{s^2(n-1)/\sigma^2(n-1)}} = \frac{(x - \mu)}{s}$$

The resulting t statistic has $n - 1$ degrees of freedom. Notice that the t probability distribution is based on normally distributed random variables. For applications, the normal Z is used when the population variance σ^2 is available, and the Student's t is used when only the sample variance s^2 is available. Statistical research using computer-generated random samples has shown that t can be used to study the distribution of sample means even if the distribution of the individual random variables is not normal.

References

1. *American Customer Satisfaction Index*. 2000. Ann Arbor: University of Michigan Business School.
2. Dabholkar, P. A., and J. J. Kellaris. 1992. Toward Understanding Marketing Students' Ethical Judgment of Controversial Personal Selling Practices. *Journal of Business Research* 24: 313–329.
3. Fiedler, Alfred W., Plant Manager. February 1999. Machine Reading Leak Rate Repeatability Studies Conducted at LDS Vacuum Products. Altamonte Springs, FL.
4. Hildebrand, David, and A. L. Ott. 1998. *Statistical Thinking for Managers*. New York: Brooks/Cole.
5. Pearson, Egon Sharpe, and R. L. Plackett, eds. 1990. *Student: A Statistical Biography of William Sealy Gosset*. Oxford, England: Clarendon Press.
6. Pearson, Egon Sharpe, and John Wishart, eds. 1958. *Development of Statistics: Student's Collected Papers*. Cambridge: . Foreword by Launce McMullen. Materials provided to the authors by Teresa O'Donnell, Guinness (GIG) Archivist, September 13, 2000.
7. "Project Romanian Rescue: Headline News," October 2000.
8. Salsburg, David. 2002. *The Lady Tasting Tea: How Statistics Revolutionized Science in the Twentieth Century*. New York: Henry Holt and Company.
9. Wessel, Harry. 2000. Lousy Service? Get Used to It. *Orlando Sentinel* November 24 p. A1.

Chapter 8

Estimation: Additional Topics

Introduction

In this chapter we consider certain additional topics in estimation. In Chapter 7 we presented confidence interval procedures to estimate certain parameters of a *single* population. In this chapter we first consider confidence interval procedures to estimate certain parameters of *two* populations. An important problem in statistical inference deals with the comparison of *two means* from normally distributed populations or the comparison of *two proportions* from large populations. For example, consider the following:

1. Corporate executives employed by retail distributors may want to estimate the difference between the mean daily sales of two retail stores.

325

2. Manufacturers may want to compare the average productivity, in units per hour, of day shift workers and night shift workers in a plant.
3. The campaign manager for a presidential candidate may want to compare the popularity rating of this candidate in two different regions of the country.
4. A clinical trial comparing carcinoma recurrence rates, side effects, and survival rates between patients receiving two different medications.
5. A chemical company receives shipments from two suppliers. Independent random samples of batches from each supplier are selected, and a comparison of impurity levels of the two batches is made.

Another estimation topic introduced in this chapter is the determination of sample size for certain situations and sampling schemes. In Section 8.4 we consider sample size, *n*, when the population size is relatively large compared to the sample size. In Section 8.5 we consider the problem of a researcher who wants to discover something about a population that is not necessarily large. We discuss other sampling methods in Chapter 17.

8.1 CONFIDENCE INTERVAL ESTIMATION OF THE DIFFERENCE BETWEEN TWO NORMAL POPULATION MEANS: DEPENDENT SAMPLES

To compare population means, random samples are drawn from the two populations. The procedure that we use to select the samples determines the appropriate method that we use to analyze inferences based on the sample results. In this section we present a sampling scheme for *dependent* samples. In Section 8.2 we will focus our attention on sampling schemes for *independent* samples.

We consider samples to be *dependent* if the values in one sample are influenced by the values in the other sample. Dependent samples are either *matched pairs* or the same individual or objects tested twice. The idea of matched pairs is that, apart from the factor under study, the members of these pairs should resemble one another as closely as possible so that the comparison of interest can be made directly. In clinical trials to compare the effectiveness of two medications, dependent samples will be selected and the members will be matched on various factors such as the patient's age or weight.

Dependent sampling also refers to two measurements taken on the same person or object. Suppose that the effectiveness of a speed-reading course is to be measured. One possible approach would be to record the number of words per minute read by a sample of students *before* taking the course and compare the data to the results for the same students *after* completing the course. In this case each pair of observations consists of "before" and "after" measurements on a single student. This type of dependent sampling is sometimes referred to as *repeated measurements*.

An interval estimate for the general case of *n* matched pairs of observations, denoted by $(x_1, y_1), (x_2, y_2),..., (x_n, y_n)$, selected from populations with means μ_X and μ_Y follows.

Confidence Intervals of Two Means: Dependent Samples (Matched Pairs)

Suppose that there is a random sample of n matched pairs of observations from normal distributions with means μ_X and μ_Y. That is, let $x_1, x_2, ..., x_n$ denote the values of the observations from the population with mean μ_X; and let $y_1, y_2,..., y_n$ denote the matched sampled values from the population with the mean μ_Y. Let $\overline{d}$ and s_d denote the observed sample mean and standard deviation for the n differences $d_i = x_i - y_i$. If the population distribution of the differences is assumed to be normal, then a $100(1 - \alpha)\%$ **confidence interval for the difference between means** $(\mu_d = \mu_X - \mu_Y)$ is given by

$$\overline{d} - t_{n-1,\alpha/2}\frac{s_d}{\sqrt{n}} < \mu_d < \overline{d} + t_{n-1,\alpha/2}\frac{s_d}{\sqrt{n}} \tag{8.1}$$

or equivalently

$$\overline{d} \pm ME$$

The standard deviation of the differences, s_d, and the margin of error, ME, are

$$s_d = \sqrt{\frac{\Sigma(d_i - \overline{d})^2}{n}}$$

$$ME = t_{n-1,\alpha/2}\frac{s_d}{\sqrt{n}} \tag{8.2}$$

and $t_{n-1,\alpha/2}$ is the number for which

$$P(t_{n-1} > t_{n-1,\alpha/2}) = \frac{\alpha}{2}$$

The random variable, t_{n-1}, has a Student's t distribution with $(n - 1)$ degrees of freedom.

Example 8.1 Cholesterol Reduction Study (Confidence Interval)

A medical study was conducted to compare the difference in effectiveness of two particular drugs in lowering cholesterol levels. The research team used a paired sample approach to control variation in reduction that might be due to factors other than the drug itself. Each member of a pair was matched by age, weight, lifestyle, and other pertinent factors. Drug X was given to one person randomly selected in each pair, and drug Y was given to the other individual in the pair. After a specified amount of time each person's cholesterol level was measured again. Suppose that a random sample of eight pairs of patients with known cholesterol problems is selected from the large populations of participants. Table 8.1 gives the number of points by which each person's cholesterol level was reduced, as well as the differences, $d_i = x_i - y_i$, for each pair. Estimate with a 99% confidence level the mean difference in the effectiveness of the two drugs, X and Y, to lower cholesterol.

Table 8.1 Cholesterol Reduction

PAIR	DRUG X	DRUG Y	DIFFERENCE ($d_i = x_i - y_i$)
1	29	26	3
2	32	27	5
3	31	28	3
4	32	27	5
5	32	30	2
6	29	26	3
7	31	33	–2
8	30	36	–6

Solution   From Table 8.1 we compute the sample mean, $\bar{d}$, and the observed sample standard deviation, s_d, of the differences in cholesterol reduction as follows:

$$\bar{d} = 1.625 \qquad \text{and} \qquad s_d = 3.777$$

From the Student's t distribution table, $t_{n-1,\alpha/2} = t_{7,0.005} = 3.499$. We use Equation 8.1 and find the 99% confidence interval for the difference between the population means:

$$\bar{d} - \frac{t_{n-1,\alpha/2}s_d}{\sqrt{n}} < \mu_x - \mu_y < \bar{d} + \frac{t_{n-1,\alpha/2}s_d}{\sqrt{n}}$$

$$1.625 - \frac{(3.499)(3.777)}{\sqrt{8}} < \mu_x - \mu_y < 1.625 + \frac{(3.499)(3.777)}{\sqrt{8}}$$

$$-3.05 < \mu_x - \mu_y < 6.30$$

Since the confidence interval contains the value of zero, we can conclude one of the following: that $\mu_x - \mu_y$ could be positive, suggesting that drug X is more effective; that $\mu_x - \mu_y$ could be negative, suggesting that drug Y is more effective; or that $\mu_x - \mu_y$ could be zero, suggesting that drug X and drug Y are equally effective. Thus, it is not possible to determine if either drug is more effective in reducing one's cholesterol level.

Example 8.2 Improve SAT Scores (Confidence Interval)

Countless Web sites, study guides, software, on-line interactive courses, books, and classes promise to increase students' vocabulary, to refresh students' math skills, and to teach test-taking strategies in order to improve SAT scores, which should help to enhance chances of college acceptance, or increase the possibilities of receiving certain scholarships. Similarly, the same types of offerings exist to improve GMAT scores, LSAT scores, MCAT scores, and other such standardized tests. One company randomly sampled 140 of its clients and collected data on each person's SAT score before taking the on-line course and each person's SAT score after taking the course. The data is stored in the data file **Improve Your Score.xls**. Estimate the difference in the mean SAT scores before and after taking this course.

Solution   Let $x_1, x_2, ..., x_n$ denote the SAT scores after each person completed the course, and let $y_1, y_2,..., y_n$ denote the SAT scores before each person took the course. The difference, $d_i = x_i - y_i$, is the After Score – Before Score for each person. This example illustrates *repeated measurements* since two scores were obtained for each individual. Using Excel, Minitab, SPSS, or some other software package, we obtain the following information:

$$\bar{d} = 77.7 \qquad \text{and} \qquad s_d = 43.68901$$

From the Student's t distribution table, $t_{n-1,\alpha/2} = t_{139,0.025} \cong 1.96$. We use Equation 8.1 and find the 95% confidence interval for the difference between the population means:

$$\bar{d} - \frac{t_{n-1,\alpha/2}s_d}{\sqrt{n}} < \mu_x - \mu_y < \bar{d} + \frac{t_{n-1,\alpha/2}s_d}{\sqrt{n}}$$

$$77.7 - \frac{(1.96)(43.68901)}{\sqrt{140}} < \mu_x - \mu_y < 77.7 + \frac{(1.96)(43.68901)}{\sqrt{140}}$$

$$70.5 < \mu_x - \mu_y < 84.9$$

Table 8.2 shows the Excel printout for this problem. Notice that the value of the margin of error appears on the line Confidence Level (95.0%). That is, the margin of error is approximately equal to 7.3 for a 95% confidence interval estimate of the difference in the after scores minus the before scores. In the long run, we estimate that the mean scores improved by as little as 70 points or by as much as 85 points following the completion of the course.

Table 8.2   Improvement in SAT Scores

Dependent Samples	
Difference = After Score – Before Score	
Mean	77.7
Standard Error	3.692395
Median	80
Mode	80
Standard Deviation	43.68901
Sample Variance	1908.729
Range	260
Minimum	-50
Maximum	210
Sum	10878
Count	140
Confidence Level (95.0%)	**7.300521**

Missing values are common in survey responses and other research. Special care must be taken if we use Excel to analyze matched pairs when there are missing data. Suppose that at least one value from the first sample is missing and *exactly* the same number of missing values occurs in the second sample (not from the same observations). Excel does not delete these observations and in this one case it will perform the calculations giving incorrect results (see Exercise 8.3). In a study of dependent samples, first delete all observations from your sample that contain missing values.

EXERCISES

Basic Exercises

8.1 A dependent random sample from two normally distributed populations gives the following results:

$$n = 15 \qquad \bar{d} = 25.4 \qquad s_d = 2.8$$

a. Find the 95% confidence interval for the difference between the means of the two populations.
b. Find the margin of error for a 95% confidence interval for the difference between the means of the two populations

8.2 A confidence interval for the difference between the means of two normally distributed populations based on the following dependent samples is desired:

Before	After
6	8
12	14
8	9
10	13
6	7

a. Find the margin of error for a 90% confidence level.
b. Find the *UCL* and the *LCL* for a 90% confidence level.
c. Find the width of a 95% confidence interval.

8.3 An educational study was designed to investigate the effectiveness of a reading program of elementary age children. Each child was given a pre-test and post-test. Higher post-test scores would indicate reading improvement. From a very large population, a random sample of scores for the pre-test and post-test are as follows:

Child	Pre-Test Score	Post-Test Score
1	40	48
2	36	42
3	32	
4	38	36
5		43
6	33	38
7	35	45

Child 3 moved from the school district and did not take the post-test. Child 5 moved into the district after the start of the study and did not take the pre-test. Find a 95% confidence interval estimate of the mean improvement in the reading scores.

Application Exercises

8.4 A random sample of 10 pairs of identical houses was chosen in a large midwestern city, and a passive solar heating system was installed in one house from each pair. The total fuel bills (in dollars) for three winter months for these homes were then determined, as shown in the accompanying table. Assuming normal population distributions, find a 90% confidence interval for the difference between the two population means.

Pair	Without Passive Solar	With Passive Solar	Pair	Without Passive Solar	With Passive Solar
1	485	452	6	386	380
2	423	386	7	426	395
3	515	502	8	473	411
4	425	376	9	454	415
5	653	605	10	496	441

8.5 A random sample of six salespersons that attended a motivational course on sales techniques was monitored three months before and three months after the course. The table shows the values of sales (in thousands of dollars) generated by these six salespersons in the two periods. Assume that the population distributions are normal. Find an 80% confidence interval for the difference between the two population means.

Salesperson	Before the Course	After the Course
1	212	237
2	282	291
3	203	191
4	327	341
5	165	192
6	198	180

8.2 CONFIDENCE INTERVAL ESTIMATION OF THE DIFFERENCE BETWEEN TWO NORMAL POPULATION MEANS: INDEPENDENT SAMPLES

In this section we develop confidence interval estimation when two samples are drawn *independently* from two normally distributed populations. We consider three situations: 1) both population variances are known; 2) both population variances are not known, but can be considered to be equal; and 3) both population variances are not known, but are not considered to be equal.

Two Means, Independent Samples, and Known Population Variances

In this scheme, samples are drawn *independently* from the two normally distributed populations so that the membership of one sample is not influenced by the membership of the other sample. Also we know the *population variances of both populations.*

Consider the case where independent samples, not necessarily of equal size, are taken from the two populations of interest. Suppose that there is a random sample of n_x observations from a population with mean μ_x and variance σ_x^2 and an independent random sample of n_y observations from a population with mean μ_y and variance σ_y^2. Let the respective sample means be $\bar{x}$ and $\bar{y}$.

As a first step, examine the situation when the two population distributions are normal with known variances. Since the object of interest is the difference between the two population means, it is natural to base an inference on the difference between the corresponding sample means. This random variable has mean

$$E(\overline{X} - \overline{Y}) = E(\overline{X}) - E(\overline{Y}) = \mu_x - \mu_y$$

and since the samples are independent,

$$Var(\overline{X} - \overline{Y}) = Var(\overline{X}) + Var(\overline{Y}) = \frac{\sigma_x^2}{n_x} + \frac{\sigma_y^2}{n_y}$$

Furthermore, it can be shown that its distribution is normal. It, therefore, follows that the random variable

$$Z = \frac{(\bar{x} - \bar{y}) - (\mu_x - \mu_y)}{\sqrt{\dfrac{\sigma_x^2}{n_x} + \dfrac{\sigma_y^2}{n_y}}}$$

has a standard normal distribution. An argument parallel to that in Chapter 7 can then be used to obtain the confidence interval for the difference between the population means.

Confidence Intervals of the Difference Between Means: Independent Samples (Normal Distributions and Known Population Variances)

Suppose that there are two **independent random samples** of n_x and n_y observations from normally distributed populations with means μ_X and μ_Y, and variances σ_X^2 and σ_Y^2. If the observed sample means are $\bar{x}$ and $\bar{y}$, then a $100(1 - \alpha)\%$ confidence interval for $(\mu_X - \mu_Y)$ is given by

$$(\bar{x} - \bar{y}) - z_{\alpha/2}\sqrt{\frac{\sigma_x^2}{n_x} + \frac{\sigma_y^2}{n_y}} < \mu_X - \mu_Y < (\bar{x} - \bar{y}) + z_{\alpha/2}\sqrt{\frac{\sigma_x^2}{n_x} + \frac{\sigma_y^2}{n_y}} \qquad (8.3)$$

or equivalently

$$(\bar{x} - \bar{y}) \pm ME$$

where the margin of error, *ME*, is given by the following:

$$ME = z_{\alpha/2}\sqrt{\frac{\sigma_x^2}{n_x} + \frac{\sigma_y^2}{n_y}} \qquad (8.4)$$

In some applications, historical variances from similar studies can be used as the true population variances.

Example 8.3 Class Preparation Time (Confidence Interval)

Independent random samples of accounting professors and information systems (IS) professors were asked to provide the number of hours they spend in preparation for each class. The sample of 321 IS professors had a mean time of 3.01 preparation hours, and the sample of 94 accounting professors had a mean time of 2.88 hours. From similar past studies the population standard deviation for the IS professors is assumed to be 1.09, and, similarly, the population standard deviation for the accounting professors is 1.01. Denoting the population mean for IS professors by μ_x and the population mean for accounting professors by μ_y, find a 95% confidence interval for $(\mu_x - \mu_y)$.

Solution   We use Equation 8.3,

$$(\bar{x} - \bar{y}) - z_{\alpha/2}\sqrt{\frac{\sigma_x^2}{n_x} + \frac{\sigma_y^2}{n_y}} < \mu_x - \mu_y < (\bar{x} - \bar{y}) + z_{\alpha/2}\sqrt{\frac{\sigma_x^2}{n_x} + \frac{\sigma_y^2}{n_y}}$$

with

$$\begin{aligned}
n_x &= 321 & \bar{x} &= 3.01 & \sigma_x &= 1.09 \\
n_y &= 94 & \bar{y} &= 2.88 & \sigma_y &= 1.01
\end{aligned}$$

And for a 95% confidence interval,

$$z_{\alpha/2} = z_{0.025} = 1.96$$

The confidence interval is then

$$(3.01 - 2.88) - 1.96\sqrt{\frac{(1.09)^2}{321} + \frac{(1.01)^2}{94}} < \mu_x - \mu_y < (3.01 - 2.88) + 1.96\sqrt{\frac{(1.09)^2}{321} + \frac{(1.01)^2}{94}}$$

or

$$-0.11 < \mu_x - \mu_y < 0.37$$

This interval includes zero, indicating an absence of strong evidence that the population means are different.

Two Means, Independent Samples, and Population Variances Assumed to Be Equal

It seems reasonable that if we do not know the population means, we most likely do not know the population variances either. Two possibilities arise: Either the unknown population variances are assumed to be equal, or they are *not* assumed to be equal. We turn our attention first to the situation where the unknown population variances are assumed to be equal. We present both of the situations but defer discussion of how to determine whether population variances are equal to Chapter 10.

Suppose again that there are two independent random samples of n_x and n_y observations from normally distributed populations with means μ_X and μ_Y, and that the populations have a common (unknown) variance σ^2—that is, $\sigma_x^2 = \sigma_y^2 = \sigma^2$. Inference about the population means is based on the difference $(\bar{x} - \bar{y})$ between the two sample means. This random variable has a normal distribution with mean $(\mu_x - \mu_y)$ and variance

$$Var(\overline{X} - \overline{Y}) = Var(\overline{X}) + Var(\overline{Y}) = \frac{\sigma^2}{n_x} + \frac{\sigma^2}{n_y}$$

It therefore follows that the random variable,

$$Z = \frac{(\bar{x} - \bar{y}) - (\mu_x - \mu_y)}{\sqrt{\frac{\sigma^2}{n_x} + \frac{\sigma^2}{n_y}}}$$

has a standard normal distribution. However, this result cannot be used as it stands because the unknown population variance is involved.

Since $\sigma_x^2 = \sigma_y^2 = \sigma^2$, then both s_x^2 and s_y^2 are estimators of the common population variance σ^2. To use only s_x^2 or only s_y^2 to estimate the common variance would ignore information from the other sample. If the sample sizes are the same $(n_x = n_y)$, then the average of s_x^2 and s_y^2 could be used to estimate the common variance. However, in the more general situation of unequal sample sizes, an estimate is needed that acknowledges the fact that more information about the common variance is obtained from the sample with the larger sample size. Thus, a weighted average of s_x^2 and s_y^2 is used. This estimator s_p^2, pools the two sets of sample information and is given in Equation 8.7.

Confidence Intervals of Two Means: Unknown Population Variances That Are Assumed to Be Equal

Suppose that there are two independent random samples with n_x and n_y observations from **normally** distributed populations with means μ_x and μ_y, and a **common, but unknown, population variance**. If the observed sample means are $\overline{x}$ and $\overline{y}$, and the observed sample variances are s_x^2 and s_y^2, then a $100(1 - \alpha)\%$ confidence interval for $(\mu_x - \mu_y)$ is given by

$$(\overline{x} - \overline{y}) - t_{n_x+n_y-2,\,\alpha/2}\sqrt{\frac{s_p^2}{n_x} + \frac{s_p^2}{n_y}} < \mu_x - \mu_y < (\overline{x} - \overline{y}) + t_{n_x+n_y-2,\,\alpha/2}\sqrt{\frac{s_p^2}{n_x} + \frac{s_p^2}{n_y}} \qquad (8.5)$$

or equivalently

$$(\overline{x} - \overline{y}) \pm ME$$

where the **margin of error**, *ME*, is

$$ME = t_{n_x+n_y-2,\,\alpha/2}\sqrt{\frac{s_p^2}{n_x} + \frac{s_p^2}{n_y}} \qquad (8.6)$$

and the **pooled sample variance**, s_p^2, is given by

$$s_p^2 = \frac{(n_x - 1)s_x^2 + (n_y - 1)s_y^2}{n_x + n_y - 2} \qquad (8.7)$$

$t_{n_x+n_y-2,\,\alpha/2}$ is the number for which

$$P\left(t_{n_x+n_y-2} > t_{n_x+n_y-2,\,\alpha/2}\right) = \frac{\alpha}{2}$$

The random variable, *t*, is approximately a Student's *t* distribution with $n_x + n_y - 2$ degrees of freedom and *t* is given by the following:

$$t = \frac{(\overline{x} - \overline{y}) - (\mu_x - \mu_y)}{s_p\sqrt{\dfrac{1}{n_x} + \dfrac{1}{n_y}}}$$

Example 8.4 Traffic Fines (Confidence Interval)

The residents of Orange City complain that traffic speeding fines given in their city are higher than the traffic speeding fines that are given in nearby DeLand. The assistant to the county manager agreed to study the problem and to indicate if the complaints were reasonable. Independent random samples of the amounts paid by residents for speeding tickets in each of the two cities over the last three months were obtained. These amounts were as follows:

Orange City	100	125	135	128	140	142	128	137	156	142
DeLand	95	87	100	75	110	105	85	95		

Assuming an equal population variance, find a 95% confidence interval for the difference in the mean costs of speeding tickets in these two cities.

Solution Let the X population be Orange City and the Y population be DeLand. First, we use a statistical package such as Minitab and conclude that normal probability plots for both samples do not indicate evidence of non-normality. Next we calculate the mean and variance of both samples and obtain results as follows:

$$n_x = 10 \qquad \bar{x} = \$133.30 \qquad s_x^2 = 218.0111$$

$$n_y = 8 \qquad \bar{y} = \$94.00 \qquad s_y^2 = 129.4286$$

The pooled sample variance is found by Equation 8.7 to be

$$s_p^2 = \frac{(n_x - 1)s_x^2 + (n_y - 1)s_y^2}{n_x + n_y - 2} = \frac{(10-1)(218.0111) + (8-1)(129.4286)}{10+8-2} = 179.2563$$

and

$$(\bar{x} - \bar{y}) = (133.30 - 94.00) = \$39.30$$

The degrees of freedom result is $n_x + n_y - 2 = 16$ and $t_{(16, 0.025)} = 2.12$.
The confidence interval is obtained by Equation 8.5 as follows:

$$(\bar{x} - \bar{y}) - t_{n_x+n_y-2, \alpha/2}\sqrt{\frac{s_p^2}{n_x} + \frac{s_p^2}{n_y}} < \mu_x - \mu_y < (\bar{x} - \bar{y}) + t_{n_x+n_y-2, \alpha/2}\sqrt{\frac{s_p^2}{n_x} + \frac{s_p^2}{n_y}}$$

$$39.3 - (2.12)\sqrt{\frac{179.2563}{10} + \frac{179.2563}{8}} < \mu_x - \mu_y < 39.3 + (2.12)\sqrt{\frac{179.2563}{10} + \frac{179.2563}{8}}$$

$$39.3 \pm 13.46$$

Figure 8.1 is the Minitab output for this example.

Figure 8.1 Traffic Fines (Confidence Interval)

	N	Mean	StDev	SE Mean
Orange City	10	133.3	14.8	4.7
DeLand	8	94.0	11.4	4.0

Difference = mu Orange City - mu DeLand
Estimate for difference: 39.30
95% CI for difference: (25.84, 52.76)

In the long run there is a difference in the cost of speeding tickets given in Orange City and those tickets given in DeLand. The mean cost of a speeding ticket in Orange City is as little as $25.84 or as much as $52.76 higher than the mean cost of a similar traffic ticket in DeLand.

Two Means, Independent Samples, and Population Variances Not Assumed to Be Equal

In many applications it is not reasonable to assume equality of population variances. In that case we do not have need for a pooled sample variance. When the population variances are unknown and not assumed to be equal, the approximate degrees of freedom is given in Equation 8.10 and is known as Satterthwaite's approximation (References 6 and 7). Most statistical packages provide both procedures (with and without equal variances) for finding confidence intervals for differences in means of independent samples.

Confidence Intervals of Two Means: Unknown Population Variances, Not Assumed to Be Equal

Suppose that there are two **independent random samples** of n_x and n_y observations from **normally** distributed populations with means μ_X and μ_Y, and it is assumed that the population variances are not equal. If the observed sample means and variances are $\bar{x}$, $\bar{y}$, and s_x^2, s_y^2, then a $100(1 - \alpha)\%$ confidence interval for $(\mu_x - \mu_y)$ is given by

$$(\bar{x} - \bar{y}) - t_{(v, \alpha/2)}\sqrt{\frac{s_x^2}{n_x} + \frac{s_y^2}{n_y}} < \mu_x - \mu_y < (\bar{x} - \bar{y}) + t_{(v, \alpha/2)}\sqrt{\frac{s_x^2}{n_x} + \frac{s_y^2}{n_y}} \qquad (8.8)$$

where the **margin of error, ME**, is

$$ME = t_{(v, \alpha/2)}\sqrt{\frac{s_x^2}{n_x} + \frac{s_y^2}{n_y}} \qquad (8.9)$$

and the degrees of freedom, v, is given by

$$v = \frac{\left[\left(\frac{s_x^2}{n_x}\right) + \left(\frac{s_y^2}{n_y}\right)\right]^2}{\left(\frac{s_x^2}{n_x}\right)^2 / (n_x - 1) + \left(\frac{s_y^2}{n_y}\right)^2 / (n_y - 1)} \qquad (8.10)$$

If the sample sizes are equal, then the degrees of freedom reduces to the following:

$$v = \left(1 + \frac{2}{\frac{s_x^2}{s_y^2} + \frac{s_y^2}{s_x^2}}\right) \times (n - 1) \qquad (8.11)$$

Example 8.5 Auditors (Confidence Interval)

The Stryker accounting firm conducted a random sample of the accounts payable for the east and the west offices of Amalgamated Distributors. From these two independent samples the company wanted to estimate the difference between the population mean values of the payables. The sample statistics obtained were as follows:

	EAST OFFICE (POPULATION X)	WEST OFFICE (POPULATION Y)
Sample mean	$290	$250
Sample size	16	11
Sample standard deviation	15	50

We do not assume that the unknown population variances are equal. Estimate the difference between the mean values of the payables for the two offices. Use a 95% confidence level.

Solution First, we calculate the degrees of freedom by using Equation 8.10:

$$v = \frac{\left[\left(\frac{s_x^2}{n_x}\right) + \left(\frac{s_y^2}{n_y}\right)\right]^2}{\left(\frac{s_x^2}{n_x}\right)^2/(n_x - 1) + \left(\frac{s_y^2}{n_y}\right)^2/(n_y - 1)} = \frac{\left[(225/16 + 2500/11)\right]^2}{\left(\frac{225}{16}\right)^2/15 + \left(\frac{2500}{11}\right)^2/10} \approx 11$$

The margin of error is now found by using Equation 8.9:

$$ME = t_{(v,\alpha/2)}\sqrt{\frac{s_x^2}{n_x} + \frac{s_y^2}{n_y}} = t_{(11,0.025)}\sqrt{\frac{225}{16} + \frac{2500}{11}} = 2.201(15.534968) = 34.19$$

Using Equation 8.8, the 95% confidence interval is as follows:

$$(290 - 250) \pm 34.19 \text{ which equals } \$5.81 < \mu_x - \mu_y < \$74.19$$

Figure 8.2 is the Minitab output for this data.

Figure 8.2 Difference in Accounts Payable (Confidence Interval)

Two-Sample T-Test and CI

Sample	N	Mean	StDev	SE Mean
1	16	290.0	15.0	3.8
2	11	250.0	50.0	15

```
Difference = mu (1) - mu (2)
Estimate for difference: 40.000
95% CI for difference: (5.8078, 74.1922)
T-Test of difference = 0 (vs not =): T-Value-3.57  P-Value = 0.026  DF = 11
```

In the long run, the mean accounts payable for the east office exceeds the mean accounts payable for the west office by as little as $5.81 or by as much as $74.19.

EXERCISES

Basic Exercises

8.6 Independent random sampling from two normally distributed populations gives the following results:

$$n_x = 64; \quad \bar{x} = 400; \quad \sigma_x = 20$$
$$n_y = 36; \quad \bar{y} = 360; \quad \sigma_y = 25$$

Find a 90% confidence interval estimate of the difference between the means of the two populations.

8.7 Independent random sampling from two normally distributed populations gives the following results:

$$n_x = 81; \quad \bar{x} = 140; \quad \sigma_x^2 = 25$$
$$n_y = 100; \quad \bar{y} = 120; \quad \sigma_y^2 = 14$$

Find a 95% confidence interval estimate of the difference between the means of the two populations.

8.8 Assuming equal population variances, determine the number of degrees of freedom for each of the following:

a. $n_1 = 12$ $s_1^2 = 30$ $n_2 = 14$ $s_2^2 = 36$
b. $n_1 = 6$ $s_1^2 = 30$ $n_2 = 7$ $s_2^2 = 36$
c. $n_1 = 9$ $s_1^2 = 16$ $n_2 = 12$ $s_2^2 = 25$

8.9 Assuming equal population variances, compute the pooled sample variance, s_p^2, for part (a) through part (c) of Exercise 8.8.

8.10 Assuming unequal population variances, determine the number of degrees of freedom for each of the following:

a. $n_1 = 12$ $s_1^2 = 6$ $n_2 = 14$ $s_2^2 = 10$
b. $n_1 = 6$ $s_1^2 = 30$ $n_2 = 10$ $s_2^2 = 36$
c. $n_1 = 9$ $s_1^2 = 16$ $n_2 = 12$ $s_2^2 = 25$
d. $n_1 = 6$ $s_1^2 = 30$ $n_2 = 7$ $s_2^2 = 36$

8.11 Determine the margin of error for a 95% confidence interval for the difference between population means for each of the following (assume equal population variances):

a. $n_1 = 12$ $s_1^2 = 6$ $\bar{x}_1 = 200$ $n_2 = 14$
$s_2^2 = 10$ $\bar{x}_2 = 160$

b. $n_1 = 6$ $s_1^2 = 6$ $\bar{x}_2 = 200$ $n_2 = 7$
$s_2^2 = 10$ $\bar{x}_2 = 160$

c. The sample sizes in part (a) are double the sample sizes in part (b). Comment on your answers to part (a) compared to your answers to part (b).

Application Exercises

8.12 A manufacturer knows that the numbers of items produced per hour by machine A and by machine B are normally distributed with a standard deviation of 8.4 items for machine A and a standard deviation of 11.3 items for machine B. The mean hourly amount produced by machine A for a random sample of 40 hours was 130 units; the mean hourly amount produced by machine B for a random sample of 36 hours was 120 units. Find the 95% confidence interval for the difference in mean parts produced per hour by these two machines.

8.13 From a random sample of six students in an introductory finance class that uses group-learning techniques, the mean examination score was found to be 76.12 and the sample standard deviation was 2.53. For an independent random sample of nine students in another introductory finance class that does not use group-learning techniques, the sample mean and standard deviation of exam scores were 74.61 and 8.61, respectively. Estimate with 95% confidence the difference between the two population mean scores; do not assume equal population variances.

8.14 🌐 Prairie Flower Cereal Inc. is a small, but growing, producer of hot and ready-to-eat breakfast cereals. Gordon Thorson, a successful grain farmer, started the company in 1910 (Reference 3). Two machines are used for packaging 18-ounce (510-gram) boxes of sugar-coated wheat cereal. Estimate the difference in the mean weights of boxes of this type of cereal packaged by the two machines. Use a 95% confidence level and the data file **Sugar Coated Wheat**. Explain your findings.

8.15 Recent business graduates currently employed in full-time positions were surveyed. Family backgrounds were self-classified as relatively high or low socioeconomic status. For a random sample of 16 high-socioeconomic-status recent business graduates, the mean total compensation was $34,500 and the sample standard deviation was $8,520. For an independent random sample of 9 low-socioeconomic-status recent business graduates, the mean total compensation was $31,499 and the sample standard deviation was $7,521. Find a 90% confidence interval for the difference between the two population means.

8.16 Suppose, for a random sample of 200 firms that revalued their fixed assets, that the mean ratio of debt to tangible assets was 0.517 and the sample standard deviation was 0.148. For an independent random sample of 400 firms that did not revalue their fixed assets, the mean ratio of debt to tangible assets was 0.489 and the sample standard deviation was 0.158. Find a 99% confidence interval for the difference between the two population means.

8.17 A researcher intends to estimate the effect of a drug on the scores of human subjects performing a task of psychomotor coordination. The members of a random sample of 9 subjects were given the drug prior to testing. The mean score in this group was 9.78, and the sample variance was 17.64. An independent random sample of 10 subjects was used as a control group and given a placebo prior to testing. The mean score in this control group was 15.10, and the sample variance was 27.01. Assuming that the population distributions are normal with equal variances, find a 90% confidence interval for the difference between the population mean scores.

8.3 CONFIDENCE INTERVAL ESTIMATION OF THE DIFFERENCE BETWEEN TWO POPULATION PROPORTIONS (LARGE SAMPLES)

Confidence intervals for a single population proportion were derived in Chapter 7. Often a comparison of two population proportions is of interest. For instance, one might want to compare the proportion of residents in one city who indicate that they will vote for a particular presidential candidate with the proportion of residents in another city who indicate the same candidate preference. Confidence intervals for the difference between two population proportions with independent large samples taken from these two populations are considered in this section.

Suppose that a random sample of n_x observations from a population with proportion P_x of "successes" yields sample proportion $\hat{p}_x$ and that an independent random sample of n_y observations from a population with proportion P_y of "successes" produces sample proportion $\hat{p}_y$. Since our concern is with the population difference $(P_x - P_y)$, it is natural to examine the random variable $(\hat{p}_x - \hat{p}_y)$. This has mean

$$E(\hat{p}_x - \hat{p}_y) = E(\hat{p}_x) - E(\hat{p}_y) = P_x - P_y$$

and, since the samples are taken independently, it has the variance

$$Var(\hat{p}_x - \hat{p}_y) = Var(\hat{p}_x) + Var(\hat{p}_y) = \frac{P_x(1 - P_x)}{n_x} + \frac{P_y(1 - P_y)}{n_y}$$

Furthermore, if the sample sizes are large, the distribution of this random variable is approximately normal, so subtracting its mean and dividing by its standard deviation gives a standard normally distributed random variable. Moreover, for large sample sizes this approximation remains valid when the unknown population proportions P_x and P_y are replaced by the corresponding sample quantities. Thus, to a good approximation, the random variable

$$Z = \frac{(\hat{p}_x - \hat{p}_y) - (P_x - P_y)}{\sqrt{\dfrac{\hat{p}_x(1 - \hat{p}_x)}{n_x} + \dfrac{\hat{p}_y(1 - \hat{p}_y)}{n_y}}}$$

has a standard normal distribution. This result allows the derivation of confidence intervals for the difference between the two population proportions when the same sample sizes are large.

Confidence Intervals of the Difference Between Population Proportions (Large Samples)

Let $\hat{p}_x$ denote the observed proportion of successes in a random sample of n_x observations from a population with proportion P_x of successes, and let $\hat{p}_y$ denote the proportion of successes observed in an independent random sample of n_y observations from a population with proportion P_Y of successes. Then, if the sample sizes are large (generally at least 40 observations in each sample), a $100(1 - \alpha)\%$ **confidence interval for the difference between population proportions**, $(P_x - P_y)$, is given by

$$(\hat{p}_x - \hat{p}_y) \pm ME \tag{8.12}$$

where the **margin of error, ME**, is as follows:

$$ME = z_{\alpha/2}\sqrt{\frac{\hat{p}_x(1 - \hat{p}_x)}{n_x} + \frac{\hat{p}_y(1 - \hat{p}_y)}{n_y}} \tag{8.13}$$

Example 8.6 Precinct Preference (Confidence Interval)

During a presidential election year many forecasts are made to determine how voters perceive a particular candidate. In a random sample of 120 registered voters in precinct A, 107 indicated that they supported the candidate in question. In an independent random sample of 141 registered voters in precinct B, only 73 indicated support for the same candidate. If the respective population proportions are denoted P_A and P_B, find a 95% confidence interval for the population difference, $(P_A - P_B)$.

Solution From the sample information it follows that

$$n_A = 120 \quad and \quad \hat{p}_A = 107/120 = 0.892; \quad n_B = 141 \quad and \quad \hat{p}_B = 73/141 = 0.518$$

For a 95% confidence interval, $\alpha = 0.05$, and so

$$z_{\alpha/2} = z_{0.025} = 1.96$$

The required interval is, therefore,

$$(0.892 - 0.518) - 1.96\sqrt{\frac{(0.892)(0.108)}{120} + \frac{(0.518)(0.482)}{141}}$$

$$< P_A - P_B < (0.892 - 0.518) + 1.96\sqrt{\frac{(0.892)(0.108)}{120} + \frac{(0.518)(0.482)}{141}}$$

$$0.274 < P_A - P_B < 0.473$$

The fact that zero is well outside this interval suggests that there is a difference in the population proportions of registered voters in precinct A and precinct B who support this presidential candidate. In the long run the difference is estimated to be as little as 27.4% or as high as 47.3%.

Figure 8.3 is the Minitab output for Example 8.6. The data suggest that there is a difference in the population proportions of registered voters in precinct A and precinct B who support this presidential candidate. In the long run about 95% of all such intervals would contain the true value of the difference.

Figure 8.3 Precinct Preference (Confidence Interval)

Sample	X	N	Sample p
1	107	120	0.891667
2	73	141	0.517730

Estimate for p(1) - p(2): 0.373936
95% CI for p(1) - p(2): **(0.274463, 0.473409)**

EXERCISES

Basic Exercises

8.18 Calculate the margin of error for each of the following:

a. $n_1 = 260$ $\hat{p}_1 = 0.75$ $n_2 = 200$ $\hat{p}_2 = 0.68$
b. $n_1 = 400$ $\hat{p}_1 = 0.60$ $n_2 = 500$ $\hat{p}_2 = 0.68$
c. $n_1 = 500$ $\hat{p}_1 = 0.20$ $n_2 = 375$ $\hat{p}_2 = 0.25$

8.19 Calculate the 95% confidence interval for the difference in population proportions for each of the following:

a. $n_1 = 370$ $\hat{p}_1 = 0.65$ $n_2 = 200$ $\hat{p}_2 = 0.68$
b. $n_1 = 220$ $\hat{p}_1 = 0.48$ $n_2 = 270$ $\hat{p}_2 = 0.52$
c. $n_1 = 500$ $\hat{p}_1 = 0.30$ $n_2 = 325$ $\hat{p}_2 = 0.25$

Application Exercises

8.20 In a random sample of 120 large retailers, 85 used regression as a method of forecasting. In an independent random sample of 163 small retailers, 78 used regression as a method of forecasting. Find a 98% confidence interval for the difference between the two population proportions.

8.21 ◒ Do seniors and freshmen have different views concerning the university's library collection? Using the data file **Library**, estimate the difference in proportions of seniors and freshmen who think that the school's library has an adequate collection of books. Use a confidence level of 90%.

8.22 "Would you use the library more if the hours were extended?" From a random sample of 138 freshmen, 80 indicated that they would use the school's library more if the hours were extended. In an independent random sample of 96 sophomores, 73 responded that they would use the library more if the hours were extended. Estimate the difference in proportion of first-year and second-year students responding affirmatively to this question. Use a 95% confidence level.

8.23 A random sample of 100 men contained 61 in favor of a state constitutional amendment to retard the rate of growth of property taxes. An independent random sample of 100 women contained 54 in favor of this amendment. The confidence interval

$$0.04 < P_x - P_y < 0.10$$

was calculated for the difference between the population proportions. What is the confidence level of this interval?

8.24 Supermarket shoppers were observed and questioned immediately after putting an item in their cart. Of a random sample of 510 choosing a product at the regular price, 320 claimed to check the price before putting the item in their cart. Of an independent random sample of 332 choosing a product at a special price, 200 made this claim. Find a 90% confidence interval for the difference between the two population proportions.

8.4 SAMPLE SIZE DETERMINATION: LARGE POPULATIONS

We have developed confidence intervals for population parameters on the basis of the information contained in a given sample. Following such a process, we may believe that the resulting confidence interval is too wide, reflecting an undesirable amount of uncertainty about the parameter being estimated. Typically, one way to obtain a narrower interval with a given confidence level is to take a larger sample.

In some circumstances we may be able to fix in advance the width of the confidence interval, choosing a sample size big enough to guarantee that width. In this section consideration of how sample size can be chosen in this way for two interval estimation problems is given. Similar procedures can be employed to solve other problems. We will concentrate on populations that are not necessarily large in Section 8.5.

Mean of a Normally Distributed Population, Known Population Variance

If a random sample of n observations is taken from a normally distributed population with mean μ and known variance σ^2, it was seen in Chapter 7 that a $100(1 - \alpha)\%$ confidence interval for the population mean is provided by

$$\bar{x} - \frac{z_{\alpha/2}\sigma}{\sqrt{n}} < \mu < \bar{x} + \frac{z_{\alpha/2}\sigma}{\sqrt{n}}$$

where $\bar{x}$ is the observed sample mean and $z_{\alpha/2}$ is the appropriate cutoff point of the standard normal distribution. This interval is centered on the sample mean and extends a distance of B, the margin of error,

$$ME = \frac{z_{\alpha/2}\sigma}{\sqrt{n}}$$

on each side of the sample mean, so that ME is half the width of the interval. Suppose, now, that the investigator wants to fix the margin of error, ME, in advance. From basic algebra it follows that,

$$\sqrt{n} = \frac{z_{\alpha/2}\sigma}{ME}$$

and by squaring both sides of the equation, the sample size n is as follows:

$$n = \frac{z_{\alpha/2}^2\sigma^2}{ME^2}$$

This choice of the sample size guarantees that the confidence interval extends a distance ME on each side of the sample mean.

Sample Size for the Mean of a Normally Distributed Population with Known Population Variance

Suppose that a random sample from a normally distributed population with known variance σ^2 is selected. Then a $100(1 - \alpha)\%$ confidence interval for the population mean extends a distance ME (sometimes called the **sampling error**) on each side of the sample mean if the sample size, n, is as follows:

$$n = \frac{z_{\alpha/2}^2\sigma^2}{ME^2} \tag{8.14}$$

Of course, the number of sample observations must necessarily be an integer. If the number n resulting from the sample size formula is not an integer, then *round up* to the next whole number in order to guarantee that our confidence interval does not exceed the required width.

Example 8.7 Length of Metal Rods (Sample Size)

The lengths of metal rods produced by an industrial process are normally distributed with a standard deviation of 1.8 millimeters. Based on a random sample of nine observations from this population, the 99% confidence interval

$$194.65 < \mu < 197.75$$

was found for the population mean length. Suppose that a production manager believes that the interval is too wide for practical use and instead requires a 99% confidence interval extending no further than 0.50 mm on each side of the sample mean. How large a sample is needed to achieve such an interval?

Solution Since

$$ME = 0.50, \sigma = 1.8 \text{ and } z_{\alpha/2} = z_{0.005} = 2.576$$

the required sample size is as follows:

$$n = \frac{z_{\alpha/2}^2\sigma^2}{ME^2}$$

$$= \frac{(2.576)^2(1.8)^2}{(0.5)^2} \approx 86$$

Therefore, to satisfy the manager's requirement, a sample of at least 86 observations is needed. This large increase in the sample size represents the additional cost of achieving the higher precision in the estimate of the true value of the population mean, reflected in a narrower confidence interval. The value 2.576, rather than 2.58, was used to determine the sample size needed.

Population Proportion

In Chapter 7 we saw that for a random sample of n observations, a $100(1 - \alpha)\%$ confidence interval for the population proportion P is

$$\hat{p} - z_{\alpha/2}\sqrt{\frac{\hat{p}(1 - \hat{p})}{n}} < P < \hat{p} + z_{\alpha/2}\sqrt{\frac{\hat{p}(1 - \hat{p})}{n}}$$

where $\hat{p}$ is the observed sample proportion. This interval is centered on the sample proportion and extends a distance (margin of error)

$$ME = z_{\alpha/2}\sqrt{\frac{\hat{p}(1 - \hat{p})}{n}}$$

on each side of the sample proportion. Now, this result *cannot* be used directly to determine the sample size necessary to obtain a confidence interval of some specific width since it involves the sample proportion, which will not be known at the outset. However, whatever the outcome, $\hat{p}(1 - \hat{p})$ cannot be bigger than 0.25, its value when the sample proportion is 0.5. Thus, the *largest* possible value for the margin of error, ME, is given by the following:

$$ME = z_{\alpha/2}\sqrt{\frac{0.25}{n}} = \frac{(0.5)z_{\alpha/2}}{\sqrt{n}}$$

Suppose, then, that a sufficiently large sample size is chosen to *guarantee* that the confidence interval extends no more than ME on each side of the sample proportion. Again using basic algebra,

$$\sqrt{n} = \frac{0.5z_{\alpha/2}}{ME}$$

and squaring yields the following:

$$n = \frac{0.25(z_{\alpha/2})^2}{(ME)^2}$$

Sample Size for Population Proportion
Suppose that a random sample is selected from a population. Then, a $100(1 - \alpha)\%$ confidence interval for the population proportion, extending a distance of at most ME on each side of the sample proportion, can be guaranteed if the sample size is as follows:

$$n = \frac{0.25(z_{\alpha/2})^2}{(ME)^2} \tag{8.15}$$

Example 8.8 Graduate Admissions Personnel (Sample Size)

In Exercise 7.33 a 95% confidence interval was calculated for the proportion of graduate admissions personnel who viewed scores on standardized exams as very important in the consideration of a candidate. Based on 142 observations the interval obtained was as follows:

$$0.533 < P < 0.693$$

Suppose, instead, that it must be ensured that a 95% confidence interval for the population proportion extends no further than 0.06 on each side of the sample proportion. How large of a sample must be taken?

Solution It is given that

$$ME = 0.06 \text{ and } z_{\alpha/2} = z_{0.025} = 1.96$$

Thus, the number of sample observations needed is as follows:

$$n = \frac{0.25z_{\alpha/2}^2}{(ME)^2} = \frac{0.25(1.96)^2}{(0.06)^2} = 266.78 \Rightarrow n = 267$$

To achieve this narrower confidence interval, a minimum of 267 sample observations is required (a significant increase over the original 142 observations).

The media frequently report the results of opinion surveys concerning issues of current interest, such as the president's rating on domestic issues or foreign policy, or people's views on some new tax proposal. These surveys generally represent the opinions of some subset of the population. Typically, these reports give estimates of the percentage of population members holding particular views. These reports often end with a statement like, "There is a plus or minus 3% sampling error," or "The poll has a 3% margin of error." Specifically, these intervals are the sample percentage, plus or minus the advertised sampling error or margin of error. However, we stress that the margin of error does not include any errors due to biased or otherwise inadequate samples.

Example 8.9 Electoral College (Sample Size)

Suppose that an opinion survey following a presidential election reported the views of a sample of U.S. citizens of voting age concerning changing the Electoral College process. The poll was said to have "a 3% margin of error." The implication is that a 95% confidence interval for the population proportion holding a particular opinion is the sample proportion plus or minus at most 3%. How many citizens of voting age need to be sampled to obtain this 3% margin of error?

Solution Using Equation 8.15,

$$n = \frac{0.25z_{\alpha/2}^2}{(ME)^2} = \frac{(0.25)(1.96)^2}{(0.03)^2} = 1067.111 \Rightarrow n = 1,068$$

Therefore, 1,068 U.S. citizens of voting age need to be sampled to achieve the desired result.

Basic Exercises

8.25 How large of a sample is needed to estimate the mean of a normally distributed population for each of the following?

   a. $ME = 5; \sigma = 40; \alpha = 0.01$
   b. $ME = 10; \sigma = 40; \alpha = 0.01$
   c. Compare and comment on your answers to parts (a) and (b).

8.26 How large of a sample is needed to estimate the population proportion for each of the following?

   a. $ME = 0.03; \alpha = 0.05$
   b. $ME = 0.05; \alpha = 0.05$
   c. Compare and comment on your answers to parts (a) and (b).

8.27 How large of a sample is needed to estimate the population proportion for each of the following?

   a. $ME = 0.05; \alpha = 0.01$
   b. $ME = 0.05; \alpha = 0.10$
   c. Compare and comment on your answers to parts (a) and (b).

Application Exercises

8.28 A research group wants to estimate the proportion of consumers who plan to buy a scanner for their PC during the next three months.

   a. How many people should be sampled so that the sampling error is at most 0.04 with a 90% confidence interval?
   b. What is the sample size required if the confidence is increased to 95%, keeping the sampling error the same?
   c. What is the required sample size if the research group extends the sampling error to 0.05 and wants a 98% confidence level?

8.29 A politician wants to estimate the proportion of constituents favoring a controversial piece of proposed legislation. Suppose that a 99% confidence interval that extends at most 0.05 on each side of the sample proportion is required. How many sample observations are needed?

8.30 The student government association at a university wants to estimate the percentage of the student body that supports a change being considered in the academic calendar of the university for the next academic year. How many students should be surveyed if a 90% confidence interval is desired and the margin of error is to be only 3%?

8.5 SAMPLE SIZE DETERMINATION: FINITE POPULATIONS

An important aspect of the planning of any survey involves the determination of an appropriate number of sample members. Several factors may be relevant. If the procedure for contacting sample members is thought likely to lead to a high rate of non-response, this eventuality should be taken into account. In many instances the resources available to the investigator, in terms of time and money, will place constraints on what can be achieved. In this section, however, we abstract from such considerations and relate sample size to the variances of the estimators of population parameters and consequently to the widths of resulting confidence intervals. To compensate for non-response or missing data, practitioners may add a certain percent (like 10%) to the sample size, n, determined by the equations in this section.

Sample Sizes for Simple Random Sampling: Estimation of the Population Mean or Total

Consider the problem of estimating the population mean from a simple random sample of n observations. If the random variable $\overline{X}$ denotes the sample mean, it is known from Chapter 6 that the variance of this random variable is as follows:

$$Var(\overline{X}) = \sigma_{\overline{X}}^2 = \frac{\sigma^2}{n} \times \frac{(N - n)}{(N - 1)}$$

If the population variance σ^2 is known, by solving the equation $Var(\overline{X})$ you can determine the sample size n that is needed to achieve any specified value of $s_{\overline{X}}^2$ for the variance of the sample mean. Similar procedures are available if the quantity of interest is the population total.

Sample Size: Population Mean or Total, Simple Random Sampling

Consider estimating the mean of a population of N members, which has variance σ^2. If the desired variance, $\sigma_{\overline{X}}^2$, of the sample mean is specified, **the required sample size to estimate the population mean through simple random sampling** is

$$n = \frac{N\sigma^2}{(N-1)\sigma_{\overline{x}}^2 + \sigma^2} \tag{8.16}$$

or, equivalently,

$$n = \frac{n_0 N}{n_0 + (N-1)} \tag{8.17}$$

where $n_0 = n$ in Equation 8.14,

$$n_0 = \frac{z_{\alpha/2}^2 \sigma^2}{ME^2}$$

1. Often it is more convenient to specify directly the width of confidence intervals for the population mean rather than $\sigma_{\overline{X}}^2$. This is easily accomplished, since, for example, a 95% confidence interval for the population mean will extend approximately $1.96\sigma_{\overline{X}}$ on each side of the sample mean.
2. If the object of interest is the **population total**, the variance of the sample estimator of this quantity is $N^2 \sigma_{\overline{X}}^2$ and a 95% confidence interval for it extends approximately $1.96N\sigma_{\overline{X}}$ on each side of $N\overline{x}$.

An obvious difficulty with the practical use of Equation 8.16 is that it involves the population variance, σ^2, which typically will be unknown. However, often an investigator will have a rough idea of the value of this quantity. Sometimes the population variance can be estimated from a preliminary sample of the population or approximated from historical data.

Example 8.10 Mortgages (Sample Size)

As in Example 7.8, suppose that in a city last year 1,118 mortgages were taken out and that a simple random sample is to be taken in order to estimate the mean amount of these mortgages. From previous experience of such populations it is estimated that the population standard deviation is approximately $20,000. A 95% confidence interval for the population mean must extend $4,000 on each side of the sample mean. How many sample observations are needed to achieve this objective?

Solution First,

$$N = 1{,}118 \qquad \sigma = 20{,}000 \qquad 1.96\sigma_{\overline{X}} = 4{,}000$$

The required sample size by using Equation 8.16 is then,

$$n = \frac{N\sigma^2}{(N-1)\sigma_{\overline{x}}^2 + \sigma^2} = \frac{(1{,}118)(20{,}000)^2}{(1{,}117)(2{,}041)^2 + (20{,}000)^2} = 88.5 \Rightarrow n = 89$$

By calculating the sample size using Equation 8.14 and Equation 8.17, we find the following:

$$n_0 = \frac{z_{\alpha/2}^2 \sigma^2}{ME^2} = \frac{(1.96)^2 (20{,}000)^2}{(4{,}000)^2} = (1.96)^2(25) = (3.8416)(25) = 96.04$$

$$n = \frac{n_0 N}{n_0 + (N-1)} = \frac{(96.04)(1118)}{96.04 + 1117} = 88.5 \Rightarrow n = 89$$

Thus, a simple random sample of 89 observations is the minimum needed to meet our objective.

Sample Sizes for Simple Random Sampling: Estimation of Population Proportion

Consider simple random sampling for the estimation of a population proportion P. Recall from earlier in the text that

$$Var(\hat{p}) = \sigma_{\hat{p}}^2 = \frac{P(1-P)}{n} \times \frac{(N-n)}{(N-1)}$$

Solving for n leads to the sample size given in Equations 8.17 and 8.18.

Sample Size: Population Proportion, Simple Random Sampling

Consider estimation of the proportion P of individuals in a population size of N who possess a certain attribute. If the desired variance, $\sigma_{\hat{p}}^2$, of the sample proportion is specified, the required sample size to estimate the population proportion through simple random sampling is as follows:

$$n = \frac{NP(1-P)}{(N-1)\sigma_{\hat{p}}^2} + P(1-P) \tag{8.18}$$

The largest possible value for this expression, whatever the value of P, is as follows:

$$n_{max} = \frac{0.25N}{(N-1)\sigma_{\hat{p}}^2} + 0.25 \tag{8.19}$$

A 95% confidence interval for the population proportion will extend approximately $1.96\sigma_p$ on each side of the sample proportion.

Example 8.11 Campus Survey (Sample Size)

As in Example 7.10, suppose that a simple random sample of the 1,395 U.S. colleges is taken to estimate the proportion for which the business statistics course is two semesters long. Whatever the true proportion, a 95% confidence interval must extend no further than 0.04 on each side of the sample proportion. How many sample observations should be taken?

Solution From the problem

$$1.96\sigma_{\hat{p}} = 0.04$$

or

$$\sigma_{\hat{p}} = 0.020408$$

the sample size needed is then,

$$n_{max} = \frac{0.25N}{(N-1)\sigma_{\hat{p}}^2 + 0.25} = \frac{(0.25)(1,395)}{(1,394)(0.020408)^2 + 0.25} = 419.88 \Rightarrow n = 420$$

Hence, a sample of 420 observations is needed.

EXERCISES

Basic Exercises

8.31 Determine the sample size needed for each of the following situations:
  a. $N = 1,650$ $\sigma = 500$ $1.96\sigma_{\bar{x}} = 50$
  b. $N = 1,650$ $\sigma = 500$ $1.96\sigma_{\bar{x}} = 100$
  c. $N = 1,650$ $\sigma = 500$ $1.96\sigma_{\bar{x}} = 200$
  d. Compare and comment on your answers to parts (a) through (c).

8.32 Determine the sample size needed for each of the following situations:
  a. $N = 3,300$ $\sigma = 500$ $1.96\sigma_{\bar{x}} = 50$
  b. $N = 4,950$ $\sigma = 500$ $1.96\sigma_{\bar{x}} = 50$
  c. $N = 5,000,000$ $\sigma = 500$ $1.96\sigma_{\bar{x}} = 50$
  d. Compare and comment on your answers to parts (a) through (c).

8.33 Determine the sample size for each of the following situations:
  a. $N = 2,500$ $\hat{p} = 0.5$ $1.96\sigma_{\hat{p}} = 0.05$
  b. $N = 2,500$ $\hat{p} = 0.5$ $1.96\sigma_{\hat{p}} = 0.03$
  c. Compare and comment on your answers to part (a) and part (b).

Application Exercises

8.34 The mean amount of the 812 mortgages taken out in a city in the past year must be estimated. Based on previous experience, a real estate broker knows that the population standard deviation is likely to be about $20,000. If a 95% confidence interval for the population mean is to extend $2,000 on each side of the sample mean, how many sample observations are needed if a simple random sample is taken?

8.35 An automobile dealer has an inventory of 400 used cars. To estimate the mean mileage of this inventory, she intends to take a simple random sample of used cars. Previous studies suggest that the population standard deviation is 10,000 miles. A 90% confidence interval for the population mean must extend 2,000 miles on each side of its sample estimate. How large of a sample size is necessary to satisfy this requirement?

8.36 A country club wants to poll a random sample of its 320 members to estimate the proportion likely to attend an early-season function. The number of sample observations should be sufficiently large to ensure that a 99% confidence interval for the population extends at most 0.05 on each side of the sample proportion. How large of a sample is necessary?

8.37 An instructor in a class of 417 students is considering the possibility of a take-home final examination. She wants to take a random sample of class members to estimate the proportion who prefer this form of examination. If a 90% confidence interval for the population proportion must extend at most 0.04 on each side of the sample proportion, how large a sample is needed?

KEY WORDS

- confidence interval for:
  - two means, independent, known variances, 332
  - two means, independent, unknown variances assumed to be equal, 334
- two means, independent, unknown variances not assumed to be equal, 336
- two means, matched, 327
- two proportions, 339
- pooled sample variance, 334

CHAPTER EXERCISES AND APPLICATIONS

8.38 Independent random samples from two normally distributed populations give the following results:

$$n_x = 15 \quad \bar{x} = 400 \quad s_x = 20$$
$$n_y = 13 \quad \bar{y} = 360 \quad s_y = 25$$

Assume that the unknown population variances are equal and find a 90% confidence interval for the difference between population means.

8.39 Independent random samples from two normally distributed populations give the following results:

$$n_x = 15 \quad \bar{x} = 400 \quad s_x = 10$$
$$n_y = 13 \quad \bar{y} = 360 \quad s_y = 40$$

If we do not assume that the unknown population variances are equal, what is the 90% confidence interval for the difference between population means?

8.40 Independent random samples from two normally distributed populations give the following results:

$$n_x = 10 \quad \bar{x} = 480 \quad s_x = 30$$
$$n_y = 12 \quad \bar{y} = 520 \quad s_y = 25$$

a. If we assume that the unknown population variances are equal, what is the 90% confidence interval for the difference of population means?

b. If we do not assume that the unknown population variances are equal, find the 90% confidence interval for the difference between the population means.

8.41 A company sends a random sample of 12 of its salespeople to a course designed to increase their motivation and, hence, presumably their effectiveness. In the following year these people generated sales with an average value of $435,000 and a sample standard deviation of $56,000. During the same period, an independently chosen random sample of 15 salespeople who had not attended the course obtained sales with an average value of $408,000 and a sample standard deviation of $43,000. Assume that the two population distributions are normal and have the same variance. Find a 95% confidence interval for the difference between their means.

8.42 Students in an introductory economics class are assigned to sections conducted by teaching assistants. For one teaching assistant the 21 students in her section obtained a mean score of 72.1 on the final examination and a standard deviation of 11.3. For a second teaching assistant the 18 students in his section obtained a mean score on the final exam of 73.8 and a standard deviation of 10.6. Assume that these data can be regarded as independent random samples from normally distributed populations with a common variance. Find an 80% confidence interval for the difference between the population means.

8.43 Several drugs are used to treat diabetes. A sales specialist for a leading pharmaceutical company randomly sampled the records of 10 sales districts to estimate the number of new prescriptions that had been written during a particular month for her company's new diabetes drug. The numbers of new prescriptions were as follows:

210, 240, 190, 275, 290, 265, 312, 284, 261, 243

a. Find a 90% confidence interval for the average number of new prescriptions written for this new drug among all the sales districts. What are the assumptions?

b. Assuming that the confidence level remains constant, what sample size is needed to reduce by half the margin of error of the confidence interval in part (a)?

8.44 A proposal for a new 1-cent tax increase to support cancer research is to appear on the ballot in one county's next election. The residents in two cities were questioned as to their level of support. In Sterling Heights a recent survey of 225 residents showed that 140 people supported the proposal, 35 were undecided, and the remainder was opposed to the new proposal. In a nearby community, Harrison Township, the results of a random sample of 210 residents found that 120 people supported the tax, 30 were opposed, and the remainder was undecided. Estimate the difference in the percentages of residents from these two communities who support this proposal. Use a 95% confidence level.

8.45 Is the average amount spent on textbooks per semester by accounting majors significantly different than the average amount spent on textbooks per semester by management majors? Answer this question with a 90% confidence interval using the following data from random samples of students majoring in accounting or management. Discuss the assumptions.

	Accounting Majors	Management Majors
Mean	$340	$285
Standard deviation	20	30
Sample size	40	50

8.46 The supervisor of an orange juice bottling company is considering the purchase of a new machine to bottle 16 fl. oz. (473 mL) bottles of 100% pure orange juice and wants an estimate of the difference in the mean filling weights between the new machine and the old machine. Random samples of bottles of orange juice that had been filled by both machines were obtained. Do the following data indicate that there is a difference in the mean filling weights between the new and the old machines? Discuss the assumptions.

	New Machine	Old Machine
Mean	470 mL	460 mL
Standard deviation	5 mL	7 mL
Sample size	15	12

8.47 Renee Payne, who is employed by a major investment firm in West Palm Beach, Florida, would like to estimate the percentage of new clients who will make a certain type of investment. If she wants a sampling error no greater than 2.5% and a confidence level of 90%, how many clients should she sample?

8.48 ⊕ An agency offers students preparation courses for a graduate school admissions test. As part of an experiment to evaluate the merits of the course, 12 students were chosen and divided into six pairs in such a way that the two members of any pair had similar academic records. Before taking the test, one member of each pair was assigned at random to take the preparation course, while the other member took no course. The achievement test scores are contained in the **Student Pair** data file. Assuming that the differences in scores are normally distributed, find a 98% confidence interval for the difference in means scores between those who took the course and those who did not.

8.49 The president's policy on domestic affairs received a 65% approval rating in a recent poll. The margin of error was given as 0.035. What sample size was used for this poll if we assume a 95% confidence level?

8.50 A newspaper article reported that 400 people in one state were surveyed and 75% were opposed to a recent court decision. The same article reported that a similar survey of 500 people in another state indicated opposition by only 45%. Construct a 95% confidence interval of the difference in population proportions based on the data.

8.51 An automobile dealer has an inventory of 328 used cars. The mean mileage of these vehicles is to be estimated. Previous experience suggests that the population standard deviation is likely to be about 12,000 miles. If a 90% confidence interval for the population mean is to extend 2,000 miles on each side of the sample mean, how large of a sample is required if simple random sampling is employed?

8.52 A simple random sample is to be taken of 527 business majors in a college to estimate the proportion favoring greater emphasis on business ethics in the curriculum. How many observations are necessary to ensure that a 95% confidence interval for the population proportion extends at most 0.06 on each side of the sample proportion?

8.53 Show algebraically that Equation 8.16 is equal to Equation 8.17—that is,

$$\frac{N\sigma^2}{(N-1)\sigma_{\bar{X}}^2 + \sigma^2} = \frac{n_0 N}{n_0 + (N-1)}$$

Appendix

Student's T-Test for Two Means with Unknown Population Variances Not Assumed to Be Equal

For the difference between two populations,

$$Z = \frac{(\bar{x} - \bar{y}) - (\mu_X - \mu_Y)}{\sqrt{\dfrac{\sigma_X^2}{n_x} + \dfrac{\sigma_Y^2}{n_y}}} \qquad \text{and} \qquad \chi^2 = \chi_X^2 + \chi_Y^2$$

is the sum of two independent chi-square random variables from the two independent random samples

$$\chi_X^2 = \frac{(n_x - 1)s_x^2}{\sigma_X^2}$$

$$\chi_Y^2 = \frac{(n_y - 1)s_y^2}{\sigma_Y^2}$$

with $(n_x - 1)$ and $(n_y - 1)$ degrees of freedom, respectively. The degrees of freedom for χ^2 is the sum of the component degrees of freedom, $v = (n_x - 1) + (n_y - 1) = n_x + n_y - 2$.

Bringing these pieces together,

$$t = \frac{\left[(\bar{x} - \bar{y}) - (\mu_X - \mu_Y)\right]/\sqrt{\sigma_X^2/n_x + \sigma_Y^2/n_y}}{\sqrt{\left[(n_x - 1)s_x^2/\sigma_X^2 + (n_y - 1)s_y^2/\sigma_Y^2\right]/(n_x + n_y - 2)}}$$

If $\sigma_X^2 = \sigma_Y^2$ then this reduces to the following:

$$t = \frac{(\bar{x} - \bar{y}) - (\mu_X - \mu_Y)}{\sqrt{\dfrac{s_p^2}{n_x} + \dfrac{s_p^2}{n_y}}}$$

References

1. Agresti, A., and B. A. Coull. 1998. Approximate Is Better than 'Exact' for Interval Estimation of Binomial Proportions. *American Statistician* 52: 119–126.

2. Agresti, A., and B. Caffo. 2000. Simple and Effective Confidence Intervals for Proportions and Differences of Proportions Result from Adding Two Successes and Two Failures. *American Statistician* 54: 280–288.

3. Carlson, William L. 1997. *Cases in Managerial Data Analysis*. Belmont, CA: Wadsworth Publishing Company.

4. Cochran, W. G. 1977. *Sampling Techniques*, 3rd ed. New York: Wiley.

5. Hogg, Robert, and Allen T. Craig. 1977. *Introduction to Mathematical Statistics*, 4th ed. New York: Macmillan.

6. Kish, Leslie. 1965. *Survey Sampling*. New York: Wiley.

7. Satterthwaite, F. E. 1946. An approximate distribution of estimates of variance components. *Biometrics Bulletin*, 2, 110–114.

8. Schaeffer, Richard L., William Mendenhall, and Lyman Ott. 1996. *Elementary Survey Sampling*, 5th ed. Belmont, CA: Duxbury Press.

Chapter 9

Hypothesis Testing: Single Population

Introduction

In this chapter we develop hypothesis-testing procedures that enable us to test the validity of some conjecture or claim by using sample data. This form of inference contrasts and complements the estimation procedures we developed in Chapters 7 and 8. The process begins with an investigator forming a hypothesis about the nature of some population. This hypothesis is stated clearly as involving two options, and then we select one option based on the results of a statistic computed from a random sample of data. Following are examples of typical problems:

1. Malt-O-Meal Inc., a producer of ready-to-eat cereal, claims that, on average, its cereal packages weigh more than 16 ounces. The company can test this claim by collecting a random sample of cereal packages, determining the weight of each one, and computing the sample mean package weight from the data.

2. An automobile parts factory wishes to monitor its manufacturing process to ensure that the diameter of pistons meets engineering tolerance specifications. It could obtain random samples every

2 hours from the production line and use them to determine if standards are being maintained.

These examples are based on a common theme. We state a hypothesis about some population parameter and then sample data are used to test the validity of our hypothesis.

9.1 Concepts of Hypothesis Testing

Here we introduce a general framework to test hypotheses by using statistics computed from random samples. Since these statistics have a sampling distribution, our decision is made in the face of random variation. Thus, clear decision rules are needed for choosing between the two choices.

The process that we develop here works as a direct analogy to a criminal jury trial. In a jury trial we assume that the accused is innocent, and the jury will decide that a person is guilty only if there is very strong evidence against the presumption of innocence. The criminal jury trial process for choosing between guilt and innocence has the following characteristics:

1. Rigorous procedures for presenting and evaluating evidence
2. A judge to enforce the rules
3. A decision process that assumes innocence unless there is evidence to prove guilt beyond a reasonable doubt

Note that this process will fail to convict a number of people who are, in fact, guilty. But if a person's innocence is rejected and the person is found guilty, we have a strong belief that the person is guilty.

We begin the hypothesis-testing procedure by considering a value for a population probability distribution parameter such as the mean, μ, the variance, σ^2, or the proportion, P. Our approach starts with a hypothesis about the parameter—called the **null hypothesis**—that will be maintained unless there is strong evidence against this null hypothesis. If we reject the null hypothesis, then the second hypothesis, named the **alternative hypothesis**, will be accepted. However, if we fail to reject the null hypothesis, we cannot necessarily conclude that the null hypothesis is correct. If we fail to reject, then either the null hypothesis is correct or the alternative hypothesis is correct, but our test procedure is not strong enough to reject the null hypothesis.

Using our Malt-O-Meal example, we could begin by assuming that the mean package weight is equal to 16 ounces, so our null hypothesis is defined as follows:

$$H_0 : \mu = 16$$

A hypothesis, whether null or alternative, might specify a single value—in this case, $\mu = 16$—for the population parameter μ. We define this hypothesis as a **simple hypothesis**, which is read as follows: "The null hypothesis is that the population parameter μ is equal to a specific value of 16." For this cereal example a possible alternative hypothesis is that the population mean package weight falls in a range of values greater than 16 ounces:

$$H_1 : \mu > 16$$

We define this alternative hypothesis as a **one-sided composite alternative hypothesis**. Another possibility would be to test the null hypothesis against the general **two-sided composite alternative hypothesis**:

$$H_1 : \mu \neq 16$$

We choose these hypotheses so that one or the other must be true. In this book we will denote the null hypothesis as H_0 and the alternative hypothesis as H_1.

Similar to a jury trial our decision to choose one or the other hypothesis follows a rigorous procedure. The decision process uses a decision statistic computed from a random sample, such as a sample mean, $\bar{x}$, a sample variance, s^2, or a sample proportion, $\hat{p}$. The decision statistic will have a known sampling distribution based on the sampling procedure and the parameter value specified by the null hypothesis. From this sampling distribution we will determine values of the decision statistic that have a small probability of occurring if the null hypothesis is true. If the decision statistic has a value that has a small probability of occurring when the null hypothesis is true, we will reject the null hypothesis and accept the alternative hypothesis. However, if the decision statistic does not have a small probability of occurring when the null hypothesis is true, then we will not reject the null hypothesis. The specification of null and alternative hypotheses depends on the problem, as indicated in the following examples.

1. Malt-O-Meal wants to determine if its mean package weight is above the label weight. Let μ denote the population mean weight (in ounces) of cereal per box. The composite null hypothesis is that this mean is at most 16 ounces:

$$H_0 : \mu \le 16$$

And the obvious alternative is that the mean weight is greater than 16 ounces:

$$H_1 : \mu > 16$$

For this problem we would seek strong evidence that the mean weight of packages is greater than 16 ounces. For example, a company might wish to avoid legal action because of low package weights. The company would have confidence in its belief if it had strong evidence that results in rejecting H_0.

2. An automobile piston factory has proposed a process to monitor the diameter of pistons on a regular schedule. Every 2 hours a random sample of $n = 6$ pistons would be selected from the production process and their diameters measured. The mean diameter for the 6 pistons would be computed and used to test the simple null hypothesis,

$$H_0 : \mu = 3.800$$

versus the alternative hypothesis,

$$H_1 : \mu \ne 3.800$$

In this case the company would continue to operate unless the null hypothesis was rejected in favor of the alternative hypothesis. Strong evidence that the pistons were not meeting the tolerance standards would result in an interruption of the production process.

Once we have specified null and alternative hypotheses and collected sample data, a decision concerning the null hypothesis must be made. We can either reject the null hypothesis and accept the alternative, or fail to reject the null hypothesis. For good reasons many statisticians prefer not to say, "accept the null hypothesis"; instead, they say, "fail to reject the null hypothesis." When we fail to reject the null hypothesis, then either the null hypothesis is true or our test procedure was not strong enough to reject it and we have committed an error. To select the hypothesis—null or alternative—we develop a decision rule based on sample evidence. Further on in this chapter we present specific decision rules for various problems. In many cases the form of the rule is fairly obvious. To test the null hypothesis that the mean weight of cereal boxes is at most 16 ounces, we obtain a random sample of boxes and compute the sample mean. If the sample mean is substantially above 16 ounces, we can reject the null hypothesis and accept the alternative hypothesis. In general, the greater the sample mean is above 16, the greater the chance is of rejecting the null hypothesis. We will develop specific decision rules next.

From our discussion of sampling distributions in Chapter 6 we know that the sample mean is different from the population mean. With only one sample mean we cannot be certain of the value of the population mean. Thus, we know that the adopted decision rule will have some chance of reaching an erroneous conclusion. Table 9.1 summarizes the possible types of error. We define **Type I error** as the probability of rejecting the null hypothesis when the null hypothesis is true. Our decision rule will be defined so that the probability of rejecting a true null hypothesis, denoted as α, is "small." We define α to be the **significance level** of the test. The probability of failing to reject the null hypothesis when it is true is $(1 - \alpha)$. We also have another possible error, called a **Type II error**, that arises when we fail to reject a false null hypothesis. For a particular decision rule the probability of making such an error when the null hypothesis is false will be denoted as β. Then the probability of rejecting a false null hypothesis is $(1 - \beta)$, which is called the *power* of the test.

We will illustrate these ideas by reference to an earlier example. A factory manager is trying to determine if the population mean package weight is greater than the package label weight. The null hypothesis is that in the population the mean package weight is less than or equal to the label weight of 16 ounces. This null hypothesis is tested against the alternative hypothesis that the mean package weight is greater than 16 ounces. To test the hypothesis, we will obtain an independent random sample of cereal packages and compute the sample mean. If the sample mean is substantially larger than 16 ounces, the null hypothesis is rejected. Otherwise, we will not reject the null hypothesis. Let $\bar{x}$ denote the sample mean. Then a possible decision rule is as follows:

$$\text{Reject } H_0 \text{ if } \bar{x} > 16.13$$

Now, suppose that the null hypothesis is true. We could still find that the sample mean is greater than 16.13, and, according to our decision rule, the null hypothesis would be rejected. In that case we would have committed a Type I error. The probability of rejection when the null hypothesis is true is the significance level α. By contrast, suppose that the null hypothesis is false and that the population mean package weight is greater than 16. We could still find that the sample mean was less than 16.13, and, according to our decision rule, the null hypothesis would not be rejected. Thus, a Type II error would have occurred. The probability of making such an error will depend on just how much the population mean exceeds 16. We will find that it is more likely that the null hypothesis would be rejected for a given sample size if the population mean was 16.5 compared to the case where the population mean was 16.1.

Table 9.1 States of Nature and Decisions on the Null Hypothesis, with Probabilities of Making the Decisions, Given the States of Nature

DECISIONS ON NULL HYPOTHESIS	STATES OF NATURE	
	NULL HYPOTHESIS IS TRUE	NULL HYPOTHESIS IS FALSE
Fail to reject H_0	Correct decision Probability = $1 - \alpha$	Type II error Probability = β
Reject H_0	Type I error Probability = α (α is called the significance level)	Correct decision Probability = $1 - \beta$ ($1 - \beta$ is called the power of the test)

Ideally, we would like to have the probabilities of both types of errors be as small as possible. However, there is a trade-off between the probabilities of the two types of errors. Given a particular sample, any reduction in the probability of Type I error, α, will result in an increase in the probability of Type II error, β, and vice versa. We need to emphasize here that there is not a direct linear substitution (e.g., a reduction of 0.02 in α does not usually result in an increase of 0.02 in β). Thus, in the previous example the probability of Type I error, α, could be reduced by changing the decision rule to the following:

$$\text{Reject } H_0 \text{ if } \bar{x} > 16.23$$

But failure to reject the null hypothesis is more likely even if the null hypothesis is false. As a result, the probability of Type II error, β, would be increased. In practice, we select a small (e.g., less than 0.10) probability of Type I error and that probability is used to set the decision rule. The probability of Type II error is then determined, as shown in Figure 9.1.

Suppose that a plant manager wished to test whether the true mean weight of cereal boxes is greater than 16 ounces. He would begin the analysis by first fixing the probability of Type I error. In a sense this is like deciding the rules for a baseball or soccer game before the game starts instead of making up the rules as the game is played. After analyzing the nature of the decision process, he might decide that the decision rule should have a probability of 0.05 or less of rejecting the null hypothesis when it is true. He would do this by selecting an appropriate number, K, according to the following decision rule: "Reject the null hypothesis if the sample mean is greater than K ounces." In the following sections we indicate the procedure to choose K. Once the number K has been chosen, the probability of Type II error can be computed—for a particular value of μ included in H_1—using the procedures to be developed in Section 9.5.

Another concept used in hypothesis testing is the **power** of the test, defined as the probability of rejecting H_0 when H_1 is true. The power is computed for particular values of μ that satisfy the null hypothesis. The power is typically different for every different value of μ. Consider the cereal problem with

$$H_0 : \mu = 16$$

$$H_1 : \mu > 16$$

Thus, for any value of μ contained in the alternative hypothesis, H_1

$$\text{Power} = P\left(\text{Reject } H_0 \,|\, \mu, (\mu \subset H_1)\right)$$

Since the decision rule is determined by the significance level chosen for the test, the concept of power does not directly affect the decision to reject or fail to reject a null hypothesis. However, by computing the power of the test for particular significance levels and values of μ included in H_1, we will have valuable information about the properties of the decision rule. For example, we will see that, by taking a larger sample size, the power of the test will be increased for a given significance level, α. Thus, we will balance the increased costs of a larger sample size against the benefits of increasing the power of the test. Another important use of power calculations occurs

Figure 9.1 Consequences of Fixing the Significance Level of a Test

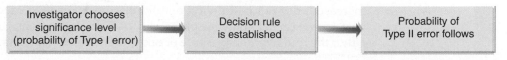

when, for a given sample size, we have a choice between two or more possible tests with the same significance levels. Then it would be appropriate to choose the test that has the smallest probability of Type II error—that is, the test with the highest power.

In Sections 9.2 to 9.4, we show how, for given significance levels, decision rules can be formulated for some important classes of hypothesis-testing problems. In Section 9.5 we show how the power of a test can be computed. A summary of the important terms and ideas that have been developed thus far is given in the following section.

Summary of Hypothesis-Testing Terminology

Null Hypothesis H_0: A hypothesis that is maintained to be true unless sufficient evidence to the contrary is obtained.

Alternative Hypothesis H_1: A hypothesis against which the null hypothesis is tested and which will be held to be true if the null is held false.

Simple Hypothesis: A hypothesis that specifies a single value for a population parameter of interest.

Composite Hypothesis: A hypothesis that specifies a range of values for a population parameter.

One-Sided Alternative: An alternative hypothesis involving all possible values of a population parameter on either one side or the other of (that is, either greater than or less than) the value specified by a simple null hypothesis.

Two-Sided Alternative: An alternative hypothesis involving all possible values of a population parameter other than the value specified by a simple null hypothesis.

Hypothesis Test Decisions: A decision rule is formulated, leading the investigator to either reject or fail to reject the null hypothesis on the basis of sample evidence.

Type I Error: The rejection of a true null hypothesis.

Type II Error: The failure to reject a false null hypothesis.

Significance Level: The probability of rejecting a null hypothesis that is true. This probability is sometimes expressed as a percentage, so a test of significance level α is referred to as a $(100-\alpha)$%-level test.

Power: The probability of rejecting a null hypothesis that is false.

We use the terms *reject* and *failure to reject* for possible decisions about a null hypothesis in formal summaries of the outcomes of tests. We will see that these terms do not adequately reflect the asymmetry of the status of null and alternative hypotheses or the consequences of a procedure in which the significance level is fixed and the probability of a Type II error is not controlled. The null hypothesis has the status of a maintained hypothesis—one held to be true—unless the data contain strong evidence to reject the hypothesis. By setting the significance level, α at a low level, we have a small probability of rejecting a true null hypothesis. When we reject a true null hypothesis, the probability of error is the significance level, α. But if there is only a small sample, then we will reject the null hypothesis only when it is wildly in error. As we increase the sample size, the probability of rejecting a false null hypothesis is increased. But failure to reject a null hypothesis leads to much greater uncertainty because we do not know the probability of Type II error. Thus, if we fail to reject, then either the null hypothesis is true or our procedure for detecting a false null hypothesis does not have sufficient power—for example, the sample size is too small. When we reject the null hypothesis, we have strong evidence that the null hypothesis is not true; and therefore, that the alternative hypothesis is true. If we seek strong evidence in favor of a particular outcome, we define that outcome as the alternative hypothesis, H_1, and the other outcome as the null hypothesis, H_0. This is called a **counterfactual argument**. When we reject H_0, there is strong evidence in favor of H_1, and we are confident that our decision is correct. But failing to reject H_0 leads to great uncertainty. We see many applications of this idea in the following sections.

The analogy to a criminal trial is apparent. An accused defendant is presumed innocent, (the null hypothesis) unless sufficient strong evidence is produced to indicate guilt beyond a reasonable doubt (rejection of the null hypothesis). The defendant may be found innocent either because he is innocent or because the evidence was not strong enough to convict. The burden of proof rests on the sample data.

EXERCISES

Basic Exercises

9.1 Mary Arnold wants to use the results of a random sample market survey to seek strong evidence that her brand of breakfast cereal has more than 20% of the total market. Formulate the null and alternative hypotheses, using P as the population proportion.

9.2 The Federal Reserve Board is meeting to decide if it should reduce interest rates in order to stimulate economic growth. State the null and alternative hypotheses regarding economic growth that the board would formulate to guide its decision.

9.3 John Stull, senior vice president of manufacturing, is seeking strong evidence to support his hope that new operating procedures have reduced the percentage of under filled cereal packages from the Ames production line. State his null and alternative hypotheses and indicate the results that would provide strong evidence.

Application Exercises

9.4 During 2000 and 2001 many people in Europe objected to purchasing genetically modified food that was produced by farmers in the United States.

The U.S. farmers argued that there was no scientific evidence to conclude that these products were not healthy. The Europeans argued that there still might be a problem with the food.

a. State the null and alternative hypotheses from the perspective of the Europeans.

b. State the null and alternative hypotheses from the perspective of the U.S. farmers.

9.5 The 2000 presidential election in the United States was very close, and the decision came down to the results of the presidential voting in the state of Florida. The election was finally decided in favor of George W. Bush over Al Gore by a U.S. Supreme Court decision that stated that it was not appropriate to hand-count ballots that had been rejected by the voting machines in various counties. At that time Bush had a small lead based on the ballots that had been counted. Imagine that you were a lawyer for George W. Bush. State your null and alternative hypotheses concerning the population vote totals for each candidate. Given your hypotheses, what would you argue about the results of the proposed recount—if it had actually occurred?

9.2 TESTS OF THE MEAN OF A NORMAL DISTRIBUTION: POPULATION VARIANCE KNOWN

In this section we present hypothesis **tests of the mean of a normal distribution (population variance known)** that have applications to business and economic problems. These procedures use a random sample of n normally distributed observations $x_1, x_2, ..., x_n$ that were obtained from a population with mean μ and known variance σ^2. We will test a hypothesis concerning the unknown population mean. Later our assumption of normality will be relaxed in many cases because of the central limit theorem.

In the discussion of hypothesis testing in Section 9.1 we noted that, if a null hypothesis is rejected using a test with significance level α, then the probability of error is known. In this case either the decision is correct or we have committed a Type I error. But if we fail to reject a null hypothesis, we do not know the probability of error. Thus, we have strong evidence to support a specific position if the null and alternative hypotheses are chosen such that rejecting the null hypothesis and accepting the alternative hypothesis lead to the support of our specific position. We demonstrate this in the following example.

Consider our previous example concerning the filling of cereal boxes. Suppose that industry regulations state that if the population mean package weight is 16.1 ounces or less for a population of packages with label weight 16 ounces, then the manufacturer will be prosecuted. Thus, our objective is to obtain strong evidence that the mean package weight, μ, is greater than 16.1 ounces. In this case we would state our null hypothesis as

$$H_0 : \mu = \mu_0 = 16.1$$

and the alternative hypothesis would be

$$H_1 : \mu > \mu_0 = 16.1$$

By designing our testing rule with significance level α, we know that rejecting the null hypothesis provides strong evidence that the mean weight is greater than 16.1 ounces because the probability of error is a small value, α.

Our test of the population mean uses the sample mean $\bar{x}$. If the sample mean is substantially greater than $\mu_0 = 16.1$, then we reject the null hypothesis. In order to obtain the appropriate decision value we use the fact that the standardized random variable

$$Z = \frac{\bar{X} - \mu_0}{\sigma/\sqrt{n}}$$

has a standard normal distribution with a mean of 0 and a variance of 1, given that H_0 is true. If α is the probability of Type I error and Z is large such that

$$P(Z > z_\alpha) = \alpha$$

then to test the null hypothesis, we can use the following decision rule:

$$\text{Reject } H_0 \text{ if } \frac{\bar{x} - \mu_0}{\sigma/\sqrt{n}} > z_\alpha$$

It follows that the probability of rejecting the null hypothesis, H_0, when it is true is the significance level α.

Note that by simple algebraic manipulation we could also state the decision rule as follows:

$$\text{Reject } H_0 \text{ if } \bar{x} > \bar{x}_c = \mu_0 + z_\alpha \sigma/\sqrt{n}$$

The value $\bar{x}_c$ is often called the **critical value** for the decision. Note that for every value z_α obtained from the standard normal distribution, there is also a value $\bar{x}_c$, and either of the previous decision rules provides exactly the same result.

Suppose that for this problem the population standard deviation is $\sigma = 0.4$ and we obtain a random sample of size 25. For a one-sided hypothesis test with significance level $\alpha = 0.05$, the value of z_α is 1.645 from the standard normal table. In this case our decision rule is as follows:

$$\text{Reject } H_0 \text{ if } \frac{\bar{x} - \mu_0}{\sigma/\sqrt{n}} = \frac{\bar{x} - 16.1}{0.4/\sqrt{25}} > 1.645$$

Figure 9.2
Normal
Probability
Density Function
Showing Both Z
and $\bar{x}$ Values for
the Decision Rule
to Test the Null
Hypothesis
$H_0 : \mu = 16.1$
versus
$H_1 : \mu > 16.1$

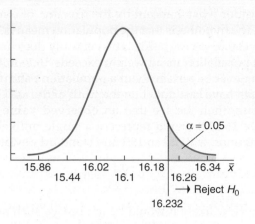
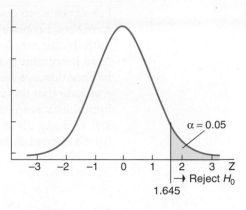

Equivalently, the rule is as follows:

$$\text{Reject } H_0 \text{ if } \bar{x} > \bar{x}_c = \mu_0 + z_\alpha \, \sigma / \sqrt{n} = 16.1 + 1.645 \times (0.4/\sqrt{25}) = 16.232$$

If we reject H_0 using this rule, then we accept the alternative hypothesis that the mean weight is greater than 16.1 ounces with the probability of Type I error 0.05 or less. This provides strong evidence to support our conclusion. But failure to reject the null hypothesis leads us to conclude that either H_0 is true or the selected testing procedure was not sensitive enough to reject H_0. The decision rules are illustrated in Figure 9.2.

We summarize the hypothesis test for a simple null hypothesis concerning the population mean in the following section.

A Test of the Mean of a Normal Population: Population Variance Known

A random sample of n observations was obtained from a normally distributed population with mean μ and known variance σ^2. If the observed sample mean is $\bar{x}$, then a test with significance level α of the null hypothesis

$$H_0 : \mu = \mu_0$$

against the alternative

$$H_1 : \mu > \mu_0$$

is obtained by using the following decision rule:

$$\text{Reject } H_0 \text{ if } \frac{\bar{x} - \mu_0}{\sigma / \sqrt{n}} > z_\alpha \qquad (9.1)$$

Or, equivalently,

$$\text{Reject } H_0 \text{ if } \bar{x} > \bar{x}_c = \mu_0 + z_\alpha \, \sigma / \sqrt{n}$$

where z_α is the number for which

$$P(Z > z_\alpha) = \alpha$$

and Z is the standard normal random variable.

Let us pause to consider what is meant by the rejection of a null hypothesis. In the cereal-box problem, the hypothesis that the population mean is 16.1 would be rejected with significance level 0.05 if $\bar{x} > 16.232$. This certainly does not mean that we would have proof that the population mean weight exceeds 16.1 units. Given only sample information, we can never be certain about a population parameter. Rather, we might conclude that the data have cast doubt on the truth of the null hypothesis. If the null hypothesis were true, then we see that an observed value of the sample mean $\bar{x} = 16.3$ (e.g., 16.3 > 16.232) would represent a single unlikely observation drawn from a normal distribution with mean 16.1 and standard deviation

$$\frac{\sigma}{\sqrt{n}} = \frac{0.4}{\sqrt{25}} = 0.08$$

We are really asking how likely it would be to observe such an extreme value if the null hypothesis were, in fact, true. We saw that the probability of observing a mean value greater than 16.232 is 0.05. Hence, in rejecting the null hypothesis, either the null hypothesis is false or we have observed an unlikely event—one that would occur only with a probability of less than that specified by the significance level. This is the sense in which the sample information has aroused doubt about the null hypothesis.

p-Value

There is another popular procedure for considering the test of the null hypothesis. Notice that in our cereal problem, the null hypothesis was rejected at significance level 0.05 but would not have been rejected at the lower 0.01 level. If we used a lower significance level, we would reduce the probability of rejecting a true null hypothesis. This would modify our decision rule to make it less likely that the null hypothesis would be rejected whether or not it is true. Obviously, the lower the significance level at which we reject a null hypothesis, the greater the doubt cast on its truth. Rather than testing hypotheses at pre-assigned levels of significance, investigators often determine the smallest level of significance at which a null hypothesis can be rejected.

The **p-value** is the probability of obtaining a value of the test statistic as extreme as, or more extreme than, the actual value obtained when the null hypothesis is true. Thus, the *p*-value is the smallest significance level at which a null hypothesis can be rejected, given the observed sample statistic. For example, suppose that in the cereal-box problem with the population mean equal to 16.1, $\sigma = 0.4$, and $n = 25$, and that under the null hypothesis we had obtained a sample mean of 16.3 ounces. Then the *p*-value would be as follows:

$$P(\bar{x} > 16.3 \mid H_0 : \mu = 16.1) = P\left(Z > \frac{16.3 - 16.1}{0.08} = 2.5\right) = 0.0062$$

From the normal probability table we find that the probability of obtaining a sample mean of 16.3 or greater from a normal distribution with a population mean of 16.1 and a standard deviation of the sample mean of 0.08 is equal to 0.0062. Thus, the *p*-value for this test is 0.0062. Now, the *p*-value (0.0062) represents the smallest significance level, α, that would lead to rejection of the null hypothesis. When the *p*-value is calculated, we could test the null hypothesis by using the following rule:

$$\text{Reject } H_0 \text{ if } p\text{-value} < \alpha$$

This rule will result in the same conclusion as obtained using Equation 9.1.

There is another, more important reason for the popularity of the p-value. The p-value provides more precise information about the strength of the rejection of the null hypothesis that results from the observed sample mean. Suppose that in the test of the cereal-box weight we had set the significance level at $\alpha = 0.05$—a popular choice. Then with a sample mean equal to 16.3 we would state that the null hypothesis was rejected at significance level 0.05. However, in fact, that sample result points to a much stronger conclusion. We could have rejected the null hypothesis at a significance level of $\alpha = 0.0063$. Alternatively, suppose that the computed p-value based on a different sample mean had been 0.07. In that case we could not reject the null hypothesis, but we would know that we were quite close to rejecting the null hypothesis. In contrast, a p-value of 0.30 would tell us that we were quite far from rejecting the null hypothesis. The popularity of the p-value is that it provides more information than merely stating that the null hypothesis was accepted or rejected at a particular significance level. The p-value is summarized next.

Interpretation of the Probability Value, or p-Value

The probability value, or p-value, is the smallest significance level at which the null hypothesis can be rejected. Consider a random sample of n observations from a population that has a normal distribution with mean μ and standard deviation σ, and the resulting computed sample mean, $\bar{x}$. The null hypothesis

$$H_0 : \mu = \mu_0$$

is tested against the alternative hypothesis

$$H_1 : \mu > \mu_0$$

The p-value for the test is

$$p\text{-}value = P\left(\frac{\bar{x} - \mu_0}{\sigma/\sqrt{n}} \geq z_p \,|\, H_0 : \mu = \mu_0 \right) \tag{9.2}$$

where z_p is the standard normal value associated with the smallest significance level at which the null hypothesis can be rejected. The p-value is regularly computed by most statistical computer programs and provides more information about the test, based on the observed sample mean. Thus, it is a popular tool for many statistical applications.

It is important to note that the p-value is an observed random variable that will be different for each random sample obtained for a statistical test. Thus, two different analysts could obtain their own random samples and sample means from a process population, and, thus, each would compute a different p-value.

Example 9.1 Evaluating a New Production Process (Hypothesis Test)

The production manager of Northern Windows Inc. has asked you to evaluate a proposed new procedure for producing its Regal line of double-hung windows. The present process has a mean production of 80 units per hour with a population standard deviation of $\sigma = 8$. The manager does not want to change to a new procedure unless there is strong evidence that the mean production level is higher with the new process.

Solution The manager will change to the new process only if there is strong evidence in its favor. Therefore, we will define the null hypothesis as

$$H_0 : \mu \le 80$$

and the alternative hypothesis as

$$H_1 : \mu > 80$$

We see that, if we define the significance level $\alpha = 0.05$ and conclude that the new process has higher productivity, then our probability of error is 0.05 or less. This would imply strong evidence in favor of our recommendation.

We obtain a random sample of $n = 25$ production hours using the proposed new process and compute the sample mean, $\bar{x}$, often using a computer. With a significance level of $\alpha = 0.05$ the decision rule is

$$\text{Reject } H_0 \text{ if } \frac{\bar{x} - 80}{8/\sqrt{25}} > 1.645$$

where $z_{0.05} = 1.645$ is obtained from the standard normal table. Alternatively, we could use the following rule:

$$\text{Reject } H_0 \text{ if } \bar{x} > \bar{x}_c = \mu_0 + z_\alpha \sigma/\sqrt{n} = 80 + 1.645 \times (8/\sqrt{25}) = 82.63$$

Suppose that the resulting sample mean was $\bar{x} = 83$. Based on that result

$$z = \frac{83 - 80}{8/\sqrt{25}} = 1.875 > 1.645$$

we would reject the null hypothesis and conclude that we have strong evidence to support the conclusion that the new process resulted in higher productivity. Given this sample mean, we could also compute the p-value as follows:

$$p\text{-value} = P(Z > 1.875) = 0.03$$

Thus we could recommend the new process to the production manager.

A Test of the Mean of a Normal Distribution (Variance Known): Composite Null and Alternative Hypotheses

The appropriate procedure for testing, at significance level α, the null hypothesis

$$H_0 : \mu \le \mu_0$$

against the alternative hypothesis

$$H_1 : \mu > \mu_0$$

is precisely the same as when the null hypothesis is $H_0 : \mu = \mu_0$. In addition, the p-values are also computed in exactly the same way.

Consider our previous example concerning the filling of cereal boxes. Suppose that industry regulations state that if the mean package weight is not 16 ounces or more for a population of packages with label weight 16 ounces, then the company will be prosecuted. In this situation we, as the regulators, could prosecute only if we found strong evidence that the mean package weight was less than 16 ounces. Thus, our objective is to prove that the mean package weight, μ, is not 16.0 ounces or more. In this case we would state the simple null hypothesis as

$$H_0 : \mu = \mu_0 = 16.0$$

or, using the composite hypothesis, as

$$H_0 : \mu \geq \mu_0 = 16.0$$

And the alternative hypothesis would be

$$H_1 : \mu < \mu_0 = 16.0$$

for either the simple or the composite hypothesis. By designing our testing rule with significance level α, we know that if we reject the null hypothesis, then we have strong evidence that the mean weight is less than 16.0 ounces because the probability of a Type I error is a small value, α.

Our test of the population mean uses the sample mean, $\bar{x}$. If the sample mean is substantially less than $\mu_0 = 16.0$, then we reject the null hypothesis. In order to obtain the appropriate decision value, we use the fact that the standard random variable

$$Z = \frac{\bar{X} - \mu_0}{\sigma/\sqrt{n}}$$

has a standard normal distribution with mean of 0 and variance of 1 when the population mean is μ_0. If z has a large negative value such that

$$P(Z < -z_\alpha) = \alpha$$

then to test the null hypothesis, we can use the following decision rule:

$$\text{Reject } H_0 \text{ if } \frac{\bar{x} - \mu_0}{\sigma/\sqrt{n}} < -z_\alpha$$

It follows that the probability of rejecting a true null hypothesis, H_0, is the significance level α.

Note that by simple algebraic manipulation we could also state the decision rule as follows:

$$\text{Reject } H_0 \text{ if } \bar{x} < \bar{x}_c = \mu_0 - z_\alpha \, \sigma/\sqrt{n}$$

The value $\bar{x}_c$ is the "critical value" for the decision. Note that for every value $-z_\alpha$ obtained from the standard normal distribution, there is also a value $\bar{x}_c$, and either of the preceding decision rules provides exactly the same result.

Suppose that for this problem the population standard deviation is $\sigma = 0.4$ and we obtain a random sample of 25. From the standard normal table with a significance level of $\alpha = 0.05$, the value of $z_\alpha = 1.645$. In this case our decision rule is

$$\text{Reject } H_0 \text{ if } \frac{\bar{x} - \mu_0}{\sigma/\sqrt{n}} = \frac{\bar{x} - 16.0}{0.4/\sqrt{25}} < -1.645$$

or we could use the following decision rule:

$$\text{Reject } H_0 \text{ if } \bar{x} < \bar{x}_c = \mu_0 - z_\alpha \, \sigma/\sqrt{n} = 16.0 - 1.645 \times (0.4/\sqrt{25}) = 15.868$$

If we reject H_0 using this rule, then we accept the alternative hypothesis that the mean weight is less than 16.0 ounces with the probability of Type I error 0.05 or less.

Figure 9.3
Normal Probability
Density Function
Showing $\bar{x}$ Values
for the Decision
Rule to Test the
Null Hypothesis
$H_0 : \mu \geq 16.0$
versus
$H_1 : \mu < 16.0$

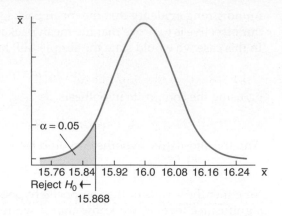

This provides strong evidence to support our conclusion. This decision rule is illustrated in Figure 9.3.

Note that this hypothesis test is the complement of the first example. The hypothesis-testing rules for alternative hypotheses dealing with the lower tail are mirror images of those dealing with the upper tail of the distribution. Computation of p-values also follows, using the lower tail instead of the upper tail probabilities. This result is summarized in Equation 9.3.

The cereal examples presented two different objectives. In the first case we wanted strong evidence that the mean weight was greater than 16.1 ounces, and, thus, we defined the null hypothesis as follows:

$$H_0 : \mu \leq 16.1$$

In the second case we wanted strong evidence that the mean was less than 16 ounces, and, therefore, we defined the null hypothesis as follows:

$$H_0 : \mu \geq 16$$

Possibilities of this type are present in many decision situations, and the decision maker is required to determine which option should be used in the particular problem being considered.

A Test of the Mean of a Normal Distribution (Variance Known): Composite or Simple Null and Alternative Hypotheses

The appropriate procedure for testing, at significance level α, the null hypothesis

$$H_0 : \mu = \mu_0 \quad \text{or} \quad \mu \geq \mu_0$$

against the alternative hypothesis

$$H_1 : \mu < \mu_0$$

uses the following decision rule:

$$\text{Reject } H_0 \text{ if } \frac{\bar{x} - \mu_0}{\sigma / \sqrt{n}} < -z_\alpha$$

Or, equivalently,

$$\text{Reject } H_0 \text{ if } \bar{x} < \bar{x}_c = \mu_0 - z_\alpha \sigma/\sqrt{n} \qquad (9.3)$$

where $-z_\alpha$ is the number for which

$$P(Z < -z_\alpha) = \alpha$$

and Z is the standard normal random variable.

In addition, the p-values can be computed by using the lower tail probabilities.

Example 9.2   Ball Bearing Production (Hypothesis Test)

The production manager of Twin Forks Ball Bearing Inc. has asked your assistance in evaluating a modified ball bearing production process. When the process is operating properly, the process produces ball bearings whose weights are normally distributed with a population mean of 5 ounces and a population standard deviation of 0.1 ounce. A new raw material supplier was used for a recent production run, and the manager wants to know if that change has resulted in a lowering of the mean weight of the ball bearings. There is no reason to suspect a problem with the new supplier, and the manager will continue to use the new supplier unless there is strong evidence that underweight ball bearings are being produced.

Solution   In this case we are interested in knowing if there is strong evidence to conclude that lower-weight bearings are being produced. Therefore, we will test the null hypothesis

$$H_0 : \mu = \mu_0 = 5$$

against the alternative hypothesis

$$H_1 : \mu < 5$$

Note how the notion of strong evidence leads us to choose the null and alternative hypotheses. We take action only if the null hypothesis is rejected and the alternative accepted. The significance level is specified as $\alpha = 0.05$, and, thus, the corresponding lower-tail value for the standard normal random variable is $z_\alpha = -1.645$ from the normal distribution table. For this problem we obtained a random sample of $n = 16$ observations and the sample mean was 4.962. Our decision rule for this problem is

$$\text{Reject } H_0 \text{ if } \frac{\bar{x} - \mu_0}{\sigma/\sqrt{n}} < -1.645$$

or

$$\text{Reject } H_0 \text{ if } \bar{x} < \bar{x}_c = \mu_0 - z_\alpha \sigma/\sqrt{n} = 5 - 1.645(0.1/\sqrt{16}) = 4.959$$

We see that we cannot reject the null hypothesis, H_0, since $\dfrac{4.962 - 5}{0.1/\sqrt{16}} = -1.52$ and $\bar{x} = 4.962 > \bar{x}_c = 4.959$. Thus, we conclude that we do not have strong evidence that the production process is producing underweight ball bearings.

We could also compute the p-value for this sample result by noting that for the standard normal distribution

$$p\text{-value} = P(Z < -1.52) = 0.0643$$

Two-Sided Alternative Hypothesis

There are some problems where deviations either too high or too low are of equal importance. For example, the diameter of an automobile engine piston cannot be too large or too small. In those situations we consider the test of the null hypothesis

$$H_0 : \mu = \mu_0$$

against the alternative hypothesis

$$H_1 : \mu \neq \mu_0$$

Here, we have no strong reason for suspecting departures either above or below the hypothesized population mean, μ_0. The null hypothesis would be doubted if the sample mean was much greater or much smaller than μ_0. Again, if the random variable has a normal distribution with known variance σ, we obtain a test with significance level α by using the result that under the null hypothesis

$$P(Z > z_{\alpha/2}) = \frac{\alpha}{2} \quad \text{and} \quad P(Z < -z_{\alpha/2}) = \frac{\alpha}{2}$$

In this case we have divided the significance level α equally between the two tails of the normal distribution. Hence, the probability that Z either exceeds $z_{\alpha/2}$ or is less than $-z_{\alpha/2}$ is α. The decision rule for a test with significance level α is

$$\text{Reject } H_0 \text{ if } \frac{\bar{x} - \mu_0}{\sigma/\sqrt{n}}$$

and is either greater than $z_{\alpha/2}$ or less than $-z_{\alpha/2}$. These results are summarized in Equation 9.4.

A Test of the Mean of a Normal Distribution Against Two-Sided Alternative (Variance Known)

The appropriate procedure for testing, at significance level α, the null hypothesis

$$H_0 : \mu = \mu_0$$

against the alternative hypothesis

$$H_1 : \mu \neq \mu_0$$

is obtained from the decision rule

$$\text{Reject } H_0 \text{ if } \frac{\bar{x} - \mu_0}{\sigma/\sqrt{n}} < -z_{\alpha/2} \quad \text{or} \quad \text{Reject } H_0 \text{ if } \frac{\bar{x} - \mu_0}{\sigma/\sqrt{n}} > z_{\alpha/2} \qquad \textbf{(9.4)}$$

Or, equivalently,

$$\text{Reject } H_0 \text{ if } \bar{x} < \mu_0 - z_{\alpha/2}\sigma/\sqrt{n} \quad \text{or} \quad \text{Reject } H_0 \text{ if } \bar{x} > \mu_0 + z_{\alpha/2}\sigma/\sqrt{n}$$

In addition, the *p*-values can be computed by noting that the corresponding tail probability would be doubled to reflect a *p*-value that refers to the sum of the upper and lower tail probabilities for the positive and negative values of *Z*. The *p*-value for the two-tailed test is

$$p\text{-value} = 2P\left(\left|\frac{\bar{x} - \mu_0}{\sigma/\sqrt{n}}\right| > z_{p/2} \,\Big|\, H_0 : \mu = \mu_0\right) \qquad (9.5)$$

where $z_{p/2}$ is the standard normal value associated with the smallest probability of rejecting the null hypothesis at either tail of the probability distribution.

Example 9.3 Analysis of Drill Hole Diameters (Hypothesis Test)

The production manager of Circuits Unlimited has asked for your assistance in analyzing a production process. This process involves drilling holes whose diameters are normally distributed with a population mean of 2 inches and a population standard deviation of 0.06 inch. A random sample of nine measurements had a sample mean of 1.95 inches. Use a significance level of $\alpha = 0.05$ to determine if the observed sample mean is unusual and suggests that the drilling machine should be adjusted.

Solution   In this case the diameter could be either too large or too small. Therefore, we perform a two-tailed hypothesis test with the null hypothesis

$$H_0 : \mu = 2.0$$

and the alternative hypothesis

$$H_1 : \mu \neq 2.0$$

The decision rule is to reject H_0 in favor of H_1 if

$$\frac{\bar{x} - \mu_0}{\sigma/\sqrt{n}} < -z_{\alpha/2} \qquad \text{or} \qquad \frac{\bar{x} - \mu_0}{\sigma/\sqrt{n}} > z_{\alpha/2}$$

and for this problem

$$\frac{\bar{x} - \mu_0}{\sigma/\sqrt{n}} = \frac{1.95 - 2.0}{0.06/\sqrt{9}} = -2.50$$

for a 5%-level test $\alpha = 0.05$ and $z_{\alpha/2} = z_{0.05/2} = 1.96$. Thus, since -2.50 is less than -1.96, we reject the null hypothesis and conclude that the drilling machine requires adjustment.

To compute the *p*-value, we first find that the probability of obtaining *Z* less than -2.50 from the normal table is 0.0062. Here, we want the *p*-value for a two-tailed test, and we must double the one-tail value. Thus, the *p*-value for this test is 0.0124, and the null hypothesis would have been rejected for a significance level above 1.24%.

We have summarized the various hypothesis-testing alternatives discussed in this section in Figure 9.10, located in the chapter appendix.

Basic Exercises

9.6 A random sample is obtained from a population with variance $\sigma^2 = 625$, and the sample mean is computed. Test the null hypothesis $H_0 : \mu = 100$ versus the alternative hypothesis $H_1 : \mu > 100$ with $\alpha = 0.05$. Compute the critical value $\bar{x}_c$ and state your decision rule for the following options:

   a. Sample size $n = 25$
   b. Sample size $n = 16$
   c. Sample size $n = 44$
   d. Sample size $n = 32$

9.7 A random sample of $n = 25$ is obtained from a population with variance σ^2, and the sample mean is computed. Test the null hypothesis $H_0 : \mu = 100$ versus the alternative hypothesis $H_1 : \mu > 100$ with $\alpha = 0.05$. Compute the critical value $\bar{x}_c$ and state your decision rule for the following options:

   a. The population variance is $\sigma^2 = 225$.
   b. The population variance is $\sigma^2 = 900$.
   c. The population variance is $\sigma^2 = 400$.
   d. The population variance is $\sigma^2 = 600$.

9.8 Using the results from Exercise 9.6 and Exercise 9.7 indicate how the critical value $\bar{x}_c$ is influenced by the sample size. Next, indicate how the critical value is influenced by the population variance, σ^2.

9.9 A random sample is obtained from a population with a variance of $\sigma^2 = 400$, and the sample mean is computed to be $\bar{x}_c = 70$. Consider the null hypothesis $H_0 : \mu = 80$ versus the alternative hypothesis $H_1 : \mu < 80$. Compute the p-value for the following options:

   a. Sample size $n = 25$
   b. Sample size $n = 16$
   c. Sample size $n = 44$
   d. Sample size $n = 32$

9.10 A random sample of $n = 25$ is obtained from a population with variance σ^2, and the sample mean is computed to be $\bar{x} = 70$. Consider the null hypothesis $H_0 : \mu = 80$ versus the alternative hypothesis $H_1 : \mu < 80$. Compute the p-value for the following options:

   a. The population variance is $\sigma^2 = 225$.
   b. The population variance is $\sigma^2 = 900$.

   c. The population variance is $\sigma^2 = 400$.
   d. The population variance is $\sigma^2 = 600$.

Application Exercises

9.11 A manufacturer of detergent claims that the contents of boxes sold weigh on average at least 16 ounces. The distribution of weight is known to be normal, with a standard deviation of 0.4 ounce. A random sample of 16 boxes yielded a sample mean weight of 15.84 ounces. Test at the 10% significance level the null hypothesis that the population mean weight is at least 16 ounces.

9.12 A company that receives shipments of batteries tests a random sample of nine of them before agreeing to take a shipment. The company is concerned that the true mean lifetime for all batteries in the shipment should be at least 50 hours. From past experience it is safe to conclude that the population distribution of lifetimes is normal with a standard deviation of 3 hours. For one particular shipment the mean lifetime for a sample of nine batteries was 48.2 hours. Test at the 10% level the null hypothesis that the population mean lifetime is at least 50 hours.

9.13 A pharmaceutical manufacturer is concerned that the impurity concentration in pills should not exceed 3%. It is known that from a particular production run impurity concentrations follow a normal distribution with a standard deviation of 0.4%. A random sample of 64 pills from a production run was checked, and the sample mean impurity concentration was found to be 3.07%.

   a. Test at the 5% level the null hypothesis that the population mean impurity concentration is 3% against the alternative that it is more than 3%.
   b. Find the p-value for this test.
   c. Suppose that the alternative hypothesis had been two-sided, rather than one-sided, with the null hypothesis $H_0 : \mu = 3$. State, without doing the calculations, whether the p-value of the test would be higher than, lower than, or the same as that found in part (b). Sketch a graph to illustrate your reasoning.
   d. In the context of this problem, explain why a one-sided alternative hypothesis is more appropriate than a two-sided alternative.

9.3 TESTS OF THE MEAN OF A NORMAL DISTRIBUTION: POPULATION VARIANCE UNKNOWN

In this section we consider the same set of hypothesis tests discussed in Section 9.2. The only difference is that the population variance is unknown, and, thus, we must use tests based on the Student's t distribution. We introduced the Student's t distribution in

Section 7.3 and showed its application for developing confidence intervals. Recall that the Student's t distribution depends on the degrees of freedom for computing the sample variance, $n - 1$. In addition, the Student's t distribution becomes close to the normal distribution as the sample size increases. Thus, for sample sizes over 100 the normal probability distribution can be used to approximate the Student's t distribution. Using the sample mean and variance, we know that the random variable

$$t_{n-1} = \frac{\bar{x} - \mu}{s/\sqrt{n}}$$

follows a Student's t distribution. The procedures for performing hypothesis **tests of the mean of a normal distribution (population variance unknown)** are defined in Equations 9.6, 9.7, and 9.8.

Tests of the Mean of a Normal Distribution: Population Variance Unknown

We are given a random sample of n observations from a normal population with mean μ. Using the sample mean and sample standard deviation, $\bar{x}$ and s respectively, we can use the following tests with significance level α.

1. To test either null hypothesis

$$H_0 : \mu = \mu_0 \quad \text{or} \quad H_0 : \mu \leq \mu_0$$

against the alternative

$$H_1 : \mu > \mu_0$$

the decision rule is as follows:

$$\text{Reject } H_0 \text{ if } t = \frac{\bar{x} - \mu_0}{s/\sqrt{n}} > t_{n-1,\alpha}$$

Or, equivalently,

$$\text{Reject } H_0 \text{ if } \bar{x} > \bar{x}_c = \mu_0 + t_{n-1,\alpha} s/\sqrt{n} \tag{9.6}$$

2. To test either null hypothesis

$$H_0 : \mu = \mu_0 \quad \text{or} \quad H_0 : \mu \geq \mu_0$$

against the alternative

$$H_1 : \mu < \mu_0$$

the decision rule is as follows:

$$\text{Reject } H_0 \text{ if } t = \frac{\bar{x} - \mu_0}{s/\sqrt{n}} < -t_{n-1,\alpha} \tag{9.7}$$

Or, equivalently,

$$\text{Reject } H_0 \text{ if } \bar{x} < \bar{x}_c = \mu_0 - t_{n-1,\alpha} s/\sqrt{n}$$

3. To test the null hypothesis

$$H_0 : \mu = \mu_0$$

against the alternative hypothesis

$$H_1 : \mu \neq \mu_0$$

the decision rule is

$$\text{Reject } H_0 \text{ if } \frac{\bar{x} - \mu_0}{s/\sqrt{n}} < -t_{n-1,\alpha/2} \quad \text{or} \quad \text{Reject } H_0 \text{ if } \frac{\bar{x} - \mu_0}{s/\sqrt{n}} > t_{n-1,\alpha/2} \qquad (9.8)$$

Or, equivalently,

$$\text{Reject } H_0 \text{ if } \bar{x} < \mu_0 - t_{n-1,\alpha/2}\, s/\sqrt{n} \quad \text{or} \quad \text{Reject } H_0 \text{ if } \bar{x} > \mu_0 + t_{n-1,\alpha/2}\, s/\sqrt{n}$$

where $t_{n-1,\alpha/2}$ is the Student's t value for $n-1$ degrees of freedom and the tail probability is $\alpha/2$.

The p-values for these tests are computed in the same way as we did for tests with known variance except that the Student's t value is substituted for the normal Z value. To obtain the p-value we often need to interpolate in the t table or use a computer package.

Example 9.4 Analysis of Weekly Sales of Frozen Broccoli (Hypothesis Test)

Grand Junction Vegetables is a producer of a wide variety of frozen vegetables. The company president has asked you to determine if the weekly sales of 16-ounce packages of frozen broccoli has increased. The mean weekly sales per store has been 2,400 packages over the past 6 months. You have obtained a random sample of sales data from 134 stores for your study. The data is contained in the data file **Broccoli**.

Solution   Given the project objectives, you decide that the null hypothesis test is that population mean sales are 2,400 versus the alternative that sales have increased using a significance level $\alpha = 0.05$. The null hypothesis is

$$H_0 : \mu = 2{,}400$$

versus the alternative hypothesis

$$H_1 : \mu > 2{,}400$$

Figure 9.4 shows the Minitab output containing the sample mean and variance. From the Minitab output we see that the sample mean is much larger than the median and that the the distance between the third quartile and the maximum sales is quite large. Thus, it is clear that the distribution of the individual observations is not a normal distribution. But the sample size is large, and, thus, by applying the central limit theorem from Chapter 6, we can assume that the sampling distribution for the sample mean is normal. Therefore, a Student's t test would be appropriate for the hypothesis test. We see that the sample mean is 3,593 and the sample standard deviation is 4,919. The *test* statistic is as follows:

$$t = \frac{3{,}593 - 2{,}400}{4{,}919/\sqrt{134}} = 2.81$$

Figure 9.4   Broccoli Sales (Descriptive Statistics)

Descriptive Statistics: Broccoli

Variable	N	N*	Mean	SE Mean	StDev	Minimum	Q1	Median	Q3	Maximum
Broccoli	134	0	3593	425	4919	156	707	2181	2300	27254

The value of t for $n - 1 = 133$ degrees of freedom and $\alpha = 0.05$ for the upper tail is approximately 1.645. Based on this result, we reject the null hypothesis and conclude that mean sales have increased.

The tests presented in this section are summarized in Figure 9.10, located in the chapter appendix.

EXERCISES

Basic Exercises

9.14 Test the hypotheses

$$H_0 : \mu \leq 100$$

$$H_1 : \mu > 100$$

using a random sample of $n = 25$, a probability of Type I error equal to 0.05, and the following sample statistics:

a. $\bar{x} = 106; s = 15$
b. $\bar{x} = 104; s = 10$
c. $\bar{x} = 95; s = 10$
d. $\bar{x} = 92; s = 18$

9.15 Test the hypotheses

$$H_0 : \mu = 100$$

$$H_1 : \mu < 100$$

using a random sample of $n = 36$, a probability of Type I error equal to 0.05, and the following sample statistics:

a. $\bar{x} = 106; s = 15$
b. $\bar{x} = 104; s = 10$
c. $\bar{x} = 95; s = 10$
d. $\bar{x} = 92; s = 18$

Application Exercises

9.16 An engineering research center claims that through the use of a new computer control system, automobiles should achieve, on average, an additional 3 miles per gallon of gas. A random sample of 100 automobiles was used to evaluate this product. The sample mean increase in miles per gallon achieved was 2.4, and the sample standard deviation was 1.8 miles per gallon. Test the hypothesis that the population mean is at least 3 miles per gallon. Find the p-value of this test, and interpret your findings.

9.17 A random sample of 1,562 undergraduates enrolled in management ethics courses was asked to respond on a scale from 1 (strongly disagree) to 7 (strongly agree) to this proposition: "Senior corporate executives are interested in social justice." The sample mean response was 4.27, and the sample standard deviation was 1.32. Test at the 1% level, against a two-sided alternative, the null hypothesis that the population mean is 4.

9.18 You have been asked to evaluate single employer plans after the establishment of the Health Benefit Guarantee Corporation. A random sample of 76 percentage changes in promised health benefits was observed. The sample mean percentage change was 0.078, and the sample standard deviation was 0.201. Find and interpret the p-value of a test of the null hypothesis that the population mean percentage change is 0 against a two-sided alternative.

9.19 A random sample of 172 marketing students was asked to rate on a scale from 1 (not important) to 5 (extremely important) health benefits as a job characteristic. The sample mean rating was 3.31, and the sample standard deviation was 0.70. Test at the 1% significance level the null hypothesis that the population mean rating is at most 3.0 against the alternative that it is bigger than 3.0.

9.20 A random sample of 170 people was provided with a forecasting problem. Each sample member was given, in two ways, the task of forecasting the next value of a retail sales variable. The previous 20 values were presented both as numbers and as points on a graph. Subjects were asked to predict the next value. The absolute forecasting errors were measured. The sample then consisted of 170 differences in absolute forecast errors (numerical minus graphical). The sample mean of these differences was –2.91, and the sample standard deviation was 11.33. Find and interpret the p-value of a test of the null hypothesis that the population mean difference is 0 against the alternative that it is negative. (The alternative can be viewed as the hypothesis that, in the aggregate, people are more successful at graphical than numerical prediction.)

9.21 The accounts of a corporation show that, on average, accounts payable are $125.32. An auditor checked a random sample of 16 of these accounts. The sample mean was $131.78 and the sample standard deviation was $25.41. Assume that the population distribution is normal. Test at the 5% significance level against a two-sided alternative the null hypothesis that the population mean is $125.32.

9.22 On the basis of a random sample the null hypothesis

$$H_0 : \mu = \mu_0$$

is tested against the alternative

$$H_1 : \mu > \mu_0$$

and the null hypothesis is not rejected at the 5% significance level.

   a. Does this necessarily imply that μ_0 is contained in the 95% confidence interval for μ?
   b. Does this necessarily imply that μ_0 is contained in the 90% confidence interval for μ if the observed sample mean is larger than μ_0?

9.23 A company selling licenses for new e-commerce computer software advertises that firms using this software obtain, on average during the first year, a yield of 10% on their initial investments. A random sample of 10 of these franchises produced the following yields for the first year of operation:

   6.1   9.2   11.5   8.6   12.1   3.9   8.4   10.1   9.4   8.9

Assuming that population yields are normally distributed, test the company's claim.

9.24 A process that produces bottles of shampoo, when operating correctly, produces bottles whose contents weigh, on average, 20 ounces. A random sample of nine bottles from a single production run yielded the following content weights (in ounces):

21.4   19.7   19.7   20.6   20.8   20.1   19.7   20.3   20.9

Assuming that the population distribution is normal, test at the 5% level against a two-sided alternative that the null hypothesis that the process is operating correctly.

9.25 A statistics instructor is interested in the ability of students to assess the difficulty of a test they have taken. This test was taken by a large group of students, and the average score was 78.5. A random sample of eight students was asked to predict this average score. Their predictions were as follows:

   72   83   78   65   69   77   81   71

Assuming a normal distribution, test the null hypothesis that the population mean prediction would be 78.5. Use a two-sided alternative and a 10% significance level.

9.26 A beer distributor claims that a new display featuring a life-size picture of a well-known rock singer will increase product sales in supermarkets by an average of 50 cases in a week. For a random sample of 20 high-volume liquor outlets, the average sales increase was 41.3 cases, and the sample standard deviation was 12.2 cases. Test at the 5% level the null hypothesis that the population mean sales increase is at least 50 cases, stating any assumptions you make.

9.27 In contract negotiations a company claims that a new incentive scheme has resulted in average weekly earnings of at least $400 for all customer service workers. A union representative takes a random sample of 15 workers and finds that their weekly earnings have an average of $381.35 and a standard deviation of $48.60. Assume a normal distribution.

   a. Test the company's claim.
   b. If the same sample results had been obtained from a random sample of 50 employees, could the company's claim be rejected at a lower significance level than that used in part (a)?

9.4 TESTS OF THE POPULATION PROPORTION (LARGE SAMPLES)

Another important set of business and economics problems involves population proportions. Business executives are interested in the percent market share for their products, and government officials are interested in the percentage of people that support a proposed new program. Inference about the population proportion based on sample proportions is an important application of hypothesis testing.

From our work in Chapters 5 and 6 we know that the distribution of the sample proportion can be approximated quite accurately by using the normal distribution. In this approximation we denote P as the population proportion and $\hat{p}$ as the sample proportion. Thus, the sample proportion $\hat{p}$ estimated from a random sample of size n has an approximate normal distribution with mean P and variance $P(1 - P)/n$. Then the standard normal statistic is as follows:

$$Z = \frac{\hat{p} - P}{\sqrt{P(1 - P)/n}}$$

If the null hypothesis is that the population proportion is

$$H_0 : P = P_0$$

it follows that, when this hypothesis is true, the random variable

$$Z = \frac{\hat{p} - P_0}{\sqrt{P_0(1 - P_0)/n}}$$

approximately follows a standard normal distribution. The procedures for **tests of a population proportion (large sample sizes)** are defined in Equations 9.9, 9.10 and 9.11.

Tests of the Population Proportion (Large Sample Sizes)

We begin by assuming a random sample of n observations from a population that has a proportion P whose members possess a particular attribute. If $nP(1 - P) > 5$ and the sample proportion is $\hat{p}$, then the following tests have significance level α.

1. To test either the hypothesis

$$H_0 : P = P_0 \quad \text{or} \quad H_0 : P \leq P_0$$

   against the alternative

$$H_1 : P > P_0$$

   the decision rule is as follows:

$$\text{Reject } H_0 \text{ if } \frac{\hat{p} - P_0}{\sqrt{P_0(1 - P_0)/n}} > z_\alpha \qquad (9.9)$$

2. To test either null hypothesis

$$H_0 : P = P_0 \quad \text{or} \quad H_0 : P \geq P_0$$

   against the alternative

$$H_1 : P < P_0$$

   the decision rule is as follows:

$$\text{Reject } H_0 \text{ if } \frac{\hat{p} - P_0}{\sqrt{P_0(1 - P_0)/n}} < -z_\alpha \qquad (9.10)$$

3. To test the null hypothesis

$$H_0 : P = P_0$$

   against the two-sided alternative

$$H_1 : P \neq P_0$$

   the decision rule is as follows:

$$\text{Reject } H_0 \text{ if } \frac{\hat{p} - P_0}{\sqrt{P_0(1 - P_0)/n}} < -z_{\alpha/2} \quad \text{or} \quad \frac{\hat{p} - P_0}{\sqrt{P_0(1 - P_0)/n}} > z_{\alpha/2} \qquad (9.11)$$

For all of these tests the p-value is the smallest significance level at which the null hypothesis can be rejected.

The tests presented here are summarized in Figure 9.11, located in the chapter appendix.

Example 9.5 Supermarket Shoppers' Price Knowledge (Hypothesis Test Using Proportions)

Market Research Inc. wants to know if shoppers are sensitive to the prices of items sold in a supermarket. It obtained a random sample of 802 shoppers and found that 378 supermarket shoppers were able to state the correct price of an item immediately after putting it into their cart. Test at the 7% level the null hypothesis that at least one-half of all shoppers are able to state the correct price.

Solution We will let P denote the population proportion of supermarket shoppers able to state the correct price in these circumstances. Test the null hypothesis

$$H_0 : P \geq P_0 = 0.50$$

against the alternative

$$H_1 : P < 0.50$$

The decision rule is to reject the null hypothesis in favor of the alternative if

$$\frac{\hat{p} - P_0}{\sqrt{P_0(1 - P_0)/n}} < -z_\alpha$$

For this example,

$$n = 802 \text{ and } \hat{p} = 378/802 = 0.471.$$

The test statistic is as follows:

$$\frac{\hat{p} - P_0}{\sqrt{P_0(1 - P_0)/n}} = \frac{0.471 - 0.5}{\sqrt{0.50(1 - 0.50)/802}} = -1.64$$

At a 7% significance level test ($\alpha = 0.07$), it follows that $z_\alpha = -1.474$ and -1.64 is less than -1.474. Thus, we reject the null hypothesis at the 7% level and conclude that less than one-half of the shoppers can correctly state the price immediately after putting an item into their supermarket cart. Using the calculated test statistic value of -1.64, we also find that the p-value for the test is 0.051.

EXERCISES

Basic Exercises

9.28 A random sample of women is obtained, and each person in the sample is asked if she would purchase a new shoe model. To determine if the new shoe model would have sales at least 25% to meet corporate profit objectives, the following hypothesis test is performed at a level of $\alpha = 0.03$ using $\hat{p}$ as the sample proportion of women who said yes.

$$H_0 : P \leq 0.25$$
$$H_1 : P > 0.25$$

What value of the sample proportion, $\hat{p}$, is required to reject the null hypothesis, given the following sample sizes?

a. $n = 400$ c. $n = 625$
b. $n = 225$ d. $n = 900$

9.29 A company is attempting to determine if it should retain a previously popular shoe model. A random sample of women is obtained, and each person in the sample is asked if she would purchase this existing shoe model. To determine if the old shoe model should be retained, the following hypothesis test is performed at a level of $\alpha = 0.05$ using $\hat{p}$ as the sample proportion of women who said yes.

$$H_0 : P \geq 0.25$$
$$H_1 : P < 0.25$$

What value of the sample proportion, $\hat{p}$, is required to reject the null hypothesis, given the following sample sizes?

a. $n = 400$ c. $n = 625$
b. $n = 225$ d. $n = 900$

Application Exercises

9.30 In a random sample of 361 owners of small businesses that had gone into bankruptcy, 105 reported conducting no marketing studies prior to opening the business. Test the hypothesis that at most 25% of all members of this population conducted no marketing studies before opening their businesses. Use $\alpha = 0.05$.

9.31 In a random sample of 998 adults in the United States, 17.3% of the sample members indicated some measure of disagreement with this statement: "Globalization is more than an economic trade system—instead it includes institutions and culture." Test at the 5% level the hypothesis that at least 25% of all U.S. adults would disagree with this statement.

9.32 In a random sample of 160 business school students, 72 sample members indicated some measure of agreement with this statement: "Scores on a standardized entrance exam are less important for a student's chance to succeed academically than is the student's high school GPA." Test the null hypothesis that one-half of all business school graduates would agree with this statement against a two-sided alternative. Find and interpret the p-value of the test.

9.33 Of a random sample of 199 auditors, 104 indicated some measure of agreement with this statement: "Cash flow is an important indication of profitability." Test at the 10% significance level against a two-sided alternative the null hypothesis that one-half of the members of this population would agree with this statement. Also find and interpret the p-value of this test.

9.34 A random sample of 50 university admissions officers was asked about expectations in application interviews. Of these sample members, 28 agreed that the interviewer usually expects the interviewee to have volunteer experience doing community projects. Test the null hypothesis that one-half of all interviewers have this expectation against the alternative that the population proportion is bigger than one-half. Use $\alpha = 0.05$.

9.35 Of a random sample of 172 elementary school educators, 118 said that parental support was the most important source of a child's success. Test the hypothesis that parental support is the most important source of a child's success for at least 75% of elementary school educators against the alternative that the population percentage is less than 75%. Use $\alpha = 0.05$.

9.36 A random sample of 202 business faculty members was asked if there should be a required foreign language course for business majors. Of these sample members, 140 felt there was a need for a foreign language course. Test the hypothesis that at least 75% of all business faculty members hold this view. Use $\alpha = 0.05$.

9.5 ASSESSING THE POWER OF A TEST

In Sections 9.2 to 9.4 we have developed various hypothesis tests with significance level α. In all of these tests we developed decision rules for rejecting the null hypothesis in favor of an alternative hypothesis. In carrying out these various tests we know that the probability of committing a Type I error when we reject the null hypothesis is a small value α or less. In addition, we may also compute the p-value for the test, and, thus, we know the smallest significance level at which the null hypothesis can be rejected. When we reject the null hypothesis, we conclude that there is strong evidence to support our conclusion. But if we fail to reject the null hypothesis, we know that either the null hypothesis is true or that we have committed a Type II error by failing to reject the null hypothesis when the alternative is true.

In this section we consider the characteristics of some of our tests when the null hypothesis is not true. We learn how to compute the probability of Type II error and also how to determine the power of the hypothesis test. Of course, a Type II error can occur only if the alternative hypothesis is true. Thus, we will consider Type II error and power for specific values of the population parameter that are included in the alternative hypothesis.

Tests of the Mean of a Normal Distribution: Population Variance Known

Following the procedures of Section 9.2, we want to test the null hypothesis that the mean of a normal population is equal to a specific value, μ_0.

Consider an example where we are testing the null hypothesis that the population mean weight of ball bearings from a production process is 5 ounces versus the alternative hypothesis that the population mean weight is greater than 5 ounces. We conduct the test with a random sample of 16 observations and a significance level of 0.05. The population distribution is assumed to be a normal distribution with a standard deviation of 0.1 ounce. Thus, the null hypothesis is

$$H_0 : \mu = 5$$

versus the alternative hypothesis

$$H_1 : \mu > 5$$

and the decision rule is as follows:

$$\text{Reject } H_0 \text{ if } \frac{\bar{x} - 5}{0.1/\sqrt{16}} > 1.645 \quad \text{or} \quad \bar{x} > 5 + 1.645(0.1/\sqrt{16}) = 5.041$$

Now, if the sample mean is less than or equal to 5.041, then, using our rule, we will fail to reject the null hypothesis.

Suppose that we want to determine the probability that the null hypothesis will not be rejected if the true mean weight is 5.05 ounces. Clearly, the alternative hypothesis is correct, and we want to determine the probability that we will fail to reject the null hypothesis and thus have a Type II error. That is, we want to determine the probability that the sample mean is less than 5.041 if the population mean is actually 5.05. Using the 16 observations we compute the probability of Type II error as follows:

$$\beta = P(\bar{x} \le 5.041 | \mu = 5.05) = P\left(z \le \frac{5.041 - 5.05}{0.1/\sqrt{16}}\right)$$

$$= P(z \le -0.36)$$

$$= 0.3594$$

Thus, using the preceding decision rule, we can show that the probability, β, of Type II error when the population mean is 5.05 ounces is 0.3594. Since the power of a test is 1 minus the probability of Type II error, when the population mean is 5.05, we have the following:

$$\text{Power} = 1 - \beta = 1 - 0.3594 = 0.6406$$

These power calculations are shown in Figure 9.5. In part (a), we see that, when the population mean is 5, the probability that the sample mean exceeds 5.041 is 0.05—the significance level of the test. Part (b) of the figure shows the density function of the sampling distribution of the sample mean when the population mean is 5.05. The shaded area in this figure shows the probability that the sample mean exceeds 5.041 when the population mean is 5.05—the power of the test. Similar calculations could be made to determine the power and probability of a Type II error for any value of μ greater than 5.0.

By computing the power of a test for all values of μ included in the null hypothesis, the **power function** can be generated, as shown in Figure 9.6.

The power function has the following features:

1. The farther the true mean is from the hypothesized mean μ_0, the greater is the power of the test—everything else being equal. Figure 9.6 illustrates this result.
2. The smaller the significance level (α) of the test, the smaller the power—everything else being equal. Thus, reducing the probability of Type I error (α) increases the probability of Type II error (β), but reducing α by 0.01 does not generally increase β by 0.01; the changes are not linear.

Figure 9.5
Sampling Distribution of Sample Mean for 16 Observations with $\sigma = 0.1$

Figure 9.6
Power Function for Test $H_0 : \mu = 5$ Against $H_1 : \mu > 5$ ($\alpha = 0.05$, $\sigma = 0.1$, $n = 16$)

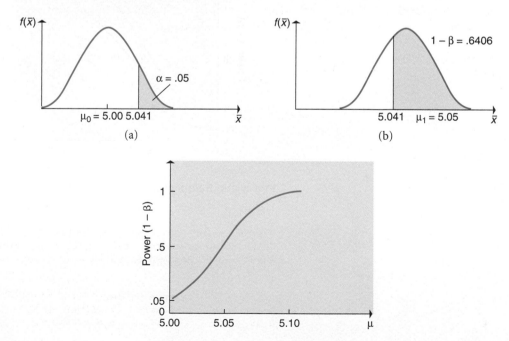

3. The larger the population variance, the lower the power of the test—everything else being equal.

4. The larger the sample size, the greater the power of the test—everything else being equal. Note that larger sample sizes reduce the variance of the sample mean and, thus, provide a greater chance that we will reject H_0 when it is not correct. Figure 9.7 presents a set of power curves at sample sizes of 4, 9, and 16 that illustrate the effect.

5. The power of the test at the critical value equals 0.5 because the probability that a sample mean is above $(\mu_0 - \bar{x}_c)$ is, of course, 0.50.

Many statistical computer packages have computational routines to compute the power of a test. For example, Figure 9.8 presents the Minitab output for the discussion example. The small differences in the power values are the result of rounding error.

Power of Population Proportion Tests (Large Samples)

In Section 9.4 we developed hypothesis tests and decision rules for testing if the population proportion had certain values. Using methods similar to those in the previous section, we can also develop the probability of Type II error for proportion tests. The probability, β, of making a Type II error for any given population proportion P_1 included in H_1 is found as follows:

1. From the test decision rule, find the range of values of the sample proportion leading to failure to reject the null hypothesis.

2. Using the value P_1 for the population proportion—where P_1 is included in the alternative hypothesis—find the probability that the sample proportion will be in the nonrejection region determined in step (1) for samples of n observations when the population proportion is P_1.

Figure 9.7
Power Functions for Test $H_0 : \mu = 5$ Against $H_1 : \mu > 5$ ($\alpha = 0.05$, $\sigma = 0.1$) for Sample Sizes 4, 9, and 16

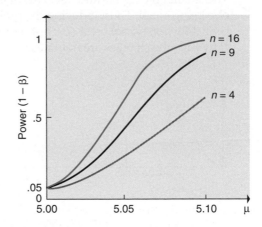

Figure 9.8
Computer Computation of Power (Minitab)

Power and Sample Size

```
1-Sample Z test

Testing mean = null (versus > null)
Calculating power for mean = null + difference
Alpha = 0.05 Assumed standard deviation = 0.1
```

Difference	Sample Size	Power
0.05	16	0.638760

We demonstrate this procedure in the following example.

Example 9.6 Forecasts of Corporate Earnings for Electronic Investors Inc. (Power and Type II Error)

The president of Electronic Investors Inc. has asked you to prepare an analysis of the forecasts of corporate earnings per share that were made by a group of financial analysts. These researchers were equally interested in the proportion of forecasts that exceeded the actual level of earnings and the proportion of forecasts that were less than the actual level of earnings.

Solution Begin your analysis by constructing a hypothesis test to determine if there was strong evidence to conclude that the proportion of forecasts that were above actual earnings was different from 50%. Using P to denote the proportion of forecasts that exceeded the actual level, the null hypothesis is

$$H_0 : P = P_0 = 0.50$$

and the alternative hypothesis is

$$H_1 : P \neq 0.50$$

The decision rule is as follows:

$$\text{Reject } H_0 \text{ if } \frac{\hat{p} - P_0}{\sqrt{P_0(1 - P_0)/n}} < -z_{\alpha/2} \quad \text{or} \quad \frac{\hat{p} - P_0}{\sqrt{P_0(1 - P_0)/n}} < -z_{\alpha/2}$$

A random sample of $n = 600$ forecasts was obtained, and it was determined that 382 exceeded actual earnings. Using a significance level of $\alpha = 0.05$, the decision rule is to reject the null hypothesis if

$$\frac{\hat{p}_x - P_0}{\sqrt{P_0(1 - P_0)/n}} < -1.96 \quad \text{or} \quad \frac{\hat{p}_x - P_0}{\sqrt{P_0(1 - P_0)/n}} > 1.96$$

Also, H_0 is rejected if

$$\hat{p}_x > 0.50 + 1.96\sqrt{0.50(1 - 0.50)/600} = 0.50 + 0.04 = 0.54$$

or

$$\hat{p}_x < 0.50 - 0.04 = 0.46$$

The observed sample proportion is

$$\hat{p}_x = \frac{382}{600} = 0.637$$

and, thus, the null hypothesis is rejected at the 5% level.

Now, we want to determine the probability of a Type II error when this decision rule is used. Suppose that the true population proportion was $P_1 = 0.55$. We want to determine the probability that the sample proportion is between 0.46 and 0.54 if the population proportion is 0.55. Thus, the probability of Type II error is as follows:

$$P(0.46 \leq \hat{p}_x \leq 0.54) = P\left[\frac{0.46 - P_1}{\sqrt{\dfrac{P_1(1 - P_1)}{n}}} \leq Z \leq \frac{0.54 - P_1}{\sqrt{\dfrac{P_1(1 - P_1)}{n}}} \right]$$

$$= P\left[\frac{0.46 - 0.55}{\sqrt{\dfrac{(0.55)(0.45)}{600}}} \leq Z \leq \frac{0.54 - 0.55}{\sqrt{\dfrac{(0.55)(0.45)}{600}}}\right]$$

$$= P(-4.43 \leq Z \leq -0.49) = 0.3121$$

Given the decision rule, the probability of a Type II error involved in failing to reject the null hypothesis when the true proportion is 0.55 is $\beta = 0.3121$. The power of the test for this value of the population proportion is as follows:

$$\text{Power} = 1 - \beta = 0.6879$$

This probability can be calculated for any proportion P_1. Figure 9.9 shows the power function for this example. Because the alternative hypothesis is two-sided, the power function differs in shape from that of Figure 9.6. Here, we are considering possible values of the population proportion on either side of the hypothesized value, 0.50. As we see, the probability of rejecting the null hypothesis when it is false increases the farther the true population proportion is from the hypothesized value.

Figure 9.9   Power Function for Test of $H_0 : P = 0.50$ versus $H_1 : P \neq 0.50$ ($\alpha = 0.05$, $n = 600$)

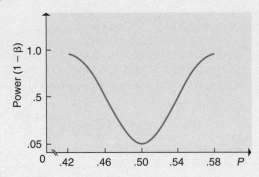

EXERCISES

Basic Exercises

9.37 Consider a problem with the hypothesis test

$$H_0 : \mu = 5$$
$$H_1 : \mu > 5$$

and the following decision rule:

Reject H_0 if $\dfrac{\bar{x} - 5}{0.1/\sqrt{16}} > 1.645$ or

$$\bar{x} > 5 + 1.645(0.1/\sqrt{16}) = 5.041$$

Compute the probability of Type II error and the power for the following true population means:

a. $\mu = 5.10$
b. $\mu = 5.03$
c. $\mu = 5.15$
d. $\mu = 5.07$

9.38 Consider Example 9.6 with the null hypothesis

$$H_0 : P = P_0 = 0.50$$

and the alternative hypothesis

$$H_0 : P \neq 0.50$$

The decision rule is

$$\frac{\hat{p}_x - 0.50}{\sqrt{0.50(1 - 0.50)/600}} < -1.96 \quad \text{or}$$

$$\frac{\hat{p}_x - 0.50}{\sqrt{0.50(1 - 0.50)/600}} > 1.96$$

with a sample size of $n = 600$. What is the probability of Type II error if the actual population proportion is

a. $P = 0.52$?   d. $P = 0.48$?
b. $P = 0.58$?   e. $P = 0.43$?
c. $P = 0.53$?

Application Exercises

9.39 A company that receives shipments of batteries tests a random sample of nine of them before agreeing to take a shipment. The company is concerned that the true mean lifetime for all batteries in the shipment should be at least 50 hours. From past experience it is safe to conclude that the population distribution of lifetimes is normal with a standard deviation of 3 hours. For one particular shipment the mean lifetime for a sample of nine batteries was 48.2 hours.

  a. Test at the 10% level the null hypothesis that the population mean lifetime is at least 50 hours.
  b. Find the power of a 10%-level test when the true mean lifetime of batteries is 49 hours.

9.40 A pharmaceutical manufacturer is concerned that the impurity concentration in pills does not exceed 3%. It is known that from a particular production run impurity concentrations follow a normal distribution with standard deviation 0.4%. A random sample of 64 pills from a production run was checked, and the sample mean impurity concentration was found to be 3.07%.

  a. Test at the 5% level the null hypothesis that the population mean impurity concentration is 3% against the alternative that it is more than 3%.
  b. Find the probability of a 5%-level test rejecting the null hypothesis when the true mean impurity concentration is 3.10%.

9.41 A random sample of 1,562 undergraduates enrolled in management ethics courses was asked to respond on a scale from 1 (strongly disagree) to 7 (strongly agree) to this proposition: "Senior corporate executives are interested in social justice." The sample mean response was 4.27, and the sample standard deviation was 1.32.

  a. Test at the 1% level against a two-sided alternative the null hypothesis that the population mean is 4.
  b. Find the probability of a 1%-level test accepting the null hypothesis when the true mean response is 3.95.

9.42 A random sample of 802 supermarket shoppers had 378 shoppers that preferred generic brand items. Test at the 10% level the null hypothesis that at least one-half of all shoppers preferred generic brand items against the alternative that the population proportion is less than one-half. Find the power of a 10%-level test if, in fact, 45% of the supermarket shoppers preferred generic brands.

9.43 In a random sample of 998 adults in the United States, 17.3% of the sample members indicated some measure of disagreement with this statement: "Globalization is more than an economic trade system—instead it includes institutions and culture."

  a. Test at the 5% level the null hypothesis that at least 25% of all U.S. adults would disagree with this statement.
  b. Find the probability of rejecting the null hypothesis with a 5%-level test if, in fact, 20% of all U.S. adults would disagree with the statement.

9.44 Of a random sample of 199 auditors, 104 indicated some measure of agreement with this statement: "Cash flow is an important indication of profitability."

  a. Test at the 10% significance level against a two-sided alternative the null hypothesis that one-half of the members of this population would agree with this statement. Also find and interpret the p-value of this test.
  b. Find the probability of accepting the null hypothesis with a 10%-level test if, in fact, 60% of all auditors agree that cash flow is an important indicator of profitability.

9.45 A fast-food chain tests each day that the average weight of its "two-pounders" is at least 32 ounces. The alternative hypothesis is that the average weight is less than 32 ounces, indicating that new processing procedures are needed. The weights of two-pounders can be assumed to be normally distributed, with a standard deviation of 3 ounces. The decision rule adopted is to reject the null hypothesis if the sample mean weight is less than 30.8 ounces.

  a. If random samples of $n = 36$ two-pounders are selected, what is the probability of a Type I error, using this decision rule?
  b. If random samples of $n = 9$ two-pounders are selected, what is the probability of a Type I error, using this decision rule? Explain why your answer differs from that in part (a).
  c. Suppose that the true mean weight is 31 ounces. If random samples of 36 two-pounders are selected, what is the probability of a Type II error, using this decision rule?

9.46 A wine producer claims that the proportion of its customers who cannot distinguish its product from frozen grape juice is, at most, 0.09. The producer decides to test this null hypothesis against the alternative that the true proportion is more than 0.09. The decision rule adopted is to reject the null hypothesis if the sample proportion of people who cannot distinguish between these two flavors exceeds 0.14.

  a. If a random sample of 100 customers is chosen, what is the probability of a Type I error, using this decision rule?
  b. If a random sample of 400 customers is selected, what is the probability of a Type I error, using this

decision rule? Explain, in words and graphically, why your answer differs from that in part (a).

c. Suppose that the true proportion of customers who cannot distinguish between these flavors is 0.20. If a random sample of 100 customers is selected, what is the probability of a Type II error?

d. Suppose that, instead of the given decision rule, it is decided to reject the null hypothesis if the sample proportion of customers who cannot distinguish between the two flavors exceeds 0.16. A random sample of 100 customers is selected.

  i. Without doing the calculations, state whether the probability of a Type I error will be higher than, lower than, or the same as in part (a).

  ii. If the true proportion is 0.20, will the probability of a Type II error be higher than, lower than, or the same as in part (c)?

9.6 TESTS OF THE VARIANCE OF A NORMAL DISTRIBUTION

In addition to the need for tests based on the sample mean, there are a number of situations where we want to determine if the population variance is a particular value or set of values. In modern quality control work this need is particularly important because a process that, for example, has an excessively large variance can produce many defective items. Here, we will develop procedures for testing the population variance, σ^2, based on the sample variance, s^2, computed using a random sample of n observations from a normally distributed population. If the null hypothesis is that the population variance is equal to some specified value, that is,

$$H_0 : \sigma^2 = \sigma_0^2$$

then when this hypothesis is true, the random variable

$$\chi_{n-1}^2 = \frac{(n-1)s^2}{\sigma^2}$$

has a chi-square distribution with $(n-1)$ degrees of freedom. Hypothesis tests are based on computed values of this statistic. If the alternative hypothesis is that the population variance is larger than, we would be suspicious of the null hypothesis if the sample variance greatly exceeded. A high computed value of χ_{n-1}^2 would result in the rejection of the null hypothesis. Conversely, an alternative hypothesis that the population variance is less than would be accepted and the null hypothesis rejected if the value of χ_{n-1}^2 was small. For a two-sided alternative that the population variance differs from, we would reject the null hypothesis if the value was either unusually high or unusually low. The chi-square distribution tests are more sensitive to the assumption of normality in the underlying distribution compared to the standard normal distribution tests. Thus, if the underlying population deviates considerably from the normal, the significance levels computed using the chi-square distribution may deviate from the correct significance levels based on the exact distribution.

The rationale for the development of appropriate tests uses the chi-square distribution notation developed in Section 7.5. We denote $\chi_{v,\alpha}^2$ as the number that is exceeded with probability α by a chi-square random variable with v degrees of freedom. That is,

$$P(\chi_v^2 > \chi_{v,\alpha}^2) = \alpha$$

or

$$P(\chi_v^2 < \chi_{v,1-\alpha}^2) = \alpha$$

and for two-tailed tests

$$P(\chi_v^2 > \chi_{v,\alpha/2}^2 \quad \text{or} \quad \chi_v^2 < \chi_{v,1-\alpha/2}^2) = \alpha$$

These probabilities are shown in Figure 7.15. The various procedures for **tests of the variance of a normal population** are summarized in Equations 9.13, 9.14, and 9.15.

It is also possible to determine p-values for the chi-square test for variances. From the general result just stated, the p-value for the chi-square test is the probability of getting a value at least as extreme as the one obtained, given the null hypothesis.

Tests of Variance of a Normal Population

We are given a random sample of n observations from a normally distributed population with variance σ^2. If we observe the sample variance s^2, then the following tests have significance level α.

1. To test either null hypothesis

$$H_0 : \sigma^2 = \sigma_0^2 \quad \text{or} \quad H_0 : \sigma^2 \leq \sigma_0^2$$

against the alternative

$$H_1 : \sigma^2 > \sigma_0^2$$

the decision rule is as follows:

$$\text{Reject } H_0 \text{ if } \quad \frac{(n-1)s^2}{\sigma_0^2} > \chi_{n-1,\alpha}^2 \tag{9.13}$$

2. To test either null hypothesis

$$H_0 : \sigma^2 = \sigma_0^2 \quad \text{or} \quad H_0 : \sigma^2 \geq \sigma_0^2$$

against the alternative

$$H_1 : \sigma^2 < \sigma_0^2$$

the decision rule is as follows:

$$\text{Reject } H_0 \text{ if } \quad \frac{(n-1)s^2}{\sigma_0^2} < \chi_{n-1,1-\alpha}^2 \tag{9.14}$$

3. To test the null hypothesis

$$H_0 : \sigma^2 = \sigma_0^2$$

against the two-sided alternative

$$H_1 : \sigma^2 \neq \sigma_0^2$$

the decision rule is

$$\text{Reject } H_0 \text{ if } \frac{(n-1)s^2}{\sigma_0^2} > \chi_{n-1,\alpha/2}^2 \quad \text{or} \quad \frac{(n-1)s^2}{\sigma_0^2} < \chi_{n-1,1-\alpha/2}^2 \tag{9.15}$$

where χ_{n-1}^2 is a chi-square random variable and $P(\chi_{n-1}^2 > \chi_{n-1,\alpha}^2) = \alpha$.

The p-value for these tests is the probability of getting a value at least as extreme as the one obtained, given the null hypothesis.

Example 9.7 Variance of Chemical Impurities (Hypothesis Tests of Population Variances)

The quality control manager of Stonehead Chemicals has asked you to determine if the variance of impurities in its shipments of fertilizer is within the established standard. This standard states that for 100-pound bags of fertilizer, the variance in the pounds of impurities cannot exceed 4.

Solution A random sample of 20 bags is obtained, and the pounds of impurities are measured for each bag. The sample variance is computed to be 6.62. In this problem we are testing the null hypothesis

$$H_0 : \sigma^2 \leq \sigma_0^2 = 4$$

against the alternative

$$H_1 : \sigma^2 > 4$$

Based on the assumption that the population has a normal distribution, the decision rule for a test of significance level α, is to reject H_0 in favor of H_1 if

$$\frac{(n-1)s^2}{\sigma_0^2} > \chi^2_{n-1,\alpha}$$

For this test, with $\alpha = 0.05$ and 19 degrees of freedom, the critical value of the chi-square variable is 30.14, from Table 7 in the appendix. Then, using the test data, we find the following:

$$\frac{(n-1)s^2}{\sigma_0^2} = \frac{(20-1)(6.62)}{4} = 31.45 > \chi^2_{n-1,\alpha} = 30.14$$

Therefore, we reject the null hypothesis and conclude that the variability of the impurities exceeds the standard. As a result, we recommend that the production process should be studied and improvements made to reduce the variability of the product components.

The p-value for this test is the probability of obtaining a chi-square statistic with 19 degrees of freedom that is greater than the observed 31.45:

$$p\text{-value} = P\left(\frac{(19)s_x^2}{\sigma_0^2} > \chi^2_{19} = 31.45 \right) = 0.036$$

The p-value of 0.036 was computed using the Minitab probability distribution function for the chi-square distribution.

EXERCISES

Basic Exercise

9.47 Test the hypotheses

$$H_0 : \sigma^2 \leq 100$$

$$H_1 : \sigma^2 > 100$$

using the following results from the following random samples:

a. $s^2 = 165; n = 25$
b. $s^2 = 165; n = 29$
c. $s^2 = 159; n = 25$
d. $s^2 = 67; n = 38$

Application Exercises

9.48 At the insistence of a government inspector, a new safety device is installed in an assembly-line operation. After the installation of this device a random sample of 8 days' output gave the following results for numbers of finished components produced:

618 660 638 625 571 598 639 582

Management is concerned about the variability of daily output and views any variance above 500 as undesirable. Test at the 10% significance level the null hypothesis that the population variance for daily output does not exceed 500.

9.49 Plastic sheets produced by a machine are periodically monitored for possible fluctuations in thickness. If the true variance in thicknesses exceeds 2.25 square millimeters, there is cause for concern about product quality. Thickness measurements for a random sample of 10 sheets produced in a particular shift were taken, giving the following results (in millimeters):

226 226 232 227 225 228 225 228 229 230

a. Find the sample variance.
b. Test at the 5% significance level the null hypothesis that the population variance is at most 2.25.

9.50 One way to evaluate the effectiveness of a teaching assistant is to examine the scores achieved by his students on an examination at the end of the course. Obviously, the mean score is of interest. However, the variance also contains useful information—some teachers have a style that works very well with more able students but is unsuccessful with less able or poorly motivated students. A professor sets a standard examination at the end of each semester for all sections of a course. The variance of the scores on this test is typically very close to 300. A new teaching assistant has a class of 30 students whose test scores had a variance of 480. Regarding these students' test scores as a random sample from a normal population, test against a two-sided alternative the null hypothesis that the population variance of their scores is 300.

9.51 A company produces electric devices operated by a thermostatic control. The standard deviation of the temperature at which these controls actually operate should not exceed 2.0 degrees Fahrenheit. For a random sample of 20 of these controls the sample standard deviation of operating temperatures was 2.36 degrees Fahrenheit. Stating any assumptions you need to make, test at the 5% level the null hypothesis that the population standard deviation is 2.0 against the alternative that it is bigger.

9.52 An instructor has decided to introduce a greater component of independent study into an intermediate microeconomics course as a way of motivating students to work independently and think more carefully about the course material. A colleague cautions that a possible consequence may be increased variability in student performance. However, the instructor responds that he would expect less variability. From his records he found that in the past, student scores on the final exam for this course followed a normal distribution with standard deviation 18.2 points. For a class of 25 students using the new approach, the standard deviation of scores on the final exam was 15.3 points. Assuming that these 25 students can be viewed as a random sample of all those who might be subjected to the new approach, test the null hypothesis that the population standard deviation is at least 18.2 points against the alternative that it is lower.

KEY WORDS

- alternative hypothesis, 354
- counterfactual argument, 359
- critical value, 360
- null hypothesis, 354
- power, 357
- power function, 379
- probability of Type II error, 378
- p-value, 362

- significance level, 356
- simple hypothesis, 354
- tests of the mean of a normal distribution (population variance known), 359
- tests of the mean of a normal distribution (population variance unknown), 371

- tests of a population proportion (large sample sizes), 375
- tests of the variance of a normal population, 385
- Type I error, 356
- Type II error, 356

CHAPTER EXERCISES AND APPLICATIONS

9.53 Explain carefully the distinction between each of the following pairs of terms:

a. Null and alternative hypotheses
b. Simple and composite hypotheses
c. One-sided and two-sided alternatives

d. Type I and Type II errors
e. Significance level and power

9.54 Carefully explain what is meant by the p-value of a test, and discuss the use of this concept in hypothesis testing.

9.55 A random sample of 10 students contains the following observations, in hours, for time spent studying in the week before final exams:

28 57 42 35 61 39 55 46 49 38

Assume that the population distribution is normal.

a. Find the sample mean and standard deviation.
b. Test at the 5% significance level the null hypothesis that the population mean is 40 hours against the alternative that it is higher.

9.56 State whether each of the following is true or false.

a. The significance level of a test is the probability that the null hypothesis is false.
b. A Type I error occurs when a true null hypothesis is rejected.
c. A null hypothesis is rejected at the 0.025 level, but is not rejected at the 0.01 level. This means that the p-value of the test is between 0.01 and 0.025
d. The power of a test is the probability of accepting a null hypothesis that is true.
e. If a null hypothesis is rejected against an alternative at the 5% level, then using the same data, it must be rejected against that alternative at the 1% level.
f. If a null hypothesis is rejected against an alternative at the 1% level, then using the same data, it must be rejected against the alternative at the 5% level.
g. The p-value of a test is the probability that the null hypothesis is true.

9.57 An insurance company employs agents on a commission basis. It claims that in their first year agents will earn a mean commission of at least $40,000 and that the population standard deviation is no more than $6,000. A random sample of nine agents found for commission in the first year,

$$\sum_{i=1}^{9} x_i = 333 \quad \text{and} \quad \sum_{i=1}^{9} (x_i - \bar{x})^2 = 312$$

where x_i is measured in thousands of dollars and the population distribution can be assumed to be normal. Test at the 5% level the null hypothesis that the population mean is at least $40,000.

9.58 Supporters claim that a new windmill can generate an average of at least 800 kilowatts of power per day. Daily power generation for the windmill is assumed to be normally distributed with a standard deviation of 120 kilowatts. A random sample of 100 days is taken to test this claim against the alternative hypothesis that the true mean is less than 800 kilowatts. The claim will not be rejected if the sample mean is 776 kilowatts or more and rejected otherwise.

a. What is the probability α of a Type I error using the decision rule if the population mean is, in fact, 800 kilowatts per day?

b. What is the probability β of a Type II error using this decision rule if the population mean is, in fact, 740 kilowatts per day?
c. Suppose that the same decision rule is used, but with a sample of 200 days rather than 100 days.
   i. Would the value of α be larger than, smaller than, or the same as that found in part (a)?
   ii. Would the value of β be larger than, smaller than, or the same as that found in part (b)?
d. Suppose that a sample of 100 observations was taken, but that the decision rule was changed so that the claim would not be rejected if the sample mean was at least 765 kilowatts.
   i. Would the value of α be larger than, smaller than, or the same as that found in part (a)?
   ii. Would the value of β be larger than, smaller than, or the same as that found in part (b)?

9.59 In a random sample of 545 accountants engaged in preparing county operating budgets for use in planning and control, 117 indicated that estimates of cash flow were the most difficult element of the budget to derive.

a. Test at the 5% level the null hypothesis that at least 25% of all accountants find cash flow estimates the most difficult estimates to derive.
b. Based on the procedure used in part (a), what is the probability that the null hypothesis would be rejected if the true percentage of those finding cash flow estimates most difficult was
   i. 20%?
   ii. 25%?
   iii. 30%?

9.60 A random sample of 104 marketing vice presidents from large Fortune 500 corporations was questioned on future developments in the business environment. Of those sample members, 50 indicated some measurement of agreement with this statement: "Firms will concentrate their efforts more on cash flow than on profits." What is the lowest level of significance at which the null hypothesis, which states that the true proportion of all such executives who would agree with this statement is one-half, can be rejected against a two-sided alternative?

9.61 In a random sample of 99 National Basketball Association games the home team won 57 games. Test the null hypothesis that the home team wins one-half of all games against the alternative that the home team wins a majority of games.

9.62 In a random sample of 150 business graduates 50 agreed or strongly agreed that businesses should focus their efforts on innovative e-commerce strategies. Test at the 5% level the null hypothesis that at most 25% of all business graduates would be in agreement with this assertion.

9.63 Of a random sample of 142 admissions counselors on college campuses 39 indicated that, on average, they spent 15 minutes or less studying each résumé. Test the null hypothesis that at most 20% of all admissions counselors spend this little time studying résumés.

9.64 Northeastern Franchisers Ltd. has a number of clients that use their process for producing exotic Norwegian dinners for customers throughout New England. The operating cost for the franchised process has a fixed cost of $1,000 per week plus $5 for every unit produced. Recently, a number of restaurant owners using the process has complained that the cost model is no longer valid and, in fact, the weekly costs are higher. Your job is to determine if there is strong evidence to support the owners' claim. To do so, you obtain a random sample of $n = 25$ restaurants and determine their costs. You also find that the number of units produced in each restaurant is normally distributed with a mean of $\mu = 400$ and a variance of $\sigma^2 = 625$. The random sample mean ($n = 25$) for weekly costs was $3,050. Prepare and implement an analysis to determine if there is strong evidence to conclude that costs are greater than those predicted by the cost model.

9.65 Prairie Flower Cereal Inc. has asked you to study the variability of the weights of cereal bags produced in plant 2, located in rural Malaysia. The package weights are known to be normally distributed. Using a random sample of $n = 71$, you find that the sample mean weight is 40 and the sample variance is 50.

The marketing vice president claims that there is a very small probability that the population mean weight is less than 39. Use an appropriate statistical analysis and comment on his claim.

9.66 ⬤ Two financial analysts were asked to predict earnings per share for a random sample of 12 corporations over the coming year. The quality of their forecasts was evaluated in terms of absolute percentage forecast error, defined as the following:

$$100 \cdot \frac{\left| \text{Actual} - \text{Predicted} \right|}{\text{Actual}}$$

The absolute percentage forecast errors made are shown in the data file **Analyst Prediction**. Stating any assumptions you make, test against a two-sided alternative the null hypothesis that the population mean absolute percentage forecast errors are the same for these two financial analysts.

9.67 ⬤ BBW Ltd. does quality control work on the final loaves of bread produced. The data file named **BBWltd**, which is stored on your data disk or local computer system, contains data collected as part of its analysis of the market. The variables in the file are

1. "Dbread," which contains a random sample of weights, in grams, of their dark bread collected from supermarket shelves.

2. "Sbread," which contains a random sample of weights, in grams, of their specialty bread collected from supermarket shelves.

3. "Csbread," which contains a random sample of weights, in grams, of their competitor's specialty bread collected from supermarket shelves.

The company guarantees that its dark bread will have a weight of 100 grams or more. Based on the sample, does the company have strong evidence, $\alpha = 0.05$, that the guarantee is being met? Provide an appropriate hypothesis test result as evidence.

9.68 ⬤ Big River Inc., a major Alaskan fish processor, is attempting to determine the weight of salmon in the Northwest Green River. A random sample of salmon was obtained and weighed. The data are stored in the file labeled **Bigfish**. Use a classical hypothesis test to determine if there is strong evidence to conclude that the population mean weight for the fish is greater than 40. Use a probability of Type I error equal to 0.05

Prepare a power curve for the test. *Hint*: Determine the population mean values for $\beta = 0.50$, $\beta = 0.25$, $\beta = 0.10$, and $\beta = 0.05$, and plot those means versus the power of the test.

9.69 A process produces cable for the local telephone company. When the process is operating correctly, cable diameter follows a normal distribution with mean 1.6 inches and standard deviation 0.05 inch. A random sample of 16 pieces of cable found diameters with a sample mean of 1.615 inches and a sample standard deviation of 0.086 inch.

a. Assuming that the population standard deviation is 0.05 inch, test at the 10% level against a two-sided alternative the null hypothesis that the population mean is 1.6 inches. Find also the lowest level of significance at which this null hypothesis can be rejected against the two-sided alternative.

b. Test at the 10% level the null hypothesis that the population standard deviation is 0.05 inch against the alternative that it is bigger.

9.70 When operating normally, a manufacturing process produces tablets for which the mean weight of the active ingredient is 5 grams, and the standard deviation is 0.025 gram. For a random sample of 12 tablets the following weights of active ingredient (in grams) were found as follows:

5.01 4.69 5.03 4.98 4.98 4.95
5.00 5.00 5.03 5.01 5.04 4.95

a. Without assuming that the population variance is known, test the null hypothesis that the population mean weight of active ingredient per tablet is 5 grams. Use a two-sided alternative and a 5% significance level. State any assumptions that you make.

b. Stating any assumptions that you make, test the null hypothesis that the population standard deviation is 0.025 gram against the alternative hypothesis that the population standard deviation exceeds 0.025 gram. Use a 5% significance level.

9.71 An insurance company employs agents on a commission basis. It claims that, in their first year, agents will earn a mean commission of at least $40,000 and that the population standard deviation is no more than $6,000. A random sample of nine agents found for commission in the first year,

$$\sum_{i=1}^{9} x_i = 333 \qquad \text{and} \qquad \sum_{i=1}^{9} (x_i - \bar{x})^2 = 312$$

measured in thousands of dollars. The population distribution can be assumed to be normal. Test at the 10% level the null hypothesis that the population standard deviation is at most $6,000.

Appendix

GUIDELINES FOR CHOOSING THE APPROPRIATE DECISION RULE

Figure 9.10
Guidelines for Choosing the Appropriate Decision Rule for a Population Mean

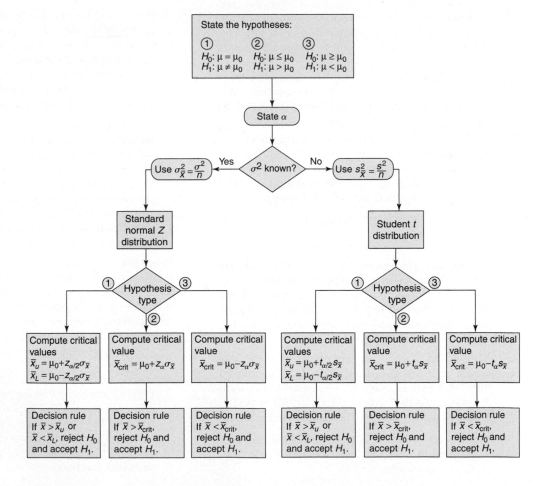

Figure 9.11
Guidelines for
Choosing the
Appropriate
Decision Rule for
a Population
Proportion

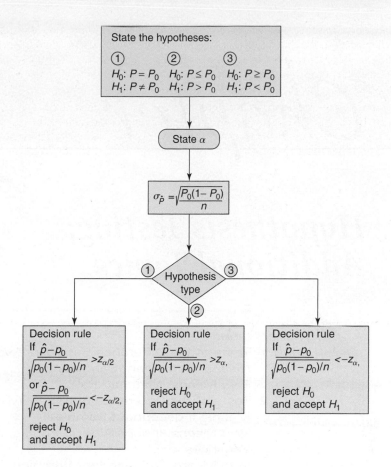

Chapter 10

Hypothesis Testing: Additional Topics

Introduction

In this chapter we develop procedures for testing the differences between two population means, proportions, and variances. This form of inference compares and complements the estimation procedures developed in Chapter 8. Our discussion in this chapter follows the development in Chapter 9, and we assume that the reader is familiar with the hypothesis testing procedure developed in Section 9.1. The process for comparing two populations begins with an investigator forming a hypothesis about the nature of the two populations and the difference between their means or proportions. The hypothesis is stated clearly as involving two options concerning the difference, and then a decision is made based on the results of a statistic computed from random samples of data from the two populations. Hypothesis tests involving variances are also becoming more important as business firms work to reduce process variability in order to ensure high quality for every unit produced. Following are two examples of typical problems:

1. An instructor is interested in determining if assigning case studies increases students' test scores in her course. She could assign cases in one section and not in the other. Then, by collecting data from each class, she could determine if there is strong evidence that the use of case studies increases exam scores.

   Suppose that the instructor conjectures that completing assigned cases does not increase overall examination scores. Let μ_1 denote the mean final examination score in the class that used case studies, and let μ_2 denote the mean final examination score in the class that did not use case studies. The **null hypothesis** is the composite hypothesis

   $$H_0 : \mu_1 - \mu_2 \leq 0$$

   The alternative topic of interest is that the use of cases actually increases the average examination score, and, thus, the **alternative hypothesis** is as follows:

   $$H_1 : \mu_1 - \mu_2 > 0$$

   In this problem the instructor would decide to assign cases only if there is strong evidence that using cases increases the mean examination score. Strong evidence results from rejecting H_0 and accepting H_1.

2. A news reporter wants to know if a tax reform appeals equally to men and women. To test this, she obtains the opinions of randomly selected men and women. These data are used to provide an answer. The reporter might hold, as a working hypothesis, that a new tax proposal is equally appealing to men and women. Using P_1, the proportion of men favoring the proposal, minus P_2, the proportion of women favoring the proposal, the null hypothesis is as follows:

   $$H_0 : P_1 - P_2 = 0$$

   If the reporter has no good reason to suspect that the bulk of support comes from either men or women, then the null hypothesis would be tested against the two-sided composite alternative hypothesis:

   $$H_1 : P_1 - P_2 \neq 0$$

   In this example rejection of H_0 would provide strong evidence that there is a difference between men and women in their response to the tax proposal.

Once we have specified the null and alternative hypotheses and collected sample data, a decision concerning the null hypothesis must be made. We can either reject the null hypothesis and accept the alternative hypothesis, or fail to reject the null hypothesis. When we fail to reject the null hypothesis, then either the null hypothesis is true or our test procedure was not strong enough to reject it and an error has been committed. To reject the null hypothesis a decision rule based on sample evidence needs to be developed. Further on in this chapter we will present specific decision rules for various problems.

10.1 Tests of the Difference between Two Normal Population Means: Dependent Samples

There are a number of applications where we wish to draw conclusions about the differences between population means instead of conclusions about the absolute levels of the means. For example, we might want to compare the output of two different production processes for which neither population mean is known. Similarly, we might want to know if one marketing strategy results in higher sales than another without knowing the population mean sales for either. These questions can be handled effectively by various different hypothesis-testing procedures.

As we saw in Section 8.1, several different assumptions can be made when confidence intervals are computed for the differences between two population means. These assumptions generally lead to specific methods for computing the population variance for the difference between sample means. There are parallel hypothesis tests that involve similar methods for obtaining the variance. We organize our discussion of the various hypothesis-testing procedures in parallel with the confidence interval estimates in Section 8.1. In Section 10.1 we will treat situations where the two samples can be assumed to be dependent. In these cases the best design, if we have control over data collection, is using two matched pairs as shown below. Then in Section 10.2 we will treat a variety of situations where the samples are independent.

Two Means, Matched Pairs

Here, we assume that a random sample of n matched pairs of observations is obtained from populations with means μ_x and μ_y. The observations will be denoted $(x_1, y_1), (x_2, y_2), ..., (x_n, y_n)$. When we have matched pairs and the pairs are positively correlated, the variance of the difference between the sample means

$$\bar{d} = \bar{x} - \bar{y}$$

will be reduced compared to using independent samples. This results because some of the characteristics of the pairs are similar, and, thus, that portion of the variability is removed from the total variability of the differences between the means. For example, when we consider measures of human behavior, differences between twins will usually be less than the differences between two randomly selected people. In general, the dimensions for two parts produced on the same specific machine will be closer than the dimensions for parts produced on two different randomly selected machines. Thus, whenever possible, we would prefer to use matched pairs of observations when comparing two populations because the variance of the difference will be smaller. With a smaller variance there is a greater probability that we will reject H_0 when the null hypothesis is not true. This principle was developed in Section 9.5 in the discussion of the power of a test. The specific decision rules for different forms of the hypothesis test are summarized in Equations 10.1, 10.2, and 10.3.

Tests of the Difference Between Population Means: Matched Pairs

Suppose that we have a random sample of n matched pairs of observations from distributions with means μ_x and μ_y. Let $\overline{d}$ and s_d denote the observed sample mean and standard deviation for the n differences $(x_i - y_i)$. If the population distribution of the differences is a normal distribution, then the following tests have significance level α:

1. To test either null hypothesis

$$H_0 : \mu_x - \mu_y = D_0 \quad \text{or} \quad H_0 : \mu_x - \mu_y \leq D_0$$

against the alternative

$$H_1 : \mu_x - \mu_y > D_0$$

the decision rule is as follows:

$$\text{Reject } H_0 \text{ if } \quad \frac{\overline{d} - D_0}{s_d / \sqrt{n}} > t_{n-1, \alpha} \tag{10.1}$$

2. To test either null hypothesis

$$H_0 : \mu_x - \mu_y = D_0 \quad \text{or} \quad H_0 : \mu_x - \mu_y \geq D_0$$

against the alternative

$$H_1 : \mu_x - \mu_y < D_0$$

the decision rule is as follows:

$$\text{Reject } H_0 \text{ if } \quad \frac{\overline{d} - D_0}{s_d / \sqrt{n}} < -t_{n-1, \alpha} \tag{10.2}$$

3. To test the null hypothesis

$$H_0 : \mu_x - \mu_y = D_0$$

against the two-sided alternative

$$H_1 : \mu_x - \mu_y \neq D_0$$

the decision rule is as follows:

$$\text{Reject } H_0 \text{ if } \quad \frac{\overline{d} - D_0}{s_d / \sqrt{n}} < -t_{n-1, \alpha/2} \quad \text{or} \quad \frac{\overline{d} - D_0}{s_d / \sqrt{n}} > t_{n-1, \alpha/2} \tag{10.3}$$

Here, $t_{n-1, \alpha}$ is the number for which

$$P(t_{n-1} > t_{n-1, \alpha}) = \alpha$$

where the random variable t_{n-1} follows a Student's t distribution with $(n - 1)$ degrees of freedom.

When we want to test the null hypothesis that the two population means are equal, we set $D_0 = 0$ in the formulas.

p-values for all of these tests are interpreted as the probability of getting a value at least as extreme as the one obtained, given the null hypothesis.

Example 10.1 Brain Activity and Recall of TV Advertising

Researchers conducted a study to estimate the relationship between a subject's brain activity while watching a television commercial and the subject's subsequent ability to recall the contents of the commercial. Subjects were shown two commercials for each of 10 products. For each commercial the ability to recall the commercial 24 hours later was measured. Each member of a pair of commercials viewed by a specific subject was then designated "high-recall" or "low-recall." Table 10.1 shows an index of the total amount of brain activity from the random sample of subjects while they were watching these commercials. Researchers wanted to know if brain wave activity was higher for high-recall ads compared to low-recall ads.

Solution Denote μ_x the population mean for high-recall commercials and μ_y the population mean for low-recall commercials. Then the differences d_i ($i = 1,..., 10$) are a random sample of 10 observations from a population with the mean of ($\mu_x - \mu_y$). Using these assumptions, we can define the null hypothesis as no difference in brain activity levels,

$$H_0 : \mu_x - \mu_y = 0$$

against the alternative that, on average, brain activity is greater for the high-recall commercials—that is,

$$H_1 : \mu_x - \mu_y > 0$$

In this test we compute the sample standard deviation of the differences, and, thus, we will use the Student's t distribution for the test.

The pattern of paired data is illustrated in Table 10.1 and contained in the data file **Response to Commercials**. Each subject was given a high-recall and a low-recall ad, and these are paired by observation number. The Minitab output for this problem is shown in Figure 10.1. The test is based on the following statistic:

$$t = \frac{\bar{d} - D_0}{s_d / \sqrt{n}} = \frac{23}{33.0 / \sqrt{10}} = 2.21$$

Table 10.1 Brain Activities of Subjects Watching 10 Pairs of Television Commercials

PRODUCT OBSERVATION	HIGH-RECALL X	LOW-RECALL Y
1	141	55
2	139	116
3	87	83
4	129	88
5	51	36
6	50	68
7	118	91
8	161	115
9	61	90
10	148	113

Paired T-Test and CI: X, Y

```
Paired T for X - Y

              N      Mean     St Dev    SE Mean
X            10    108.500    42.506     13.441
Y            10     85.500    26.471      8.371
Difference   10     23.0000   32.9848    10.4307

95% lower bound for mean difference: 3.8793
T-Test of mean difference = 0 (vs > 0): T-Value = 2.21  P-Value = 0.027
```

We found the value $t_{9, 0.05} = 1.833$ in Table 8 of the appendix. Since 2.21 exceeds this value, we reject the null hypothesis and accept the alternative hypothesis. Thus, we conclude that there is substantial evidence to conclude that brain activity is higher for the high-recall compared to the low-recall group. We note that the p-value for this test is 0.027, as shown in the Minitab output.

Finally, we note that missing data are a problem that often occurs in applied statistical work. For example, suppose that the brain wave measurement was lost for one of the two ads for a particular subject. Standard procedure would argue that the entire observation should be removed and the analysis carried out with nine paired observations.

EXERCISES

Basic Exercises

10.1 You have been asked to determine if two different production processes have different mean numbers of units produced per hour. Process 1 has a mean defined as μ_1 and process 2 has a mean defined as μ_2. The null and alternative hypotheses are as follows:

$$H_0 : \mu_1 - \mu_2 = 0$$
$$H_1 : \mu_1 - \mu_2 > 0$$

Using a random sample of 25 paired observations, the sample means are 50 and 60 for populations 1 and 2. Can you reject the null hypothesis using a probability of Type I error $\alpha = 0.05$ if

a. the sample standard deviation of the difference is 20?

b. the sample standard deviation of the difference is 30?

c. the sample standard deviation of the difference is 15?

d. the sample standard deviation of the difference is 40?

10.2 You have been asked to determine if two different production processes have different mean numbers of units produced per hour. Process 1 has a mean defined as μ_1 and process 2 has a mean

defined as μ_2. The null and alternative hypotheses are as follows:

$$H_0 : \mu_1 - \mu_2 \geq 0$$
$$H_1 : \mu_1 - \mu_2 < 0$$

Using a random sample of 25 paired observations, the sample means are 56 and 50 for populations 1 and 2. Can you reject the null hypothesis using a probability of Type I error $\alpha = 0.05$ if

a. the sample standard deviation of the difference is 20?

b. the sample standard deviation of the difference is 30?

c. the sample standard deviation of the difference is 15?

d. the sample standard deviation of the difference is 40?

Application Exercises

10.3 In a study comparing banks in Germany and Great Britain, a sample of 145 matched pairs of banks was formed. Each pair contained one bank from Germany and one from Great Britain. The pairings were made in such a way that the two members were as similar as possible in regard to such factors as size and age. The ratio of total loans outstanding to total assets was calculated for each of the banks. For this ratio, the sample mean difference (German – Great Britain) was 0.0518, and the sample standard deviation of the differences was 0.3055. Test against a two-sided alternative the null hypothesis that the two population means are equal.

10.4   ● A college placement office wants to determine whether male and female economics graduates receive, on average, different salary offers for their first position after graduation. The placement officer randomly selected eight pairs of business graduates in such a way that the qualifications, interests, and backgrounds of the members of any pair were as similar as possible. The data file **Salary Pair** contains the highest salary offer received by each sample member at the end of the recruiting round. Assuming that the distributions

are normal, test the null hypothesis that the population means are equal against the alternative that the true mean for males is higher than for females.

10.5   ● An agency offers students preparation courses for a graduate school admissions test. As part of an experiment to evaluate the merits of the course, 12 students were chosen and divided into six pairs in such a way that the members of any pair had similar academic records. Before taking the test, one member of each pair was assigned at random to take the preparation course, while the other member did not take a course. The achievement test scores are contained in the **Student Pair** data file. Assuming that the differences in scores follow a normal distribution, test at the 5% level the null hypothesis that the two population means are equal against the alternative that the true mean is higher for students taking the preparation course.

10.2 TESTS OF THE DIFFERENCE BETWEEN TWO NORMAL POPULATION MEANS: INDEPENDENT SAMPLES

Two Means, Independent Samples, Known Population Variances

Now we will consider the case where we have independent random samples from two normally distributed populations. The first population has a mean of μ_x and a variance of σ_x^2, and we obtain a random sample of size n_x. The second population has a mean of μ_y and a variance of σ_y^2, and a random sample of size n_y is obtained.

In Section 8.1, we showed that if the sample means are denoted by $\bar{x}$ and $\bar{y}$, then the random variable

$$Z = \frac{(\bar{x} - \bar{y}) - (\mu_x - \mu_y)}{\sqrt{\dfrac{\sigma_x^2}{n_x} + \dfrac{\sigma_y^2}{n_y}}}$$

has a standard normal distribution. If the two population variances are known, tests of the difference between the population means can be based on this result, using the same arguments as before. Generally, we are comfortable using known population variances if the process being studied has been stable over some time and we have obtained similar variance measurements over this time. And because of the central limit theorem, the results presented here hold for large sample sizes even if the populations are not normal. For large sample sizes the approximation is quite satisfactory when sample variances are used for population variances. Of course, we can also perform a hypothesis test of the variance, as shown in Section 9.6. This allows the derivation of tests of wide applicability, as summarized in Equations 10.4, 10.5, and 10.6.

Tests of the Difference Between Population Means: Independent Samples (Known Variances)

Suppose that we have independent random samples of n_x and n_y observations from normal distributions with means μ_x and μ_y and variances σ_x^2 and σ_y^2, respectively. If the observed sample means are $\bar{x}$ and $\bar{y}$, then the following tests have significance level α:

1. To test either null hypothesis

$$H_0 : \mu_x - \mu_y = D_0 \quad \text{or} \quad H_0 : \mu_x - \mu_y \leq D_0$$

against the alternative

$$H_1 : \mu_x - \mu_y > D_0$$

the decision rule is as follows:

$$\text{Reject } H_0 \text{ if } \quad \frac{\bar{x} - \bar{y} - D_0}{\sqrt{\dfrac{\sigma_x^2}{n_x} + \dfrac{\sigma_y^2}{n_y}}} > z_\alpha \tag{10.4}$$

2. To test either null hypothesis

$$H_0 : \mu_x - \mu_y = D_0 \quad \text{or} \quad H_0 : \mu_x - \mu_y \geq D_0$$

against the alternative

$$H_1 : \mu_x - \mu_y < D_0$$

the decision rule is as follows:

$$\text{Reject } H_0 \text{ if } \quad \frac{\bar{x} - \bar{y} - D_0}{\sqrt{\dfrac{\sigma_x^2}{n_x} + \dfrac{\sigma_y^2}{n_y}}} < -z_\alpha \tag{10.5}$$

3. To test the null hypothesis

$$H_0 : \mu_x - \mu_y = D_0$$

against the two-sided alternative

$$H_1 : \mu_x - \mu_y \neq D_0$$

the decision rule is as follows:

$$\text{Reject } H_0 \text{ if } \quad \frac{\bar{x} - \bar{y} - D_0}{\sqrt{\dfrac{\sigma_x^2}{n_x} + \dfrac{\sigma_y^2}{n_y}}} < -z_{\alpha/2} \quad \text{or} \quad \frac{\bar{x} - \bar{y} - D_0}{\sqrt{\dfrac{\sigma_x^2}{n_x} + \dfrac{\sigma_y^2}{n_y}}} > z_{\alpha/2} \tag{10.6}$$

If the sample sizes are large ($n > 100$), then a good approximation at significance level α can be made if we replace the population variances with the sample variances. In addition, the central limit theorem leads to good approximations even if the populations are not normally distributed. p-values for all of these tests are interpreted as the probability of getting a value at least as extreme as the one obtained, given the null hypothesis.

Example 10.2 Comparison of Alternative Fertilizers (Hypothesis Test for Differences Between Means)

Shirley Brown, an agricultural economist, wants to compare cow manure and turkey dung as fertilizers. Historically, farmers had used cow manure on their cornfields. Recently, a major turkey farmer offered to sell composted turkey dung at a favorable price. The farmers decided that they would use this new fertilizer only if there was strong evidence that productivity increased over the productivity that occurred with cow manure. Shirley was asked to conduct the research and statistical analysis in order to develop a recommendation to the farmers.

Solution To begin the study, Shirley specified a hypothesis test with

$$H_0 : \mu_x - \mu_y \leq 0$$

versus the alternative that

$$H_1 : \mu_x - \mu_y > 0$$

where μ_x is the population mean productivity using turkey dung and μ_y is the population mean productivity using cow manure. H_1 indicates that turkey dung results in higher productivity. The farmers will not change their fertilizer unless there is strong evidence in favor of increased productivity. She decided before collecting the data that a significance level of $\alpha = 0.05$ would be used for this test.

Using this design, Shirley implemented an experiment to test the hypothesis. Cow manure was applied to one set of $n_y = 25$ randomly selected fields. The sample mean productivity was $\bar{y} = 100$ From past experience the variance in productivity for these fields was assumed to be $\sigma_y^2 = 400$. Turkey dung was applied to a second random sample of $n_x = 25$ fields, and the sample mean productivity was $\bar{x} = 115$ Based on published research reports, the variance for these fields was assumed to be $\sigma_x^2 = 625$. The two sets of random samples were independent. The decision rule is to reject H_0 in favor of H_1 if

$$\frac{\bar{x} - \bar{y}}{\sqrt{\dfrac{\sigma_x^2}{n_x} + \dfrac{\sigma_y^2}{n_y}}} > z_\alpha$$

The computed statistics for this problem are as follows:

$$n_x = 25 \quad \bar{x} = 115 \quad \sigma_x^2 = 625$$

$$n_y = 25 \quad \bar{y} = 100 \quad \sigma_y^2 = 400$$

$$z = \frac{115 - 100}{\sqrt{\dfrac{625}{25} + \dfrac{400}{25}}} = 2.34$$

Comparing the computed value of $z = 2.34$ with $z_{0.05} = 1.645$, Shirley concluded that the null hypothesis is clearly rejected. In fact, we found that the p-value for this test is 0.0096. As a result, there is overwhelming evidence that turkey dung results in higher productivity than cow manure.

Two Means, Independent Samples, Unknown Population Variances Assumed to Be Equal

In those cases where the population variances are not known and the sample sizes are under 100, we need to use the Student's t distribution. There are some theoretical problems when we use the Student's t distribution for differences between sample means. However, these problems can be solved using the procedure that follows if we can assume that the population variances are equal. This assumption is realistic in many cases where we are comparing groups. In Section 10.4 we present a procedure for testing the equality of variances from two normal populations.

The major difference is that this procedure uses a commonly pooled estimator of the equal population variance. This estimator is as follows:

$$s_p^2 = \frac{(n_x - 1)s_x^2 + (n_y - 1)s_y^2}{(n_x + n_y - 2)}$$

The hypothesis test is performed using the Student's t statistic for the difference between two means:

$$t = \frac{(\bar{x} - \bar{y}) - (\mu_x - \mu_y)}{\sqrt{\dfrac{s_p^2}{n_x} + \dfrac{s_p^2}{n_y}}}$$

Note that the form for the test statistic is similar to that of the Z statistic, which is used when the population variances are known. The various tests using this procedure are summarized below.

Tests of the Difference Between Population Means: Population Variances Unknown and Equal

In these tests it is assumed that we have independent random sample of size n_x and n_y observations drawn from normally distributed populations with means μ_x and μ_y and a common variance. The sample variances s_x^2 and s_y^2 are used to compute a pooled variance estimator:

$$s_p^2 = \frac{(n_x - 1)s_x^2 + (n_y - 1)s_y^2}{(n_x + n_y - 2)} \tag{10.7}$$

We emphasize here that s_p^2 is the weighted average of the two sample variances, s_x^2 and s_y^2.

Then, using the observed sample means $\bar{x}$ and $\bar{y}$ the following tests have significance level α:

1. To test either null hypothesis

$$H_0 : \mu_x - \mu_y = D_0 \quad \text{or} \quad H_0 : \mu_x - \mu_y \leq D_0$$

against the alternative

$$H_1 : \mu_x - \mu_y > D_0$$

the decision rule is as follows:

$$\text{Reject } H_0 \text{ if } \frac{\bar{x} - \bar{y} - D_0}{\sqrt{\dfrac{s_p^2}{n_x} + \dfrac{s_p^2}{n_y}}} > t_{n_x + n_y - 2, \alpha} \tag{10.8}$$

---

2. To test either null hypothesis

$$H_0 : \mu_x - \mu_y = D_0 \quad \text{or} \quad H_0 : \mu_x - \mu_y \geq D_0$$

against the alternative

$$H_1 : \mu_x - \mu_y < D_0$$

the decision rule is as follows:

$$\text{Reject } H_0 \text{ if } \quad \frac{\bar{x} - \bar{y} - D_0}{\sqrt{\dfrac{s_p^2}{n_x} + \dfrac{s_p^2}{n_y}}} < -t_{n_x + n_y - 2, \alpha} \tag{10.9}$$

3. To test the null hypothesis

$$H_0 : \mu_x - \mu_y = D_0$$

against the two-sided alternative

$$H_1 : \mu_x - \mu_y \neq D_0$$

the decision rule is as follows:

$$\text{Reject } H_0 \text{ if } \quad \frac{\bar{x} - \bar{y} - D_0}{\sqrt{\dfrac{s_p^2}{n_x} + \dfrac{s_p^2}{n_y}}} < -t_{n_x + n_y - 2, \alpha/2} \quad \text{or} \quad \frac{\bar{x} - \bar{y} - D_0}{\sqrt{\dfrac{s_p^2}{n_x} + \dfrac{s_p^2}{n_y}}} > t_{n_x + n_y - 2, \alpha/2} \tag{10.10}$$

Here, $t_{n_x + n_y - 2, \alpha}$ is the number for which

$$P(t_{n_x + n_y - 2} > t_{n_x + n_y - 2, \alpha}) = \alpha$$

p-values for all of these tests are interpreted as the probability of getting a value as extreme as the one obtained, given the null hypothesis.

Example 10.3   Retail Sales Patterns (Hypothesis Test for Differences Between Means)

A sporting goods store operates in a medium-sized shopping mall. In order to plan staffing levels, the manager has asked for your assistance to determine if there is strong evidence that Monday sales are higher than Saturday sales.

Solution   To answer the question, you decide to gather random samples of 25 Saturdays and 25 Mondays from a population of several years of data. The samples are drawn independently. You decide to test the null hypothesis

$$H_0 : \mu_M - \mu_S \leq 0$$

against the alternative hypothesis

$$H_1 : \mu_M - \mu_S > 0$$

where the subscripts M and S refer to Monday and Saturday sales. The sample statistics are as follows:

$$\bar{x}_M = 1078 \qquad s_M = 633 \qquad n_M = 25$$
$$\bar{y}_S = 908.2 \qquad s_S = 469.8 \qquad n_S = 25$$

The pooled variance estimate is as follows:

$$s_p^2 = \frac{(25 - 1)(633)^2 + (25 - 1)(469.8)^2}{25 + 25 - 2} = 310{,}700$$

The test statistic is then computed as follows:

$$t = \frac{\bar{x}_M - \bar{y}_s}{\sqrt{\dfrac{s_p^2}{n_x} + \dfrac{s_p^2}{n_y}}} = \frac{1078 - 908.2}{\sqrt{\dfrac{310{,}700}{25} + \dfrac{310{,}700}{25}}} = 1.08$$

Using a significance level of $\alpha = 0.05$ and 48 degrees of freedom, we find that the critical value of t is 1.677. Therefore, we conclude that there is not sufficient evidence to reject the null hypothesis, and, thus, there is no reason to conclude that mean sales on Mondays are higher.

Example 10.4   Brain Activity Study (Hypothesis Test for Differences Between Means)

In this example we examine the effect of using different assumptions for Student's t tests for differences between population means. Recall that in Example 10.1 we prepared the analysis assuming that the sample observations were paired. We found that there was evidence to reject the hypothesis that there was no difference between the population means, and to accept the hypothesis that the high-recall ads had a higher population mean brain activity. Here, we will revisit Example 10.1 using other assumptions (use the data file **Response to Commercials**).

Solution   First, we drop the assumption that the sample observations are matched pairs and correlated. We will, however, assume that the two population variances are equal. We are testing the same hypothesis that was tested in Example 10.1. The Minitab results are shown in Figure 10.2. The computed Student's t value is 1.45, the p-value is 0.082, and the degrees of freedom are 18. Thus, with a significance level of 0.05 we cannot reject the null hypothesis, and there is no strong evidence to support a difference in brain wave activity. Without the assumption of paired and positively correlated samples the variance of the difference is too large to conclude that the difference is significant.

Figure 10.2   Brain Wave Study: Independent Samples, Population Variances Equal (Minitab Output)

Two-Sample T-Test and CI: X,Y

```
Two-sample T for X vs Y


          N      Mean    St Dev  SE Mean
X        10     108.5      42.5       13
Y        10      85.5      26.5      8.4

Difference = mu (X) - mu (Y)
Estimate for difference:    23.0000
95% lower bound for difference:   -4.4587
T-Test of difference = 0 (vs >): T-Value = 1.45   P-Value = 0.082   DF = 18
Both use Pooled StDev = 35.4079
```

Two Means, Independent Samples, Unknown Population Variances Not Assumed to Be Equal

Hypothesis tests of differences between population means when the individual variances are unknown and not equal require modification of the variance computation and the degrees of freedom. The computation of sample variance for the difference between sample means is changed. There are substantial complexities in the determination of degrees of freedom for the critical value of the Student's t statistic. The specific computational forms were presented in Section 8.2. Equations 10.11–10.14 below summarize the procedures.

Tests of the Difference Between Population Means: Population Variances Unknown and Not Equal

These tests assume that we have independent random sample of size n_x and n_y observations from normal populations with means μ_x and μ_y and unequal variances. The sample variances s_x^2 and s_y^2 are used. The degrees of freedom v for the Student's t statistic is given by the following:

$$v = \frac{\left[\left(\frac{s_x^2}{n_x}\right) + \left(\frac{s_y^2}{n_y}\right)\right]^2}{\left(\frac{s_x^2}{n_x}\right)^2 / (n_x - 1) + \left(\frac{s_y^2}{n_y}\right)^2 / (n_y - 1)} \quad (10.11)$$

Then, using the observed sample means $\bar{x}$ and $\bar{y}$ the following tests have significance level α:

1. To test either null hypothesis

$$H_0 : \mu_x - \mu_y = D_0 \quad \text{or} \quad H_0 : \mu_x - \mu_y \leq D_0$$

against the alternative

$$H_1 : \mu_x - \mu_y > D_0$$

the decision rule is as follows:

$$\text{Reject } H_0 \text{ if } \quad \frac{\bar{x} - \bar{y} - D_0}{\sqrt{\frac{s_x^2}{n_x} + \frac{s_y^2}{n_y}}} > t_{v,\alpha} \quad (10.12)$$

2. To test either null hypothesis

$$H_0 : \mu_x - \mu_y = D_0 \quad \text{or} \quad H_0 : \mu_x - \mu_y \geq D_0$$

against the alternative

$$H_1 : \mu_x - \mu_y < D_0$$

the decision rule is as follows:

$$\text{Reject } H_0 \text{ if } \quad \frac{\bar{x} - \bar{y} - D_0}{\sqrt{\frac{s_x^2}{n_x} + \frac{s_y^2}{n_y}}} < -t_{v,\alpha} \quad (10.13)$$

3. To test the null hypothesis

$$H_0 : \mu_x - \mu_y = D_0$$

against the two-sided alternative

$$H_1 : \mu_x - \mu_y \neq D_0$$

the decision rule is as follows:

$$\text{Reject } H_0 \text{ if } \quad \frac{\bar{x} - \bar{y} - D_0}{\sqrt{\dfrac{s_x^2}{n_x} + \dfrac{s_y^2}{n_y}}} < -t_{v,\alpha/2} \quad \text{or} \quad \frac{\bar{x} - \bar{y} - D_0}{\sqrt{\dfrac{s_x^2}{n_x} + \dfrac{s_y^2}{n_y}}} > t_{v,\alpha/2} \quad \textbf{(10.14)}$$

Here, $t_{v,\alpha}$ is the number for which

$$P(t_v > t_{v,\alpha}) = \alpha$$

The analysis for Example 10.4 was run again without assuming equal population variances. The Excel results are shown in Figure 10.3. Here, the only important change is that the degrees of freedom are lower, resulting in a slightly higher p-value.

Figure 10.3
Brain Wave Study:
Independent
Samples (Excel
Output)

t-Test: Two-Sample Assuming Unequal Variances		
	Variable 1	Variable 2
Mean	108.5	85.5
Variance	1806.72222	700.7222222
Observations	10	10
Hypothesized Mean Difference	0	
df	15	
t Stat	1.45248674	
P(T<= t) one-tail	0.0834817	
t Critical one-tail	1.75305104	
P(T<= t) two tail	0.1669634	
t Critical two-tail	2.13145086	

EXERCISES

Basic Exercises

10.6 You have been asked to determine if two different production processes have different mean numbers of units produced per hour. Process 1 has a mean defined as μ_1 and process 2 has a mean defined as μ_2. The null and alternative hypotheses are as follows:

$$H_0 : \mu_1 - \mu_2 = 0$$
$$H_1 : \mu_1 - \mu_2 > 0$$

Using a random sample of 25 observations from process 1 and 28 observations from process 2, and the known variance for process 1 equal to 900 and the known variance for process 2 equal to 1,600. Can you reject the null hypothesis using a probability of Type I error $\alpha = 0.05$ if

a. the process means are 50 and 60?

b. the difference in process means is 20?

c. the process means are 45 and 50?

d. the difference in process means is 15?

10.7 You have been asked to determine if two different production processes have different mean numbers of units produced per hour. Process 1 has a mean defined as μ_1 and process 2 has a mean defined as μ_2. The null and alternative hypotheses are as follows:

$$H_0 : \mu_1 - \mu_2 \leq 0$$
$$H_1 : \mu_1 - \mu_2 > 0$$

The process variances are unknown but assumed to be equal. Using a random samples of 25 observations from process 1 and 36 observations from process 2, the sample means are 56 and 50 for populations 1 and 2. Can you reject the null hypothesis using a probability of Type I error $\alpha = 0.05$ if

a. the sample standard deviation from process 1 is 30 and from process 2 is 28?
b. the sample standard deviation from process 1 is 22 and from process 2 is 33?
c. the sample standard deviation from process 1 is 30 and from process 2 is 42?
d. the sample standard deviation from process 1 is 15 and from process 2 is 36?

Application Exercises

10.8 A screening procedure was designed to measure attitudes toward minorities as managers. High scores indicate negative attitudes and low scores indicate positive attitudes. Independent random samples were taken of 151 male financial analysts and 108 female financial analysts. For the former group the sample mean and standard deviation scores were 85.8 and 19.13, while the corresponding statistics for the latter group were 71.5 and 12.2. Test the null hypothesis that the two population means are equal against the alternative that the true mean score is higher for male than for female financial analysts.

10.9 For a random sample of 125 British entrepreneurs the mean number of job changes was 1.91 and the sample standard deviation was 1.32. For an independent random sample of 86 British corporate managers the mean number of job changes was 0.21 and the sample standard deviation was 0.53. Test the null hypothesis that the population means are equal against the alternative that the mean number of job changes is higher for British entrepreneurs than for British corporate managers.

10.10 A political science professor is interested in comparing the characteristics of students who do and do not vote in national elections. For a random sample of 114 students who claimed to have voted in the last presidential election, she found a mean grade point average of 2.71 and a standard deviation of 0.64. For an independent random sample of 123 students who did not vote, the mean grade point average was 2.79 and the standard deviation was 0.56. Test against a two-sided alternative the null hypothesis that the population means are equal.

10.11 In light of a recent large corporation bankruptcy, auditors are becoming increasingly concerned about the possibility of fraud. Auditors might be helped in determining the chances of fraud if they carefully measure cash flow. To evaluate this possibility, samples of midlevel auditors from CPA firms were presented with cash-flow information from a fraud case, and they were asked to indicate the chance of material fraud on a scale from 0 to 100. A random sample of 36 auditors used the cash-flow information. Their mean assessment was 36.21, and the sample standard deviation was 22.93. For an independent random sample of 36 auditors not using the cash-flow information, the sample mean and standard deviation were respectively 47.56 and 27.56. Assuming that the two population distributions are normal with equal variances, test against a two-sided alternative the null hypothesis that the population means are equal.

10.12 Initial public offerings' prospectuses were examined. In a random sample of 70 prospectuses in which sales forecasts were disclosed, the mean debt-to-equity ratio prior to the offering issue was 3.97, and the sample standard deviation was 6.14. For an independent random sample of 51 prospectuses in which sales earnings forecasts were not disclosed, the mean debt-to-equity ratio was 2.86, and the sample standard deviation was 4.29. Test against a two-sided alternative the null hypothesis that population mean debt-to-equity ratios are the same for disclosers and nondisclosers of earnings forecasts.

10.13 A publisher is interested in the effects on sales of college texts that include more than 100 data files. The publisher plans to produce 20 texts in the business area and randomly chooses 10 to have more than 100 data files. The remaining 10 are produced with at most 100 data files. For those with more than 100, first-year sales averaged 9,254, and the sample standard deviation was 2,107. For the books with at most 100, average first-year sales were 8,167, and the sample standard deviation was 1,681. Assuming that the two population distributions are normal with the same variance, test the null hypothesis that the population means are equal against the alternative that the true mean is higher for books with more than 100 data files.

10.3 TESTS OF THE DIFFERENCE BETWEEN TWO POPULATION PROPORTIONS (LARGE SAMPLES)

Next, we will develop procedures for comparing two population proportions. We will consider a standard model with a random sample of n_x observations from a population with a proportion P_x of "successes" and a second independent random sample of n_y observations from a population with a proportion P_y of "successes."

In Chapter 5 we saw that, for large samples, proportions can be normally distributed random variables, and, as a result,

$$Z = \frac{(\hat{p}_x - \hat{p}_y) - (P_x - P_y)}{\sqrt{\dfrac{P_x(1 - P_x)}{n_x} + \dfrac{P_y(1 - P_y)}{n_y}}}$$

has a standard normal distribution.

We want to test the hypothesis that the population proportions P_x and P_y equal. Denote their common value by P_0. Then under this hypothesis

$$Z = \frac{(\hat{p}_x - \hat{p}_y)}{\sqrt{\dfrac{P_0(1 - P_0)}{n_x} + \dfrac{P_0(1 - P_0)}{n_y}}}$$

follows to a close approximation a standard normal distribution.

Finally, the unknown proportion P_0 can be estimated by a pooled estimator defined as follows:

$$\hat{p}_0 = \frac{n_x \hat{p}_x + n_y \hat{p}_y}{n_x + n_y}$$

The null hypothesis in these tests assumes that the population proportions are equal. If the null hypothesis is true, then an unbiased and efficient estimator for P_0 can be obtained by combining the two random samples, and, as a result, $\hat{p}_0$ is computed using this equation. Then we can replace the unknown P_0 by $\hat{p}_0$ to obtain a random variable that has a distribution close to the standard normal for large sample sizes.

The tests are summarized as follows.

Testing the Equality of Two Population Proportions (Large Samples)

We are given independent random samples of size n_x and n_y with proportion of successes $\hat{p}_x$ and $\hat{p}_y$. When we assume that the population proportions are equal, an estimate of the common proportion is as follows:

$$\hat{p}_0 = \frac{n_x \hat{p}_x + n_y \hat{p}_y}{n_x + n_y}$$

For large sample sizes—$nP_0(1 - P_0) > 5$—the following tests have significance level α:

1. To test either null hypothesis

$$H_0 : P_x - P_y = 0 \quad \text{or} \quad H_0 : P_x - P_y \leq 0$$

against the alternative

$$H_1 : P_x - P_y > 0$$

the decision rule is as follows:

$$\text{Reject } H_0 \text{ if } \frac{(\hat{p}_x - \hat{p}_y)}{\sqrt{\dfrac{\hat{p}_0(1 - \hat{p}_0)}{n_x} + \dfrac{\hat{p}_0(1 - \hat{p}_0)}{n_y}}} > z_\alpha \tag{10.15}$$

2. To test either null hypothesis

$$H_0 : P_x - P_y = 0 \quad \text{or} \quad H_0 : P_x - P_y \geq 0$$

against the alternative

$$H_1 : P_x - P_y < 0$$

the decision rule is as follows:

$$\text{Reject } H_0 \text{ if } \frac{(\hat{p}_x - \hat{p}_y)}{\sqrt{\dfrac{\hat{p}_0(1 - \hat{p}_0)}{n_x} + \dfrac{\hat{p}_0(1 - \hat{p}_0)}{n_y}}} < -z_\alpha \tag{10.16}$$

3. To test the null hypothesis

$$H_0 : P_x - P_y = 0$$

against the two-sided alternative

$$H_1 : P_x - P_y \neq 0$$

the decision rule is as follows:

$$\text{Reject } H_0 \text{ if } \frac{(\hat{p}_x - \hat{p}_y)}{\sqrt{\dfrac{\hat{p}_0(1 - \hat{p}_0)}{n_x} + \dfrac{\hat{p}_0(1 - \hat{p}_0)}{n_y}}} < -z_{\alpha/2} \quad \text{or}$$

$$\frac{(\hat{p}_x - \hat{p}_y)}{\sqrt{\dfrac{\hat{p}_0(1 - \hat{p}_0)}{n_x} + \dfrac{\hat{p}_0(1 - \hat{p}_0)}{n_y}}} > z_{\alpha/2} \tag{10.17}$$

It is also possible to compute and interpret p-values as the probability of getting a value at least as extreme as the one obtained, given the null hypothesis.

Example 10.5   Change in Customer Recognition of New Products After an Advertising Campaign (Hypothesis Tests of Differences Between Proportions)

Northern States Marketing Research has been asked to determine if an advertising campaign for a new cell phone increased customer recognition of the new **World A** phone. A random sample of 270 residents of a major city were asked if they knew about the World A phone before the advertising campaign. In this survey 50 respondents had heard of World A. After the advertising campaign a second random sample of 203 residents were asked exactly the same question using the same protocol. In this case 81 respondents had heard of the World A phone. Do these results provide evidence that customer recognition increased after the advertising campaign?

Solution Define P_x and P_y as the population proportions that recognized the World A phone before and after the advertising campaign, respectively. The null hypothesis is

$$H_0 : P_x - P_y \geq 0$$

and the alternative hypothesis is

$$H_1 : P_x - P_y < 0$$

The decision rule is to reject H_0 in favor of H_1 if

$$\frac{(\hat{p}_x - \hat{p}_y)}{\sqrt{\dfrac{P_0(1 - P_0)}{n_x} + \dfrac{P_0(1 - P_0)}{n_y}}} < -z_\alpha$$

The data for this problem are as follows:

$$n_x = 270 \quad \hat{p}_x = 50/270 = 0.185 \quad n_y = 203 \quad \hat{p}_y = 81/203 = 0.399$$

The estimate of the common variance P_0 under the null hypothesis is as follows:

$$\hat{p}_0 = \frac{n_x \hat{p}_x + n_y \hat{p}_y}{n_x + n_y} = \frac{(270)(0.185) + (203)(0.399)}{270 + 203} = 0.277$$

The test statistic is as follows:

$$\frac{(\hat{p}_x - \hat{p}_y)}{\sqrt{\dfrac{\hat{p}_0(1 - \hat{p}_0)}{n_x} + \dfrac{\hat{p}_0(1 - \hat{p}_0)}{n_y}}} = \frac{0.185 - 0.399}{\sqrt{\dfrac{(0.277)(1 - 0.277)}{270} + \dfrac{(0.277)(1 - 0.277)}{203}}} = -5.15$$

For a one-tailed test with $\alpha = 0.05$, the $-z_{0.05}$ value is -1.645. Thus, we reject the null hypothesis and conclude that customer recognition did increase after the advertising campaign.

EXERCISES

Basic Exercise

10.14   Test the hypotheses

$$H_0 : P_x - P_y = 0$$
$$H_1 : P_x - P_y < 0$$

using the following statistics from random samples:

a. $\hat{p}_x = 0.42, n_x = 500$;
   $\hat{p}_y = 0.50, n_y = 600$

b. $\hat{p}_x = 0.60, n_x = 500$;
   $\hat{p}_y = 0.64, n_y = 600$

c. $\hat{p}_x = 0.42, n_x = 500$;
   $\hat{p}_y = 0.49, n_y = 600$

d. $\hat{p}_x = 0.25, n_x = 500$;
   $\hat{p}_y = 0.34, n_y = 600$

e. $\hat{p}_x = 0.39, n_x = 500$;
   $\hat{p}_y = 0.42, n_y = 600$

Application Exercises

10.15   Random samples of 900 people in the United States and in Great Britain indicated that 60% of the people in the United States were positive about the future economy, while 66% of the people in Great Britain were positive about the future economy. Does this provide strong evidence that the people in Great Britain are more optimistic about the economy?

10.16 A random sample of 1,556 people in country A were asked to respond to this statement: "Increased world trade can increase our per capita prosperity." Of these sample members, 38.4% agreed with the statement. When the same statement was presented to a random sample of 1,108 people in country B, 52.0% agreed. Test the null hypothesis that the population proportions agreeing with this statement were the same in the two countries against the alternative that a higher proportion agreed in country B.

10.17 Small-business telephone users were surveyed 6 months after access to carriers other than AT&T became available for wide-area telephone service. Of a random sample of 368 users, 92 said they were attempting to learn more about their options, as did 37 of an independent random sample of 116 users of alternate carriers. Test at the 5% significance level, against a two-sided alternative, the null hypothesis that the two population proportions are the same.

10.18 Employees of a building materials chain facing a shutdown were surveyed on a prospective employee ownership plan. Some employees pledged $10,000 to this plan, putting up $800 immediately, while others indicated that they did not intend to pledge. Of a random sample of 175 people who had pledged, 78 had already been laid off, while 208 of a random sample of 604 people who had not pledged had already been laid off. Test at the 5% level, against a two-sided alternative, the null

hypothesis that the population proportions already laid off were the same for people who pledged as for those who did not.

10.19 Of a random sample of 381 high-quality investment equity options, 191 had less than 30% debt. Of an independent random sample of 166 high-risk investment equity options, 145 had less than 30% debt. Test against a two-sided alternative the null hypothesis that the two population proportions are equal.

10.20 Independent random samples of consumers were asked about satisfaction with their computer system in two slightly different ways. The options available for answer were the same in the two cases. When asked how *satisfied* they were with their computer system, 138 of 240 sample members opted for "very satisfied." When asked how *dissatisfied* they were with their computer system, 128 of 240 sample members opted for "very satisfied." Test at the 5% significance level, against the obvious one-sided alternative, the null hypothesis that the two population proportions are equal.

10.21 Of a random sample of 1,200 people in Denmark, 480 had a positive attitude toward car salesmen. Of an independent random sample of 1,000 people in France, 790 had a positive attitude toward car salesmen. Test at the 1% level the null hypothesis that the population proportions are equal against the alternative that a higher proportion of French have a positive attitude toward car salesmen.

10.4 TESTS OF THE EQUALITY OF THE VARIANCES BETWEEN TWO NORMALLY DISTRIBUTED POPULATIONS

There are a number of situations where we are interested in comparing the variances from two normally distributed populations. For example, the Student's t test in Section 10.2 assumed equal variances and used the two sample variances to compute a pooled estimator for the common variances. We will see that comparisons of variances are also important inferential procedures for regression analysis—see Chapters 11 and 12—and for analysis of variance—see Chapter 15. Quality control studies are often concerned with the question of which process has the smaller variance.

In this section we develop a procedure for testing the assumption that population variances from independent samples are equal. To perform such tests, we introduce the F probability distribution. We begin by letting s_x^2 be the sample variance for a random sample of n_x observations from a normally distributed population with population variance σ_x^2. A second independent random sample of size n_y provides a sample variance of s_y^2 from a normal population with population variance σ_y^2. Then the random variable

$$F = \frac{s_x^2/\sigma_x^2}{s_y^2/\sigma_y^2}$$

follows a distribution known as the F distribution. This family of distributions, which is widely used in statistical analysis, is identified by the degrees of freedom for the numerator and the degrees of freedom for the denominator. The degrees of freedom for the numerator are associated with the sample variance s_x^2 and equal to $(n_x - 1)$. Similarly, the degrees of freedom for the denominator are associated with the sample variance s_y^2 and equal to $(n_y - 1)$.

The F distribution is constructed as the ratio of two chi-square random variables, each divided by its degrees of freedom. The chi-square distribution relates the sample and population variances for a normally distributed population. Hypothesis tests that use the F distribution depend on the assumption of a normal distribution. The characteristics of the F distribution are summarized below.

The F Distribution

We have two independent random samples with n_x and n_y observations from two normal populations with variances σ_x^2 and σ_y^2. If the sample variances are s_x^2 and s_y^2, then the random variable

$$F = \frac{s_x^2/\sigma_x^2}{s_y^2/\sigma_y^2} \qquad (10.18)$$

has an F distribution with numerator degrees of freedom $(n_x - 1)$ and denominator degrees of freedom $(n_y - 1)$.

An F distribution with numerator degrees of freedom v_1 and denominator degrees of freedom v_2 will be denoted F_{v_1, v_2}. We denote as $F_{v_1, v_2, \alpha}$ the number for which

$$P(F_{v_1, v_2} > F_{v_1, v_2, \alpha}) = \alpha$$

We need to emphasize that this test is quite sensitive to the assumption of normality.

The cutoff points for $F_{v_1, v_2, \alpha}$, for α equal to 0.05 and 0.01, are provided in Table 9 of the appendix. For example, for 10 numerator degrees of freedom and 20 denominator degrees of freedom, we see from the table that

$$F_{10,20,0.05} = 2.35 \quad \text{and} \quad F_{10,20,0.01} = 3.37$$

Hence,

$$P(F_{10,20} > 2.35) = 0.05 \quad \text{and} \quad P(F_{10,20} > 3.37) = 0.01$$

Figure 10.4 presents a schematic description of the F distribution for this example.

Figure 10.4
F Probability Density Function with 10 Numerator Degrees of Freedom and 20 Denominator Degrees of Freedom

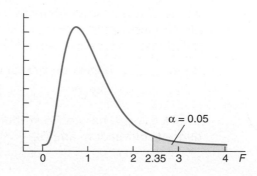

In practical applications we usually arrange the F ratio so that the larger sample variance is in the numerator and the smaller is in the denominator. Thus, we only need to use the upper cutoff points to test the hypothesis of equality of variances. When the population variances are equal, the F random variable becomes

$$F = \frac{s_x^2}{s_y^2}$$

and this ratio of sample variances becomes the test statistic. The intuition for this test is quite simple: If one of the sample variances greatly exceeds the other, then we must conclude that the population variances are not equal. The hypothesis tests of equality of variances are summarized as follows.

Tests of Equality of Variances from Two Normal Populations

Let s_x^2 and s_y^2 be observed sample variances from independent random samples of size n_x and n_y from normally distributed populations with variances σ_x^2 and σ_y^2. Use s_x^2 to denote the larger variance. Then the following tests have significance level α:

1. To test either null hypothesis

$$H_0 : \sigma_x^2 = \sigma_y^2 \quad \text{or} \quad H_0 : \sigma_x^2 \leq \sigma_y^2$$

against the alternative

$$H_1 : \sigma_x^2 > \sigma_y^2$$

the decision rule is as follows:

$$\text{Reject } H_0 \text{ if} \quad F = \frac{s_x^2}{s_y^2} > F_{n_x-1, n_y-1, \alpha} \tag{10.19}$$

2. To test the null hypothesis

$$H_0 : \sigma_x^2 = \sigma_y^2$$

against the two-sided alternative

$$H_1 : \sigma_x^2 \neq \sigma_y^2$$

the decision rule is as follows:

$$\text{Reject } H_0 \text{ if} \quad F = \frac{s_x^2}{s_y^2} > F_{n_x-1, n_y-1, \alpha/2} \tag{10.20}$$

where s_x^2 is the larger of the two sample variances. Since either sample variance could be larger, this rule is actually based on a two-tailed test, and, hence, we use $\alpha/2$ as the upper tail probability.

Here, F_{n_x-1, n_y-1} is the number for which

$$P(F_{n_x-1, n_y-1, \alpha} > F_{n_x-1, n_y-1, \alpha}) = \alpha$$

where F_{n_x-1, n_y-1} has an F distribution with $(n_x - 1)$ numerator degrees of freedom and $(n_y - 1)$ denominator degrees of freedom.

For all of these tests a p-value is the probability of getting a value at least as extreme as the one obtained, given the null hypothesis. Because of the complexity of the F distribution, critical values are computed for only a few special cases. Thus, p-values will be typically computed using a statistical package such as Minitab.

Example 10.6 Study of Maturity Variances by Investors Now (Hypothesis Tests for the Equality of Two Variances)

The research staff of Investors Now, an on-line financial trading firm, was interested in determining if there is a difference in the variance of the maturities of AAA-rated industrial bonds compared to CCC-rated industrial bonds.

Solution This question requires that we design a study that compares the population variances of maturities for the two different bonds. We will test the null hypothesis

$$H_0 : \sigma_x^2 = \sigma_y^2$$

against the alternative hypothesis

$$H_1 : \sigma_x^2 \neq \sigma_y^2$$

where σ_x^2 is the variance in maturities for AAA-rated bonds and σ_y^2 is the variance in maturities for CCC-rated bonds. The significance level of the test was chosen as $\alpha = 0.02$.

The decision rule is to reject H_0 in favor of H_1 if

$$\frac{s_x^2}{s_y^2} > F_{n_x-1, n_y-1, \alpha/2}$$

Note here that either sample variance could be larger and we place the larger sample variance in the numerator. Hence, the probability for this upper tail is $\alpha/2$. A random sample of 17 AAA-rated bonds resulted in a sample variance $s_x^2 = 123.35$, and an independent random sample of 11 CCC-rated bonds resulted in a sample variance $s_y^2 = 8.02$. The test statistic is as follows:

$$\frac{s_x^2}{s_y^2} = \frac{123.35}{8.02} = 15.38$$

Given a significance level of $\alpha = 0.02$, we find that the critical value of F, from interpolation in Table 9 of the appendix, is as follows:

$$F_{16, 10, 0.01} = 4.53$$

Clearly, the computed value of F (15.38) exceeds the critical value (4.53), and we reject H_0 in favor of H_1. Thus, there is strong evidence that variances in maturities are different for these two types of bonds.

Basic Exercise

10.22 Test the hypothesis

$$H_0 : \sigma_x^2 = \sigma_y^2$$

$$H_1 : \sigma_x^2 > \sigma_y^2$$

using the following data:

a. $s_x^2 = 125, n_x = 45; s_y^2 = 51, n_y = 41$

b. $s_x^2 = 125, n_x = 45; s_y^2 = 235, n_y = 44$

c. $s_x^2 = 134, n_x = 48; s_y^2 = 51, n_y = 41$

d. $s_x^2 = 88, n_x = 39; s_y^2 = 167, n_y = 25$

Application Exercises

10.23 It is hypothesized that the more expert a group of people examining personal income tax filings, the more variable the judgments will be about the accuracy. Independent random samples, each of 30 individuals, were chosen from groups with different levels of expertise. The "low-expertise" group consisted of people who had just completed their first intermediate accounting course. Members of the "high-expertise" group had completed undergraduate studies and were employed by reputable CPA firms. The sample members were asked to judge the accuracy of personal income tax filings. For the low-expertise group the sample variance was 451.770, while for the high-expertise group it was 1,614.208. Test the null hypothesis that the two population variances are equal against the alternative that the true variance is higher for the high-expertise group.

10.24 It is hypothesized that the total sales of a corporation should vary more in an industry with active price competition than in one with duopoly and tacit collusion. In a study of the merchant ship production industry it was found that in 4 years of active price competition the variance of company A's total sales was 114.09. In the following 7 years, during which there was duopoly and tacit collusion, this variance was 16.08. Assume that the data can be regarded as an independent random sample from two normal distributions. Test at the 5% level the null hypothesis that the two population variances are equal against the alternative that the variance of total sales is higher in years of active price competition.

10.25 In Exercise 10.11 it was assumed that population variances for assessments of the chance of material fraud were the same for auditors using cash-flow information as for auditors not using cash-flow information. Test this assumption against a two-sided alternative hypothesis.

10.26 In Exercise 10.13 it was assumed that population variances were equal for first-year sales of textbooks with more than 100 data files and those with at most 100 data files. Test this assumption against a two-sided alternative.

10.27 A university research team was studying the relationship between idea generation by groups with and without a moderator. For a random sample of four groups with a moderator the mean number of ideas generated per group was 78.0, and the standard deviation was 24.4. For a random sample of four groups without a moderator the mean number of ideas generated was 63.5, and the standard deviation was 20.2. Test the assumption that the two population variances were equal against the alternative that the population variance is higher for groups with a moderator.

10.5 SOME COMMENTS ON HYPOTHESIS TESTING

In this chapter we have presented several important applications of hypothesis-testing methodology. In an important sense, this methodology is fundamental to decision making and analysis in the face of random variability. As a result, the procedures have great applicability to a number of research and management decisions. The procedures are relatively easy to use, and various computer processes minimize the computational effort. Thus, we have a tool that is appealing and quite easy to use. However, there are some subtle problems and areas of concern that we need to consider in order to avoid serious mistakes.

The null hypothesis plays a crucial role in the hypothesis-testing framework. In a typical investigation we set the significance level, α, at a small probability value.

Then, we obtain a random sample and use the data to compute a test statistic. If the test statistic is outside of the acceptance region (depending on the direction of the test), the null hypothesis is rejected and the alternative hypothesis is accepted. When we do reject the null hypothesis, we have strong evidence—a small probability of error—in favor of the alternative hypothesis. In some cases we may fail to reject a drastically false null hypothesis simply because we have only limited sample information or because the test has low power. There may be important cases where this outcome is appropriate. For example, we would not change an existing process that is working effectively unless we had strong evidence that a new process clearly would be even better. In other cases, however, the special status of the null hypothesis is neither warranted nor appropriate. In those cases we might consider the costs of making both Type I and Type II errors in a decision process. We might also consider a different specification of the null hypothesis—noting that rejection of the null provides strong evidence in favor of the alternative. When we have two alternatives, we could initially choose either as the null hypothesis. In the cereal-package weight example at the beginning of Chapter 9 the null hypothesis could be either that

$$H_0 : \mu \geq 16$$

or that

$$H_0 : \mu \leq 16$$

In the first case rejection would provide strong evidence that the population mean weight is less than 16. In the latter case rejection would provide strong evidence that the population mean weight is greater than 16. As we have indicated, failure to reject either of these null hypotheses would not provide strong evidence. There are also procedures for controlling both Type I and Type II errors simultaneously (see, for example, Reference 1).

On some occasions very large amounts of sample information are available, and we reject the null hypothesis even when differences are not practically important. Thus, we need to contrast statistical significance with a broader definition of significance. Suppose that very large samples are used to compare annual mean family incomes in two cities. One result might be that the sample means differ by $2.67, and that difference might lead us to reject a null hypothesis and thus conclude that one city has a higher mean family income than the other. While that result might be statistically significant, it clearly has no practical significance with respect to consumption or quality of life.

In specifying a null hypothesis and a testing rule, we are defining the test conditions before we look at the sample data that were generated by a process that includes a random component. Thus, if we look at the data before defining the null and alternative hypotheses, we no longer have the stated probability of error, and the concept of "strong evidence" resulting from rejecting the null hypothesis is not valid. For example, if we decide on the significance level of our test after we have seen the p-values, then we cannot interpret our results in probability terms. Suppose that an economist compares each of five different income-enhancing programs against a standard minimal level using a hypothesis test. After collecting the data and computing p-values, she determines that the null hypothesis—income not above the standard minimal level—can be rejected for one of the five programs with a significance level of $\alpha = 0.20$. Clearly, this result violates the proper use of hypothesis testing. But we have seen this done by supposedly professional economists.

As statistical computing tools have become more powerful, there are a number of new ways to violate the principle of specifying the null hypothesis before seeing the data. The recent popularity of data mining—using a computer program to search for relationships between variables in a very large data set—introduces new possibilities for abuse. Data mining can provide a description of subsets and differences in a particularly large sample of data. However, after seeing the results from a data mining operation, analysts may be tempted to define hypothesis tests that will use random samples from the same data set. This clearly violates the principle of defining the hypothesis test before seeing the data. A drug company may screen large numbers of medical treatment cases and discover that 5 out of 100 drugs have significant effects for the treatment of previously unintended diseases. Such a result might legitimately be used to identify potential research questions for a new research study with new random samples. However, if the original data are then used to test a hypothesis concerning the treatment benefits of the five drugs, we have a serious violation of the proper application of hypothesis testing, and none of the probabilities of error are correct.

Defining the null and alternative hypotheses requires careful consideration of the objectives of the analysis. For example, we might be faced with a proposal to introduce a specific new production process. In one case the present process might include considerable new equipment, well-trained workers, and a belief that the process performs very well. In that case we would define the productivity for the present process as the null hypothesis and the new process as the alternative. Then, we would adopt the new process only if there is strong evidence—rejecting the null hypothesis with a small α— that the new process has higher productivity. Alternatively, the present process might be old and include equipment that needs to be replaced and a number of workers that require supplementary training. In that case we might choose to define the new process productivity as the null hypothesis. Thus, we would continue with the old process only if there is strong evidence that the old process's productivity is higher.

When we establish control charts for monitoring process quality using acceptance intervals as in Chapter 6 we set the desired process level as the null hypothesis and we also set a very small significance level—$\alpha < 0.01$. Thus, we reject only when there is very strong evidence that the process is no longer performing properly. However, these control chart hypothesis tests are established only after there has been considerable work to bring the process under control and minimize its variability. Therefore, we are quite confident that the process is working properly, and we do not wish to change in response to small variations in the sample data. But if we do find a test statistic from sample data outside the acceptance interval and hence reject the null hypothesis, we can be quite confident that something has gone wrong and we need to fix the process immediately.

The tests developed in this chapter are based on the assumption that the underlying distribution is normal or that the central limit theorem applies for the distribution of sample means or proportions. When the normality assumption no longer holds, those probabilities of error may not be valid. Since we cannot be sure that most populations are precisely normal, we might have some serious concerns about the validity of our tests. Considerable research has shown that tests involving means do not strongly depend on the normality assumption. These tests are said to be "robust" with respect to normality. However, tests involving variances are not robust. Thus, greater caution is required when using hypothesis tests based on variances. In Chapter 5 we showed how we can use normal probability plots to quickly check to determine if a sample is likely to have come from a normally distributed population. This should be part of good practice in any statistical study of the types discussed in this textbook.

Figure 10.5 Flow Chart for Selecting the Appropriate Hypothesis Test When Comparing Two Population Means

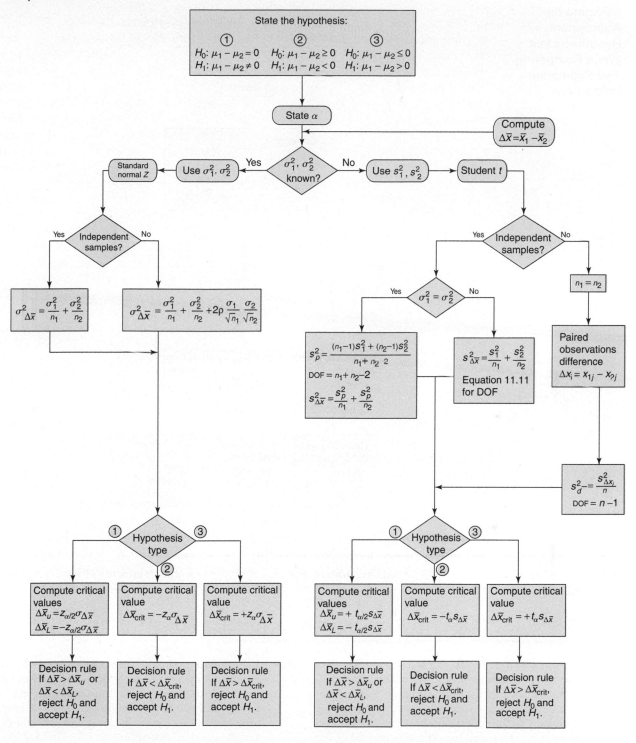

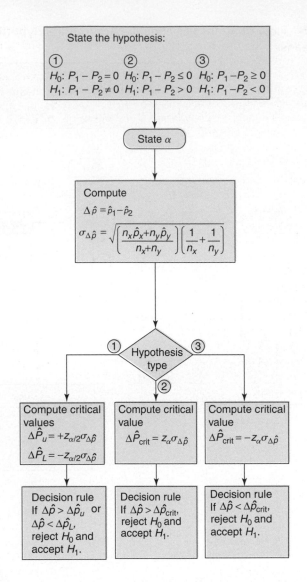

Figure 10.6
Flow Chart for Selecting the Appropriate Hypothesis Test When Comparing Two Population Proportions

State the hypothesis:

① $H_0: P_1 - P_2 = 0$ ② $H_0: P_1 - P_2 \leq 0$ ③ $H_0: P_1 - P_2 \geq 0$
   $H_1: P_1 - P_2 \neq 0$ $H_1: P_1 - P_2 > 0$ $H_1: P_1 - P_2 < 0$

State α

Compute

$\Delta \hat{p} = \hat{p}_1 - \hat{p}_2$

$\sigma_{\Delta \hat{p}} = \sqrt{\left(\dfrac{n_x \hat{p}_x + n_y \hat{p}_y}{n_x + n_y} \right)\left(\dfrac{1}{n_x} + \dfrac{1}{n_y} \right)}$

Hypothesis type

① Compute critical values

$\Delta \hat{P}_u = +z_{\alpha/2} \sigma_{\Delta \hat{p}}$

$\Delta \hat{P}_L = -z_{\alpha/2} \sigma_{\Delta \hat{p}}$

② Compute critical value

$\Delta \hat{P}_{\text{crit}} = z_\alpha \sigma_{\Delta \hat{p}}$

③ Compute critical value

$\Delta \hat{P}_{\text{crit}} = -z_\alpha \sigma_{\Delta \hat{p}}$

Decision rule
If $\Delta \hat{p} > \Delta \hat{p}_u$ or $\Delta \hat{p} < \Delta \hat{p}_L$, reject H_0 and accept H_1.

Decision rule
If $\Delta \hat{p} > \Delta \hat{p}_{\text{crit}}$, reject H_0 and accept H_1.

Decision rule
If $\Delta \hat{p} < \Delta \hat{p}_{\text{crit}}$, reject H_0 and accept H_1.

KEY WORDS

- alternative hypothesis, 393
- F distribution, 411

- null hypothesis, 393

- tests of equality of variances from two normal populations, 412

CHAPTER EXERCISES AND APPLICATIONS

Note: If the probability of Type I error is not indicated, select a level that is appropriate for the situation described.

10.28 A statistician tests the null hypothesis that the proportion of men favoring a tax reform proposal is the same as the proportion of women. Based on sample data, the null hypothesis is rejected at the 5% significance level. Does this imply that the probability is at least 0.95 that the null hypothesis is false? If not, provide a valid probability statement.

10.29 In a study of performance ratings of ex-smokers a random sample of 34 ex-smokers had a mean rating of 2.21 and a sample standard deviation of 2.21. For an independent random sample of 86 long-term ex-smokers the mean rating was 1.47 and the sample standard deviation was 1.69. Find the lowest level of significance at which the null hypothesis of equality of the two population means can be rejected against a two-sided alternative.

10.30 Independent random samples of business managers and college economics faculty were asked to respond on a scale from 1 (strongly disagree) to 7 (strongly agree) to this statement: "Grades in advanced economics are good indicators of students' analytical skills." For a sample of 70 business managers the mean response was 4.4 and the sample standard deviation was 1.3. For a sample of 106 economics faculty the mean response was 5.3 and the sample standard deviation was 1.4.

a. Test at the 5% level the null hypothesis that the population mean response for business managers would be at most 4.0.

b. Test at the 5% level the null hypothesis that the population means are equal against the alternative that the population mean response is higher for economics faculty than for business managers.

10.31 Independent random samples of bachelor's and master's degree holders in statistics, whose initial job was with a major actuarial firm and who subsequently moved to an insurance company, were questioned. For a sample of 44 bachelor's degree holders the mean number of months before the first job change was 35.02 and the sample standard deviation was 18.20. For a sample of 68 master's degree holders the mean number of months before the first job change was 36.34 and the sample standard deviation was 18.94. Test at the 10% level, against a two-sided alternative, the null hypothesis that the population mean numbers of months before the first job change are the same for the two groups.

10.32 A study was aimed at assessing the effects of group size and group characteristics on the generation of advertising concepts. To assess the influence of group size, groups of four and eight members were compared. For a random sample of four 4-member groups the mean number of advertising concepts generated per group was 78.0 and the sample standard deviation was 24.4. For an independent random sample of four 8-member groups, the mean number of advertising concepts generated per group was 114.7 and the sample standard deviation was 14.6. (In each case, the groups had a moderator.) Stating any assumptions that you need to make, test at the 1% level the null hypothesis that the population means are the same against the alternative that the mean is higher for 8-member groups.

10.33 An index of reading difficulty of a written text is calculated through the following steps:

i. Find the average number of words per sentence.

ii. Find the percentage of words with four or more syllables.

iii. The index is 40% of the sum of (i) and (ii).

A random sample of six advertisements taken from magazine A had the following indices:

15.75 10.55 10.16 9.92 9.23 8.20

An independent random sample of six advertisements from magazine B had the following indices:

9.17 8.44 6.10 5.78 5.58 5.36

Stating any assumptions you need to make, test at the 5% level the null hypothesis that the population mean indices are the same against the alternative that the true mean is higher for magazine A than for magazine B.

10.34 From Exercise 10.33 the indices for a random sample of six advertisements in magazine C were as follows:

9.50 8.60 8.59 6.50 4.79 4.29

For an independent random sample of six advertisements in magazine D, the indices were as follows:

10.21 9.66 7.67 5.12 4.88 3.12

Stating any assumptions you need to make, test against a two-sided alternative the null hypothesis that the two population mean indices are the same.

10.35 Independent random samples of business and economics faculty were asked to respond on a scale from 1 (strongly disagree) to 4 (strongly agree) to this statement: "The threat and actuality of takeovers of publicly held companies provide discipline for boards and managers to maximize the value of the company to shareholders." For a sample of 202 business faculty the mean response was 2.83 and the sample standard deviation was 0.89. For a sample of 291 economics faculty the mean response was 3.00 and the sample standard deviation was 0.67. Test the null hypothesis that the population means are equal against the alternative that the mean is higher for economics faculty.

10.36 Independent random samples of patients who had received knee and hip replacement were asked to assess the quality of service on a scale from 1 (low) to 7 (high). For a sample of 83 knee patients the mean rating was 6.543 and the sample standard deviation was 0.649. For a sample of 54 hip patients the mean rating was 6.733 and the sample standard deviation was 0.425. Test against a two-sided alternative the null hypothesis that the population mean ratings for these two types of patients are the same.

10.37 Of a random sample of 148 accounting majors, 75 rated a sense of humor as a very important trait to their career performance. This same view was held by 81 of an independent random sample of 178 finance majors.

a. Test at the 5% level the null hypothesis that at least one-half of all finance majors rate a sense of humor as very important.

b. Test at the 5% level against a two-sided alternative the null hypothesis that the population proportions of accounting and finance majors who rate a sense of humor as very important are the same.

10.38 Aimed at finding substantial earnings decreases, a random sample of 23 firms with substantial earnings decreases showed that the mean return on assets 3 years previously was 0.058 and the sample standard deviation was 0.055. An independent random sample of 23 firms without substantial earnings decreases showed a mean return of 0.146 and a standard deviation 0.058 for the same period. Assume that the two population distributions are normal with equal standard deviations. Test at the 5% level the null hypothesis that the population mean returns on assets are the same against the alternative that the true mean is higher for firms without substantial earnings decrease.

10.39 Random samples of employees in fast-food restaurants where the employer provides a training program were drawn. Of a sample of 67 employees who had not completed high school, 11 had participated in a training program provided by their current employer. Of an independent random sample of 113 employees who had completed high school but had not attended college, 27 had participated. Test at the 1% level the null hypothesis that the participation rates are the same for the two groups against the alternative that the rate is lower for those who have not completed high school.

10.40 Of a random sample of 69 health insurance firms 47 did public relations in-house, as did 40 of an independent random sample of 69 casualty insurance firms. Find and interpret the p-value of a test of equality of the population proportions against a two-sided alternative.

10.41 Independent random samples were taken of male and female clients of University Entrepreneurship Centers. These clients were considering starting a business. Of 94 male clients 53 actually started a business venture, as did 47 of 68 female clients. Find and interpret the p-value of a test of equality of the population proportions against the alternative that the proportion of female clients actually starting a business is higher than the proportion of male clients.

10.42 An index of reading difficulty of a written text is calculated through the following steps:

i. Find the average number of words per sentence.
ii. Find the percentage of words with four or more syllables.
iii. The index is 40% of the sum of (i) and (ii).

A random sample of six advertisements taken from magazine A had the following indices:

15.75 10.55 10.16 9.92 9.23 8.20

An independent random sample of six advertisements from magazine B had the following indices:

9.17 8.44 6.10 5.78 5.58 5.36

Test against a two-sided alternative the null hypothesis that the population standard deviation of the index of advertisements in magazine A is the same as the population standard deviation of the index of advertisements in magazine B.

10.43 Two financial analysts were asked to predict earnings per share for a random sample of 12 corporations over the coming year. The quality of their forecasts was evaluated in terms of absolute percentage forecast error, defined as

$$100 \cdot \frac{\left|\text{Actual} - \text{Predicted}\right|}{\text{Actual}}$$

The absolute percentage forecast errors made are shown in the data file **Analyst Prediction**.
Test the null hypothesis of equality of population variances for absolute percentage forecast errors for the two analysts.

10.44 You are in charge of rural economic development in a rapidly developing country that is using its newfound oil wealth to develop the entire country. As part of your responsibility you have been asked to determine if there is evidence that the new rice-growing procedures have increased output per hectare. A random sample of 27 fields was planted using the old procedure, and the sample mean output was 60 per hectare with a sample variance of 100. During the second year the new procedure was applied to the same fields and the sample mean output was 64 per hectare, with a sample variance of 150. The sample correlation between the two fields was 0.38. The population variances are assumed to be equal, and that assumption should be used for the problem analysis.

a. Use a hypothesis test with a probability of Type I error = 0.05 to determine if there is strong evidence to support the conclusion that the new process leads to higher output per hectare, and interpret the results.

b. Under the assumption that the population variances are equal, construct a 95% acceptance interval for the ratio of the sample variances. Do the observed sample variances lead us to conclude that the population variances are the same? Please explain.

10.45 The president of Amalgamated Retailers International, Samiha Peterson, has asked for your assistance in studying the market penetration for the company's new cell phone. You are asked to study two markets and determine if the difference in market share remains the same. Historically, in market 1 in western Poland, Amalgamated has had a 30% market share. Similarly, in market 2 in southern Austria, Amalgamated has had a 35% market share. You obtain a random sample of potential customers from each area. From market 1, 258 out of a total sample of 800 indicate they will purchase from Amalgamated. From market 2, 260 out of 700 indicate they will purchase from Amalgamated.

a. Using a probability of error $\alpha = 0.03$, test the hypothesis that the market shares are equal versus the hypothesis that they are not equal (market 2 – market 1).

b. Using a probability of error $\alpha = 0.03$, test the hypothesis that the market shares are equal versus the hypothesis that the share in market 2 is larger.

10.46 In an agricultural experiment two expensive, high-yield varieties of corn are to be tested and the yield improvements measured. The experiment is arranged so that each variety is planted in 10 pairs of similar plots. The data contained in data file **Corn Yield** are the percentage yield increases obtained for these two varieties. Stating any assumptions you make, test at the 10% level the null hypothesis that the two population mean percentage yield increases are the same. Use a two-sided alternative hypothesis.

10.47 You are the product manager for brand 4 in a large food company. The company president has complained that a competing brand, called brand 2, has higher average sales. The data services group has stored the latest product sales ("saleb2" and "saleb4") and price data ("apriceb2" and "apriceb4") in a file named **Storet**, which is contained on your data disk or local computer system.

a. Based on a statistical hypothesis test, does the president have strong evidence to support her complaint? Show all statistical work and reasoning.

b. After analyzing the data, you note that a large outlier of value 971 is contained in the sample for brand 2. Repeat part (a) with this extreme observation removed. What do you now conclude about the president's complaint?

10.48 Joe Ortega is the product manager for Ole ice cream. You have been asked to determine if Ole ice cream has greater sales than Carl's ice cream, which is a strong competitor. The **data file Ole** contains weekly sales and price data for the competing brands over the year in three different supermarket chains. These sample data represent a random sample of all ice cream sales for the two brands.

a. Design and implement an analysis to determine if there is strong evidence to conclude that Ole ice cream has higher mean sales than Carl's ice cream ($\alpha = 0.05$). Explain your procedure and show all computations. You may include Minitab output if appropriate to support your analysis. Explain your conclusions.

b. Design and implement an analysis to determine if the prices charged for the two brands are different ($\alpha = 0.05$). Carefully explain your analysis, show all computations, and interpret your results.

10.49 Mary Peterson is in charge of preparing blended flour for exotic bread making. The process is to take two different types of flour and mix them together in order to achieve high-quality breads. For one of the products flour A and flour B are mixed together. The package of flour A comes from a packing process that has a population mean weight of 8 ounces with a population variance of 0.04. The package of flour B has a population mean weight of 8 ounces and a population variance of 0.06. The package weights have a correlation of 0.40. The A and B packages are mixed together to obtain a 16-ounce package of special exotic flour. Every 60 minutes a random sample of four packages of exotic flour are selected from the process, and the mean weight for the four packages is computed. Prepare a 99% acceptance interval for a quality control chart for the sample means from the sample of four packages. Show all of your work and explain your reasoning. Explain how this acceptance chart would be used to ensure that the package weights continue to meet the standard.

10.50 A study was conducted to determine if there was a difference in humor content in British and American trade magazine advertisements. In an independent random sample of 270 American trade magazine advertisements, 56 were humorous. An independent random sample of 203 British trade magazine advertisements contained 52 humorous ads. Do these data provide evidence that there is a difference in the proportion of humorous ads in British versus American trade magazines?

REFERENCE

1. Carlson, W. L., and B. Thorne. 1997. *Applied Statistical Methods*. Upper Saddle River, NJ: Prentice Hall, 539–53.

Chapter 11

Simple Regression

Introduction

Our study to this point has focused on analysis and inference related to a single variable. In this chapter we will extend our analysis to relationships between variables. Our analysis will build on the descriptive relationships using scatter plots and covariance/correlation coefficients developed in Chapter 2. We assume that the reader is familiar with that material.

The analysis of business and economic processes makes extensive use of relationships between variables. These relationships are expressed mathematically as

$$Y = f(X)$$

where the function can follow linear and nonlinear forms. In many applications the form of the relationship is not precisely known. Here we will develop analyses based on linear models that are developed using least squares regression. In many cases linear relationships provide a good model of the process. In other cases we are interested in a limited portion of a nonlinear relationship that can be approximated by a linear relationship. In Section 12.7 we will show how some important nonlinear relationships can also be analyzed using regression analysis. Thus, the regression procedures have wide application to a broad range of problems.

Linear relationships are very useful for many business and economic applications as indicated in the following examples:

- The president of Amalgamated Materials, a manufacturer of sheetrock building material, believes that the mean annual quantity of sheetrock sold in his region is a linear function of the total value of building permits issued during the previous year.
- A grain dealer wants to know the effect of total output on price per ton so that he can develop a prediction model using historical data.
- The marketing department analysts need to know how gasoline price affects total sales of gasoline. By using weekly price and sales data, they plan to develop a linear model that will tell them how much sales change as the result of price changes.

With the advent of many high-quality statistical packages and spreadsheets such as Excel it is now possible for almost anyone to compute correlation and regression statistics. Unfortunately we also know that it is not possible for everyone to interpret and use these computer results correctly. Here you will learn key insights that will guide your use of regression analysis.

11.1 OVERVIEW OF LINEAR MODELS

In Chapter 2 we saw how the relationship between two variables can be described by using scatter plots to provide a picture of the relationship, and correlation coefficients to provide a numerical measure. In many economic and business problems a specific functional relationship is needed to obtain numerical results.

- A manager would like to know what mean level of sales can be expected if the price is set at $10 per unit.
- If 250 workers are employed in a factory, how many units would be produced during an average day?
- If a developing country increases its fertilizer production by 1,000,000 tons, how much increase in grain production should be expected?

In many cases we can adequately approximate the desired functional relationships by a linear equation,

$$Y = \beta_0 + \beta_1 X$$

where Y is the dependent or endogenous variable, X is the independent or exogenous variable, β_0 is the Y-intercept, and β_1 is the slope of the line, or the change in Y for every unit change in X. The assumption made in developing the least squares regression procedure is that different values of X can be set, and there will be a corresponding mean value of Y that results because of the underlying linear relationship in the process being studied. The linear equation model computes the mean of Y for every value of X and is the basis for obtaining many economic and business relationships including demand functions, production functions, consumption functions, and sales forecasts.

Figure 11.1
Linear Function
and Data Points

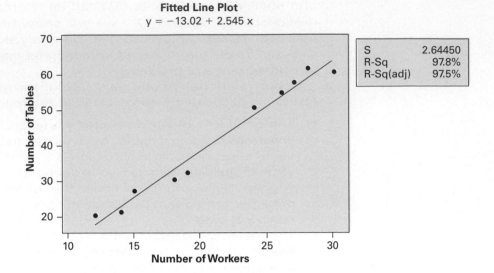

The slope coefficient β_1 is extremely important for many business and economic applications since it indicates the change in an output or endogenous variable for each unit change in an input or exogenous variable. If the linear relationship describes the relationship between the number of cell phones assembled Y as a function of the number of labor hours X used then β_1 indicates the increase in the number of cell phones assembled for each additional labor hour. Thus management can determine if the value of the increased output is greater than the cost of an additional hour of labor. The constant β_0 provides a measure of the mean level of output over all levels of the input variable.

We use regression to determine the best linear relationship between Y and X for a particular application. This requires us to find the best values for the coefficients β_0 and β_1. We use the data available from the process to compute "estimates" or numerical values for the coefficients, β_0, and β_1. These estimates—defined as b_0 and b_1—are computed by using **Least Squares Regression**, a technique widely implemented in statistical packages such as Minitab and in spreadsheets such as Excel. Regression is a procedure that computes coefficients for the best fit line given a set of data points. Consider a typical plot of points from a process that has a linear relationship as shown in Figure 11.1.

Least Squares Regression

The **least squares regression line** based on sample data is

$$\hat{y} = b_0 + b_1 x \qquad (11.1)$$

b_1 is the **slope** of the line, or change in y for every unit change in x, and calculated as

$$b_1 = \frac{Cov(x, y)}{s_x^2} \qquad (11.2)$$

and b_0 is the **y-intercept** calculated as

$$b_0 = \bar{y} - b_1 \bar{x} \qquad (11.3)$$

Example 11.1 Manufacturing Plant (Regression Line)

The Rising Hills Manufacturing Company in Redwood Falls regularly collects data to monitor its operations. This data is stored in the data file **Rising Hills**. The number of workers, X, and the number of tables, Y, produced per hour for a sample of 10 workers is shown in Figure 11.1. If management decides to employ 25 workers, estimate the expected number of tables that are likely to be produced.

Solution   Using the data, we computed the descriptive statistics:

$$Cov(x, y) = 106.93, \; s_x^2 = 42.01, \; \bar{y} = 41.2, \; \bar{x} = 21.3$$

From the covariance we see that the direction of the relationship is *positive*. Using the descriptive statistics, we compute the sample regression coefficients:

$$b_1 = \frac{Cov(x, y)}{s_x^2} = \frac{106.93}{42.01} = 2.545$$

$$b_0 = \bar{y} - b_1\bar{x} = 41.2 - 2.545(21.3) = -13.02$$

From this, the sample regression line is as follows:

$$\hat{y} = b_0 + b_1 x = -13.02 + 2.545x$$

For 25 employees we would expect to produce

$$\hat{y} = -13.02 + 2.545(25) = 50.615$$

or approximately 51 tables. We can also use a statistical software package such as Minitab or a spreadsheet such as Excel to obtain the same regression coefficients and regression line for most realistic data as the sample size generally makes computation tedious.

We can *always* substitute *any* value for x into a least squares line and make a meaningful decision. Sometimes the relationship is merely spurious or the value of x may be outside an acceptable range of values. For example, since the numbers of workers in the Rising Hill Manufacturing Plant ranged from 12 to 30, we cannot predict the number of tables produced per hour if 100 workers were employed.

EXERCISES

Basic Exercises

11.1 Complete the following for the (x, y) pairs of data points (1,5), (3,7), (4,6), (5,8), and (7,9):

a. Prepare a scatter plot of these data points.
b. Compute b_1.
c. Compute b_0.
d. What is the equation of the regression line?

11.2 The following data gives X, the price charged per piece of plywood and Y, the quantity sold (in thousands).

Price per Piece, X	Thousands of Pieces Sold, Y
$6	80
7	60
8	70
9	40
10	0

a. Prepare a scatter plot of these data points.
b. Compute the covariance.
c. Compute and interpret b_1.

d. Compute b_0.

e. What quantity of plywood would you expect to sell if the price were $7 per piece?

11.3 A random sample of data for 7 days of operation produced the following (price, quantity) data values:

Price per Gallon of Paint, X	Quantity Sold, Y
10	100
8	120
5	200
4	200
10	90
7	110
6	150

a. Prepare a scatter plot of the data.

b. Compute and interpret b_1.

c. Compute and interpret b_0.

d. How many gallons of paint would you expect to sell if the price is $7 per gallon?

Application Exercises

11.4 A large consumer goods company has been studying the effect of advertising on total profits. As part of this study, data on advertising expenditures and total sales were collected for a 6-month period and are as follows:

(10, 100) (15, 200) (7, 80) (12, 120) (14, 150)

The first number is advertising expenditures and the second is total sales.

a. Plot the data.

b. Does the plot provide evidence that advertising has a positive effect on sales?

c. Compute the regression coefficients, b_0 and b_1.

11.5 Abdul Hassan, president of Floor Coverings Unlimited, has asked you to study the relationship between market price and the tons of rugs supplied by his competitor, Best Floor Inc. He supplies you with the following observations of price per ton and number of tons, obtained from his secret files:

(2, 5) (4, 10) (3, 8) (6, 18) (3, 6) (5, 15) (6, 20) (2, 4)

The first number for each observation is price and the second is quantity.

a. Prepare a scatter plot.

b. Determine the regression coefficients, b_0 and b_1.

c. Write a short explanation of the regression equation that tells Abdul how the equation can be used to describe his competition. Include an indication of the range over which the equation can be applied.

11.6 A random sample of 12 college baseball players participated in a special weight-training program in an attempt to improve their batting averages. The program lasted for 20 weeks immediately prior to the start of the baseball season. The average number of hours per week and the change in their batting averages from the preceding season are as follows:

(8.0, 10) (20.0, 100) (5.4, −10) (12.4, 79) (9.2, 50) (15.0, 89) (6.0, 34) (8.0, 30) (18.0, 68) (25.0, 110) (10.0, 34) (5.0, 10)

a. Plot the data. Does it appear that the weight-training program was successful?

b. Estimate the regression equation.

11.2 LINEAR REGRESSION MODEL

From our study of economics we know that the quantity of goods purchased, Y, in a specific market can be modeled as a linear function of the disposable income, X. If income is a specific level, x_i, purchasers respond by purchasing a quantity, y_i. In the real world we know there are other factors that influence the actual quantity purchased. These include identifiable factors such as the price of the goods in question, advertising, and the prices of competing goods. In addition, there are other unknown factors that can influence the actual quantity purchased. In a simple linear equation we model the effect of these factors, other than income, by an error term labeled as ε. Thus, the model is as follows:

$$Y = \beta_0 + \beta_1 X + \varepsilon$$

Least squares regression provides us with an estimated model of the linear relationship between an independent or exogenous variable and a dependent or endogenous variable. We begin the process of regression modeling by assuming a population model that has predetermined X values, and for every X there is a mean value of Y plus a random error term. We use the estimated regression equation—as shown in Figure 11.1—to estimate the mean value of Y for every value of X. Individual points vary about this line because of a random error term that has a mean of 0 and a common variance for all values of X. The random error represents all of the influences on Y that are not represented by the linear relationship between Y and X. Effects of these factors, which are assumed to be independent of X, behave like a random variable whose population mean is 0. The random deviations ε_i about the linear model are shown in Figure 11.2, and they are combined with the mean of Y_i for every X_i to obtain the observed value y_i.

Figure 11.2 presents an example of a set of observations that were generated by an underlying linear model of a process. The mean level of Y, for every X, is represented by the population equation

$$Y = \beta_0 + \beta_1 X$$

The linear regression model provides the expected value of the random variable Y when X takes on a specific value. The assumption of linearity implies that this expectation can be written as

$$E(Y \mid X = x) = \beta_0 + \beta_1 X$$

where β_0 represents the Y intercept of the equation and β_1 is the slope. The actual observed value of Y for a given value of X is modeled as being equal to the expected value or population mean plus a random error, ε, that has a mean of 0 and a variance of σ^2:

$$y = \beta_0 + \beta_1 X_i + \varepsilon$$

The random error term ε represents the variation in y that is not explained by the linear relationship. The following assumptions are used to make inferences about the population linear model by using the estimated model coefficients.

Figure 11.2
Population Model
for Linear
Regression

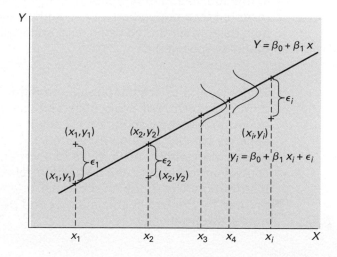

Linear Regression Assumptions

1. The *Y*s are linear functions of *X* plus a random error term

$$y_i = \beta_0 + \beta_1 x_i + \varepsilon_i$$

2. The *x* values are fixed numbers, or they are realizations of random variable *X* that are independent of the error terms, ε_i $(i = 1, \cdots, n)$. In the latter case inference is carried out conditionally on the observed values of x_i $(i = 1, \cdots, n)$.

3. The error terms are random variables with a mean of 0 and the same variance, σ^2. The latter is called homoscedasticity or uniform variance:

$$E[\varepsilon_i] = 0 \quad \text{and} \quad E[\varepsilon_i^2] = \sigma^2 \quad \text{for} \quad (i = 1, \ldots, n)$$

4. The random error terms, ε_i, are not correlated with one another, so that

$$E[\varepsilon_i \varepsilon_j] = 0 \quad \text{for all } i \neq j$$

The linear equation represented by the line is the best fit linear equation. We see that individual data points are above and below the line and that the line has points with both positive and negative deviations. The distance—in the Y or vertical dimension—of each point (x_i, y_i) from the linear equation is defined as the residual, e_i. We would like to choose the equation so that some function of the positive and negative residuals is as small as possible. In this way we find estimates for the coefficients, β_0 and β_1, which we label as b_0 and b_1. Equations to compute these estimates are developed using the least squares regression procedure. Least squares regression chooses b_0 and b_1 such that the sum of the squared residuals is minimized. The least squares procedure is intuitively rational and provides estimators that have good statistical properties.

Linear Regression Population Equation Model

In the application of regression analysis the process being studied is represented by a population model, and an estimated model, utilizing available data, is computed using least squares regression. The population model is specified as

$$y_i = \beta_0 + \beta_1 x_i + \varepsilon_i \tag{11.4}$$

where β_0 and β_1 are the population model coefficients and ε is a random error term. For every observed value, x_i, an observed value, y_i, is generated by the population model. For purposes of statistical inference, as we will develop in Section 11.5, ε is assumed to have a normal distribution with a mean of 0 and a variance of σ^2. Later we see that the central limit theorem can be used to relax the assumption of a normal distribution. The model of the linear relationship between *Y* and *X* is defined by the two coefficients, β_0 and β_1. Figure 11.2 represents the model schematically.

In the least squares regression model we assume that values of the independent variable, x_i, are selected, and for each x_i there is a population mean of Y. The observed values of y_i contain the mean and the random deviation ε_i. A set of n (x_i, y_i) points is observed and used to obtain estimates of the model coefficients using the least squares procedure. We extend the concepts of classical inference developed in Chapters 7–10 to make inferences about the underlying population model by using the estimated regression model. In Chapter 12 we will see how several independent variables can be considered simultaneously using multiple regression.

The estimated regression model as shown schematically in Figure 11.3 is given by the equation

$$y_i = b_0 + b_1 x_i + e_i$$

where b_0 and b_1 are the estimated values of the coefficients and e is the difference between the predicted value of Y on the regression line, defined as

$$\hat{y}_i = b_0 + b_1 x_i$$

and the observed value y_i. The difference between y_i and $\hat{y}_i$ for each value of X is defined as the residual

$$e_i = y_i - \hat{y}_i$$
$$= y_i - (b_0 + b_1 x_i)$$

Thus, for each observed value of X there is a predicted value of Y from the estimated model and an observed value. The difference between the observed and predicted values of Y is defined as the residual, e_i. The residual, e_i, is not the model error, ε, but is the combined measure of the model error and errors that result because b_0 and b_1 are sample results and, thus, subject to random variation or error, in turn, this leads to variation or error in estimating the predicted value.

We determine the estimated regression model by obtaining estimates, b_0 and b_1, of the population coefficients using the process called least squares analysis, which we will develop in Section 11.3. These coefficients are, in turn, used to obtain predicted values of Y for every value of X.

Figure 11.3
Estimated
Regression Model

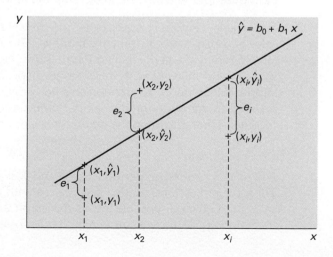

Early mathematicians struggled with the problem of developing a procedure for estimating the coefficients for the linear equation. Simply minimizing the deviations was not useful because the deviations have both positive and negative signs. Various procedures using absolute values have also been developed but none has proven as useful or as popular as least squares regression. We will learn later that the coefficients developed using this procedure also have very useful statistical properties. One important caution for least squares is that extreme outlier points can have such a strong influence on the regression line that the line is shifted toward this point. Thus, you should always examine scatter plots to be sure that the regression relationship is not based on just a few extreme points.

Our discussion continues with an example that indicates a typical application of regression analysis and the kind of results that can be obtained.

Example 11.2 Sales Prediction for Northern Household Goods (Regression Model Estimation)

The president of Northern Household Goods has asked you to develop a model that will predict total sales for proposed new retail store locations. Northern is a rapidly expanding general retailer, and it needs a rational strategy for determining where new stores should be located. As part of the project you need to estimate a linear equation that predicts retail sales per household as a function of household disposable income. The company has obtained data from a national sampling survey of households, and the variables retail sales (Y) and income (X) per household will be used to develop the model.

Solution Figure 11.4 is a scatter plot that shows the relationship between retail sales and disposable income for families. The actual data are shown in Table 11.1 and stored in a data file named **Retail Sales**. From economic theory we know that sales should increase with increases in disposable income, and the plot strongly supports that theory. Regression analysis provides us with a linear model that can be used to compute retail sales per household for various levels of disposable income. A line drawn on the graph represents the simple regression model

$$Y = 559 + 0.3815X$$

where Y is retail sales per household and X is disposable income per household. Thus, the regression equation provides us with the best linear model for predicting sales for a given disposable income based on the data. Notice that this model tells us that every \$1 increase in per capita disposable family income, X, is associated

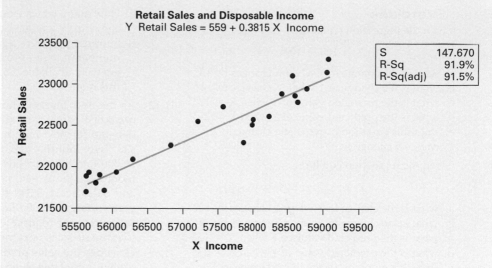

Figure 11.4 Retail Sales per Household versus Per Capita Disposable Income

Table 11.1 Data on Disposable Income per Household (*X*) and Retail Sales per Household (*Y*)

YEAR	INCOME (*X*)	RETAIL SALES (*Y*)	YEAR	INCOME (*X*)	RETAIL SALES (*Y*)
1	$55,641	$21,886	12	$57,850	$22,301
2	$55,681	$21,934	13	$57,975	$22,518
3	$55,637	$21,699	14	$57,992	$22,580
4	$55,825	$21,901	15	$58,240	$22,618
5	$55,772	$21,812	16	$58,414	$22,890
6	$55,890	$21,714	17	$58,561	$23,112
7	$56,068	$21,932	18	$59,066	$23,315
8	$56,299	$22,086	19	$58,596	$22,865
9	$56,825	$22,265	20	$58,631	$22,788
10	$57,205	$22,551	21	$58,758	$22,949
11	$57,562	$22,736	22	$59,037	$23,149

with an increase in the expected value of retail sales, *Y*, of $0.38. Clearly, that result is important for forecasting retail sales. For example, we find that a family income of $50,000 would predict retail sales at $19,075 ($559 + $50,000 × 0.3815).

At this point we need to emphasize that the regression results summarize the information contained in the data and do not "prove" that increased income "causes" increased sales. Economic theory suggests that there is causation, and the estimated regression model supports that theory. Scatter plots, correlations, and regression equations cannot prove causation, but they can provide supporting evidence. Thus, in order to establish conclusions, we need a combination of theory— experience in business management and economics—and good statistical analysis.

Basic Exercises

11.7 Given the regression equation

$$Y = 100 + 10X$$

a. what is the change in Y when X changes by +3?
b. what is the change in Y when X changes by –4?
c. what is the predicted value of Y when $X = 12$?
d. what is the predicted value of Y when $X = 23$?
e. does this equation prove that a change in X causes a change in Y?

11.8 Given the regression equation

$$Y = -50 + 12X$$

a. what is the change in Y when X changes by +3?
b. what is the change in Y when X changes by –4?
c. what is the predicted value of Y when $X = 12$?
d. what is the predicted value of Y when $X = 23$?
e. does this equation prove that a change in X causes a change in Y?

11.9 Given the regression equation

$$Y = 43 + 10X$$

a. what is the change in Y when X changes by +8?
b. what is the change in Y when X changes by –6?
c. what is the predicted value of Y when $X = 11$?
d. what is the predicted value of Y when $X = 29$?
e. does this equation prove that a change in X causes a change in Y?

11.10 Given the regression equation

$$Y = 100 + 21X$$

a. what is the change in Y when X changes by +5?
b. what is the change in Y when X changes by –7?
c. what is the predicted value of Y when $X = 14$?
d. what is the predicted value of Y when $X = 27$?
e. does this equation prove that a change in X causes a change in Y?

Application Exercises

11.11 In Example 11.1 a linear regression model was developed. Use that model to answer the following:

a. Interpret the coefficient $b_1 = 2.545$ for the plant manager.

b. How many tables would be produced on average with 19 workers?
c. Suppose you were asked to estimate the number of tables produced if only five workers were available. Discuss your response to this request.

11.12 As the new Market Manger for Blue Crunchies breakfast cereal you are asked to estimate the demand for next month using regression analysis. Two months ago the target market had 20,000 families and sales were 3,780 boxes, one month ago the target market was 40,000 families and sales were 5,349 boxes. Next month you plan to target 75,000 families. How would you respond to the request to use regression analysis to estimate sales next month?

11.13 Consider the sales prediction model developed for Northern Household Goods in Example 11.2.

a. Estimate per capita sales if the mean disposable income is $46,000?
b. Interpret the coefficients, b_0 and b_1 for Northern's management.
c. You have been asked to estimate per capita sales if mean disposable income grows to $64,000. Discuss how you would proceed and indicate your cautions.

11.14 What is the difference between a population linear model and an estimated linear regression model?

11.15 Explain the difference between the residual e_i and the model error ε_i.

11.16 Suppose that we obtained an estimated equation for the regression of weekly sales of "palm pilots" and the price charged during the week. Interpret the constant b_0 for the product brand manager.

11.17 A regression model of total grocery sales on disposable income was estimated using data from small isolated towns in the western United States. Prepare a list of factors that might contribute to the random error term.

11.3 LEAST SQUARES COEFFICIENT ESTIMATORS

The population regression line is a useful theoretical construct, but for applications we need to determine an estimate of the model using available data. Suppose that we have n pairs of observations, $(x_1, y_1), (x_2, y_2), ..., (x_n, y_n)$. We would like to find the straight line that best fits these points. To do this, we need to find estimators of the unknown coefficients β_0 and β_1 of the population regression line.

We obtain the coefficient estimators b_0 and b_1 with equations derived by using the least squares procedure. As shown in Figure 11.3, there is a deviation, e_i, between the observed value, y_i, and the predicted value, $\hat{y}_i$, in the estimated regression equation for each value of X, where $e_i = y_i - \hat{y}_i$. We then compute a mathematical function that represents the effect of squaring all of the residuals and computing the sum of the squared residuals. This function—whose left side is labeled SSE—includes the coefficients b_0 and b_1. The quantity SSE is defined as the *error sum of squares*. The coefficient estimators b_0 and b_1 are selected as the estimators that minimize the error sum of squares.

Least Squares Procedure

The least squares procedure obtains estimates of the linear equation coefficients b_0 and b_1 in the model

$$\hat{y}_i = b_0 + b_1 x_i \tag{11.5}$$

by minimizing the sum of the squared residuals e_i:

$$SSE = \sum_{i=1}^{n} e_i^2$$

$$= \sum_{i=1}^{n} \left(y_i - \hat{y}_i \right)^2 \tag{11.6}$$

The coefficients b_0 and b_1 are chosen so that the quantity

$$SSE = \sum_{i=1}^{n} e_i^2$$

$$= \sum_{i=1}^{n} (y_i - (b_0 + b_1 x_i))^2 \tag{11.7}$$

is minimized. We use differential calculus to obtain the coefficient estimators that minimize SSE. The derivation of the estimators using calculus is presented in the chapter appendix.

The resulting coefficient estimator is as follows:

$$b_1 = \frac{\sum_{i=1}^{n} (x_i - \bar{x})(y_i - \bar{y})}{\sum_{i=1}^{n} (x_i - \bar{x})^2}$$

$$= \frac{Cov(x, y)}{s_x^2}$$

$$= \frac{\sum_{i=1}^{n} (x_i - \bar{x}) y_i}{\sum_{i=1}^{n} (x_i - \bar{x}) x_i}$$

Note that the numerator of the estimator is the sample covariance of X and Y and the denominator is the sample variance of X. The third line shows that the coefficient b_1 is a linear function of the Y's. We spend considerable time with the slope coefficient because for many applications this is the key result. The slope coefficient b_1 is an estimate of the change in Y when X changes by one unit. For example, if Y is total output and X is number of workers, then b_1 is an estimate of the marginal increase in output for each new worker. Results such as this explain why regression has become such an important analysis tool.

With some algebraic manipulations we can show that the coefficient estimator is also equal to

$$b_1 = r_{xy} \frac{s_Y}{s_X}$$

where r_{xy} is the sample correlation and s_y and s_x are the sample standard deviations for X and Y. This is an important result because it indicates how the standardized relationship between X and Y, the correlation r_{xy}, is directly related to the slope coefficient.

In the chapter appendix we also show that the constant estimator is as follows:

$$b_0 = \bar{y} - b_1 \bar{x}$$

Substituting this value for b_0 into the linear equation, we have the following:

$$y = \bar{y} - b_1 \bar{x} + b_1 x$$
$$y - \bar{y} = b_1(x - \bar{x})$$

From this equation we see that, when $x = \bar{x}$ then $y = \bar{y}$ and that the regression equation always passes through the point $(\bar{x}, \bar{y})$. The estimated value of the dependent variable, $\hat{y}_i$, is then obtained by using

$$\hat{y}_i = b_0 + b_1 x_i$$

or by using

$$\hat{y}_i = \bar{y} + b_1(x_i - \bar{x})$$

This latter form emphasizes that the regression line goes through the means of X and Y.

Least Squares Derived Coefficient Estimators
The slope coefficient estimator is

$$b_1 = \frac{\sum_{i=1}^{n} (x_i - \bar{x})(y_i - \bar{y})}{\sum_{i=1}^{n} (x_i - \bar{x})^2} = r_{xy} \frac{s_Y}{s_X}$$

and the constant or intercept estimator is

$$b_0 = \bar{y} - b_1 \bar{x}$$

We also note that the regression line always goes through the mean $(\bar{X}, \bar{Y})$.

The least squares procedure could be used to compute coefficient estimates b_0 and b_1, using any set of paired data. However, in most applications we want to make inferences about the underlying population

> model that is part of our economic or business problem. In order to make inferences it is necessary that we agree on the linear regression assumptions given in Section 11.2. Given these assumptions, it can be shown that the least squares coefficient estimators are unbiased and have minimum variance.

The second of these assumptions—where x values are fixed and independent of the model error—is generally, with justification, taken to be true, although in some advanced econometric work, it is untenable. (The assumption fails to hold, for example, when the x_i cannot be measured precisely or when the regression is part of a system of interdependent equations.) Here, however, we will take this assumption as given.

Assumptions 3 and 4 concern the error terms, ε_i, in the regression equation. The expected error term is 0, and all error terms have the same variance. Thus, we do not expect the variances of the error terms to be higher for some observations than for others. Figure 11.2 shows this pattern with the errors for all X values being sampled from populations with the same variance. Finally, it is assumed that the instances of ε_i $(i = 1, \cdots, n)$ are not correlated with one another. Thus, for example, the occurrence of a large positive discrepancy at one observation point does not help us predict the values of any of the other error terms. Assumptions 3 and 4 will be satisfied if the error terms, ε_i, can be viewed as a random sample from a population with a mean of 0. In the remainder of this chapter, these assumptions will hold. With larger sample sizes we can show that the central limit theorem can be applied to the coefficient estimators and they can be treated just as we did sample means in various forms of inference in Chapters 7–10. Thus, the assumption of normality can be relaxed. The possibility for relaxing some of these assumptions will be considered in Chapter 13.

Computer Computation of Regression Coefficient

Extensive application of regression analysis has been made possible by statistical computer packages and Excel. As you might suspect, the computations to obtain the regression coefficient estimates are tedious. The estimator equations and other important statistical computations are included in computer packages and Excel and are used to compute the coefficient estimates for specific problems. Excel can be used to obtain the basic regression output without too much difficulty. But if you wish to use some of the advanced applied regression analysis procedures or insightful graphical analysis, then you should use a good statistical computer package. Since we are primarily interested in applications, our most important task is proper analysis of the regression computations for these applications. This analysis should be guided by knowing the estimator equations and the related discussion. We do not, however, use these estimator equations to actually compute the estimates or other regression statistics. *We assign the computation to computers—our tasks are to think, analyze, and make recommendations.*

Figure 11.5 presents a portion of the Minitab output for the retail sales example. Note the location of the estimates for the constant, b_0, and the slope coefficient, b_1, in the computer output. The remaining items on each line help interpret the quality of the estimates and are developed in subsequent sections.

Figure 11.5
Regression
Analysis for Retail
Sales Using
Minitab

Regression Analysis: Y Retail Sales versus X Income

```
The regression equation is
Y  Retail Sales = 559 + 0.382 X  Income                    Coefficients b₀, b₁

Predictor        Coef   SE Coef        T       P
Constant          559      1451     0.39   0.704
X  Income     0.38152   0.02529    15.08   0.000


S = 147.670    R-Sq = 91.9%    R-Sq(adj) = 91.5%


Analysis of Variance

Source           DF         SS         MS        F       P
Regression        1    4961434    4961434   227.52   0.000
Residual Error   20     436127      21806
Total            21    5397561


Unusual Observations

                       Y  Retail
Obs   X  Income          Sales        Fit   SE Fit   Residual   St Resid
 12       57850        22301.0    22630.2     34.0     -329.2      -2.29R


R denotes an observation with a large standardized residual
```

In this regression the estimated constant, b_0, is 559 and the estimated slope coefficient, b_1, is 0.382. These values were computed using the coefficient estimator equations previously developed. The estimated equation can be written as

$$\hat{y}_i = 559 + 0.382x$$

or, using the means $\overline{X} = 57{,}342$ and $\overline{Y} = 22{,}436$, as

$$\hat{y}_i = 22{,}436 + 0.382(x_i - 57{,}342)$$

Typically, regression models should be used only over the range of the observed X values where we have information about the relationship because the relationship may not be linear outside this range. The second form of the regression model is centered on the data means with a rate of change equal to b_1. By using this form, we focus on the mean location of the regression model and not on the intercept with the Y axis. Naïve users of regression analysis will sometimes attempt interpretations of the constant b_0, claiming certain conclusions about the dependent variable when the independent variable has a value of 0. Consider the example regression of retail sales on disposable income. Would we really claim that retail sales are $559 when disposable income is 0? In fact, we simply do not have data to support any sales amount when disposable income is 0. This is another example of the importance of good analysis instead of silly interpretations. As professional analysts we must be careful not to claim results that simply do not exist.

EXERCISES

Basic Exercise

11.18 Compute the coefficients for a least squares regression equation and write the equation, given the following sample statistics:

a. $\overline{x} = 50$, $\overline{y} = 100$, $s_x = 25$, $s_y = 75$, $r_{xy} = 0.6$, $n = 60$.
b. $\overline{x} = 60$, $\overline{y} = 210$, $s_x = 35$, $s_y = 65$, $r_{xy} = 0.7$, $n = 60$.
c. $\overline{x} = 20$, $\overline{y} = 100$, $s_x = 60$, $s_y = 78$, $r_{xy} = 0.75$, $n = 60$.

d. $\bar{x} = 10$, $\bar{y} = 50$, $s_x = 100$, $s_y = 75$, $r_{xy} = 0.4$, n = 60.

e. $\bar{x} = 90$, $\bar{y} = 200$, $s_x = 80$, $s_y = 70$, $r_{xy} = 0.6$, n = 60.

Application Exercises

11.19 A company sets different prices for a particular DVD system in eight different regions of the country. The accompanying table shows the numbers of units sold and the corresponding prices (in dollars).

Sales	420	380	350	400	440	380	450	420
Price	104	195	148	204	96	256	141	109

a. Plot these data, and estimate the linear regression of sales on price.

b. What effect would you expect a $50 increase in price to have on sales?

11.20 For a sample of 20 monthly observations a financial analyst wants to regress the percentage rate of return (Y) of the common stock of a corporation on the percentage rate of return (X) of the Standard and Poor's 500 index. The following information is available:

$$\sum_{i=1}^{20} y_i = 22.6 \quad \sum_{i=1}^{20} x_i = 25.4 \quad \sum_{i=1}^{20} x_i^2 = 145.7 \quad \sum_{i=1}^{20} x_i y_i = 150.5$$

a. Estimate the linear regression of Y on X.

b. Interpret the slope of the sample regression line.

c. Interpret the intercept of the sample regression line.

11.21 A corporation administers an aptitude test to all new sales representatives. Management is interested in the extent to which this test is able to predict sales representatives' eventual success. The accompanying table records average weekly sales (in thousands of dollars) and aptitude test scores for a random sample of eight representatives.

Weekly sales	10	12	28	24	18	16	15	12
Test score	55	60	85	75	80	85	65	60

a. Estimate the linear regression of weekly sales on aptitude test scores.

b. Interpret the estimated slope of the regression line.

11.22 It was hypothesized that the number of bottles of an imported premium beer sold per evening in the restaurants of a city depends linearly on the average costs of meals in the restaurants. The following results were obtained for a sample of n = 17 restaurants of approximately equal size where

y = number of bottles sold per evening

x = average cost, in dollars, of a meal

$$\bar{x} = 25.5 \quad \bar{y} = 16.0 \quad \frac{\sum_{i=1}^{n}(x_i - \bar{x})^2}{n-1} = 350$$

$$\frac{\sum_{i=1}^{n}(x_i - \bar{x})(y_i - \bar{y})}{n-1} = 180$$

a. Find the sample regression line.

b. Interpret the slope of the sample regression line.

c. Is it possible to provide a meaningful interpretation of the intercept of the sample regression line? Explain.

It is recommended that the following exercises be solved by using a computer.

11.23 Refer to the data file **Dow Jones**, which contains percentage change (X) in the Dow Jones index over the first five trading days of the year and percentage change (Y) in the index over the whole year.

a. Estimate the linear regression of Y on X.

b. Provide interpretations of the intercept and slope of the sample regression line.

11.24 On Friday, November 13, 1989, prices on the New York Stock Exchange fell steeply; the Standard and Poor's 500-share index was down 6.1% on that day. The data file **New York Stock Exchange Gains and Losses** shows the percentage *losses* (y) of the 25 largest mutual funds on November 13, 1989. Also shown are the percentage *gains* (x), assuming reinvested dividends and capital gains, for these same funds for 1989 through November 11.

a. Estimate the linear regression of November 13 losses on pre–November 13, 1989, gains.

b. Interpret the slope of the sample regression line.

11.25 Ace Manufacturing is studying worker absence. The data in the file **Employee Absence** were found for annual change in overall absentee rate and annual change in mean employee absence rate due to own illness.

a. Estimate the linear regression of change in mean employee absence rate due to own illness on change in absentee rate.

b. Interpret the estimated slope of the regression line.

11.4 The Explanatory Power of a Linear Regression Equation

The estimated regression model that we have developed can be viewed as a method for explaining the changes in a dependent variable Y that results from changes in an independent variable X. If we had observations only of the dependent variable, Y, then the central tendency of Y would be represented by the mean $\bar{y}$ and the total variability about the central tendency Y would be represented by the numerator of the sample variance estimator, $\sum(y_i - \bar{y})^2$. When we also have measures of X, we have shown that the central tendency of Y can now be expressed as a function of X. We expect that the linear equation would be closer to the individual values of Y, and, thus, the variability about the linear equation would be smaller than the variability about the mean.

Now we are ready to develop measures that indicate how effectively the variable X explains the behavior of Y. In our retail sales example shown in Figure 11.4, retail sales, Y, tends to increase with disposable income, X, and, thus, disposable income explains some of the differences in retail sales. The points, however, are not all on the line, so the explanation is not perfect. Here, we will develop measures based on the partitioning of variability that measure the capability of X to explain Y in a specific regression application.

The analysis of variance, ANOVA, for least squares regression is developed by partitioning the total variability of Y into an explained component and an error component. In Figure 11.6 we show that the deviation of an individual Y value from its mean can be partitioned into the deviation of the predicted value from the mean and the deviation of the observed value from the predicted value:

$$y_i - \bar{y} = (\hat{y}_i - \bar{y}) + (y_i - \hat{y}_i)$$

We square each side of the equation—because the sum of deviations about the mean is equal to 0—and sum the result over all n points:

$$\sum_{i=1}^{n}(y_i - \bar{y})^2 = \sum_{i=1}^{n}(\hat{y}_i - \bar{y})^2 + \sum_{i=1}^{n}(y_i - \hat{y})^2$$

Figure 11.6
Partitioning of
Variability

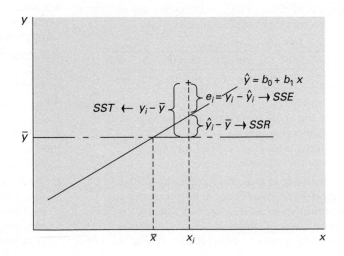

Some of you may note the squaring of the right-hand side should include the cross product of the two terms in addition to their squared quantities. It can be shown that the cross-product term goes to 0. This equation is expressed as follows:

$$SST = SSR + SSE$$

Here, we see that the total variability—SST—can be partitioned into a component—SSR—that represents variability that is explained by the slope of the regression equation. (The mean of Y is different at different levels of X.) The second component—SSE—results from the random or unexplained deviation of points from the regression line. This variability provides an indication of the uncertainty that is associated with the regression model. We define the left side as the *total sum of squares*:

$$SST = \sum_{i=1}^{n} (y_i - \bar{y})^2$$

The amount of variability explained by the regression equation is defined as the *regression sum of squares* and computed as follows:

$$SSR = \sum_{i=1}^{n} (\hat{y}_i - y)^2 = b_1^2 \sum_{i=1}^{n} (x_i - \bar{x})^2$$

We see that the variability explained by the regression depends directly on the size of the coefficient b_1 and on the spread of the independent, X, variable data. The deviations about the regression line, e_i, that are used to compute the unexplained or *error sum of squares* can be defined using the following algebraic forms:

$$SSE = \sum_{i=1}^{n} (y_i - (b_0 + b_1 x_i))^2 = \sum_{i=1}^{n} (y_i - \hat{y}_i)^2 = \sum_{i=1}^{n} e_i^2$$

For a given set of observed values of the dependent variables, Y, the SST is fixed as the total variability of all observations from the mean. We see that in this partitioning, larger values of SSR and hence smaller values of SSE indicate a regression equation that "fits" or comes closer to the observed data. This partitioning is shown graphically in Figure 11.6. From the equation for SSR we see that explained variability, SSR, is directly related to the spread of the independent or X variable. Thus, as we are thinking about regression applications, we know that we should try to obtain data that have a large range for the independent variable so that the resulting regression model will have a smaller unexplained variability.

Analysis of Variance

The total variability in a regression analysis, SST, can be partitioned into a component explained by the regression, SSR, and a component due to unexplained error, SSE,

$$SST = SSR + SSE \qquad\qquad (11.8)$$

with the components defined as follows:
Total sum of squares

$$SST = \sum_{i=1}^{n} (y_i - \bar{y})^2 \qquad\qquad (11.9)$$

Error sum of squares

$$SSE = \sum_{i=1}^{n} (y_i - (b_0 + b_1 x_i))^2 = \sum_{i=1}^{n} (y_i - \hat{y}_i)^2 = \sum_{i=1}^{n} e_i^2 \qquad (11.10)$$

Regression sum of squares

$$SSR = \sum_{i=1}^{n}(\hat{y}_i - \bar{y})^2 = b_1^2 \sum_{i=1}^{n}(x_i - \bar{x})^2 \qquad (11.11)$$

With this background let us return to our retail sales example (Example 11.2) with data file **Retail Sales** and look at how we use the partitioned variability to determine how well our model explains the process being studied. Table 11.2 shows the detailed calculations of residuals, e_i; deviations of Y from the mean, and deviations of predicted values of Y from the mean. These provide us with the components to compute SSE, SST, and SSR. The sum of squared deviations for column 5 is $SSE = 436,127$. The sum of squared deviations for column 6 is $SST = 5,397,565$. Finally, the sum of squared deviations for column 7 is $SSR = 4,961,438$. Figure 11.7 presents the Minitab and Excel regression outputs with the analysis of variance section included.

Table 11.2 Actual and Predicted Values for Retail Sales per Household and Residuals from Its Linear Regression on Income per Household

Year	Income (X)	Retail Sales (Y)	Predicted Retail Sales	Residual	Observed Deviation from the Mean	Predicted Deviation from the Mean
1	55,641	21,886	21,787	99	-550	-649
2	55,681	21,934	21,803	131	-502	-633
3	55,637	21,699	21,786	-87	-737	-650
4	55,825	21,901	21,858	43	-535	-578
5	55,772	21,812	21,837	-25	-624	-599
6	55,890	21,714	21,882	-168	-722	-554
7	56,068	21,932	21,950	-18	-504	-486
8	56,299	22,086	22,039	48	-350	-398
9	56,825	22,265	22,239	26	-171	-197
10	57,205	22,551	22,384	167	115	-52
11	57,562	22,736	22,520	216	300	84
12	57,850	22,301	22,630	-329	-135	194
13	57,975	22,518	22,678	-160	82	242
14	57,992	22,580	22,684	-104	144	248
15	58,240	22,618	22,779	-161	182	343
16	58,414	22,890	22,845	45	454	409
17	58,561	23,112	22,902	211	676	465
18	59,066	23,315	23,094	221	879	658
19	58,596	22,865	22,915	-50	429	479
20	58,631	22,788	22,928	-140	352	492
21	58,758	22,949	22,977	-28	513	541
22	59,037	23,149	23,083	-66	713	647
			Sum of squared values	436,127	5,397,565	4,961,438

Figure 11.7
Regression
Analysis for Retail
Sales on
Disposable
Income

Regression Analysis: Y Retail Sales versus X Income

```
The regression equation is
Y  Retail Sales = 559 + 0.382 X  Income

Predictor      Coef   SE Coef      T      P
Constant        559      1451   0.39  0.704
X  Income    0.38152   0.02529  15.08  0.000
```

s_e, Standard error of the estimate

```
S = 147.670    R-Sq = 91.9%   R-Sq(adj) = 91.5%
```

R^2, Coefficient of determination

```
Analysis of Variance

Source           DF        SS        MS       F      P
Regression        1   4961434   4961434  227.52  0.000
Residual Error   20    436127     21806
Total            21   5397561
```

s_e^2, Model error variance

$SSR = 4,961,434$
$SSE = 436,127$
$SST = 5,397,561$

```
Unusual Observations

                    Y  Retail
Obs   X  Income       Sales      Fit   SE Fit  Residual  St Resid
 12       57850     22301.0  22630.2     34.0    -329.2    -2.29R
```

```
R denotes an observation with a large standardized residual.
```

Coefficient of Determination R^2

We have seen that the fit of the regression equation to the data is improved as SSR increases and SSE decreases. The ratio of the regression sum of squares, SSR, divided by the total sum of squares, SST, provides a descriptive measure of the proportion or percent of the total variability that is explained by the regression model. This measure is called the *coefficient of determination*—or, more generally, R^2:

$$R^2 = \frac{SSR}{SST} = 1 - \frac{SSE}{SST}$$

The coefficient of determination is often interpreted as the percent of variability in y that is explained by the regression equation. Previously, we showed that SSR increases directly with the spread of the independent variable X:

$$SSR = \sum_{i=1}^{n} (\hat{y}_i - \bar{y})^2 = b_1^2 \sum_{i=1}^{n} (x_i - \bar{x})^2$$

Thus, we see that R^2 also increases directly with the spread of the independent variable. When you are seeking data to estimate a regression model, it is important to choose the observations of the independent variable that provide the largest possible spread in X so that we obtain a regression model with the highest R^2.

Coefficient of Determination R^2

The coefficient of determination for a regression equation is defined as follows:

$$R^2 = \frac{SSR}{SST} = 1 - \frac{SSE}{SST} \tag{11.12}$$

This quantity varies from 0 to 1, and higher values indicate a better regression. Caution should be used in making general interpretations of R^2 because a high value can result from either a small SSE or a large SST or both.

R^2 can vary from 0 to 1, since SST is fixed and $0 < SSR < SST$. A larger R^2 implies a better regression, everything else being equal. In the regression output—Figure 11.7—we see that the R^2 for the retail sales regression is 0.919 or 91.9%. One popular interpretation is that R^2 is the *percent explained variability*.

The second form of the equation emphasizes that R^2 depends on the ratio of SSE divided by SST. We can have a high R^2 because there is a small SSE—the desired goal—or because there is a large SST or both. General interpretations of R^2 that apply to all regression equations are dangerous. Two regression models with the same set of observed y_i values can always be compared using R^2, and the model with the larger R^2 provides a better explanation of Y. But global comparisons of R^2—stating that a model is good because its R^2 is above a particular value—are misleading. Generally, experienced analysts have found that R^2 is 0.80 and above for models based on time series data. Cross-section data models (e.g., cities, states, firms) have values in the 0.40 to 0.60 range, and models based on data from individual people often have R^2 in the 0.10 to 0.20 range.

To illustrate the problem of global interpretations of R^2, consider two regression models—whose plots are shown in Figure 11.8—each of which is based on a total of 25 observations. Both models have SSE equal to 17.89, so the fit of the regression equation to the data points is the same. But the first model has a total sum of squares equal to 5,201.05, while the second has SST equal to 68.22. The R^2 values for the two models are as follows:

Model 1

$$R^2 = 1 - \frac{SSE}{SST} = 1 - \frac{17.89}{5,201.05} = 0.997$$

Model 2

$$R^2 = 1 - \frac{SSE}{SST} = 1 - \frac{17.89}{68.22} = 0.738$$

Since both models have the same SSE, and thus the same goodness of fit, one cannot claim that Model 1 fits the data better. Yet Model 1 has a substantially higher R^2 compared to Model 2. As we see here, one should be very careful about global interpretations of R^2. Note that the two different vertical axis intervals in Figure 11.8 result from different values for SST.

The correlation coefficient can also be linked with R^2, as shown, by noting that the correlation squared is equal to the coefficient of determination. Another interpretation of the correlation is that it is the square root of the percent explained variability.

Correlation and R^2

The coefficient of determination, R^2, for simple regression is equal to the simple correlation squared:

$$R^2 = r_{xy}^2 \tag{11.13}$$

This provides an important link between correlation and the regression model.

The error sum of squares can be used to obtain an estimate of the variance of the model error ε_i. As we will see, the estimator for the variance of the model error will be used for regression model statistical inference. Recall that we have assumed that the population error, ε_i, is a random error with a mean of 0 and a variance of σ^2. The estimator for σ^2 is computed in the following section.

Figure 11.8
Comparison of R^2 for Two Regression Models

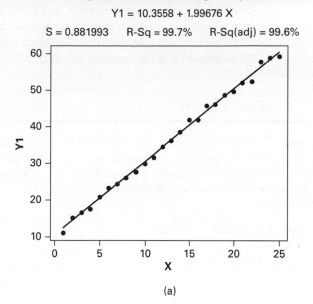

Regression Model with High R Squared

Y1 = 10.3558 + 1.99676 X

S = 0.881993   R-Sq = 99.7%   R-Sq(adj) = 99.6%

(a)

Regression Model with Low R Squared

Y2 = 10.3558 + 1.96759 X

S = 0.881993   R-Sq = 73.8%   R-Sq(adj) = 72.6%

(b)

Estimation of Model Error Variance

The quantity *SSE* is a measure of the total squared deviation about the estimated regression line and e_i is the residual. An estimator for the variance of the population model error is as follows:

$$\hat{\sigma}^2 = s_e^2 = \; = \frac{\sum_{i=1}^{n} e_i^2}{n-2} = \frac{SSE}{n-2}$$

(11.14)

Division by $n - 2$ instead of $n - 1$ results because the simple regression model uses two estimated parameters, b_0 and b_1, instead of one. In the next section we see that this variance estimator is the basis for statistical inference in the regression model.

EXERCISES

Basic Exercise

11.26 Compute SSR, SSE, s^2_e, and the coefficient of determination, given the following statistics computed from a random sample of pairs of X and Y observations:

a. $\sum_{i=1}^{n}(y_i - \bar{y})^2 = 100{,}000$, $R^2 = 0.50$, $n = 52$

b. $\sum_{i=1}^{n}(y_i - \bar{y})^2 = 90{,}000$, $R^2 = 0.70$, $n = 52$

c. $\sum_{i=1}^{n}(y_i - \bar{y})^2 = 240$, $R^2 = 0.80$, $n = 52$

d. $\sum_{i=1}^{n}(y_i - \bar{y})^2 = 200{,}000$, $R^2 = 0.30$, $n = 74$

e. $\sum_{i=1}^{n}(y_i - \bar{y})^2 = 60{,}000$, $R^2 = 0.90$, $n = 40$

Application Exercises

11.27 Let the sample regression line be

$$y_i = b_0 + b_1x_i + e_i = \hat{y}_i + e_i \ (i = 1, 2, ..., n)$$

and let $\bar{x}$ and $\bar{y}$ denote the sample means for the independent and dependent variables, respectively.

a. Show that

$$e_i = y_i - \bar{y} - b(x_i - \bar{x})$$

b. Using the result in part (a), show that

$$\sum_{i=1}^{n} e_i = 0$$

c. Using the result in part (a), show that

$$\sum_{i=1}^{n} e_i^2 = \sum_{i=1}^{n}(y_i - \bar{y})^2 - b^2 \sum_{i=1}^{n}(x_i - \bar{x})^2$$

d. Show that

$$\hat{y}^i - \bar{y} = b_i(x_i - \bar{x})$$

e. Using the results in parts (c) and (d), show that

$$SST = SSR + SSE$$

f. Using the result in part (a), show that

$$\sum_{i=1}^{n} e_i(x_i - \bar{x}) = 0$$

11.28 Let

$$R^2 = \frac{SSR}{SST}$$

denote the coefficient of determination for the sample regression line.

a. Using part (d) of Exercise 11.27, show that

$$R^2 = b_1^2 \frac{\sum_{i=1}^{n}(x_i - \bar{x})^2}{\sum_{i=1}^{n}(y_i - \bar{y})^2}$$

b. Using the result in part (a), show that the coefficient of determination is equal to the square of the sample correlation between X and Y.

c. Let b_1 be the slope of the least squares regression of Y on X, b_1^* the slope of the least squares regression of X on Y, and r the sample correlation between X and Y. Show that $b_1 \cdot b_1^* = r^2$

11.29 Find and interpret the coefficient of determination for the regression of DVD system sales on price, using the following data:

Sales	420	380	350	400	440	380	450	420
Price	98	194	244	207	89	261	149	198

11.30 ⬤ Find and interpret the coefficient of determination for the regression of the percentage change in the Dow Jones index in a year on the percentage change in the index over the first 5 trading days of the year. Compare your answer with the sample correlation found for these data. Use the data file **Dow Jones**.

11.31 ⬤ Find the proportion of the sample variability in mutual fund percentage losses on November 13, 1989, explained by their linear dependence on 1989 percentage gains through November 12, based on the data in the data file **New York Stock Exchange Gains and Losses**.

11.32 ⬤ Refer to the data on employee absence rate in Exercise 11.25. Use data file **Employee Absence**.

a. Find the predicted values, $\hat{y}_i$, and the residuals, e_i, for the least squares regression of, Y, change in mean employee absence rate due to own illness, on, X, change in unemployment rate.

b. Find the sums of squares SST, SSR, and SSE, and verify that

$$SST = SSR + SSE$$

c. Using the results in part (b), find and interpret the coefficient of determination.

11.33 Refer to the data on weekly sales and aptitude test scores achieved by sales representatives given in Exercise 11.21.

a. Find the predicted values, , and residuals, e_i, for the least squares regression of weekly sales on aptitude test scores.

b. Find the sums of squares SST, SSR, and SSE, and verify that

$$SST = SSR + SSE$$

c. Using the results in part (b), find and interpret the coefficient of determination.

d. Find directly the sample correlation coefficient between sales and aptitude test scores, and verify that its square is equal to the coefficient of determination.

11.34 In a study it was shown that for a sample of 353 college faculty the correlation was 0.11 between annual raises and teaching evaluations. What would be the coefficient of determination of a regression of annual raises on teaching evaluations for this sample? Interpret your result.

11.5 STATISTICAL INFERENCE: HYPOTHESIS TESTS AND CONFIDENCE INTERVALS

Now that we have developed the coefficient estimators and an estimator for σ^2, we are ready to make population model inferences. The basic approach follows that developed in Chapters 7 through 10. We develop variance estimators for the coefficient estimators, b_0 and b_1, and then use the estimated parameters and variances to test hypotheses and compute confidence intervals using the Student's t distribution. Inferences from regression analysis will help us understand the process being modeled and make decisions about the process. Initially, we assume that random model errors, ε, are normally distributed. Later this assumption will be replaced by the central limit theorem assumption. We begin by developing variance estimators and useful test forms. Then we apply these using our retail sales data.

In Section 11.2 we defined the population model for simple regression as

$$y_i = \beta_0 + \beta_1 x_i + \varepsilon_i$$

with the instances of x_i being predetermined values and not random variables. From our work in Chapters 4 and 5 on linear functions of random variables, we know that, if ε_i is a normally distributed random variable with variance σ^2, then y_i is also normally distributed with the same variance. The right-hand side is a linear function of X except for the random variable ε_i. If we add a function of X to a random variable, we do not change the variance. In Section 11.3 we found that the estimator for the slope coefficient, b_1, is

$$b_1 = \frac{\sum_{i=1}^{n}(x_i - \bar{x})(y_i - \bar{y})}{\sum_{i=1}^{n}(x_i - \bar{x})^2}$$

$$= \sum \left(\frac{(x_i - \bar{x})}{\sum(x_i - \bar{x})^2} \right) y_i$$

$$= \sum a_i y_i$$

where

$$a_i = \frac{(x_i - \bar{x})}{\sum_{i=1}^{n}(x_i - \bar{x})^2}$$

In this estimator we see that b_1 is a linear function of the random variable y_i whose variance is σ^2. The instances of y_i are independent random variables. Thus, the variance of b_1 is a simple transformation of the variance of Y. Using the results from Chapter 5, the linear function can be written as follows:

$$b_1 = \sum_{i=1}^{n} a_i y_i$$

$$a_i = \frac{(x_i - \bar{x})}{\sum_{i=1}^{n}(x_i - \bar{x})^2}$$

$$\sigma_{b_1}^2 = \sum_{i=1}^{n} a_i^2 \sigma^2$$

$$\sigma_{b_1}^2 = \sum_{i=1}^{n} \left(\frac{(x_i - \bar{x})}{\sum_{i=1}^{n}(x_i - \bar{x})^2} \right)^2 \sigma^2$$

$$= \frac{\sum_{i=1}^{n}(x_i - \bar{x})^2}{\left(\sum_{i=1}^{n}(x_i - \bar{x})^2 \right)^2} \sigma^2$$

$$= \frac{\sigma^2}{\sum_{i=1}^{n}(x_i - \bar{x})^2}$$

Since y_i is normally distributed and b_1 is a linear function of independent normal variables, this linear function implies that b_1 is also normally distributed. From this analysis we can derive the population and sample variances.

Sampling Distribution of the Least Squares Coefficient Estimator

If the standard least squares assumptions hold, then b_1 is an unbiased estimator for β_1 and has a population variance

$$\sigma_{b_1}^2 = \frac{\sigma^2}{\sum_{i=1}^{n}(x_i - \bar{x})^2} = \frac{\sigma^2}{(n-1)s_x^2} \qquad (11.15)$$

and an unbiased sample variance estimator

$$s_{b_1}^2 = \frac{s_e^2}{\sum_{i=1}^{n}(x_i - \bar{x})^2} = \frac{s_e^2}{(n-1)s_x^2} \qquad (11.16)$$

The regression constant estimator, b_0, is also a linear function of the random variable y_i, and, thus, it can be shown to be normally distributed, and its variance estimator can be derived as

$$s_{b_0}^2 = \left(\frac{1}{n} + \frac{\bar{x}^2}{(n-1)s_x^2} \right) s_e^2$$

It is important to observe that the variance of the slope coefficient, b_1, depends on two important quantities:

1. The distance of the points from the regression line measured by s_e^2. Higher values imply greater variance for b_1.
2. The total deviation of the X values from the mean is measured by $(n-1)s_x^2$. The greater the spread in the X values implies a smaller variance for the slope coefficient.

These two results are very important as one is thinking about choices of data for a regression model. Previously, we noted that a wider spread in the independent, X, variable resulted in a higher R^2, indicating a stronger relationship. Now, we see that a wider spread in the independent variable—measured by s_x^2—results in a smaller variance for the estimated slope coefficient, b_1. It follows that smaller variance slope coefficient estimators imply a better regression model. We need to also add that many research conclusions and policy decisions are based on the change in Y that results from a change in X, as estimated by b_1. Thus, we would like to have the variance of this important decision variable, b_1, be as small as possible.

The equation that computes the estimated coefficients for b_1 assumes that the variances of the error terms ε_i are uniform or equal over the range of the independent variables. This is the condition defined as homoscedasticity. However, there are a number of situations where homoscedasticity does not apply and we say that the errors are defined as heteroscedastic, that is the variances of the instances of ε_i are not uniform. For example, the variation in annual household consumption generally increases with increasing levels of household disposable income, because with higher incomes households have greater flexibility between consumption and saving. A plot of annual household consumption versus disposable income would show the data "fanning out" around a linear trend as disposable income increases. Similarly, the variance in factory output could increase as additional workers are added if the additional workers have less experience and training. When the variance of the instances of ε_i are not uniform or heteroscedastic we can show that the estimated coefficients are still unbiased. However, the estimated coefficient variances, $\sigma_{b_i}^2$, are not correct and need to be adjusted. In Section 13.6 we discuss heteroscedasticity and indicate modifications to the inference procedures when the errors "fan out" or the variances of the instances of ε_i are not uniform.

In applied regression analysis we first would like to know if there is a relationship. In the regression model we see that if β_1 is 0, then there is no linear relationship—Y would not continuously increase or decrease with increases in X. To determine if there is a linear relationship, we can test the hypothesis

$$H_0 : \beta_1 = 0$$

versus

$$H_1 : \beta_1 \neq 0$$

Given that b_1 is normally distributed, we can test this hypothesis using the Student's t statistic

$$t = \frac{b_1 - \beta_1}{s_{b_1}} = \frac{b_1 - 0}{s_{b_1}} = \frac{b_1}{s_{b_1}}$$

that is distributed as Student's t with $n - 2$ degrees of freedom. The hypothesis test can also be performed for values of β_1 other than 0. One rule of thumb is to conclude that a relationship exists if the absolute value of the t statistic is greater than 2. This result holds exactly for a two-tailed test with $\alpha = 0.05$ and 60 degrees of freedom and provides a close approximation for $n > 30$.

Basis for Inference about the Population Regression Slope

Let β_1 be a population regression slope and b_1 its least squares estimate based on n pairs of sample observations. Then, if the standard regression assumptions hold and it can also be assumed that the errors, ε_i, are normally distributed, the random variable

$$t = \frac{b_1 - \beta_1}{s_{b_1}} \tag{11.17}$$

is distributed as Student's t with $(n - 2)$ degrees of freedom. In addition, the central limit theorem enables us to conclude that this result is approximately valid for a wide range of non-normal distributions and large enough sample sizes, n.

The coefficient standard deviation and Student's t statistic—for $\beta_1 = 0$—are routinely computed in most regression programs. Example output from Minitab is shown in Figure 11.9

For the retail sales model the slope coefficient is $b_1 = 0.382$ with a standard deviation of $S_{b_1} = 0.02529$. To decide if there is a relationship between retail sales, Y, and disposable income, X, we can test the hypothesis

$$H_0 : \beta_1 = 0$$

versus

$$H_1 : \beta_1 \neq 0$$

Under the null hypothesis the ratio of the coefficient estimator, b_1, to its standard deviation has a Student's t distribution. For the retail sales example we find that the computed Student's t statistic is as follows:

$$t = \frac{b_1 - \beta_1}{s_{b_1}} = \frac{b_1 - 0}{s_{b_1}} = \frac{0.38152 - 0}{0.02529} = 15.08$$

The resulting Student's t statistic, $t = 15.08$, as shown in the regression output, provides strong evidence to reject the null hypothesis and conclude that there is a strong relationship between retail sales and disposable income. We also note that the p-value for b_1 is 0.000, providing alternative evidence that β_1 is not equal to 0. Recall from Chapter 9 that the p-value is the smallest significance level at which the null hypothesis can be rejected or the p-value is the probability that the null hypothesis is true.

Figure 11.9
Retail Sales
Model: Coefficient
Variance
Estimators
(Minitab Output)

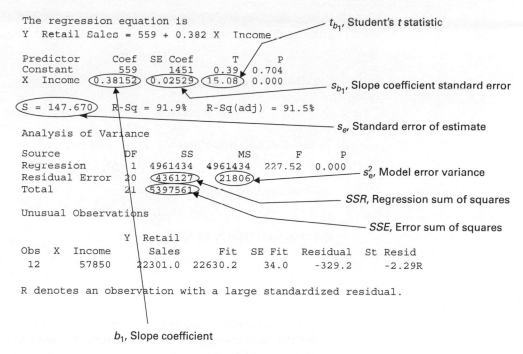

The regression equation is
Y Retail Sales = 559 + 0.382 X Income

t_{b_1}, Student's t statistic

Predictor	Coef	SE Coef	T	P
Constant	559	1451	0.39	0.704
X Income	0.38152	0.02529	15.08	0.000

s_{b_1}, Slope coefficient standard error

S = 147.670   R-Sq = 91.9%   R-Sq(adj) = 91.5%

s_e, Standard error of estimate

Analysis of Variance

Source	DF	SS	MS	F	P
Regression	1	4961434	4961434	227.52	0.000
Residual Error	20	436127	21806		
Total	21	5397561			

s_e^2, Model error variance

SSR, Regression sum of squares

SSE, Error sum of squares

Unusual Observations

Obs	X Income	Y Retail Sales	Fit	SE Fit	Residual	St Resid
12	57850	22301.0	22630.2	34.0	-329.2	-2.29R

R denotes an observation with a large standardized residual.

b_1, Slope coefficient

Hypothesis tests could also be performed on the equation constant, b_0, using the standard deviation previously developed and shown in the Minitab output. However, because we are usually interested in rates of change—measured by b_1—tests involving the constant are generally less important.

If the sample size is large enough for the central limit theorem to apply, then we can perform such hypothesis tests even if the errors, ε_i, are not normally distributed. The key question concerns the distribution of b_1. If b_1 has an approximately normal distribution, then the hypothesis test can be performed.

Tests of the Population Regression Slope

If the regression errors, ε_i, are normally distributed and the standard least squares assumptions hold (or if the distribution of b_1 is approximately normal), the following tests have significance level α:

1. To test either null hypothesis

$$H_0 : \beta_1 = \beta_1^* \quad \text{or} \quad H_0 : \beta_1 \leq \beta_1^*$$

against the alternative

$$H_1 : \beta_1 > \beta_1^*$$

the decision rule is as follows:

$$\text{Reject } H_0 \text{ if } \frac{b_1 - \beta_1^*}{s_{b_1}} \geq t_{n-2,\alpha} \tag{11.18}$$

2. To test either null hypothesis

$$H_0 : \beta_1 = \beta_1^* \quad \text{or} \quad H_0 : \beta_1 \geq \beta_1^*$$

against the alternative

$$H_1 : \beta_1 < \beta_1^*$$

the decision rule is as follows:

$$\text{Reject } H_0 \text{ if } \frac{b_1 - \beta_1^*}{s_b} \leq -t_{n-2,\alpha} \tag{11.19}$$

3. To test the null hypothesis

$$H_0 : \beta_1 = \beta_1^*$$

against the two-sided alternative

$$H_1 : \beta_1 \neq \beta_1^*$$

the decision rule is as follows:

$$\text{Reject } H_0 \text{ if } \frac{b_1 - \beta_1^*}{s_{b_1}} \geq t_{n-2,\alpha/2} \quad \text{or} \quad \frac{b_1 - \beta_1^*}{s_{b_1}} \leq -t_{n-2,\alpha/2} \tag{11.20}$$

We can derive confidence intervals for the slope β_1 of the population regression line by using the coefficient and variance estimators we have developed and the rationale presented in Chapter 7.

Confidence Intervals for the Population Regression Slope b_1

If the regression errors, ε_i, are normally distributed and the standard regression assumptions hold, a $100(1 - \alpha)\%$ confidence interval for the population regression slope β_1 is given by

$$b_1 - t_{(n-2,\alpha/2)}s_{b_1} < \beta_1 < b_1 + t_{(n-2,\alpha/2)}s_{b_1} \tag{11.21}$$

where $t_{n-2,\alpha/2}$ is the number for which

$$P(t_{n-2} > t_{n-2,\alpha/2}) = \alpha/2$$

and the random variable t_{n-2} follows a Student's t distribution with $(n - 2)$ degrees of freedom.

From the regression output for the retail sales on disposable income regression in Figure 11.9, we know that

$$n = 22 \quad b_1 = 0.3815 \quad S_{b_1} = 0.0253$$

For a 99% confidence interval for β_1 we have $1 - \alpha = 0.99$, and $n - 2 = 20$ degrees of freedom, and, thus, from Table 8 in the appendix

$$t_{n-2,\alpha/2} = t_{20,0.005} = 2.845$$

Therefore, we have the 99% confidence interval

$$0.3815 - (2.845)(0.0253) < \beta_1 < 0.3815 + (2.845)(0.0253)$$

or

$$0.3095 < \beta_1 < 0.4535$$

Figure 11.10

Confidence Intervals for the Retail Sales Population Regression Slope at Confidence Levels, 90%, 95%, and 99%

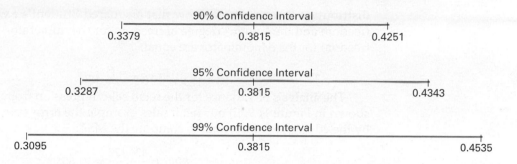

We see that the 99% confidence interval for the expected increase in retail sales per household associated with a $1 increase in disposable income per household covers the range from $0.3095 to $0.4353. Figure 11.10 shows the 90%, 95%, and 99% confidence intervals for the population regression slope.

Hypothesis Test for Population Slope Coefficient Using the *F* Distribution

There is an alternative test for the hypothesis that the slope coefficient, β_1, is equal to 0:

$$H_0 : \beta_1 = 0$$

$$H_1 : \beta_1 \neq 0$$

This test is based on the partitioning of variability that we developed in Section 11.4. The assumption for this test is that, if the null hypothesis is true, then both *SSE* and *SSR* can be used to obtain independent estimators of the model error variance σ^2. To perform this test, we obtain two sample estimates of the population standard deviation σ. These are defined as mean square terms. The regression sum of squares, *SSR*, has one degree of freedom, since it refers to the single slope coefficient, and the mean square for regression, *MSR*, is as follows:

$$MSR = \frac{SSR}{1} = SSR$$

If the null hypothesis—no relationship—is true, then *MSR* is an estimate of the overall model variance, σ^2. We also use the error sum of squares as before to obtain the mean square for error, *MSE*:

$$MSE = \frac{SSE}{n-2} = s_e^2$$

In Section 10.4 we introduced the *F* distribution as the ratio of independent sample estimates of variance, given equal population variances. It can be shown that *MSR* and *MSE* are independent and that under H_0 both are estimates of the population variance, σ^2. Thus, if H_0 is true, then we can show that the ratio

$$F = \frac{MSR}{MSE} = \frac{SSR}{s_e^2}$$

has an *F* distribution with 1 degree of freedom for the numerator and $n - 2$ degrees of freedom for the denominator. It should also be noted that the *F* statistic is equal to the squared *t* statistic for the slope coefficient. This can be shown algebraically. From distribution theory we can show that a squared Student's t with $n - 2$ degrees of freedom and the F with 1 degree of freedom for the numerator, and $n - 2$ degrees of freedom for the denominator are equal:

$$F_{1,n-2,\alpha} = t^2_{n-2,\alpha/2}$$

The analysis of variance for the retail sales regression from the Minitab output is shown in Figure 11.9. In our retail sales example the error sum of squares is divided by the 20 degrees of freedom to compute the MSE:

$$MSE = \frac{436,127}{20} = 21,806$$

Then the F ratio is computed as the ratio of the two mean squares:

$$F = \frac{MSR}{MSE} = \frac{4,961,434}{21,806} = 227.52$$

This F ratio is substantially larger than the critical value for $\alpha = 0.01$ with 1 degree of freedom for the numerator and 20 degrees of freedom for the denominator ($F_{1,20,0.01} = 8.10$) from Table 9 in the appendix. The Minitab output—Figure 11.9—for the retail sales regression shows the p-value for this computed F as 0.000, providing alternative evidence to reject H_0. Also note that the F statistic is equal to t^2 where the Student's t statistic is computed for the slope coefficient, b_1:

$$F = t^2$$

$$227.52 = 15.08^2$$

F Test for Simple Regression Coefficient

We can test the hypothesis

$$H_0 : \beta_1 = 0$$

against the alternative

$$H_1 : \beta_1 \neq 0$$

using the F statistic

$$F = \frac{MSR}{MSE} = \frac{SSR}{s_e^2} \qquad (11.22)$$

The decision rule is as follows:

$$\text{Reject } H_0 \text{ if } F \geq F_{1,n-2,\alpha} \qquad (11.23)$$

We can also show that the F statistic is

$$F = t^2_{b_1} \qquad (11.24)$$

for any simple regression analysis.

From this result we see that hypothesis tests relating to the population slope coefficient will provide exactly the same result when using either the Student's t or the F distribution. We will learn in Chapter 13 that the F distribution—when used in a multiple regression analysis—also provides the opportunity for testing the hypothesis that several population slope coefficients are simultaneously equal to 0.

EXERCISES

Basic Exercises

11.35 Given the simple regression model

$$Y = \beta_0 + \beta_1 X$$

and the regression results that follow, test the null hypothesis that the slope coefficient is 0 versus the alternative hypothesis of greater than zero using probability of Type I error equal to 0.05, and determine the two-sided 95% and 99% confidence intervals.

a. A random sample of size n = 38 with
   $b_1 = 5 \quad s_{b_1} = 2.1$
b. A random sample of size n = 46 with
   $b_1 = 5.2 \quad s_{b_1} = 2.1$
c. A random sample of size n = 38 with
   $b_1 = 2.7 \quad s_{b_1} = 1.87$
d. A random sample of size n = 29 with
   $b_1 = 6.7 \quad s_{b_1} = 1.8$

11.36 Use a simple regression model to test the hypothesis

$$H_0 : \beta_1 - 0$$

versus

$$H_1 : \beta_1 \neq 0$$

with $\alpha = 0.05$, given the following regression statistics:

a. The sample size is 35, $SST = 100{,}000$, and the correlation between X and Y is 0.46.
b. The sample size is 61, $SST = 123{,}000$, and the correlation between X and Y is 0.65.
c. The sample size is 25, $SST = 128{,}000$, and the correlation between X and Y is 0.69.

Application Exercises

11.37 Mumbai Electronics is planning to extend its marketing region from the western United States to include the midwestern states. In order to predict its sales in this new region the company has asked you to develop a linear regression of DVD system sales on price, using the following data supplied by the marketing department:

Sales	418	384	343	407	432	386	444	427
Price	98	194	231	207	89	255	149	195

a. Use an unbiased estimation procedure to find an estimate of the variance of the error terms in the population regression.

b. Use an unbiased estimation procedure to find an estimate of the variance of the least squares estimator of the slope of the population regression line.
c. Find a 90% confidence interval for the slope of the population regression line.

11.38 A fast-food chain decided to carry out an experiment to assess the influence of advertising expenditure on sales. Different relative changes in advertising expenditure, compared to the previous year, were made in eight regions of the country, and resulting changes in sales levels were observed. The accompanying table shows the results.

Increase in advertising expenditure (%)	0	4	14	10	9	8	6	1
Increase in sales (%)	2.4	7.2	10.3	9.1	10.2	4.1	7.6	3.5

a. Estimate by least squares the linear regression of increase in sales on increase in advertising expenditure.
b. Find a 90% confidence interval for the slope of the population regression line.

11.39 A liquor wholesaler is interested in assessing the effect of the price of a premium scotch whiskey on the quantity sold. The results in the accompanying table on price, in dollars, and sales, in cases, were obtained from a sample of 8 weeks of sales records.

Price	19.2	20.5	19.7	21.3	20.8	19.9	17.8	17.2
Sales	25.4	14.7	18.6	11.4	11.1	15.7	29.2	35.2

Find a 95% confidence interval for the expected change in sales resulting from a $1 increase in price.

It is recommended that a computer be used for the following exercises.

11.40 ◉ Continue the analysis of Exercise 11.30 of the regression of the percentage change in the Dow Jones index in a year on the percentage change in the index over the first 5 trading days of the year. Use the data file **Dow Jones**.

a. Use an unbiased estimation procedure to find a point estimate of the variance of the error terms in the population regression.

b. Use an unbiased estimation procedure to find a point estimate of the variance of the least squares estimator of the slope of the population regression line.

c. Find and interpret a 95% confidence interval for the slope of the population regression line.

d. Test at the 10% significance level, against a two-sided alternative, the null hypothesis that the slope of the population regression line is 0.

11.41 Estimate a linear regression model for mutual fund losses on November 13, 1989, using the data file **New York Stock Exchange Gains and Losses**.

a. Use an unbiased estimation procedure to obtain a point estimate of the variance of the error terms in the population regression.

b. Use an unbiased estimation procedure to obtain a point estimate of the variance of the least squares estimator of the slope of the population regression line.

c. Find 90%, 95%, and 99% confidence intervals for the slope of the population regression line.

11.6 PREDICTION

Regression models can be used to compute predictions or forecasts for the dependent variable, given an assumed future value for the independent variable. Suppose that we are interested in forecasting the value of the dependent variable, given that the independent variable is equal to a specified value, x_{n+1}, and that the linear relationship between dependent and independent variables continues to hold. The corresponding value of the dependent variable will then be

$$y_{n+1} = \beta_0 + \beta_1 x_{n+1} + \varepsilon_{n+1}$$

which, given x_{n+1}, has expectation

$$E[y_{n+1} | x_{n+1}] = \beta_0 + \beta_1 x_{n+1}$$

Two distinct options are of interest:

1. We might want to estimate or predict the actual value that will result for a single observation, y_{n+1}. This option used in forecasting or predicting the result of a single outcome is shown in Figure 11.11.

2. Alternatively we might want to estimate the conditional expected value, $E[y_{n+1} | x_{n+1}]$—that is, the average value of the dependent variable when the independent variable is fixed at x_{n+1}. This option is shown in Figure 11.12.

You should note that the range of errors or variance is larger when forecasting a single value as shown in Figure 11.11 compared to forecasting the mean as shown in Figure 11.12.

Given that the standard regression assumptions continue to hold, the same point estimate results for either option. We simply replace the unknown β_0 and β_1 by their least squares estimates, b_0 and b_1. That is, $(\beta_0 + \beta_1 x_{n+1})$ is estimated by $(b_0 + b_1 x_{n+1})$. We know that the corresponding estimator is the best linear unbiased estimator for Y, given X. With the first option we are interested in the best forecast for a single occurrence of the process. But for the second option we are interested in the expected value or long-term average for the process. For both options, an appropriate point estimate under our assumptions is as follows:

$$\hat{y}_{n+1} = b_0 + b_1 x_{n+1}$$

This follows because we do not know anything useful about the random variable, ε_{n+1}, except that its mean is 0. Thus, without other information we will use 0 as its point estimate.

Figure 11.11

Least Squares
Estimated
Regression Line of
Retail Sales on
Disposable
Income for a
Single Observed
Value

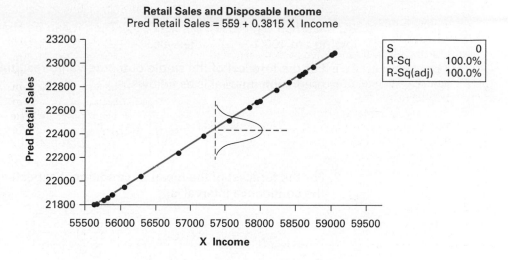

Retail Sales and Disposable Income
Pred Retail Sales = 559 + 0.3815 X Income

Figure 11.12

Least Squares
Estimated
Regression Line of
Retail Sales on
Disposable
Income for the
Expected Value

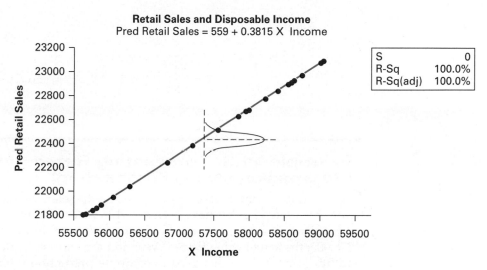

Retail Sales and Disposable Income
Pred Retail Sales = 559 + 0.3815 X Income

However, we usually want intervals in addition to point estimates, and for that purpose the two options are different. This is because the variance estimators are different for the two different quantities being estimated. The results for these different variance estimators lead to the two different intervals. The interval for the first option is generally defined as a prediction interval because we are predicting the value for a single point. The interval for the second option is referred to as a confidence interval because it is the interval for the expected value.

Forecast Confidence Intervals and Prediction Intervals

Suppose that the population regression model is

$$y_i = \beta_0 + \beta_1 x_i + \varepsilon_i \quad (i = 1,...,n + 1)$$

that the standard regression assumptions hold, and that the ε_i are normally distributed. Let b_0 and b_1 be the least squares estimates of β_0 and

β_1, based on (x_1, y_1), (x_2, y_2), ...,(x_n, y_n). Then it can be shown that the following are $100(1 - \alpha)\%$ intervals.

1. For the forecast of the single outcome value resulting for Y_{n+1}, the prediction interval is as follows:

$$\hat{y}_{n+1} \pm t_{n-2,\alpha/2} \sqrt{\left[1 + \frac{1}{n} + \frac{(x_{n+1} - \bar{x})^2}{\sum_{i=1}^{n}(x_i - \bar{x})^2} \right]} s_e \qquad (11.25)$$

2. For the forecast of the mean or conditional expectation $E(Y_{n+1} \mid x_{n+1})$, the confidence interval is

$$\hat{y}_{n+1} \pm t_{n-2,\alpha/2} \sqrt{\left[\frac{1}{n} + \frac{(x_{n+1} - \bar{x})^2}{\sum_{i=1}^{n}(x_i - \bar{x})^2} \right]} s_e \qquad (11.26)$$

where

$$\bar{x} = \frac{\sum_{i=1}^{n} x_i}{n} \quad \text{and} \quad \hat{y}_{n+1} = b_0 + b_1 x_{n+1}$$

Example 11.3 Forecasting Retail Sales (Regression Model Forecasting)

We illustrate the interval computation using the retail sales and disposable income from Example 11.2. We have been asked to determine the following forecast values for retail sales per household when disposable income per household is $58,000: the actual value for next year and the expected value for the long run. In addition, we have been asked to compute prediction intervals and confidence intervals for these forecasts. Use the data file **Retail Sales**.

Solution The forecast values for next year and for the long run are both as follows:

$$\hat{y}_{n+1} = b_0 + b_1 x_{n+1}$$

$$= 559 + (0.3815)(58,000) = 22,686$$

Thus, we find that the estimated sales are $22,686 when disposable income is $58,000. We have also found that

$$n = 22 \quad \bar{x} = 57,342 \quad \sum(x_i - \bar{x})^2 = 34,084,596 \quad s_e^2 = 21,806$$

Hence, the standard error for a predicted single observation of Y is as follows:

$$\sqrt{\left[1 + \frac{1}{n} + \frac{(x_{n+1} - \bar{x})^2}{\sum_{i=1}^{n}(x_i - \bar{x})^2} \right]} s_e = \sqrt{\left[1 + \frac{1}{22} + \frac{(58,000 - 57,342)^2}{34,084,596} \right]} \sqrt{21,806} = 151.90$$

Similarly, we find that the standard error for the expected value of Y is as follows:

$$\sqrt{\left[\frac{1}{n}+\frac{(x_{n+1}-\bar{x})^2}{\sum_{i=1}^{n}(x_i-\bar{x})^2}\right]}s_e = \sqrt{\left[\frac{1}{22}+\frac{(58,000-57,342)^2}{34,084,596}\right]}\sqrt{21,806}=35.61$$

Suppose that 95% intervals are required for the forecasts with $\alpha=0.05$ and

$$t_{n-2,\alpha/2} = t_{20,0.025} = 2.086$$

Using these results, we find that the 95% prediction interval for next year's retail sales when disposable income is $58,000 is computed as follows:

$$22,686 \pm (2.086)(151.90)$$
$$22,686 \pm 317$$

Thus, the 95 prediction interval for sales in a single year in which income is $58,000 runs from $22,369 to $23,003.

For the confidence interval for the expected value of retail sales when disposable income is $58,000, we have the following:

$$22,686 \pm (2.086)(35.61)$$
$$22,686 \pm 74$$

Hence, the 95% confidence interval for the expected value runs from $22,612 to $23,760.

The distinction between these two interval estimation problems is illustrated in Figures 11.11 and 11.12. We see in each figure the estimated regression line for our retail sales—disposable income data. Also, in Figure 11.11 we see a probability density function representing our uncertainty about the value that retail sales will take in any specific year in which disposable income is $58,000. The probability density function in Figure 11.12 represents our uncertainty about expected, or average, retail sales in years when disposable income is $58,000. Of course, we would be less certain about sales in a single specific year than about average sales, and this is reflected in the shapes of the two density functions. We see that both are centered on retail sales of $22,686, but that the density function for the prediction of a single outcome in Figure 11.11 has greater dispersion. As a result, the prediction interval for a specific value is wider than the confidence interval for expected retail sales.

We can obtain some further insights by studying the general forms of the prediction and confidence intervals. As we have seen, the wider the interval, the greater the uncertainty surrounding the point forecast. From these formulas we make four observations:

1. All other things being equal, the larger the sample size n, the narrower are both the prediction interval and the confidence interval. Thus, we see that the more sample information we have available, the more confident we will be of our inference.
2. All other things being equal, the larger s_e^2 is, the wider are both the prediction interval and the confidence interval. Again, this is to be expected, since s_e^2 is an estimate of σ^2, the variance of the regression errors, ε_i. Since these errors

$$\varepsilon_i = y_i - \beta_0 - \beta_1 x_i$$

represent the discrepancy between the observed values of the dependent variables and their expectations, given the independent variables, the bigger the magnitude of discrepancy, the more imprecise will be our inference.

3. Consider now the quantity $\left(\sum_{i=1}^{n} \left(x_i - \bar{x} \right)^2 \right)$. This is simply a multiple of the sample variance of the observations of the independent variable. A large variance implies that we have information for a wide range of values of this variable, which allows more precise estimates of the population regression line and correspondingly narrower confidence intervals and narrower prediction intervals.

4. We also see that larger values of the quantity $(x_{n+1}-\bar{x})^2$ result in wider confidence intervals and wider prediction intervals. Thus, both intervals become wider as we move from the mean of the independent variable, X. Since our sample data are centered at the mean $\bar{x}$, we would expect to be more definitive about our inference when the independent variable is relatively close to this central value than when it is some distance away.

Extrapolation of the regression equation outside the range of the data used for estimation is not recommended. Suppose that you are asked to predict retail sales per household in a year when disposable income is $70,000. Referring to the data in Table 11.1 and the regression line in Figure 11.12, we see that $70,000 is well outside the range of the data used to develop the regression model. An inexperienced analyst might use the procedures previously developed to estimate a prediction or a confidence interval. From the equations we can see that the resulting intervals would be very wide, and, thus, the forecast would be of limited value. However, there is a more fundamental problem with forecasts made outside the range of the original data: We simply have no evidence to indicate the nature of the relationship outside of the range of the data. There is no reason in economic theory that requires absolutely that the relationship will remain linear with the same rate of change when we move outside of the range of the data used to estimate the regression model coefficients. Any extrapolation of the model outside of the range of the data to obtain predicted values must be based on knowledge or evidence beyond that contained in the regression analysis on the available data. Major errors can result when analysts have attempted this kind of extrapolation.

EXERCISES

Basic Exercises

11.42 Given a simple regression analysis, suppose that we have obtained a fitted regression model

$$\hat{y}_i = 12+5x_i$$

and also

$$s_e = 9.67 \quad \bar{x}=8 \quad n = 32 \quad \sum_{i=1}^{n}(x_i - \bar{x})^2 = 500$$

Find the 95% confidence interval and 95% prediction interval for the point where $x = 13$.

11.43 Given a simple regression analysis, suppose that we have obtained a fitted regression model

$$\hat{y}_i = 14+7x_i$$

and also

$$s_e = 7.45 \quad \bar{x}=8 \quad n = 25 \quad \sum_{i=1}^{n}(x_i - \bar{x})^2 = 300$$

Find the 95% confidence interval and 95% prediction interval for the point where $x = 11$.

11.44 Given a simple regression analysis, suppose that we have obtained a fitted regression model

$$\hat{y}_i = 22+8x_i$$

and also

$$s_e = 3.45 \quad \bar{x}=11 \quad n = 22 \quad \sum_{i=1}^{n}(x_i - \bar{x})^2 = 400$$

Find the 95% confidence interval and 95% prediction interval for the point where $x = 17$.

11.45 Given a simple regression analysis, suppose that we have obtained a fitted regression model

$$\hat{y}_i = 8 + 10\,x_i$$

and also

$$s_e = 11.23 \qquad \bar{x} = 8 \qquad n = 44 \qquad \sum_{i=1}^{n}(x_i - \bar{x})^2 = 800$$

Find the 95% confidence interval and 95% prediction interval for the point where $x = 17$.

Application Exercises

11.46 A sample of 25 blue-collar employees at a production plant was taken. Each employee was asked to assess his own job satisfaction (x) on a scale from 1 to 10. In addition, the numbers of days absent (y) from work during the last year were found for these employees. The sample regression line

$$\hat{y}_i = 11.6 - 1.2x$$

was estimated by least squares for these data. Also found were

$$\bar{x} = 6.0 \qquad \sum_{i=1}^{25}(x_i - \bar{x})^2 = 130.0 \quad SSE = 80.6$$

a. Test at the 1% significance level against the appropriate one-sided alternative the null hypothesis that job satisfaction has no linear effect on absenteeism.

b. A particular employee has job satisfaction level 4. Find a 90% interval for the number of days this employee would be absent from work in a year.

11.47 Doctors are interested in the relationship between the dosage of a medicine and the time required for a patient's recovery. The following table shows, for a sample of ten patients, dosage levels (in grams) and recovery times (in hours). These patients have similar characteristics except for medicine dosages.

Dosage level	1.2	1.3	1.0	1.4	1.5	1.8	1.2	1.3	1.4	1.3
Recovery time	25	28	40	38	10	9	27	30	16	18

a. Estimate the linear regression of recovery time on dosage level.

b. Find and interpret a 90% confidence interval for the slope of the population regression line.

c. Would the sample regression derived in part (a) be useful in predicting recovery time for a patient given 2.5 grams of this drug? Explain your answer.

11.48 For a sample of 20 monthly observations a financial analyst wants to regress the percentage rate of return (Y) of the common stock of a corporation on the percentage rate of return (X) of the Standard and Poor's 500 index. The following information is available:

$$\sum_{i=1}^{20} y_i = 22.6 \quad \sum_{i=1}^{20} x_i = 25.4 \quad \sum_{i=1}^{20} x_i^2 = 145.7$$

$$\sum_{i=1}^{20} x_i y_i = 150.5 \quad \sum_{i=1}^{20} y_i^2 = 196.2$$

a. Test the null hypothesis that the slope of the population regression line is 0 against the alternative that it is positive.

b. Test against the two-sided alternative the null hypothesis that the slope of the population regression line is 1.

11.49 Using the data of Exercise 11.21, test the null hypothesis that representatives' weekly sales are not linearly related to their aptitude test scores against the alternative that there is positive association.

11.50 Refer to the data of Exercise 11.41. Test against a two-sided alternative the null hypothesis that mutual fund losses on Friday, November 13, 1989, did not depend linearly on previous gains in 1989.

11.51 Denote by r the sample correlation between a pair of random variables.

a. Show that

$$\frac{1 - r^2}{n - 2} = \frac{s_e^2}{SST}$$

b. Using the result in part (a), show that

$$\frac{r}{\sqrt{(1 - r^2)/(n - 2)}} = \frac{b}{s_e / \sqrt{\sum(x_i - \bar{x})^2}}$$

11.52 It was hypothesized that the number of bottles of craft beer sold per evening in the restaurants of a city depends linearly on the average costs of meals in the restaurants. The following results were obtained for a sample of $n = 17$ restaurants, of approximately equal size, where

y = number of bottles sold per evening
x = average cost, in dollars, of a meal

$$\bar{x} = 25.5 \quad \bar{y} = 16.0 \quad \frac{\sum_{i=1}^{n}(x_i - \bar{x})^2}{n - 1} = 350$$

$$\frac{\sum_{i=1}^{n}(x_i - \bar{x})(y_i - \bar{y})}{n - 1} = 180$$

$$\frac{\sum(y_i - \bar{y})^2}{n - 1} = 250$$

Test against a two-sided alternative the null hypothesis that the slope of the population regression line is 0.

11.53 For a sample of 74 monthly observations the regression of the percentage return on gold (y) against the percentage change in the consumer price index (x) was estimated. The sample regression line, obtained through least squares, was as follows:

$$y = -0.003 + 1.11x$$

The estimated standard deviation of the slope of the population regression line was 2.31. Test the null hypothesis that the slope of the population regression line is 0 against the alternative that the slope is positive.

11.54 A liquor wholesaler is interested in assessing the effect of the price of a premium scotch whiskey on the quantity sold. The results in the accompanying table on price, in dollars, and sales, in cases, were obtained from a sample of eight weeks of sales records.

Price	19.2	20.5	19.7	21.3	20.8	19.9	17.8	17.2
Sales	25.4	14.7	18.6	11.4	11.1	15.7	29.2	35.2

Test at the 5% level against the appropriate one-sided alternative the null hypothesis that sales do not depend linearly on price for this premium scotch whiskey.

11.55 Refer to the data of Exercise 11.29.
   a. Find a point estimate for the volume of sales when the price of the DVD system is $480 in a given region.
   b. If the price of the system is set at $480, find 95% confidence intervals for the actual volume of sales in a particular region and the expected number of sales in that region.

11.56 ⬤ The data file **Dow Jones** shows percentage changes (x_i) in the Dow Jones index over the first 5 trading days of each of 13 years and also the corresponding percentage changes (y_i) in the index over the whole year. If the Dow Jones index increases by 1.0% in the first 5 trading days of a year, find 90% confidence intervals for the *actual* and also the *expected* percentage changes in the index over the whole year. Discuss the distinction between these intervals.

11.57 ⬤ Refer to the data in Exercise 11.25 (data file **Employee Absence**). For a year in which there is no change in the unemployment rate, find 90% confidence intervals for the *actual* and also the *expected* changes in, Y, mean employee absence rate due to own illness.

11.58 Use the data of Exercise 11.20 to find 90% and 95% confidence intervals for the expected return on the corporation's stock when the rate of return on the Standard and Poor's 500 index is 1%.

11.59 A new sales representative for the corporation of Exercise 11.21 scores 70 on the aptitude test. Find 80% and 90% confidence intervals for the value of weekly sales he will achieve.

11.7 CORRELATION ANALYSIS

In this section we use correlation coefficients to study relationships between variables. In Chapter 2 the sample correlation coefficient was used to describe the relationship between variables indicated in the data. In Chapters 4 and 5 we learned about the population correlation. Here, we develop inference procedures that use the correlation coefficient for studying linear relationships between variables.

In principle, there are any number of ways in which a pair of random variables might be related to each other. As we begin our analysis, it is helpful to postulate some functional form for their relationship. It is often reasonable to conjecture, as a good approximation, that the association is linear. If the pair of linearly related random variables X and Y is being considered, a scatter plot of the joint observations on this pair will tend to be clustered around a straight line. Conversely, if a linear relationship does not exist, then the scatter plot will not follow a straight line. Not all of the relationships that we will study will be tightly clustered about a straight line. Many important relationships will have scatter plots that show a tendency toward a linear relationship, but with considerable deviation from a straight line. We saw a number of such examples in previous sections of this chapter.

Correlations have wide applications in business and economics. In many applied economic problems we argue that there is an independent or exogenous variable X, whose values are determined by activities outside of the economic system being modeled, and that there is a dependent or endogenous variable Y, whose value depends on the value of X. If we ask if sales increase when prices are reduced, we are thinking about a situation in which a seller deliberately and independently adjusts prices up or down and observes changes in sales. Now suppose that prices and quantities sold result from equilibriums of supply and demand as proposed by the basic economic model. Then we could model prices and quantities both as random variables and ask if these two random variables are related to each other. The correlation coefficient can be used to determine if there is a relationship between variables in either of these situations.

Suppose that both X and Y are determined simultaneously by factors that are outside of the economic system being modeled. Therefore, a model in which both X and Y are random variables is often more realistic. In Chapter 4 the correlation coefficient, ρ_{xy}, was developed as a measure of the relationship between two random variables, X and Y. In those cases the population correlation coefficient, ρ_{xy}, was used to indicate a linear relationship without implying that one variable is independent and the other is dependent. In situations where one variable is logically dependent on a second variable, we can use regression analysis to develop a linear model. Here, we develop statistical inference procedures that use sample correlations to determine characteristics of population correlations.

Hypothesis Test for Correlation

The sample correlation coefficient

$$r = \frac{s_{xy}}{s_x s_y}$$

$$s_{xy} = \frac{\sum_{i=1}^{n}\left(x_i - \bar{x}\right)\left(y_i - \bar{y}\right)}{n - 1}$$

is useful as a descriptive measure of the strength of linear association in a sample. We can also use the correlation to test the hypothesis that there is no linear association in the population between a pair of random variables—that is,

$$H_0 : \rho = 0$$

This particular null hypothesis of no linear relationship between a pair of random variables is of great interest in a number of applications. When we compute the sample correlation from data, the result is likely to be different from 0 even if the population correlation is 0. Thus, we would like to know how large a difference from 0 is required for a sample correlation to provide evidence that the population correlation is not 0.

We can show that, when the null hypothesis is true and the random variables have a joint normal distribution, then the random variable

$$t = \frac{r\sqrt{(n - 2)}}{\sqrt{(1 - r^2)}}$$

follows a Student's t distribution with $(n - 2)$ degrees of freedom. The appropriate hypothesis tests are shown in Equations 11.27 through 11.29.

Tests for Zero Population Correlation

Let r be the sample correlation coefficient, calculated from a random sample of n pairs of observations from a joint normal distribution. The following tests of the null hypothesis

$$H_0 : \rho = 0$$

have a significance value α. We emphasize that all of the following hypothesis tests are based on the assumption that the correlation is 0.

1. To test H_0 against the alternative

$$H_1 : \rho > 0$$

the decision rule is as follows:

$$\text{Reject } H_0 \text{ if } \quad \frac{r\sqrt{(n-2)}}{\sqrt{(1-r^2)}} > t_{n-2,\alpha} \qquad \text{(11.27)}$$

2. To test H_0 against the alternative

$$H_1 : \rho < 0$$

the decision rule is as follows:

$$\text{Reject } H_0 \text{ if } \quad \frac{r\sqrt{(n-2)}}{\sqrt{(1-r^2)}} < -t_{n-2,\alpha} \qquad \text{(11.28)}$$

3. To test H_0 against the two-sided alternative

$$H_1 : \rho \neq 0$$

the decision rule is as follows:

$$\text{Reject } H_0 \text{ if } \quad \frac{r\sqrt{(n-2)}}{\sqrt{(1-r^2)}} < -t_{n-2,\alpha/2} \quad \text{ or } \quad \frac{r\sqrt{(n-2)}}{\sqrt{(1-r^2)}} > t_{n-2,\alpha/2} \quad \text{(11.29)}$$

Here, $t_{n-2,\alpha}$ is the number for which

$$P(t_{n-2} > t_{n-2,\alpha}) = \alpha$$

where the random variable t_{n-2} follows a Student's t distribution with $(n-2)$ degrees of freedom.

4. If we set $t_{n-2,\alpha/2} = 2.0$ in Equation 11.3, an approximate "rule to remember" for testing the previous hypothesis that the population correlation is 0 can be shown to be

$$|r| > \frac{2}{\sqrt{n}}$$

Example 11.4 Political Risk Score (Hypothesis Test for Correlation)

A research team was attempting to determine if political risk in countries is related to inflation for these countries. In this research a survey of political risk analysts produced a mean political risk score for each of 49 countries. (Data are from Reference 2.)

Solution The political risk score is scaled such that the higher the score, the greater the political risk. The sample correlation between political risk score and inflation for these countries was 0.43.

We wish to determine if the population correlation, ρ, between these measures is different from 0. Specifically, we want to test

$$H_0 : \rho = 0$$

against

$$H_1 : \rho > 0$$

using the sample information

$$n = 49 \quad r = 0.43$$

The test is based on the statistic

$$t = \frac{r\sqrt{(n-2)}}{\sqrt{(1-r^2)}} = \frac{0.43\sqrt{(49-2)}}{\sqrt{1-(0.43)^2}} = 3.265$$

Since there are $(n - 2) = 47$ degrees of freedom, we have from the Student's t Table 8 in the appendix,

$$t_{47, 0.005} < 2.704$$

Therefore, we can reject the null hypothesis at the 0.5% significance level. As a result, we have strong evidence of a positive linear relationship between inflation and experts' judgments of political riskiness of countries. Note that from this result we cannot conclude that one variable caused the other, but only that they are related.

We noted previously that the null hypothesis $H_0 : \rho = 0$ can be rejected by using the approximate rule of thumb $|r| > \dfrac{2}{\sqrt{n}}$. This result provides a quick test to determine if two variables are linearly related when one or more sample correlations are being examined. Thus, for a sample size of $n = 25$ the absolute value of the sample correlation would have to exceed $\dfrac{2}{\sqrt{25}} = 0.40$. But for a sample of size $n = 64$ the absolute value of the sample correlation would have to exceed only $\dfrac{2}{\sqrt{64}} = 0.25$. This result has been found to be useful in many statistical applications.

EXERCISES

Basic Exercises

11.60 Given the following pairs of (x, y) observations, compute the sample correlation.

a. (2, 5), (5, 8), (3, 7), (1, 2), (8, 15)
b. (7, 5), (10, 8), (8, 7), (6, 2), (13, 15)
c. (12, 4), (15, 6), (16, 5), (21, 8), (14, 6)
d. (2, 8), (5, 12), (3, 14), (1, 9), (8, 22)

11.61 Test the null hypothesis

$$H_0 : \rho = 0$$

versus

$$H_1 : \rho \neq 0$$

given the following:

a. A sample correlation of 0.35 for a random sample of size $n = 40$

b. A sample correlation of 0.50 for a random sample of size $n = 60$

c. A sample correlation of 0.62 for a random sample of size $n = 45$

d. A sample correlation of 0.60 for a random sample of size $n = 25$

11.62 An instructor in a statistics course set a final examination and also required the students to do a data analysis project. For a random sample of 10 students, the scores obtained are shown in the table. Find the sample correlation between the examination and project scores.

Examination	81	62	74	78	93	69	72	83	90	84
Project	76	71	69	76	87	62	80	75	92	79

Application Exercises

11.63 In the study of 49 countries discussed in Example 11.4, the sample correlation between the experts' political riskiness score and the infant mortality rate in these countries was 0.75. Test the null hypothesis of no correlation between these quantities against the alternative of positive correlation.

11.64 For a random sample of 353 high school teachers the correlation between annual raises and teaching evaluations was found to be 0.11. Test the null hypothesis that these quantities are uncorrelated in the population against the alternative that the population correlation is positive.

11.65 The sample correlation for 68 pairs of annual returns on common stocks in country A and country B was found to be 0.51. Test the null hypothesis that the population correlation is 0 against the alternative that it is positive.

It is recommended that the following exercises be solved by using the computer.

11.66 The accompanying table and the data file **Dow Jones** show percentage changes (x_i) in the Dow Jones index over the first 5 trading days of each of 13 years and also the corresponding percentage changes (y_i) in the index over the whole year.

a. Calculate the sample correlation.

b. Test at the 10% significance level, against a two-sided alternative, the null hypothesis that the population correlation is 0.

x	y	x	y
1.5	14.9	5.6	2.3
0.2	−9.2	−1.4	11.9
−0.1	19.6	1.4	27.0
2.8	20.3	1.5	−4.3
2.2	−3.7	4.7	20.3
−1.6	27.7	1.1	4.2
−1.3	22.6		

11.67 A college administers for all its courses a student evaluation questionnaire. For a random sample of 12 courses the accompanying table and the data file **Student Evaluation** show both the average student ratings of the instructor (on a scale from 1 to 5), and the average expected grades of the students (on a scale from A = 4 to F = 0).

Instructor rating	2.8	3.7	4.4	3.6	4.7	3.5	4.1	3.2	4.9	4.2	3.8	3.3
Expected grade	2.6	2.9	3.3	3.2	3.1	2.8	2.7	2.4	3.5	3.0	3.4	2.5

a. Find the sample correlation between instructor ratings and expected grades.

b. Test at the 10% significance level the hypothesis that the population correlation coefficient is zero against the alternative that it is positive.

11.68 In an advertising study the researchers wanted to determine if there was a relationship between the per capita cost and the per capita revenue. The following variables were measured for a random sample of advertising programs:

x_i = Cost of Advertisement ÷ Number of Inquiries Received

y_i = Revenue from Inquiries ÷ Number of Inquiries Received

The sample data results are shown in the data file **Advertising Revenue**. Find the sample correlation, and test against a two-sided alternative the null hypothesis that the population correlation is 0.

11.8 BETA MEASURE OF FINANCIAL RISK

The financial discipline has developed a number of measures and analysis procedures to help investors measure and control financial risk in the development of investment portfolios. Risk can be identified as diversifiable risk and nondiversifiable risk. Diversifiable risk is that risk associated with specific firms and industries and includes labor conflicts, new competition, consumer market changes, and many other factors. This risk can be controlled by larger portfolio sizes and by including stocks whose returns have negative correlations. We developed these procedures in Chapter 5. Nondiversifiable risk is that risk associated with the entire economy. Shifts in the economy resulting from business cycles, international crisis, the evolving world energy demands, or others affect all firms but do not have the same effect on each firm. The overall effect is measured by the average return on stocks such as measured by the Standard and Poor's 500-stock composite index (S & P 500). The effect on individual firms is measured by the beta coefficient.

The beta coefficient for a specific firm is the slope coefficient that is obtained when the returns for a particular firm is regressed on the return for a broad index such as the S & P 500. This slope coefficient indicates how responsive the returns for a particular firm are to the overall market returns. In most cases the beta is positive, but in some limited cases a firms returns will move in the opposite direction compared to the overall economy. If the firms return follows the market exactly then the beta coefficient would be 1. If the firms returns are more responsive to the market then the beta would be larger than 1 and if the firms returns are less responsive to the market then the beta would be less than 1. Using financial analysis based on the Capital Asset Pricing Model the required return on an investment is given by the following:

$$\begin{pmatrix} Required\ Return \\ on\ Investment \end{pmatrix} = \begin{pmatrix} Risk-free \\ Rate \end{pmatrix} + \left[\begin{pmatrix} Beta\ for \\ Investment \end{pmatrix} \times \left(\begin{pmatrix} Market \\ Return \end{pmatrix} - \begin{pmatrix} Risk-free \\ rate \end{pmatrix} \right) \right]$$

From the previous result we see that a higher value of beta results in the need for a higher required return on investment. This higher required return would adjust for the fact that the stock return is influenced more heavily by the nondiversifiable market risk. Diversification through larger portfolios cannot adjust for overall shifts in the market.

A financial manager might be only concerned about the actual value of the beta. However, a statistical analyst would also be concerned about the "quality" of the regression model that provides the estimate of beta and thus standard error of the coefficient, Student's t, R-squared and other measures become appropriate. A statistical analyst would also be concerned about the time period represented by the data. We would like the period to be as long as possible to obtain an estimate with a low variance. However, we also know that major changes occur over time that may result in a "sea change" in the economy. In those cases we might be mixing data from two different kinds of economy and the resulting estimated beta might not be appropriate for present decisions. Thus, it is important that the statistical analyst work closely with experienced financial analysts and fund managers who can help reflect on overall economic conditions.

Example 11.5 will show how we can estimate beta using our present knowledge of regression analysis.

Example 11.5 Estimation of Beta Coefficients

The research department of Blue Star Investments has been asked to determine the beta coefficients for the firms Pearson PLC and Infosys and you have been assigned the project. Both firms are large multinational organizations. Pearson is a wide range publisher and provider of various media, while Infosys is a large computer software and information services firm with headquarters in India.

Solution   After discussions with a number of analysts you decide that you will use monthly data going back 60 months from April 2008. The measure is month end proportion change in stock value and the data is contained in the data file **Return on Stock Price 60 Month**. The regression analysis results and scatter plot for the Pearson analysis is shown in Figure 11.13, and the analysis for Infosys is shown in Figure 11.14.

As indicated in Figure 11.13 the Pearson return has a beta of 1.10 with a coefficient Student's t = 5.61 and an overall R-squared of 35.2%. Thus, we see that the nondiversifiable risk for Pearson follows the market quite closely. For the 60 month period the monthly return for Pearson was 0.6%.

The Infosys return has a beta of 1.87 with a coefficient Student's t = 4.49 and an overall R-squared of 25.8%. Thus, we see that the nondiversifiable risk response for Infosys is substantially above the overall market. For the 60-month period the monthly return for Infosys was 1.96%. Recall the previous discussion from the Capital Asset Pricing Model, which indicated that a higher beta would require a higher market return to adjust for the risk. In fact, we see that the Infosys return was over three times that of Pearson.

Figure 11.13 Computation of Beta for Pearson

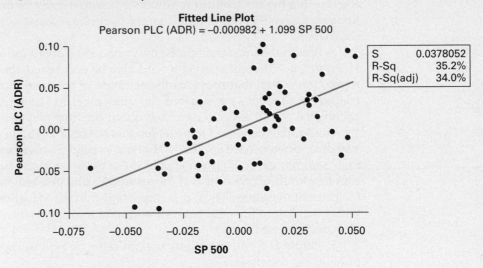

Regression Analysis: Pearson PLC (ADR) versus SP 500

```
The regression equation is
Pearson PLC (ADR) = - 0.00098 + 1.10 SP 500

Predictor       Coef    SE Coef       T      P
Constant    -0.000982   0.005046   -0.19  0.846
SP 500        1.0991     0.1960     5.61  0.000
```

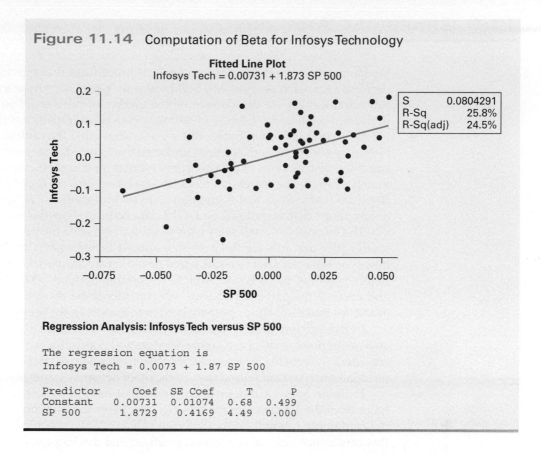

Figure 11.14 Computation of Beta for Infosys Technology

Fitted Line Plot
Infosys Tech = 0.00731 + 1.873 SP 500

S	0.0804291
R-Sq	25.8%
R-Sq(adj)	24.5%

Regression Analysis: Infosys Tech versus SP 500

```
The regression equation is
Infosys Tech = 0.0073 + 1.87 SP 500

Predictor      Coef   SE Coef      T      P
Constant    0.00731   0.01074   0.68  0.499
SP 500       1.8729    0.4169   4.49  0.000
```

EXERCISES

11.69 As part of a process to build a new automotive portfolio you have been asked to determine the beta coefficients for AB Volvo and General Motors. Data for this task is contained in the data file **Return on Stock Price 60 Months**. Compare the required return on the two stocks to compensate for the risk.

11.70 In this exercise you are asked to determine the beta coefficient for Senior Housing Properties Trust. Data for this task is contained in the data file **Return on Stock Price 60 Months**. Interpret this coefficient.

11.71 An investor is considering the possibility of including TCF Financial in his portfolio. Data for this task is contained in the data file **Return on Stock Price 60 Months**. Compare the mean and variance of the monthly return with the Standard and Poor's 500 index mean and variance. Then, estimate the beta coefficient. Based on this analysis what would you recommend to the investor.

11.72 Allied Financial is considering the possibility of adding one or more computer industry stocks to its portfolio. You are asked to consider the possibility of Seagate, Microsoft, and Tata Information systems. Data for this task is contained in the data file **Return on Stock Price 60 Months**. Compare the return on these three stocks by computing the beta coefficients and the mean and variance of the returns. What is your recommendation regarding these three stocks.

11.73 Charlie Ching has asked you to analyze the possibility of including Seneca Foods and Safeco in his portfolio. Data for this task is contained in the data file **Return on Stock Price 60 Months**. Compute the beta coefficients for the stock price growth for each stock. Then construct a portfolio that includes equal dollar value for both stocks. Compute the beta coefficient for that portfolio. Compare the mean and variance for the portfolio with the Standard and Poor's 500. What is your recommendation regarding the inclusion of these two stocks in Charlie's portfolio?

We have developed the theory and analysis procedures that provide the capability to perform regression analysis and build linear models. Using hypothesis tests and confidence intervals, we can determine the quality of our model and identify certain important relationships. These inferential procedures initially assume that the model errors are normally distributed. But we also know that the central limit theorem will help us perform hypothesis tests and construct confidence intervals as long as the sampling distributions of the coefficient estimators and predicted values are approximately normal. The regression model is also based on a set of assumptions. However, there are many ways that regression analysis applications can go wrong, including assumptions that are not satisfied if the data do not follow the assumed patterns.

The example of retail sales regressed on disposable income—Figure 11.2—has a scatter plot that follows the pattern assumed in regression analysis. That pattern, however, does not always occur when new data are studied. One of the best ways to detect potential problems for simple regression analysis is to prepare scatter plots and observe the pattern. Here, we will consider some analysis tools and regression examples that can help us prepare better regression analysis applications.

In this section, graphical analysis will be used to show the effect on regression analysis of points that have extreme X values and points that have Y values that deviate considerably from the least squares regression equation. In later chapters we show how residuals analysis can be used to examine other deviations from standard data patterns.

Extreme points are defined as points that have X values that deviate substantially from the X values for the other points. Refer to Equation 11.26, which presents the confidence interval for the expected value of Y at a specific value of X. Central to this confidence interval is a term typically called the *leverage*, h_i, for a point, which is defined as follows:

$$h_i = \frac{1}{n} + \frac{(x_i - \bar{x})^2}{\sum_{i=1}^{n}(x_i - \bar{x})^2}$$

This leverage term will increase the standard deviation of the expected value as data points are farther from the mean of X and, thus, lead to a wider confidence interval. A point i is defined as an extreme point if its value of h is substantially different from the h values for all other data points. We see in the following example that Minitab will identify points that have a high leverage with an X if $h_i > 3\,p/n$, where p is the number of predictors including the constant. The same feature is available in most good statistical packages, but not in Excel. Using this capability, extreme points can be identified, as shown in Example 11.6.

Outlier points are defined as those that deviate substantially in the Y direction from the predicted value. Typically, these points are identified by computing the standardized residual as follows:

$$e_{is} = \frac{e_i}{s_e\sqrt{1-h_i}}$$

That is, the standardized residual is the residual divided by the standard error of the residual. Note that in the previous equation points with high leverage—large h_i—will have a smaller standard error of the residual. This occurs because points with high leverage are likely to influence the location of the estimated regression line, and, hence, the observed and expected values of Y will be closer. Minitab will mark observations that have an absolute value of the standardized residual greater than 2.0 with an R to indicate that they are outliers. This capability is also available in most good statistical packages, but not in Excel. Using this capability outlier points can be identified, as shown in Example 11.6.

In the next two examples we will see that extreme points and outliers have a great influence on the estimated regression equation compared to other observations. In any applied analysis either these unusual points are part of the data that represent the process being studied, or they are not. In the former case they should be included in the data set, and in the latter case they should not. The analyst must decide! Typically, these decisions require a good understanding of the process and good judgment. First, the individual points should be examined carefully and their source checked. These unusual points could have resulted from measurement or recording errors and, thus, would be eliminated or corrected. Further investigation may reveal unusual circumstances that are not expected to be part of the standard process, and this would indicate exclusion of the data points. Decisions concerning what a standard process is and other related decisions require careful judgment and examination of other information about the process being studied. A good analyst uses the previously mentioned statistical computations to identify observations that should be examined more carefully, but does not rely exclusively on these measures for unusual observations to make the final decision.

Example 11.6   The Effect of Extreme X Values (Scatter Plot Analysis)

We are interested in determining the effect of extreme X values on the regression. In this example the effect of points with X values that are substantially different from the other points will be investigated using two samples that differ in only two points. These comparative examples, while somewhat unusual, are used to emphasize the effect of extreme points on a regression analysis.

Solution   Figure 11.15 is a scatter plot with a regression line drawn on the points, and Figure 11.16 is the output from the regression analysis computed with the data. The regression slope is positive and $R^2 = 0.632$. But note that two extreme

Figure 11.15   Scatter Plot with Two Extreme X Points: Positive Slope

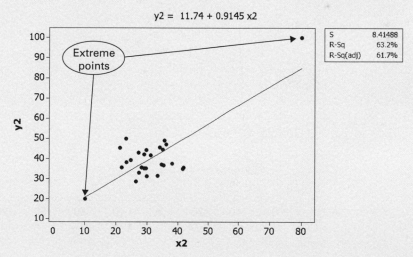

Figure 11.16 Regression Analysis with Two Extreme X Points: Positive Slope (Minitab Output)

Regression Analysis: Y2 versus x2

```
The regression equation is
Y2 = 11.74 + 0.9145 x2


S = 8.41488   R-Sq = 63.2%   R-Sq(adj) = 61.7%

Analysis of Variance

Source       DF        SS       MS       F       P
Regression    1    3034.80  3034.80   42.86   0.000
Error        25    1770.26    70.81
Total        26    4805.05
```

Fitted Line: y2 versus x2

points seem to determine the regression relationship. Now let us consider the effect of changing the two extreme data points, as shown in Figures 11.17 and 11.18.

As a result of changing only two data points, the relationship now has a statistically significant negative slope, and the predictions would be substantially different. Without examining the scatter plots we would not know why we had either a positive or a negative slope. We might have thought that our results represented a standard regression situation such as we saw in the retail sales scatter plot. Note that in Figure 11.17 that observation 26 has been labeled as an extreme observation by the symbol *X*.

Figure 11.17 Scatter Plot with Extreme *X* Points: Negative Slope

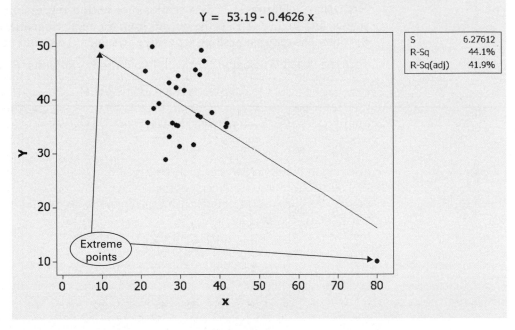

$$Y = 53.19 - 0.4626\,x$$

S	6.27612
R-Sq	44.1%
R-Sq(adj)	41.9%

Extreme points

Regression Analysis: Y versus X

```
The regression equation is
Y1 = 53.2 - 0.463 X

Predictor        Coef     SE Coef       T        P
Constant       53.195       3.518   15.12    0.000
X1            -0.4626       0.1042   -4.44    0.000


s = 6.27612   R-Sq = 44.1%   R-Sq(adj) = 41.9%


Analysis of Variance

Source           DF          SS        MS       F       P
Regression        1      776.56    776.56   19.71   0.000
Residual Error   25      984.74     39.39
Total            26     1761.30
```

Observation 26 is an extreme point with large influence.

```
Unusual Observations

Obs    X      Y     Fit   Se Fit   Residual   St Resid
 7   35.5  49.14  36.78    1.27      12.37        2.01R
26   80.0  10.00  16.19    5.17      -6.19       -1.74 X


R denotes an observation with a large standardized residual.
X denotes an observation whose X value gives it large influence.
```

This example demonstrates a common problem when historical data are used. Suppose that *X* is the number of workers employed on a production shift and *Y* is the number of units produced on that shift. Most of the time the factory operates with a relatively stable workforce, and output depends in large part on the amount of raw materials available and the sales requirements. The operation adjusts up or down over a narrow range in response to demands and to the available workforce, *X*. Thus, we see that in most cases the scatter plot covers a narrow range for the *X* variable. But occasionally there is a very large or small workforce—or the number of workers has been recorded incorrectly. On those days the production might be unusually high or low—or might be recorded incorrectly. As a result, we have extreme points that can have a major influence on the regression model. These few days determine the regression results. Without the extreme points the regression would indicate little or no relationship. If these extreme points represent extensions of the relationship, then the estimated model is useful. But if these points result from unusual conditions or recording errors, the estimated model is misleading.

In a particular application we may find that these outlier points are correct and should be used to determine the regression line. But the analyst needs to make that decision knowing that all of the other data points do not support a significant relationship. In fact, you do need to think carefully in order to understand the system and process that generated the data and to evaluate the available data.

Example 11.7 The Effect of Outliers in the Y Variable (Scatter Plot Analysis)

In this example we consider the effect of outliers in the y or vertical direction. recall that the regression analysis model assumes that all of the variation is in the Y direction. Thus, we know that outliers in the Y direction will have large residuals, and these will result in a higher estimate of the model error. In this example we will see that the effects can be even more extreme.

Solution To begin, observe the scatter plot and regression analysis in Figures 11.19 and 11.20. In this example we have a strong relationship between the X and Y variables. The scatter plot clearly supports a linear relationship with $b_1 = 11.88$. In addition, the regression model R^2 is close to 1, and the Student's t statistic is very large. Clearly, we have strong evidence to support a linear model.

Figure 11.19 Scatter Plot with Anticipated Pattern

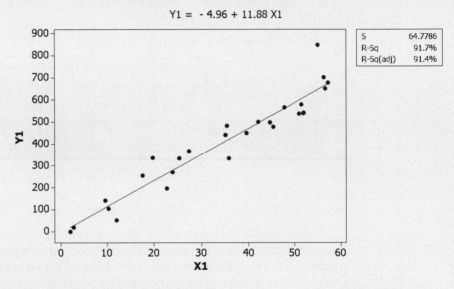

$$Y1 = -4.96 + 11.88\ X1$$

S	64.7786
R-Sq	91.7%
R-Sq(adj)	91.4%

Figure 11.20 Regression with Anticipated Pattern (Minitab Output)

Regression Analysis: Y1 versus X1

```
The regression equation is
Y1 = -4.96 + 11.88 X1



s = 64.7786  R-Sq = 91.7%  R-Sq(adj) = 91.4%



Analysis of Variance

Source       DF        SS        MS       F       P
Regression    1   1160171   1160171  276.48   0.000
Error        25    104907      4196
Total        26   1265077
```

Fitted Line: Y1 versus X1

Figure 11.21 Scatter Plot with Y Outlier Points

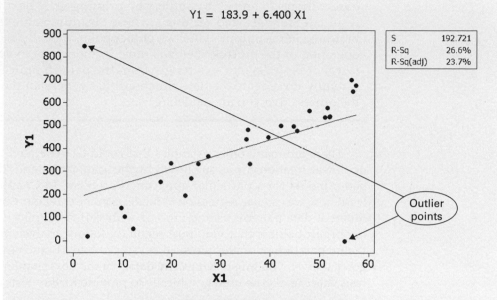

$$Y1 = 183.9 + 6.400\ X1$$

S	192.721
R-Sq	26.6%
R-Sq(adj)	23.7%

Outlier points

Now let us consider the effect of changing two observations to outlier data points, as shown in Figure 11.21. This could occur because of a data recording error or because of a very unusual condition in the process being studied.

The regression slope is still positive, but now $b_1 = 6.40$, and the slope estimate has a larger standard error, as shown in Figure 11.22. The confidence interval is much wider, and the predicted value from the regression line is not as

Figure 11.22 Regression with Y Outlier Points (Minitab Output)

Regression Analysis: Y1 versus X1

```
The regression equation is
Y1 = 184 + 6.40 X1

Predictor      Coef      SE Coef      T         P
Constant       183.92    82.10        2.24      0.034
X1             6.400     2.126        3.01      0.006


S = 192.721  R-Sq = 26.6%  R-Sq(adj) = 23.7%

Analysis of Variance

Source          DF        SS           MS        F        P
Regression      1         336540       336540    9.06     0.006
Residual Error  25        928537       37141
Total           26        1265077

Unusual Observations

Obs   X1     Y1      Fit     Se Fit   Residual   St Resid
26    2.0    850.0   196.7   78.3     653.3      3.71R
27    55.0   0.0     535.9   57.3     -535.9     -2.91R

R denotes an observation with a large standardized residual.
```

Outliers marked with R

accurate. The correct regression model is now not as clear. Minitab identifies observations 26 and 27 as outliers by printing an R next to the standardized residual. Standardized residuals whose absolute value is greater than 2 are indicated in the output. If the two outlier points actually occurred in the normal operation of the process, then you must include them in your analysis. But the fact that they deviate so strongly from the pattern indicates that you should carefully investigate the data situations that generated those points and study the process that you are modeling.

There are many other examples that could be generated. You might find that a nonlinear relationship is suggested by the scatter plot and, thus, would provide a better model for a particular application problem. In Chapters 12 and 13 we will learn how we can use regression to model nonlinear relationships. You will see many different data patterns as you proceed with various applications of regression. The important point is that you must regularly follow analysis procedures—including the preparation of scatter plots—that can provide as much insight as possible. As a good analyst, you must **"Know thy data!"** In the next chapter we will consider how residuals can also be used graphically to provide further tests of regression models.

EXERCISES

Basic Exercise

11.74 Frank Anscombe, senior research executive, has asked you to analyze the following four linear models using data contained in the data file **Anscombe**:

$$Y_1 = \beta_0 + \beta_1 X_1$$
$$Y_2 = \beta_0 + \beta_1 X_2$$
$$Y_3 = \beta_0 + \beta_1 X_3$$
$$Y_4 = \beta_0 + \beta_1 X_4$$

Use your computer package to obtain a linear regression estimate for each model. Prepare a scatter plot for the data used in each model. Write a report, including regression and graphical outputs, that compares and contrasts the four models.

Application Exercise

11.75 John Foster, president of Public Research Inc., has asked for your assistance in a study of the occurrence of crimes in different states before and after a large federal government expenditure to reduce crime. As part of this study he wants to know if the crime rate for selected crimes after the expenditure can be predicted using the crime rate before the expenditure. He has asked you to test the hypothesis that crime before predicts crime after for Total Crime rate and for the Murder, Rape, and Robbery rates. The data for your analysis are contained in the data file **Crime Study**. Perform appropriate analysis and write a report that summarizes your results.

KEY WORDS

- analysis of variance, 439
- basis for inference about the population regression slope, 448
- coefficient estimators, 432
- coefficient of determination, R^2, 441
- confidence intervals for predictions, 455
- confidence intervals for the population regression slope b_1, 450
- correlation and R^2, 442

- estimation of model error variance, 443
- F test for simple regression coefficient, 452
- least squares coefficient estimators, 432
- least squares procedure, 433
- least squares regression line, 424
- linear regression outcomes, 430

- linear regression population equation model, 428
- sampling distribution of the least squares coefficient estimator, 446
- slope, 424
- tests for zero population correlation, 462
- tests of the population regression slope, 449
- y-intercept, 424

11.76 What is meant by the statement that a pair of random variables are positively correlated? Give examples of pairs of random variables for which you would expect the following:

  a. Positive correlation
  b. Negative correlation
  c. Zero correlation

11.77 A random sample of five sets of observations for a pair of random variables yielded the results given in the following table:

X	4	1	0	1	4
Y	-2	-1	0	1	2

  a. Find the sample correlation coefficient.
  b. In light of the fact that each y_i value is the square of the corresponding x_i value, comment on your answer in part (a).

11.78 For a random sample of 53 building supply stores in a chain the correlation between annual euro sales per square meter of floor space and annual euro rent per square meter of floor space was found to be 0.37. Test the null hypothesis that these two quantities are uncorrelated in the population against the alternative that the population correlation is positive.

11.79 For a random sample of 526 firms the sample correlation between the proportion of a firm's officers who are directors and a risk-adjusted measure of return on the firm's stock was found to be 0.1398. Test against a two-sided alternative the null hypothesis that the population correlation is 0.

11.80 For a sample of 66 months the correlation between the returns on Canadian and Singapore 10-year bonds was found to be 0.293. Test the null hypothesis that the population correlation is 0 against the alternative that it is positive.

11.81 For a random sample of 192 female employees, a sample correlation of –0.18 was found between age and a measure of willingness to relocate. Given only this information, derive all the conclusions you can about the regression of willingness to relocate on age.

11.82 Based on a sample on n observations, (x_1, y_1), (x_2, y_2), ..., (x_n, y_n), the sample regression of y on x is calculated. Show that the sample regression line passes through the point $(x = \bar{x}, y = \bar{y})$, where $\bar{x}$ and $\bar{y}$ are the sample means.

11.83 🌐 A company routinely administers an aptitude test to all new management trainees. At the end of the first year with the company, these trainees are graded by their immediate supervisors. For a random sample of 12 trainees, the results shown in the data file **Employee Test** were obtained.

  a. Estimate the regression of supervisor's grade on aptitude score.
  b. Interpret the slope of the sample regression line.
  c. Is it possible to give a useful interpretation of the intercept of the sample regression line? Explain.
  d. Find and interpret the coefficient of determination for this regression.
  e. Test against the obvious one-sided alternative the null hypothesis that the slope of the population regression line is 0.
  f. Find a 95% confidence interval for the supervisor's grade that would be obtained by a particular trainee who had an aptitude score of 70.

11.84 An attempt was made to evaluate the inflation rate as a predictor of the spot rate in the German treasury bill market. For a sample of 79 quarterly observations the estimated linear regression

$$\hat{y} = 0.0027 + 0.7916x$$

was obtained, where

y = actual change in the spot rate
x = change in the spot rate predicted by the inflation rate

The coefficient of determination was 0.097, and the estimated standard deviation of the estimator of the slope of the population regression line was 0.2759.

  a. Interpret the slope of the estimated regression line.
  b. Interpret the coefficient of determination.
  c. Test the null hypothesis that the slope of the population regression line is 0 against the alternative that the true slope is positive, and interpret your result.
  d. Test against a two-sided alternative the null hypothesis that the slope of the population regression line is 1, and interpret your result.

11.85 The following table shows, for eight vintages of select wine, purchases per buyer (y) and the wine buyer's rating in a year (x):

x	3.6	3.3	2.8	2.6	2.7	2.9	2.0	2.6
y	24	21	22	22	18	13	9	6

a. Estimate the regression of purchases per buyer on the buyer's rating.

b. Interpret the slope of the estimated regression line.

c. Find and interpret the coefficient of determination.

d. Find and interpret a 90% confidence interval for the slope of the population regression line.

e. Find a 90% confidence interval for expected purchases per buyer for a vintage for which the buyer's rating is 2.0.

11.86   For a sample of 306 students in a basic business statistics course the sample regression line

$$y = 58.813 + 0.2875x$$

was obtained. Here,

y = final student score at the end of the course
x = score on a diagnostic statistics test given at the beginning of the course

The coefficient of determination was 0.1158, and the estimated standard deviation of the estimator of the slope of the population regression line was 0.04566.

a. Interpret the slope of the sample regression line.

b. Interpret the coefficient of determination.

c. The information given allows the null hypothesis that the slope of the population regression line is 0 to be tested in two different ways against the alternative that it is positive. Carry out these tests and show that they reach the same conclusion.

11.87   Based on a sample of 30 observations, the population regression model

$$y_i = \beta_0 + \beta_1 x_i + \varepsilon_i$$

was estimated. The least squares estimates obtained were as follows:

$$b_0 = 10.1 \quad \text{and} \quad b_1 = 8.4$$

The regression and error sums of squares were as follows:

$$SSR = 128 \quad \text{and} \quad SSE = 286$$

a. Find and interpret the coefficient of determination.

b. Test at the 10% significance level against a two-sided alternative the null hypothesis that β_1 is 0.

c. Find

$$\sum_{i=1}^{30} \left(x_i - \bar{x} \right)^2$$

11.88   Based on a sample of 25 observations, the population regression model

$$y_i = \beta_0 + \beta_1 x_1 + \varepsilon_i$$

was estimated. The least squares estimates obtained were as follows:

$$b_0 = 15.6 \quad \text{and} \quad b_1 = 1.3$$

The total and error sums of squares were as follows:

$$SST = 268 \quad \text{and} \quad SSE = 204$$

a. Find and interpret the coefficient of determination.

b. Test against a two-sided alternative at the 5% significance level the null hypothesis that the slope of the population regression line is 0.

c. Find a 95% confidence interval for β_1.

11.89   An analyst believes that the only important determinant of banks' returns on assets (Y) is the ratio of loans to deposits (x). For a random sample of 20 banks the sample regression line

$$Y = 0.97 + 0.47x$$

was obtained with coefficient of determination 0.720.

a. Find the sample correlation between returns on assets and the ratio of loans to deposits.

b. Test against a two-sided alternative at the 5% significance level the null hypothesis of no linear association between the returns and the ratio.

c. Find

$$\frac{s_e}{\sqrt{\sum \left(x_i - \bar{x} \right)^2}}$$

11.90   If a regression of the yield per acre of corn on the quantity of fertilizer used is estimated using fertilizer quantities in the range typically used by farmers, the slope of the estimated regression line will certainly be positive. However, it is well known that, if an enormously high amount of fertilizer is used, corn yield will be very low. Discuss the benefits of applying regression analysis to a data set that includes a few cases of excessive fertilizer use combined with data from typical operations.

The following exercises require the use of a computer.

11.91   ⊙ A college's Economics Department is attempting to determine if verbal or mathematical proficiency is more important for predicting academic success in the study of economics. The department faculty have decided to use the grade point average (GPA) in economics courses for graduates as a measure of success. Verbal proficiency is measured by the SAT verbal and the ACT English entrance examination test scores. Mathematical proficiency is measured by the SAT mathematics and the ACT mathematics entrance examination scores. The data for 112 students are available in a data file named **Student GPA**, which is available on your data disk. The designation of the variable columns is presented at the beginning of the data file. You should use your local statistical computer program to perform the analysis for this problem.

a. Prepare a graphical plot of the economics GPA versus each of the two verbal proficiency scores and each of the two mathematical proficiency scores. Which variable is a better predictor? Note any unusual patterns in the data.

b. Compute the linear model coefficients and the regression analysis statistics for the models that predict economics GPA as a function of each verbal and each mathematics score. Using both the SAT mathematics and verbal measures and the ACT mathematics and English measures, determine whether mathematical or verbal proficiency is the best predictor of economics GPA.

c. Compare the descriptive statistics—mean, standard deviation, upper and lower quartiles, and range—for the predictor variables. Note the differences and indicate how these differences affect the capability of the linear model to predict.

11.92 The administrator of the National Highway Traffic Safety Administration (NHTSA) wants to know if the different types of vehicles in a state have a relationship to the highway death rate in the state. She has asked you to perform several regression analyses to determine if average vehicle weight, percentage imported cars, percentage light trucks, or average car age is related to crash deaths in automobiles and pickups. The data for the analyses are in the data file named **Crash**, which is located on your data disk. The variable descriptions and locations are contained in the data file catalog in the chapter appendix.

a. Prepare graphical plots of crash deaths versus each of the potential predictor variables. Note the relationship and any unusual patterns in the data points.

b. Prepare a simple regression analysis of crash deaths on the potential predictor variables. Determine which, if any, of the regressions indicate a significant relationship.

c. State the results of your analysis and rank the predictor variables in terms of their relationship to crash deaths.

11.93 The Department of Transportation wishes to know if states with a larger percentage of urban

population have higher automobile and pickup crash death rates. In addition, it wants to know if either, the average speed on rural roads, or the percentage of rural roads that are surfaced, are related to crash death rates. Data for this study are included in the data file **Crash**, stored on your data disk.

a. Prepare graphical plots of crash deaths versus each of the potential predictor variables. Note the relationship and any unusual patterns in the data points.

b. Prepare a simple regression analysis of crash deaths on the potential predictor variables. Determine which, if any, of the regressions indicate a significant relationship.

c. State the results of your analysis and rank the predictor variables in terms of their relationship to crash deaths.

11.94 An economist wishes to predict the market value of owner-occupied homes in small midwestern cities. He has collected a set of data from 45 small cities for a 2-year period and wants you to use this as the data source for the analysis. The data are stored in the file **Citydat**, which is located on your data disk. He wants you to develop two prediction equations: one that uses the size of the house as a predictor and a second that uses the tax rate as a predictor.

a. Plot the market value of houses (hseval) versus the size of houses (sizense), and then versus the tax rates (taxrate). Note any unusual patterns in the data.

b. Prepare regression analyses for the two predictor variables. Which variable is the stronger predictor of the value of houses?

c. A business developer in a midwestern state has stated that local property tax rates in small towns need to be lowered because if they are not, no one will purchase a house in these towns. Based on your analysis in this problem, evaluate the business developer's claim.

11.95 Stuart Wainwright, the vice president of purchasing for a large national retailer, has asked you to prepare an analysis of retail sales by state. He wants to know if either the percent of unemployment or the per capita personal income is related to per capita retail sales. Data for this study are stored in the data file named **Retail**, which is located on your data disk and described in the data file catalog in the chapter appendix.

a. Prepare graphical plots and regression analyses to determine the relationships between per capita retail sales and unemployment and personal income. Compute 95% confidence intervals for the slope coefficients in each regression equation.

b. What is the effect of a $1,000 decrease in per capita income on per capita sales?

c. For the per capita income regression equation what is the 95% confidence interval for retail sales at the mean per capita income and at $1,000 above the mean per capita income?

11.96 • A major national supplier of building materials for residential construction is concerned about total sales for next year. It is well known that the company's sales are directly related to the total national residential investment. Several New York bankers are predicting that interest rates will rise about two percentage points next year. You have been asked to develop a regression analysis that can be used to predict the effect of interest rate changes on residential investment. The time series data for this study are contained in the data file named **Macro2008**, which is located on your data disk and described in the Chapter 13 appendix.

a. Develop two regression models to predict residential investment, using the prime interest rate for one and the federal funds interest rate for the other. Analyze the regression statistics and indicate which equation provides the best predictions.

b. Determine the 95% confidence interval for the slope coefficient in both regression equations.

c. Based on each model, predict the effect of a two-percentage-point increase in interest rates on residential investment.

d. Using both models, compute 95% confidence intervals for the change in residential investment that results from a two-percentage-point increase in interest rates.

Appendix

DERIVATION OF LEAST SQUARES ESTIMATORS

In this appendix we derive the least squares estimators of the population regression parameters. We want to find the values b_0 and b_1 for which the sum of squared discrepancies

$$SSE = \sum_{i=1}^{n} e_i^2 = \sum_{i=1}^{n} (y_i - b_0 - b_1 x_i)^2$$

is as small as possible.

As a first step, we keep b_1 constant and differentiate with respect to b_0, giving

$$\frac{\partial SSE}{\partial b_0} = 2 \sum_{i=1}^{n} (y_i - b_0 - b_1 x_i)$$

$$= -2 \left(\sum y_i - n b_0 - b_1 \sum x_i \right)$$

Since this derivative must be 0 for a minimum, we have the following:

$$\sum y_i - n b_0 - b_1 \sum x_i = 0$$

Hence, dividing through by n yields

$$b_0 = \bar{y} - b_1 \bar{x}$$

Substituting this expression for b_0 gives

$$SSE = \sum_{i=1}^{n} [(y_i - \bar{y}) - b_1 (x_i - \bar{x})]^2$$

Differentiating this expression with respect to b_1 then gives

$$\frac{\partial SSE}{\partial b_1} = -2\sum_{i=1}^{n}(x_i - \bar{x})[(y_i - \bar{y}) - b_1(x_i - \bar{x})^2]$$

$$= 2\left(\sum (x_i - \bar{x})(y_i - \bar{y}) - b_1\sum(x_i - \bar{x})^2\right)$$

This derivative must be 0 for a minimum, so we have the following:

$$\sum(x_i - \bar{x})(y_i - \bar{y}) = b_1\sum(x_i - \bar{x})^2$$

Hence,

$$b_1 = \frac{\sum(x_i - \bar{x})(y_i - \bar{y})}{\sum(x_i - \bar{x})^2}$$

DATA FILE DESCRIPTIONS

Retail

This small data file contains observations for 50 states and the District of Columbia. The data for the year 1984 were obtained from the 1986 Statistical Abstract.

VARIABLE	DESCRIPTION
Perinc84	Per capita personal income for 1984
Retsal84	Per capita retail sales for 1984
Totpop84	Total population for 1984
Unemp84	Percent unemployment for 1984

Crash

This data file contains observations by state, with one state missing. The data were used to develop regression models to predict motor vehicle death rate per state as a function of the characteristics of the state population, road system, and motor vehicle mix. A variety of interesting models can be developed using these data. All of the data were collected for the year 1976.

VARIABLE	DESCRIPTION
PrurPop	Proportion rural population
Deaths	Crash deaths in automobiles and pickups divided by population
Lghttrks	Percent light trucks
Impcars	Percent imported automobiles
Popdens	Population per square mile
DRm76Mi	Deaths per mile driven in 1976
Hschool	Percent high school graduates
Doctors	Physicians per 100,000 population
Ruspeed	Average measured speed on rural two-lane roads
Prsurf	Proportion of rural roads surfaced
Tpopdeth	Total motor vehicle deaths divided by population times 100

REFERENCES

1. Dhalla, N. K. 1979. Short-Term Forecasts of Advertising Expenditures. *Journal of Advertising Research* 19 (1): 7–14.
2. Mampower, J. L., S. Livingston, and T. J. Lee. 1987. Expert Judgments of Political Risk. *Journal of Forecasting* 6:51–65.

Chapter 12

Multiple Regression

Introduction

In Chapter 11 we developed simple regression as a procedure for obtaining a linear equation that predicts a dependent or endogenous variable as a function of a single independent or exogenous variable—for example, total number of items sold as a function of price. However, in many situations several independent variables jointly influence a dependent variable. Multiple regression enables us to determine the simultaneous effect of several independent variables on a dependent variable using the least squares principle.

Many important applications of multiple regression occur in business and economics. These applications include the following:

1. The quantity of goods sold is a function of price, income, advertising, price of substitute goods, and other variables.
2. Capital investment occurs when a business person believes that a profit can be made. Thus, capital investment is a function of variables related to the potential for profit, including interest rate, gross domestic product, consumer expectations, disposable income, and technological level.
3. Salary is a function of experience, education, age, and job rank.
4. Large retail, hotel, and restaurant companies decide on locations for new outlets based on the anticipated sales revenue and/or profitability. Using data from previous successful and unsuccessful locations, analysts can build models that predict sales or profit for a potential new location.

Business and economic analysis has some unique characteristics compared to analysis in other disciplines. Natural scientists work in a laboratory where many—but not all—variables can be controlled. In contrast, the economist's and manager's laboratory is the world, and conditions cannot be controlled. Thus, we need tools such as multiple regression to estimate the simultaneous effect of several variables. Multiple regression as a "lab tool" is very important for the work of managers and economists. In this chapter we will see many specific applications in discussion examples and problem exercises.

The methods for fitting multiple regression models are based on the same least squares principle presented in Chapter 11, and, thus, the insights gained there will extend directly to multiple regression. However, there are complexities introduced because of the relationships between the various exogenous variables. These require additional insights that are developed in this chapter.

12.1 THE MULTIPLE REGRESSION MODEL

Our objective here is to learn how to use multiple regression for creating and analyzing models. Thus, we learn how multiple regression works and some guidelines for interpretation. A good understanding provides the capability for solving a wide range of applied problems. This study of multiple regression methods will parallel the study of simple regression. The first step in model development is model specification, which includes the selection of model variables and the model form. Next, we study the least squares process, followed by an analysis of variability to identify the effects of each predictor variable. Then we study estimation, confidence intervals, and hypothesis testing. Computer applications are used extensively to indicate how the theory is applied to realistic problems. Your study of this material will be aided if you relate the ideas in this chapter to those presented in Chapter 11.

Model Specification

We begin with an application that illustrates the important task of regression model specification. Model specification includes selection of the exogenous variables and the functional form of the model.

Example 12.1 Process Manufacturing (Regression Model Specification)

The production manager for Flexible Circuits Inc. has asked for your assistance in studying a manufacturing process. Flexible circuits are produced from a continuous roll of flexible resin with a thin film of copper conducting material bonded to its surface. Copper is bonded to the resin by passing the resin through a copper-based solution. The thickness of the copper is critical for high-quality circuits. Copper thickness depends, in part, on the temperature of the copper solution, speed of the production line, density of the solution, and thickness of the flexible resin. To control the thickness of the bonded copper, the production manager needs to know the effect of each of these variables. You have been asked for assistance to develop a multiple regression model.

Solution   Multiple regression can be used to provide estimates of the effect of each variable in combination with the other variables. Model development begins with a careful analysis of the problem context. The first step for this example would be an extended discussion with product design and manufacturing engineers so that the process being modeled is understood in detail. In some cases existing literature related to the process would be studied. The process must be understood and agreed to by all concerned before a useful model can be developed using multiple regression analysis. In this example the dependent variable, Y, is the copper thickness. Independent variables include temperature of the copper solution, X_1; speed of the production line, X_2; density of the solution, X_3; and thickness of the flexible resin, X_4. These variables were identified as potential predictors of copper thickness, Y, by engineers and scientists that understand the technology of the plating process. Based on the study of the process, the resulting model specification is as follows:

$$Y = \beta_0 + \beta_1 X_1 + \beta_2 X_2 + \beta_3 X_3 + \beta_4 X_4$$

In the previous linear model the β_js are constant linear coefficients of the independent variables X_j that indicate the conditional effect of each independent variable on the determination of the dependent variable, Y, in the population. Thus, the coefficients β_j are parameters in the linear regression model. A series of production runs would then be made to obtain measurements of various combinations of independent and dependent variables. (See the discussion of experimental design in Section 13.2.)

Example 12.2 Store Location (Model Specification)

The director of planning for a large retailer was dissatisfied with the company's new-store development experience. In the past 4 years 25% of new stores failed to obtain their projected sales within the 2-year trial period and were closed with substantial economic losses. The director wanted to develop better criteria for choosing store locations and decided that the historical experience of successful and unsuccessful stores should be studied.

Solution   Discussion with a consultant indicated that data from stores that met and that did not meet anticipated sales could be used to develop a multiple regression model. The consultant suggested that the second year's sales should be used as the dependent variable, Y. A regression model would be used to predict second-year sales as a function of several independent variables that define the area surrounding the store. Stores would be located only where the predicted sales exceeded a minimum level. The model would also indicate the effect of various independent variables on sales.

After considerable discussion with people in the company the consultant recommended the following independent variables:

1. X_1 = Size of store
2. X_2 = Traffic volume on highway in front of store
3. X_3 = Stand-alone store versus shopping mall location
4. X_4 = Location of competing store within 1/4 mile
5. X_5 = Per capita income of population within 5 miles
6. X_6 = Total number of people within 5 miles
7. X_7 = Per capita income of population within 10 miles
8. X_8 = Total number of people within 10 miles

Multiple regression was used to obtain estimates of the sales prediction model coefficients from data collected for all stores opened during the past 8 years. The data set included both stores that were still operating and those that were closed. A model was developed that could be used to predict second-year sales. This model included coefficient estimators, b_j, for the model parameters, β_j. To apply the model

$$\hat{y}_i = b_0 + \sum_{j=1}^{8} b_j x_{ji}$$

measurements of the independent variables were collected for each proposed new store location and the predicted sales were computed for that location. A predicted sales level was used, along with the judgment of marketing analysts and a committee of successful store managers, as input to the store location decision process.

The strategy for model specification will be influenced by the model objectives. One objective is prediction of a dependent or outcome variable. Applications include predicting or forecasting sales, output, total consumption, total investment, and many other business and economic performance criteria. A second objective is estimating the marginal effect of each independent variable. Economists and managers need to know how changes of independent variables, X_j, where $j = 1, ..., K$, change performance measures, Y. For example consider the following:

1. How do sales change as a result of a price increase and advertising expenditures?
2. How does output change when the amounts of labor and capital are changed?
3. Does infant mortality become lower when health care expenditures and local sanitation are increased?

Regression Objectives

Multiple regression provides two important results:

1. An estimated linear equation that predicts the dependent variable, Y, as a function of K observed independent variables, X_j, where $j = 1, \ldots, K$:

$$\hat{y}_i = b_0 + b_1 x_{1i} + b_2 x_{2i} + \cdots + b_K x_{Ki}$$

where $i = 1, \ldots, n$ observations.

2. The marginal change in the dependent variable, Y, that is related to changes in the independent variables—estimated by the coefficients, b_j. In multiple regression these coefficients depend on what other variables are included in the model. The coefficient b_j indicates the change in Y, given a unit change in X_j, while controlling for the simultaneous effect of the other independent variables.

In some problems both results are equally important. However, usually one will predominate (e.g., prediction of store sales, Y, in the store location example).

Marginal change is more difficult to estimate because the independent variables are related not only to the dependent variables but also to each other. If two or more independent variables change in a direct linear relationship with each other, it is difficult to determine the individual effect of each independent variable on the dependent variable.

Consider in detail the model in Example 12.2. The coefficient of x_1—that is, b_1—indicates change in second-year sales for each unit change in size of store. The coefficient of x_5 indicates the change in sales for each unit change in the per capita income of the population within 5 miles, while that of x_7 indicates the sales change for change in per capita income of the population within 10 miles. It is, of course, likely that the variables x_5 and x_7 are correlated. Thus, to the extent that these variables both change at the same time it is difficult to determine the contribution of each variable to change in store sales revenue. This correlation between independent variables introduces a complexity to the model. It is important to understand that the model predicts store sales revenue using the particular combination of variables contained in the model. The effect of a predictor variable is the effect of that variable when combined with the other variables. Thus, in general, the coefficient of a variable does not provide an indication of that variable's effect under all conditions. These complexities will be explored further as we develop the multiple regression model.

Model Development

When applying multiple regression, we construct a model to explain variability in the dependent variable. In order to do this we want to include the simultaneous and individual influences of several independent variables. For example, suppose that we wanted to develop a model that would predict the annual profit margin for savings and loan associations using data collected over a period of years. An initial model specification indicated that the annual profit margin was related to the net revenue per deposit dollar and the number of savings and loan offices. The net revenue is expected to increase the annual profit margin, and the number of savings and loan offices is anticipated to decrease the annual profit margin because of increased competition. This would lead us to specify a population regression model:

$$Y = \beta_0 + \beta_1 X_1 + \beta_2 X_2 + \varepsilon$$

where

Y = annual profit margin

X_1 = net annual revenue per deposit dollar

X_2 = number of savings and loan offices for that year

Table 12.1 and the data file named **Savings and Loan** contain 25 observations by year of these variables. These data will be used to develop a linear model that predicts annual profit margin as a function of revenue per deposit dollar and number of offices (Reference 4).

But before we can estimate the model, we need to develop and understand the multiple regression procedure. To begin, let us consider the general multiple regression model and note the differences from the simple regression model. The multiple regression model is

$$y_i = \beta_0 + \beta_1 x_{1i} + \beta_2 x_{2i} + \ldots + \beta_K x_{Ki} + \varepsilon_i$$

where ε_i is the random error term with a mean of 0 and a variance of σ^2, and the β_j terms are the coefficients or marginal effects of the independent or exogenous variables, X_{ji}, where $j = 1, \ldots, K$, given the effects of the other independent variables. The i terms indicate the observations with $i = 1, \ldots, n$. We use lowercase letters x_{ji} to denote specific values of variable X_j at observation i. We assume that the random errors ε are independent of the variables X_j and of each other to ensure proper

Table 12.1 Savings and Loan Associations Operating Data

Year	Revenue per Dollar	Number of Offices	Profit Margin	Year	Revenue per Dollar	Number of Offices	Profit Margin
1	3.92	7,298	0.75	14	3.78	6,672	0.84
2	3.61	6,855	0.71	15	3.82	6,890	0.79
3	3.32	6,636	0.66	16	3.97	7,115	0.7
4	3.07	6,506	0.61	17	4.07	7,327	0.68
5	3.06	6,450	0.7	18	4.25	7,546	0.72
6	3.11	6,402	0.72	19	4.41	7,931	0.55
7	3.21	6,368	0.77	20	4.49	8,097	0.63
8	3.26	6,340	0.74	21	4.70	8,468	0.56
9	3.42	6,349	0.9	22	4.58	8,717	0.41
10	3.42	6,352	0.82	23	4.69	8,991	0.51
11	3.45	6,361	0.75	24	4.71	9,179	0.47
12	3.58	6,369	0.77	25	4.78	9,318	0.32
13	3.66	6,546	0.78				

estimates of the coefficients and their variances. In Chapter 13 we will indicate the effect of relaxing these assumptions.

The sample estimated model is

$$y_i = b_0 + b_1 x_{1i} + b_2 x_{2i} + \ldots + b_K x_{Ki} + e_i$$

where e_i is the residual or difference between the observed value of Y and the estimated value of Y obtained by using the estimated coefficients, b_j, where $j = 1, \ldots, K$. The regression procedure obtains simultaneous estimates, b_j, of the population model coefficients, β_j, using the least squares procedure.

In our savings and loan associations example the population model for individual data points is as follows:

$$y_i = \beta_0 + \beta_1 x_{1i} + \beta_2 x_{2i} + \varepsilon_i$$

This reduced model with only two predictor variables provides the opportunity for developing additional insights into the regression procedure. The regression function can be depicted graphically in three dimensions, as shown in Figure 12.1. The regression function is shown as a plane whose Y values are a function of the independent variable values of X_1 and X_2. For each possible pair, x_{1i}, x_{2i}, the expected value of the dependent variable, Y, is on the plane. Figure 12.2 specifically illustrates the savings and loan example. An increase in X_1 leads to an increase in the expected value of Y, conditional on the effect of X_2. Similarly, an increase in X_2 leads to a decrease in the expected value of Y, conditional on the effect of X_1.

To complete our model, we add an error term defined as ε. This error term recognizes that no postulated relationship will hold exactly and that there are likely to be additional variables that also affect the observed value of Y. Thus, in the application setting we observe the expected value of the dependent variable, Y—as depicted by the plane in Figure 12.2—plus a random error term, ε, that represents the portion of Y not included in the expected value. As a result, the data model has the form

$$y_i = \beta_0 + \beta_1 x_{1i} + \beta_2 x_{2i} + \ldots + \beta_K x_{Ki} + \varepsilon_i$$

Figure 12.1 The Plane Is the Expected Value of Y as a Function of X_1 and X_2

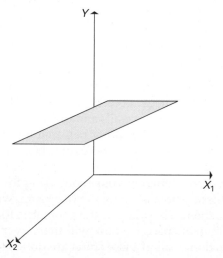

Figure 12.2 Comparison of the Observed and Expected Values of Y as a Function of Two Independent Variables

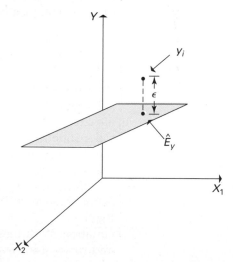

For the savings and loan example, with two independent variables, the population regression model is as follows:

$$y_i = \beta_0 + \beta_1 x_{1i} + \beta_2 x_{2i} + \varepsilon_i$$

Given particular values of the net revenue, x_{1i}, and the number of savings and loan offices, x_{2i}, the observed profit margin, y_i, is the sum of two parts: the expected value, $\beta_0 + \beta_1 x_{1i} + \beta_2 x_{2i}$, and the random error term, ε_i. The random error term can be regarded as the combination of the effects of numerous other unidentified factors that affect profit margins. Figure 12.2 illustrates the model, with the plane indicating the expected value for various combinations of the independent variables and with the ε_i, shown as the deviation between the expected value, and the observed value of Y, marked by a large dot, for a particular data point. In general, the observed values of Y will not lie on the plane but instead will be above or below the plane because of the positive or negative error terms, ε_i.

Simple regression, developed in the previous chapter, is merely a special case of multiple regression with only one predictor variable, and, hence, the plane is reduced to a line. Thus, the theory and analysis developed for simple regression also apply to multiple regression. However, there are some additional interpretations that we will develop in our study of multiple regression. One of the important interpretations is illustrated in the following discussion of three-dimensional graphing.

Three-Dimensional Graphing

Your understanding of the multiple regression procedure might be helped by considering a simplified graphical image. Look at the corner of the room in which you are sitting. The lines formed by the two walls and the floor represent the axes for two independent variables, X_1 and X_2. The corner between the two walls is the axis for the dependent variable, Y. To estimate a regression line, we collect sets of points (x_{1i}, x_{2i}, and y_i).

Now, picture these points plotted in your room using the wall and floor corners as the three axes. With these points hanging in your room, we find a plane in space that comes close to all of them. This plane is the geometric form of the least squares equation. With these points in space we now will maneuver a plane up and down and rotate it in two directions—all of these shifts are done simultaneously until we have a plane that is "close" to all of the points. Recall that we did this with a straight line in two dimensions in Chapter 11 to obtain an equation

$$\hat{y} = b_0 + b_1 x$$

Then, we extend that idea to three dimensions to obtain an equation

$$\hat{y} = b_0 + b_1 x_1 + b_2 x_2$$

This process is, of course, more complicated compared to simple regression. But real problems are complicated, and regression provides a way to better analyze the complexity of these problems. We want to know how Y changes with changes in X_1. But we know that these changes are, in turn, influenced by the way X_2 changes. And if X_1 and X_2 always change together, we cannot tell how much each variable contributes to changes in Y.

Geometric interpretations of multiple regression become increasingly complex as the number of independent variables increases. However, the analogy to simple regression is extremely useful. We estimate the coefficients by minimizing the sum of squared deviations in the Y dimension about a linear function of the independent variables. In simple regression the function is a straight line on a two-dimensional graph. With two independent variables the function is a plane in three-dimensional space. Beyond two independent variables we have various complex hyperplanes that are impossible to visualize.

EXERCISES

Basic Exercises

12.1 Given the estimated linear model

$$\hat{y} = 10 + 3x_1 + 2x_2 + 4x_3$$

  a. compute $\hat{y}$ when $x_1 = 20$, $x_2 = 11$, and $x_3 = 10$.
  b. compute $\hat{y}$ when $x_1 = 15$, $x_2 = 14$, and $x_3 = 20$.
  c. compute $\hat{y}$ when $x_1 = 35$, $x_2 = 19$, and $x_3 = 25$.
  d. compute $\hat{y}$ when $x_1 = 10$, $x_2 = 17$, and $x_3 = 30$.

12.2 Given the estimated linear model

$$\hat{y} = 10 + 5x_1 + 4x_2 + 2x_3$$

  a. compute $\hat{y}$ when $x_1 = 20$, $x_2 = 11$, and $x_3 = 10$.
  b. compute $\hat{y}$ when $x_1 = 15$, $x_2 = 14$, and $x_3 = 20$.
  c. compute $\hat{y}$ when $x_1 = 35$, $x_2 = 19$, and $x_3 = 25$.
  d. compute $\hat{y}$ when $x_1 = 10$, $x_2 = 17$, and $x_3 = 30$.

12.3 Given the estimated linear model

$$\hat{y} = 10 + 2x_1 + 12x_2 + 8x_3$$

  a. compute $\hat{y}$ when $x_1 = 20$, $x_2 = 11$, $x_3 = 10$.
  b. compute $\hat{y}$ when $x_1 = 15$, $x_2 = 24$, $x_3 = 20$.
  c. compute $\hat{y}$ when $x_1 = 20$, $x_2 = 19$, $x_3 = 25$.
  d. compute $\hat{y}$ when $x_1 = 10$, $x_2 = 9$, $x_3 = 30$.

12.4 Given the following estimated linear model

$$\hat{y} = 10 + 2x_1 + 12x_2 + 8x_3$$

  a. what is the change in $\hat{y}$ when x_1 increases by 4?
  b. what is the change in $\hat{y}$ when x_3 increases by 1?
  c. what is the change in $\hat{y}$ when x_2 increases by 2?

12.5 Given the following estimated linear model

$$\hat{y} = 10 - 2x_1 - 14x_2 + 6x_3$$

  a. what is the change in $\hat{y}$ when x_1 increases by 4?
  b. what is the change in $\hat{y}$ when x_3 decreases by 1?
  c. what is the change in $\hat{y}$ when x_2 decreases by 2?

Application Exercises

12.6 An aircraft company wanted to predict the number of worker-hours necessary to finish the design of a new plane. Relevant explanatory variables were thought to be the plane's top speed, its weight, and the number of parts it had in common with other models built by the company. A sample of 27 of the company's planes was taken, and the following model was estimated:

$$y_i = \beta_0 + \beta_1 x_{1i} + \beta_2 x_{2i} + \beta_3 x_{3i} + \varepsilon_i$$

where

  y_i = design effort, in millions of worker-hours
  x_{1i} = plane's top speed, in miles per hour
  x_{2i} = plane's weight, in tons
  x_{3i} = percentage number of parts in common with other models

The estimated regression coefficients were as follows:

$$b_1 = 0.661 \quad b_2 = 0.065 \quad b_3 = -0.018$$

Interpret these estimates.

12.7 In a study of the influence of financial institutions on bond interest rates in Germany, quarterly data over a period of 12 years were analyzed. The postulated model was

$$y_i = \beta_0 + \beta_1 x_{1i} + \beta_2 x_{2i} + \varepsilon_i$$

where

y_i = change over the quarter in the bond interest rates

x_{1i} = change over the quarter in bond purchases by financial institutions

x_{2i} = change over the quarter in bond sales by financial institutions

The estimated partial regression coefficients were as follows:

$$b_1 = 0.057 \quad b_2 = -0.065$$

Interpret these estimates.

12.8 The following model was fitted to a sample of 30 families in order to explain household milk consumption:

$$y_i = \beta_0 + \beta_1 x_{1i} + \beta_2 x_{2i} + \varepsilon_i$$

where

y_i = milk consumption, in quarts per week
x_{1i} = weekly income, in hundreds of dollars
x_{2i} = family size

The least squares estimates of the regression parameters were as follows:

$$b_0 = -0.025 \quad b_1 = 0.052 \quad b_2 = 1.14$$

a. Interpret the estimates b_1 and b_2.
b. Is it possible to provide a meaningful interpretation of the estimate b_0?

12.9 The following model was fitted to a sample of 25 students using data obtained at the end of their freshman year in college. The aim was to explain students' weight gains:

$$y_i = \beta_0 + \beta_1 x_{1i} + \beta_2 x_{2i} + \beta_3 x_{3i} \varepsilon_i$$

where

y_i = weight gained, in pounds, during freshman year
x_{1i} = average number of meals eaten per week
x_{2i} = average number of hours of exercise per week
x_{3i} = average number of beers consumed per week

The least squares estimates of the regression parameters were as follows:

$$b_0 = 7.35 \quad b_1 = 0.653 \quad b_2 = -1.345 \quad b_3 = 0.613$$

a. Interpret the estimates b_1, b_2, and b_3.
b. Is it possible to provide a meaningful interpretation of the estimate b_0?

12.2 ESTIMATION OF COEFFICIENTS

Multiple regression coefficients are computed using estimators obtained by the least squares procedure. This least squares procedure is similar to that presented in Chapter 11 for simple regression. However, the estimators are complicated by the relationships between the independent X_j variables that occur simultaneously with the relationships between the independent and dependent variables. For example, if two independent variables increase or decrease linearly with each other—a positive or negative correlation—while at the same time there are increases or decreases in the dependent variable, we cannot identify which independent variable is actually related to the change in the dependent variable. As a result, we will find that the estimated regression coefficients are less reliable if there are high correlations between two or more independent variables. The estimates of coefficients and their variances are always obtained using a computer. However, we will spend considerable effort studying the algebra and computational forms in least squares regression. This effort will provide you with the background to understand the procedure and to determine how different data patterns influence the results. We begin with the standard assumptions for the multiple regression model.

Standard Multiple Regression Assumptions

The population multiple regression model is

$$y_i = \beta_0 + \beta_1 x_{1i} + \beta_2 x_{2i} + \cdots + \beta_K x_{Ki} + \varepsilon_i$$

and we assume that n sets of observations are available. The following standard assumptions are made for the model:

1. The x_{ji} terms are fixed numbers, or they are realizations of random variables, X_j, that are independent of the error terms, ε_i. In the latter case, inference is carried out conditionally on the observed values of the x_{ji}'s.
2. The expected value of the random variable Y is a linear function of the independent X_j variables.
3. The error terms are normally distributed random variables with a mean of 0 and the same variance, σ^2. The latter is called homoscedasticity or uniform variance.

$$E[\varepsilon_i] = 0 \text{ and } E[\varepsilon_i^2] = \sigma^2 \text{ for } (i = 1, \ldots, n)$$

4. The random error terms, ε_i, are not correlated with one another, so that

$$E[\varepsilon_i \varepsilon_j] = 0 \text{ for all } i = j$$

5. It is not possible to find a set of non-zero numbers, $c_0, c_1, \ldots, c_K$, such that

$$c_0 + c_1 x_{1i} + c_2 x_{2i} + \cdots + c_K x_{Ki} = 0$$

This is the property of no linear relationship between the X_j variables.

The first four assumptions are essentially the same as those made for simple regression. The error terms in assumption 3 are assumed to be normally distributed for statistical inference. But we will see that just as with simple regression the central limit theorem allows us to relax that assumption if the sample size is large enough. Assumption 5 excludes certain cases in which there are linear relationships between the predictor variables. For example, suppose we are interested in explaining the variability in rates charged for shipping corn. One obvious explanatory variable would be the distance the corn is shipped. Distance could be measured in several different units such as miles or kilometers. But it would not make sense to use both distance in miles and distance in kilometers as predictor variables. These two measures are linear functions of each other and would not satisfy assumption 5. In addition, it would be foolish to try to assess their separate effects. As we shall see, the equations to compute the coefficient estimates and the computer programs will not work if assumption 5 is not satisfied. In most cases proper model specification will avoid violating assumption 5.

Least Squares Procedure

The least squares procedure for multiple regression computes the estimated coefficients so as to minimize the sum of the residuals squared. Recall that the residual is defined as

$$e_i = y_i - \hat{y}_i$$

where y_i is the observed value of Y and $\hat{y}_i$ is the value of Y predicted from the regression. Formally, we minimize SSE:

$$SSE = \sum_{i=1}^{n} e_i^2$$

$$= \sum_{i=1}^{n} (y_i - \hat{y}_i)^2$$

$$= \sum_{i=1}^{n} (y_i - (b_0 + b_1 x_{1i} + \cdots + b_K x_{Ki}))^2$$

This minimization is the process of finding a plane that best represents a set of points in space, as we considered in our discussion of three-dimensional graphing. To carry out the process formally, we use partial derivatives to develop a set of simultaneous normal equations that are then solved to obtain the coefficient estimators. For those with strong mathematical insights the chapter appendix presents some of the details of the process. However, one can obtain great insights by realizing that we want an equation that best represents the observed data. Fortunately, for the applications studied in this book, the complex computations are always performed using a statistical computer package such as Minitab, *SAS*, or *SPSS*. Our objective here is to understand how to interpret the regression results and use them to solve problems. We will do this by examining some of the intermediate algebraic results to help understand the effects of various data patterns on the coefficient estimators.

Least Squares Estimation and the Sample Multiple Regression

We begin with a sample of n observations denoted as $x_{1i}, x_{2i}, \ldots, x_{Ki}, y_i$, where $i = 1, \ldots, n$, measured for a process whose population multiple regression model is as follows:

$$y_i = \beta_0 + \beta_1 x_{1i} + \beta_2 x_{2i} + \ldots + \beta_K x_{Ki} + \varepsilon_i$$

The least squares estimates of the coefficients $\beta_1, \beta_2, \ldots, \beta_K$, are the values $b_0, b_1, \ldots, b_k$ for which the sum of the squared deviations

$$SSE = \sum_{i=1}^{n} (y_i - b_0 - b_1 x_{1i} - b_2 x_{2i} - \ldots b_K x_{Ki})^2 \tag{12.2}$$

is a minimum.

The resulting equation

$$\hat{y}_i = b_0 + b_1 x_{1i} + b_2 x_{2i} + \ldots b_K x_{Ki} \tag{12.3}$$

is the sample multiple regression of Y on $X_1, X_2, \ldots, X_K$.

Let us consider again the regression model with only two predictor variables.

$$\hat{y}_i = b_0 + b_1 x_{1i} + b_2 x_{2i}$$

The coefficient estimators can be solved using the following forms:

$$b_1 = \frac{s_y(r_{x_1 y} - r_{x_1 x_2} r_{x_2 y})}{s_{x_1}(1 - r_{x_1 x_2}^2)} \tag{12.4}$$

$$b_2 = \frac{s_y(r_{x_2y} - r_{x_1x_2}r_{x_1y})}{s_{x_2}(1 - r_{x_1x_2}^2)} \qquad (12.5)$$

$$b_0 = \bar{y} - b_1\bar{x}_1 - b_2\bar{x}_2 \qquad (12.6)$$

where

r_{x_1y} is the sample correlation between X_1 and Y
r_{x_2y} is the sample correlation between X_2 and Y
$r_{x_1x_2}$ is the sample correlation between X_1 and X_2
s_{x_1} is the sample standard deviation for X_1
s_{x_2} is the sample standard deviation for X_2

In the equations for the coefficient estimators we see that the slope coefficient estimate, b_1, not only depends on the correlation between Y and X_1, but also is affected by the correlation between X_1 and X_2 and the correlation between X_2 and Y. If the correlation between X_1 and X_2 is equal to 0, then the coefficient estimators, b_1 and b_2, will be the same as the coefficient estimator for simple regression—we should note that this hardly ever happens in business and economic analysis. Conversely, if the correlation between the independent variables is equal to 1, the coefficient estimators will be undefined, but this will result only from poor model specification and will violate multiple regression assumption 5. If the independent variables are perfectly correlated, then they both experience simultaneous relative changes. We see that in that case it is not possible to tell which variable predicts the change in Y. In Example 12.3 we see the effect of the correlations between independent variables by considering the savings and loan association problem, whose data are shown in Table 12.1.

Example 12.3 Profit Margins of Savings and Loan Associations (Regression Coefficient Estimation)

The director of the savings and loan association has asked you to identify variables that affect the percent profit margin.

Solution As a first step we develop a multiple regression model specification that predicts profit as a linear function of the percent of net revenue per deposit dollar and the number of offices. Using the data in Table 12.1 that are stored in the **Savings and Loan** data file, we have estimated a multiple regression model, as seen in the Minitab and Excel outputs in Figure 12.3.

The estimated coefficients are identified in the computer output. We see that each unit increase in revenue, X_1, results in a 0.237 increase in percent profit—if the other variable does not change—and a unit increase in the number of offices decreases profit by 0.000249. Now consider the two simple regression models in Figures 12.4 and 12.5 with Y regressed on each independent variable by itself. First, consider Y regressed on revenue, X_1, in Figure 12.4. In this simple regression the coefficient for X_1 is –0.169, which is clearly different from +0.237 in multiple regression. Next we see that the correlation between X_1 and X_2 is 0.941. This large correlation has a major impact on the coefficient of X_1 in the multiple regression equation.

Figure 12.3 Regression Equation for Savings and Loan Association Profit (Minitab and Excel Output)

Regression Analysis: Y profit versus X1 revenue, X2 offices

```
The regression equation is
Y profit = 1.56 + 0.237 X1 revenue - 0.000249 X2 offices
```
→ Regression coefficients b_0, b_1, b_2

```
Predictor          Coef      SE Coef       T       P
Constant         1.56450     0.07940    19.70   0.000
X1 revenue       0.23720     0.05556     4.27   0.000
X2 offices     -0.00024908  0.00003205  -7.77   0.000

S = 0.0533022  R-Sq = 86.5%   R-Sq(adj) = 85.3%

Analysis of Variance

Source           DF        SS        MS       F       P
Regression        2     0.40151   0.20076  70.66   0.000
Residual Error   22     0.06250   0.00284
Total            24     0.46402
```

SUMMARY OUTPUT						
Regression Statistics						
Multiple R	0.930212915					
R Square	0.865296068					
Adjusted R Square	0.853050256					
Standard Error	0.053302217					
Observations	25					
ANOVA						
	df	*SS*	*MS*	*F*	*Significance F*	
Regression	2	0.40151122	0.20075561	70.66057082	2.64962E-10	
Residual	22	0.06250478	0.002841126			
Total	24	0.464016				
	Coefficients	*Standard Errors*	*t Stat*	*P-value*	*Lower 95%*	*Upper 95%*
Intercept	1.564496771	0.079395981	19.70498685	1.81733E-15	1.399839407	1.72915414
X1 revenue	0.237197475	0.055559366	4.269261695	0.000312567	0.121974278	0.35242067
X2 offices	–0.000249079	3.20485E-05	–7.771949195	9.50879E-08	–0.000315544	–0.00018261

Regression coefficients
b_0, b_1, b_2

Next, consider the regression of Y on X_2 alone in Figure 12.5. In this simple regression the slope coefficient for number of offices, X_2, is –0.000120 in contrast to –0.000249 for the multiple regression coefficient. This change in coefficients, while not quite as dramatic compared to the coefficient for X_1, also results from the high correlation between the independent variables.

The correlations between the three variables are as follows:

	Y Profit	X1 Revenue
X1 revenue	–0.704	
X2 offices	–0.868	0.941

Figure 12.4 Savings and Loan Profit Regressed on Revenue

Regression Analysis: Y profit versus X1 revenue

```
The regression equation is
Y profit = 1.33 - 0.169 X1 revenue


Predictor              Coef        SE Coef       T       P
Constant             1.3262        0.1386      9.57   0.000
X1 revenue          -0.16913       0.03559    -4.75   0.000
                                                              Regression
S = 0.100891   R-Sq = 49.5%   R-Sq(adj) = 47.4%              coefficient b₁

Analysis of Variance

Source          DF         SS          MS       F       P
Regression       1     0.22990     0.22990    22.59   0.000
Residual Error  23     0.23412     0.01018
Total           24     0.46402
```

Figure 12.5 Savings and Loan Profit Regressed on Number of Offices

Regression Analysis: Y profit versus X2 revenue

```
The regression equation is
Y profit = 1.55 - 0.000120 X2 offices


Predictor              Coef        SE Coef       T       P
Constant             1.5460        0.1048      14.75   0.000
X2 offices          -0.00012033  0.00001434    -8.39   0.000
                                                              Regression
S = 0.0704917   R-Sq = 75.4%   R-Sq(adj) = 74.3%            coefficient b₂

Analysis of Variance

Source          DF         SS          MS       F       P
Regression       1     0.34973     0.34973    70.38   0.000
Residual Error  23     0.11429     0.00497
Total           24     0.46402
```

We see that the correlation between X_1 and X_2 is 0.941. Thus, the two variables tend to move together, and it is not surprising that the multiple regression coefficients are different from the simple regression coefficients. We should note that the multiple regression coefficients are *conditional coefficients*; that is, the estimated coefficient b_1 depends on the other variables included in the model. This will always be the case in multiple regression unless two independent variables have a sample correlation of zero—a very unlikely event.

These relationships can also be studied by using a "matrix plot" from Minitab, as shown in Figure 12.6. Matrix plots are not available in Excel. Note that the simple relationship between Y and X_2 is clearly linear, while the simple relationship between Y and X_1 is somewhat curvilinear. This nonlinear relationship between X_1 and Y explains in part why the coefficient of X_1 changed so dramatically from simple to multiple regression. We see from this example that correlations between independent variables can have a major influence on the estimated coefficients. Thus, if one has a choice, highly correlated independent variables should be avoided. But in many cases we do not have that choice. Regression coefficient estimates are always conditional on the other predictor variables in the model. In this example, profit

Figure 12.6
Matrix Plots for
Savings and Loan
Variables

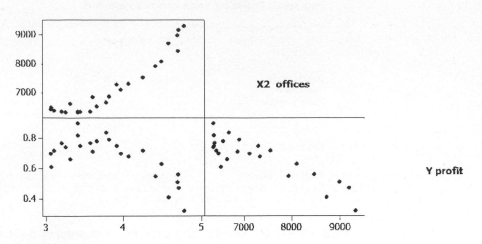

Matrix Plot of X1 revenue, X2 offices, Y profit

increases as a function of percent revenue per deposit dollar. However, the simultaneous increase in number of offices—which reduced profit—would hide the profit increase if a simple regression analysis was used. Thus, proper model specification—that is, choice of predictor variables—is very important. Model specification requires an understanding of the problem context and appropriate theory.

EXERCISES

Basic Exercise

12.10 Compute the Coefficients b_1 and b_2 for the regression model

$$\hat{y}_i = b_0 + b_1 x_{1i} + b_2 x_{2i}$$

given the following summary statistics:

a. $r_{x_1 y} = 0.60$, $r_{x_2 y} = 0.70$, $r_{x_1 x_2} = 0.50$
   $s_{x_1} = 200$, $s_{x_2} = 100$, $s_y = 400$

b. $r_{x_1 y} = -0.60$, $r_{x_2 y} = 0.70$, $r_{x_1 x_2} = -0.50$
   $s_{x_1} = 200$, $s_{x_2} = 100$, $s_y = 400$

c. $r_{x_1 y} = 0.40$, $r_{x_2 y} = 0.450$, $r_{x_1 x_2} = 0.80$
   $s_{x_1} = 200$, $s_{x_2} = 100$, $s_y = 400$

d. $r_{x_1 y} = 0.60$, $r_{x_2 y} = -0.50$, $r_{x_1 x_2} = -0.60$
   $s_{x_1} = 200$, $s_{x_2} = 100$, $s_y = 400$

Application Exercises

12.11 Consider the following estimated linear regression equations:

$$Y = a_0 + a_1 X_1 \quad Y = b_0 + b_1 X_1 + b_2 X_2$$

a. Show in detail the coefficient estimators for a_1 and b_1 when the correlation between X_1 and X_2 is equal to 0.

b. Show in detail the coefficient estimators for a_1 and b_1 when the correlation between X_1 and X_2 is equal to 1.

The following exercises require the use of a computer.

12.12 Amalgamated Power Inc. has asked you to estimate a regression equation to determine the effect of various predictor variables on the demand for electricity sales. You will prepare a series of regression estimates and discuss the results using the quarterly data for electrical sales during the past 17 years in the data file **Power Demand**.

a. Estimate a regression equation with electricity sales as the dependent variable using the number of customers and the price as predictor variables. Interpret the coefficients.

b. Estimate a regression equation (electricity sales) using only number of customers as a predictor variable. Interpret the coefficient and compare the result to the result from part (a).

c. Estimate a regression equation (electricity sales) using the price and degree days as predictor variables. Interpret the coefficients. Compare the coefficient for price with that obtained in part (a).

d. Estimate a regression equation (electricity sales) using disposable income and degree days as predictor variables. Interpret the coefficients.

12.13 Transportation Research Inc. has asked you to prepare some multiple regression equations to estimate the effect of variables on fuel economy. The data for this study are contained in the data file **Motors**, and the dependent variable is miles per gallon—milpgal—as established by the Department of Transportation certification.

a. Prepare a regression equation that uses vehicle horsepower—horsepower—and vehicle weight—weight—as independent variables. Interpret the coefficients.

b. Prepare a second regression equation that adds the number of cylinders—cylinder—as an independent variable to the equation from part (a). Interpret the coefficients.

c. Prepare a regression equation that uses number of cylinders and vehicle weight as independent variables. Interpret the coefficients and compare the results with those from parts (a) and (b).

d. Prepare a regression equation that uses vehicle horsepower, vehicle weight, and price as predictor variables. Interpret the coefficients.

e. Write a short report that summarizes your results.

12.14 Transportation Research Inc. has asked you to prepare some multiple regression equations to estimate the effect of variables on vehicle horsepower. The data for this study are contained in the data file **Motors**, and the dependent variable is vehicle horsepower—horsepower—as established by the Department of Transportation certification.

a. Prepare a regression equation that uses vehicle weight—weight—and cubic inches of cylinder displacement—displacement—as predictor variables. Interpret the coefficients.

b. Prepare a regression equation that uses vehicle weight, cylinder displacement, and number of cylinders—cylinder—as predictor variables. Interpret the coefficients and compare the results with those in part (a).

c. Prepare a regression equation that uses vehicle weight, cylinder displacement, and miles per gallon—milpgal—as predictor variables. Interpret the coefficients and compare the results with those in part (a).

d. Prepare a regression equation that uses vehicle weight, cylinder displacement, miles per gallon, and price as predictor variables. Interpret the coefficients and compare the results with those in part (c).

e. Write a short report that presents the results of your analysis of this problem.

12.3 EXPLANATORY POWER OF A MULTIPLE REGRESSION EQUATION

Multiple regression uses independent variables to explain the behavior of the dependent variable. We find that variability in the dependent variable can, in part, be explained by the linear function of the independent variables. In this section we develop a measure of the proportion of the variability in the dependent variable that can be explained by the multiple regression model.

The estimated regression model from the sample is

$$y_i = b_0 + b_1 x_{1i} + b_2 x_{2i} + \cdots + b_K x_{Ki} + e_i$$

Alternatively, we can write

$$y_i = \hat{y}_i + e_i$$

where

$$\hat{y}_i = b_0 + b_1 x_{1i} + b_2 x_{2i} + \cdots + b_K x_{Ki}$$

is the predicted value of the dependent variable and the residual, e_i, is the difference between the observed and the predicted values. Table 12.2 contains these quantities for the savings and loan example in the first three columns.

We can subtract the sample mean of the dependent variable from both sides, giving

$$(y_i - \bar{y}) = (\hat{y}_i - \bar{y}) + e_i$$
$$= (\hat{y}_i - \bar{y}) + (y_i - \hat{y}_i)$$

Table 12.2

Actual Values, Predicted Values, and Residuals for Savings and Loan Regression

y_i	$\hat{y}_i$	$e_i = y_i - \hat{y}_i$	$y_i - \bar{y}$	$\hat{y}_i - \bar{y}$
0.75	0.677	0.073	0.076	0.003
0.71	0.713	−0.003	0.036	0.039
0.66	0.699	−0.039	−0.014	0.025
0.61	0.672	−0.062	−0.064	−0.002
0.7	0.684	0.016	0.026	0.010
0.72	0.708	0.012	0.046	0.034
0.77	0.740	0.030	0.096	0.066
0.74	0.759	−0.019	0.066	0.085
0.9	0.794	0.106	0.226	0.120
0.82	0.794	0.026	0.146	0.120
0.75	0.798	−0.048	0.076	0.124
0.77	0.827	−0.057	0.096	0.153
0.78	0.802	−0.022	0.106	0.128
0.84	0.799	0.041	0.166	0.125
0.79	0.754	0.036	0.116	0.080
0.7	0.734	−0.034	0.026	0.060
0.68	0.705	−0.025	0.006	0.031
0.72	0.693	0.027	0.046	0.019
0.55	0.635	−0.085	−0.124	−0.039
0.63	0.613	0.017	−0.044	−0.061
0.56	0.570	−0.010	−0.114	−0.104
0.41	0.480	−0.070	−0.264	−0.194
0.51	0.437	0.073	−0.164	−0.237
0.47	0.395	0.075	−0.204	−0.279
0.32	0.377	−0.057	−0.354	−0.297
Sum of squares:		0.0625 (SSE)	0.4640 (SST)	0.4015 (SSR)

which can be stated as follows:

Observed Deviation from Mean = Predicted Deviation from Mean + Residual

Then by squaring both sides and summing over the index, i, we have

$$\sum_{i=1}^{n}(y_i - \bar{y})^2 = \sum_{i=1}^{n}(\hat{y}_1 - \bar{y} + y_i - \hat{y}_1)^2$$

$$= \sum_{i=1}^{n}(\hat{y}_i - \bar{y})^2 + \sum_{i=1}^{n}e_i^2$$

which is the sum of squares decomposition presented in Chapter 11:

$$SST = SSR + SSE$$

Total Sum of Squares = Regression Sum of Squares + Error Sum of Squares

This simplified decomposition occurs because y and $\hat{y}$ are independent, and, thus,

$$\sum_{i=1}^{n}(\hat{y}_i - \bar{y})(y_i - \hat{y}_i) = 0$$

Sum of Squares Decomposition and the Coefficient of Determination

We begin with the multiple regression model fitted by least squares

$$y_i = b_0 + b_1 x_{1i} + b_2 x_{2i} + \cdots + b_K x_{Ki} + e_i = \hat{y}_i + e_i$$

where the b_j terms are the least squares estimates of the coefficients of the population regression model and the e terms are the residuals from the estimated regression model.

The model variability can be partitioned into the components

$$SST = SSR + SSE \qquad (12.7)$$

where these components are defined as follows:
Total sum of squares

$$SST = \sum_{i=1}^{n}(y_i - \bar{y})^2 \qquad (12.8)$$

$$= \sum_{i=1}^{n}(\hat{y}_i - \bar{y})^2 + \sum_{i=1}^{n}(y_i - \hat{y}_i)^2 \qquad (12.9)$$

Error sum of squares

$$SSE = \sum_{i=1}^{n}(y_i - \hat{y}_i)^2 = \sum_{i=1}^{n}e_i^2 \qquad (12.10)$$

Regression sum of squares

$$SSR = \sum_{i=1}^{n}(\hat{y}_i - \bar{y})^2 \qquad (12.11)$$

This decomposition can be interpreted as follows:

Total Sample Variability = Explained Variability + Unexplained Variability

The coefficient of determination, R^2, of the fitted regression is defined as the proportion of the total sample variability explained by the regression

$$R^2 = \frac{SSR}{SST} = 1 - \frac{SSE}{SST} \qquad (12.12)$$

and it follows that

$$0 \leq R^2 \leq 1$$

The sum of squared errors is also used to compute the estimation for the variance of population model errors, as shown in Equation 12.12. As with simple regression, the variance of population errors is used for multiple regression statistical inference.

Estimation of Error Variance

Given the population multiple regression model

$$y_i = \beta_0 + \beta_1 x_{1i} + \beta_2 x_{2i} + \ldots + \beta_K x_{Ki} + \varepsilon_i$$

and the standard regression assumptions, let σ^2 denote the common variance of the error term, ε_i. Then an unbiased estimate of that variance is

$$s_e^2 = \frac{\sum_{i=1}^{n} e_i^2}{n-K-1} = \frac{SSE}{n-K-1} \qquad (12.13)$$

where K is the number of independent variables in the regression model. The square root of the variance, s_e, is also called the **standard error of the estimate**.

At this point we can also compute the mean square regression as follows:

$$MSR = \frac{SSR}{K}$$

We use MSR as a measure of the explained variability adjusted for the number of independent variables.

The sample mean for the savings and loan profit dependent variable is $\bar{y} = 0.674$, and we have used this value to compute the last two columns of Table 12.2. Using the data in Table 12.2 and the components, we can show that

$$SSE = 0.0625 \quad SST = 0.4640 \quad R^2 = 0.87$$

From these results we find that for this sample 87% of the variability in the savings and loan association's profit is explained by the linear relationships with net revenues and number of offices. Note that we could also compute the regression sum of squares from the identity

$$SSR = SST - SSE = 0.4640 - 0.0625 = 0.4015$$

We can also compute an estimate for the error variance σ^2 by using Equation 12.13:

$$s_e^2 = \frac{\sum_{i=1}^{n} e_i^2}{n-K-1} = \frac{SSE}{n-K-1} = \frac{0.0625}{25-1-2} = 0.00284$$

Figure 12.7 presents the regression output from Minitab for the savings and loan association problem, with the various computed sums of squares indicated. These quantities are routinely computed by statistical computer packages, and the detail in Table 12.2 is included only to indicate how the sums of squares are computed. In all of the work that follows, we assume that the sums of squares are calculated by a computer package.

The components of variability have associated degrees of freedom. The SST quantity has $n-1$ degrees of freedom because the mean of Y is required for its computation. The SSR component has K degrees of freedom because K coefficients are required for its computation. Finally, the SSE component has $n-K-1$ degrees of freedom because K coefficients and the mean are required for its computation. Note that in Figure 12.7 the output includes the degrees of freedom (DF) associated with each component.

Figure 12.7
Regression Output
for the Savings
and Loan
Association
Problem

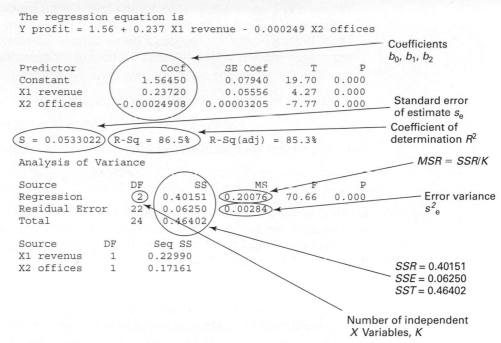

Regression Analysis: Y profit versus X1 revenue, X2 offices

```
The regression equation is
Y profit = 1.56 + 0.237 X1 revenue - 0.000249 X2 offices
```

Coefficients b_0, b_1, b_2

```
Predictor             Coef      SE Coef       T       P
Constant           1.56450      0.07940   19.70   0.000
X1 revenue         0.23720      0.05556    4.27   0.000
X2 offices       -0.00024908    0.00003205 -7.77   0.000
```

Standard error of estimate s_e

Coefficient of determination R^2

```
S = 0.0533022   R-Sq = 86.5%   R-Sq(adj) = 85.3%
```

$MSR = SSR/K$

```
Analysis of Variance

Source            DF       SS        MS        F       P
Regression         2    0.40151   0.20076   70.66   0.000
Residual Error    22    0.06250   0.00284
Total             24    0.46402

Source          DF    Seq SS
X1 revenus       1    0.22990
X2 offices       1    0.17161
```

Error variance s_e^2

$SSR = 0.40151$
$SSE = 0.06250$
$SST = 0.46402$

Number of independent X Variables, K

INTERPRETATION

We use the coefficient of determination, R^2, routinely as a descriptive statistic to describe the strength of the linear relationship between the independent X variables and the dependent variable, Y. It is important to emphasize that R^2 can only be used to compare regression models that have the same set of sample observations of y_i, where $i = 1, \ldots, n$. This result is seen from the equation form as follows:

$$R^2 = 1 - \frac{SSE}{SST}$$

Thus, we see that R^2 can be large either because SSE is small—indicating that the observed points are close to the predicted points—or because SST is large. We have seen that SSE and s_e^2 indicate the closeness of the observed points to the predicted points. With the same SST for two or more regression equations R^2 provides a comparable measure of the goodness of fit for the equations.

There is a potential problem with using R^2 as an overall measure of the quality of a fitted equation. As additional independent variables are added to a multiple regression model—in essentially all applied situations—the explained sum of squares, SSR, will increase even if the additional independent variable is not an important predictor variable. Thus, we might find that R^2 has increased spuriously after one or more nonsignificant predictor variables have been added to the multiple regression model. In such a case the increased value of R^2 would be misleading. To avoid this problem, the adjusted coefficient of determination can be computed as shown in Equation 12.14.

Adjusted Coefficient of Determination
The **adjusted coefficient of determination**, $\bar{R}^2$, is defined as follows:

$$\bar{R}^2 = 1 - \frac{SSE/(n-K-1)}{SST/(n-1)}$$

(12.14)

We use this measure to correct for the fact that nonrelevant independent variables will result in some small reduction in the error sum of squares. Thus, the adjusted $\overline{R}^2$, provides a better comparison between multiple regression models with different numbers of independent variables.

Returning to our savings and loan example, we see that

$$n = 25 \quad K = 2 \quad SSE = 0.0625 \quad SST = 0.4640$$

and, thus, the adjusted coefficient of determination is as follows:

$$\overline{R}^2 = 1 - \frac{0.0625/22}{0.4640/24} = 0.853$$

In this example the difference between R^2 and $\overline{R}^2$ is not very large. However, if the regression model had contained a number of independent variables that were not important conditional predictors, then the difference would be substantial. Another measure of relationship in multiple regression is the coefficient of multiple correlation.

Coefficient of Multiple Correlation

The **coefficient of multiple correlation** is the correlation between the predicted value and the observed value of the dependent variable

$$R = r(\hat{y}, y) = \sqrt{R^2} \qquad (12.15)$$

and is equal to the square root of the multiple coefficient of determination. We use R as another measure of the strength of the relationship between the dependent variable and the independent variables. Thus, it is comparable to the correlation between Y and X in simple regression.

EXERCISES

Basic Exercises

12.15 A regression analysis has produced the following analysis of variance table:

Analysis of Variance			
Source	DF	SS	MS
Regression	3	4500	
Residual Error	26	500	

a. Compute s_e and s_e^2
b. Compute SST.
c. Compute R^2 and the adjusted coefficient of determination.

12.16 A regression analysis has produced the following analysis of variance table:

Analysis of Variance			
Source	DF	SS	MS
Regression	2	7000	
Residual Error	29	2500	

a. Compute s_e and s_e^2
b. Compute SST.
c. Compute R^2 and the adjusted coefficient of determination.

12.17 A regression analysis has produced the following analysis of variance table:

Analysis of Variance			
Source	DF	SS	MS
Regression	4	40,000	
Residual Error	45	10,000	

a. Compute s_e and s_e^2.
b. Compute SST.
c. Compute R^2 and the adjusted coefficient of determination.

12.18 A regression analysis has produced the following analysis of variance table:

Analysis of Variance			
Source	DF	SS	MS
Regression	5	80,000	
Residual Error	200	15,000	

a. Compute s_e and s_e^2.
b. Compute SST.
c. Compute R^2 and the adjusted coefficient of determination.

Application Exercises

12.19 In the study of Exercise 12.6, where the least squares estimates were based on 27 sets of sample observations, the total sum of squares and regression sum of squares were found to be as follows:

$$SST = 3.881 \quad \text{and} \quad SSR = 3.549$$

a. Find and interpret the coefficient of determination.
b. Find the error sum of squares.
c. Find the adjusted coefficient of determination.
d. Find and interpret the coefficient of multiple correlation.

12.20 In the study of Exercise 12.8, where the least squares estimates were based on 30 sets of sample observations, the total sum of squares and regression sum of squares were found to be as follows:

$$SST = 162.1 \quad \text{and} \quad SSR = 88.2$$

a. Find and interpret the coefficient of determination.
b. Find the adjusted coefficient of determination.
c. Find and interpret the coefficient of multiple correlation.

12.21 In the study of Exercise 12.9, 25 observations were used to calculate the least squares estimates. The regression sum of squares and error sum of squares were found to be as follows:

$$SSR = 79.2 \quad \text{and} \quad SSE = 45.9$$

a. Find and interpret the coefficient of determination.
b. Find the adjusted coefficient of determination.
c. Find and interpret the coefficient of multiple correlation.

12.22 Refer to the savings and loan association data given in Table 12.1.

a. Estimate by least squares the regression of profit margin on number of offices.
b. Estimate by least squares the regression of net revenues on number of offices.
c. Estimate by least squares the regression of profit margin on net revenues.
d. Estimate by least squares the regression of number of offices on net revenues.

12.4 CONFIDENCE INTERVALS AND HYPOTHESIS TESTS FOR INDIVIDUAL REGRESSION COEFFICIENTS

In Section 12.2 we developed and discussed the point estimators for the parameters of the multiple regression model:

$$y_i = \beta_0 + \beta_1 x_{1i} + \beta_2 x_{1i} + \cdots + \beta_K x_{Ki} + \varepsilon_i$$

Now, we will develop confidence intervals and tests of hypotheses for the estimated regression coefficients. These confidence intervals and hypothesis tests depend on the variance of the coefficients and the probability distribution of the coefficients. In Section 12.5 we showed that the simple regression coefficient is a linear function of the dependent variable, Y. Multiple regression coefficients, denoted by b_j, are also linear functions of the dependent variable, Y, but the algebra is somewhat more complex and will not be presented here. In the previous multiple regression equation we see that the dependent variable, Y, is a linear function of the X variables plus the random error, ε. For a given set of X terms the function

$$\beta_0 + \beta_1 x_{1i} + \beta_2 x_{2i} + \cdots + \beta_K x_{Ki}$$

is actually a constant. We also know from Chapters 4 and 5 that adding a constant to a random variable ε results in the random variable Y having the same probability distribution and variance as the original random variable ε. As a result, the dependent variable, Y, has the same normal distribution and variance as the error term, ε. Then it follows that the regression coefficients, b_j—which are linear functions of Y—also have a normal distribution, and their variance can be derived by using the linear relationship between the regression coefficients and the dependent variable. This computation would follow the same process as used for simple regression in Section 11.5, but the algebra is more complex.

Based on the linear relationship between the coefficients and Y, we know that the coefficient estimates are normally distributed if the model error, ε, is normally distributed. Because of the central limit theorem, we generally find that the coefficient estimates are approximately normally distributed even if ε is not normally distributed. Thus, the hypothesis tests and confidence intervals we develop are not seriously affected by departures from normality in the distribution of the error terms.

We can think of the error term, ε, in the population regression model as including the combined influences on the dependent variable of a multitude of factors not included in the list of independent variables. These factors individually may not have an important influence, but in combination their effect can be important. The fact that the error term is made up of a large number of components whose effects are random provides an intuitive argument for assuming that the coefficient errors are also normally distributed.

As we have seen previously, the coefficient estimators, b_j, are linear functions of Y, and the predicted value of Y is a linear function of the regression coefficient estimators. The computer does the computations resulting from the complex relationships. However, these relationships can sometimes cause interpretation problems. Thus, we will spend time gaining important insights into the variance computations. If we do not understand how the variances are computed, we will not be able to adequately understand hypothesis tests and confidence intervals.

The variance of a coefficient estimate is affected by the sample size, the spread of the X variables, the correlations between the independent variables, and the model error term. Thus, these correlations affect both confidence intervals and tests of hypotheses. Previously, we saw how the correlations between the independent variables influence the coefficient estimators. These correlations between independent variables also increase the variance of the coefficient estimators. An important conclusion is that the variance of the coefficient estimators, in addition to the coefficient estimators, is conditional on the entire set of independent variables in the regression model.

The previous discussion under three-dimensional graphing emphasized the complex effects of several variables on the coefficient variance. As the relationships between independent variables become stronger, estimates of coefficients become more unstable—that is, they have higher variance. The following discussion provides a more formal discussion of these complexities. To obtain good coefficient estimates—those that are low in variance—you should seek a wide range for the independent variables, choose independent variables that are not strongly related to each other, and find a model that is close to all data points. The reality of applied statistical work in business and economics is that we often must use data that are less than ideal, such as the data for the savings and loan example. But by knowing the effects discussed here, we can make good judgments about the applicability of our models.

To gain some understanding of the effect of independent variable correlations, we consider the variance estimators from the estimated multiple regression model with two predictor variables:

$$\hat{y}_i = b_0 + b_1 x_{1i} + b_2 x_{2i}$$

The coefficient variance estimators are

$$s_{b_1}^2 = \frac{s_e^2}{(n-1)s_{x_1}^2(1-r_{x_1 x_2}^2)} \tag{12.16}$$

$$s_{b_2}^2 = \frac{s_e^2}{(n-1)s_{x_2}^2(1-r_{x_1 x_2}^2)} \tag{12.17}$$

and the square roots of these variance estimators, s_{b_1} and s_{b_2}, are called the *coefficient standard errors*.

The variance of the coefficient estimators increases directly with the distance the points are from the line, measured by s_e^2 the estimated error variance. In addition, a wider spread of the independent variable values—measured by $s_{x_1}^2$ or by $s_{x_2}^2$—decreases the coefficient variance. Recall that these results are also applied for simple regression coefficient estimato--rs. We also see that the variance of the coefficient estimators increases with increases in the correlation between the independent variables in the model. As the correlation increases between two independent variables, it becomes more difficult to separate the effect of the individual variables for predicting the dependent variables. As the number of independent variables in a model increases, the influences on the coefficient variance continue to be important, but the algebraic structure becomes very complex and will not be presented here. The correlation effect leads to the result that coefficient variance estimators are conditional on the other independent variables in the model. Recall that the actual coefficient estimators are also conditional on the other independent variables in the model, again because of the effect of correlations between the independent variables.

The basis for inference about population regression coefficients is summarized next. We are typically more interested in the regression coefficients β_j than in the constant or intercept β_0. Thus, we will concentrate on the former, noting that inference about the latter proceeds along similar lines.

Basis for Inference about the Population Regression Parameters

Let the population regression model be as follows:

$$y_i = \beta_0 + \beta_1 x_{1i} + \beta_2 x_{1i} + \cdots + \beta_K x_{Ki} + \varepsilon_i$$

Let $b_0, b_1, \ldots, b_K$ be the least squares estimates of the population parameters and $s_{b_0}, s_{b_1}, \ldots, s_{b_K}$ be the estimated standard deviations of the least squares estimators. Then, if the standard regression assumptions hold and if the error terms, ε_i, are normally distributed,

$$t_{b_j} = \frac{b_j - \beta_j}{s_{b_j}} \quad (j = 1, 2, \ldots, K) \tag{12.18}$$

is distributed as a Student's t distribution with $(n-K-1)$ degrees of freedom.

Confidence Intervals

Confidence intervals for the β_j can be derived by using Equation 12.19.

Confidence Intervals for Regression Coefficients

If the population regression errors, ε_i, are normally distributed and the standard regression assumptions hold, the $100(1-\alpha)\%$ two-sided confidence intervals for the regression coefficients, β_j, are given by

$$b_j - t_{n-K-1,\,\alpha/2} s_{b_j} < \beta_j < b_j + t_{n-K-1,\,\alpha/2} s_{b_j} \tag{12.19}$$

where $t_{n-K-1,\alpha/2}$ is the number for which

$$P(t_{n-K-1} > t_{n-K-1,\alpha/2}) = \frac{\alpha}{2}$$

and the random variable t_{n-K-1} follows a Student's t distribution with $(n-K-1)$ degrees of freedom.

Example 12.4 Developing the Savings and Loan Model (Confidence Interval Estimation)

We have been asked to determine confidence intervals for the coefficients of the savings and loan regression model developed in Example 12.3.

Solution The Minitab regression output for the savings and loan regression model is shown in Figure 12.8. The coefficient estimators and their standard deviations for the revenue, b_1, and number of offices, b_2, predictor variables are computed as follows:

$$b_1 = 0.2372, \quad s_{b_1} = 0.0556; \quad b_2 = -0.000249 \text{ and } s_{b_2} = 0.00003205$$

Thus, we see that the standard deviation of the sampling distribution of the least squares estimator for β_1 is estimated as 0.05556 and for β_2 is estimated as 0.00003205.

To obtain the 99% confidence intervals for β_1 and β_2, we use the Student's t value from Table 8 in the appendix.

$$t_{n-K-1,\alpha/2} = t_{22,0.005} = 2.819$$

Using these results, we find that the 99% coefficient confidence interval for β_1 is

$$0.237 - (2.819)(0.05556) < \beta_1 < 0.237 + (2.819)(0.05556)$$

or

$$0.080 < \beta_1 < 0.394$$

Thus, the 99% confidence interval for the expected increase in the savings and loan profit margin resulting from a 1-unit increase in net revenue, given a fixed number of offices, runs from 0.080 to 0.394. The 99% coefficient confidence interval for β_2 is

$$-0.000249 - (2.819)(0.0000320) < \beta_2 < -0.000249 + (2.819)(0.0000320)$$

or

$$-0.000339 < \beta_2 < -0.000159$$

Therefore, we see that the 99% confidence interval for the expected decrease in the profit margin resulting from an increase of 1,000 offices, for a fixed level of net revenue, runs from 0.159 to 0.339.

Figure 12.8   Savings and Loan Regression: Minitab Output

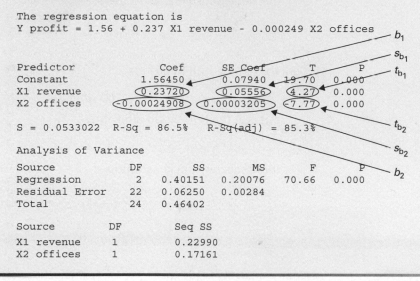

Regression Analysis: Y profit versus X1 revenue, X2 offices

```
The regression equation is
Y profit = 1.56 + 0.237 X1 revenue - 0.000249 X2 offices


Predictor             Coef      SE Coef        T         P
Constant           1.56450      0.07940    19.70     0.000
X1 revenue         0.23720      0.05556     4.27     0.000
X2 offices      -0.00024908   0.00003205    -7.77     0.000

S = 0.0533022  R-Sq = 86.5%    R-Sq(adj) = 85.3%

Analysis of Variance

Source             DF         SS        MS        F        P
Regression          2    0.40151   0.20076    70.66    0.000
Residual Error     22    0.06250   0.00284
Total              24    0.46402

Source         DF       Seq SS
X1 revenue      1      0.22990
X2 offices      1      0.17161
```

Tests of Hypotheses

Tests of hypotheses for regression coefficients can be developed using the coefficient variance estimates. Of particular interest is the hypothesis test

$$H_0 : \beta_j = 0$$

which is frequently used to determine if a specific independent variable is conditionally important in a multiple regression model.

Tests of Hypotheses for the Regression Coefficients

If the regression errors, ε_i, are normally distributed and the standard regression assumptions hold, then the following hypothesis tests have significance level α:

1. To test either null hypothesis

$$H_0 : \beta_j = \beta^* \quad \text{or} \quad H_0 : \beta_j \le \beta^*$$

against the alternative

$$H_1 : \beta_j > \beta^*$$

the decision rule is as follows:

$$\text{Reject } H_0 \text{ if } \quad \frac{b_j - \beta^*}{s_{b_j}} > t_{n-K-1,\alpha} \tag{12.20}$$

2. To test either null hypothesis

$$H_0 : \beta_j = \beta^* \quad \text{or} \quad H_0 : \beta_j \geq \beta^*$$

against the alternative

$$H_1 : \beta_j < \beta^*$$

the decision rule is as follows:

$$\text{Reject } H_0 \text{ if} \quad \frac{b_j - \beta^*}{s_{b_j}} < -t_{n-K-1,\alpha} \tag{12.21}$$

3. To test the null hypothesis

$$H_0 : \beta_j = \beta^*$$

against the two-sided alternative

$$H_1 : \beta_j \neq \beta^*$$

the decision rule is as follows:

$$\text{Reject } H_0 \text{ if} \quad \frac{b_j - \beta_*}{s_{b_j}} > t_{n-K-1,\alpha/2} \quad \text{or} \quad \frac{b_j - \beta_*}{s_{b_j}} < -t_{n-K-1,\alpha/2} \tag{12.22}$$

INTERPRETATION

Many analysts argue that if we cannot reject the conditional hypothesis that the coefficient is 0, then we must conclude that the variable should not be included in the regression model. The Student's t statistic for this test is typically computed in most regression programs and is printed next to the coefficient variance estimate; in addition, the p-value for the hypothesis test is typically included. These are shown in the Minitab output in Figure 12.8. Using the printed Student's t statistic or the p-value, we can immediately conclude whether or not a particular predictor variable is conditionally significant, given the other variables in the regression model.

There are clearly other procedures for deciding if an independent variable should be included in a regression model. We see that the preceding selection procedure ignores Type II error—the population coefficient is not equal to 0, but we fail to reject the null hypothesis that it is equal to 0. This is a particular problem when a model based on economic or another theory that is carefully specified to include certain independent variables. Then, because of a large error, ε, or correlations between independent variables, or both, we cannot reject the hypothesis that the coefficient is 0. In this case many analysts will include the independent variable in the model because the original model specification based on economic theory or experience is believed to dominate. This is a difficult issue and requires good judgment based on both statistical results and theory concerning the underlying relationship being modeled.

Example 12.5 Developing the Savings and Loan Model (Coefficient Hypothesis Tests)

We have been asked to determine if the coefficients in the savings and loan regression model are conditionally significant predictors of profit.

Solution The hypothesis test for this question will use the Minitab regression results shown in Figure 12.8. First, we wish to determine if the variable, total revenue, has a significant effect on increasing profit, conditional on or controlling for the effect of the variable, number of offices. The null hypothesis is

$$H_0 : \beta_1 = 0$$

versus the alternative hypothesis

$$H_1 : \beta_1 > 0$$

The test can be performed by computing the Student's t statistic associated with the coefficient, given H_0:

$$t_{b_1} = \frac{b_1 - \beta_1}{s_{b_1}} = \frac{0.237 - 0}{0.05556} = 4.27$$

From the Student's t Table 8 in the appendix at the end of the book, we can determine that the critical value for the Student's t statistic is as follows:

$$t_{22, 0.005} = 2.819$$

Figure 12.8 also indicates that the p-value for the hypothesis test is less than 0.005. Based on this evidence, we reject H_0 and accept H_1 and conclude that total revenue is a statistically significant predictor of increased profit for savings and loans, given that we have controlled for the effect of the number of offices.

Similarly, we can determine if the total number of offices has a significant effect on reducing profit margins. The null hypothesis is

$$H_0 : \beta_2 = 0$$

versus the alternative hypothesis

$$H_1 : \beta_2 < 0$$

The test can be performed by computing the Student's t statistic associated with the coefficient, given H_0:

$$t_{b_2} = \frac{b_2 - \beta_2}{s_{b_2}} = \frac{-0.000249 - 0}{0.0000320} = -7.77$$

From Table 8 of the appendix we can find that the critical value for the Student's t statistic is as follows:

$$t_{22, 0.005} = 2.819$$

Figure 12.8 also indicates that the p-value for the hypothesis test is less than 0.005. Based on this evidence, we reject H_0 and accept H_1 and conclude that number of offices is a statistically significant predictor of lower profit for savings and loans, given that we have controlled for the effect of total revenue.

It is important to emphasize that both of the hypothesis tests are based on the particular set of variables included in the regression model. If, for example, additional predictor variables were included, then these tests would no longer be valid. With additional variables in the model the coefficient estimates and their estimated standard deviations would be different, and, thus, the Student's t statistics would also be different.

Note that in the Minitab regression output for this problem, shown in Figure 12.8, the Student's t statistic for the null hypothesis—$H_0 : \beta_j = 0$—is computed as the ratio of the estimated coefficient divided by the estimated coefficient standard error—contained in the two columns to the left of the Student's t. The probability or p-value for the two-tailed hypothesis test—$H_j : \beta_j \neq 0$—is also displayed. Thus, an analyst can perform these hypothesis tests directly by examining the multiple regression output. The Student's t and the p-value are computed in every modern statistical package. Most analysts routinely look for these test results as they examine regression output from a computer statistical package.

Example 12.6 Factors Affecting Property Tax Rate (Analysis of Regression Coefficients)

A group of city managers commissioned a study to determine the factors that influence urban property tax rates for cities with populations between 100,000 and 200,000.

Solution Using a sample of 20 U.S. cities, the following regression model was estimated:

$$\hat{y} = 1.79 + \underset{(0.000139)}{0.000567x_1} + \underset{(0.0082)}{0.0183x_2} - \underset{(0.000446)}{0.000191x_3}$$

$$R^2 = 0.71 \qquad\qquad n = 20$$

where

y = effective property tax rate (actual levies divided by market value of the tax base)
x_1 = number of housing units per square mile
x_2 = percentage of total city revenue represented by grants from state and federal governments
x_3 = median per capita personal income, in dollars

The numbers in parentheses under the coefficients are the estimated coefficient standard errors.

The aforementioned presentation provides a good format for displaying the results of a regression analysis model. The results indicate that the conditional estimates of the effects of the three predictor variables are as follows:

1. An increase of one housing unit per square mile increases the effective property tax rate by 0.000567. Note that property tax rates are typically expressed in terms of dollars per $1,000 of assessed property value. Thus, an increase of 0.000567 indicates that property tax rates are higher by $0.567 per $1,000 of assessed property value.
2. An increase of 1% of the total city revenue from state and federal grants increases the effective tax rate by 0.0183.
3. An increase of $1 in median per capita personal income leads to an expected decrease in the effective tax rate by 0.000191.

We emphasize again that these coefficient estimates are valid only for a model with all three of the predictor variables included.

To better understand the accuracy of these effects, we will construct conditional 95% confidence intervals. For the estimated regression model there are $(20-3-1) = 16$ degrees of freedom for error. Thus, the Student's t statistic for computing confidence intervals is, from the appendix, $t_{16,0.025} = 2.12$. The format for confidence intervals is as follows:

$$b_j - t_{n-K-1,\alpha/2}s_{bj} < \beta_j < b_j + t_{n-K-1,\alpha/2}s_{bj}$$

Thus, the coefficient for the number of housing units per square mile has a 95% confidence interval of

$$0.000567 - (2.12)(0.000139) < \beta_1 < 0.000567 + (2.12)(0.000139)$$
$$0.000272 < \beta_1 < 0.000862$$

The coefficient for the percentage of revenue represented by grants has a 95% confidence interval of

$$0.0183 - (2.12)(0.0082) < \beta_2 < 0.0183 + (2.12)(0.0082)$$
$$0.0009 < \beta_2 < 0.0357$$

Finally, the coefficient for median per capita personal income has a 95% confidence interval of

$$-0.000191 - (2.12)(0.000446) < \beta_3 < -0.000191 + (2.12)(0.000446)$$
$$-0.001137 < \beta_3 < 0.000755$$

Again, we emphasize that these intervals are conditional on all three predictor variables being included in the model.

We see that the 95% confidence interval for β_3 includes 0, and, thus, we could not reject the two-tailed hypothesis that this coefficient is 0. Based on this confidence interval, we conclude that X_3 is not a statistically significant predictor variable in the multiple regression model. However, the confidence intervals for the other two variables do not include 0, and, thus, we conclude that they are statistically significant.

Example 12.7 Effects of Fiscal Factors on Housing Prices (Regression Model Coefficient Estimation)

Northern City, Minnesota, was interested in the effect of local property development on the market price of houses in the city. Northern City is one of many small, non-metropolitan, midwestern cities with populations in the range from 6,000 to 40,000. One of the objectives was to determine how increased commercial property development would influence the value of local housing. Data are stored in the data file **Citydat**.

Solution   To answer this question, data were collected from a number of cities and used to construct a regression model that estimates the effect of key variables on housing price. For this study the following variables were obtained for each city:

Y (hseval) = Mean market price for houses in the city
X_1 (sizehse) = Mean number of rooms in houses
X_2 (incom72) = Mean household income
X_3 (taxrate) = Tax rate per thousand dollars of assessed value for houses
X_4 (Comper) = Percentage of taxable property that is commercial property

The multiple regression output, prepared using Minitab, is shown in Figure 12.9. The coefficient for the mean number of rooms in city houses is 7.878 with a coefficient standard deviation of 1.809. In this study housing values are in units of $1,000 with a mean of $21,000 over all cities. Thus, if the mean number of rooms in a city's houses was larger by 1.0, then the mean price would be larger by $7,878. The resulting Student's t statistic is 4.35 and the p-value is 0.000. Thus, the conditional hypothesis that this coefficient is equal to 0 is rejected. The same result occurs for the income and tax rate variables. The incom72 variable is in units of dollars, and, thus, if a city's mean income is higher by $1,000, then the coefficient of 0.003666 indicates that mean housing price will be $3,666 higher. If the tax rate increases by 1%, mean housing price is reduced by $1,720. We see that the regression analysis leads to the conclusion that each of these three variables is a significant predictor of the mean house price in the cities included in this study. However, we see that the coefficient for the percent commercial property, "comper," is −10.614 with a coefficient standard deviation of 6.491, resulting in a Student's t statistic equal to −1.64. Note that here is an important area for judgment. The coefficient would have a single-tail p-value of 0.053 or a two-tailed p-value of 0.106. Thus, it appears to have some effect in reducing the mean price of houses. Given that the effects of house size, income, and tax rate on the market price for houses have been included, we see that the percent commercial property does not increase housing prices. Thus, the argument that the market value of houses will increase if more commercial property is developed is not supported by this analysis. That conclusion is true only for a model that includes these four predictor variables. Note also that the values of $R^2 = 47.4\%$ and s_e (standard error of the regression) = 3.677 are included in the regression output.

Figure 12.9 Housing Price Regression Model (Minitab Output)

Regression Analysis: hseval versus sizehse, income72, taxrate, Comper

```
The regression equation is
hseval = -28.1 + 7.88 sizehse + 0.00367 incom72 - 172 taxrate -10.6 Comper

Predictor          Coef      SE Coef         T        P
Constant        -28.075        9.766     -2.87    0.005
sizehse           7.878        1.809      4.35    0.000
incom72        0.003666     0.001344      2.73    0.008
taxrate         -171.80        43.09     -3.99    0.000
Comper          -10.614        6.491     -1.64    0.106


S = 3.67686    R-Sq = 47.4%   R-Sq(adj) = 45.0%

Analysis of Variance

Source            DF         SS        MS        F       P
Regression         4    1037.49    259.37    19.19   0.000
Residual Error    85    1149.14     13.52
Total             89    2186.63
```

The advocates of increased commercial development also claimed that increasing the amount of commercial property would decrease the taxes paid on owner-occupied houses. This claim was tested using the regression output in Figure 12.10, prepared using Excel. The coefficient estimators and their standard errors are indicated. The Student's t statistics for the size of house and the tax rate coefficients are 2.65 and 6.36, indicating that these variables are important predictors. The Student's t statistic for income is 1.83 with a p-value of 0.07 for a two-tailed test. Thus, income has some influence as a predictor, but its effect is not as strong as the previous two variables. Again, we see a place for good judgment that considers the problem context. The conditional hypothesis that increased commercial property decreases taxes on owner-occupied houses can be tested using the conditional Student's t statistic for the variable "Comper" in the regression output. The conditional Student's t statistic is -1.03 with a p-value of 0.308. Thus, the hypothesis that increased commercial property does not decrease house taxes cannot be rejected. There is no evidence from this analysis that house taxes would be lowered if there was additional commercial development.

Figure 12.10 House Tax Regression Model (Excel Output)

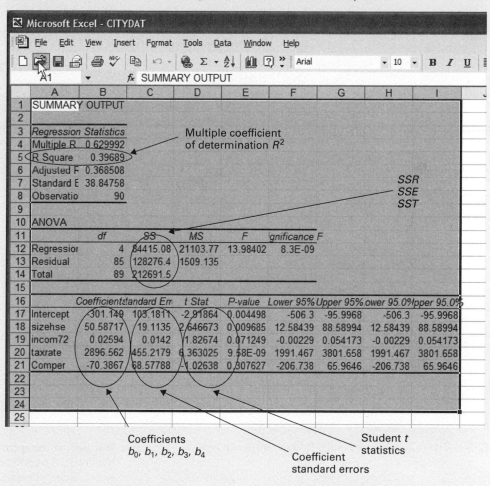

Based on the regression analyses performed in this study, the consultants concluded that there was no evidence that increased commercial property would either increase the market value of houses or lower the property taxes for a house.

EXERCISES

Basic Exercises

12.23 The following are results from a regression model analysis:

$$\hat{y} = 1.50 + 4.8x_1 + 6.9x_2 - 7.2x_3$$
$$\phantom{\hat{y} = 1.50 +}(2.1)\quad(3.7)\quad(2.8)$$
$$R^2 = 0.71 \qquad n = 24$$

The numbers below the coefficient estimates are the sample standard errors of the coefficient estimates.

a. Compute two-sided 95% confidence intervals for the three regression slope coefficients.
b. For each of the slope coefficients test the hypotheses

$$H_0 : \beta_j = 0 \quad \text{versus} \quad H_1 : \beta_j > 0$$

12.24 The following are results from a regression model analysis:

$$\hat{y} = 2.50 + 6.8x_1 - 6.9x_2 - 7.2x_3$$
$$\phantom{\hat{y} = 2.50 +}(3.1)\quad(3.7)\quad(3.2)$$
$$R^2 = 0.85 \qquad n = 34$$

The numbers below the coefficient estimates are the estimated coefficient standard errors.

a. Compute two-sided 95% confidence intervals for the three regression slope coefficients.
b. For each of the slope coefficients test the hypothesis

$$H_0 : \beta_j = 0 \quad \text{versus} \quad H_1 : \beta_j > 0$$

12.25 The following are results from a regression model analysis:

$$\hat{y} = -101.50 + 34.8x_1 + 56.9x_2 - 57.2x_3$$
$$\phantom{\hat{y} = -101.50 +}(12.1)\quad(23.7)\quad(32.8)$$
$$R^2 = 0.71 \qquad n = 65$$

The numbers in parentheses under the coefficients are the estimated coefficient standard errors.

a. Compute two-sided 95% confidence intervals for the three regression slope coefficients.
b. For each of the slope coefficients test the hypothesis

$$H_0 : \beta_j = 0 \quad \text{versus} \quad H_1 : \beta_j > 0$$

12.26 The following are results from a regression model analysis:

$$\hat{y} = -9.50 + 17.8x_1 + 26.9x_2 - 9.2x_3$$
$$\phantom{\hat{y} = -9.50 +}(7.1)\quad(13.7)\quad(3.8)$$
$$R^2 = 0.71 \qquad n = 39$$

The numbers in parentheses under the coefficients are the estimated coefficient standard errors.

a. Compute two-sided 95% confidence intervals for the three regression slope coefficients.

b. For each of the slope coefficients test the hypothesis

$$H_0 : \beta_j = 0 \quad \text{versus} \quad H_1 : \beta_j > 0$$

Application Exercises

12.27 In the study of Exercise 12.6, the estimated standard errors were as follows:

$$s_{b_1} = 0.099 \qquad s_{b_2} = 0.032 \qquad s_{b_3} = 0.0023$$

a. Find 90% and 95% confidence intervals for β_1.
b. Find 95% and 99% confidence intervals for β_2.
c. Test against a two-sided alternative the null hypothesis that, all else being equal, the plane's weight has no linear influence on its design effort.
d. The error sum of squares for this regression was 0.332. Using the same data, a simple linear regression of design effort on percentage number of common parts was fitted, yielding an error sum of squares of 3.311. Test at the 1% level the null hypothesis that, taken together, the variable's top speed and weight contribute nothing in a linear sense to explanation of changes in the variable, design effort, given that the variable percentage number of common parts is also used as an explanatory variable.

12.28 In the study of Exercise 12.8, where the sample regression was based on 30 observations, the estimated standard errors were as follows:

$$s_{b_1} = 0.023 \qquad s_{b_2} = 0.35$$

a. Test against the appropriate one-sided alternative the null hypothesis that, for fixed family size, milk consumption does not depend linearly on income.
b. Find 90%, 95%, and 99% confidence intervals for β_2.

12.29 In the study of Exercises 12.9 and 12.21, where the sample regression was based on 25 observations, the estimated standard errors were as follows:

$$s_{b_1} = 0.189 \qquad s_{b_2} = 0.565 \qquad s_{b_3} = 0.243$$

a. Test against the appropriate one-sided alternative the null hypothesis that, all else being equal, hours of exercise do not linearly influence weight gain.
b. Test against the appropriate one-sided alternative the null hypothesis that, all else being equal, beer consumption does not linearly influence weight gain.
c. Find 90%, 95%, and 99% confidence intervals for β_1.

12.30 Refer to the data of Example 12.6.

    a. Test against a two-sided alternative the null hypothesis that, all else being equal, median per capita personal income has no influence on the effective property tax rate.

    b. Test the null hypothesis that, taken together, the three independent variables do not linearly influence the effective property tax rate.

12.31 ⬤ Refer to the data of Example 12.7 with data file **Citydat**.

    a. Find 95% and 99% confidence intervals for the expected change in the market price for houses resulting from a 1-unit increase in the mean number of rooms when the values of all other independent variables remain unchanged.

    b. Test the null hypothesis that, all else being equal, mean household income does not influence the market price against the alternative that the higher the mean household income, the higher the market price.

12.32 In a study of revenue generated by national lotteries, the following regression equation was fitted to data from 29 countries with lotteries:

$$y = -31.323 + 0.4045x_1 + 0.8772x_2 - 365.01x_3 - 9.9298x_4$$
$$ {\scriptstyle (0.00755)} \quad {\scriptstyle (0.3107)} \quad {\scriptstyle (263.88)} \quad {\scriptstyle (3.4520)}$$

$$R^2 = .51$$

where

    y = dollars of net revenue per capita per year generated by the lottery

    x_1 = mean per capita personal income of the country

    x_2 = number of hotel, motel, inn, and resort rooms per thousand persons in the country

    x_3 = spendable revenue per capita per year generated by parimutuel betting, racing, and other legalized gambling

    x_4 = percentage of the nation's border contiguous with a state or states with a lottery

The numbers in parentheses under the coefficients are the estimated coefficient standard errors.

    a. Interpret the estimated coefficient on x_1.

    b. Find and interpret a 95% confidence interval for the coefficient on x_2, in the population regression.

    c. Test the null hypothesis that the coefficient on x_3 in the population regression is 0 against the alternative that this coefficient is negative. Interpret your findings.

12.33 A study was conducted to determine whether certain features could be used to explain variability in the prices of furnaces. For a sample of 19 furnaces the following regression was estimated:

$$y = -68.236 + 0.0023x_1 + 19.729x_2 + 7.653x_3 \quad R^2 = 0.84$$
$$ {\scriptstyle (0.005)} \qquad {\scriptstyle (8.992)} \qquad {\scriptstyle (3.082)}$$

where

    y = price, in dollars

    x_1 = rating of furnace, in BTU per hour

    x_2 = energy efficiency ratio

    x_3 = number of settings

The numbers in parentheses under the coefficients are the estimated coefficient standard errors.

    a. Find a 95% confidence interval for the expected increase in price resulting from an additional setting when the values of the rating and the energy efficiency ratio remain fixed.

    b. Test the null hypothesis that, all else being equal, the energy efficiency ratio of furnaces does not affect their price against the alternative that the higher the energy efficiency ratio, the higher the price.

12.34 In a study of the demand for imports in Nigeria the following model was fitted to 19 years of data:

$$y = -58.9 + 0.20x_1 - 0.10x_2 \qquad \overline{R}^2 = 0.96$$
$$ {\scriptstyle (0.0092)} \quad {\scriptstyle (0.084)}$$

where

    y = quantity of imports

    x_1 = personal consumption expenditures

    x_2 = price of imports ÷ domestic prices

The numbers in parentheses under the coefficients are the estimated coefficient standard errors.

    a. Find a 95% confidence interval for β_1.

    b. Test against the appropriate one-sided alternative the null hypothesis that $\beta_2 = 0$.

12.35 In a study of foreign holdings in British banks the following sample regression was obtained, based on 14 annual observations:

$$y = -3.248 + 0.101x_1 - 0.244x_2 + 0.057x_3 \qquad R^2 = 0.93$$
$$ {\scriptstyle (0.023)} \quad {\scriptstyle (0.080)} \quad {\scriptstyle (0.00925)}$$

where

    y = year-end share of assets in British bank subsidiaries held by foreigners, as a percentage of total assets

    x_1 = annual change, in billions of pounds, in foreign direct investment in Great Britain (excluding finance, insurance and real estate)

    x_2 = bank price-earnings ratio

    x_3 = index of the exchange value of the pound

The number in parentheses under the coefficients are the estimated coefficient standard errors.

a. Find a 90% confidence interval for β_1 and interpret your result.

b. Test the null hypothesis that β_2 is 0 against the alternative that it is negative, and interpret your result.

c. Test the null hypothesis that β_3 is 0 against the alternative that it is positive and interpret your result.

12.36 In a study of differences in levels of community demand for firefighters, the following sample regression was obtained, based on data from 39 towns in Maryland:

$$y = -0.00232 - 0.00024x_1 - 0.00002x_2 + 0.00034x_3 + 0.48122x_4$$
$$(0.00010)\quad(0.000018)\quad(0.00012)\quad(0.77954)$$
$$+\,0.04950x_5 - 0.00010x_6 + 0.00645x_7 \quad \overline{R}^2 = 0.3572$$
$$(0.01172)\quad(0.00005)\quad(0.00306)$$

where

y = number of full-time firefighters per capita

x_1 = maximum base salary of firefighters, in thousands of dollars

x_2 = percentage of population

x_3 = estimated per capita income, in thousands of dollars

x_4 = population density

x_5 = amount of intergovernmental grants per capita, in thousands of dollars

x_6 = number of miles from the regional city

x_7 = percentage of the population that is male and between 12 and 21 years of age

The numbers in parentheses under the coefficients are the estimated coefficient standard errors.

a. Find and interpret a 99% confidence interval for β_5.

b. Test against a two-sided alternative the null hypothesis that β_4 is 0, and interpret your result.

c. Test against a two-sided alternative the null hypothesis that β_7 is 0, and interpret your result.

12.5 TESTS ON REGRESSION COEFFICIENTS

In the previous section we showed how a conditional hypothesis test can be conducted to determine if a specific variable coefficient is conditionally significant in a regression model. There are, however, situations where we are interested in the effect of the combination of several variables. For example, in a model that predicts quantity sold, we might be interested in the combined effect of both the seller's price and the competitor's price. In other cases we might be interested in knowing if the combination of all variables is a useful predictor of the dependent variable.

Tests on All Coefficients

First, we present hypothesis tests to determine if sets of several coefficients are all simultaneously equal to 0. Consider again the model:

$$y_i = \beta_0 + \beta_1 x_{1i} + \beta_2 x_{1i} + \cdots + \beta_K x_{Ki} + \varepsilon_i$$

We begin by considering the null hypothesis that all of the coefficients are simultaneously equal to zero:

$$H_0 : \beta_1 = \beta_2 = \cdots = \beta_K = 0$$

Accepting this hypothesis would lead us to conclude that none of the predictor variables in the regression model is statistically significant and, thus, that they provide no useful information. If this were to occur, then we would need to go back to the model specification process and develop a new set of predictor variables. Fortunately, in most applied regression situations this hypothesis is rejected because the specification process usually leads to identification of at least one significant predictor variable.

To test the previous hypothesis, we can use the partitioning of variability developed in Section 12.3:

$$SST = SSR + SSE$$

Recall that SSR is the amount of variability explained by the regression and that SSE is the amount of unexplained variability. Also recall that the variance of the regression model can be estimated by using the following:

$$s_e^2 = \frac{SSE}{(n - K - 1)}$$

If the null hypothesis that all coefficients are equal to 0 is true, then *the mean square regression*

$$MSR = \frac{SSR}{K}$$

is also a measure of error with K degrees of freedom. As a result, the ratio of

$$F = \frac{SSR / K}{SSE / (n - K - 1)}$$
$$= \frac{MSR}{s_e^2}$$

has an F distribution with K degrees of freedom for the numerator and $n - K - 1$ degrees of freedom for the denominator. If the null hypothesis is true, then both the numerator and the denominator provide estimates of the population variance. As noted in Section 11.4 the ratio of independent sample variances from populations with equal population variances follows an F distribution if the populations are normally distributed. The computed value of F is compared with the critical value of F from Table 9 in the appendix at a significance level α. If the computed value exceeds the critical value from the table, we reject the null hypothesis and conclude that at least one coefficient is not equal to 0. This test procedure is summarized in Equation 12.23.

Test on All the Coefficients of a Regression Model

Consider the multiple regression model:

$$y_i = \beta_0 + \beta_1 x_{1i} + \beta_2 x_{2i} + \cdots + \beta_K x_{Ki} + \varepsilon_i$$

To test the null hypothesis

$$H_0 : \beta_1 = \beta_2 = \cdots = \beta_K = 0$$

against the alternative hypothesis

$$H_1 : \text{At least one } \beta_j \neq 0$$

at a significance level α, we use the decision rule

$$\text{Reject } H_0 : \text{if} \qquad F_{K, n-K-1} = \frac{MSR}{s_e^2} > F_{K, n-K-1, \alpha} \qquad (12.23)$$

where $F_{K, n-K-1, \alpha}$ is the critical value of F from Table 9 in the appendix at the end of the book for which

$$P(F_{K, n-K-1} > F_{K, n-K-1, \alpha}) = \alpha$$

The computed random variable $F_{K, n-K-1}$ follows an F distribution with numerator degrees of freedom K and denominator degrees of freedom $(n - K - 1)$.

Example 12.8 Housing Price Prediction Model (Simultaneous Coefficient Testing)

During the development of the housing price prediction model for Northern City the analysts wanted to know if there was evidence that the combination of four predictor variables was not a significant predictor of housing price. That is, they wanted to test the hypothesis

$$H_0 : \beta_1 = \beta_2 = \beta_3 = \beta_4 = 0$$

Solution This testing procedure can be illustrated by the housing price regression in Figure 12.9 prepared using the **Citydat** data file. In the analysis of variance table, the computed F statistic is 19.19 with 4 degrees of freedom for the numerator and 85 degrees of freedom for the denominator. The computation of F is as follows:

$$F = \frac{259.37}{13.52} = 19.19$$

This exceeds the critical value of $F = 3.55$ for $\alpha = 0.01$ from Table 9 in the appendix. In addition, note that Minitab—and most statistics packages—compute the p-value, which in this example is equal to 0.000. Thus, we would reject the hypothesis that all coefficients are equal to zero.

Test on a Subset of Regression Coefficients

In the previous sections we have developed hypothesis tests for individual regression parameters and for all regression parameters taken together. Next, we develop a hypothesis test for a subset of regression parameters, such as the combined price example previously discussed. We use this test to determine if the combined effect of several independent variables is significant in a regression model.

Consider a regression model that contains independent variables designated as X_j and Z_j terms:

$$y_i = \beta_0 + \beta_1 x_{1i} + \cdots + \beta_K x_{Ki} + \alpha_1 z_{1i} + \cdots + \alpha_r z_{ri} + \varepsilon_i$$

and the null hypothesis to be tested is as follows:

$$H_0 : \alpha_1 = \alpha_2 = \cdots = \alpha_r = 0 \text{ given } \beta_j \neq 0, \quad j = 1, \ldots, K$$

If H_0 is true, then the Z_j variables should not be included in the regression model because they provide nothing further to explain the behavior of the dependent variable beyond what the X_j variables provided. The procedure for performing this test is summarized in Equation 12.24, following a detailed discussion of the testing procedure.

The test is conducted by comparing the error sum of squares, SSE, from the complete regression model, which includes both the X and the Z variables, with the $SSE(r)$ from a restricted model that includes only the X variables. First, we run a regression on the complete regression model and obtain the error sum of squares, designated as SSE. Next, we run the restricted regression, which excludes the Z variables (note that the coefficients α_j are all restricted to values of 0 in this regression):

$$y_i = \beta_0 + \beta_1 x_{1i} + \cdots + \beta_K x_{Ki} + \varepsilon_i^*$$

From this regression we obtain the restricted error sum of squares, designated as $SSE(r)$. Then we compute the F statistic with r degrees of freedom for the numerator, r is the number of variables removed simultaneously from the restricted model, and $n - K - r - 1$ degrees of freedom for the denominator, the degrees of freedom for error in the model that includes both the X and the Z independent variables. The F statistic is

$$F = \frac{(SSE(r) - SSE)/r}{s_e^2}$$

where s_e^2 is the estimated variance of the error for the complete model. This statistic follows an F distribution with r degrees of freedom in the numerator and $n - K - r - 1$ degrees of freedom in the denominator. If the computed F is greater than the critical value of F, then the null hypothesis is rejected, and we conclude that the Z variables as a set should be included in the model. Note that this test does not imply that individual Z variables should not be excluded by, for example, using the Student's t test discussed previously. In addition, the test for all Z's does not imply that a subset of the Z variables cannot be excluded by using this test procedure with a different subset of Z variables.

Test on a Subset of the Regression Parameters

Given a regression model with the independent variables partitioned into X and Z subsets,

$$y_i = \beta_0 + \beta_1 x_{1i} + \cdots + \beta_K x_{Ki} + \alpha_1 z_{1i} + \cdots + \alpha_r z_{ri} + \varepsilon_i$$

To test the null hypothesis

$$H_0: \alpha_1 = \alpha_2 = \cdots = \cdots = \alpha_r = 0$$

which states that the regression parameters in a particular subset are simultaneously equal to 0, against the alternative hypothesis

$$H_1: \text{At least one } \alpha_j \neq 0 \ (j = 1, ..., r)$$

We compare the error sum of squares for the complete model with the error sum of squares for the restricted model. First, run a regression for the complete model, which includes all independent variables, and obtain the error sum of squares, *SSE*. Next, run a restricted regression, which excludes the Z variables whose coefficients are the αs—the number of variables excluded is r. From this regression obtain the restricted error sum of squares, *SSE(r)*. Then compute the F statistic and apply the decision rule for significance level α:

$$\text{Reject } H_0 \text{ if } F = \frac{(SSE(r) - SSE)/r}{s_e^2} > F_{r, n-K-r-1, \alpha} \qquad (12.24)$$

Comparison of F and t Tests

If we used Equation 12.24 with $r = 1$, we could test the hypothesis that a single variable, X_j, does not improve the prediction of the dependent variable, given the other independent variables in the model. Thus, we have the following hypothesis test:

$$H_0: \beta_j = 0 \mid \beta_l \neq 0, \qquad j \neq l \qquad l = 1, \ldots, K$$
$$H_1: \beta_j \neq 0 \mid \beta_l \neq 0, \qquad j \neq l \qquad l = 1, \ldots, K$$

Previously, we have seen that this test could also be performed using a Student's t test. Using methods beyond this book, we can show that the corresponding F and t tests provide exactly the same conclusions regarding the hypothesis test for a single variable. In addition, the computed t statistic for the coefficient b_j is equal to the square root of the corresponding computed F statistic. That is,

$$t_{b_j}^2 = F_{x_j}$$

where F_{x_j} is the F statistic computed using Equation 12.24 when variable x_j is excluded from the model and, thus, $r = 1$. We show this numerical result in Example 12.9.

Statistical distribution theory also shows that an F random variable with 1 degree of freedom in the numerator is the square of a t random variable with the same degrees of freedom as the denominator of the F random variable. Thus, the F and t tests will always provide the same conclusions regarding the hypothesis test for a single independent variable in a multiple regression model.

Example 12.9 Housing Price Prediction for Small Cities (Hypothesis Tests for Coefficient Subsets)

The developers of the housing price prediction model from Example 12.8 wanted to determine if the combined effect of tax rate and percent commercial property contributes to the prediction after the effects of house size and income have been previously included.

Solution Continuing with the problem from Examples 12.7 and 12.8, we have a conditional test of the hypothesis that two variables are not significant predictors, given that the other two are significant predictors:

$$H_0 : \beta_3 = \beta_4 = 0 \mid \beta_1, \beta_2 \neq 0$$

This test will be conducted using the procedure in Equation 12.24. Figure 12.9 presents the regression for the complete model with all four predictor variables. In that regression $SSE = 1{,}149.14$. In Figure 12.11 we have the reduced regression with only house size and income as predictor variables. In that regression $SSE = 1{,}426.93$. The hypothesis is tested by first computing the F statistic whose numerator is the error sum of squares for the reduced model [$SSE(r)$] minus the SSE for the complete model:

$$F = \frac{(1426.93 - 1149.14)/2}{13.52} = 10.27$$

The F statistic has 2 degrees of freedom—for the two variables being tested simultaneously—for the numerator and 85 degrees of freedom for the denominator. Note that the variance estimator, $s_e^2 = 13.52$, is obtained from the complete model in Figure 12.9, which has 85 degrees of freedom for error. The critical value for F with $\alpha = 0.01$ and 2 and 85 degrees of freedom, from Table 9 in the appendix, is approximately 4.9. Since the computed value of F exceeds the critical value, we reject the null hypothesis that tax rate and percent commercial property are not in combination conditionally significant. The combined effect of these two variables does improve the model that predicts housing price. Therefore, tax rate and percent commercial property should be included in the model.

Figure 12.11 Housing Price Regression: Reduced Model (Minitab Output)

Regression Analysis: hseval versus sizehse, income72

```
The regression equation is
hseval = -42.2 + 9.14 sizehse + 0.00393 incom72


Predictor         Coef     SE Coef        T       P
Constant       -42.208       9.810    -4.30   0.000
sizehse          9.135       1.940     4.71   0.000
incom72       0.003927    0.001473     2.67   0.009


S = 4.04987     R-Sq = 34.7%   R-Sq(adj) = 33.2%

Analysis of Variance

Source            DF        SS        MS       F       P
Regression         2    759.70    379.85   23.16   0.000
Residual Error    87   1426.93     16.40
Total             89   2186.63


Source     DF    Seq SS                         SSE(r)
sizehse     1    643.12
incom72     1    116.58
```

We also computed this regression with the variable "Comper" excluded and found that the resulting *SSE* was as follows:

$$SSE(1) = 1,185.29$$

Then the computed *F* statistic for this variable was as follows:

$$F = \frac{(1185.29 - 1149.14)/1}{13.52} = 2.674$$

The square root of 2.674 is 1.64, which is the computed *t* statistic for the variable "Comper" in the regression output in Figure 12.9. Using either the computed *F* or the computed *t*, we would obtain this result for the hypotheses for this variable:

$$H_0 : \beta_{Comper} = 0 \mid \beta_l \neq 0, l \neq Comper$$

$$H_1 : \beta_{Comper} \neq 0 \mid \beta_l \neq 0, l \neq Comper$$

EXERCISES

Basic Exercise

12.37 Suppose that you have estimated coefficients for the following regression model:

$$Y = \beta_0 + \beta_1 X_1 + \beta_2 X_2 + \beta_3 X_3$$

Test the hypothesis that all three of the predictor variables are equal to 0, given the following analysis of variance tables:

a. Analysis of Variance

Source	DF	SS	MS
Regression	3	4,500	
Residual Error	26	500	

b. Analysis of Variance

Source	DF	SS	MS
Regression	3	9,780	
Residual Error	26	2,100	

c. Analysis of Variance

Source	DF	SS	MS
Regression	3	46,000	
Residual Error	26	25,000	

d. Analysis of Variance

Source	DF	SS	MS
Regression	3	87,000	
Residual Error	26	48,000	

Application Exercises

12.38 Refer to the study on aircraft design effort in Exercises 12.6 and 12.19.

a. Test the null hypothesis:

$$H_0 : \beta_1 = \beta_2 = \beta_3 = 0$$

b. Set out the analysis of variance table.

12.39 For the study on the influence of financial institutions on share prices of Exercise 12.7, 48 quarterly observations were used, and the corrected coefficient of determination was found to be $\overline{R}^2 = 0.463$. Test the null hypothesis:

$$H_0 : \beta_1 = \beta_2 = 0$$

12.40 Refer to the study on milk consumption, described in Exercises 12.8, 12.20, and 12.28.

a. Test the null hypothesis:

$$H_0 : \beta_1 = \beta_2 = 0$$

b. Set out the analysis of variance table.

12.41 Refer to the study on weight gains described in Exercises 12.9, 12.21, and 12.29.

a. Test the null hypothesis:

$$H_0 : \beta_1 = \beta_2 = \beta_3 = 0$$

b. Set out the analysis of variance table.

12.42 Refer to Exercise 12.32. Test the null hypothesis that, taken together, the four independent variables do not linearly influence revenue generated by state lotteries.

12.43 Refer to Exercise 12.33. Test the null hypothesis that, taken together, the three independent variables do not linearly influence the price of furnaces.

12.44 Refer to the study of Exercise 12.34. Test the null hypothesis that, taken together, personal consumption expenditures and the relative price of imports do not linearly affect the demand for imports in Nigeria.

12.45 Refer to the study on the determinants of community demand for firefighters discussed in Exercise 12.36. Test the null hypothesis

$$H_0 : \beta_1 = \beta_2 = \beta_3 = \beta_4 = \beta_5 = \beta_6 = \beta_7 = 0$$

and interpret your findings.

12.46 A dependent variable is regressed on K independent variables, using n sets of sample observations. We denote SSE as the error sum of squares and R^2 as the coefficient of determination for this estimated regression. We want to test the null hypothesis that K_1 of these independent variables, taken together, do not linearly affect the dependent variable, given that the other $(K - K_1)$ independent variables are also to be used. Suppose that the regression is re-estimated with the K_1 independent variables of interest excluded. Let SSE^* denote the error sum of squares and R^{*2} the coefficient of determination for this regression. Show that the statistic for testing our null hypothesis, introduced in Section 12.5, can be expressed as follows:

$$\frac{(SSE^* - SSE) / K_1}{SSE / (n - K - 1)} = \frac{R^2 - R^{*2}}{1 - R^2} \cdot \frac{n - K - 1}{K_1}$$

12.47 In the study in Exercises 12.8, 12.20, and 12.28 on milk consumption, a third independent variable—number of preschool children in the household—was added to the regression model. The sum of squared errors when this augmented model was estimated by least squares was found to be 83.7. Test the null hypothesis that, all other things being equal, the number of preschool children in the household does not linearly affect milk consumption.

12.48 Suppose that a dependent variable is related to K independent variables through a multiple regression model. Let R^2 denote the coefficient of determination and $\overline{R}^2$ the corrected coefficient. Suppose that n sets of observations are used to fit the regression.

a. Show that

$$\overline{R}^2 = \frac{(n - 1)R^2 - K}{n - K - 1}$$

b. Show that

$$R^2 = \frac{(n - K - 1)\overline{R}^2 + K}{n - 1}$$

c. Show that the statistic for testing the null hypothesis that all the regression coefficients are 0 can be written as

$$\frac{SSR / K}{SSE / (n - K - 1)} = \frac{n - K - 1}{K} \cdot \frac{\overline{R}^2 + A}{1 - \overline{R}^2}$$

where

$$A = \frac{K}{n - K - 1}$$

An important application of regression models is to predict or forecast values of the dependent variable, given values for the independent variables. Forecasts can be computed directly from the estimated regression model using the coefficient estimates in that model, as shown in Equation 12.25.

Predictions from the Multiple Regression Models

Given that the population regression model

$$y_i = \beta_0 + \beta_1 x_{1i} + \beta_2 x_{1i} + \cdots + \beta_K x_{Ki} + \varepsilon_i$$

holds and that the standard regression assumptions are valid, let b_0, b_1, ..., b_k be the least squares estimates of the model coefficients, β_j, where $j = 1, ..., K$, based on the $x_{1i}, x_{2i} \ldots, x_{Ki}$ ($i = 1, ..., n$) data points. Then, given a new observation of a data point, $x_{1,n+1}, x_{2,n+1}, ..., x_{K,n+1}$ the best linear unbiased forecast of y_{n+1} is

$$\hat{y}_i = b_0 + b_1 x_{1i} + b_2 x_{1i} + \cdots + b_K x_{Ki} \quad i = n + 1 \qquad (12.25)$$

It is very risky to obtain forecasts that are based on X values outside the range of the data used to estimate the model coefficients because we do not have data evidence to support the linear model at those points.

In addition to the predicted value of Y for a particular set of x_j terms, we are often interested in a confidence interval or a prediction interval associated with the prediction. As we discussed in Section 11.6, the confidence interval includes the expected value of Y with probability $1 - \alpha$. In contrast, the prediction interval includes individual predicted values—expected values of Y plus the random error term. To obtain these intervals, we need to compute estimates of the standard deviations for the expected value of Y and for the individual points. These computations are similar in form to those used in simple regression, but the estimator equations are much more complicated. The standard deviations for predicted values, $s_{\hat{y}}$, are a function of the standard error of the estimate, s_e; the standard deviation of the predictor variables; the correlations between the predictor variables; and the square of the distance between the mean of the independent variables and the X terms for the prediction. This standard deviation is similar to the standard deviation for simple regression predictions in Chapter 11. However, the equations for multiple regression are very complex and will not be presented here—instead, we will compute the values using Minitab. The standard deviations for the prediction interval, the confidence interval, and the corresponding intervals are computed by most good statistics packages. Excel does not have the capability to compute the standard deviation of the predicted variables.

Example 12.10 Forecast of Savings and Loan Profit Margin (Regression Model Forecasts)

You have been asked to forecast the savings and loan profit margin for a year in which the percentage net revenue is 4.50 and there are 9,000 offices, using the savings and loan regression model. Data are stored in the file **Savings and Loan**.

Solution Using the notation from Equation 12.25, we have the following variables:

$$x_{1,n+1} = 4.50 \quad x_{2,n+1} = 9{,}000$$

Using these values, we find that our point predictor of profit margin is as follows:

$$\hat{y}_{n+1} = b_0 + b_1 x_{1,n+1} + b_{2,n+1}$$
$$= 1.565 + (0.237)(4.50) - (0.000249)(9{,}000) = 0.39$$

Thus, for a year when the percentage net revenue per deposit dollar is 4.50 and the number of offices is 9,000, we predict that the percentage profit margin for savings and loan associations will be 0.39.

Predicted values, confidence intervals, and prediction intervals can be computed directly in the Minitab regression routine.

The regression output is shown in Figure 12.12. The predicted value, $\hat{y} = 0.39$, and its standard deviation, 0.0277, are presented, along with the confidence

Figure 12.12 Forecasts and Forecast Intervals for Multiple Regression (Minitab Output)

Regression Analysis: Y profit versus X1 revenue, X2 offices

```
The regression equation is
Y profit = 1.56 + 0.237 X1 revenue - 0.000249 X2 offices


Predictor         Coef     SE Coef       T       P
Constant       1.56450     0.07940   19.70   0.000
X1 revenue     0.23720     0.05556    4.27   0.000
X2 offices  -0.00024908  0.00003205   -7.77   0.000


S = 0.0533022   R-Sq = 86.5%   R-Sq(adj) = 85.3%


Analysis of Variance

Source        DF       SS        MS       F       P
Regression     2  0.40151   0.20076   70.66   0.000
Residual Error22  0.06250   0.00284
Total         24  0.46402


Predicted Values for New Observations

New
Obs   Fit   SE Fit      95% CI            95% PI
 1 0.3902  0.0277  (0.3327, 0.4476) (0.2656, 0.5148)


Values of Predictors for New Observations

New                    X2
Obs  X1 revenue   offices
 1         4.50      9000
```

Predicted value

Standard error for predicted value

Prediction interval

Confidence interval

Prediction variable values

interval and the prediction interval. The confidence interval—CI—provides an interval for the expected value of Y on the linear function defined by the values of the independent variables. This interval is a function of the standard error of the regression model, the distance that the x_j values are from their individual sample means, and the correlation between the x_j variables used to fit the model. The prediction interval—PI—provides an interval for a single observed value. Thus, it includes the variability associated with the expected value plus the variability of a single point about the predicted value.

EXERCISES

Basic Exercise

12.49 Given the estimated multiple regression equation

$$\hat{y} = 6 + 5x_1 + 4x_2 + 7x_3 + 8x_4$$

what is the predicted value of Y when

a. $x_1 = 10, x_2 = 23, x_3 = 9$, and $x_4 = 12$?
b. $x_1 = 23, x_2 = 18, x_3 = 10$, and $x_4 = 11$?
c. $x_1 = 10, x_2 = 23, x_3 = 9$, and $x_4 = 12$?
d. $x_1 = -10, x_2 = 13, x_3 = -8$, and $x_4 = -16$?

Application Exercises

12.50 Using the information in Exercise 12.9, predict the weight gain for a freshman who eats an average of 20 meals per week, exercises an average of 10 hours per week, and consumes an average of 6 beers per week.

12.51 Using the information in Exercise 12.8, predict the weekly milk consumption of a family of four with an income of $600 per week.

$$b_0 = 0.578$$

12.52 For the regression on aircraft design effort in Exercise 12.6, the estimated intercept was 2.0.

Predict design effort for a plane with a top speed of Mach 1.0, weighing 7 tons, and having 50% of its parts in common with other models.

12.53 A real estate agent hypothesizes that in her town the selling price of a house in dollars (y) depends on its size in square feet of floor space (x_1), the lot size in square feet (x_2), the number of bedrooms (x_3), and the number of bathrooms (x_4). For a random sample of 20 house sales the following least squares estimated model was obtained:

$$\hat{y} = 1998.5 + 22.352x_1 + 1.4686x_2 + 6767.3x_3 + 2701.1x_4$$
$$\quad\quad\;\; (2.5543)\quad\;\; (1.4492)\quad\;\; (1820.8)\quad\;\; (1996.2)$$

$R^2 = 0.9843$

The numbers in parentheses under the coefficients are the estimated coefficient standard errors.

a. Interpret in the context of this model the estimated coefficient on x_2.
b. Interpret the coefficient of determination.
c. Assuming that the model is correctly specified, test at the 5% level against the appropriate one-sided alternative the null hypothesis that, all else being equal, selling price does not depend on number of bathrooms.
d. Estimate the selling price of a house with 1,250 square feet of floor space, a lot of 4,700 square feet, 3 bedrooms, and 1 bathroom.

12.7 TRANSFORMATIONS FOR NONLINEAR REGRESSION MODELS

We have seen how regression analysis can be used to estimate linear relationships that predict a dependent variable as a function of one or more independent variables. These applications are very important. However, in addition, there are a number of economic and business relationships that are not strictly linear. In this section we develop procedures for modifying certain nonlinear model formats so that multiple regression procedures can be used to estimate the model coefficients. Thus, our objective in Sections 12.7 and 12.8 is to expand the range of problems that are adaptable to regression analysis. In this way we see that regression analysis has even broader applications.

By examining the least squares algorithm, we will see that, with careful manipulation of nonlinear models, it is possible to use least squares for a broader set of

Figure 12.13 Examples of Quadratic Functions

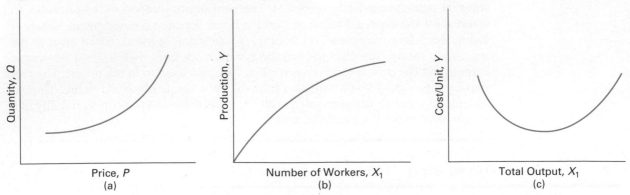

applied problems. The assumptions concerning independent variables in multiple regression are not very restrictive. Independent variables define points at which we measure a random variable Y. We assume that there is a linear relationship between the levels of the independent variables X_j, where $j = 1, ..., K$, and the expected value of the dependent variable Y. We can take advantage of this freedom to expand the set of models that can be estimated. Thus, we can move beyond linear models in our multiple regression applications. Three examples are shown in Figure 12.13:

1. Supply functions may be nonlinear.
2. The increase in total output with increases in the number of workers may become flatter as more workers are added.
3. Average cost per unit produced is often minimized at an intermediate level of production.

Quadratic Transformations

We have spent considerable time developing regression analysis to estimate linear equations that represent various business and economic processes. There are also many processes that can best be represented by nonlinear equations. Total revenue has a quadratic relationship with price, with maximum revenue occurring at an intermediate price level if the demand function has a negative slope. In many cases the minimum production cost per unit occurs at an intermediate level of output, with cost per unit decreasing as we approach the minimum cost per unit and then increasing after passing the minimum unit cost level. We can model a number of these economic and business relationships by using a quadratic model:

$$Y = \beta_0 + \beta_1 X_1 + \beta_2 X_1^2 + \varepsilon$$

To estimate the coefficients of a quadratic model for applications such as these, we can transform or modify the variables, as shown in Equations 12.26 and 12.27. In this way a nonlinear quadratic model is converted to a model that is linear in a modified set of variables.

Quadratic Model Transformations
The quadratic function

$$Y = \beta_0 + \beta_1 X_1 + \beta_2 X_1^2 + \varepsilon \qquad \text{(12.26)}$$

can be transformed into a linear multiple regression model by defining new variables:

$$z_1 = x_1$$
$$z_2 = x_1^2$$

and then specifying the model as

$$y_i = \beta_0 + \beta_1 z_{1i} + \beta_2 z_{2i} + \varepsilon_i \tag{12.27}$$

which is linear in the transformed variables. Transformed quadratic variables can be combined with other variables in a multiple regression model. Thus, we can fit a multiple quadratic regression using transformed variables. The goal is to find models that are linear in other mathematical forms of a variable.

INTERPRETATION

By transforming the variables, we can estimate a linear multiple regression model and use the results as a nonlinear model. Inference procedures for transformed quadratic models are the same as those that we have previously developed for linear models. In this way we avoid confusion that would result if different statistical procedures were used for linear versus quadratic models. The coefficients must be combined for interpretation. Thus, if we have a quadratic model, then the effect of a variable, X, is indicated by the coefficients of both the linear and the quadratic terms. We can also perform a simple hypothesis test to determine if a quadratic model is an improvement over a linear model. The Z_2 or X_1^2 variable is merely an additional variable whose coefficient can be tested—$H_0 : \beta_2 = 0$—using the conditional Student's t or F statistic. If a quadratic model fits the data better than a linear model, then the coefficient of the quadratic variable—$Z_2 = X_1^2$—will be significantly different from 0. The same approach applies if we have variables such as $Z_3 = X_1^3$ or $Z_4 = X_1^2 X_2$.

Example 12.11 Production Costs (Quadratic Model Estimation)

Arnold Sorenson, production manager of New Frontiers Instruments Inc., was interested in estimating the mathematical relationship between the number of electronic assemblies produced during an 8-hour shift and the average cost per assembly. This function would then be used to estimate cost for various production order bids and to determine the production level that would minimize average cost. Data are found in the data file **Production Cost**.

Solution Arnold collected data from nine shifts during which the number of assemblies ranged from 100 to 900. In addition, he obtained the average cost per unit for those days from the accounting department. These data are presented in a scatter plot prepared using Excel, shown in Figure 12.14. As a result of his study of economics and his experience, Arnold suspected that the function might be quadratic with an intermediate minimum average cost. He designed his analysis to consider both a linear and a quadratic average production cost function.

Figure 12.15 is the simple regression of cost as a linear function of the number of units. We see that the linear relationship is almost flat, indicating no linear

Figure 12.14 Mean Production Cost as a Function of Number of Units

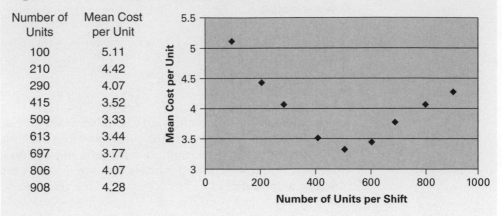

Number of Units	Mean Cost per Unit
100	5.11
210	4.42
290	4.07
415	3.52
509	3.33
613	3.44
697	3.77
806	4.07
908	4.28

Figure 12.15 Linear Regression Average Cost on Number of Units

Regression Analysis: Mean Cost per Unit versus Number of Units

```
The regression equation is
Mean Cost per Unit = 4.43 - 0.000855 Number of Units


Predictor                Coef      SE Coef       T       P
Constant               4.4330       0.3994   11.10   0.000
Number of Units    -0.0008547       0.0007029   -1.22   0.263


S = 0.547614    R-Sq = 17.4%    R-Sq(adj) = 5.6%

Analysis of Variance

Source            DF        SS         MS       F       P
Regression         1     0.4433     0.4433    1.48   0.263
Residual Error     7     2.0992     0.2999
Total              8     2.5425
```

Figure 12.16 Quadratic Model Analysis for Average Cost on Number of Units

Regression Analysis: Mean Cost per Unit versus Number of Units, No Units Squared

```
The regression equation is
Mean Cost per Unit = 5.91 - 0.00884 Number of Units + 0.000008
No Units Squared

Predictor                Coef      SE Coef       T       P
Constant               5.9084       0.1614   36.60   0.000
Number of Units    -0.0088415       0.0007344  -12.04   0.000
No Units Squared   -0.00000793      0.00000071   11.15   0.000

S = 0.126875    R-Sq = 96.2%    R-Sq(adj) = 94.9%

Analysis of Variance

Source            DF        SS         MS       F       P
Regression         2     2.4459     1.2230   75.97   0.000
Residual Error     6     0.0966     0.0161
Total              8     2.5425
```

relationship between average cost and number of units produced. If Arnold had simply used this relationship, he would have been led to serious errors in his cost estimation procedures.

Figure 12.16 presents the quadratic regression that shows mean cost per unit as a nonlinear function of the number of units produced. Note that b_2 is different from 0 and thus should be included in the model. In addition, note that R^2 for the quadratic model is 0.962 compared to 0.174 for the linear model. By using the quadratic model, Arnold has produced a substantially more useful mean cost model.

Logarithmic Transformations

A number of economic relationships can be modeled by exponential functions. For example, if the percent change in quantity of goods sold changes linearly in response to percent changes in the price, then the demand function will have an exponential form:

$$Q = \beta_0 P^{\beta_1}$$

where Q is the quantity demanded and P is the price per unit. Exponential demand functions have constant elasticity, and, thus, a 1% change in price results in the same percent change in quantity demanded for all price levels. In contrast, linear demand models indicate that a unit change in the price variable will result in the same change in quantity demanded for all price levels. Exponential demand models are widely used in the analysis of market behavior. One important feature of exponential models is that the coefficient β_1 is the constant elasticity, e, of demand Q with respect to price P:

$$e = \frac{\partial Q/Q}{\partial P/P} = \beta_j$$

This result is developed in most microeconomics textbooks. Exponential model coefficients are estimated using logarithmic transformations, as shown in Equation 12.29.

The logarithmic transformation assumes that the random error term multiplies the true value of Y to obtain the observed value. Thus, in the exponential model the error is a percentage of the true value, and the variance of the error distribution increases with increases in Y. If this result is not true, the log transformation is not correct. In that case a much more complex nonlinear estimation technique must be used. Those techniques are considerably beyond the scope of this book.

Exponential Model Transformations
Coefficients for exponential models of the form

$$Y = \beta_0 X_1^{\beta_1} X_2^{\beta_2} \varepsilon \tag{12.28}$$

can be estimated by first taking the logarithm of both sides in order to obtain an equation that is linear in the logarithms of the variables:

$$\log(Y) = \log(\beta_0) + \beta_1 \log(X_1) + \beta_2 \log(X_2) + \log(\varepsilon) \tag{12.29}$$

Using this form, we can regress the logarithm of Y on the logarithms of the two X variables and obtain estimates for the coefficients β_1 and β_2 directly from the regression analysis. Since the coefficients are elasticities, many economists use this model form where they can assume that elasticities are constant over the range of the data. Note that this estimation procedure requires that the random errors are multiplicative in the original exponential model. Thus, the error term, ε, is expressed as a percentage increase or decrease instead of the addition or subtraction of a random error, as we have seen for linear regression models.

Another important application of exponential models is the Cobb-Douglas production function, which has the form

$$Q = \beta_0 L^{\beta_1} K^{\beta_2}$$

where Q is the quantity produced, L is the amount of labor used, and K is the amount of capital. β_1 and β_2 are the relative contributions of changes in labor and changes in capital to changes in quantity produced. In one special case the sum of the coefficients is restricted to equal 1, and we have constant returns to scale. In that case β_1 and β_2 are the percent contributions of labor and capital to productivity increase.

The estimation of the coefficients when their sum is equal to 1 is one example of restricted estimation in regression models. Equation 12.29 is modified by the restriction

$$\beta_1 + \beta_2 = 1$$

and, therefore, substitution of the form

$$\beta_2 = 1 - \beta_1$$

is included, and the new estimation equation becomes

$$\log(Y) = \log(\beta_0) + \beta_1 \log(X_1) + (1 - \beta_1) \log(X_2) + \log(\varepsilon)$$

$$\log(Y) - \log(X_2) = \log(\beta_0) + \beta_1 [\log(X_1) - \log(X_2)] + \log(\varepsilon)$$

$$\log\left(\frac{Y}{X_2}\right) = \log(\beta_0) + \beta_1 \log\left(\frac{X_1}{X_2}\right) + \log(\varepsilon) \qquad \text{(12.30)}$$

Thus, we see that the β_1 coefficient is obtained by regressing $\log(Y/X_2)$ on $\log(X_1/X_2)$. Then β_2 is computed by subtracting β_1 from 1.0.

All quality computer-based statistical packages have the capabilities to easily compute the required transformations of the data for logarithmic models. In the following example we used Minitab, but similar results could be obtained using many other packages.

Example 12.12 Production Function for Minong Boat Works (Exponential Model Estimation)

The Minong Boat Works began producing small fishing boats in the early 1970s for northern Wisconsin fishermen. The owners developed a low-cost production method for producing quality boats. As a result, they have experienced increased demand over the years. The production method uses a workstation with a set of jigs and power tools that can be operated by a varying number of workers. Over the years the number of workstations (units of capital) has grown from 1 to 20 to meet the demand for boats. At the same time the workforce has grown from 2 to 25 full time workers. The owners are now considering expanding their sales to potential markets in Michigan and Minnesota. Therefore, they need to decide how much to increase the number of workstations and number of workers to achieve various levels of increased production.

Solution Their daughter, a senior economics major, suggests that they estimate a restricted Cobb-Douglas production function using data from previous years of operation. She explains that this production function will enable them to predict the number of boats produced for different levels of workstations and workers. The owners agree that such an analysis is a good idea and ask their daughter to prepare the analysis. She begins the analysis by collecting the production data, contained in the data file **Boat Production**, from old company records. To obtain the coefficient estimates, she first must transform the original model specification to a form that can be estimated by least squares regression. The Cobb-Douglas production function model is

$$Y = \beta_0 K^{\beta_1} L^{\beta_2}$$

with the restriction

$$\beta_1 = 1 - \beta_2$$

where Y is the number of boats produced each year, K is the number of production stations (units of capital) used each year, and L is the number of workers used each year.

The restricted Cobb-Douglas production function was transformed to the estimation form,

$$\log\left(\frac{Y}{K}\right) = \log(\beta_0) + \beta_2 \log\left(\frac{L}{K}\right)$$

for least squares estimation.

The regression model estimate is shown in Figure 12.17 with the resulting equation:

$$\log\left(\frac{Y}{K}\right) = 3.02 + 0.845 \log\left(\frac{L}{K}\right) \tag{12.31}$$

From this result we see that the estimated model coefficient, b_2, is 0.845. Therefore, $b_1 = 1 - 0.845 = 0.155$. Finally, $\log(b_0) = 3.02$. This analysis shows that 84.5% of the value of production comes from labor and 15.5% from capital. After applying the appropriate algebraic transformations, the production function model is as follows:

$$Y = 20.49 K^{0.155} L^{0.845} \tag{12.32}$$

This production function can be used as a tool for predicting the expected output obtained by using various levels of capital and labor.

Figure 12.18 presents a comparison of the observed number of boats and the forecast number of boats from the transformed regression equation. The forecast number of boats was computed using Equation 12.32. That analysis also indicates that the R^2 for the regression of the number of boats on the predicted number of boats is 0.987. This R^2 can be interpreted just as you would an R^2 for any linear regression model, and, thus, we see that the predicted number of boats provides a good fit for the observed boat production data. The R^2 for the transformed regression data in Figure 12.17 cannot be easily interpreted as an indicator of the relationship between the number of boats produced and the independent variables of labor and capital because the units are in logarithms of ratios.

Figure 12.17 Restricted Production Function Regression Analysis (Minitab Output)

```
The regression equation is
logbotunit = 3.02 + 0.845 logworunit


Predictor       Coef      SE Coef      T      P
Constant      3.02325     0.04387    68.92   0.000
logworun      0.84479     0.09062     9.32   0.000


S = 0.1105    R-Sq = 79.8%   R-Sq(adj) = 78.9%

Analysis of Variance

Source          DF        SS        MS       F      P
Regression       1     1.0618    1.0618   86.90   0.000
Residual Error  22     0.2688    0.0122
Total           23     1.3306
```

Figure 12.18 Comparison of Observed and Predicted Production

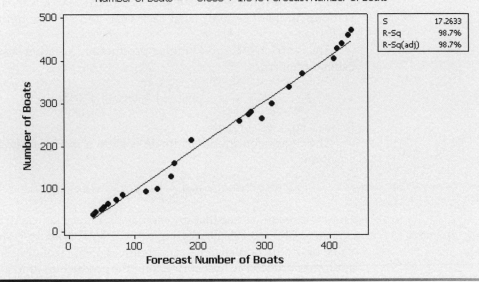

Fitted Line Plot
Number of Boats = − 8.306 + 1.045 Forecast Number of Boats

EXERCISES

Basic Exercises

12.54 Consider the following two equations estimated using the procedures developed in this section:

i. $y_i = 4x^{1.5}$

ii. $y_i = 1 + 2x_i + 2x_i^2$

Compute values of y_i when $x_i = 1, 2, 4, 6, 8, 10$.

12.55 Consider the following two equations estimated using the procedures developed in this section:

i. $y_i = 4x^{1.8}$

ii. $y_i = 1 + 2x_i + 2x_i^2$

Compute values of y_i when $x_i = 1, 2, 4, 6, 8, 10$.

12.56 Consider the following two equations estimated using the procedures developed in this section:

i. $y_i = 4x^{1.5}$

ii. $y_i = 1 + 2x_i + 1.7\, x_i^2$

Compute values of y_i when $x_i = 1, 2, 4, 6, 8, 10$.

12.57 Consider the following two equations estimated using the procedures developed in this section.

i. $y_i = 3x^{1.2}$

ii. $y_i = 1 + 5x_i - 1.5x_i^2$

Compute values of y_i when $x_i = 1, 2, 4, 6, 8, 10$.

Application Exercises

12.58 Describe an example from your experience in which a quadratic model would be better than a linear model.

12.59 John Swanson, president of Market Research Inc., has asked you to estimate the coefficients of the model

$$Y = \beta_0 + \beta_1 X_1 + \beta_2 X_1^2 + \beta_3 X_2$$

where Y is the expected sales of office supplies for a large retail distributor of office supplies, X_1 is the total disposable income of residents within 5 miles of the store, and X_2 is the total number of persons employed in information-based businesses within 5 miles of the store. Recent work by a national consulting firm has concluded that the coefficients in the model must have the following restriction:

$$\beta_1 + \beta_2 = 2$$

Describe how you would estimate the model coefficients using least squares.

12.60 In a study of the determinants of household expenditures on vacation travel, data were obtained from a sample of 2,246 households. (See Reference 2.) The model estimated was

$$\log y = -4.054 + 1.1556 \log x_1 - 0.4408 \log x_2$$
$$\quad\quad\quad\quad (0.0546) \quad\quad\quad (0.0490)$$

$$R^2 = .168$$

where

y = expenditure on vacation travel
x_1 = total annual consumption expenditure
x_2 = number of members in household

The numbers in parentheses under the coefficients are the estimated coefficient standard errors.

a. Interpret the estimated regression coefficients.
b. Interpret the coefficient of determination.
c. All else being equal, find a 95% confidence interval for the percentage increase in expenditures on vacation travel resulting from a 1% increase in total annual consumption expenditures.
d. Assuming that the model is correctly specified, test at the 1% significance level the null hypothesis that, all else being equal, the number of members in a household does not affect expenditures on vacation travel against the alternative that the greater the number of household members, the lower the vacation travel expenditures.

12.61 The following model was estimated for a sample of 322 supermarkets in large metropolitan areas (see Reference 3):
where

y = store size
x = median income in zip code area in which store is located

The number in parentheses under the coefficient is the estimated coefficient standard error.

a. Interpret the estimated coefficient on $\log x$.
b. Test the null hypothesis that income has no impact on store size against the alternative that higher income tends to be associated with larger store size.

12.62 An agricultural economist believes that the amount of beef consumed (y) in tons in a year in the United States depends on the price of beef (x_1) in dollars per pound, the price of pork (x_2) in dollars per pound, the price of chicken (x_3) in dollars per pound, and the income per household (x_4) in thousands of dollars. The following sample regression was obtained through least squares, using 30 annual observations:

$$\log y = -0.024 - 0.529 \log x_1 + 0.217 \log x_2 + 0.193 \log x_3$$
$$\quad\quad\quad\quad (0.168) \quad\quad\quad (0.103) \quad\quad\quad (0.106)$$

$$+ 0.416 \log x_4 \quad\quad R^2 = 0.683$$
$$(.163)$$

The numbers in parentheses under the coefficients are the estimated coefficient standard errors.

a. Interpret the coefficient on $\log x_1$.
b. Interpret the coefficient on $\log x_2$.
c. Test at the 1% significance level the null hypothesis that the coefficient on $\log x_4$ in the population regression is 0 against the alternative that it is positive.
d. Test the null hypothesis that the four variables ($\log x_1, \log x_2, \log x_3, \log x_4$) do not, as a set, have any linear influence on $\log y$.
e. The economist is also concerned that over the years the increasing awareness of the effects of heavy red meat consumption on health may have influenced the demand for beef. If this is indeed the case, how would this influence your view of the original estimated regression?

12.63 You have been asked to develop an exponential production function—Cobb-Douglas form—that will predict the number of microprocessors produced by a manufacturer, Y, as a function of the units of capital, X_1; the units of labor, X_2; and the number of computer science staff involved in basic research, X_3. Specify the model form and then carefully and completely indicate how you would estimate the coefficients. Do this first using an unrestricted model and then a second time including the restriction that the coefficients of the three variables should sum to 1.

12.64 Consider the following nonlinear model with multiplicative errors:

$$Y = \beta_0 X_1^{\beta_1} X_2^{\beta_2} X_3^{\beta_3} X_4^{\beta_4} \varepsilon$$
$$\beta_1 + \beta_2 = 1$$
$$\beta_3 + \beta_4 = 1$$

a. Show how you would obtain the coefficient estimates. Coefficient restrictions must be satisfied. Show all of your work and explain what you are doing.

b. What is the constant elasticity for Y versus X_4? Show all of your work.

The following exercises require the use of a computer.

12.65 ◑ Angelica Chandra, president of Benefits Research Inc., has asked you to study the salary structure of her firm. Benefits Research provides consulting and management for employee health care and retirement programs. Its clients are mid- to large-sized firms. As a first step you are asked to estimate a regression model that estimates expected salary as a function of years of experience in the firm. You are to consider linear, quadratic, and cubic models and determine which one would be most suitable. Estimate appropriate regression models and write a short report that recommends the best model. Use the data contained in the file **Benefits Research**.

12.66 ◑ The data file *German Imports* shows German real imports (y), real private consumption (x_1), and real exchange rate (x_2), in terms of U.S. dollars per mark, over a period of 31 years. Estimate the model

$$\log y_t = \beta_0 + \beta_1 \log x_{1t} + \beta_2 \log x_{2t} + \varepsilon_i$$

and write a report on your findings.

12.8 DUMMY VARIABLES FOR REGRESSION MODELS

In the discussion of multiple regression up to this point we have assumed that the independent variables, x_j, have existed over a range and contained many different values. However, in the multiple regression assumptions the only restriction on the independent variables is that they are fixed values. Thus, we could have an independent variable that took on only two values: $x_j = 0$ and $x_j = 1$. This structure is commonly defined as a *dummy variable*, and we will see that it provides a valuable tool for applying multiple regression to situations involving categorical variables. One important example is a linear function that shifts in response to some influence. Consider first a simple regression equation:

$$Y = \beta_0 + \beta_1 X_1$$

Now, suppose that we introduce a dummy variable, X_2, that has values 0 and 1 and that the resulting equation is as follows:

$$Y = \beta_0 + \beta_1 X_1 + \beta_2 X_2$$

When $X_2 = 0$ in this equation, the constant is β_0, but when $X_2 = 1$, the constant is $\beta_0 + \beta_2$. Thus, we see that the dummy variable shifts the linear relationship between Y and X_1 by the value of the coefficient β_2. In this way we can represent the effect of shifts in our regression equation. Dummy variables are also called *indicator variables*. We begin our discussion with an example of an important application.

Example 12.13 Wage Discrimination Analysis (Dummy Variable Model Estimation)

The president of Investors Ltd. wants to determine if there is any evidence of wage discrimination in the salaries of male and female financial analysts. Figure 12.19 presents an example of annual wages versus years of experience for the analysts. See the data file **Gender and Salary**.

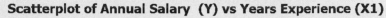

Figure 12.19 Example of Data Pattern Indicating Wage Discrimination

Scatterplot of Annual Salary (Y) vs Years Experience (X1)

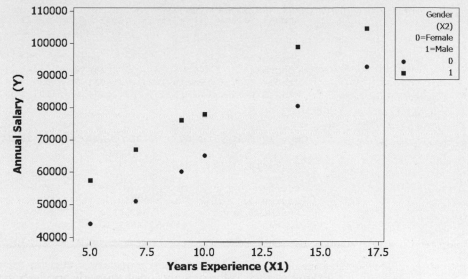

Solution Examining the data and the graph, we see two different subsets of salaries, and that salaries for males appears to be uniformly higher across the years of experience.

| 0 | Female Employees |
| 1 | Male Employees |

This problem can be analyzed by estimating a multiple regression model of salary, Y, versus years of experience, X_1, with a second variable, X_2, that is coded as follows:
The resulting multiple regression model

$$\hat{y} = b_0 + b_1 x_1 + b_2 x_2$$

can be estimated using the procedures we have learned, noting that the coefficient b_1 is an estimate of the expected annual increase in salary per year of experience and b_2 is the shift in mean salary from male to female employees. If b_2 is positive, we have an indication that male salaries are uniformly higher.

Figure 12.20 presents the multiple regression analysis from Minitab for this problem. From this analysis we see that the coefficient of x_2—gender—has a Student's t statistic equal to 14.88 and a p-value of 0, which leads us to reject the null hypothesis that the coefficient is equal to 0. This result indicates that male salaries are significantly higher. We also see that $b_1 = 4{,}076.5$, indicating that the expected value for the annual increase is $4,076.50, and that $b_2 = 14{,}683.7$, indicating that the male salaries are, on average, $14,683.70 higher. Analyses such as these have been used successfully in a number of wage discrimination lawsuits. As a result, most companies perform an analysis similar to this to determine if there is any evidence of salary discrimination.

Figure 12.20 Regression Analysis for Wage Discrimination Example
Regression Analysis: Annual Salary versus Gender (X2), Years Experience

```
The regression equation is
Annual Salary (Y) = 23608 + 14684 Gender (X2) 0=Female 1=Male
                         + 4076 Years Experience (X1)


Predictor                           Coef  SE Coef      T      P
Constant                           23608     1434  16.46  0.000
Gender (X2) 0=Female 1=Male      14683.7    987.0  14.88  0.000
Year Experience (X1)              4076.5    121.3  33.61  0.000



S = 1709.48     R-Sq = 99.3%    R-Sq(adj) = 99.2%

Analysis of Variance

Source            DF          SS          MS        F      P
Regression         2  3948240796  1974120398  675.53  0.000
Residual Error     9    26300913     2922324
Total             11  3974541710
```

Examples such as the previous one have wide application to a number of problems including the following:

1. The relationship between the number of units sold and the price is likely to shift if a new competitor moves into the market.
2. The relationship between aggregate consumption and aggregate disposable income may shift in time of war or other major national event.
3. The relationship between total output and number of workers may shift as the result of the introduction of new production technology.
4. The demand function for a product may shift because of a new advertising campaign or a news release relating to the product.

This discussion has introduced the concept of dummy variable regression as a procedure for extending our analysis capability. The procedure is summarized next.

Dummy Variable Regression Analysis

The relationship between Y and X_1

$$Y = \beta_0 + \beta_1 X_1 + \varepsilon$$

can shift in response to a changed condition. The shift effect can be estimated by using a dummy variable that has values of 0 (condition not present) and 1 (condition present). As shown in Figure 12.19, all of the observations from the upper set of data points have dummy variable $x_2 = 1$, and the observations for the lower points have $x_2 = 0$. In these cases the relationship between Y and X_1 is specified by the multiple regression model:

$$\hat{y}_i = b_0 + b_2 x_{2i} + b_1 x_{1i} \tag{12.33}$$

The coefficient b_2 represents the shift of the function between the upper and lower sets of points in Figure 12.19. The functions for each set of points are

$$\hat{y} = b_0 + b x_1 \qquad \text{when } x_2 = 0$$

and

$$\hat{y} = (b_0 + b_2 x_2) + b_1 x_1 \qquad \text{when } x_2 - 1$$

In the first function the constant is b_0, while in the second the constant is $b_0 + b_2$. In Chapter 13 we will show how dummy variables can be used to analyze problems with more than two discrete categories.

This simple specification of the regression model is a very powerful tool for problems that involve a shift of the linear function by identifiable discrete factors. In addition, the multiple regression structure provides a direct procedure for performing a hypothesis test, as we did in Example 12.13. The hypothesis test is as follows:

$$H_0 : \beta_2 = 0 \mid \beta_1 \neq 0$$
$$H_1 : \beta_2 \neq 0 \mid \beta_1 \neq 0$$

Rejection of the null hypothesis, H_0, leads to the conclusion that the constant is different between the two subsets of data. In Example 12.13 we saw that this difference in the constant led to the conclusion that there was a significant difference in wages between the male and female subgroups after the effect of years of experience has been removed.

Differences in Slope

We can also use dummy variables to model and test for differences in the slope coefficient by adding an interaction variable. Figure 12.21 presents a typical example. To test for both differences in the constant and differences in the slope, we use a more complex regression model.

Dummy Variable Regression for Differences in Slope

To determine if there are significant differences in slopes between two discrete conditions, we need to expand our regression model to a more complex form:

$$Y = \beta_0 + \beta_2 X_2 + (\beta_1 + \beta_3 X_2) X_1 \tag{12.34}$$

Now, we see that the slope coefficient of X_1 contains two components, β_1 and $\beta_3 X_2$. When X_2 equals 0, the slope is the usual β_1. However, when X_2 equals 1, the slope is equal to the algebraic sum of $\beta_1 + \beta_3$. To estimate the model, we actually need to create a new set of transformed variables that are linear. Therefore, the model actually used for estimation is as follows:

$$\hat{y} = b_0 + b_2 x_{2i} + b_1 x_{1i} + b_3 x_{2i} x_{1i} \tag{12.35}$$

The resulting regression model is now linear with three variables. The new variable, $x_1 x_2$, is often called an *interaction variable*. Note that when the dummy variable $x_2 = 0$, this variable has a value of 0, but when $x_2 = 1$, this variable has the value of x_1. The coefficient b_3 is an estimate of the difference in the coefficient of x_1 when $x_2 = 1$ compared to $x_2 = 0$. Thus, the Student's t statistic for b_3 can be used to test the following hypotheses:

$$H_0 : \beta_3 = 0 \mid \beta_1 \neq 0, \beta_2 \neq 0$$
$$H_1 : \beta_3 \neq 0 \mid \beta_1 \neq 0, \beta_2 \neq 0$$

If we reject the null hypothesis, we conclude that there is a difference in the slope coefficient for the two subgroups. In many cases we will be interested in both the difference in the constant and the difference in the slope and will test both of the hypotheses presented in this section.

Example 12.14 Salary Model for Systems Inc. (Dummy Variable Model Estimation)

The president of Systems Inc. is interested in knowing if the annual salary increases for the female engineers in the company have maintained the same level as those for the male engineers. There have been some complaints from both male and female engineers that the salaries for female engineers have not increased at the same rate as those for male engineers.

Figure 12.21 Regression Analysis for Annual Salary versus Experience and Gender

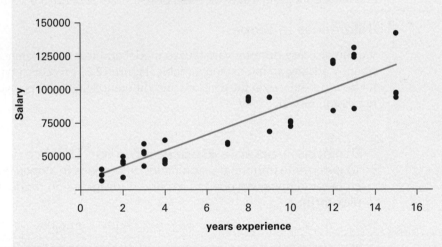

Regression Analysis: Salary versus years experi, Gender, gender-exper

```
The regression equation is
Salary = 36990 + 4216 years experience + 4806 Gender + 2487 gender-experience

Predictor             Coef    SE Coef       T       P
Constant           36989.6      827.2   44.72   0.000
years experience   4215.79       92.15  45.75   0.000
Gender                4806       1188    4.04   0.000
gender-experience   2487.1       133.3  18.66   0.000


S = 1964.98   R-Sq = 99.6%   R-Sq(adj) = 99.6%


Analysis of Variance

Source         DF          SS           MS       F       P
Regression      3  32062830877  10687610292  2768.00  0.000
Residual Error 34    131278408      3861130
Total          37  32194109284
```

Solution The scatter plot and regression analysis output are shown in Figure 12.21. The scatter plot suggests that the slope is higher for the upper subgroup, representing male engineers. A multiple regression analysis was run to estimate the effect of experience and gender on annual salary. This multiple regression analysis can be used to test the hypothesis that the rates of increase are the same for both subgroups of engineers. From this analysis we see that the "gender-experience" variable, which is an estimate of the difference between male and female annual salary increases, has a coefficient of 2,487, a Student's t statistic of 18.66, and a p-value of 0. Thus we estimate that the annual salary increases for males are \$2,487 larger than the increases for females. We reject the null hypothesis that, as their experience increases, the salaries of both male and female engineers have increased at the same rate. In addition we see that the "gender" variable has a coefficient of 4,806 with a Student's t statistic of 4.04 indicating that on average male salaries are \$4,806 higher. Thus, it will be important to take steps to deal with the salary discrimination that is evident in the data. The data are stored in the file **Gender and Salary Increase**.

EXERCISES

Basic Exercises

12.67 What is the model constant when the dummy variable equals 1 in the following equations, where x_1 is a continuous variable and x_2 is a dummy variable with a value of 0 or 1.

a. $\hat{y} = 4 + 8x_1 + 3x_2$
b. $\hat{y} = 7 + 6x_1 + 5x_2$
c. $\hat{y} = 4 + 8x_1 + 3x_2 + 4x_1x_2$

12.68 What are the model constant and the slope coefficient of x_1 when the dummy variable equals 1 in the following equations, where x_1 is a continuous variable and x_2 is a dummy variable with a value of 0 or 1.

a. $\hat{y} = 4 + 9x_1 + 1.78x_2 + 3.09x_1x_2$
b. $\hat{y} = -3 + 7x_1 + 4.15x_2 + 2.51x_1x_2$
c. $\hat{y} = 10 + 5x_1 + 3.67x_2 + 3.98x_1x_2$

Application Exercises

12.69 The following model was fitted to observations from 1972 to 1979 in an attempt to explain pricing behavior:

$$\hat{y} = 37x_1 + 5.22x_2$$
$$\quad\; (0.029) \quad (0.50)$$

where

$\hat{y}$ = difference between price in the current year and price in the previous year in dollars per barrel

x_1 = difference between spot price in the current year and spot price in the previous year

x_2 = dummy variable taking the value 1 in 1974 and 0 otherwise to represent the specific effect of the oil embargo of that year

The numbers in parentheses under the coefficients are the estimated coefficient standard errors.

Interpret verbally and graphically the estimated coefficient on the dummy variable.

12.70 The following model was fitted to explain the selling prices of condominiums in a sample of 815 sales:

$$\hat{y} = -1264 + 48.18x_1 + 3382x_2 - 1859x_3 + 3219x_4 + 2005x_5$$
$$\qquad\qquad (0.91) \qquad (515) \qquad (488) \qquad (947) \qquad (768)$$

$\overline{R}^2 = 0.86$

where

$\hat{y}$ = selling price of condo in dollars
x_1 = square footage of living area
x_2 = size of garage in number of cars
x_3 = age of condo in years
x_4 = dummy variable taking the value 1 if the condo has a fireplace and 0 otherwise
x_5 = dummy variable taking the value 1 if the condo has hardwood floors and 0 if it has vinyl floors

a. Interpret the estimated coefficient of x_4.
b. Interpret the estimated coefficient of x_5.
c. Find a 95% confidence interval for the impact of a fireplace on selling price, all other things being equal.
d. Test the null hypothesis that type of flooring has no impact on selling price against the alternative that, all other things equal, condos with hardwood floors have a higher selling price than those with vinyl flooring.

12.71 The following model was fitted to data on 32 insurance companies:

$$\hat{y} = 7.62 - 0.16x_1 + 1.23x_2 \qquad R^2 = 0.37$$
$$\qquad\quad (0.008) \quad\; (0.496)$$

where

$\hat{y}$ = price-earnings ratio
x_1 = size of insurance company assets, in billions of dollars
x_2 = dummy variable taking the value 1 for regional companies and 0 for national companies

The numbers in parentheses under the coefficients are the estimated coefficient standard errors.

a. Interpret the estimated coefficient on the dummy variable.
b. Test against a two-sided alternative the null hypothesis that the true coefficient on the dummy variable is 0.
c. Test at the 5% level the null hypothesis $\beta_1 = \beta_2 = 0$, and interpret your result.

12.72 A business school dean wanted to assess the importance of factors that might help in predicting success in law school. For a random sample of 50 students, data were obtained when students graduated from law school, and the following model was fitted:

$$y_i = \alpha + \beta_1 x_{1i} + \beta_2 x_{2i} + \beta_3 x_{3i} + \varepsilon_i$$

where

y_i = score reflecting overall performance while in law school
x_{1i} = undergraduate grade point average
x_{2i} = score on GMAT
x_{3i} = dummy variable taking the value 1 if a student's letters of recommendation are unusually strong and 0 otherwise

Use the portion of the computer output from the estimated regression shown here to write a report summarizing the findings of this study.

Source	DF	Sum of Squares	Mean Square	F Value	R-Square
Model	3	641.04	212.68	8.48	0.356
Error	46	1,159.66	25.21		
Total	49	1,800.70			

Parameter	Estimate	t for H$_0$: $\beta_j = 0$	Std. Error of Estimate
Intercept	6.512		
X1	3.502	1.45	2.419
X2	0.491	4.59	0.107
X3	10.327	2.45	4.213

12.73 The following model was fitted to data on 50 states:

$$\hat{y} = 13{,}472 + 547x_1 + 5.48x_2 + 493x_3 + 32.7x_4 + 5{,}793x_5$$
$$\qquad\quad (124.3) \quad (1.858) \quad\; (208.9) \quad\; (234) \quad\; (2{,}897)$$
$$- 3{,}100x_6 \qquad R^2 = .54$$
$$\;\;(1{,}761)$$

where

$\hat{y}$ = annual salary of the attorney general of the state
x_1 = average annual salary of lawyers in thousands of dollars
x_2 = number of bills enacted in previous legislative session
x_3 = number of due process reviews by state courts that resulted in overturn of legislation in previous 40 years
x_4 = length of term of the attorney general of the state
x_5 = dummy variable taking value 1 if justices of the state supreme court can be removed from office by the governor, judicial review board, or majority vote of the supreme court and 0 otherwise
x_6 = dummy variable taking value 1 if supreme court justices are elected on partisan ballots and 0 otherwise

The numbers in parentheses under the coefficients are the estimated coefficient standard errors.

a. Interpret the estimated coefficient on the dummy variable x_5.
b. Interpret the estimated coefficient on the dummy variable x_6.
c. Test at the 5% level the null hypothesis that the true coefficient on the dummy variable x_5 is 0 against the alternative that it is positive.
d. Test at the 5% level the null hypothesis that the true coefficient on the dummy variable x_6 is 0 against the alternative that it is negative.
e. Find and interpret a 95% confidence level for the parameter β_1.

12.74 A consulting group offers courses in financial management for executives. At the end of these courses participants are asked to provide overall ratings of the value of the course. For a sample of 25 courses the following regression was estimated by least squares:

$$\hat{y} = 42.97 + 0.38x_1 + 0.52x_2 - 0.08x_3 + 6.21x_4 \qquad R^2 = 0.569$$
$$\qquad\quad (0.29) \quad\; (0.21) \quad\; (0.11) \quad\; (0.359)$$

where

$\hat{y}$ = average rating by participants of the course
x_1 = percentage of course time spent in group discussion sessions
x_2 = money, in dollars, per course member spent on preparing course material

x_3 = money, in dollars, per course member spent on food and drinks

x_4 = dummy variable taking the value 1 if a visiting guest lecturer is brought in and 0 otherwise

The numbers in parentheses under the coefficients are the estimated coefficient standard errors.

a. Interpret the estimated coefficient on x_4.

b. Test against the alternative that it is positive the null hypothesis that the true coefficient on x_4 is 0.

c. Interpret the coefficient of determination, and use it to test the null hypothesis that, taken as a group, the four independent variables do not linearly influence the dependent variable.

d. Find and interpret a 95% confidence interval for β_2.

12.75   A regression model was estimated to compare performance of students taking a business statistics course—either as a standard 14-week course or as an intensive 3-week course. The following model was estimated from observations of 350 students (see Reference 5):

$$\hat{y} = -.7052 + 1.4170x_1 + 2.1624x_2 + .8680x_3 + 1.0845x_4$$
$$\quad\quad (0.4568) \quad\ (0.3287) \quad\ (.4393) \quad\ (0.3766)$$

$$+ 0.4694x_5 + 0.0038x_6 + 0.0484x_7 \quad R^2 = 0.344$$
$$\quad (0.0628) \quad\quad (0.0094) \quad\quad (0.0776)$$

where

$\hat{y}$ = score on a standardized test of understanding of statistics after taking the course

x_1 = dummy variable taking the value 1 if the 3-week course was taken and 0 if the 14-week course was taken

x_2 = student's grade point average

x_3 = dummy variable taking the value 0 or 1, depending on which of two teachers had taught the course

x_4 = dummy variable taking the value 1 if the student is male and 0 if female

x_5 = score on a standardized test of understanding of mathematics before taking the course

x_6 = number of semester credit hours the student had completed

x_7 = age of student

The numbers in parentheses under the coefficients are the estimated coefficient standard errors.

Write a report discussing what can be learned from this fitted regression.

The following exercises will require a computer.

12.76   In a survey of 27 undergraduates at the University of Illinois the accompanying results were obtained with grade point averages (y), the number of hours per week spent studying (x_1), the average number of hours spent preparing for tests (x_2), the number of hours per week spent in bars (x_3), whether students take notes or mark highlights when reading texts (x_4 = 1 if yes, 0 if no), and the average number of credit hours taken per semester (x_5). Estimate the regression of grade point average on the five independent variables, and write a report on your findings. The data are in the data file **Student Performance** located on your data disk.

12.77   You have been asked to develop a model to analyze salary in a large business organization. The data for this model are stored in a file named **Salorg**.

a. Using the data in the file, develop a regression model that predicts salary as a function of the variables you select. Compute the conditional F and conditional t statistics for the coefficient of each predictor variable included in the model. Show all work and carefully explain your analysis process.

b. Test the hypothesis that female employees have a lower annual salary conditional on the variables in your model. The variable "Gender_1F" is coded 1 for female employees and 0 for male employees.

c. Test the hypothesis that the female employees have had a lower rate of salary increase conditional on the variables in the model developed for part (b).

12.9 MULTIPLE REGRESSION ANALYSIS APPLICATION PROCEDURE

In this section we present an extended case study that indicates how a statistical study would be conducted. Careful study of this example can provide guidance in using many of the analysis procedures developed in this chapter and previous chapters.

The objective in this study is to produce a multiple regression model to predict sales of cotton fabric. Data for the project are obtained from the data file **Cotton**, which is included on the data disk for this textbook. The variables in the data file are as follows:

QUARTER	QUARTER OF YEAR
year	Year of observation
cottonq	Quantity of cotton fabric produced
whoprice	Wholesale price index
impfab	Quantity of imported fabric
expfab	Quantity of exported fabric

Model Specification

The first step in model development is the selection of an appropriate economic theory that provides a rationale for the model analysis. This process of identifying a set of likely predictor variables and the mathematical form of the model is known as *model specification*. In this case the appropriate theory is based on that of economic demand models. Economic theory indicates that price should have an important effect—increased price reduces the quantity demanded. In addition, there are likely to be other variables that influence the quantity of cotton demanded. We would anticipate that the quantity of cotton fabric imported is likely to reduce the demand for domestic fabric and that the quantity of cotton fabric exported is likely to increase the demand for domestic fabric. In economic language, imports and exports of fabric shift the demand function. Based on this analysis, our original specification includes price with a negative coefficient, exported fabric with a positive coefficient, and imported fabric with a negative coefficient. All coefficients are initially specified as having linear effects. Thus, the model has the form

$$y_i = \beta_0 + \beta_1 x_{1i} + \beta_2 x_{2i} + \beta_3 x_{3i} + \varepsilon_i$$

where x_1 is the wholesale price, x_2 is the quantity of imported fabric, and x_3 is the quantity of exported fabric.

There is also the possibility that the quantity demanded varies over time, and, thus, the model should include the possibility of a time variable to reduce unexplained variability. For this analysis we wish to use a variable that represents time. Because time is indicated by a combination of year and quarter, we used the transformation

$$\text{Time} = \text{Year} + 0.25 * \text{Quarter}$$

to produce a new variable for time that is continuously increasing with each quarter.

The next step in the analysis is to prepare a statistical description of the variables and their relationships. We exclude year and quarter from this analysis because they have been replaced by time and their inclusion would only add confusion to the analysis. We use Minitab to produce measures of central tendency and dispersion and also to obtain some understanding of the pattern of the observations. Figure 12.22 contains the output produced using Minitab. Examination of the mean, the standard deviation, and the minimum and maximum indicates the potential application region for the model. The estimated regression model always passes through the mean of the model variables. Predicted values of the dependent variable, cottonq, are usable over the range of the independent variables.

The next step is to examine the simple relationships between the variables, using both the correlation matrix and the matrix plots option. These should be examined together to determine the strength of the linear relationships (correlations) and to determine the form of the relationships (matrix plot).

Figure 12.22
Minitab Output for
Descriptive
Statistics for
Cotton Market
Variables

Results for: Cotton.MtW
Descriptive Statistics: conttonq. whoprice, impfab, expfab, time

Variable	N	N*	Mean	SE Mean	StDev	Minimum	Q1	Median	Q3
cottonq	28	0	1779.8	54.9	290.5	1277.0	1535.3	1762.5	2035.0
whoprice	28	0	106.81	1.16	6.11	98.00	100.45	107.40	112.20
impfab	28	0	7.52	1.38	7.33	1.30	2.78	4.85	9.05
expfab	28	0	274.0	20.3	107.7	80.0	190.5	277.1	358.1
time	28	0	69.625	0.389	2.056	66.250	67.813	69.625	71.438

Variable	Maximum
cottonq	2287.0
whoprice	115.80
impfab	27.00
expfab	477.0
time	73.000

Figure 12.23 contains the correlation matrix for the variables in the study prepared using Minitab. The *p*-value shown with each correlation indicates the probability that the hypothesis of 0 correlation between the two variables is true. Using our screening rule based on hypothesis testing, we can conclude that a *p*-value less than 0.05 provides evidence for a strong linear relationship between the two variables. Examining the first column, we see that there are strong linear relationships between cottonq and both whoprice and time. The variable expfab has a possible marginally significant simple relationship. A good rule to remember, as shown in Section 11.7, for examining correlation coefficients is that the absolute value of the correlation should be greater than 2 divided by the square root of the sample size, *n*. For this problem the screening value is $2 / \sqrt{28} = 0.38$.

The second task is to determine if there are strong simple relationships between the pairs of possible predictor variables. We see a very high correlation between time and whoprice and significant relationships between impfab and both time and whoprice. These high correlations will lead to a high variance for the coefficient estimators for both time and whoprice if they are both included as predictor variables.

We can also examine the relationships between variables by using matrix plots shown in Figure 12.24. The individual scatter plots show the relationships between a number of different variables simultaneously. Thus, they provide a display format that is similar to a correlation matrix. The advantage of the scatter plot is that it includes all of the data points. Thus, one can also see if there is a simple nonlinear

Figure 12.23
Minitab Output:
Correlations for
Cotton Variables

Correlations: cottonq, whoprice, impfab, expfab, time

	cottonq	whoprice	impfab	expfab
whoprice	-0.950			
	0.000			
impfab	0.291	-0.439		
	0.133	0.019		
expfab	0.370	-0.285	0.181	
	0.052	0.142	0.357	
time	-0.950	0.992	-0.392	-0.238
	0.000	0.000	0.039	0.222

Cell Contents: Pearson correlation
                P-Value

Figure 12.24
Matrix Plots for
Variables in the
Study (Minitab
Output)

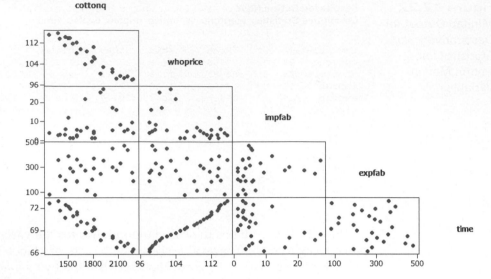

relationship between variables and/or if there is some strange grouping of observations. All variables except year and quarter are included in the same order as in the correlation matrix so that there is a direct comparison between the correlation matrix and the matrix plots.

Note the correspondence between the correlations and the scatter plots. Both whoprice and time have strong negative linear relationships with cottonq. However, the strong positive linear relationship between whoprice and time will have a major influence on the estimated coefficients, as shown in Section 12.2, and on the coefficient standard errors, as shown in Section 12.4. There are no other strong simple relationships between the potential predictor variables. Neither imports nor exports are correlated with wholesale price, time, or each other.

Multiple Regression

The next step is to estimate the first multiple regression model. The economic theory for this analysis suggests that the quantity of cotton fabric produced should be inversely related to price and to the amount of fabric imported and directly related to the amount of fabric exported. In addition, the strong correlation between time and cotton fabric production indicates that production declined linearly over time, but that wholesale price also increased linearly over time. The resulting very high positive correlation between time and wholesale price influences both coefficients in a multiple regression equation. We select cottonq as the dependent variable and whoprice, impfab, expfab, and time, in that order, as the independent variables. The first multiple regression analysis is shown in Figure 12.25.

Analysis of the regression statistics indicates a high R^2, and the standard error of the estimate (S) equals 78.91 compared to the standard deviation of 290.5 (Figure 12.22) for cottonq by itself. The variables impfab and expfab are both conditionally significant with signs corresponding to economic theory. The small Student's t statistics for whoprice and time indicate that, in fact, there is a serious problem. Both variables cannot be included as predictors because they both represent the same effect.

INTERPRETATION

The rules for dropping variables are based on a combination of both theories for the model and statistical indicators. The statistical rule would be to drop the variable with the smallest absolute Student's t, that is, time. Economic theory would argue for

Figure 12.25
Initial Multiple
Regression Model
(Minitab Output)

Regression Analysis: cottonq versus whoprice, impfab, expfab, time

The regression equation is
cottonq =8876 - 24.3 whoprice - 5.57 impfab + 0.376 expfab - 65.5 time

Predictor	Coef	SE Coef	T	P
Constant	8876	2295	3.87	0.001
whoprice	-24.31	24.45	-0.99	0.331
impfab	-5.565	2.527	-2.20	0.038
expfab	0.3758	0.1595	2.36	0.027
time	-65.51	70.24	-0.93	0.361

S = 78.9141   R-Sq = 93.7%   R-Sq(adj) = 92.6%

Analysis of Variance

Source	DF	SS	MS	F	P
Regression	4	2134572	533643	85.69	0.000
Residual Error	23	143231	6227		
Total	27	2277803			

Source	DF	Seq SS
whoprice	1	2055110
impfab	1	44905
expfab	1	29141
time	1	5417

Note
This table indicates the conditional explained variability for each variable, given the order of entry used for this regression analysis.

Unusual Observations

Obs	Whoprice	Cottonq	Fit	SE Fit	Residual	St Resid
18	110	1810.0	1663.3	29.6	146.7	2.00R

R denotes an observation with a large standardized residual.

including a price variable in a model to predict quantity produced or quantity demanded. We see that in this case both rules lead to the same conclusion. This is not always the case, and, thus, good judgment and clear thinking about model objectives are very important.

It is important that one clearly state the rationale for variable selection before examining the statistical output. In economic demand or supply models such as the one considered here, we would have a very strong desire to follow economic theory and include price unless the statistical results were very strong against that prior judgment. For example, if the absolute value of the Student's t for time was above 2.5 or 3 and the absolute value of the Student's t for wholesale price was less than 1, there would be strong evidence against the theory that price is an important variable.

Based on this analysis, a second regression model is estimated, as shown in Figure 12.26, with time excluded as a predictor variable. We see now that whoprice is highly significant and that the s and R^2 statistics are essentially the same as those in the first regression analysis (Figure 12.25). Note also that the explained regression sum of squares (SSR) and the residual error sum of squares (SSE) are essentially the same. The standard deviation for the whoprice coefficient has dropped from 24.45 to 2.835, and as a result, the Student's t is substantially larger. As we learned in Section 12.4, high correlations between independent variables result in much larger variances for the coefficient estimator. We see that effect here. Note also that for this regression model the wholesale price coefficient estimate changed from -24.31 to -46.956. In Section 12.2 we saw that correlations between predictor variables have a complex effect on coefficient

Figure 12.26
Final Regression
Analysis Model
(Minitab Output)

Regression Analysis: cottonq versus whoprice, impfab, expfab, time

```
The regression equation is
cottonq = 6757 - 47.0 whoprice - 6.52 impfab + 0.319 expfab


Predictor    Coef   SE Coef       T      P
Constant   6757.0     322.2   20.97  0.000
whoprice  -46.956     2.835  -16.56  0.000
impfab     -6.517     2.306   -2.83  0.009
expfab      0.3190   0.1471    2.17  0.040


S = 78.6998   R-Sq = 93.5%  R-Sq(adj) = 92.7%


Analysis of Variance


Source             DF        SS       MS       F      P
Regression          3   2129156   709719  114.59  0.000
Residual Error     24    148648     6194
Total              27   2277803


Source     DF    Seq SS
whoprice    1   2055110
impfab      1     44905
expfab      1     29141
```

> **Note**
> These sequential conditional explained sums of squares are the same as those for the regression in Figure 13.26, which included time as a predictor variable.

```
Unusual Observations

Obs  Whoprice  Cottonq     Fit  SE Fit  Residual  St Resid
18        110   1810.0  1642.0    18.7     168.0      2.20R

R denotes an observation with a large standardized residual.
```

estimates, so there will not always be a difference that is this large. However, correlations between independent variables always increase the coefficient standard error. The standard errors for the other two coefficients have not changed substantially because the correlations with time were not large.

Minitab also provides a list of observations with extreme residuals. We see in observation 18 that the observed value of cottonq is substantially above the value predicted by the equation. In this case we might decide to go back to the original data and try to determine if there was an error in the reported data. Such an investigation might also provide some important insights into the process being studied using multiple regression.

Effect of Dropping a Statistically Significant Variable

In this section we will consider the effect of removing a conditionally significant variable from the regression model. We saw in Figure 12.26 that expfab is a statistically significant predictor of the quantity of cotton produced. However, the regression analysis in Figure 12.27 has expfab removed from the regression model in Figure 12.26.

INTERPRETATION

Note that, as a result of removing expfab, the standard error of the estimate has increased from 78.70 to 84.33 and R^2 has decreased from 93.5% to 92.2%. These results indicate that the model error term is now larger and, thus, the quality of the model has been reduced.

The conditional F statistic for expfab can be computed using the analysis of variance tables from the models in Figures 12.26 and 12.27. In the following equation we

Figure 12.27
Minitab Output:
Regression
Analysis with
Exported Fabric
Eliminated

Regression Analysis: cottonq versus whoprice, impfab, expfab, time

```
The regression equation is
cottonq = 6995 - 48.4 whoprice - 6.20 impfab


Predictor    Coef  SE Coef      T      P
Constant   6994.8    324.6  21.55  0.000
whoprice  -48.388    2.955 -16.38  0.000
impfab     -6.195    2.465  -2.51  0.019


S = 84.3299   R-Sq = 92.2%  R-Sq(adj) = 91.6%

Analysis of Variance

Source          DF       SS      MS       F      P
Regression       2  2100015 1050007  147.65  0.000
Residual Error  25   177788    7112
Total           27  2277803
```

define the final regression from Figure 12.26 as model 1 and the regression from Figure 12.27, with expfab removed, as model 2. Using these conventions, the conditional F statistic for the variable expfab, X_3, under the null hypothesis that its coefficient is 0, can be computed as follows:

$$F_{x_3} = \frac{SSR_1 - SSR_2}{s_e^2} = \frac{(2,129,156 - 2,100,015)}{6,194} = 4.705$$

We can also compute the conditional Student's t statistic for variable x_3 by taking the square root of the conditional F_{x_3}

$$t_{x_3} = \sqrt{4.705} = 2.169$$

and, of course, we see that this is the same as the Student's t statistic for the expfab (x_3) variable in Figure 12.26. The conditional F test for a single independent variable is always exactly the same as the conditional F because an F with 1 degree of freedom for the numerator is exactly equal to t^2.

Analysis of Residuals

After fitting the regression model, it is valuable to examine the residuals to determine how the model actually fits the data and the regression assumptions. In Section 11.9 we discussed the analysis of outliers and extreme points in simple regression. Those ideas carry over directly to multiple regression and should be part of your analysis of residuals. Recall that the residuals are computed as follows:

$$e_i = y_i - \hat{y}_i$$

A variable that contains the residuals for a particular regression analysis can be computed in Minitab or any other good statistical package. This has been done for the final regression model in Figure 12.26. The first step is to examine the pattern of the residuals by constructing a histogram, as shown in Figure 12.28. We see that the distribution of the residuals is approximately symmetric. The distribution also appears to be somewhat uniform. Note that this results in part from the small sample size used to construct the histogram.

Preparing a normal probability plot, as shown in Figure 12.29, is useful in determining the pattern of the residuals. The plot indicates an approximate linear relationship, and, thus, it is not possible to reject the assumption of normally distributed residuals.

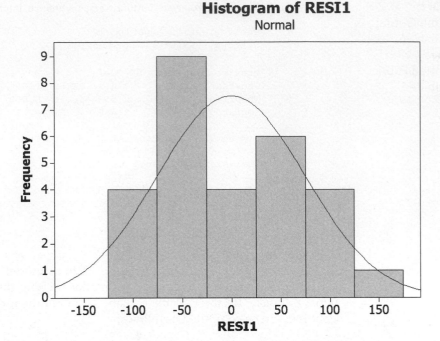

Figure 12.28
Histogram for Residuals from Final Regression Model

Histogram of RESI1
Normal

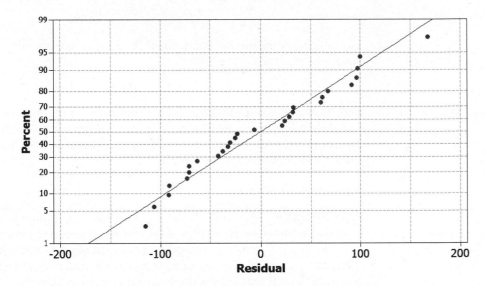

Figure 12.29
Normal Probability Plot for Model Residuals

It is also a good practice to plot the residuals against each of the independent variables included in the analysis. This provides a check that there were not a few unusual data points or a complex conditional nonlinear relationship for one of the independent variables. If the model has been correctly specified and estimated, we expect that there is no pattern of relationship between the independent variables and the residuals. Figure 12.30 presents the plot of residuals versus the wholesale price variable. We do not see any unusual patterns in this plot except the large positive outlier when the wholesale price is approximately 110.

In Figure 12.31 we show the plot of residuals versus imported fabric. Again, we do not see any unusual residual patterns, but we do observe that most of the imports are concentrated between 0 and 10. Thus, the larger values of imported fabric could be

Figure 12.30
Scatterplot of
Residuals versus
Wholesale Price

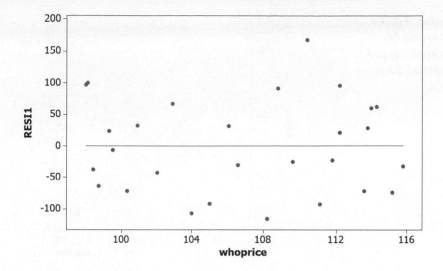

Figure 12.31
Scatterplot of
Residuals versus
Imported Fabric

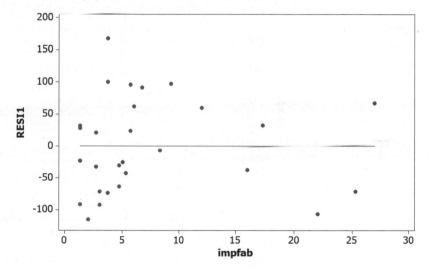

having a large effect on the regression slope coefficient. Finally, in Figure 12.32 we see a plot of residuals versus exported fabric. Again, the pattern of residuals does not suggest an alternative to the linear relationship.

The final residuals analysis examines the relationship between the residuals and the dependent variable. We consider a plot of the residuals versus the observed value of the dependent variable in Figure 12.33 and versus the predicted value of the dependent variable in Figure 12.34. We can see in Figure 12.33 that there is a positive relationship between the residuals and the observed value of cottonq. There are more negative residuals at low values of cottonq and more positive residuals at high values of cottonq. It is possible to show mathematically that there is always a positive correlation between the residuals and the observed values of the dependent variable. Therefore, a plot of the residuals versus the observed value does not provide any useful information. However, one should always plot the residuals versus the predicted or fitted values of the dependent variable. This provides a way to determine if the model errors are stable over the range of predicted values. In this example note that there is not a relationship between the residuals and the predicted values. Thus, the model errors are stable over the range.

Figure 12.32
Scatterplot of
Residuals versus
Exported Fabric

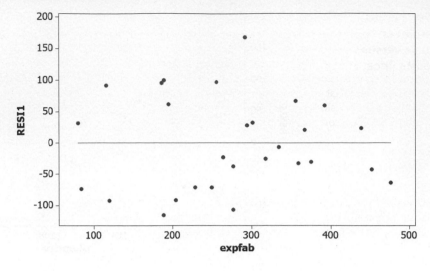

Figure 12.33
Scatterplot of
Residuals versus
Observed Value of
Cotton

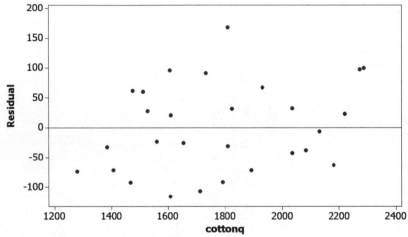

Figure 12.34
Scatterplot of
Residuals versus
Predicted Value of
Cotton

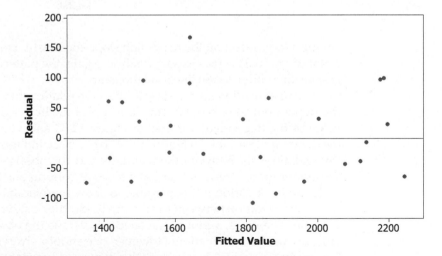

In Chapter 13 we will use residuals analysis to identify two regression model situations, heteroscedasticity and autocorrelation, that violate the regression assumption that the error variance is the same over the range of the model.

EXERCISES

Basic Exercises

12.78 Suppose that two independent variables are included as predictor variables in a multiple regression analysis. What can you expect will be the effect on the estimated slope coefficients when these two variables have a correlation equal to

a. 0.78?
b. 0.08?
c. 0.94?
d. 0.33?

12.79 Consider a regression analysis with $n = 34$ and four potential independent variables. Suppose that one of the independent variables has a correlation of 0.23 with the dependent variable. Does this imply that this independent variable will have a very small Student's t statistic in the regression analysis with all four predictor variables?

12.80 Consider a regression analysis with $n = 47$ and three potential independent variables. Suppose that one of the independent variables has a correlation of 0.95 with the dependent variable. Does this imply that this independent variable will have a very large Student's t statistic in the regression analysis with all three predictor variables?

12.81 Consider a regression analysis with $n = 49$ and two potential independent variables. Suppose that one of the independent variables has a correlation of 0.56 with the dependent variable. Does this imply that this independent variable will have a very small Student's t statistic in the regression analysis with both predictor variables?

Application Exercises

12.82 In order to assess the effect in one state of a casualty insurance company's economic power on its political power, the following model was hypothesized and fitted to data from all 50 states:

$$Y = \beta_0 + \beta_1 X_1 + \beta_2 X_2 + \beta_3 X_3 + \beta_4 x_4 + \beta_5 X_5 + \varepsilon$$

where

Y = ratio of company's payments for state and local taxes, in thousands of dollars, to total state and local tax revenues in millions of dollars

X_1 = insurance company state concentration ratio (a measure of the concentration of banking resources)

X_2 = per capita income in the state in thousands of dollars

X_3 = ratio of nonfarm income to the sum of farm and nonfarm income

X_4 = ratio of insurance company's net after-tax income to insurance reserves (multiplied by 1,000)

X_5 = average of insurance reserves (divided by 10,000)

Part of the computer output from the estimated regression is shown here. Write a report summarizing the findings of this study.

$$R\text{-Square} = 0.515$$

Parameter	Estimate	Student's t for H_0: Parameter $= 0$	Std. Error of Estimate
Intercept	10.60	2.41	4.40
X1	−0.90	−0.69	1.31
X2	0.14	0.50	0.28
X3	−12.85	−2.83	4.18
X4	0.080	0.50	0.160
X5	0.100	5.00	0.020

12.83 A random sample of 93 freshmen at the University of Illinois was asked to rate on a scale from 1 (low) to 10 (high) their overall opinion of residence hall life. They were also asked to rate their levels of satisfaction with roommates, with the floor, with the hall, and with the resident advisor. (Information on satisfaction with the room itself was obtained, but this was later discarded as it provided no useful additional power in explaining overall opinion.) The following model was estimated:

$$Y = \beta_0 + \beta_1 X_1 + \beta_2 X_2 + \beta_3 X_3 + \beta_4 X_4 + \varepsilon$$

where

Y = overall opinion of residence hall
X_1 = satisfaction with roommates
X_2 = satisfaction with floor
X_3 = satisfaction with hall
X_4 = satisfaction with resident advisor

Use the accompanying portion of the computer output from the estimated regression to write a report summarizing the findings of this study.

Dependent Variable: Y Overall Opinion

Source	DF	Sum of Squares	Mean Square	F Value	R-Square
Model	4	37.016	9.2540	9.958	0.312
Error	88	81.780	0.9293		
Total	92	118.79			

Parameter	Estimate	Student's t for H$_0$: Parameter = 0	Std. Error of Estimate
Intercept	3.950	5.84	0.676
X$_1$	0.106	1.69	0.063
X$_2$	0.122	1.70	0.072
X$_3$	0.092	1.75	0.053
X$_4$	0.169	2.64	0.064

12.84 The following model was fitted to 47 monthly observations in an attempt to explain the difference between certificate of deposit rates and commercial paper rates:

$$Y = \beta_0 + \beta_1 X_1 + \beta_2 X_2 + \varepsilon$$

where

Y = commercial paper certificate of deposit rate less commercial paper rate

X_1 = commercial paper rate

X_2 = ratio of loans and investments to capital

Use the part of the computer output from the estimated regression shown here to write a report summarizing the findings of this analysis.

R-Square = 0.730

Parameter	Estimate	Student's t for H$_0$: parameter = 0	Std. Error of Estimate
Intercept	−5.559	−4.14	1.343
X$_1$	0.186	5.64	0.033
X$_2$	0.450	2.08	0.216

12.85 🌐 You have been asked to develop a multiple regression model to predict the annual number of traffic deaths in the United States as a function of total miles traveled and average travel speed. The

data file **Traffic Death Rate** contains 10 years of annual data on the death rates per 100 million vehicle miles (y), total travel in billion vehicle miles (x_1), and average speed in miles per hour of all vehicles (x_2). Compute the multiple regression of y on x_1 and x_2, and write a report discussing your findings.

12.86 🌐 The data file **Household Income** contains data for the 50 states in the United States. The variables included in the data file are the percentage of females that are in the labor force (y), the median household personal income (x_1), the mean years of education completed by females (x_2), and the unemployment rate of women (x_3). Compute the multiple regression of y on x_1, x_2, and x_3, and write a report on your findings.

12.87 🌐 You have been asked to develop a multiple regression model that predicts real money supply in Germany as a function of income and interest rate. The data file **Real Money** contains 12 annual observations on real money per capita (y), real income per capita (x_1), and interest rates (x_2) in Germany. Use these data to develop a model that predicts per capita real money as a function of per capita income and interest rate, and write a report on your findings.

12.88 🌐 The United Nations has hired you as a consultant to help identify factors that predict manufacturing growth in developing countries. You have decided to use multiple regression to develop a model and identify important variables that predict growth. You have collected the data in the data file **Developing Country** from 48 countries. The variables included are percentage manufacturing growth (y), percentage agricultural growth (x_1), percentage exports growth (x_2), and percentage rate of inflation (x_3) in 48 developing countries. Develop the multiple regression model and write a report on your findings.

KEY WORDS

12.89 The method of least squares is used far more often than any alternative procedure to estimate the parameters of a multiple regression model. Explain the basis for this method of estimation, and discuss why its use is so widespread.

12.90 It is common practice to compute an analysis of variance table in conjunction with an estimated multiple regression. Carefully explain what can be learned from such a table.

12.91 State whether each of the following statements is true or false.

a. The error sum of squares must be smaller than the regression sum of squares.
b. Instead of carrying out a multiple regression, we can get the same information from simple linear regressions of the dependent variable on each independent variable.
c. The coefficient of determination cannot be negative.
d. The adjusted coefficient of determination cannot be negative.
e. The coefficient of multiple correlation is the square root of the coefficient of determination.

12.92 If an additional independent variable, however irrelevant, is added to a multiple regression model, a smaller sum of squared errors will result. Explain why this is so, and discuss the consequences for the interpretation of the coefficient of determination.

12.93 A dependent variable is regressed on two independent variables. It is possible that the hypotheses $H_0 : \beta_1 = 0$ and $H_0 : \beta_2 = 0$ cannot be rejected at low significance levels, yet the hypothesis $H_0 : \beta_1 = \beta_2 = 0$ can be rejected at a very low significance level. In what circumstances might this result arise?

12.94 [*This exercise requires the material in the chapter appendix.*] Suppose that the regression model

$$y_i = \beta_0 + \beta_1 x_{1i} + \beta_2 x_{2i} + \varepsilon_i$$

is estimated by least squares. Show that the residuals, e_i, from the fitted model sum to 0.

12.95 A study was conducted to assess the influence of various factors on the start of new firms in the computer chip industry. For a sample of 70 countries the following model was estimated:

$$\hat{y} = -59.31 + 4.983x_1 + 2.198x_2 + 3.816x_3 - 0.310x_4$$
$$\phantom{\hat{y} = -59.31 +} (1.156) \quad (0.210) \quad (2.063) \quad (0.330)$$

$$-0.886x_5 + 3.215x_6 + 0.85x_7 \quad R^2 = 0.766$$
$$(3.055) \quad (1.568) \quad (0.354)$$

where

$\hat{y}$ = new business starts in the industry
x_1 = population in millions

x_2 = industry size
x_3 = measure of economic quality of life
x_4 = measure of political quality of life
x_5 = measure of environmental quality of life
x_6 = measure of health and educational quality of life
x_7 = measure of social quality of life

The numbers in parentheses under the coefficients are the estimated coefficient standard errors.

a. Interpret the estimated regression coefficients.
b. Interpret the coefficient of determination.
c. Find a 90% confidence interval for the increase in new business starts resulting from a 1-unit increase in the economic quality of life, with all other variables unchanged.
d. Test against a two-sided alternative at the 5% level the null hypothesis that, all else remaining equal, the environmental quality of life does not influence new business starts.
e. Test against a two-sided alternative at the 5% level the null hypothesis that, all else remaining equal, the health and educational quality of life does not influence new business starts.
f. Test the null hypothesis that, taken together, these seven independent variables do not influence new business starts.

12.96 A survey research group conducts regular studies of households through mail questionnaires and is concerned about the factors influencing the response rate. In an experiment, 30 sets of questionnaires were mailed to potential respondents. The regression model fitted to the resulting data set was as follows:

$$Y = \beta_0 + \beta_1 X_1 + \beta_2 X_2 + \varepsilon$$

where

Y = percentage of responses received
X_1 = number of questions asked
X_2 = length of questionnaire in number of words

Part of the SAS computer output from the estimate regression is shown next.

$$R\text{-Square} = 0.637$$

Parameter	Estimate	Student's t for H$_0$: Parameter = 0	Std. Error of Estimate
Intercept	74.3652		
X1	−1.8345	−2.89	0.6349
X2	−0.0162	−1.78	0.0091

a. Interpret the estimated regression coefficients.

b. Interpret the coefficient of determination.

c. Test at the 1% significance level the null hypothesis that, taken together, the two independent variables do not linearly influence the response rate.

d. Find and interpret a 99% confidence interval for β_1.

e. Test the null hypothesis
$$H_0 : \beta_2 = 0$$
against the alternative
$$H_1 : \beta_2 < 0$$
and interpret your findings.

12.97 A consulting group offers courses in financial management for executives. At the end of these courses participants are asked to provide overall ratings of the value of the course. To assess the impact of various factors on ratings, the model
$$Y = \beta_0 + \beta_1 X_1 + \beta_2 X_2 + \beta_3 X_3 + \varepsilon$$
was fitted for 25 such courses, where

Y = average rating by participants of the course
X_1 = percentage of course time spent in group discussion sessions
X_2 = amount of money (in dollars) per course member spent on the preparation of subject matter material
X_3 = amount of money per course member spent on the provision of non-course-related material (food, drinks, and so forth)

Part of the SAS computer output for the fitted regression is shown next.

R-Square = 0.579

Parameter	Estimate	Student's t for H_0: Parameter = 0	Std. Error of Estimate
Intercept	42.9712		
X1	0.3817	1.89	0.2018
X2	0.5172	2.64	0.1957
X3	0.0753	1.09	0.0693

a. Interpret the estimated regression coefficients.

b. Interpret the coefficient of determination.

c. Test at the 5% level the null hypothesis that, taken together, the three independent variables do not linearly influence the course rating.

d. Find and interpret a 90% confidence interval for β_1.

e. Test the null hypothesis
$$H_0 : \beta_2 = 0$$
against the alternative
$$H_1 : \beta_2 > 0$$
and interpret your result.

f. Test at the 10% level the null hypothesis
$$H_0 : \beta_3 = 0$$
against the alternative
$$H_1 : \beta_3 \neq 0$$
and interpret your result.

12.98 At the end of classes professors are rated by their students on a scale from 1 (poor) to 5 (excellent). Students are also asked what course grades they expect, and these are coded as A = 4, B = 3, and so on. The data file **Teacher Rating** contains, for a random sample of 20 classes, ratings of professors, the average expected grades, and the numbers of students in the classes. Compute the multiple regression of rating on expected grade and number of students, and write a report on your findings.

12.99 Flyer Computer Inc. wishes to know the effect of various variables on labor efficiency. Based on a sample of 64 observations, the following model was estimated by least squares:
$$\hat{y} = -16.528 + 28.729x_1 + .022x_2 - 0.023x_3 - 0.054x_4$$
$$- 0.077x_5 + 0.411x_6 + 0.349x_7 + 0.028x_8 \quad R^2 = .467$$
where

$\hat{y}$ = index of direct labor efficiency in production plant
x_1 = ratio of overtime hours to straight-time hours worked by all production workers
x_2 = average number of hourly workers in the plant
x_3 = percentage of employees involved in some quality-of-worklife program
x_4 = number of grievances filed per 100 workers
x_5 = disciplinary action rate
x_6 = absenteeism rate for hourly workers
x_7 = salaried workers' attitudes, from low (dissatisfied) to high, as measured by questionnaire
x_8 = percentage of hourly employees submitting at least one suggestion in a year to the plant's suggestion program

Also obtained by least squares from these data was the fitted model:
$$\hat{y} = 9.062 - 10944x_1 + 0.320x_2 + 0.019x_3 \quad R^2 = 0.242$$
The variables $x_4, x_5, x_6, x_7,$ and x_8 are measures of the performance of a plant's industrial relations system. Test at the 1% level the null hypothesis that they do not contribute to explaining direct labor efficiency, given that $x_1, x_2,$ and x_3 are also to be used.

12.100 Based on 107 students' scores on the first examination in a course on business statistics, the following model was estimated by least squares:
$$\hat{y} = 2.178 + 0.469x_1 + 3.369x_2 + 3.054x_3$$
$$\quad\quad\quad (0.090) \quad\quad (0.456) \quad\quad (1.457)$$
$$R^2 = .686$$

where

$\hat{y}$ = student's actual score on the examination
x_1 = student's expected score on the examination
x_2 = hours per week spent working on the course
x_3 = student's grade point average

The numbers in parentheses under the coefficients are the estimated coefficient standard errors.

a. Interpret the estimate of β_1.
b. Find and interpret a 95% confidence interval for β_2.
c. Test against a two-sided alternative the null hypothesis that β_3 is 0, and interpret your result.
d. Interpret the coefficient of determination.
e. Test the null hypothesis that $\beta_1 = \beta_2 = \beta_3 = 0$.
f. Find and interpret the coefficient of multiple correlation.
g. Predict the score of a student who expects a score of 80, works 8 hours per week on the course, and has a grade point average of 3.0.

12.101 Based on 25 years of annual data, an attempt was made to explain savings in India. The model fitted was as follows:

$$y_i = \beta_0 + \beta_1 x_{1i} + \beta_2 x_{2i} + \varepsilon_i$$

where

y = change in real deposit rate
x_1 = change in real per capita income
x_2 = change in real interest rate

The least squares parameter estimates (with standard errors in parentheses) were (Reference 1) as follows:

$$b_1 = 0.0974 \ (0.0215) \quad b_2 = 0.374 \ (0.209)$$

The corrected coefficient of determination was as follows:

$$\overline{R}^2 = .91$$

a. Find and interpret a 99% confidence interval for β_1.
b. Test against the alternative that it is positive the null hypothesis that β_2 is 0.
c. Find the coefficient of determination.
d. Test the null hypothesis that $\beta_1 = \beta_2 = 0$.
e. Find and interpret the coefficient of multiple correlation.

12.102 Based on data on 2,679 high school basketball players, the following model was fitted:

$$y_i = \beta_0 + \beta_1 x_{1i} + \beta_2 x_{2i} + \ldots + \beta_9 x_{9i} + \varepsilon_i$$

where

y = minutes played in season
x_1 = field goal percentage
x_2 = free throw percentage
x_3 = rebounds per minute
x_4 = points per minute

x_5 = fouls per minute
x_6 = steals per minute
x_7 = blocked shots per minute
x_8 = turnovers per minute
x_9 = assists per minute

The least squares parameter estimates (with standard errors in parentheses) were as follows:

$b_0 = 358.848 \ (44.695) \quad b_1 = 0.6742 \ (0.0639) \quad b_2 = 0.2855 \ (0.0388)$

$b_3 = 303.81 \ (77.73) \quad b_4 = 504.95 \ (43.26) \quad b_5 = -3923.5 \ (120.6)$

$b_6 = 480.04 \ (224.9) \quad b_7 = 1350.3 \ (212.3) \quad b_8 = -891.67 \ (180.87)$

$b_9 = 722.95 \ (110.98)$

The coefficient of determination was as follows:

$$R^2 = 0.5239$$

a. Find and interpret a 90% confidence interval for β_6.
b. Find and interpret a 99% confidence interval for β_7.
c. Test against the alternative that it is negative the null hypothesis that β_8 is 0. Interpret your result.
d. Test against the alternative that it is positive the null hypothesis that β_9 is 0. Interpret your result.
e. Interpret the coefficient of determination.
f. Find and interpret the coefficient of multiple correlation.

12.103 Based on data from 63 counties, the following model was estimated by least squares:

$$\hat{y} = 0.58 - .052x_1 - .005x_2 \qquad R^2 = .17$$
$$\phantom{\hat{y} = 0.58} (.019) \quad (.042)$$

where

$\hat{y}$ = growth rate in real gross domestic product
x_1 = real income per capita
x_2 = average tax rate, as a proportion of gross national product

The numbers in parentheses under the coefficients are the estimated coefficient standard errors.

a. Test against a two-sided alternative the null hypothesis that β_1 is 0. Interpret your result.
b. Test against a two-sided alternative the null hypothesis that β_2 is 0. Interpret your result.
c. Interpret the coefficient of determination.
d. Find and interpret the coefficient of multiple correlation.

12.104 The following regression model was fitted to data on 60 U.S. female amateur golfers:

$$\hat{y} = 164{,}683 + 341.10x_1 + 170.02x_2 + 495.19x_3 - 4.23x_4$$
$$\phantom{\hat{y} = 164{,}683} (100.59) \quad (167.18) \quad (305.48) \quad (90.0)$$

$$-136{,}040x_5 - 35{,}549x_6 + 202.52x_7$$
$$(25.634) \quad (16{,}240) \quad (106.20)$$

$$\overline{R}^2 = .516$$

where

$\hat{y}$ = winnings per tournament in dollars
x_1 = average length of drive in yards
x_2 = percentage times drive ends in fairway
x_3 = percentage times green reached in regulation
x_4 = percentage times par saved after hitting into sand trap
x_5 = average number of putts taken on greens reached in regulation
x_6 = average number of putts taken on greens not reached in regulation
x_7 = number of years the golfer has played

The numbers in parentheses under the coefficients are the estimated coefficient standard errors. Write a report summarizing what can be learned from these results.

12.105　The Economics Department wishes to develop a multiple regression model to predict student GPA for economics courses. Department faculty have collected data for 112 graduates, which include the variables economics GPA, SAT verbal, SAT mathematics, ACT English, ACT social science, and high school percentile rank. The data are stored in a file named **Student GPA** on your data disk.

　　a. Use the SAT variables and class rank to determine the best prediction model. Remove any independent variables that are not significant. What are the coefficients, their Student's t statistics, and the model?

　　b. Use the ACT variables and class rank to determine the best prediction model. Remove any independent variables that are not significant. What are the coefficients, their Student's t statistics, and the model?

　　c. Which model predicts an economics GPA better? Present the evidence to support your conclusion.

12.106　The data file **Salary Model** contains a dependent variable and seven independent variables. You are to obtain the "best" regression model that predicts Y as a function of the seven independent variables. The data are stored on your data disk.

　　　　The dependent variable is named "Y" in the file, and the independent variables are also appropriately labeled. Use regression analysis to determine which variables should be in the final model and to estimate the coefficients. Show the conditional F test and the conditional t test for any variables removed. Analyze the model residuals using plots. Show your results and discuss your conclusions. Transform variables if the residuals indicate a nonlinear relationship. Present your final model clearly, showing the coefficients and the coefficient Student's t statistics.

12.107　Use the data in the file **Citydat** to estimate a regression equation that can be used to determine the marginal effect of the percent of commercial property on the market value per owner-occupied residence. Include the percent of owner-occupied residences, the percent of industrial property, the median of rooms per residence, and the per capita income as additional predictor variables in your multiple regression equation. The variables are included on your data disk and described in the chapter appendix. Indicate which of the variables are conditionally significant. Your final equation should include only significant variables. Discuss and interpret your final regression model, including an indication of how you would select a community for your house.

12.108　The administrator of the National Highway Traffic Safety Administration (NHTSA) wants to know if the different types of vehicles in a state have a relationship to the highway death rate in the state. She has asked you to develop multiple regression analyses to determine if the average vehicle weight, the percentage of imported cars, the percentage of light trucks, and the average car age are related to crash deaths in automobiles and pickups. The data for the analysis are located in the data file named **Crash**, which is located on your data disk. A description of the variables is contained in the Chapter 11 appendix.

　　a. Prepare a correlation matrix for crash deaths and the predictor variables. Note the simple relationships between crash deaths and the predictor variables. In addition, indicate any potential multicollinearity problems between the predictor variables.

　　b. Prepare a multiple regression analysis of crash deaths on the potential predictor variables. Remove any nonsignificant predictor variables, one at a time, from the regression model. Indicate your best final model.

　　c. State the conclusions from your analysis and discuss the conditional importance of the variables in terms of their relationship to crash deaths.

12.109　The Department of Transportation wishes to know if states with a larger percentage of urban population have higher automobile and pickup crash death rates. In addition, it wants to know if the variable, average speed on rural roads, or the variable, percentage of rural roads that are surfaced is conditionally related to crash death rates, given percentage of urban population. Data for this study are included in the file **Crash**, which is stored on your data disk and the variables are defined in the Chapter 11 appendix.

　　a. Prepare a correlation matrix and descriptive statistics for crash deaths and the potential predictor variables. Note the relationships and any potential problems of multicollinearity.

b. Prepare a multiple regression analysis of crash deaths on the potential predictor variables. Determine which of the variables should be retained in the regression model because they have a conditionally significant relationship.

c. State the results of your analysis in terms of your final regression model. Indicate which variables are conditionally significant.

12.110 An economist wishes to predict the market value of owner-occupied homes in small midwestern cities. He has collected a set of data from 45 small cities for a 2-year period and wants you to use this as the data source for the analysis. The data are in the file **Citydat**, which is stored on your data disk and the variables are described in the chapter appendix. He wants you to develop a multiple regression prediction equation. The potential predictor variables include the size of the house, tax rate, percent commercial property, per capita income, and total city government expenditures.

a. Compute the correlation matrix and descriptive statistics for the market value of residences and the potential predictor variables. Note any potential problems of multicollinearity. Define the approximate range for your regression model by the variable means ±2 standard deviations.

b. Prepare multiple regression analyses using the predictor variables. Remove any variables that are not conditionally significant. Which variable, size of house or tax rate, has the stronger conditional relationship to the value of houses?

c. A business developer in a midwestern state has stated that local property tax rates in small towns need to be lowered because, if they are not, no one will purchase a house in these towns. Based on your analysis in this problem, evaluate the business developer's claim.

12.111 Stuart Wainwright, the vice president of purchasing for a large national retailer, has asked you to prepare an analysis of retail sales by state. He wants to know if the percent of unemployment and the per capita personal income are jointly related to the per capita retail sales. Data for this study are in the data file named **Retail**, which is stored on your data disk and the variables are described in the Chapter 11 appendix.

a. Prepare a correlation matrix, compute descriptive statistics, and obtain a regression analysis of per capita retail sales on unemployment and personal income. Compute 95% confidence intervals for the slope coefficients in each regression equation.

b. What is the conditional effect of a $1,000 decrease in per capita income on per capita sales?

c. Would the prediction equation be improved by adding the state population as an additional predictor variable?

12.112 A major national supplier of building materials for residential construction is concerned about total sales for next year. It is well known that the company's sales are directly related to the total national residential investment. Several New York bankers are predicting that interest rates will rise about two percentage points next year. You have been asked to develop a regression analysis that can be used to predict the effect of interest rate changes on residential investment. In addition to interest rate, you believe that the GNP, money supply, government spending, and price index for finished goods might be predictors of residential investment. Therefore, you decide that two multiple regression models will be needed. One will include prime interest rate and important additional variables. The second will include federal funds interest rate and important additional variables. The time-series data for this study are contained in the data file named **Macro2008**, which is stored on your data disk and described in the Chapter 13 appendix.

a. Develop two multiple regression models to predict residential investment using prime interest rate for one and federal funds interest rate for the other. The final regression models should include only predictor variables that have a significant conditional effect. Analyze the regression statistics and indicate which equation provides the best predictions.

b. Determine the 95% confidence interval for the interest rate conditional slope coefficient in both regression equations.

12.113 The Congressional Budget Office (CBO) is interested in determining if state-level infant death rates are related to the level of medical resources available in the state. Data for the study are contained in the data file named **State**, which is stored on your data disk. The variables are described in the chapter appendix. The measure of infant deaths is infant deaths under 1 year per 100 live births. The set of possible predictor variables includes physicians per 100,000 population, per capita personal income, and total expenditures for hospitals (this variable should be expressed on a per capita basis by dividing by the state population).

a. Prepare the multiple regression analysis and determine which of the predictor variables should be included in the multiple regression model. Interpret your final regression model, including a discussion of the coefficients, their Student's t's, the standard error of the estimate, and R^2.

b. Identify two additional variables that might be additional predictors if added to the multiple regression model. Test their effect in a multiple regression analysis and indicate if your initial suspicions were correct.

12.114 ● Develop a multiple regression model to predict salary as a function of other independent variables, using the data in the file **Salary Model**, which is stored on your data disk. For this problem do not use years of experience; instead, use age as a surrogate for experience.

a. Describe the steps used to obtain the final regression model.

b. Test the hypothesis that the rate of change in female salaries as a function of age is less than the rate of change for male salaries as a function of age. Your hypothesis test should be set up to provide strong evidence of discrimination against females if it exists. [*Note:* Females are indicated by a "1" for the variable "sex" in column 5. The test should be made conditional on the other significant predictor variables from part (a).]

12.115 ● A group of activists in Peaceful, Montana, are seeking increased development for this pristine enclave, which has received some national recognition on the television program *Four Dirty Old Men*. The group claims that increased commercial and industrial development will bring new prosperity and lower taxes to Peaceful. Specifically, it claims that an increased percentage of commercial and industrial development will decrease the property tax rate and increase the market value for owner-occupied residences.

You have been hired to analyze their claims. For this purpose you have obtained the data file **Citydat**, which contains data from 45 small cities. The variables are described in the chapter appendix. From these data you will first develop regression models that predict the average value of owner-occupied housing and the property tax rate. Then you will determine if and how the addition of percent commercial property and then percent industrial property affects the variability in these regression models. The basic model for predicting market value of houses (c10) includes the size of house (c4), the tax rate (c7), the per capita income (c9), and the percent of owner-occupied residences (c12) as independent variables. The basic model for predicting tax rate (c7) includes the tax assessment base (c6), current city expenditures per capita

(c5/c8), and the percent of owner-occupied residences (c12) as independent variables.

Determine if the percent of commercial (c14) and the percent of industrial (c15) variables improve the explained variability in each of the two models. Perform a conditional F test for each of these additional variables. First, estimate the conditional effect of percent commercial property by itself and then the conditional effect of percent industrial property by itself. Carefully explain the results of your analysis. Include in your report an explanation of why it was important to include all of the other variables in the regression model instead of just examining the effect of the direct and simple relationship between percent commercial property and percent industrial property on the tax rate and market value of housing.

12.116 ● Use the data in the data file named **Student GPA**, which is stored on your data disk, to develop a model to predict a student's grade point average in economics. Begin with the variables ACT scores, gender, and HSpct.

a. Use appropriate statistical procedures to choose a subset of statistically significant predictor variables. Describe your strategy and carefully define your final model.

b. Discuss how this model might be used as part of the college's decision process to select students for admission.

12.117 For a random sample of 50 observations, an economist estimated the following regression model:

$$\log y_i = \alpha + \beta_1 \log x_{1i} + \beta_2 \log x_{2i} + \beta_3 \log x_{3i} + \beta_4 \log x_{4i} + \varepsilon_i$$

where
   y = revenue from a medical practice
   x_{1i} = average number of hours worked by physicians in the practice
   x_{2i} = number of physicians in the practice
   x_{3i} = number of allied health personnel (such as nurses) employed in the practice
   x_{4i} = number of rooms used in the practice

Use the portion of the computer output shown next to write a report on these results.

R-Square = 0.927

Parameter	Estimate	Student's t for H_0: Parameter = 0	Std. Error of Estimate
Intercept	2.347	–	
Log X1	0.239	3.27	0.073
Log X2	0.673	8.31	0.081
Log X3	0.279	6.64	0.042
Log X4	0.082	1.61	0.051

Appendix: Mathematical Derivations

1 LEAST SQUARES DERIVATION OF ESTIMATORS

The derivation of coefficient estimators for a model with two predictor variables is as follows:

$$\hat{y}_i = b_0 + b_1 x_{1i} + b_2 x_{2i}$$

Minimize

$$SSE = \sum_{i=1}^{n} [y_i - (b_0 + b_1 x_{1i} + b_2 x_{2i})]^2$$

Applying differential calculus, we obtain a set of three normal equations that can be solved for the coefficient estimators:

$$\frac{\partial SSE}{\partial b_0} = 0$$

$$2 \sum_{i=1}^{n} \left[y_i - \left(b_0 + b_1 x_{1i} + b_2 x_{2i} \right) \right] (-1) = 0$$

$$\sum_{i=1}^{n} y_i - n b_0 - b_1 \sum_{i=1}^{n} x_{1i} - b_2 \sum_{i=1}^{n} x_{2i} = 0$$

$$n b_0 + b_1 \sum_{i=1}^{n} x_{1i} + b_2 \sum_{i=1}^{n} x_{2i} = \sum_{i=1}^{n} y_i$$

$$\frac{\partial SSE}{\partial b_1} = 0$$

$$2 \sum_{i=1}^{n} \left[y_i - \left(b_0 + b_1 x_{1i} + b_2 x_{2i} \right) \right] (-x_{1i}) = 0$$

$$\sum_{i=1}^{n} x_{1i} y_i - b_0 \sum_{i=1}^{n} x_{1i} - b_1 \sum_{i=1}^{n} x_{1i}^2 - b_2 \sum_{i=1}^{n} x_{1i} x_{2i} = 0$$

$$b_0 \sum_{i=1}^{n} x_{1i} + b_1 \sum_{i=1}^{n} x_{1i}^2 + b_2 \sum_{i=1}^{n} x_{1i} x_{2i} = \sum_{i=1}^{n} x_{1i} y_i$$

$$\frac{\partial SSE}{\partial b_2} = 0$$

$$2 \sum_{i=1}^{n} \left[y_i - \left(b_0 + b_1 x_{1i} + b_2 x_{2i} \right) \right] (-x_{2i}) = 0$$

$$\sum_{i=1}^{n} x_{2i} y_i - b_0 \sum_{i=1}^{n} x_{2i} - b_1 \sum_{i=1}^{n} x_{1i} x_{2i} - b_2 \sum_{i=1}^{n} x_{2i}^2 = 0$$

$$b_0 \sum_{i=1}^{n} x_{2i} + b_1 \sum_{i=1}^{n} x_{1i} x_{2i} + b_2 \sum_{i=1}^{n} x_{2i}^2 = \sum_{i=1}^{n} x_{2i} y_i$$

As a result of applying the least squares algorithm, we have a system of three linear equations in three unknowns:

$$b_0, b_1, b_2$$

$$nb_0 + b_1 \sum_{i=1}^{n} x_{1i} + b_2 \sum_{i=1}^{n} x_{2i} = \sum_{i=1}^{n} y_i$$

$$b_0 \sum_{i=1}^{n} x_{1i} + b_1 \sum_{i=1}^{n} x_{1i}^2 + b_2 \sum_{i=1}^{n} x_{1i}x_{2i} = \sum_{i=1}^{n} x_{1i}y_i$$

$$b_0 \sum_{i=1}^{n} x_{2i} + b_1 \sum_{i=1}^{n} x_{1i}x_{2i} + b_2 \sum_{i=1}^{n} x_{2i}^2 = \sum_{i=1}^{n} x_{2i}y_i$$

The normal equations are solved for the desired coefficients by first computing the various X and Y squared and cross-product terms.

The intercept term is estimated by the following:

$$b_0 = \bar{y} - b_1\bar{x}_1 - b_2\bar{x}_2$$

2 TOTAL EXPLAINED VARIABILITY

The explained variability SSR term in multiple regression is more complex than the SSR term in simple regression.

For the two-independent-variable regression model

$$Y = \beta_0 + \beta_1 X_1 + \beta_2 X_2$$

we find that

$$SSR = \sum_{i=1}^{n} \left(\hat{y}_i - \bar{y} \right)^2$$

$$= \sum_{i=1}^{n} \left[b_0 + b_1 x_{1i} + b_2 x_{2i} - \left(b_0 + b_1 \bar{x}_1 + b_2 \bar{x}_2 \right) \right]^2$$

$$= \sum_{i=1}^{n} \left[b_1^2 \left(x_{1i} - \bar{x}_1 \right)^2 + b_2^2 \left(x_{2i} - \bar{x}_2 \right)^2 + 2b_1 b_2 \left(x_{1i} - \bar{x}_1 \right)\left(x_{2i} - \bar{x}_2 \right) \right]$$

$$= (n - 1)\left(b_1^2 s_{x_1}^2 + b_2^2 s_{x_2}^2 + 2r_{x_1 x_2} b_1 b_2 s_{x_1} s_{x_2} \right)$$

We see that the explained variability has a portion directly associated with each of the independent variables and a portion associated with the correlation between the two variables.

DATA FILE DESCRIPTIONS

Data File Citydat	
This data file contains a cross-section database for project analysis. The file contains data from 45 nonmetropolitan Minnesota cities for the years 1973 and 1974. The data were collected in 1976 as part of a research project to determine the effect of economic growth on local city expenditures, tax rates, and housing values. The file contains a total of 90 observations.	
C1	Observation sequential number
County	County code
City	MCD code
Sizehse	Median rooms per owner-occupied house
Totexp	Total current city government expenditures
Taxbase	Assessment base in millions of 1972 dollars

Taxrate	Tax levy divided by total assessment
Pop73	1973 population estimate
Incom72	1972 per capita income
Hseval	Market value per owner-occupied residence
Taxhse	Average tax per owner-occupied residence
Homper	Percent of property value:owner-occupied residence
Rentper	Percent of property value: rental residence
Comper	Percent of property value: commercial
Indper	Percent of property value: industrial property
Utilper	Percent of property value: public utility
Year	Year represented by data

Data File	State
State	Name of state
Code	Code number assigned to state
Totpop84	Total state population 1984
Birth83	Registered births/1000 population by place of residence, excludes births to non-U.S. residents, 1983
Infmrt82	Infant deaths under 1 year per 100 live births, excludes fetal deaths, 1982
Helexp82	Personal health care expenditures per capita 1982
Phys82	Physicians per 100,000 population, 1982, American Medical Association
Tecsal85	Average teacher salaries, public elementary and secondary schools, 1985, National Education Association
Pupexp85	Current expenditures per pupil in attendance,1985, National Education Association
Welper84	Public aid recipients as percent of population, 1984, ADC + FSSI payments
Emper84	Civilian employment as percent of civilian noninstitutional population, 1984, BLS
Unemp84	Unemployment percentage of civilian labor force, 1984, BLS
Perinc84	Per capita personal income, 1984
Peren84	Per capita energy consumption, 1983, U.S. Energy Information Administration
Vehdet82	Motor vehicle death rate per 100,000 population, 1982, U.S. Center for Health Statistics
Retsal84	Retail sales per capita, 1984
Totcri82	Total reported crime per 100,000 population,1982
Totcri84	Total reported crime per 100,000 population, 1984
Heart82	Deaths per 100,000 population, heart disease, 1982
Acid82	Deaths per 100,000 population, accidents, 1982
Pulmon82	Deaths per 100,000 population, chronic obstructive pulmonary diseases and allied conditions, 1982
Suicid82	Deaths per 100,000 population, suicide, 1982

Cirrh82	Deaths per 100,000 population, chronic liver disease, cirrhosis, 1982
Homici82	Deaths per 100,000 population, homicide and legal intervention, 1982
Police83	Police per 100,000 population, 1983
Enfexp83	Police and prison expenditures per capita, 1983
Reven83	Total revenue per capita, 1983
Educ83	Total expenditures for education, million
Hiway83	Total expenditures for highways, million
Pubwel83	Total expenditures for public welfare, million
Hosp83	Total expenditures for hospitals, million

REFERENCES

1. Ghatak, S., and D. Deadman. 1989. Money, Prices and Stabilization Policies in Some Developing Countries. *Applied Economics* 21: 853–865.

2. Hagermann, R. P. 1981. The Determinants of Household Vacation Travel: Some Emperical Evidence. *Applied Economics* 13: 225–234.

3. MacDonald, J. M., and P. E. Nelson. 1991. Do the Poor Still Pay More? Food Price Variations in Large Metropolitan Areas. *Journal of Urban Economics* 30: 344–359.

4. Spellman, L. J. 1978. Entry and Profitability in a Rate-free Savings and Loan Market. *Quarterly Review of Economics and Business* 18 (2): 87–95.

5. Van Scyoc, L. J., and J. Gleason. 1993. Traditional or Intensive Course Lengths? A Comparison of Outcomes in Economics Learning. *Journal of Economic Education* 24: 15–22.

Chapter 13

Additional Topics in Regression Analysis

Introduction

In Chapters 11 and 12 we developed simple and multiple regression as tools to estimate the coefficients for linear models for business and economic applications. We now understand that the purpose of fitting a regression equation is to use information about the independent variables to explain the behavior of the dependent variables and to derive predictions of the dependent variable. The model coefficients can also be used to estimate the rate of change of the dependent variable as the result of changes in an independent variable, conditional on the particular set of other independent variables included in the model remaining fixed. In this chapter we study a set of alternative specifications. In addition, we consider situations in which the basic regression assumptions are violated.

The topics in this chapter can be selected individually to supplement your study of regression analysis. Almost everyone will be interested in the model-building discussion in the next section. The process of model building is fundamental to all regression applications, and, thus, we begin with those ideas. The section dealing with dummy variables and experimental design provides methods for extending the model applications. Sections such as those dealing with heteroscedasticity and autocorrelations indicate how to deal with violations of assumptions.

Regression models are developed in business and economic applications to increase understanding and guide decisions. Developing these models requires a good understanding of the system and process being studied. Statistical theory provides a link between the underlying process and the data observed from that process. This linking of the problem context and good statistical analysis usually requires an interdisciplinary team that can provide expertise on all aspects of the problem. In the authors' experience, these teams will be successful only when all team members learn from each other—production specialists need to have a basic understanding of statistical procedures and statisticians need to understand the production process.

13.1 MODEL-BUILDING METHODOLOGY

Here, a general strategy for constructing regression models is developed. We live in a complex world, and no one believes that we can capture precisely the complexities of economic and business behavior in one or more equations. Our goal is to use a relatively simple model that provides a sufficiently close approximation of the complex reality that it provides useful insights. The art of model building recognizes the impossibility of representing all of the many individual influences on a dependent variable and tries to pick out the most influential variables. Next, it is necessary to formulate a model to depict relationships between these factors. We want to build a simple model that is easy to interpret but not so oversimplified that important influences are ignored.

The process of statistical model building is problem-specific. Our approach will depend on what is known about the behavior of the quantities under study and what data are available. We present the various stages of model building depicted in Figure 13.1.

Model Specification

Analysis begins with the development of the model specification. This includes selection of the dependent and independent variables and the algebraic form of the model. We seek a specification that provides an adequate representation of the system and process under study. The examples in Chapters 11 and 12 that dealt with retail sales, profitability of savings and loan associations, and cotton production all postulated a linear relationship between the dependent variable and the independent variables. Linear models often provide a good approximation for the problem of interest. But we will not always find this to be true.

Figure 13.1
The Stages of
Statistical Model
Building

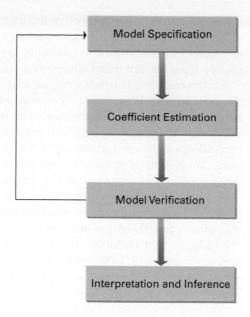

Model specification begins with an understanding of the theory that provides the context for the model. We should carefully study the existing literature and learn what is known about the situation that we are working to model. This background study should include consultation with those that have knowledge of the context. Included would be those who have done research in the problem area and those who have developed similar models. For applied work one should also contact experienced practitioners who have working knowledge of the system being modeled.

Model specification typically requires considerable thinking about the system and the process that underlies the problem. When we have complex problems involving a number of factors, it is important that the interdisciplinary team carefully analyze all aspects of the problem. It may be necessary to do additional research and perhaps include others that have important insights. Specification requires serious study and analysis. If not done properly, the entire model development will be seriously compromised. This is also the time when we need to determine the required data for the study. In many cases this may involve deciding if the available data—or data that could be obtained—will be adequate for model estimation. If we do not know what we want to do or understand the context of the problem, then sophisticated analysis tools and competent analysts will not give us the best possible answer. Inexperienced analysts often run computer-based computations before thinking carefully about the problem. Professional analysts know that such an approach leads to inferior results.

Coefficient Estimation

A statistical model, once specified, typically involves a number of unknown coefficients, or parameters. The next stage of the model-building exercise is to employ available data in the estimation of these coefficients. Both point estimates and interval estimates should be obtained for the multiple regression model:

$$y_i = \beta_0 + \beta_1 x_{1i} + \beta_2 x_{2i} + \cdots + \beta_k x_{ki} + \varepsilon_i$$

From a statistical perspective the regression model objectives can be divided into either a prediction of the mean of the dependent variable, Y, or an estimation of one or more of the individual coefficients, β_j. In many cases the objectives are not completely separate, but these alternatives identify important options.

If the objective is prediction, we want a model that has a small standard error of the estimate, s_e. We are not as concerned about correlated independent variables because we know that a number of different combinations of correlated variables will result in the same prediction precision. However, we do need to know that the correlations between independent variables will continue to hold in future populations. We also need to have a wide spread for the independent variables to ensure a small prediction variance over the desired range of the model application.

Alternatively, estimation of the slope coefficients leads us to consider a wider range of issues. The estimated standard deviation, s_{b_j}, of the slope coefficients is influenced directly by the standard error of the model and inversely by the spread of the independent variables and the correlations between independent variables, as seen in Section 12.4. Multicollinearity—correlations between independent variables—is a critical issue, as we will discuss in Section 13.5. Also, we will see in Section 13.4 that failure to include important predictor variables results in a biased estimator of the coefficients for predictor variables included in the model. These two results lead to a classic statistical problem. Do we include a predictor variable that is highly correlated with the other predictor variables and, thus, avoid a biased coefficient estimate but also substantially increase the variance of the coefficient estimator? Or do we exclude a correlated predictor variable to reduce the coefficient estimator variance but increase the bias? Selecting the proper balance of estimator bias and variance is often a problem in applied model building.

Model Verification

When developing the model specification, we incorporate insights concerning the behavior of the underlying system and process. Certain simplifications and assumptions occur when translating these insights into algebraic forms and when selecting data for model estimation. Since some of these might prove untenable, it is important to check the adequacy of the model.

After estimating a regression equation, we may find that the estimates do not make sense, given what we know about the process. For example, suppose the model indicates that the demand for cars increases as prices increase, which is counter to basic economic theory. Such a result may occur because of inadequate data or because of some high correlations between price and other predictor variables. These are possible reasons for the wrong coefficient sign. But the problem may also result from faulty model specification. Failure to include the proper set of predictor variables can lead to coefficient bias and incorrect signs. We also need to check the assumptions made about the random variables in the model. For example, the basic regression assumptions state that the error terms all have the same variance and are uncorrelated with one another. In Sections 13.6 and 13.7 we see how these assumptions can be checked by using the available data.

If we find implausible results, then it is necessary to examine our assumptions, model specification, and the data. This may lead us to consider a different model specification. Thus, in Figure 13.1 we indicate a feedback loop in the model-building process. As we develop experience with model building and other difficult problem solving, we will discover that these processes tend to be iterative, with considerable cycling back to earlier stages until a satisfactory model and problem solution are developed.

Model Interpretation and Inference

Once a model has been constructed, it can be used to learn something about the system and process being studied. In regression analysis this may involve finding confidence intervals for the model parameters, testing hypotheses of interest, or forecasting future values of the dependent variable, given assumed values of the independent variables. It is important to recognize that inference of this sort is based on the assumption of appropriate model specification and estimation. The more severe any specification or estimation errors, the less reliable any inferences derived from the estimated model.

We should also recognize that some of the results from our analysis using the available data may not agree with previous understandings. When this occurs, we will need to carefully compare our results with past understandings. Differences may result from a different or improper specification of the model, errors in the data, or some other shortcoming. But we might also have discovered some important new results because of a superior problem specification or because of new data that represent a change in the environment being studied. In any case we must be prepared to either make corrections or present our new results in a logical manner.

13.2 DUMMY VARIABLES AND EXPERIMENTAL DESIGN

Dummy variables were introduced in Section 12.8 in applications involving regression models applied to two different subsets of data. For example, we saw how they could be used to test for gender discrimination in the salary example.

In this section we expand the potential applications of dummy variables. First, we present an application in which a regression model is applied to more than two subsets of data. Next, we show how dummy variables can be used to estimate the seasonal effects on a regression model applied to time-series data. Finally, we show how dummy variables can be used to analyze data from experimental situations, which are defined by multiple-level categorical variables. We also provide an example that shows how dummy variables can be used for public policy analysis.

Example 13.1   Demand for Wool Products (Dummy Variable Model Analysis)

A senior marketing analyst for the American Wool Producers Association is interested in estimating the demand for wool products in various cities as a function of total disposable income in the city. Data were gathered from 30 randomly selected Standard Metropolitan Statistical Areas (SMSAs). As a first step the analyst specifies a regression model for the relationship between sales and disposable income:

$$Y = \beta_0 + \beta_1 X_1$$

where X_1 is the per capita annual disposable income for a city and Y is the per capita sales of wool products in the city. After some additional discussions, the analyst wonders if overall sales levels differ among different geographic regions: north, central, and south.

Figure 13.2 Per Capita Wool Sales Versus Per Capita Disposable Income

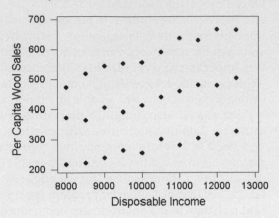

Solution The analysis begins by placing each of the cities in one of the three regions. Figure 13.2 is a scatter plot of per capita sales versus disposable income. The data appear to be separated into three distinct subgroups corresponding to geographic regions. Two dummy variables are used to identify each of the three regions:

North: $x_2 = 0$, $x_3 = 1$
Central: $x_2 = 1$, $x_3 = 0$
South: $x_2 = 0$, $x_3 = 0$

In general, k distinct regions or subsets can be identified uniquely with $k - 1$ dummy variables. If we try to use k dummy variables to represent k distinct subsets, then a linear relationship between predictor variables will result, and estimation of coefficients will be impossible, as discussed in Section 12.2. This is sometimes referred to as the "dummy variable trap."

Shifts in the model constant could be estimated using the following model:

$$Y = \beta_0 + \beta_2 X_2 + \beta_3 X_3 + \beta_1 X_1$$

Applying this model to the north, it becomes

$$Y = \beta_0 + \beta_2(0) + \beta_3(1) + \beta_1 X_1$$

$$= (\beta_0 + \beta_3) + \beta_1 X_1$$

In the central region we find the following:

$$Y = \beta_0 + \beta_2(1) + \beta_3(0) + \beta_1 X_1$$

$$= (\beta_0 + \beta_2) + \beta_1 X_1$$

Finally, for the southern region the model is as follows:

$$Y = \beta_0 + \beta_2(0) + \beta_3(0) + \beta_1 X_1$$

$$= \beta_0 + \beta_1 X_1$$

Summarizing these results, the constants for the various regions are as follows:

North: $\beta_0 + \beta_3$
Central: $\beta_0 + \beta_2$
South: β_0

This formulation defines the south as the "base" constant, with β_3 and β_2 defining the shift of the function for northern and central cities, respectively. Hypothesis tests, using the coefficient Student's t statistic, could be used to determine if there are significant differences between the constants for the different regions compared, in this case, to the constant for the southern region. For additional regions, constants could be modeled by using dummy variables that continue this pattern. We could specify the dummy variables so that any level would be the base level to which the other levels are compared. In this problem specifying the south as the base condition is natural, given the problem objectives.

The model with differences in slope coefficients and constants is as follows:

$$Y = \beta_0 + \beta_2 X_2 + \beta_3 X_3 + (\beta_1 + \beta_4 X_2 + \beta_5 X_3)X_1$$

$$= \beta_0 + \beta_2 X_2 + \beta_3 X_3 + \beta_1 X_1 + \beta_4 X_2 X_1 + \beta_5 X_3 X_1$$

Applying this model to the northern region, we see that

$$Y = \beta_0 + \beta_2(0) + \beta_3(1) + (\beta_1 + \beta_4(0) + \beta_5(1))X_1$$

$$= (\beta_0 + \beta_3) + (\beta_1 + \beta_5)X_1$$

For the central region the model is as follows:

$$Y = \beta_0 + \beta_2(1) + \beta_3(0) + (\beta_1 + \beta_4(1) + \beta_5(0))X_1$$

$$= (\beta_0 + \beta_2) + (\beta_1 + \beta_4)X_1$$

Finally, for the southern region

$$Y = \beta_0 + \beta_2(0) + \beta_3(0) + (\beta_1 + \beta_4(0) + \beta_5(0))X_1$$

$$= \beta_0 + \beta_1 X_1$$

The X_1 slope coefficient for cities in different regions are as follows:

North: $\beta_1 + \beta_5$
Central: $\beta_1 + \beta_4$
South: β_1

Again, the south is the base condition with slope β_1. Hypothesis tests can be used to determine the statistical significance of slope coefficient differences compared to the base condition—in this case the southern region. Using this dummy variable regression model, the analyst can estimate the relationship between sales and disposable income by region of the country.

Using the sample of 30 SMSAs divided equally among the three geographic regions, a dummy variable multiple regression model was estimated using Minitab. The results are contained in Figure 13.3. From the regression model we

Figure 13.3 Dummy Variable Multiple Regression Model to Estimate Per Capita Wool Consumption (Minitab Output)

```
The regression equation is
Per Capita Wool Sales = 12.7 + 138 North X3 + 96.3 Central X2
          + 0.0252 Disposable Income + 0.0168 NorX3Inc + 0.00608 CentX2Inc


Predictor            Coef        StDev       T        P
Constant            12.73        27.74     0.53    0.600
North X3           138.46        39.22     3.53    0.022
Central X2          96.33        39.22     2.46    0.002
Disposab          0.025231     0.002680   9.42    0.000
NorX3 Inc         0.016839     0.003790   4.44    0.000
CentX2 In         0.006085     0.003790   1.61    0.121


S = 12.17     R-Sq = 99.4%    R-Sq(adj) = 99.2%

Analysis of Variance


Source          DF        SS        MS        F        P
Regression       5     553704    110741    747.71   0.000
Residual Error  24       3555       148
Total           29     557259
```

can determine characteristics of the wool purchase patterns. Conditional hypothesis tests of the form

$$H_0: \beta_j = 0 \mid \beta_l \neq 0, l = 1, ..., K, l \neq j$$
$$H_1: \beta_i \neq 0 \mid \beta_l \neq 0, l = 1, ..., K, l \neq j$$

can be used to determine the conditional effects of the various factors on the demand for wool. The coefficient for the X_3 dummy variable, $\beta_3 = 138.46$, indicates that people in the north spend an average of $138.46 more than people in the south. Similarly, people in the central region spend an average of $96.33 more than people in the south. These coefficients are each conditionally significant. The coefficient for disposable income is 0.0252, indicating that for people in the south each dollar of increased per capita income increases the purchase of wool products by 0.025, and this result is conditionally significant. For people in the north each dollar of increased income increases expenditure for wool products by 0.042 (0.0252 + 0.0168), and the difference in the increased slope is conditionally significant. The estimated rate of increase in purchase per dollar of increased income is also greater for people in the central region compared to the south. However, that difference is not conditionally significant. Using these results, sales by region can be predicted more precisely compared to a model that combines all regions and uses only per capita income.

Example 13.2 Forecasting Sale of Wool Products (Seasonal Dummy Variables)

After finishing the regional sales analysis, the analyst decided to study the relationship between sales and disposable income using time-series data. After some discussion he realized that sales are different for each quarter of the year. For example, during the fourth quarter sales were high in anticipation of holiday-season gifts and colder weather. Your assistance with the study is requested.

Solution   After discussing the problem, you recommend that the four quarters for each year be represented by three dummy variables. In this way the multiple regression model can be used to estimate differences in sales between the different quarters. Specifically, you propose a structure that is similar to the regional dummy variable model:

First quarter: $x_2 = 0, x_3 = 0, x_4 = 0$
Second quarter: $x_2 = 1, x_3 = 0, x_4 = 0$
Third quarter: $x_2 = 0, x_3 = 1, x_4 = 0$
Fourth quarter: $x_2 = 0, x_3 = 0, x_4 = 1$

The dummy variable coefficients are estimates of shifts in the wool consumption function between quarters in the following data model:

$$Y = \beta_0 + \beta_2 X_2 + \beta_3 X_3 + \beta_4 X_4 + \beta_1 X_1$$

where Y is the total sales of wool products and X_1 is disposable income. The constants for the various quarters are as follows:

First quarter: β_0
Second quarter: $\beta_0 + \beta_2$
Third quarter: $\beta_0 + \beta_3$
Fourth quarter: $\beta_0 + \beta_4$

Experimental Design Models

Experimental design procedures have been a major area of statistical research and practice for a number of years. Early work dealt with agricultural research. The efforts of statisticians such as R. A. Fisher and O. L. Davies in England during the 1920s provided the foundation for experimental design methodology and for statistical practice in general. Agricultural experiments require an entire growing season to obtain data. Thus, it was important to develop procedures that could answer a number of questions and ensure great precision. In addition, most of the experiments defined activity using variables with discrete as opposed to continuous levels. Experimental design methods have also been used extensively in the study of human behavior and in various industrial experiments. The recent emphasis on improving quality and productivity has spawned increased activity in this area of statistics, with important contributions from groups such as the Center for Quality and Productivity at the University of Wisconsin.

Experimental Design
Dummy variable regression can be used as a tool in experimental design work. The experiments have a single outcome variable that contains all of the random error. Each experimental outcome is measured at discrete combinations of experimental (independent) variables, X_j.

There is an important difference in philosophy for experimental designs in comparison to most of the problems we have considered.

Experimental design attempts to identify causes for the changes in the dependent variable. This is done by pre-specifying combinations of discrete independent variables at which the dependent variable will be measured. An important objective is to choose experimental points, defined by independent variables, that provide minimum variance estimators. The order in which the experiments are performed is chosen randomly to avoid biases from variables not included in the experiment.

Experimental outcomes, Y, are measured at specific combinations of levels for treatment and blocking variables. A *treatment variable* represents a variable whose effect we are interested in estimating with minimum variance. For example, we might wish to know which of four different production machines will provide the highest productivity per hour. In that case the treatment is the production machines represented by a four-level categorical variable, Z_j. A *blocking variable* represents a variable that is part of the environment, and, thus, we cannot preselect the variable level. But we want to include the level of the blocking variable in our model so that we can remove the variability in the outcome variable, Y, that is associated with different levels of the blocking variables. We can represent a K level treatment or blocking variable by using $K - 1$ dummy variables. Let us consider a simple example that has one four-level treatment variable, Z_1, and one three-level blocking variable, Z_2. These variables could be represented by dummy variables, as shown in Table 13.1. Then, by using these dummy variables, the experimental design model could be estimated by the multiple regression model:

$$y_i = \beta_0 + \beta_1 x_{1i} + \beta_2 x_{2i} + \beta_3 x_{3i} + \beta_4 x_{4i} + \beta_5 x_{5i} + \varepsilon_i$$

In this model, for example, the coefficient β_3 is an estimate of the amount by which the productivity for treatment level 4 exceeds that for treatment level 1, for categorical treatment variable, Z_1. Of course, if β_3 is negative, we know that treatment level 1 has a higher productivity than treatment level 4. Following the logic of multiple regression, we know that variables X_4 and X_5 have the effect of explaining some of the variability in Y and hence result in a smaller variance estimator. This model can easily be expanded to include several treatment variables simultaneously

Table 13.1 Example of Dummy Variable Specification for Treatment and Blocking Variables

Z_1	X_1	X_2	X_3
1	0	0	0
2	1	0	0
3	0	1	0
4	0	0	1
Z_2	X_4	X_5	
1	0	0	
2	1	0	
3	0	1	

with several other blocking variables. In addition, if there is a continuous variable—for example, ambient temperature—that affects productivity, then that variable can also be added directly to the regression model. In many cases several replications of the basic design are conducted to provide sufficient degrees of freedom for error. This process is demonstrated in Example 13.3.

Example 13.3 Worker Training Program (Dummy Variable Model Specification)

Mary Cruz is the production manager for a large auto parts factory. She is interested in determining the effect of a new training program on worker productivity. Considerable research supports the conclusion that productivity is influenced by the machine type and by the amount of education a worker has received.

Solution Mary defines the following variables for the experiment:

Y The number of units produced per 8-hour shift
Z_1 The type of training

1. Traditional classroom lecture and film presentation
2. Interactive Computer-Assisted Instruction (CAI)

Z_2 Machine type

1. Machine type 1
2. Machine type 2
3. Machine type 3

Z_3 Workers' educational level

1. High school education
2. At least one year of post-high school education

The variable Z_1 is called a *treatment variable* because the major study objective is an evaluation of the training program. The variables Z_2 and Z_3 are called *blocking variables* because they are included to help reduce or block out some of the unexplained variability. In this way the variance is reduced, and the test for the main treatment effects has greater power. The term *blocking variable* is a carryover from the agricultural experiments where fields were separated into small blocks, each of which had different soil conditions. It is also possible to estimate the effect of these blocking variables. Thus, one does not lose information by calling certain variables blocking variables instead of treatment variables.

Experimental design observations are predefined using the independent variables. Table 13.2 presents a listing of the observations with each observation designated using levels of the Z variables. In this design, which is called a full factorial design, there are 12 observations, one for each combination of the treatment and blocking variables. The Y_i observations represent the measured responses at each of the experimental conditions. In the data, model Y_i contains the effect of the treatment and blocking variables plus random error. In many experimental designs this pattern of 12 observations is replicated (repeated) to provide more degrees of freedom for error and lower variance estimates of the effects of the design variables. This design can also be analyzed using analysis of variance procedures. However, we will show here how the analysis can be performed using dummy variable regression.

Table 13.2 Experimental Design for Productivity Study

PRODUCTION Y	TRAINING Z_1	MACHINE Z_2	EDUCATION Z_3
Y_1	1	1	1
Y_2	1	1	2
Y_3	1	2	1
Y_4	1	2	2
Y_5	1	3	1
Y_6	1	3	2
Y_7	2	1	1
Y_8	2	1	2
Y_9	2	2	1
Y_{10}	2	2	2
Y_{11}	2	3	1
Y_{12}	2	3	2

The levels for each of the three design variables—Z_1, Z_2, and Z_3—can be expressed as a set of dummy variables. Define the following dummy variables:

$$z_1 = 1 \rightarrow x_1 = 0$$

$$z_1 = 2 \rightarrow x_1 = 1$$

$$z_2 = 1 \rightarrow x_2 = 0 \; \& \; x_3 = 0$$

$$z_2 = 2 \rightarrow x_2 = 1 \; \& \; x_3 = 0$$

$$z_2 = 3 \rightarrow x_2 = 0 \; \& \; x_3 = 1$$

$$z_3 = 1 \rightarrow x_4 = 0$$

$$z_3 = 2 \rightarrow x_4 = 1$$

Using these relationships, the experimental design model in Table 13.2, which uses the Z variables, can be represented by dummy variables, as shown in Table 13.3. Using these dummy variables, we can define a multiple regression model:

$$Y = \beta_0 + \beta_1 X_1 + \beta_2 X_2 + \beta_3 X_3 + \beta_4 X_4$$

The regression coefficients are estimated using the variables as previously specified. The 12 experiments or observations defined in Tables 13.2 and 13.3 are defined as one replication of the experimental design. A replication contains all of the individual experiments that are included in the experimental design. Often several replications of the design are made to provide greater accuracy for the coefficient estimates and to provide sufficient degrees of freedom for estimating the variance. In the dummy variable model we estimate four coefficients and a constant, leaving $n - 4 - 1$ degrees of freedom for estimating the variance. With one replication $n = 12$, we have 7 degrees of freedom for estimating the variance.

Table 13.3 Experimental Design for Productivity Study Using Dummy Variables

PRODUCTIVITY Y	X_1	X_2	X_3	X_4
Y_1	0	0	0	0
Y_2	0	0	0	1
Y_3	0	1	0	0
Y_4	0	1	0	1
Y_5	0	0	1	0
Y_6	0	0	1	1
Y_7	1	0	0	0
Y_8	1	0	0	1
Y_9	1	1	0	0
Y_{10}	1	1	0	1
Y_{11}	1	0	1	0
Y_{12}	1	0	1	1

With two replications of the design $n = 24$, we have 19 degrees of freedom for estimating the variance, and with three replications we have 31 degrees of freedom. Usually, at least 15 or 20 degrees of freedom are required to obtain stable estimates of variance. Using the definitions of the dummy variables, we find that the estimated regression coefficients are interpreted as follows:

1. b_1 is the productivity increase for the new CAI training compared to the standard classroom training.
2. b_2 is the productivity increase for machine type 2 compared to machine type 1.
3. b_3 is the productivity increase for machine type 3 compared to machine type 1.
4. b_4 is the productivity increase for the post-high school education compared to high school alone.

Any of these "increases" could be negative, implying a decrease.

The significance of each of these effects can be tested using our standard hypothesis-testing procedures. Note that, if an experimental observation is lost or fails, the same regression model can still be used to estimate the coefficients. However, we then have a larger variance, and, hence, the hypothesis tests have lower power.

It is also possible to add continuous variables or covariates to the model. Suppose that Mary suspects that the number of years of worker experience and the ambient temperature also influence productivity. These two continuous variables can be measured for each experiment and added to the dummy variable regression model. The regression model then becomes

$$Y = \beta_0 + \beta_1 X_1 + \beta_2 X_2 + \beta_3 X_3 + \beta_4 X_4 + \beta_5 X_5 + \beta_6 X_6$$

where X_5 is the years of experience and X_6 is the ambient temperature. If these latter variables are important, they will reduce the variance and increase the power of the hypothesis tests for the effects of other variables.

Another possible extension is the inclusion of interaction effects. Suppose that Mary suspects that the CAI training provides greater benefits for workers working with machine type 3. To test for this effect, she can include an interaction variable, $X_7 = X_1 X_3$. The values for X_7 are the product of the X_1 and the X_3 variables. Thus, in Table 13.3 we would add a column for X_7, which has 1s for the 11th and 12th observations and 0s for the remaining observations. If she also suspects that the CAI training benefits workers with more education, she can define another interaction variable, $X_8 = X_1 X_4$. This variable adds another column to Table 13.3 with 1s for the 8th, 10th, and 12th observations and 0s for the remaining observations. It is possible to add other variables and interaction terms. Thus, the number of options with these experimental designs is very large.

With all of these additions the regression model is as follows:

$$Y = \beta_0 + \beta_1 X_1 + \beta_2 X_2 + \beta_3 X_3 + \beta_4 X_4 + \beta_5 X_5 + \beta_6 X_6 + \beta_7 X_7 + \beta_8 X_8$$

In this equation there are eight coefficients and a constant to estimate, leaving only 3 degrees of freedom for estimating the variance if only one replication of the design is performed. In situations where measurements can be made accurately and the various effects are large, this design, with even one replication, can provide useful information about the factors that influence productivity. In most cases more than one replication is desirable. More observations provide better coefficient estimates and a smaller coefficient variance. However, in an industrial situation experiments may involve the entire factory and, thus, can be very expensive. Analysts try to maximize the understanding gained from each set of experiments.

In this section we introduced experimental designs and their analysis using dummy variables. Experimental design is a major area for applied statistics that can be studied in many other courses and books. Statistical software, such as Minitab, typically contains an extensive set of routines for developing various sophisticated experimental design models. These should be used only after you have learned about their specific details and interpretations. However, even with the introduction presented here, you have a powerful tool for handling some important productivity problems.

Applications of experimental design have become increasingly important in manufacturing and other business operations. Experiments to identify variables related to increased production and decreased defects are important in efforts to improve production operations. The use of dummy variables and multiple regression for experimental design analysis extends the problem types that you can handle without learning additional analysis techniques. This is an important additional advantage for dummy variable procedures.

Public Sector Applications

Applications of dummy variable regression have become increasingly popular in numerous areas of public sector research and policy analysis. Many of these projects make use of discrete policy options and work with specific subgroups. Many of these studies make use of extensive data files collected by government agencies as part of their programs to identify various public health and safety issues and to provide information for policy and legislative development. The following example from published research provides an indication of the kind of research pursued and the size of the studies.

Example 13.4 Food Source Makes a Difference in Diet Quality

In a study to examine the relationship between diet quality and source of food, Andrea Carlson and Shirley Gerrior (2006) analyzed data from 9,407 adults contained in the 1994 Continuing Survey of Food Intake by Individuals (SFII) using the Healthy Eating Index as the measure of diet quality. The authors grouped the participants in 10 different groups or clusters based on where they purchased the food that they reported eating during a 24-hour period. Home Cookers represented 46.5% of the sample. They estimated a large multiple regression model that included nine sources of food intake represented as dummy variables with home cookers specified as the base condition. In addition they included a number of other variables that have been traditionally known to predict the quality of diet. These factors where included to reduce error variance and, thus, to provide more efficient coefficient estimators. The estimated coefficients and their standard errors are shown in Figure 13.4. The coefficients of the various food sources provide a comparison with the home cooker source of food. Note that all of these other sources have coefficients that indicate a significantly lower quality on the Healthy Eating Index with the fast food source being the lowest quality. For our purposes this example indicates the extensive possibilities that result from carefully specified dummy variable regression models.

Figure 13.4 Multivariate Linear Prediction of Total HEI Score

Cluster	Coefficient	Standard Error	Cluster	Coefficient	Standard Error
Home Cookers	(omitted)		Homemaker	0.35	0.53
Carry Out	−2.25	0.42*	Person is retired	2.11	0.47*
High Service	−3.15	0.44*	Person is a student	2.21	0.94*
Guests	−2.26	0.55*	Annual income: total	8.43E−05	0.00*
Fast Food	−3.97	0.67*	Income squared	−4.40E−10	0.00*
Vending	−2.94	0.76*	**Health Behaviors**		
Office	−1.97	0.77*	Consumed any alcohol day 1	1.24	0.28*
Coffee and Receptions	−2.05	0.87*	Body Mass index	−0.13	0.03*
Gardeners	−0.05	0.92	Exercise 1 time per week	1.36	0.53*
Bars and Taverns	−2.56	1.14*	Exercise 2–6 times per week	2.11	0.33*
Age and Sex			Exercise every day	1.53	0.36*
Person is female	2.54	0.28*	Little or no exercise	(omitted)	
Person is male	(omitted)		Mean hours of tv	−0.19	−0.06*
age	−0.06	0.05	Person currently smokes	−4.32	0.32*
age squared	2.94E−04	0.00	**Geographic**		
Education			Central City	−0.13	0.31
Less than a high school degree	−2.57	0.37*	Suburb	(omitted)	
High school degree	(omitted)		Rural, non MSA area	−2.09	0.34*
At least 4 years of college	3.39	0.35*	Midwest region	1.71	0.35*
Employment and Income			Northeast region	2.23	0.38*
Employed full or part time	(omitted)		Southeast region	(omitted)	
Person is looking for work	−1.34	0.92	West region	2.20	0.36*

*Indicates the coefficient is significant (p<0.05). Omitted variables from the referent group.

EXERCISES

Basic Exercises

13.1 Write the model specification and define the variables for a multiple regression model to predict college GPA as a function of entering SAT scores and the year in college: freshman, sophomore, junior, and senior.

13.2 Write the model specification and define the variables for a multiple regression model to predict wages in U.S. dollars as a function of years of experience and country of employment, indicated as Germany, Great Britain, Japan, United States, and Turkey.

13.3 Write the model specification and define the variables for a multiple regression model to predict the cost per unit produced as a function of factory type (indicated as classic technology, computer-controlled machines, and computer-controlled material handling), and as a function of country (indicated as Colombia, South Africa, and Japan).

13.4 An economist wants to estimate a regression equation relating demand for a product (Y) to its price (X_1) and income (X_2). It is to be based on 12 years of quarterly data. However, it is known that demand for this product is seasonal; that is, it is higher at certain times of the year than others.

a. One possibility for accounting for seasonality is to estimate the model

$$y_t = \beta_0 + \beta_1 x_{1t} + \beta_2 x_{2t} + \beta_3 x_{3t} + \beta_4 x_{4t} + \beta_5 x_{5t} + \beta_6 x_{6t} + \varepsilon_t$$

where x_{3t}, x_{4t}, x_{5t}, and x_{6t} are dummy variable values, with

$x_{3t} = 1$ in first quarter of each year,
0 otherwise

$x_{4t} = 1$ in second quarter of each year,
0 otherwise

$x_{5t} = 1$ in third quarter of each year,
0 otherwise

$x_{6t} = 1$ in fourth quarter of each year,
0 otherwise

Explain why this model cannot be estimated by least squares.

b. A model that can be estimated is as follows:

$$y_t = \beta_0 + \beta_1 x_{1t} + \beta_2 x_{2t} + \beta_3 x_{3t} + \beta_4 x_{4t} + \beta_5 x_{5t} + \varepsilon_t$$

Interpret the coefficients on the dummy variables in this model.

Application Exercises

13.5 Sharon Parsons, president of Gourmet Box Mini Pizza, has asked for your assistance in developing a model that predicts the demand for the new snack lunch pizza named Pizza1. This product competes in a market with three other brands that are named B2, B3, and B4 for identification. At present the products are sold by three major distribution chains identified as 1, 2, and 3. These three chains have different market sizes, and, thus, sales for each distributor are likely to be different. The data file **Market** contains weekly data collected over the past 52 weeks from the three distribution chains. The variables in the data file are defined next.

Use multiple regression to develop a model that predicts the quantity of Pizza1 sold per week by each distributor. The model should contain only important predictor variables.

Distributor	Numerical identifier of the distributor 1, 2, or 3
Weeknum	Sequential number of the week in which data were collected
Sales Pizza1	Number of units of Pizza1 sold by the distributor during the week
Price Pizza1	Retail price for Pizza1 charged by the distributor during that week
Promotion	Level of promotion for the week, designated as 0 No promotion; 1 television ad; 2 store display; 3 both television and store display
Sales B2	Number of units of brand 2 sold by the distributor during the week
Price B2	Retail price for brand 2 charged by the distributor during that week
Sales B3	Number of units of brand 3 sold by the distributor during the week
Price B3	Retail price for brand 3 charged by the distributor during that week
Sales B4	Number of units of brand 4 sold by the distributor during the week
Price B4	Retail price of brand 4 charged by the distributor during that week

13.6 You have been asked to develop a multiple regression model to predict per capita sales of cold cereal in cities with populations over 100,000. As a first step you hold a meeting with the key marketing managers that have experience with cereal sales. From this meeting you discover that per capita sales are expected to be influenced by the cereal price, price of competing cereals, mean per capita income, percentage of college graduates, mean annual temperature, and mean annual rainfall.

You also learn that the linear relationship between price and per capita sales is expected to have a different slope for cities east of the Mississippi River. Per capita sales are expected to be higher in cities with high and low per capita income compared to cities with intermediate per capita income. Per capita sales are also expected to be different in the following four sectors of the country: Northwest, Southwest, Northeast, Southeast.

Prepare a model specification whose coefficients can be estimated using multiple regression. Define each variable completely and indicate the mathematical form of the model. Discuss your specification, indicate which variables you expect to be statistically significant, and explain the rationale for your expectation.

13.7 Maxine Makitright, president of Good Parts Ltd., has asked you to develop a model that predicts the number of defective parts per 8-hour work shift in her factory. She believes that there are differences among the three daily shifts and among the four raw material suppliers. In addition, higher production and a higher number of workers are thought to be related to increased number of defectives. Maxine visits the factory at various times, including all three shifts, to observe operations and to offer operating advice. She has provided you with a list of the shifts that she has visited and wants to know if the number of defectives increases or decreases when she visits the factory.

Prepare a written description of how you would develop a model to estimate and test for the various factors that might influence the number of defective parts produced per shift. Carefully define each coefficient in your model and define the test you would use. Indicate how you would collect the data and how you would define each variable used in the model. Discuss the interpretations that you would make from your model specification.

13.8 Custom Woodworking Inc. has been in business for 40 years. The company produces high-quality custom-made wooden furniture and very high-quality interior cabinet and interior woodwork for expensive homes and offices. It has been very successful in large part because of the highly skilled craftworkers who design and produce its products in consultation with customers. Many of the company's products have won national awards for quality design and workmanship. Each custom-made product is produced by a team of two or more craftworkers who first meet with the customer, prepare an initial design, review the design with the customer, and then build the product. Customers may also meet with the craftworkers at various times during the production.

The craftworkers are well educated and have developed excellent woodworking skills. Most have liberal arts degrees and have trained with skilled craftworkers. Employees are classified at three levels: 1. apprentice, 2. professional, and 3. master. Levels 2 and 3 pay higher wages, and workers typically move through the levels as they gain experience and skill. The company now has a diverse workforce, which includes white, black, and Latino workers, and both men and women. When the business started 40 years ago, all workers were white. About 20 years ago the company began to hire black and Latino craftworkers, and about 10 years ago they hired women craftworkers. The male white workers tend to be overrepresented in the higher job classifications because, in part, they have the most experience. At present, the workforce contains 40% white males, 30% black and Latino males, 15% white females, and 15% black and Latino females.

Recently, serious concerns have been expressed concerning wage discrimination. Specifically, it is alleged that women and nonwhite workers are not receiving fair compensation based on their experience. The company management claims that every person is paid fairly based on years of experience, job classification level, and individual ability. It claims that there are no differences in wages based on either race or gender in terms of either base wage or increment for each year of experience.

Explain how you would carry out an analysis to determine if management's claim is true. Show the details of your analysis and provide a clear rationale. Indicate the data that should be collected and the names and descriptions of the variables you will use in the analysis. Clearly indicate the statistical tests that would be used to determine the true situation and indicate the decision rules based on the hypothesis tests and results from the data.

13.9 You have been asked to serve as a consultant and expert witness for a wage discrimination lawsuit. A group of Latino and black women have filed the suit against their company, Amalgamated Distributors Inc. The women, who have between 5 and 25 years of service with the company, allege that the average rate of their annual wage increase has been significantly less than that of a group of white males and a group of white females. The jobs for all three groups contain a variety of administrative, analytical, and managerial components. All of the employees began with a bachelor's degree, and years of experience is an important factor for predicting job performance and worker productivity. You have been provided with the present monthly wage and the number of years of experience for all workers in the three groups. In addition, the data indicate those in all three groups who have obtained an MBA degree. Note that you do not perform any data analysis for this problem.

a. Develop a statistical model and analysis that can be used to analyze the data. Indicate hypothesis tests that can be used to provide strong evidence of wage discrimination if wage discrimination exists. The company has also hired a statistician as a consultant and expert witness. Describe your analysis completely and clearly.

b. Assume that your hypothesis tests result in strong evidence that supports your clients' claim. Briefly summarize the key points that you will make in your expert witness testimony to the court. The company's lawyer can be expected to cross-examine you with the help of a statistician who teaches statistics at a prestigious liberal arts college.

13.3 LAGGED VALUES OF THE DEPENDENT VARIABLES AS REGRESSORS

In this section we consider lagged dependent variables, an important topic when time-series data are analyzed—that is, when measurements on the quantities of interest are taken over time. For example, we might have monthly observations, quarterly observations, or annual observations. Economists regularly use time-series variables such as interest rates, inflation measures, aggregate investment, and aggregate consumption for various analysis and modeling projects. We specify time-series observations using the subscript t to denote time instead of the i used to denote cross-section data. Thus, a multiple regression model would be as follows:

$$y_t = \beta_0 + \beta_t x_{1t} + \beta_2 x_{2t} + \cdots + \beta_K x_{Kt} + \varepsilon_t$$

In many time-series applications the dependent variable in time period t is also often related to the value taken by this variable in the previous time period—that is to y_{t-1}. The value of the dependent variable in an earlier time period is called a *lagged dependent variable*.

> ## Regressions Involving Lagged Dependent Variables
> Consider the following regression model linking a dependent variable, Y, and K independent variables:
>
> $$y_t = \beta_0 + \beta_t x_{1t} + \beta_2 x_{2t} + \cdots + \beta_K x_{Kt} + \gamma y_{t-1} + \varepsilon_t \qquad (13.1)$$
>
> where $\beta_0, \beta_1, \ldots, \beta_K, \gamma$ are fixed coefficients. By using data generated by this model,
>
> 1. the coefficients $\beta_0, \beta_1, \ldots, \beta_K, \gamma$ can be estimated by least squares in the usual manner.
> 2. confidence intervals and hypothesis tests for the regression coefficients can be computed precisely the same as for the ordinary multiple regression model. (Strictly speaking, when the regression equation contains lagged dependent variables, these procedures are only approximately valid. The quality of the approximation improves, all other things being equal, as the number of sample observations increases.)

3. an increase of 1 unit in the independent variable X_j in time period t, with all other independent variables held fixed, leads to an expected increase in the dependent variable of β_j in period t, $\beta_j\gamma$ in period $(t + 1)$, $\beta_j\gamma^2$ in period $(t + 2)$, $\beta_j\gamma^3$ in period $(t + 3)$, and so on. The total expected increase over all current and future time periods is as follows:

$$\frac{\beta_j}{(1 - \gamma)}.$$

4. caution should be expressed when using confidence intervals and hypothesis tests with time-series data. There is the possibility that the equation errors, ε_i, are no longer independent of one another. We consider this in Section 13.7 under autocorrelations. In particular, when the errors are correlated, the coefficient estimates are unbiased, but not efficient. Thus, confidence intervals and hypothesis tests are no longer valid. Econometricians have developed procedures for obtaining estimates under these conditions, and these are introduced in Section 13.7.

To illustrate the calculation of regression estimates and inference based on the fitted regression equation when the model includes lagged dependent variables, we consider extended Example 13.5 (Reference 1).

Example 13.5 Advertising Expenditures as a Function of Retail Sales (Lagged Variable Regression Model)

A researcher was interested in forecasting advertising expenditures as a function of retail sales, while knowing that the previous year's advertising also had an influence.

Solution It was believed that local advertising per household would depend on retail sales per household. Also, since advertisers may be unwilling or unable to adjust their plans to sudden changes in the level of retail sales, the value of local advertising expenditures per household in the previous year was added to the model. Thus, advertising expenditures in the current year are related to retail sales (x_t) in the current year and advertising expenditures (y_{t-1}) in the previous year. The model to be fitted is then

$$y_t = \beta_0 + \beta_1 x_{1t} + \gamma y_{t-1} + \varepsilon_t$$

where

$y_t =$ local advertising per household in year t
$x_t =$ retail sales per household in year t

INTERPRETATION

The data for advertising and retail sales are stored in a Minitab data file labeled **Advertising Retail**. The lagged value y_{t-1} can be generated in Minitab using the lag function under the calculator routines and in all other good statistical packages using similar procedures. After completing the lag transformation, the data file will include the lagged variable. Observation 1 for the lagged variable is missing, and the data set has only 21 observations. This will always be the case when lagged variables are created. Of course, you might have access to data from the previous year—year 0 in this example—and that value could replace the missing value. The data are now ready for you to run multiple regression using the conventional Minitab commands. The resulting regression output is shown in Figure 13.5.

The resulting regression for this problem (with the first observation missing) is as follows:

$$\hat{y}_t = -43.8 + \underset{(0.0029)}{0.0188}x_t + \underset{(0.087)}{0.479}y_{t-1}$$

The numbers below the regression coefficients are the coefficient standard deviations. The Student's t statistic for each coefficient is quite large, and the resulting p-values are 0.00, indicating that we can reject the null hypothesis that the coefficients are 0. With 18 degrees of freedom for error, the critical value for a Student's t statistic for a two-tailed hypothesis with $\alpha = 0.05$ is $t = 2.101$.

In time-series models the coefficient of determination R^2 can be somewhat misleading. For example, the high value for $R^2 = 96.3\%$ in the present problem does not necessarily indicate a strong relationship between local advertising and retail sales. Rather, it is a well-known empirical fact that the time plots of many business and economic time series exhibit a rather smooth evolutionary pattern over time. This fact alone is enough to ensure a high value for the coefficient of determination

Figure 13.5
Advertising Expenditure as a Function of Retail Sales and Lagged Advertising Expenditure (Minitab Output)

```
The regression equation is
Advertising Y(t) = -43.8 + 0.0188 Retail Sales X(t) + 0.479 lag advertising

21 cases used 1 cases contain missing values

Predictor        Coef      SE Coef        T        P
Constant      -43.766        9.843    -4.45    0.000
Retail S     0.018777     0.002855     6.58    0.000
lag adve      0.47906      0.08732     5.49    0.000


S = 3.451      R-Sq = 96.3%    R-Sq(adj) = 95.9%

Analysis of Variance

Source             DF          SS        MS        F        P
Regression          2      5559.1    2779.5   233.43    0.000
Residual Error     18       214.3      11.9
Total              20      5773.4

Source          DF     Seq SS
Retail S         1     5200.7
lag adve         1      358.4

Unusual observations
 obs    Retail S   Advertis        Fit    SE Fit   Residual   St Resid
   4        5507    119.220    112.716     1.222      6.504       2.02R
  20        6394    145.370    151.853     1.774     -6.483      -2.19R

R denotes an observation with a large standardized residual
```

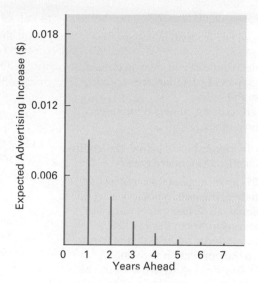

Figure 13.6
Expected Future Increases in Local Advertising per Household

when a lagged dependent variable is included in the regression model. As a practical matter, you are advised to pay relatively little attention to the value of R^2 for such models.

The estimated regression for this problem can be interpreted as follows. Suppose that retail sales per household increase by $1 in the current year. The expected impact on local advertising per household is an increase of 0.0188 in the current year, a further increase of

$$(0.479)(0.0188) = \$0.0090$$

next year, a further increase of

$$(0.479)^2 (0.0188) = \$0.0043$$

in two years, and so on. The total effect on all future advertising expenditures per household is an expected increase of

$$\frac{0.0188}{1 - 0.479} = \$0.0361$$

Thus, we see that the expected effect of an increase in sales is an immediate increase in advertising expenditures, a smaller increase in the following year, a yet smaller increase two years ahead, and so on. Figure 13.6 illustrates this geometrically decreasing effect of an increase in sales in the current year on advertising in future years.

EXERCISES

Basic Exercises

13.10 Consider the following models estimated using regression analysis applied to time-series data.

What is the long-term effect of a 1-unit increase in x in period t?

    a. $y_t = 10 + 2x_t + 0.34y_{t-1}$
    b. $y_t = 10 + 2.5x_t + 0.24y_{t-1}$
    c. $y_t = 10 + 2x_t + 0.64y_{t-1}$
    d. $y_t = 10 + 4.3x_t + 0.34y_{t-1}$

13.11 A market researcher is interested in the average amount of money spent per year by college students on clothing. From 25 years of annual data the following estimated regression was obtained through least squares:

$$y_t = 50.72 + 0.142x_{1t} + 0.027x_{2t} + 0.432y_{t-1}$$
$$(0.047) \phantom{x_{1t}} (0.021) \phantom{x_{2t}} (0.136)$$

where

y = expenditure per student, in dollars, on clothes

x_1 = disposable income per student, in dollars, after the payment of tuition, fees, and room and board

x_2 = index of advertising, aimed at the student market, on clothes

The numbers in parentheses below the coefficients are the coefficient standard errors.

a. Test at the 5% level, against the obvious one-sided alternative, the null hypothesis that, all else being equal, advertising does not affect expenditures on clothes in this market.

b. Find a 95% confidence interval for the coefficient on x_1 in the population regression.

c. With advertising held fixed, what would be the expected impact over time of a $1 increase in disposable income per student on clothing expenditure?

Application Exercises

13.12 ● Use the data from the **Retail Sales** file to estimate the regression model

$$y_t = \beta_0 + \beta_1 x_t + \gamma y_{t-1} + \varepsilon_t$$

and test the null hypothesis that $\gamma = 0$, where

y_t = ratail sales per household

x_t = disposable income per household

13.13 ● The data file **Money UK** contains observations from the United Kingdom on the quantity of money in millions of pounds (Y); income, in millions of pounds (X_1); and the local authority interest rate (X_2). Estimate the model (Reference 5)

$$y_t = \beta_0 + \beta_1 x_{1t} + \beta_2 x_{2t} + \gamma y_{t-1} + \varepsilon_t$$

and write a report on your findings.

13.14 ● The data file **Pension Funds** contains data on the market return (X) of stocks and the percentage (Y) of portfolios in common stocks at market value at the end of the year for private pension funds. Estimate the model

$$y_t = \beta_0 + \beta_1 x_t + \gamma y_{t-1} + \varepsilon_t$$

and write a report on your findings.

13.15 ● The data file **Income Canada** shows quarterly observations on income (Y) and money supply (X) in Canada. Estimate the model (Reference 3)

$$y_t = \beta_0 + \beta_1 x_t + \gamma y_{t-1} + \varepsilon_t$$

and write a report on your findings.

13.16 ● The data file **Births Australia** shows annual observations on the first confinement resulting in a live birth of the current marriage (Y) and the number of first marriages (for females) in the previous year (X) in Australia. Estimate the model (Reference 4)

$$y_t = \beta_0 + \beta_1 x_t + \gamma y_{t-1} + \varepsilon_t$$

and write a report on your findings.

13.17 ● The data file **Pinkham Sales** shows annual observations on unit sales (Y) and advertising expenditure (X), both in thousands of dollars, of Lydia E. Pinkham. Estimate the model

$$\log y_t = \beta_0 + \beta_1 \log x_t + \gamma \log y_{t-1} + \varepsilon_t$$

and write a report on your findings (Reference 2).

13.18 ● The data file **Thailand Consumption** shows 29 annual observations on private consumption (Y) and disposable income (X) in Thailand. Fit the regression model

$$\log y_t = \beta_0 + \beta_1 \log x_{1t} + \gamma \log y_{t-1} + \varepsilon_t$$

and write a report on your findings.

13.4 SPECIFICATION BIAS

The specification of a statistical model that adequately depicts real-world behavior is a delicate and difficult task. We know that no simple model can describe perfectly the nature of a process and the determinants of process outcomes. Our objective in model building is to discover a straightforward formulation that adequately models the underlying process for the questions of interest. However, we should also note that there are certain cases where substantial divergence of the model from reality can result in conclusions that are seriously in error.

We have seen previously some techniques for specifying a model that more appropriately models the process. Our use of dummy variables in Sections 12.8 and 13.2 and transformations of nonlinear models to linear forms in Section 12.7 are important examples. In this section we consider the implications of not including important predictor variables in our regression model.

In formulating a regression model, an investigator attempts to relate the dependent variable of interest to all of its important determinants. Thus, if we adopt a linear model, we want to include as independent variables all variables that might markedly influence the dependent variable of interest. In formulating the regression model

$$y_i = \beta_0 + \beta_1 x_{1i} + \beta_2 x_{2i} + \cdots + \beta_K x_{Ki} + \varepsilon_i$$

we implicitly assume that the set of independent variables, $X_1, X_2, ..., X_K$, contains all quantities that significantly affect the behavior of the dependent variable, Y. We know that in any real applied problem there will be other factors that also affect the dependent variable. The joint influence of these factors is absorbed within the error term, ε_i. However, a serious problem can occur if an important variable is omitted from the list of independent variables.

Bias from Excluding Significant Predictor Variables
When significant predictor variables are omitted from the model, the least squares estimates of coefficients included in the model are usually biased, and the usual inferential statements from hypothesis tests or confidence intervals can be seriously misleading. In addition, the estimated model error includes the effect of the missing variables and, thus, is larger. In the rare case where omitted variables are uncorrelated with the independent variables included in the regression model, this bias in the estimation of coefficients does not occur.

A simple example involves the retail market for gasoline. Suppose that you are the owner of store A, which sells gasoline, and store B, 50 yards down the street, also sells gasoline. You strongly believe that if you lowered your price, unit sales would increase, and if you raised your price, unit sales would decrease. But if store B raised and lowered its price, the change in your unit sales would also be influenced by the price set at store B. Thus, if you ignored the prices set by store B and considered only your prices in attempting to predict unit sales, you would usually have serious errors in your estimate of the relationship between your price and your unit sales. First, we will show this result mathematically, and then present a numerical example.

We illustrate how the bias in estimating regression coefficients results by showing the effect of omitting a variable from a model with two independent variables:

$$y_i = \beta_0 + \beta_1 x_{1i} + \beta_2 x_{2i} + \varepsilon_i$$

Suppose that in this situation the analyst leaves out variable x_2 and instead estimates the following regression model:

$$y_i = \alpha_0 + \alpha_1 x_{1i} + \mu_i$$

Note that we have used two different symbols to emphasize the fact that the coefficient estimators will be different. For the simple regression model the estimator for the coefficient of x_1 is as follows:

$$\hat{\alpha}_1 = \frac{\sum_{i=1}^{n}(x_{1i} - \bar{x}_1)y_i}{\sum_{i=1}^{n}(x_{1i} - \bar{x}_1)^2}$$

By substituting the correct model with two predictor variables and determining the expected value, we find that

$$E[\hat{\alpha}_1] = E\left[\frac{\sum_{i=1}^{n}(x_{1i} - \bar{x}_1)y_i}{\sum_{i=1}^{n}(x_{1i} - \bar{x}_1)^2}\right] = E\left[\frac{\sum_{i=1}^{n}(x_{1i} - \bar{x}_1)(\beta_0 + \beta_1 x_{1i} + \beta_2 x_{2i} + \varepsilon_i)}{\sum_{i=1}^{n}(x_{1i} - \bar{x}_1)^2}\right]$$

When we compute the expected value, we find that

$$E[\hat{\alpha}_1] = \beta_1 + \beta_2\left[\frac{\sum_{i=1}^{n}(x_{1i} - \bar{x}_1)x_{2i}}{\sum_{i=1}^{n}(x_{1i} - \bar{x}_1)^2}\right]$$

Thus, we see that the coefficient of the X_1 variable is biased unless the correlation between X_1 and X_2 is 0.

The previous mathematical results show the bias in coefficient estimates that occurs when an important variable is omitted. In Chapter 12 we showed mathematically and intuitively that the coefficient estimates in a multiple regression model are influenced by all of the independent variables included in the model. Thus, it follows that if we omit an important independent variable, then the estimated coefficients of the remaining variables will be different. Example 13.6 shows this result numerically and should be carefully studied.

Example 13.6 Savings and Loan Regression Model with Omitted Variable (Model Specification Error)

Consider the savings and loan example used in Chapter 12. In that example the annual percentage profit margin (Y) of savings and loan associations was regressed on their percentage net revenue per deposit dollar (X_1), and the number of offices (X_2). In Example 12.3 we estimated the regression coefficients and found that the model was as follows:

$$\hat{y} = 1.565 + 0.237x_1 - 0.000249x_2 \qquad R^2 = 0.865$$
$$\phantom{\hat{y} = 1.565 +} (0.0555) \quad\;\; (0.0000320)$$

One conclusion that follows from this analysis is that for a fixed number of offices, a 1-unit increase in net revenue per deposit dollar leads to an expected increase of 0.237 unit in profit margin. What would happen if we regressed profit margin on only the net revenue per deposit dollar using the data stored in the file **Savings and Loan**?

Solution Using the data, we ran the regression of profit margin (Y) on net revenue per deposit dollar (X_1) and found the model was as follows:

$$\hat{y} = 1.326 - 0.169x_1 \quad R^2 = 0.50$$
$$\text{(0.036)}$$

Comparing the two fitted models, we notice that one consequence of ignoring X_2 is that the percent explained variability, R^2, is substantially reduced.

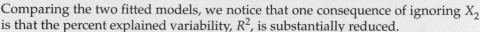**INTERPRETATION**   There is, however, a more serious effect on the coefficient of net revenue. In the multiple regression model a 1-unit increase in net revenue increased profit by 0.237, while in the simple regression model the effect was a decrease of 0.169. This result is clearly counterintuitive—we should not expect an increase in net revenue to decrease profit margin. In both models we would reject the null hypothesis that there is not a relationship. Here, we see the result of the biased estimator for the coefficient that occurs when a significant variable, X_2, is not included in the model. Without including the conditional effect of the number of offices, we obtain a biased estimator.

This example nicely illustrates the point. If an important explanatory variable is not included in the regression model, any conclusions drawn about the effects of other independent variables can be seriously misleading. In this particular case we have seen that adding a relevant variable could well alter the conclusion of a significant negative association to that of a significant positive association. Further insight can be gained from inspection of the data in Table 12.1. Over the latter part of the period, at least, the profit margin fell and net revenue rose, suggesting a negative association between these variables. However, a further look at the data reveals an increase in the number of offices over this same period, suggesting the possibility that this factor could be the cause of the declining profit margin. The only legitimate way to disentangle the separate effects of the two independent variables on the dependent variable is to model them jointly in a regression equation. This example illustrates the importance of using the multiple regression model rather than simple linear regression equations when there is more than one relevant independent variable.

EXERCISES

Basic Exercises

13.19 Suppose that the true linear model for a process was

$$Y = \beta_0 + \beta_1 X_1 + \beta_2 X_2 + \beta_3 X_3$$

and you incorrectly estimated the model

$$Y = \alpha_0 + \alpha_1 X_2$$

Interpret and contrast the coefficients for X_2 in the two models. Show the bias that results from using the second model.

13.20 Suppose that a regression relationship is given by the following:

$$Y = \beta_0 + \beta_1 X_1 + \beta_2 X_2$$

If the simple linear regression of Y on X_1 is estimated from a sample of n observations, the resulting slope estimate is generally biased for β_1. However, in the special case where the sample correlation between X_1 and X_2 is 0, this will not be so. In fact, in that case the same estimate results whether or not X_2 is included in the regression equation.

a. Explain verbally why this statement is true.
b. Show algebraically that this statement is true.

Application Exercises

13.21 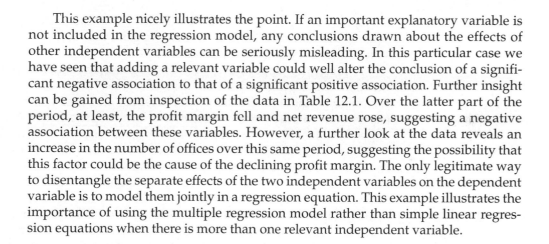 Transportation Research Inc. has asked you to prepare some multiple regression equations to estimate the effect of variables on fuel economy.

The data for this study are contained in the data file **Motors**, and the dependent variable is miles per gallon—milpgal—as established by the Department of Transportation certification.

a. Prepare a regression equation that uses vehicle horsepower—horspwer—and vehicle weight—weight—as independent variables. Interpret the coefficients.

b. Prepare a second biased regression with vehicle weight not included. What can you conclude about the coefficient of horsepower?

13.22   Use the data in the file **Citydat** to estimate a regression equation that can be used to determine the marginal effect of the percent commercial property on the market value per owner-occupied residence (Hseval). Include the percent owner-occupied residences (Homper), percent industrial property (Indper), the median rooms per residence (sizehse), and per capita income (Incom 72) as additional predictor variables in your multiple regression equation. The variables are included on your data disk and described in the Chapter 12 appendix. Indicate which of the variables are conditionally significant. Your final equation should include only significant variables. Run a second regression with median rooms per residence excluded. Interpret the new coefficient for percent commercial property that results from the second regression. Compare the two coefficients.

13.5 MULTICOLLINEARITY

If a regression model is correctly specified and the assumptions are satisfied, the least squares estimates are the best that can be achieved. Nevertheless, in some circumstances they may not be very good!

To illustrate, suppose that we wish to develop a model to predict unit sales as a function of our price and the competitor's price. Imagine, now, that you are in the fortunate position of the laboratory scientist and that you are able to design the experiment to study this problem. The best approach to selecting observations depends somewhat on the objectives of the analysis, but there are best strategies.

There are, however, choices that we would not make. For example, we would not choose the same values of the independent variables for all of the observations. Another bad choice would be to select independent variables that are highly correlated. In Section 12.2 we saw that it would be impossible to estimate the coefficients if the independent variables were perfectly correlated. And in Section 12.4 we saw that the variance of coefficient estimators increases as the correlation moves away from 0. In Figure 13.7 we see examples of perfect correlation between the variables X_1 and X_2. From these plots we see that changes in one variable are directly related to changes in the other variable. Now suppose that we were attempting to use

Figure 13.7
Two Designs with Perfect Multicollinearity

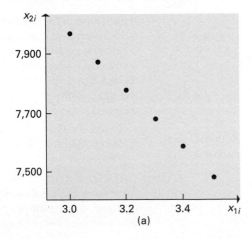

(a)

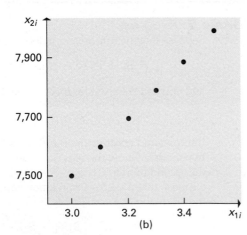

(b)

independent variable values such as these to estimate the coefficients of the regression model:

$$y_i = \beta_0 + \beta_1 x_{1i} + \beta_2 x_{2i} + \varepsilon_i$$

The futility of such a task is apparent. If a change in X_1 occurs simultaneously with a change in X_2, then we cannot tell which of the independent variables actually is related to the change in Y. If we want to assess the separate effects of the independent variables, it is essential that they not move exactly in unison through the experiment. The standard assumptions for multiple regression analysis exclude cases of perfect correlation between independent variables.

The use of the independent variables in Figure 13.7 would be a bad design choice. A slightly less extreme case is illustrated in Figure 13.8. Here, the design points do not lie on single straight lines but are very close to doing so. In this situation the results provide some information about the separate influences of the independent variables, but not very much. It will be possible to calculate least squares estimates of the coefficients, but these coefficient estimates will have high variance. In addition the point estimate of a coefficient can be quite different from the actual mean value of the coefficient—even resulting in a coefficient estimate that has an incorrect sign. As a result, the estimated coefficients will not be statistically significant and could be misleading even when the actual effect of the independent variable on the dependent variable might be quite strong. This phenomenon is referred to as **multicollinearity**. A classic example of multicollinearity often occurs when data from a competitive product market are used to estimate the relationship between quantity sold and price when the competitor's price is also included. Because both competitors are operating in the same market they will tend to adjust prices when the competitor makes a price adjustment. Driving past several gasoline stations on an urban street makes this behavior quite clear. We also discussed the effects of correlated independent variables extensively in Chapter 12.

In the vast majority of practical cases involving business and economic applications, we are not able to control the choice of variable observations. Rather, we are constrained to work with the particular data set that fate has given us. In this context, then, multicollinearity is a problem arising not from a bad choice of data but from the data that are available for our analysis. The savings and loan example in Chapter 12 had a high correlation between the independent variables—but that was the reality of the problem environment. More generally, in regression equations involving several independent variables, the multicollinearity problem arises from patterns of strong

Figure 13.8
Illustrations of
Designs with
Multicollinearity

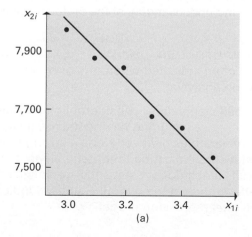

(a)

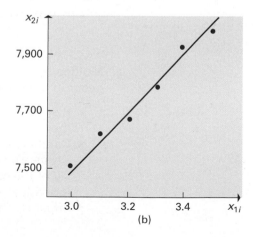

(b)

intercorrelations among the independent variables. Perhaps the most frustrating aspect of the problem, which can be summarized as having data that are not very informative about the parameters of interest, is that typically little can be done about it. It is, however, still important to be aware of the problem and watch for its occurrence.

There are a number of indicators of multicollinearity. First, of course, you should always examine a simple correlation matrix of the independent variables to determine if any of the independent variables are individually correlated. We did this in the extended application example in Section 12.9. Another indication of the likely presence of multicollinearity occurs when, taken as a group, a set of independent variables appears to exert considerable influence on the dependent variable, but when looked at separately, through tests of hypotheses, all appear individually to be insignificant. In this case a linear function of the several variables might be used to compute a new variable to replace several correlated variables. Another strategy is to regress individual independent variables on all of the other independent variables in the model. This can indicate complex examples of multicollinearity. Given multicollinearity, it would be unwise in these circumstances to jump to the conclusion that a particular independent variable did not affect the dependent variable. Rather, it is preferable to acknowledge that the group as a whole is clearly influential, but the data are not sufficiently informative to allow the disentangling, with any precision, of its members' separate effects.

Another related problem occurs if redundant or irrelevant predictor variables are included in a model. If these unnecessary variables are correlated with the other predictor variables—and they often are—then the variance of the coefficient estimates for the important variables will be increased, as noted in Section 12.4. As a result, the overall efficiency of the coefficient estimates will be reduced. Care should be taken to avoid including irrelevant predictor variables.

There are several approaches that can be used in situations where multicollinearity is a problem. But they all require careful thinking and judgment about the objectives of the model and the problem environment that it represents. First, one can remove an independent variable that is highly correlated with one or more other independent variables. This will reduce the variance of the coefficient estimate, but, as shown in Section 12.4, you could introduce a bias in the coefficient estimate if the omitted variable is important in the model. You might be able to construct a new independent variable that is a function of several highly correlated independent variables. You might be able to substitute a new independent variable that represents the same influence but is not correlated with other independent variables. None of these is always the perfect solution. Multicollinearity and omitted variables from the previous section are both issues that require good model specification based on good judgment, experience, and understanding of the problem context.

Indicators of Multicollinearity

Multicollinearity is often indicated when one or more of the following occur in a regression analysis:

a. Regression coefficients differ considerably from values indicated by theory or experience including having incorrect signs.
b. Coefficients of variables believed to be a strong influence have small Student's t statistics indicating that their values do not differ from 0.
c. All of the coefficient student t statistics are small, indicating no individual effect, and yet the overall F statistic indicates a strong effect for the total regression model.

d. High correlations between individual independent variables or one or more of the independent variables have a strong linear regression relationship to the other independent variables or a combination of both.

Corrections for Multicollinearity

a. Remove one or more of the highly correlated independent variables. But as shown in Section 13.4 this might lead to a bias in coefficient estimation.
b. Change the model specification, including possibly a new independent variable that is a function of several correlated independent variables.
c. Obtain additional data that does not have the same strong correlations between the independent variables.

Note that you may not find that any of these corrections work and, thus, your regression model may not be suitable for its intended purpose. Consequently, a new analysis strategy may be needed.

EXERCISES

Application Exercises

13.23 In the regression model

$$Y = \beta_0 + \beta_1 X_1 + \beta_2 X_2$$

the extent of any multicollinearity can be evaluated by finding the correlation between X_1 and X_2 in the sample. Explain why this is so.

13.24 An economist estimates the following regression model:

$$y_i = \beta_0 + \beta_1 x_{1i} + \beta_2 x_{2i} + \varepsilon_i$$

The estimates of the parameters β_1 and β_2 are not very large compared with their respective standard errors. But the size of the coefficient of determination indicates quite a strong relationship between the dependent variable and the pair of independent variables. Having obtained these results, the economist strongly suspects the presence of multicollinearity. Since his chief interest is in the influence of X_1 on the dependent variable, he decides that he will avoid the problem of multicollinearity by regressing Y on X_1 alone. Comment on this strategy.

13.25 Based on data from 63 counties, the following model was estimated by least squares:

$$\hat{y} = 0.58 - 0.052x_1 - 0.005x_2 \qquad R^2 = 0.17$$
$$\phantom{\hat{y} = 0.58 - }{}_{(0.019)} \qquad {}_{(0.042)}$$

where

$\hat{y}$ = growth rate in real gross domestic product
x_1 = real income per capita
x_2 = average tax rate, as a proportion of gross national product

The numbers below the coefficients are the coefficient standard errors. After the independent variable X_1, real income per capita, was dropped from the model, the regression of growth rate in real gross domestic product on X_2, average tax rate, was estimated. This yielded the following fitted model:

$$\hat{y} = 0.060 - 0.074x_2 \qquad R^2 = 0.072$$
$$\phantom{\hat{y} = 0.060 - }{}_{(0.34)}$$

Comment on this result.

13.6 HETEROSCEDASTICITY

The least squares estimation method and its inferential procedures are based on the standard regression assumptions. When these assumptions hold, least squares regression provides a powerful set of analysis tools. However, when one or more of these assumptions are violated, the estimated coefficients can be inefficient, and the inferences drawn can be misleading.

In this and the next section we consider the problems associated with the assumptions concerning the distribution of error terms ε_i in the following model:

$$y_i = \beta_0 + \beta_1 x_{1i} + \beta_2 x_{2i} + \cdots + \beta_K x_{Ki} + \varepsilon_i$$

Specifically, we have assumed that these errors have uniform variance and are uncorrelated with each other. In the following section we examine the possibility of correlated errors. Here, we consider the assumption of uniform variance.

There are many examples that suggest the possibility of nonuniform variance. Consider a situation in which we are interested in factors affecting output from a particular industry. We collect data from several different firms that include measures of output and likely predictor variables. If these firms have different sizes, then total output will vary. In addition, it is likely that the larger firms have greater variance in their output measure compared to small firms. This results from the observation that there are more factors that affect the error terms in a large firm than there are in a small firm. Hence, the error terms will be larger in both positive and negative terms.

Models in which the error terms do not all have the same variance are said to exhibit **heteroscedasticity**. When this phenomenon is present, least squares is not the most efficient procedure for estimating the coefficients of the regression model. Moreover, the usual procedures for deriving confidence intervals and tests of hypotheses for these coefficients are no longer valid. Thus, we need procedures that test for heteroscedasticity. Most of the common procedures check the assumption of constant error variance against some plausible alternative. We may find that the size of the error variance is directly related to one of the independent predictor variables. Another possibility is that the variance increases with the expected value of the dependent variable.

In our estimated regression model we can obtain estimates of the expected values of the dependent variable by using the following:

$$\hat{y} = b_0 + b_1 x_{1i} + b_2 x_{2i} + \cdots + b_K x_{Ki}$$

And, in turn, we can estimate the error terms, ε_i, by the residuals:

$$e_i = y_i - \hat{y}_i$$

We often find that graphical techniques are useful for detecting heteroscedasticity. In practice, we prepare scatter plots of the residuals versus the independent variables and the predicted values $\hat{y}_i$, from the regression. For example, consider Figure 13.9, which shows possible plots of the residual, e_i, against the independent variable X_{1i}. In part (a) of the figure, we see that the magnitude of the errors tends to increase with increasing values of X_1, indicating that the error variances are not constant. This

Figure 13.9
Plots of Residuals
Against an
Independent
Variable

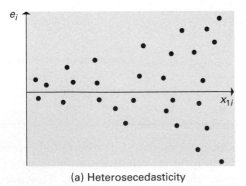

(a) Heterosecedasticity

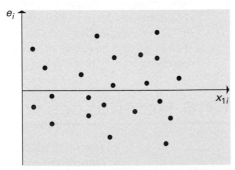

(b) No Apparent Heterosecedasticity

"fanning out" of the residuals will result in an inefficient estimate of the error term, but the effect can be removed by an appropriate transformation as we will show next. In contrast, part (b) of the figure shows no systematic relationship between the errors and X_1. Thus, in part (b) there is no evidence of nonuniform variance.

In Chapter 12 we developed a least squares regression model to estimate the relationship between the savings and loan profit margin (Y), the net revenue per deposit dollar (X_1), and the number of offices (X_2) through the following model:

$$\hat{y} = b_0 + b_1 x_{1i} + b_2 x_{2i}$$

Consider the estimated regression model from Figure 12.3. We computed the residuals for all observations using the procedure in the extended example problem in Section 12.9. In Figures 13.10 and 13.11 we present scatter plots of the residuals versus the revenue per deposit dollar and versus the number of offices. Examination of these plots indicates that there does not appear to be any relationship between the magnitude of the residuals and either of the independent variables. Figure 13.12 presents a scatter plot of the residuals versus the predicted value of the dependent variable. Again, there does not appear to be any relationship between the predicted value of Y and the magnitude of the residuals. Based on an examination of the residual plots, we find no evidence of heteroscedasticity.

We now consider a more formal procedure for detecting heteroscedasticity and for estimating the coefficients of regression models when it is strongly suspected that the assumption of constant error variance is violated. There are many possible forms for heteroscedasticity that can be detected with a variety of procedures. We

Figure 13.10
Plot of Residuals versus Revenues per Deposit Dollar

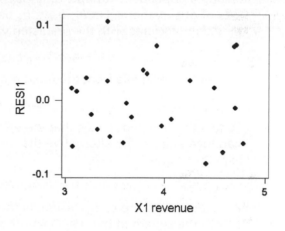

Figure 13.11
Plot of Residuals versus Number of Offices

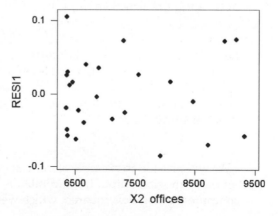

Figure 13.12
Plot of Residuals
versus Predicted
Profit Margin

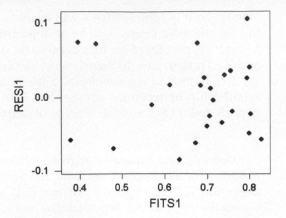

will consider one such procedure that can be used to detect heteroscedasticity when the variance of the error term has a linear relationship with the predicted value of the dependent variable.

Test for Heteroscedasticity

Consider a regression model

$$y_i = \beta_0 + \beta_1 x_{1i} + \beta_2 x_{2i} + \cdots + \beta_K x_{Ki} + \varepsilon_i$$

linking a dependent variable to K independent variables and based on n sets of observations. Let b_0, b_1,..., b_K be the least squares estimate of the model coefficients with the predicted values

$$\hat{y}_i = b_0 + b_1 x_{1i} + b_2 x_{2i} + \cdots + b_K x_{Ki}$$

and let the residuals from the fitted model be as follows:

$$e_i = y_i - \hat{y}_i$$

To test the null hypothesis that the error terms, ε_i, all have the same variance against the alternative that their variances depend on the expected values

$$\hat{y}_i = b_0 + b_1 x_{1i} + b_2 x_{2i} + \cdots + b_K x_{Ki}$$

we estimate a simple regression. In this regression the dependent variable is the square of the residuals—that is, e_i^2—and the independent variable is the predicted value, $\hat{y}_i$,

$$e_i^2 = a_0 + a_1 \hat{y}_i \tag{13.2}$$

Let R^2 be the coefficient of determination of this auxiliary regression. Then, for a test of significance level α, the null hypothesis is rejected if nR^2 is bigger than $\chi_{1,\alpha}^2$, where $\chi_{1,\alpha}^2$ is the critical value of the chi-square random variable with 1 degree of freedom and probability of error α and n is the sample size.

We will provide an example of this test using the savings and loan example. A subset of the regression output from Minitab is shown in Figure 13.13. Minitab was used to compute the residuals squared, which were then regressed on the predicted value.

```
The regression equation is
ResSquared = 0.00621 - 0.00550 FITS1

Predictor          Coef        SE Coef          T          P
Constant         0.006211     0.002970       2.09       0.048
FITS1           -0.005503     0.004327      -1.27       0.216


S = 0.002742    R-Sq = 6.6%     R-Sq(adj) = 2.5%

Analysis of Variance

Source              DF           SS              MS         F        P
Regression           1    0.000012158     0.000012158     1.62     0.216
Residual Error      23    0.000172939     0.000007519
Total               24    0.000185097
```

From the regression of the squared residuals on the predicted values, we obtain the following estimated model:

$$e^2 = 0.00621 + 0.00550\,\hat{y} \qquad R^2 = 0.066$$
$$\text{(0.00433)}$$

The regression includes $n = 25$ observations, and, thus, the test statistic is as follows:

$$nR^2 = (25)(0.066) = 1.65$$

From Table 7 in the appendix, we find, for a 10% significance level test

$$\chi^2_{1,0.10} = 2.71$$

Therefore, we cannot reject the null hypothesis that the regression model has uniform variance over the predicted values. This confirms our initial conclusions based on examining the scatter plots of residuals in Figures 13.10, 13.11, and 13.12.

Now suppose that we had rejected the null hypothesis that the variance was uniform. Then ordinary least squares would not be the appropriate estimation procedure for the initial model. There are a number of estimation strategies depending on the nature of the nonuniform error. Most procedures involve transforming the model variables so that the error terms have a uniform magnitude over the range of the model. Consider the example where the variance of the error terms is directly proportional to the square of the expected value of the dependent variable. In this case we could approximate the model error term as

$$\varepsilon_i = \hat{y}_i \delta_i$$

where δ_i is a random variable with uniform variance over the range of the regression model. Using this error term, the regression model would be as follows:

$$y_i = \beta_0 + \beta_1 x_{1i} + \beta_2 x_{2i} + \cdots + \beta_K x_{Ki} + \hat{y}_i \delta_i$$

In this approximation the error term fans out or increases linearly with the expected value—implying that the variance increases with the square of the expected value. Here, we can obtain an error term whose magnitude is uniform over the model by dividing every term on both sides of the equation by $\hat{y}_i$. When this particular form is assumed, a simple two-stage procedure is used to estimate the parameters of the regression model. At the first stage the model is estimated by least squares in the usual way, and the predicted values, $\hat{y}_i$, of the dependent variable are recorded. At the second stage we estimate the regression equation

$$\frac{y_i}{\hat{y}_i} = \beta_0 \frac{1}{\hat{y}_i} + \beta_1 \frac{x_{1i}}{\hat{y}_i} + \beta_2 \frac{x_{2i}}{\hat{y}_i} + \cdots + \beta_K \frac{x_{Ki}}{\hat{y}_i} + \delta_i$$

with an error term that meets the standard regression assumptions. In this model we regress $y_i / \hat{y}_i$ on the independent variables $1 / \hat{y}_i, x_{1i} / \hat{y}_i, x_{2i} / \hat{y}_i, ..., x_{Ki} / \hat{y}_i$. This model does not include a constant or Y-intercept term, and most statistical packages have an option that provides for coefficient estimates with the constant term excluded. The estimated coefficients are the estimates for the original model coefficients. Many additional similar procedures can be found in any good econometrics textbook under the heading of "weighted least squares."

The appearance of heteroscedastic errors can also result if a linear regression model is estimated in circumstances where a log linear model is appropriate. When the process is such that a log linear model is appropriate, we should make the transformations and estimate a log linear model. Taking logarithms will dampen the influence of large observations, especially if the large observations result from percentage growth from previous states—an exponential growth pattern. The resulting model will often appear to be free from heteroscedasticity. Log linear models are often appropriate when the data under study are time series of economic variables, such as consumption, income, and money, that tend to grow exponentially over time.

EXERCISES

Application Exercises

13.26 In Chapter 11, the regression of retail sales per household on disposable income per household was estimated by least squares. The data are given in Table 11.1, and Table 11.2 shows the residuals and the predicted values of the dependent variable.

a. Graphically check for heteroscedasticity in the regression errors.
b. Check for heteroscedasticity by using a formal test.

13.27 Consider a regression model that uses 48 observations. Let e_i denote the residuals from the fitted regression and $\hat{y}_i$ the in-sample predicted values of the dependent variable. The least squares regression of e_i^2 on $\hat{y}_i$ has coefficient of determination 0.032. What can you conclude from this finding?

13.28 The data file **Household Income** contains data for 50 states in the United States. The variables included in the data file are the percentage of females that are in the labor force (Y), median household personal income (X_1), mean years of education completed by females (X_2), and the unemployment rate of women (X_3).

a. Compute the multiple regression of Y on X_1, X_2, and X_3.
b. Graphically check for heteroscedasticity in the regression errors.
c. Use a formal test to check for heteroscedasticity.

13.29 You have been asked by East Anglica Realty Ltd. to provide a linear model that will estimate the selling price of homes as a function of family. There is particular concern for obtaining the most efficient estimate of the relationship between income and house price. East Anglica has collected data on their sales experience over the past 5 years and the data is contained in the file **East Anglica Realty Ltd**.

a. Estimate the regression of house price on family income.
b. Graphically check for heteroscedasticity.
c. Use a formal test of hypothesis to check for heteroscedasticity.
d. If you establish that there is heteroscedasticity in b and c, perform another regression that corrects for heteroscedasticity.

13.7 AUTOCORRELATED ERRORS

In this section we will examine the effects on the regression model if the error terms in a regression model are correlated with one another. Up to this point we have assumed that the random errors for our model are independent. However, in many business and economic problems we use time-series data. When time-series data are analyzed, the error term represents the effect of all factors, other than the independent variables, that influence the dependent variable. In time-series data the behavior of many of these factors might be quite similar over several time periods, and the result would be a correlation between the error terms that are close together in time.

For example, suppose you were estimating consumption of durable goods as a function of disposable income, interest rate, and possibly some other variables. However, other factors such as consumer concern about future employment, world conflicts, global warming, and other similar concerns would likely also effect consumption. Since these factors are not included as predictor variables in the model their effect would be included in the error term. And it is likely that these effects would continue over several time periods and, thus, the effects on the error term would be correlated over several time periods. These correlations between error terms from adjacent time periods are, thus, common in many models constructed using time-series data.

To emphasize time-series observations, we will subscript the observations by t and write the regression model as follows:

$$y_t = \beta_0 + \beta_1 x_{1t} + \beta_2 x_{2t} + \cdots + \beta_K x_{Kt} + \varepsilon_t$$

The hypothesis tests and confidence intervals in multiple regression assume that the errors are independent. If the errors are not independent, then the estimated standard errors for the coefficients are biased. For example, it can be shown that, if there is a positive correlation between the error terms from adjacent time-series observations, then the least squares estimate of the coefficient standard error is too small. As a result, the computed Student's t statistic for the coefficient will be too large. This could lead us to conclude that certain coefficients are significantly different from 0—by rejecting the null hypothesis $\beta_j = 0$—when, in fact, the null should not be rejected. In addition, estimated confidence intervals would be too narrow.

It is therefore critically important in regressions with time-series data to test the hypothesis that the error terms are not correlated with one another. Correlations between first-order errors through time are defined as **autocorrelated errors**. As we study this problem, it is useful to have in mind some autocorrelation structure. One appealing model is that the error in time t, ε_t, is highly correlated with the error in the previous time period, ε_{t-1}, but less correlated with errors two or more periods previous in the time series. We will define

$$\text{Corr}(\varepsilon_t, \varepsilon_{t-1}) = \rho$$

where ρ is a correlation coefficient and, thus, exists over the range from -1 to $+1$, as discussed in Chapter 11. In most applications we are most concerned about positive values of the correlation coefficient. For errors that are separated by l periods the autocorrelation can be modeled as follows:

$$\text{Corr}(\varepsilon_t, \varepsilon_{t-1}) = \rho^l$$

As a result, the correlation decays rapidly as the number of periods of separation grows. We see then that the correlation between errors far apart in time is relatively weak, while that between errors closer to one another is possibly quite strong.

Now, if we assume that the errors ε_t all have the same variance, it is possible to show that the autocorrelation structure corresponds to the model

$$\varepsilon_t = \rho \varepsilon_{t-1} + u_t$$

where the random variable u_t has a mean of 0 and a constant variance of σ^2, and is not autocorrelated. This is defined as the first-order autoregressive model of autocorrelated behavior. Looking at this equation, we see that the value taken by the error at time t, ε_t, depends on its value in the previous time period (the strength of that dependence being determined by the correlation coefficient ρ) and on a second random term μ_t. This model is illustrated in Figure 13.14, which shows time plots of errors generated by the model for values of $\rho = 0, 0.3, 0.6$, and 0.9. The case $\rho = 0$ corresponds to no autocorrelation in the errors. In part (a) of the figure, it can be seen that there is no apparent pattern in the progression through time of the errors. The value taken by one does not influence the values of the others. As we move from relatively weak autocorrelation ($\rho = 0.3$) to quite strong autocorrelation ($\rho = 0.9$), in parts (b), (c), and (d), the pattern that emerges through time of the errors becomes increasingly less jagged, so that in part (d) it is quite clear that an error is likely to be relatively close in value to its immediate neighbor.

Examination of Figure 13.14 suggests that graphical methods might be useful in detecting the presence of autocorrelated errors. Ideally, we would like to plot the model errors, ε_i, but these are unknown, so we typically examine the plot of residuals from the regression model. In particular, we could examine a time plot of residuals such as that shown in Figure 13.15 for the savings and loan regression. This time-series plot was prepared using Minitab.

Examining the time series plot in Figure 13.15, we do not see any autocorrelation in the residuals but instead have the jagged pattern seen in Figure 13.14(a). This evidence argues against autocorrelation. However, since the problem is so important, it is desirable to have a more formal test of the hypothesis of no autocorrelation in the errors of a regression model.

Figure 13.14
Time Plots of
Residuals from
Regressions
Whose Error
Terms Follow a
First-Order
Autoregressive
Process

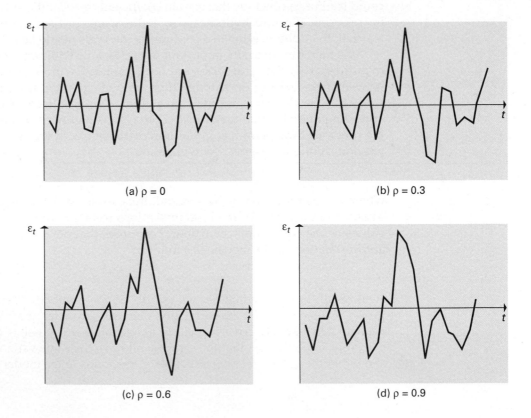

(a) $\rho = 0$

(b) $\rho = 0.3$

(c) $\rho = 0.6$

(d) $\rho = 0.9$

Figure 13.15
Time-Series Plot
of Residuals from
Savings and Loan
Regression

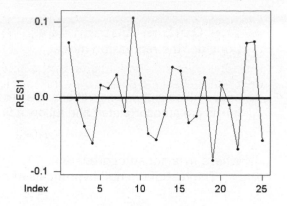

The test that is most often used is the **Durbin–Watson test**, based on the model residuals, e_t. The test statistic, d, is calculated by

$$d = \frac{\sum_{t=2}^{n}(e_t - e_{t-1})^2}{\sum_{t=1}^{n}e_t^2}$$

and the test procedure is described next.

We can show that the Durbin–Watson statistic can be written approximately as

$$d = 2(1 - r)$$

where r is the sample estimate of the population correlation, ρ, between adjacent errors. If the errors are not autocorrelated, then r is approximately 0 and d is approximately 2. In contrast, positive correlation leads to small values of d with 0 being the lower limit, and negative correlation leads to large values of d with 4 being the upper limit. There is a theoretical difficulty involved in basing tests for autocorrelated errors on the Durbin–Watson statistic. The problem is that the actual sampling distribution of d, even when the hypothesis of no autocorrelation is true, depends on the particular values of the independent variables. It is obviously infeasible to tabulate the distribution for every possible set of values of the independent variables. Fortunately, it is known that, whatever the independent variables the distribution of d lies between the distributions of two other random variables whose percentage points can be tabulated. For tests of significance levels 1% and 5%, cutoff points for these random variables are tabulated in Table 12 of the appendix. For various combinations of n and K the table gives values of d_L and d_U. The null hypothesis of no autocorrelation is rejected against the alternative of positive autocorrelation if the calculated d is less than d_L. The null hypothesis is accepted if d is larger than d_U and less than $4 - d_U$, while the test is inconclusive if d lies between d_L and d_U. Finally, if the d statistic is greater than $4 - d_L$, we would conclude that there is negative autocorrelation. This complex pattern is illustrated in Figure 13.16.

Figure 13.16
Decision Rule for
the Durbin–
Watson Test

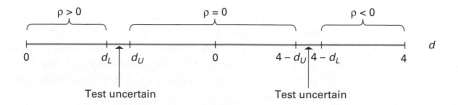

The Durbin–Watson Test

Consider the regression model

$$y_t = \beta_0 + \beta_1 x_{1t} + \beta_2 x_{2t} + \cdots + \beta_K x_{Kt} + \varepsilon_t$$

based on sets of n observations. We are interested in determining if the error terms are autocorrelated and follow a first-order autoregressive model

$$\varepsilon_t = \rho \varepsilon_{t-1} + u_t$$

where u_t is not autocorrelated.

The test of the null hypothesis of no autocorrelation

$$H_0 : \rho = 0$$

is based on the Durbin–Watson statistic

$$d = \frac{\sum_{t=2}^{n}(e_t - e_{t-1})^2}{\sum_{t=1}^{n} e_t^2} \tag{13.3}$$

where the e_t are the residuals when the regression equation is estimated by least squares. When the alternative hypothesis is of positive autocorrelation in errors—that is,

$$H_1 : \rho > 0$$

the decision rule is as follows:

Reject H_0 if $d < d_L$
Accept H_0 if $d > d_U$
Test inconclusive if $d_L < d < d_U$

where d_L and d_U are tabulated for values of n and K and for significance levels of 1% and 5% in Table 12 of the appendix.

Occasionally, one wants to test against the alternative of negative autocorrelation—that is,

$$H_1 : \rho < 0$$

Then the decision rule is as follows:

Reject H_0 if $d > 4 - d_L$
Accept H_0 if $d < 4 - d_U$
Test inconclusive if $4 - d_L > d > 4 - d_U$

The Durbin–Watson d statistic can be computed by most computer programs in the regression procedure by request. Figure 13.17 shows the Minitab output for the savings and loan example with the Durbin–Watson d statistic computed. The computed Durbin–Watson d statistic is 1.95, and from the appendix with $\alpha = 0.01$, $k = 2$, and $n = 25$ the critical values are $d_L = 0.98$ and $d_U = 1.30$. Thus, $H_0 : \rho = 0$ cannot be rejected, and we conclude that the error terms are not autocorrelated.

Figure 13.17
Durbin–Watson d
Statistic
Calculation

```
The regression equation is
Y profit = 1.56 + 0.237 X1 revenue -0.000249 X2 offices

Predictor        Coef        StDev         T         P
Constant      1.56450      0.07940     19.70     0.000
X1 reven      0.23720      0.05556      4.27     0.000
X2 offic   -0.00024908   0.00003205   -7.77     0.000


S = 0.05330    R-Sq = 86.5%   R-Sq(adj) = 85.3%

Analysis of Variance

Source            DF         SS         MS         F        P
Regression         2      0.40151    0.20076    70.66    0.000
Residual Error    22      0.06250    0.00284
Total             24      0.46402


Durbin-Watson statistic = 1.95
```

Estimation of Regressions with Autocorrelated Errors

When we conclude, based on the Durbin–Watson test, that we do have autocorrelated errors, we need to modify the regression procedure to remove the effect of these autocorrelated errors. Typically, this is done by an appropriate transformation of the variables used in the regression estimation procedure. We develop the basic method in the steps that follow. First, consider a multiple regression model with autocorrelated errors:

$$y_t = \beta_0 + \beta_1 x_{1t} + \beta_2 x_{2t} + \cdots + \beta_K x_{Kt} + \varepsilon_t$$

The same regression model at time $t - 1$ follows:

$$y_{t-1} = \beta_0 + \beta_1 x_{1t-1} + \beta_2 x_{2t-1} + \cdots + \beta_K x_{Kt-1} + \varepsilon_{t-1}$$

Multiplying both sides of this equation by ρ, the correlation between adjacent errors gives the following:

$$\rho y_{t-1} = \beta_0\rho + \beta_1\rho x_{1t-1} + \beta_2\rho x_{2t-1} + \cdots + \beta_K\rho x_{Kt-1} + \rho\varepsilon_{t-1}$$

Then we subtract this equation from the first equation to obtain

$$y_t - \rho y_{t-1} = \beta_0(1 - \rho) + \beta_1(x_{1t} - \rho x_{1t-1}) + \beta_2(x_{2t} - \rho x_{2t-1}) + \cdots + \beta_K(x_{Kt} - \rho x_{Kt-1}) + \mu_t$$

where

$$u_t = \varepsilon_t - \rho\varepsilon_{t-1}$$

and the random variable u_t has uniform variance and is not autocorrelated. We see that now we have a regression model linking the dependent variable $(y_t - \rho y_{t-1})$ and the independent variables $(x_{1t} - \rho x_{1,t-1})$, $(x_{2t} - \rho x_{2,t-1}),..., (x_{Kt} - \rho x_{K,t-1})$. The parameters of this model are precisely the same as those of the original model except that the constant term is $\beta_0(1 - \rho)$ instead of β_0. More important is the fact that in this model the errors are not autocorrelated, and, thus, least squares multiple regression can be used to estimate the model coefficients. The least squares inferential procedures for confidence intervals and hypothesis tests are appropriate for this transformed model.

Based on this analysis, we see that the problem of autocorrelated errors can be avoided by estimating the least squares regression using the dependent variable $(y_t - \rho y_{t-1})$ and the independent variables $(x_{1t} - \rho x_{1,t-1})$, $(x_{2t} - \rho x_{2,t-1}),...,$

$(x_{Kt} - \rho x_{K,t-1})$. Unfortunately, this approach faces a problem in practice because we do not know the value of ρ. Various procedures for obtaining an estimate for ρ are used in different computer programs. Here, we demonstrate a simple procedure where we use

$$r = 1 - \frac{d}{2}$$

to estimate ρ.

Estimation of Regression Models with Autocorrelated Errors

Suppose that we want to estimate the coefficients of the regression model

$$y_t = \beta_0 + \beta_1 x_{1t} + \beta_2 x_{2t} + \cdots + \beta_K x_{Kt} + \varepsilon_t$$

when the error term ε_t is autocorrelated.

This can be accomplished in two stages, as follows:

1. Estimate the model by least squares, obtaining the Durbin–Watson d statistic and hence the estimate

$$r = 1 - \frac{d}{2} \tag{13.4}$$

of the autocorrelation parameter.

2. Estimate by least squares a second regression in which the dependent variable is $(y_t - ry_{t-1})$ and the independent variables are $(x_{1t} - rx_{1,t-1})$, $(x_{2t} - rx_{2,t-1}),\ldots, (x_{Kt} - rx_{K,t-1})$.

The parameters $\beta_1, \beta_2, \ldots, \beta_k$ are estimated regression coefficients from this second model. An estimate of β_0 is obtained by dividing the estimated intercept for the second model by $(1 - r)$. Hypothesis tests and confidence intervals for the regression coefficients can be carried out using the output from the second regression.

Example 13.7   Time-Series Regression Model (Regression Analysis with Correlated Errors)

In this extended example we demonstrate how to carry out a regression analysis, using Minitab, when the errors are autocorrelated. In this example we wish to develop a model that predicts the aggregate consumption of durable goods as a function of disposable income and the federal funds interest rate.

Solution   The data for this project are contained in a file named **Macro2008**. The variables for this data file are described in the chapter appendix. We will use the following variables:

CD   Personal Consumption Expenditures: Durable Goods (2000 real dollars)
YPDI   Disposable Personal Income (2000 real dollars)
FFED   Federal Funds Effective Rate

The data file contains quarterly data from 1947.1 (1st quarter) through 2008.2 (1st quarter), but we wish to estimate the model using data from 1980.1 through 2008.1. Therefore, our first task is to obtain a subset of the larger data by using Minitab.

We then run the multiple regression and obtain the output in Figure 13.18.

The Durbin–Watson statistic for this model is 0.2015, indicating positive autocorrelation. Thus, it is necessary to use transformations to obtain appropriate variables for running the regression. An estimated value for serial correlation, r, is computed using the relationship in Equation 13.4:

$$r = 1 - \frac{d}{2} = 1 - \frac{0.20}{2} = 0.90$$

Transformed variables are then computed in Minitab using the estimated value $r = 0.90$. Since the transformation uses a lagged value of each variable, we lose the first observation in the data set. Figure 13.19 presents the regression model prepared using the modified variables.

Figure 13.18 Multiple Regression to Predict Consumption of Durables: Original Data (Minitab Output)

Regression Analysis: Durable good versus Disposable P, Federal Fund

```
The regression equation is
Durable goods = - 755 + 0.223 Disposable Personal Income
                + 10.4 Federal Funds Rate


Predictor                        Coef    SE Coef       T      P
Constant                      -755.03      40.29  -18.74  0.000
Disposable Personal Income   0.223353   0.004958   45.05  0.000
Federal Funds Rate             10.439      1.998    5.22  0.000


S = 50.3072   R-Sq = 97.4%   R-Sq(adj) = 97.3%


Analysis of Variance

Source            DF        SS       MS        F      P
Regression         2  10241668  5120834  2023.39  0.000
Residual Error   110    278390     2531
Total            112  10520058


Source                       DF    Seq SS
Disposable Personal Income    1  10172578
Federal Funds Rate            1     69089


Unusual Observations

       Disposable
         Personal  Durable
Obs        Income    goods     Fit   SE Fit  Residual  St Resid
  6          3760   258.40  257.79    14.72      0.61      0.01 X
  7          3838   266.76  287.73    16.92    -20.96     -0.44 X
  8          3838   246.97  285.78    16.56    -38.81     -0.82 X

X denotes an observation whose X value gives it large leverage.


Durbin-Watson statistic = 0.201535
```

Figure 13.19 Regression Analysis Using Transformed Variables Without Autocorrelation (Minitab Output)

Regression Analysis: Durable cons versus Disposable I, Fed Funds Ad

```
The regression equation is
Durable cons adj = - 51.8 + 0.195 Disposable Income adj - 0.93 Fed Funds Adj


112 cases used, 1 cases contain missing values


Predictor                    Coef   SE Coef       T      P
Constant                  -51.820     7.599   -6.82  0.000
Disposable Income adj     0.19540   0.01124   17.38  0.000
Fed Funds Adj              -0.933     1.817   -0.51  0.609


S = 18.8067   R-Sq = 74.5%   R-Sq(adj) = 74.0%


Analysis of Variance

Source            DF       SS      MS       F      P
Regression         2   112686   56343  159.30  0.000
Residual Error   109    38552     354
Total            111   151238


Source                  DF   Seq SS
Disposable Income adj     1   112593
Fed Funds Adj             1       93


Unusual Observations

      Disposable   Durable
Obs   Income adj  cons adj     Fit   SE Fit   Residual   St Resid
  5          362     33.99   12.37    11.62      21.62       1.46 X
  9          378     33.19   24.20     6.56       8.99       0.51 X
 12          396     38.14   27.43     6.16      10.71       0.60 X
 88          616    161.72   68.95     2.53      92.77       4.98R
 89          918     85.43  128.55     4.24     -43.12      -2.35R
104          919     76.62  126.99     3.78     -50.37      -2.73R
105          878    156.42  118.95     3.41      37.47       2.03R

R denotes an observation with a large standardized residual.
X denotes an observation whose X value gives it large leverage.


Durbin-Watson statistic = 2.52246
```

Comparing the regression outputs in Figures 13.18 and 13.19 clearly indicates the problems associated with regression models that have autocorrelated errors. The first regression analysis is as follows:

$$\text{Durable Goods} = -755 + 0.223 \text{ Disposable Personal Income}$$
$$+ 10.4 \text{ Federal Funds Rate}$$
$$R^2 = 97.4\%$$
$$D.W. = 0.2015$$

The first regression has a Durbin–Watson d statistic of 0.2015, indicating strong positive autocorrelation. Based on the regression statistics for the estimated coefficients we conclude that both disposable income ($b_1 = 0.223$) and federal funds interest rate ($b_2 = 10.439$) are statistically significant predictors of consumption expenditures for durable goods.

However, the second regression analysis—using data for the model without autocorrelated errors—provides a different conclusion:

$$\text{Durable cons adj} = -51.8 + 0.195 \text{ Disposable Income adj} -$$
$$0.93 \text{ Fed Funds Adj} \qquad R^2 = 74.55\% \qquad \text{D.W.} = 2.52$$

Notice that the variable names have been modified to reflect the fact that they have been transformed to variables that will produce a model that does not have autocorrelation. In addition, note that the Durbin–Watson d statistic is 2.52, indicating that autocorrelation does not exist. We see that the estimated coefficient for disposable income, $b_1 = 0.195$, is similar to that from the first regression and that the coefficient standard error is 0.01124. The resulting Student's t statistic, 17.38, leads us to conclude that disposable income is a significant predictor of durable goods consumption. In contrast, the coefficient of federal funds interest rate is $b_2 = -0.93$ with a Student's t statistic of -0.51. Thus, we cannot reject the null hypothesis that the coefficient for federal funds interest rate is 0 and that we should eliminate that variable as a predictor in the regression model.

In this example we have seen that autocorrelation led to an incorrect conclusion concerning the importance of the federal funds interest rate. Without adjusting the data to remove the correlation we would have used the Student's t statistic from the model with the original data, and that Student's t statistic from the unadjusted regression overestimates the Student's t statistic from the adjusted regression. The Student's t for the disposable income coefficient in the first regression is also overestimated. However, after adjustment to the correct estimator we find that the coefficient is still substantially different from 0.

A number of statistical packages such as Eviews3 and SAS, which are designed for working with time-series data, have built-in routines that automatically estimate the autocorrelation coefficient and adjust for autocorrelation. Many of these routines have iterative computational routines and as a result generate improved estimates of model coefficients and variances compared to the routine demonstrated here. Thus, if you have access to such a package, you will find the estimation easier than using Minitab or Excel in a parallel procedure. In general, those other computer packages provide more efficient estimates of the coefficients.

Autocorrelated Errors in Models with Lagged Dependent Variables

When we have a regression model with lagged dependent variables on the right-hand side and also have autocorrelated errors, the usual least squares procedures can result in even more severe problems. In addition to the usual problems concerning the estimation of coefficient errors we also know that the coefficient estimators are biased and not consistent. This occurs because there is a correlation between the model error and a predictor variable, and that introduces a bias in the coefficient estimate. Unfortunately, in this situation of lagged dependent variables, the previously discussed procedures for testing for autocorrelated errors are not valid. So we will briefly introduce an appropriate procedure.

Consider the model

$$y_t = \beta_0 + \beta_1 x_{1t} + \beta_2 x_{2t} + \cdots + \beta_K x_{Kt} + \gamma y_{t-1} + \varepsilon_t$$

Suppose that this model is fitted to n sets of sample observations by least squares. Let d be the usual Durbin–Watson statistic with

$$r = 1 - \frac{d}{2}$$

and let s_c denote the estimated standard deviation of the estimated coefficient γ for the lagged dependent variable. Our null hypothesis is that the autoregressive parameter ρ is 0. A test of this hypothesis, approximately valid in large samples, is based on Durbin's h statistic:

$$h = r\sqrt{n/(1 - ns_c^2)}$$

Under the null hypothesis this statistic has a distribution that is well approximated in large samples by the standard normal. Thus, for example, the null hypothesis of no autocorrelation is rejected against the alternative that ρ is positive at the 5% significance level if the h statistic exceeds 1.645.

If the autoregressive error is

$$u_t = \varepsilon_t - \rho\varepsilon_{t-1}$$

then, using a modification of the procedure previously developed for autocorrelation adjustment, we can develop the following model:

$$y_t - \rho y_{t-1} = \beta_0(1 - \rho) + \beta_1(x_{1t} - \rho x_{1t-1}) + \beta_2(x_2 - \rho x_{2t-1}) + \cdots + \beta_K(x_{Kt} - \rho x_{Kt-1}) + \gamma(y_{t-1} - \rho y_{t-2}) + \delta_t$$

One possible approach to parameter estimation, which requires only an ordinary least squares estimation program, is to substitute, in turn, possible values of ρ—say, 0.1, 0.3, 0.5, 0.7, and 0.9—in the preceding equation. Then the regression of the dependent variable $(y_t - \rho y_{t-1})$ and the independent variables $(x_{1t} - \rho x_{1,t-1})$, $(x_{2t} - \rho x_{2,t-1})$,...., $(x_{Kt} - \rho x_{K,t-1})$, $(y_{t-1} - \rho y_{t-2})$ is fitted by least squares for each possible ρ value. The value of ρ chosen is that for which the resulting sum of squared errors is smallest. Inference about the β_j is then based on the corresponding fitted regression.

EXERCISES

Basic Exercises

13.30 Suppose that a regression was run with three independent variables and 30 observations. The Durbin–Watson statistic was 0.50. Test the hypothesis that there was no autocorrelation. Compute an estimate of the autocorrelation coefficient if the evidence indicates that there was autocorrelation.

   a. Repeat with the Durbin–Watson statistic equal to 0.80.
   b. Repeat with the Durbin–Watson statistic equal to 1.10.
   c. Repeat with the Durbin–Watson statistic equal to 1.25.
   d. Repeat with the Durbin–Watson statistic equal to 1.70.

13.31 Suppose that a regression was run with two independent variables and 28 observations. The Durbin–Watson statistic was 0.50. Test the hypothesis that there was no autocorrelation. Compute an estimate of the autocorrelation coefficient if the evidence indicates that there was autocorrelation.

   a. Repeat with the Durbin–Watson statistic equal to 0.80.
   b. Repeat with the Durbin–Watson statistic equal to 1.10.
   c. Repeat with the Durbin–Watson statistic equal to 1.25.
   d. Repeat with the Durbin–Watson statistic equal to 1.70.

Application Exercises

13.32 In a regression based on 30 annual observations, U.S. farm income was related to four independent variables—grain exports, federal government subsidies, population, and a dummy variable for bad weather years. The model was fitted by least squares, resulting in a Durbin–Watson statistic of 1.29. The regression of e_i^2 on $\hat{y}_i$ yielded a coefficient of determination of 0.043.

    a. Test for heteroscedasticity.
    b. Test for autocorrelated errors.

13.33 Consider the following regression model:

$$y_t = \beta_0 + \beta_1 x_{1t} + \beta_2 x_{2t} + \cdots + \beta_K x_{Kt} + \varepsilon_t$$

Show that if

$$\text{Var}(\varepsilon) = Kx_i^2 \qquad (K > 0)$$

then

$$\text{Var}\left[\frac{\varepsilon_i}{x_i}\right] = K$$

Discuss the possible relevance of this result in treating a form of heteroscedasticity.

13.34 Refer to Exercise 13.13. Let e_i denote the residuals from the fitted regression and $\hat{y}_i$ the in-sample predicted values. The least squares regression of e_i^2 on $\hat{y}_i$ has coefficient of determination of 0.087. What can you conclude from this finding?

13.35 ⬤ Refer to Exercise 13.13 on money supply in the United Kingdom. What can be concluded from the Durbin–Watson statistic for the fitted regression? (Use the data file, **Money UK**.)

13.36 ⬤ Refer to Exercise 13.18 on Thailand consumption. Test the null hypothesis of no autocorrelated errors against the alternative of positive autocorrelation. (Use the data file, **Thailand Consumption**.)

13.37 A factory operator hypothesized that his unit output costs (y) depend on wage rate (x_1), other input costs (x_2), overhead costs (x_3), and advertising expenditures (x_4). A series of 24 monthly observations was obtained, and a least squares estimate of the model yielded the following results:

$$\hat{y}_i = 0.75 + 0.24x_{1t} + 0.56x_{2t} - 0.32x_{3t} + 0.23x_{4t}$$
$$\quad\;\; (0.07) \qquad (0.12) \qquad (0.23) \qquad (0.5)$$
$$R^2 = 0.79 \qquad d = 0.85$$

The figures in parentheses below the estimated coefficients are their estimated standard errors.

What can you conclude from these results?

13.38 ⬤ The data file **Advertising Retail** shows, for a consumer goods corporation, 22 consecutive years of data on sales (y) and advertising (x).

    a. Estimate the regression:

$$y_t = \beta_0 + \beta_1 x_t + \varepsilon_t$$

    b. Check for autocorrelated errors in this model.
    c. If necessary, re-estimate the model, allowing for autocorrelated errors.

13.39 The omission of an important independent variable from a time-series regression model can result in the appearance of autocorrelated errors. In Example 13.5 we estimated the model

$$y_t = \beta_0 + \beta_1 x_{1t} + \varepsilon_t$$

relating profit margin to net revenue for our savings and loan data. Carry out a Durbin–Watson test on the residuals from this model. What can you infer from the results?

13.40 Refer to Exercise 13.11 on money spent by students on clothing. The Durbin–Watson statistic for the fitted regression model is 1.82. Test the null hypothesis of no autocorrelated errors against the alternative of positive autocorrelation.

Key Words

Chapter Exercises and Applications

13.41 Write brief reports, including examples, explaining the use of each of the following in specifying regression models:

    a. Dummy variables
    b. Lagged dependent variables
    c. The logarithmic transformation

13.42 Consider the fitting of the following model:

$$Y = \beta_0 + \beta_1 X_1 + \beta_2 X_2 + \beta_3 X_3$$

where

Y = tax ravenues as a percentage of gross national product in a country

X_1 = exports as a percentage of gross national product in the country

X_2 = income per capita in the country

X_3 = dummy variable taking the value 1 if the country participates in some form of economic integration, 0 otherwise

This provides a means of allowing for the effects on tax revenue of participation in some form of economic integration. Another possibility would be to estimate the regression

$$Y = \beta_0 + \beta_1 X_1 + \beta_2 X_2$$

separately for countries that did and did not participate in some form of economic integration. Explain how these approaches to the problem differ.

13.43 Discuss the following statement: "In many practical regression problems, multicollinearity is so severe that it would be best to run separate simple linear regressions of the dependent variable on each independent variable."

13.44 Explain the nature of and the difficulties caused by each of the following:

a. Heteroscedasticity
b. Autocorrelated errors

13.45 The following model was fitted to data on 90 German chemical companies:

$$\hat{y} = 0.819 + \underset{(1.79)}{2.11x_1} + \underset{(1.94)}{0.96x_2} - \underset{(0.144)}{0.059x_3} + \underset{(4.08)}{5.87x_4} +$$

$$\underset{(0.00115)}{0.00226x_5} \qquad \overline{R}^2 = .410$$

where the numbers in parentheses are estimated coefficient standard errors and

y = share price
x_1 = earnings per share
x_2 = funds flow per share
x_3 = dividends per share
x_4 = book value per share
x_5 = a measure of growth

a. Test at the 10% level the null hypothesis that the coefficient on x_1 is 0 in the population regression against the alternative that the true coefficient is positive.

b. Test at the 10% level the null hypothesis that the coefficient on x_2 is 0 in the population

regression against the alternative that the true coefficient is positive.

c. The variable X_2 was dropped from the original model, and the regression of Y on (X_1, X_3, X_4, X_5) was estimated. The estimated coefficient on X_1 was 2.95 with standard error 0.63. How can this result be reconciled with the conclusion of part (a).

13.46 The following model was fitted to data from 28 countries in 1989 in order to explain the market value of their debt at that time:

$$\hat{y} = 77.2 - \underset{(8.0)}{9.6x_1} - \underset{(2.73)}{17.2x_2} - \underset{(0.056)}{0.15x_3} + \underset{(1.0)}{2.2x_4}$$

$$R^2 = 0.84$$

where

y = secondary market price, in dollars, in 1989 of $100 of the country's debt

x_1 = 1 if U.S. bank regulators have mandated write-down for the country's assets on books of U.S. banks, 0 otherwise

x_2 = 1 if the country suspended interest payments in 1989, 2 if the country suspended interest payments before 1989 and was still in suspension, and 0 otherwise

x_3 = debt-to-gross-national-product ratio

x_4 = rate of real gross national product growth, 1980−1985

The numbers below the coefficients are the coefficient standard errors.

a. Interpret the estimated coefficient on x_1.
b. Test the null hypothesis that, all else being equal, debt-to-gross-national-product ratio does not linearly influence the market value of a country's debt against the alternative that the higher this ratio, the lower the value of the debt.
c. Interpret the coefficient of determination.
d. The specification of the dummy variable x_2 is unorthodox. An alternative would be to replace x_2 by the pair of variables (x_5, x_6), defined as follows:

x_5 = 1 if the country suspended interest payments in 1989, 0 otherwise

x_6 = 1 if the country suspended interest payments before 1989 and was still in suspension, 0 otherwise

Compare the implications of these two alternative specifications.

13.47 An attempt was made to construct a regression model explaining student scores in intermediate economics courses (Reference 6). The population regression model assumed that

Y = total student score in intermediate economics courses

X_1 = mathematics score on Scholastic Aptitude Test

X_2 = verbal score on Scholastic Aptitude Test

X_3 = grade in college algebra (A = 4, B = 3, C = 2, D = 1)

X_4 = grade in college principles of economics course

X_5 = dummy variable taking the value 1 if the student is female, and 0 if male

X_6 = dummy variable taking the value 1 if the instructor is male, and 0 if female

X_7 = dummy variable taking the value 1 if the student and instructor are the same gender, and 0 otherwise

This model was fitted to data on 262 students. Next we report t-ratios, so that t_i is the ratio of the estimate of β_i to its associated estimated standard error. These ratios are as follows:

$t_1 = 4.69,\quad t_2 = 2.89,\quad t_3 = 0.46,\quad t_4 = 4.90,$
$t_5 = 0.13,\quad t_6 = -1.08,\quad t_7 = 0.88$

The objective of this study was to assess the impact of the gender of student and instructor on performance. Write a brief report outlining what has been learned about this issue.

13.48 The following regression was fitted by least squares to 32 annual observations on time-series data:

$$\log y_t = 4.52 - \underset{(0.28)}{0.62} \log x_{1t} + \underset{(0.38)}{0.92} \log x_{2t} +$$
$$\underset{(0.21)}{0.61} \log x_{3t} + \underset{(0.12)}{0.16} \log x_{4t}$$
$$\overline{R}^2 = 0.683 \qquad d = 0.61$$

where

y_t = quantity of U.S. wheat exported

x_{1t} = price of U.S. wheat on world market

x_{2t} = quantity of U.S. wheat harvested

x_{3t} = measure of income in countries importing U.S. wheat

x_{4t} = price of barley on world market

The numbers below the coefficients are the coefficient standard errors.

a. Interpret the estimated coefficient on $\log x_{1t}$ in the context of the assumed model.

b. Test at the 5% level the null hypothesis that, all else being equal, income in importing countries has no effect on U.S. wheat exports against the alternative that higher income

leads to higher expected exports. (Ignore, for now, the Durbin–Watson d statistic.)

c. What null hypothesis can be tested by the d statistic? Carry out this test for the present problem, using a 1% significance level.

d. In view of your finding in part (c), comment on your conclusion in part (b). How might you proceed to test the null hypothesis of part (b)?

13.49 The following regression was fitted by least squares to 30 annual observations on time-series data:

$$\log y_t = 4.31 + \underset{(0.17)}{0.27} \log x_{1t} + \underset{(0.21)}{0.53} \log x_{2t} - \underset{(0.30)}{0.82} \log x_{3t}$$
$$\overline{R}^2 = .615 \qquad d = .49$$

where

y_t = number of business failures

x_{1t} = rate of unemployment

x_{2t} = short-term interest rate

x_{3t} = value of new business orders placed

The numbers below the coefficients are the coefficient standard errors.

a. Interpret the estimated coefficient on $\log x_{3t}$ in the context of the assumed model.

b. What null hypothesis can be tested by the d statistic? Carry out this test for the present problem, using a 1% significance level.

c. Given your results in part (b), is it possible to test, with the information given, the null hypothesis that, all else being equal, short-term interest rates do not influence business failures?

d. Estimate the correlation between adjacent error terms in the regression model.

13.50 A stockbroker is interested in the factors influencing the rate of return on the common stock of banks. For a sample of 30 banks the following regression was estimated by least squares:

$$\hat{y} = 2.37 + \underset{(0.39)}{0.84} x_1 + \underset{(0.12)}{0.15} x_2 - \underset{(0.09)}{0.13} x_3 + \underset{(1.97)}{1.67} x_4$$
$$R^2 = 0.317$$

where

y = percentage rate of return on common stock of bank

x_1 = percentage rate of growth of bank's earnings

x_2 = percentage rate of growth of bank's assets

x_3 = loan losses as percentage of bank's assets

x_4 = 1 if bank head office is in New York City, and 0 otherwise

The numbers below the coefficients are the coefficient standard errors.

a. Interpret the estimated coefficient on x_4.

b. Interpret the coefficient of determination, and use it to test the null hypothesis that, taken as a group, the four independent variables do not linearly influence the dependent variable.

c. Let e_i denote the residuals from the fitted regression and $\hat{y}_i$ the in-sample predicted values of the dependent variable. The least squares regression of e_i^2 on $\hat{y}_i$ yielded coefficient of determination 0.082. What can be concluded from this finding?

13.51 A market researcher is interested in the average amount of money per year spent by students on entertainment. From 30 years of annual data, the following regression was estimated by least squares:

$$\hat{y}_t = 40.93 + 0.253x_t + 0.546y_{t-1} \qquad d = 1.86$$
$$\quad\quad\quad\;\; (0.106) \quad\;\; (0.134)$$

where

y_t = expenditure per student, in dollars, on entertainment

x_t = disposable income per student, in dollars, after payment of tuition, fees, and room, and board

The numbers below the coefficients are the coefficient standard errors.

a. Find a 95% confidence interval for the coefficient on x_t in the population regression.

b. What would be the expected impact over time of a $1 increase in disposable income per student on entertainment expenditure?

c. Test the null hypothesis of no autocorrelation in the errors against the alternative of positive autocorrelation.

13.52 A local public utility would like to be able to predict a dwelling unit's average monthly electricity bill. The company statistician estimated by least squares the following regression model:

$$y_t = \beta_0 + \beta_1 x_{1t} + \beta_2 x_{2t} + \varepsilon_t$$

where

y_t = average monthly electricity bill, in dollars

x_{1t} = average bimonthly automobile gasoline bill, in dollars

x_{2t} = number of rooms in dwelling unit

From a sample of 25 dwelling units, the statistician obtained the following output from the SAS program:

Parameter	Estimate	Student's t for H_0: parameter = 0	Std. error of estimate
Intercept	−10.8030		
X1	−0.0247	−0.956	0.0259
X2	10.9409	18.517	0.5909

a. Interpret, in the context of the problem, the least squares estimate of β_2.

b. Test against a two-sided alternative the null hypothesis

$$H_0: \beta_1 = 0$$

c. The statistician is concerned about the possibility of multicollinearity. What information is needed to assess the potential severity of this problem?

d. It is suggested that household income is an important determinant of size of electricity bill. If this is so, what can you say about the regression estimated by the statistician?

e. Given the fitted model, the statistician obtains the predicted electricity bills, $\hat{y}_t$, and the residuals, e_t. He then regresses e_t^2 on $\hat{y}_t$, finding that the regression has a coefficient of determination of 0.0470. Interpret this finding.

13.53 ⬤ The data file **Indonesia Revenue** shows 15 annual observations from Indonesia on total government tax revenues other than from oil (y), national income (x_1), and the value added by oil as a percentage of gross domestic product (x_2). Estimate by least squares the following regression:

$$\log y_t = \beta_0 + \beta_1 \log x_{1t} + \beta_2 \log x_{2t} + \varepsilon_t$$

Write a report summarizing your findings, including a test for autocorrelated errors.

13.54 ⬤ The data file **German Income** shows 22 annual observations from the Federal Republic of Germany on percentage change in wages and salaries (y), productivity growth (x_1), and the rate of inflation (x_2), as measured by the gross national product price deflator. Estimate by least squares the following regression:

$$y_t = \beta_0 + \beta_1 x_{1t} + \beta_2 x_{2t} + \varepsilon_t$$

Write a report summarizing your findings, including a test for heteroscedasticity and a test for autocorrelated errors.

13.55 ⬤ The data file **Japan Imports** shows 35 quarterly observations from Japan on quantity of imports (y), ratio of import prices to domestic prices (x_1), and real gross national product (x_2). Estimate by least squares the following regression:

$$\log y_t = \beta_0 + \beta_1 \log x_{1t} + \beta_2 \log x_{2t} + \gamma \log y_{t-1} + \varepsilon_t$$

Write a report summarizing your findings, including a test for autocorrelated errors.

13.56 A study was conducted on the labor-hour costs of Federal Deposit Insurance Corporation (FDIC) audits of banks. Data were obtained on 91 such audits. Some of these were conducted by the FDIC alone and some jointly with state auditors.

Auditors rated banks' management as good, satisfactory, fair, or unsatisfactory. The model estimated was

$$\log y = 2.41 + \underset{(0.0477)}{0.3674} \log x_1 + \underset{(0.0628)}{0.2217} \log x_2 +$$
$$\underset{(0.0287)}{0.0803} \log x_3 - \underset{(0.2905)}{0.1755} x_4 + \underset{(0.1044)}{0.2799} x_5 +$$
$$\underset{(0.1657)}{0.5634} x_6 - \underset{(0.0787)}{0.2572} x_7 \qquad R^2 = 0.766$$

where

y = FDIC auditor labor-hours
x_1 = total assets of bank
x_2 = total number of offices in bank
x_3 = ratio of classified loans to total loans for bank
x_4 = 1 if management rating was "good," 0 otherwise
x_5 = 1 if management rating was "fair," 0 otherwise
x_6 = 1 if management rating was "unsatisfactory," 0 otherwise
x_7 = 1 if audit was conducted jointly with the state, 0 otherwise

The numbers in parentheses beneath coefficient estimates are the associated standard errors.

Write a report on these results.

13.57 The data file **Britain Sick Leave** shows data from Great Britain on the days of sick leave per person (Y), unemployment rate (X_1), ratio of benefits to earnings (X_2), and the real wage rate (X_3). Estimate the model

$$\log y_t = \beta_0 + \beta_1 \log x_{1t} + \beta_2 \log x_{2t} + \beta_3 \log x_{3t} + \varepsilon_t$$

and write a report on your findings. Include in your analysis a check on the possibility of autocorrelated errors and, if necessary, a correction for this problem.

13.58 The U.S. Department of Commerce has asked you to develop a regression model to predict quarterly investment in production and durable equipment. The suggested predictor variables include GDP, prime interest rate, per capita income lagged, federal government spending, and state and local government spending. The data for your analysis are found in the data file **Macro2008**, which is stored on your data disk and described in the data dictionary in the chapter appendix. Use data from the time period 1980.1 through 2008.1.

a. Estimate a regression model using only interest rate to predict the investment. Use the Durbin–Watson statistic to test for autocorrelation.

b. Find the best multiple regression equation to predict investment using the predictor variables previously indicated. Use the Durbin–Watson statistic to test for autocorrelation.

c. What are the differences between the regression models in parts (a) and (b) in terms of goodness of fit, prediction capability, autocorrelation, and contributions to understanding the investment problem?

13.59 An economist has asked you to develop a regression model to predict consumption of service goods as a function of Disposable Personal Income and other important variables. The data for your analysis are found in the data file **Macro2008**, which is stored on your data disk and described in the data dictionary in the chapter appendix. Use data from the period 1980.1 through 2008.1.

a. Estimate a regression model using only Disposable Personal Income to predict consumption of service goods. Test for autocorrelation using the Durbin–Watson statistic.

b. Estimate a multiple regression model using Disposable Personal Income, total consumption lagged 1 period, and prime interest rate as additional predictors. Test for autocorrelation. Does this multiple regression model reduce the problem of autocorrelation?

13.60 Jack Wong, a Tokyo investor, is considering plans to develop a primary steel plant in Japan. After reviewing the initial design proposal, he is concerned about the proposed mix of capital and labor. He has asked you to prepare several production functions using some historical data from the United States. The data file **Metals** contains 27 observations of the value-added output, labor input, and gross value of plant and equipment per factory.

a. Use multiple regression to estimate a linear production function with value-added output regressed on labor and capital.

b. Plot the residuals versus labor and equipment. Note any unusual patterns.

c. Use multiple regression with transformed variables to estimate a Cobb–Douglas production function of the form

$$Y = \beta_0 L^{\beta_1} K^{\beta_2}$$

where y is the value added, L is the labor input, and K is the capital input.

d. Use multiple regression transformed variables to estimate a Cobb–Douglas production function with constant returns to scale. Note that this production function has the same form as the function estimated in part (c), but it has the additional restriction that $\beta_1 + \beta_2 = 1$. To develop the transformed regression model, substitute β_2 as a function of β_1 and convert to a regression format.

e. Compare the three production functions using residual plots and a standard error of the estimate that is expressed in the same scale. You will need to convert the predicted values from parts (c) and (d), which are in logarithms, back to the original units. Then you can subtract the predicted values from the original values of Y to obtain the residuals. Use the residuals to compute comparable standard errors of the estimate.

13.61 The administrator of a small city has asked you to identify variables that influence the mean market value of houses in small midwestern cities. You have obtained data from a number of small cities, which are stored in the data file **Citydat**. The candidate predictor variables are the median size of the house (sizehse), the property tax rate (taxrate) (tax levy divided by total assessment), the total expenditures for city services (totexp), and the percent commercial property (comper).

a. Estimate the multiple regression model using all of the indicated predictor variables. Select only statistically significant variables for your final equation.

b. An economist stated that, since the data came from cities of different populations, your model is likely to contain heteroscedasticity. He argued that mean housing prices from larger cities would have a smaller variance because the number of houses used to compute the mean housing prices would be larger. Test for heteroscedasticity.

c. Estimate the multiple regression equation using weighted least squares with population as the weighting variable. Compare the coefficients for the weighted and unweighted multiple regression models.

13.62 The chief financial officer of a major service company has asked you to develop a regression model to predict consumption of service goods as a function of GDP and other important variables. The data for your analysis are found in the data file **Macro2008**, which is stored on your data disk and described in the data dictionary in the chapter appendix. Use data from the period 1980.1 through 2008.1.

a. Estimate a regression model using only GDP to predict consumption of service goods. Test for autocorrelation using the Durbin–Watson statistic.

b. Estimate a multiple regression model using GDP, total consumption lagged 1 period, imports or services, and prime interest rate as additional predictors. Test for autocorrelation. Does this multiple regression model reduce the problem of autocorrelation?

13.63 The marketing vice president of Consolidated Appliances has asked you to develop a regression model to predict consumption of durable goods as a function of Disposable Personal Income and other important variables. The data for your analysis are found in the data file **Macro2008**, which is stored on your data disk and described in the data dictionary in the chapter appendix. Use data from the period 1976.1 through 2008.1.

a. Estimate a regression model using only Disposable Personal Income to predict consumption of durable goods. Test for autocorrelation using the Durbin–Watson statistic.

b. Estimate a multiple regression model using Disposable Personal Income, total consumption lagged 1 period, imports of goods, population, and prime interest rate as additional predictors. Test for autocorrelation. Does this multiple regression model reduce the problem of autocorrelation?

Appendix

Data File Macro2008

Economic Series in Real Dollars

Quarterly data are available from the first quarter of 1947 through the first quarter of 2008 except where indicated. The data are in 2,000 dollars. Index numbers, [2000=100] Seasonally adjusted Bureau of Economic Analysis

Downloaded on 6/28/2008 At 9:59:43 AM Last Revised June 26, 2008

Code	Description	Start Date
FFED	Effective Federal Funds Rate	1954 03
FBPR	Bank Prime Loan Rate	1949 01

FM2	M2 Money Stock	1959 01
GDP	Gross Domestic Product	1947 01
C	Personal Consumption Expenditures	1947 01
CD	Durable Goods	1947 01
CN	Nondurable Goods	1947 01
CS	Services	1947 01
I	Gross Private Domestic Investment	1947 01
IF	Fixed Investment	1947 01
IN	Nonresidential	1947 01
IS	Structures	1947 01
IES	Equipment And Software	1947 01
IR	Residential	1947 01
X	Exports	1947 01
XG	Goods	1947 01
XS	Services	1947 01
M	Imports	1947 01
MG	Goods	1947 01
MS	Services	1947 01
G	Government Spending	1947 01
GF	Federal	1947 01
GD	National defense	1947 01
GN	Nondefense	1947 01
GSL	State and local	1947 01
YPI	Personal income	1947 01
YTAX	Less: Personal Current Taxes	1947 01
YDPI	Equals: Disposable Personal Income	1947 01
YPO	Less: Personal Outlays	1947 01
YPCE	Personal Consumption Expenditures	1947 01
YPS	Equals: Personal Saving	1947 01
POP	Population (Midperiod, Thousands)	1947 01
YPCI	Per Capita Income (Thousands)	1947 01

REFERENCES

Dhalla, N. K. 1979. Short-Term Forecasts of Advertising Expenditures. *Journal of Advertising Research* 19 (1): 7–13.

Carlson, A. & Gerrior G. 2006. Food Source Makes a Difference in Diet Quality. *Journal of Nutrition Education and Behavior* 38(4): 238–243.

Erikson, G. M. 1981. Using Ridge Regression to Estimate Directly Lagged Effects in Marketing. *Journal of American Statistical Association* 76:766–773.

Hsiao, C. 1979 Autoregressive Modeling of Canadian Money and Income Data. *Journal of American Statistical Association* 74:553–560.

McDonald, J. 1981. Modeling Demographic Relationships: An Analysis of Forecast Functions for Australian Births. *Journal of the American Statistical Association* 76:782–792.

Mills, T. C. 1978. The Functional Form of the UK Demand for Money. *Applied Statistics* 27:52–57.

Waldauer, C., V. G. Duggal, and M. L. Willliams. 1992. Gender Differences in Economic Knowledge: A Further Extension of the Analysis. *Quarterly Review of Economics and Finance* 32 (4): 138–143.

Chapter 14

Analysis of Categorical Data

Introduction

In this chapter we introduce *nonparametric* tests that are often the appropriate procedure needed to make statistical conclusions about qualitative data (nominal or ordinal data), or numerical data when the normality assumption cannot be made about the probability distribution of the population. Such data are frequently obtained in many settings including marketing research studies, business surveys, and questionnaires.

First we discuss certain tests that are based on the chi-square distribution such as a test of the hypothesis that data are generated by a *fully specified* probability distribution. This technique is often used by market researchers to determine if products are equally preferred by potential customers or to check if the market shares for several brands of a product have changed over a given period of time.

Next, we test the hypothesis that data are generated by some distribution, such as the binomial, the Poisson, or the normal, without assuming the parameters of that distribution to be known. In these circumstances the available data can be used to estimate the unknown population parameters. A goodness-of-fit test is used when population parameters are estimated. The chi-square test can be extended to deal with a problem in which a sample is taken from a population, each of whose members can be uniquely cross-classified according to a pair of characteristics. The hypothesis to be tested is of no association in the population between possessions of these characteristics. Marketing professionals use this procedure frequently. For larger contingency tables it is convenient to use a software package to determine the test-statistic and *p*-value.

Finally we consider nonparametric alternatives to various procedures introduced earlier in the book. It is not our intention here to attempt to describe the entire wide array of such nonparametric procedures that are available. Rather, our objective is the more modest one of providing a flavor of selected nonparametric procedures including the Sign test, the Wilcoxon signed rank test, the Mann–Whitney *U* test, the Wilcoxon rank sum test, and the Spearman rank correlation test.

14.1 GOODNESS-OF-FIT TESTS: SPECIFIED PROBABILITIES

The most straightforward test of this type is illustrated with a study that observed a random sample of 300 subjects purchasing a soft drink. Of these subjects, 75 selected brand A, 110 selected brand B, and the remainder selected brand C. This information is displayed in Table 14.1.

More generally, consider a random sample of n observations that can be classified according to K categories. If the number of observations falling into each category is $O_1, O_2,..., O_K$, the setup is as shown in Table 14.2.

The sample data are to be used to test a null hypothesis specifying the probabilities that an observation falls in each of the categories. In the example of 300 subjects purchasing a soft drink, the null hypothesis (H_0) might be that a randomly chosen subject is equally likely to select any of the three different varieties. This null hypothesis, then, specifies that the probability is $1/3$ that a sample observation falls into each of the three categories. To test this hypothesis, it is natural to compare the sample numbers *observed* with what would be *expected* if the null hypothesis were true. Given a total of 300 sample observations, the expected number of subjects in each category under the null hypothesis would be $(300)(1/3) = 100$. This information is summarized in Table 14.3.

Table 14.1 Brand Selection

CATEGORY (BRAND)	A	B	C	TOTAL
Number of subjects	75	110	115	300

Table 14.2 Classification of *n* Observations into *K* Categories

CATEGORY	1	2	...	K	TOTAL
Number of observations	O_1	O_2	...	O_K	n

Table 14.3 Observed and Expected Number of Purchases for Three Brands of Soft Drink

CATEGORY (BRAND)	A	B	C	TOTAL
Observed number of subjects	75	110	115	300
Probability (under H_0)	1/3	1/3	1/3	1
Expected number of subjects (under H_0)	100	100	100	300

In the general case of *K* categories, suppose that the null hypothesis specifies P_1, P_2, ..., P_K for the probabilities that an observation falls into the categories. Assume that these possibilities are mutually exclusive and collectively exhaustive—that is, each sample observation must belong to one of the categories and cannot belong to more than one. In this case, the hypothesized probabilities must sum to 1—that is,

$$P_1 + P_2 + \cdots + P_K = 1$$

Then, if there are *n* sample observations, the expected numbers in each category, under the null hypothesis, will be as follows:

$$E_i = nP_i \ (i = 1, 2, ..., K)$$

This is shown in Table 14.4.

The null hypothesis about the population specifies the probabilities that a sample observation will fall into each possible category. The sample observations are to be used to check this hypothesis. If the null hypothesis were true, we would think that the observed data in each category would be close in value to the expected numbers in each category. In such circumstances the data provide a close *fit* to the assumed population distribution of probabilities. Tests of the null hypothesis are based on an assessment of the closeness of this fit and are generally referred to as **goodness-of-fit-tests**.

Now, in order to test the null hypothesis, it is natural to look at the magnitudes of the discrepancies between what is observed and what is expected. The larger these discrepancies are in absolute value, the more suspicious we are of the null hypothesis. The random variable in Equation 14.2 is known as the chi-square random variable.

Table 14.4 Observed and Expected Numbers for *n* Observations and *K* Categories

CATEGORY	1	2	...	K	TOTAL
Observed number	O_1	O_2	...	O_K	n
Probability (under H_0)	P_1	P_2	...	P_K	1
Expected number (under H_0)	$E_1 = nP_1$	$E_2 = nP_2$	...	$E_K = nP_K$	n

Chi-Square Random Variable

A random sample of n observations, each of which can be classified into exactly one of K categories, is selected. Suppose the observed numbers in each category are $O_1, O_2,..., O_K$. If a null hypothesis (H_0) specifies probabilities $P_1, P_2,..., P_K$ for an observation falling into each of these categories, the expected numbers in the categories, under H_0, would be as follows:

$$E_i = nP_i \ (i = 1, 2,..., K) \qquad (14.1)$$

If the null hypothesis is true and the sample size is large enough that the expected values are at least 5, then the random variable associated with

$$\chi^2 = \sum_{i=1}^{K} \frac{(O_i - E_i)^2}{E_i} \qquad (14.2)$$

has, to a good approximation, a chi-square distribution with $(K-1)$ degrees of freedom.

Intuitively, the number of degrees of freedom follows from the fact that the O_i must sum to n. Hence, if the number of sample members, n, and the numbers of observations falling in any $(K–1)$ of the categories are known, then the number in the Kth category is also known. The null hypothesis will be rejected when the observed numbers differ substantially from the expected numbers—that is, for unusually large values of the statistic in Equation 14.2. The appropriate goodness-of-fit test follows.

A Goodness-of-Fit Test: Specified Probabilities

A **goodness-of-fit test**, of significance level α, of H_0 against the alternative that the **specified probabilities** are not correct is based on the decision rule

$$\text{Reject } H_0 \text{ if } \sum_{i=1}^{K} \frac{(O_i - E_i)^2}{E_i} > \chi^2_{K-1,\alpha}$$

where $\chi^2_{K-1,\alpha}$ is the number for which

$$P(\chi^2_{K-1} > \chi^2_{K-1,\alpha}) = \alpha$$

and the random variable χ^2_{K-1} follows a chi-square distribution with $(K-1)$ degrees of freedom.

To illustrate this test, consider again the data of Table 14.3 on brand selection. The null hypothesis is that the probabilities are the same for the three categories. The test of this hypothesis is based on the following:

$$\chi^2 = \sum_{i=1}^{3} \frac{(O_i - E_i)^2}{E_i} = \frac{(75 - 100)^2}{100} + \frac{(110 - 100)^2}{100} + \frac{(115 - 100)^2}{100} = 9.50$$

There are $K = 3$ categories, so $K - 1 = 2$ degrees of freedom are associated with the chi-square distribution. From Table 7 in the appendix,

$$\chi^2_{2,0.01} = 9.21$$

Therefore, according to our decision rule, the null hypothesis is rejected at the 1% significance level. These data contain strong evidence against the hypothesis that a randomly chosen subject is equally likely to select any of the three soft drink brands.

Example 14.1 Do Customers Have a Preference for Any of Four Hershey Chocolate Bars? (Chi-Square)

Suppose that the Hershey Company wants to determine if customers have a preference for any of the following four candy bars: A. Mr. Goodbar; B. Hershey's Milk Chocolate; C. Hershey's Special Dark Mildly Sweet Chocolate; or D. Krackel. From a random sample of 200 people it was found that 43 preferred Mr. Goodbar; 53 preferred Hershey's Milk Chocolate; 60 preferred Hershey's Special Dark Mildly Sweet Chocolate, and the remainder preferred Krackel. Test the null hypothesis that customers have no preference for any of the four candy bars.

Solution The null hypothesis states that customers have **no preference** for any of the four candy bars (A, B, C, and D). That is, all four candy bars are equally preferred:

$$H_0 : P_A = P_B = P_C = P_D = 0.25$$

Since the null hypothesis states that each candy bar is preferred by 25% of the customers, it follows that each of the expected values will be 50:

$$E_i = nP_i = 200(0.25) = 50$$

The chi-square test statistic is calculated in Table 14.5.

Table 14.5 Do Customers Have a Preference for Any of Four Hershey Chocolate Bars?

TYPE OF CANDY BAR	O_i	E_i	$(O_i - E_i)$	$(O_i - E_i)^2$	$(O_i - E_i)^2 / E_i$
A. Mr. Goodbar	43	50	−7	49	49/50 = 0.98
B. Hershey's Milk Chocolate	53	50	3	9	9/50 = 0.18
C. Hershey's Special Dark	60	50	10	100	100/50 = 2.00
D. Krackel	44	50	−6	36	36/50 = 0.72
					$\chi^2 = 3.88$

The chi-square test statistic is $\chi^2 = \Sigma (O_i - E_i)^2 / E_i = 3.88$. From Table 7 in the appendix with df = K − 1 = 3, we find that the test-statistic falls between 0.584 and 6.25. Thus, we conclude 0.100 < p-value < 0.900. That is, we fail to reject the null hypothesis and conclude that the data is not statistically significant to conclude that customers have a preference for at least one of these candy bars. We must be careful not to conclude that all four candy bars are equally preferred; we can only state that the evidence does not support a preference. Perhaps a more extensive study would lead to a different conclusion.

Another marketing question that Hershey might address concerns whether the current customer preferences differ from historically known preferences.

Example 14.2 Is There a Change in Customer Preferences? (Chi-Square)

From historical data, such as sales records, the Hershey Company knows that 30% of its customers prefer Mr. Goodbar, 50% prefer Hershey's Milk Chocolate, 15% prefer Hershey's Special Dark Mildly Sweet Chocolate, and the remainder prefer Krackel. Suppose that marketing analysts sample 200 people and find that 50 prefer Mr. Goodbar, 93 prefer Hershey's Milk Chocolate, 45 prefer Hershey's Special Dark Mildly Sweet Chocolate, and the remainder prefers Krackel. Have current preferences for these products changed from the known preferences?

Solution The null hypothesis is that current customer preferences follow the same pattern. That is, the customer preferences do not differ from that known to the Hershey Company:

$$H_0 : P_A = 0.30; P_B = 0.50; P_C = 0.15; P_D = 0.05$$

The expected number of customers who prefer Mr. Goodbar is as follows:

$$E_A = nP_A = 200(0.30) = 60$$

The expected number of customers who prefer each of the other candy bars is computed similarly and the test-statistic (Table 14.6) is found to be as follows:

$$\chi^2 = \sum_{i=1}^{K} \frac{(O_i - E_i)^2}{E_i} = 10.06$$

Table 14.6 Have Customer Preferences Changed?

TYPE OF CANDY BAR	O_i	E_i	$(O_i - E_i)$	$(O_i - E_i)^2$	$(O_i - E_i)^2 / E_i$
A. Mr. Goodbar	50	60	−10	100	$100/60 = 1.67$
B. Hershey's Milk Chocolate	93	100	−7	49	$49/100 = 0.49$
C. Hershey's Special Dark	45	30	15	225	$225/30 = 7.50$
D. Krackel	12	10	2	4	$4/10 = 0.40$
					$\chi^2 = 10.06$

From Table 7 in the appendix with df $= K - 1 = 3$, we find that the test-statistic falls between 9.35 and 11.34. Thus, we conclude that

$$0.010 < \text{p-value} < 0.025$$

and reject the null hypothesis. The data is statistically significant to conclude that current customer preferences differ from the given pattern of preferences. Market researchers could now look into the specific differences and perhaps recommend appropriate marketing strategies.

Example 14.3   Gas Company (Chi-Square)

A gas company has determined from past experience that at the end of winter 80% of its accounts are fully paid, 10% are 1 month in arrears, 6% are 2 months in arrears, and 4% are more than 2 months in arrears. At the end of this winter the company checked a random sample of 400 of its accounts, finding 287 to be fully paid, 49 to be 1 month in arrears, 30 to be 2 months in arrears, and 34 to be more than 2 months in arrears. Do these data suggest that the pattern of previous years is not being followed this winter?

Solution   Under the null hypothesis that the proportions in the present winter conform to the historical record, the respective probabilities for the four categories are 0.80, 0.10, 0.06, and 0.04. Under that hypothesis the expected numbers of accounts in each category, for a random sample of 400 accounts, would be as follows:

$$400(0.80) = 320; \qquad 400(0.10) = 40; \qquad 400(0.06) = 24; \qquad 400(0.04) = 16$$

The observed and expected numbers are as follows:

NUMBER OF MONTHS IN ARREARS	0	1	2	MORE THAN 2	TOTAL
Observed number	287	49	30	34	400
Probability (under H_0)	0.80	0.10	0.06	0.04	1
Expected number (under H_0)	320	40	24	16	400

The test of the null hypothesis (H_0) is based on the following:

$$\chi^2 = \sum_{i=1}^{4} \frac{(O_i - E_i)^2}{E_i} = \frac{(287 - 320)^2}{320} + \frac{(49 - 40)^2}{40} + \frac{(30 - 24)^2}{24} + \frac{(34 - 16)^2}{16} = 27.178$$

Here there are $K = 4$ categories, so there are $K - 1 = 3$ degrees of freedom. From Table 7 in the appendix we have the following:

$$\chi^2_{3,0.005} = 12.84$$

Since 27.178 is much bigger than 12.84, the null hypothesis is very clearly rejected, even at the 0.5% significance level. Certainly, these data provide considerable evidence to suspect that the pattern of payments of gas bills this year differs from the historical norm. Inspection of the numbers in the table shows that more accounts are in arrears over a longer time period than is usually the case.

A word of caution is in order. The figures used in calculating the test-statistic in Equation 14.2 must be the *observed* and *expected numbers* in each category. It is not correct, for example, to use instead the percentages of sample members in each category.

EXERCISES

Application Exercises

14.1   A professor is planning to use a new book for a financial accounting course and is considering three possibilities: *Financial Accounting Made Easy*, *Financial Accounting Without Tears*, and *Financial Accounting for Profit and Pleasure*. The professor contacted a random sample of 60 students who had already taken this course and asked each to review the three books, indicating a first preference. The results obtained are shown in the following table. Test the null hypothesis that for this population their first preferences are evenly distributed over the three books.

Book	Made Easy	Without Tears	Profit and Pleasure
Number of first preferences	17	25	18

14.2 A random sample of 75 mutual funds whose performance ranked in the top 20% of all funds from 2002–2004 was selected. Their performance was observed over the next 3 years. In this later period suppose that 13 of the sample funds ranked in the top 20% of all funds, 20 in the second 20%, 18 in the third 20%, 11 in the fourth 20%, and the remainder in the bottom 20%. Test the null hypothesis that a randomly chosen top 20% fund from 2002–2004 is equally likely to fall into each of the five possible performance categories over the following 3 years.

14.3 An insurance company in Chattanooga, Tennessee, wanted to determine the importance of price as a factor in choosing a hospital in that region. A random sample of 450 consumers was asked to select "not important," "important," or "very important" as an answer. Respective numbers selecting these answers were 142, 175, and 133. Test the null hypothesis that a randomly chosen consumer is equally likely to select each of these three answers.

14.4 Production records indicate that in normal operation for a certain electronic component, 93% have no faults, 5% have one fault, and 2% have more than one fault. For a random sample of 500 of these components from a week's output, 458 were found to have no faults, 30 to have one fault, and 12 to have more than one fault. Test at the 5% level the null hypothesis that the quality of the output from this week conforms to the usual pattern.

14.5 A charity solicits donations by telephone. It has been found that 60% of all calls result in a refusal to donate; 30% result in a request for more information through the mail, with a promise to at least consider donating; and 10% generate an immediate credit card donation. For a random sample of 100 calls made in the current week, 65 resulted in a refusal to donate, 31 in a request for more information through the mail, and 4 in an immediate credit card donation. Test at the 10%

level the null hypothesis that the usual pattern of outcomes is being followed in the current week.

14.6 A campus administrator has found that 60% of all students view courses as very useful, 20% as somewhat useful, and 20% as worthless. Of a random sample of 100 students taking business courses, 68 found the course in question very useful, 18 somewhat useful, and 14 worthless. Test the null hypothesis that the population distribution for business courses is the same as that for all courses.

14.7 Several types of yogurt are sold in a small general store in New England. From a past study of customer selections the owner knows that 20% of the customers ordered flavor A, 35% flavor B, 18% flavor C, 12% flavor D, and the remainder flavor E. Now the owner, who thinks that the customer preferences have changed, randomly samples 80 customers and finds that 12 prefer A, 16 prefer B, 30 prefer C, 7 prefer E, and the remainder prefer D. Determine if the customers' preferences have changed from the last study.

14.8 In a recent market survey five different soft drinks were tested to determine if consumers have a preference for any of the soft drinks. Each person was asked to indicate her favorite drink. The results were as follows: drink A, 20; drink B, 25; drink C, 28; drink D, 15; and drink E, 27. Is there a preference for any of these soft drinks?

14.9 A team of marketing research students was asked to determine the pizza best liked by students enrolled in the team's college. Two years ago a similar study was conducted, and it was found that 40% of all students at this college preferred Bellini's pizza, 25% chose Anthony's pizza as the best, 20% selected Ferrara's pizza, and the rest selected Marie's pizza. To see if preferences have changed, 180 students were randomly selected and asked to indicate their pizza preferences. The results were as follows: 40 selected Ferrara's as their favorite, 32 students chose Marie's, 80 students preferred Bellini's, and the remainder selected Anthony's. Do the data indicate that the preferences today differ from those from the last study?

14.10 A random sample of statistics professors was asked to complete a survey including questions on curriculum content, computer integration, and software preferences. Of the 250 responses, 100 professors indicated that they preferred software package M and 80 preferred software package E, while the remainder were evenly split between preference for software package S and software package P. Do the data indicate that professors have a preference for any of these software packages?

14.2 GOODNESS-OF-FIT TESTS: POPULATION PARAMETERS UNKNOWN

In Section 14.1 the hypothesis concerned data that are generated by a *fully specified* probability distribution. The null hypothesis in this test specifies the probability that a sample observation will fall in any category. However, it often is required to test the hypothesis that data are generated by some distribution, such as the binomial, the Poisson, or the normal, without assuming the parameters of that distribution to be known. In these circumstances Section 14.1 is not applicable, but the available data can be used to estimate the unknown population parameters. The goodness-of-fit test used when population parameters are estimated is stated next.

Goodness-of-Fit Tests When Population Parameters Are Estimated

Suppose that a null hypothesis specifies category probabilities that depend on the estimation (from the data) of m unknown population parameters. The appropriate **goodness-of-fit test when population parameters are estimated** is precisely as in Section 14.1, except that the number of degrees of freedom for the chi-square random variable is

$$\text{Degrees of Freedom} = (K - m - 1) \tag{14.3}$$

where K is the number of categories, and m is the number of unknown population parameters.

A Test for the Poisson Distribution

Consider a test to determine if data are generated by the Poisson distribution. One procedure for attempting to resolve questions of disputed authorship is to count the number of occurrences of particular words in blocks of text. These can be compared with results from passages whose authorship is known; often this comparison can be achieved through the assumption that the number of occurrences follows a Poisson distribution. An example of this type of research involves the study of *The Federalist Papers* (Reference 22).

Example 14.4 Federalist Papers (Chi-Square)

For a sample of 262 blocks of text (each approximately 200 words in length) from *The Federalist Papers* (Reference 22), the mean number of occurrences of the word *may* was 0.66. Table 14.7 shows the observed frequencies of occurrence of this word in the 262 sampled blocks of text. Test the null hypothesis that the population distribution of occurrences is Poisson, without assuming prior knowledge of the mean of this distribution.

Table 14.7 Occurrences of the Word "may" in 262 Blocks of Text in *The Federalist Papers*

NUMBER OF OCCURRENCES	0	1	2	3 OR MORE
Observed frequency	156	63	29	14

Solution   Recall that, if the Poisson distribution is appropriate, the probability of x occurrences is

$$P(x) = \frac{e^{-\lambda}\lambda^x}{x!}$$

where λ is the mean number of occurrences. Although this population mean is unknown, it can be estimated by the sample mean 0.66. It is then possible, by substituting 0.66 for λ, to estimate the probability for any number of occurrences under the null hypothesis that the population distribution is Poisson. For example, the probability of two occurrences is as follows:

$$P(2) = \frac{e^{-0.66}(0.66)^2}{2!}$$

$$= \frac{(0.5169)(0.66)^2}{2} = 0.1126$$

Similarly, the probabilities for zero and one occurrence can be found, so the probability of three or more occurrences is as follows:

$$P(X \geq 3) = 1 - P(0) - P(1) - P(2)$$

These probabilities are shown in the second row of Table 14.8.

Table 14.8 Observed and Expected Frequencies for *The Federalist Papers*

NUMBER OF OCCURENCES	0	1	2	3 OR MORE	TOTAL
Observed frequencies	156	63	29	14	262
Probabilities	0.5169	0.3411	0.1126	0.0294	1
Expected frequencies under H_0	135.4	89.4	29.5	7.7	262

Then, exactly as before, the expected frequencies under the null hypothesis are obtained from the following:

$$E_i = nP_i \ (i = 1, 2,..., K)$$

Thus, for example, the expected frequency of two occurrences of the word *may* in 262 blocks of text is $(262)(0.1126) = 29.5$. Even though the variable itself is an integer, it is best not to round these expected values to integer values. The bottom row of Table 14.8 shows these expected frequencies. The test-statistic is then as follows:

$$\chi^2 = \sum_{i=1}^{4} \frac{(O_i - E_i)^2}{E_i} = \frac{(156 - 135.4)^2}{135.4} + \frac{(63 - 89.4)^2}{89.4} + \frac{(29 - 29.5)^2}{29.5} + \frac{(14 - 7.7)^2}{7.7} = 16.08$$

Since there are four categories and one parameter has been estimated, the approximate number of degrees of freedom for the test is 2. From Table 7 in the appendix we have the following:

$$\chi^2_{2,0.005} = 10.60$$

Thus, the null hypothesis that the population distribution is Poisson can be rejected at the 0.5% significance level. The evidence in the data against that hypothesis is, then, very strong indeed.

A Test for the Normal Distribution

The normal distribution plays an important role in statistics, and many practical procedures rely for their validity, or for particular optimality properties, on an assumption that sample data are from a normal distribution. In Chapter 5 we looked at the normal probability plot to check for evidence of non-normality. Also, in Chapter 7 (Figure 7.2 and Figure 7.9) we visually tested for evidence of non-normality by determining if the dots in the normal probability plots were "close" to the straight line. Next, we consider a test of the normality assumption through an adaptation of the chi-square procedure. This test is both easy to carry out and likely to be more powerful.

The **Jarque–Bera test for normality**, which is an adaptation of the chi-square procedure, relies on two descriptive measures, skewness (Equation 14.5) and kurtosis (Equation 14.6). We discussed skewness in the appendix to Chapter 2. Skewness, a measure of symmetry, is known to be 0 for the normal distribution. Kurtosis provides a measure of the weight in the tails of a probability density function. It is known that for the normal distribution the population kurtosis is 3. Therefore, the Jarque–Bera test for a normal distribution is based on the closeness to 0 of the sample skewness and the closeness to 3 of the sample kurtosis. The Jarque–Bera test-statistic is given in Equation 14.4.

Jarque–Bera Test for Normality

Suppose that we have a random sample $x_1, x_2, \cdots, x_n$ of n observations from a population. The test-statistic for the **Jarque–Bera test for normality** is

$$JB = n\left[\frac{(Skewness)^2}{6} + \frac{(Kurtosis - 3)^2}{24}\right] \tag{14.4}$$

where using sample information, **skewness** of a population is estimated by

$$Skewness = \frac{\sum_{i=1}^{n}(x_i - \bar{x})^3}{ns^3} \tag{14.5}$$

and **kurtosis** is estimated by

$$Kurtosis = \frac{\sum_{i=1}^{n}(x_i - \bar{x})^4}{ns^4} \tag{14.6}$$

It is known that, as the number of sample observations becomes very large, this statistic has, under the null hypothesis that the population distribution is normal, a chi-square distribution with 2 degrees of freedom. The null hypothesis is, of course, rejected for large values of the test-statistic.

Unfortunately, the chi-square approximation to the distribution of the Jarque–Bera test-statistic, JB, is close only for very large sample sizes. Table 14.9 (Reference 2) shows significance points appropriate for a range of sample sizes for tests at the 5% and 10% levels. The recommended procedure, then, is to calculate the statistic, JB, in Equation 14.4 and reject the null hypothesis of normality if the test-statistic exceeds the appropriate value tabulated in Table 14.9.

Table 14.9 Significance Points of the Jarque–Bera Statistic (Reference 2)

SAMPLE SIZE n	10% POINT	5% POINT	SAMPLE SIZE n	10% POINT	5% POINT
20	2.13	3.26	200	3.48	4.43
30	2.49	3.71	250	3.54	4.51
40	2.70	3.99	300	3.68	4.60
50	2.90	4.26	400	3.76	4.74
75	3.09	4.27	500	3.91	4.82
100	3.14	4.29	800	4.32	5.46
125	3.31	4.34	∞	4.61	5.99
150	3.43	4.39			

Example 14.5 Daily Stock Market Rates of Return: Dell Inc. (Test of the Normal Distribution)

Daily closing prices of shares of Dell Inc. stock for 2007 are contained in the data file **Dell 2007**. The sample has $n = 251$ trading days. Compute the daily rates of return and test the null hypothesis that the true distribution for these rates of return is normal.

Solution From the data file **Dell 2007**, we first calculate the daily rates of return, r_i, for each of the $n = 251$ trading days as follows:

$$r_i = \frac{p_i - p_{i-1} + d_i}{p_{i-1}} \text{ for } i = 1,...,n \tag{14.7}$$

where p_i is the closing price on day i and d_i is any dividend paid on day i. No dividends were paid in 2007. Once the daily rates of return are calculated, the following intermediate calculations are found:

$$\sum_{i=1}^{251}(r_i - \bar{r})^2 = 0.0835496$$

$$\sum_{i=1}^{251}(r_i - \bar{r})^3 = -0.002158324$$

$$\sum_{i=1}^{251}(r_i - \bar{r})^4 = 0.000329593$$

From Equation 14.5, skewness is calculated as follows:

$$\text{Skewness} = \frac{\sum_{i=1}^{n}(r_i - \bar{r})^3}{ns^3} = \frac{-0.002158324}{251(0.00000610951)} \cong -1.41$$

and by Equation 14.6 kurtosis is as follows:

$$\text{Kurtosis} = \frac{\sum_{i=1}^{n}(r_i - \bar{r})^4}{ns^4} = \frac{0.000329593}{251(0.000000111688)} \cong 11.76$$

Next, we find the Jarque–Bera test-statistic, JB:

$$JB \cong 251\left[\frac{(-1.41)^2}{6} + \frac{(8.76)^2}{24}\right] \cong 886$$

Comparison of this result with the significance points in Table 14.9 certainly provides ground to think that the population distribution is not normal.

It is often the case with real data that questions arise concerning unusual data points, such as the outlier seen in the normal probability plot in Figure 14.1. So what can we say about that point? Did it really happen or was there a recording error? Except for this outlier, the other rates of return fluctuate between -0.05 and +0.05. If no recording error occurred, analysts would look for extenuating circumstances or very unusual conditions that might lead to this unusually low rate of return. This outlier occurred on November 30, 2007 when the closing price of shares of Dell stock was $24.54 down from $28.14 the preceding day. Closing prices go up or down reflecting market concerns such as news about a company or threats to the economy. On November 30, 2007 Gaffen (Reference 9) posted "Learning to Sell Dell" on MarketBeat, *Wall Street Journal*'s online inside look at the markets. According to Gaffen, "The day's sport has been to smack Michael Dell around, along with his PC company, which is off by 13.5% after the company said its outlook remains clouded, and profitability figures show the firm remains in a transitional period" (Reference 9).

Figure 14.1 Daily Rates of Return: Dell Inc. 2007 (Probability Plot)

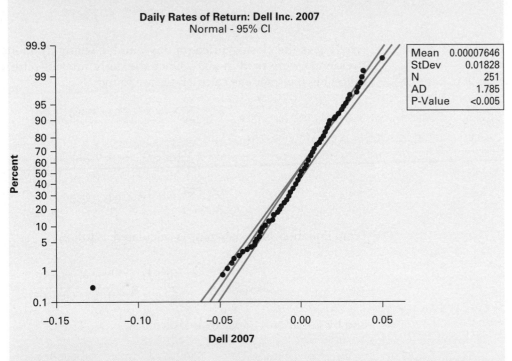

Figure 14.1 was *Reproduced with permission of Yahoo! Inc. ©2008 Yahoo! Inc. YAHOO! and the YAHOO! logo are registered trademarks of Yahoo! Inc.*

Skewness and kurtosis are included in the standard output of most statistical software packages, However, alternative formulas to Equation 14.5 and Equation 14.6 may be used. Other nonparametric tests of normality such as the Kolmogorov–Smirnov test, Anderson–Darling test, Ryan–Joiner test, Shapiro–Wilk test, and the Lilliefors test are beyond the scope of this book (References 2, 6, 14, 19, 24).

EXERCISES

Application Exercises

14.11 The number of times a machine broke down each week was observed over a period of 100 weeks and recorded in the accompanying table. It was found that the average number of breakdowns per week over this period was 2.1. Test the null hypothesis that the population distribution of breakdown is Poisson.

Number of Breakdowns	0	1	2	3	4	5 or More
Number of weeks	10	24	32	23	6	5

14.12 In a period of 100 minutes there were a total of 190 arrivals at a highway toll booth. The accompanying table shows the frequency of arrivals per minute over this period. Test the null hypothesis that the population distribution is Poisson.

Number of Arrivals in Minutes	0	1	2	3	4 or More
Observed Frequency	10	26	35	24	5

14.13 A random sample of 50 students was asked to estimate how much money they spent on textbooks in a year. The sample skewness of these amounts was found to be 0.83 and the sample kurtosis was 3.98. Test at the 10% level the null hypothesis that the population distribution of amounts spent is normal.

14.14 A random sample of 100 measurements of the resistance of electronic components produced in a period of 1 week was taken. The sample skewness was 0.63 and the sample kurtosis was 3.85. Test the null hypothesis that the population distribution is normal.

14.15 Select a stock such as Apple, Dell, or Microsoft and use the Jarque–Bera test to determine if the annual daily rates of return for a particular year follow a normal distribution.

14.16 A random sample of 125 monthly balances for holders of a particular credit card indicated that the sample skewness was 0.55 and the sample kurtosis was 2.77. Test the null hypothesis that the population distribution is normal.

14.3 CONTINGENCY TABLES

Suppose that a sample is taken from a population and the members can be uniquely cross-classified according to a pair of characteristics, A and B. The hypothesis to be tested is of no association or dependence in the population between possession of characteristic A and possession of characteristic B. For example, a travel agency may want to know if there is any relationship between a client's gender and the method used to make an airline reservation. An accounting firm may want to examine the relationship between the age of people and the type of income tax return filed by these individuals. Or perhaps, in a medical study, a pharmaceutical company may want to know if the success of a drug used to control cholesterol is dependent on a person's weight. A marketing research company may test if a customer's choice of cereal is in some way dependent on the color of the cereal box. Perhaps there is an association between political affiliation and support for a particular amendment that is to appear on the next election's ballot.

Assume that there are r categories for A and c categories for B, so a total of rc cross-classifications is possible. The number of sample observations belonging to both the ith category of A and the jth category of B will be denoted as O_{ij}, where $i = 1, 2,...,r$ and $j = 1, 2,..., c$. Table 14.10 is called an $r \times c$ contingency table. For

Table 14.10 Cross-Classification of n Observations in an $r \times c$ Contingency Table

	CHARACTERISTIC B				
Characteristic A	1	2	...	c	Total
1	O_{11}	O_{12}	...	O_{1c}	R_1
2	O_{21}	O_{22}	...	O_{2c}	R_2
:	:	:	...	:	:
r	O_{r1}	O_{r2}	...	O_{rc}	R_r
Total	C_1	C_2	...	C_c	n

convenience, row and column totals were added to Table 14.10, denoted respectively as $R_1, R_2, ..., R_r$ and $C_1, C_2, ..., C_c$.

To test the null hypothesis of no association between characteristics A and B, we ask how many observations we would expect to find in each cross-classification if that hypothesis was true. This question becomes meaningful when the row and column totals are *fixed*. Consider, then, the joint classification corresponding to the ith row and jth column of the table. There are a total of C_j observations in the jth column, and, given no association, we would expect each of these column totals to be distributed among the rows in proportion to the total number of observations in each ith row. Thus, we would expect a proportion R_i/n of these C_j observations to be in the ith row. Hence, the estimated expected number of observations in the cross-classifications is

$$E_{ij} = \frac{R_i C_j}{n} \quad \text{for } (i = 1, 2, ..., r; \ j = 1, 2, ..., c)$$

where R_i and C_j are the corresponding row and column totals.

Our test of the null hypothesis of no association is based on the magnitudes of the discrepancies between the observed numbers and those that would be expected if that hypothesis was true. The random variable given in Equation 14.8 is a generalized version of that introduced in Section 14.1.

> ### Chi-Square Random Variable for Contingency Tables
> It can be shown that under the null hypothesis the random variable associated with
>
> $$\chi^2 = \sum_{i=1}^{r} \sum_{j=1}^{c} \frac{(O_{ij} - E_{ij})^2}{E_{ij}} \tag{14.8}$$
>
> has, to a good approximation, a chi-square distribution with $(r - 1)(c - 1)$ degrees of freedom. The approximation works well if no more than 20% of the estimated expected numbers E_{ij} is less than 5. Sometimes adjacent classes can be combined in order to meet this assumption.

The double summation in Equation 14.8 implies that the summation extends over all rc cells of the table. Clearly, the null hypothesis of no association will be rejected for large absolute discrepancies between observed and expected numbers—that is, for high values of the statistic in Equation 14.8. The test procedure is summarized as follows.

A Test of Association in Contingency Tables

Suppose that a sample of n observations is cross-classified according to two characteristics in an $r \times c$ contingency table. Denote by O_{ij} the number of observations in the cell that is in the ith row and jth column. If the null hypothesis is H_0: No association exists between the two characteristics in the population then the estimated expected number of observations in each cell under H_0 is

$$E_{ij} = \frac{R_i C_j}{n} \tag{14.9}$$

where R_i and C_j are the corresponding row and column totals. A **test of association** at a significance level α is based on the following decision rule:

$$\text{Reject } H_0 \text{ if } = \sum_{i=1}^{r} \sum_{j=1}^{c} \frac{(O_{ij} - E_{ij})^2}{E_{ij}} > \chi^2_{(r-1)(c-1), \alpha}$$

Example 14.6 Market Differentiation (Test of Association)

When marketers position products or establish new brands, they aim to differentiate their product from its competition. To investigate the consumer's perception, spontaneous associations are frequently used. That means consumers are exposed to different products and asked what comes to their mind when they see or hear of this product. For example, suppose a study was conducted to determine whether "safety" or "sporty" comes to a person's mind when they see or hear of a particular type of automobile: BMW, Mercedes, or Lexus. Associations and products can be organized in a cross table, such as Table 14.11. The number in the cells thereby equals the frequency a certain combination occurred (e.g., 256 people named BMW as sporty). Use a chisquare test to evaluate whether the products mentioned differ in their associations and are, thus, perceived as dissimilar (which is most likely desired by the marketer).

Table 14.11 Automobile by Consumer Perception

AUTOMOBILE	SPORTY	SAFETY	TOTAL
BMW	256	74	330
Mercedes	41	42	83
Lexus	66	34	100
Total	**363**	**150**	**513**

Solution The null hypothesis to be tested implies that, in the population, the three types of automobiles are perceived as similar; that is, there is no association between the automobile type and customers' perception of the car as being known for being sporty or being known for its safety. To test the null hypothesis of no association, we again ask how many observations we would *expect* to find in each cross-classification if that hypothesis were true.

For example, if there were no association between these characteristics, the expected number of customers who perceived a BMW as sporty would be as follows:

$$E_{11} = \frac{(330)(363)}{513} = 233.5$$

The other expected numbers are calculated in the same way and are shown in Table 14.12 alongside the corresponding observed numbers.

Table 14.12 Observed (and Expected) Number of Customers in Each Cross-Classification

Automobile	Sporty	Safety	Total
BMW	256 (233.5)	74 (96.5)	330
Mercedes	41 (58.7)	42 (24.3)	83
Lexus	66 (70.8)	34 (29.2)	100

The test of the null hypothesis of no association is based on the magnitudes of the discrepancies between the observed numbers and those that would be expected if that hypothesis was true. Extending Equation 14.2 to include each of the six cross-classifications gives the following value of the chi-square test statistic:

$$\chi^2 = \frac{(256 - 233.5)^2}{233.5} + \frac{(74 - 96.5)^2}{96.5} + \frac{(41 - 58.7)^2}{58.7} + \frac{(42 - 24.3)^2}{24.3}$$

$$+ \frac{(66 - 70.8)^2}{70.8} + \frac{(34 - 29.2)^2}{29.2} = 26.8$$

The degrees of freedom are $(r - 1)(c - 1)$. Here, there are $r = 3$ rows and $c = 2$ columns in the table, so the appropriate number of degrees of freedom are as follows:

$$(r - 1)(c - 1) = (3 - 1)(2 - 1) = 2$$

From Table 7 in the appendix, we find the following:

$$\chi^2_{2,0.005} = 10.60$$

Therefore, the null hypothesis of no association is very clearly rejected, even at the 0.5% level. The evidence against this hypothesis is overwhelming.

It should be noted, as was the case for the goodness-of-fit tests in earlier sections, that the figures used in calculating the statistic must be the *actual numbers* observed and not, for example, percentages of the total.

Example 14.7 Sarbanes-Oxley Act of 2002

Regulatory Agencies and the U.S. Congress are recognizing both the values and emerging issues for small firms as the Sarbanes-Oxley Act of 2002 (SOX) is implemented. On April 23, 2006 the Advisory Committee on Smaller Public Companies issued a final report to the Security and Exchange Commission assessing the impact of Sarbanes-Oxley Act of 2002 on smaller public companies (Final Report of the Advisory Committee on Smaller Public Companies to the U.S. Securities and Exchange Commission, April 23, 2006). In Example 1.4 we introduced a study that was conducted among a random sample of CEOs, CFOs, and board members of corporations since the implementation of the Sarbanes-Oxley Act of 2002

(Reference 21). Based on the data contained in Table 14.13, is there an association between the firm's opinion as to the overall impact of Sarbanes-Oxley implementation and the firm's size.

Table 14.13 Overall Impact of Sarbanes-Oxley Implementation and Size of the Firm

IMPACT OF SOX	SMALL FIRMS	MEDIUM SIZE FIRMS	LARGE FIRMS
Little or No Impact	17	13	6
Moderate to Very Major Impact	13	41	22

Solution In this study the size of the firm was measured by annual revenue, not number of employees or some other factor. Small firms are corporations with annual revenue not exceeding $250 million; large firms had annual revenue above $750 million. We calculate each of the expected number of firms for each cell as

$$E_{11} = \frac{(36)(30)}{112} = 9.64$$

and then use Equation 14.8 to obtain a test-statistic of 11.358. With 2 degrees of freedom and $\chi^2_{2,0.005} = 10.60$ (Table 7 in the appendix), we conclude that the data is statistically significant to indicate that the p-value < 0.005 and that there is an association between opinion on overall impact of the Sarbanes-Oxley Act of 2002 and the size of the firm. From Figure 14.2 (obtained using SPSS), we see the same conclusion with p-value $= 0.003$.

Figure 14.2 Overall Impact of Sarbanes-Oxley Act of 2002 by Size of Firm (SPSS)

			Size			Total
Overall Impact of SOX			Small	Medium	Large	
Little or no impact	Count		17	13	6	36
	Expected Count		9.6	17.4	9.0	36.0
Major impact	Count		13	41	22	76
	Expected Count		20.4	36.6	19.0	76.0
Total	Count		30	54	28	112

Chi-Square Tests

	Value	df	Asymp. Sig. (2-sided)
Pearson Chi-Square	**11.358(a)**	2	**.003**
Likelihood Ratio	10.900	2	.004
Linear-by-Linear Association	7.907	1	.005
N of Valid Cases	112		

a 0 cells (.0%) have expected count less than 5. The minimum expected count is 9.00

Although the use of chi-square test for association may indicate that there is a relationship between two variables, this procedure does not indicate the direction or strength of the relationship.

Application Exercises

14.17 Do commercial-free cable programs promote better citizenship among our school-aged children (Reference 15)? Many teachers and administrators believe that the use of commercial-free cable programs can enhance a student's interest in the democratic process in the years prior to the voting age. Other educators think that television is the enemy of education. Suppose that in a study in Texas a random sample of 150 high school history teachers was asked "Would you like to use commercial-free cable programs in your classroom?" The following contingency table gives the teachers' responses to this question as well as their opinions concerning whether or not such programming enhances citizenship. Is there evidence of a relationship between the responses to these two questions?

Effect	Use Commercial-Free Cable Programs?	
	Yes	No
Promotes better citizenship	78	25
Doesn't promote better citizenship	37	10

14.18 University administrators have collected the following information concerning student grade point average and the school of the student's major.

School	GPA < 3.0	GPA 3.0 or Higher
Arts & Sciences	50	35
Business	45	30
Music	15	25

Determine if there is any association between GPA and major.

14.19 Should all college students be required to own a laptop computer? Although this policy does exist at many universities, the added expense for students at small private schools should be considered. One business school recently surveyed its students to determine their reaction to this possible policy. The responses are given in the following table along with students' majors.

Major	Laptop Required?	
	Yes	No
Accounting	68	42
Finance	40	15
Management	60	50
Marketing	30	25

Do the data indicate that there is an association between one's major and the response to this question?

14.20 How do customers first hear about a new product? A random sample of 200 users of a new product was surveyed to determine the answer to this question. Other demographic data such as age were also collected. The respondents included 50 people under the age of 21 and 90 people between the ages of 21 and 35; the remainder were over 35 years of age. Of those under 21, 60% heard about the product from a friend, and the remainder saw an advertisement in the local paper. One-third of the people in the age category from 21 to 35 saw the advertisement in the local paper. The other two-thirds heard about it from a friend. Of those over 35, only 30% heard about it from a friend, while the remainder saw the local newspaper advertisement. Set up the contingency table for the variables age and method of learning about the product. Is there an association between the consumer's age and the method by which the customer heard about the new product?

14.21 Following a presidential debate, people were asked how they might vote in the forthcoming election. Is there any association between one's gender and choice of presidential candidate?

Candidate Preference	Gender	
	Male	Female
Candidate A	150	130
Candidate B	100	120

14.4 NONPARAMETRIC TESTS FOR PAIRED OR MATCHED SAMPLES

The simplest nonparametric test to carry out is the **sign test**. It is most frequently employed in testing hypotheses about analyzing data from paired or matched samples. The sign test is used in market research studies to determine if consumer preference exists for one of two products. Since respondents simply name their preference, the data are nominal and lend themselves to nonparametric procedures. The sign test is also useful to test the median of a population.

Sign Test for Paired or Matched Samples

Suppose that paired or matched samples are taken from a population and the differences equal to 0 are discarded, leaving n observations. The sign test can be used to test the null hypothesis that the population median of the differences is 0 (which would be true, for example, if the differences came from a population whose distribution was symmetric about a mean of 0). Let + indicate a positive difference and − indicate a negative difference. If the null hypothesis was true, our sequence of + and − differences could be regarded as a random sample from a population in which the probabilities for + and − were each 0.5. In that case the observations would constitute a random sample from a binomial population in which the probability of + was 0.5. Thus, if P denotes the true proportion of +'s in the population (that is, the true proportion of positive differences), the null hypothesis is simply

$$H_0 : P = 0.5$$

The sign test is then based on the fact that the number of positive observations, S, in the sample has a binomial distribution (with $P = 0.5$ under the null hypothesis).

> ### Sign Test for Paired Samples
> Suppose that paired or matched random samples are taken from a population and the differences equal to 0 are discarded, leaving n observations. Calculate the difference for each pair of observations and record the sign of this difference. The sign test is used to test
>
> $$H_0 : P = 0.5$$
>
> where P is the proportion of non-zero observations in the population that are positive. The test-statistic S for the sign test for paired samples is simply
>
> $$S = \text{the number of pairs with a positive difference}$$
>
> where S has a binomial distribution with $P = 0.5$ and $n =$ the number of non-zero differences.

After determining the null and alternative hypotheses and finding a test-statistic, the next step is to determine the p-value and draw conclusions based on a decision rule.

> ### Determining p-Value for a Sign Test
> The **p-value for a sign test** is found using the binomial distribution with n = number of non-zero differences, S = number of positive differences, and $P = 0.5$.
>
> a. For an upper tail test
>
> $$H_1 : P > 0.5 \quad p\text{-value} = P(x \geq S) \tag{14.10}$$

b. For a lower tail test

$$H_1 : P < 0.5 \quad p\text{-value} = P(x \le S) \tag{14.11}$$

c. For a two-tail test, let $S = \max(S_+, S_-)$ where S_+ is the number of positive differences and S_- is the number of negative differences. Then,

$$H_1 : P \ne 0.5 \quad p\text{-value} = 2P(x \ge S) \tag{14.12}$$

Example 14.8 Product Preference (Sign Test)

An Italian restaurant, close to a college campus, contemplated a new recipe for the sauce used on its pizza. A random sample of eight students was chosen, and each was asked to rate on a scale from 1 to 10 the tastes of the original sauce and the proposed new one. The scores of the taste comparison are shown in Table 14.14 with higher numbers indicating a greater liking of the product.

Do the data indicate an overall tendency to prefer the new pizza sauce to the original pizza sauce?

Solution Also shown in Table 14.14 are the differences in the scores for every taster and the signs of these differences. Thus, a + is assigned if the original product is preferred, a – if the new product is preferred, and 0 if the two products are rated equally. In this particular experiment, two tasters preferred the original pizza sauce, five preferred the new recipe, and one rated them equal.

The null hypothesis of interest is that in the population at large there is no overall tendency to prefer one product to the other. In assessing this hypothesis, we compare the numbers expressing a preference for each product, discarding those who rated the products equally. In the present example, the values for taster G are omitted in further analysis and the effective sample size is reduced to $n = 7$. The only sample information on which our test is based is that two of the seven tasters preferred the original product. Hence, the test-statistic is $S = 2$.

Table 14.14 Student Ratings for Pizza Sauce

| | RATING | | | |
| | ORIGINAL PIZZA | NEW PIZZA | DIFFERENCE | SIGN OF |
STUDENT	SAUCE	SAUCE	(ORIGINAL – NEW)	DIFFERENCE
A	6	8	–2	–
B	4	9	–5	–
C	5	4	1	+
D	8	7	1	+
E	3	9	–6	–
F	6	9	–3	–
G	7	7	0	0
H	5	9	–4	–

The null hypothesis can be viewed as the hypothesis that the population median of the differences is 0. If the null hypothesis was true, our sequence of + and – differences could be regarded as a random sample from a population in which the probabilities for + and – were each 0.5. In that case the observations would constitute a random sample from a binomial population in which the probability of + was 0.5. Thus, if P denotes the true proportion of + signs in the population (that is, the true proportion of the population that prefers the original pizza sauce), the null hypothesis is simply as follows:

$H_0: P = 0.5$ *There is no overall tendency to prefer one sauce to the other.*

A one-tailed test is used to determine if there is an overall tendency to prefer the new pizza sauce to the original pizza sauce. The alternative of interest is that in the population the majority of preferences are for the new product. This alternative is expressed as follows:

$H_1: P < 0.5$ *Fewer than 50% prefer the old pizza sauce.*

Next, we find the probability of observing a sample result as extreme as or more extreme than that found if the null hypothesis was, in fact, true. This value is the p-value of the test. If we denote by $P(x)$ the probability of observing x "successes" (+) in $n = 7$ binomial trials, each with probability of success 0.5, then the cumulative binomial probability of observing two or fewer + signs can be obtained by Table 3, in the appendix. Thus, the p-value is as follows:

$$p\text{-value} = P(x \le 2) = 0.227$$

With a p-value this large we are unable to reject the null hypothesis, and we conclude that the data are not sufficient to suggest that the students have a preference for the new sauce. Similarly, we could have said that if we adopt the decision rule "Reject H_0 if two or fewer + signs occur in the sample," then the probability is 0.2266 that the null hypothesis will be rejected when it is, in fact, true. Hence, such a test has a p-value of 22.66%. Since the p-value is the smallest significance level at which the null hypothesis can be rejected, for the present example the null hypothesis can be rejected at 22.66% or higher. It is unlikely that one would be willing to accept such a high significance level. Again, we conclude that the data are not statistically significant to recommend a change in the pizza sauce. Perhaps our decision is a consequence of our having such a small number of sample observations.

Wilcoxon Signed Rank Test for Paired or Matched Samples

One disadvantage of the sign test is that it takes into account only a very limited amount of information—namely, the signs of the differences. For example, in Table 14.14 the sign test simply records which product is preferred, *ignoring the strengths of the preferences.* When the sample size is small, it might be suspected that the test would not be very powerful. The Wilcoxon signed rank test provides a method to incorporate information about the magnitude of the differences between matched pairs. It is still a distribution-free test. Like many nonparametric tests, it is based on *ranks*.

The Wilcoxon Signed Rank Test for Paired Samples
The **Wilcoxon signed rank test** can be employed when a random sample of matched pairs of observations is available. Assume that the population distribution of the differences in these **paired samples** is symmetric and

that we want to test the null hypothesis that this distribution is centered at 0. Discarding pairs for which the difference is 0, we rank the remaining n absolute differences in ascending order with ties assigned the average of the ranks they occupy. The sums of the ranks corresponding to positive and negative differences are calculated, and the smaller of these sums is the Wilcoxon signed rank statistic T—that is,

$$T = min(T_+, T_-)$$ (14.13)

where

T_+ = sum of the positive ranks
T_- = sum of the negative ranks
n = number of non-zero differences

The null hypothesis is rejected if T is less than or equal to the value in Table 10 in the appendix.

Example 14.9 Product Preference (Wilcoxon Signed Rank Test)

Consider again Example 14.8, the student ratings for pizza sauce. Use the Wilcoxon signed rank test to determine if the data indicate an overall tendency to prefer the new pizza sauce to the original pizza sauce?

Solution   As with the sign test, we ignore any difference of 0, so taster G is removed from the study and the sample size is reduced to $n = 7$. The non-zero absolute differences are then ranked in ascending order of magnitude. That is, the smallest absolute value is given a rank of "1." If two or more values are equal, they are assigned the average of the next available ranks. In our example the two smallest absolute differences are equal. The rank assigned to them is, therefore, the average of ranks 1 and 2—that is, 1.5. The next absolute value is assigned rank 3, and so on. We rank all differences and obtain Table 14.15.

Table 14.15 Calculation of Wilcoxon Test Statistic for Taste Preference Data

TASTER	DIFFERENCE	RANK (+)	RANK (−)
A	−2		3
B	−5		6
C	1	1.5	
D	1	1.5	
E	−6		7
F	−3		4
G	0		
H	−4		5
		Rank sum 3	**25**
Wilcoxon signed rank statistic T = minimum (3, 25) = 3			

The ranks for positive and negative differences are summed separately. The smaller of these sums is the Wilcoxon signed rank statistic T. Here, $T = 3$.

We will now suppose that the population distribution of the paired differences is symmetric. The null hypothesis to be tested is that the center of this distribution is 0. In our example, then, we are assuming that differences in the ratings of the two products have a symmetric distribution, and we want to test whether that distribution is centered on 0—that is, no difference between ratings. We would be suspicious of the null hypothesis if the sum of the ranks for positive differences was very different from that for negative differences. Hence, the null hypothesis will be rejected for low values of the statistic T.

Cutoff points for the distribution of this random variable are given in Table 10 in the appendix for tests against a one-sided alternative that the population distribution of the paired differences is specified either to be centered on some number bigger than 0 or to be centered on some number less than 0. For sample size n Table 10 shows, for selected probabilities α, the number T_α such that $P(T < T_\alpha) = \alpha$. For example, if we let $\alpha = 0.05$, we read in the table for $n = 7$ that $P(T \leq 4) = 0.05$. Since the Wilcoxon signed rank test statistic is $T = 3$, the null hypothesis is rejected against the one-sided alternative at the 5% level. It appears likely that, overall, ratings are higher for the new product.

Normal Approximation to the Sign Test

As a consequence of the central limit theorem the normal distribution can be used to approximate the binomial distribution if the sample size is large. Experts differ on the exact definition of "large." We suggest that the normal approximation is acceptable if the sample size exceeds 20. A continuity correction factor in the test-statistic compensates for estimating discrete data with a continuous distribution and provides a closer approximation to the p-value.

The Sign Test: Normal Approximation (Large Samples)

If the number n of non-zero sample observations is large, then the sign test is based on the **normal approximation** to the binomial with the following mean and standard deviation:

Mean: $\mu = np = 0.5n$; Standard Deviation:

$$\sigma = \sqrt{np(1-p)} = \sqrt{0.2n} = 0.5\sqrt{n}$$

The test-statistic is

$$Z = \frac{S^* - \mu}{\sigma} = \frac{S^* - 0.5n}{0.5\sqrt{n}} \tag{14.14}$$

where S^* is the test-statistic corrected for continuity defined as follows:

a. For a two-tail test

$$S^* = S + 0.5 \text{ if } S < \mu \quad \text{or} \quad S^* = S - 0.5 \text{ if } S > \mu \tag{14.15}$$

b. For an upper tail test

$$S^* = S - 0.5 \tag{14.16}$$

c. For a lower tail test

$$S^* = S + 0.5 \tag{14.17}$$

Example 14.10 Ice Cream (Sign Test: Normal Approximation)

A random sample of 100 children was asked to compare two new ice cream flavors—peanut butter ripple and bubblegum surprise. Fifty-six sample members preferred peanut butter ripple, 40 preferred bubblegum surprise, and 4 expressed no preference. Use the *normal approximation* to determine if there is an overall preference for either flavor. Compare your result to the binomial probabilities obtained using both Excel and Minitab.

Solution To test if there is an overall preference in this population for one flavor over the other, the hypotheses are as follows:

$$H_0 : P = 0.5 \text{ Children have no preference for either flavor.}$$

$$H_1 : P \neq 0.5 \text{ Children have a preference for one flavor.}$$

Let P be the population proportion that prefers bubblegum surprise, giving $S = 40$ (we could just as well have chosen P to be the population proportion that prefers peanut butter ripple with $S = 56$). Using Equation 14.14 and Equation 14.15,

$$\mu = np = 0.5n = 0.5(96) = 48$$

$$\sigma = 0.5\sqrt{96} = 4.899$$

$$z = \frac{S^* - \mu}{\sigma} = \frac{40.5 - 48}{4.899} = -1.53 \quad \text{since} \quad 40 < 48, S^* = 40.5$$

From the standard normal distribution, it follows that the approximate p-value $= 2(0.0630) = 0.126$. Hence, the null hypothesis can be rejected at all significance levels greater than 12.6%. If no continuity correction factor is used, the value Z becomes $Z = -1.633$, giving a slightly smaller p-value of 0.1024.

Normal Approximation to the Wilcoxon Signed Rank Test

When the number n of non-zero differences in the sample is large ($n > 20$), the normal distribution provides a good approximation to the distribution of the Wilcoxon statistic T under the null hypothesis that the population differences are centered on 0. When this hypothesis is true, the mean and variance of this distribution are given in Equation 14.18 and Equation 14.19.

The Wilcoxon Signed Rank Test: Normal Approximation (Large Samples)

Under the null hypothesis that the population differences are centered on 0, the Wilcoxon signed rank test has mean and variance given by

$$E(T) = \mu_T = \frac{n(n + 1)}{4} \tag{14.18}$$

and

$$Var(T) = \sigma_T^2 = \frac{n(n + 1)(2n + 1)}{24} \tag{14.19}$$

Then, for large n, the distribution of the random variable, Z, is approximately standard normal where

$$Z = \frac{T - \mu_T}{\sigma_T}$$ (14.20)

If the number, n, of non-zero differences is large and T is the observed value of the Wilcoxon statistic, then the following tests have significance level α.

1. If the alternative hypothesis is one-sided, reject the null hypothesis if

$$\frac{T - \mu_T}{\sigma_T} < -z_\alpha$$

2. If the alternative hypothesis is two-sided, reject the null hypothesis if

$$\frac{T - \mu_T}{\sigma_T} < -z_{\alpha/2}$$

Example 14.11 Postaudit Procedures (Wilcoxon Signed Rank Test)

A study compared firms with and without sophisticated postaudit procedures. A sample of 31 matched pairs of firms was examined. For each firm the ratio of market valuation to replacement cost of assets was computed as a measure of firm performance. In each of the 31 pairs one firm employed sophisticated postaudit procedures and the other did not. The 31 differences in ratios were calculated and the absolute differences were ranked. The smaller of the rank sums, 189, was for those pairs where the ratio was higher for the firm without sophisticated postaudit procedures. Test the null hypothesis that the distribution of differences in ratios is centered on 0 against the alternative that the ratio of market valuation to replacement cost of assets tends to be lower for firms without sophisticated postaudit procedures (Reference 20).

Solution Given a sample of $n = 31$ pairs, the Wilcoxon statistic has, under the null hypothesis, the mean

$$\mu_T = \frac{n(n + 1)}{4} = \frac{(31)(32)}{4} = 248$$

and variance

$$Var(T) = \sigma_T^2 = \frac{n(n + 1)(2n + 1)}{24} = \frac{(31)(32)(63)}{24} = 2{,}604$$

so that the standard deviation is as follows:

$$\sigma_T = 51.03$$

The observed value of the statistic is $T = 189$. It follows from Equation 14.18 through Equation 14.20 that the null hypothesis is rejected against the one-sided alternative if

$$Z = \frac{T - \mu_T}{\sigma_T} = \frac{189 - 248}{51.03} = \frac{-59}{51.03} = -1.16 < z_\alpha$$

For $\alpha = 0.05$

$$z_\alpha = -1.645$$

The test result is not sufficient to reject the null hypothesis. Using the standard normal distribution, the null hypothesis could only be rejected at all significance levels of 12.3% or higher. Such a large p-value indicates that the data is not statistically significant to indicate that the ratio of market valuation to replacement cost of assets tends to be lower for firms without sophisticated postaudit procedures.

Sign Test for Single Population Median

The sign test can also be used to test hypotheses about the central location (median) of a population distribution.

Example 14.12   Starting Incomes of Recent College Graduates (Sign Test)

The starting incomes of a random sample of 23 recent graduates are as follows:

29,250	29,900	28,070	31,400	31,100	29,000	33,000	50,000	28,500	31,000
34,800	42,100	33,200	36,000	65,800	34,000	29,900	32,000	31,500	29,900
32,890	36,000	35,000							

Do the data indicate that the median starting income differs from \$35,000? The data for this problem can be found in the data file **Income**.

Solution   Since the distribution of incomes is often skewed, the sign test will be used. The null and alternative hypotheses are as follows:

$$H_0 : \text{Median} = \$35{,}000$$

$$H_1 : \text{Median} \neq \$35{,}000$$

Here, we test the null hypothesis using a binomial distribution with $P = 0.50$. First, we approximate the answer using Equation 14.14 and Equation 14.15. Notice that there are 17 students who indicated income less than \$35,000 and 5 who indicated income greater than \$35,000 and 1 student with a starting income of \$35,000. The sample size is reduced to $n = 22$ and $S = 5$. The mean and the standard deviation are found to be as follows:

$$\mu = np = 0.5n = 0.5(22) = 11$$

$$\sigma = 0.5\sqrt{22} = 2.345$$

Since $S = 5 < \mu = 11$, the test-statistic for the normal approximation is as follows:

$$Z = \frac{5.5 - 11}{2.345} = -2.35$$

Using the table for the standard normal distribution, the *approximate p*-value is $2(0.0094) = 0.0188$. Therefore, the null hypothesis is rejected at 1.88% or higher.

EXERCISES

Application Exercises

14.22 A random sample of 12 financial analysts was asked to predict the percentage increases in the prices of two common stocks over the next year. The results obtained are shown in the table. Use the sign test to test the null hypothesis that for the population of analysts there is no overall preference for increases in one stock over the other.

Analyst	Stock 1	Stock 2
A	6.8	7.2
B	9.8	12.3
C	2.1	5.3
D	6.2	6.8
E	7.1	7.2
F	6.5	6.2
G	9.3	10.1
H	1.0	2.7
I	–0.2	1.3
J	9.6	9.8
K	12.0	12.0
L	6.3	8.9

14.23 An organization offers a program designed to increase the level of comprehension achieved by students when reading technical material quickly. Each member of a random sample of 10 students was given 30 minutes to read an article. A test of the level of comprehension achieved was then administered. This process was repeated after these students had completed the program. The accompanying table shows comprehension scores before and after completion of the program. Use the sign test to test the null hypothesis that for this population there is no overall improvement in comprehension levels following completion of the program.

Student	Before	After
A	62	69
B	63	72
C	84	80
D	70	70
E	60	69
F	53	61
G	49	63
H	58	59
I	83	87
J	92	98

14.24 A sample of 11 managers in retail stores having self-checkout was asked if customers have a positive attitude about the scanning process. Seven managers answered "yes," and four answered "no." Test against a two-sided alternative the null hypothesis that, for the population of managers, responses would be equally divided between "yes" and "no."

14.25 A sample of 60 corporations buying back franchises was examined. Of these cases, returns on common stock around the buy-back announcement date were positive 39 times, negative 18 times, and zero 3 times. Test the null hypothesis that positive and negative returns are equally likely against the alternative that positive returns are more likely (Reference 4).

14.26 Of a random sample of 130 voters, 44 favored a state tax increase to raise funding for education, 68 opposed the tax increase, and 18 expressed no opinion. Test against a two-sided alternative the null hypothesis that voters in the state are evenly divided on the issue of this tax increase.

14.27 A random sample of 60 professional economists was asked to predict whether next year's inflation rate would be higher than, lower than, or about the same as that in the current year. The results are shown in the following table. Test the null hypothesis that the profession is evenly divided on the question.

Prediction	Number
Higher	20
Lower	29
About the same	11

14.28 Irvine and Rosenfeld (Reference 11) studied the "impact of selling Monthly Income Preferred Stock (MIPS) on the common share prices of the issuing firms." The IRS has allowed dividends of MIPS to be tax deductible from the time that Goldman Sachs first introduced them in 1993. Thus, "issuing MIPS enables the firm to increase its equity base at an after-tax cost nearly equal to that of long-term debt." One aspect of their study concerned a comparison of selected financial characteristics of firms that had issued MIPS (a total of 185) with those of comparable firms that had not issued MIPS before January 1, 1999. The MIPS-issuing firms were also divided between publicly traded industrials and public utilities, such as telephone, electric, gas, and water. The following table is a partial listing of selected findings of this study:

	MIPS Firms' N	MIPS Firms' Mean	Comparable Firms	Sign Test	Sign Rank Test
Total Assets (billions)					
All firms issuing MIPS	185	26.47	19.42	0.01	0.01
Utilities	83	10.45	8.65	0.01	0.01
Industrials	102	39.60	28.26	0.01	0.01
Interest Coverage					
All firms issuing MIPS	164	5.53	7.71	0.04	0.01
Utilities	83	4.44	5.15	0.01	0.01
Industrials	81	6.63	10.25	0.06	0.01
Long-Term Debt to Total Assets (%)					
All firms issuing MIPS	185	23.5	21.4	0.06	0.03
Utilities	83	32.6	29.3	0.03	0.01
Industrials	102	16.1	14.9	0.19	0.28

Discuss the findings of this portion of the study.

14.29 A random sample of 10 students was asked to rate, in a blind taste test, the quality of two brands of ice cream, one reduced-sugar and one regular ice cream. Ratings were based on a scale from 1 (poor) to 10 (excellent). The accompanying table gives the results. Use the Wilcoxon test to test the null hypothesis that the distribution of the paired differences is centered on 0 against the alternative that the population of all student ice cream consumers prefer the regular brand.

Student	Reduced Sugar	Regular
A	2	6
B	3	5
C	7	6
D	8	8
E	7	5
F	4	8
G	3	9
H	4	6
I	5	4
J	6	9

14.30 Sixteen freshmen on a college campus were grouped into eight pairs in such a way that the two members of any pair were as similar as possible in academic backgrounds—as measured by high school class rank and achievement test scores—and also in social backgrounds. The major difference within pairs was that one student was an in-state student and the other was from out-of-state. At the end of the first year of college, grade point averages of these students were recorded, yielding the results shown in the table. Use the Wilcoxon test to analyze the data. Discuss the implications of the test results.

Pair	In-State	Out-of-State
A	3.4	2.8
B	3.0	3.1
C	2.4	2.7
D	3.8	3.3
E	3.9	3.7
F	2.3	2.8
G	2.6	2.6
H	3.7	3.3

14.31 A random sample of 40 business majors who had just completed introductory courses in both statistics and accounting was asked to rate each class in terms of level of interest on a scale from 1 (very uninteresting) to 10 (very interesting). The 40 differences in the pairs of ratings were calculated and the absolute differences ranked. The smaller of the rank sums, which was for those finding accounting the more interesting, was 281. Test the null hypothesis that the population of business majors would rate these courses equally against the alternative that the statistics course is viewed as the more interesting.

14.32 A consultant is interested in the impact of the introduction of a total quality management program on job satisfaction of employees. A random sample of 30 employees was asked to assess level of satisfaction on a scale from 1 (very dissatisfied) to 10 (very satisfied) three months before the introduction of the program. These same sample members were asked to make this assessment again three months after the introduction of the program. The 30 differences in the pairs of ratings were calculated and the absolute differences ranked. The smaller of the rank sums, which was for those more satisfied before the introduction of the program, was 169. What can be concluded from this finding?

14.33 A random sample of 80 owners of videocassette recorders was taken. Each sample member was asked to assess the amounts of time in a month spent watching material he or she had recorded from television broadcasts and watching purchased or rented commercially recorded tapes. The 80 differences in times spent were then calculated and their absolute values ranked. The smaller of the rank sums, for material recorded from television, was 1,502. Discuss the implications of this sample result.

14.5 NONPARAMETRIC TESTS FOR INDEPENDENT RANDOM SAMPLES

In this section we introduce two tests that compare the central locations of two population distributions when *independent random samples* are taken from the two populations. The two tests are the Mann–Whitney U test and the Wilcoxon rank sum test.

Mann–Whitney U Test

The distribution of the Mann–Whitney statistic, U, approaches the normal distribution quite rapidly as the number of sample observations increases. The approximation is adequate if each sample contains at least 10 observations. Thus, we will only consider here samples with $n_1 \geq 10$ and $n_2 \geq 10$. To test the null hypothesis that the central locations of the two population distributions are the same, we assume that, apart from any possible differences in central location, the two population distributions are identical.

The Mann–Whitney U Statistic

Assume that, apart from any possible differences in central location, the two population distributions are identical. Suppose that n_1 observations are available from the first population and n_2 observations from the second. The two samples are pooled, and the observations are ranked in ascending order with ties assigned the average of the next available ranks. Let R_1 denote the sum of the ranks of the observations from the first population. The **Mann–Whitney U statistic** is then defined as follows:

$$U = n_1 n_2 + \frac{n_1(n_1 + 1)}{2} - R_1 \qquad (14.21)$$

It can be shown then that, if the null hypothesis is true, the random variable U has mean and variance as defined in Equation 14.22 and Equation 14.23.

Mann–Whitney U Test: Normal Approximation

Assuming as the null hypothesis that the central locations of the two population distributions are the same, the **Mann–Whitney U** has the following mean and variance:

$$E(U) = \mu_U = \frac{n_1 n_2}{2} \qquad (14.22)$$

$$Var(U) = \sigma_U^2 = \frac{n_1 n_2 (n_1 + n_2 + 1)}{12} \qquad (14.23)$$

Then, for large sample sizes (both at least 10), the distribution of the random variable

$$Z = \frac{U - \mu_U}{\sigma_U} \qquad (14.24)$$

is approximated by the normal distribution.

Example 14.13 Hours of Study (Mann–Whitney U Test)

Table 14.16 shows the numbers of hours per week students claim to spend studying for introductory finance and accounting courses. The data are from independent random samples of 10 finance students and 12 accounting students.

Do the data indicate a difference in the median number of hours per week that students spend studying for introductory finance and accounting courses? The name of the data file is **Hours**.

Solution Our null hypothesis is that the central locations (medians) of the two population distributions are identical.

H_0 : Median (1) = Median (2); *Students spend the same amount of time studying for introductory finance and accounting courses.*

The two samples are pooled, and the observations are ranked in ascending order with ties being treated in the same way as previously. These ranks are shown in Table 14.17.

Now, if the null hypothesis was true, we would expect the average ranks for the two samples to be quite close. In the particular example the average rank for the finance students is 9.35, while that for the accounting students is 13.29. As usual, when testing hypotheses, we want to know how likely a discrepancy of this magnitude would be if the null hypothesis were true.

Table 14.16 Number of Hours per Week Spent Studying for Introductory Finance and Accounting Courses

| Finance | 10 | 6 | 8 | 10 | 12 | 13 | 11 | 9 | 5 | 11 | | |
| Accounting | 13 | 17 | 14 | 12 | 10 | 9 | 15 | 16 | 11 | 8 | 9 | 7 |

Table 14.17 Number of Hours per Week Spent Studying for Introductory Finance and Accounting Courses

FINANCE	(RANK)	ACCOUNTING	(RANK)
10	(10)	13	(17.5)
6	(2)	17	(22)
8	(4.5)	14	(19)
10	(10)	12	(15.5)
12	(15.5)	10	(10)
13	(17.5)	9	(7)
11	(13)	15	(20)
9	(7)	16	(21)
5	(1)	11	(13)
11	(13)	8	(4.5)
		9	(7)
		7	(3)
RANK SUM 93.5		**RANK SUM 159.5**	

It is not necessary to calculate both rank sums, for if we know one, we can deduce the other. In this example, for instance, the ranks must sum to the sum of the integers 1 through 22—that is, to 253. Thus, any test of the hypothesis can be based on just one of the rank sums. If finance is the first sample, then

$$n_1 = 10 \quad n_2 = 12 \quad R_1 = 93.5$$

so the value observed for the Mann–Whitney statistic is, by Equation 14.21,

$$U = n_1 n_2 + \frac{n_1(n_1 + 1)}{2} - R_1 = (10)(12) + \frac{(10)(11)}{2} - 93.5 = 81.5$$

Using the null hypothesis that the central locations of the two population distributions are the same and Equation 14.22, the distribution of the statistic has mean

$$E(U) = \mu_U = \frac{n_1 n_2}{2} = \frac{(10)(12)}{2} = 60$$

and variance

$$\text{Var}(U) = \sigma_U^2 = \frac{n_1 n_2 (n_1 + n_2 + 1)}{12} = \frac{(10)(12)(23)}{12} = 230$$

It follows that

$$Z = \frac{U - \mu_U}{\sigma_U} = \frac{81.5 - 60}{\sqrt{230}} = 1.42 \text{ and } p\text{-}value = 0.1556.$$

With the usual 0.05 significance level, the test result is not sufficient to conclude that students spend more time studying for one of these subjects than the other. We could have used a continuity correction factor in the normal approximation. The p-value will be slightly higher than 0.1556.

If accounting is population 1 with $n_1 = 12$ and $R_1 = 159.5$, the outcome will be the same, since $Z = -1.42$. The p-value will still be 0.1556.

Wilcoxon Rank Sum Test

The **Wilcoxon rank sum test** is similar to the Mann–Whitney U test. The results will be the same for both tests. We include it here for completeness, since this test may be preferred for its ease. Similar to the Mann–Whitney U test, the distribution of the Wilcoxon rank sum test approaches the normal distribution quite rapidly as the number of sample observations increases. The approximation is adequate if each sample contains at least 10 observations.

Wilcoxon Rank Sum Statistic T

Suppose that n_1 observations are available from the first population and n_2 observations from the second. The two samples are pooled, and the observations are ranked in ascending order with ties assigned the average of the next available ranks. Let T denote the sum of the ranks of the observations from the first population (T in the Wilcoxon rank sum test is the same as R_1 in the Mann–Whitney U test). Assuming that the null hypothesis to be true, the Wilcoxon rank sum statistic, T, has mean

$$E(T) = \mu_T = \frac{n_1(n_1 + n_2 + 1)}{2} \tag{14.25}$$

$$\text{Var}(T) = \sigma_T^2 = \frac{n_1 n_2 (n_1 + n_2 + 1)}{12} \qquad (14.26)$$

Then, for large samples ($n_1 \geq 10$ and $n_2 \geq 10$), the distribution of the random variable

$$Z = \frac{T - \mu_T}{\sigma_T} \qquad (14.27)$$

is approximated by the normal distribution. For a large number of ties Equation 14.26 may not be correct (Reference 17).

For the data in Table 14.17, $T = R_1 = 93.5$ with

$$E(T) = \mu_T = \frac{n_1(n_1 + n_2 + 1)}{2} = \frac{10(23)}{2} = 115$$

and

$$\text{Var}(T) = \sigma_T^2 = \frac{n_1 n_2 (n_1 + n_2 + 1)}{12} = 230$$

Notice that the variance of the sampling distribution of the Wilcoxon rank sum statistic, T, is the same as the variance of the sampling distribution of the Mann–Whitney statistic, U. It follows that

$$Z = \frac{T - \mu_T}{\sigma_T} = \frac{93.5 - 115}{\sqrt{230}} = -1.42 \implies p\text{-}value = 0.1556.$$

Example 14.14   Earnings for Two Firms (Wilcoxon Rank Sum Test)

In a study designed to compare the performance of firms that give management forecasts of earnings with the performances of those that do not, independent random samples of 80 firms from each of the populations were taken. The variability of the growth rate of earnings over the previous 10 periods was measured for each of the 160 firms, and these variabilities were ranked. The sum of the ranks for firms not disclosing management earnings forecasts was 7,287 (Reference 12). Test against a two-sided alternative the null hypothesis that the central locations of the population distributions of earnings variabilities are the same for these two types of firms. Show that the results are the same with both the Mann–Whitney U test and the Wilcoxon rank sum test.

Solution   Since we have $n_1 = 80, n_2 = 80$, and $R_1 = 7,287$, the calculated value of the Mann–Whitney statistic is as follows:

$$U = n_1 n_2 + \frac{n_1(n_1 + 1)}{2} - R_1 = (80)(80) + \frac{(80)(81)}{2} - 7,287 = 2,353$$

Under the null hypothesis the Mann–Whitney statistic has mean

$$\mu_U = \frac{n_1 n_2}{2} = \frac{(80)(80)}{2} = 3,200$$

and variance

$$\sigma_U^2 = \frac{n_1 n_2 (n_1 + n_2 + 1)}{12} = \frac{(80)(80)(161)}{12} = 85{,}867$$

Here, we have the following:

$$Z = \frac{2{,}353 - 3{,}200}{\sqrt{85{,}867}} = -2.89$$

From the standard normal distribution Table 1 in the appendix, we see that the value of $\alpha/2$ corresponding to a Z-value of 2.89 is 0.0019, so p-value is 0.0038. Hence, the null hypothesis can be rejected at all levels higher than 0.38%.

The Wilcoxon rank sum test uses Equation 14.25 through Equation 14.27. The mean of T is as follows:

$$E(T) = \frac{n_1 (n_1 + n_2 + 1)}{2} = \frac{80(161)}{2} = 6{,}440$$

The variance of T is the same as the variance of U (Equation 14.23 is the same as Equation 14.26). Thus, by Equation 14.27,

$$Z = \frac{T - \mu_T}{\sigma_T} = \frac{7{,}287 - 6{,}440}{\sqrt{85{,}867}} = 2.89$$

and, again, the null hypothesis can be rejected at all levels higher than 0.38%. The results are the same whether using either the Mann–Whitney U test or the Wilcoxon rank sum test. These data, then, present very strong evidence against the hypothesis that the central locations of the distributions of population variability in earnings growth rates are the same for firms that give management earnings forecasts as for those that do not.

Now, if we had been given the actual data rather than just the ranks, we could have carried out a test of the null hypothesis using the methods of Chapter 10. However, using the Mann–Whitney test, we have found that the null hypothesis can be rejected *without the assumption of population normality*.

EXERCISES

Application Exercises

14.34 A study compared firms with and without an audit committee. For samples of firms of each type the extent of directors' ownership was measured as number of shares owned by the board as a proportion of the total number of shares issued. In the sample, directors' ownership was, overall, higher for firms without an audit committee. To test for statistical significance, the Mann–Whitney U statistic was calculated. It follows that $(U - \mu_U)/\sigma_U$ was found to be 2.01 (Reference 3). What can we conclude from this result?

14.35 A stock market analyst produced at the beginning of the year a list of stocks to buy and another list of stocks to sell. For a random sample of 10 stocks

from the "buy list," percentage returns over the year were as follows:

9.6	5.8	13.8	17.2	11.6
4.2	3.1	11.7	13.9	12.3

For an independent random sample of 10 stocks from the "sell list," percentage returns over the year were as follows:

22.7	6.2	8.9	11.3	2.1
3.9	22.4	1.3	7.9	10.2

Use the Mann–Whitney test to interpret these data.

14.36 For a random sample of 12 business graduates from a technical college, the starting salaries accepted for employment on graduation (in thousands of dollars) were the following:

26.2	29.3	31.3	28.7	27.4	25.1
26.0	27.2	27.5	29.8	32.6	34.6

For an independent random sample of 10 graduates from a state university, the corresponding figures were as follows:

25.3	28.2	29.2	27.1	26.8
26.5	30.7	31.3	26.3	24.9

Analyze the data using the Mann–Whitney test, and comment on the results.

14.37 A corporation interviews both marketing and finance majors for general management positions. A random sample of 10 marketing majors and an independent random sample of 14 finance majors were subjected to intensive interviewing and testing by a team of the corporation's senior managers. The candidates were then ranked from 1 (most suitable for employment) to 24, as shown in the accompanying table. Test the null hypothesis that, overall, the corporation's senior management has no preference between marketing and finance majors against the alternative that finance majors are preferred.

1. finance	9. marketing	17. marketing
2. finance	10. marketing	18. marketing
3. marketing	11. finance	19. finance
4. finance	12. finance	20. finance
5. finance	13. marketing	21. finance
6. marketing	14. finance	22. marketing
7. finance	15. finance	23. marketing
8. marketing	16. finance	24. finance

14.38 A random sample of 15 male students and an independent random sample of 15 female students were asked to write essays at the conclusion of a writing course. These essays were then ranked from 1 (best) to 30 (worst) by a professor. The following rankings resulted:

Male	26	24	15	16	8	29	12	6	18
	11	13	19	10	28	7
Female	22	2	17	25	14	21	5	30	3	9
	4	1	27	23	20

Test the null hypothesis that in the aggregate the two genders are equally ranked against a two-sided alternative.

14.39 A newsletter rates mutual funds. Independent random samples of 10 funds with the highest rating and 10 funds with the lowest rating were chosen. The following figures are percentage rates of return achieved by these 20 funds in the next year.

Highest rated	8.1	12.7	13.9	2.3	16.1	5.4	7.3
	9.8	14.3	4.1
Lowest rated	3.5	14.0	11.1	4.7	6.2	13.3	7.0
	7.3	4.6	10.0

Test the null hypothesis of no difference between the central locations of the population distributions of rates of return against the alternative that the highest-rated funds tended to achieve higher rates of return than the lowest-rated funds.

14.40 A random sample of 50 students was asked what salary the college should be prepared to pay to attract the right individual to coach the football team. An independent random sample of 50 faculty members was asked the same question. The 100 salary figures were then pooled and ranked in order (with rank 1 assigned to the lowest salary). The sum of the ranks for faculty members was 2,024. Test the null hypothesis that there is no difference between the central locations of the distributions of salary proposals of students and faculty members against the alternative that in the aggregate students would propose a higher salary to attract a football coach.

14.41 The time taken in days from year-end for a random sample of 120 Australian companies with clean audit reports to release a preliminary profit report was compared with the time taken for an independent random sample of 86 companies whose reports had a "subject to" qualification. The times taken for the 206 companies were pooled and ranked, with shortest time assigned rank 1. The sum of the ranks for companies with a "subject to" qualification was 9,686 (Reference 28). Test the null hypothesis that the central locations of the two population distributions are identical against the alternative that companies with "subject to" qualifications tend to take longer to produce their preliminary profit reports.

14.42 Starting salaries of MBA graduates from two leading business schools were compared. Independent random samples of 30 students from each school were taken, and the 60 starting salaries were pooled and ranked. The sum of the ranks for students from one of these schools was 1,243. Test the null hypothesis that the central locations of the population distributions are identical.

14.6 SPEARMAN RANK CORRELATION

The sample correlation coefficient can be seriously affected by odd extreme observations. Moreover, tests based on it rely for their validity on an assumption of normality. A measure of correlation that is not susceptible to serious influence by extreme values and on which valid tests can be based for very general population distributions is obtained through the use of ranks. The resulting test will then be nonparametric.

Spearman Rank Correlation

Suppose that a random sample $(x_1, y_1),...,(x_n, y_n)$ of n pairs of observations is taken. If the x_i and y_i are each ranked in ascending order and the sample correlation of these ranks is calculated, the resulting coefficient is called the **Spearman rank correlation coefficient**. If there are no tied ranks, an equivalent formula for computing this coefficient is

$$r_s = 1 - \frac{6 \sum_{i=1}^{n} d_i^2}{n(n^2 - 1)} \qquad (14.28)$$

where the d_i are the differences of the ranked pairs.

The following tests of the null hypothesis H_0 of no association in the population have a significance level α.

1. To test against the alternative of positive association, the decision rule is as follows:

$$\text{Reject } H_0 \text{ if } r_s > r_{s,\alpha} \qquad (14.29)$$

2. To test against the alternative of negative association, the decision rule is as follows:

$$\text{Reject } H_0 \text{ if } r_s < -r_{s,\alpha} \qquad (14.30)$$

3. To test against the two-sided alternative of some association, the decision rule is as follows:

$$\text{Reject } H_0 \text{ if } r_s < -r_{s,\alpha/2} \quad \text{or} \quad r_s > r_{s,\alpha/2} \qquad (14.31)$$

Example 14.15   Cruise Industry Promotion (Spearman Rank Correlation)

To promote the cruise industry in Florida, suppose that James Thorne of the Cruise Emporium of Ormond Beach ran an advertisement in 17 tourism magazines. Readers were invited to write for additional brochures and literature. The two variables to be related are

   X: Cost of advertising and circulation, in thousands of dollars
   Y: Return-on-inquiry cost

where the latter is defined as

   Y = (Estimated Revenue from Inquiries – Cost of Advertisement) ÷ Cost of Advertisement

Table 14.18 lists the ranks of these two variables for the 17 magazine advertisements. Calculate the Spearman rank correlation coefficient and test for association between the variables.

Table 14.18 Rank Correlation Calculations for the Cruise Example

MAGAZINE	RANK (x_i)	RANK (y_i)	$d_i = \text{RANK}(x_i) - \text{RANK}(y_i)$	d_i^2
1	14	2	12	144
2	8	4	4	16
3	1	16	−15	225
4	16	1	15	225
5	17	5	12	144
6	13	6	7	49
7	15	8	7	49
8	2	11	−9	81
9	7	9	−2	4
10	3	13	−10	100
11	6	12	−6	36
12	9	17	−8	64
13	5	3	2	4
14	4	7	−3	9
15	11	14	−3	9
16	12	15	−3	9
17	10	10	0	0
				Sum 1,168

Solution Since there are no ties in the ranks, we use Equation 14.28 and obtain the following:

$$r_s = 1 - \frac{6\sum_{i=1}^{n} d_i^2}{n(n^2 - 1)} = 1 - \frac{6(1,168)}{17[(17)^2 - 1]} = -0.431$$

Since there are 17 pairs of observations, the cutoff points (see Table 11 in the appendix) for 10% level and 5% level tests are, respectively, as follows:

$$r_{s,0.05} = 0.412 \quad \text{and} \quad r_{s,0.025} = 0.49$$

The null hypothesis of no association can be rejected against the two-sided alternative, according to the decision rule, at the 10% level but not at the 5% level. Our conclusions are not based on the assumption of population normality. The negative correlation coefficient indicates that the more one spends for advertising the lower the rate of return.

If there are no ties in the ranks, then to calculate the Spearman rank correlation with either Minitab or Excel is straightforward. If there are ties, we compute the simple correlation (Section 11.7) between the ranks.

Application Exercises

14.43 Students in an e-business technology course were given a written final examination as well as a project to complete as part of their final grade. For a random sample of 10 students, the scores on both the exam and the project are as follows:

Exam	81	62	74	78	93	69	72	83	90	84
Project	76	71	69	76	87	62	80	75	92	79

    a. Find the Spearman rank correlation coefficient.
    b. Test for association.

14.44 The accompanying table shows, for a random sample of 20 long-term growth mutual funds, percentage return over a period of 12 months and total assets (in millions of dollars).

Return	Assets	Return	Assets	Return	Assets
29.3	300	16.0	421	12.9	75
27.6	70	15.5	99	11.3	610

Return	Assets	Return	Assets	Return	Assets
23.7	3,004	15.2	756	9.9	264
22.3	161	15.0	730	7.9	27
22.0	827	14.4	436	6.7	71
19.6	295	14.0	143	3.3	719
17.6	29	13.7	117		

    a. Calculate the Spearman rank correlation coefficient.

    b. Carry out a nonparametric test of the null hypothesis of no association in the population against a two-sided alternative.

    c. Discuss the advantages of a nonparametric test for these data.

KEY WORDS

- Chi-Square random variable, 617
- goodness-of-fit test, 616
- goodness-of-fit test when population parameters are estimated, 622
- goodness-of-fit test: specified probabilities, 617
- Jarque–Bera test for normality, 624
- Mann–Whitney U test, 643
- sign test, 632
- Spearman rank correlation coefficient, 649
- test of association, 629
- Wilcoxon rank sum test, 645
- Wilcoxon signed rank test, 635

CHAPTER EXERCISES AND APPLICATIONS

14.45 Suppose that a random sample of firms with impaired assets was classified according to whether discretionary write-downs of these assets were taken, and also according to whether there was evidence of subsequent merger or acquisition activity. Using the data in the accompanying table, test the null hypothesis of no association between these characteristics.

Write-Down	Merger or Acquisition Activity?	
	No	
Yes	32	48
No	25	57

14.46 A manufacturer of a certain product has three factories located across the United States. There are three major causes of defects in this product, which we will identify as A, B, and C. During a recent week the reported occurrences of product defects in the three factories were as follows:

Factory 1	A, 15;	B, 25;	C, 23
Factory 2	A, 10;	B, 12;	C, 21
Factory 3	A, 32;	B, 28;	C, 44

Based on these frequencies, can we conclude that the defect patterns in the different factories are the same?

14.47 The human resources department is attempting to determine if employees' undergraduate majors influence their performance. The majors considered are business, economics, mathematics, and all others. Personnel ratings are grouped as excellent, strong, and average. The classifications are based on employees with two to four years of experience, as follows:

Business major	excellent, 21;	strong, 18;	average, 10
Economics major	excellent, 19;	strong, 15;	average, 5
Mathematics major	excellent, 10;	strong, 5;	average, 5
Other major	excellent, 5;	strong, 15;	average, 13

Do these data indicate that there is a difference in ratings based on undergraduate major?

14.48 A random sample of people from three different job classifications labeled A, B, and C was asked to indicate preferences for three brands of camping lanterns: Big Star, Lone Star, and Bright Star. The preferences were as follows:

Group A	Big Star, 54;	Lone Star, 67;	Bright Star, 39
Group B	Big Star, 23;	Lone Star, 13;	Bright Star, 44
Group C	Big Star, 69;	Lone Star, 53;	Bright Star, 59

Do these data indicate that there is a difference in ratings for the three different groups?

14.49 A liberal arts college was interested in determining if there were different graduate school patterns for students with undergraduate majors in history and economics. The college surveyed a random sample of recent graduates and found that a large number obtained graduate degrees in business, law, and theology. The frequency of persons in the various combinations is shown next. Based on these results, is there evidence that undergraduate economics and history majors pursue different graduate school programs?

	Graduate Studies		
Undergraduate	Business	Law	Theology
Economics	30	20	10
History	6	34	20

14.50 Suppose that you have collected market survey data for gender and product purchase. Perform a chi-square test to determine if there is a different probability of purchase among men and women. Include in your answer the expected cell values under the null hypothesis.

	Gender	
Decision	Male	Female
Purchase	150	150
No purchase	50	250

14.51 Sally Smith is a long-time political campaign manager from Chicago. In the primary election there are four candidates. She wishes to determine if voter preference is different over the four major districts. A random sample survey results in the candidate preference frequencies by district and is shown in the following contingency table. Perform an appropriate statistical test to determine if candidate preference is related to the district.

	Preference for Candidates in Primary Election				
District	A	B	C	D	Total
1	52	34	80	34	200
2	33	15	78	24	150
3	66	54	141	39	300

14.52 A manufacturer of household appliances wanted to determine if there was a relationship between family size and the size of washing machine purchased. The manufacturer was preparing guidelines for sales personnel and wanted to know if the sales staff should make specific recommendations to customers. A random sample of 300 families was asked about family size and size of washing machine. For the 40 families with one or two people, 25 had an 8-pound washer, 10 had a 10-pound washer, and 5 had a 12-pound washer. The 140 families with three or four people included 37 with the 8-pound washer, 62 with the 10-pound washer, and 41 with the 12-pound washer. For the remaining 120 families with five or more people, 8 had an 8-pound washer, 53 had a 10-pound washer, and 59 had a 12-pound washer. Based on these results, what can be concluded about family size and size of washer? Construct a two-way table, state the hypothesis, compute the statistics, and state your conclusion.

14.53 The gear-cutting department in a large manufacturing firm produces high-quality gears. The number produced per hour by a single machinist is 1, 2, or 3, as shown in the table. Company management is interested in determining the effect of worker experience on the number of units produced per hour. Worker experience is classified in three subgroups: 1 year or less, 2 to 5 years, and more than 5 years. Use the data in the table to determine if experience and number of parts produced per hour are independent.

	Units Produced/Hour			
Experience	1	2	3	Total
≤ 1 year	10	30	10	50
2–5 years	10	20	20	50
> 5 years	10	10	30	50
Total	30	60	60	150

14.54 Aurica Sabou has been working on a plan for new store locations as part of her regional expansion. In the city proposed for expansion there are three possible locations: north, east, and west. From past experience she knows that the three major profit centers in her stores are tools, lumber, and paint. In selecting a location, the demand patterns in the different parts of the city were important. She commissioned a sampling study of the city that resulted in a two-way table for the variables residential location and product purchased. This table was prepared by the market research department using data obtained from the random sample of households in the three major residential areas of the city. Each residential area had a separate phone number prefix, and the last four digits were chosen using a computer random number generator. Is there a difference in the demand patterns for the three major items among the different areas of the city?

	Product Demand		
Area	Tools	Lumber	Paint
East	100	50	50
North	50	95	45
West	65	70	75

14.55 The Speedi-Flex delivery service is conducting a study of its delivery operations. As part of this study it collected data on package type by originating source for one day's operation for one district office in the Southeast. These data are shown in the table. The major originating sources were identified as (1) small cities (towns), (2) central business districts (CBDs), (3) light manufacturing districts (factories), and (4) suburban residential communities (suburbs). Three major size and rate categories classify the items handled. Overnight envelopes must weigh 3 pounds or less and have a fixed charge of $12 anywhere in the United States. Small packages weigh from 4 to 10 pounds and have dimension restrictions. Large packages can weigh from 11 to 75 pounds and have the lowest rate per pound and the longest delivery time.

	Package Size (LB)			
Package Source	≤ 3	4–10	11–75	Total
Towns	40	40	20	100
CBDs	119	63	18	200
Factories	18	71	111	200
Suburbs	69	64	17	150

a. Are there any differences in the patterns of packages originated at the various locations?
b. Which two combinations have the largest percentage deviation from a uniform pattern?

14.56 A travel agent randomly sampled individuals in her target market and asked, "Did you use a travel agent to book your last airline flight?" By cross-referencing the answers to this question with the responses to the rest of the questionnaire, the agent obtained data such as that in the following contingency table:

	Did You Use a Travel Agent to Book Your Last Flight?	
Age	Yes	No
Under 30	15	30
30 to 39	20	42
40 to 49	47	42
50 to 59	36	50
60 or older	45	20

Determine if there is an association between the respondent's age and use of a travel agent to make reservations for the respondent's last flight.

14.57 When the law was passed to give the same legal status to e-signatures as to handwritten signatures, nearly 60% of small business owners thought that digital signatures would not help them do business on-line (Reference 26). Suppose that the following data were obtained in a similar study of small business owners classified by the number of years that the company has existed and the CEO's opinion on the ability of e-signatures to increase business.

	Will Digital Signatures Have a Positive Effect on Your Business?		
Age of Company	Yes	No	Uncertain
Less than 5 years	80	68	10
5 to 10 years	60	90	15
More than 10 years	72	63	12

Is there any relationship between the age of the company and the owner's opinion concerning the effectiveness of e-signatures?

14.58 The American Society for Quality (ASQ) offers its members exclusive recruiting tools available on-line: "Only members seeking to hire quality professionals can post jobs to these free bulletins and only members have access to these jobs online" (Reference 5). Suppose that a random sample of companies was surveyed and asked to indicate if they had used an Internet career service site to search for prospective employees. The companies were also asked questions concerning the posting fee for use of such a site. Is there a relationship between use of such a site and management's opinion on the posting fee?

	Have You Used an Internet Career Service Site?	
Posting Fee	Yes	No
Fee is too high	36	50
Fee is about right	82	28

14.59 *Business Florida* is the official guide to business growth and development in Florida. It is published annually by Enterprise Florida Inc., the Florida Economic Development Council Inc., and *Florida Trend* magazine. In *Business Florida 2001* (Reference 25), 10 reasons are given to encourage a company to select Florida as "a site for business development and expansion." Suppose that in a follow-up study a random sample of businesses that located in Florida within the last three years is surveyed. Do the data in the following contingency table show any relationship between the primary reason for the company's move to Florida and the industry type?

	Industry Type		
Primary Reason	Manufacturing	Retail	Tourism
Emerging technology	53	25	10
Tax credits	67	36	20
Labor force	30	40	33

14.60 Should large retailers offer banking services? Retail giants, such as Nordstrom and Federated Department Stores (corporate parent of Macy's and Bloomingdale's), began offering various banking services by the end of 2000 (Reference 7). Some incentives to attract customers included longer grace periods for late payments, reduced fees for such services as wire transfers, and auto or home improvement loans. Small community banks may be concerned about their future if more retailers enter the world of banking. Suppose that a market research company conducted a national survey for one retailer that is considering offering banking services to its customers. The respondents were asked to indicate the provider (bank, retail store, other) that they most likely would use for certain banking services (assuming that rate is not a factor). Is there a relationship between these two variables?

	Provider		
Service	Bank	Retail Store	Other
Checking account	100	45	10
Savings account	85	25	45
Home mortgage	30	10	80

14.61 Many easy weight-loss products are just gimmicks that attract people with the hope of a fast way to a slimmer body. Diet industry groups, health professionals, and federal officials warn that deceptive advertising can lure consumers into danger (Reference 8). Suppose that a random sample of residents in one community was asked if they had ever tried a quick weight-loss product. They were also asked if they thought that there should be stricter advertising controls to prohibit deceptive weight-loss advertising.

	Used a Quick Weight-Loss Product?	
Advertising	Yes	No
Stricter controls needed	85	40
Stricter controls not needed	25	64

Are respondents' views on advertising controls dependent on whether or not they had ever used a quick weight-loss product?

14.62 "Rattled by the trembling stock market, online enterprises began what will no doubt be a long run of layoffs" (Reference 10). Although the economy is new, apparently the same old downsizing is taking place among dot-com companies. These e-companies claim that firings are necessary to increase profits and save costs. Suppose that the following contingency table shows the number of layoffs in three dot-com companies and the months of service by those employees that were laid off. Is there any relationship between theses two variables?

	Dot-Com Company		
Age	A	B	C
Less than 6 months	23	40	12
6 months to 1 year	15	21	12
More than 1 year	12	9	6

14.63 Some marketing research studies indicate the "positive impact of store brand penetration on store profitability as measured by market share" (Reference 16). Two years ago the manager of a local supermarket that sells three national brands

(brands A, B, and C) and one store brand (brand D) of orange juice found that brands A and C were equally preferred, 33% preferred brand B, and 27% preferred the store brand, D. Now, the manager thinks that there has been a change in customer preferences and that the preference for store brand orange juice has increased and perhaps will positively contribute to increased profits. The results from a recent random sample of shoppers indicate the following preferences.

Favorite Brand	A	B	C	D (Store Brand)
Number	56	70	28	126

Has there been a change in customer preferences from the study 2 years ago?

14.64 By late fall 2000, customers who wanted wireless Internet service could choose from four basic categories of hardware: Palm handhelds and their off-spring that use the Palm operating system, Pocket PCs, Web-enabled phones, and mobile e-mail devices (Reference 23). Analyzing the following data taken from a survey of wireless Internet service users, does satisfaction depend on the hardware category selected?

Hardware Category	Are You Satisfied with Your Purchase?	
	Yes	No
Palm handhelds	128	40
Pocket PCs	45	15
Web-enabled phones	30	8
Mobile e-mail devices	30	6

14.65 🌐 As part of an exploratory market study, students on one college campus were asked to answer a brief survey concerning their college library (Reference 27). One question asked if students thought that the library hours should be extended.
   a. Test for a relationship between students' responses to this question and their class standing. The data are stored in the data file **Library**.
   b. What recommendations would you suggest to the library staff?

14.66 🌐 Can a student easily find books in the college library? This question was also included in the college library survey (Reference 27).
   a. Test for any relationship between students' responses to this question and their class standing. The data are stored in the data file **Library**.

b. What recommendations would you suggest to the library staff?

14.67 🌐 The Institutional Research Office (IRO) at a major university annually conducts surveys of freshmen, sophomores, and juniors to determine levels of satisfaction with student services, facilities, and policies of the university. Seniors are surveyed separately in the Senior Survey. Suppose that the director of the IRO at one university provides university administrators/faculty/staff with analyses of trends, comparisons, and other output useful for purpose of continuous improvement.

The 2002 Student Satisfaction Survey, conducted in the spring of 2002 from mid-March to early May, was mailed to a random sample of 600 students (200 freshmen, 200 sophomores, and 200 juniors). The response rate was 248, or 42.5% (after adjusting for undeliverable or unclaimed surveys). Demographic information included respondent's school or college of major, age, and gender. Suppose that selected data collected from the 2002 Student Satisfaction Survey are included in the data file **IRO**. Students were asked to indicate if they were satisfied with, neutral toward, or dissatisfied with on-line registration, the university bookstore, food service, the student accounts/billing office, student financial planning, the work-study program, and various other service providers on campus. From the data, numerous relationships can be investigated. Analyze the data, select and test several possible relationships, and write a summary of findings to be submitted to the university president. Include in your report discussion of any relationship between a student's satisfaction with library hours and the student's class standing, a student's satisfaction level with faculty advising, availability of internships, on-line registration, and overseas programs. Your report can be enhanced by descriptive measures, graphs, and estimations.

14.68 A recent study of computer usage (Reference 18) found that "children ages 2 to 5 averaged 27 minutes a day at the computer, while children 6 to 11 spent 49 minutes a day, and those 12 to 17 averaged 63 minutes a day." Most schools are now wired to the Internet, but how these computers are used in the classroom varies. According to Jay Becker, a professor at the University of California at Irvine, "schools serving poor children were more likely to emphasize word processing and other simple tasks while those serving more affluent students taught computer skills to promote problem-solving and a deeper understanding of an area of study." Suppose that a team of educational researchers under the direction of Dr. Joy Haugaard conducted a survey to test this hypothesis. The study involved 225 schools from both poorer communities and more affluent districts. The following table gives their responses to the question "Concerning computer usage, is your school more likely to emphasize basic tasks such as word processing or computer skills involving problem-solving?"

Content Emphasis	Economic Status	
	Poor Community	Affluent Community
Basic tasks (word processing)	75	40
Computer skills (problem solving)	30	80

Do the data from this study agree with Becker's conclusions?

14.69 There are several forms that people can use to file their federal income tax returns. One standard method is the 1040 form. Some people use other forms such as the telefile process. Others simply file for an extension (to extend the deadline beyond April 15). Suppose that in a particular locality a study of 200 randomly selected people filing returns was conducted. The filer's age was an important variable in this study. Proportional to the age demographics of the area, the study included 50 people under 25 and 90 people between the ages of 25 and 45; the remainder were over 45. Of those under the age of 25, 35 used a 1040 form, 8 used another form, and the remainder filed for an extension. Two-thirds of the people in the age category from 25 to 45 used the 1040 form, 20 used a different form, and the remainder filed for an extension. Seventy-five percent of the people over 45 used the 1040 form, 4 people filed for an extension, and the remainder used a different process. Determine if there is any association between a person's age and the method used to file income tax returns.

14.70 In Example 14.2 a random sample of 200 people was asked to indicate candy bar preference. Suppose that we also gathered demographic data such as gender. From the 50 who preferred Mr. Goodbar, it was found that 20% were female; from the 93 who preferred Hershey's Milk Chocolate, 70 were female; from the 45 who preferred Hershey's Special Dark, 80% were male; and from the remainder who preferred Krackel, two-thirds were male. Do the data indicate that there is an association between candy bar preference and gender?

14.71 What does it mean to say that a test is nonparametric? What are the relative advantages of such tests?

14.72 Construct a realistic example of a statistical problem in the business area where a nonparametric test would be preferred to the alternative parametric test.

14.73 In a random sample of 12 analysts, 7 believed that automobile sales in the United States were likely to be significantly higher next year than in the present year, 2 believed that sales would be significantly lower, and the others anticipated that next year's sales would be roughly the same as those in the current year. What can we conclude from these data?

14.74 In a random sample of 16 exchange rate analysts, 8 believed that the Japanese yen would be an excellent investment this year, 5 believed that it would be a poor investment, and 3 had no strong opinion on the question. What conclusions can be drawn from these data?

14.75 Of a random sample of 100 college students, 35 expected to achieve a higher standard of living than their parents, 43 expected a lower standard of living, and 22 expected about the same standard of living as their parents. Do these data present strong evidence that, for the population of students, more expect a lower standard of living compared with their parents than expect a higher standard of living?

14.76 Of a random sample of 120 business school professors, 48 believed students' analytical skills had improved over the last decade, 35 believed these skills had deteriorated, and 37 saw no discernible change. Evaluate the strength of the sample evidence suggesting that, for all business school professors, more believe that analytical skills have improved than believe that these skills have deteriorated.

14.77 A random sample of 10 corporate analysts was asked to rate, on a scale from 1 (very poor) to 10 (very high), the prospects for their own corporations and for the economy at large in the current year. The results obtained are shown in the accompanying table. Using the Wilcoxon test, discuss the proposition that in the aggregate corporate analysts are more optimistic about the prospects for their own companies than for the economy at large.

Analyst	Own Corporation	Economy at Large
1	8	8
2	7	5
3	6	7
4	5	4
5	8	4
6	6	9
7	7	7
8	5	2
9	4	6
10	9	6

14.78 Nine pairs of hypothetical profiles were constructed for corporate employees applying for admission to an executive MBA program. Within each pair these profiles were identical, except that one candidate was male and the other female. For interviews for employment of these graduates, evaluations on a scale of 1 (low) to 10 (high) were made of the candidates' suitability for employment. The results are shown in the accompanying table. Analyze these data using the Wilcoxon test.

Interview	Male	Female
1	8	8
2	9	10
3	7	5
4	4	7
5	8	8
6	9	9
7	5	3
8	4	5
9	6	2

14.79 American Traveler Survey conducts research on business and leisure travel habits (Reference 13). Suppose that a random sample of 513 individuals were randomly sampled and information was collected about the method a subject used to make an airline reservation (last reservation for either business or pleasure) and the subject's gender. Test the null hypothesis of no association between these two characteristics. The data is summarized as follows:

Reservation Method	Female	Male
Used a travel agent	56	74
Booked on the Internet	148	142
Called the airline's toll-free number	66	34

REFERENCES

1. Anderson, T. W.; Darling, D. A. 1952. Asymptotic theory of certain "goodness-of-fit" criteria based on stochastic processes. *Annals of Mathematical Statistics* **23**:193–212.

2. Bera, A. K., and C. M. Jarque. 1981. An Efficient Large-Sample Test for Normality of Observations and Regression Residuals. *Working Papers in Economics and Econometrics* 40, Australian National University.

3. Brandbury, M. E. 1990. The Incentives for Voluntary Audit Committee Formation. *Journal of Accounting and Public Policy* 9:19–36.

4. Brickley, F. H. Dark, and M. S. Weisbach. 1991. An Agency Perspective on Franchising. *Financial Management* 20 (1): 27–35.

5. "Career Services Program Updated." *On Q* (American Society for Quality) 15, no. 4 (Fall 2000).

6. Conover, W. J. 1999. *Practical Nonparametric Statistics*, 3ʳᵈ edition. New York, Wiley.

7. Coolidge, Carrie. 2000. Socks and Bonds. *Forbes* (July 3): 62.

8. "Dieter Hunger for Gimmicks." *New York Times* article appearing in *Orlando Sentinel*, October 29, 2000, p. A11.

9. Gaffen, David. Learning to Sell Dell. MARKETBEAT, November 30, 2007 3:21 pm. http:// blogs.wsj.com/marketbeat/2007/11/30/ (accessed 11/14/08).

10. Godwin, Jennifer. 2000. New Economy, Same Old Downsizing. *Forbes* (July 3): 60.

11. Irvine, Paul, and James Rosenfeld. 2000. Raising Capital Using Monthly Income Preferred Stock: Market Reaction and Implications for Capital Structure Theory. *Financial Management* 29:5–20.

12. Jaggi, B., and P. Grier. 1980. A Comparative Analysis of Forecast Disclosing and Nondisclosing Firms. *Financial Management* 9 (2): 38–43.

13. Jamison, Jane. 1999. Survey Highlights Agents' Strength. *Travel Weekly* (October 25): 10–47.

14. Jarque, Carlos M. and Anil K. Bera. 1980. Efficient tests for normality, homoscedasticity and serial independence of regression residuals. *Economics Letters* 6 (3): 255–259.

15. Keveney, Bill. 2000. Classroom TV Brings Election to Students: Commercial-free Cable Programs Promote Citizenship. *USA Today* (October 30): 4D.

16. Lal, Rajiv, and Marcel CorstJensrajiv Lal. 2000. Building Store Loyalty Through Store Brands. *Journal of Marketing Research* 37 (3): 281.

17. Lehman, E. L. 1975. *Nonparametrics: Statistical Methods Based on Ranks*. San Francisco: Holden-Day.

18. Lewin, Tamara. 2001. Children's Computer Use Grows, but Gap Persist, Study Says. *New York Times* (January 22): A11.

19. Lilliefors, H. 1967. On the Kolmogorov-Smirnov test for normality with mean and variance unknown. *Journal of the American Statistical Association*, Vol. 62. (June): 399–402.

20. Meyers, M. D., L. A. Gordon, and M. M. Hamer. 1991. Postauditing Capital Assets and Firm Performance: An Empirical Investigation. *Managerial and Decision Economics* 12: 317–327.

21. Michelson, Stuart, J. Stryker and B. Thorne. "The Sarbanes-Oxley Act of 2002: What Impact Has It Had on Small Business Firms? Submitted for publication, 2008.

22. Mosteller, F., and D. L. Wallace. *Interference and Disputed Authorship: The Federalist* © 1964, Addison-Wesley, Reading, Mass., Tables 2.3 and 2.4. Reprinted with permission.

23. Nadeau, Michael. 2000. Cut the Cord. Access: *America's Guide to the Internet*. Special Magazine Supplement to *Orlando Sentinel* (October 29): 12–14. www.accessmagazine.com.

24. Shapiro, S. S. and Wilk, M. B. 1965. An analysis of variance test for normality (complete samples). *Biometrika*, 52, 3 and 4:591–611.

25. Shepherd, Gary. 2001. 10 Reasons Why Your Business Belongs in Florida. *Business Trend's Business Florida 2001*, www.businessflorida.com.

26. "Sign Here Please," *USA Today*, October 30, 2000, p.1B. *www.office.com*.

27. Thorne, J. Renee, et al. "University Library Study," unpublished paper. Data available in data file **Library**.

28. Whittred, G. P. 1980. Audit Qualification and the Timeliness of Corporate Annual Reports. *Accounting Review* 55:563–577.

Chapter 15

Analysis of Variance

Introduction

In modern business applications of statistical analysis there are a number of situations that require comparisons of processes at more than two levels. For example, the manager of Integrated Circuits Inc. would like to determine if any of five different processes for assembling components results in higher productivity per hour and in fewer defective components. Analyses to answer such questions come under the general heading of experimental design. An important tool for organizing and analyzing the data from this experiment is called *analysis of variance*, the subject of this chapter. The experiment might also be extended to a design that includes the question of which of four sources of raw materials leads to the highest productivity in combination with the different manufacturing processes. This question could be answered by using two-way analysis of variance. In another example the president of Prairie Flower Cereal is interested in comparing product sales per week of four different brands over three different stores. Again we have a problem design that can be analyzed using analysis of variance. In Section 13.2 we showed that dummy variables could also be used for analysis of experimental design problems.

In Sections 10.1 and 10.2 we saw how to test the hypothesis of equality of two population means. In fact, two distinct tests were developed, the appropriate test depending on the mechanism employed in the generation of sample observations. Specifically, our tests assumed either paired observations or independent random samples. This distinction is important, and, to clarify it, we pause to consider a simple illustration. Suppose that it is our objective to compare the fuel consumption recorded for two different makes of automobile, A-cars and B-cars. We could randomly select 10 people to drive these cars over a specified distance, each driver being assigned to a car of each type, so that any particular driver will drive both an A-car and a B-car. The 20 resulting fuel consumption figures obtained will consist of 10 pairs, each pair corresponding to a single driver. This is the matched pairs design, and its attraction lies in its ability to produce a comparison between the quantities of interest (in this case fuel consumption for the two types of car), while making allowance for the possible importance of an additional relevant factor (individual driver differences). Thus, if a significant difference between the performance of A-cars and that of B-cars is found, we have some assurance that this is not a result of differences in driver behavior. An alternative design would be to take 20 drivers and randomly assign 10 of them to A-cars and 10 to B-cars (though, in fact, there is no need to have equal numbers of trials for each type of car). The 20 resulting fuel consumption figures would then constitute a pair of independent random samples of 10 observations each on A-cars and B-cars.

For these two types of design, we discussed in Chapter 10 the appropriate procedures for testing the null hypothesis of equality of a pair of population means. In this chapter our aim is to extend these procedures to the development of tests for the equality of several population means. Suppose, for example, that our study included a third make of automobile, the C-car. The null hypothesis of interest would then be that the population mean fuel consumption is the same for all three makes of car. We show how tests for such hypotheses can be constructed, beginning with the case where independent random samples are taken. In Section 15.5 the extension of the test based on matched pairs will be discussed.

Suppose that out of 20 drivers 7 are randomly assigned to A-cars, 7 to B-cars, and 6 to C-cars. Using the data in Table 15.1, we computed the following:

$$\text{Sample mean for A-cars} = \frac{146.3}{7} = 20.9$$

$$\text{Sample mean for B-cars} = \frac{162.4}{7} = 23.2$$

$$\text{Sample mean for C-cars} = \frac{137.4}{6} = 22.9$$

Naturally, these sample means are not all the same. As always, however, when testing hypotheses, we are interested in the likelihood of such differences arising by chance if, in fact, the null hypothesis was true. If it is concluded that such discrepancies would be very unlikely to arise by chance, considerable skepticism about the truth of the null hypothesis would arise.

To clarify the issues involved, consider Figure 15.1, which depicts two hypothetical sets of data. The sample means in part (a) of the figure are precisely the same as those in part (b). The crucial difference is that in the former the observations are

Table 15.1 Fuel Consumption Figures from Three Independent Random Samples, in Miles per Gallon

	A-Cars	B-Cars	C-Cars
	22.2	24.6	22.7
	19.9	23.1	21.9
	20.3	22.0	23.2
	21.4	23.5	24.1
	21.2	23.6	22.1
	21.0	22.1	23.4
	20.3	23.5	—
Sums	**146.3**	**162.4**	**137.4**

Figure 15.1 Two Sets of Sample Fuel Consumption Data on Three Makes of Automobile

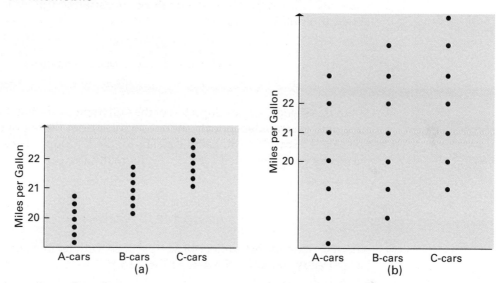

tightly clustered about their respective sample means, while in the latter there is much greater dispersion. Visual inspection of part (a) suggests very strongly the conjecture that the data, in fact, arise from three populations with different means. Looking at part (b) of the figure, by contrast, we would not be terribly surprised to learn that these data came from a common population.

INTERPRETATION

This illustration serves to point out the very essence of the test for equality of population means. The critical factor is the *variability* involved in the data. If the variability *around* the sample means is small compared with the variability *among* the sample means, as in Figure 15.1(a), we are inclined to doubt the null hypothesis that the population means are equal. If, as in Figure 15.1(b), the variability around the sample means is large compared with the variability among them, the evidence against the null hypothesis is rather weak. This being the case, it seems reasonable to expect that an appropriate test will be based on assessments of variation. This is indeed the case, and for this reason the general technique employed is referred to as the analysis of variance.

15.2 ONE-WAY ANALYSIS OF VARIANCE

The problem introduced in Section 15.1 can be treated quite generally. Suppose that we want to compare the means of K populations, *each of which is assumed to have the same variance.* Independent random samples of $n_1, n_2, \ldots, n_k$ observations are taken from these populations. We use the symbol x_{ij} to denote the jth observation in the ith population. Then, using the format of Table 15.1, we can display the sample data as in Table 15.2.

The procedure for testing the equality of population means in this setup is called one-way analysis of variance, a term that will become clearer when we discuss other analysis of variance models.

> **The Framework for One-Way Analysis of Variance**
> Suppose that we have independent random samples of $n_1, n_2, \ldots, n_k$ observations from K populations. If the population means are denoted $\mu_1, \mu_2, \ldots, \mu_K$, the one-way analysis of variance framework is designed to test the null hypothesis:
>
> $$H_0 : \mu_1 = \mu_2 = \ldots = \mu_k$$
>
> $$H_1 : \mu_i \neq \mu_j \text{ For at least one pair } \mu_i, \mu_j$$

In this section we develop a test of the null hypothesis that the K population means are equal, given independent random samples from those populations. The obvious first step is to calculate the sample means for the K groups of observations. These sample means will be denoted $\bar{x}_1, \bar{x}_2, \ldots, \bar{x}_K$. Formally, then

$$\bar{x}_i = \frac{\sum_{j=1}^{n_i} x_{ij}}{n_i} \quad (i = 1, 2, \ldots, K)$$

where n_i denotes the number of sample observations in group i. In this notation we have already found for the data of Table 15.1:

$$\bar{x}_1 = 20.9 \qquad \bar{x}_2 = 23.2 \qquad \bar{x}_3 = 22.9$$

Table 15.2 Sample Observations from Independent Random Samples of K Populations

	POPULATION		
1	2	$\ldots$	K
x_{11}	x_{21}	$\ldots$	x_{K1}
x_{12}	x_{22}	$\ldots$	x_{K2}
.	.		.
.	.		.
.	.		.
x_{1n}	x_{2n}	$\ldots$	x_{Kn}

Now, the null hypothesis of interest specifies that the K populations have a common mean. A logical step, then, is to form an estimate of that common mean from the sample observations. This is just the sum of all of the sample values divided by their total number. If we let n denote the total number of sample observations, then

$$n = \sum_{i=1}^{K} n_i$$

In our example $n = 20$. The overall mean of the sample observations can then be expressed as

$$\bar{\bar{x}} = \frac{\sum_{i=1}^{K} \sum_{j=1}^{n_i} x_{ij}}{n}$$

where the double summation notation indicates that we sum over all observations within each group and over all groups; that is, we sum all of the available observations. An equivalent expression is as follows:

$$\bar{\bar{x}} = \frac{\sum_{i=1}^{K} n_i \bar{x}_i}{n}$$

For the fuel consumption data of Table 15.1 the overall mean is as follows:

$$\bar{x} = \frac{(7)(20.9) + (7)(23.2) + (6)(22.9)}{20} = 22.3$$

Hence, if, in fact, the population mean fuel consumption is the same for A-cars, B-cars, and C-cars, we estimate that common mean to be 22.3 miles per gallon.

As indicated in Section 15.1, the test of equality of population means is based on a comparison of two types of variability exhibited by the sample members. The first is variability about the individual sample means within the K groups of observations. It is convenient to refer to this as *within-groups variability*. Second, we are interested in the variability among the K group means. This is called *between-groups variability*. We now seek measures, based on the sample data, of these two types of variability.

To begin, consider variability within groups. To measure variability in the first group, we calculate the sum of squares deviations of the observations about their sample mean $\bar{x}_1$ that is,

$$SS_1 = \sum_{j=1}^{n_1} (x_{1j} - \bar{x}_1)^2$$

Similarly, for the second group, whose sample mean is $\bar{x}_2$, we calculate

$$SS_2 = \sum_{j=1}^{n_2} (x_{2j} - \bar{x}_2)^2$$

and so on. The total within-groups variability, denoted SSW, is then the sum of the sums of squares over all K groups—that is,

$$SSW = SS_1 + SS_2 + \cdots + SS_K$$

or

$$SSW = \sum_{i=1}^{K} \sum_{j=1}^{n_i} (x_{ij} - \bar{x}_i)^2$$

For the data on fuel consumption we have the following:

$$SS_1 = (22.2 - 20.9)^2 + (19.9 - 20.9)^2 + \cdots + (20.3 - 20.9)^2 = 3.76$$

$$SS_2 = (24.6 - 23.2)^2 + (23.1 - 23.2)^2 + \cdots + (23.5 - 23.2)^2 = 4.96$$

$$SS_3 = (22.7 - 22.9)^2 + (21.9 - 22.9)^2 + \cdots + (23.4 - 22.9)^2 = 3.46$$

The within-group sum of squares is, therefore,

$$SSW = SS_1 + SS_2 + SS_3 = 3.76 + 4.96 + 3.46 = 12.18$$

Next, we need a measure of variability between groups. A natural measure is based on the discrepancies between the individual group means and the overall mean. In fact, as before, these discrepancies are squared, giving

$$(\bar{x}_1 - \bar{x})^2, (\bar{x}_2 - \bar{x})^2, \ldots, (\bar{x}_K - \bar{x})^2$$

In computing the total between-group sum of squares, SSG, we weight each squared discrepancy by the number of sample observations in the corresponding group (so that the most weight is given to the squared discrepancies in groups with most observations), giving

$$SSG = \sum_{i=1}^{K} n_i (\bar{x}_i - \bar{x})^2$$

Thus, for our fuel consumption data

$$SSG = (7)(20.9 - 22.3)^2 + (7)(23.2 - 22.3)^2 + (6)(22.9 - 22.3)^2$$
$$= 21.55$$

Another sum of squares is often calculated. This is the sum of squared discrepancies of *all* the sample observations about their *overall* mean. This is called the *total sum of squares* and is expressed as follows:

$$SST = \sum_{i=1}^{K} \sum_{j=1}^{n_i} (x_{ij} - \bar{x})^2$$

In fact, we show in the appendix to this chapter that the total sum of squares is the sum of the within-group and between-group sums of squares—that is,

$$SST = SSW + SSG$$

Hence, for the fuel consumption data we have the following:

$$SST = 12.18 + 21.55 = 33.73$$

Sum of Squares Decomposition for One-Way Analysis of Variance

Suppose that we have independent random samples of $n_1, n_2, \ldots, n_k$ observations from K populations. Denote by $\bar{x}_1, \bar{x}_2, \ldots, \bar{x}_K$ the K group sample means and by $\bar{x}$ the overall sample mean. We define the following **sums of squares**:

$$\text{WITHIN-GROUPS}: SSW = \sum_{i=1}^{K} \sum_{j=1}^{n_i} (x_{ij} - \bar{x}_i)^2 \tag{15.1}$$

$$\text{BETWEEN-GROUPS: } SSG = \sum_{i=1}^{K} n_i (\bar{x}_i - \bar{x})^2 \qquad (15.2)$$

$$\text{TOTAL: } SST = \sum_{i=1}^{K} \sum_{j=1}^{n_i} (x_{ij} - \bar{x})^2 \qquad (15.3)$$

where x_{ij} denotes the jth sample observation in the ith group.
Then,

$$SST = SSW + SSG \qquad (15.4)$$

The decomposition of the total sum of squares into the sum of two components—within-groups and between-groups sums of squares—provides the basis for the analysis of variance test of equality of group population means. We can view this decomposition as expressing the total variability of all the sample observations about their overall mean as the sum of variability within groups and variability between groups. Schematically, this is shown in Figure 15.2.

Our test of the equality of population means is based on the assumption that the K populations have a common variance. If the null hypothesis that the population means are all the same is true, each of the sums of squares, SSW and SSG, can be used as the basis for an estimate of the common population variance. To obtain these estimates, the sums of squares must be divided by the appropriate number of degrees of freedom.

First, we show in the chapter appendix that an unbiased estimator of the population variance results if SSW is divided by $(n - K)$. The resulting estimate is called the *within-groups mean square*, denoted MSW, so that

$$MSW = \frac{SSW}{n - K}$$

For our data we have the following:

$$MSW = \frac{12.18}{20 - 3} = 0.71647$$

If the population means are equal, another unbiased estimator of the population variance is obtained by dividing SSG by $(K - 1)$, also shown in the chapter appendix. The resulting quantity is called the *between-groups mean square*, denoted MSG, and, hence,

$$MSG = \frac{SSG}{K - 1}$$

For the fuel consumption data

$$MSG = \frac{21.55}{3 - 1} = 10.775$$

When the population means are *not* equal, the between-groups mean square does *not* provide an unbiased estimate of the common population variance. Rather, the expected

Figure 15.2
Sum of Squares
Decomposition for
One-Way Analysis
of Variance

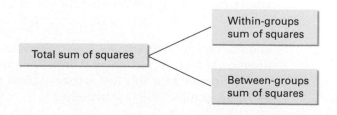

value of the corresponding random variable exceeds the common population variance, as it also carries information about the squared differences of the true population means.

If the null hypothesis was true, we would now be in possession of two unbiased estimates of the same quantity, the common population variance. It would be reasonable to expect these estimates to be quite close to each other. The greater the discrepancy between these two estimates, all else being equal, the stronger our suspicion that the null hypothesis is not true. The test of the null hypothesis is based on the ratio of mean squares (see the chapter appendix):

$$F = \frac{MSG}{MSW}$$

If this ratio is quite close to 1, there is little cause to doubt the null hypothesis of equality of population means. However, as already noted, if the variability between groups is large compared to the variability within groups, we suspect the null hypothesis to be false. This is the case where a value considerably larger than 1 arises for the F ratio. The null hypothesis is rejected for large values of this ratio.

A formal test follows from the fact that, if the null hypothesis of equality of population means is true, the random variable follows the F distribution (discussed in Section 10.4) with numerator degrees of freedom $(K - 1)$ and denominator degrees of freedom $(n - K)$, assuming the population distributions to be normal.

Hypothesis Test for One-Way Analysis of Variance

Suppose that we have independent random samples of $n_1, n_2, \ldots, n_k$ observations from K populations. Denote by n the total sample size, so that

$$n = n_1 + n_2 + \cdots + n_K$$

We define the **mean squares** as follows:

$$\text{WITHIN-GROUPS}: MSW = \frac{SSW}{n - K} \tag{15.5}$$

$$\text{BETWEEN-GROUPS}: MSG = \frac{SSG}{K - 1} \tag{15.6}$$

The null hypothesis to be tested is that the K population means are equal—that is,

$$H_0 : \mu_1 = \mu_2 = \cdots = \mu_K$$

We make the following additional assumptions:

1. The population variances are equal.
2. The population distributions are normal.

A test of significance level α is provided by the decision rule

$$\text{Reject } H_0 \text{ if } \frac{MSG}{MSW} > F_{K-1,n-K,\alpha} \tag{15.7}$$

where $F_{K-1,n-K,\alpha}$ is the number for which

$$P(F_{K-1,n-K} > F_{K-1,n-K,\alpha}) = \alpha$$

and the random variable $F_{K-1,\,n-k}$ follows an F distribution with numerator degrees of freedom $(K - 1)$ and denominator degrees of freedom $(n - K)$.

The p-value for this test is the smallest significance value that would allow us to reject the null hypothesis.

For the fuel consumption data, we find the following:

$$\frac{MSG}{MSW} = \frac{10.775}{0.71647} = 15.04$$

The numerator and denominator degrees of freedom are, respectively, $(K-1) = 2$ and $(n-K) = 17$. Thus, for a 1% significance level test, from Table 9 in the appendix, we have the following:

$$F_{2,17,0.01} = 6.11$$

Hence, these data allow us to reject, at the 1% significance level, the null hypothesis that population mean fuel consumption is the same for all three types of automobiles.

The computations involved in carrying out this test are very conveniently summarized in a **one-way analysis of variance table**. The general form of the table is set out in Table 15.3. For the fuel consumption data the analysis of variance is set out in Table 15.4. Note that in some expositions the within-groups sum of squares is referred to as the *error sum of squares*.

Table 15.3   General Format of One-Way Analysis of Variance Table

SOURCE OF VARIATION	SUM OF SQUARES	DEGREES OF FREEDOM	MEAN SQUARES	F RATIO
Between groups	SSG	$K-1$	$MSG = \dfrac{SSG}{K-1}$	$\dfrac{MSG}{MSW}$
Within groups	SSW	$n-K$	$MSW = \dfrac{SSW}{n-K}$	
Total	SST	$n-1$		

Table 15.4   One-Way Analysis of Variance Table for Fuel Consumption Data

SOURCE OF VARIATION	SUM OF SQUARES	DEGREES OF FREEDOM	MEAN SQUARES	F RATIO
Between groups	21.55	2	10.78	15.05
Within groups	12.18	17	0.7165	
Total	33.73	19		

Example 15.1   Reading Difficulty of Magazine Advertisements (One-Way Analysis of Variance)

The *fog index* is used to measure the reading difficulty of a written text: The higher the value of the index, the more difficult the reading level. We want to know if the reading difficulty index is different for three magazines: *Scientific American*, *Fortune*, and the *New Yorker*.

Solution   Independent random samples of 6 advertisements were taken from *Scientific American*, *Fortune*, and the *New Yorker*, and the fog indices for the 18 advertisements were measured, as recorded in Table 15.5 (Reference 2).

From these data we can derive the analysis of variance table using a statistical program such as Minitab. Figure 15.3 contains the analysis of variance output. To test the null hypothesis that the population mean fog indices are the same, the computed F ratio—F = 6.97—in the analysis of variance table must be compared with tabulated values of the F distribution with (2, 15) degrees of freedom. From Table 9 in the appendix we find the following:

$$F_{2,15,0.01} = 6.36$$

INTERPRETATION

Thus, the null hypothesis of equality of the three population mean fog indices is rejected at the 1% significance level. Note also that the computed p-value as found in Figure 15.3 is 0.007. We have strong evidence that the reading difficulty is different, with *New Yorker* having the lowest index. Note that the Minitab output provides a graphical display of subgroup means and their confidence intervals. This output provides a visual display of the differences between subgroup means, noting in this case that the *New Yorker* differs substantially from *Scientific American* and *Fortune*.

Table 15.5 Fog Index of Reading Difficulty for Three Magazines

SCIENTIFIC AMERICAN	FORTUNE	NEW YORKER
15.75	12.63	9.27
11.55	11.46	8.28
11.16	10.77	8.15
9.92	9.93	6.37
9.23	9.87	6.37
8.20	9.42	5.66

Figure 15.3 One-Way Analysis of Variance for Reading Difficulty in *Scientific American*, *Fortune*, and the *New Yorker* (Minitab Output)

One-way ANOVA: SCIENTIFIC AMERICAN, FORTUNE, NEW YORKER

```
Source    DF       SS     MS      F      P
Factor     2    48.53  24.26   6.97  0.007
Error     15    52.22   3.48
Total     17   100.75

S = 1.866    R-Sq = 48.17%    R-Sq(adj) = 41.26%


                                   Individual 95% CIs For Mean Based on
                                   Pooled StDev
Level               N    Mean   StDev    -+--------+--------+--------+----
SCIENTIFIC AMERI    6  10.968   2.647                   (------*------)
FORTUNE             6  10.680   1.202                 (------*------)
NEW YORKER          6   7.350   1.412      (------*------)
                                         -+--------+--------+--------+----
                                         6.0      8.0     10.0     12.0

Pooled StDev = 1.866
```

Multiple Comparisons Between Subgroup Means

After we have concluded that subgroup means are different by rejecting the null hypothesis one might naturally ask which subgroup means are different from others. Thus, we would like to have a minimal interval that could be used to decide if two subgroup means are different in a statistical sense. Or more precisely can we reject a hypothesis that certain of the subgroup means are not different from others when we have concluded that at least one of the subgroup means is different from others. This is an important question for applied analysis, but one that leads to certain additional complications.

If we have two subgroups then we can use the hypothesis testing methods developed in Chapter 10 to compute a minimum significant difference (MSD) between two sample means that would lead us to reject the hypothesis that the population means are equal and, thus, that we have evidence to conclude that the population means are different. In those cases we would compute a common estimate of variance s_p and the resulting MSD can be computed as follows:

$$MSD = t_{\frac{\alpha}{2}} s_p \sqrt{\frac{2}{n}}$$

While this procedure, based on hypothesis tests with probability of error α, works well for two subgroups it does not work well when there are k subgroups. In that case the number of paired comparisons can be computed using the combinations equation developed in Chapter 3:

$$C_2^k = \frac{k!}{(k-2)!2!}$$

and, thus, the probability of error α would no longer hold.

A number of procedures have been developed to deal with the multiple comparisons question. Essentially they involve developing intervals that are somewhat wider than those for the two subgroup case. These intervals are developed using advanced mathematical statistics analysis that provides intervals with the correct α levels for many subgroups. We will present here a procedure developed by John Tukey, which uses an extended form of the Student's t distribution. Factors identified as q are presented in Table 13 in the appendix for various numbers of subgroups, degrees of freedom, and α equal to 0.01 and 0.05.

Multiple Comparison Procedure
The minimum significant difference between K subgroups is computed using

$$MSD(k) = q \frac{s_p}{\sqrt{n}}$$

$$with$$

$$s_p = \sqrt{MSW}$$

with the factor q selected from Table 13 for the appropriate level of α (0.01, 0.05), the number of subgroups K, and the degrees of freedom for MSW. To obtain the value of q from Table 13 note that in Table 13 the columns are based on the number of subgroups and the rows indicate the degrees of freedom for error. The resulting MSD can be used to indicate which subgroup means are different and, thus, provides a very useful screening device that can be used to extend the results from the analyses we have discussed here.

Addendum to Example 15.1 Application of Multiple Comparisons

In Example 15.1 we compared the reading difficulty of three magazines and the degrees of freedom for error was 15. For $\alpha = 0.05$ the value of q from Table 13 is 3.67. Thus, the minimum significant difference is as follows:

$$MSD(3) = 3.67 \frac{1.87}{\sqrt{18}}$$

$$= 1.62$$

with

$$s_p = \sqrt{3.48} = 1.87$$

Using this value of 1.62 and the subgroup means in Figure 15.3 we can see that the *New Yorker* mean is significantly different from both *Scientific American* and *Fortune*, but the later two are not different.

Population Model for One-Way Analysis of Variance

It is instructive to view the one-way analysis of variance model in a different light. Let the random variable X_{ij} denote the jth observation from the ith population, and let μ_i stand for the mean of this population. Then X_{ij} can be viewed as the sum of two parts—its mean and a random variable ε_{ij} having a mean of 0. Therefore, we can write the following:

$$X_{ij} = \mu_i + \varepsilon_{ij}$$

Now, because independent random samples are taken, the random variables ε_{ij} will be uncorrelated with one another. Moreover, given our assumption that the population variances are all the same, it follows that the ε_{ij} all have the same variances. Hence, these random variables satisfy the standard assumptions (see Section 12.3) imposed on the error terms of a multiple regression model. This equation can be viewed as such a model, with unknown parameters $\mu_1, \mu_2, \ldots, \mu_K$. The null hypothesis of interest is as follows:

$$H_0 : \mu_1 = \mu_2 = \cdots = \mu_K$$

A test on these parameters is facilitated by the further assumption of normality.

The model can be written in a slightly different manner. Let μ denote the overall mean of the K combined populations and G_i the discrepancy between the population mean for the ith group and this overall mean, so that

$$G_i = \mu_i - \mu \quad \text{or} \quad \mu_i = \mu + G_i$$

Substituting into the original equation gives

$$X_{ij} = \mu + G_i + \varepsilon_{ij}$$

so that an observation is made up of the sum of an overall mean μ, a group-specific term G_i, and a random error ε_{ij}. Then our null hypothesis is that every population mean μ_i is the same as the overall mean, or

$$H_0 : G_1 = G_2 = \cdots = G_K = 0$$

Figure 15.4
Illustration of the
Population Model
for the One-Way
Analysis of
Variance

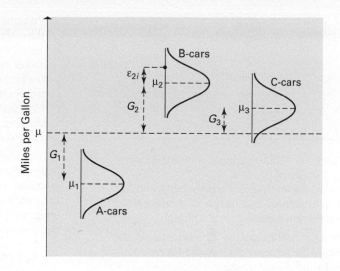

This population model and some of the assumptions are illustrated in Figure 15.4. For each type of car, actual fuel consumption recorded in any trial can be represented by a normally distributed random variable. The population means of fuel consumption, μ_1, μ_2, and μ_3, for A-cars, B-cars, and C-cars, respectively, determine the centers of these distributions. According to our assumption these population distributions must have the same variances. Figure 15.4 also shows the mean μ of the three combined populations and the differences G_j between the individual population means and the overall mean. Finally, for B-cars, we have marked by a dot the ith sample observation. The random variable ε_{ji} is then the difference between the observed value and the mean of the sub-population j from which it is drawn.

EXERCISES

Basic Exercises

15.1 Given the following analysis of variance table compute mean squares for between groups and within groups. Compute the F ratio and test the hypothesis that the group means are equal.

Source of Variation	Sum of Squares	Degrees of Freedom
Between groups	1,000	4
Within groups	750	15
Total	1,750	19

15.2 Given the following analysis of variance table compute mean squares for between groups and within groups. Compute the F ratio and test the hypothesis that the group means are equal.

Source of Variation	Sum of Squares	Degrees of Freedom
Between groups	879	3
Within groups	798	16
Total	1,677	19

15.3 Given the following analysis of variance table compute mean squares for between groups and within groups. Compute the F ratio and test the hypothesis that the group means are equal.

Source of Variation	Sum of Squares	Degrees of Freedom
Between groups	1,000	2
Within groups	743	15
Total	1,743	17

Application Exercises

15.4 A manufacturer of cereal is considering three alternative box colors—red, yellow, and blue. To check whether such a consideration has any effect on sales, 16 stores of approximately equal size are chosen. Red boxes are sent to 6 of these stores, yellow boxes to 5 others, and blue boxes to the remaining 5. After a few days a check is made on the number of sales in each store. The results (in tens of boxes) shown in the following table were obtained.

Red	Yellow	Blue
43	52	61
52	37	29
59	38	38
76	64	53
61	74	79
81		

a. Calculate the within-groups, between-groups, and total sum of squares.

b. Complete the analysis of variance table, and test the null hypothesis that the population mean sales levels are the same for all three box colors.

15.5 An instructor has a class of 23 students. At the beginning of the semester each student is randomly assigned to one of four teaching assistants—Smiley, Haydon, Alleline, or Bland. The students are encouraged to meet with their assigned teaching assistant to discuss difficult course material. At the end of the semester a common examination is administered. The scores obtained by students working with these teaching assistants are shown in the accompanying table.

Smiley	Haydon	Alleline	Bland
72	78	80	79
69	93	68	70
84	79	59	61
76	97	75	74
64	88	82	85
	81	68	63

a. Calculate the within-groups, between-groups, and total sum of squares.

b. Complete the analysis of variance table and test the null hypothesis of equality of population mean scores for the teaching assistants.

15.6 Three suppliers provide parts in shipments of 500 units. Random samples of six shipments from each of the three suppliers were carefully checked, and the numbers of parts not conforming to standards were recorded. These numbers are listed in the following table:

Supplier A	Supplier B	Supplier C
28	22	33
37	27	29
34	29	39
29	20	33
31	18	37
33	30	38

a. Prepare the analysis of variance table for these data.

b. Test the null hypothesis that the population mean numbers of parts per shipments not conforming to standards are the same for all three suppliers.

c. Compute the minimum significant difference and indicate which subgroups have different means.

15.7 A corporation is trying to decide which of three makes of automobile to order for its fleet—domestic, Japanese, or European. Five cars of each type were ordered, and, after 10,000 miles of driving, the operating cost per mile of each was assessed. The accompanying results in cents per mile were obtained.

Domestic	Japanese	European
18.0	20.1	19.3
15.6	15.6	15.4
15.4	16.1	15.1
19.1	15.3	18.6
16.9	15.4	16.1

a. Prepare the analysis of variance table for these data.

b. Test the null hypothesis that the population mean operating costs per mile are the same for these three types of car.

c. Compute the minimum significant difference and indicate which subgroups have different means.

15.8 Random samples of seven freshmen, seven sophomores, and seven juniors taking a business statistics class were drawn. The accompanying table shows scores on the final examination.

Freshmen	Sophomores	Juniors
82	71	64
93	62	73
61	85	87
74	94	91
69	78	56
70	66	78
53	71	87

a. Prepare the analysis of variance table.

b. Test the null hypothesis that the three population mean scores are equal.

c. Compute the minimum significant difference and indicate which subgroups have different means.

15.9 Samples of four salespeople from each of four regions were asked to predict percentage increases in sales volume for their territories in the next 12 months. The predictions are shown in the accompanying table.

West	Midwest	South	East
6.8	7.2	4.2	9.0
4.2	6.6	4.8	8.0
5.4	5.8	5.8	7.2
5.0	7.0	4.6	7.6

a. Prepare the analysis of variance table.
b. Test the null hypothesis that the four population mean sales growth predictions are equal.

15.10 Independent random samples of six assistant professors, four associate professors, and five full professors were asked to estimate the amount of time outside the classroom spent on teaching responsibilities in the last week. Results, in hours, are shown in the accompanying table.

Assistant	Associate	Full
7	15	11
12	12	7
11	15	6
15	8	9
9		7
14		

a. Prepare the analysis of variance table.
b. Test the null hypothesis that the three population mean times are equal.

15.11 Two tutoring services offer crash courses in preparation for the CPA exam. To check on the effectiveness of these services, 15 students were chosen. Five students were randomly assigned to service A, 5 were assigned to service B, and the remaining 5 did not take a crash course. Their scores on the examination, expressed as percentages, are given in the table.

Service A Course	Service B Course	No Course
79	74	72
74	69	71
92	87	81
67	81	61
85	64	63

a. Prepare the analysis of variance table.
b. Test the null hypothesis that the three population mean scores are the same.
c. Compute the minimum significant difference and indicate which subgroups have different means.

15.12 In the study of Example 15.1 independent random samples of six advertisements from *True Confessions*, *People Weekly*, and *Newsweek* were taken. The fog indices for these advertisements are given in the accompanying table. Test the null hypothesis that the population mean fog indices are the same for advertisements in these three magazines and compute the minimum significant difference and indicate which subgroups have different means.

True Confessions	People Weekly	Newsweek
12.89	9.50	10.21
12.69	8.60	9.66
11.15	8.59	7.67
9.52	6.50	5.12
9.12	4.79	4.88
7.04	4.29	3.12

15.13 For the one-way analysis of variance model we write the jth observation from the ith group as

$$X_{ij} = \mu + G_i + \varepsilon_{ij}$$

where μ is the overall mean, G_i is the effect specific to the ith group, and ε_{ij} is a random error for the jth observation from the ith group. Consider the data of Example 15.1.

a. Estimate μ.
b. Estimate G_i for each of the three magazines.
c. Estimate ε_{32}, the error term corresponding to the second observation (8.28) for the *New Yorker*.

15.14 Use the model for the one-way analysis of variance for the data of Exercise 15.12.

a. Estimate μ
b. Estimate G_j for each of the three magazines.
c. Estimate ε_{13}, the error term corresponding to the third observation (11.15) for *True Confessions*.

15.3 THE KRUSKAL–WALLIS TEST

As we have already noted, the one-way analysis of variance test of Section 15.2 generalizes to the multipopulation case for the t test comparing two population means when independent random samples are available. The test is based on an assumption that the underlying population distributions are normal. In Section 14.6 we introduced the Mann–Whitney test, a nonparametric test that is valid for the comparison of the central locations of two populations based on independent random samples, even when the

Table 15.6 Fuel Consumption Figures (in Miles per Gallon) and Ranks from Three Independent Random Samples

A-Cars	Rank	B-Cars	Rank	C-Cars	Rank
22.2	11	24.6	20	22.7	12
19.9	1	23.1	13	21.9	7
20.3	2.5	22.0	8	23.2	14
21.4	6	23.5	16.5	24.1	19
21.2	5	23.6	18	22.1	9.5
21.0	4	22.1	9.5	23.4	15
20.3	2.5	23.5	16.5		
Rank sum	**32**		**101.5**		**76.5**

population distributions are not normal. It is also possible to develop a nonparametric alternative to the one-way analysis of variance test. This is known as the **Kruskal–Wallis test**, employed when an investigator has strong grounds for suspecting that the parent population distributions may be markedly different from the normal.

Like the majority of the nonparametric tests we have already encountered, the Kruskal–Wallis test is based on the *ranks* of the sample observations. We will illustrate the computation of the test-statistic by reference to the fuel consumption data of Table 15.1. The sample values are all pooled together and ranked in ascending order, as in Table 15.6, using the average of adjacent ranks in the case of ties.

The test is based on the sums of the ranks $R_1, R_2, \ldots, R_K$ for the K samples. In the fuel consumption example

$$R_1 = 32 \quad R_2 = 101.5 \quad R_3 = 76.5$$

Now, the null hypothesis to be tested is that the three population means are the same. We would be suspicious of that hypothesis if there were substantial differences among the average ranks for the K samples. In fact, our test is based on the statistic where n_i are the sample sizes in the K groups and n is the total number of sample observations. Define W as follows:

$$W = \frac{12}{n(n+1)} \sum_{i=1}^{K} \frac{R_i^2}{n_i} - 3(n+1)$$

The null hypothesis would be in doubt if a large value for W was observed. The basis for the test follows from the fact that, unless the sample sizes are very small, the random variable corresponding to the test statistic has, under the null hypothesis, a distribution that is well approximated by the χ^2 distribution with $(K-1)$ degrees of freedom.

The Kruskal–Wallis Test

Suppose that we have independent random samples of $n_1, n_2, \ldots n_k$ observations from K populations. Let

$$n = n_1 + n_2 + \cdots + n_K$$

denote the total number of sample observations. Denote by $R_1, R_2, \ldots,$ R_k the sums of ranks for the K samples when the sample observations are pooled together and ranked in ascending order. The test of the null hypothesis, H_0, of equality of the population means is based on the statistic

$$W = \frac{12}{n(n+1)} \sum_{i=1}^{K} \frac{R_i^2}{n_i} - 3(n+1) \qquad (15.8)$$

A test of significance level α is given by the decision rule

$$\text{Reject } H_0 \text{ if } W > \chi^2_{K-1,\alpha} \qquad (15.9)$$

where $\chi^2_{K-1,\alpha}$ is the number that is exceeded with probability α by a χ^2 random variable with $(K-1)$ degrees of freedom.

This test procedure is approximately valid, provided that the sample contains at least five observations from each population.

For our fuel consumption data we find the following:

$$W = \frac{12}{(20)(21)} \left[\frac{(32)^2}{7} + \frac{(101.5)^2}{7} + \frac{(76.5)^2}{6} \right] - (3)(21) = 11.10$$

Here, we have $(K-1) = 2$ degrees of freedom, so for a 0.5% significance level test, we find from Table 7 in the appendix that

$$\chi^2_{2,.005} = 10.60$$

Hence, the null hypothesis that the population mean fuel consumption is the same for the three types of automobiles can be rejected even at the 0.5% significance level. Of course, we also rejected this hypothesis using the analysis of variance test of Section 15.2. However, here we have been able to do so without imposing the assumption of normality of the population distributions.

Example 15.2 Importance of Brand Names (Kruskal–Wallis Test)

A research study was designed to determine if women from different occupational subgroups assign different levels of importance to brand names when purchasing soft drinks.

Solution Independent random samples of 101 clerical, 112 administrative, and 96 professional women were asked to rate, on a scale from 1 to 7, the importance attached to brand name when purchasing soft drinks. The value of the Kruskal–Wallis statistic for this study was reported as 25.22. Test the null hypothesis that the population mean ratings are the same for these three subgroups.

The calculated test statistic is as follows:

$$W = 25.22$$

Since there are $K = 3$ groups, we have for a 0.5% test

$$\chi^2_{K-1,\alpha} = \chi^2_{2,.005} = 10.60$$

Thus, the null hypothesis that the three population mean ratings are the same is very clearly rejected on the evidence of this sample, even at the 0.5% level of significance. We have strong evidence that women from different occupational subgroups assign different levels of importance to brand names.

Exercises

Basic Exercises

15.15 Consider a problem with three subgroups with the sum of ranks in each of the subgroups equal to 45, 98, and 88, and with subgroup sizes equal to 6, 6, and 7. Complete the Kruskal–Wallis test and test the null hypothesis of equal subgroup ranks.

15.16 Consider a problem with four subgroups with the sum of ranks in each of the subgroups equal to 49, 84, 76, and 81, and with subgroup sizes equal to 4, 6, 7, and 6. Complete the Kruskal–Wallis test and test the null hypothesis of equal subgroup ranks.

15.17 Consider a problem with four subgroups with the sum of ranks in each of the subgroups equal to 71, 88, 82, and 79, and with subgroup sizes equal to 5, 6, 6, and 7. Complete the Kruskal–Wallis test and test the null hypothesis of equal subgroup ranks.

Application Exercises

15.18 For the data of Exercise 15.4 use the Kruskal–Wallis test of the null hypothesis that the population mean sales levels are identical for three box colors.

15.19 Using the data of Exercise 15.5, perform a Kruskal–Wallis test of the null hypothesis that the population mean test scores are the same for students assigned to the four teaching assistants.

15.20 Using the data of Exercise 15.6, carry out a test of the null hypothesis of equality of the three population mean numbers of parts per shipment not conforming to standards without assuming normality of population distributions.

15.21 For the data of Exercise 15.7 test the null hypothesis that the population mean operating costs per mile are the same for all three types of automobiles without assuming normal population distributions.

15.22 Using the data of Exercise 15.8, carry out a nonparametric test of the null hypothesis of equality of population mean examination scores for freshmen, sophomores, and juniors.

15.23 Based on the data of Exercise 15.9, use the Kruskal–Wallis method to test the null hypothesis of equality of population mean sales growth predictions for the four regions.

15.24 Refer to Exercise 15.10. Without assuming normal population distributions test the null hypothesis that the population mean times spent outside the classroom on teaching responsibilities are the same for assistant, associate, and full professors.

15.25 Based on the data of Exercise 15.11, perform the Kruskal–Wallis test of the null hypothesis of equal population mean scores on the CPA exam for students using no tutoring services and using services A and B.

15.26 Independent random samples of 101 college sophomores, 112 college juniors, and 96 college seniors were asked to rate, on a scale from 1 to 7, the importance attached to brand name when purchasing a car. The value of the Kruskal–Wallis statistic obtained was 0.15.

   a. What null hypothesis can be tested using this information?
   b. Carry out this test.

15.4 Two-Way Analysis of Variance: One Observation per Cell, Randomized Blocks

Although our primary interest lies in the analysis of one particular feature of an experiment, we may suspect that a second factor could exert an important influence on the outcome. In the earliest sections of this chapter we discussed an experiment in which the objective was to compare the fuel consumption of three types of automobiles. Data were collected from three independent random samples of trials and analyzed through a one-way analysis of variance. It was assumed that the variability in the sample data was due to two causes—genuine differences between the performance characteristics of these three types of car and random variation. In fact, we might suspect that part of the observed random variability could be explained by differences in driver habits. Now, if this last factor could be isolated, the amount of random variability in the experiment would be reduced accordingly. This might, in turn, make it easier to detect differences in the performance of the automobiles. In other words, by designing an experiment to account for differences in driver characteristics, we hope to achieve a more powerful test of the null hypothesis that population mean fuel consumption is the same for all types of automobiles.

In fact, it is quite straightforward to design an experiment in such a way that the influence of a second factor of this kind can be taken into account. Suppose, once again, that we have three makes of automobile (say, α-cars, β-cars, and γ-cars) whose fuel economies we wish to compare. We consider an experiment in which six trials are to be run with each type of car. If these trials are conducted using six drivers, each of whom drives a car of all three types, it will be possible, since every car type will have been tested by every driver, to extract from the results information about driver variability as well as information about the differences among the three types of car. The additional variable—in this case drivers—is sometimes called a *blocking variable*. The experiment is said to be arranged in *blocks*; in our example there would be six blocks, one for each driver.

This kind of blocked design can be used to obtain information about two factors simultaneously. For example, suppose that we want to compare fuel economy obtained not only by different types of automobiles, but also by different types of drivers. In particular, we may be interested in the effect of driver age on fuel economy. To do this, drivers can be subdivided into age categories. We might use the following six age classes (in years):

1. 25 and under
2. 26–35
3. 36–45
4. 46–55
5. 56–65
6. Over 65

Then we can arrange our experiment so that an automobile from each group is driven by a driver from each age class. In this way, in addition to testing the hypothesis that population mean fuel consumption is the same for each automobile type, we can test the hypothesis that population mean fuel consumption is the same for each age class.

In fact, whether a car of each type is driven by each of six drivers or a car of each type is driven by a driver from each of six age classes, the procedure for testing equality of population mean fuel consumption for the automobile types is the same. In this section we use the latter design for purposes of illustration.

Table 15.7 gives results for an experiment involving three automobile types and six driver age classes. The comparison of automobile types is the main focus of interest, and driver ages are used as a blocking variable.

This kind of design is called a **randomized blocks design**. The randomization arises because we randomly select one driver from the first age class to drive an

Table 15.7 Sample Observations on Fuel Consumption Recorded for Three Types of Automobiles Driven by Drivers in Six Classes

	Automobile Type			
Driver Class	α-Cars	β-Cars	γ-Cars	Sum
1	25.1	23.9	26.0	75.0
2	24.7	23.7	25.4	73.8
3	26.0	24.4	25.8	76.2
4	24.3	23.3	24.4	72.0
5	23.9	23.6	24.2	71.7
6	24.2	24.5	25.4	74.1
Sum	148.2	143.4	151.2	442.8

α-car, one driver from the second age class to drive an α-car, and so on. This procedure is repeated for each driver class and for each of the car types. If possible, the trials should be carried out in random order rather than block by block.

Suppose that we have K groups and that there are H blocks. We will use x_{ij} to denote the sample observation corresponding to the ith group and the jth block. Thus, the sample data may be set out as in Table 15.8. Notice that the format here is simply an extension of the experimental form used for the paired observations test of Section 10.1, where we had only two groups to allow us to test the equality of several mean populations.

To develop a test of the hypothesis that the population means are the same for all K groups we require the sample means for these groups. For the mean of the ith group, we use the notation $\bar{x}_{i\cdot}$, so

$$\bar{x}_{i\cdot} = \frac{\sum\limits_{j=1}^{H} x_{ij}}{H} \qquad (i = 1, 2, \cdots, K)$$

From Table 15.7 we obtain the following:

$$\bar{x}_{1\cdot} = \frac{148.2}{6} = 24.7 \qquad \bar{x}_{2\cdot} = \frac{143.4}{6} = 23.9 \qquad \bar{x}_{3\cdot} = \frac{151.2}{6} = 25.2$$

We are also interested in the differences in the population block means. Hence, we require the sample means for the H blocks. We use $\bar{x}_{\cdot j}$ to denote the sample mean for the jth block, so

$$\bar{x}_{\cdot j} = \frac{\sum\limits_{i=1}^{K} x_{ij}}{K} \qquad (j = 1, 2, \cdots, H)$$

For the fuel consumption data of Table 15.7 we have the following:

$$\bar{x}_{\cdot 1} = \frac{75.0}{3} = 25.0 \quad \bar{x}_{\cdot 2} = \frac{73.8}{3} = 24.6 \quad \bar{x}_{\cdot 3} = \frac{76.2}{3} = 25.4$$

$$\bar{x}_{\cdot 4} = \frac{72.0}{3} = 24.0 \quad \bar{x}_{\cdot 5} = \frac{71.7}{3} = 23.9 \quad \bar{x}_{\cdot 6} = \frac{74.1}{3} = 24.7$$

Finally, we require the overall mean of the sample observations. If n denotes the total number of observations, then

$$n = HK$$

Table 15.8 Sample Observation on K Groups and H Blocks

	GROUP			
BLOCK	1	2	...	K
1	x_{11}	x_{21}	...	x_{k1}
2	x_{12}	x_{22}	...	x_{k2}
.	.	.		.
.	.	.		.
.	.	.		.
H	x_{1H}	x_{2H}	...	x_{KH}

and the sample mean observation is as follows:

$$\bar{x} = \frac{\sum_{i=1}^{K}\sum_{j=1}^{H} x_{ij}}{n} = \frac{\sum_{i=1}^{K} \bar{x}_{i\cdot}}{K} = \frac{\sum_{j=1}^{H} x_{\cdot j}}{H}$$

For the data of Table 15.7,

$$\bar{x} = \frac{442.8}{18} = 24.6$$

Before proceeding to consider the form of an appropriate test for the hypothesis of interest, it is useful to examine the population model that is implicitly being assumed. Let the random variable X_{ij} correspond to the observation for the ith group and jth block. This value is then regarded as the sum of the following four components:

1. An "overall" mean μ
2. A parameter G_i, which is specific to the ith group and measures the discrepancy between the mean for that group and the overall mean
3. A parameter B_j, which is specific to the ith block and measures the discrepancy between the mean for that block and the overall mean
4. A random variable ε_{ij}, which represents experimental error, or that part of the observation not explained by either the overall mean or the group or block membership

We can therefore write the following:

$$X_{ij} = \mu + G_i + B_j + \varepsilon_{ij}$$

The error term ε_{ij} is taken to obey the standard assumptions of the multiple regression model. In particular, then, we assume independence and equality of variances.

We can now write this as follows:

$$X_{ij} - \mu = G_i + B_j + \varepsilon_{ij}$$

Now, given sample data, the overall mean μ is estimated by the overall sample mean $\bar{x}$, so an estimate of the left-hand side is provided by $(x_{ij} - \bar{x})$. The difference G_j between the population mean for the ith group and the overall population mean is estimated by the corresponding difference in sample means, $(\bar{x}_{i\cdot} - \bar{x})$. Similarly, B_j is estimated by $(\bar{x}_{\cdot j} - \bar{x})$. Finally, by subtraction, we estimate the error term by

$$(x_{ij} - \bar{x}) - (\bar{x}_{i\cdot} - \bar{x}) - (\bar{x}_{\cdot j} - \bar{x}) = x_{ij} - \bar{x}_{i\cdot} - \bar{x}_{\cdot j} + \bar{x}$$

Thus, we have for the sample members

$$(x_{ij} - \bar{x}) = (\bar{x}_{i\cdot} - \bar{x}) - (\bar{x}_{\cdot j} - \bar{x}) + (x_{ij} - \bar{x}_{i\cdot} - \bar{x}_{\cdot j} + \bar{x})$$

To illustrate, consider the fuel consumption recorded by a driver from the third class with an α-car. From Table 15.7,

$$x_{13} = 26.0$$

The term on the left-hand side is as follows:

$$x_{13} - \bar{x} = 26.0 - 24.6 = 1.4$$

For the group (automobile) effect, we have the following:

$$\bar{x}_1 - \bar{x} = 24.7 - 24.6 = 0.1$$

(Notice that this term will result whenever the α-car is driven.) For the block (driver) effect, we have the following:

$$\bar{x}_{\cdot 3} - \bar{x} = 25.4 - 24.6 = 0.8$$

Finally, the error term is as follows:

$$x_{13} - \bar{x}_{1\cdot} - \bar{x}_{\cdot 3} + \bar{x} = 26.0 - 24.7 - 25.4 + 24.6 = 0.5$$

Thus, we have for this observation

$$1.4 = 0.1 + 0.8 + 0.5$$

We can interpret this equation as follows: When a driver from the third age class tested the α-car, he consumed 1.4 miles per gallon more than the average for all cars and drivers. Of this amount it is estimated that 0.1 is due to the automobile, 0.8 is due to the driver age class, and the remaining 0.5 resulted from other factors, which we put down to chance variability or experimental error.

Now, if both sides are squared and summed over all n sample observations, it can be shown that the result is as follows:

$$\sum_{i=1}^{K}\sum_{j=1}^{H}(x_{ij} - \bar{x})^2 = H\sum_{i=1}^{K}(\bar{x}_{i\cdot} - \bar{x})^2 + K\sum_{j=1}^{H}(\bar{x}_{\cdot j} - \bar{x})^2 + \sum_{i=1}^{K}\sum_{j=1}^{H}(x_{ij} - \bar{x}_{i\cdot} - \bar{x}_{\cdot j} + \bar{x})^2$$

This equation expresses the total sample variability of the observations about their overall mean as the sum of variabilities due to differences among groups, differences among blocks, and error, respectively. It is on the decomposition of these sums of squares that the analysis of experiments of this type is based. The analysis is called two-way analysis of variance, since the data are categorized in two ways, according to groups and blocks.

We illustrate this important sum of squares decomposition in Figure 15.5. Notice, by contrast with the decomposition for the one-way analysis of variance, that the total sum of squares of the sample observations about their overall mean is here broken down into *three* components. We summarize the components in Equations 15.10 to 15.14; the extra component arises because of our ability to extract from the data information about differences among blocks.

For the fuel consumption data of Table 15.7 we find

$$SST = (25.1 - 24.6)^2 + (24.7 - 24.6)^2 + \cdots + (25.4 - 24.6)^2 = 11.88$$
$$SSG = 6[(24.7 - 24.6)^2 + (23.9 - 24.6)^2 + (25.2 - 24.6)^2] = 5.16$$
$$SSB = 3[(25.0 - 24.6)^2 + (24.6 - 24.6)^2 + \cdots + (24.7 - 24.6)^2] = 4.98$$

so, by subtraction,

$$SSE = SST - SSG - SSB = 11.88 - 5.16 - 4.98 = 1.74$$

Figure 15.5
Sum of Squares Decomposition for Two-Way Analysis of Variance with One Observation per Cell

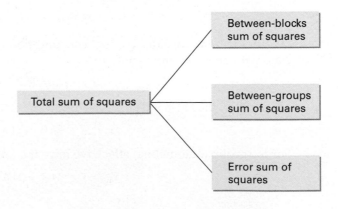

Sum of Squares Decomposition for Two-Way Analysis of Variance

Suppose that we have a sample of observations with x_{ij} denoting the observation in the ith group and jth block. Suppose that there are K groups and H blocks, for a total of

$$n = KH$$

observations. Denote the group sample means by $\bar{x}_{i\cdot}$ ($i = 1, 2,...,K$), the block sample means by $\bar{x}_{\cdot j}$ ($j = 1, 2,...,H$), and the overall sample mean by $\bar{x}$.

We define the following sum of squares:

$$\text{TOTAL}: SST = \sum_{i=1}^{K}\sum_{j=1}^{H}(x_{ij} - \bar{x})^2 \tag{15.10}$$

$$\text{BETWEEN-GROUPS}: SSG = H\sum_{i=1}^{K}(\bar{x}_{i\cdot} - \bar{x})^2 \tag{15.11}$$

$$\text{BETWEEN-BLOCKS}: SSB = K\sum_{j=1}^{H}(\bar{x}_{\cdot j} - \bar{x})^2 \tag{15.12}$$

$$\text{ERROR}: SSE = \sum_{i=1}^{K}\sum_{j=1}^{H}(x_{ij} - \bar{x}_{i\cdot} - \bar{x}_{\cdot j} + \bar{x})^2 \tag{15.13}$$

Then,

$$SST = SSG + SSB + SSE \tag{15.14}$$

From this point the tests associated with the two-way analysis of variance proceed in a fashion similar to the one-way analysis of Section 15.2. First, the mean squares are obtained by dividing each sum of squares by the appropriate number of degrees of freedom. For the total sum of squares the degrees of freedom are 1 less than the total number of observations, that is, $(n - 1)$. For the sum of squares between groups the degrees of freedom are 1 less than the number of groups, or $(K - 1)$. Similarly, for the sum of squares between blocks, the number of degrees of freedom is $(H - 1)$. Hence, by subtraction, the degrees of freedom associated with the sum of squared errors are as follows:

$$(n - 1) - (K - 1) - (H - 1) = n - K - H + 1$$
$$= KH - K - H + 1$$
$$= (K - 1)(H - 1)$$

The null hypothesis that the population group means are equal can then be tested through the ratio of the mean square for groups to the mean square error, as shown in Equation 15.18. Very often a blocking variable is included in the analysis simply to reduce variability due to experimental error. However, sometimes the hypothesis that the block population means are equal is also of interest. This can be tested through the ratio of the mean square for blocks to the mean square error from Equation 15.19. As in the case of the one-way analysis of variance, the relevant standard for comparison is obtained from a tail probability of the F distribution.

For the fuel consumption data the mean squares are as follows:

$$MSG = \frac{SSG}{K - 1} = \frac{5.16}{2} = 2.58$$

$$MSB = \frac{SSB}{H - 1} = \frac{4.98}{5} = 0.996$$

$$MSE = \frac{SSE}{(k - 1)(H - 1)} = \frac{1.74}{10} = 0.174$$

To test the null hypothesis that the population mean fuel consumption is the same for all three types of automobiles, we require the following:

$$\frac{MSG}{MSE} = \frac{2.58}{0.174} = 14.83$$

For a 1% significance level test we have from Table 9 in the appendix,

$$F_{K-1,(K-1)(H-1),\alpha} = F_{2,10,0.01} = 7.56$$

Hypothesis Tests for Two-Way Analysis of Variance

Suppose that we have a sample observation for each group-block combination in a design containing K groups and H blocks

$$x_{ij} = \mu + G_j + B_i + \varepsilon_{ji}$$

where G_j is the group effect and B_i is the block effect.
   Define the following mean squares:

$$\text{BETWEEN-GROUPS}: MSG = \frac{SSG}{K-1} \tag{15.15}$$

$$\text{BETWEEN-BLOCKS}: MSB = \frac{SSB}{H-1} \tag{15.16}$$

$$\text{ERROR}: MSE = \frac{SSE}{(K-1)(H-1)} \tag{15.17}$$

We assume that the error terms ε_{ji} in the model are independent of one another and have the same variance. It is further assumed that these errors are normally distributed.
   Then, a test of significance level α of the null hypothesis, H_0, that the K population group means are all the same is provided by the following decision rule:

$$\text{Reject } H_0 \text{ if } \frac{MSG}{MSE} > F_{K-1,(K-1)(H-1),\alpha} \tag{15.18}$$

A test of significance level α of the null hypothesis, H_0, that the H population block means are all the same is provided by the decision rule

$$\text{Reject } H_0 \text{ if } \frac{MSB}{MSE} > F_{H-1,(K-1)(H-1),\alpha} \tag{15.19}$$

Here, $F_{v_1,v_2,\alpha}$ is the number exceeded with probability α by a random variable following an F distribution with numerator degrees of freedom v_1 and denominator degrees of freedom v_2.

Therefore, on the evidence of these data, the hypothesis of equal mean population performances for the three types of automobiles is clearly rejected at the 1% significance level.
   In this particular example the null hypothesis of equality of the population block means is the hypothesis that population values of mean fuel consumption are the same for each driver age class. The test is based on the following:

$$\frac{MSB}{MSE} = \frac{.996}{.174} = 5.72$$

For a 1% test we have from Table 9 in the appendix,

$$F_{H-1,(K-1)(H-1),\alpha} = F_{5,10,0.01} = 5.64$$

Hence, the null hypothesis of equal population means for the six driver age classes is also rejected at the 1% significance level.

Once again, it is very convenient to summarize the computations in tabular form. The general setup for the **two-way analysis of variance table** is shown in Table 15.9. For the fuel consumption data this analysis of variance is set out in Figure 15.6. The numbers of degrees of freedom are determined by the numbers of groups and blocks. The mean squares are obtained by dividing the sums of squares by their associated degrees of freedom. The mean square error is then the denominator in the calculation of the two F ratios on which our tests are based.

Table 15.9 General Format of Two-Way Analysis of Variance Table

SOURCE OF VARIATION	SUM OF SQUARES	DEGREES OF FREEDOM	MEAN SQUARES	F RATIO
Between groups	SSG	$K-1$	$MSG = \dfrac{SSG}{K-1}$	$\dfrac{MSG}{MSE}$
Between blocks	SSB	$H-1$	$MSB = \dfrac{SSB}{H-1}$	$\dfrac{MSB}{MSE}$
Error	SSE	$(K-1)(H-1)$	$MSE = \dfrac{SSE}{(K-1)(H-1)}$	
Total	SST	$N-1$		

Figure 15.6
Example 15.3
Results for Two-Way Analysis of Variance (Minitab Output)

```
Two-way ANOVA: Mileage versus Car, Driver

Source   DF      SS      MS      F       P
Car       2    5.16   2.580   14.83   0.001
Driver    5    4.98   0.996    5.72   0.009
Error    10    1.74   0.174
Total    17   11.88

S = 0.4171     R-Sq = 85.35%     R-Sq(adj) = 75.10%


              Individual 95% CIs For Mean Based on
              Pooled StDev
Car   Mean    -------+--------+--------+--------+-
1     24.7                (-----*-----)
2     23.9       (-----*-----)
3     25.2                      (-----*-----)
              -------+--------+--------+--------+-
                  24.00    24.60    25.20    25.80


              Individual 95% CIs For Mean Based on
              Pooled StDev
Driver Mean   -----+--------+--------+--------+---
1      25.0              (------ *------ )
2      24.6          (------*-----·)
3      25.4                    (-----*------ )
4      24.0     (------*------ )
5      23.9    (------*-----·)
6      24.7                  (------*------·)
              -----+--------+--------+--------+---
                 23.80    24.50    25.20    25.90
```

EXERCISES

Basic Exercises

15.27 Consider a two-way analysis of variance with one observation per cell and randomized blocks with the following results:

Source of Variation	Sum of Squares	Degrees of Freedom
Between groups	231	4
Between blocks	348	5
Error	550	20
Total	1,129	29

Compute the mean squares and test the hypotheses that between-group means are equal and between-block means are equal.

15.28 Consider a two-way analysis of variance with one observation per cell and randomized blocks with the following results:

Source of Variation	Sum of Squares	Degrees of Freedom
Between groups	380	6
Between blocks	232	5
Error	387	30
Total	989	41

Compute the mean squares and test the hypotheses that between-group means are equal and between-block means are equal.

15.29 Consider a two-way analysis of variance with one observation per cell and randomized blocks with the following results:

Source of Variation	Sum of Squares	Degrees of Freedom
Between groups	131	3
Between blocks	287	6
Error	360	18
Total	778	27

Compute the mean squares and test the hypotheses that between-group means are equal and between-block means are equal.

Application Exercises

15.30 Four financial analysts were asked to predict earnings growth over the coming year for five oil companies. Their forecasts, as projected percentage increases in earnings, are given in the accompanying table.
   a. Prepare the two-way analysis of variance table.
   b. Test the null hypothesis that the population mean growth forecasts are the same for all oil companies.

| Oil Company | Analyst | | | |
	A	B	C	D
1	8	12	7	13
2	9	9	8	12
3	12	10	9	10
4	11	10	10	12
5	9	8	10	14

15.31 An agricultural experiment designed to assess differences in yields of corn for four different varieties, using three different fertilizers, produced the results (in bushels per acre) shown in the following table:

Fertilizer	Variety			
	A	B	C	D
1	86	88	77	84
2	92	91	81	93
3	75	80	83	79

a. Prepare the two-way analysis of variance table.
b. Test the null hypothesis that the population mean yields are identical for all four varieties of corn.
c. Test the null hypothesis that population mean yields are the same for all three brands of fertilizer.

15.32 A company has test-marketed three new types of soup in selected stores over a period of 1 year. The following table records sales achieved (in thousands of dollars) for each of the three soups in each quarter of the year.

Quarter	Soup		
	A	B	C
1	47	57	65
2	63	63	76
3	79	67	54
4	52	50	49

a. Prepare the two-way analysis of variance table.
b. Test the null hypothesis that population mean sales are the same for all three types of soup.

15.33 A diet soda manufacturer wants to compare the effects on sales of three can colors—red, yellow, and blue. Four regions are selected for the test, and three stores are randomly chosen from each region, each to display one color of cans. The accompanying table shows sales (in tens of cans) at the end of the experimental period.

Region	Can Color		
	Red	Yellow	Blue
East	47	52	60
South	56	54	52
Midwest	49	63	55
West	41	44	48

a. Prepare the appropriate analysis of variance table.
b. Test the null hypothesis that population mean sales are the same for each can color.

15.34 An instructor in an economics class is considering three different texts. He is also considering three types of examinations—multiple choice, essay, and a mix of multiple choice and essay questions. During the year he teaches nine sections of the course and randomly assigns a text–examination type combination of each section. At the end of the course he obtained students' evaluations for each section. These ratings are shown in the accompanying table.

Examination	Text		
	A	B	C
Multiple choice	4.8	5.3	4.9
Essays	4.6	5.0	4.3
Mix	4.6	5.1	4.8

a. Prepare the analysis of variance table.
b. Test the null hypothesis of equality of population mean ratings for the three texts.
c. Test the null hypothesis of equality of population mean ratings for the three examination types.

15.35 We introduced for the two-way analysis of variance the population model

$$X_{ij} - \mu = G_i + \beta_j + \varepsilon_{ij}$$

For the data of Exercise 15.33, obtain sample estimates for each term on the right-hand side of this equation for the east region–red can combination.

15.36 For the data of Exercise 15.34, obtain sample estimates for each term on the right-hand side of the equation used in the previous exercise for the text C–multiple choice combination.

15.37 Four real estate agents were asked to appraise the values of 10 houses in a particular neighborhood. The appraisals were expressed in thousands of dollars, with the results shown in the following table.

Source of Variation	Sum of Squares
Between agents	268
Between houses	1,152
Error	2,352

a. Complete the analysis of variance table.
b. Test the null hypothesis that population mean assessments are the same for these four real estate agents.

15.38 Four brands of fertilizer were evaluated. Each brand was applied to each six plots of land containing soils of different types. Percentage increases in corn yields were then measured for the 24 brand-soil type combinations. The results obtained are summarized in the accompanying table.

Source of Variation	Sum of Squares
Between fertilizers	135.6
Between soil types	81.7
Error	111.3

a. Complete the analysis of variance table.
b. Test the null hypothesis that population mean yield increases are the same for the four fertilizers.
c. Test the null hypothesis that population mean yield increases are the same for the six soil types.

15.39 Three television pilot shows for potential situation comedy series were shown to audiences in four regions of the country—the East, the South, the Midwest, and the West Coast. Based on audience reactions, a score (on a scale from 0 to 100) was obtained for each show. The sums of squares between groups (shows) and between blocks (regions) were found to be

$$SSG = 95.2 \quad \text{and} \quad SSB = 69.5$$

and the error sum of squares was as follows:

$$SSE = 79.3$$

Prepare the analysis of variance table, and test the null hypothesis that the population mean scores for audience reactions are the same for all three shows.

15.40 Suppose that, in the two-way analysis of variance setup with one observation per cell, there are just two groups. Show in this case that the F ratio for testing the equality of the group population means is precisely the square of the test-statistic discussed in Section 11.1 for testing equality of population means, given a sample of matched pairs. Hence, deduce that the two tests are equivalent in this particular case.

15.5 TWO-WAY ANALYSIS OF VARIANCE: MORE THAN ONE OBSERVATION PER CELL

In the two-way analysis of variance layout of Section 15.4 we can view the tabulated raw data (as in Tables 15.7 and 15.8) as being broken down into cells, where each cell refers to a particular group-block combination. Thus, for example, the results obtained when a driver from the fourth age class drives a β-car constitute a single cell. A feature of the design analyzed in Section 15.4 is that each cell contains just a single sample observation. Thus, a driver from the fourth age class tests a β-car only once.

In this section we consider the possibility of replicating the experiment so that, for example, β-cars would be driven by more than one driver from the fourth age class. The data resulting from such a design would then involve more than just a single observation per cell. There are two major advantages in extending the sample in this way. First, when more sample data are available, the resulting estimates will be more precise, and we will be better able to distinguish differences among the population means. Second, a design with more than one observation per cell allows the isolation of a further source of variability—the **interaction** between groups and blocks. Such interactions occur when differences in group effects are not distributed uniformly across blocks. For example, drivers who achieve better than average fuel consumption figures may be considerably more successful in getting better fuel economy than other drivers when driving an α-car than when driving a β-car. Thus, this better than average performance is not uniformly spread over all types of cars but rather is more manifest in some types than others. This possibility of driver-car interaction can be taken into account in an analysis based on more than one observation per cell.

To illustrate the kind of data that can be analyzed, Table 15.10 contains results on fuel consumption recorded for drivers from five age classes with three types of automobiles: X-cars, Y-cars, and Z-cars. The three observations in each cell refer to independent trials by drivers from a given age class with automobiles of a particular type.

To denote the individual sample observations, we require a triple subscript, so x_{ijl} will denote the lth observation in the ijth cell—that is, the lth observation in the cell corresponding to the ith group and the jth block. As before, we will let K denote

Table 15.10 Sample Observations on Fuel Consumption Recorded for Three Types of Automobiles Driven by Five Classes of Drivers; Three Observations per Cell

DRIVER CLASS	X-CARS			Y-CARS			Z-CARS		
1	25.0	25.4	25.2	24.0	24.4	23.9	25.9	25.8	25.4
2	24.8	24.8	24.5	23.5	23.8	23.8	25.2	25.0	25.4
3	26.1	26.3	26.2	24.6	24.9	24.9	25.7	25.9	25.5
4	24.1	24.4	24.4	23.9	24.0	23.8	24.0	23.6	23.5
5	24.0	23.6	24.1	24.4	24.4	24.1	25.1	25.2	25.3

the number of groups and H the number of blocks. We denote by L the number of observations per cell. Hence, in the example of Table 15.10, $K = 3$, $H = 5$, and $L = 3$. This notation is illustrated in Table 15.11.

Based on the results of an experiment of this type, there are three null hypotheses that can be tested: no difference between group means, no difference between block means, and no group-block interaction. In order to carry out these tests we will again calculate various sample means, defined and calculated as follows:

1. *Group Means*

   The mean of *all* the sample observations in the ith group is denoted $\bar{x}_{i\cdot\cdot}$, so

$$\bar{x}_{i\cdot\cdot} = \frac{\displaystyle\sum_{j=1}^{H}\sum_{l=1}^{L} x_{ijl}}{HL}$$

From Table 15.10 we find the following:

$$\bar{x}_{1\cdot\cdot} = \frac{25.0 + 25.4 + \cdots + 23.6 + 24.1}{15} = 24.86$$

$$\bar{x}_{2\cdot\cdot} = \frac{24.0 + 24.4 + \cdots + 24.4 + 24.1}{15} = 24.16$$

$$\bar{x}_{3\cdot\cdot} = \frac{25.9 + 25.8 + \cdots + 25.2 + 25.3}{15} = 25.10$$

Table 15.11 Sample Observations on K Groups and H Blocks; L Observations per Cell

BLOCK	GROUP			
	1	2	. . .	K
1	$x_{111}x_{112}\cdots x_{11L}$	$x_{211}x_{212}\cdots x_{21L}$	$\cdots$	$x_{K11}x_{K12}\cdots x_{K1L}$
2	$x_{121}x_{122}\cdots x_{12L}$	$x_{221}x_{222}\cdots x_{22L}$		$x_{K21}x_{K22}\cdots x_{K2L}$
.	.	.		.
.	.	.		.
.	.	.		.
H	$x_{1H1}x_{1H2}\cdots x_{1HL}$	$x_{2H1}x_{2H2}\cdots x_{2HL}$	$\cdots$	$x_{KH1}x_{KH2}\cdots x_{KHL}$

2. *Block Means*

The mean for all the sample observations in the *j*th block is denoted $\bar{x}_{\cdot j \cdot}$, so

$$\bar{x}_{\cdot j \cdot} = \frac{\sum_{i=1}^{K} \sum_{l=1}^{L} x_{ijl}}{KL}$$

From Table 15.10 we find the following:

$$\bar{x}_{\cdot 1 \cdot} = \frac{25.0 + 25.4 + \cdots + 25.8 + 25.4}{9} = 25.00$$

$$\bar{x}_{\cdot 2 \cdot} = \frac{24.8 + 24.8 + \cdots + 25.0 + 25.4}{9} = 24.53$$

$$\bar{x}_{\cdot 3 \cdot} = \frac{26.1 + 26.3 + \cdots + 25.9 + 25.5}{9} = 25.57$$

$$\bar{x}_{\cdot 4 \cdot} = \frac{24.1 + 24.4 + \cdots + 23.6 + 23.5}{9} = 23.97$$

$$\bar{x}_{\cdot 5 \cdot} = \frac{24.0 + 23.6 + \cdots + 25.2 + 25.3}{9} = 24.47$$

3. *Cell Means*

To check the possibility of group–block interactions, it is necessary to calculate the sample mean for each cell. Let $\bar{x}_{ij \cdot}$ denote the sample mean for the (*ij*)th cell. Then,

$$\bar{x}_{ij \cdot} = \frac{\sum_{l=1}^{L} x_{ijl}}{L}$$

Hence, we find for the data from Table 15.10,

$$\bar{x}_{11 \cdot} = \frac{25.0 + 25.4 + 25.2}{3} = 25.2$$

$$\bar{x}_{12 \cdot} = \frac{24.8 + 24.8 + 24.5}{3} = 24.7$$

and, similarly,

$$\bar{x}_{13 \cdot} = 26.2 \quad \bar{x}_{14 \cdot} = 24.3 \quad \bar{x}_{15 \cdot} = 23.9$$

$$\bar{x}_{21 \cdot} = 24.1 \quad \bar{x}_{22 \cdot} = 23.7 \quad \bar{x}_{23 \cdot} = 24.8 \quad \bar{x}_{24 \cdot} = 23.9 \quad \bar{x}_{25 \cdot} = 24.3$$

$$\bar{x}_{31 \cdot} = 25.7 \quad \bar{x}_{32 \cdot} = 25.2 \quad \bar{x}_{33 \cdot} = 25.7 \quad \bar{x}_{34 \cdot} = 23.7 \quad \bar{x}_{35 \cdot} = 25.2$$

4. *Overall Mean*

We denote the mean of all the sample observations by $\bar{x}$, so

$$\bar{x} = \frac{\sum_{i=1}^{K} \sum_{j=1}^{H} \sum_{l=1}^{L} x_{ijl}}{KHL}$$

For our data this quantity is simplest to calculate as the average of the three group sample means, as follows:

$$\bar{x} = \frac{24.86 + 24.16 + 25.10}{3} = 24.71$$

Now, to get a feeling for the analysis, it is convenient to think in terms of the assumed population model. Let X_{jil} denote the random variable corresponding to the lth observation in the ijth cell. Then the model assumed in our analysis is as follows:

$$X_{ijl} = \mu + G_i + B_j + I_{ij} + \varepsilon_{ijl}$$

The first three terms on the right-hand side are precisely the same as those in the model without replication. As before, they represent an overall mean, a group-specific factor, and a block-specific factor. The next term, I_{ij}, represents the effect of being in the jith cell, given that the overall, group, and block effects are already accounted for. If there was no group-block interaction, this term would be 0. Its presence in the model allows us to test for interaction. Finally, the error term, ε_{ijl}, is a random variable representing experimental error.

We will rewrite the model in deviation form:

$$X_{ijl} - \mu = G_i + B_j + I_{ij} + \varepsilon_{ijl}$$

It is shown that the total sum of squares can be decomposed as the sum of four terms, representing variability due to groups, blocks, interaction between groups and blocks, and error.

Without providing detailed derivations the decomposition on which the tests are based is shown in Equations 15.20 to 15.25.

Two-Way Analysis of Variance: Several Observations per Cell

Suppose that we have a sample of observations on K groups and H blocks, with L observations per cell. Let x_{ijl} denote the lth observation in the cell for the ith group and jth block. Let $\bar{x}$ denote the overall sample mean, $\bar{x}_{i\cdot\cdot}$ the group sample means, $\bar{x}_{\cdot j\cdot}$ the block sample means, and $\bar{x}_{ij\cdot}$ the cell sample means.

Then we define the following sums of squares and associated degrees of freedom:

	Sum of Squares	Degrees of Freedom	
Total:	$SST = \sum_i \sum_j \sum_l (x_{ijl} - \bar{x})^2$	$KHL - 1$	(15.20)
Between-groups:	$SSG = HL \sum_{i=1}^{K} (\bar{x}_{i\cdot\cdot} - \bar{x})^2$	$K - 1$	(15.21)
Between-blocks:	$SSB = KL \sum_{i=1}^{H} (\bar{x}_{\cdot j\cdot} - \bar{x})^2$	$H - 1$	(15.22)
Interaction:	$SSI = L \sum_{i=1}^{K} \sum_{j=1}^{H} (\bar{x}_{ij\cdot} - \bar{x}_{i\cdot\cdot} - \bar{x}_{\cdot j\cdot} + \bar{x})$	$(K - 1)(H - 1)$	(15.23)
Error:	$SSE = \sum_i \sum_j \sum_l (x_{ijl} - \bar{x}_{ij\cdot})^2$	$KH(L - 1)$	(15.24)

Then,

$$SST = SSG + SSB + SSI + SSE \qquad (15.25)$$

Division of the component sums of squares by their corresponding degrees of freedom yields the mean squares *MSG, MSB, MSI,* and *MSE.*

Tests of the hypotheses of no effects for groups, blocks, and interaction are based on the respective *F* ratios:

$$\frac{MSG}{MSE} \quad \frac{MSB}{MSE} \quad \frac{MSI}{MSE}$$

The tests are carried out with reference to the *F* distributions with the corresponding numerator and denominator degrees of freedom. Their validity rests on the assumption that the ε_{ijl} behave as a random variable from a normal distribution.

Figure 15.7 depicts the decomposition of the total sum of squares of the sample observations about their overall mean as the sum of four components. It differs from Figure 15.5 in that, as the experiment is replicated, we are now able to isolate an interaction sum of squares.

As before, the calculations involved can be conveniently summarized in an analysis of variance table. The general form of the table when there are *L* observations per cell in a two-way analysis of variance is shown in Table 15.12.

In fact, formulas that are computationally simpler exist for the calculation of the various sums of squares. Nevertheless, the arithmetic involved is still rather tedious and should be performed using a computer. We will not go into further detail here but will simply report in Figure 15.8 the results of the calculations for our data. In practice, analysis of variance computations are typically carried out using a statistical computer package such as Minitab. Thus, considerations of arithmetic complexity rarely impose any constraint on practical analyses.

The degrees of freedom in Figure 15.8 follow from the fact that for these data we have the following:

$$K = 3 \quad H = 5 \quad L = 3$$

The mean squares are obtained by dividing the sums of squares by their associated degrees of freedom. Finally, the *F* ratios follow from dividing, in turn, each of the first three mean squares by the error mean square.

Using the material in Figure 15.8, we can test the three null hypotheses of interest. First, we test the null hypothesis of no interaction between drivers and automobile type. This test is based on the calculated *F* ratio 21.35 and the *p*-value

Figure 15.7
Sum of Squares Decomposition for a Two-Way Analysis of Variance with More than One Observation per Cell

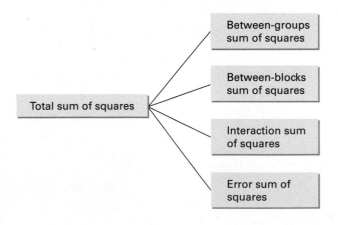

Table 15.12 General Format of the Two-Way Analysis of Variance Table with *L* Observations per Cell

Source of Variation	Sum of Squares	Degrees of Freedom	Mean Squares	*F* Ratio
Between groups	SSG	$K - 1$	$MSG = \dfrac{SSG}{K - 1}$	$\dfrac{MSG}{MSE}$
Between blocks	SSB	$H - 1$	$MSB = \dfrac{SSB}{H - 1}$	$\dfrac{MSB}{MSE}$
Interaction	SSI	$(K - 1)(H - 1)$	$MSI = \dfrac{SSI}{(K - 1)(H - 1)}$	$\dfrac{MSI}{MSE}$
Error	SSE	$KH(L - 1)$	$MSI = \dfrac{SSE}{KH(L - 1)}$	
Total	SST			

Figure 15.8
Minitab Analysis
of Variance Output
for Fuel
Consumption Data
of Table 17.10

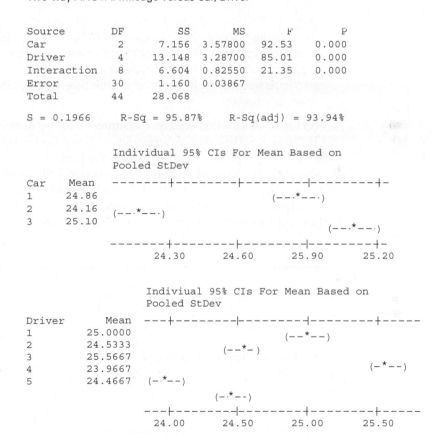

```
Two-way ANOVA: Mileage versus Car, Driver

Source        DF        SS        MS        F        P
Car            2     7.156   3.57800    92.53    0.000
Driver         4    13.148   3.28700    85.01    0.000
Interaction    8     6.604   0.82550    21.35    0.000
Error         30     1.160   0.03867
Total         44    28.068

S = 0.1966    R-Sq = 95.87%    R-Sq(adj) = 93.94%


                    Individual 95% CIs For Mean Based on
                    Pooled StDev
Car     Mean    -------+---------+---------+---------+-
1      24.86                            (--.*--.)
2      24.16    (--.*--.)
3      25.10                                  (--.*--.)
                -------+---------+---------+---------+-
                   24.30     24.60     25.90     25.20


                    Indiviual 95% CIs For Mean Based on
                    Pooled StDev
Driver     Mean   ---+---------+---------+---------+-----
1        25.0000                       (--*--)
2        24.5333                (--*-)
3        25.5667                            (-*--)
4        23.9667   (-.*--)
5        24.4667           (-.*--)
                  ---+---------+---------+---------+-----
                  24.00     24.50     25.00     25.50
```

of 0.000. Since the numerator and denominator degrees of freedom are 8 and 30, respectively, we have from the appendix

$$F_{8,30,0.01} = 3.17$$

The null hypothesis of no interaction between car type and driver is very clearly rejected at the 1% level of significance.

Next, we test the null hypothesis that the population mean fuel consumption is the same for X-cars, Y-cars, and Z-cars. The test is based on the calculated F ratio 92.53. From Table 9 in the appendix we find for a 1% test with numerator and denominator degrees of freedom 2 and 30, respectively,

$$F_{2,30,0.01} = 5.39$$

Hence, the null hypothesis of equality of the population means for automobile types is overwhelmingly rejected at the 1% significance level.

Finally, we test the null hypothesis that the population mean fuel consumption is the same for all five driver age classes. From Figure 15.8 the test is based on the calculated F ratio 85.01. Hence, the numerator and denominator degrees of freedom are 4 and 30, respectively, so for a 1% significance level test

$$F_{4,30,0.01} = 4.02$$

The null hypothesis of equality of population means for the driver age classes is very clearly rejected at the 1% significance level.

The evidence of our data points very firmly to the following three conclusions:

1. Average fuel consumption is not the same for X-cars, Y-cars, and Z-cars.
2. The average performance levels are not the same for all driver classes.
3. The differences in driver performance are not spread evenly over all three types of automobiles. Rather, compared with other drivers, a driver from a particular age class is likely to do relatively better in one automobile type than in another.

So far in this section we have assumed that the number of observations in each cell is the same. However, this restriction is not necessary and may, on occasion, be inconvenient for an investigator. In fact, the formulas for the computation of sums of squares can be modified to allow for unequal cell contents. We are not concerned here with the technical details of the calculation of appropriate sums of squares. Generally, an investigator will have available a computer package for this purpose. Rather, our interest lies in the analysis of the results.

Example 15.4 Worker Satisfaction Level (Two-Way Analysis of Variance)

A study (Reference 1) was designed to compare the satisfaction levels of introverted and extroverted workers performing stimulating and nonstimulating tasks. For the purpose of this study there are two worker types and two task types, producing four combinations. The sample mean satisfaction levels reported by workers in these four combinations were as follows:

Introverted worker, nonstimulating task (16 observations):	2.78
Extroverted worker, nonstimulating task (15 observations):	1.85
Introverted worker, stimulating task (17 observations):	3.87
Extroverted worker, stimulating task (19 observations):	4.12

The following table shows the calculated sums of squares and associated degrees of freedom. Complete the analysis of variance table and analyze the results of this experiment.

Source of Variation	Sum of Squares	Degrees of Freedom
Task	62.04	1
Worker type	0.06	1
Interaction	1.85	1
Error	23.31	63
Total	87.26	66

Solution Once again, the mean squares are obtained from division of the sums of squares by their associated degrees of freedom. The F ratios then follow from division of the task, worker type, and interaction mean squares by the error mean square. The analysis of variance table may now be completed as shown.

Source of Variation	Sum of Squares	Degrees of Freedom	Mean Squares	F ratios
Task	62.04	1	62.04	167.68
Worker type	0.06	1	0.06	0.16
Interaction	1.85	1	1.85	5.00
Error	23.31	63	0.37	
Total	87.26	66		

The analysis of variance table can be used as the basis for testing three null hypotheses. For the null hypothesis of equal mean population satisfaction levels with the two types of task, the calculated F ratio is 167.68. We have numerator degrees of freedom 1 and denominator degrees of freedom 63, so from the appendix for a 1% test

$$F_{1,63,0.01} = 7.06$$

Hence, the null hypothesis of equal population mean satisfaction levels for stimulating and nonstimulating tasks is very clearly rejected. This result is not surprising. We would naturally expect workers to be more satisfied when performing stimulating rather than nonstimulating tasks.

Next, we test the null hypothesis that the population mean satisfaction levels are the same for introverted and extroverted workers. Here, the calculated F ratio is 0.16. Again, the degrees of freedom are 1 and 63, so for a 5% test

$$F_{1,63,0.05} = 4.00$$

The null hypothesis of equal mean levels of satisfaction for introverted and extroverted workers cannot be rejected at the 5% level of significance.

In many studies the interaction term is not, in itself, of any great importance. The main reason for including it in the analysis is to "soak up" some of the variability in the data, rendering any differences between population means easier to detect. However, in this particular study the interaction is of major interest. The null hypothesis of no interaction between task and worker type in determining worker satisfaction levels is tested through the calculated F ratio 5.00. Once again, the numerator and denominator degrees of freedom are 1 and 63, respectively. Hence, comparison with the tabulated values of the F distribution reveals that the null hypothesis of no interaction can be rejected at the 5% level but not at the 1% level of significance.

Basic Exercises

15.41 Consider an experiment with treatment factors A and B with factor A having four levels and factor B having three levels. The results of the experiment are summarized in the following analysis of variance table.

Compute the mean squares and test the null hypotheses of no effect from either treatment and no interaction effect.

Source of Variation	Sum of Squares	Degrees of Freedom
Treatment A groups	71	3
Treatment B groups	63	2
Interaction	50	6
Error	280	60
Total	464	71

15.42 Consider an experiment with treatment factors A and B with factor A having five levels and factor B having six levels. The results of the experiment are summarized in the following analysis of variance table:

Source of Variation	Sum of Squares	Degrees of Freedom
Treatment A groups	86	4
Treatment B groups	75	5
Interaction	75	20
Error	300	90
Total	536	119

Compute the mean squares and test the null hypotheses of no effect from either treatment and no interaction effect.

15.43 Consider an experiment with treatment factors A and B with factor A having three levels and factor B having seven levels. The results of the experiment are summarized in the following analysis of variance table:

Source of Variation	Sum of Squares	Degrees of Freedom
Treatment A groups	37	2
Treatment B groups	58	6
Interaction	57	12
Error	273	84
Total	425	104

Compute the mean squares and test the null hypotheses of no effect from either treatment and no interaction effect.

Application Exercises

15.44 Suppose that scores given by judges to competitors in the ski-jumping events of the Winter Olympics were analyzed. For the men's ski-jumping competition, suppose there were 22 contestants and nine judges. Each judge in seven sub-events assessed each contestant. The scores given can, thus, be treated in the framework of a two-way analysis of variance with 198 contestant-judge cells, seven observations per cell. The sums of squares are given in the following table:

Source of Variation	Sum of Squares
Between contestants	364.50
Between judges	0.81
Interaction	4.94
Error	1,069.94

a. Complete the analysis of variance table.
b. Carry out the associated F tests and interpret your findings.

15.45 Refer to Exercise 15.44. Twelve pairs were entered in the ice-dancing competition. Once again, there were nine judges, and contestants were assessed in seven sub-events. The sums of squares between groups (pairs of contestants) and between blocks (judges) were found to be

$$SSG = 60.10 \quad \text{and} \quad SSB = 1.65$$

while the interaction and error sums of squares were as follows:

$$SSI = 3.35 \quad \text{and} \quad SSE = 31.61$$

Analyze these results and verbally interpret the conclusions.

15.46 A psychologist is working with three types of aptitude tests that may be given to prospective management trainees. In deciding how to structure the testing process, an important issue is the possibility of interaction between test takers and test type. If there was no interaction, only one type of test would be needed. Three tests of each type are given to members of each of four groups of subject type. These were distinguished by ratings of poor, fair, good, and excellent in preliminary interviews. The scores obtained are listed in the following table:

Subject Type	Test Type								
	Profile Fit			Mindbender			Psych Out		
Poor	65	68	62	69	71	67	75	75	78
Fair	74	79	76	72	69	69	70	69	65
Good	64	72	65	68	73	75	78	82	80
Excellent	83	82	84	78	78	75	76	77	75

a. Set up the analysis of variance table.
b. Test the null hypothesis of no interaction between subject type and test type.

15.47 Random samples of two freshman, two sophomores, two juniors, and two seniors each from four dormitories were asked to rate on a scale from 1 (poor) to 10 (excellent) the quality of the dormitory environment for studying. The results are shown in the following table:

Year	Dormitory							
	A		B		C		D	
Freshman	7	5	8	6	9	8	9	9
Sophomore	6	8	5	5	7	8	8	9
Junior	5	4	7	6	6	7	7	8
Senior	7	4	6	8	7	5	6	7

a. Set up the analysis of variance table.
b. Test the null hypothesis that the population mean ratings are the same for the four dormitories.
c. Test the null hypothesis that the population mean ratings are the same for the four student years.
d. Test the null hypothesis of no interaction between student year and dormitory rating.

15.48 In some experiments with several observations per cell the analyst is prepared to assume that there is no interaction between groups and blocks. Any apparent interaction found is then attributed to random error. When such an assumption is made, the analysis is carried out in the usual way, except that what were previously the interaction and error sums of squares are now added together to form a new error sum of squares. Similarly, the corresponding degrees of freedom are added. If the assumption of no interaction is correct, this approach has the advantage of providing more error degrees of freedom and hence more powerful tests of the equality of group and block means. For the study of Exercise 15.47, suppose that we now make the assumption of no interaction between dormitory ratings and student years.

a. State, in your own words, what is implied by this assumption.
b. Given this assumption, set up the new analysis of variance table.
c. Test the null hypothesis that the population mean ratings are the same for all dormitories.
d. Test the null hypothesis that the population mean ratings are the same for all four student years.

15.49 Refer to Exercise 15.31. Having carried out the experiment to compare mean yields per acre of four varieties of corn and three brands of fertilizer, an agricultural researcher suggested that there might be some interaction between variety and fertilizer. To check this possibility, another set of trials was carried out, producing the yields in the table.

Fertilizer	Variety			
	A	B	C	D
1	80	88	73	88
2	94	91	79	93
3	81	78	83	83

a. What would be implied by an interaction between variety and fertilizer?
b. Combine the data from the two sets of trials and set up an analysis of variance table.
c. Test the null hypothesis that the population mean yield is the same for all four varieties of corn.
d. Test the null hypothesis that the population mean yield is the same for all three brands of fertilizer.
e. Test the null hypothesis of no interaction between variety of corn and brand of fertilizer.

15.50 Refer to Exercise 15.33. Suppose that a second store for each region–can color combination is added to the study, yielding the results shown in the following table. Combining these results with those of Exercise 15.33, carry out the analysis of variance calculations and discuss your findings.

Region	Can Color		
	Red	Yellow	Blue
East	45	50	54
South	49	51	58
Midwest	43	60	50
West	38	49	44

15.51 Having carried out the study of Exercise 15.34, the instructor decided to replicate the study the following year. The results obtained are shown in the table. Combining these results with those of Exercise 15.34, carry out the analysis of variance calculations and discuss your findings.

Examination	Text		
	A	B	C
Multiple choice	4.7	5.1	4.8
Essays	4.4	4.6	4.0
Mix	4.5	5.3	4.9

CHAPTER EXERCISES AND APPLICATIONS

15.52 Carefully distinguish between the one-way analysis of variance framework and the two-way analysis of variance framework. Give examples different from those discussed in the text and exercises of business problems for which each might be appropriate.

15.53 Carefully explain what is meant by the interaction effect in the two-way analysis of variance with more than one observation per cell. Give examples of this effect in business-related problems.

15.54 Consider a study to assess the readability of financial report messages. The effectiveness of the written message is assessed using a standard procedure. Financial reports were given to independent random samples from three groups—certified public accountants, chartered financial analysts, and commercial bank loan officer trainees. The procedure was then administered, and the scores for the sample members were recorded. The null hypothesis of interest is that the population mean scores for the three groups are identical. Test this hypothesis, given the information in the accompanying table.

Source of Variation	Sum of Squares	Degrees of Freedom
Between groups	5,165	2
Within groups	120,802	1,005
Total	125,967	1,007

15.55 In an experiment designed to assess aids to the success of interviews of graduate students carried out by faculty mentors, interviewers were randomly assigned to one of three interview modes—feedback, feedback and goal setting, and control. For the feedback mode interviewers had the opportunity to examine and discuss their graduate students' reactions to previous interviews. In the feedback-and-goal-setting mode faculty mentors were encouraged to set goals for the forthcoming interview. For the control group interviews were carried out in the usual way, without feedback or goal setting. After the interviews were completed, the satisfaction levels of the graduate students with the interviews were assessed. For the 45 people in the feedback group, the mean satisfaction level was 13.98. The 49 people in the feedback-and-goal-setting group had a mean satisfaction level of 15.12, while the 41 control group members had a mean satisfaction level of 13.07. The F ratio computed from the data was 4.12.

a. Prepare the complete analysis of variance table.
b. Test the null hypothesis that the population mean satisfaction levels are the same for all three types of interview.

15.56 A study classified each of 134 lawyers into one of four groups based on observation and an interview. The 62 lawyers in group A were categorized as having high levels of stimulation and support and average levels of public spirit. The 52 lawyers in group B had low stimulation, average support, and high public spirit. Group C contained 7 lawyers with average stimulation, low support, and low public spirit. The 13 lawyers in group D were assessed as low on all three criteria. Salary levels for these four groups were compared. The sample means were 7.87 for group A, 7.47 for group B, 5.14 for group C, and 3.69 for group D. The F ratio calculated from these data was 25.60.

a. Prepare the complete analysis of variance table.
b. Test the null hypothesis that the population mean salaries are the same for lawyers in these four groups.

15.57 In a study to estimate the effects of smoking on routine health risk, employees were classified as continuous smokers, recent ex-smokers, long-term ex-smokers, and those who never smoked. Samples of 96, 34, 86, and 206 members of these groups were taken. Sample mean numbers of medical contacts per month were found to be 2.15, 2.21, 1.47, and 1.69, respectively. The F ratio calculated from these data was 2.56.

a. Prepare the complete analysis of variance table.
b. Test the null hypothesis of equality of the four population mean health risk rates.

15.58 Michigan has had restrictions on price advertising for wine. However, for a period these restrictions were lifted. Data were collected on total wine sales over three periods of time—under restricted price advertising, with restrictions lifted, and after the re-imposition of restrictions. The accompanying table shows sums of squares and degrees of freedom. Assuming that the usual requirements for the analysis of variance are met—in particular, that sample observations are independent of one another—test the null hypothesis of equality of population mean sales in these three time periods.

Source of Variation	Sum of Squares	Degrees of Freedom
Between groups	11,438.3028	2
Within groups	109,200.0000	15
Total	120,638.3028	17

15.59 Independent random samples of the selling prices of houses in four districts were taken. The selling prices (in thousands of dollars) are shown in the accompanying table. Test the null hypothesis that population mean selling prices are the same in all four districts.

District A	District B	District C	District D
73	85	97	61
63	59	86	67
89	84	76	84
75	70	78	67
70	80	76	69

15.60 For the data of Exercise 15.59 use the Kruskal–Wallis test to test the null hypothesis that the population mean selling prices of houses are the same in the four districts.

15.61 A study was aimed at assessing the class schedule satisfaction levels, on a scale from 1 (very dissatisfied) to 7 (very satisfied), of nontenured faculty who were job-sharers, full-time, or part-time. For a sample of 25 job-sharers the mean satisfaction level was 6.60; for a sample of 24 full-time faculty the mean satisfaction level was 5.37; for a sample of 20 part-time faculty the mean satisfaction level was 5.20. The F ratio calculated from these data was 6.62.

a. Prepare the complete analysis of variance table.

b. Test the null hypothesis of equality of the three population mean satisfaction levels.

15.62 Consider the one-way analysis of variance setup.

a. Show that the within-groups sum of squares can be written as follows:

$$SSW = \sum_{i=1}^{K}\sum_{j=1}^{n_i} x_{ij}^2 - \sum_{i=1}^{K} n_i \bar{x}_i^2$$

b. Show that the between-groups sum of squares can be written as follows:

$$SSG = \sum_{i=1}^{K} n_i \bar{x}_i^2 - n\bar{x}^2$$

c. Show that the total sum of squares can be written as follows:

$$SST = \sum_{i=1}^{K}\sum_{j=1}^{n_i} x_{ij}^2 - n\bar{x}^2$$

15.63 Consider the two-way analysis of variance setup, with one observation per cell.

a. Show that the between-groups sum of squares can be written as follows:

$$SSG = H\sum_{i=1}^{K} \bar{x}_{i\cdot}^2 - n\bar{x}^2$$

b. Show that the between-blocks sum of squares can be written as follows:

$$SSB = K\sum_{j=1}^{H} \bar{x}_{\cdot j}^2 - n\bar{x}^2$$

c. Show that the total sum of squares can be written as follows:

$$SST = \sum_{i=1}^{K}\sum_{j=1}^{H} x_{ij}^2 - n\bar{x}^2$$

d. Show that the error sum of squares can be written as follows:

$$SSE = \sum_{i=1}^{K}\sum_{j=1}^{H} x_{ij}^2 - H\sum_{i=1}^{K} \bar{x}_{i\cdot}^2 - K\sum_{j=1}^{H} \bar{x}_{\cdot j}^2 + n\bar{x}^2$$

15.64 Information on consumer satisfactions of three price groupings for beer—high, medium, and low—were obtained from a random sample of 125 consumers. The sums of squares for these satisfaction measures are given in the accompanying table. Complete the analysis of variance table, and test the null hypothesis that the population mean satisfaction levels are the same for all three price groupings.

Source of Variation	Sum of Squares
Between consumers	37,571.5
Between brands	32,987.3
Error	55,710.7

15.65 Three real estate agents were each asked to assess the values of five houses in a neighborhood. The results, in thousands of dollars, are given in the table. Prepare the analysis of variance table, and test the null hypothesis that population mean valuations are the same for the three real estate agents.

House	Agent		
	A	B	C
1	210	218	226
2	192	190	198
3	183	187	185
4	227	223	237
5	242	240	237

15.66 Students were classified according to three parental income groups and also according to three possible score ranges on the SAT examination. One student was chosen randomly from each of the nine cross-classifications, and the grade point averages of those sample members at the end of the sophomore year were recorded. The results are shown in the accompanying table.

Sat Score	Income Group		
	High	Moderate	Low
Very high	3.7	3.6	3.6
High	3.4	3.5	3.2
Moderate	2.9	2.8	3.0

a. Prepare the analysis of variance table.
b. Test the null hypothesis that the population mean grade point averages are the same for all three income groups.
c. Test the null hypothesis that the population mean grade point averages are the same for all three SAT score groups.

15.67 For the two-way analysis of variance model with one observation per cell, write the observation from the ith group and jth block as

$$X_{ij} = \mu + G_i + B_j + \varepsilon_{ij}$$

Refer to Exercise 15.65 and consider the observation on agent B and house 1 ($x_{21} = 218$).

a. Estimate μ.
b. Estimate and interpret G_2.
c. Estimate and interpret B_1.
d. Estimate ε_{21}.

15.68 Refer to Exercise 15.66 and consider the observation on moderate-income group and high SAT score ($x_{22} = 3.5$).

a. Estimate μ.
b. Estimate and interpret G_2.
c. Estimate and interpret B_1.
d. Estimate ε_{21}.

15.69 Consider the two-way analysis of variance setup, with L observations per cell.

a. Show that the between-groups sum of squares can be written as follows:

$$SSG = HL \sum_{i=1}^{K} \bar{x}_{i\cdot\cdot}^2 - HKL\bar{x}^2$$

b. Show that the between-blocks sum of squares can be written as follows:

$$SSB = KL \sum_{j=1}^{H} \bar{x}_{\cdot j\cdot}^2 - HKL\bar{x}^2$$

c. Show that the error sum of squares can be written as follows:

$$SSE = \sum_{i=1}^{K}\sum_{j=1}^{H}\sum_{l=1}^{L} x_{ijl}^2 - L\sum_{i=1}^{K}\sum_{j=1}^{H} \bar{x}_{ij\cdot}^2$$

d. Show that the total sum of squares can be written as follows:

$$SST = \sum_{i=1}^{K}\sum_{j=1}^{H}\sum_{l=1}^{L} x_{ijl}^2 - HKL\bar{x}^2$$

e. Show that the interaction sum of squares can be written as follows:

$$SSI = L\sum_{i=1}^{K}\sum_{j=1}^{H} \bar{x}_{ij\cdot}^2 - HL\sum_{i=1}^{K} \bar{x}_{i\cdot\cdot}^2 - KL\sum_{j=1}^{H} \bar{x}_{\cdot j\cdot}^2 + HKL\bar{x}^2$$

15.70 Purchasing agents were given information about a cellular phone system and asked to assess its quality. The information given was identical except for two factors—price and country of origin. For price there were three possibilities: $150, $80, and no price given. For country of origin there were also three possibilities: United States, Taiwan, and no country given. Part of the analysis of variance table for the quality assessments of the purchasing agents is shown here. Complete the analysis of variance table and provide a full analysis of these data.

Source of Variation	Sum of Squares	Degrees of Freedom
Between prices	0.178	2
Between countries	4.365	2
Interaction	1.262	4
Error	93.330	99

15.71 In the study of Exercise 15.70, information on the cellular phone system was also shown to MBA students. Part of the analysis of variance table for their quality assessments is shown here.

Complete the analysis of variance table and provide a full analysis of these data.

Source of Variation	Sum of Squares	Degrees of Freedom
Between prices	0.042	2
Between countries	17.319	2
Interaction	2.235	4
Error	70.414	45

15.72 Having carried out the study of Exercise 15.66, the investigator decided to take a second independent random sample of one student from each of the nine income–SAT score categories. The grade point averages found are given in the accompanying table.

Sat Score	Income Group		
	High	Moderate	Low
Very high	3.9	3.7	3.8
High	3.2	3.6	3.4
Moderate	2.7	3.0	2.8

a. Prepare the analysis of variance table.
b. Test the null hypothesis that the population mean grade point averages are the same for all three income groups.
c. Test the null hypothesis that the population mean grade point averages are the same for all three SAT score groups.
d. Test the null hypothesis of no interaction between income group and SAT score.

15.73 An experiment was carried out to test the effects on yields of five varieties of corn and five types of fertilizer. For each variety-fertilizer combination, six plots were used and the yields recorded, with the results shown in the following table:

Fertilizer Type	Variety of Corn									
	A		B		C		D		E	
1	75	77	74	67	93	90	79	83	72	77
	79	83	73	65	87	82	87	88	79	83
	85	78	79	80	86	88	86	90	78	86
2	80	72	71	69	84	88	77	82	70	75
	76	73	75	62	90	79	84	87	80	80
	70	74	77	63	83	80	82	83	74	81
3	85	87	76	73	88	94	81	86	77	83
	80	79	77	70	89	86	90	90	87	79
	87	80	83	80	89	93	87	88	86	88
4	80	79	74	77	86	87	80	77	79	85
	82	77	69	78	90	85	90	84	88	80
	85	80	74	76	83	88	80	88	87	82
5	75	79	75	80	92	88	82	78	80	87
	86	82	84	80	89	94	85	86	90	83
	79	83	72	77	86	90	82	89	86	83

a. Test the null hypothesis that the population mean yields are the same for all five varieties of corn.
b. Test the null hypothesis that the population mean yields are the same for all five brands of fertilizer.
c. Test the null hypothesis of no interaction between variety and fertilizer.

Appendix: Mathematical Derivations

1 TOTAL SUM OF SQUARES

$$SST = \sum_{i=1}^{K}\sum_{j=1}^{n_i}(x_{ij} - \bar{x})^2$$

$$= \sum_{i=1}^{K}\sum_{j=1}^{n_i}(x_{ij} - \bar{x}_i + \bar{x}_i - \bar{x})^2$$

$$= \sum_{i=1}^{K}\sum_{j=1}^{n_i}(x_{ij} - \bar{x}_i)^2 + \sum_{i=1}^{K}\sum_{j=1}^{n_i}(\bar{x}_i - \bar{x})^2 + 2\sum_{i=1}^{K}(\bar{x}_i - \bar{x})\sum_{j=1}^{n_i}(x_{ij} - \bar{x}_i)$$

$$= \sum_{i=1}^{K}\sum_{j=1}^{n_i}(x_{ij} - \bar{x}_i)^2 + \sum_{i=1}^{K}n_i(\bar{x}_i - \bar{x})^2$$

$$SST = SSW + SSG$$

$$\text{Note: } \sum_{j=1}^{n_i}(x_{ij} - \bar{x}) = 0$$

2   WITHIN-GROUPS MEAN SQUARE (MSW)

For each subgroup i

$$\sigma^2 = E\left[\frac{\sum_{j=1}^{n_i}(x_{ij} - \mu_i)^2}{n_i}\right]$$

$$= E\left[\frac{\sum_{j=1}^{n_i}(x_{ij} - \bar{x}_i + \bar{x}_i - \mu_i)^2}{n_i}\right]$$

$$= E\left[\frac{\sum_{j=1}^{n_i}(x_{ij} - \bar{x}_i)^2}{n_i}\right] + \frac{\sigma^2}{n_i}$$

$$\frac{(n_i - 1)\sigma^2}{n_i} = E\left[\frac{\sum_{j=1}^{n_i}(x_{ij} - \bar{x}_i)^2}{n_i}\right]$$

$$\hat{\sigma}^2 = \frac{\sum_{j=1}^{n_i}(x_{ij} - \bar{x}_i)^2}{n_i - 1}$$

Summing over K subgroups

$$\hat{\sigma}^2 = \frac{\sum_{i=1}^{K}\sum_{j=1}^{n_i}(x_{ij} - \bar{x}_i)^2}{n - K} = \frac{SSW}{n - K}$$

$$\hat{\sigma}^2 = MSW$$

3   BETWEEN-GROUPS MEAN SQUARE (MSG)

$$\mu_i = \mu \quad i = 1, \ldots, K$$

Then,

$$\hat{\sigma}^2 = E\left[\frac{\sum_{i=1}^{K}\sum_{j=1}^{n_i}(x_{ij} - \bar{x})^2}{n - 1}\right]$$

$$= E\left[\frac{\sum_{i=1}^{K}\sum_{j=1}^{n_i}(x_{ij} - \bar{x}_i + \bar{x}_i - \bar{x})^2}{n - 1}\right]$$

$$= E\left[\frac{\sum_{i=1}^{K}\sum_{j=1}^{n_i}(x_{ij} - \bar{x}_i)^2}{n - 1} + \frac{\sum_{i=1}^{K}\sum_{j=1}^{n_i}(\bar{x}_i - \bar{x})^2}{n - 1}\right]$$

$$= \frac{(n - K)\hat{\sigma}^2}{n - 1} + \frac{\sum_{i=1}^{K}n_i(\bar{x}_i - \bar{x})^2}{n - 1}$$

$$\frac{(K-1)\hat{\sigma}^2}{n-1} = \frac{\sum_{i=1}^{K} n_i(\bar{x}_i - \bar{x})^2}{n-1}$$

$$\hat{\sigma}^2 = \frac{\sum_{i=1}^{K} n_i(\bar{x}_i - \bar{x})^2}{K-1}$$

$$\hat{\sigma}^2 = MSG = \frac{SSG}{K-1}$$

4   RATIO OF MEAN SQUARES

If

$$H_0 : \mu_1 = \mu_2 = \cdots = \mu_K$$

is true, then MSG—with $K-1$ degrees of freedom—is an estimator of σ^2 and

$$\chi_{K-1}^2 = \frac{(K-1)MSG}{\sigma^2}$$

In addition, MSW with $n-K$ degrees is an estimator of σ^2, and, therefore,

$$\chi_{n-K}^2 = \frac{(n-K)MSW}{\sigma^2}$$

Thus,

$$F_{K-1,n-K} = \frac{\dfrac{\chi_{K-1}^2}{K-1}}{\dfrac{\chi_{n-K}^2}{n-K}} = \frac{MSG}{MSW}$$

REFERENCES

1. Kim, J. S. 1980. Relationships of Personality of Perceptual and Behavioral Responses in Stimulating and Nonstimulating Tasks. *Academy of Management Journal* 23:307–319.
2. Shuptrine, F. K., and D. D. McVicker. 1981. Readability Levels of Magazine Advertisements. *Journal of Advertising Research* 21 (5): 45–50.

Chapter 16

Time-Series Analysis and Forecasting

Introduction

In this chapter we develop procedures for analyzing data sets that contain measurements over time for various variables. Examples of time-series data include monthly product sales and interest rates, quarterly corporate earnings and aggregate consumption, and daily closing prices for shares of common stock.

Time Series

A **time series** is a set of measurements, ordered over time, on a particular quantity of interest. In a time series the sequence of the observations is important, in contrast to cross-section data for which the sequence of observations is not important.

Time-series data typically possess special characteristics—associated with the sequence of the observations—that necessitate the development of special statistical analysis methods. Virtually all of the procedures of data analysis and inference that we have developed are based on the assumption that samples are random—in particular, that the observations errors are independent. Only very rarely will the assumption of independence be realistic for time-series data. For example, consider a series of monthly sales for a manufactured product and note possible reasons for lack of independence. If sales were higher than average last month, then it is reasonable to expect that high sales will continue because the strong underlying economic and business conditions are not likely to change abruptly. Thus, we can expect similarity in sales during adjacent months. We also note that sales of many products have a seasonal pattern—shorts and swimsuits have higher sales in spring and early summer compared to winter. Many retail stores have peak sales during the fourth quarter because of Christmas gift purchases. These and many other examples establish the case for lack of independence.

The lack of independence between time-series observations leads to serious problems if conventional statistical procedures—which assume independence—are used with time-series data. We saw the problem in Section 13.7 when examining the problems of using conventional regression procedures when the errors are correlated between observations. The independence assumption is crucial, and other serious problems can occur if conventional procedures are used when the observations are dependent. In this chapter we focus on examining time-series analysis procedures that apply to a single time series.

We have considered the negative aspect of the kinds of dependency patterns likely to occur in time-series data. These are real problems and require special procedures. However, this dependency can also be exploited to produce lower variance forecasts of future time-series values. For example, if there is a correlation between adjacent month errors in a retail series, then that correlation can be used to provide a better forecast for the next month compared to a forecast based on a random sample. We will develop procedures based on the assumption that past patterns of relationship between measurements in a time series will continue into the future and can be used for forecasting—this is rather like arguing that we can, in fact, learn from a study of history.

In the first section we develop index numbers, which are used in a number of economic writings. The time-series analysis procedures contained in subsequent sections do not require a knowledge of index numbers. They are included here to provide a complete presentation of topics related to time-series analysis.

Our discussion begins with the development of index numbers. To motivate our discussion, consider the following question: What changes have occurred in the price of automobiles built in the United States in the past 10 years? It almost goes without saying that the price has risen, but how can this price rise be described quantitatively? On the surface this question may not seem very difficult to answer. As a first step, one could collect price information about these automobiles in each of the past 10 years and graph it using a time plot.

However, thinking about the problem carefully may lead to a number of questions. First, we note that automobiles are not homogeneous, and, thus, we need to be more specific in our definition of the particular type of automobile. There is clearly a wide range of prices and quality, and the change in average price of all automobiles sold may merely reflect a change in the pattern of purchase: Do sales consist of more higher-priced automobiles? In the latter case the average price would increase because we have more higher-priced cars. Other changes in the market mix could result in other movements of the mean. Table 16.1 provides a simple hypothetical example of a market with only a low-priced and a high-priced automobile. Note that the average price decreased but that this was the result of more low-priced cars and fewer high-priced cars in the mix. This is not a particularly useful way to compare the price of automobiles over two different years.

Another possible solution is to compute the average price of a single car of each type, as shown in Table 16.2. This procedure is also flawed because we have a market in which subcompact cars are considerably more popular than luxury cars. The price of subcompact cars is the same over the two years, while the price of luxury cars doubles. As a result, the average based on a single car of each type is considerably higher in the second year. But this does not provide an accurate picture because it gives equal weight to each car type, when, in fact, subcompact cars are purchased much more frequently.

Table 16.1 Hypothetical Data on Automobile Prices and Sales

YEAR	SUBCOMPACT CARS PRICE (THOUSAND DOLLARS)	SUBCOMPACT CARS NUMBER SOLD (THOUSANDS)	LUXURY CARS PRICE (THOUSAND DOLLARS)	LUXURY CARS NUMBER SOLD (THOUSANDS)	ALL CARS AVERAGE PRICE (THOUSAND DOLLARS)
1	10	5	30	15	25.0
2	11	15	33	5	16.5

Table 16.2 Hypothetical Data on Automobile Prices and Sales: Equal Weighting

YEAR	SUBCOMPACT CARS PRICE (THOUSAND DOLLARS)	SUBCOMPACT CARS NUMBER SOLD (THOUSANDS)	LUXURY CARS PRICE (THOUSAND DOLLARS)	LUXURY CARS NUMBER SOLD (THOUSANDS)	ALL CARS AVERAGE PRICE OF A SINGLE CAR OF EACH TYPE (THOUSAND DOLLARS)
1	10	100	24	1	17
2	10	100	48	1	29

These examples demonstrate that to form a reliable picture of the overall price pattern over time, it is necessary to take carefully into account the quantities purchased in each time period. We will see how appropriate weighted averages can be formed.

Another similar confusion occurs if consumers purchase more cars with optional extra equipment in the second year compared to the first. In that case consumers are implicitly purchasing higher-quality cars compared to the previous year. We could possibly look only at prices for cars without any extra equipment in order to obtain a valid comparison.

Difficulties also occur because of technological improvements. It is not surprising to note that present cars have higher fuel efficiency and last longer than cars produced in the 1970s and 1980s. Thus, price increases might be highly influenced by changes in quality. Accounting for changes in quality is of major importance and should not be ignored in judging price comparisons, but techniques for analyzing the effect of quality changes are beyond the scope of our work here.

We have used examples of a single product to illustrate the problem, but such comparisons are typically of interest only to those directly related to purchasing and selling that product. Thus, we will direct our concern to comparing the price changes of individual products with those of other products.

The index number problem examined next is directed toward comparing the movement of prices for a group of commodities. For example, the price of common stock in each company whose shares are traded on the New York Stock Exchange will change over a 1-month period. We would like to produce a measure of the aggregate change in prices. **Index numbers** are designed to solve such problems.

Price Index for a Single Item

We begin our discussion of index numbers with a simple case. Figure 16.1 is an Excel spreadsheet that shows the computation of a price index for Ford Motor Company stock over a 12-week period. The second column contains the actual stock price. Interpreting these numbers is a bit confusing, but this task can be simplified by computing a price index with the first-week price being the base period. In the third column we see the computed price index. Thus, for the second week the price index is

$$100\left(\frac{19.875}{20.25}\right) = 98.1$$

Figure 16.1
Prices and Price Index for Ford Motor Company Stock Over 12 Weeks

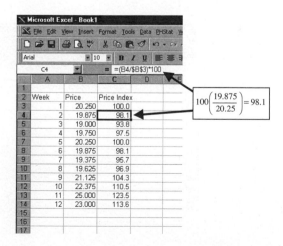

based on the second-week price of 19.875. The percentages calculated in this fashion are called *index numbers of price*. The choice of the base period is arbitrary. We could have chosen any other week as our base and expressed all prices as a percentage of the price for that week.

The advantage of using index numbers here lies in the greater ease of interpretation of the numbers. We see immediately from Figure 16.1, for instance, that the price of Ford Motor Company stock was 13.6% higher in week 12 than in week 1.

Calculating Price Indices for a Single Item

Suppose that we have a series of observations over time on the price of a single item. To form a price index, one time period is chosen as a base, and the price for every period is expressed as a percentage of the base period price. Thus, if p_0 denotes the price in the base period and p_1 the price in a second period, the price index for this second period is as follows:

$$100\left(\frac{p_1}{p_0}\right)$$

Unweighted Aggregate Price Index

Next, we consider how to represent aggregate price movements for a group of items. Figure 16.2 is an Excel spreadsheet that shows the prices paid to U.S. farmers, in dollars per bushel, for wheat, corn, and soybeans over 10 crop years. The table also shows one way of achieving an aggregate price index for these crops. We compute the average price for each year and then use that average to construct an index for the average, using the first year as a base.

The resulting unweighted aggregate index of prices is easy to calculate, as shown in Figure 16.2. It expresses the average price in each year as a percentage of the average price in the base year. However, no account is taken of the differences in quantities of these crops produced. The computation equation in Figure 16.2 indicates division of the sums of prices. This is, of course, the same as dividing by the averages of these prices. The averages would result from dividing the sums in the numerator and the denominator by 3.

Figure 16.2
Prices per Bushel of Three Crops in 10 Years: Unweighted Aggregate Index of Prices

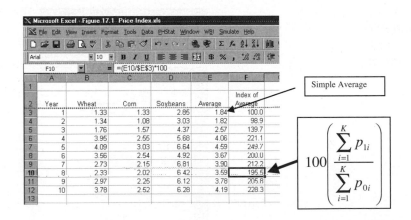

Suppose that we have a series of observations over time on the prices of a group of K items. As before, one time is chosen as a base.

The **unweighted aggregate index of prices** is obtained by calculating the average price of these items in each time period and then calculating an index for these average prices. That is, the average price in every period is expressed as a percentage of the average price in the base period. Let p_{0i} denote the price of the ith item in the base period and p_{1i} the price of this item in the second period. The unweighted aggregate index of prices for this second period is as follows:

$$100\left(\frac{\sum_{i=1}^{K} p_{1i}}{\sum_{i=1}^{K} p_{0i}}\right)$$

Weighted Aggregate Price Index

In general, we would like to weight the individual prices by some measures of the quantity sold. One possibility is to use average quantities over some or all of the time periods in question. In many cases quantities are expensive to obtain and instead the indices are based on quantities in a single time period. When these quantities are from the base period, the resulting index is called a *Laspeyres price index*.

The Laspeyres index, in effect, compares the total cost of purchasing the base-period quantities in the base period with what would have been the total cost of purchasing these same quantities in other periods. To illustrate, consider using the crop price data from Figure 16.2 with the additional information that production in year 1 was 1,352 million bushels of wheat, 4,152 million bushels of corn, and 1,127 million bushels of soybeans. Hence, the cost, in millions of dollars, of the year 1 total output was as follows:

$$(1{,}352)(1.33) + (4{,}152)(1.33) + (1{,}127)(2.85) = 10{,}532$$

In year 2, at the prices then prevailing, the total cost of purchasing the base-year quantities would have been

$$(1{,}352)(1.34) + (4{,}152)(1.08) + (1{,}127)(3.03) = 9{,}711$$

The Laspeyres price index for year 2 is, therefore,

$$100\left(\frac{9{,}711}{10{,}532}\right) = 92.2$$

Figure 16.3 shows the complete index, calculated in this way, for these data.

Figure 16.3
Laspeyres Price
Index for Three
Crops

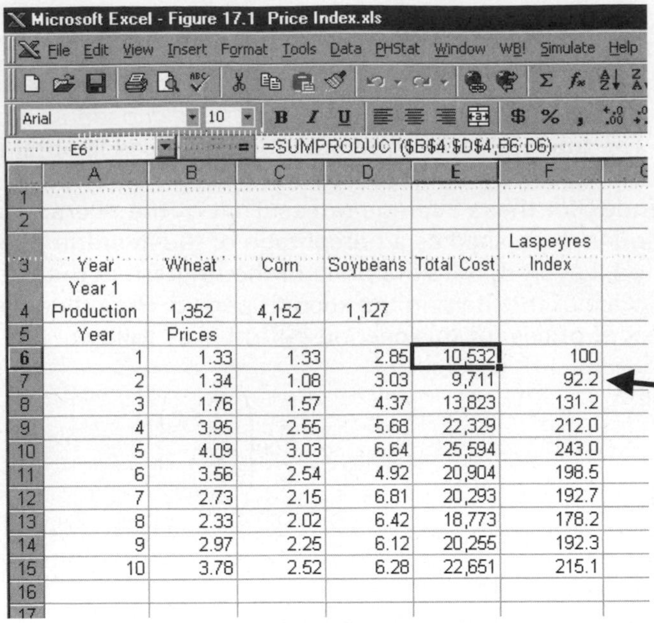

The spreadsheet cell formula bar reads: E6 = SUMPRODUCT($B$4:$D$4,B6:D6)

Year	Wheat	Corn	Soybeans	Total Cost	Laspeyres Index
Year 1 Production	1,352	4,152	1,127		
Year	Prices				
1	1.33	1.33	2.85	10,532	100
2	1.34	1.08	3.03	9,711	92.2
3	1.76	1.57	4.37	13,823	131.2
4	3.95	2.55	5.68	22,329	212.0
5	4.09	3.03	6.64	25,594	243.0
6	3.56	2.54	4.92	20,904	198.5
7	2.73	2.15	6.81	20,293	192.7
8	2.33	2.02	6.42	18,773	178.2
9	2.97	2.25	6.12	20,255	192.3
10	3.78	2.52	6.28	22,651	215.1

$$100\left(\frac{9{,}711}{10{,}532}\right) = 92.2$$

The Laspeyres Price Index

Suppose that we have a group of K commodities for which price information is available over a period of time. One period is selected as the base for an index. The **Laspeyres price index** in any period is the total cost of purchasing the quantities traded in the base period at prices in the period of interest, expressed as a percentage of the total cost of purchasing these same quantities in the base period.

Let p_{0i} denote the price and q_{0i} the quantity purchased of the ith item in the base period. If p_{1i} is the price of the ith item in the second period, the Laspeyres price index for the period is as follows:

$$100\left(\frac{\sum_{i=1}^{K} q_{0i}\,p_{1i}}{\sum_{i=1}^{K} q_{0i}\,p_{0i}}\right)$$

Comparison of the formula for the Laspeyres price index with that for the unweighted aggregate index of prices is instructive. The difference is that, in forming the Laspeyres index, the price of each item is weighted by the quantity traded in the base period.

We see that the Laspeyres price index uses quantity information from only the base period. This is valuable when it is difficult to obtain that information for every period. This could be a disadvantage if the base period quantities were not representative of the time series being considered. Thus, the Laspeyres index could become outdated. One way around this problem is to construct a moving Laspeyres price index, in which the base period is changed from time to time through the acquisition of quantity information for new base periods. Many published national price indices, such as the Consumer Price Index, are constructed in essentially this way.

Weighted Aggregate Quantity Index

Price indices provide a representation of the changes over time in aggregate prices of a group of commodities. We might also want a picture of the evolution of overall quantities traded. Again, any reasonable approach to this problem is likely to result in a weighted quantity index, since we would presumably want to give more weight to a change in the quantity purchased of a very expensive item than to a change by the same amount in purchases of an inexpensive item. One procedure for achieving this is through the *Laspeyres quantity index*, which we illustrate for the quantities produced of wheat, corn, and soybeans given in Figure 16.4.

The Laspeyres quantity index weights the individual quantities by the base period prices. The price weights are 1.33, 1.33, and 2.85 for wheat, corn, and soybeans, resulting in a total value for year 1 of 10,532 million dollars. To obtain a quantity index for year 2, we compare this with the total value of year 2 production, had year 1 prices prevailed—that is,

$$(1{,}618)(1.33) + (5{,}641)(1.33) + (1{,}176)(2.85) = 13{,}006$$

The Laspeyres quantity index for year 2 is, therefore,

$$100\left(\frac{13{,}006}{10{,}532}\right) = 123.5$$

Figure 16.4 shows the quantities produced and the quantity index for a 10-year period.

The Laspeyres Quantity Index

We have quantity data for a set of items collected over a set of K years. One period is selected as a base period. The **Laspeyres quantity index** in any period is then the total cost of the quantities traded in that period,

Figure 16.4 Production, in Millions of Bushels, and Quantity Index

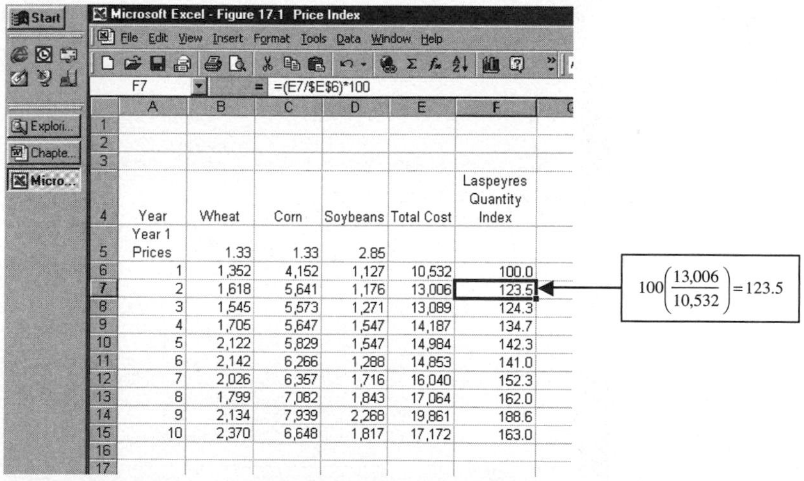

Year	Wheat	Corn	Soybeans	Total Cost	Laspeyres Quantity Index
Year 1 Prices	1.33	1.33	2.85		
1	1,352	4,152	1,127	10,532	100.0
2	1,618	5,641	1,176	13,006	123.5
3	1,545	5,573	1,271	13,089	124.3
4	1,705	5,647	1,547	14,187	134.7
5	2,122	5,829	1,547	14,984	142.3
6	2,142	6,266	1,288	14,853	141.0
7	2,026	6,357	1,716	16,040	152.3
8	1,799	7,082	1,843	17,064	162.0
9	2,134	7,939	2,268	19,861	188.6
10	2,370	6,648	1,817	17,172	163.0

based on the base period prices, expressed as a percentage of the total cost of the base period quantities.

Let q_{0i} and p_{0i} denote the quantity and price of the ith item in the base period and q_{1i} the quantity of that item in the period of interest. The Laspeyres quantity index for that period is then as follows:

$$100\left(\frac{\sum_{i=1}^{K} q_{1i} p_{0i}}{\sum_{i=1}^{K} q_{0i} p_{0i}}\right)$$

Change in Base Period

Officially published series of index numbers are updated at various times by bringing forward the base period. In these circumstances the value of the original index at the new base point is typically given. As an illustration, note the calculation in column F in Figure 16.5, showing the price indices for wheat, corn, and soybeans. Column F shows the price index for crop years 1 through 6, using year 1 as a base beginning with row 14 of column F. Column H gives the Laspeyres price index for years 6 through 10, using year 6 as the base. These indices are plotted in Figure 16.6, where the discontinuity in year 6 is obvious.

Examining Figure 16.6, it is difficult to obtain a clear understanding of the price patterns over the entire time period. Thus, we would prefer to examine a **spliced price index** that has year 6 as the base year. In the original index based on year 1, the index for year 6 was 198.5 as seen in Figure 16.5. To transform the year 6 index based on year 1 to a year 6 index based on year 6, we divide by 198.5 and multiply by 100. Similarly, all of the other indices based on year 1 can be converted to a year 6 base by

Figure 16.5
Aggregate Laspeyres Price Indices Using Different Base Years

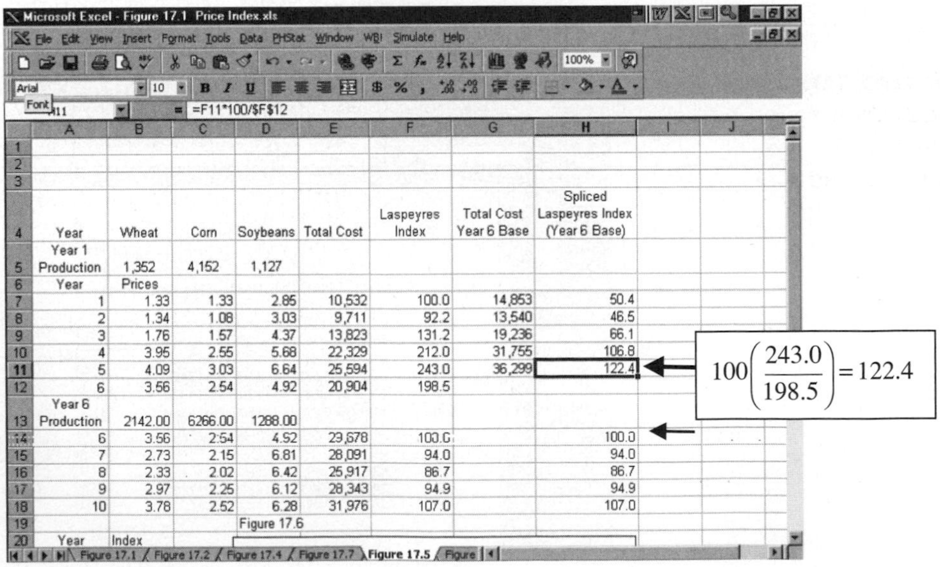

$$100\left(\frac{243.0}{198.5}\right) = 122.4$$

Figure 16.6
Time Plots of
Laspeyres
Aggregate Price
Indices With Years
1–6 (Base Year 1)
and Years 6–10
(Base Year 6)

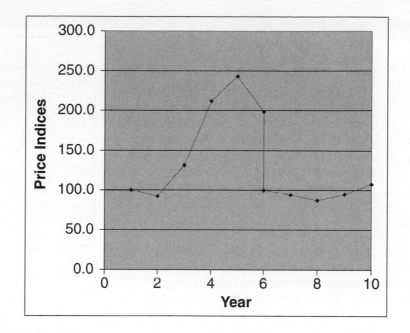

dividing by 198.5 and multiplying by 100. For example, the new index for year 5 is as follows:

$$100\left(\frac{243.0}{198.5}\right) = 122.4$$

The spliced index obtained using a year 6 base is plotted in Figure 16.7. This graph presents a clearer picture of the pattern of price variation over the 10-year period.

Figure 16.7
Spliced Aggregate
Laspeyres Price
Index for Wheat,
Corn, and
Soybeans
(Year 6 = 100)

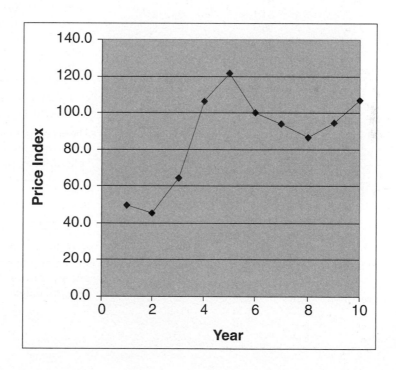

EXERCISES

Basic Exercises

16.1 Suppose that you are analyzing a market and find a Laspeyres price index that was developed with the year 2000 as the base period. Interpret the results when the index for 2003 is as follows:

   a. 134.5
   b. 97.4
   c. 101.7

16.2 Refer to Figure 16.4. Compute the revised Laspeyres quantity index for years 1 through 6 if the year 1 prices are 1.45 (wheat), 1.21 (corn), and 2.98 (soybeans).

16.3 Universities incur many costs in their operation, including the costs of energy, books, laboratory, and other equipment, stationery, and labor. Suppose that you are asked to show how price levels faced by your university have changed over the past 10 years. What difficulties would you expect to encounter, and how would you attempt to proceed?

Application Exercises

Note: Exercises 16.4 through 16.7 should be completed using Excel.

16.4 The accompanying table shows the price per share of stock in Bank of New York Inc. for 12 weeks.

Week	Price	Week	Price	Week	Price
1	35	5	35	9	34 6/8
2	35 7/8	6	34 7/8	10	35 2/8
3	34 6/8	7	35	11	38 6/8
4	34 3/8	8	34 6/8	12	37 1/8

   a. Form a price index with week 1 as the base.
   b. Form a price index with week 4 as the base.

16.5 A restaurant offers three "specials"—steak, seafood, and chicken. Their average prices (in dollars) for the 12 months of last year are shown in the following table:

Month	Steak	Seafood	Chicken
January	7.12	6.45	5.39
February	7.41	6.40	5.21
March	7.45	6.25	5.25
April	7.70	6.60	5.40
May	7.72	6.70	5.45
June	7.75	6.85	5.60
July	8.10	6.90	5.54
August	8.15	6.84	5.70
September	8.20	6.96	5.72
October	8.30	7.10	5.69
November	8.45	7.10	5.85
December	8.65	7.14	6.21

The following base table shows numbers of orders of these specials in each month. Take January as the base.

Month	Steak	Seafood	Chicken
January	123	169	243
February	110	160	251
March	115	181	265
April	101	152	231
May	118	140	263
June	100	128	237
July	92	129	221
August	87	130	204
September	123	164	293
October	131	169	301
November	136	176	327
December	149	193	351

   a. Find the unweighted aggregate price index.
   b. Find the Laspeyres price index.
   c. Find the Laspeyres quantity index.

16.6 The accompanying table shows hourly wage rates over 6 years for three types of employees in a small company.

Year	Manual	Clerical	Supervisory
1	10.60	8.40	16.40
2	11.10	8.70	16.50
3	11.80	9.10	16.90
4	11.90	9.20	18.80
5	12.30	9.60	16.00
6	12.50	9.70	16.30

Take year 1 as base. In that year there were 72 manual employees, 23 clerical employees, and 10 supervisory employees.

   a. Find the unweighted index of hourly wage rates.
   b. Find the Laspeyres index for hourly wage rates.

16.7 The accompanying table shows a price index for a group of commodities over 6 years. Obtain a spliced index with year 4 as base.

Year	1	2	3	4	5	6
Base year 1	100	108.4	114.3	120.2		
Base year 2				100	103.5	107.8

16.8 Explain why it is useful to develop a price index for a group of products—for example, an index of energy prices. What are the advantages of a *weighted* index of prices?

16.2 A NONPARAMETRIC TEST FOR RANDOMNESS

The first step in our process of analyzing time-series data will be to consider a test for randomness in time series. We will develop the *runs test*, which is a nonparametric test that is particularly easy to perform.

To demonstrate the test, we will first look at a series of 16 daily observations on an index of the volume of shares traded on the New York Stock Exchange. The data are shown in Table 16.3 and graphed in Figure 16.8. A line has been drawn on this figure at the median. For an even number of observations the median is the average of the middle pair when the observations are arranged in ascending order. Here, that is

$$\text{Median} = \frac{107 + 108}{2} = 107.5$$

If this series was random, then the volume traded on one day would be independent of the volume traded on any other day. In particular, a high-volume day would be no more likely to be followed by another high-volume day than would any other day. The runs test developed here separates the observations into a subgroup above the median and a subgroup below the median, as shown in Figure 16.8, with the median at 107.5. Then letting a + denote observations above the median and a − denote observations below the median, we find the following pattern over the sequential days:

$$- - - - + + - - + - + + + + + -$$

This sequence consists of a run of four "−" signs, followed by a run of two "+" signs, a run of two "−" signs, a run of one "+" sign, a run of one "−" sign, a run of five "+" signs, and finally a run of one "−" sign. In total, there are $R = 7$ runs.

Table 16.3   Index of Volume of Shares Traded

Day	Volume	Day	Volume	Day	Volume	Day	Volume
1	98	5	113	9	114	13	109
2	93	6	111	10	107	14	108
3	82	7	104	11	111	15	128
4	103	8	103	12	109	16	92

Figure 16.8
Index of Volume
of Shares Traded
versus Day

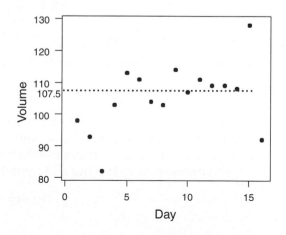

If, as might be suspected here, there was a positive association between adjacent observations in time, we would expect to find relatively few runs. In our example we ask how likely it is to observe seven or fewer runs if the series is truly random. This requires knowledge of the distribution of the number of runs when the null hypothesis of randomness is true. The cumulative distribution is tabulated in Table 14 of the appendix. From that table we see that, for $n = 16$ observations, the probability under the null hypothesis of finding 7 or fewer runs is 0.214. Therefore, the null hypothesis of randomness can be rejected only against the alternative of positive association between adjacent observations at the $\alpha = 0.214$ significance level. This is not small enough to reasonably reject the null hypothesis, nor is it large enough to provide strong support in favor of the null hypothesis. We have merely failed to find strong evidence to reject it. Tests of randomness based on small samples such as this have quite low power.

The Runs Test

Suppose that we have a time series of n observations. Denote observations above the median with "+" signs and observations below the median with "−" signs. Use these signs to define the sequence of observations in the series. Let R denote the number of runs in the sequence. The null hypothesis is that the series is a set of random variables. Table 14 in the appendix gives the smallest significance level at which this null hypothesis can be rejected against the alternative of positive association between adjacent observations, as a function of R and n.

If the alternative is the two-sided hypothesis on nonrandomness, the significance level must be doubled if it is less than 0.5. Alternatively, if the significance level read from the table is bigger than 0.5, the appropriate significance level for the test against the two-sided alternative is $2(1 - \alpha)$.

For time series with $n > 20$, the distribution of the number of runs under the null hypothesis can be approximated by a normal distribution. It can be shown that under the null hypothesis

$$Z = \frac{R - \dfrac{n}{2} - 1}{\sqrt{\dfrac{n^2 - 2n}{4(n - 1)}}}$$

has a standard normal distribution. This result provides a test for randomness.

The Runs Test: Large Samples

Given that we have a time series with n observations and $n > 20$, define the number of runs, R, as the number of sequences above or below the median. We want to test the null hypothesis

$$H_0 : \text{The series is random}$$

The following tests have significance level α.

1. If the alternative hypothesis is positive association between adjacent observations, the decision rule is as follows:

$$\text{Reject } H_0 \text{ if } Z = \frac{R - \dfrac{n}{2} - 1}{\sqrt{\dfrac{n^2 - 2n}{4(n-1)}}} < -z_\alpha \qquad (16.1)$$

2. If the alternative is a two-sided hypothesis of nonrandomness, the decision rule is as follows:

$$\text{Reject } H_0 \text{ if } Z = \frac{R - \dfrac{n}{2} - 1}{\sqrt{\dfrac{n^2 - 2n}{4(n-1)}}} < -z_{\alpha/2} \quad \text{or} \quad Z = \frac{R - \dfrac{n}{2} - 1}{\sqrt{\dfrac{n^2 - 2n}{4(n-1)}}} > z_{\alpha/2} \quad (16.2)$$

Example 16.1   Analysis of Sales Data (Runs Test)

You have been asked to determine if the 30 years of annual sales follow a random pattern from one observation to the next in a time series.

Solution The data for this study are contained in a data file named **Pinkham Sales Data,** stored on the data disk. Figure 16.9 is a time-series plot of the data with the median drawn on the graph. Examination of the plot suggests that the observations are not independent since they appear to follow a pattern. The runs test-statistics can be computed using Minitab or another computer package. From either a computer analysis or an inspection of Figure 16.9 we find that the series has eight runs and that the null hypothesis of a random time series is rejected with p-value = 0.0030.

Figure 16.9   Lydia Pinkham Sales Data over Time

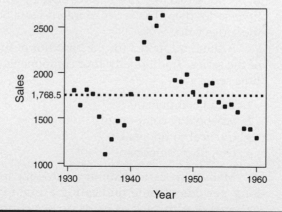

We could also use the number of runs and the test-statistic to compute the Z value for the test as

$$Z = \frac{R - \dfrac{n}{2} - 1}{\sqrt{\dfrac{n^2 - 2n}{4(n - 1)}}} = \frac{8 - 15 - 1}{\sqrt{\dfrac{900 - 60}{116}}} = -2.97$$

and the resulting p-value for a two-tailed test is 0.0030 from Table 1 in the appendix. Thus, we see the evidence in favor of a nonrandom series is quite overwhelming.

EXERCISES

Basic Exercises

16.9 A time series contains 18 observations. What is the probability that the number of runs

  a. is fewer than 5?
  b. exceeds 11?
  c. is fewer than 8?

16.10 A time series contains 50 observations. What is the probability that the number of runs

  a. is fewer than 14?
  b. is fewer than 17?
  c. is greater than 38?

16.11 A time series contains 100 observations. What is the probability that the number of runs

  a. is fewer than 25?
  b. is fewer than 41?
  c. is greater than 90?

Application Exercises

16.12 🔵 The data file **Exchange Rate** shows an index of the value of the U.S. dollar against trading partners' currencies over 12 consecutive months. Use the runs test to test this series for randomness.

16.13 🔵 The data file **Inventory Sales** shows the inventory-sales ratio for manufacturing and trade in the United States over a period of 12 years. Test this series for randomness using the runs test.

16.14 🔵 The data file **Stock Market Index** shows annual returns on a stock market index over 14 years. Test for randomness using the runs test.

16.15 🔵 The data file **Gold Price** shows the year-end price of gold (in dollars) over 14 consecutive years. Use the runs test to test this series for randomness.

16.3 COMPONENTS OF A TIME SERIES

In Sections 16.3 through 16.5 we develop some descriptive procedures for analyzing time-series data. The series of interest will be denoted by $X_1, X_2,..., X_n$, and at time t the series value is X_t.

A standard model for the behavior of time series identifies various components of the series. Traditionally, four components are represented, at least in part, in most time series:

1. Trend component
2. Seasonality component
3. Cyclical component
4. Irregular component

Many time series exhibit a tendency to grow or decrease rather steadily over long periods of time, indicating a trend component. For example, measures of national wealth such as gross domestic product have typically grown over time.

Figure 16.10
Gross Domestic
Product by Time
Indicating a Trend

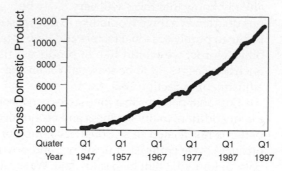

Time Series Plot of Gross Domestic Product

Trends often hold up over time, and, when they do, this provides an important component for developing forecasts. Figure 16.10 shows the time series for quarterly gross domestic product for over 50 years, from the data file **Macro2008** contained on the data disk. This pattern clearly shows a strong upward trend component that is stronger in some periods than in others. This time plot reveals a major trend component that is important for initial analysis and is usually followed by more sophisticated analyses, as we show in future sections.

Another important component is the seasonal pattern. Figure 16.11 shows quarterly earnings per share of a corporation. The fourth quarter earnings are substantially higher and the second quarter earnings are somewhat higher compared to the other periods. Note how this pattern continues to repeat over the four-quarter cycle representing each year. In addition to the seasonality component there is also a noticeable upward trend in earnings per share. Our treatment of seasonality depends on our objectives. For example, if it is important to forecast each quarter as precisely as possible, then we include a seasonality component in our model. In Section 13.2, for instance, we showed how dummy variables can be used to estimate a seasonality component in a time series. Thus, if we anticipate that the seasonality pattern will continue, then the seasonality component estimation must be included in our forecasting model.

For some other purposes seasonality can be a nuisance. In many applications the analyst requires an assessment of overall movements in a time series, uncontaminated by the influence of seasonal factors. For instance, suppose that we have just received

Figure 16.11
Quarterly
Earnings per
Share of a
Corporation
Indicating a
Seasonality
Component

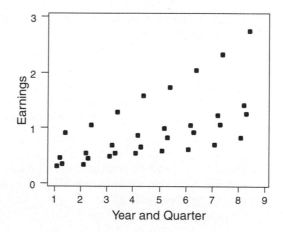

16.3 Components of a Time Series   **717**

the most recent fourth-quarter earnings figures of the corporation in Figure 16.11. We already know that these will very likely be a good deal higher than those of the previous quarter. What we would like to do is assess how much of this increase in earnings is due to purely seasonal factors and how much represents real underlying growth. In other words, we would like to produce a time series free from seasonal influence. Such a series is said to be seasonally adjusted. We will say a little more about seasonal adjustment in Section 16.5.

Seasonal patterns in a time series constitute one form of regular, oscillatory behavior. In addition, many business and economic time series exhibit oscillatory or cyclical patterns not related to seasonal behavior. For example, many economic series follow business cycle patterns of upswings and downswings. In Figure 16.9 we see a cyclical pattern for Lydia Pinkham sales data. We see a decrease in sales to a trough in 1936, followed by an upswing to a peak in the mid-1940s, and thereafter a steady decline. This pattern is a common business-cycle time series, and we can describe historical behavior by cyclical movements. However, we are not suggesting that there is sufficient regularity in such historical patterns to allow the reliable prediction of future peaks and troughs. Indeed, the available evidence suggests that this is not the case.

We have discussed three sources of variability in a time series. If we could characterize time series primarily in terms of trend, seasonal, and cyclical components, then the series would vary smoothly over time, and forecasts could be made using these components. However, actual data do not behave in that way. In addition to the major components the series will exhibit irregular components, induced by a multitude of factors influencing the behavior of any actual series and exhibiting patterns that look rather unpredictable on the basis of past experience. These patterns can be thought of as similar to the random error term in a regression model. In all of the component examples that we have plotted so far, we can see the irregular component clearly on top of the structural components.

Time Series Component Analysis

A time series can be described by models based on the following components:

T_t	Trend component
S_t	Seasonality component
C_t	Cyclical component
I_t	Irregular component

Using these components, we can define a time series as the sum of its components or as an additive model:

$$X_t = T_t + S_t + C_t + I_t$$

Alternatively, in other circumstances we might define a time series as the product of its components or as a multiplicative model—often represented as a logarithmic additive model:

$$X_t = T_t S_t C_t I_t$$

We do not have to restrict ourselves to these two structural forms. For example, in some cases we might have a combination of additive and multiplicative forms.

Much of the early work in time-series analysis concentrated on the isolation of the individual components from a series. Thus, at any point in time the series value could be expressed as a function of the components. Often this approach was achieved by the use of moving averages, as we discuss in the next two sections. This approach has been replaced in large part by more modern approaches. An exception is the problem of seasonal adjustment, which requires the extraction of the seasonality component from the series and which we discuss in Section 16.5.

The more modern approach to time-series analysis involves the construction of a formal model, in which various components are either explicitly or implicitly present, to describe the behavior of a data series. In model building there are two possible treatments of series components. One is to regard them as being fixed over time, so that a trend might be represented by a straight line. This approach is often valuable in the analysis of physical data but is far less appropriate in business and economic applications, where experience suggests that any apparently fixed regularities are all too often illusory on closer examination. To illustrate the point, suppose that we consider the Lydia Pinkham data for the years 1936 through 1943 only. We see in Figure 16.9 that over this period there appears to be a steady, fixed upward trend. However, had this "trend" been projected forward a few years from 1943, the resulting forecasts of future sales would have been highly inaccurate. It is only when we look at the picture in future years that we see just how inappropriate a fixed-trend model would have been.

For business and economic data another treatment of the regular components of a time series is preferable. Rather than regarding them as being fixed for all time, it is generally more sensible to think of them as steadily evolving over time. Thus, we need not be committed to fixed trend or seasonal patterns but can allow for the possibility that these components change with time. Models of this sort will be considered after we have looked at moving averages.

EXERCISES

Application Exercises

16.16 ⊙ The data file **Housing Starts** shows private housing units started per thousand of population in the United States over a period of 24 years.

    a. Use the large-sample variant of the runs test to test this series for randomness.

    b. Draw a time plot of this series and comment on the components of the series revealed by this plot.

16.17 ⊙ The data file **Earnings per Share** shows earnings per share of a corporation over a period of 28 years.

    a. Use the large-sample variant of the runs test to test this series for randomness.

    b. Draw a time plot of this series and comment on the components of the series revealed by this plot.

16.4 MOVING AVERAGES

The irregular component in some time series may be so large that it obscures any underlying regularities, thus, rendering difficult any visual interpretation of the time plot. In these circumstances the actual plot will appear rather jagged, and we may want to smooth it to achieve a clearer picture. We can reduce this problem by using a moving average.

We can smooth using the method of moving averages based on the idea that any large irregular component at any point in time will exert a smaller effect if we average the point with its immediate neighbors. The simplest procedure we can use is a simple centered $(2m + 1)$-point moving average. That is, we replace each observation x_t by the average of itself and its neighbors so

$$x_t^* = \frac{1}{2m + 1} \sum_{j=-m}^{m} x_{t+j}$$

$$= \frac{x_{t-m} + x_{t-m+1} + \cdots + x_t + \cdots + x_{t+m-1} + x_{t+m}}{2m + 1}$$

For example, if we set m at 2, the 5-point moving average is as follows:

$$x_t^* = \frac{x_{t-2} + x_{t-1} + x_t + x_{t+1} + x_{t+2}}{5}$$

Since the first observation is x_1, the first moving average term would be as follows:

$$x_3^* = \frac{x_1 + x_2 + x_3 + x_4 + x_5}{5}$$

This is the average of the first five observations. For the Lydia Pinkham sales data of Example 16.1 we have for 1933

$$x_3^* = \frac{1,806 + 1,644 + 1,814 + 1,770 + 1,518}{5} = 1,710.4$$

Similarly, x_4^* is the average of the second through the sixth observation, and so on. Table 16.4 gives the original and smoothed series. Notice that for centered moving averages we lose the first and last m observations. Thus, while the original series runs from 1931 through 1960, the smoothed series goes from 1933 through 1958.

Table 16.4
Annual Sales of Lydia Pinkham with the Simple Centered 5-Point Moving Average

Year	Sales	Aver1	Year	Sales	Aver1
1931	1806*		1946	2177	2232.4
1932	1644*		1947	1920	2125.6
1933	1814	1710.4	1948	1910	1955.6
1934	1770	1569.8	1949	1984	1858
1935	1518	1494.2	1950	1787	1847.2
1936	1103	1426	1951	1689	1844.4
1937	1266	1356.6	1952	1866	1784.4
1938	1473	1406.4	1953	1896	1753.6
1939	1423	1618	1954	1684	1747.2
1940	1767	1832	1955	1633	1687.8
1941	2161	2057.8	1956	1657	1586.6
1942	2336	2276.8	1957	1569	1527.2
1943	2602	2450.8	1958	1390	1458.4
1944	2518	2454	1959	1387*	
1945	2637	2370.8	1960	1289*	

Simple Centered ($2m + 1$)-Point Moving Averages

Let $x_1, x_2, x_3, ..., x_n$ be n observations on a time series of interest. A smoothed series can be obtained by using a simple centered ($2m + 1$)-point moving average:

$$x_t^* = \frac{1}{2m + 1} \sum_{j=-m}^{m} x_{t+j} \qquad (t = m + 1, m + 2, ..., n - m) \tag{16.3}$$

A moving average can be generated using Minitab, as shown in Figure 16.12. We see both the original series and the smoothed series—the 5-point moving average series—plotted versus time. As we can see, the moving average series is indeed smoother than the original series. Thus, the moving average series has removed the underlying irregular component from the series to reveal better the structural components.

The kind of moving average discussed in this section is just one of many that might have been used. It is often deemed desirable to use a weighted average, in which most weight is given to the central observation, with weights for other values decreasing as their distance from the central observation increases. For example, we might use a weighted average such as

$$x_t^* = \frac{x_{t-2} + 2x_{t-1} + 4x_t + 2x_{t+1} + x_{t+2}}{10}$$

In any event the objective in using moving averages remains the smoothing out of the irregular component in order to allow us to form a clearer picture of the underlying irregularities in a time series. The technique is perhaps of most value for descriptive purposes, in the production of graphs such as Figure 16.12.

Extraction of the Seasonal Component through Moving Averages

We now move to develop a procedure for using moving averages to extract seasonal components from business and economic series. Seasonal components can be a nuisance, and the analyst may want to remove them from the series to obtain a keener appreciation of the behavior of other components. Recall also that in Section 13.2 we showed how dummy variables could be used to estimate and control seasonal effects.

Figure 16.12
Simple Centered
5-Point Moving
Average of Lydia
Pinkham Sales
Data

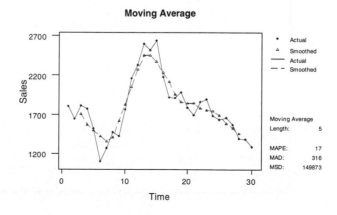

Consider a quarterly time series with a seasonal component. Our strategy to remove seasonality will be to produce four-period moving averages so that the various seasonal values are brought together in a single seasonal moving average. For example, using the earnings per share data in Table 16.5, the first member of the series would be

$$\frac{0.300 + 0.460 + 0.345 + 0.910}{4} = 0.50375$$

and the second member would be

$$\frac{0.460 + 0.345 + 0.910 + 0.330}{4} = 0.51125$$

The complete series is shown in Table 16.5.

Table 16.5
Actual Earnings per Share of a Corporation and Centered 4-Point Moving Average

YEAR QUARTER	EARNINGS	4-POINT MOVING AVERAGES	CENTERED 4-POINT MOVING AVERAGES
1.1	0.3	*	*
1.2	0.46	*	*
1.3	0.345	0.50375	0.5075
1.4	0.91	0.51125	0.5219
2.1	0.33	0.53250	0.5444
2.2	0.545	0.55625	0.5725
2.3	0.44	0.58875	0.6094
2.4	1.04	0.63000	0.6469
3.1	0.495	0.66375	0.6769
3.2	0.68	0.69000	0.7206
3.3	0.545	0.75125	0.7581
3.4	1.285	0.76500	0.7888
4.1	0.55	0.81250	0.8269
4.2	0.87	0.84125	0.8781
4.3	0.66	0.91500	0.9200
4.4	1.58	0.92500	0.9400
5.1	0.59	0.95500	0.9763
5.2	0.99	0.99750	1.0163
5.3	0.83	1.03500	1.0375
5.4	1.73	1.04000	1.0475
6.1	0.61	1.05500	1.0663
6.2	1.05	1.07750	1.1163
6.3	0.92	1.15500	1.1663
6.4	2.04	1.17750	1.2000
7.1	0.7	1.22250	1.2400
7.2	1.23	1.25750	1.2925
7.3	1.06	1.32750	1.3425
7.4	2.32	1.35750	1.3800
8.1	0.82	1.40250	1.4263
8.2	1.41	1.45000	1.5013
8.3	1.25	1.55250	*
8.4	2.73	*	*

This new series of moving averages should be free from seasonality, but there is still a problem. The location in time of the members of the series of moving averages does not correspond precisely with that of the members of the original series. The first term is the average of the first four observations, and, thus, we might regard it as being centered between the second and third observations:

$$x_{2.5}^* = \frac{x_1 + x_2 + x_3 + x_4}{4}$$

Similarly, the second term could be written as follows:

$$x_{3.5}^* = \frac{x_2 + x_3 + x_4 + x_5}{4}$$

This problem can be overcome by centering our series of 4-point moving averages. This can be done by calculating the averages of adjacent pairs, which for the first value is as follows:

$$x_3^* = \frac{x_{2.5}^* + x_{3.5}^*}{2} = \frac{0.50375 + 0.51125}{2} = 0.5075$$

This value is the centered moving average corresponding to the third observation of the original series. The remainder of the series of centered moving averages is in the final column of Table 16.5. Note again that this procedure results in the loss of two observations from each end of the series.

The series of centered moving averages is plotted in Figure 16.13 along with the original series. Clearly, the seasonality component has been removed. In addition, because we have used moving averages, the irregular component has also been smoothed. The resulting picture, thus, allows us to judge the nonseasonal regularities in the data. We see that the smoothed series is dominated by an upward trend. Closer examination reveals steady earnings growth in the early part of the series, a central portion of rather slower growth, and resumption in the last part of the period of a pattern similar to the early one.

Figure 16.13
Centered 4-Point
Moving Averages
and Original
Series for
Earnings per
Share of a
Corporation

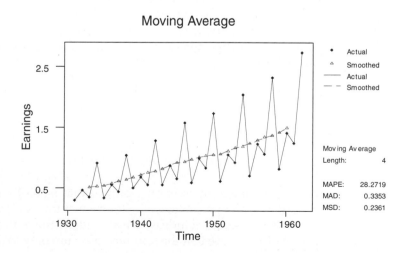

A Simple Moving Average Procedure for Seasonal Adjustment

Let x_t ($t = 1, 2, ..., n$) be a seasonal time series of period s ($s = 4$ for quarterly data and $s = 12$ for monthly data). A centered s-point moving average series, x_t^*, is obtained through the following steps, where it is assumed that s is even:

1. Form the s-point moving averages

$$x_{t+0.5}^* = \frac{\sum_{j=-(s/2)+1}^{s/2} x_{t+j}}{s} \qquad \left(t = \frac{s}{2}, \frac{s}{2} + 1,...,n - \frac{s}{2} \right) \qquad (16.4)$$

2. Form the centered s-point moving averages

$$x_t^* = \frac{x_{t-0.5}^* + x_{t+0.5}^*}{2} \qquad \left(t = \frac{s}{2} + 1, \frac{s}{2} + 2,...,n - \frac{s}{2} \right) \qquad (16.5)$$

We have seen that the series of centered s-point moving averages can be a useful tool for gaining descriptive insight into the structure of a time series. Since it is largely free from seasonality and embodies a smoothing of the irregular component, it is well suited for the identification of a trend and/or cyclical component. This series of moving averages also forms the basis for many practical seasonal adjustment procedures. The specific procedure depends on a number of factors, including the amount of stability one assumes in the seasonal pattern and whether seasonality is viewed as additive or multiplicative. In the later case we often take logarithms of the data.

Next, we discuss a seasonal adjustment approach that is based on the implicit assumption of a stable seasonal pattern over time. The procedure is known as the *seasonal index method*. We assume that for any month or quarter, in each year, the effect of seasonality is to increase or decrease the series by the same percentage.

We will illustrate the seasonal index method using the corporate earnings data. The seasonally adjusted series is computed in Table 16.6. The first two columns contain the original series and the centered 4-point moving average. To assess the influence of seasonality, we express the original series as a percentage of the centered 4-point moving average series. Thus, for example, for the third quarter of year 1, we have the following:

$$100 \left(\frac{x_3}{x_3^*} \right) = 100 \left(\frac{0.345}{0.5075} \right) = 67.98$$

These percentages are also entered into Table 16.7, where the calculation of the seasonal index is shown. To assess the effect of seasonality in the first quarter, we find the median of the seven percentages for that quarter. This is the fourth value when they are arranged in ascending order—that is, 60.43. In a similar way we find the median of x_t as a percentage of x_t^* for each of the other quarters.

To obtain seasonal indices, we also adjust the indices so that their average is 100. In Table 16.7 we see that the four medians sum only to 395.88. We can obtain the final

Table 16.6

Seasonal Adjustment of Earnings per Share of a Corporation by the Seasonal Index Method

YEAR QUARTER	x_t	x_t^*	$100\left(\dfrac{x_t}{x_t^*}\right)$	SEASONAL INDEX	ADJUSTED SERIES
1.1	0.300*			61.06	0.4913
1.2	0.460*			96.15	0.4784
1.3	0.345	0.5075	67.98	72.95	0.4729
1.4	0.910	0.5219	174.36	169.84	0.5358
2.1	0.330	0.5444	60.62	61.06	0.5405
2.2	0.545	0.5725	95.20	96.15	0.5668
2.3	0.440	0.6094	72.20	72.95	0.6032
2.4	1.040	0.6469	160.77	169.84	0.6123
3.1	0.495	0.6769	73.13	61.06	0.8107
3.2	0.680	0.7206	94.37	96.15	0.7072
3.3	0.545	0.7581	71.89	72.95	0.7471
3.4	1.285	0.7888	162.91	169.84	0.7566
4.1	0.550	0.8269	66.51	61.06	0.9008
4.2	0.870	0.8781	99.08	96.15	0.9048
4.3	0.660	0.9200	71.74	72.95	0.9047
4.4	1.580	0.9400	168.09	169.84	0.9303
5.1	0.590	0.9763	60.43	61.06	0.9663
5.2	0.990	1.0163	97.41	96.15	1.0296
5.3	0.830	1.0375	80.00	72.95	1.1378
5.4	1.730	1.0475	165.16	169.84	1.0186
6.1	0.610	1.0663	57.21	61.06	0.9990
6.2	1.050	1.1163	94.06	96.15	1.0920
6.3	0.920	1.1663	78.88	72.95	1.2611
6.4	2.040	1.2000	170.00	169.84	1.2011
7.1	0.700	1.2400	56.45	61.06	1.1464
7.2	1.230	1.2925	95.16	96.15	1.2793
7.3	1.060	1.3425	78.96	72.95	1.4531
7.4	2.320	1.3800	168.12	169.84	1.3660
8.1	0.820	1.4263	57.49	61.06	1.3429
8.2	1.410	1.5013	93.92	96.15	1.4665
8.3	1.250*			72.95	1.7135
8.4	2.730*			169.84	1.6074

Table 16.7

Calculation of Seasonal Index for Earnings per Share Data of a Corporation

	QUARTER				
YEAR	1	2	3	4	SUMS
1			67.98	174.36	
2	60.62	95.20	72.20	160.77	
3	73.13	94.37	71.89	162.91	
4	66.51	99.08	71.74	168.09	
5	60.43	97.41	80.00	165.16	
6	57.21	94.06	78.88	170.00	
7	56.45	95.16	78.96	168.12	
8	57.49	93.92			
Median	60.43	95.16	72.20	168.09	395.88
Seasonal index	61.06	96.15	72.95	169.84	400

indices—that have a mean of 100—by multiplying each median by (400/395.88). For the first quarter we have

$$\text{Seasonal Index} = 60.43\left(\frac{400}{395.88}\right) = 61.06$$

We interpret this figure as estimating that the effect of seasonality is to lower first quarter earnings to 61.06% of what they would have been in the absence of seasonal factors.

The seasonal indices, from the last row of Table 16.7, are entered in the fifth column of Table 16.6. Notice that the same index is used for any particular quarter in every year. Finally, we obtain our seasonally adjusted value as follows:

$$\text{Adjusted value} = \text{Original value}\left(\frac{100}{\text{Seasonal Index}}\right)$$

For example, for the third quarter of year 1 the seasonally adjusted value is as follows:

$$0.345\left(\frac{100}{72.95}\right) = 0.4729$$

The complete seasonally adjusted series obtained in this way is given in the final column of Table 16.6 and graphed in Figure 16.14. Notice that there is a suggestion of a little remaining seasonality in the latter part of the period. This suggests that a more elaborate approach, allowing for changing seasonal patterns, may be desirable.

The seasonal index method presented here provides one simple solution to the index problem. Many important time series—such as gross domestic product and its components, employment and unemployment, prices, and wages—have strong seasonal components. Generally, data on such quantities are published by government agencies in both unadjusted and adjusted forms. Although they are more complex than the method described here, official adjustment procedures are typically based on moving averages. The seasonal adjustment procedure most commonly employed in official U.S. government publications is the Census X-11 method. It differs from the seasonal index method in allowing for a steadily evolving seasonal pattern over time. It can be shown that in its additive version X-11 estimates the seasonal component of a monthly time series to a close approximation by

$$S_t = \frac{z_{t-36} + 2z_{t-24} + 3z_{t-12} + 3z_t + 3z_{t+12} + 2z_{t+24} + z_{t+36}}{15}$$

Figure 16.14
Seasonally
Adjusted Earnings
per Share of a
Corporation

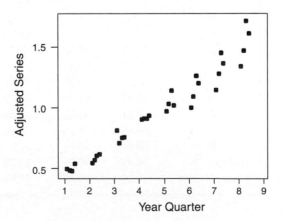

where

$$z_t = x_t - x_t^*$$

with x_t the original value of the series at time t and x_t^* the corresponding centered 12-point moving average. Of course, if such a procedure is used, some special treatment is needed for values toward the end of the series, as the expression for the seasonal factor will involve values in the time series that have not yet occurred. A possible way of accomplishing this is to replace unknown future values of a series in the moving average by forecasts based on the available data.

EXERCISES

Application Exercises

16.18 ● The data file **Quarterly Earnings 16.18** shows quarterly sales of a corporation over a period of 6 years.

    a. Draw a time plot of this series and discuss its features.

    b. Use the seasonal index method to seasonally adjust this series. Graph the seasonally adjusted series and discuss its features.

16.19 ● The data file **Quarterly Sales** shows quarterly sales of a corporation over a period of 6 years.

    a. Draw a time plot of this series and discuss its features.

    b. Use the seasonal index method to seasonally adjust this series. Graph the seasonally adjusted series and discuss its features.

16.20 ● Compute a simple centered 3-point moving average series for the gold price data of Exercise 16.15. Plot the smoothed series and discuss the resulting graph.

16.21 ● Compute a simple centered 5-point moving average series for the housing starts data of Exercise 16.16. Draw a time plot of the smoothed series and comment on your results.

16.22 ● Compute a simple centered 7-point moving average series for the corporate earnings data of Exercise 16.17. Based on a time plot of the smoothed series, what can be said about its regular components?

16.23 Let

$$x_t^* = \frac{1}{2m+1} \sum_{j=-m}^{m} x_{t+j}$$

be a simple centered $(2m + 1)$-point moving average. Show that

$$x_{t+1}^* = x_t^* \frac{x_{t+m+1} - x_{t-m}}{2m + 1}$$

How might this result be used in the efficient computation of series of centered moving averages?

16.24 ● The data file **Quarterly Earnings 16.24** shows earnings per share of a corporation over a period of 7 years.

    a. Draw a time plot of these data. Does your graph suggest the presence of a strong seasonal component in this earnings series?

    b. Using the seasonal index method, obtain a seasonally adjusted earnings series. Graph this series and comment on its behavior.

16.25 a. Show that the centered s-point moving average series of Section 16.4 can be written as follows:

$$x_t^* = \frac{x_{t-(s/2)} + 2\left(x_{t-(s/2)+1} + \cdots + x_{t+(s/2)-1}\right) + x_{t+(s/2)}}{2s}$$

    b. Show that

$$x_{t+1}^* = x_t^* + \frac{x_{t+(s/2)+1} + x_{t+(s/2)} - x_{t-(s/2)+1} - x_{t-(s/2)}}{2s}$$

Discuss the computational advantages of this formula in the seasonal adjustment of monthly time series.

16.26 ● The data file **Monthly Sales** shows monthly product sales over a period of 3 years. Use the seasonal index method to obtain a seasonally adjusted series.

16.5 EXPONENTIAL SMOOTHING

We now examine some procedures for using the current and past values of a time series to forecast future values of the series. This easily stated problem can be very difficult to resolve satisfactorily. A vast array of forecasting methods are in common use, and, to a great extent, the eventual choice will be problem-specific, depending on the resources and objectives of the analyst and the nature of the available data.

Our aim is to use the available observations, $x_1, x_2, ..., x_t$, on a series to predict the unknown future values $x_{t+1}, x_{t+2}, ...$. Forecasting is of crucial importance in the business environment as a rational basis for decision making. For example, monthly product sales are predicted as a basis for inventory control policy. Forecasts of future earnings are used when making investment decisions.

In this section we introduce a forecasting method known as **simple exponential smoothing** that performs quite effectively in a number of forecasting applications. In addition, it forms the basis for some more-elaborate forecasting methods. Exponential smoothing is appropriate when the series is nonseasonal and has no consistent upward or downward trend.

In the absence of trend and seasonality the objective is to estimate the current level of the time series and then use this estimate to forecast future values. Our position is that we are standing at time t, we are looking back on the series of observations $x_t, x_{t-1}, x_{t-2}, ...,$ and we want to form an assessment of the current level of the series. As a prelude, we consider two extreme possibilities. First, we might simply use the most recent observation to forecast all future observations. In some cases, such as prices in speculative markets, this may be the best we can do, but the result is not very successful. However, in many series with irregular components we would likely want to use a number of previous observations in the series. This would identify any patterns that might exist in the time series and avoid using only a random fluctuation as the basis of our forecast.

At the opposite extreme we might use the average of all past values as our estimate of the current level. A moment's reflection suggests that often this would not be useful because all past values would be treated equally. Thus, for example, if we tried to predict future sales by this procedure, we would be assigning equal importance to sales many years ago and to recent sales. It seems reasonable that more recent experience should have a greater impact on our forecast.

Simple exponential smoothing allows a compromise between these extremes, providing a forecast based on a weighted average of current and past values. In forming this average, most weight is given to the most recent observation, rather less to the immediately preceding value, less to the one before that, and so on. We estimate the level at the current time t by

$$\hat{x}_t = \alpha x_t + \alpha(1-\alpha)x_{t-1} + \alpha(1-\alpha)^2 x_{t-2} + \cdots$$

where α is a number between 0 and 1. For example, with $\alpha = 0.5$ the forecast of future observations is

$$\hat{x}_t = .5x_t + .25x_{t-1} + .125x_{t-2} + \cdots$$

so that a weighted average, with declining weights, is applied to current and past observations in computing the forecasts.

From this model we see that the forecast of the series at any time t is estimated by

$$\hat{x}_t = \alpha x_t + \alpha(1-\alpha)x_{t-1} + \alpha(1-\alpha)^2 x_{t-2} + \cdots$$

and, similarly, the level at the previous time period $(t-1)$ would be estimated by

$$\hat{x}_{t-1} = \alpha x_{t-1} + \alpha(1-\alpha)x_{t-2} + \alpha(1-\alpha)^2 x_{t-3} + \cdots$$

Multiplying through by $1-\alpha$, we have the following:

$$(1-\alpha)\hat{x}_{t-1} = \alpha(1-\alpha)x_{t-1} + \alpha(1-\alpha)^2 x_{t-2} + \alpha(1-\alpha)^3 x_{t-3} + \cdots$$

Hence, on subtracting these two equations we obtain the following:

$$\hat{x}_t - (1-\alpha)\hat{x}_{t-1} = \alpha x_t$$

And by simple manipulation we have the equation for computing the simple exponential smoothing forecast:

$$\hat{x}_t = (1-\alpha)\hat{x}_{t-1} + \alpha x_t \quad \text{for } 0 < \alpha < 1$$

This provides a convenient recursive algorithm for calculating forecasts. The forecast value, $\hat{x}_t$, at time t is a weighted average of the previous period forecast $\hat{x}_{t-1}$ and the latest observation x_t. The weights given to each depend on the choice of α, which is defined as the smoothing constant. Note that a small value of α gives greater weight to $\hat{x}_{t-1}$, which is based on the past history of the series, and less weight to x_t, which represents the most recent data.

We can illustrate the procedure using the Lydia Pinkham sales data with a value of $\alpha = 0.6$. The process begins by setting the first element of the series:

$$\hat{x}_1 = x_1 = 1{,}806$$

The second value in the forecast would be as follows:

$$\hat{x}_2 = .4\hat{x}_1 + .6x_2$$
$$= (.4)(1{,}806) + (.6)(1{,}644) = 1{,}708.8$$

And this process continues through the series so that

$$\hat{x}_3 = .4\hat{x}_2 + .6x_3$$
$$= (.4)(1{,}708.8) + (.6)(1{,}814) = 1{,}771.9$$

Forecasting Through Simple Exponential Smoothing

Let $x_1, x_2, \ldots, x_n$ be a set of observations on a nonseasonal time series with no consistent upward or downward trend. The **simple exponential smoothing method of forecasting** then proceeds as follows:

1. Obtain the smoothed series $\hat{x}_t$, as

$$\hat{x}_1 = x_1$$

$$\hat{x}_t = (1-\alpha)\hat{x}_{t-1} + \alpha x_t \quad (0 < \alpha < 1; t = 2, 3, \ldots, n) \tag{16.6}$$

where α is a smoothing constant whose value is fixed between 0 and 1.

2. Standing at time n, we obtain forecasts of future values, x_{n+h}, of the series by

$$\hat{x}_{n+h} = \hat{x}_n \qquad (h = 1, 2, 3, \ldots)$$

So far we have said little about the choice of the smoothing constant, α, in practical applications. In applications this choice may be based on either subjective or objective grounds. One possibility is to rely on experience or judgment. For instance, an analyst who wants to predict product demand may have had considerable experience in working with data on similar product lines and may use that experience to select an appropriate α. Visual inspection of a graph of the available data can also be useful in suggesting an appropriate value for the smoothing constant. If the series appears to contain a substantial irregular element, we do not want to give too much weight to the most recent observation alone since it might not indicate what we expect in the future. This would suggest a relatively low value for the smoothing constant, α. But if the series is rather smooth, we would use a higher value for α in order to give more weight to the most recent observation.

A more objective approach is to try several different values and see which would have been most successful in predicting historical movements in the time series. We might, for example, compute the smoothed series at values of α of 0.8, 0.6, 0.4, and 0.2 and choose the value that provides the best forecast in the historical series. We would compute the error for each forecast as follows:

$$e_t = x_t - \hat{x}_{t-1}$$

One possibility is to compute, for each trial value of α, the sum of squared forecast errors:

$$SS = \sum_{t=2}^{n} e_t^2 = \sum_{t=2}^{n} \left(x_t - \hat{x}_{t-1} \right)^2$$

The value of α that minimizes the sum of squared forecast errors will be used for future predictions. Simple exponential smoothing can be performed using Minitab. Figure 16.15 shows a plot of the original and smoothed series using $\alpha = 0.9$, which was established by trying different values and finding the value that provided a satisfactory fit. The reported MSD in Figure 16.15 is the sum of squared forecast errors divided by the number of observations.

Whatever value of the smoothing constant is used, Equation 16.6 can be regarded as an updating mechanism. At time $(t - 1)$ the level of the series is estimated by $\hat{x}_{t-1}$. Then in the next period the new observation x_t is used to update this estimate so that the new estimate of level is a weighted average of the previous estimate and the new observation.

The Holt–Winters Exponential Smoothing Forecasting Model

Many business forecasting procedures are based on extensions of simple exponential smoothing. The Holt–Winters Exponential Smoothing procedure allows for trend, and possibly also seasonality, in a time series.

First, we consider a nonseasonal time series. We want to estimate not only the current level of the series but also the trend—regarded as the difference between the current level and the preceding level.

Figure 16.15
Lydia Pinkham
Sales Data with
Original and
Simple
Exponential
Smoothing Values

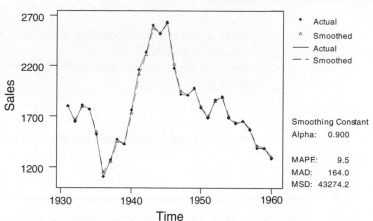

We denote x_t as the observed value and $\hat{x}_t$ as the estimate of the level. The trend estimate is represented as T_t. The principle behind the estimation of these two quantities is much the same as in the simple exponential smoothing algorithm. The two estimating equations are

$$\hat{x}_t = (1 - \alpha)(\hat{x}_{t-1} + T_{t-1}) + \alpha x_t \qquad (0 < \alpha < 1)$$
$$T_t = (1 - \beta)T_{t-1} + \beta(\hat{x}_t - \hat{x}_{t-1}) \qquad (0 < \beta < 1)$$

where α and β are smoothing constants whose values are set between 0 and 1.

Comparable to simple exponential smoothing the Holt–Winters procedure uses these equations to update previous estimates using a new observation. The estimate of level $\hat{x}_{t-1}$ made at time $(t - 1)$, taken in conjunction with the trend estimate, T_{t-1}, suggests for time t a level $(\hat{x}_{t-1} + T_{t-1})$. This estimate is modified, in light of the new observation, x_t, to obtain an updated estimate of level, $\hat{x}_t$, using the given equation.

Similarly, trend at time $(t - 1)$ is estimated as T_{t-1}. However, once the new observation, x_t, is available, an estimate of trend is suggested as the difference between the two most recent estimates of level. The trend estimate at time t is then the weighted average as given.

We begin the computations by setting the following:

$$T_2 = x_2 - x_1 \qquad \text{and} \qquad \hat{x}_2 = x_2$$

Then, the previous equations are applied, in turn, for $t = 3, 4, ..., n$. We demonstrate these calculations in Example 16.2. The entire procedure is summarized next.

Forecasting with the Holt–Winters Method: Nonseasonal Series

Let $x_1, x_2,..., x_n$ be a set of observations on a nonseasonal time series. The **Holt–Winters method: nonseasonal series** of forecasting proceeds as follows.

1. Obtain estimates of level $\hat{x}_t$ and trend T_t as

$$\hat{x}_2 = x_2 \qquad T_2 = x_2 - x_1$$
$$\hat{x}_t = (1 - \alpha)(\hat{x}_{t-1} + T_{t-1}) + \alpha x_t \qquad (0 < \alpha < 1; t = 3, 4, ...,n)$$

$$T_t = (1-\beta)T_{t-1} + (\beta\hat{x}_t - \hat{x}_{t-1}) \qquad (0 < \beta < 1; t = 3,4,\dots,n) \qquad \text{(16.7)}$$

where α and β are smoothing constants whose values are fixed between 0 and 1.

2. Standing at time n, we obtain forecasts of future values, x_{n+h}, of the series by

$$\hat{x}_{n+h} = \hat{x}_n + hT_n \qquad \text{(16.8)}$$

where h is the number of periods in the future.

Example 16.2 Forecasting Consumer Credit (Holt–Winters Exponential Smoothing)

You are asked to obtain a forecast for outstanding consumer credit using the Holt–Winters exponential smoothing procedure.

Solution The calculations that follow use the consumer credit data in Table 16.8, which also includes the calculations for the Holt–Winters procedure.

The initial estimates of level and trend in year 2 are

$$\hat{x}_2 = x_2 = 155$$

and

$$T_2 = x_2 - x_1 = 155 - 133 = 22$$

This smoothing application will use $\alpha = 0.7$, $\beta = 0.6$, and the following equations:

$$\hat{x}_t = 0.3(\hat{x}_{t-1} + T_{t-1}) + 0.7x_t$$
$$T_t = 0.4T_{t-1} + 0.6(\hat{x}_t - \hat{x}_{t-1})$$

Table 16.8 Holt–Winters Calculations for Consumer Credit Outstanding ($\alpha = 0.7$, $\beta = 0.6$)

t	x_t	$\hat{x}_t$	T_t
1	133		
2	155	155	22
3	165	169	17
4	171	175	11
5	194	192	14
6	231	223	25
7	274	266	36
8	312	309	40
9	313	324	25
10	333	338	18
11	343	347	13

Then for $t = 3$

$$\hat{x}_3 = 0.3(\hat{x}_2 + T_2) + 0.7x_3$$
$$= (0.3)(155 + 22) + (0.7)(165)$$
$$= 168.6$$

and, in addition,

$$T_3 = 0.4T_2 + 0.6(\hat{x}_3 - \hat{x}_2)$$
$$= (0.4)(22) + (0.6)(168.6 - 155)$$
$$= 16.96$$

Then for $t = 4$

$$\hat{x}_4 = 0.3(\hat{x}_3 + T_3) + 0.7x_4$$
$$= (0.3)(168.6 + 16.96) + (0.7)(171)$$
$$= 175.4$$

and, in addition,

$$T_4 = 0.4T_3 + 0.6(\hat{x}_4 - \hat{x}_3)$$
$$= (0.4)(16.96) + (0.6)(175.4 - 168.6)$$
$$= 10.86$$

The remaining calculations continue in the same way, setting, in turn, $t = 5, 6, ..., 11$. The results of these calculations are shown in Table 16.8.

Now let us use these level and trend estimates to forecast future observations. Given a series $x_1, x_2, ..., x_n$, the most recent level and trend estimates are $\hat{x}_t$ and T_n, respectively. In the production of forecasts it is assumed that this latest trend will continue from the most recent level. Thus, we forecast using the relationship

$$\hat{x}_{n+1} = \hat{x}_n + T_n$$

and for the following one

$$\hat{x}_{n+2} = \hat{x}_n + 2T_n$$

and in general for h periods ahead

$$\hat{x}_{n+h} = \hat{x}_n + hT_n$$

From Table 16.8 the most recent level and trend estimates are as follows:

$$\hat{x}_{11} = 347 \qquad T_{11} = 13$$

Then the forecasts for the next three periods are as follows:

$$\hat{x}_{12} = 347 + 13 = 360$$
$$\hat{x}_{13} = 347 + (2)(13) = 373$$
$$\hat{x}_{14} = 347 + (3)(13) = 386$$

The Holt–Winters procedure can be computed in Minitab, and Figure 16.16 presents the time-series graph and the forecasts. The Minitab procedure differs slightly

Figure 16.16 Consumer Credit Outstanding Observed and Forecasts Using Minitab Calculations

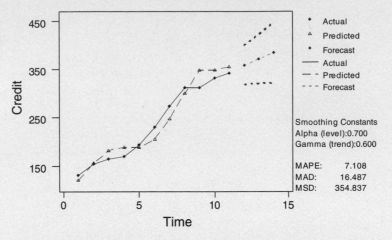

from the procedure just described. Minitab computes an estimate for the first period using the following procedure:

1. Minitab fits a linear regression model to time-series data (y variable) versus time (x variable).
2. The constant from this regression is the initial estimate of the level component; the slope coefficient is the initial estimate of the trend component.

As a result, the values calculated by the Minitab program will differ slightly from those in Table 16.8. The comparable values computed by the Minitab procedure are shown in Table 16.9. The Minitab procedure will generally provide slightly better forecasts compared to the more simplified procedure we have shown. For

Table 16.9 Minitab Calculations for Consumer Credit Outstanding ($\alpha = 0.7$, $\beta = 0.6$)

TIME	OBSERVED CONSUMER CREDIT	LEVEL EXPECTED VALUE	TREND	FORECASTS
1	133	130	28	
2	155	156	27	
3	165	170	19	
4	171	177	12	
5	194	192	14	
6	231	224	24	
7	274	266	35	
8	312	309	40	
9	313	324	25	
10	333	338	18	
11	343	347	13	
12				360
13				373
14				385

other statistical packages check the specific computational algorithms to ensure that you understand what is being computed. Usually this can be done by clicking the Help option.

Forecasting Seasonal Time Series

We will now examine an extension of the Holt–Winters method that allows for seasonality. In most practical problems the seasonal factor is taken to be multiplicative, so that, for example, in dealing with monthly sales figures, we might think of January in terms of a proportion of average monthly sales. As before, the trend component is assumed to be additive.

Similar to the nonseasonal case, we will use x_t, $\hat{x}_t$, and T_t to denote, respectively, the observed value and the level and trend estimates at time t. The seasonal factor is denoted F_t, so if the time series contains s periods per year, the seasonal factor for the corresponding period in the previous year will be F_{t-s}.

In the Holt–Winters model the estimates of level, trend, and the seasonal factor are updated by the following three equations

$$\hat{x}_t = (1-\alpha)(\hat{x}_{t-1}+T_{t-1})+\alpha\frac{x_t}{F_{t-s}} \qquad (0 < \alpha < 1)$$
$$T_t = (1-\beta)T_{t-1}+\beta(\hat{x}_t-\hat{x}_{t-1}) \qquad (0 < \beta < 1)$$
$$F_t = (1-\gamma)F_{t-s}+\gamma\frac{x_t}{\hat{x}_t} \qquad (0 < \gamma < 1)$$

where α, β, and γ are smoothing constants with values between 0 and 1.

The term $(\hat{x}_{t-1}+T_{t-1})$ is an estimate of the level at time t computed at the previous time period $t-1$. This estimate is then updated when x_t becomes available. But we also remove the influence of seasonality by deflating it by the latest available estimate, F_{t-s}, of the seasonal factor for that period. The updating equation for trend, T_t, is the same as used previously.

Finally, the seasonal factor, F_t, is estimated using the third equation. The most recent estimate of the factor, available from the previous year, is F_{t-s}. However, dividing the new observation, x_t, by the level estimate, $\hat{x}_t$, suggests a seasonal factor $x_t/\hat{x}_t$. The new estimate of the seasonal factor is then a weighted average of these two quantities.

Forecasting with the Holt–Winters Method: Seasonal Series

Let $x_1, x_2,..., x_t$ be a set of observations on a seasonal time series of period s (with $s = 4$ for quarterly data and $s = 12$ for monthly data). The **Holt–Winters method: seasonal series** of forecasting uses a set of recursive estimates from the historical series. These estimates utilize a level factor, α; a trend factor, β; and a multiplicative seasonal factor, γ. The recursive estimates are based on the following equations:

$$\hat{x}_t = (1-\alpha)(\hat{x}_{t-1}+T_{t-1})+\alpha\frac{x_t}{F_{t-s}} \qquad (0 < \alpha < 1)$$
$$T_t = (1-\beta)T_{t-1}+\beta(\hat{x}_t-\hat{x}_{t-1}) \qquad (0 < \beta < 1)$$
$$F_t = (1-\gamma)F_{t-s}+\gamma\frac{x_t}{\hat{x}_t} \qquad (0 < \gamma < 1) \qquad (16.9)$$

where $\hat{x}_t$ is the smoothed level of the series, T_t is the smoothed trend of the series, and F_t is the smoothed seasonal adjustment for the series. The computational details are tedious and best left to a computer. We have demonstrated the algorithm used by Minitab, but numerous quality statistical packages have similar procedures. These computer procedures may differ in the way they handle the generation of factors for the initial periods of an observed time series, and, thus, you should consult the documentation for the package to determine the exact procedure used. Minitab uses a dummy variable regression procedure to obtain estimates for the initial periods.

After the initial procedure generates the level, trend, and seasonal factors from a historical series, we can use the results to forecast future values at h time periods ahead from the last observation, x_n, in the historical series. The forecast equation is as follows:

$$\hat{x}_{n+h} = (\hat{x}_n + hT_n)F_{n+h-s} \tag{16.10}$$

We note that the seasonal factor, F, is the one generated for the most recent seasonal time period.

The procedure that we have developed here can be implemented using the Minitab procedure labeled "Winters method" smoothing forecast. Specifically, the method described here uses the "multiplicative" option. The Winters method employs a level component, a trend component, and a seasonal component at each period. It uses three weights, or smoothing parameters, to update the components at each period. Initial values for the level and trend components are obtained from a linear regression on time. Initial values for the seasonal component are obtained from a dummy variable regression using detrended data. The Winters method smoothing equations for the multiplicative model are those previously used.

This procedure will be demonstrated using the corporate earnings per share in Minitab. A plot of observed and fitted values, along with forecasts for the next four periods, is shown in Figure 16.17. Forecasts are obtained by using the most recent

Figure 16.17
History and Forecast of Corporate Earnings Using Holt–Winters Method: Seasonal Series

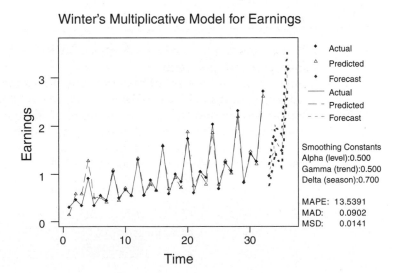

Winter's Multiplicative Model for Earnings

Smoothing Constants
Alpha (level):0.500
Gamma (trend):0.500
Delta (season):0.700

MAPE: 13.5391
MAD: 0.0902
MSD: 0.0141

trend and level estimates and then adjusting for the particular seasonal factor. Given a season containing s time periods, the forecast for one period ahead would be as follows:

$$\hat{x}_{n+1} = (\hat{x}_n + T_n)F_{n+1-s}$$

Our example data contain 32 time periods and a seasonal factor $s = 4$, indicating quarterly data. Thus, to forecast the next observation beyond the end of the series, we use the following:

$$\hat{x}_{33} = (\hat{x}_{32} + T_{32})F_{29}$$

Table 16.10

Computational Results: Minitab Application of Holt–Winters Smoothing Procedure: Seasonal Series

Year Quarter	Corporate Earnings	Smoothed Value	Level Estimate	Trend Estimate	Seasonal Estimate	Forecast
1.1	0.300	0.043	0.387	0.242	0.713	
1.2	0.460	0.360	0.562	0.208	0.851	
1.3	0.345	0.433	0.609	0.128	0.628	
1.4	0.910	1.055	0.631	0.075	1.529	
2.1	0.330	0.450	0.584	0.014	0.609	
2.2	0.545	0.498	0.619	0.024	0.872	
2.3	0.440	0.389	0.672	0.039	0.646	
2.4	1.040	1.028	0.696	0.031	1.505	
3.1	0.495	0.424	0.770	0.053	0.633	
3.2	0.680	0.671	0.801	0.042	0.856	
3.3	0.545	0.518	0.843	0.042	0.646	
3.4	1.285	1.269	0.869	0.034	1.486	
4.1	0.550	0.550	0.886	0.025	0.624	
4.2	0.870	0.758	0.964	0.052	0.888	
4.3	0.660	0.623	1.019	0.053	0.648	
4.4	1.580	1.514	1.067	0.051	1.482	
5.1	0.590	0.666	1.032	0.008	0.588	
5.2	0.990	0.916	1.077	0.026	0.910	
5.3	0.830	0.697	1.193	0.071	0.681	
5.4	1.730	1.767	1.215	0.047	1.441	
6.1	0.610	0.714	1.150	−0.009	0.548	
6.2	1.050	1.047	1.147	−0.006	0.914	
6.3	0.920	0.782	1.246	0.046	0.721	
6.4	2.040	1.795	1.354	0.077	1.487	
7.1	0.700	0.741	1.355	0.039	0.526	
7.2	1.230	1.238	1.370	0.027	0.902	
7.3	1.060	0.988	1.433	0.045	0.734	
7.4	2.320	2.131	1.519	0.066	1.515	
8.1	0.820	0.799	1.572	0.059	0.523	
8.2	1.410	1.419	1.597	0.042	0.889	
8.3	1.250	1.172	1.671	0.058	0.744	
8.4	2.730	2.531	1.765	0.076	1.537	
9.1						0.963
9.2						1.705
9.3						1.48
9.4						3.18

This forecast is for the first quarter; thus, we use the most recent first quarter seasonal factor, and that is F_{29}. In general, if we are forecasting h periods into the future, we obtain the forecast as follows:

$$\hat{x}_{n+h} = (\hat{x}_n + hT_n)F_{n+h-s}$$

The forecast here uses a level factor, $\alpha = 0.5$; a trend factor, $\beta = 0.5$; and a seasonal factor, $\gamma = 0.7$.

Finally, in Table 16.10 we show the detailed results of the computation of trend, level, and seasonal factors for each period.

The actual forecasts obtained through the Holt–Winters approach will depend on the specific values chosen for the smoothing constants. As in our earlier discussion of exponential smoothing, this choice could be based on either subjective or objective criteria. The analyst's experience with similar data sets might suggest suitable values of the smoothing constants. Alternatively, several different sets of possible values could be tried on the available historical data, and the set that would have yielded the best forecasts for that data could be used to generate the forecasts. This strategy is easy to implement by using a statistical computer package, as shown by the example we demonstrated using Minitab.

EXERCISES

Application Exercises

16.27 ◐ Based on the data of Exercise 16.13, use the method of simple exponential smoothing to obtain forecasts of the inventory-sales ratio over the next 4 years. Use a smoothing constant of $\alpha = 0.6$. Graph the observed time series and the forecasts.

16.28 ◐ Use the method of simple exponential smoothing, with a smoothing constant of $\alpha = 0.7$, to obtain forecasts of the price of gold in the next 5 years, based on the data of Exercise 16.15.

16.29 ◐ Using the data of Exercise 16.16, employ the method of simple exponential smoothing with smoothing constant $\alpha = 0.5$ to predict housing starts in the next 3 years.

16.30 ◐ The data file **Earnings per Share 16.30** shows earnings per share of a corporation over a period of 18 years.

a. Using smoothing constants $\alpha = 0.8, 0.6, 0.4,$ and 0.2, find forecasts based on simple exponential smoothing.

b. Which of the forecasts would you choose to use?

16.31 a. If forecasts are based on simple exponential smoothing with $\hat{x}_t$ denoting the smoothed value of the series at time t, show that the error made in forecasting x_t, standing at time $(t-1)$, can be written as follows:

$$e_t = x_t - \hat{x}_{t-1}$$

b. Hence, show that we can write $\hat{x}_t = x_t - (1-\alpha)e_t$, from which we see that the most recent observation and the most recent forecast error are used to compute the next forecast.

16.32 Suppose that in the simple exponential smoothing method the smoothing constant α is set equal to 1. What forecasts will result?

16.33 Comment on the following statement: "We know that all business and economic time series exhibit variability through time. Yet if simple exponential smoothing is used, the same forecast results for all future values of the time series. Since we know that all future values will not be the same, this is absurd."

16.34 ◐ The data file **Industrial Production Canada** shows an index of industrial production for Canada over a period of 15 years. Use the Holt–Winters procedure with smoothing constants $\alpha = 0.7$ and $\beta = 0.5$ to obtain forecasts over the next 5 years.

16.35 ◐ The data file **Hourly Earnings** shows manufacturing hourly earnings in the United States over 24 months. Use the Holt–Winters procedure with smoothing constants $\alpha = 0.7$ and $\beta = 0.6$ to obtain forecasts for the next 3 months.

16.36 ◐ The data file **Food Prices** shows an index of food prices, seasonally adjusted, over a period of 14 months in the United States. Use the Holt–Winters method with smoothing constants $\alpha = 0.5$ and $\beta = 0.5$ to obtain forecasts for the next 3 months.

16.37 ● The data file **Profit Margins** shows percentage profit margins of a corporation over a period of 11 years. Obtain forecasts for the next 2 years, using the Holt–Winters method with smoothing constants $\alpha = 0.4$ and $\beta = 0.4$.

16.38 ● Use the Holt–Winters seasonal method to obtain forecasts of sales up to eight quarters ahead, based on the data of Exercise 16.18.

Employ smoothing constants $\alpha = 0.4$, $\beta = 0.5$, and $\gamma = 0.6$. Graph the data and the forecasts.

16.39 ● Use the Holt–Winters seasonal method to obtain forecasts of sales up to eight quarters ahead based on the data of Exercise 16.19. Employ smoothing constants $\alpha = 0.5$, $\beta = 0.6$, and $\gamma = 0.7$. Graph the data and the forecasts.

16.6 AUTOREGRESSIVE MODELS

In this section we present a different approach to time-series forecasting. This approach involves using the available data to estimate parameters of a model of the process that might have generated the time series. In this section we consider one widely used procedure, *autoregressive models*, that is based on the model-building approach.

In Section 13.3 we introduced the use of lagged dependent variables in multiple regression models, and that approach is the basis of the models we discuss here. Essentially, the idea is to regard a time series as a series of random variables. For practical purposes we might often be prepared to assume that these random variables all have the same means and variances. However, we cannot assume that they are independent of each other. Certainly, if we consider a series of product sales, it is very likely that sales in adjacent periods are correlated with each other. Correlation patterns such as those between adjacent periods are sometimes referred to as *autocorrelation*.

In principle, any number of autocorrelation patterns is possible. However, some are considerably more likely to arise than others. A particularly attractive possibility arises when we think of a fairly strong correlation between adjacent observations in time: a less strong correlation between observations two time periods apart, a weaker correlation yet between values three time periods apart, and so on. A very simple autocorrelation pattern of this sort arises when the correlation between adjacent values in the time series is some number—say, $\phi_1 (0 \leq |\phi_1| \leq 1)$—that between values two time periods apart is ϕ_1^2, that between values three time periods apart is ϕ_1^3, and so on. Thus, if we let x_t denote the value of the series at time t, we have under this model of autocorrelation

$$\text{Corr}(x_t, x_{t-j}) = \phi_1^j \qquad (j = 1, 2, 3, \ldots)$$

This autocorrelation structure gives rise to a time-series model of the form

$$x_t = \gamma + \phi_1 x_{t-1} + \varepsilon_t$$

where γ and ϕ_1 are fixed parameters and the random variables ε_t have means 0 and fixed variances for all t and are not correlated with each other. The purpose of the parameter γ is to allow for the possibility that the series x_t has some mean other than 0. Otherwise, this is the model we used in Section 13.7 to represent autocorrelation in the error terms of a regression equation. It is called a *first-order autoregressive model*.

The first-order autoregressive model expresses the current value, x_t, of a series in terms of the previous value, x_{t-1}, and a nonautocorrelated random variable, ε_t. Since the random variable ε_t is not autocorrelated, it is unpredictable. For series generated by the first-order autoregressive model, forecasts of future values depend only on the most recent value of the series. However, in many applications we would want to use more than this one observation as a basis for forecasting. An obvious extension of the model would be to make the current value of the series dependent on the two most recent observations. Thus, we could use a model

$$x_t = \gamma + \phi_1 x_{t-1} + \phi_2 x_{t-2} + \varepsilon_t$$

where γ, ϕ_1, and ϕ_2 are fixed parameters. This is called a *second-order autoregressive model*.

More generally, for any positive integer p, the current value of the series can be made (linearly) dependent on the p previous values through the autoregressive model of order p:

$$x_t = \gamma + \phi_1 x_{t-1} + \phi_2 x_{t-2} + \cdots + \phi_p x_{t-p} + \varepsilon_t$$

where γ, ϕ_1, ϕ_2,..., ϕ_p are fixed parameters. This equation depicts the general autoregressive model. In the remainder of this section we consider the fitting of such models and their use in forecasting future values.

Suppose that we have a series of observations x_1, x_2,..., x_n. We want to use these to estimate the unknown parameters γ, ϕ_1, ϕ_2,..., ϕ_p for which the sum of squared discrepancies

$$SS = \sum_{t=p+1}^{n} (x_t - \gamma - \phi_1 x_{t-1} - \phi_2 x_{t-2} - \cdots - \phi_p x_{t-p})^2$$

is smallest. Hence, the estimation can be carried out using a multiple regression program. We demonstrate this procedure in Example 16.3 for the Lydia Pinkham sales data.

Autoregressive Models and Their Estimation

Let x_t ($t = 1, 2,..., n$) be a time series. A model that can often be used effectively to represent that series is the autoregressive model of order p:

$$x_t = \gamma + \phi_1 x_{t-1} + \phi_2 x_{t-2} + \cdots + \phi_p x_{t-p} + \varepsilon_t \tag{16.11}$$

where γ, ϕ_1, ϕ_2,..., ϕ_p are fixed parameters and the ε_t are random variables that have means 0 and constant variances and are uncorrelated with one another.

The parameters of the autoregressive model are estimated through a least squares algorithm, as the values of γ, ϕ_1, ϕ_2,..., ϕ_p for which the sum of squares

$$SS = \sum_{t=p+1}^{n} (x_t - \gamma - \phi_1 x_{t-1} - \phi_2 x_{t-2} - \cdots - \phi_0 x_{t-p})^2 \tag{16.12}$$

is a minimum.

Example 16.3   Forecasting Sales Data (Autoregressive Model)

You have been asked to develop an autoregressive model to forecast the Lydia **Pinkham Sales Data**.

Solution To use an autoregressive model to generate forecasts of future values, it is necessary to fix a value for p, the order of the autoregression. In making this choice we must choose p large enough to account for all of the important autocorrelation behavior of the series. But in addition we do not want p to be so large that we are including irrelevant parameters, and as a result having inefficient estimation of the important parameters. In general, parsimonious—simple but sufficient to accomplish the objective—models are preferred for good time-series forecasting.

One possibility is to fix the value of p arbitrarily, perhaps on the basis of past experience, with similar data sets. An alternative approach is to set some maximal order, K, of the autoregression and fit, in turn, models of order $p = K, K-1, K-2,...$. For each value of p, the null hypothesis that the final autoregression parameter, ϕ_p, of the model is 0 is tested against a two-sided alternative. The procedure terminates when we find a value of p for which this null hypothesis is not rejected. Our aim, then, is to test the null hypothesis

$$H_0 : \phi_p = 0$$

against the alternative

$$H_1 : \phi_p \neq 0$$

In Chapter 11 we developed procedures for testing the null hypothesis, H_0. Basically, we know that the ratio of the coefficient estimate divided by the coefficient standard error follows a Student's t distribution. The Minitab regression output (and the regression output from any statistical package) includes that Student's t calculation and in addition the probability of the null hypothesis being true (the p-value for the null hypothesis) given the computed Student's t.

Forecasting from Estimated Autoregressive Models

Suppose that we have observations $x_1, x_2,..., x_t$ from a time series and that an autoregressive model of order p has been fitted to these data. Write the estimated model as follows:

$$x_t = \hat{\gamma} + \hat{\phi}_1 x_{t-1} + \hat{\phi}_2 x_{t-2} + \cdots + \hat{\phi}_p x_{t-p} + \varepsilon_t \tag{16.13}$$

Standing at time n, we obtain forecasts of future values of the series from

$$\hat{x}_{n+h} = \hat{\gamma} + \hat{\phi}_1 \hat{x}_{n+h-1} + \hat{\phi}_2 \hat{x}_{n+h-2} + \cdots + \cdots \hat{\phi}_p \hat{x}_{n+h-p} \quad (h = 1, 2, 3,...) \tag{16.14}$$

where for $h > 0$, $\hat{x}_{n+h}$ is the forecast of x_{t+h} standing at time n, and for $h \leq 0$, $\hat{x}_{t+h}$ is simply the observed value of x_{t+h}.

Figure 16.18 presents abbreviated copies of Minitab regression output for autoregressive models using the Lydia Pinkham sales data with $p = 1, 2, 3, 4$.

We will apply this approach for the Pinkham sales data, using a 10% significance level for our tests. Using the results in Figure 16.18, we begin with the regression with $p = 4$. We find that the coefficient of x_{t-4} has a Student's t statistic of -1.39 and a

Figure 16.18

Autoregressive
Models for the
Lydia Pinkham
Sales Data
(Minitab Output)

Regression with p = 1

```
Sales = 193 + 0.883 Salelag1
29 cases used 1 cases contain missing values

Predictor          Coef          StDev            T            P
Constant          193.3          189.0          1.02        0.316
Salelag1         0.8831         0.1024          8.62        0.000

S = 207.0     R-Sq = 73.4%     R-Sq(adj) = 72.4%
```

Regression with p = 2

```
Sales = 314 + 1.18 Salelag1 - 0.358 Salelag2
28 cases used 2 cases contain missing values

Predictor          Coef          StDev            T            P
Constant          313.7          192.5          1.63        0.116
Salelag1         1.1801         0.1870          6.31        0.000
Salelag2        -0.3578         0.1914         -1.87        0.073

S = 199.6     R-Sq = 76.9%     R-Sq(adj) = 75.1%
```

Regression with p = 3

```
Sales = 322 + 1.19 Salelag1 - 0.317 Salelag2 - 0.057 Salelag3
27 cases used 3 cases contain missing values

Predictor          Coef          StDev            T            P
Constant          322.3          215.7          1.49        0.149
Salelag1         1.1881         0.2065          5.75        0.000
Salelag2        -0.3168         0.3081         -1.03        0.315
Salelag3        -0.0574         0.2098         -0.27        0.787

S = 203.0     R-Sq = 78.1%     R-Sq(adj) = 75.2%
```

Regression with p = 4

```
Sales = 446 + 1.19 Salelag1 - 0.439 Salelag2 + 0.286 Salelag3 - 0.291
Salelag4
26 cases used 4 cases contain missing values
Predictor          Coef          StDev            T            P
Constant          446.2          232.8          1.92        0.069
Salelag1         1.1937         0.2108          5.66        0.000
Salelag2        -0.4391         0.3238         -1.36        0.190
Salelag3         0.2859         0.3174          0.90        0.378
Salelag4        -0.2914         0.2101         -1.39        0.180
S = 202.6         R-Sq = 80.1%        R-Sq(adj) = 76.3%
```

p-value of 0.180. Thus, we cannot reject the null hypothesis that the coefficient is 0, and we move on to the regression with $p = 3$. Here, we see that the coefficient of x_{t-3} has a Student's t statistic equal to -0.27 and a p-value of 0.787. Again, we cannot reject the null hypothesis that this coefficient is 0. For the regression model with $p = 2$ we see that the coefficient of x_{t-2} has a Student's t statistic of -1.87 and a p-value of 0.073. Thus, we can reject the null hypothesis that the coefficient of x_{t-2} is 0. Our chosen model then is the one with two lagged values, $p = 2$. The final equation is as follows:

$$\hat{x}_t = 313.7 + 1.1801x_{t-1} - 0.3578x_{t-2}$$

Now that we have the model, we want to apply it to obtain forecasts for the Lydia Pinkham sales data. We begin by noting that the last two values in the data series are as follows:

$$x_{29} = 1{,}387 \quad \text{and} \quad x_{30} = 1{,}289$$

We can now predict the next value x_{31} as follows:

$$\hat{x}_{31} = 313.69 + 1.180x_{30} - 0.358x_{29}$$
$$= 313.69 + (1.180)(1{,}289) - (0.358)(1{,}387) = 1{,}338.2$$

Figure 16.19
Predicted Values
from
Autoregressive
Model for
Pinkham Sales
Data

```
Sales = 314 + 1.18 Salelag1 - 0.358 Salelag2

28 cases used 2 cases contain missing values

Predictor        Coef        StDev          T          P
Constant        313.7        192.5       1.63      0.116
Salelag1       1.1801       0.1870       6.31      0.000
Salelag2      -0.3578       0.1914      -1.87      0.073

S = 199.6      R-Sq = 76.9%      R-Sq(adj) = 75.1%


Predicted Values

     Fit   StDev Fit          95.0% CI              95.0% PI
  1338.6        63.5    ( 1207.7,  1469.4)    (  907.1,  1770.1)
```

Figure 16.20
Sales of Lydia
Pinkham and
Forecasts Based
on a Fitted
Second-Order
Autoregressive
Model

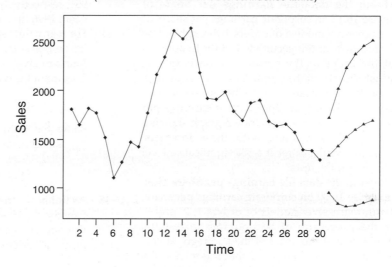

Time Series Plot for Sales
(with forecasts and their 95% confidence limits)

We recognize that the predicted value of the error term, ε_t, is 0. Now, we can forecast the next value in the series following the same procedure, except that we must use the forecast value for x_{31}—that is, $\hat{x}_t$

$$\hat{x}_{32} = 313.7 + 1.180\,\hat{x}_{31} - 0.358x_{30}$$
$$= 313.69 + (1.180)(1{,}338.2) - (0.358)(1{,}289) = 1{,}431.30$$

These calculations can be performed directly by Minitab—or any other good statistical package—and the results are shown in Figure 16.19.

We can continue with this process and obtain predictions for as many future periods as we like. The sales time series and the forecasts for six periods are shown in Figure 16.20.

EXERCISES

Application Exercises

16.40 Using the data of Table 16.10, estimate a first-order autoregressive model for the index of volume of shares traded. Use the fitted model to obtain forecasts for the next 4 days.

16.41 The data file **Trading Volume** shows the volume of transactions (in hundreds of thousands) in shares of a corporation over a period of 12 weeks. Using these data, estimate a first-order autoregressive model, and use the fitted model to obtain forecasts of volume for the next 3 weeks.

16.42 🌐 Using the data file **Housing Starts** of Exercise 16.16, estimate autoregressive models of orders 1 through 4. Use the method of this section to test the hypothesis that the order of the autoregression is $(p - 1)$ against the alternative that the order is p, with a significance level of 10%. Select one of these models, and calculate forecasts of housing starts for the next 5 years. Draw a time plot showing the original observations together with the forecasts. Would different forecasts result if a significance level of 5% was used for the tests of autoregressive order?

16.43 🌐 From the data file **Earnings per Share** of Exercise 16.17 on corporate earnings per share, fit autoregressive models of orders 1 through 4. Use the procedure of this section to test the hypothesis that the order of the autoregression is $(p - 1)$ against the alternative that the true order is p, with a 10% significance level. Choose one of these models, and compute forecasts of earnings per share for the next 5 years. Draw a graph showing the original data along with these forecasts. Would the results differ if a 5% significance level was used for the tests?

16.44 🌐 Refer to the data file **Earnings per Share 16.30** of Exercise 16.30 on corporate earnings per share. Fit autoregressive models of orders 1, 2, and 3. Use the procedure of Section 16.6 to test the hypothesis that the order of the autoregression is $(p - 1)$ against the alternative that it is p, at a 10% significance level, and thereby select a value for autoregressive order. Use the selected model to generate earnings-per-share forecasts up to 4 years ahead. Draw a time plot of the observations and forecasts. Would different results be obtained with 5% significance tests?

16.45 🌐 In Figure 16.18, fitted autoregressive models of orders 1 through 4 are given for annual sales data. We then selected a model by testing the null hypothesis of autoregression of order $(p - 1)$ against the alternative of autoregression of order p at the 10% significance level. Repeat this procedure, but test at the 5% significance level.

a. What autoregressive model is now selected?
b. Obtain forecasts of sales for the next 3 years, based on this selected model.

16.46 For a certain product it was found that annual sales volume could be well described by a third-order autoregressive model. The estimated model obtained was as follows:

$$x_t = 202 + 1.10x_{t-1} - 0.48x_{t-2} + 0.17x_{t-3} + \varepsilon_t$$

For 1993, 1994, and 1995, sales were 867, 923, and 951, respectively. Calculate sales forecasts for the years 1996 through 1998.

16.47 For many time series, particularly prices in speculative markets, the *random walk* model has been found to give a good representation of actual data. This model is written as follows:

$$x_t = x_{t-1} + \varepsilon_t$$

Show that, if this model is appropriate, forecasts of x_{n+h} standing at time n, are given by the following:

$$\hat{x}_{n+h} = x_n \qquad (h = 1, 2, 3, \ldots)$$

16.48 🌐 Refer to the data file **Hourly Earnings** of Exercise 16.35, showing earnings over 24 months. Denote the observations x_t ($t = 1, 2, \ldots, 24$). Now, form the series of first differences:

$$z_t = x_t - x_{t-1} \quad (t = 2, 3, \ldots, 24)$$

Fit autoregressive models of orders 1 through 4 to the series z_t. Using the approach of this section for testing the hypothesis that the autoregressive order is $(p - 1)$ against the alternative of order p, with a 10% significance level, select one of these models. Using the selected model, find forecasts for z_t, where $t = 25, 26$, and 27. Hence, obtain forecasts of earnings for the next 3 months.

16.7 AUTOREGRESSIVE INTEGRATED MOVING AVERAGE MODELS

In this section we briefly introduce an approach to time-series forecasting that is widely used in business applications. The models to be discussed include, as special cases, the autoregressive models discussed in Section 16.6.

In a classic book, George Box and Gwilyn Jenkins introduced a methodology sufficiently versatile to provide a moderately skillful user with good results for a wide range of forecasting problems that occur in practice (Reference 1). The Box–Jenkins approach requires that we first define a very broad class of models from which forecasts can be derived. Next we develop a methodology for picking, on the basis of the characteristics of the available data, a suitable model for any forecasting problem.

The general class of models is the class of autoregressive integrated moving average models, or **ARIMA models**. These are rather natural extensions of the autoregressive models of Section 16.6. Moreover, the simple exponential smoothing and Holt–Winters predictors of Section 16.5 can be derived from specific members of this general class, as can many other widely used forecasting algorithms. The models and the Box–Jenkins time-series analysis techniques can be generalized to allow for seasonality and also to deal with related time series so that future values of one series can be predicted from information not only on its own past but also on the past of other relevant series. This last possibility allows an approach to forecasting that generalizes the regression procedures discussed in Chapters 11 through 13.

It is not possible in the space available to provide a full discussion of the Box–Jenkins methodology. (For an introduction to this methodology, see Reference 3.) In essence, it involves three stages:

1. Based on summary statistics that are readily calculated from the available data, the analyst selects a specific model that might be appropriate from the general class. This is not simply a matter of automatically following a set of rules, but rather requires a certain amount of judgment and experience. However, one is not forever committed to the model chosen at this stage but can abandon it in favor of some alternative at a later stage of the analysis if that appears desirable.
2. The specific model chosen will almost invariably have some unknown coefficients. These must be estimated from the available data using efficient statistical techniques, such as least squares.
3. Finally, checks are applied to determine whether the estimated model provides an adequate representation of the available time-series data. Any inadequacies revealed at this stage may suggest some alternative specification, and the process of model selection, coefficient estimation, and model checking is iterated until a satisfactory model is found.

The Box–Jenkins approach to forecasting has the great advantage of flexibility— a wide range of predictors is available, and choice among them is based on data evidence. Moreover, when this approach to forecasting has been compared with other methods, using actual economic and business time series, it has usually been found to perform very well. Thus, the procedure can be said to have survived the acid test: In practice, it works!

In concluding this brief discussion, note that computer programs for performing a time-series analysis through the fitting to data of ARIMA models are widely available—including a set of procedures in Minitab. However, the method does have a drawback compared with other simpler procedures discussed in earlier sections of this chapter. Because flexibility is allowed in choosing an appropriate model from the general class, the Box–Jenkins approach is more costly in terms of skilled worker time than methods that force a single model structure onto every time series.

KEY WORDS

CHAPTER EXERCISES AND APPLICATIONS

16.49   Refer to Exercise 16.35 and the data file **Hourly Earnings**, which shows monthly hourly earnings in manufacturing.

a. Obtain an index with month 1 as base.
b. Obtain an index with month 5 as base.

16.50   A library purchases both books and journals. The accompanying table and data file **Library Purchases** show the average prices (in dollars) paid for each and the quantities purchased over a period of 6 years. Use year 1 as base.

	Books		Journals	
Year	Price	Quantity	Price	Quantity
1	20.4	694	30.1	155
2	22.3	723	33.4	159
3	23.3	687	36.0	160
4	24.6	731	39.8	163
5	27.0	742	45.7	160
6	29.2	748	50.7	155

a. Find the unweighted aggregate index of prices.
b. Find the Laspeyres price index.
c. Find the Laspeyres quantity index.

16.51   Explain the statement that a time series can be viewed as being made up of a number of components. Provide examples of business and economic time series for which you would expect particular components to be important.

16.52   In many business applications, forecasts for future values of time series, such as sales and earnings, are made exclusively on the basis of past information on the time series in question. What features of time-series behavior are exploited in the production of such forecasts?

16.53   A manager in charge of inventory control requires sales forecasts for several products, on a monthly basis, over the next 6 months. This manager has available monthly sales records over the past 4 years for each of these products. He decides to use, as forecasts for each of the next 6 months, the average monthly sales over the previous 4 years. Do you think this is a good strategy? Provide reasons.

16.54   What is meant by the seasonal adjustment of a time series? Explain why government agencies expend a large amount of effort on the seasonal adjustment of economic time series.

16.55   The data file **US Industrial Production** shows an index of U.S. industrial production over 14 years.

a. Test this series for randomness using the runs test.
b. Draw a time plot of these data and discuss the features revealed by the graph.
c. Compute the series of simple centered 3-point moving averages. Graph this smoothed series, and discuss its behavior.

16.56   The data file **Product Sales** shows 24 annual observations on sales of a product.

a. Use the large-sample variant of the runs test to test this series for randomness.
b. Draw a time plot of the data and discuss the characteristics of the series shown by this graph.
c. Compute the series of simple centered 5-point moving averages. Graph this smoothed series and discuss its behavior.

16.57   The data file **Quarterly Earnings 16.57** shows quarterly earnings per share of a corporation over 7 years.

a. Draw a time plot of these data. Does this graph suggest the presence of a strong seasonal component?
b. Use the seasonal index method to obtain a seasonally adjusted series.

16.58   The data file **Price Index** shows 15 monthly values on the price index of a commodity.

a. Calculate the series of simple centered 3-point moving averages.
b. Draw a time plot of the smoothed series and comment on its characteristics.

16.59   Refer to Exercise 16.56 and the data file **Product Sales**. Use simple exponential smoothing with smoothing constant $\alpha = 0.5$ to obtain forecasts of sales for the next 3 years.

16.60   Refer to Exercise 16.58 and the data file **Price Index**. Use the Holt–Winters method with smoothing constants $\alpha = 0.7$ and $\beta = 0.6$ to obtain forecasts of the price index for the next 4 months.

16.61 ⊘ Refer to Exercise 16.57 and the data file **Quarterly Earnings 16.57**. Use the Holt-Winters seasonal method with smoothing constants $\alpha = 0.6$, $\beta = 0.6$, and $\gamma = 0.8$ to obtain forecasts of this earnings-per-share series for the next four quarters.

16.62 ⊘ Using the data file **Product Sales** of Exercise 16.59, estimate autoregressive models of orders 1 through 4 for product sales. Using the procedure of Section 16.6 for testing the hypothesis that the autoregressive order is $(p - 1)$ against the alternative that the order is p, with a significance level of 10%, choose one of these models. Compute forecasts for the next 3 years from the chosen model.

REFERENCES

1. Box, G. E. P., and G. M. Jenkins. 1970. *Time Series Analysis, Forecasting, and Control*. San Francisco: Holden-Day.

2. Granger, C. W., and P. Newbold. 1986. *Forecasting Economic Time Series*, 2nd ed. Orlando, FL: Academic Press.

3. Newbold, P., and T. Bos. 1994. *Introductory Business Forecasting*, 2nd ed. Cincinnati, OH: South-Western.

Chapter 17

Additional Topics in Sampling

Introduction

In some situations it is desirable to break down the population into sub-groups called strata, so that each individual member of the population belongs to one, and only one, of the strata. The basis of the stratum might be some particular identifiable characteristic of the population of special interest to the researcher. This type of sampling is called stratified sampling. In this chapter we introduce confidence interval estimation of a population mean, population total, and population proportion for stratified sampling, and we consider allocation of sample size under proportional and optimal allocation. A brief discussion of cluster sampling, two-phase sampling, and non-probabilistic sampling methods is also presented.

17.1 STRATIFIED SAMPLING

Suppose that you decide to investigate the views of students on your campus concerning some sensitive topic, and the framing of appropriately worded questions could be difficult. It is likely that you would want to ask several questions of every sample member and so, given limited resources, would be able to take only a fairly small sample. You would presumably select a simple random sample of, say, 100 students from a list of all students on campus. Suppose, however, that, on closer inspection of the records of the sample members, you find that only two of them are business majors, though the population proportion of business majors is far higher than this. Your problem at this stage is twofold. First, you may well be interested in comparing the views of business majors with those of the rest of the student population. This is hardly feasible, given their minimal representation in your sample. Second, you may suspect that the views of business majors on this question will differ from those of their fellow students. If that was the case, you would worry about the reliability of inference based on a sample in which this group is seriously underrepresented.

You could perhaps console yourself with the thought that, since you have taken a random sample, any estimators derived in the usual way will be unbiased, and the resulting inference, in the statistical sense, will be strictly valid. However, a little reflection should convince you that this is scant consolation indeed! All that unbiasedness indicates is that, if the sampling procedure is repeated a very large number of times and the estimator calculated, its average will be equal to the corresponding population value. But, in fact, you are *not* going to repeat the sampling procedure a large number of times. You have to base your conclusions on *just a single sample*, and the fact that business majors could have been overrepresented in other samples you might have drawn, so that things "average out" in the long run, is not terribly useful.

There is a second tempting possibility, one that is in many ways preferable to proceeding with the original sample. You could simply discard the original sample and take another. If the constitution of the sample achieved at the second attempt looks more representative of the population at large, you may well be better off to proceed with it. The difficulty now is that the sampling procedure you have adopted—where the population is to be sampled until you achieve a sample you like the looks of—is very difficult to formalize and, consequently, the sample results are very hard to analyze with any statistical validity. This is no longer simple random sampling, and the procedures of Chapter 7 are, therefore, not strictly valid.

Fortunately, a third alternative sampling scheme exists to afford protection against just this type of problem. If it is suspected at the outset that particular identifiable characteristics of population members are germane to the subject of inquiry or if particular subgroups of the population are of special interest to the investigator, it is not necessary (and probably not desirable) to be content with simple random sampling as a means of selecting the sample members. Instead, the population can be broken down into subgroups, or *strata*, and a simple random sample taken from each stratum. The only requirement is that each individual member of the population be identifiable as belonging to one, and only one, of the strata.

Stratified Random Sampling
Suppose that a population of N individuals can be subdivided into K mutually exclusive and collectively exhaustive groups, or strata. **Stratified random sampling** is the selection of independent simple random samples from each stratum of the population. If the K strata in the population contain N_1, N_2,..., N_K members, then

$$N_1 + N_2 + \cdots + N_K = N$$

There is no need to take the same number of sample members from every stratum. Denote the numbers in the sample by $n_1, n_2,..., n_K$. Then the total number of sample members is as follows:

$$n_1 + n_2 + \cdots + n_K = n$$

The population of students whose views are to be canvassed could be divided into two strata—business majors and non-business majors. Less straightforward stratification is also possible. Suppose that, on some other topic, you believe that a student's gender and class year (senior, junior, sophomore, or freshman) are both potentially relevant. In that case, to satisfy the requirement that the strata be mutually exclusive and collectively exhaustive, eight strata—senior women, senior men, and so on—are needed.

Later in this section the question of how to allocate the sampling effort among the strata is considered. An attractive possibility, often employed in practice, is *proportional allocation*: The proportion of sample members from any stratum is the same as the proportion of population members in that stratum.

Analysis of Results from Stratified Random Sampling

The analysis of the results of a stratified random sample is relatively straightforward. Let $\mu_1, \mu_2,... \mu_K$ denote the population means in the K strata and $\bar{x}_1, \bar{x}_2,... \bar{x}_K$ the corresponding sample means. Consider a particular stratum—say, the jth stratum. Then, since a simple random sample has been taken in this stratum, the stratum sample mean is an unbiased estimator of the population mean μ_j. Also, from an unbiased estimation procedure for the variance of the stratum sample mean, the point estimate is

$$\hat{\sigma}_{\bar{x}_j}^2 = \frac{s_j^2}{n_j} \times \frac{(N_j - n_j)}{N_j - 1}$$

where s_j^2 is the sample variance in the jth stratum. Inference about individual strata can therefore be made in the same way as in Section 7.6.

Generally, inferences about the overall population mean μ are of interest where

$$\mu = \frac{N_1\mu_1 + N_2\mu_2 + \cdots + N_K\mu_K}{N} = \frac{1}{N}\sum_{j=1}^{K} N_j\mu_j$$

A natural point estimate is provided by the following:

$$\bar{x}_{st} = \frac{1}{N}\sum_{j=1}^{K} N_j\bar{x}_j$$

An unbiased estimator of the variance of the estimator of μ follows from the fact that the samples in each stratum are independent of one another, and the point estimate is given by the following:

$$\hat{\sigma}_{\bar{x}_{st}}^2 = \frac{1}{N^2}\sum_{j=1}^{K} N_j^2\, \hat{\sigma}_{\bar{x}_j}^2$$

Inferences about the overall population mean can be based on these results.

Estimation of the Population Mean, Stratified Random Sample

Suppose that random samples of n_j individuals are taken from strata containing N_j individuals ($j = 1, 2,..., K$). Let

$$\sum_{j=1}^{K} N_j = N \qquad \text{and} \qquad \sum_{j=1}^{K} n_j = n$$

Denote the sample means and variances in the strata by $\bar{x}_j$ and s_j^2 ($j = 1, 2,..., K$) and the overall population mean by μ.

1. An unbiased estimation procedure for the overall population mean μ yields the following point estimate:

$$\bar{x}_{st} = \frac{1}{N} \sum_{j=1}^{K} N_j \bar{x}_j \qquad (17.1)$$

2. An unbiased estimation procedure for the variance of our estimator of the overall population mean yields the point estimate

$$\hat{\sigma}_{\bar{x}_{st}}^2 = \frac{1}{N^2} \sum_{j=1}^{K} N_j^2 \hat{\sigma}_{\bar{x}_j}^2 \qquad (17.2)$$

where

$$\hat{\sigma}_{\bar{x}_j}^2 = \frac{s_j^2}{n_j} \times \frac{(N_j - n_j)}{N_j - 1} \qquad (17.3)$$

3. Provided the sample size is large, $100(1 - \alpha)\%$ **confidence intervals for the population mean for stratified random samples** are obtained from the following:

$$\bar{x}_{st} - z_{\alpha/2} \hat{\sigma}_{\bar{x}_{st}} < \mu < \bar{x}_{st} + z_{\alpha/2} \hat{\sigma}_{\bar{x}_{st}} \qquad (17.4)$$

Example 17.1   Restaurant Chain (Estimation)

A restaurant chain has 60 restaurants in Illinois, 50 in Indiana, and 45 in Ohio. Management is considering adding a new item to the menus. To test the likely demand for this item, it was introduced on the menus of random samples of 12 restaurants in Illinois, 10 in Indiana, and 9 in Ohio. Using the subscripts 1, 2, and 3 to denote Illinois, Indiana, and Ohio, respectively, the sample means and standard deviations for numbers of orders received for this item per restaurant in the three states in a week were as follows:

$$\bar{x}_1 = 21.2 \quad s_1 = 12.8$$

$$\bar{x}_2 = 13.3 \quad s_2 = 11.4$$

$$\bar{x}_3 = 26.1 \quad s_3 = 9.2$$

Estimate the mean number of weekly orders per restaurant, μ, for all restaurants in this chain.

Solution   It is known that

$$N_1 = 60 \quad N_2 = 50 \quad N_3 = 45 \quad N = 155$$

$$n_1 = 12 \quad n_2 = 10 \quad n_3 = 9 \quad n = 31$$

Our estimate of the population mean is as follows:

$$\bar{x}_{st} = \frac{1}{N} \sum_{j=1}^{K} N_j \bar{x}_j = \frac{(60)(21.2) + (50)(13.3) + (45)(26.1)}{155} = 20.1$$

Thus, the estimated mean number of weekly orders per restaurant is 20.1.

The next step is to calculate the quantities:

$$\hat{\sigma}_{\bar{x}_1}^2 = \frac{s_1^2}{n_1} \times \frac{(N_1 - n_1)}{N_1 - 1} = \frac{(12.8)^2}{12} \times \frac{48}{59} = 11.108$$

$$\hat{\sigma}_{\bar{x}_2}^2 = \frac{s_2^2}{n_2} \times \frac{(N_2 - n_2)}{N_2 - 1} = \frac{(11.4)^2}{10} \times \frac{40}{49} = 10.609$$

$$\hat{\sigma}_{\bar{x}_3}^2 = \frac{s_3^2}{n_3} \times \frac{(N_3 - n_3)}{N_3 - 1} = \frac{(9.2)^2}{9} \times \frac{36}{44} = 7.695$$

Together with the individual stratum sample means, these quantities can be used to compute confidence intervals for the population means of the three strata, exactly as in Example 7.8 (although in this case the sample sizes are too small for comfort). Our concentration is on the overall population mean. To obtain confidence intervals for this quantity,

$$\hat{\sigma}_{\bar{x}_{st}}^2 = \frac{1}{N^2} \sum_{j=1}^{K} N_j^2 \sigma_{\bar{x}_j}^2$$

$$= \frac{(60)^2 (11.108) + (50)^2 (10.609) + (45)^2 (7.695)}{(155)^2} = 3.417$$

and on taking the square root

$$\hat{\sigma}_{\bar{x}_{st}} = 1.85$$

Thus, the 95% confidence interval for the mean number of orders per restaurant received in a week is

$$20.1 - (1.96)(1.85) < \mu < 20.1 + (1.96)(1.85)$$

or

$$16.5 < \mu < 23.7$$

The 95% confidence interval runs from 16.5 to 23.7 orders per restaurant.

Since the population total is the product of the population mean and the number of population members, these procedures can readily be modified to allow its estimation, as described next.

Estimation of the Population Total, Stratified Random Sample

Suppose that random samples of n_j individuals from strata containing N_j individuals ($j = 1, 2,..., K$) are selected and that the quantity to be estimated is the population total, $N\mu$.

1. An unbiased estimation procedure for $N\mu$ leads to the following point estimate:

$$N\bar{x}_{st} = \sum_{j=1}^{K} N_j \bar{x}_j \qquad (17.5)$$

2. An unbiased estimation procedure for the variance of our estimator of the population total yields the following estimate:

$$N^2 \hat{\sigma}_{\bar{x}_{st}}^2 = \sum_{j=1}^{K} N_j^2 \hat{\sigma}_{\bar{x}_j}^2 \qquad (17.6)$$

3. Provided the sample size is large, $100(1 - \alpha)\%$ **confidence intervals for the population total for stratified random samples** are obtained from the following:

$$N\bar{x}_{st} - z_{\alpha/2} N\hat{\sigma}_{\bar{x}_{st}} < N\mu < N\bar{x}_{st} + z_{\alpha/2} N\hat{\sigma}_{\bar{x}_{st}} \qquad (17.7)$$

Example 17.2 Total Annual Enrollment in Business Statistics (Estimation)

Of the 1,395 colleges in the United States, 364 have 2-year programs and 1,031 are 4-year schools. A simple random sample of 40 two-year schools and an independent simple random sample of 60 four-year schools were taken. The sample means and standard deviations of numbers of students enrolled in the past year in business statistics courses are given in the table. Estimate the total annual enrollment in business statistics courses.

	2-Year Schools	4-Year Schools
Mean	154.3	411.8
Standard Deviation	87.3	219.9

Solution   It is known that

$$N_1 = 364 \quad n_1 = 40 \quad \bar{x}_1 = 154.3 \quad s_1 = 87.3$$
$$N_2 = 1,031 \quad n_2 = 60 \quad \bar{x}_2 = 411.8 \quad s_2 = 219.9$$

Our estimate of the population total is as follows:

$$N\bar{x}_{st} = \sum_{j=1}^{K} N_j \bar{x}_j = (364)(154.3) + (1,031)(411.8) = 480,731$$

Next,

$$\hat{\sigma}_{\bar{x}_1}^2 = \frac{s_1^2}{n_1} \times \frac{(N_1 - n_1)}{N_1 - 1} = \frac{(87.3)^2}{40} \times \frac{324}{363} = 170.06$$

$$\hat{\sigma}^2_{\bar{x}_2} = \frac{s^2_2}{n_2} \times \frac{(N_2 - n_2)}{N_2 - 1} = \frac{(219.9)^2}{60} \times \frac{971}{1,030} = 759.77$$

Finally,

$$N^2 \hat{\sigma}^2_{\bar{x}_{st}} = \sum_{j=1}^{K} N_j^2 \hat{\sigma}^2_{\bar{x}_{st}} = (364)^2(170.06) + (1,031)^2(759.77) = 830,138,148.73 \quad \text{and, on}$$

taking the square root,

$$N \hat{\sigma}^2_{\bar{x}_{st}} = 28,812$$

For a 95% confidence interval,

$$z_{\alpha/2} = z_{0.025} = 1.96$$

The required 95% interval is, therefore,

$$480,731 - (1.96)(28,812) < N\mu < 480,731 + (1.96)(28,812)$$

or

$$424,259 < N\mu < 537,203$$

Thus, our 95% confidence interval runs from 424,259 to 537,203 students enrolled.

Next, consider the problem of estimating a population proportion based on a stratified random sample. Let $P_1, P_2,...,P_k$ be the population proportions in the K strata and $\hat{p}_1, \hat{p}_2,..., \hat{p}_k$ the corresponding sample proportions. If P denotes the overall population proportion, its estimate is based on the fact that

$$P = \frac{N_1 P_1 + N_2 P_2 + \cdots + N_K P_K}{N} = \frac{1}{N} \sum_{j=1}^{K} N_j P_j$$

Procedures to develop an **estimation of the population proportion from a stratified** random sample follow.

Estimation of the Population Proportion, Stratified Random Sample

Suppose that random samples of n_j individuals from strata containing N_j individuals ($j = 1, 2,..., K$) are obtained. Let P_j be the population proportion and $\hat{p}_j$ the sample proportion, in the jth stratum, of those possessing a particular characteristic. If P is the overall population proportion then,

1. an unbiased estimation procedure for P yields the following:

$$\hat{p}_{st} = \frac{1}{N} \sum_{j=1}^{K} N_j \hat{p}_j \tag{17.8}$$

2. an unbiased estimation procedure for the variance of our estimator of the overall population proportion is

$$\hat{\sigma}^2_{\hat{p}_{st}} = \frac{1}{N^2} \sum_{j=1}^{K} N_j^2 \hat{\sigma}^2_{\hat{p}_j} \tag{17.9}$$

where

$$\hat{\sigma}_{\hat{p}_j}^2 = \frac{\hat{p}_j(1 - \hat{p}_j)}{n_j - 1} \times \frac{(N_j - n_j)}{N_j - 1} \tag{17.10}$$

is the estimate of the variance of the sample proportion in the *j*th stratum.

3. Provided the sample size is large, $100(1 - \alpha)\%$ **confidence intervals for the population proportion for stratified random samples** are obtained from the following:

$$\hat{p}_{st} - z_{\alpha/2}\hat{\sigma}_{\hat{p}_{st}} < P < \hat{p}_{st} + z_{\alpha/2}\sigma_{\hat{p}_{st}} \tag{17.11}$$

Example 17.3 Statistics Taught in Economics Departments (Estimation)

In the study of Example 17.2, suppose that it was found that business statistics was taught by members of the economics department in 7 of the 2-year colleges and 13 of the 4-year colleges in the sample. Estimate the proportion of all colleges in which this course is taught in the economics department.

Solution   It is known that

$$N_1 = 364 \qquad n_1 = 40 \qquad \hat{p}_1 = \frac{7}{40} = 0.175$$

$$N_2 = 1{,}031 \qquad n_2 = 60 \qquad \hat{p}_2 = \frac{13}{60} = 0.217$$

Our estimate of the population proportion is as follows:

$$\hat{p}_{st} = \frac{1}{N}\sum_{j=1}^{K} N_j\hat{p}_j = \frac{(364)(0.175) + (1{,}031)(0.217)}{1{,}395} = 0.206$$

Thus, it is estimated that in 20.6% of all colleges, the economics department teaches the course.

Next,

$$\hat{\sigma}_{\hat{p}_1}^2 = \frac{\hat{p}_1(1 - \hat{p}_1)}{n_1 - 1} \times \frac{(N_1 - n_1)}{N_1 - 1} = \frac{(0.175)(0.825)}{39} \times \frac{324}{363} = 0.003304$$

$$\hat{\sigma}_{\hat{p}_2}^2 = \frac{\hat{p}_2(1 - \hat{p}_2)}{n_2 - 1} \times \frac{(N_2 - n_2)}{N_2 - 1} = \frac{(0.217)(0.783)}{59} \times \frac{971}{1{,}030} = 0.002715$$

Together with the individual stratum sample proportions, these values can be used to calculate confidence intervals for the two stratum population proportions, exactly as in Example 7.10. Here, focus is given to interval estimation for the overall population proportion, for which

$$\hat{\sigma}_{\hat{p}_{st}}^2 = \frac{1}{N^2}\sum_{j=1}^{K} N_j^2\hat{\sigma}_{\hat{p}_j}^2 = \frac{(364)^2(0.003304) + (1{,}031)^2(0.002715)}{(1{,}395)^2} = 0.001708$$

so taking the square root yields the following:

$$\hat{\sigma}_{\hat{p}_{st}} = 0.0413$$

For a 90% confidence level,

$$z_{\alpha/2} = z_{0.05} = 1.645$$

and the 90% confidence interval for the population proportion from a stratified random sample is as follows:

$$(0.206) - (1.645)(0.0413) < P < (0.206) + (1.645)(0.0413)$$
$$0.138 < P < 0.274$$

This interval runs from 13.8% to 27.4% of all colleges.

Allocation of Sample Effort Among Strata

The question of the allocation of the sample effort among the various strata remains to be discussed. Assuming that a total of n sample members is to be selected, how many of these sample observations should be allocated to each stratum? In fact, the survey in question may have multiple objectives, meaning that no clear-cut answer is available. Nevertheless, it is possible to specify criteria for choice that the investigator might keep in mind. If little or nothing is known beforehand about the population and if there are no strong requirements for the production of information about sparsely populated individual strata, a natural choice is *proportional allocation*.

Proportional Allocation: Sample Size

The proportion of sample members in any stratum is the same as the proportion of population members in that stratum. Thus, for the jth stratum

$$\frac{n_j}{n} = \frac{N_j}{N} \tag{17.12}$$

so that the **sample size for the jth stratum using proportional allocation** is as follows:

$$n_j = \frac{N_j}{N} \times n \tag{17.13}$$

This intuitively reasonable allocation mechanism is frequently employed and generally provides a satisfactory analysis. Notice that proportional allocation was used in Example 17.1. A total of $N=155$ restaurants was divided into three strata (Illinois, Indiana, and Ohio). A sample of $n = 31$ was selected with

$$n_1 = \frac{60}{155} \times 31 = 12 \qquad n_2 = \frac{50}{155} \times 31 = 10 \qquad n_3 = \frac{45}{155} \times 31 = 9$$

Sometimes strict adherence to proportional allocation will produce relatively few observations in strata in which the investigator is particularly interested. In that case inference about the population parameters of these particular strata could be quite imprecise. In these circumstances one might prefer to allocate more observations to such strata than is dictated by proportional allocation. In

Example 17.2 and Example 17.3, 364 of the 1,395 colleges are 2-year schools, and a sample of 100 observations is to be taken. If proportional allocation had been used, the number of 2-year schools in the sample would have been as follows:

$$n_1 = \frac{N_1}{N} \times n = \frac{364}{1,395} \times 100 = 26$$

Since the publisher was particularly interested in acquiring information about this market, it was thought that a sample of only 26 observations would be inadequate. For this reason, 40 of the 100 sample observations were allocated to this stratum.

If the sole objective of a survey is to estimate as precisely as possible an overall population parameter, such as the mean, total, or proportion, and if enough is known about the population, it is possible to derive an *optimal allocation*.

Optimal Allocation: Sample Size for *j*th Stratum, Overall Population Mean or Total

If it is required to estimate an overall population mean or total and if the population variances in the individual strata are denoted σ_j^2, it can be shown that the most precise estimators are obtained with optimal allocation. The **sample size for the *j*th stratum using optimal allocation** is as follows:

$$n_j = \frac{N_j \sigma_j}{\sum\limits_{i=1}^{K} N_i \sigma_i} \times n \qquad (17.14)$$

This formula is intuitively plausible. Compared with proportional allocation, it allocates relatively more sample effort to strata in which the population variance is highest. That is to say, a larger sample size is required where the greater population variability exists. Thus, in Example 17.1, where proportional allocation was used, if the differences observed in the sample standard deviations correctly reflect differences in the population quantities, it would have been preferable to take fewer observations in the third stratum and more in the first.

An immediate objection arises to the use of Equation 17.14. It requires knowledge of the population standard deviations, σ_j, whereas very often one will not even have worthwhile estimates of these values before the sample is taken. This point is considered in the final section of the chapter.

Now, consider the sample size required under optimal allocation for a population proportion.

Optimal Allocation: Sample Size for *j*th Stratum, Population Proportion

For estimating the overall population proportion, estimators with the smallest possible variance are obtained by optimal allocation. The **sample size for the *j*th stratum for population proportion using optimal allocation** is as follows:

$$n_j = \frac{N_j \sqrt{P_j(1 - P_j)}}{\sum\limits_{i=1}^{K} N_i \sqrt{P_i(1 - P_i)}} \times n \qquad (17.15)$$

Compared with the proportional allocation, Equation 17.15 allocates more sample observations to strata in which the true population proportions are closest to 0.50. The difficulty in using Equation 17.15 is that it involves the unknown proportions P_j for ($j = 1, 2,..., K$), the very quantities that the survey is designed to estimate.

Nevertheless, sometimes prior knowledge about the population can provide at least a rough idea as to which strata have proportions closest to 0.5. In Example 17.3 the sample proportions suggest that the number of 2-year colleges in the sample should have been less than the number resulting from proportional allocation. The same conclusion holds for this study when one compares the sample standard deviations of Example 17.2 with Equation 17.14. In spite of this, it was decided that *more*, rather than fewer, 2-year colleges should be included in the sample. The reason for this decision was that, in this particular study, the publisher was eager to obtain reliable information about both the 2-year and the 4-year college markets.

This illustration serves as an example of an important point. Although the division of sample effort suggested by Equation 17.14 and Equation 17.15 is often referred to as the *optimum allocation*, it is optimal only with regard to the narrow criterion of efficient estimation of overall population parameters. Frequently, surveys have broader objectives than this, in which case it may well be reasonable to depart from the optimum allocation.

Determining Sample Sizes for Stratified Random Sampling with Specified Degree of Precision

It is also possible to derive formulas for the sample size needed to yield a specified degree of precision when stratified random sampling is employed.

Variance of Estimator of Population Mean, Stratified Sampling

Let the random variable $\overline{X}_{st}$ denote the **estimator of the population mean from stratified sampling** and $\overline{X}_j$ ($j = 1, 2,..., K$) the sample means for the individual strata. It then follows, since

$$\overline{X}_{st} = \frac{1}{N}\sum_{j=1}^{K} N_j \overline{X}_j \tag{17.16}$$

that the **variance** of $\overline{X}_{st}$ is

$$\text{Var}(\overline{X}_{st}) = \sigma_{\overline{X}_{st}}^2 = \frac{1}{N^2}\sum_{j=1}^{K} N_j^2 \, \text{Var}(\overline{X}_j) = \frac{1}{N^2}\sum_{j=1}^{K} N_j^2 \frac{\sigma_j^2}{n_j} \times \frac{(N_j - n_j)}{N_j - 1} \tag{17.17}$$

where the σ_j^2 are the population variances for the K strata.

Now, for any choice of $n_1, n_2,...,n_K$, Equation 17.17 can be used to derive the corresponding variance of the estimator of the population mean. However, the actual total sample size, n, required to achieve a particular value for this variance will depend on the manner in which the sample observations are allocated among the strata. We have already discussed two frequently used procedures, proportional allocation and optimum allocation. In either case, by substituting for n_j in Equation 17.17, you can solve the resulting equation and obtain the sample size, n. The results are given in Equation 17.18 and Equation 17.19.

Total Sample Size to Estimate Overall Mean (Stratum Population Variances Specified), Stratified Random Sampling

Suppose that a population of N members is subdivided in K strata containing N_1, N_2,..., N_K members. Let σ_j^2 denote the population variance in the jth stratum, and suppose that an **estimate of the overall population mean** is desired. If the desired variance, $\sigma_{\bar{X}_{st}}^2$, of the sample estimator is specified, the required total sample size, n, is as follows:

1. **Proportional allocation**

$$n = \frac{\sum\limits_{j=1}^{K} N_j \sigma_j^2}{N \sigma_{\bar{X}_{st}}^2 + \dfrac{1}{N}\sum\limits_{j=1}^{K} N_j \sigma_j^2} \qquad (17.18)$$

2. **Optimal allocation**

$$n = \frac{\dfrac{1}{N}\left(\sum\limits_{j=1}^{K} N_j \sigma_j\right)^2}{N \sigma_{\bar{X}_{st}}^2 + \dfrac{1}{N}\sum\limits_{j=1}^{K} N_j \sigma_j^2} \qquad (17.19)$$

Example 17.4 Restaurant in Three States (Sample Size)

As in Example 17.1, take a stratified random sample to estimate the mean number of orders per restaurant of a new food item when the numbers of restaurants in the three states are as follows:

$$N_1 = 60 \quad N_2 = 50 \quad N_3 = 45$$

Suppose also that the experience of the restaurant chain suggests that the population standard deviations for the three states are likely to be approximately

$$\sigma_1 = 13 \quad \sigma_2 = 11 \quad \sigma_3 = 9$$

If a 95% confidence interval is required for the population mean that extends three orders per restaurant on each side of the sample point estimate, how many sample observations in total are needed?

Solution Note that

$$1.96\sigma_{\bar{X}_{st}} = 3, \qquad so \qquad \sigma_{\bar{X}_{st}} = 1.53$$

$$\sum_{j=1}^{K} N_j \sigma_j^2 = (60)(13)^2 + (50)(11)^2 + (45)(9)^2 = 19{,}835$$

and

$$\frac{1}{N}\left(\sum_{j=1}^{K} N_j \sigma_j\right)^2 = \frac{[(60)(13) + (50)(11) + (45)(9)]^2}{155} = 19{,}421$$

For **proportional allocation** the sample size needed is as follows:

$$n = \frac{\displaystyle\sum_{j=1}^{K} N_j \sigma_j^2}{N\sigma_{\bar{X}_{st}}^2 + \dfrac{1}{N}\displaystyle\sum_{j=1}^{K} N_j \sigma_j^2} = \frac{19{,}835}{(155)(1.53)^2 + 19{,}835/155} = 40.4$$

Thus, a sample of 41 observations will suffice to produce the required level of precision.

If **optimal allocation** is to be used, the sample size needed is

$$n = \frac{\dfrac{1}{N}\left(\displaystyle\sum_{j=1}^{K} N_j \sigma_j\right)^2}{N\sigma_{\bar{X}_{st}}^2 + \dfrac{1}{N}\displaystyle\sum_{j=1}^{K} N_j \sigma_j^2} = \frac{19{,}421}{(155)(1.53)^2 + 19{,}835/155} = 39.6$$

so the same degree of reliability can be obtained with 40 observations if this method of allocation is used. In this particular case, since the population standard deviations are quite close, this represents only a very small savings compared with proportional allocation.

EXERCISES

Application Exercises

17.1 A small town contains a total of 1,800 households. The town is divided into three districts, containing 820, 540, and 440 households, respectively. A stratified random sample of 300 households contains 120, 90, and 90 households, respectively, from these three districts. Sample members were asked to estimate their total energy bills for the winter months. The respective sample means were $290, $352, and $427, and the respective sample standard deviations were $47, $61, and $93.

    a. Use an unbiased estimation procedure to estimate the mean winter energy bill for all households in this town.

    b. Use an unbiased estimation procedure to find an estimate of the variance of the estimator of part (a).

    c. Find a 95% confidence interval for the population mean winter energy bill for households in this town.

17.2 A college has 152 assistant professors, 127 associate professors, and 208 full professors. The college

administration is investigating the amount of time these faculty members spend in meetings in a semester. Random samples of 40 assistant professors, 40 associate professors, and 50 full professors were asked to keep records of time spent in meetings during a semester. The sample means were 27.6 hours for assistant professors, 39.2 hours for associate professors, and 43.3 hours for full professors. The sample standard deviations were 7.1 hours for assistant professors, 9.9 hours for associate professors, and 12.3 hours for full professors.

    a. Find a 90% confidence interval for the mean time spent in meetings by full professors at this college during the semester.

    b. Using an unbiased estimation procedure, estimate the mean time spent in meetings by all faculty members at this college during the semester.

    c. Find 90% and 95% confidence intervals for the mean time spent in meetings by all faculty members at this college during the semester.

17.3 A local bus company is planning a new route to serve four housing subdivisions. Random samples of households are taken from each subdivision, and sample members are asked to rate on a scale from 1 (strongly opposed) to 5 (strongly in favor) their reaction to the proposed service. The results are summarized in the accompanying table.

	Subdivision 1	Subdivision 2	Subdivision 3	Subdivision 4
N_i	240	190	350	280
n_i	40	40	40	40
$\bar{x}_i$	2.5	3.6	3.9	2.8
s_i	0.8	0.9	1.2	0.7

a. Find a 90% confidence interval for the mean reaction of households in subdivision 1.
b. Using an unbiased estimation procedure, estimate the mean reaction of all households to be served by the new route.
c. Find 90% and 95% confidence intervals for the mean reaction of all households to be served by the new route.

17.4 In a stratified random sample of students on a small campus, sample members were asked to rate, on a scale from 1 (poor) to 5 (excellent), opportunities for extracurricular activities. The results are shown in the accompanying table.

	Freshmen and Sophomores	Juniors and Seniors
N_i	632	529
n_i	50	50
$\bar{x}_i$	3.12	3.37
s_i	1.04	0.86

a. Find a 95% confidence interval for the mean rating that would be given by all freshmen and sophomores on this campus.
b. Find a 95% confidence interval for the mean rating that would be given by all juniors and seniors on this campus.
c. Find a 95% confidence interval for the mean rating that would be given by all undergraduate students on this campus.

17.5 Refer to Exercise 17.2.

a. Find a 90% confidence interval for the total amount of time spent in meetings by all full professors in this college in the semester.
b. Find a 90% confidence interval for the total amount of time spent in meetings by all faculty members in this college in the semester.

17.6 A company has three divisions, and auditors are attempting to estimate the total amounts of the company's accounts receivable. Random samples of these accounts were taken for each of the three divisions, yielding the results shown in the following table:

	Division 1	Division 2	Division 3
N_i	120	150	180
n_i	40	45	50
$\bar{x}_i$	$237	$198	$131
s_i	$93	$64	$47

a. Using an unbiased estimation procedure, find a point estimate of the total value of all accounts receivable for this company.
b. Find a 95% confidence interval for the total value of all accounts receivable for this company.

17.7 Of the 1,395 colleges in the United States, 364 have 2-year schools. In a random sample of 40 two-year schools it was found that the text *Statistics Can Be Fun* was used in 10 of the schools. In an independent random sample of 60 four-year schools, this text was used by 8 of the sample members.

a. Find an estimate of the proportion of all colleges using this text, using an unbiased estimation procedure.
b. Find a 95% confidence interval for the proportion of all colleges using this text.

17.8 A consulting company has developed a short course on modern business forecasting methods for corporate executives. The first course was attended by 150 executives. From the information they supplied, it was concluded that the technical skills of 100 course members were more than adequate to follow the course material, while those of the remaining 50 were judged barely adequate. After the completion of the course, questionnaires were sent to independent random samples of 25 people from each of these two groups in order to obtain feedback that could lead to improved presentation in subsequent courses. Six of the more skilled group and 14 of the less skilled group indicated that they believed the course had been too theoretical.

a. Find an estimate of the proportion of all course members with this opinion, using an unbiased estimation procedure.
b. Find 90% and 95% confidence intervals for this population proportion.

17.9 A college has 152 assistant professors, 127 associate professors, and 208 full professors. A journalist with the student newspaper was interested in whether faculty members were actually in their offices during posted office hours. The student journalist decided to investigate samples of 40 assistant professors, 40 associate professors, and 50 full professors. Student volunteers were sent to knock on the doors of these sample members during their posted office hours. It was found that 31 of the assistant professors, 29 of the associate professors, and 34 of the full professors were actually in their offices at these times.

a. Using an unbiased estimation procedure, find a point estimate of the proportion of all faculty members who are in their offices during posted office hours.
b. Find 90% and 95% confidence intervals for the proportion of all faculty members who are in their offices during posted office hours.

17.10 Refer to Exercise 17.2. If a total sample of 130 faculty members is to be taken, determine how many of these should be full professors under each of the following schemes:

a. Proportional allocation
b. Optimum allocation, assuming the stratum population standard deviations are the same as the corresponding sample values

17.11 Refer to the data of Exercise 17.3. If a total sample of 160 households is to be taken, determine how many of these should be from subdivision 1 under each of the following schemes:

a. Proportional allocation
b. Optimum allocation, assuming the stratum population standard deviations are the same as the corresponding sample values

17.12 Refer to the data of Exercise 17.4. If a total sample of 100 students is to be taken, determine how many of these should be freshmen and sophomores under each of the following schemes:

a. Proportional allocation
b. Optimum allocation, assuming the stratum population standard deviations are the same as the corresponding sample values

17.13 Refer to the data of Exercise 17.6. If a total sample of 135 accounts receivable is to be taken, determine how many of these should be from Division 1 under each of the following schemes:

a. Proportional allocation
b. Optimum allocation, assuming the stratum population standard deviations are the same as the corresponding sample values

17.14 Refer to the data of Example 17.2. If a total sample of 100 colleges is to be taken, determine how many of these should be 4-year schools under each of the following schemes:

a. Proportional allocation
b. Optimum allocation, assuming the stratum population standard deviations are the same as the corresponding sample values

17.15 An auditor wants to estimate the mean value of a corporation's accounts receivable. The population is divided into four strata, containing 500, 400, 300, and 200 accounts, respectively. On the basis of past experience, it is estimated that the standard deviations of values in these strata will be $150, $200, $300, and $400, respectively. If a 90% confidence interval for the overall population mean is to extend $25 on each side of the sample estimate, determine the total sample size needed under both proportional allocation and optimal allocation.

17.16 Mean household income must be estimated for a town that can be divided into three districts. The relevant information is shown in the table.

District	Population Size	Estimated Standard Deviation ($)
1	1,150	4,000
2	2,120	6,000
3	930	8,000

If a 95% confidence interval for the population mean extending $500 on each side of the sample estimate is required, determine how many sample observations in total are needed under proportional allocation and optimal allocation.

17.2 OTHER SAMPLING METHODS

Simple random sampling and stratified random sampling have been discussed briefly. These are not the only procedures used for choosing a sample. Some alternative methods are discussed in this section.

Cluster Sampling

Suppose that an investigator wants to survey a population spread over a wide geographical area, such as a large city or a state. If either a simple random sample or a stratified random sample is to be used, two immediate problems will arise. First, in order to draw the sample, the investigator will need a reasonably accurate listing of the population members. Such a list may not be available or could perhaps be obtained only at a prohibitively high cost. Second, even if the investigator does possess a list of the population, the resulting sample members will almost inevitably be thinly spread over a large area. In that case, having interviewers contact each individual sample member will be quite costly. Of course, if a mail questionnaire is to be used, this latter problem does not arise. However, this means of contact may lead to an unacceptably high rate of nonresponse, leading the investigator to prefer personal interviews.

Faced with the dilemma of either not having a reliable population listing or wanting to set up personal interviews with sample members when budget resources are tight, the investigator may use an alternative sampling procedure known as **cluster sampling**. This approach is attractive when a population can conveniently be subdivided into relatively small, geographically compact units called *clusters*. For example, a city might be subdivided into political wards or residential blocks. This can generally be achieved even when a complete listing of residents or households is unavailable.

In cluster sampling a simple random sample of clusters is selected from the population, and every individual in each of the sampled clusters is contacted; that is, a complete census is carried out in each of the chosen clusters. In the following equations procedures for deriving valid inferences about the population mean and proportion from the results of a cluster sample are given.

Estimators for Cluster Sampling

A population is subdivided into M clusters, a simple random sample of m of these clusters is selected, and information is obtained from every member of the sampled clusters. Let $n_1, n_2, ..., n_m$ denote the numbers of population members in the m sampled clusters. Denote the means of these clusters by $\bar{x}_1, \bar{x}_2, ..., \bar{x}_m$ and the proportions of cluster members possessing an attribute of interest by $\hat{p}_1, \hat{p}_2, ..., \hat{p}_m$. The objective is to estimate the overall population mean μ and proportion P.

1. Unbiased estimation procedures give

$$\bar{x}_c = \frac{\sum_{i=1}^{m} n_i \bar{x}_i}{\sum_{i=1}^{m} n_i} \tag{17.20}$$

and

$$\hat{p}_c = \frac{\sum_{i=1}^{m} n_i \hat{p}_i}{\sum_{i=1}^{m} n_i} \tag{17.21}$$

2. Estimates of the variance of these estimators, following from unbiased estimation procedures, are

$$\hat{\sigma}^2_{\bar{x}_c} = \frac{M - m}{Mm\bar{n}^2} \left(\frac{\sum_{i=1}^{m} n_i^2 (\bar{x}_i - \bar{x}_c)^2}{m - 1} \right) \tag{17.22}$$

and

$$\hat{\sigma}^2_{\hat{p}_c} = \frac{M - m}{Mm\bar{n}^2} \left(\frac{\sum_{i=1}^{m} n_i^2 (\hat{p}_i - \hat{p}_c)^2}{m - 1} \right) \tag{17.23}$$

where $\bar{n} = \sum_{i=1}^{m} n_i/m$ is the average number of individuals in the sampled clusters.

Based on these estimators, the confidence intervals with cluster sampling follow.

Estimation of Population Mean, Cluster Sampling
Provided the sample size is large, a $100(1 - \alpha)\%$ **confidence interval for the population mean using cluster sampling** is as follows:

$$\bar{x}_c - z_{\alpha/2}\hat{\sigma}_{\bar{x}_c} < \mu < \bar{x}_c + z_{\alpha/2}\hat{\sigma}_{\bar{x}_c} \tag{17.24}$$

Similarly, confidence intervals for the population proportion based on cluster sampling are established.

Estimation of Population Proportion, Cluster Sampling
Provided the sample size is large, a $100(1 - \alpha)\%$ **confidence interval for the population proportion using cluster sampling** is as follows:

$$\hat{p}_c - z_{\alpha/2}\hat{\sigma}_{\hat{p}_c} < P < \hat{p}_c + z_{\alpha/2}\hat{\sigma}_{\hat{p}_c} \tag{17.25}$$

Notice that inferences can be made with relatively little prior information about the population. All that is required is a breakdown into identifiable clusters. It is not necessary to know the total number of population members. It is sufficient to know the numbers in each of the *sampled* clusters, and these can be determined during the course of the survey, since a full census is taken in each cluster in the sample. In addition, since sample members will be geographically close to one another within clusters, their contact by interviewers is relatively inexpensive.

Example 17.5 Cluster Sampling for Family Incomes (Estimation)

A simple random sample of 20 blocks is taken from a residential area containing a total of 1,000 blocks. Each household in the sampled blocks is then contacted, and information is obtained about family incomes. The mean annual incomes and the proportion of families with incomes below $15,000 per year in the sampled blocks are contained in the data file **Income Clusters**. For this residential area estimate the mean family income and the proportion of families with incomes below $15,000 per year.

Solution   It is known that

$$m = 20 \quad \text{and} \quad M = 1,000$$

The total number of households in the sample is as follows:

$$\sum_{i=1}^{m} n_i = (23 + 31 + \cdots + 41) = 607$$

To obtain point estimates,

$$\sum_{i=1}^{m} n_i \bar{x}_i = (23)(26,823) + (31)(19,197) + \cdots + (41)(16,493) = 15,848,158$$

and

$$\sum_{i=1}^{m} n_i \hat{p}_i = (23)(0.1304) + (31)(0.4516) + \cdots + (41)(0.3659) = 153$$

Our point estimates are, therefore,

$$\bar{x}_c = \frac{\sum_{i=1}^{m} n_i \bar{x}_i}{\sum_{i=1}^{m} n_i} = \frac{15,848,158}{607} = 26,109$$

$$\hat{p}_c = \frac{\sum_{i=1}^{m} n_i \hat{p}_i}{\sum_{i=1}^{m} n_i} = \frac{153}{607} = 0.2521$$

Thus, on the basis of this sample evidence it is estimated that for this residential area, mean annual household income is $26,109 and 25.21% of households have incomes below $15,000 per year.

To obtain interval estimates of the population mean, the average cluster size is needed where

$$\bar{n} = \frac{\sum_{i=1}^{m} n_i}{m} = \frac{607}{20} = 30.35$$

Also,

$$\frac{\sum_{i=1}^{m} n_i^2 (\bar{x}_i - \bar{x}_c)^2}{m - 1} = \frac{(23)^2 (26,283 - 26,109)^2 + \cdots + (41)^2 (16,493 - 26,109)^2}{19} = 69,270,562,244$$

so

$$\sigma_{\bar{x}_c}^2 = \frac{M-m}{Mm\bar{n}^2} \times \frac{\sum\limits_{i=1}^{m} n_i^2 (\bar{x}_i - \bar{x}_c)^2}{m-1} = \frac{(980)(69,270,562,244)}{(1,000)(20)(30.35)^2} = 3,684,914$$

and taking the square root,

$$\hat{\sigma}_{\bar{x}} = 1,920$$

A 95% confidence interval for the population mean is

$$26,109 - (1.96)(1,920) < \mu < 26,109 + (1.96)(1,920)$$

or

$$22,346 < \mu < 29,872$$

A 95% confidence interval for the mean income of all families in this area, therefore, runs from \$22,346 to \$29,872.

To obtain interval estimates for the population proportion,

$$\frac{\sum\limits_{i=1}^{m} n_i^2 (\hat{p}_i - \hat{p}_c)^2}{m-1} = \frac{(23)^2 (0.1304 - 0.2521)^2 + \cdots + (41)^2 (0.3659 - 0.2521)^2}{19} = 38.1547$$

Then,

$$\hat{\sigma}_{\hat{p}_c}^2 = \frac{M-m}{Mm\bar{n}^2} \left(\frac{\sum\limits_{i=1}^{m} n_i^2 (\hat{p}_i - \hat{p}_c)^2}{m-1} \right)$$

$$= \frac{(980)(38.1547)}{(1,000)(20)(30.35)^2} = 0.0020297$$

and taking the square root,

$$\hat{\sigma}_{\hat{p}_c} = 0.0451$$

The 95% confidence interval for the population proportion is

$$0.2521 - (1.96)(0.0451) < P < 0.2521 + (1.96)(0.0451)$$

or

$$0.164 < P < 0.340$$

Our 95% confidence interval for the percentage of households with annual incomes below \$15,000 runs from 16.4% to 34.0%.

Cluster sampling has a superficial resemblance to stratified sampling. In both, the population is first divided into subgroups. However, the similarity is rather illusory. In stratified random sampling a sample is taken from *every stratum* of the population in an attempt to ensure that important segments of the population are given due weight. By contrast, in cluster sampling a random sample of *clusters* is taken, so that some clusters will have no members in the sample. Since, within clusters, population members will probably be fairly homogeneous, the danger is that important subgroups of the population may be either not represented at all or grossly underrepresented in the final sample. In consequence, while the great advantage of cluster sampling lies in its convenience, this convenience may well be at the cost of additional imprecision in the sample estimates. A further distinction between cluster sampling and stratified sampling is that in the former a *complete census* of cluster members is taken, while in the latter a *random sample* of stratum members is drawn. This difference, however, is not essential. Indeed, on occasions an investigator may draw a random sample of cluster members rather than take a full census.

Two-Phase Sampling

In many investigations the population is not surveyed in a single step. Rather, it is often convenient to carry out an initial pilot study in which a relatively small proportion of the sample members are contacted. The results obtained are then analyzed prior to conducting the bulk of the survey. The chief disadvantage of such a procedure is that it can be quite time-consuming. However, this factor may be outweighed by several advantages. One important benefit is that the investigator is able, at modest cost, to try out the proposed questionnaire in order to ensure that the various questions can be thoroughly understood. The pilot study may also suggest additional questions whose potential importance had previously been overlooked. Moreover, this study should also provide an estimate of the likely rate of nonresponse. Should this prove unacceptably high, some modification in the method of soliciting responses might appear desirable.

Conducting a survey in two stages, beginning with a pilot study, is known as **two-phase sampling**. This approach has two further advantages. First, if stratified random sampling is employed, the pilot study can be used to provide estimates of the individual stratum variances. These, in turn, can be employed to estimate the optimum allocation of the sample among the various strata. Second, the results of the pilot study can be used to estimate the number of observations needed to obtain estimators of population parameters with a specified level of precision. The following examples serve to illustrate these points. Consider a straightforward situation in which a simple random sample is to be used to estimate a population mean. At the outset relatively little is known about this population, so an initial pilot survey is to be carried out to get some idea of the sample size required.

Example 17.6 Mean Value of Accounts Receivable (Sample Size)

An auditor wishes to estimate the mean value of accounts receivable in a total population of 1,120 accounts. He wants to produce a 95% confidence interval for the population mean extending approximately $4 on each side of the sample mean. To begin, he takes a simple random sample of 100 accounts, finding a sample standard deviation of $30.27. How many more accounts should be sampled?

Solution   From Section 8.6 the sample size needed was found to be

$$n = \frac{N\sigma^2}{(N-1)\sigma_{\bar{X}}^2 + \sigma^2}$$

where $N = 1,120$ is the number of population members in this case. In order for the 95% confidence interval to be the required width,

$$1.96\sigma_{\bar{x}} = 4$$

so that $\sigma_{\bar{x}}$, the standard deviation of the sample mean, must be as follows:

$$\sigma_{\bar{x}} = \frac{4}{1.96} = 2.04$$

The population standard deviation, σ, is unknown. However, as a result of the initial study of 100 accounts receivable, it is estimated to be 30.27. The total number of sample observations needed is, therefore,

$$n = \frac{N\sigma^2}{(N-1)\sigma_{\bar{x}}^2 + \sigma^2} = \frac{(1,120)(30.27)^2}{(1,119)(2.04)^2 + (30.27)^2} = 184.1$$

Since 100 observations have already been taken, an additional 85 will suffice to satisfy the auditor's objective.

Example 17.7   Income (Sample Size)

An investigator intends to take a stratified random sample to estimate mean family income in a town where the numbers in the three stratum districts are as follows:

$$N_1 = 1,150 \quad N_2 = 2,120 \quad N_3 = 930$$

To begin, the investigator conducts a pilot study, sampling 30 households from each district and obtaining the sample standard deviations $3,657, $6,481, and $8,403, respectively. Suppose that the objective is to obtain, with as small a size as possible, a 95% confidence interval for the population mean extending $500 on each side of the sample estimate. How many additional observations should be taken in each district?

Solution   The requirement that a specified degree of precision be obtained with as few sample observations as possible implies that optimal allocation must be used. Recall from Equation 17.14 that the numbers n_1, n_2, and n_3 to be sampled in the three strata are as follows:

$$n_j = \frac{N_j\sigma_j}{\displaystyle\sum_{i=1}^{K} N_i\sigma_i} \times n \qquad (j = 1, 2, 3)$$

where the σ_i are the stratum population standard deviations. Using our sample estimates in place of these quantities,

$$n_1 = \frac{(1,150)(3,657)}{(1,150)(3,657) + (2,120)(6,481) + (930)(8,403)} \times n = 0.163n$$

$$n_2 = \frac{(2,120)(6,481)}{(1,150)(3,657) + (2,120)(6,481) + (930)(8,403)} \times n = 0.533n$$

$$n_3 = \frac{(930)(8,403)}{(1,150)(3,657) + (2,120)(6,481) + (930)(8,403)} \times n = 0.303n$$

The properties of the total sample to be allocated to each stratum under the optimal scheme are now specified. It remains to determine the total number n of sample observations.

Nonprobabilistic Sampling Methods

Various sampling schemes for which it is possible to specify the probability that any particular sample will be drawn from the population have been considered. Because of this feature of the sampling methods, valid statistical inferences based on the sample results can be made. Otherwise, the derivation of unbiased point estimates and confidence intervals with specified probability content could not be achieved with strict statistical validity.

Nevertheless, in many practical applications, **nonprobabilistic methods** are used for selecting sample members, primarily as a matter of convenience. For example, suppose that you want to assess the reactions of students on your campus to some issue of topical interest. One possibility would be to ask all your friends how they feel about it. This group would not constitute a random sample from the population of all students. Accordingly, if you proceed to analyze the data as if they were obtained from a random sample, the resulting inference would lack proper statistical validity.

A more sophisticated version of the approach just described, called **quota sampling**, is commonly used by polling organizations. Interviewers are assigned to a particular locale and instructed to contact specified numbers of people of certain age, race, and gender characteristics. These assigned quotas represent what are thought to be appropriate proportions for the population at large. However, once the quotas are determined, interviewers are granted flexibility in the choice of sample members. Their choice is typically not random. Quota sampling can, and often does, produce quite accurate estimates of population parameters. The drawback is that, since the sample is not chosen using probabilistic methods, there is no valid way of determining the reliability of the resulting estimates.

EXERCISES

Application Exercises

17.17 A market research organization wants to estimate the mean amounts of time in a week that television sets are in use in households in a city that contains 65 precincts. A simple random sample of 10 precincts was selected, and every household in each sampled precinct was questioned. The following results were obtained:

a. Find a point estimate of the population mean amount of time that televisions are in use in this city.

b. Find a 90% confidence interval for the population mean.

Sampled Precinct	Number of Households	Mean Time Television in Use (Hours)
1	28	29.6
2	35	18.4
3	18	32.7
4	52	26.3
5	41	22.4
6	38	31.6
7	36	19.7
8	30	23.8
9	23	25.4
10	42	24.1

17.18 A union executive wants to estimate the mean value of bonus payments made to a corporation's clerical employees in the first month of a new plan. This corporation has 52 subdivisions, and a simple random sample of 8 of these is taken. Information is then obtained from the payroll records of every clerical worker in each of the sampled subdivisions. The results obtained are shown in the following table:

Sampled Subdivision	Number of Clerical Employees	Mean Bonus (Dollars)
1	69	83
2	75	64
3	41	42
4	36	108
5	59	136
6	82	102
7	64	95
8	71	98

a. Find a point estimate of the population mean bonus per clerical employee for this month.
b. Find a 99% confidence interval for the population mean.

17.19 In the survey of Exercise 17.17, the households were asked if they had cable television. The numbers having cable are given in the accompanying table.

Precinct	1	2	3	4	5	6	7	8	9	10
Number	12	11	10	29	15	13	20	14	9	26

a. Find a point estimate of the proportion of all households in the city having cable television.
b. Find a 90% confidence interval for this population proportion.

17.20 In the survey of Exercise 17.18, the clerical employees in the 8 sampled subdivisions were asked if they were satisfied with the operation of the bonus plan. The results obtained are listed in the following table:

Subdivision	1	2	3	4	5	6	7	8
Number satisfied	24	25	11	21	35	44	30	34

a. Find a point estimate of the proportion of all clerical employees satisfied with the bonus plan.
b. Find a 95% confidence interval for this population proportion.

17.21 A city is divided into 50 geographic subdivisions. An estimate was required of the proportion of households in the city interested in a new lawn-care service. A random sample of three subdivisions contained 611, 521, and 734 households, respectively. The numbers expressing interest in the service were 128, 131, and 172, respectively. Find a 90% confidence interval for the proportion of all households in this city interested in the lawn-care service.

17.22 A bank holds 720 delinquent mortgages in residential properties. It required an estimate of the mean current appraised value of these properties. Initially, a random sample of 20 was appraised, and a sample standard deviation of $37,600 was found. If the bank requires a 90% confidence interval for the population mean extending $5,000 on each side of the sample mean, how many more properties must be appraised?

17.23 A college has 3,200 undergraduate students and 800 graduate students. Researchers are interested in the amount of money spent in a year on textbooks by these students. Initially, simple random samples of 30 undergraduate students and 30 graduate students were taken. The sample standard deviations for amounts spent were $40 and $58, respectively. A 90% confidence interval for the overall population mean that extends $5 on each side of the sample point estimate is required. Estimate the smallest total number of additional sample observations needed to achieve this goal.

17.24 A corporation has a fleet of 480 company cars—100 compact, 180 mid-size, and 200 full-size. To estimate the overall mean annual repair costs for these cars, a preliminary random sample of 10 cars of each type is selected. The sample standard deviations for repair costs were $105 for compact cars, $162 for mid-size cars, and $183 for full-size cars. A 95% confidence interval for the overall population mean annual repair cost per car that extends $20 on each side of the sample point estimate is required. Estimate the smallest total number of additional sample observations that must be taken.

KEY WORDS

17.25 Carefully explain the distinction between stratified random sampling and cluster sampling. Provide illustrations of sampling problems where each of these techniques might be useful.

17.26 The U.S. Senate has 100 members. Information was obtained from the individuals responsible for managing correspondence in 61 senators' offices. Of these, 38 specified a minimum number of letters that must be received on an issue before a form letter in response is created.

   a. Assume these observations constitute a random sample from the population, and find a 90% confidence interval for the proportion of all senators' offices with this policy.
   b. In fact, information was *not* obtained from a random sample of senate offices. Questionnaires were sent to *all* 100 offices, but only 61 responded. How does this information influence your view of the answer to part (a) (Reference 2)?

17.27 A company has three subdivisions, employing a total of 970 managers. Independent random samples of managers were taken from each subdivision, and the number of years with the company was determined for each sample member. The results are summarized in the accompanying table.

	Subdivision 1	Subdivision 2	Subdivision 3
N_i	352	287	331
n_i	30	20	30
$\bar{x}_i$	9.2	12.3	13.5
s_i	4.9	6.4	7.6

   a. Find a 99% confidence interval for the mean number of years with the company for managers in subdivision 1.
   b. Find a 99% confidence interval for the mean number of years with the company for all managers.

17.28 Of the 300 pages in a particular book, 180 pages are primarily nontechnical, while the remainder is technical. Independent random samples of technical and nontechnical pages were taken, and the numbers of errors per page were recorded. The results are summarized in the following table:

	Technical	Nontechnical
N_i	120	180
n_i	20	20
$\bar{x}_i$	1.6	0.74
s_i	0.98	0.56

   a. Find a 95% confidence interval for the mean number of errors per page in this book.
   b. Find a 99% confidence interval for the total number of errors in the book.

17.29 In the analysis of Exercise 17.28, it was found that 9 of the sampled technical pages and 15 of the sampled nontechnical pages contained no errors. Find a 90% confidence interval for the proportion of all pages in this book that have no errors.

17.30 Refer to the data of Exercise 17.27. If a total of 80 managers was sampled, determine how many sample members would be from subdivision 1 under each of the following schemes:

   a. Proportional allocation
   b. Optimum allocation, assuming that the stratum population standard deviations are the same as the corresponding sample quantities

17.31 Refer to the data of Exercise 17.28. If a total of 40 pages are to be sampled, determine how many sampled pages would be technical under each of the following schemes:

   a. Proportional allocation
   b. Optimum allocation, assuming that the stratum population standard deviations are the same as the corresponding sample quantities

17.32 You intend to sample the students in your university to assess their views on the adequacy of space in the library. You decide to use a stratified sample by year—freshmen, sophomores, and so forth. Discuss the factors you would take into account in deciding how many sample observations to take in each stratum.

17.33 Suppose that you were asked by your state office of elections to assist in resolving an election dispute between two candidates or, perhaps, you were asked to be a statistical expert in a lawsuit concerning the outcome of a close election (such as the 2000 U.S. presidential election). Many questions arise. Should all ballots in the state be recounted? Should only ballots in certain counties be recounted? If only certain ballots are recounted, which ballots? These and other similar questions were asked during the 2000 U.S. presidential election. Discuss the advantages and disadvantages of various sampling designs that might be used to select ballots to be recounted.

References

1. Cochran, W. G. 1977. *Sampling Techniques*, 3rd ed. New York: Wiley.
2. Culnan, M. J. 1992. Processing Unstructured Organizational Transactions: Mail Handling in the U.S. Senate. *Organizational Science* 3:117–37.
3. Deming, W. E. 1960. *Sample Design in Business Research*. New York: Wiley.
4. Hogg, Robert, and Allen T. Craig. 1977. *Introduction to Mathematical Statistics*, 4th ed. New York: Macmillan.
5. Kish, Leslie. 1965. *Survey Sampling*. New York: Wiley.
6. Levy, Paul S., and Stanley Lemeshow. 1991. *Sampling of Populations: Methods and Applications*. New York: Wiley.
7. Schaeffer, Richard L., William Mendenhall, and Lyman Ott. 1996. *Elementary Survey Sampling*, 5th ed. Belmont, CA: Duxbury Press.

Chapter 18

Statistical Decision Theory

Introduction

The topic of this chapter could be characterized as capturing the essence of management problems in any organization. Indeed, the applicability of the subject matter extends further, touching many aspects of our everyday lives. We will consider situations in which an individual, a group, or a corporation has available several alternative feasible courses of action. The decision as to which course to follow must be made in a world in which there is uncertainty about the future behavior of the factors that will determine the consequences stemming from the action taken. In this chapter four criteria for decision making are discussed. The maximin criterion and the minimax regret criterion are nonprobabilistic decision-making criteria. That is, these decision criteria "do not take into account the probability associated with the outcomes for each alternative; they merely focus on the dollar value of the outcomes" (Reference 3). Two decision-making criteria that include information about the chances of each outcome's occurrence are the expected monetary value criterion and the expected utility criterion.

We are all constrained to operate in an environment whose future direction is uncertain. For example, you may consider attending a baseball game but are apprehensive because of the possibility of rain. If you *knew* that it was not going to rain, you would go to the game; if you were *certain* that heavy rain was going to fall for several hours, you would not go. But you are unable to predict the weather with complete assurance, and your decision must be made while contemplating an uncertain future. As another example, at some stage during your final year in college, you will have to decide what to do upon graduation. It is possible that you will have offers of employment from several sources. Graduate school, too, may be a possibility. The decision as to your initial career direction is clearly an important one. Certainly, you will have acquired information about the alternatives. You will know what starting salaries are offered, and you will have learned something about the business operations of your future potential employers and how you might fit into these operations.

However, one really does not have a very clear picture of where one will be in a year or two if a particular offer is accepted. This important decision, then, is made in the face of uncertainty about the future.

In the business world, circumstances of this type often arise, as the following examples illustrate:

1. In a recession a company must decide whether to lay off employees. If the downturn in business activity is to be short-lived, it may be preferable to retain these workers, who might be difficult to replace when demand improves. If the recession is to be prolonged, however, their retention would be costly. Unfortunately, the art of economic forecasting has not reached the stage where it is possible to predict with great certainty the length or severity of a recession.
2. An investor may believe that interest rates are currently at a peak. In that case long-term bonds would appear to be very attractive. However, it is impossible to be sure about the future direction of interest rates, and if they were to continue to rise, the decision to tie up funds in long-term bonds would have been suboptimal.
3. Contractors are often required to submit bids for a program of work. The decision to be made is the level at which the bid should be pitched. Two areas of uncertainty may be relevant here. First, the contractor will not know how low a bid will have to be in order to secure the work. Second, the contractor cannot be sure precisely how much it will cost to fulfill the contract. Again, in spite of this uncertainty, some decision must be made.
4. The cost of drilling exploratory offshore oil wells is enormous, and, in spite of excellent geological advice, oil companies will not know, before a well is drilled, whether commercially viable quantities of oil will be discovered. The decision as to whether and where to drill in a particular field is one that must be made in an uncertain environment.

Our objective is to study methods for attacking decision-making problems of the type just described. A decision maker is faced with a finite number, K, of possible *actions*, which will be labeled $a_1, a_2,..., a_K$. At the time a particular action must be selected, the decision maker is uncertain about the future of some factor that will determine the consequences of the chosen action. It is assumed that a finite number, H, of possible *states of nature* can characterize the possibilities for this factor. These will be denoted $s_1, s_2,..., s_H$. Finally, it is assumed that the decision maker is able to specify the monetary reward, or *payoff*, for each action–state of nature combination. Let M_{ij} represent the payoff for action a_i in the event of the occurrence of state of nature s_j. Actions, states of nature, monetary payoffs, and payoff tables are part of the general framework for any decision-making problem.

Framework for a Decision-Making Problem

1. The decision maker has available K possible courses of **action**: a_1, $a_2,..., a_K$. Actions are sometimes called *alternatives*.
2. There are H possible uncertain **states of nature**: $s_1, s_2,..., s_H$. States of nature are the possible outcomes over which the decision maker has no control. Sometimes states of nature are called *events*.
3. For each possible action–state of nature combination there is an associated outcome representing either profit or loss, called the monetary **payoff**, M_{ij}, that corresponds to action a_i and state of nature s_j. The table of all such outcomes for a decision problem is called a **payoff table**.

The general form of a payoff table is shown in Table 18.1.

When a decision maker is faced with alternative courses of action, the appropriate choice will depend to a considerable extent on the objectives. It is possible to describe various lines of attack that have been employed in the solution of business decision-making problems. However, it must be kept in mind that each individual problem has its own special features and that the objectives of decision makers may vary considerably and indeed be rather complex. A situation of this sort arises when one contemplates the position of a middle manager in a large corporation. In practice, this manager's objectives may differ somewhat from those of the corporation. In making decisions the manager is very likely to be conscious of his own position as well as the overall good of the corporation.

In spite of the individual nature of decision-making problems, it may be possible to eliminate some actions from further consideration under any circumstances.

Table 18.1 Payoff Table for a Decision Problem with K Possible Actions and H Possible States of Nature

ACTION	STATE OF NATURE			
A_I/S_I	s_1	s_2	...	s_H
a_1	M_{11}	M_{12}		M_{1H}
a_2	M_{21}	M_{22}	...	M_{2H}
.	.	.	.	.
.	.	.	.	.
.	.	.	.	.
a_K	M_{K1}	M_{K2}	...	M_{KH}

The following example is used throughout this chapter.

Example 18.1   Cellular Phone Manufacturer (Admissible Actions)

Consider a manufacturer planning to introduce a new cellular phone. The manufacturer has available four alternative production processes, denoted by A, B, C, and D, ranging in scope from a relatively minor modification of existing facilities to a major extension of the plant. The decision as to which course of action to follow must be made at a time when the eventual demand for the product will be unknown. For convenience, this potential demand is characterized as "low," "moderate," or "high." It will also be assumed that the manufacturer is able to calculate, for each production process, the profit over the lifetime of the investment for each of the three levels of demand. Table 18.2 shows these profit levels (in dollars) for each production process–level of demand combination. Determine if there are any inadmissible actions.

Solution   In this example there are four possible actions corresponding to the four possible production processes and three possible states of nature corresponding to the three possible levels of demand for the product.

Referring to Table 18.2, consider production process D. The payoff from this process will be precisely the same as that from process C if there is a low level of demand and lower than that from process C if the level of demand is either moderate or high. It therefore makes no sense to choose option D, since there is another available choice through which the payoffs can be no lower and could be higher. Since action C is necessarily at least as rewarding as and possibly more rewarding

Table 18.2   Estimated Profits of a Cellular Phone Manufacturer for Different Process-Demand Combinations

ACTION	STATE OF NATURE		
PRODUCTION PROCESS	LOW DEMAND	MODERATE DEMAND	HIGH DEMAND
Process A	70,000	120,000	200,000
Process B	80,000	120,000	180,000
Process C	100,000	125,000	160,000
Process D	100,000	120,000	150,000

than action D, then action C is said to *dominate* action D. Since production process D is dominated by another available alternative, production process C, production process D is said to be *inadmissible*. This action should be removed from further consideration, as it would be suboptimal to adopt it. Accordingly, this possibility will be dropped from further consideration, and, in our subsequent analysis of this problem, only the possibility of adoption of process A, B, or C is considered.

The decision-making problem as outlined is essentially discrete in character. That is to say, there are only a finite number of available alternatives and a finite number of possible states of nature. However, many practical problems are continuous. The state of nature, for instance, may be more appropriately measured on a continuum than depicted by a number of discrete possibilities. In the cellular phone manufacturer example it may be possible to anticipate a range of potential demand levels rather than simply to specify three levels. Also, in some problems the available actions are most appropriately represented by a continuum. This would be the case, for example, when a contractor must decide on the level at which to bid for a contract. The remainder of this chapter focuses on the discrete case. The *principles* involved in the analysis of the continuous case are no different. However, the details of that analysis are based on calculus and will not be considered further here.

EXERCISES

Basic Exercises

18.1 An investor is considering three alternatives—a certificate of deposit, a low-risk stock fund, and a high-risk stock fund—for a $20,000 investment. The investor considers three possible states of nature:

s_1: Strong stock market
s_2: Moderate stock market
s_3: Weak stock market

The payoff table (in dollars) is as follows:

Action	State of Nature		
Possible Investment Alternative	s_1	s_2	s_3
Certificate of deposit	1,200	1,200	1,200
Low-risk stock fund	4,300	1,200	−600
High-risk stock fund	6,600	800	−1,500

Are any of these actions inadmissible?

18.2 A manufacturer of deodorant is about to expand production capacity to make a new product. Four alternative production processes are available. The accompanying table shows estimated profits in dollars for these processes for each of three possible demand levels for the product.

Action	State of Nature		
Production Process	Low Demand	Moderate Demand	High Demand
A	100,000	350,000	900,000
B	150,000	400,000	700,000
C	250,000	400,000	600,000
D	250,000	400,000	550,000

Are any of these actions inadmissible?

18.2 SOLUTIONS NOT INVOLVING SPECIFICATION OF PROBABILITIES

Before deciding which production process to employ, our manufacturer of cellular phones is likely to ask, "What are the chances of each of these levels of demand actually materializing?" The bulk of this chapter discusses solutions to a decision-making problem that require the specification of outcome probabilities for the various states of

Table 18.3 Maximin Criterion Output for Example 18.1

ACTION	STATE OF NATURE			MINIMUM PAYOFF
PRODUCTION PROCESS	LOW DEMAND	MODERATE DEMAND	HIGH DEMAND	MINIMUM PAYOFF FOR EACH PROCESS
A	70,000	120,000	200,000	70,000
B	80,000	120,000	180,000	80,000
C	100,000	125,000	160,000	**100,000 (Maximum)**

nature. However, in this section two choice criteria that are not based on such probabilities and, in fact, have no probabilistic content are presented. Rather, these approaches (and others of the same type) depend only on the structure of the payoff table.

The two procedures considered in this section are called the *maximin criterion* and the *minimax regret criterion*. Each criterion is discussed in relation to the payoff table for the cellular phone manufacturer in Example 18.1, with the inadmissible strategy of choosing production process D ignored. The manufacturer must, therefore, select from among three available actions, faced with three possible states of nature.

Maximin Criterion

Consider the worst possible outcome for each action, whatever state of nature materializes. This *worst outcome* is simply the smallest payoff that could conceivably result. The **maximin criterion** selects the action for which the minimum payoff is highest; that is, we *maximize* the *minimum* payoff.

For the cellular phone manufacturer's problem, the smallest payoff, whatever production process is used, occurs at the low level of demand. Clearly, as set out in Table 18.3, the maximum value of these minimum payoffs is $100,000. This will occur if production process C is used. Thus, maximin criterion selects production process C.

Since the maximum value of the minimum payoff for each production process is $100,000, it follows that production process C is selected as the course of action under the maximin criterion.

Example 18.2 Investment Opportunity (Maximin)

An investor wishes to choose between investing $10,000 for one year at an assured interest rate of 12% and investing the same amount over that period in a portfolio of common stocks. If the fixed-interest choice is made, the investor will be assured of a payoff of $1,200. If the portfolio of stocks is chosen, the return will depend on the performance of the market over the year. If the market is buoyant, a profit of $2,500 is expected; if the market is steady, the expected profit is $500; and for a depressed market, a loss of $1,000 is expected. Set up the payoff table for this investor, and find the maximin choice of action.

Solution   Table 18.4 shows the payoffs (in dollars), with a negative payoff indicating a loss.

The minimum payoff for the fixed-interest investment is $1,200, as this will occur whatever happens in the stock market. The minimum payoff from the stock portfolio

Table 18.4 Maximin Criterion Output for Example 18.2

ACTION	STATE OF NATURE			MINIMUM PAYOFF
INVESTMENT OPTION	BUOYANT STATE	STEADY STATE	DEPRESSED STATE	MINIMUM PAYOFF FOR EACH INVESTMENT OPTION
Fixed interest	1,200	1,200	−1,200	**1,200 (Maximum)**
Stock Portfolio	2,500	1,500	−1,000	−1,000

is a loss of $1,000, or −$1,000, which occurs when the market is depressed. Since the largest minimum payoff arises from the fixed-interest investment, it follows that fixed interest is selected as the course of action under the maximin criterion.

From these illustrations the general form of the decision rule based on the maximin criterion is clear. The objective of the maximin criterion is to *maximize* the *minimum* payoff.

Decision Rule Based on Maximin Criterion

Suppose that a decision maker has to choose from K admissible actions a_1, a_2,..., a_K, given H possible states of nature $s_1, s_2,..., s_H$. Let M_{ij} denote the payoff corresponding to the ith action and jth state of nature. For each action seek the smallest possible payoff. For the action a_1, for example, this is the smallest of $M_{11, 12},...,M_{1H}$. Let us denote this minimum M_1^* where

$$M_1^* = Min\ (M_{11}, M_{12},... M_{1H})$$

More generally, the smallest possible payoff for action a_i is given by the following:

$$M_i^* = Min\ (M_{i1}, M_{i2},... M_{iH})$$

The **maximin criterion** then selects the action a_i for which the corresponding M_1^* is largest (that is, the action for which the minimum payoff is highest).

The positive feature of the maximin criterion for decision making is that it produces the largest possible payoff that can be *guaranteed*. If production process C is used, the cellular phone manufacturer is *assured* a payoff of at least $100,000, whatever the level of demand turns out to be. Similarly, for the investor of Example 18.2, the choice of fixed interest makes a *certain* profit of $1,200. In neither example can any available alternative action *guarantee* as much.

However, it is precisely within this guarantee that reservations about the maximin criterion arise because one must often pay a price for such a guarantee. The price here lies in the forgoing of opportunities to receive a larger payoff, through the choice of some other action, *however unlikely* the worst-case situation seems to be. Thus, for example, the cellular phone manufacturer may be virtually certain that a high level of demand will result, in which case production process C would be a poor choice, since it yields the lowest payoff at this demand level.

The maximin criterion, then, can be thought of as providing a very cautious strategy for choosing among alternative actions. Such a strategy may, in certain circumstances, be appropriate, but only an extreme pessimist would use it invariably. For this reason it is sometimes called the *criterion of pessimism*: "Maximin is often used in situations where the planner feels he or she cannot afford to be wrong. Defense planning might be an example, as would investing your life savings. The planner chooses a decision that does as well as possible in the worst possible (most pessimistic) case" (Reference 1).

Minimax Regret Criterion

The decision maker wanting to use the *minimax regret criterion* must imagine being in the position where a choice of action has been made and one of the states of nature has occurred. The decision maker can look back on the choice made either with satisfaction or with disappointment because, as things turned out, some alternative action would have been preferable. The decision maker then determines the *regret*, or *opportunity loss*, of not making the best decision for a given state of nature and establishes a regret table.

Regret or Opportunity Loss Table
Suppose that a payoff table is arranged as a rectangular array with rows corresponding to actions and columns to states of nature. If each payoff in the table is subtracted from the largest payoff *in its column*, the resulting array is called a **regret table**, or an **opportunity loss table**.

By considering the difference between the actual monetary payoff that occurs for a decision and the optimal payoff for the same state of nature, the decision maker can select the action that <u>mini</u>mizes the <u>maximum loss or regret</u>.

Decision Rule Based on Minimax Regret Criterion
Given the regret table, the actions dictated by the **minimax regret criterion** are found as follows:

1. For each row (action), find the maximum regret.
2. Choose the action corresponding to the *minimum* of these *maximum* regrets.

The **minimax regret criterion** selects the action for which the maximum regret is smallest; that is, the minimax regret criterion produces the smallest possible opportunity loss that can be guaranteed.

Consider again the cellular phone manufacturer in Example 18.1. It will be shown that process B is selected by the minimax regret criterion. Suppose that the level of demand for the new product turns out to be low. In that case the best choice of action would have been production process C, yielding a payoff of $100,000. Had this choice been made, the manufacturer would have had 0 regret. Had process A been chosen, the resulting profit would have been only $70,000. The extent of the manufacturer's regret, in this eventuality, is the difference between the best payoff that could have been obtained ($100,000) and that resulting from what turned out to be an inferior

Table 18.5 Minimax Regret Criterion Output for Example 18.1

ACTION	STATE OF NATURE			H
PRODUCTION PROCESS	LOW DEMAND	MODERATE DEMAND	HIGH DEMAND	MAXIMUM REGRET FOR EACH PROCESS
A	30,000	5,000	0	30,000
B	20,000	5,000	20,000	**20,000 (Minimum)**
C	0	0	40,000	40,000

choice of action. Thus, the regret would be $100,000 – $70,000 = $30,000. Similarly, given low demand, if process B had been chosen, the regret would be as follows:

$$\$100,000 - \$80,000 = \$20,000$$

Continuing in this way the regrets involved for moderate and high levels of demand are calculated. In each case the regret is 0 for what would have turned out to be the best choice of action (process C for moderate demand and process A for high demand). These regrets, or opportunity losses from not making the best decision for a given state of nature, are given in Table 18.5, with the largest amount of regret for a given process included in the last column.

Clearly, the minimax regret criterion selects production process B, since the maximum regret for this process is the smallest of processes A, B, and C.

Neither the maximin criterion nor the minimax regret criterion allows the decision maker to inject personal views as to the likelihood of occurrence of states of nature into the decision-making process. Since most practical business problems occur in an environment with which the decision maker is at least moderately familiar, this represents a waste of expertise. The probabilities associated with the outcomes for each alternative action are considered in the next section.

EXERCISES

Basic Exercises

18.3 Consider Exercise 18.1, where an investor is considering three alternatives—a certificate of deposit, a low-risk stock fund, and a high-risk stock fund—for a $20,000 investment. She considers three possible states of nature:

s_1: Strong stock market
s_2: Moderate stock market
s_3: Weak stock market

The payoff table (in dollars) is as follows:

Action	State of Nature		
Possible Investment Alternative	s_1	s_2	s_3
Certificate of deposit	1,200	1,200	1,200
Low-risk stock fund	4,300	1,200	–600
High-risk stock fund	6,600	800	–1,500

a. Which action is selected by the maximin criterion?
b. Which action is selected by the minimax regret criterion?

18.4 Consider the manufacturer of deodorant in Exercise 18.2 who is about to expand production capacity to make a new product. Four alternative production processes are available. The accompanying table shows estimated profits, in dollars, for these processes for each of three possible demand levels for the product.

Action	State of Nature		
Production Process	Low Demand	Moderate Demand	High Demand
A	100,000	350,000	900,000
B	150,000	400,000	700,000
C	250,000	400,000	600,000
D	250,000	400,000	550,000

a. Which action is chosen by the maximin criterion?

b. Which action is chosen by the minimax regret criterion?

18.5 Another criterion for selecting a decision is the *maximax criterion*, sometimes known as the *criterion of optimism*. This criterion chooses the action with the largest possible payoff.

   a. What action would be chosen by the cellular phone manufacturer with the payoffs of Table 18.2, according to this criterion?

   b. The investor of Example 18.2 according to this criterion would choose what action?

Application Exercises

18.6 The cellular phone manufacturer in Example 18.1 has three admissible actions—processes A, B, and C. When these are considered together, process B is chosen by the minimax regret criterion. Suppose now that a fourth admissible alternative, production process E, is available. Estimated payoffs for this action are $60,000 under low demand, $115,000 for moderate demand, and $220,000 for high demand. Show that when production processes A, B, C, and E are considered together, process A is chosen by the minimax regret criterion. Thus, while adding process E to the available actions does not result in the selection of that process, it does lead to the choice of a different action than would otherwise have been the case. Comment on the intuitive appeal of the minimax regret criterion in light of this example.

18.7 Consider a decision problem with two possible actions and two states of nature.

   a. Give an example of a payoff table where both actions are admissible and the same action is chosen by both the maximin criterion and the minimax regret criterion.

   b. Give an example of a payoff table according to which different actions are chosen by the maximin criterion and the minimax regret criterion.

18.8 Consider a decision problem with two admissible actions and two possible states of nature. Formulate a description of the form that the payoff table must take for the same action to be chosen by the maximin criterion and by the minimax regret criterion.

18.9 The prospective operator of a shoe store has the opportunity to locate in an established and successful shopping center. Alternatively, at lower cost, she can locate in a new center whose development has recently been completed. If the new center turns out to be very successful, it is expected that annual store profits from location in it would be $130,000. If the center is only moderately successful, annual profits would be $60,000. If the new center is unsuccessful, an annual loss of $10,000 would be expected. The profits to be expected from location in the established center will also depend to some extent on the degree of success of the new center, as potential customers may be drawn to it. If the new center was unsuccessful, annual profits for the shoe store located in the established center would be expected to be $90,000. However, if the new center was moderately successful, the expected profits would be $70,000, while they would be $30,000 if the new center turned out to be very successful.

   a. Set up the payoff table for the decision-making problem of this shoe store operator.

   b. Which action is chosen by the maximin criterion?

   c. Which action is chosen by the minimax regret criterion?

18.3 EXPECTED MONETARY VALUE

An important ingredient in the analysis of many business decision-making problems is likely to be the decision maker's assessment of the chances that various states of nature relevant in the determination of the eventual payoff will occur. The criteria discussed in Section 18.2 do not allow the incorporation of this kind of assessment into the decision-making process. However, a manager will almost invariably have a good feeling for the environment in which the decision is to be made and will want this expertise to be taken into account before deciding on a course of action. The discussion in this section assumes that a *probability* of occurrence can be attached to each state of nature, and it will be shown how these probabilities are employed in arriving at an eventual decision.

In general, when there are H possible states of nature, a probability must be attached to each. These probabilities are denoted by $P_1, P_2, \ldots, P_H$, so that probability P_j corresponds to state of nature s_j. The general setup for this decision-making problem is shown in Table 18.6.

Table 18.6 Payoffs with State-of-Nature Probabilities

ACTION	STATE OF NATURE			
a_i/s_i	$s_1(P_1)$	$s_2(P_2)$	...	$s_H(P_H)$
a_1	M_{11}	M_{12}	...	M_{1H}
a_2	M_{21}	M_{22}	...	M_{2H}
.	.	.	.	.
.	.	.	.	.
.	.	.	.	.
a_K	M_{K1}	M_{K2}	...	M_{KH}

Since one, and only one, of the states of nature must occur, these probabilities necessarily sum to 1, so that

$$\sum_{j=1}^{H} P_j = 1$$

When choosing an action, the decision maker will see each particular choice as having a specific probability of receiving the associated payoff and will, therefore, be able to calculate the *expected payoff* arising from each action. The expected payoff for this action is then the sum of the individual payoffs, weighted by their associated probabilities. These expected payoffs are often called the **expected monetary values** of the actions.

Expected Monetary Value (EMV) Criterion

Suppose that a decision maker has K possible actions, $a_1, a_2, ..., a_K$, and is faced with H states of nature. Let M_{ij} denote the payoff corresponding to the ith action and jth state, and P_j the probability of occurrence of the jth state of nature, with $\sum_{j=1}^{H} P_j = 1$. The **expected monetary value**, or **EMV**, of action a_i, $EMV(a_i)$, is as follows:

$$EMV(a_i) = P_1 M_{i1} + P_2 M_{i2} + \cdots + P_H M_{iH} = \sum_{j=1}^{H} P_j M_{ij} \qquad (18.1)$$

The **expected monetary value criterion** adopts the action with the largest expected monetary value; that is, given a choice among alternative actions, the *EMV* criterion dictates the choice of the action for which the *EMV* is highest.

Let us return to the cellular phone manufacturer in Example 18.1 and calculate the *EMV* for each of the production processes. The cellular phone manufacturer will presumably have some experience with the market for this product and, on the basis of that experience, will be able to form a view as to the likelihood of occurrence of low, moderate, or high demand. Suppose that the cellular phone manufacturer knows that, of all previous introductions of this type of product, 10% have had low demand, 50% moderate demand, and 40% high demand. In the absence of any further information it is then reasonable to postulate, for this particular market introduction, the following probabilities for the states of nature:

$$P_1 = P(s_1) = \text{Probability of Low Demand} = 0.1$$
$$P_2 = P(s_2) = \text{Probability of Moderate Demand} = 0.5$$
$$P_3 = P(s_3) = \text{Probability of High Demand} = 0.4$$

Since one, and only one, of the states of nature must occur, these probabilities necessarily sum to 1; that is, the states of nature are mutually exclusive and collectively exhaustive. These probabilities are added to the payoff table (Table 18.2), which produces Table 18.7.

If the cellular phone manufacturer adopts production process A, she will receive a payoff of $70,000 with probability 0.1, $120,000 with probability 0.5, and $200,000 with probability 0.4. For the cellular phone manufacturer the expected monetary values for the three admissible actions are as follows:

$$EMV(\text{Process A}) = (0.1)(70{,}000) + (0.5)(120{,}000) + (0.4)(200{,}000) = \$147{,}000$$
$$EMV(\text{Process B}) = (0.1)(80{,}000) + (0.5)(120{,}000) + (0.4)(180{,}000) = \$140{,}000$$
$$EMV(\text{Process C}) = (0.1)(100{,}000) + (0.5)(125{,}000) + (0.4)(160{,}000) = \$136{,}500$$

The cellular phone manufacturer would choose production process A. It is interesting to note that neither the maximin criterion nor the minimax regret criterion led to this particular choice. However, the information that a high level of demand appears much more likely than a low level has been added. This renders process A as a relatively attractive option.

Decision Trees

The analysis of a decision problem by means of the expected monetary value criterion can be conveniently set out diagrammatically through a mechanism called a **decision tree**. When faced with analyzing decisions under risk, the tree diagram is a graphical device that forces the decision maker "to examine all possible outcomes, including unfavorable ones. He or she is also forced to make decisions in a logical, sequential manner" (Reference 3). Decision trees are especially helpful when a sequence of decisions must be made. All decision trees contain the following:

☐ **Decision (or action) nodes.** These squares indicate that a decision must be made and are sometimes called square nodes.

○ **Event (state of nature) nodes.** These circular junctions, from which *branches* emerge, represent a possible state of nature, to which the associated probability is attached. These nodes are sometimes called circular nodes.

❘ **Terminal nodes.** A vertical bar represents the end of the decision-event branch. Originally, a triangle was used to designate this point. Sometimes no designation is given.

After carefully defining a problem, the decision maker draws the decision tree, assigns probabilities to the possible events (states of nature), and estimates the payoff for each possible decision-event combination (every combination of action and state of nature). Now the decision maker is ready to find the optimal decision. This is called "solving the tree" (Reference 1). To solve a decision tree, one must work backward (called *folding back* the tree). Compute the expected monetary value (*EMV*) for each state of nature by starting at the far right of the decision tree and working back to decision nodes on the left.

Table 18.7
Payoffs and State-
of-Nature
Probabilities for
Cellular Phone
Manufacturer in
Example 18.1

ACTION	STATE OF NATURE		
PRODUCTION PROCESS	LOW DEMAND ($P = 0.10$)	MODERATE DEMAND ($P = 0.50$)	HIGH DEMAND ($P = 0.40$)
A	70,000	120,000	200,000
B	80,000	120,000	180,000
C	100,000	125,000	160,000

A tree diagram for the cellular phone manufacturer is given in Figure 18.1. The following steps were taken to choose the action with the largest *EMV*:

1. Beginning at the left-hand side of the figure, branches emerge from the **decision node** (square junction) representing the three possible actions: process A, process B, and process C. Next, come **event nodes** (circular junctions), from which branches representing possible states of nature (levels of demand emerge).

2. The *associated probability* is attached to each state of nature (low, moderate, or high).

3. The *payoffs* corresponding to the action–state of nature combinations are inserted at the far right of the tree.

4. The computations proceed from *right to left*, beginning with these payoffs. For each circular junction the sum of the probability times the payoff for each emerging branch is found. This provides the *EMV* for each action.

5. The *optimal decision* has the highest *EMV* and is indicated at the left square junction. Process A is, therefore, chosen by the expected monetary value criterion. This choice of action results in an expected monetary value, or expected profit, of $147,000 for the cellular phone manufacturer.

Figure 18.1
Decision Tree for
Cellular Phone
Manufacturer
(*Action with
Maximum *EMV*)

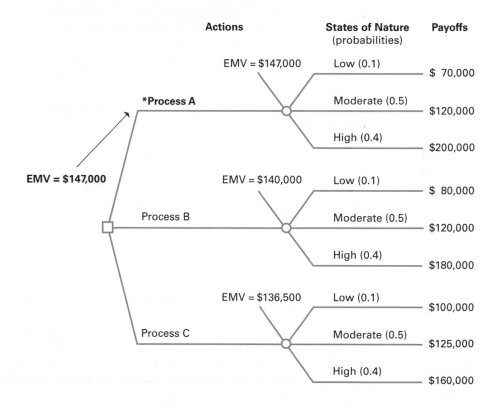

Example 18.3 Investment Opportunity (EMV Criterion)

The investor in Example 18.2 needed to decide between a fixed-interest-rate investment and a portfolio of stocks. Let us assume that this investor is, in fact, very optimistic about the future course of the stock market, believing that the probability of a buoyant market is 0.6, while the probability is 0.2 for each of the other two states. The payoffs and state-of-nature probabilities are, therefore, those given in the following table:

| Action | State of Nature | | |
Investment	Buoyant State $(P = 0.60)$	Steady State $(P = 0.20)$	Depressed State $(P = 0.20)$
Fixed interest	1,200	1,200	1,200
Stock portfolio	2,500	500	−1,000

Which investment should be chosen according to the expected monetary value criterion?

Solution Since a payoff of $1,200 will result from the fixed-interest investment, whatever happens in the stock market, the expected monetary value of this investment is $1,200. The *EMV* for the stock portfolio is as follows:

$$EMV \text{ (Stock Portfolio)} = (0.6)(2,500) + (0.2)(500) + (0.2)(-1,000) = \$1,400$$

Since this is the higher expected monetary value, the investor would choose the *portfolio of common stocks*, according to the expected monetary value criterion.

The completed decision tree for Example 18.3 is Figure 18.2.

A problem that requires a *sequence* of decisions is considered next.

Figure 18.2 Decision Tree for Example 18.3; Optimal Decision: Select the Stock Portfolio

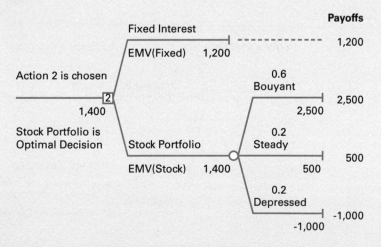

Example 18.4 Drug Manufacturer (EMV Criterion)

A drug manufacturer holds the patent rights to a new formula for lowering cholesterol levels. The manufacturer is able to sell the patent for $50,000 or to proceed with intensive tests of the drug's efficacy. The cost of carrying out these tests is $10,000. If the drug is found to be ineffective, it will not be marketed, and the cost of the tests will be written off as a loss. In the past, tests of drugs of this type have shown 60% to be effective and 40% ineffective.

If the tests should now reveal the drug to be effective, the manufacture has the option either to sell the patent rights and test results for $120,000 or to market the drug. If the drug is marketed, it is estimated that profits on sales (exclusive of the cost of the tests) will amount to $180,000 if the sales campaign is highly successful, but only $90,000 if it is just moderately successful. It is estimated that these two levels of market penetration are equally likely. According to the expected monetary value criterion, how should the drug manufacturer proceed?

Solution It is best to attack this problem through the construction of a decision tree. The completed tree is shown in Figure 18.3.

The manufacturer may decide either to sell the patent, in which case there is nothing further to be done, or to retain it and carry out tests on the drug's efficacy. There are two possible states of nature—the drug is either effective (with probability 0.6) or ineffective (with probability 0.4). In the latter case, the story ends. However, if the drug proves to be effective, a second decision must be made—whether to market it or to sell the patent rights and test results. If the former option is adopted, then the level of marketing success determines the eventual outcome, which could be either moderate or high (each with probability 0.5).

Figure 18.3 Decision Tree for Example 18.4; Optimal Decision: Retain Patent, and, If Test Shows Drug to Be Effective, Then Market the Drug (EMV = $71,000)

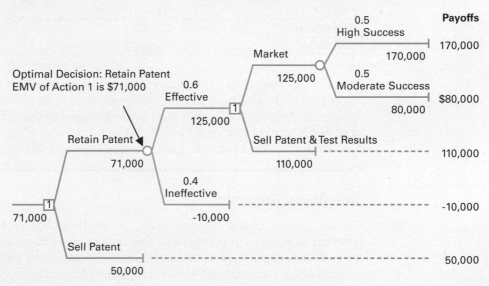

Next, the payoffs resulting from all action–state of nature combinations are considered. Begin at the bottom of the decision tree. If the manufacturer's original decision is to sell the patent, the manufacturer receives $50,000. If the patent is kept but the drug turns out to be ineffective, the manufacturer sustains a loss of $10,000, the cost of carrying out the tests. This is shown as a negative payoff in that amount. If the drug is found to be effective and the patent and test results are then sold, the manufacturer receives $120,000, from which must be subtracted the cost of the tests, leaving a payoff of $110,000. Finally, if the drug is marketed, the payoffs for moderate and high success are, respectively, $90,000 and $180,000, less the cost of the tests, leaving $80,000 and $170,000, respectively.

Having reached this point, the decision problem is solved by working backward from right to left along the tree. This is necessary because the appropriate action at the first decision point cannot be determined until the expected monetary value of the best available option at the second decision point is found.

Therefore, begin by supposing that initially the patent was retained and that the tests proved the drug to be effective. If the patent and test results are sold, then a profit of $110,000 will result. The expected monetary value from marketing the drug is as follows:

$$EMV = (0.5)(170,000) + (0.5)(80,000) = \$125,000$$

Since this exceeds $110,000, the better option at this stage, by the expected monetary value criterion, is to market the drug. This amount is, therefore, entered at the square junction of the second decision point and is treated as the payoff that results if the manufacturer's initial decision is to retain the patent, and the tests indicate that the drug is effective. Hence, for the initial decision the payoff table with state-of-nature probabilities is as shown here. The expected monetary value of selling the patent is the assured $50,000, while the expected monetary value of retaining it is $(0.6)(125,000) + (0.4)(-10,000) = \$71,000$. Then, by the expected monetary value criterion, the patent should be retained.

	State of Nature	
Action	Effective Drug ($P = 0.60$)	Ineffective Drug ($P = 0.40$)
Retain patent	125,000	−10,000
Sell patent	50,000	50,000

If the manufacturer's objective is to maximize expected monetary value (that is, expected profit), then the manufacturer should retain the patent. If the tests prove the drug to be effective, then the manufacturer should market it. This strategy yields an expected profit of $71,000.

By use of a decision tree, the same result appears in Figure 18.3.

Sensitivity Analysis

For the cellular phone manufacturer, production process A was selected by the expected monetary value criterion. This decision was based on the estimated payoff for each action–state of nature combination and on the estimated probability of occurrence for each state of nature. However, often a decision maker will be uncertain about such estimates, so it is useful to ask under what range of specifications of a decision problem a particular action will be optimal under the expected monetary value criterion. **Sensitivity analysis** seeks to answer such questions, the most straightforward case being where a single problem specification is allowed to vary, while all other specifications are held fixed.

To illustrate, suppose that the cellular phone manufacturer agrees with the assessment that the probability of high demand is 0.4 but is less sure of the assessments for the other two states of nature. Let P denote the probability of low demand so that the probability of moderate demand must be $(0.6 - P)$. According to the expected monetary value criterion, under what range of values of P would the adoption of process A be optimal? Using the payoffs of Table 18.7, the expected monetary values are as follows:

$$EMV(A) = (P)(70,000) + (0.6 - P)(120,000) + (0.4)(200,000) = 152,000 - 50,000P$$
$$EMV(B) = (P)(80,000) + (0.6 - P)(120,000) + (0.4)(180,000) = 144,000 - 40,000P$$
$$EMV(C) = (P)(100,000) + (0.6 - P)(125,000) + (0.4)(160,000) = 139,000 - 25,000P$$

Choice of process A will remain optimal provided the associated EMV is higher than that of each of the other two processes. Thus, for process A to be preferred to process B, it must follow that

$$152,000 - 50,000P > 144,000 - 40,000P$$

or

$$8,000 > 10,000P$$

so

$$P < 0.8$$

This must be so, since, by our assumptions, the probability of low demand cannot exceed 0.6. Similarly, for process A to be preferred to process C, then

$$152,000 - 50,000P > 139,000 - 25,000P$$

or

$$13,000 > 25,000P$$

so

$$P < 0.52$$

If the payoffs are as postulated in Table 18.7 and the probability of high demand is 0.4, then production process A is the best choice under the expected monetary value criterion, provided that the probability of low demand is less than 0.52.

Now suppose that the cellular phone manufacturer is uncertain about the estimated payoff of $200,000 for process A under high demand. Consider under what range of payoffs process A will be the optimal choice, when all other problem specifications are kept at their initial levels, given in Table 18.7. If M is the payoff for process A under high demand, then the expected monetary value for this process is as follows:

$$EMV(A) = (0.1)(70,000) + (0.5)(120,000) + 0.4M = 67,000 + 0.4M$$

The expected monetary values for processes B and C are, as before, $140,000 and $136,500. Therefore, process A will be the best choice according to the expected monetary value criterion, provided that

$$67,000 + 0.4M > 140,000$$

or

$$0.4M > 73,000$$

or

$$M > 182,500$$

If all other specifications are as originally given in Table 18.7, then production process A will be selected by the expected monetary value criterion, provided that the payoff for process A under high demand exceeds $182,500.

EXERCISES

Application Exercises

18.10 A student already has offers of employment. She must now decide whether to visit another potential employer for further interviews. She views the time and effort of doing so as having a cost of $500, which will be incurred whether or not she takes a job with this employer. If the employer offers a position preferable to her other alternatives, this would be viewed as a benefit worth $5,000 (from which the $500 cost must be subtracted). Otherwise, her time and effort would have been wasted.

   a. Set up the payoff table for the student's decision-making problem.
   b. Suppose the student believes that the probability is 0.05 that she would be offered a position preferable to her other alternatives by this employer. According to the expected monetary value criterion, should she visit this potential employer?

18.11 A manager has to choose between two actions, a_1 and a_2. There are two possible states of nature, s_1 and s_2. The payoffs are shown in the accompanying table. If the manager believes that each state of nature is equally likely to occur, which action should be chosen, according to the expected monetary value criterion?

| | State of Nature | |
Action	s_1	s_2
a_1	72,000	51,000
a_2	78,000	47,000

18.12 The investor of Exercise 18.1 believes that the probability of a strong stock market is 0.2, the probability of a moderate stock market is 0.5, and the probability of a weak stock market is 0.3.

   a. Which action should be chosen, according to the expected monetary value criterion?
   b. Draw the decision tree for the investor's problem.

18.13 The deodorant manufacturer in Exercise 18.2 knows that historically 30% of new products of this type have met high demand, 40% have met moderate demand, and 30% have met low demand.

   a. According to the expected monetary value criterion, which production process should be used?
   b. Draw the decision tree for this manufacturer's problem.

18.14 Consider a decision problem with two admissible actions and two possible states of nature, each of which is equally likely to occur.

   a. Determine whether each of the following statements is true or false for such problems:
      i. The action chosen by the expected monetary value criterion will always be the same as the action chosen by the maximin criterion.
      ii. The action chosen by the expected monetary value criterion will always be the same as the action chosen by the minimax regret criterion.
      iii. The action chosen by the expected monetary value criterion will always be that for which the average possible payoff is higher.
   b. Would your answer regarding statement (iii) in part (a) be the same if the two states of nature were not equally likely to occur?

18.15 A decision problem has K possible actions and H possible states of nature. If one of these actions is inadmissible, show that it cannot be chosen by the expected monetary value criterion.

18.16 The shoe store operator of Exercise 18.9 believes that the probability is 0.4 that the new shopping center will be very successful, 0.4 that it will be moderately successful, and 0.2 that it will be unsuccessful.

   a. According to the expected monetary value criterion, where should the shoe store be located?
   b. Draw the decision tree.

18.17 Refer to the decision-making problem in Exercises 18.1, 18.3, and 18.12. This investor is comfortable with the assessment of a probability of 0.2 for a strong market. However, she is less sure of the probability assessments for the other two states of nature. Under what range of probabilities for a weak stock market does the expected monetary value criterion give the choice of action found in Exercise 18.12?

18.18 Refer to the problem of the deodorant manufacturer of Exercises 18.2, 18.4, and 18.13.

   a. The manufacturer is comfortable with an assessment that the probability of low demand is 0.3 but is less secure about the probabilities for the other two demand levels. Under what range of probabilities for moderate demand will the expected monetary value criterion yield the choice of action found in Exercise 18.13?

   b. Take the remaining problem specifications to be as given in Exercises 18.2 and 18.13. Under what range of profits for high demand when process A is used will the expected monetary value criterion give the choice of action found in Exercise 18.13?

18.19 Refer to the problem of the shoe store operator of Exercises 18.9 and 18.16.

   a. The shoe store operator is happy with the assessment that the probability is 0.2 that the new shopping center will be unsuccessful but is less sure about the probability assessments for the other two states of nature. Under what range of probabilities that the new shopping center will be very successful will the expected monetary value criterion lead to the choice of action found in Exercise 18.16?

   b. Assuming that the other problem specifications are as in Exercises 18.9 and 18.16, under what range of profit levels for location in the new center if it turns out to be very successful will the expected monetary value criterion lead to the choice of action found in Exercise 18.16?

18.20 A manufacturer receives regular contracts for large consignments of parts for the automobile industry. This manufacturer's production process is such that, when it is operating correctly, 10% of all parts produced do not meet industry specifications. However, the production process is prone to a particular malfunction, whose presence can be checked at the beginning of a production run. When the process is operated with this malfunction, 30% of the parts produced fail to meet industry specifications. The manufacturer supplies parts under a contract that will yield a profit of $20,000 if only 10% of the parts are defective and a profit of $12,000 if 30% of the parts are defective. The cost of checking for the malfunction is $1,000, and, if it turns out that repair is needed, this costs a further $2,000. If incurred, these costs must be subtracted from the profit of the contract. Historically, it has been found that the production process functions correctly 80% of the time. The manufacturer must decide whether to check the process at the beginning of a production run.

   a. According to the expected monetary value criterion, what is the optimal decision?
   b. Draw the decision tree.
   c. Suppose that the proportion of occasions on which the production process operates correctly is unknown. Under what range of values for this proportion would the decision selected in part (a) be optimal, according to the expected monetary value criterion?

18.21 A contractor has to decide whether to submit a bid for a construction project. It will cost $16,000 to prepare the bid. This cost would be incurred whether or not the bid was accepted. The contractor intends to bid at a level that will produce a $110,000 profit (less the cost of preparing the bid). The contractor knows that 20% of bids prepared in this way have been successful.

   a. Set up the payoff table.
   b. Should a bid be prepared and submitted, according to the expected monetary value criterion?
   c. Under what range of probabilities that the bid will be successful should a bid be prepared and submitted, according to the expected monetary value criterion?

18.22 On Thursday evening the manager of a small branch of a car rental agency finds that she has six cars available for rental on the following day. However, she is able to request delivery of additional cars at a cost of $20 each from the regional depot. Each car that is rented produces an expected profit of $40. (The cost of delivery of the car must be subtracted from this profit.) Each potential customer requesting a car when none is available is counted as a $10 loss in goodwill. On reviewing the records for previous Fridays, the manager finds that the number of cars requested has ranged from 6 to 10; the percentages are shown in the accompanying table. The manager must decide how many cars, if any, to order from the regional depot.

Number of requests	6	7	8	9	10
Percent	10	30	30	20	10

   a. Set up the payoff table.
   b. If the expected monetary value criterion is used, how many cars should be ordered?

18.23 A contractor has decided to place a bid for a project. Bids are to be set in multiples of $20,000. It is estimated that the probability that a bid of $240,000 will secure the contract is 0.2, the probability that a bid of $220,000 will be successful is 0.3, and the probability that a bid of $200,000 will be accepted is 0.5. It is thought that any bid under $200,000 is certain to succeed and any bid over $240,000 is certain to fail. If the manufacturer wins the contract, he must solve a design problem with two possible choices at this stage. The contractor can hire outside consultants, who will guarantee a satisfactory solution, for a price of $80,000. Alternatively, he can invest $30,000 of his own resources in an attempt to solve the problem internally; if this effort fails, he must then engage the consultants. It is estimated that the probability of successfully solving the problem internally is 0.6. Once this problem has been solved, the additional cost of fulfilling the contract is $140,000.

a. Potentially, this contractor has two decisions to make. What are they?

b. Draw the decision tree.

c. What is the optimal course of action, according to the expected monetary value criterion?

18.24 Consider a decision problem with two actions, a_1 and a_2, and two states of nature, s_1 and s_2. Let M_{ij} denote the payoff corresponding to action a_i and state of nature s_j. Assume that the probability of occurrence of state of nature s_1 is P, so the probability of state s_2 is $(1 - P)$.

a. Show that action a_1 is selected by the *EMV* criterion if

$$P(M_{11} - M_{21}) > (1 - P)(M_{22} - M_{12})$$

b. Hence, show that if a_1 is an admissible action, there is some probability, P, for which it will be chosen. However, if a_1 is not admissible, it cannot be chosen, whatever the value of P.

18.4 SAMPLE INFORMATION: BAYESIAN ANALYSIS AND VALUE

Decisions made in the business world can often involve considerable amounts of money, and the cost of making a suboptimal choice may turn out to be substantial. This being the case, it could well pay the decision maker to make an effort to obtain as much relevant information as possible before the decision is made. In particular, a decision maker will want to become as thoroughly informed as possible about the chances of occurrence of the various states of nature that determine the eventual payoff.

This feature of any careful analysis of a decision problem has not been apparent in our discussion so far. The cellular phone manufacturer, in Section 18.3, assessed the probabilities of low, moderate, and high levels of demand for a new cellular phone as 0.1, 0.5, and 0.4, respectively. However, this assessment reflected no more than the historical proportions achieved by previous products. In practice, a decision maker might well want to carry out some market research on the prospects for the new product. Given such research, these initial or *prior probabilities* may be modified, yielding new probabilities, called *posterior probabilities*, for the three demand levels. The information (in this case the market research results) leading to the modification of probabilities for the states of nature will be referred to as *sample information*.

Use of Bayes' Theorem

In Chapter 3 the mechanism for modifying prior probabilities to produce posterior probabilities was given. This is accomplished through **Bayes' theorem**, which, for your convenience, is restated in the framework of our decision-making problem.

Let $s_1, s_2, ..., s_H$ be H mutually exclusive and collectively exhaustive events, corresponding to the H states of nature of a decision problem. Let A be some other event. Denote the conditional probability that s_i will occur, given that A occurs, by $P(s_i|A)$ and the probability of A, given s_i, by $P(A|s_i)$. **Bayes' theorem** states that the conditional probability of s_i, given A, can be expressed as follows:

$$P(s_i|A) = \frac{P(A|s_i)P(s_i)}{P(A)}$$

$$= \frac{P(A|s_i)P(s_i)}{P(A|s_1)P(s_1) + P(A|s_2)P(s_2) + \cdots + P(A|s_H)P(s_H)} \quad (18.2)$$

In the terminology of this section $P(s_i)$ is the **prior probability** of s_i and is modified to the **posterior probability**, $P(s_i|A)$, given the **sample information** that event A has occurred.

Now, suppose that the cellular phone manufacturer hires a market research organization to predict the level of demand for this new product. Of course, there will be a fee for this service. Later in this chapter the question of whether the return merits the cost involved is discussed. The organization provides a rating of "poor," "fair," or "good," on the basis of its research. A review of the market research company's records reveals the quality of its past predictions in this field. Table 18.8 shows, for each level of demand outcome, the proportion of poor, fair, and good assessments.

For example, on 10% of occasions that demand was high, the assessment was "poor." Thus, in the notation of conditional probability, denoting low, moderate, and high demand levels by s_1, s_2, and s_3, respectively, it follows that

$$P(\text{Poor} \mid s_1) = 0.6 \quad P(\text{Poor} \mid s_2) = 0.3 \quad P(\text{Poor} \mid s_3) = 0.1$$

It is only a coincidence that the sum of $P(\text{Poor} \mid s_1) = 0.6$, $P(\text{Poor} \mid s_2) = 0.3$, and $P(\text{Poor} \mid s_3) = 0.1$ is 1.0. It is not necessary that these conditional probabilities sum to 1. Take "fair," for example; notice that the sum of $P(\text{Fair} \mid s_1) = 0.2$, $P(\text{Fair} \mid s_2) = 0.4$, and $P(\text{Fair} \mid s_3) = 0.2$ is only 0.8 and not 1.0.

Suppose now that the market research firm is consulted and produces an assessment of "poor" for the prospects of the cellular phone. Given this new information, the prior probabilities

$$P(s_1) = 0.1 \quad P(s_2) = 0.5 \quad P(s_3) = 0.4$$

Table 18.8 Proportion of Assessments of Each Type Provided by a Market Research Organization for Cellular Phones Achieving Given Levels of Demand

ACTION	STATE OF NATURE		
ASSESSMENT	LOW DEMAND (S_1)	MODERATE DEMAND (S_2)	HIGH DEMAND (S_3)
Poor	0.6	0.3	0.1
Fair	0.2	0.4	0.2
Good	0.2	0.3	0.7

for the three demand levels can be modified using Bayes' theorem. For a low level of demand, the posterior probability is as follows:

$$P(s_1 | \text{Poor}) = \frac{P(\text{Poor} | s_1) P(s_1)}{P(\text{Poor} | s_1) P(s_1) + P(\text{Poor} | s_2) P(s_2) + P(\text{Poor} | s_3) P(s_3)}$$

$$= \frac{(0.6)(0.1)}{(0.6)(0.1) + (0.3)(0.5) + (0.1)(0.4)} = \frac{0.06}{0.25} = 0.24$$

Similarly, for the other two demand levels the posterior probabilities are as follows:

$$P(s_2 | \text{Poor}) = \frac{(0.3)(0.5)}{0.25} = 0.6$$

$$P(s_3 | \text{Poor}) = \frac{(0.1)(0.4)}{0.25} = 0.16$$

The posterior probabilities can then be employed to calculate the expected monetary values. Table 18.9 shows the payoffs (without the fee of the organization), together with the posterior probabilities for the three demand levels. This is simply a modification of Table 18.7, with the posterior probabilities replacing the prior probabilities of that table.

The expected monetary values for the three production processes can be found in precisely the same manner as before. These are as follows:

EMV (Process A) = (0.24)(70,000) + (0.60)(120,000) + (0.16)(200,000) = $120,800
EMV (Process B) = (0.24)(80,000) + (0.60)(120,000) + (0.16)(180,000) = $120,000
EMV (Process C) = (0.24)(100,000) + (0.60)(125,000) + (0.16)(160,000) = $124,600

If the assessment of market prospects is "poor," then, according to the expected monetary value criterion, production process C should be used. The market research group's assessment has rendered low demand much more likely and high demand considerably less likely than was previously the case. This shift in the view of market prospects is sufficient to induce the cellular phone manufacturer to switch preference from process A (based on the prior probabilities) to process C.

Following the same line of argument, one can determine the decisions that would be made if the prospects for the cellular phone's market success were rated either "fair" or "good." Again, the posterior probabilities for the three levels of

Table 18.9 Payoffs for Cellular Phone Manufacturer and Posterior Probabilities for States of Nature, Given an Assessment of "Poor" by Market Research Organization

ACTION	STATE OF NATURE		
PRODUCTION PROCESS	LOW DEMAND ($P = 0.24$)*	MODERATE DEMAND ($P = 0.60$)*	HIGH DEMAND ($P = 0.16$)*
A	70,000	120,000	200,000
B	80,000	120,000	180,000
C	100,000	125,000	160,000

*Posterior probabilities

Table 18.10 *EMVs* for Cellular Phone Manufacturer for Three Possible Assessments by a Market Research Firm

ACTION	STATE OF NATURE		
PRODUCTION PROCESS	POOR ASSESSMENT	FAIR ASSESSMENT	GOOD ASSESSMENT
A	120,800	138,000	167,556
B	120,000	133,333	155,556
C	124,600	132,667	145,667

demand can be obtained through Bayes' theorem. For a "fair" assessment, these are as follows:

$$P(s_1 \mid \text{Fair}) = \frac{1}{15} \qquad P(s_2 \mid \text{Fair}) = \frac{10}{15} \qquad P(s_3 \mid \text{Fair}) = \frac{4}{15}$$

For a "good" assessment

$$P(s_1 \mid \text{Good}) = \frac{2}{45} \qquad P(s_2 \mid \text{Good}) = \frac{15}{45} \qquad P(s_3 \mid \text{Good}) = \frac{28}{45}$$

Using these posterior probabilities, we obtained the expected monetary values of each of the production processes for each given assessment. Table 18.10 contains these EMVs. The calculated EMVs in Table 18.10 could vary depending on the number of decimal places used to express the posterior probabilities.

As has been shown previously, if the assessment is "poor," then process C is preferred by the expected monetary value criterion. If any other assessment is made, then production process A would be chosen, according to this criterion.

Recall that, for the cellular phone manufacturer's problem when the prior probabilities for levels of demand were used, the optimal decision according to the expected monetary value criterion was to use process A. It can be the case (if an assessment of "poor" is obtained) that a different decision will be made when these prior probabilities are modified by sample information. Hence, it turns out that consulting the market research organization could be valuable for the manufacturer. Of course, if the choice of process A had proved optimal, whatever the assessment, the sample information could not possibly be of value.

Example 18.5 Drug Manufacturer Revisited (Expected Monetary Value)

In Example 18.4 a drug manufacturer had to decide whether to sell the patent for a cholesterol-lowering formula before subjecting the drug to thorough testing. (Subsequently, if the patent was retained and the drug was found to be effective, a second decision—to market the drug or to sell the patent and test results—also had to be made.) For the initial decision, the two states of nature were s_1: Drug is effective; and s_2: Drug is ineffective. The associated prior probabilities, formed on the basis of previous experience, are as follows:

$$P(s_1) = 0.6 \quad \text{and} \quad P(s_2) = 0.4$$

The drug manufacturer has the option of carrying out, at modest cost, an initial test before the first decision is made. The test is not infallible. For drugs that have subsequently proved effective, the preliminary test result was positive on 60% of occasions and negative on the remainder. For ineffective drugs a positive preliminary test result was obtained 30% of the time, the other results being negative. Given the results of the preliminary test, how should the drug manufacturer proceed? Assume that it is still possible to sell the patent for $50,000 if the preliminary test result is negative.

Solution First, notice that, if the patent is retained and the exhaustive tests prove the drug to be effective, then in the absence of any sample information on market conditions, the optimal decision at this stage, as in Example 18.4, is to market the drug. The information provided by the preliminary test is irrelevant in that particular decision. However, it could conceivably influence the initial decision as to whether to sell the patent. Accordingly, only this decision is considered.

The conditional probabilities of the sample outcomes, given the states of nature, are as follows:

$$P(Positive \mid s_1) = 0.6 \qquad P(Negative \mid s_1) = 0.4$$

$$P(Positive \mid s_2) = 0.3 \qquad P(Negative \mid s_2) = 0.7$$

If the result of the preliminary test is positive, then the posterior probability for the state s_1 (effective), given this information, is as follows:

$$P(s_1 \mid Positive) = \frac{P(Positive \mid s_1)P(s_1)}{P(Positive \mid s_1)P(s_1) + P(Positive \mid s_2)P(s_2)} = \frac{(0.6)(0.6)}{(0.6)(0.6) + (0.3)(0.4)} = 0.75$$

Further, since the two posterior probabilities must sum to 1, then $P(s_2 \mid Positive) = 0.25$. The accompanying payoff table is the same as in Example 18.4, with these posterior probabilities added.

	State of Nature	
Action	Effective Drug ($P = 0.75$)*	Ineffective Drug ($P = 0.25$)*
Retain patent	125,000	−10,000
Sell patent	50,000	50,000

*Posterior probabilities

The expected monetary value, if the patent is sold, is $50,000, while if the patent is retained, the expected monetary value is as follows:

$$(0.75)(125,000) + (0.25)(-10,000) = \$91,250$$

Therefore, if the initial test result is positive, the patent should be retained, according to this criterion.

Next, consider the case where the preliminary test result is negative. The posterior probability for the state s_1 is, by Bayes' theorem, as follows:

$$P(s_1 \mid Negative) = \frac{P(Negative \mid s_1)P(s_1)}{P(Negative \mid s_1)P(s_1) + P(Negative \mid s_2)P(s_2)} = \frac{(0.4)(0.6)}{(0.4)(0.6) + (0.7)(0.4)} = 0.4615$$

Hence, the posterior probability for the state s_2 is as follows:

$$P(s_2 \mid Negative) = 0.5385$$

Once more, if the patent is sold, the expected monetary value is the $50,000 that will be received. If the patent is retained, the expected monetary value of this decision is as follows:

$$(0.4615)(125,000) + (0.5385)(-10,000) = \$52,302.50$$

Thus, even if the preliminary test result is negative, the optimal decision, by the expected monetary value criterion, is to retain the patent.

In this particular example, then, whatever the sample information, the chosen action is the same. The manufacturer should retain the patent in the event of either result emerging from the preliminary test. Since the sample information cannot possibly affect the decision, there is, of course, no point in gathering it. In fact, since performing the preliminary test will not be costless, it will be suboptimal to do so. Thus, according to the expected monetary value criterion, the drug manufacturer should retain the patent, and if the thorough tests prove the drug to be effective, then the manufacturer should market it. The preliminary test should not be carried out.

The Value of Sample Information

It has been shown how sample information can be incorporated into the decision-making process. The potential value of such information lies, of course, in its provision of a better feel for the chances of occurrence of the relevant states of nature. This, in turn, can provide firmer ground on which to base a decision. This section shows how a *monetary* value can be attached to the sample information. This is important, since there will typically be some cost involved in obtaining the sample information, and the decision maker will want to know whether the expected benefits exceed this cost.

Example 18.5 illustrates a situation where the same action was optimal, whatever the sample result. In such a case the sample information clearly has no value, since the same action would have been taken without it. This is a general rule: If the sample information cannot affect the choice of action, then it has a value of 0.

Accordingly, the remainder of this section concerns only circumstances in which the sample result can affect the choice of action. Our example of the cellular phone manufacturer planning to introduce a new product is such a case. This manufacturer has to choose from three production processes and is faced with three states of nature, representing different levels of demand for the product. Section 18.3 showed that, in the absence of sample information and using only the prior probabilities, process A with an expected monetary value of $147,000 is selected.

Now, in practice, having obtained sample information, the decision maker will typically not know which state of nature will occur but will have more firmly grounded probabilistic assessments for these states. However, before discussing the value of sample information in this general framework, it is useful to consider the extreme case where **perfect information** is obtainable—that is, the case where the decision maker is able to gain information that will tell *with certainty* which state will occur. What is the value to the decision maker of having such perfect information?

Let us return again to the cellular phone manufacturer and calculate the *EVPI*. In the context of this manufacturer perfect information corresponds to knowledge of which of the three possible demand levels will actually result. In the absence of any sample information and on the basis of the prior probabilities only, process A will be chosen. However, referring to Table 18.7, if the level of demand is low, then the best choice will be process C. Since this has a payoff that exceeds by $30,000 that of process A, the value of knowing that demand will be low is $30,000. Similarly, if it is known that moderate demand will result, process C will again be chosen. Here, the payoff from the best available choice exceeds that of process A by $5,000, which is, accordingly, the value of knowing that demand will be moderate. If it is known that high demand will occur, then process A will be chosen. Thus, this particular knowledge is of no value, since the same decision would have been made without it. The value of perfect information depends on the information. Using the prior probabilities of the various states of nature, the expected value of perfect information is found.

For the cellular phone manufacturer, the prior probabilities are 0.1 for low, 0.5 for moderate, and 0.4 for high demand. It, therefore, follows that to this manufacturer the value of perfect information is $30,000 with probability 0.1, $5,000 with probability 0.5, and $0 with probability 0.4. The expected value of perfect information is, accordingly, as follows:

$$EVPI = (0.1)(30,000) + (0.5)(5,000) + (0.4)(0) = \$5,500$$

This dollar amount, then, represents the expected value to the cellular phone manufacturer of knowing what level of demand will result.

Although perfect information will not be available typically, the calculation of the expected value of perfect information can be useful. Since, of course, no sample information can be better than perfect, its expected value cannot be higher than that of the expected value of perfect information. Thus, the expected value of perfect information provides an *upper limit* for the expected value of any sample information. For example, if the cellular phone manufacturer is offered information at a cost of $6,000, it is not necessary to inquire further about the quality of this information. It should not be purchased, however reliable, according to the expected monetary value criterion, since its expected value cannot be more than $5,500.

Consider now the more general problem of assessing the value of sample information that is not necessarily perfect. Again, consider the decision-making problem of the cellular phone manufacturer who has the option of obtaining an assessment from a market research organization of the prospects for the new cellular phone. These prospects will be rated "poor," "fair," or "good." In Section 18.4 it was shown that, in the last two of the three eventualities, process A will still be chosen. Thus, if a "fair" or "good" rating is obtained, the initial choice of action will remain unchanged, and nothing will have been gained from consulting the market research company.

However, if the prospects are rated "poor," then Table 18.10 shows that the optimal choice is process C. This optimal choice would yield an expected monetary value of $124,600, whereas process A, which otherwise would have been used, gives an expected monetary value of $120,800. The difference in these amounts, $3,800, represents the gain from the sample information *if the assessment is "poor."* The gains from the sample information are $0 for ratings of "good" or "fair" and $3,800 for a rating of "poor."

We now need to know how likely these gains are to materialize, so in our example we must find the probability of a "poor" assessment. In general, if A denotes a piece of sample information and $s_1, s_2,..., s_H$ the H possible states of nature, then

$$P(A) = P(A \mid s_1)P(s_1) + P(A \mid s_2)P(s_2) + \cdots + P(A \mid s_H)P(s_H)$$

For the cellular phone example, with s_1, s_2, and s_3 denoting low, moderate, and high levels of demand, respectively, then

$$P(s_1) = 0.1 \qquad P(s_2) = 0.5 \qquad P(s_3) = 0.4$$
$$P(\text{Poor} \mid s_1) = 0.6 \qquad P(\text{Poor} \mid s_2) = 0.3 \qquad P(\text{Poor} \mid s_3) = 0.1$$

Therefore, the probability of a "poor" assessment is as follows:

$$P(\text{Poor}) = P(\text{Poor} \mid s_1)(P(s_1) + P(\text{Poor} \mid s_2)P(s_2) + P(\text{Poor} \mid s_3)P(s_3)$$
$$= (0.6)(0.1) + (0.3)(0.5) + (0.1)(0.4) = 0.25$$

In the same way, using the conditional probabilities of Table 18.8, the probabilities for the other two assessments are as follows:

$$P(\text{Fair}) = 0.30 \quad P(\text{Good}) = 0.45$$

Thus, the value of the sample information is $3,800 with a probability of 0.25, $0 with a probability of 0.30, and $0 with a probability of 0.45. It, therefore, follows that the **expected value of the sample information** is

$$EVSI = (0.25)(3,800) + (0.30)(0) + (0.45)(0) = \$950$$

This dollar amount, then, represents the expected value of the sample information to the decision maker. In terms of the expected monetary value criterion this sample information will be worth acquiring if its cost is less than its expected value. The **expected net value of sample information** is the difference between its expected value and its cost.

Suppose that the market research group charges a fee of $750 for its assessment. The expected net value of this assessment to the cellular phone manufacturer is then $950 − $750 = $200. Thus, the manufacturer's expected payoff will be $200 higher if the sample information is purchased than if it is not. This amount represents the expected worth of having that information, taking into account its cost. In this case the manufacturer's optimal strategy is to purchase the market research report and then use production process A if the assessment is either "good" or "fair" and process C if the assessment is "poor." The *EMV* of this strategy is $147,200—that is, the $147,000 that would result from no sample information plus the expected net value of the sample information.

Expected Value of Sample Information, EVSI

Suppose that a decision maker has to choose from K possible actions in the face of H states of nature, $s_1, s_2, ..., s_H$. The decision maker may obtain sample information. Let there be M possible sample results, $A_1, A_2, ..., A_M$.

The expected value of sample information is obtained as follows:

1. Determine which action would be chosen if only the prior probabilities were used.
2. Determine the probabilities of obtaining each sample result:

$$P(A_i) = P(A_i \mid s_1)P(s_1) + P(A_i \mid s_2)P(s_2) + \cdots + P(A_i \mid s_H)P(s_H)$$

3. For each possible sample result A_i, find the difference, V_i, between the expected monetary value for the optimal action and that for the action chosen if only prior probabilities are used. This is the **value of the sample information,** given that A_i was observed.
4. The **expected value of sample information,** or **EVSI**, is then

$$EVSI = P(A_1)V_1 + P(A_2)V_2 + \cdots + P(A_M)V_M \qquad (18.4)$$

The Value of Sample Information Viewed by Means of Decision Trees

The expected value of sample information can be computed in an alternative (but equivalent) manner, which is arithmetically slightly more cumbersome but does provide a convenient way of representing the problem in terms of a sequence of decisions through the construction of a decision tree. The first decision to make is whether to obtain the sample information. Next, it is necessary to decide which of the alternative actions should be followed.

To illustrate, consider again the problem of the cellular phone manufacturer. Figure 18.4 shows the decision trees following from the three possible market research appraisals. These trees have the same general structure as Figure 18.1. The essential difference is that the probabilities associated with the three states of nature are the appropriate *posterior probabilities,* given the specific sample information. These posterior probabilities were found in Section 18.4. The payoffs are now weighted by the posterior probabilities, yielding the expected monetary value of each action, given each possible sample result. These are the expected monetary values shown in Table 18.10. Finally, at the left of each part of Figure 18.4 is the highest possible expected monetary value for each sample outcome.

This information is transferred to the right of Figure 18.5, in which the decision whether to purchase the market research study is analyzed. If this information is not bought, then the bottom part of Figure 18.5 shows an expected monetary value of $147,000. This results from using the prior probabilities and is taken from Figure 18.1.

We turn now to the upper part of Figure 18.5; the expected monetary value that results will depend on the sample outcome. The probabilities are 0.25 for "poor," 0.30 for "fair," and 0.45 for "good." Thus, since $124,600 can be expected with probability 0.25, $138,000 with probability 0.30, and $167,556 with probability 0.45, the expected payoff if the sample information is purchased is as follows:

$$(0.25)(124,600) + (0.30)(138,000) + (0.45)(167,556) = \$147,950$$

However, it is necessary to subtract from this amount the $750 cost of the sample information, leaving $147,200. Since this is more than the expected payoff when no sample information is obtained, the best strategy, according to the expected monetary value criterion, is to purchase the services of the market research group. The optimal decision has, as indicated at the left of Figure 18.5, an expected monetary value of $147,200.

Figure 18.4
Decision Trees for the Cellular Phone Manufacturer, Given the Market Research Organization Assessments of (a) Poor, (b) Fair, and (c) Good (*Action with Maximum EMV)

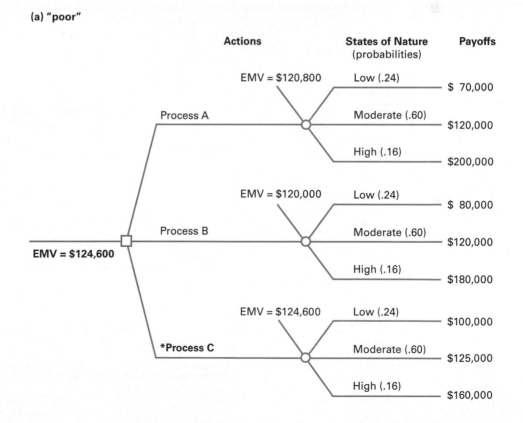

(a) "poor"

(b) "fair"

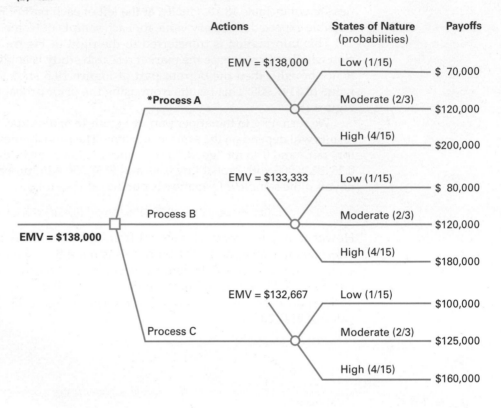

(c) "good"

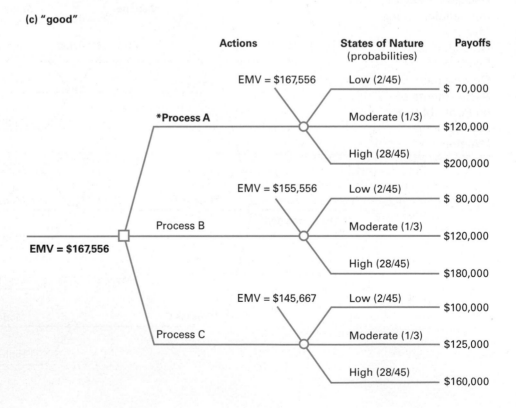

Figure 18.5
Cellular Phone
Manufacturer's
Decision to
Purchase the
Services of the
Market Research
Organization
(*Action with
Maximum EMV)

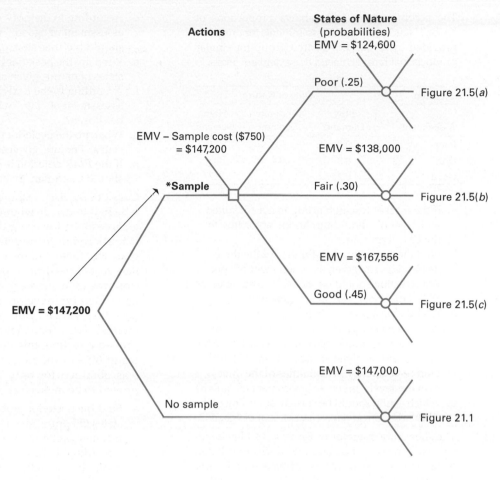

EXERCISES

Application Exercises

18.25 A manufacturer must decide whether to mount, at a cost of $100,000, an advertising campaign for a product whose sales have been rather flat. It is estimated that a highly successful campaign would add $400,000 (from which the campaign's costs must be subtracted) to profits, and a moderately successful campaign would add $100,000, but an unsuccessful campaign would add nothing. Historically, 40% of all similar campaigns have been very successful, 30% have been moderately successful, and the remainder have been unsuccessful. This manufacturer contacts a media consultant for a judgment on the potential effectiveness of the campaign. This consultant's record is such that she has reported favorably on 80% of campaigns that turned out to be highly successful, 40% of those that were moderately successful, and 10% of unsuccessful campaigns.

a. Find the prior probabilities for the three states of nature.

b. In the absence of any report from the media consultant, should this advertising campaign be mounted, according to the *EMV* criterion?

c. Find the posterior probabilities for the three states of nature, given that the media consultant reports favorably.

d. Given a favorable report from the consultant, should the advertising campaign be mounted, according to the *EMV* criterion?

e. Find the posterior probabilities for the three states of nature, given that the media consultant does not report favorably.

f. If the consultant's report is not favorable, should the advertising campaign be mounted, according to the *EMV* criterion?

18.26 Refer to Exercise 18.2. The deodorant manufacturer has four possible production processes from which to choose, depending on the view that is taken of future demand levels. On the basis of past experience the prior probabilities are 0.3 for high demand, 0.4 for moderate demand, and 0.3 for low demand.

The accompanying table shows proportions of "poor," "fair," and "good" assessments for prospects provided by a market research group for similar products that have achieved these demand levels.

Action	State of Nature		
Assessment	Low Demand	Moderate Demand	High Demand
Poor	0.5	0.3	0.1
Fair	0.3	0.4	0.2
Good	0.2	0.3	0.7

a. If the market research group is not consulted, which action should be chosen, according to the *EMV* criterion?

b. Find the posterior probabilities of the three demand levels, given an assessment of "poor."

c. Which action should be chosen, according to the *EMV* criterion, given an assessment of "poor"?

d. Find the posterior probabilities of the three demand levels, given an assessment of "fair."

e. Which action should be chosen, according to the *EMV* criterion, given an assessment of "fair"?

f. Find the posterior probabilities of the three demand levels, given an assessment of "good."

g. Which action should be chosen, according to the *EMV* criterion, given an assessment of "good"?

18.27 The shoe store operator of Exercise 18.9 has available two courses of action. Her decision is based on her view of the likely level of success of the new shopping center. Historically, 40% of new centers of this type have been very successful, 40% have been moderately successful, and 20% have been unsuccessful. A consulting group sells assessments of the prospects of this type of shopping center. The table given here shows the proportion of "good," "fair," and "poor" assessments, given the particular outcome actually resulting.

Action	State of Nature (Success Level)		
Assessment	Very Successful	Moderately Successful	Unsuccessful
Good	0.6	0.3	0.2
Fair	0.3	0.4	0.3
Poor	0.1	0.3	0.5

a. What are the prior probabilities for the three states of nature?

b. If the shoe store operator does not seek advice from the consulting group, what action should she take, according to the *EMV* criterion?

c. What are the posterior probabilities of the three states of nature, given an assessment of "good"?

d. According to the *EMV* criterion, given an assessment of "good," what course of action should the shoe store operator adopt?

e. What are the posterior probabilities of the three states of nature, given an assessment of "fair"?

f. According to the *EMV* criterion, given an assessment of "fair," which action should be chosen?

g. What are the posterior probabilities of the three states of nature, given an assessment of "poor"?

h. If the *EMV* criterion is followed, which action should be chosen, given a forecast of "poor"?

18.28 Consider the drug manufacturer of Example 18.5, who had to decide whether to sell the patent for a cholesterol-lowering drug before subjecting it to thorough testing. In the example we saw that, whatever the result of a certain preliminary test of the drug's efficacy, the optimal decision was to retain the patent. Subsequently, this manufacturer developed a superior preliminary test, which again could be carried out at modest cost. For drugs that subsequently proved effective, this new test gave a positive result 80% of the time, while a positive result was obtained for only 10% of the drugs that proved to be ineffective.

a. Find the posterior probabilities of the two states of nature, given a positive result from this new preliminary test.

b. According to the *EMV* criterion, should the patent be sold if the new test result is positive?

c. Find the posterior probabilities of the two states of nature, given a negative result from the new preliminary test.

d. According to the *EMV* criterion, should the patent be sold if the new test result is negative?

18.29 In Exercise 18.20, a supplier of parts to the automobile industry had to decide whether to check the production process for a certain malfunction before starting a production run. The two states of nature were as follows:

s_1: Repair not needed (10% of all parts produced fail to meet specifications)

s_2: Repair needed (30% of all parts produced fail to meet specifications)

The prior probabilities, derived from the historical record for this production process, are as follows:

$$P(s_1) = 0.8 \quad \text{and} \quad P(s_2) = 0.2$$

The manufacturer can, before beginning a full production run, produce a single part and check whether it meets specifications, basing a decision on whether to check the production process on the resulting sample information.

   a. If the single part checked meets specifications, what are the posterior probabilities of the states of nature?

   b. If the single part checked meets specifications, should the production process be checked according to the *EMV* criterion?

   c. If the single part checked does not meet specifications, what are the posterior probabilities of the states of nature?

   d. If the single part checked does not meet specifications, should the production process be checked, according to the *EMV* criterion?

18.30 Continuing Exercise 18.29, suppose now that, before making a decision on whether to check the production process, *two* parts are made and examined.

   a. If, in fact, repair is not needed, what are the probabilities that both parts, just one part, or neither part will fail to meet specifications?

   b. Compute the same probabilities as in part (a), given that repair of the production process is, in fact, needed.

   c. Compute the posterior probabilities of the states of nature, and determine the optimal action under the expected monetary value criterion, given each of the following circumstances:

     i. Both parts fail to meet specifications.
     ii. Just one part fails to meet specifications.
     iii. Neither part fails to meet specifications.

18.31 The Watts New Lightbulb Corporation ships large consignments of lightbulbs to big industrial users. When the production process is functioning correctly (which is 90% of the time), 10% of all bulbs produced are defective. However, the process is susceptible to an occasional malfunction, leading to a defective rate of 20%. The Watts New Lightbulb Corporation counts the cost, in terms of goodwill, of a shipment with the higher defective rate to an industrial user as $5,000. If a consignment is suspected of containing this larger proportion of defectives, it can instead be sold to a chain of discount stores, though this involves a reduction of $600 in profits, whether or not the consignment does indeed contain a large proportion of defective bulbs. Decisions by this company are made through the *EMV* criterion.

   a. A consignment is produced. In the absence of any further information should it be shipped to an industrial user or to the discount chain?

   b. Suppose that a single bulb from the consignment is checked. Determine where the

consignment should be shipped under each of the following circumstances:

     i. This bulb is defective.
     ii. This bulb is not defective.

   c. Suppose that two bulbs from the consignment are checked. Determine where the consignment should be shipped for each of the following situations:

     i. Both bulbs are defective.
     ii. Just one bulb is defective.
     iii. Neither bulb is defective.

   d. Without doing the calculations indicate how the decision problem could be attacked if 100 bulbs were checked prior to shipping the consignment.

18.32 Refer to the problem of the investor of Exercise 18.1.

   a. Explain what is meant by "perfect information" in the context of this investor's problem.

   b. The prior probabilities are 0.2 for a strong stock market, 0.5 for a moderate stock market, and 0.3 for a weak stock market. What is the expected value of perfect information to this investor?

18.33 For the deodorant manufacturer of Exercise 18.2, the prior probabilities are 0.3 for high demand, 0.4 for moderate demand, and 0.3 for low demand. Find the *EVPI* to this manufacturer.

18.34 For the shoe store operator of Exercise 18.9, the prior probabilities are 0.4 that the new shopping center will be very successful, 0.4 that it will be moderately successful, and 0.2 that it will be unsuccessful. What is the expected value of perfect information to this shoe store operator?

18.35 The manufacturer of automobile parts of Exercise 18.20 must decide whether to check the production process before beginning a full production run. Given that the production process functions correctly 80% of the time, what is the value of perfect information to this manufacturer?

18.36 Before showing how to find the expected value of sample information, we discussed separately the determination of the expected value of perfect information. In fact, this was not necessary because perfect information is just a special kind of sample information. Given the general procedure for finding the expected value of sample information, show how to specialize this to the case of perfect information.

18.37 Refer to Exercise 18.25. The manufacturer is considering an advertising campaign and first seeks the advice of a media consultant.

   a. What is the expected value to the manufacturer of the media consultant's advice?

b. The media consultant charges a fee of $5,000. What is the expected net value of the consultant's advice?

c. This manufacturer faces a two-stage decision problem. First, the manufacturer must decide whether to purchase advice from the media consultant. Next, the manufacturer must decide whether to mount the advertising campaign. Draw the complete decision tree, and indicate how the manufacturer should proceed.

18.38 Refer to Exercise 18.26. Find the largest fee the deodorant manufacturer should pay to the market research group, according to the expected monetary value criterion.

18.39 Refer to Exercise 18.27. Find the expected value to the shoe store operator of an assessment of the shopping center's prospects provided by the consulting group.

18.40 Refer to Exercise 18.28. Before deciding whether to sell the patent of the new cholesterol-lowering formula, the drug manufacturer carries out the new preliminary test. Find the expected value to the manufacturer of the test result.

18.41 Refer to Exercise 18.29. The supplier of automobile parts is able to produce and examine a single part before deciding whether to check the production process. What is the *EVSI*?

18.42 Consider the Watts New Lightbulb Corporation of Exercise 18.31. The corporation can check one or more lightbulbs before deciding whether to ship a consignment to an industrial user or to a discount chain.

a. What is the expected value to the corporation of checking a single lightbulb?

b. What is the expected value to the corporation of checking two lightbulbs?

c. What is the difference between expected values of checking two bulbs and one bulb?

d. If the first bulb checked turns out to be defective, what is the expected value of checking the second?

e. If the first bulb checked turns out not to be defective, what is the expected value of checking the second?

18.5 ALLOWING FOR RISK: UTILITY ANALYSIS

The expected monetary value criterion provides a framework for decision making that has wide practical applicability. That is to say, in many instances, an individual or corporation will believe that the action offering the highest expected monetary value is the preferred course. However, this is not invariably the case, as the following examples illustrate.

1. Many individuals purchase term life insurance through which, for a relatively modest outlay, the insured person's estate is generously compensated in the event of death during the term of the policy. Now, insurance companies are able to calculate the death probability of an individual of any given age during a specified period of time. Accordingly, their rates are set in such a way that the price of a policy exceeds the amount of money that is expected to be paid out. The amount of this excess covers the insurance company's costs and provides, on the average, a margin of profit. It then follows that, for the person insured, the expected payoff from the life insurance policy is less than its cost. Therefore, if everyone based decisions on the expected monetary value criterion, term life insurance would not be purchased. Nevertheless, many people do buy this form of insurance, demonstrating a willingness to sacrifice something in expected returns for the assurance that heirs will be provided a financial cushion in the event of death.

2. Suppose that an investor is considering purchasing shares in one or more of a group of corporations. In principle, it is possible to postulate the various states of nature that will influence the returns from investment in each of these corporations. In this way the expected monetary value of an investment of a fixed amount in each corporation could be determined. According to the expected monetary value criterion, the investor should then put all available capital into

the corporation for which the expected monetary value is highest. In fact, a great many investors in the stock market do not follow such a strategy. Rather, they spread their cash over a portfolio of stocks. The abandonment of the option of "putting all one's eggs in a single basket," while leading to a lower expected return, provides a hedge against the possibility of losing a good deal of money if the single stock with the highest expected return happens to perform badly. In opting for a portfolio of stocks the investor is asserting a willingness to sacrifice something in expected monetary value for a smaller chance of a large financial loss.

In each of these examples, the decision maker has exhibited a preference for a criterion of choice other than expected monetary value, and in each circumstance this preference seems to be extremely reasonable. The two examples involve a common ingredient in addition to expected returns. In both cases the decision maker wants to take *risk* into account. The purchaser of term life insurance is prepared to accept a negative expected return as the price to be paid for the chance of a large positive return in the event of death. In doing so, this purchaser is expressing a **preference for risk** (of course, guarding against the risk that the purchaser's family will be financially ill-prepared at the time of the purchaser's death). By contrast, the investor who spreads an investment over a portfolio of stocks, accepts a lower expected return in order to reduce the chances of a large loss is expressing an **aversion to risk**.

The expected monetary value criterion is inappropriate for decision makers who either prefer or are averse to risk. Fortunately, it is not too difficult to modify this criterion to handle situations in which risk is a relevant factor. Essentially, the idea is to replace the monetary payoffs by quantities that reflect not only the dollar amounts to be received but also the decision maker's attitude to risk.

The Concept of Utility

Example 18.3 considered the problem of an investor choosing between a guaranteed fixed-interest investment and a portfolio of stocks. The former would yield a payoff of $1,200, while gains of $2,500 and $500 would result for the latter if the stock market was buoyant or steady, but a loss of $1,000 would result if it was depressed. This investor believed that the respective probabilities for these three states of nature were 0.6, 0.2, and 0.2. In that event the expected monetary value from choosing the stock portfolio was $1,400, exceeding by $200 that of the fixed-interest investment. At this juncture we need to inquire whether this higher expected return merits the risk of losing $1,000, as would occur if the market was depressed. A very wealthy investor, who could quite comfortably sustain such a loss, would almost certainly decide that it does. However, the position of a relatively poor person, to whom a loss of $1,000 would be quite disastrous, may well be different. For such an investor the payoffs must be replaced by some other quantities that more adequately reflect the calamitous nature of a loss of $1,000. These quantities must measure the value, or *utility*, to the investor of a loss of $1,000 as compared with, for example, a gain of $500 or $2,500.

The early works of researchers such as Von Neumann and Morgenstern (Reference 4) enhanced the concept of utility, which even today plays a central role in economics. Utility analysis provides the basis for the solution of decision-making problems in the presence of risk preference or aversion. To employ it, only fairly mild and usually quite reasonable assumptions are needed. Suppose that an individual is faced with several possible payoffs, which may or may not be monetary. It is assumed that the individual can rank in order (possibly with ties) the utility, or satisfaction, that would be derived from each. Thus, if payoff A is preferred to B and B is preferred to C, then A must be preferred to C.

Also assume that, if payoff A is preferred to B and B is preferred to C, then there exists a gamble, which offers A with probability P and C with probability $(1 - P)$, such that the decision maker will be indifferent between taking this gamble and receiving B with certainty. Given these and certain other, generally innocuous assumptions whose details need not detain us, it is possible to show that the rational decision maker will choose the action for which expected utility is highest. Consequently, the decision problem is analyzed precisely as in the preceding sections, *but with utilities instead of payoffs.* That is to say, a utility table rather than a payoff table is constructed, and then the state-of-nature probabilities to compare expected utilities are employed.

Now consider how the utilities corresponding to the various payoffs are determined. The possible payoffs in ascending order for our investor are –$1,000, $500, $1,200, and $2,500. The first step is to obtain a utility function.

Obtaining a Utility Function

Suppose that a decision maker may receive several alternative payoffs. The transformation from payoffs to **utilities** is made as follows:

1. The units in which utility is measured are arbitrary. Accordingly, a scale can be fixed in any convenient fashion. Let L be the lowest and H the highest of all the payoffs. Assign utility 0 to payoff L and utility 100 to payoff H.
2. Let I be any payoff between L and H. Determine the probability P such that the decision maker is indifferent between the following alternatives:

   a. Receive payoff I with certainty.
   b. Receive payoff H with probability P and payoff L with probability $(1 - P)$.

3. The utility to the decision maker of payoff I is then $100P$. The curve relating utility to payoff is called a **utility function**.

The first step is straightforward and simply provides us with a convenient metric for measuring utility. The choice of the numbers 0 and 100 to represent the utilities of the lowest and highest payoffs is entirely arbitrary. Any other pair of numbers could equally well be used, as long as the utility of the highest payoff is greater than that of the lowest, without affecting the remaining analysis.

As a practical matter, the second step is the most difficult, partly because it presupposes that the decision maker can manipulate probabilities in a coherent way. In practice, the probability must be determined by trial and error, through the asking of questions such as "Would you prefer to receive I with certainty or a gamble in which you could obtain H with probability 0.9 and L with probability 0.1?" Or perhaps, the question "Would you prefer to receive I with certainty or a gamble in which you could obtain H with probability 0.8 and L with probability 0.2?" This process is continued until the point of indifference is reached.

The logic of the final step is quite straightforward. Since H has utility 100 and L has utility 0, the *expected utility* if H is obtained with probability P and L with probability $(1 - P)$ is as follows:

$$100P + 0(1 - P) = 100P$$

Since the decision maker is indifferent between this gamble and receiving I with certainty, the utility $100P$ is associated with the payoff I.

Return now to our investor. At the first step we attach utility 0 to the lowest payoff, –$1,000, and utility 100 to the highest, $2,500.

It remains to determine the utilities for the intermediate payoffs, $500 and $1,200. This is achieved by posing to the decision maker a series of questions, such as "Would you prefer to receive $500 with certainty or a gamble in which you could obtain a gain of $2,500 with probability P and a loss of $1,000 with probability $(1 - P)$?" Different values of the probability P are tried until the value at which the decision maker is indifferent between the two alternatives is found. This process is repeated for the payoff of $1,200.

Suppose that the investor is indifferent between a payoff of $500 and the gamble with $P = 0.6$ and between a payoff of $1,200 and the gamble with $P = 0.8$. The utilities for the intermediate payoffs are then as follows:

Payoff $500	Utility = (100)(0.6) = 60
Payoff $1,200	Utility = (100)(0.8) = 80

The four utilities for this investor are plotted against the corresponding payoffs as points in Figure 18.6.

A curve is drawn through these points to indicate the general shape of this investor's utility function. The shape of this curve is interesting, since it characterizes the investor's attitude to risk. As must be the case, utility increases as the payoff increases. However, notice that the *rate of increase* of utility is highest at the lowest payoffs and decreases as payoff increases. This implies a distaste for the lowest payoffs that is more than commensurate with their monetary amounts, indicating *aversion* to risk. This aversion can be seen from the investor's attitude to the gambles offered. For example, the investor is indifferent between a sure payoff of $500 and a gamble in which $2,500 might be won with probability 0.6 and $1,000 lost with probability 0.4. The expected monetary value of this gamble is

$$(0.6)(2,500) + (0.4)(-1,000) = \$1,100$$

which considerably exceeds the equally preferred sure payoff of $500. The amount of this difference provides a measure of the extent of the aversion to risk.

The shape of Figure 18.6 is typical of risk aversion.

Figure 18.6
Utility Function
for an Investor

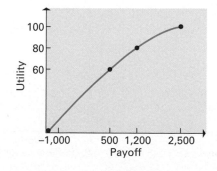

Friedman and Savage suggested, "An important class of reactions of individuals to risk can be rationalized by a rather simple extension of orthodox utility analysis" (Reference 2). They developed graphs of utility functions similar to the three types of utility functions shown in Figure 18.7.

The function in part (a) of Figure 18.7, where utility increases at a *decreasing* rate as payoff increases, has the same shape as Figure 18.6, once again reflecting an *aversion* to risk. In part (b) of Figure 18.7, utility increases at an *increasing* rate as the payoffs become higher. This implies a taste for the highest payoffs that is more than commensurate with the monetary amounts involved, thus showing *preference* for risk. Finally, part (c) of Figure 18.7 shows the intermediate case with utility increasing at a *constant* rate for all payoffs. In this case the monetary values of the payoffs provide a true measure of their utility to the decision maker, who thus demonstrates **indifference to risk**.

The three curves of Figure 18.7 characterize aversion for, preference for, and indifference to risk. However, it is not necessarily the case that a decision maker will exhibit just one of these attitudes over the whole range of possible payoffs.

Figure 18.8 illustrates a more complex situation.

Here, for payoffs in the range between M_1 and M_2 the utility function has the shape of Figure 18.7(a), indicating aversion to risk in this payoff range. However, for payoffs of monetary amounts between M_2 and M_3, this utility function has the shape of Figure 18.7(b). Hence, for this range of payoffs the decision maker exhibits a preference for risk. Finally, in the range of highest payoffs, between M_3 and M_4, the position is once again reversed, the decision maker being averse to risk in this region. Such a utility function can arise in practical problems. For example, an investor may well be averse to sustaining a substantial loss, while being prepared to accept some risk to obtain a fairly high positive return rather than a modest one. However, if a satisfactorily high return can be achieved at modest risk, the investor may be reluctant to risk much more for the possibility of an even higher return.

Expected Utility Criterion for Decision Making

Having determined the appropriate utilities, it remains only to solve the decision-making problem by finding that course of action with the highest expected utility. These expected utilities are obtained in the usual manner, employing the probabilities of the states of nature, as given in Equation 18.5.

Figure 18.7 Utility functions: (a) Risk Aversion; (b) Preference for Risk; (c) Indifference to Risk

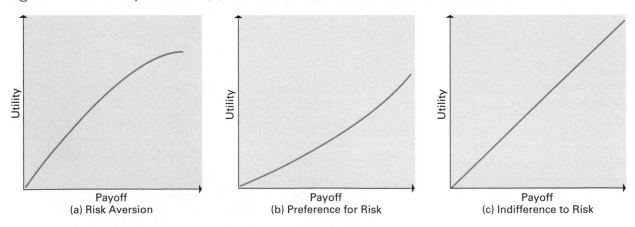

(a) Risk Aversion (b) Preference for Risk (c) Indifference to Risk

Figure 18.8
Utility Function
Showing Aversion
to Risk Between
Payoffs M_1 and M_2
and Payoffs M_3
and M_4 and
Preference for
Risk Between
Payoffs M_2 and M_3

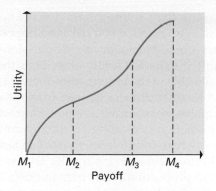

The Expected Utility Criterion

Suppose that a decision maker has K possible actions, $a_1, a_2, ..., a_K$, and is faced with H states of nature. Let U_{ij} denote the utility corresponding to the ith action and jth state, and P_j the probability of occurrence of the jth state of nature. Then the **expected utility**, $EU(a_i)$, of the action a_i is as follows:

$$EU(a_i) = P_1 U_{i1} + P_2 U_{i2} + \cdots + P_H U_{iH} = \sum_{j=1}^{H} P_j U_{ij} \tag{18.5}$$

Given a choice between alternative actions, the **expected utility criterion** dictates the choice of the action for which expected utility is highest. Under generally reasonable assumptions it can be shown that the rational decision maker should adopt this criterion.

If the decision maker is indifferent to risk, the expected utility criterion and the expected monetary value criterion are equivalent.

Table 18.11 shows the utilities and state-of-nature probabilities for our investor.

If the fixed-interest investment is chosen, a utility of 80 is assured, whichever state of nature prevails. For the portfolio of stocks the expected utility is as follows:

$$(0.6)(100) + (0.2)(60) + (0.2)(0) = 0.72$$

Since this is less than 80, this investor should elect to make the fixed-interest investment, according to the expected utility criterion.

In Example 18.3, investment in the portfolio of stocks was selected by the expected monetary value criterion. However, the incorporation into the analysis of another factor—the extent of this investor's aversion to risk—leads to the conclusion

Table 18.11 Utilities and State-of-Nature Probabilities for an Investor

ACTION	STATE OF THE MARKET		
INVESTMENT	BUOYANT STATE ($P = 0.60$)	STEADY STATE ($P = 0.20$)	DEPRESSED STATE ($P = 0.20$)
Fixed interest	80	80	80
Stock portfolio	100	60	0

that the fixed-interest option is the better choice. This example serves to illustrate that on occasion, when risk is an important factor, the expected monetary value criterion is inadequate for solving decision-making problems.

The expected utility criterion is the most generally applicable and intellectually defensible of the criteria introduced for attacking decision-making problems.

Its chief drawback arises from the difficulty of eliciting information about which gambles are regarded as equally attractive as particular assured payoffs. This type of information is essential in the determination of utilities. For a wide range of problems where indifference to risk can safely be assumed, the expected monetary value criterion remains applicable. This would typically be the case, for example, in a small proportion of the corporation's total revenue. If, however (as may be the case in the development of a new commercial airliner, for example), possible losses from a project could threaten a corporation with insolvency, the utilities should appropriately reflect an aversion to risk. A company may attempt to spread this risk by forming partnerships with other firms in the industry or with possible customers.

EXERCISES

Application Exercises

18.43 A decision maker faces a problem in which the possible payoffs (in dollars) are as follows:

1,000   3,000   6,000   9,000   10,000   12,000

Utility 0 is assigned to a payoff of $1,000 and utility 100 to a payoff of $12,000. This decision maker is indifferent to risk for payoffs in this range.

a. Find the utilities for the four intermediate payoffs.
b. For each intermediate payoff, I, find the probability P such that the decision maker is indifferent between receiving I with certainty and a wager in which $12,000 is received with probability P and $1,000 with probability $(1 - P)$.

18.44 The shoe store operator of Exercise 18.9 has six possible payoffs (in dollars):

−10,000   30,000   60,000   70,000   90,000   130,000

Assign utility 0 to a loss of $10,000 and utility 100 to a profit of $130,000. For each intermediate payoff, I, the probabilities P such that the shoe store operator is indifferent between receiving I with certainty and a gamble in which $130,000 would be gained with probability P and $10,000 lost with

probability $(1 - P)$ are shown in the accompanying table.

Payoff	30,000	60,000	70,000	90,000
P	0.35	0.60	0.70	0.85

a. What are the utilities for the intermediate payoffs?
b. Suppose that the probabilities that the new shopping center will be very successful, will be moderately successful, and will be unsuccessful are 0.4, 0.4, and 0.2, respectively. Which action should be taken if expected utility is to be maximized?

18.45 The shoe store operator of Exercise 18.44 is unsure what value P to attach to indifference between receiving $30,000 with certainty and a gamble in which $130,000 would be gained with probability P and $10,000 lost with probability $(1-P)$. Assuming that the remaining problem specifications are as in Exercise 18.44, under what range of values for this probability will the expected utility criterion yield the same choice of action?

18.46 Consider the contractor of Exercise 18.21. In fact, this contractor is indifferent between submitting and not submitting a bid. What does this imply about the contractor's utility function?

KEY WORDS

- action, 775
- admissible action, 776
- aversion to risk, 807
- Bayes' theorem, 792
- decision nodes, 784
- decision trees, 784
- EMV, 783
- event nodes, 785
- EVPI, 798

CHAPTER EXERCISES AND APPLICATIONS

18.47 A consultant is considering submitting detailed bids for two possible contracts. The bid for the first contract costs $100 to prepare, while that for the second contract costs $150 to prepare. If the bid for the first contract is accepted and the work is carried out, a profit of $800 will result. If the bid for the second contract is accepted and the work is carried out, a profit of $1,200 will result. Any costs of bid preparation must be subtracted from these profits. The consultant can submit bids for both contracts. However, the consultant does not have the resources to carry out both pieces of work simultaneously. If a bid is submitted and accepted and the consultant is then unable to carry out the work, the consultant counts this as a cost of $200 in lost goodwill. For the decision-making process, there are four possible states of nature:

s_1: Both bids rejected
s_2: Bid for the first contract accepted, bid for the second contract rejected
s_3: Bid for the second contract accepted, bid for the first contract rejected
s_4: Both bids accepted

a. The consultant has four possible courses of action. What are they?
b. Construct the payoff table for this consultant's decision-making problem.
c. Which action is chosen by the maximin criterion?
d. Which action is chosen by the minimax regret criterion?

18.48 Refer to Exercise 18.47. The consultant believes that the probability is 0.7 that a bid for the first contract would be accepted, that the probability is 0.4 that a bid for the second contract would be accepted, and that the acceptance of one bid is independent of the acceptance of the other bid.

a. What are the probabilities for the four states of nature?

b. According to the expected monetary value criterion, which action should the consultant adopt, and what is the expected monetary value of this action?
c. Draw the decision tree for the consultant's problem.
d. What is the expected value of perfect information to this consultant?
e. The consultant is offered "inside information" on the prospects of the bid for the first contract. This information is entirely reliable in the sense that it would allow the consultant to know for sure whether the bid would be accepted. However, no further information is available on the prospects of the bid for the second contract. What is the expected value of this "inside information"?

18.49 Refer to Exercises 18.47 and 18.48. There are nine possible payoffs for this consultant, as follows (in dollars):

−250	−150	−100	0	550
700	750	950	1,050	

A utility of 0 is assigned to a loss of $250 and a utility of 100 to a profit of $1,050. For each intermediate payoff, *I*, the probabilities *P* such that the consultant is indifferent between payoff *I* with certainty and a gamble in which $1,050 is gained with probability *P* and $250 lost with probability (1 − *P*) are shown in the accompanying table. According to the expected utility criterion, which action should the consultant choose, and what is the expected utility of this action?

Payoff	−150	−100	0	550	700	750	950
P	0.05	0.10	0.20	0.65	0.70	0.75	0.85

REFERENCES

1. Eppen, G. D., F. J. Gould, et al. 1998. *Introductory Management Science: Decision Modeling with Spreadsheets*, 5th ed. Upper Saddle River, NJ: Prentice Hall.

2. Friedman, Milton, and L. J. Savage. 1948. The Utility Analysis of Choices Involving Risk. *Journal of Political Economy* 56:279–304.

3. Render, Barry, and Ralph M. Stair, Jr. 2000. *Quantitative Analysis for Management*, 7th ed. Upper Saddle River, NJ: Prentice Hall.

4. Von Neumann, John, and Oskar Morgenstern. 1953. *The Theory of Games and Economic Behavior*, 3rd ed. Princeton, NJ: Princeton University Press.

APPENDIX TABLES

Table 1   Cumulative Distribution Function of the Standard Normal Distribution

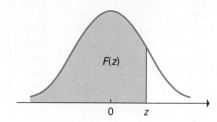

z	F(z)	z	F(z)	z	F(z)	z	F(z)	z	F(z)	z	F(z)
.00	.5000										
.01	.5040	.31	.6217	.61	.7291	.91	.8186	1.21	.8869	1.51	.9345
.02	.5080	.32	.6255	.62	.7324	.92	.8212	1.22	.8888	1.52	.9357
.03	.5120	.33	.6293	.63	.7357	.93	.8238	1.23	.8907	1.53	.9370
.04	.5160	.34	.6331	.64	.7389	.94	.8264	1.24	.8925	1.54	.9382
.05	.5199	.35	.6368	.65	.7422	.95	.8289	1.25	.8944	1.55	.9394
.06	.5239	.36	.6406	.66	.7454	.96	.8315	1.26	.8962	1.56	.9406
.07	.5279	.37	.6443	.67	.7486	.97	.8340	1.27	.8980	1.57	.9418
.08	.5319	.38	.6480	.68	.7517	.98	.8365	1.28	.8997	1.58	.9429
.09	.5359	.39	.6517	.69	.7549	.99	.8389	1.29	.9015	1.59	.9441
.10	.5398	.40	.6554	.70	.7580	1.00	.8413	1.30	.9032	1.60	.9452
.11	.5438	.41	.6591	.71	.7611	1.01	.8438	1.31	.9049	1.61	.9463
.12	.5478	.42	.6628	.72	.7642	1.02	.8461	1.32	.9066	1.62	.9474
.13	.5517	.43	.6664	.73	.7673	1.03	.8485	1.33	.9082	1.63	.9484
.14	.5557	.44	.6700	.74	.7704	1.04	.8508	1.34	.9099	1.64	.9495
.15	.5596	.45	.6736	.75	.7734	1.05	.8531	1.35	.9115	1.65	.9505
.16	.5636	.46	.6772	.76	.7764	1.06	.8554	1.36	.9131	1.66	.9515
.17	.5675	.47	.6803	.77	.7794	1.07	.8577	1.37	.9147	1.67	.9525
.18	.5714	.48	.6844	.78	.7823	1.08	.8599	1.38	.9162	1.68	.9535
.19	.5753	.49	.6879	.79	.7852	1.09	.8621	1.39	.9177	1.69	.9545
.20	.5793	.50	.6915	.80	.7881	1.10	.8643	1.40	.9192	1.70	.9554
.21	.5832	.51	.6950	.81	.7910	1.11	.8665	1.41	.9207	1.71	.9564
.22	.5871	.52	.6985	.82	.7939	1.12	.8686	1.42	.9222	1.72	.9573
.23	.5910	.53	.7019	.83	.7967	1.13	.8708	1.43	.9236	1.73	.9582
.24	.5948	.54	.7054	.84	.7995	1.14	.8729	1.44	.9251	1.74	.9591
.25	.5987	.55	.7088	.85	.8023	1.15	.8749	1.45	.9265	1.75	.9599
.26	.6026	.56	.7123	.86	.8051	1.16	.8770	1.46	.9279	1.76	.9608
.27	.6064	.57	.7157	.87	.8078	1.17	.8790	1.47	.9292	1.77	.9616
.28	.6103	.58	.7190	.88	.8106	1.18	.8810	1.48	.9306	1.78	.9625
.29	.6141	.59	.7224	.89	.8133	1.19	.8830	1.49	.9319	1.79	.9633
.30	.6179	.60	.7257	.90	.8159	1.20	.8849	1.50	.9332	1.80	.9641

z	F(z)	z	F(z)	z	F(z)	z	F(z)	z	F(z)	z	F(z)
1.81	.9649	2.21	.9864	2.61	.9955	3.01	.9987	3.41	.9997	3.81	.9999
1.82	.9656	2.22	.9868	2.62	.9956	3.02	.9987	3.42	.9997	3.82	.9999
1.83	.9664	2.23	.9871	2.63	.9957	3.03	.9988	3.43	.9997	3.83	.9999
1.84	.9671	2.24	.9875	2.64	.9959	3.04	.9988	3.44	.9997	3.84	.9999
1.85	.9678	2.25	.9878	2.65	.9960	3.05	.9989	3.45	.9997	3.85	.9999
1.86	.9686	2.26	.9881	2.66	.9961	3.06	.9989	3.46	.9997	3.86	.9999
1.87	.9693	2.27	.9884	2.67	.9962	3.07	.9989	3.47	.9997	3.87	.9999
1.88	.9699	2.28	.9887	2.68	.9963	3.08	.9990	3.48	.9997	3.88	.9999
1.89	.9706	2.29	.9890	2.69	.9964	3.09	.9990	3.49	.9998	3.89	1.0000
1.90	.9713	2.30	.9893	2.70	.9965	3.10	.9990	3.50	.9998	3.90	1.0000
1.91	.9719	2.31	.9896	2.71	.9966	3.11	.9991	3.51	.9998	3.91	1.0000
1.92	.9726	2.32	.9898	2.72	.9967	3.12	.9991	3.52	.9998	3.92	1.0000
1.93	.9732	2.33	.9901	2.73	.9968	3.13	.9991	3.53	.9998	3.93	1.0000
1.94	.9738	2.34	.9904	2.74	.9969	3.14	.9992	3.54	.9998	3.94	1.0000
1.95	.9744	2.35	.9906	2.75	.9970	3.15	.9992	3.55	.9998	3.95	1.0000
1.96	.9750	2.36	.9909	2.76	.9971	3.16	.9992	3.56	.9998	3.96	1.0000
1.97	.9756	2.37	.9911	2.77	.9972	3.17	.9992	3.57	.9998	3.97	1.0000
1.98	.9761	2.38	.9913	2.78	.9973	3.18	.9993	3.58	.9998	3.98	1.0000
1.99	.9767	2.39	.9916	2.79	.9974	3.19	.9993	3.59	.9998	3.99	1.0000
2.00	.9772	2.40	.9918	2.80	.9974	3.20	.9993	3.60	.9998		
2.01	.9778	2.41	.9920	2.81	.9975	3.21	.9993	3.61	.9998		
2.02	.9783	2.42	.9922	2.82	.9976	3.22	.9994	3.62	.9999		
2.03	.9788	2.43	.9925	2.83	.9977	3.23	.9994	3.63	.9999		
2.04	.9793	2.44	.9927	2.84	.9977	3.24	.9994	3.64	.9999		
2.05	.9798	2.45	.9929	2.85	.9978	3.25	.9994	3.65	.9999		
2.06	.9803	2.46	.9931	2.86	.9979	3.26	.9994	3.66	.9999		
2.07	.9808	2.47	.9932	2.87	.9979	3.27	.9995	3.67	.9999		
2.08	.9812	2.48	.9934	2.88	.9980	3.28	.9995	3.68	.9999		
2.09	.9817	2.49	.9936	2.89	.9981	3.29	.9995	3.69	.9999		
2.10	.9821	2.50	.9938	2.90	.9981	3.30	.9995	3.70	.9999		
2.11	.9826	2.51	.9940	2.91	.9982	3.31	.9995	3.71	.9999		
2.12	.9830	2.52	.9941	2.92	.9982	3.32	.9996	3.72	.9999		
2.13	.9834	2.53	.9943	2.93	.9983	3.33	.9996	3.73	.9999		
2.14	.9838	2.54	.9945	2.94	.9984	3.34	.9996	3.74	.9999		
2.15	.9842	2.55	.9946	2.95	.9984	3.35	.9996	3.75	.9999		
2.16	.9846	2.56	.9948	2.96	.9985	3.36	.9996	3.76	.9999		
2.17	.9850	2.57	.9949	2.97	.9985	3.37	.9996	3.77	.9999		
2.18	.9854	2.58	.9951	2.98	.9986	3.38	.9996	3.78	.9999		
2.19	.9857	2.59	.9952	2.99	.9986	3.39	.9997	3.79	.9999		
2.20	.9861	2.60	.9953	3.00	.9986	3.40	.9997	3.80	.9999		

Table 2 Probability Function of the Binomial Distribution

The table shows the probability of x successes in n independent trials, each with probability of success P. For example, the probability of four successes in eight independent trials, each with probability of success .35, is .1875.

n	x	.05	.10	.15	.20	.25	.30	.35	.40	.45	.50
							P				
1	0	.9500	.9000	.8500	.8000	.7500	.7000	.6500	.6000	.5500	.5000
	1	.0500	.1000	.1500	.2000	.2500	.3000	.3500	.4000	.4500	.5000
2	0	.9025	.8100	.7225	.6400	.5625	.4900	.4225	.3600	.3025	.2500
	1	.0950	.1800	.2550	.3200	.3750	.4200	.4550	.4800	.4950	.5000
	2	.0025	.0100	.0225	.0400	.0625	.0900	.1225	.1600	.2025	.2500
3	0	.8574	.7290	.6141	.5120	.4219	.3430	.2746	.2160	.1664	.1250
	1	.1354	.2430	.3251	.3840	.4219	.4410	.4436	.4320	.4084	.3750
	2	.0071	.0270	.0574	.0960	.1406	.1890	.2389	.2880	.3341	.3750
	3	.0001	.0010	.0034	.0080	.0156	.0270	.0429	.0640	.0911	.1250
4	0	.8145	.6561	.5220	.4096	.3164	.2401	.1785	.1296	.0915	.0625
	1	.1715	.2916	.3685	.4096	.4219	.4116	.3845	.3456	.2995	.2500
	2	.0135	.0486	.0975	.1536	.2109	.2646	.3105	.3456	.3675	.3750
	3	.0005	.0036	.0115	.0256	.0469	.0756	.1115	.1536	.2005	.2500
	4	.0000	.0001	.0005	.0016	.0039	.0081	.0150	.0256	.0410	.0625
5	0	.7738	.5905	.4437	.3277	.2373	.1681	.1160	.0778	.0503	.0312
	1	.2036	.3280	.3915	.4096	.3955	.3602	.3124	.2592	.2059	.1562
	2	.0214	.0729	.1382	.2048	.2637	.3087	.3364	.3456	.3369	.3125
	3	.0011	.0081	.0244	.0512	.0879	.1323	.1811	.2304	.2757	.3125
	4	.0000	.0004	.0022	.0064	.0146	.0284	.0488	.0768	.1128	.1562
	5	.0000	.0000	.0001	.0003	.0010	.0024	.0053	.0102	.0185	.0312
6	0	.7351	.5314	.3771	.2621	.1780	.1176	.0754	.0467	.0277	.0156
	1	.2321	.3543	.3993	.3932	.3560	.3025	.2437	.1866	.1359	.0938
	2	.0305	.0984	.1762	.2458	.2966	.3241	.3280	.3110	.2780	.2344
	3	.0021	.0146	.0415	.0819	.1318	.1852	.2355	.2765	.3032	.3125
	4	.0001	.0012	.0055	.0154	.0330	.0595	.0951	.1382	.1861	.2344
	5	.0000	.0001	.0004	.0015	.0044	.0102	.0205	.0369	.0609	.0938
	6	.0000	.0000	.0000	.0001	.0002	.0007	.0018	.0041	.0083	.0156
7	0	.6983	.4783	.3206	.2097	.1335	.0824	.0490	.0280	.0152	.0078
	1	.2573	.3720	.3960	.3670	.3115	.2471	.1848	.1306	.0872	.0547
	2	.0406	.1240	.2097	.2753	.3115	.3177	.2985	.2613	.2140	.1641
	3	.0036	.0230	.0617	.1147	.1730	.2269	.2679	.2903	.2918	.2734
	4	.0002	.0026	.0109	.0287	.0577	.0972	.1442	.1935	.2388	.2734
	5	.0000	.0002	.0012	.0043	.0115	.0250	.0466	.0774	.1172	.1641
	6	.0000	.0000	.0001	.0004	.0013	.0036	.0084	.0172	.0320	.0547
	7	.0000	.0000	.0000	.0000	.0001	.0002	.0006	.0016	.0037	.0078
8	0	.6634	.4305	.2725	.1678	.1001	.0576	.0319	.0168	.0084	.0039
	1	.2793	.3826	.3847	.3355	.2670	.1977	.1373	.0896	.0548	.0312
	2	.0515	.1488	.2376	.2936	.3115	.2965	.2587	.2090	.1569	.1094
	3	.0054	.0331	.0839	.1468	.2076	.2541	.2786	.2787	.2568	.2188
	4	.0004	.0046	.0185	.0459	.0865	.1361	.1875	.2322	.2627	.2734
	5	.0000	.0004	.0026	.0092	.0231	.0467	.0808	.1239	.1719	.2188
	6	.0000	.0000	.0002	.0011	.0038	.0100	.0217	.0413	.0703	.1094
	7	.0000	.0000	.0000	.0001	.0004	.0012	.0033	.0079	.0164	.0312
	8	.0000	.0000	.0000	.0000	.0000	.0001	.0002	.0007	.0017	.0039
9	0	.6302	.3874	.2316	.1342	.0751	.0404	.0207	.0101	.0046	.0020
	1	.2985	.3874	.3679	.3020	.2253	.1556	.1004	.0605	.0339	.0176
	2	.0629	.1722	.2597	.3020	.3003	.2668	.2162	.1612	.1110	.0703
	3	.0077	.0446	.1069	.1762	.2336	.2668	.2716	.2508	.2119	.1641
	4	.0006	.0074	.0283	.0661	.1168	.1715	.2194	.2508	.2600	.2461
	5	.0000	.0008	.0050	.0165	.0389	.0735	.1181	.1672	.2128	.2461
	6	.0000	.0001	.0006	.0028	.0087	.0210	.0424	.0743	.1160	.1641
	7	.0000	.0000	.0000	.0003	.0012	.0039	.0098	.0212	.0407	.0703

Table 2 Probability Function of the Binomial Distribution Continued

n	x	P									
		.05	.10	.15	.20	.25	.30	.35	.40	.45	.50
	8	.0000	.0000	.0000	.0000	.0001	.0004	.0013	.0035	.0083	.0176
	9	.0000	.0000	.0000	.0000	.0000	.0000	.0001	.0003	.0008	.0020
10	0	.5987	.3487	.1969	.1074	.0563	.0282	.0135	.0060	.0025	.0010
	1	.3151	.3874	.3474	.2684	.1877	.1211	.0725	.0403	.0207	.0098
	2	.0746	.1937	.2759	.3020	.2816	.2335	.1757	.1209	.0763	.0439
	3	.0105	.0574	.1298	.2013	.2503	.2668	.2522	.2150	.1665	.1172
	4	.0010	.0112	.0401	.0881	.1460	.2001	.2377	.2508	.2384	.2051
	5	.0001	.0015	.0085	.0264	.0584	.1029	.1536	.2007	.2340	.2461
	6	.0000	.0001	.0012	.0055	.0162	.0368	.0689	.1115	.1596	.2051
	7	.0000	.0000	.0001	.0008	.0031	.0090	.0212	.0425	.0746	.1172
	8	.0000	.0000	.0000	.0001	.0004	.0014	.0043	.0106	.0226	.0439
	9	.0000	.0000	.0000	.0000	.0000	.0001	.0004	.0016	.0042	.0098
	10	.0000	.0000	.0000	.0000	.0000	.0000	.0000	.0001	.0003	.0010
11	0	.5688	.3138	.1673	.0859	.0422	.0198	.0088	.0036	.0014	.0005
	1	.3293	.3835	.3248	.2362	.1549	.0932	.0518	.0266	.0125	.0054
	2	.0867	.2131	.2866	.2953	.2581	.1998	.1395	.0887	.0513	.0269
	3	.0137	.0710	.1517	.2215	.2581	.2568	.2254	.1774	.1259	.0806
	4	.0014	.0158	.0536	.1107	.1721	.2201	.2428	.2365	.2060	.1611
	5	.0001	.0025	.0132	.0388	.0803	.1321	.1830	.2207	.2360	.2256
	6	.0000	.0003	.0023	.0097	.0268	.0566	.0985	.1471	.1931	.2256
	7	.0000	.0000	.0003	.0017	.0064	.0173	.0379	.0701	.1128	.1611
	8	.0000	.0000	.0000	.0002	.0011	.0037	.0102	.0234	.0462	.0806
	9	.0000	.0000	.0000	.0000	.0001	.0005	.0018	.0052	.0126	.0269
	10	.0000	.0000	.0000	.0000	.0000	.0000	.0002	.0007	.0021	.0054
	11	.0000	.0000	.0000	.0000	.0000	.0000	.0000	.0000	.0002	.0005
12	0	.5404	.2824	.1422	.0687	.0317	.0138	.0057	.0022	.0008	.0002
	1	.3413	.3766	.3012	.2062	.1267	.0712	.0368	.0174	.0075	.0029
	2	.0988	.2301	.2924	.2835	.2323	.1678	.1088	.0639	.0339	.0161
	3	.0173	.0852	.1720	.2362	.2581	.2397	.1954	.1419	.0923	.0537
	4	.0021	.0213	.0683	.1329	.1936	.2311	.2367	.2128	.1700	.1208
	5	.0002	.0038	.0193	.0532	.1032	.1585	.2039	.2270	.2225	.1934
	6	.0000	.0005	.0040	.0155	.0401	.0792	.1281	.1766	.2124	.2256
	7	.0000	.0000	.0006	.0033	.0015	.0291	.0591	.1009	.1489	.1934
	8	.0000	.0000	.0001	.0005	.0024	.0078	.0199	.0420	.0762	.1208
	9	.0000	.0000	.0000	.0001	.0004	.0015	.0048	.0125	.0277	.0537
	10	.0000	.0000	.0000	.0000	.0000	.0002	.0008	.0025	.0068	.0161
	11	.0000	.0000	.0000	.0000	.0000	.0000	.0001	.0003	.0010	.0029
	12	.0000	.0000	.0000	.0000	.0000	.0000	.0000	.0000	.0001	.0002
13	0	.5133	.2542	.1209	.0550	.0238	.0097	.0037	.0013	.0004	.0001
	1	.3512	.3672	.2774	.1787	.1029	.0540	.0259	.0113	.0045	.0016
	2	.1109	.2448	.2937	.2680	.2059	.1388	.0836	.0453	.0220	.0095
	3	.0214	.0997	.1900	.2457	.2517	.2181	.1651	.1107	.0660	.0349
	4	.0028	.0277	.0838	.1535	.2097	.2337	.2222	.1845	.1350	.0873
	5	.0003	.0055	.0266	.0691	.1258	.1803	.2154	.2214	.1989	.1571
	6	.0000	.0008	.0063	.0230	.0559	.1030	.1546	.1968	.2169	.2095
	7	.0000	.0001	.0011	.0058	.0186	.0442	.0833	.1312	.1775	.2095
	8	.0000	.0000	.0001	.0011	.0047	.0142	.0336	.0656	.1089	.1571
	9	.0000	.0000	.0000	.0001	.0009	.0034	.0101	.0243	.0495	.0873
	10	.0000	.0000	.0000	.0000	.0001	.0006	.0022	.0065	.0162	.0349
	11	.0000	.0000	.0000	.0000	.0000	.0001	.0003	.0012	.0036	.0095
	12	.0000	.0000	.0000	.0000	.0000	.0000	.0000	.0001	.0005	.0016
	13	.0000	.0000	.0000	.0000	.0000	.0000	.0000	.0000	.0000	.0001
14	0	.4877	.2288	.1028	.0440	.0178	.0068	.0024	.0008	.0002	.0001
	1	.3593	.3559	.2539	.1539	.0832	.0407	.0181	.0073	.0027	.0009
	2	.1229	.2570	.2912	.2501	.1802	.1134	.0634	.0317	.0141	.0056

Table 2   Probability Function of the Binomial Distribution Continued

n	x	P									
		.05	.10	.15	.20	.25	.30	.35	.40	.45	.50
	3	.0259	.1142	.2056	.2501	.2402	.1943	.1366	.0845	.0462	.0222
	4	.0037	.0348	.0998	.1720	.2202	.2290	.2022	.1549	.1040	.0611
	5	.0004	.0078	.0352	.0860	.1468	.1963	.2178	.2066	.1701	.1222
	6	.0000	.0013	.0093	.0322	.0734	.1262	.1759	.2066	.2088	.1833
	7	.0000	.0002	.0019	.0092	.0280	.0618	.1082	.1574	.1952	.2095
	8	.0000	.0000	.0003	.0020	.0082	.0232	.0510	.0918	.1398	.1833
	9	.0000	.0000	.0000	.0003	.0018	.0066	.0183	.0408	.0762	.1222
	10	.0000	.0000	.0000	.0000	.0003	.0014	.0049	.0136	.0312	.0611
	11	.0000	.0000	.0000	.0000	.0000	.0002	.0010	.0033	.0093	.0222
	12	.0000	.0000	.0000	.0000	.0000	.0000	.0001	.0005	.0019	.0056
	13	.0000	.0000	.0000	.0000	.0000	.0000	.0000	.0001	.0002	.0009
	14	.0000	.0000	.0000	.0000	.0000	.0000	.0000	.0000	.0000	.0001
15	0	.4633	.2059	.0874	.0352	.0134	.0047	.0016	.0005	.0001	.0000
	1	.3658	.3432	.2312	.1319	.0668	.0305	.0126	.0047	.0016	.0005
	2	.1348	.2669	.2856	.2309	.1559	.0916	.0476	.0219	.0090	.0032
	3	.0307	.1285	.2184	.2501	.2252	.1700	.1110	.0634	.0318	.0139
	4	.0049	.0428	.1156	.1876	.2252	.2186	.1792	.1268	.0780	.0417
	5	.0006	.0105	.0449	.1032	.1651	.2061	.2123	.1859	.1404	.0916
	6	.0000	.0019	.0132	.0430	.0917	.1472	.1906	.2066	.1914	.1527
	7	.0000	.0003	.0030	.0138	.0393	.0811	.1319	.1771	.2013	.1964
	8	.0000	.0000	.0005	.0035	.0131	.0348	.0710	.1181	.1647	.1964
	9	.0000	.0000	.0001	.0007	.0034	.0116	.0298	.0612	.1048	.1527
	10	.0000	.0000	.0000	.0001	.0007	.0030	.0096	.0245	.0515	.0916
	11	.0000	.0000	.0000	.0000	.0001	.0006	.0024	.0074	.0191	.0417
	12	.0000	.0000	.0000	.0000	.0000	.0001	.0004	.0016	.0052	.0139
	13	.0000	.0000	.0000	.0000	.0000	.0000	.0001	.0003	.0010	.0032
	14	.0000	.0000	.0000	.0000	.0000	.0000	.0000	.0000	.0001	.0005
	15	.0000	.0000	.0000	.0000	.0000	.0000	.0000	.0000	.0000	.0000
16	0	.4401	.1853	.0743	.0281	.0100	.0033	.0010	.0003	.0001	.0000
	1	.3706	.3294	.2097	.1126	.0535	.0228	.0087	.0030	.0009	.0002
	2	.1463	.2745	.2775	.2111	.1336	.0732	.0353	.0150	.0056	.0018
	3	.0359	.1423	.2285	.2463	.2079	.1465	.0888	.0468	.0215	.0085
	4	.0061	.0514	.1311	.2001	.2552	.2040	.1553	.1014	.0572	.0278
	5	.0008	.0137	.0555	.1201	.1802	.2099	.2008	.1623	.1123	.0667
	6	.0001	.0028	.0180	.0550	.1101	.1649	.1982	.1983	.1684	.1222
	7	.0000	.0004	.0045	.0197	.0524	.1010	.1524	.1889	.1969	.1746
	8	.0000	.0001	.0009	.0055	.0197	.0487	.0923	.1417	.1812	.1964
	9	.0000	.0000	.0001	.0012	.0058	.0185	.0442	.0840	.1318	.1746
	10	.0000	.0000	.0000	.0002	.0014	.0056	.0167	.0392	.0755	.1222
	11	.0000	.0000	.0000	.0000	.0002	.0013	.0049	.0142	.0337	.0667
	12	.0000	.0000	.0000	.0000	.0000	.0002	.0011	.0040	.0115	.0278
	13	.0000	.0000	.0000	.0000	.0000	.0000	.0002	.0008	.0029	.0085
	14	.0000	.0000	.0000	.0000	.0000	.0000	.0000	.0001	.0005	.0018
	15	.0000	.0000	.0000	.0000	.0000	.0000	.0000	.0000	.0001	.0002
	16	.0000	.0000	.0000	.0000	.0000	.0000	.0000	.0000	.0000	.0000
17	0	.4181	.1668	.0631	.0225	.0075	.0023	.0007	.0002	.0000	.0000
	1	.3741	.3150	.1893	.0957	.0426	.0169	.0060	.0019	.0005	.0001
	2	.1575	.2800	.2673	.1914	.1136	.0581	.0260	.0102	.0035	.0010
	3	.0415	.1556	.2359	.2393	.1893	.1245	.0701	.0341	.0144	.0052
	4	.0076	.0605	.1457	.2093	.2209	.1868	.1320	.0796	.0411	.0182
	5	.0010	.0175	.0068	.1361	.1914	.2081	.1849	.1379	.0875	.0472
	6	.0001	.0039	.0236	.0680	.1276	.1784	.1991	.1839	.1432	.0944
	7	.0000	.0007	.0065	.0267	.0668	.1201	.1685	.1927	.1841	.1484
	8	.0000	.0001	.0014	.0084	.0279	.0644	.1134	.1606	.1883	.1855
	9	.0000	.0000	.0003	.0021	.0093	.0276	.0611	.1070	.1540	.1855

Table 2 Probability Function of the Binomial Distribution Continued

n	x	.05	.10	.15	.20	.25	.30	.35	.40	.45	.50
							P				
	10	.0000	.0000	.0000	.0004	.0025	.0095	.0263	.0571	.1008	.1484
	11	.0000	.0000	.0000	.0001	.0005	.0026	.0090	.0242	.0525	.0944
	12	.0000	.0000	.0000	.0000	.0001	.0006	.0024	.0081	.0215	.0472
	13	.0000	.0000	.0000	.0000	.0000	.0001	.0005	.0021	.0068	.0182
	14	.0000	.0000	.0000	.0000	.0000	.0000	.0001	.0004	.0016	.0052
	15	.0000	.0000	.0000	.0000	.0000	.0000	.0000	.0001	.0003	.0010
	16	.0000	.0000	.0000	.0000	.0000	.0000	.0000	.0000	.0000	.0001
	17	.0000	.0000	.0000	.0000	.0000	.0000	.0000	.0000	.0000	.0000
18	0	.3972	.1501	.0536	.0180	.0056	.0016	.0004	.0001	.0000	.0000
	1	.3763	.3002	.1704	.0811	.0338	.0126	.0042	.0012	.0003	.0001
	2	.1683	.2835	.2556	.1723	.0958	.0458	.0190	.0069	.0022	.0006
	3	.0473	.1680	.2406	.2297	.1704	.1046	.0547	.0246	.0095	.0031
	4	.0093	.0700	.1592	.2153	.2130	.1681	.1104	.0614	.0291	.0117
	5	.0014	.0218	.0787	.1507	.1988	.2017	.1664	.1146	.0666	.0327
	6	.0002	.0052	.0301	.0816	.1436	.1873	.1941	.1655	.1181	.0708
	7	.0000	.0010	.0091	.0350	.0820	.1376	.1792	.1892	.1657	.1214
	8	.0000	.0002	.0022	.0120	.0376	.0811	.1327	.1734	.1864	.1669
	9	.0000	.0000	.0004	.0033	.0139	.0386	.0794	.1284	.1694	.1855
	10	.0000	.0000	.0001	.0008	.0042	.0149	.0385	.0771	.1248	.1669
	11	.0000	.0000	.0000	.0001	.0010	.0046	.0151	.0374	.0742	.1214
	12	.0000	.0000	.0000	.0000	.0002	.0012	.0047	.0145	.0354	.0708
	13	.0000	.0000	.0000	.0000	.0000	.0002	.0012	.0044	.0134	.0327
	14	.0000	.0000	.0000	.0000	.0000	.0000	.0002	.0011	.0039	.0117
	15	.0000	.0000	.0000	.0000	.0000	.0000	.0000	.0002	.0009	.0031
	16	.0000	.0000	.0000	.0000	.0000	.0000	.0000	.0000	.0001	.0006
	17	.0000	.0000	.0000	.0000	.0000	.0000	.0000	.0000	.0000	.0001
	18	.0000	.0000	.0000	.0000	.0000	.0000	.0000	.0000	.0000	.0000
19	0	.3774	.1351	.0456	.0144	.0042	.0011	.0003	.0001	.0000	.0000
	1	.3774	.2852	.1529	.0685	.0268	.0093	.0029	.0008	.0002	.0000
	2	.1787	.2852	.2428	.1540	.0803	.0358	.0138	.0046	.0013	.0003
	3	.0533	.1796	.2428	.2182	.1517	.0869	.0422	.0175	.0062	.0018
	4	.0112	.0798	.1714	.2182	.2023	.1419	.0909	.0467	.0203	.0074
	5	.0018	.0266	.0907	.1636	.2023	.1916	.1468	.0933	.0497	.0222
	6	.0002	.0069	.0374	.0955	.1574	.1916	.1844	.1451	.0949	.0518
	7	.0000	.0014	.0122	.0443	.0974	.1525	.1844	.1797	.1443	.0961
	8	.0000	.0002	.0032	.0166	.0487	.0981	.1489	.1797	.1771	.1442
	9	.0000	.0000	.0007	.0051	.0198	.0514	.0980	.1464	.1771	.1762
	10	.0000	.0000	.0001	.0013	.0066	.0220	.0528	.0976	.1449	.1762
	11	.0000	.0000	.0000	.0003	.0018	.0077	.0233	.0532	.0970	.1442
	12	.0000	.0000	.0000	.0000	.0004	.0022	.0083	.0237	.0529	.0961
	13	.0000	.0000	.0000	.0000	.0001	.0005	.0024	.0085	.0233	.0518
	14	.0000	.0000	.0000	.0000	.0000	.0001	.0006	.0024	.0082	.0222
	15	.0000	.0000	.0000	.0000	.0000	.0000	.0001	.0005	.0022	.0074
	16	.0000	.0000	.0000	.0000	.0000	.0000	.0000	.0001	.0005	.0018
	17	.0000	.0000	.0000	.0000	.0000	.0000	.0000	.0000	.0001	.0003
	18	.0000	.0000	.0000	.0000	.0000	.0000	.0000	.0000	.0000	.0000
	19	.0000	.0000	.0000	.0000	.0000	.0000	.0000	.0000	.0000	.0000
20	0	.3585	.1216	.0388	.0115	.0032	.0008	.0002	.0000	.0000	.0000
	1	.3774	.2702	.1368	.0576	.0211	.0068	.0020	.0005	.0001	.0000
	2	.1887	.2852	.2293	.1369	.0669	.0278	.0100	.0031	.0008	.0002
	3	.0596	.1901	.2428	.2054	.1339	.0716	.0323	.0123	.0040	.0011
	4	.0133	.0898	.1821	.2182	.1897	.1304	.0738	.0350	.0139	.0046
	5	.0022	.0319	.1028	.1746	.2023	.1789	.1272	.0746	.0365	.0148
	6	.0003	.0089	.0454	.1091	.1686	.1916	.1712	.1244	.0746	.0370
	7	.0000	.0020	.0160	.0545	.1124	.1643	.1844	.1659	.1221	.0739
	8	.0000	.0004	.0046	.0222	.0609	.1144	.1614	.1797	.1623	.1201

Table 2
Probability Function of the Binomial Distribution Continued

n	x	P									
		.05	.10	.15	.20	.25	.30	.35	.40	.45	.50
	9	.0000	.0001	.0011	.0074	.0271	.0654	.1158	.1597	.1771	.1602
	10	.0000	.0000	.0002	.0020	.0099	.0308	.0686	.1171	.1593	.1762
	11	.0000	.0000	.0000	.0005	.0030	.0120	.0336	.0710	.1185	.1602
	12	.0000	.0000	.0000	.0001	.0008	.0039	.0136	.0355	.0727	.1201
	13	.0000	.0000	.0000	.0000	.0002	.0010	.0045	.0146	.0366	.0739
	14	.0000	.0000	.0000	.0000	.0000	.0002	.0012	.0049	.0150	.0370
	15	.0000	.0000	.0000	.0000	.0000	.0000	.0003	.0013	.0049	.0148
	16	.0000	.0000	.0000	.0000	.0000	.0000	.0000	.0003	.0013	.0046
	17	.0000	.0000	.0000	.0000	.0000	.0000	.0000	.0000	.0002	.0011
	18	.0000	.0000	.0000	.0000	.0000	.0000	.0000	.0000	.0000	.0002
	19	.0000	.0000	.0000	.0000	.0000	.0000	.0000	.0000	.0000	.0000
	20	.0000	.0000	.0000	.0000	.0000	.0000	.0000	.0000	.0000	.0000

Reproduced with permission from National Bureau of Standards, *Tables of the Binomial Probability Distribution*, United States Department of Commerce (1950).

Table 3 Cumulative Binomial Probabilities

The table shows the probability of x or fewer successes in n independent trials each with probability of success P. For example, the probability of two or less successes in four independent trials, each with probability of success, 0.35 is 0.874.

n	x	.05	.10	.15	.20	.25	.30	.35	.40	.45	.500
2	0	.902	.81	.722	.64	.562	.49	.422	.36	.302	.25
	1	.998	.99	.978	.96	.937	.91	.877	.84	.797	.75
	2	1.00	1.00	1.00	1.00	1.00	1.00	1.00	1.00	1.00	1.00
3	0	.857	.729	.614	.512	.422	.343	.275	.216	.166	.125
	1	.993	.972	.939	.896	.844	.784	.718	.648	.575	.500
	2	1.00	.999	.997	.992	.984	.973	.957	.936	.909	.875
	3	1.00	1.00	1.00	1.00	1.00	1.00	1.00	1.00	1.00	1.000
4	0	.815	.656	.522	.41	.316	.24	.179	.13	.092	.062
	1	.986	.948	.89	.819	.738	.652	.563	.475	.391	.312
	2	1.00	.996	.988	.973	.949	.916	.874	.821	.759	.687
	3	1.00	1.00	.999	.998	.996	.992	.985	.974	.959	.937
	4	1.00	1.00	1.00	1.00	1.00	1.00	1.00	1.00	1.00	1.000
5	0	.774	.59	.444	.328	.237	.168	.116	.078	.05	.031
	1	.977	.919	.835	.737	.633	.528	.428	.337	.256	.187
	2	.999	.991	.973	.942	.896	.837	.765	.683	.593	.500
	3	1.00	1.00	.998	.993	.984	.969	.946	.913	.869	.812
	4	1.00	1.00	1.00	1.00	.999	.998	.995	.99	.982	.969
	5	1.00	1.00	1.00	1.00	1.00	1.00	1.00	1.00	1.00	1.000
6	0	.735	.531	.377	.262	.178	.118	.075	.047	.028	.016
	1	.967	.886	.776	.655	.534	.42	.319	.233	.164	.109
	2	.998	.984	.953	.901	.831	.744	.647	.544	.442	.344
	3	1.00	.999	.994	.983	.962	.93	.883	.821	.745	.656
	4	1.00	1.00	1.00	.998	.995	.989	.978	.959	.931	.891
	5	1.00	1.00	1.00	1.00	1.00	.999	.998	.996	.992	.984
	6	1.00	1.00	1.00	1.00	1.00	1.00	1.00	1.00	1.00	1.000
7	0	.698	.478	.321	.21	.133	.082	.049	.028	.015	.008
	1	.956	.85	.717	.577	.445	.329	.234	.159	.102	.062
	2	.996	.974	.926	.852	.756	.647	.532	.42	.316	.227
	3	1.00	.997	.988	.967	.929	.874	.80	.71	.608	.500
	4	1.00	1.00	.999	.995	.987	.971	.944	.904	.847	.773
	5	1.00	1.00	1.00	1.00	.999	.996	.991	.981	.964	.937
	6	1.00	1.00	1.00	1.00	1.00	1.00	.999	.998	.996	.992
	7	1.00	1.00	1.00	1.00	1.00	1.00	1.00	1.00	1.00	1.000
8	0	.663	.43	.272	.168	.10	.058	.032	.017	.008	.004
	1	.943	.813	.657	.503	.367	.255	.169	.106	.063	.035
	2	.994	.962	.895	.797	.679	.552	.428	.315	.22	.145
	3	1.00	.995	.979	.944	.886	.806	.706	.594	.477	.363
	4	1.00	1.00	.997	.99	.973	.942	.894	.826	.74	.637
	5	1.00	1.00	1.00	.999	.996	.989	.975	.95	.912	.855
	6	1.00	1.00	1.00	1.00	1.00	.999	.996	.991	.982	.965
	7	1.00	1.00	1.00	1.00	1.00	1.00	1.00	.999	.998	.996
	8	1.00	1.00	1.00	1.00	1.00	1.00	1.00	1.00	1.00	1.000
9	0	.63	.387	.232	.134	.075	.04	.021	.01	.005	.002
	1	.929	.775	.599	.436	.30	.196	.121	.071	.039	.020
	2	.992	.947	.859	.738	.601	.463	.337	.232	.15	.090
	3	.999	.992	.966	.914	.834	.73	.609	.483	.361	.254
	4	1.00	.999	.994	.98	.951	.901	.828	.733	.621	.500
	5	1.00	1.00	.999	.997	.99	.975	.946	.901	.834	.746
	6	1.00	1.00	1.00	1.00	.999	.996	.989	.975	.95	.910
	7	1.00	1.00	1.00	1.00	1.00	1.00	.999	.996	.991	.980
	8	1.00	1.00	1.00	1.00	1.00	1.00	1.00	1.00	.999	.998
	9	1.00	1.00	1.00	1.00	1.00	1.00	1.00	1.00	1.00	1.000

Table 3 Cumulative Binomial Probabilities Continued

n	x	.05	.10	.15	.20	.25	.30	.35	.40	.45	.500
10	0	.599	.349	.197	.107	.056	.028	.013	.006	.003	.001
	1	.914	.736	.544	.376	.244	.149	.086	.046	.023	.011
	2	.988	.93	.82	.678	.526	.383	.262	.167	.10	.055
	3	.999	.987	.95	.879	.776	.65	.514	.382	.266	.172
	4	1.00	.998	.99	.967	.922	.85	.751	.633	.504	.377
	5	1.00	1.00	.999	.994	.98	.953	.905	.834	.738	.623
	6	1.00	1.00	1.00	.999	.996	.989	.974	.945	.898	.828
	7	1.00	1.00	1.00	1.00	1.00	.998	.995	.988	.973	.945
	8	1.00	1.00	1.00	1.00	1.00	1.00	.999	.998	.995	.989
	9	1.00	1.00	1.00	1.00	1.00	1.00	1.00	1.00	1.00	.999
	10	1.00	1.00	1.00	1.00	1.00	1.00	1.00	1.00	1.00	1.000
11	0	.569	.314	.167	.086	.042	.02	.009	.004	.001	.000
	1	.898	.697	.492	.322	.197	.113	.061	.03	.014	.006
	2	.985	.91	.779	.617	.455	.313	.20	.119	.065	.033
	3	.998	.981	.931	.839	.713	.57	.426	.296	.191	.113
	4	1.00	.997	.984	.95	.885	.79	.668	.533	.397	.274
	5	1.00	1.00	.997	.988	.966	.922	.851	.753	.633	.500
	6	1.00	1.00	1.00	.998	.992	.978	.95	.901	.826	.726
	7	1.00	1.00	1.00	1.00	.999	.996	.988	.971	.939	.887
	8	1.00	1.00	1.00	1.00	1.00	.999	.998	.994	.985	.967
	9	1.00	1.00	1.00	1.00	1.00	1.00	1.00	.999	.998	.994
	10	1.00	1.00	1.00	1.00	1.00	1.00	1.00	1.00	1.00	1.000
	11	1.00	1.00	1.00	1.00	1.00	1.00	1.00	1.00	1.00	1.000
12	0	.54	.282	.142	.069	.032	.014	.006	.002	.001	.000
	1	.882	.659	.443	.275	.158	.085	.042	.02	.008	.003
	2	.98	.889	.736	.558	.391	.253	.151	.083	.042	.019
	3	.998	.974	.908	.795	.649	.493	.347	.225	.134	.073
	4	1.00	.996	.976	.927	.842	.724	.583	.438	.304	.194
	5	1.00	.999	.995	.981	.946	.882	.787	.665	.527	.387
	6	1.00	1.00	.999	.996	.986	.961	.915	.842	.739	.613
	7	1.00	1.00	1.00	.999	.997	.991	.974	.943	.888	.806
	8	1.00	1.00	1.00	1.00	1.00	.998	.994	.985	.964	.927
	9	1.00	1.00	1.00	1.00	1.00	1.00	.999	.997	.992	.981
	10	1.00	1.00	1.00	1.00	1.00	1.00	1.00	1.00	.999	.997
	11	1.00	1.00	1.00	1.00	1.00	1.00	1.00	1.00	1.00	1.000
	12	1.00	1.00	1.00	1.00	1.00	1.00	1.00	1.00	1.00	1.000
13	0	.513	.254	.121	.055	.024	.01	.004	.001	.00	.000
	1	.865	.621	.398	.234	.127	.064	.03	.013	.005	.002
	2	.975	.866	.692	.502	.333	.202	.113	.058	.027	.011
	3	.997	.966	.882	.747	.584	.421	.278	.169	.093	.046
	4	1.00	.994	.966	.901	.794	.654	.501	.353	.228	.133
	5	1.00	.999	.992	.97	.92	.835	.716	.574	.427	.291
	6	1.00	1.00	.999	.993	.976	.938	.871	.771	.644	.50
	7	1.00	1.00	1.00	.999	.994	.982	.954	.902	.821	.709
	8	1.00	1.00	1.00	1.00	.999	.996	.987	.968	.93	.867
	9	1.00	1.00	1.00	1.00	1.00	.999	.997	.992	.98	.954
	10	1.00	1.00	1.00	1.00	1.00	1.00	1.00	.999	.996	.989
	11	1.00	1.00	1.00	1.00	1.00	1.00	1.00	1.00	.999	.998
	12	1.00	1.00	1.00	1.00	1.00	1.00	1.00	1.00	1.00	1.000
14	0	.488	.229	.103	.044	.018	.007	.002	.001	.00	.000
	1	.847	.585	.357	.198	.101	.047	.021	.008	.003	.001
	2	.97	.842	.648	.448	.281	.161	.084	.04	.017	.006
	3	.996	.956	.853	.698	.521	.355	.22	.124	.063	.029
	4	1.00	.991	.953	.87	.742	.584	.423	.279	.167	.090
	5	1.00	.999	.988	.956	.888	.781	.641	.486	.337	.212

Table 3 Cumulative Binomial Probabilities Continued

n	x	.05	.10	.15	.20	.25	.30	.35	.40	.45	.500
							P				
	6	1.00	1.00	.998	.988	.962	.907	.816	.692	.546	.395
	7	1.00	1.00	1.00	.998	.99	.969	.925	.85	.741	.605
	8	1.00	1.00	1.00	1.00	.998	.992	.976	.942	.881	.788
	9	1.00	1.00	1.00	1.00	1.00	.998	.994	.982	.957	.910
	10	1.00	1.00	1.00	1.00	1.00	1.00	.999	.996	.989	.971
	11	1.00	1.00	1.00	1.00	1.00	1.00	1.00	.999	.998	.994
	12	1.00	1.00	1.00	1.00	1.00	1.00	1.00	1.00	1.00	.999
	13	1.00	1.00	1.00	1.00	1.00	1.00	1.00	1.00	1.00	1.000
15	0	.463	.206	.087	.035	.013	.005	.002	.00	.00	.000
	1	.829	.549	.319	.167	.08	.035	.014	.005	.002	.000
	2	.964	.816	.604	.398	.236	.127	.062	.027	.011	.004
	3	.995	.944	.823	.648	.461	.297	.173	.091	.042	.018
	4	.999	.987	.938	.836	.686	.515	.352	.217	.12	.059
	5	1.00	.998	.983	.939	.852	.722	.564	.403	.261	.151
	6	1.00	1.00	.996	.982	.943	.869	.755	.61	.452	.304
	7	1.00	1.00	.999	.996	.983	.95	.887	.787	.654	.500
	8	1.00	1.00	1.00	.999	.996	.985	.958	.905	.818	.696
	9	1.00	1.00	1.00	1.00	.999	.996	.988	.966	.923	.849
	10	1.00	1.00	1.00	1.00	1.00	.999	.997	.991	.975	.941
	11	1.00	1.00	1.00	1.00	1.00	1.00	1.00	.998	.994	.982
	12	1.00	1.00	1.00	1.00	1.00	1.00	1.00	1.00	.999	.996
	13	1.00	1.00	1.00	1.00	1.00	1.00	1.00	1.00	1.00	1.000
16	0	.44	.185	.074	.028	.01	.003	.001	.00	.00	.000
	1	.811	.515	.284	.141	.063	.026	.01	.003	.001	.000
	2	.957	.789	.561	.352	.197	.099	.045	.018	.007	.002
	3	.993	.932	.79	.598	.405	.246	.134	.065	.028	.011
	4	.999	.983	.921	.798	.63	.45	.289	.167	.085	.038
	5	1.00	.997	.976	.918	.81	.66	.49	.329	.198	.105
	6	1.00	.999	.994	.973	.92	.825	.688	.527	.366	.227
	7	1.00	1.00	.999	.993	.973	.926	.841	.716	.563	.402
	8	1.00	1.00	1.00	.999	.993	.974	.933	.858	.744	.598
	9	1.00	1.00	1.00	1.00	.998	.993	.977	.942	.876	.773
	10	1.00	1.00	1.00	1.00	1.00	.998	.994	.981	.951	.895
	11	1.00	1.00	1.00	1.00	1.00	1.00	.999	.995	.985	.962
	12	1.00	1.00	1.00	1.00	1.00	1.00	1.00	.999	.997	.989
	13	1.00	1.00	1.00	1.00	1.00	1.00	1.00	1.00	.999	.998
	14	1.00	1.00	1.00	1.00	1.00	1.00	1.00	1.00	1.00	1.000
17	0	.418	.167	.063	.023	.008	.002	.001	.00	.00	.000
	1	.792	.482	.252	.118	.05	.019	.007	.002	.001	.000
	2	.95	.762	.52	.31	.164	.077	.033	.012	.004	.001
	3	.991	.917	.756	.549	.353	.202	.103	.046	.018	.006
	4	.999	.978	.901	.758	.574	.389	.235	.126	.06	.025
	5	1.00	.995	.968	.894	.765	.597	.42	.264	.147	.072
	6	1.00	.999	.992	.962	.893	.775	.619	.448	.29	.166
	7	1.00	1.00	.998	.989	.96	.895	.787	.641	.474	.315
	8	1.00	1.00	1.00	.997	.988	.96	.901	.801	.663	.500
	9	1.00	1.00	1.00	1.00	.997	.987	.962	.908	.817	.685
	10	1.00	1.00	1.00	1.00	.999	.997	.988	.965	.917	.834
	11	1.00	1.00	1.00	1.00	1.00	.999	.997	.989	.97	.928
	12	1.00	1.00	1.00	1.00	1.00	1.00	.999	.997	.991	.975
	13	1.00	1.00	1.00	1.00	1.00	1.00	1.00	1.00	.998	.994
	14	1.00	1.00	1.00	1.00	1.00	1.00	1.00	1.00	1.00	.999
	15	1.00	1.00	1.00	1.00	1.00	1.00	1.00	1.00	1.00	1.00
18	0	.397	.15	.054	.018	.006	.002	.00	.00	.00	.000
	1	.774	.45	.224	.099	.039	.014	.005	.001	.00	.000

Table 3 Cumulative Binomial Probabilities Continued

n	x	.05	.10	.15	.20	.25	.30	.35	.40	.45	.500
	2	.942	.734	.48	.271	.135	.06	.024	.008	.003	.001
	3	.989	.902	.72	.501	.306	.165	.078	.033	.012	.004
	4	.998	.972	.879	.716	.519	.333	.189	.094	.041	.015
	5	1.00	.994	.958	.867	.717	.534	.355	.209	.108	.048
	6	1.00	.999	.988	.949	.861	.722	.549	.374	.226	.119
	7	1.00	1.00	.997	.984	.943	.859	.728	.563	.391	.240
	8	1.00	1.00	.999	.996	.981	.94	.861	.737	.578	.407
	9	1.00	1.00	1.00	.999	.995	.979	.94	.865	.747	.593
	10	1.00	1.00	1.00	1.00	.999	.994	.979	.942	.872	.760
	11	1.00	1.00	1.00	1.00	1.00	.999	.994	.98	.946	.881
	12	1.00	1.00	1.00	1.00	1.00	1.00	.999	.994	.982	.952
	13	1.00	1.00	1.00	1.00	1.00	1.00	1.00	.999	.995	.985
	14	1.00	1.00	1.00	1.00	1.00	1.00	1.00	1.00	.999	.996
	15	1.00	1.00	1.00	1.00	1.00	1.00	1.00	1.00	1.00	.999
	16	1.00	1.00	1.00	1.00	1.00	1.00	1.00	1.00	1.00	1.000
19	0	.377	.135	.046	.014	.004	.001	.00	.00	.00	.000
	1	.755	.42	.198	.083	.031	.01	.003	.001	.00	.000
	2	.933	.705	.441	.237	.111	.046	.017	.005	.002	.000
	3	.987	.885	.684	.455	.263	.133	.059	.023	.008	.002
	4	.998	.965	.856	.673	.465	.282	.15	.07	.028	.010
	5	1.00	.991	.946	.837	.668	.474	.297	.163	.078	.032
	6	1.00	.998	.984	.932	.825	.666	.481	.308	.173	.084
	7	1.00	1.00	.996	.977	.923	.818	.666	.488	.317	.180
	8	1.00	1.00	.999	.993	.971	.916	.815	.667	.494	.324
	9	1.00	1.00	1.00	.998	.991	.967	.913	.814	.671	.500
	10	1.00	1.00	1.00	1.00	.998	.989	.965	.912	.816	.676
	11	1.00	1.00	1.00	1.00	1.00	.997	.989	.965	.913	.820
	12	1.00	1.00	1.00	1.00	1.00	.999	.997	.988	.966	.916
	13	1.00	1.00	1.00	1.00	1.00	1.00	.999	.997	.989	.968
	14	1.00	1.00	1.00	1.00	1.00	1.00	1.00	.999	.997	.990
	15	1.00	1.00	1.00	1.00	1.00	1.00	1.00	1.00	.999	.998
	16	1.00	1.00	1.00	1.00	1.00	1.00	1.00	1.00	1.00	1.000
20	0	.358	.122	.039	.012	.003	.001	.00	.00	.00	.000
	1	.736	.392	.176	.069	.024	.008	.002	.001	.00	.000
	2	.925	.677	.405	.206	.091	.035	.012	.004	.001	.000
	3	.984	.867	.648	.411	.225	.107	.044	.016	.005	.001
	4	.997	.957	.83	.63	.415	.238	.118	.051	.019	.006
	5	1.00	.989	.933	.804	.617	.416	.245	.126	.055	.021
	6	1.00	.998	.978	.913	.786	.608	.417	.25	.13	.058
	7	1.00	1.00	.994	.968	.898	.772	.601	.416	.252	.132
	8	1.00	1.00	.999	.99	.959	.887	.762	.596	.414	.252
	9	1.00	1.00	1.00	.997	.986	.952	.878	.755	.591	.412
	10	1.00	1.00	1.00	.999	.996	.983	.947	.872	.751	.588
	11	1.00	1.00	1.00	1.00	.999	.995	.98	.943	.869	.748
	12	1.00	1.00	1.00	1.00	1.00	.999	.994	.979	.942	.868
	13	1.00	1.00	1.00	1.00	1.00	1.00	.998	.994	.979	.942
	14	1.00	1.00	1.00	1.00	1.00	1.00	1.00	.998	.994	.979
	15	1.00	1.00	1.00	1.00	1.00	1.00	1.00	1.00	.998	.994
	16	1.00	1.00	1.00	1.00	1.00	1.00	1.00	1.00	1.00	.999
	17	1.00	1.00	1.00	1.00	1.00	1.00	1.00	1.00	1.00	1.000

Table 4 Values of $e^{-\lambda}$

λ	$e^{-\lambda}$	λ	$e^{-\lambda}$	λ	$e^{-\lambda}$	λ	$e^{-\lambda}$
0.00	1.000000	2.60	.074274	5.10	.006097	7.60	.000501
0.10	.904837	2.70	.067206	5.20	.005517	7.70	.000453
0.20	.818731	2.80	.060810	5.30	.004992	7.80	.000410
0.30	.740818	2.90	.055023	5.40	.004517	7.90	.000371
0.40	.670320	3.00	.049787	5.50	.004087	8.00	.000336
0.50	.606531	3.10	.045049	5.60	.003698	8.10	.000304
0.60	.548812	3.20	.040762	5.70	.003346	8.20	.000275
0.70	.496585	3.30	.036883	5.80	.003028	8.30	.000249
0.80	.449329	3.40	.033373	5.90	.002739	8.40	.000225
0.90	.406570	3.50	.030197	6.00	.002479	8.50	.000204
1.00	.367879	3.60	.027324	6.10	.002243	8.60	.000184
1.10	.332871	3.70	.024724	6.20	.002029	8.70	.000167
1.20	.301194	3.80	.022371	6.30	.001836	8.80	.000151
1.30	.272532	3.90	.020242	6.40	.001661	8.90	.000136
1.40	.246597	4.00	.018316	6.50	.001503	9.00	.000123
1.50	.223130	4.10	.016573	6.60	.001360	9.10	.000112
1.60	.201897	4.20	.014996	6.70	.001231	9.20	.000101
1.70	.182684	4.30	.013569	6.80	.001114	9.30	.000091
1.80	.165299	4.40	.012277	6.90	.001008	9.40	.000083
1.90	.149569	4.50	.011109	7.00	.000912	9.50	.000075
2.00	.135335	4.60	.010052	7.10	.000825	9.60	.000068
2.10	.122456	4.70	.009095	7.20	.000747	9.70	.000061
2.20	.110803	4.80	.008230	7.30	.000676	9.80	.000056
2.30	.100259	4.90	.007447	7.40	.000611	9.90	.000050
2.40	.090718	5.00	.006738	7.50	.000553	10.00	.000045
2.50	.082085						

Table 5 Individual Poisson Probabilities

	MEAN ARRIVAL RATE λ									
	0.1	0.2	0.3	0.4	0.5	0.6	0.7	0.8	0.9	1.0
0	.9048	.8187	.7408	.6703	.6065	.5488	.4966	.4493	.4066	.3679
1	.0905	.1637	.2222	.2681	.3033	.3293	.3476	.3595	.3659	.3679
2	.0045	.0164	.0333	.0536	.0758	.0988	.1217	.1438	.1647	.1839
3	.0002	.0011	.0033	.0072	.0126	.0198	.0284	.0383	.0494	.0613
4	.0	.0001	.0003	.0007	.0016	.0030	.0050	.0077	.0111	.0153
5	.0	.0	.0	.0001	.0002	.0004	.0007	.0012	.0020	.0031
6	.0	.0	.0	.0	.0	.0	.0001	.0002	.0003	.0005
7	.0	.0	.0	.0	.0	.0	.0	.0	.0	.0001

	MEAN ARRIVAL RATE λ									
	1.1	1.2	1.3	1.4	1.5	1.6	1.7	1.8	1.9	2.0
0	.3329	.3012	.2725	.2466	.2231	.2019	.1827	.1653	.1496	.1353
1	.3662	.3614	.3543	.3452	.3347	.3230	.3106	.2975	.2842	.2707
2	.2014	.2169	.2303	.2417	.2510	.2584	.2640	.2678	.2700	.2707
3	.0738	.0867	.0998	.1128	.1255	.1378	.1496	.1607	.1710	.1804
4	.0203	.0260	.0324	.0395	.0471	.0551	.0636	.0723	.0812	.0902
5	.0045	.0062	.0084	.0111	.0141	.0176	.0216	.0260	.0309	.0361
6	.0008	.0012	.0018	.0026	.0035	.0047	.0061	.0078	.0098	.0120
7	.0001	.0002	.0003	.0005	.0008	.0011	.0015	.0020	.0027	.0034
8	.0	.0	.0001	.0001	.0001	.0002	.0003	.0005	.0006	.0009
9	.0	.0	.0	.0	.0	.0	.0001	.0001	.0001	.0002

	MEAN ARRIVAL RATE λ									
	2.1	2.2	2.3	2.4	2.5	2.6	2.7	2.8	2.9	3.0
0	.1225	.1108	.1003	.0907	.0821	.0743	.0672	.0608	.0550	.0498
1	.2572	.2438	.2306	.2177	.2052	.1931	.1815	.1703	.1596	.1494
2	.2700	.2681	.2652	.2613	.2565	.2510	.2450	.2384	.2314	.2240
3	.1890	.1966	.2033	.2090	.2138	.2176	.2205	.2225	.2237	.2240
4	.0992	.1082	.1169	.1254	.1336	.1414	.1488	.1557	.1622	.1680
5	.0417	.0476	.0538	.0602	.0668	.0735	.0804	.0872	.0940	.1008
6	.0146	.0174	.0206	.0241	.0278	.0319	.0362	.0407	.0455	.0504
7	.0044	.0055	.0068	.0083	.0099	.0118	.0139	.0163	.0188	.0216
8	.0011	.0015	.0019	.0025	.0031	.0038	.0047	.0057	.0068	.0081
9	.0003	.0004	.0005	.0007	.0009	.0011	.0014	.0018	.0022	.0027
10	.0001	.0001	.0001	.0002	.0002	.0003	.0004	.0005	.0006	.0008
11	.0	.0	.0	.0	.0	.0001	.0001	.0001	.0002	.0002
12	.0	.0	.0	.0	.0	.0	.0	.0	.0	.0001

	MEAN ARRIVAL RATE λ									
	3.1	3.2	3.3	3.4	3.5	3.6	3.7	3.8	3.9	4.0
0	.0450	.0408	.0369	.0334	.0302	.0273	.0247	.0224	.0202	.0183
1	.1397	.1304	.1217	.1135	.1057	.0984	.0915	.0850	.0789	.0733
2	.2165	.2087	.2008	.1929	.1850	.1771	.1692	.1615	.1539	.1465
3	.2237	.2226	.2209	.2186	.2158	.2125	.2087	.2046	.2001	.1954
4	.1733	.1781	.1823	.1858	.1888	.1912	.1931	.1944	.1951	.1954
5	.1075	.1140	.1203	.1264	.1322	.1377	.1429	.1477	.1522	.1563
6	.0555	.0608	.0662	.0716	.0771	.0826	.0881	.0936	.0989	.1042
7	.0246	.0278	.0312	.0348	.0385	.0425	.0466	.0508	.0551	.0595
8	.0095	.0111	.0129	.0148	.0169	.0191	.0215	.0241	.0269	.0298
9	.0033	.0040	.0047	.0056	.0066	.0076	.0089	.0102	.0116	.0132
10	.0010	.0013	.0016	.0019	.0023	.0028	.0033	.0039	.0045	.0053
11	.0003	.0004	.0005	.0006	.0007	.0009	.0011	.0013	.0016	.0019
12	.0001	.0001	.0001	.0002	.0002	.0003	.0003	.0004	.0005	.0006
13	.0	.0	.0	.0	.0001	.0001	.0001	.0001	.0002	.0002
14	.0	.0	.0	.0	.0	.0	.0	.0	.0	.0001

Table 5 Individual Poisson Probabilities Continued

	MEAN ARRIVAL RATE λ									
	4.1	4.2	4.3	4.4	4.5	4.6	4.7	4.8	4.9	5.0
0	.0166	.0150	.0136	.0123	.0111	.0101	.0091	.0082	.0074	.0067
1	.0679	.0630	.0583	.0540	.0500	.0462	.0427	.0395	.0365	.0337
2	.1393	.1323	.1254	.1188	.1125	.1063	.1005	.0948	.0894	.0842
3	.1904	.1852	.1798	.1743	.1687	.1631	.1574	.1517	.1460	.1404
4	.1951	.1944	.1933	.1917	.1898	.1875	.1849	.1820	.1789	.1755
5	.1600	.1633	.1662	.1687	.1708	.1725	.1738	.1747	.1753	.1755
6	.1093	.1143	.1191	.1237	.1281	.1323	.1362	.1398	.1432	.1462
7	.0640	.0686	.0732	.0778	.0824	.0869	.0914	.0959	.1002	.1044
8	.0328	.0360	.0393	.0428	.0463	.0500	.0537	.0575	.0614	.0653
9	.0150	.0168	.0188	.0209	.0232	.0255	.0281	.0307	.0334	.0363
10	.0061	.0071	.0081	.0092	.0104	.0118	.0132	.0147	.0164	.0181
11	.0023	.0027	.0032	.0037	.0043	.0049	.0056	.0064	.0073	.0082
12	.0008	.0009	.0011	.0013	.0016	.0019	.0022	.0026	.0030	.0034
13	.0002	.0003	.0004	.0005	.0006	.0007	.0008	.0009	.0011	.0013
14	.0001	.0001	.0001	.0001	.0002	.0002	.0003	.0003	.0004	.0005

	MEAN ARRIVAL RATE λ									
	5.1	5.2	5.3	5.4	5.5	5.6	5.7	5.8	5.9	6.0
0	.0061	.0055	.0050	.0045	.0041	.0037	.0033	.0030	.0027	.0025
1	.0311	.0287	.0265	.0244	.0225	.0207	.0191	.0176	.0162	.0149
2	.0793	.0746	.0701	.0659	.0618	.0580	.0544	.0509	.0477	.0446
3	.1348	.1293	.1239	.1185	.1133	.1082	.1033	.0985	.0938	.0892
4	.1719	.1681	.1641	.1600	.1558	.1515	.1472	.1428	.1383	.1339
5	.1753	.1748	.1740	.1728	.1714	.1697	.1678	.1656	.1632	.1606
6	.1490	.1515	.1537	.1555	.1571	.1584	.1594	.1601	.1605	.1606
7	.1086	.1125	.1163	.1200	.1234	.1267	.1298	.1326	.1353	.1377
8	.0692	.0731	.0771	.0810	.0849	.0887	.0925	.0962	.0998	.1033
9	.0392	.0423	.0454	.0486	.0519	.0552	.0586	.0620	.0654	.0688
10	.0200	.0220	.0241	.0262	.0285	.0309	.0334	.0359	.0386	.0413
11	.0093	.0104	.0116	.0129	.0143	.0157	.0173	.0190	.0207	.0225
12	.0039	.0045	.0051	.0058	.0065	.0073	.0082	.0092	.0102	.0113
13	.0015	.0018	.0021	.0024	.0028	.0032	.0036	.0041	.0046	.0052
14	.0006	.0007	.0008	.0009	.0011	.0013	.0015	.0017	.0019	.0022

	MEAN ARRIVAL RATE λ									
	6.1	6.2	6.3	6.4	6.5	6.6	6.7	6.8	6.9	7.0
0	.0022	.0020	.0018	.0017	.0015	.0014	.0012	.0011	.0010	.0009
1	.0137	.0126	.0116	.0106	.0098	.0090	.0082	.0076	.0070	.0064
2	.0417	.0390	.0364	.0340	.0318	.0296	.0276	.0258	.0240	.0223
3	.0848	.0806	.0765	.0726	.0688	.0652	.0617	.0584	.0552	.0521
4	.1294	.1249	.1205	.1162	.1118	.1076	.1034	.0992	.0952	.0912
5	.1579	.1549	.1519	.1487	.1454	.1420	.1385	.1349	.1314	.1277
6	.1605	.1601	.1595	.1586	.1575	.1562	.1546	.1529	.1511	.1490
7	.1399	.1418	.1435	.1450	.1462	.1472	.1480	.1486	.1489	.1490
8	.1066	.1099	.1130	.1160	.1188	.1215	.1240	.1263	.1284	.1304
9	.0723	.0757	.0791	.0825	.0858	.0891	.0923	.0954	.0985	.1014
10	.0441	.0469	.0498	.0528	.0558	.0588	.0618	.0649	.0679	.0710
11	.0244	.0265	.0285	.0307	.0330	.0353	.0377	.0401	.0426	.0452
12	.0124	.0137	.0150	.0164	.0179	.0194	.0210	.0227	.0245	.0263
13	.0058	.0065	.0073	.0081	.0089	.0099	.0108	.0119	.0130	.0142
14	.0025	.0029	.0033	.0037	.0041	.0046	.0052	.0058	.0064	.0071

Table 5 Individual Poisson Probabilities Continued

					Mean Arrival Rate λ					
	7.1	7.2	7.3	7.4	7.5	7.6	7.7	7.8	7.9	8.0
0	.0008	.0007	.0007	.0006	.0006	.0005	.0005	.0004	.0004	.0003
1	.0059	.0054	.0049	.0045	.0041	.0038	.0035	.0032	.0029	.0027
2	.0208	.0194	.0180	.0167	.0156	.0145	.0134	.0125	.0116	.0107
3	.0492	.0464	.0438	.0413	.0389	.0366	.0345	.0324	.0305	.0286
4	.0874	.0836	.0799	.0764	.0729	.0696	.0663	.0632	.0602	.0573
5	.1241	.1204	.1167	.1130	.1094	.1057	.1021	.0986	.0951	.0916
6	.1468	.1445	.1420	.1394	.1367	.1339	.1311	.1282	.1252	.1221
7	.1489	.1486	.1481	.1474	.1465	.1454	.1442	.1428	.1413	.1396
8	.1321	.1337	.1351	.1363	.1373	.1381	.1388	.1392	.1395	.1396
9	.1042	.1070	.1096	.1121	.1144	.1167	.1187	.1207	.1224	.1241
10	.0740	.0770	.08	.0829	.0858	.0887	.0914	.0941	.0967	.0993
11	.0478	.0504	.0531	.0558	.0585	.0613	.0640	.0667	.0695	.0722
12	.0283	.0303	.0323	.0344	.0366	.0388	.0411	.0434	.0457	.0481
13	.0154	.0168	.0181	.0196	.0211	.0227	.0243	.0260	.0278	.0296
14	.0078	.0086	.0095	.0104	.0113	.0123	.0134	.0145	.0157	.0169
15	.0037	.0041	.0046	.0051	.0057	.0062	.0069	.0075	.0083	.0090
16	.0016	.0019	.0021	.0024	.0026	.0030	.0033	.0037	.0041	.0045
17	.0007	.0008	.0009	.0010	.0012	.0013	.0015	.0017	.0019	.0021
18	.0003	.0003	.0004	.0004	.0005	.0006	.0006	.0007	.0008	.0009
19	.0001	.0001	.0001	.0002	.0002	.0002	.0003	.0003	.0003	.0004

					Mean Arrival Rate λ					
	8.1	8.2	8.3	8.4	8.5	8.6	8.7	8.8	8.9	9.0
0	.0003	.0003	.0002	.0002	.0002	.0002	.0002	.0002	.0001	.0001
1	.0025	.0023	.0021	.0019	.0017	.0016	.0014	.0013	.0012	.0011
2	.01	.0092	.0086	.0079	.0074	.0068	.0063	.0058	.0054	.0050
3	.0269	.0252	.0237	.0222	.0208	.0195	.0183	.0171	.0160	.0150
4	.0544	.0517	.0491	.0466	.0443	.0420	.0398	.0377	.0357	.0337
5	.0882	.0849	.0816	.0784	.0752	.0722	.0692	.0663	.0635	.0607
6	.1191	.1160	.1128	.1097	.1066	.1034	.1003	.0972	.0941	.0911
7	.1378	.1358	.1338	.1317	.1294	.1271	.1247	.1222	.1197	.1171
8	.1395	.1392	.1388	.1382	.1375	.1366	.1356	.1344	.1332	.1318
9	.1256	.1269	.1280	.1290	.1299	.1306	.1311	.1315	.1317	.1318
10	.1017	.1040	.1063	.1084	.1104	.1123	.1140	.1157	.1172	.1186
11	.0749	.0776	.0802	.0828	.0853	.0878	.0902	.0925	.0948	.0970
12	.0505	.0530	.0555	.0579	.0604	.0629	.0654	.0679	.0703	.0728
13	.0315	.0334	.0354	.0374	.0395	.0416	.0438	.0459	.0481	.0504
14	.0182	.0196	.0210	.0225	.0240	.0256	.0272	.0289	.0306	.0324
15	.0098	.0107	.0116	.0126	.0136	.0147	.0158	.0169	.0182	.0194
16	.0050	.0055	.0060	.0066	.0072	.0079	.0086	.0093	.0101	.0109
17	.0024	.0026	.0029	.0033	.0036	.0040	.0044	.0048	.0053	.0058
18	.0011	.0012	.0014	.0015	.0017	.0019	.0021	.0024	.0026	.0029
19	.0005	.0005	.0006	.0007	.0008	.0009	.0010	.0011	.0012	.0014

					Mean Arrival Rate λ					
	9.1	9.2	9.3	9.4	9.5	9.6	9.7	9.8	9.9	10.0
0	.0001	.0001	.0001	.0001	.0001	.0001	.0001	.0001	.0001	.0000
1	.0010	.0009	.0009	.0008	.0007	.0007	.0006	.0005	.0005	.0005
2	.0046	.0043	.0040	.0037	.0034	.0031	.0029	.0027	.0025	.0023
3	.0140	.0131	.0123	.0115	.0107	.01	.0093	.0087	.0081	.0076
4	.0319	.0302	.0285	.0269	.0254	.0240	.0226	.0213	.0201	.0189
5	.0581	.0555	.0530	.0506	.0483	.0460	.0439	.0418	.0398	.0378
6	.0881	.0851	.0822	.0793	.0764	.0736	.0709	.0682	.0656	.0631
7	.1145	.1118	.1091	.1064	.1037	.1010	.0982	.0955	.0928	.0901
8	.1302	.1286	.1269	.1251	.1232	.1212	.1191	.1170	.1148	.1126

Table 5   Individual Poisson Probabilities Continued

| | \multicolumn{10}{c|}{MEAN ARRIVAL RATE λ} |
	9.1	9.2	9.3	9.4	9.5	9.6	9.7	9.8	9.9	10.0
9	.1317	.1315	.1311	.1306	.13	.1293	.1284	.1274	.1263	.1251
10	.1198	.1210	.1219	.1228	.1235	.1241	.1245	.1249	.1250	.1251
11	.0991	.1012	.1031	.1049	.1067	.1083	.1098	.1112	.1125	.1137
12	.0752	.0776	.0799	.0822	.0844	.0866	.0888	.0908	.0928	.0948
13	.0526	.0549	.0572	.0594	.0617	.0640	.0662	.0685	.0707	.0729
14	.0342	.0361	.0380	.0399	.0419	.0439	.0459	.0479	.05	.0521
15	.0208	.0221	.0235	.0250	.0265	.0281	.0297	.0313	.0330	.0347
16	.0118	.0127	.0137	.0147	.0157	.0168	.0180	.0192	.0204	.0217
17	.0063	.0069	.0075	.0081	.0088	.0095	.0103	.0111	.0119	.0128
18	.0032	.0035	.0039	.0042	.0046	.0051	.0055	.0060	.0065	.0071
19	.0015	.0017	.0019	.0021	.0023	.0026	.0028	.0031	.0034	.0037

| | \multicolumn{10}{c|}{MEAN ARRIVAL RATE λ} |
	10.1	10.2	10.3	10.4	10.5	10.6	10.7	10.8	10.9	11.0
0	.00	.00	.00	.00	.00	.00	.00	.00	.00	.0000
1	.0004	.0004	.0003	.0003	.0003	.0003	.0002	.0002	.0002	.0002
2	.0021	.0019	.0018	.0016	.0015	.0014	.0013	.0012	.0011	.0010
3	.0071	.0066	.0061	.0057	.0053	.0049	.0046	.0043	.0040	.0037
4	.0178	.0168	.0158	.0148	.0139	.0131	.0123	.0116	.0109	.0102
5	.0360	.0342	.0325	.0309	.0293	.0278	.0264	.0250	.0237	.0224
6	.0606	.0581	.0558	.0535	.0513	.0491	.0470	.0450	.0430	.0411
7	.0874	.0847	.0821	.0795	.0769	.0743	.0718	.0694	.0669	.0646
8	.1103	.1080	.1057	.1033	.1009	.0985	.0961	.0936	.0912	.0888
9	.1238	.1224	.1209	.1194	.1177	.1160	.1142	.1124	.1105	.1085
10	.1250	.1249	.1246	.1241	.1236	.1230	.1222	.1214	.1204	.1194
11	.1148	.1158	.1166	.1174	.1180	.1185	.1189	.1192	.1193	.1194
12	.0966	.0984	.1001	.1017	.1032	.1047	.1060	.1072	.1084	.1094
13	.0751	.0772	.0793	.0814	.0834	.0853	.0872	.0891	.0909	.0926
14	.0542	.0563	.0584	.0604	.0625	.0646	.0667	.0687	.0708	.0728
15	.0365	.0383	.0401	.0419	.0438	.0457	.0476	.0495	.0514	.0534
16	.0230	.0244	.0258	.0272	.0287	.0303	.0318	.0334	.0350	.0367
17	.0137	.0146	.0156	.0167	.0177	.0189	.0200	.0212	.0225	.0237
18	.0077	.0083	.0089	.0096	.0104	.0111	.0119	.0127	.0136	.0145
19	.0041	.0045	.0048	.0053	.0057	.0062	.0067	.0072	.0078	.0084
20	.0021	.0023	.0025	.0027	.0030	.0033	.0036	.0039	.0043	.0046

| | \multicolumn{10}{c|}{MEAN ARRIVAL RATE λ} |
	11.1	11.2	11.3	11.4	11.5	11.6	11.7	11.8	11.9	12.0
0	.0000	.0000	.0000	.0000	.0000	.0000	.0000	.0000	.0000	.0000
1	.0002	.0002	.0001	.0001	.0001	.0001	.0001	.0001	.0001	.0001
2	.0009	.0009	.0008	.0007	.0007	.0006	.0006	.0005	.0005	.0004
3	.0034	.0032	.0030	.0028	.0026	.0024	.0022	.0021	.0019	.0018
4	.0096	.0090	.0084	.0079	.0074	.0069	.0065	.0061	.0057	.0053
5	.0212	.0201	.0190	.0180	.0170	.0160	.0152	.0143	.0135	.0127
6	.0393	.0375	.0358	.0341	.0325	.0310	.0295	.0281	.0268	.0255
7	.0623	.0600	.0578	.0556	.0535	.0514	.0494	.0474	.0455	.0437
8	.0864	.0840	.0816	.0792	.0769	.0745	.0722	.0700	.0677	.0655
9	.1065	.1045	.1024	.1003	.0982	.0961	.0939	.0917	.0895	.0874
10	.1182	.1170	.1157	.1144	.1129	.1114	.1099	.1082	.1066	.1048
11	.1193	.1192	.1189	.1185	.1181	.1175	.1169	.1161	.1153	.1144
12	.1104	.1112	.1120	.1126	.1131	.1136	.1139	.1142	.1143	.1144
13	.0942	.0958	.0973	.0987	.1001	.1014	.1025	.1036	.1046	.1056
14	.0747	.0767	.0786	.0804	.0822	.0840	.0857	.0874	.0889	.0905

Table 5 Individual Poisson Probabilities Continued

					Mean Arrival Rate λ					
	11.1	11.2	11.3	11.4	11.5	11.6	11.7	11.8	11.9	12.0
15	.0553	.0572	.0592	.0611	.0630	.0649	.0668	.0687	.0706	.0724
16	.0384	.0401	.0418	.0435	.0453	.0471	.0489	.0507	.0525	.0543
17	.0250	.0264	.0278	.0292	.0306	.0321	.0336	.0352	.0367	.0383
18	.0154	.0164	.0174	.0185	.0196	.0207	.0219	.0231	.0243	.0255
19	.0090	.0097	.0104	.0111	.0119	.0126	.0135	.0143	.0152	.0161
20	.0050	.0054	.0059	.0063	.0068	.0073	.0079	.0084	.0091	.0097

					Mean Arrival Rate λ					
	12.1	12.2	12.3	12.4	12.5	12.6	12.7	12.8	12.9	13.0
4	.0050	.0046	.0043	.0041	.0038	.0035	.0033	.0031	.0029	.0027
5	.0120	.0113	.0107	.0101	.0095	.0089	.0084	.0079	.0074	.0070
6	.0242	.0230	.0219	.0208	.0197	.0187	.0178	.0169	.0160	.0152
7	.0419	.0402	.0385	.0368	.0353	.0337	.0323	.0308	.0295	.0281
8	.0634	.0612	.0591	.0571	.0551	.0531	.0512	.0493	.0475	.0457
9	.0852	.0830	.0808	.0787	.0765	.0744	.0723	.0702	.0681	.0661
10	.1031	.1013	.0994	.0975	.0956	.0937	.0918	.0898	.0878	.0859
11	.1134	.1123	.1112	.1100	.1087	.1074	.1060	.1045	.1030	.1015
12	.1143	.1142	.1139	.1136	.1132	.1127	.1121	.1115	.1107	.1099
13	.1064	.1072	.1078	.1084	.1089	.1093	.1096	.1098	.1099	.1099
14	.0920	.0934	.0947	.0960	.0972	.0983	.0994	.1004	.1013	.1021
15	.0742	.0759	.0777	.0794	.0810	.0826	.0841	.0856	.0871	.0885
16	.0561	.0579	.0597	.0615	.0633	.0650	.0668	.0685	.0702	.0719
17	.0399	.0416	.0432	.0449	.0465	.0482	.0499	.0516	.0533	.0550
18	.0268	.0282	.0295	.0309	.0323	.0337	.0352	.0367	.0382	.0397
19	.0171	.0181	.0191	.0202	.0213	.0224	.0235	.0247	.0259	.0272
20	.0103	.0110	.0118	.0125	.0133	.0141	.0149	.0158	.0167	.0177

					Mean Arrival Rate λ					
	13.1	13.2	13.3	13.4	13.5	13.6	13.7	13.8	13.9	14.0
5	.0066	.0062	.0058	.0055	.0051	.0048	.0045	.0042	.0040	.0037
6	.0144	.0136	.0129	.0122	.0115	.0109	.0103	.0097	.0092	.0087
7	.0269	.0256	.0245	.0233	.0222	.0212	.0202	.0192	.0183	.0174
8	.0440	.0423	.0407	.0391	.0375	.0360	.0345	.0331	.0318	.0304
9	.0640	.0620	.0601	.0582	.0563	.0544	.0526	.0508	.0491	.0473
10	.0839	.0819	.0799	.0779	.0760	.0740	.0720	.0701	.0682	.0663
11	.0999	.0983	.0966	.0949	.0932	.0915	.0897	.0880	.0862	.0844
12	.1091	.1081	.1071	.1060	.1049	.1037	.1024	.1011	.0998	.0984
13	.1099	.1098	.1096	.1093	.1089	.1085	.1080	.1074	.1067	.1060
14	.1028	.1035	.1041	.1046	.1050	.1054	.1056	.1058	.1060	.1060
15	.0898	.0911	.0923	.0934	.0945	.0955	.0965	.0974	.0982	.0989
16	.0735	.0751	.0767	.0783	.0798	.0812	.0826	.0840	.0853	.0866
17	.0567	.0583	.0600	.0617	.0633	.0650	.0666	.0682	.0697	.0713
18	.0412	.0428	.0443	.0459	.0475	.0491	.0507	.0523	.0539	.0554
19	.0284	.0297	.0310	.0324	.0337	.0351	.0365	.0380	.0394	.0409
20	.0186	.0196	.0206	.0217	.0228	.0239	.0250	.0262	.0274	.0286

					Mean Arrival Rate λ					
	14.1	14.2	14.3	14.4	14.5	14.6	14.7	14.8	14.9	15.0
6	.0082	.0078	.0073	.0069	.0065	.0061	.0058	.0055	.0051	.0048
7	.0165	.0157	.0149	.0142	.0135	.0128	.0122	.0115	.0109	.0104
8	.0292	.0279	.0267	.0256	.0244	.0234	.0223	.0213	.0204	.0194
9	.0457	.0440	.0424	.0409	.0394	.0379	.0365	.0351	.0337	.0324
10	.0644	.0625	.0607	.0589	.0571	.0553	.0536	.0519	.0502	.0486
11	.0825	.0807	.0789	.0771	.0753	.0735	.0716	.0698	.0681	.0663

Table 5 Individual Poisson Probabilities Continued

					MEAN ARRIVAL RATE λ					
	14.1	14.2	14.3	14.4	14.5	14.6	14.7	14.8	14.9	15.0
12	.0970	.0955	.0940	.0925	.0910	.0894	.0878	.0861	.0845	.0829
13	.1052	.1043	.1034	.1025	.1014	.1004	.0992	.0981	.0969	.0956
14	.1060	.1058	.1057	.1054	.1051	.1047	.1042	.1037	.1031	.1024
15	.0996	.1002	.1007	.1012	.1016	.1019	.1021	.1023	.1024	.1024
16	.0878	.0889	.0900	.0911	.0920	.0930	.0938	.0946	.0954	.0960
17	.0728	.0743	.0757	.0771	.0785	.0798	.0811	.0824	.0836	.0847
18	.0570	.0586	.0602	.0617	.0632	.0648	.0663	.0677	.0692	.0706
19	.0423	.0438	.0453	.0468	.0483	.0498	.0513	.0528	.0543	.0557
20	.0298	.0311	.0324	.0337	.0350	.0363	.0377	.0390	.0404	.0418
21	.0200	.0210	.0220	.0231	.0242	.0253	.0264	.0275	.0287	.0299
22	.0128	.0136	.0143	.0151	.0159	.0168	.0176	.0185	.0194	.0204
23	.0079	.0084	.0089	.0095	.0100	.0106	.0113	.0119	.0126	.0133
24	.0046	.0050	.0053	.0057	.0061	.0065	.0069	.0073	.0078	.0083

					MEAN ARRIVAL RATE λ					
	15.1	15.2	15.3	15.4	15.5	15.6	15.7	15.8	15.9	16.0
7	.0098	.0093	.0088	.0084	.0079	.0075	.0071	.0067	.0063	.0060
8	.0186	.0177	.0169	.0161	.0153	.0146	.0139	.0132	.0126	.0120
9	.0311	.0299	.0287	.0275	.0264	.0253	.0243	.0232	.0223	.0213
10	.0470	.0454	.0439	.0424	.0409	.0395	.0381	.0367	.0354	.0341
11	.0645	.0628	.0611	.0594	.0577	.0560	.0544	.0527	.0512	.0496
12	.0812	.0795	.0778	.0762	.0745	.0728	.0711	.0695	.0678	.0661
13	.0943	.0930	.0916	.0902	.0888	.0874	.0859	.0844	.0829	.0814
14	.1017	.1010	.1001	.0993	.0983	.0974	.0963	.0953	.0942	.0930
15	.1024	.1023	.1021	.1019	.1016	.1012	.1008	.1003	.0998	.0992
16	.0966	.0972	.0977	.0981	.0984	.0987	.0989	.0991	.0992	.0992
17	.0858	.0869	.0879	.0888	.0897	.0906	.0914	.0921	.0928	.0934
18	.0720	.0734	.0747	.0760	.0773	.0785	.0797	.0808	.0819	.0830
19	.0572	.0587	.0602	.0616	.0630	.0645	.0659	.0672	.0686	.0699
20	.0432	.0446	.0460	.0474	.0489	.0503	.0517	.0531	.0545	.0559
21	.0311	.0323	.0335	.0348	.0361	.0373	.0386	.0400	.0413	.0426
22	.0213	.0223	.0233	.0244	.0254	.0265	.0276	.0287	.0298	.0310
23	.0140	.0147	.0155	.0163	.0171	.0180	.0188	.0197	.0206	.0216
24	.0088	.0093	.0099	.0105	.0111	.0117	.0123	.0130	.0137	.0144
25	.0053	.0057	.0061	.0064	.0069	.0073	.0077	.0082	.0087	.0092

					MEAN ARRIVAL RATE λ					
	16.1	16.2	16.3	16.4	16.5	16.6	16.7	16.8	16.9	17.0
7	.0057	.0054	.0051	.0048	.0045	.0043	.0040	.0038	.0036	.0034
8	.0114	.0108	.0103	.0098	.0093	.0088	.0084	.0080	.0076	.0072
9	.0204	.0195	.0187	.0178	.0171	.0163	.0156	.0149	.0142	.0135
10	.0328	.0316	.0304	.0293	.0281	.0270	.0260	.0250	.0240	.0230
11	.0481	.0466	.0451	.0436	.0422	.0408	.0394	.0381	.0368	.0355
12	.0645	.0628	.0612	.0596	.0580	.0565	.0549	.0534	.0518	.0504
13	.0799	.0783	.0768	.0752	.0736	.0721	.0705	.0690	.0674	.0658
14	.0918	.0906	.0894	.0881	.0868	.0855	.0841	.0828	.0814	.0800
15	.0986	.0979	.0971	.0963	.0955	.0946	.0937	.0927	.0917	.0906
16	.0992	.0991	.0989	.0987	.0985	.0981	.0978	.0973	.0968	.0963
17	.0939	.0944	.0949	.0952	.0956	.0958	.0960	.0962	.0963	.0963
18	.0840	.0850	.0859	.0868	.0876	.0884	.0891	.0898	.0904	.0909
19	.0712	.0725	.0737	.0749	.0761	.0772	.0783	.0794	.0804	.0814
20	.0573	.0587	.0601	.0614	.0628	.0641	.0654	.0667	.0679	.0692
21	.0439	.0453	.0466	.0480	.0493	.0507	.0520	.0533	.0547	.0560

Table 5 Individual Poisson Probabilities Continued

	MEAN ARRIVAL RATE λ									
	16.1	16.2	16.3	16.4	16.5	16.6	16.7	16.8	16.9	17.0
22	.0322	.0333	.0345	.0358	.0370	.0382	.0395	.0407	.0420	.0433
23	.0225	.0235	.0245	.0255	.0265	.0276	.0287	.0297	.0309	.0320
24	.0151	.0159	.0166	.0174	.0182	.0191	.0199	.0208	.0217	.0226
25	.0097	.0103	.0108	.0114	.0120	.0127	.0133	.0140	.0147	.0154

	MEAN ARRIVAL RATE λ									
	17.1	17.2	17.3	17.4	17.5	17.6	17.7	17.8	17.9	18.0
8	.0068	.0064	.0061	.0058	.0055	.0052	.0049	.0046	.0044	.0042
9	.0129	.0123	.0117	.0112	.0107	.0101	.0097	.0092	.0088	.0083
10	.0221	.0212	.0203	.0195	.0186	.0179	.0171	.0164	.0157	.0150
11	.0343	.0331	.0319	.0308	.0297	.0286	.0275	.0265	.0255	.0245
12	.0489	.0474	.0460	.0446	.0432	.0419	.0406	.0393	.0380	.0368
13	.0643	.0628	.0612	.0597	.0582	.0567	.0553	.0538	.0524	.0509
14	.0785	.0771	.0757	.0742	.0728	.0713	.0699	.0684	.0669	.0655
15	.0895	.0884	.0873	.0861	.0849	.0837	.0824	.0812	.0799	.0786
16	.0957	.0951	.0944	.0936	.0929	.0920	.0912	.0903	.0894	.0884
17	.0963	.0962	.0960	.0958	.0956	.0953	.0949	.0945	.0941	.0936
18	.0914	.0919	.0923	.0926	.0929	.0932	.0934	.0935	.0936	.0936
19	.0823	.0832	.0840	.0848	.0856	.0863	.0870	.0876	.0882	.0887
20	.0704	.0715	.0727	.0738	.0749	.0760	.0770	.0780	.0789	.0798
21	.0573	.0586	.0599	.0612	.0624	.0637	.0649	.0661	.0673	.0684
22	.0445	.0458	.0471	.0484	.0496	.0509	.0522	.0535	.0547	.0560
23	.0331	.0343	.0354	.0366	.0378	.0390	.0402	.0414	.0426	.0438
24	.0236	.0246	.0255	.0265	.0275	.0286	.0296	.0307	.0318	.0328
25	.0161	.0169	.0177	.0185	.0193	.0201	.0210	.0218	.0227	.0237

	MEAN ARRIVAL RATE λ									
	18.1	18.2	18.3	18.4	18.5	18.6	18.7	18.8	18.9	19.0
9	.0079	.0075	.0072	.0068	.0065	.0061	.0058	.0055	.0053	.0050
10	.0143	.0137	.0131	.0125	.0120	.0114	.0109	.0104	.0099	.0095
11	.0236	.0227	.0218	.0209	.0201	.0193	.0185	.0178	.0171	.0164
12	.0356	.0344	.0332	.0321	.0310	.0299	.0289	.0278	.0269	.0259
13	.0495	.0481	.0468	.0454	.0441	.0428	.0415	.0403	.0390	.0378
14	.0640	.0626	.0611	.0597	.0583	.0569	.0555	.0541	.0527	.0514
15	.0773	.0759	.0746	.0732	.0719	.0705	.0692	.0678	.0664	.0650
16	.0874	.0864	.0853	.0842	.0831	.0820	.0808	.0796	.0785	.0772
17	.0931	.0925	.0918	.0912	.0904	.0897	.0889	.0881	.0872	.0863
18	.0936	.0935	.0934	.0932	.0930	.0927	.0924	.0920	.0916	.0911
19	.0891	.0896	.0899	.0902	.0905	.0907	.0909	.0910	.0911	.0911
20	.0807	.0815	.0823	.0830	.0837	.0844	.0850	.0856	.0861	.0866
21	.0695	.0706	.0717	.0727	.0738	.0747	.0757	.0766	.0775	.0783
22	.0572	.0584	.0596	.0608	.0620	.0632	.0643	.0655	.0666	.0676
23	.0450	.0462	.0475	.0487	.0499	.0511	.0523	.0535	.0547	.0559
24	.0340	.0351	.0362	.0373	.0385	.0396	.0408	.0419	.0431	.0442
25	.0246	.0255	.0265	.0275	.0285	.0295	.0305	.0315	.0326	.0336

	MEAN ARRIVAL RATE λ									
	19.1	19.2	19.3	19.4	19.5	19.6	19.7	19.8	19.9	20.0
10	.0090	.0086	.0082	.0078	.0074	.0071	.0067	.0064	.0061	.0058
11	.0157	.0150	.0144	.0138	.0132	.0126	.0121	.0116	.0111	.0106
12	.0249	.0240	.0231	.0223	.0214	.0206	.0198	.0191	.0183	.0176
13	.0367	.0355	.0344	.0333	.0322	.0311	.0301	.0291	.0281	.0271
14	.0500	.0487	.0474	.0461	.0448	.0436	.0423	.0411	.0399	.0387
15	.0637	.0623	.0610	.0596	.0582	.0569	.0556	.0543	.0529	.0516
16	.0760	.0748	.0735	.0723	.0710	.0697	.0684	.0671	.0659	.0646

Table 5 Individual Poisson Probabilities Continued

	MEAN ARRIVAL RATE λ									
	19.1	19.2	19.3	19.4	19.5	19.6	19.7	19.8	19.9	20.0
17	.0854	.0844	.0835	.0825	.0814	.0804	.0793	.0782	.0771	.0760
18	.0906	.0901	.0895	.0889	.0882	.0875	.0868	.0860	.0852	.0844
19	.0911	.0910	.0909	.0907	.0905	.0903	.0900	.0896	.0893	.0888
20	.0870	.0874	.0877	.0880	.0883	.0885	.0886	.0887	.0888	.0888
21	.0791	.0799	.0806	.0813	.0820	.0826	.0831	.0837	.0842	.0846
22	.0687	.0697	.0707	.0717	.0727	.0736	.0745	.0753	.0761	.0769
23	.0570	.0582	.0594	.0605	.0616	.0627	.0638	.0648	.0659	.0669
24	.0454	.0466	.0477	.0489	.0500	.0512	.0523	.0535	.0546	.0557
25	.0347	.0358	.0368	.0379	.0390	.0401	.0412	.0424	.0435	.0446

	MEAN ARRIVAL RATE λ									
	20.1	20.2	20.3	20.4	20.5	20.6	20.7	20.8	20.9	21.0
10	.0055	.0053	.0050	.0048	.0045	.0043	.0041	.0039	.0037	.0035
11	.0101	.0097	.0092	.0088	.0084	.0080	.0077	.0073	.0070	.0067
12	.0169	.0163	.0156	.0150	.0144	.0138	.0132	.0127	.0122	.0116
13	.0262	.0253	.0244	.0235	.0227	.0219	.0211	.0203	.0195	.0188
14	.0376	.0365	.0353	.0343	.0332	.0322	.0311	.0301	.0292	.0282
15	.0504	.0491	.0478	.0466	.0454	.0442	.0430	.0418	.0406	.0395
16	.0633	.0620	.0607	.0594	.0581	.0569	.0556	.0543	.0531	.0518
17	.0748	.0736	.0725	.0713	.0701	.0689	.0677	.0665	.0653	.0640
18	.0835	.0826	.0817	.0808	.0798	.0789	.0778	.0768	.0758	.0747
19	.0884	.0879	.0873	.0868	.0861	.0855	.0848	.0841	.0834	.0826
20	.0888	.0887	.0886	.0885	.0883	.0881	.0878	.0875	.0871	.0867
21	.0850	.0854	.0857	.0860	.0862	.0864	.0865	.0866	.0867	.0867
22	.0777	.0784	.0791	.0797	.0803	.0809	.0814	.0819	.0824	.0828
23	.0679	.0688	.0698	.0707	.0716	.0724	.0733	.0741	.0748	.0756
24	.0568	.0579	.0590	.0601	.0611	.0622	.0632	.0642	.0652	.0661
25	.0457	.0468	.0479	.0490	.0501	.0512	.0523	.0534	.0545	.0555

Table 6 Cumulative Poisson Probabilities

					Mean Arrival Rate λ					
	0.1	0.2	0.3	0.4	0.5	0.6	0.7	0.8	0.9	1.0
0	.9048	.8187	.7408	.6703	.6065	.5488	.4966	.4493	.4066	.3679
1	.9953	.9825	.9631	.9384	.9098	.8781	.8442	.8088	.7725	.7358
2	.9998	.9989	.9964	.9921	.9856	.9769	.9659	.9526	.9371	.9197
3	1.0000	.9999	.9997	.9992	.9982	.9966	.9942	.9909	.9865	.9810
4	1.0000	1.0000	1.0000	.9999	.9998	.9996	.9992	.9986	.9977	.9963
5	1.0000	1.0000	1.0000	1.0000	1.0000	1.0000	.9999	.9998	.9997	.9994
6	1.0000	1.0000	1.0000	1.0000	1.0000	1.0000	1.0000	1.0000	1.0000	.9999
7	1.0000	1.0000	1.0000	1.0000	1.0000	1.0000	1.0000	1.0000	1.0000	1.0000

					Mean Arrival Rate λ					
	1.1	1.2	1.3	1.4	1.5	1.6	1.7	1.8	1.9	2.0
0	.3329	.3012	.2725	.2466	.2231	.2019	.1827	.1653	.1496	.1353
1	.6990	.6626	.6268	.5918	.5578	.5249	.4932	.4628	.4337	.4060
2	.9004	.8795	.8571	.8335	.8088	.7834	.7572	.7306	.7037	.6767
3	.9743	.9662	.9569	.9463	.9344	.9212	.9068	.8913	.8747	.8571
4	.9946	.9923	.9893	.9857	.9814	.9763	.9704	.9636	.9559	.9473
5	.9990	.9985	.9978	.9968	.9955	.9940	.9920	.9896	.9868	.9834
6	.9999	.9997	.9996	.9994	.9991	.9987	.9981	.9974	.9966	.9955
7	1.0000	1.0000	.9999	.9999	.9998	.9997	.9996	.9994	.9992	.9989
8	1.0000	1.0000	1.0000	1.0000	1.0000	1.0000	.9999	.9999	.9998	.9998
9	1.0000	1.0000	1.0000	1.0000	1.0000	1.0000	1.0000	1.0000	1.0000	1.0000

					Mean Arrival Rate λ					
	2.1	2.2	2.3	2.4	2.5	2.6	2.7	2.8	2.9	3.0
0	.1225	.1108	.1003	.0907	.0821	.0743	.0672	.0608	.0550	.0498
1	.3796	.3546	.3309	.3084	.2873	.2674	.2487	.2311	.2146	.1991
2	.6496	.6227	.5960	.5697	.5438	.5184	.4936	.4695	.4460	.4232
3	.8386	.8194	.7993	.7787	.7576	.7360	.7141	.6919	.6696	.6472
4	.9379	.9275	.9162	.9041	.8912	.8774	.8629	.8477	.8318	.8153
5	.9796	.9751	.9700	.9643	.9580	.9510	.9433	.9349	.9258	.9161
6	.9941	.9925	.9906	.9884	.9858	.9828	.9794	.9756	.9713	.9665
7	.9985	.9980	.9974	.9967	.9958	.9947	.9934	.9919	.9901	.9881
8	.9997	.9995	.9994	.9991	.9989	.9985	.9981	.9976	.9969	.9962
9	.9999	.9999	.9999	.9998	.9997	.9996	.9995	.9993	.9991	.9989
10	1.0000	1.0000	1.0000	1.0000	.9999	.9999	.9999	.9998	.9998	.9997
11	1.0000	1.0000	1.0000	1.0000	1.0000	1.0000	1.0000	1.0000	.9999	.9999
12	1.0000	1.0000	1.0000	1.0000	1.0000	1.0000	1.0000	1.0000	1.0000	1.0000

					Mean Arrival Rate λ					
	3.1	3.2	3.3	3.4	3.5	3.6	3.7	3.8	3.9	4.0
0	.0450	.0408	.0369	.0334	.0302	.0273	.0247	.0224	.0202	.0183
1	.1847	.1712	.1586	.1468	.1359	.1257	.1162	.1074	.0992	.0916
2	.4012	.3799	.3594	.3397	.3208	.3027	.2854	.2689	.2531	.2381
3	.6248	.6025	.5803	.5584	.5366	.5152	.4942	.4735	.4532	.4335
4	.7982	.7806	.7626	.7442	.7254	.7064	.6872	.6678	.6484	.6288
5	.9057	.8946	.8829	.8705	.8576	.8441	.8301	.8156	.8006	.7851
6	.9612	.9554	.9490	.9421	.9347	.9267	.9182	.9091	.8995	.8893
7	.9858	.9832	.9802	.9769	.9733	.9692	.9648	.9599	.9546	.9489
8	.9953	.9943	.9931	.9917	.9901	.9883	.9863	.9840	.9815	.9786
9	.9986	.9982	.9978	.9973	.9967	.9960	.9952	.9942	.9931	.9919
10	.9996	.9995	.9994	.9992	.9990	.9987	.9984	.9981	.9977	.9972
11	.9999	.9999	.9998	.9998	.9997	.9996	.9995	.9994	.9993	.9991
12	1.0000	1.0000	1.0000	.9999	.9999	.9999	.9999	.9998	.9998	.9997
13	1.0000	1.0000	1.0000	1.0000	1.0000	1.0000	1.0000	1.0000	.9999	.9999
14	1.0000	1.0000	1.0000	1.0000	1.0000	1.0000	1.0000	1.0000	1.0000	1.0000

Table 6 Cumulative Poisson Probabilities Continued

					Mean Arrival Rate λ					
	4.1	4.2	4.3	4.4	4.5	4.6	4.7	4.8	4.9	5.0
0	.0166	.0150	.0136	.0123	.0111	.0101	.0091	.0082	.0074	.0067
1	.0845	.0780	.0719	.0663	.0611	.0563	.0518	.0477	.0439	.0404
2	.2238	.2102	.1974	.1851	.1736	.1626	.1523	.1425	.1333	.1247
3	.4142	.3954	.3772	.3594	.3423	.3257	.3097	.2942	.2793	.2650
4	.6093	.5898	.5704	.5512	.5321	.5132	.4946	.4763	.4582	.4405
5	.7693	.7531	.7367	.7199	.7029	.6858	.6684	.6510	.6335	.6160
6	.8786	.8675	.8558	.8436	.8311	.8180	.8046	.7908	.7767	.7622
7	.9427	.9361	.9290	.9214	.9134	.9049	.8960	.8867	.8769	.8666
8	.9755	.9721	.9683	.9642	.9597	.9549	.9497	.9442	.9382	.9319
9	.9905	.9889	.9871	.9851	.9829	.9805	.9778	.9749	.9717	.9682
10	.9966	.9959	.9952	.9943	.9933	.9922	.9910	.9896	.9880	.9863
11	.9989	.9986	.9983	.9980	.9976	.9971	.9966	.9960	.9953	.9945
12	.9997	.9996	.9995	.9993	.9992	.9990	.9988	.9986	.9983	.9980
13	.9999	.9999	.9998	.9998	.9997	.9997	.9996	.9995	.9994	.9993
14	1.0000	1.0000	1.0000	.9999	.9999	.9999	.9999	.9999	.9998	.9998

					Mean Arrival Rate λ					
	5.1	5.2	5.3	5.4	5.5	5.6	5.7	5.8	5.9	6.0
0	.0061	.0055	.0050	.0045	.0041	.0037	.0033	.0030	.0027	.0025
1	.0372	.0342	.0314	.0289	.0266	.0244	.0224	.0206	.0189	.0174
2	.1165	.1088	.1016	.0948	.0884	.0824	.0768	.0715	.0666	.0620
3	.2513	.2381	.2254	.2133	.2017	.1906	.1800	.1700	.1604	.1512
4	.4231	.4061	.3895	.3733	.3575	.3422	.3272	.3127	.2987	.2851
5	.5984	.5809	.5635	.5461	.5289	.5119	.4950	.4783	.4619	.4457
6	.7474	.7324	.7171	.7017	.6860	.6703	.6544	.6384	.6224	.6063
7	.8560	.8449	.8335	.8217	.8095	.7970	.7841	.7710	.7576	.7440
8	.9252	.9181	.9106	.9027	.8944	.8857	.8766	.8672	.8574	.8472
9	.9644	.9603	.9559	.9512	.9462	.9409	.9352	.9292	.9228	.9161
10	.9844	.9823	.9800	.9775	.9747	.9718	.9686	.9651	.9614	.9574
11	.9937	.9927	.9916	.9904	.9890	.9875	.9859	.9841	.9821	.9799
12	.9976	.9972	.9967	.9962	.9955	.9949	.9941	.9932	.9922	.9912
13	.9992	.9990	.9988	.9986	.9983	.9980	.9977	.9973	.9969	.9964
14	.9997	.9997	.9996	.9995	.9994	.9993	.9991	.9990	.9988	.9986

					Mean Arrival Rate λ					
	6.1	6.2	6.3	6.4	6.5	6.6	6.7	6.8	6.9	7.0
0	.0022	.0020	.0018	.0017	.0015	.0014	.0012	.0011	.0010	.0009
1	.0159	.0146	.0134	.0123	.0113	.0103	.0095	.0087	.0080	.0073
2	.0577	.0536	.0498	.0463	.0430	.0400	.0371	.0344	.0320	.0296
3	.1425	.1342	.1264	.1189	.1118	.1052	.0988	.0928	.0871	.0818
4	.2719	.2592	.2469	.2351	.2237	.2127	.2022	.1920	.1823	.1730
5	.4298	.4141	.3988	.3837	.3690	.3547	.3406	.3270	.3137	.3007
6	.5902	.5742	.5582	.5423	.5265	.5108	.4953	.4799	.4647	.4497
7	.7301	.7160	.7017	.6873	.6728	.6581	.6433	.6285	.6136	.5987
8	.8367	.8259	.8148	.8033	.7916	.7796	.7673	.7548	.7420	.7291
9	.9090	.9016	.8939	.8858	.8774	.8686	.8596	.8502	.8405	.8305
10	.9531	.9486	.9437	.9386	.9332	.9274	.9214	.9151	.9084	.9015
11	.9776	.9750	.9723	.9693	.9661	.9627	.9591	.9552	.9510	.9467
12	.9900	.9887	.9873	.9857	.9840	.9821	.9801	.9779	.9755	.9730
13	.9958	.9952	.9945	.9937	.9929	.9920	.9909	.9898	.9885	.9872
14	.9984	.9981	.9978	.9974	.9970	.9966	.9961	.9956	.9950	.9943

Table 6   Cumulative Poisson Probabilities Continued

	MEAN ARRIVAL RATE λ									
	7.1	7.2	7.3	7.4	7.5	7.6	7.7	7.8	7.9	8.0
0	.0008	.0007	.0007	.0006	.0006	.0005	.0005	.0004	.0004	.0003
1	.0067	.0061	.0056	.0051	.0047	.0043	.0039	.0036	.0033	.0030
2	.0275	.0255	.0236	.0219	.0203	.0188	.0174	.0161	.0149	.0138
3	.0767	.0719	.0674	.0632	.0591	.0554	.0518	.0485	.0453	.0424
4	.1641	.1555	.1473	.1395	.1321	.1249	.1181	.1117	.1055	.0996
5	.2881	.2759	.2640	.2526	.2414	.2307	.2203	.2103	.2006	.1912
6	.4349	.4204	.4060	.3920	.3782	.3646	.3514	.3384	.3257	.3134
7	.5838	.5689	.5541	.5393	.5246	.5100	.4956	.4812	.4670	.4530
8	.7160	.7027	.6892	.6757	.6620	.6482	.6343	.6204	.6065	.5925
9	.8202	.8096	.7988	.7877	.7764	.7649	.7531	.7411	.7290	.7166
10	.8942	.8867	.8788	.8707	.8622	.8535	.8445	.8352	.8257	.8159
11	.9420	.9371	.9319	.9265	.9208	.9148	.9085	.9020	.8952	.8881
12	.9703	.9673	.9642	.9609	.9573	.9536	.9496	.9454	.9409	.9362
13	.9857	.9841	.9824	.9805	.9784	.9762	.9739	.9714	.9687	.9658
14	.9935	.9927	.9918	.9908	.9897	.9886	.9873	.9859	.9844	.9827
15	.9972	.9969	.9964	.9959	.9954	.9948	.9941	.9934	.9926	.9918
16	.9989	.9987	.9985	.9983	.9980	.9978	.9974	.9971	.9967	.9963
17	.9996	.9995	.9994	.9993	.9992	.9991	.9989	.9988	.9986	.9984
18	.9998	.9998	.9998	.9997	.9997	.9996	.9996	.9995	.9994	.9993
19	.9999	.9999	.9999	.9999	.9999	.9999	.9998	.9998	.9998	.9997
20	1.0000	1.0000	1.0000	1.0000	1.0000	1.0000	.9999	.9999	.9999	.9999

	MEAN ARRIVAL RATE λ									
	8.1	8.2	8.3	8.4	8.5	8.6	8.7	8.8	8.9	9.0
0	.0003	.0003	.0002	.0002	.0002	.0002	.0002	.0002	.0001	.0001
1	.0028	.0025	.0023	.0021	.0019	.0018	.0016	.0015	.0014	.0012
2	.0127	.0118	.0109	.0100	.0093	.0086	.0079	.0073	.0068	.0062
3	.0396	.0370	.0346	.0323	.0301	.0281	.0262	.0244	.0228	.0212
4	.0940	.0887	.0837	.0789	.0744	.0701	.0660	.0621	.0584	.0550
5	.1822	.1736	.1653	.1573	.1496	.1422	.1352	.1284	.1219	.1157
6	.3013	.2896	.2781	.2670	.2562	.2457	.2355	.2256	.2160	.2068
7	.4391	.4254	.4119	.3987	.3856	.3728	.3602	.3478	.3357	.3239
8	.5786	.5647	.5507	.5369	.5231	.5094	.4958	.4823	.4689	.4557
9	.7041	.6915	.6788	.6659	.6530	.6400	.6269	.6137	.6006	.5874
10	.8058	.7955	.7850	.7743	.7634	.7522	.7409	.7294	.7178	.7060
11	.8807	.8731	.8652	.8571	.8487	.8400	.8311	.8220	.8126	.8030
12	.9313	.9261	.9207	.9150	.9091	.9029	.8965	.8898	.8829	.8758
13	.9628	.9595	.9561	.9524	.9486	.9445	.9403	.9358	.9311	.9261
14	.9810	.9791	.9771	.9749	.9726	.9701	.9675	.9647	.9617	.9585
15	.9908	.9898	.9887	.9875	.9862	.9848	.9832	.9816	.9798	.9780
16	.9958	.9953	.9947	.9941	.9934	.9926	.9918	.9909	.9899	.9889
17	.9982	.9979	.9977	.9973	.9970	.9966	.9962	.9957	.9952	.9947
18	.9992	.9991	.9990	.9989	.9987	.9985	.9983	.9981	.9978	.9976
19	.9997	.9997	.9996	.9995	.9995	.9994	.9993	.9992	.9991	.9989
20	.9999	.9999	.9998	.9998	.9998	.9998	.9997	.9997	.9996	.9996

	MEAN ARRIVAL RATE λ									
	9.1	9.2	9.3	9.4	9.5	9.6	9.7	9.8	9.9	10.0
0	.0001	.0001	.0001	.0001	.0001	.0001	.0001	.0001	.0001	.0000
1	.0011	.0010	.0009	.0009	.0008	.0007	.0007	.0006	.0005	.0005
2	.0058	.0053	.0049	.0045	.0042	.0038	.0035	.0033	.0030	.0028
3	.0198	.0184	.0172	.0160	.0149	.0138	.0129	.0120	.0111	.0103
4	.0517	.0486	.0456	.0429	.0403	.0378	.0355	.0333	.0312	.0293
5	.1098	.1041	.0986	.0935	.0885	.0838	.0793	.0750	.0710	.0671
6	.1978	.1892	.1808	.1727	.1649	.1574	.1502	.1433	.1366	.1301

Table 6 Cumulative Poisson Probabilities Continued

					Mean Arrival Rate λ					
	9.1	9.2	9.3	9.4	9.5	9.6	9.7	9.8	9.9	10.0
7	.3123	.3010	.2900	.2792	.2687	.2584	.2485	.2388	.2294	.2202
8	.4426	.4296	.4168	.4042	.3918	.3796	.3676	.3558	.3442	.3328
9	.5742	.5611	.5479	.5349	.5218	.5089	.4960	.4832	.4705	.4579
10	.6941	.6820	.6699	.6576	.6453	.6329	.6205	.6080	.5955	.5830
11	.7932	.7832	.7730	.7626	.7520	.7412	.7303	.7193	.7081	.6968
12	.8684	.8607	.8529	.8448	.8364	.8279	.8191	.8101	.8009	.7916
13	.9210	.9156	.9100	.9042	.8981	.8919	.8853	.8786	.8716	.8645
14	.9552	.9517	.9480	.9441	.9400	.9357	.9312	.9265	.9216	.9165
15	.9760	.9738	.9715	.9691	.9665	.9638	.9609	.9579	.9546	.9513
16	.9878	.9865	.9852	.9838	.9823	.9806	.9789	.9770	.9751	.9730
17	.9941	.9934	.9927	.9919	.9911	.9902	.9892	.9881	.9870	.9857
18	.9973	.9969	.9966	.9962	.9957	.9952	.9947	.9941	.9935	.9928
19	.9988	.9986	.9985	.9983	.9980	.9978	.9975	.9972	.9969	.9965
20	.9995	.9994	.9993	.9992	.9991	.9990	.9989	.9987	.9986	.9984

					Mean Arrival Rate λ					
	10.1	10.2	10.3	10.4	10.5	10.6	10.7	10.8	10.9	11.0
0	.0000	.0000	.0000	.0000	.0000	.0000	.0000	.0000	.0000	.0000
1	.0005	.0004	.0004	.0003	.0003	.0003	.0003	.0002	.0002	.0002
2	.0026	.0023	.0022	.0020	.0018	.0017	.0016	.0014	.0013	.0012
3	.0096	.0089	.0083	.0077	.0071	.0066	.0062	.0057	.0053	.0049
4	.0274	.0257	.0241	.0225	.0211	.0197	.0185	.0173	.0162	.0151
5	.0634	.0599	.0566	.0534	.0504	.0475	.0448	.0423	.0398	.0375
6	.1240	.1180	.1123	.1069	.1016	.0966	.0918	.0872	.0828	.0786
7	.2113	.2027	.1944	.1863	.1785	.1710	.1636	.1566	.1498	.1432
8	.3217	.3108	.3001	.2896	.2794	.2694	.2597	.2502	.2410	.2320
9	.4455	.4332	.4210	.4090	.3971	.3854	.3739	.3626	.3515	.3405
10	.5705	.5580	.5456	.5331	.5207	.5084	.4961	.4840	.4719	.4599
11	.6853	.6738	.6622	.6505	.6387	.6269	.6150	.6031	.5912	.5793
12	.7820	.7722	.7623	.7522	.7420	.7316	.7210	.7104	.6996	.6887
13	.8571	.8494	.8416	.8336	.8253	.8169	.8083	.7995	.7905	.7813
14	.9112	.9057	.9	.8940	.8879	.8815	.8750	.8682	.8612	.8540
15	.9477	.9440	.9400	.9359	.9317	.9272	.9225	.9177	.9126	.9074
16	.9707	.9684	.9658	.9632	.9604	.9574	.9543	.9511	.9477	.9441
17	.9844	.9830	.9815	.9799	.9781	.9763	.9744	.9723	.9701	.9678
18	.9921	.9913	.9904	.9895	.9885	.9874	.9863	.9850	.9837	.9823
19	.9962	.9957	.9953	.9948	.9942	.9936	.9930	.9923	.9915	.9907
20	.9982	.9980	.9978	.9975	.9972	.9969	.9966	.9962	.9958	.9953

					Mean Arrival Rate λ					
	11.1	11.2	11.3	11.4	11.5	11.6	11.7	11.8	11.9	12.0
0	.0000	.0000	.0000	.0000	.0000	.0000	.0000	.0000	.0000	.0000
1	.0002	.0002	.0002	.0001	.0001	.0001	.0001	.0001	.0001	.0001
2	.0011	.0010	.0009	.0009	.0008	.0007	.0007	.0006	.0006	.0005
3	.0046	.0042	.0039	.0036	.0034	.0031	.0029	.0027	.0025	.0023
4	.0141	.0132	.0123	.0115	.0107	.0100	.0094	.0087	.0081	.0076
5	.0353	.0333	.0313	.0295	.0277	.0261	.0245	.0230	.0217	.0203
6	.0746	.0708	.0671	.0636	.0603	.0571	.0541	.0512	.0484	.0458
7	.1369	.1307	.1249	.1192	.1137	.1085	.1035	.0986	.0940	.0895
8	.2232	.2147	.2064	.1984	.1906	.1830	.1757	.1686	.1617	.1550
9	.3298	.3192	.3089	.2987	.2888	.2791	.2696	.2603	.2512	.2424
10	.4480	.4362	.4246	.4131	.4017	.3905	.3794	.3685	.3578	.3472
11	.5673	.5554	.5435	.5316	.5198	.5080	.4963	.4847	.4731	.4616
12	.6777	.6666	.6555	.6442	.6329	.6216	.6102	.5988	.5874	.5760
13	.7719	.7624	.7528	.7430	.7330	.7230	.7128	.7025	.6920	.6815
14	.8467	.8391	.8313	.8234	.8153	.8069	.7985	.7898	.7810	.7720

Table 6 Cumulative Poisson Probabilities Continued

	MEAN ARRIVAL RATE λ									
	11.1	11.2	11.3	11.4	11.5	11.6	11.7	11.8	11.9	12.0
15	.9020	.8963	.8905	.8845	.8783	.8719	.8653	.8585	.8516	.8444
16	.9403	.9364	.9323	.9280	.9236	.9190	.9142	.9092	.9040	.8987
17	.9654	.9628	.9601	.9572	.9542	.9511	.9478	.9444	.9408	.9370
18	.9808	.9792	.9775	.9757	.9738	.9718	.9697	.9674	.9651	.9626
19	.9898	.9889	.9879	.9868	.9857	.9845	.9832	.9818	.9803	.9787
20	.9948	.9943	.9938	.9932	.9925	.9918	.9910	.9902	.9893	.9884

	MEAN ARRIVAL RATE λ									
	12.1	12.2	12.3	12.4	12.5	12.6	12.7	12.8	12.9	13.0
5	.0191	.0179	.0168	.0158	.0148	.0139	.0130	.0122	.0115	.0107
6	.0433	.0410	.0387	.0366	.0346	.0326	.0308	.0291	.0274	.0259
7	.0852	.0811	.0772	.0734	.0698	.0664	.0631	.0599	.0569	.0540
8	.1486	.1424	.1363	.1305	.1249	.1195	.1143	.1093	.1044	.0998
9	.2338	.2254	.2172	.2092	.2014	.1939	.1866	.1794	.1725	.1658
10	.3368	.3266	.3166	.3067	.2971	.2876	.2783	.2693	.2604	.2517
11	.4502	.4389	.4278	.4167	.4058	.3950	.3843	.3738	.3634	.3532
12	.5645	.5531	.5417	.5303	.5190	.5077	.4964	.4853	.4741	.4631
13	.6709	.6603	.6495	.6387	.6278	.6169	.6060	.5950	.5840	.5730
14	.7629	.7536	.7442	.7347	.7250	.7153	.7054	.6954	.6853	.6751
15	.8371	.8296	.8219	.8140	.8060	.7978	.7895	.7810	.7724	.7636
16	.8932	.8875	.8816	.8755	.8693	.8629	.8563	.8495	.8426	.8355
17	.9331	.9290	.9248	.9204	.9158	.9111	.9062	.9011	.8959	.8905
18	.9600	.9572	.9543	.9513	.9481	.9448	.9414	.9378	.9341	.9302
19	.9771	.9753	.9734	.9715	.9694	.9672	.9649	.9625	.9600	.9573
20	.9874	.9863	.9852	.9840	.9827	.9813	.9799	.9783	.9767	.9750
21	.9934	.9927	.9921	.9914	.9906	.9898	.9889	.9880	.9870	.9859
22	.9966	.9963	.9959	.9955	.9951	.9946	.9941	.9936	.9930	.9924
23	.9984	.9982	.9980	.9978	.9975	.9973	.9970	.9967	.9964	.9960

	MEAN ARRIVAL RATE λ									
	13.1	13.2	13.3	13.4	13.5	13.6	13.7	13.8	13.9	14.0
5	.0101	.0094	.0088	.0083	.0077	.0072	.0068	.0063	.0059	.0055
6	.0244	.0230	.0217	.0204	.0193	.0181	.0171	.0161	.0151	.0142
7	.0513	.0487	.0461	.0438	.0415	.0393	.0372	.0353	.0334	.0316
8	.0953	.0910	.0868	.0828	.0790	.0753	.0718	.0684	.0652	.0621
9	.1593	.1530	.1469	.1410	.1353	.1297	.1244	.1192	.1142	.1094
10	.2432	.2349	.2268	.2189	.2112	.2037	.1964	.1893	.1824	.1757
11	.3431	.3332	.3234	.3139	.3045	.2952	.2862	.2773	.2686	.2600
12	.4522	.4413	.4305	.4199	.4093	.3989	.3886	.3784	.3684	.3585
13	.5621	.5511	.5401	.5292	.5182	.5074	.4966	.4858	.4751	.4644
14	.6649	.6546	.6442	.6338	.6233	.6128	.6022	.5916	.5810	.5704
15	.7547	.7456	.7365	.7272	.7178	.7083	.6987	.6890	.6792	.6694
16	.8282	.8208	.8132	.8054	.7975	.7895	.7813	.7730	.7645	.7559
17	.8849	.8791	.8732	.8671	.8609	.8545	.8479	.8411	.8343	.8272
18	.9261	.9219	.9176	.9130	.9084	.9035	.8986	.8934	.8881	.8826
19	.9546	.9516	.9486	.9454	.9421	.9387	.9351	.9314	.9275	.9235
20	.9732	.9713	.9692	.9671	.9649	.9626	.9601	.9576	.9549	.9521
21	.9848	.9836	.9823	.9810	.9796	.9780	.9765	.9748	.9730	.9712
22	.9917	.9910	.9902	.9894	.9885	.9876	.9866	.9856	.9845	.9833
23	.9956	.9952	.9948	.9943	.9938	.9933	.9927	.9921	.9914	.9907

	MEAN ARRIVAL RATE λ									
	14.1	14.2	14.3	14.4	14.5	14.6	14.7	14.8	14.9	15.0
6	.0134	.0126	.0118	.0111	.0105	.0098	.0092	.0087	.0081	.0076
7	.0299	.0283	.0268	.0253	.0239	.0226	.0214	.0202	.0191	.0180
8	.0591	.0562	.0535	.0509	.0484	.0460	.0437	.0415	.0394	.0374

Table 6 Cumulative Poisson Probabilities Continued

					MEAN ARRIVAL RATE λ					
	14.1	14.2	14.3	14.4	14.5	14.6	14.7	14.8	14.9	15.0
9	.1047	.1003	.0959	.0918	.0878	.0839	.0802	.0766	.0732	.0699
10	.1691	.1628	.1566	.1507	.1449	.1392	.1338	.1285	.1234	.1185
11	.2517	.2435	.2355	.2277	.2201	.2127	.2054	.1984	.1915	.1848
12	.3487	.3391	.3296	.3203	.3111	.3021	.2932	.2845	.2760	.2676
13	.4539	.4434	.4330	.4227	.4125	.4024	.3925	.3826	.3728	.3632
14	.5598	.5492	.5387	.5281	.5176	.5071	.4967	.4863	.4759	.4657
15	.6594	.6494	.6394	.6293	.6192	.6090	.5988	.5886	.5783	.5681
16	.7472	.7384	.7294	.7204	.7112	.7020	.6926	.6832	.6737	.6641
17	.8200	.8126	.8051	.7975	.7897	.7818	.7737	.7656	.7573	.7489
18	.8770	.8712	.8653	.8592	.8530	.8466	.8400	.8333	.8265	.8195
19	.9193	.9150	.9106	.9060	.9012	.8963	.8913	.8861	.8807	.8752
20	.9492	.9461	.9430	.9396	.9362	.9326	.9289	.9251	.9211	.9170
21	.9692	.9671	.9650	.9627	.9604	.9579	.9553	.9526	.9498	.9469
22	.9820	.9807	.9793	.9779	.9763	.9747	.9729	.9711	.9692	.9673
23	.9899	.9891	.9882	.9873	.9863	.9853	.9842	.9831	.9818	.9805
24	.9945	.9941	.9935	.9930	.9924	.9918	.9911	.9904	.9896	.9888
25	.9971	.9969	.9966	.9963	.9959	.9956	.9952	.9947	.9943	.9938

					MEAN ARRIVAL RATE λ					
	15.1	15.2	15.3	15.4	15.5	15.6	15.7	15.8	15.9	16.0
7	.0170	.0160	.0151	.0143	.0135	.0127	.0120	.0113	.0106	.0100
8	.0355	.0337	.0320	.0304	.0288	.0273	.0259	.0245	.0232	.0220
9	.0667	.0636	.0607	.0579	.0552	.0526	.0501	.0478	.0455	.0433
10	.1137	.1091	.1046	.1003	.0961	.0921	.0882	.0845	.0809	.0774
11	.1782	.1718	.1657	.1596	.1538	.1481	.1426	.1372	.1320	.1270
12	.2594	.2514	.2435	.2358	.2283	.2209	.2137	.2067	.1998	.1931
13	.3537	.3444	.3351	.3260	.3171	.3083	.2996	.2911	.2827	.2745
14	.4554	.4453	.4353	.4253	.4154	.4056	.3959	.3864	.3769	.3675
15	.5578	.5476	.5374	.5272	.5170	.5069	.4968	.4867	.4767	.4667
16	.6545	.6448	.6351	.6253	.6154	.6056	.5957	.5858	.5759	.5660
17	.7403	.7317	.7230	.7141	.7052	.6962	.6871	.6779	.6687	.6593
18	.8123	.8051	.7977	.7901	.7825	.7747	.7668	.7587	.7506	.7423
19	.8696	.8638	.8578	.8517	.8455	.8391	.8326	.8260	.8192	.8122
20	.9128	.9084	.9039	.8992	.8944	.8894	.8843	.8791	.8737	.8682
21	.9438	.9407	.9374	.9340	.9304	.9268	.9230	.9190	.9150	.9108
22	.9652	.9630	.9607	.9583	.9558	.9532	.9505	.9477	.9448	.9418
23	.9792	.9777	.9762	.9746	.9730	.9712	.9694	.9674	.9654	.9633
24	.9880	.9871	.9861	.9851	.9840	.9829	.9817	.9804	.9791	.9777
25	.9933	.9928	.9922	.9915	.9909	.9902	.9894	.9886	.9878	.9869

					MEAN ARRIVAL RATE λ					
	16.1	16.2	16.3	16.4	16.5	16.6	16.7	16.8	16.9	17.0
8	.0208	.0197	.0186	.0176	.0167	.0158	.0149	.0141	.0133	.0126
9	.0412	.0392	.0373	.0355	.0337	.0321	.0305	.0290	.0275	.0261
10	.0740	.0708	.0677	.0647	.0619	.0591	.0565	.0539	.0515	.0491
11	.1221	.1174	.1128	.1084	.1041	.0999	.0959	.0920	.0883	.0847
12	.1866	.1802	.1740	.1680	.1621	.1564	.1508	.1454	.1401	.1350
13	.2664	.2585	.2508	.2432	.2357	.2285	.2213	.2144	.2075	.2009
14	.3583	.3492	.3402	.3313	.3225	.3139	.3054	.2971	.2889	.2808
15	.4569	.4470	.4373	.4276	.4180	.4085	.3991	.3898	.3806	.3715
16	.5560	.5461	.5362	.5263	.5165	.5067	.4969	.4871	.4774	.4677
17	.6500	.6406	.6311	.6216	.6120	.6025	.5929	.5833	.5737	.5640
18	.7340	.7255	.7170	.7084	.6996	.6908	.6820	.6730	.6640	.6550
19	.8052	.7980	.7907	.7833	.7757	.7681	.7603	.7524	.7444	.7363
20	.8625	.8567	.8508	.8447	.8385	.8321	.8257	.8191	.8123	.8055
21	.9064	.9020	.8974	.8927	.8878	.8828	.8777	.8724	.8670	.8615
22	.9386	.9353	.9319	.9284	.9248	.9210	.9171	.9131	.9090	.9047

Table 6 Cumulative Poisson Probabilities Continued

	MEAN ARRIVAL RATE λ									
	16.1	16.2	16.3	16.4	16.5	16.6	16.7	16.8	16.9	17.0
23	.9611	.9588	.9564	.9539	.9513	.9486	.9458	.9429	.9398	.9367
24	.9762	.9747	.9730	.9713	.9696	.9677	.9657	.9637	.9616	.9594
25	.9859	.9849	.9839	.9828	.9816	.9804	.9791	.9777	.9763	.9748
26	.9920	.9913	.9907	.9900	.9892	.9884	.9876	.9867	.9858	.9848

	MEAN ARRIVAL RATE λ									
	17.1	17.2	17.3	17.4	17.5	17.6	17.7	17.8	17.9	18.0
8	.0119	.0112	.0106	.0100	.0095	.0089	.0084	.0079	.0075	.0071
9	.0248	.0235	.0223	.0212	.0201	.0191	.0181	.0171	.0162	.0154
10	.0469	.0447	.0426	.0406	.0387	.0369	.0352	.0335	.0319	.0304
11	.0812	.0778	.0746	.0714	.0684	.0655	.0627	.0600	.0574	.0549
12	.1301	.1252	.1206	.1160	.1116	.1074	.1033	.0993	.0954	.0917
13	.1944	.1880	.1818	.1758	.1699	.1641	.1585	.1531	.1478	.1426
14	.2729	.2651	.2575	.2500	.2426	.2354	.2284	.2215	.2147	.2081
15	.3624	.3535	.3448	.3361	.3275	.3191	.3108	.3026	.2946	.2867
16	.4581	.4486	.4391	.4297	.4204	.4112	.4020	.3929	.3839	.3751
17	.5544	.5448	.5352	.5256	.5160	.5065	.4969	.4875	.4780	.4686
18	.6458	.6367	.6275	.6182	.6089	.5996	.5903	.5810	.5716	.5622
19	.7281	.7199	.7115	.7031	.6945	.6859	.6773	.6685	.6598	.6509
20	.7985	.7914	.7842	.7769	.7694	.7619	.7542	.7465	.7387	.7307
21	.8558	.8500	.8441	.8380	.8319	.8255	.8191	.8126	.8059	.7991
22	.9003	.8958	.8912	.8864	.8815	.8765	.8713	.8660	.8606	.8551
23	.9334	.9301	.9266	.9230	.9193	.9154	.9115	.9074	.9032	.8989
24	.9570	.9546	.9521	.9495	.9468	.9440	.9411	.9381	.9350	.9317
25	.9732	.9715	.9698	.9680	.9661	.9641	.9621	.9599	.9577	.9554
26	.9838	.9827	.9816	.9804	.9791	.9778	.9764	.9749	.9734	.9718
27	.9905	.9898	.9891	.9883	.9875	.9866	.9857	.9848	.9837	.9827

	MEAN ARRIVAL RATE λ									
	18.1	18.2	18.3	18.4	18.5	18.6	18.7	18.8	18.9	19.0
9	.0146	.0138	.0131	.0124	.0117	.0111	.0105	.0099	.0094	.0089
10	.0289	.0275	.0262	.0249	.0237	.0225	.0214	.0203	.0193	.0183
11	.0525	.0502	.0479	.0458	.0438	.0418	.0399	.0381	.0363	.0347
12	.0881	.0846	.0812	.0779	.0748	.0717	.0688	.0659	.0632	.0606
13	.1376	.1327	.1279	.1233	.1189	.1145	.1103	.1062	.1022	.0984
14	.2016	.1953	.1891	.1830	.1771	.1714	.1658	.1603	.1550	.1497
15	.2789	.2712	.2637	.2563	.2490	.2419	.2349	.2281	.2214	.2148
16	.3663	.3576	.3490	.3405	.3321	.3239	.3157	.3077	.2998	.2920
17	.4593	.4500	.4408	.4317	.4226	.4136	.4047	.3958	.3870	.3784
18	.5529	.5435	.5342	.5249	.5156	.5063	.4970	.4878	.4786	.4695
19	.6420	.6331	.6241	.6151	.6061	.5970	.5879	.5788	.5697	.5606
20	.7227	.7146	.7064	.6981	.6898	.6814	.6729	.6644	.6558	.6472
21	.7922	.7852	.7781	.7709	.7636	.7561	.7486	.7410	.7333	.7255
22	.8494	.8436	.8377	.8317	.8256	.8193	.8129	.8065	.7998	.7931
23	.8944	.8899	.8852	.8804	.8755	.8704	.8652	.8600	.8545	.8490
24	.9284	.9249	.9214	.9177	.9139	.9100	.9060	.9019	.8976	.8933
25	.9530	.9505	.9479	.9452	.9424	.9395	.9365	.9334	.9302	.9269
26	.9701	.9683	.9665	.9646	.9626	.9606	.9584	.9562	.9539	.9514
27	.9816	.9804	.9792	.9779	.9765	.9751	.9736	.9720	.9704	.9687

	MEAN ARRIVAL RATE λ									
	19.1	19.2	19.3	19.4	19.5	19.6	19.7	19.8	19.9	20.0
10	.0174	.0165	.0157	.0149	.0141	.0134	.0127	.0120	.0114	.0108
11	.0331	.0315	.0301	.0287	.0273	.0260	.0248	.0236	.0225	.0214
12	.0580	.0556	.0532	.0509	.0488	.0467	.0446	.0427	.0408	.0390
13	.0947	.0911	.0876	.0842	.0809	.0778	.0747	.0717	.0689	.0661

Table 6 Cumulative Poisson Probabilities Continued

	MEAN ARRIVAL RATE λ									
	19.1	19.2	19.3	19.4	19.5	19.6	19.7	19.8	19.9	20.0
14	.1447	.1397	.1349	.1303	.1257	.1213	.1170	.1128	.1088	.1049
15	.2084	.2021	.1959	.1899	.1840	.1782	.1726	.1671	.1617	.1565
16	.2844	.2768	.2694	.2621	.2550	.2479	.2410	.2342	.2276	.2211
17	.3698	.3613	.3529	.3446	.3364	.3283	.3203	.3124	.3047	.2970
18	.4604	.4514	.4424	.4335	.4246	.4158	.4071	.3985	.3899	.3814
19	.5515	.5424	.5333	.5242	.5151	.5061	.4971	.4881	.4792	.4703
20	.6385	.6298	.6210	.6122	.6034	.5946	.5857	.5769	.5680	.5591
21	.7176	.7097	.7016	.6935	.6854	.6772	.6689	.6605	.6521	.6437
22	.7863	.7794	.7724	.7653	.7580	.7507	.7433	.7358	.7283	.7206
23	.8434	.8376	.8317	.8257	.8196	.8134	.8071	.8007	.7941	.7875
24	.8888	.8842	.8795	.8746	.8697	.8646	.8594	.8541	.8487	.8432
25	.9235	.9199	.9163	.9126	.9087	.9048	.9007	.8965	.8922	.8878
26	.9489	.9463	.9437	.9409	.9380	.9350	.9319	.9288	.9255	.9221
27	.9670	.9651	.9632	.9612	.9591	.9570	.9547	.9524	.9500	.9475

	MEAN ARRIVAL RATE λ									
	20.1	20.2	20.3	20.4	20.5	20.6	20.7	20.8	20.9	21.0
10	.0102	.0097	.0092	.0087	.0082	.0078	.0074	.0070	.0066	.0063
11	.0204	.0194	.0184	.0175	.0167	.0158	.0150	.0143	.0136	.0129
12	.0373	.0356	.0340	.0325	.0310	.0296	.0283	.0270	.0257	.0245
13	.0635	.0609	.0584	.0560	.0537	.0515	.0493	.0473	.0453	.0434
14	.1010	.0973	.0938	.0903	.0869	.0836	.0805	.0774	.0744	.0716
15	.1514	.1464	.1416	.1369	.1323	.1278	.1234	.1192	.1151	.1111
16	.2147	.2084	.2023	.1963	.1904	.1847	.1790	.1735	.1682	.1629
17	.2895	.2821	.2748	.2676	.2605	.2536	.2467	.2400	.2334	.2270
18	.3730	.3647	.3565	.3484	.3403	.3324	.3246	.3168	.3092	.3017
19	.4614	.4526	.4438	.4351	.4265	.4179	.4094	.4009	.3926	.3843
20	.5502	.5413	.5325	.5236	.5148	.5059	.4972	.4884	.4797	.4710
21	.6352	.6267	.6181	.6096	.6010	.5923	.5837	.5750	.5664	.5577
22	.7129	.7051	.6972	.6893	.6813	.6732	.6651	.6569	.6487	.6405
23	.7808	.7739	.7670	.7600	.7528	.7456	.7384	.7310	.7235	.7160
24	.8376	.8319	.8260	.8201	.8140	.8078	.8016	.7952	.7887	.7822
25	.8833	.8787	.8739	.8691	.8641	.8591	.8539	.8486	.8432	.8377
26	.9186	.9150	.9114	.9076	.9037	.8997	.8955	.8913	.8870	.8826
27	.9449	.9423	.9395	.9366	.9337	.9306	.9275	.9242	.9209	.9175

	MEAN ARRIVAL RATE λ									
	21.1	21.2	21.3	21.4	21.5	21.6	21.7	21.8	21.9	22.0
11	.0123	.0116	.0110	.0105	.0099	.0094	.0090	.0085	.0080	.0076
12	.0234	.0223	.0213	.0203	.0193	.0184	.0175	.0167	.0159	.0151
13	.0415	.0397	.0380	.0364	.0348	.0333	.0318	.0304	.0291	.0278
14	.0688	.0661	.0635	.0610	.0586	.0563	.0540	.0518	.0497	.0477
15	.1072	.1034	.0997	.0962	.0927	.0893	.0861	.0829	.0799	.0769
16	.1578	.1528	.1479	.1432	.1385	.1340	.1296	.1253	.1211	.1170
17	.2206	.2144	.2083	.2023	.1965	.1907	.1851	.1796	.1743	.1690
18	.2943	.2870	.2798	.2727	.2657	.2588	.2521	.2454	.2389	.2325
19	.3760	.3679	.3599	.3519	.3440	.3362	.3285	.3209	.3134	.3060
20	.4623	.4537	.4452	.4367	.4282	.4198	.4115	.4032	.3950	.3869
21	.5490	.5403	.5317	.5230	.5144	.5058	.4972	.4887	.4801	.4716
22	.6322	.6238	.6155	.6071	.5987	.5902	.5818	.5733	.5648	.5564
23	.7084	.7008	.6930	.6853	.6774	.6695	.6616	.6536	.6455	.6374
24	.7755	.7687	.7619	.7550	.7480	.7409	.7337	.7264	.7191	.7117
25	.8321	.8264	.8206	.8146	.8086	.8025	.7963	.7900	.7836	.7771
26	.8780	.8734	.8686	.8638	.8588	.8537	.8486	.8433	.8379	.8324
27	.9139	.9103	.9065	.9027	.8988	.8947	.8906	.8863	.8820	.8775

Table 7 Cutoff Points of the Chi-Square Distribution Function

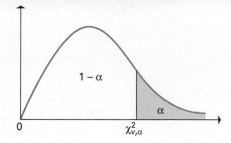

For selected probabilities α, the table shows the values $\chi^2_{v,\alpha}$ such that $P(\chi^2_v > \chi^2_{v,\alpha}) = \alpha$, where χ^2_v is a chi-square random variable with v degrees of freedom. For example, the probability is .100 that a chi-square random variable with 10 degrees of freedom is greater than 15.99.

v	α									
	.995	.990	.975	.950	.900	.100	.050	.025	.010	.005
1	0.0^4393	0.0^3157	0.0^3982	0.0^2393	0.0158	2.71	3.84	5.02	6.63	7.88
2	0.0100	0.0201	0.0506	0.103	0.211	4.61	5.99	7.38	9.21	10.60
3	0.072	0.115	0.216	0.352	0.584	6.25	7.81	9.35	11.34	12.84
4	0.207	0.297	0.484	0.711	1.064	7.78	9.49	11.14	13.28	14.86
5	0.412	0.554	0.831	1.145	1.61	9.24	11.07	12.83	15.09	16.75
6	0.676	0.872	1.24	1.64	2.20	10.64	12.59	14.45	16.81	18.55
7	0.989	1.24	1.69	2.17	2.83	12.02	14.07	16.01	18.48	20.28
8	1.34	1.65	2.18	2.73	3.49	13.36	15.51	17.53	20.09	21.96
9	1.73	2.09	2.70	3.33	4.17	14.68	16.92	19.02	21.67	23.59
10	2.16	2.56	3.25	3.94	4.87	15.99	18.31	20.48	23.21	25.19
11	2.60	3.05	3.82	4.57	5.58	17.28	19.68	21.92	24.73	26.76
12	3.07	3.57	4.40	5.23	6.30	18.55	21.03	23.34	26.22	28.30
13	3.57	4.11	5.01	5.89	7.04	19.81	22.36	24.74	27.69	29.82
14	4.07	4.66	5.63	6.57	7.79	21.06	23.68	26.12	29.14	31.32
15	4.60	5.23	6.26	7.26	8.55	22.31	25.00	27.49	30.58	32.80
16	5.14	5.81	6.91	7.96	9.31	23.54	26.30	28.85	32.00	34.27
17	5.70	6.41	7.56	8.67	10.09	24.77	27.59	30.19	33.41	35.72
18	6.26	7.01	8.23	9.39	10.86	25.99	28.87	31.53	34.81	37.16
19	6.84	7.63	8.91	10.12	11.65	27.20	30.14	32.85	36.19	38.58
20	7.43	8.26	9.59	10.85	12.44	28.41	31.41	34.17	37.57	40.00
21	8.03	8.90	10.28	11.59	13.24	29.62	32.67	35.48	38.93	41.40
22	8.64	9.54	10.98	12.34	14.04	30.81	33.92	36.78	40.29	42.80
23	9.26	10.20	11.69	13.09	14.85	32.01	35.17	38.08	41.64	44.18
24	9.89	10.86	12.40	13.85	15.66	33.20	36.42	39.36	42.98	45.56
25	10.52	11.52	13.12	14.61	16.47	34.38	37.65	40.65	44.31	46.93
26	11.16	12.20	13.84	15.38	17.29	35.56	38.89	41.92	45.64	48.29
27	11.81	12.88	14.57	16.15	18.11	36.74	40.11	43.19	46.96	49.64
28	12.46	13.56	15.31	16.93	18.94	37.92	41.34	44.46	48.28	50.99
29	13.12	14.26	16.05	17.71	19.77	39.09	42.56	45.72	49.59	52.34
30	13.79	14.95	16.79	18.49	20.60	40.26	43.77	46.98	50.89	53.67
40	20.71	22.16	24.43	26.51	29.05	51.81	55.76	59.34	63.69	66.77
50	27.99	29.71	32.36	34.76	37.69	63.17	67.50	71.42	76.15	79.49
60	35.53	37.48	40.48	43.19	46.46	74.40	79.08	83.30	88.38	91.95
70	43.28	45.44	48.76	51.74	55.33	85.53	90.53	95.02	100.4	104.2
80	51.17	53.54	57.15	60.39	64.28	96.58	101.9	106.6	112.3	116.3
90	59.20	61.75	65.65	69.13	73.29	107.6	113.1	118.1	124.1	128.3
100	67.33	70.06	74.22	77.93	82.36	118.5	124.3	129.6	135.8	140.2

Reproduced with permission from C. M. Thompson, "Tables of percentage points of the chi-square distribution," *Biometrika* 32 (1941).

Table 8 Cutoff Points for the Student's *t* Distribution

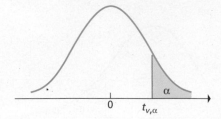

For selected probabilities, α, the table shows the values $t_{v,\alpha}$ such that $P(t_v > t_{v,\alpha}) = \alpha$, where t_v is a Student's *t* random variable with *v* degrees of freedom. For example, the probability is .10 that a Student's *t* random variable with 10 degrees of freedom exceeds 1.372.

v	α				
	0.100	0.050	0.025	0.010	0.005
1	3.078	6.314	12.706	31.821	63.657
2	1.886	2.920	4.303	6.965	9.925
3	1.638	2.353	3.182	4.541	5.841
4	1.533	2.132	2.776	3.747	4.604
5	1.476	2.015	2.571	3.365	4.032
6	1.440	1.943	2.447	3.143	3.707
7	1.415	1.895	2.365	2.998	3.499
8	1.397	1.860	2.306	2.896	3.355
9	1.383	1.833	2.262	2.821	3.250
10	1.372	1.812	2.228	2.764	3.169
11	1.363	1.796	2.201	2.718	3.106
12	1.356	1.782	2.179	2.681	3.055
13	1.350	1.771	2.160	2.650	3.012
14	1.345	1.761	2.145	2.624	2.977
15	1.341	1.753	2.131	2.602	2.947
16	1.337	1.746	2.120	2.583	2.921
17	1.333	1.740	2.110	2.567	2.898
18	1.330	1.734	2.101	2.552	2.878
19	1.328	1.729	2.093	2.539	2.861
20	1.325	1.725	2.086	2.528	2.845
21	1.323	1.721	2.080	2.518	2.831
22	1.321	1.717	2.074	2.508	2.819
23	1.319	1.714	2.069	2.500	2.807
24	1.318	1.711	2.064	2.492	2.797
25	1.316	1.708	2.060	2.485	2.787
26	1.315	1.706	2.056	2.479	2.779
27	1.314	1.703	2.052	2.473	2.771
28	1.313	1.701	2.048	2.467	2.763
29	1.311	1.699	2.045	2.462	2.756
30	1.310	1.697	2.042	2.457	2.750
40	1.303	1.684	2.021	2.423	2.704
60	1.296	1.671	2.000	2.390	2.660
∞	1.282	1.645	1.960	2.326	2.576

Table 9 Cutoff Points for the F Distribution

For probabilities $\alpha = 0.5$ and $\alpha = .01$, the tables show the values $F_{\nu_1,\nu_2,\alpha}$ such that $P(F_{\nu_1,\nu_1} > F_{\nu_1,\nu_2,\alpha}) = \alpha$, where F_{ν_1,ν_2} is an F random variable, with numerator degrees of freedom ν_1 and denominator degrees of freedom ν_2. For example, the probability is .05 that an $F_{3,7}$ random variable exceeds 4.35.

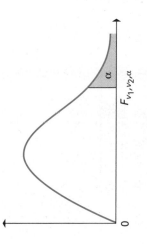

$\alpha = .05$

DENOMINATOR ν_2	NUMERATOR ν_1																		
	1	2	3	4	5	6	7	8	9	10	12	15	20	24	30	40	60	120	∞
1	161.4	199.5	215.7	224.6	230.2	234.0	236.8	238.9	240.5	241.9	243.9	245.9	248.0	249.1	250.1	251.1	252.2	253.3	254.3
2	18.51	19.00	19.16	19.25	19.30	19.33	19.35	19.37	19.38	19.40	19.41	19.43	19.45	19.45	19.46	19.47	19.48	19.49	19.50
3	10.13	9.55	9.28	9.12	9.01	8.94	8.89	8.85	8.81	8.79	8.74	8.70	8.66	8.64	8.62	8.59	8.57	8.55	8.53
4	7.71	6.94	6.59	6.39	6.26	6.16	6.09	6.04	6.00	5.96	5.91	5.86	5.80	5.77	5.75	5.72	5.69	5.66	5.63
5	6.61	5.79	5.41	5.19	5.05	4.95	4.88	4.82	4.77	4.74	4.68	4.62	4.56	4.53	4.50	4.46	4.43	4.40	4.36
6	5.99	5.14	4.76	4.53	4.39	4.28	4.21	4.15	4.10	4.06	4.00	3.94	3.87	3.84	3.81	3.77	3.74	3.70	3.67
7	5.59	4.74	4.35	4.12	3.97	3.87	3.79	3.73	3.68	3.64	3.57	3.51	3.44	3.41	3.38	3.34	3.30	3.27	3.23
8	5.32	4.46	4.07	3.84	3.69	3.58	3.50	3.44	3.39	3.35	3.28	3.22	3.15	3.12	3.08	3.04	3.01	2.97	2.93
9	5.12	4.26	3.86	3.63	3.48	3.37	3.29	3.23	3.18	3.14	3.07	3.01	2.94	2.90	2.86	2.83	2.79	2.75	2.71
10	4.96	4.10	3.71	3.48	3.33	3.22	3.14	3.07	3.02	2.98	2.91	2.85	2.77	2.74	2.70	2.66	2.62	2.58	2.54
11	4.84	3.98	3.59	3.36	3.20	3.09	3.01	2.95	2.90	2.85	2.79	2.72	2.65	2.61	2.57	2.53	2.49	2.45	2.40
12	4.75	3.89	3.49	3.26	3.11	3.00	2.91	2.85	2.80	2.75	2.69	2.62	2.54	2.51	2.47	2.43	2.38	2.34	2.30
13	4.67	3.81	3.41	3.18	3.03	2.92	2.83	2.77	2.71	2.67	2.60	2.53	2.46	2.42	2.38	2.34	2.30	2.25	2.21
14	4.60	3.74	3.34	3.11	2.96	2.85	2.76	2.70	2.65	2.60	2.53	2.46	2.39	2.35	2.31	2.27	2.22	2.18	2.13
15	4.54	3.68	3.29	3.06	2.90	2.79	2.71	2.64	2.59	2.54	2.48	2.40	2.33	2.29	2.25	2.20	2.16	2.11	2.07
16	4.49	3.63	3.24	3.01	2.85	2.74	2.66	2.59	2.54	2.49	2.42	2.35	2.28	2.24	2.19	2.15	2.11	2.06	2.01
17	4.45	3.59	3.20	2.96	2.81	2.70	2.62	2.55	2.49	2.45	2.38	2.31	2.23	2.19	2.15	2.10	2.06	2.01	1.96
18	4.41	3.55	3.16	2.93	2.77	2.66	2.58	2.51	2.46	2.41	2.34	2.27	2.19	2.15	2.11	2.06	2.02	1.97	1.92
19	4.38	3.52	3.13	2.90	2.74	2.63	2.54	2.48	2.42	2.38	2.31	2.23	2.16	2.11	2.07	2.03	1.98	1.93	1.88

Table 9 Cutoff Points for the *F* Distribution Continued

$\alpha = .05$

Denominator v_2	Numerator v_1																		
	1	2	3	4	5	6	7	8	9	10	12	15	20	24	30	40	60	120	∞
20	4.35	3.49	3.10	2.87	2.71	2.60	2.51	2.45	2.39	2.35	2.28	2.20	2.12	2.08	2.04	1.99	1.95	1.90	1.84
21	4.32	3.47	3.07	2.84	2.68	2.57	2.49	2.42	2.37	2.32	2.25	2.18	2.10	2.05	2.01	1.96	1.92	1.87	1.81
22	4.30	3.44	3.05	2.82	2.66	2.55	2.46	2.40	2.34	2.30	2.23	2.15	2.07	2.03	1.98	1.94	1.89	1.84	1.78
23	4.28	3.42	3.03	2.80	2.64	2.53	2.44	2.37	2.32	2.27	2.20	2.13	2.05	2.01	1.96	1.91	1.86	1.81	1.76
24	4.26	3.40	3.01	2.78	2.62	2.51	2.42	2.36	2.30	2.25	2.18	2.11	2.03	1.98	1.94	1.89	1.84	1.79	1.73
25	4.24	3.39	2.99	2.76	2.60	2.49	2.40	2.34	2.28	2.24	2.16	2.09	2.01	1.96	1.92	1.87	1.82	1.77	1.71
26	4.23	3.37	2.98	2.74	2.59	2.47	2.39	2.32	2.27	2.22	2.15	2.07	1.99	1.95	1.90	1.85	1.80	1.75	1.69
27	4.21	3.35	2.96	2.73	2.57	2.46	2.37	2.31	2.25	2.20	2.13	2.06	1.97	1.93	1.88	1.84	1.79	1.73	1.67
28	4.20	3.34	2.95	2.71	2.56	2.45	2.36	2.29	2.24	2.19	2.12	2.04	1.96	1.91	1.87	1.82	1.77	1.71	1.65
29	4.18	3.33	2.93	2.70	2.55	2.43	2.35	2.28	2.22	2.18	2.10	2.03	1.94	1.90	1.85	1.81	1.75	1.70	1.64
30	4.17	3.32	2.92	2.69	2.53	2.42	2.33	2.27	2.21	2.16	2.09	2.01	1.93	1.89	1.84	1.79	1.74	1.68	1.62
40	4.08	3.23	2.84	2.61	2.45	2.34	2.25	2.18	2.12	2.08	2.00	1.92	1.84	1.79	1.74	1.69	1.64	1.58	1.51
60	4.00	3.15	2.76	2.53	2.37	2.25	2.17	2.10	2.04	1.99	1.92	1.84	1.75	1.70	1.65	1.59	1.53	1.47	1.39
120	3.92	3.07	2.68	2.45	2.29	2.17	2.09	2.02	1.96	1.91	1.83	1.75	1.66	1.61	1.55	1.50	1.43	1.35	1.25
∞	3.84	3.00	2.60	2.37	2.21	2.10	2.01	1.94	1.88	1.83	1.75	1.67	1.57	1.52	1.46	1.39	1.32	1.22	1.00

Table 9 Cutoff Points for the F Distribution Continued

$\alpha = .01$

Denominator v_2	Numerator v_1 1	2	3	4	5	6	7	8	9	10	12	15	20	24	30	40	60	120	∞
1	4052	4999.5	5403	5625	5764	5859	5928	5982	6022	6056	6106	6157	6209	6235	6261	6287	6313	6339	6366
2	98.50	99.00	99.17	99.25	99.30	99.33	99.36	99.37	99.39	99.40	99.42	99.43	99.45	99.46	99.47	99.47	99.48	99.48	99.50
3	34.12	30.82	29.46	28.71	28.24	27.91	27.67	27.49	27.35	27.23	27.05	26.87	26.69	26.60	26.50	26.41	26.32	26.22	26.13
4	21.20	18.00	16.69	15.98	15.52	15.21	14.98	14.80	14.66	14.55	14.37	14.20	14.02	13.93	13.84	13.75	13.65	13.56	13.46
5	16.26	13.27	12.06	11.39	10.97	10.67	10.46	10.29	10.16	10.05	9.89	9.72	9.55	9.47	9.38	9.29	9.20	9.11	9.02
6	13.75	10.92	9.78	9.15	8.75	8.47	8.26	8.10	7.98	7.87	7.72	7.56	7.40	7.31	7.23	7.14	7.06	6.97	6.88
7	12.25	9.55	8.45	7.85	7.46	7.19	6.99	6.84	6.72	6.62	6.47	6.31	6.16	6.07	5.99	5.91	5.82	5.74	5.65
8	11.26	8.65	7.59	7.01	6.63	6.37	6.18	6.03	5.91	5.81	5.67	5.52	5.36	5.28	5.20	5.12	5.03	4.95	4.86
9	10.56	8.02	6.99	6.42	6.06	5.80	5.61	5.47	5.35	5.26	5.11	4.96	4.81	4.73	4.65	4.57	4.48	4.40	4.31
10	10.04	7.56	6.55	5.99	5.64	5.39	5.20	5.06	4.94	4.85	4.71	4.56	4.41	4.33	4.25	4.17	4.08	4.00	3.91
11	9.65	7.21	6.22	5.67	5.32	5.07	4.89	4.74	4.63	4.54	4.40	4.25	4.10	4.02	3.94	3.86	3.78	3.69	3.60
12	9.33	6.93	5.95	5.41	5.06	4.82	4.64	4.50	4.39	4.30	4.16	4.01	3.86	3.78	3.70	3.62	3.54	3.45	3.36
13	9.07	6.70	5.74	5.21	4.86	4.62	4.44	4.30	4.19	4.10	3.96	3.82	3.66	3.59	3.51	3.43	3.34	3.25	3.17
14	8.86	6.51	5.56	5.04	4.69	4.46	4.28	4.14	4.03	3.94	3.80	3.66	3.51	3.43	3.35	3.27	3.18	3.09	3.00
15	8.68	6.36	5.42	4.89	4.56	4.32	4.14	4.00	3.89	3.80	3.67	3.52	3.37	3.29	3.21	3.13	3.05	2.96	2.87
16	8.53	6.23	5.29	4.77	4.44	4.20	4.03	3.89	3.78	3.69	3.55	3.41	3.26	3.18	3.10	3.02	2.93	2.84	2.75
17	8.40	6.11	5.18	4.67	4.34	4.10	3.93	3.79	3.68	3.59	3.46	3.31	3.16	3.08	3.00	2.92	2.83	2.75	2.65
18	8.29	6.01	5.09	4.58	4.25	4.01	3.84	3.71	3.60	3.51	3.37	3.23	3.08	3.00	2.92	2.84	2.75	2.66	2.57
19	8.18	5.93	5.01	4.50	4.17	3.94	3.77	3.63	3.52	3.43	3.30	3.15	3.00	2.92	2.84	2.76	2.67	2.58	2.49
20	8.10	5.85	4.94	4.43	4.10	3.87	3.70	3.56	3.46	3.37	3.23	3.09	2.94	2.86	2.78	2.69	2.61	2.52	2.42
21	8.02	5.78	4.87	4.37	4.04	3.81	3.64	3.51	3.40	3.31	3.17	3.03	2.88	2.80	2.72	2.64	2.55	2.46	2.36
22	7.95	5.72	4.82	4.31	3.99	3.76	3.59	3.45	3.35	3.26	3.12	2.98	2.83	2.75	2.67	2.58	2.50	2.40	2.31
23	7.88	5.66	4.76	4.26	3.94	3.71	3.54	3.41	3.30	3.21	3.07	2.93	2.78	2.70	2.62	2.54	2.45	2.35	2.26
24	7.82	5.61	4.72	4.22	3.90	3.67	3.50	3.36	3.26	3.17	3.03	2.89	2.74	2.66	2.58	2.49	2.40	2.31	2.21
25	7.77	5.57	4.68	4.18	3.85	3.63	3.46	3.32	3.22	3.13	2.99	2.85	2.70	2.62	2.54	2.45	2.36	2.27	2.17
26	7.72	5.53	4.64	4.14	3.82	3.59	3.42	3.29	3.18	3.09	2.96	2.81	2.66	2.58	2.50	2.42	2.33	2.23	2.13
27	7.68	5.49	4.60	4.11	3.78	3.56	3.39	3.26	3.15	3.06	2.93	2.78	2.63	2.55	2.47	2.38	2.29	2.20	2.10
28	7.64	5.45	4.57	4.07	3.75	3.53	3.36	3.23	3.12	3.03	2.90	2.75	2.60	2.52	2.44	2.35	2.26	2.17	2.06
29	7.60	5.42	4.54	4.04	3.73	3.50	3.33	3.20	3.09	3.00	2.87	2.73	2.57	2.49	2.41	2.33	2.23	2.14	2.03
30	7.56	5.39	4.51	4.02	3.70	3.47	3.30	3.17	3.07	2.98	2.84	2.70	2.55	2.47	2.39	2.30	2.21	2.11	2.01
40	7.31	5.18	4.31	3.83	3.51	3.29	3.12	2.99	2.89	2.80	2.66	2.52	2.37	2.29	2.20	2.11	2.02	1.92	1.80
60	7.08	4.98	4.13	3.65	3.34	3.12	2.95	2.82	2.72	2.63	2.50	2.35	2.20	2.12	2.03	1.94	1.84	1.73	1.60
120	6.85	4.79	3.95	3.48	3.17	2.96	2.79	2.66	2.56	2.47	2.34	2.19	2.03	1.95	1.86	1.76	1.66	1.53	1.38
∞	6.63	4.61	3.78	3.32	3.02	2.80	2.64	2.51	2.41	2.32	2.18	2.04	1.88	1.79	1.70	1.59	1.47	1.32	1.00

Table 10 Cutoff Points for the Distribution of the Wilcoxon Test Statistic

For sample size n, the table shows, for selected probabilities α, the numbers T_α such that $P(T \leq T_\alpha) = \alpha$, where the distribution of the random variable T is that of the Wilcoxon test statistic under the null hypothesis.

n	α				
	.005	.010	.025	.050	.100
4	0	0	0	0	1
5	0	0	0	1	3
6	0	0	1	3	4
7	0	1	3	4	6
8	1	2	4	6	9
9	2	4	6	9	11
10	4	6	9	11	15
11	6	8	11	14	18
12	8	10	14	18	22
13	10	13	18	22	27
14	13	16	22	26	32
15	16	20	26	31	37
16	20	24	30	36	43
17	24	28	35	42	49
18	28	33	41	48	56
19	33	38	47	54	63
20	38	44	53	61	70

Reproduced with permission from R. L. McCormack, "Extended tables of the Wilcoxon matched pairs signed rank statistics," *Journal of the American Statistical Association* 60 (1965).

Table 11 Cutoff Points for the Distribution of Spearman Rank Correlation Coefficient

For sample size n, the table shows, for selected probabilities α, the numbers $r_{s,\alpha}$ such that $P(r_s > r_{s,\alpha}) = \alpha$, where the distribution of the random variable r_s is that of Spearman rank correlation coefficient under the null hypothesis of no association.

n	α			
	.050	.025	.010	.005
5	.900	—	—	—
6	.829	.886	.943	—
7	.714	.786	.893	—
8	.643	.738	.833	.881
9	.600	.683	.783	.833
10	.564	.648	.745	.794
11	.523	.623	.736	.818
12	.497	.591	.703	.780
13	.475	.566	.673	.745
14	.457	.545	.646	.716
15	.441	.525	.623	.689
16	.425	.507	.601	.666
17	.412	.490	.582	.645
18	.399	.476	.564	.625
19	.388	.462	.549	.608
20	.377	.450	.534	.591
21	.368	.438	.521	.576
22	.359	.428	.508	.562
23	.351	.418	.496	.549
24	.343	.409	.485	.537
25	.336	.400	.475	.526
26	.329	.392	.465	.515
27	.323	.385	.456	.505
28	.317	.377	.448	.496
29	.311	.370	.440	.487
30	.305	.364	.432	.478

Reproduced with permission from E. G. Olds, "Distribution of sums of squares of rank differences for small samples," *Annals of Mathematical Statistics* 9 (1938).

Table 12 Cutoff Points for the Distribution of the Durbin-Watson Test Statistic

Let d_α be the number such that $P(d < d_\alpha) = \alpha$, where the random variable d has the distribution of the Durbin-Watson statistic under the null hypothesis of no autocorrelation in the regression errors. For probabilities $\alpha = .05$ and $\alpha = .01$, the tables show, for numbers of independent variables, K, values d_L and d_U such that $d_L \leq d_\alpha \leq d_U$, for numbers n of observations.

	$\alpha = .05$									
	K									
n	1		2		3		4		5	
	d_L	d_U	d_L	d_U	d_L	d_U	d_L	d_U	d_L	d_U
15	1.08	1.36	0.95	1.54	0.82	1.75	0.69	1.97	0.56	2.21
16	1.10	1.37	0.98	1.54	0.86	1.73	0.74	1.93	0.62	2.15
17	1.13	1.38	1.02	1.54	0.90	1.71	0.78	1.90	0.67	2.10
18	1.16	1.39	1.05	1.53	0.93	1.69	1.82	1.87	0.71	2.06
19	1.18	1.40	1.08	1.53	0.97	1.68	0.86	1.85	0.75	2.02
20	1.20	1.41	1.10	1.54	1.00	1.68	0.90	1.83	0.79	1.99
21	1.22	1.42	1.13	1.54	1.03	1.67	0.93	1.81	0.83	1.96
22	1.24	1.43	1.15	1.54	1.05	1.66	0.96	1.80	0.86	1.94
23	1.26	1.44	1.17	1.54	1.08	1.66	0.99	1.79	0.90	1.92
24	1.27	1.45	1.19	1.55	1.10	1.66	1.01	1.78	0.93	1.90
25	1.29	1.45	1.21	1.55	1.12	1.66	1.04	1.77	0.95	1.89
26	1.30	1.46	1.22	1.55	1.14	1.65	1.06	1.76	0.98	1.88
27	1.32	1.47	1.24	1.56	1.16	1.65	1.08	1.76	1.01	1.86
28	1.33	1.48	1.26	1.56	1.18	1.65	1.10	1.75	1.03	1.85
29	1.34	1.48	1.27	1.56	1.20	1.65	1.12	1.74	1.05	1.84
30	1.35	1.49	1.28	1.57	1.21	1.65	1.14	1.74	1.07	1.83
31	1.36	1.50	1.30	1.57	1.23	1.65	1.16	1.74	1.09	1.83
32	1.37	1.50	1.31	1.57	1.24	1.65	1.18	1.73	1.11	1.82
33	1.38	1.51	1.32	1.58	1.26	1.65	1.19	1.73	1.13	1.81
34	1.39	1.51	1.33	1.58	1.27	1.65	1.21	1.73	1.15	1.81
35	1.40	1.52	1.34	1.58	1.28	1.65	1.22	1.73	1.16	1.80
36	1.41	1.52	1.35	1.59	1.29	1.65	1.24	1.73	1.18	1.80
37	1.42	1.53	1.36	1.59	1.31	1.66	1.25	1.72	1.19	1.80
38	1.43	1.54	1.37	1.59	1.32	1.66	1.26	1.72	1.21	1.79
39	1.43	1.54	1.38	1.60	1.33	1.66	1.27	1.72	1.22	1.79
40	1.44	1.54	1.39	1.60	1.34	1.66	1.29	1.72	1.23	1.79
45	1.48	1.57	1.43	1.62	1.38	1.67	1.34	1.72	1.29	1.78
50	1.50	1.59	1.46	1.63	1.42	1.67	1.38	1.72	1.34	1.77
55	1.53	1.60	1.49	1.64	1.45	1.68	1.41	1.72	1.38	1.77
60	1.55	1.62	1.51	1.65	1.48	1.69	1.44	1.73	1.41	1.77
65	1.57	1.63	1.54	1.66	1.50	1.70	1.47	1.73	1.44	1.77
70	1.58	1.64	1.55	1.67	1.52	1.70	1.49	1.74	1.46	1.77
75	1.60	1.65	1.57	1.68	1.54	1.71	1.51	1.74	1.49	1.77
80	1.61	1.66	1.59	1.69	1.56	1.72	1.53	1.74	1.51	1.77
85	1.62	1.67	1.60	1.70	1.57	1.72	1.55	1.75	1.52	1.77
90	1.63	1.68	1.61	1.70	1.59	1.73	1.57	1.75	1.54	1.78
95	1.64	1.69	1.62	1.71	1.60	1.73	1.58	1.75	1.56	1.78
100	1.65	1.69	1.63	1.72	1.61	1.74	1.59	1.76	1.57	1.78

Table 12 Cutoff Points for the Distribution of the Durbin-Watson Test Statistic Continued

							$\alpha = .01$				
						K					
n	1		2		3		4		5	
	d_L	d_U	d_L	d_U	d_L	d_U	d_L	d_U	d_L	d_U
15	0.81	1.07	0.70	1.25	0.59	1.46	0.49	1.70	0.39	1.96
16	0.84	1.09	0.74	1.25	0.63	1.44	0.53	1.66	0.44	1.90
17	0.87	1.10	0.77	1.25	0.67	1.43	0.57	1.63	0.48	1.85
18	0.90	1.12	0.80	1.26	0.71	1.42	0.61	1.60	0.52	1.80
19	0.93	1.13	0.83	1.26	0.74	1.41	0.65	1.58	0.56	1.77
20	0.95	1.15	0.86	1.27	0.77	1.41	0.68	1.57	0.60	1.74
21	0.97	1.16	0.89	1.27	0.80	1.41	0.72	1.55	0.63	1.71
22	1.00	1.17	0.91	1.28	0.83	1.40	0.75	1.54	0.66	1.69
23	1.02	1.19	0.94	1.29	0.86	1.40	0.77	1.53	0.70	1.67
24	1.04	1.20	0.96	1.30	0.88	1.41	0.80	1.53	0.72	1.66
25	1.05	1.21	0.98	1.30	0.90	1.41	0.83	1.52	0.75	1.65
26	1.07	1.22	1.00	1.31	0.93	1.41	0.85	1.52	0.78	1.64
27	1.09	1.23	1.02	1.32	0.95	1.41	0.88	1.51	0.81	1.63
28	1.10	1.24	1.04	1.32	0.97	1.41	0.90	1.51	0.83	1.62
29	1.12	1.25	1.05	1.33	0.99	1.42	0.92	1.51	0.85	1.61
30	1.13	1.26	1.07	1.34	1.01	1.42	0.94	1.51	0.88	1.61
31	1.15	1.27	1.08	1.34	1.02	1.42	0.96	1.51	0.90	1.60
32	1.16	1.28	1.10	1.35	1.04	1.43	0.98	1.51	0.92	1.60
33	1.17	1.29	1.11	1.36	1.05	1.43	1.00	1.51	0.94	1.59
34	1.18	1.30	1.13	1.36	1.07	1.43	1.01	1.51	0.95	1.59
35	1.19	1.31	1.14	1.37	1.08	1.44	1.03	1.51	0.97	1.59
36	1.21	1.32	1.15	1.38	1.10	1.44	1.04	1.51	0.99	1.59
37	1.22	1.32	1.16	1.38	1.11	1.45	1.06	1.51	1.00	1.59
38	1.23	1.33	1.18	1.39	1.12	1.45	1.07	1.52	1.02	1.58
39	1.24	1.34	1.19	1.39	1.14	1.45	1.09	1.52	1.03	1.58
40	1.25	1.34	1.20	1.40	1.15	1.46	1.10	1.52	1.05	1.58
45	1.29	1.38	1.24	1.42	1.20	1.48	1.16	1.53	1.11	1.58
50	1.32	1.40	1.28	1.45	1.24	1.49	1.20	1.54	1.16	1.59
55	1.36	1.43	1.32	1.47	1.28	1.51	1.25	1.55	1.21	1.59
60	1.38	1.45	1.35	1.48	1.32	1.52	1.28	1.56	1.25	1.60
65	1.41	1.47	1.38	1.50	1.35	1.53	1.31	1.57	1.28	1.61
70	1.43	1.49	1.40	1.52	1.37	1.55	1.34	1.58	1.31	1.61
75	1.45	1.50	1.42	1.53	1.39	1.56	1.37	1.59	1.34	1.62
80	1.47	1.52	1.44	1.54	1.42	1.57	1.39	1.60	1.36	1.62
85	1.48	1.53	1.46	1.55	1.43	1.58	1.41	1.60	1.39	1.63
90	1.50	1.54	1.47	1.56	1.45	1.59	1.43	1.61	1.41	1.64
95	1.51	1.55	1.49	1.57	1.47	1.60	1.45	1.62	1.42	1.64
100	1.52	1.56	1.50	1.58	1.48	1.60	1.46	1.63	1.44	1.65

Reproduced with permission from J. Durbin and G. S. Watson, "Testing for serial correlation in least squares regression, II," *Biometrika* 38 (1951).

Table 13 Critical Values[a] of the Studentized Range Q

Upper 5% points ($\alpha = .05$)

ν	η																		
	2	3	4	5	6	7	8	9	10	11	12	13	14	15	16	17	18	19	20
1	18.0	27.0	32.8	37.1	40.4	43.1	45.4	47.4	49.1	50.6	52.0	53.2	54.3	55.4	56.3	57.2	58.0	58.8	59.6
2	6.09	8.3	9.8	10.9	11.7	12.4	13.0	13.5	14.0	14.4	14.7	15.1	15.4	15.7	15.9	16.1	16.4	16.6	16.8
3	4.50	5.91	6.82	7.50	8.04	8.48	8.85	9.18	9.46	9.72	9.95	10.15	10.35	10.52	10.69	10.84	10.98	11.11	11.24
4	3.93	5.04	5.76	6.29	6.71	7.05	7.35	7.60	7.83	8.03	8.21	8.37	8.52	8.66	8.79	8.91	9.03	9.13	9.23
5	3.64	4.60	5.22	5.67	6.03	6.33	6.58	6.80	6.99	7.17	7.32	7.47	7.60	7.72	7.83	7.93	8.03	8.12	8.21
6	3.46	4.34	4.90	5.31	5.63	5.89	6.12	6.32	6.49	6.65	6.79	6.92	7.03	7.14	7.24	7.34	7.43	7.51	7.59
7	3.34	4.16	4.68	5.06	5.36	5.61	5.82	6.00	6.16	6.30	6.43	6.55	6.66	6.76	6.85	6.94	7.02	7.09	7.17
8	3.26	4.04	4.53	4.89	5.17	5.40	5.60	5.77	5.92	6.05	6.18	6.29	6.39	6.48	6.57	6.65	6.73	6.80	6.87
9	3.20	3.95	4.42	4.76	5.02	5.24	5.43	5.60	5.74	5.87	5.98	6.09	6.19	6.28	6.36	6.44	6.51	6.58	6.64
10	3.15	3.88	4.33	4.65	4.91	5.12	5.30	5.46	5.60	5.72	5.83	5.93	6.03	6.11	6.20	6.27	6.34	6.40	6.47
11	3.11	3.82	4.26	4.57	4.82	5.03	5.20	5.35	5.49	5.61	5.71	5.81	5.90	5.99	6.06	6.14	6.20	6.26	6.33
12	3.08	3.77	4.20	4.51	4.75	4.95	5.12	5.27	5.40	5.51	5.62	5.71	5.80	5.88	5.95	6.03	6.09	6.15	6.21
13	3.06	3.73	4.15	4.45	4.69	4.88	5.05	5.19	5.32	5.43	5.53	5.63	5.71	5.79	5.86	5.93	6.00	6.05	6.11
14	3.03	3.70	4.11	4.41	4.64	4.83	4.99	5.13	5.25	5.36	5.46	5.55	5.64	5.72	5.79	5.85	5.92	5.97	6.03
15	3.01	3.67	4.08	4.37	4.60	4.78	4.94	5.08	5.20	5.31	5.40	5.49	5.58	5.65	5.72	5.79	5.85	5.90	5.96
16	3.00	3.65	4.05	4.33	4.56	4.74	4.90	5.03	5.15	5.26	5.35	5.44	5.52	5.59	5.66	5.72	5.79	5.84	5.90
17	2.98	3.63	4.02	4.30	4.52	4.71	4.86	4.99	5.11	5.21	5.31	5.39	5.47	5.55	5.61	5.68	5.74	5.79	5.84
18	2.97	3.61	4.00	4.28	4.49	4.67	4.82	4.96	5.07	5.17	5.27	5.35	5.43	5.50	5.57	5.63	5.69	5.74	5.79
19	2.96	3.59	3.98	4.25	4.47	4.65	4.79	4.92	5.04	5.14	5.23	5.32	5.39	5.46	5.53	5.59	5.65	5.70	5.75
20	2.95	3.58	3.96	4.23	4.45	4.62	4.77	4.90	5.01	5.11	5.20	5.28	5.36	5.43	5.49	5.55	5.61	5.66	5.71
24	2.92	3.53	3.90	4.17	4.37	4.54	4.68	4.81	4.92	5.01	5.10	5.18	5.25	5.32	5.38	5.44	5.50	5.54	5.59
30	2.89	3.49	3.84	4.10	4.30	4.46	4.60	4.72	4.83	4.92	5.00	5.08	5.15	5.21	5.27	5.33	5.38	5.43	5.48
40	2.86	3.44	3.79	4.04	4.23	4.39	4.52	4.63	4.74	4.82	4.91	4.98	5.05	5.11	5.16	5.22	5.27	5.31	5.36
60	2.83	3.40	3.74	3.98	4.16	4.31	4.44	4.55	4.65	4.73	4.81	4.88	4.94	5.00	5.06	5.11	5.16	5.20	5.24
120	2.80	3.36	3.69	3.92	4.10	4.24	4.36	4.48	4.56	4.64	4.72	4.78	4.84	4.90	4.95	5.00	5.05	5.09	5.13
∞	2.77	3.31	3.63	3.86	4.03	4.17	4.29	4.39	4.47	4.55	4.62	4.68	4.74	4.80	4.85	4.89	4.93	4.97	5.01

Table 13 Critical Values[a] of the Studentized Range Q (continued)

Upper 1% points (α = .01)

ν \ η	2	3	4	5	6	7	8	9	10	11	12	13	14	15	16	17	18	19	20
1	90.0	135	164	186	202	216	227	237	246	253	260	266	272	277	282	286	290	294	298
2	14.0	19.0	22.3	24.7	26.6	28.2	29.5	30.7	31.7	32.6	33.4	34.1	34.8	35.4	36.0	36.5	37.0	37.5	37.9
3	8.26	10.6	12.2	13.3	14.2	15.0	15.6	16.2	16.7	17.1	17.5	17.9	18.2	18.5	18.8	19.1	19.3	19.5	19.8
4	6.51	8.12	9.17	9.96	10.6	11.1	11.5	11.9	12.3	12.6	12.8	13.1	13.3	13.5	13.7	13.9	14.1	14.2	14.4
5	5.70	6.97	7.80	8.42	8.91	9.32	9.67	9.97	10.24	10.48	10.70	10.89	11.08	11.24	11.40	11.55	11.68	11.81	11.93
6	5.24	6.33	7.03	7.56	7.97	8.32	8.61	8.87	9.10	9.30	9.49	9.65	9.81	9.95	10.08	10.21	10.32	10.43	10.54
7	4.95	5.92	6.54	7.01	7.37	7.68	7.94	8.17	8.37	8.55	8.71	8.86	9.00	9.12	9.24	9.35	9.46	9.55	9.65
8	4.74	5.63	6.20	6.63	6.96	7.24	7.47	7.68	7.87	8.03	8.18	8.31	8.44	8.55	8.66	8.76	8.85	8.94	9.03
9	4.60	5.43	5.96	6.35	6.66	6.91	7.13	7.32	7.49	7.65	7.78	7.91	8.03	8.13	8.23	8.32	8.41	8.49	8.57
10	4.48	5.27	5.77	6.14	6.43	6.67	6.87	7.05	7.21	7.36	7.48	7.60	7.71	7.81	7.91	7.99	8.07	8.15	8.22
11	4.39	5.14	5.62	5.97	6.25	6.48	6.67	6.84	6.99	7.13	7.25	7.36	7.46	7.56	7.65	7.73	7.81	7.88	7.95
12	4.32	5.04	5.50	5.84	6.10	6.32	6.51	6.67	6.81	6.94	7.06	7.17	7.26	7.36	7.44	7.52	7.59	7.66	7.73
13	4.26	4.96	5.40	5.73	5.98	6.19	6.37	6.53	6.67	6.79	6.90	7.01	7.10	7.19	7.27	7.34	7.42	7.48	7.55
14	4.21	4.89	5.32	5.63	5.88	6.08	6.26	6.41	6.54	6.66	6.77	6.87	6.96	7.05	7.12	7.20	7.27	7.33	7.39
15	4.17	4.83	5.25	5.56	5.80	5.99	6.16	6.31	6.44	6.55	6.66	6.76	6.84	6.93	7.00	7.07	7.14	7.20	7.26
16	4.13	4.78	5.19	5.49	5.72	5.92	6.08	6.22	6.35	6.46	6.56	6.66	6.74	6.82	6.90	6.97	7.03	7.09	7.15
17	4.10	4.74	5.14	5.43	5.66	5.85	6.01	6.15	6.27	6.38	6.48	6.57	6.66	6.73	6.80	6.87	6.94	7.00	7.05
18	4.07	4.70	5.09	5.38	5.60	5.79	5.94	6.08	6.20	6.31	6.41	6.50	6.58	6.65	6.72	6.79	6.85	6.91	6.96
19	4.05	4.67	5.05	5.33	5.55	5.73	5.89	6.02	6.14	6.25	6.34	6.43	6.51	6.58	6.65	6.72	6.78	6.84	6.89
20	4.02	4.64	5.02	5.29	5.51	5.69	5.84	5.97	6.09	6.19	6.29	6.37	6.45	6.52	6.59	6.65	6.71	6.76	6.82
24	3.96	4.54	4.91	5.17	5.37	5.54	5.69	5.81	5.92	6.02	6.11	6.19	6.26	6.33	6.39	6.45	6.51	6.56	6.61
30	3.89	4.45	4.80	5.05	5.24	5.40	5.54	5.65	5.76	5.85	5.93	6.01	6.08	6.14	6.20	6.26	6.31	6.36	6.41
40	3.82	4.37	4.70	4.93	5.11	5.27	5.39	5.50	5.60	5.69	5.77	5.84	5.90	5.96	6.02	6.07	6.12	6.17	6.21
60	3.76	4.28	4.60	4.82	4.99	5.13	5.25	5.36	5.45	5.53	5.60	5.67	5.73	5.79	5.84	5.89	5.93	5.98	6.02
120	3.70	4.20	4.50	4.71	4.87	5.01	5.12	5.21	5.30	5.38	5.44	5.51	5.56	5.61	5.66	5.71	5.75	5.79	5.83
∞	3.64	4.12	4.40	4.60	4.76	4.88	4.99	5.08	5.16	5.23	5.29	5.35	5.40	5.45	5.49	5.54	5.57	5.61	5.65

[a] $\text{Range}/S_\gamma \sim Q_{1-\alpha; \eta, \nu}.$ η is the size of the sample from which the range is obtained, and ν is the number of degrees of freedom of S_γ.

Source: Reprinted from E. S. Pearson and H. O. Hartley, eds., Table 29 of *Biometrika Tables for Statisticians*, Vol. 1, 3rd ed., 1966, by permission of the *Biometrika* Trustees, London.

Table 14 Cumulative Distribution Function of the Runs Test Statistic

For a given number n of observations, the table shows the probability, for a random time series, that the number of runs will not exceed K.

n											K								
	2	3	4	5	6	7	8	9	10	11	12	13	14	15	16	17	18	19	20
6	.100	.300	.700	.900	1.000														
8	.029	.114	.371	.629	.886	.971	1.000												
10	.008	.040	.167	.357	.643	.833	.960	.992	1.000										
12	.002	.013	.067	.175	.392	.608	.825	.933	.987	.998	1.000								
14	.001	.004	.025	.078	.209	.383	.617	.791	.922	.975	.996	.999	1.000						
16	.000	.001	.009	.032	.100	.214	.405	.595	.786	.900	.968	.991	.999	1.000	1.000				
18	.000	.000	.003	.012	.044	.109	.238	.399	.601	.762	.891	.956	.988	.997	1.000	1.000	1.000		
20	.000	.000	.001	.004	.019	.051	.128	.242	.414	.586	.758	.872	.949	.981	.996	.999	1.000	1.000	1.000

Reproduced with permission from F. Swed and C. Eisenhart, "Tables for testing randomness of grouping in a sequence of alternatives," *Annals of Mathematical Statistics* 14 (1943).

ANSWERS TO SELECTED EVEN-NUMBERED EXERCISES

Chapter 1

1.2 a. Categorical—nominal
b. Categorical—ordinal
c. Numerical—discrete

1.4 a. Categorical—Qualitative—ordinal
b. Numerical—Quantitative—discrete
c. Categorical—Qualitative—nominal
d. Categorical—Qualitative—nominal

1.6 a. Categorical—Qualitative—nominal
b. Numerical—Quantitative—discrete
c. Categorical—Qualitative—nominal; yes/no response
d. Categorical—Qualitative—ordinal

1.8 a. Various answers—Categorical variable with ordinal responses:
Health consciousness
b. Various answers—Categorical variable with nominal responses: Gender

1.10

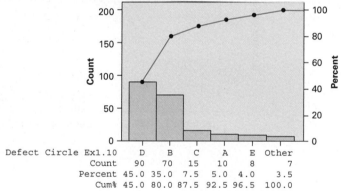

Pareto Chart of Defect code_Ex1.10

Defect Circle Ex1.10	D	B	C	A	E	Other
Count	90	70	15	10	8	7
Percent	45.0	35.0	7.5	5.0	4.0	3.5
Cum%	45.0	80.0	87.5	92.5	96.5	100.0

1.12

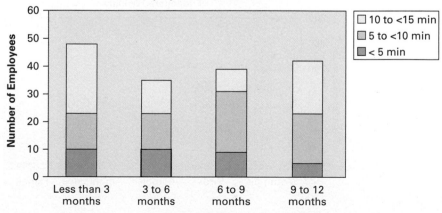

1.14 a.

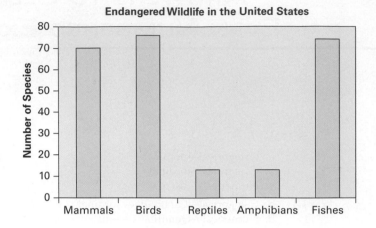

Endangered Wildlife in the United States

b.

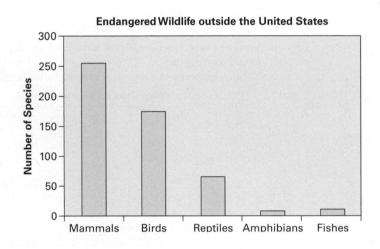

Endangered Wildlife outside the United States

c.

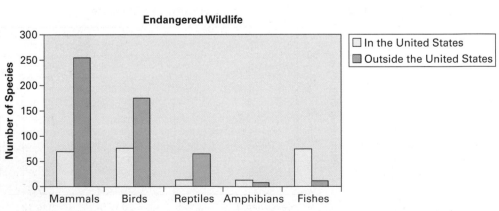

Endangered Wildlife

1.16 Describe the data graphically.

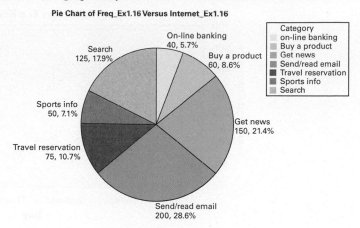

1.18 a.

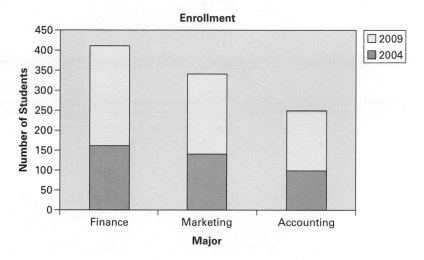

b.

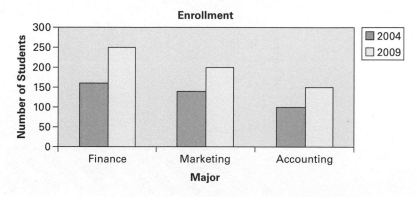

1.20

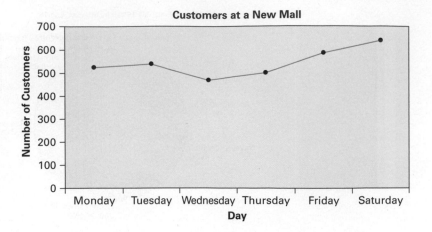

1.22 a.

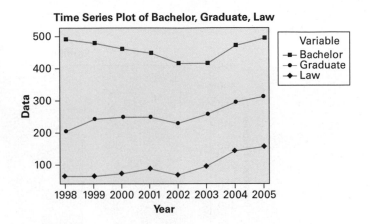

b. The number of law and graduate degrees awarded is increasing. The number of bachelor degrees awarded declined from 1998 to 2002, leveled off in 2003, then began an upward trend in 2004. Enrollment restrictions may be in order if class sizes are becoming too large or if crowding conditions occur.

1.24 a.

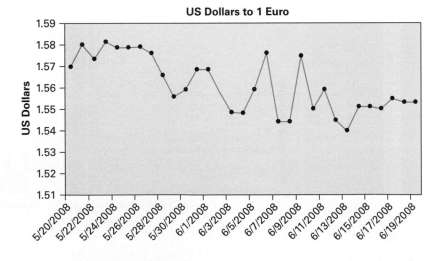

b. Answers may vary.

1.26

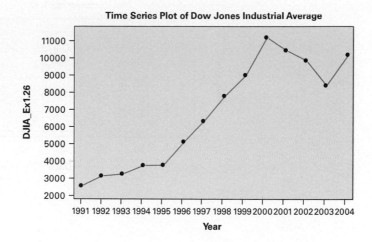

1.28

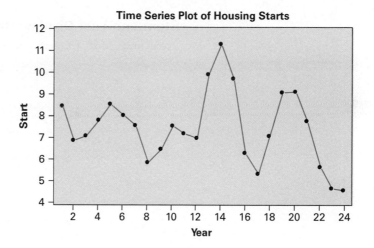

1.30 a. 5 – 7 classes
      b. 7 – 8 classes
      c. 8 – 10 classes
      d. 8 – 10 classes
      e. 10 – 11 classes

1.32 a.

Classes	Frequency
10 < 20	5
20 < 30	3
30 < 40	7
40 < 50	4
50 < 60	5
60 < 70	4

b. histogram and c. ogive

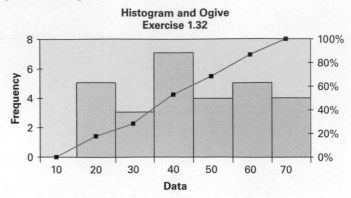

d.

Stem-and-Leaf Display: Data_Ex1.32

```
Stem-and-leaf of Data N = 28
Leaf Unit = 1.0

   5    1   23557
   8    2   148
  (7)   3   2567799
  13    4   0144
   9    5   14699
   4    6   2455
```

1.34

Classes	Frequency	a. Relative Frequency	b. Cumulative Frequency	c. Relative Cumulative Frequency
0<10	8	16.33%	8	16.33%
10<20	10	20.41%	18	36.74%
20<30	13	26.53%	31	63.27%
30<40	12	24.49%	43	87.76%
40<50	6	12.24%	49	100.00%
Total	49	100.00%		

1.36 Various answers—one possibility is to use 7 classes with a width of 0.1.

Classes	Frequency	Cumulative %
3.5 < 3.6	1	1.33%
3.6 < 3.7	8	12.00%
3.7 < 3.8	29	50.67%
3.8 < 3.9	22	80.00%
3.9 < 4.0	13	97.33%
4.0 < 4.10	1	98.67%
4.10 < 4.20	1	100.00%

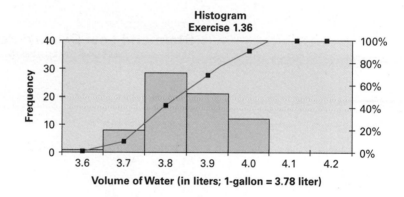

**Histogram
Exercise 1.36**

Volume of Water (in liters; 1-gallon = 3.78 liter)

Stem-and-Leaf Display: Weights
```
Stem-and-leaf of Weights  N = 28
Leaf Unit = 0.010

    1    35   7
    3    36   34
    9    36   577799
   21    37   111122344444
  (17)   37   55566777777889999
   37    38   0111112222244
   24    38   556677899
   15    39   01334444
    7    39   56689
    2    40
    2    40   6
    1    41   1
```

1.38   a. Histogram and c. Ogive of the **Returns** data

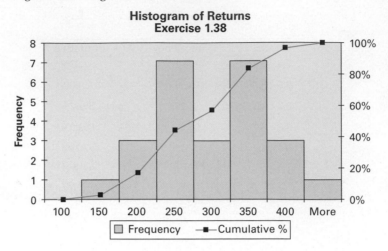

Histogram of Returns
Exercise 1.38

b.

Stem-and-Leaf Display: Returns
```
Stem-and-leaf of Weights N = 25
Leaf Unit = 10

  1    1   3
  4    1   899
 11    2   0014444
 (3)   2   589
 11    3   0000122
  4    3   689
  1    4
  1    4
  1    5   0
```

1.40

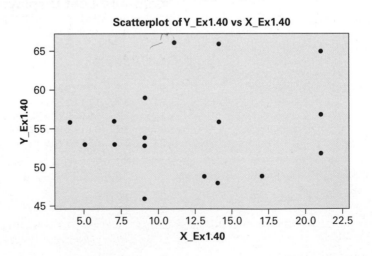

Scatterplot of Y_Ex1.40 vs X_Ex1.40

1.42 a.

Subcontractor	Defective Parts	Non-Defective Parts	Parts Supplied
A	4	54	58
B	10	60	70
C	6	66	72
Total	20	180	200

b.

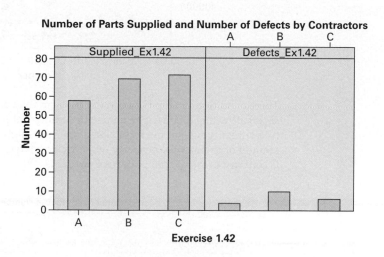

1.44

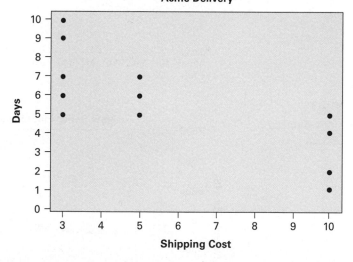

The relationship appears to be negative; however there is significant variability in delivery time at each of the three shipping costs—regular, $3; fast, $5; and lightning, $10.

1.46

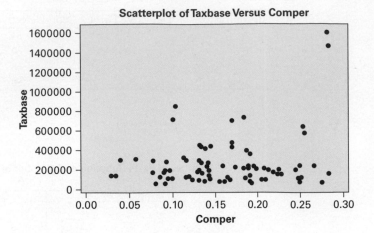

There is no relationship between the two variables and hence no evidence that emphasis on attracting a larger percentage of commercial property increases the tax base. The two outlier points on the right side of the plot might be used to argue that a very high amount of commercial property will provide a larger tax base. That argument, however, is contrary to the overall pattern of the data.

1.48 a.

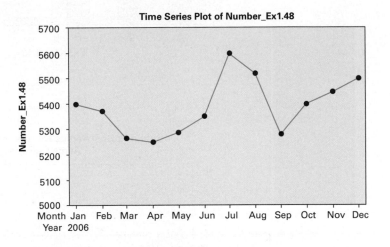

b.

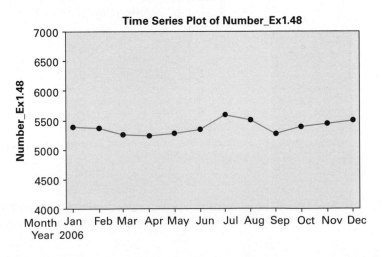

c. Differences between the two graphs include the variability of the data series. One graph suggests greater variability in the data series while the other one suggests a relatively flat line with less variability. Keep in mind the scale on which the measurements are made.

1.50

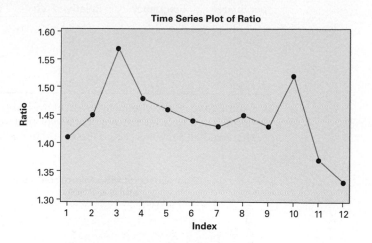

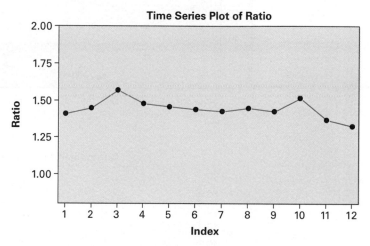

Differences between the two graphs include the variability of the data series. One graph suggests greater variability in the data series, while the other one suggests a relatively flat line with less variability. Keep in mind the scale on which the measurements are made.

1.52   a.

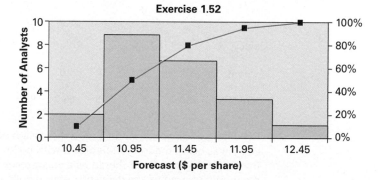

Answer to b., c. and d. are as follows:

Forecast of Earnings per Share	(b) Frequency	(c) Relative Freq.	(d) Cumulative Freq.	Cumulative %
9.95	2	0.1	2	10.00%
10.45	8	0.4	10	50.00%
10.95	6	0.3	16	80.00%
11.45	3	0.15	19	95.00%
11.95	1	0.05	20	100.00%

d. Cumulative relative frequencies are in the last column of the previous table. These numbers indicate the percent of analysts who forecast that level of earnings per share and all previous classes, up to and including the current class.

1.54

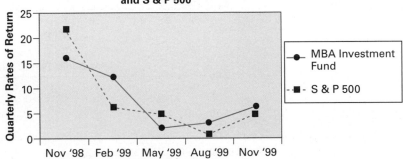

1.56 a.

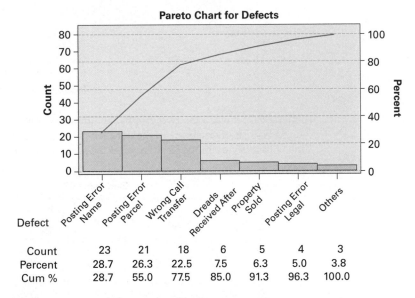

Defect	Posting Error Name	Posting Error Parcel	Wrong Call Transfer	Dreads Received After	Property Sold	Posting Error Legal	Others
Count	23	21	18	6	5	4	3
Percent	28.7	26.3	22.5	7.5	6.3	5.0	3.8
Cum %	28.7	55.0	77.5	85.0	91.3	96.3	100.0

b. Recommendations should include a discussion of the data entry process. The data entry was being made by individuals with no knowledge of the data. Training of the data entry personnel should be a major recommendation. Increasing the size of the monitors used by the data entry staff would also reduce the number of errors.

1.58

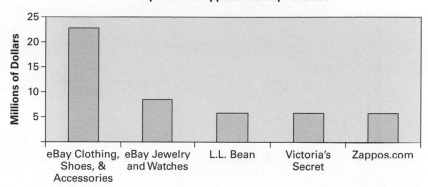

Weekly traffic increases from 2003 to 2004 could come about because the total number of users of the Internet has increased, an increasing awareness of health Internet sites, or an aging baby boom population that is more concerned about health issues.

1.60

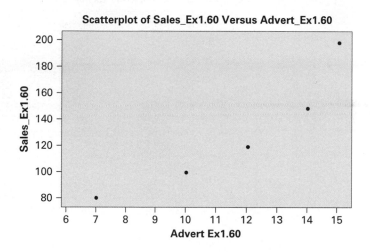

1.62

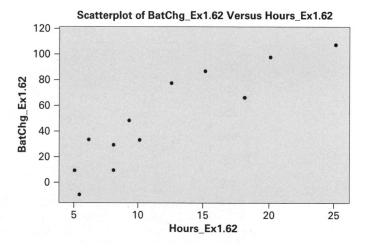

It appears that the number of hours spent per week in a special weight-training program is positively related to the change in batting averages from the previous season.

1.64 a.

Age	Friend	Newspaper	Subtotal
<21 years	30	20	50
21–35	60	30	90
>35	18	42	60
Subtotal	108	92	200

b.

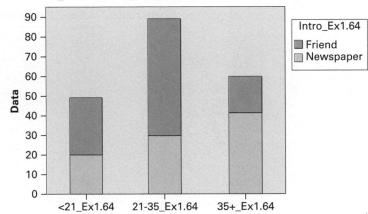

1.66 a.

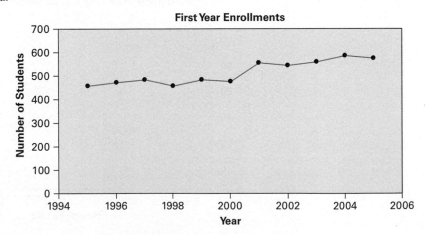

b.

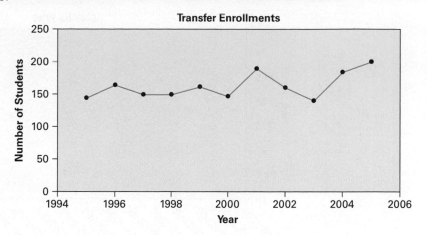

1.68   a.

Payment	M	T	W	Th	F	S	Total
Am Ex	7	0	3	4	3	6	23
MC	1	4	4	2	4	9	24
Visa	6	6	4	5	8	10	39
Cash	3	1	0	0	3	9	16
Other	2	0	4	4	7	6	23
Subtotal	19	11	15	15	25	40	125

b.

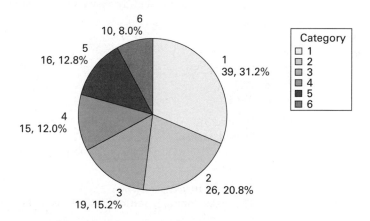

1.70

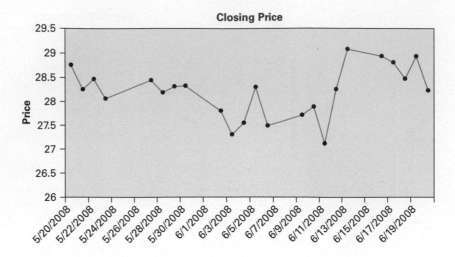

Chapter 2

2.2 a. 12   b. 13   c. 8

2.4 a. 5.94   b. 6.35
    c. The distribution is relatively symmetric since the mean of 5.94 is relatively close to the median of 6.35. Since the mean is slightly less than the median, the distribution is slightly skewed to the left.

2.6 a. 53.57. The mean demand for one-gallon bottles is 53.57, which is the balancing point of the distribution. The median of 55 indicates that half of the distribution had larger sales than 55 bottles and half had smaller sales. No unique mode exists in the distribution.
    b. Comment on symmetry or skewness. Since the mean is slightly less than the median, the distribution is slightly skewed to the left.

2.8 a. 25.58   b. 22.50   c. 22

2.10 a. 8.545   b. 9.0
    c. The distribution is slightly skewed to the left since the mean is less than the median.

2.12 $s^2 = 5.143$ and $s = 2.268$

2.14 $\bar{x} = 9$; $s^2 = 2.5$; $s = 1.581$; $CV = 17.57$

2.16 a. IQR = 24.25; $Q_1 = 49.5$; $Q_3 = 73.75$
    b. 77.2
    c. 83.64

2.18 a. 190 and 310. At least 88.9% of the observations are within 3 standard deviations from the mean.
    b. 210 and 290. At least 75% of the observations are within 2 standard deviations from the mean.

2.20 a. $\mu_{stocks} = 8.16$, $\mu_{Tbills} = 5.786$
    The mean annual % return on stocks is higher than the return for U.S. Treasury bills.

b. $\sigma_{stocks} = 20.648$, $\sigma_{Tbills} = 1.362$
The variability of the U.S. Treasury bills is much smaller than the return on stocks.

2.22 a. range = 0.54, standard deviation = 0.1024, variance = 0.010486
b. Five number summary:

Min	Q1	Median	Q3	Max
3.57	3.74	3.79	3.87	4.11

c. IQR = 0.13. This tells that the range of the middle 50% of the distribution is 0.13.
d. 0.02689 or 2.689%

2.24 a. s = 3.8696
b. The distribution is mounded. Therefore, the empirical rule applies. Approximately 95% of the distribution is expected to be within +/− 2 standard deviations of the mean.

2.26 a. 4.2   b. 4.583

2.28 32,299.519

2.30 a. 1.40   b. $s^2 = 3.0612$, s = 1.7496

2.32 a. 11.025   b. 0.520

2.34 a. 261.54545   b. 17.370

2.36 a. 1392.5   b. 0.9930

2.38 a. 4.268
b. 0.128
c. Weak positive association between the number of drug units and the number of days to complete recovery. Recommend low or no dosage units.

2.40 a. −20.75   b. −0.937

2.42

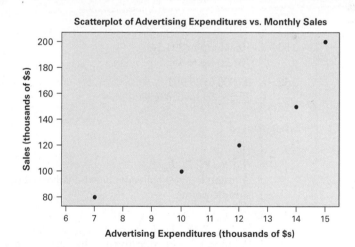

Scatterplot of Advertising Expenditures vs. Monthly Sales

Correlation = .93002

2.44 a. 18.1325   b. Sample variance = 204.7017,   s = 14.307

2.46 Variance = 123.78
Standard deviation = 11.13

2.48   a.

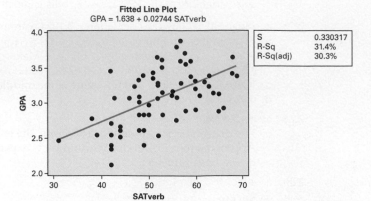

Fitted Line Plot
GPA = 1.638 + 0.02744 SATverb

S	0.330317
R-Sq	31.4%
R-Sq(adj)	30.3%

b. Describe the data numerically:

Covariances: GPA, SATverb

```
                  GPA SATverb
GPA          0.169284
SATverb      1.791637  65.293985
```

Correlations: GPA, SATverb

```
Pearson correlation of GPA and SATverb=0.560
P-Value=0.000
```

Regression Analysis: GPA versus SATverb

```
The regression equation is
GPA=1.64 + 0.0274 SATverb
```

c. 3.06

2.50   a. 195.46 up to 394.54
        b. 137.50 up to 452.50

2.52   a. 23,000 to 35,000
        b. 15,583.59 to 42,416.41

Chapter 3

3.2   a. (E_3, E_9)
        b. $(E_1, E_2, E_3, E_7, E_8, E_9)$
        c. A union B is not collectively exhaustive—it does not contain all of the possible sample points.

3.4   a. (E_3, E_6)
        b. $(E_3, E_4, E_5, E_6, E_9, E_{10})$
        c. A union B is not collectively exhaustive—it does not contain all of the possible sample points.

3.6   a. $(A \cap B)$ is the event that the Dow Jones average rises on both days, which is O_1. $(\overline{A} \cap B)$ is the event the Dow Jones average does not rise on the first day but it rises on the second day, which is O_3. The union between these two will be O_1 or O_3 either of which by definition is event B: The Dow Jones average rises on the second day.
        b. Since $(\overline{A} \cap B)$ is the event the Dow Jones average does not rise on the first day but rises on the second day, which is O_3, and because A is the event that the Dow Jones average rises on the first day, then the union will be O_2: either the Dow Jones average does not rise on the first day but rises on the second day or the Dow Jones average rises on the first day or both. This is the definition of A∪B.

3.8   .53

3.10 .3709

3.12 .0123

3.14 a. .54   b. .18
     c. A complement is the event that the rate of return is not more than 10%.
     d. .46
     e. The intersection between more than 10% and return will be negative is the null or
        empty set.
     f. 0
     g. The union of A and B is the event that the rates of return of are less than -10%,
        -10% to 0%, 10% to 20%, and more than 20%.
     h. .72
     i. A and B are mutually exclusive because their intersection is the null set.
     j. A and B are not collectively exhaustive because their union does not equal 1.

3.16 Note that A and B of exercise 3.2 are not mutually exclusive. So, we want to show that
     $P(A \cup B) \neq P(A) + P(B)$. Since $A = [E_1, E_3, E_7, E_9]$ and $B = [E_2, E_3, E_8, E_9]$, $A \cup B =$
     $[E_1, E_2, E_3, E_7, E_8, E_9]$. We also know that $P(A) = P(E_1) + P(E_3) + P(E_7) + P(E_9)$
     and $P(B) = P(E_2) + P(E_3) + P(E_8) + P(E_9)$. However, $P(A \cup B) = P(E_1) + P(E_2) +$
     $P(E_3) + P(E_7) + P(E_8) + P(E_9)$, which does not equal $P(A) + P(B) = P(E_1) + P(E_2) +$
     $2P(E_3) + P(E_7) + P(E_8) + 2P(E_9)$.

3.18 a. .87
     b. .35
     c. By the third probability postulate, the sum of the probabilities of all outcomes in the
        sample space must sum to 1.

3.20 0

3.22 .75

3.24 .80, A and B are independent since the P(A I B) of .80 equals the P(A) of .80.

3.26 .625, A and B are not independent since the P(A I B) of .625 does not equal the P(A) of .70.

3.28 a. 5,040
     b. 0.0001984

3.30 .00833

3.32 .0167

3.34 28

3.36 a. 150   b. .2667   c. .20

3.38 .35

3.40 a. No, the two events are not mutually exclusive because $P(A \cap B) \neq 0$.
     b. No, the two events are not collectively exhaustive because $P(A \cup B) \neq 1$.
     c. No, the two events are not statistically independent because $P(A \cap B) = .15 \neq .06 =$
        P(A)P(B).

3.42 a. .069

3.44 a. .5556   b. .8333

3.46 .1292

3.48 a. .9   b. .88   c. .925

3.50 a. 0.867
     b. Check if $P(A \cap B) = P(A)P(B)$. Since $.04 \neq .06$, the two events are not independent
        events.

3.52 .2

3.54 .05

3.56 .05

3.58 .1667

3.60 .40

3.62 Odds $= \dfrac{.5}{1-.5} = 1$ to 1 odds

3.64 2.00

3.66 a. .12
      b. .7037
      c. Check if $P(F \cap N) = P(F)P(N)$. Since .19 ≠ .2133, the two events are not independent.
      d. .3333
      e. Check if $P(I \cap O) = P(I)P(O)$. Since .07 ≠ .0399, the two events are not independent.
      f. .79
      g. .27
      h. .87

3.68 a. .25   b. .32   c. .16   d. .125   e. .2121

3.70 a. .32   b. .25   c. .375   d. .48   e. .4375
      f. No, since $P(A \cap Y)$ which is .12 ≠ $P(A)P(Y)$ which is .08

3.72 a. .76   b. .77   c. .4348

3.74 a. .025   b. .445   c. .2697

3.76 a. .475   b. .3684   c. .8571

3.78 .375

3.80 .3636

3.82 .6667

3.84 .6923

3.86 .444

3.88 Mutually exclusive events are events such that if one event occurs, the other event cannot occur. For example, a U.S. Senator voting in favor of a tax cut cannot also vote against it. Independent events are events such that the occurrence of one event has no effect on the probability of the other event. For example, whether or not you ate breakfast this morning is unlikely to have any effect on the probability of a U.S. Senator voting in favor of a tax cut.

3.90 Conditional probability is understanding the probability of one event given that another event has occurred. This is utilizing prior information that a specific event has occurred and then analyzing how that impacts the probability of another event. The importance is incorporating information about a known event. This has the impact of reducing the sample space in an experiment.

3.92 a. True   b. True   c. True   d. True
      e. False   f. False   g. False

3.94 a. False   b. False   c. True   d. False   e. False

3.96 a. .08   b. No   c. .267   d. .58

3.98 a. .105   b. .2625   c. .645   d. .5917
      e. No   f. No   g. No

3.100 a. .11   b. .69   c. .1833   d. No

3.102 a. .12   b. .7   c. No   d. .3333   e. .355

3.104 a. 66   b. .1667

3.106 a. .5192   b. .6482
       c. The probability of renewals in February have increased; however, the conditional probability of renewal fell in each of the categories.

3.108 .4828

3.110 a. .5138   b. .4629

3.112 a. .5   b. .84   c. No   d. .9898

3.114 a. .52   b. .8846

3.116 a. .43
       b. Not likely since wearing gloves reduces her probability.

3.118 .875

Chapter 4

4.2   Discrete random variable

4.4   Discrete random variable

4.6   Total sales, advertising expenditures, competitor's sales

4.8   Discrete

4.10 Probability distribution of number of heads in one toss

X-number of heads	P(x)
0	.5
1	.5

4.12 Various answers OK

X – # of Times Missing Class	P(x)	F(x)
0	.65	.65
1	.15	.80
2	.10	.90
3	.09	.99
4	.01	1.00

4.14 a. Cumulative probability function: OK

X	0	1	2	3	4	5	6	7	8	9
P(x)	.10	.08	.07	.15	.12	.08	.10	.12	.08	.10
F(x)	.10	.18	.25	.40	.52	.60	.70	.82	.90	1.00

       b. .48
       c. .57

4.16   a. Probability distribution function

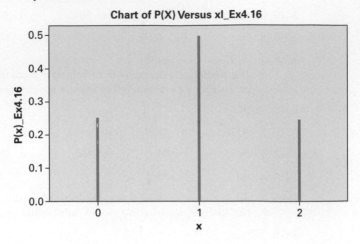

b. Cumulative probability function

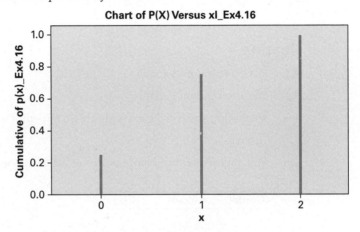

c. $\mu_x = 1.00$ d. $\sigma^2{}_x = 0.50$

4.18   a.

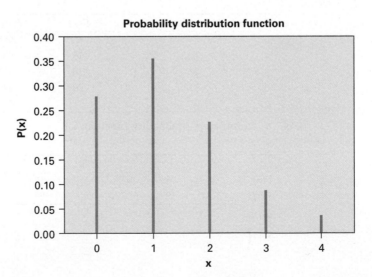

b.

x	F(x)
0	0.28
1	0.64
2	0.87
3	0.96
4	1.00

Cumulative distribution function

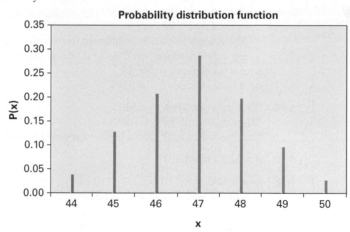

c. 1.25 returns
d. 1.1675

4.20 a. Probability function

Probability distribution function

b. Cumulative probability function

x	F(x)
44	0.04
45	0.17
46	0.38
47	0.67
48	0.87
49	0.97
50	1.00

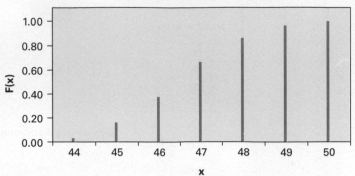

Cumulative distribution function

c. 0.7

d. 0.8556

e. $\mu_x = 46.9$ pounds per bag, $\sigma_x = 1.3964$ pounds per bag

f. $\mu = \$.812$, $\sigma_\pi = \$.0279$

4.22 a. Probability function

X	0	1	2
P(x)	0.81	0.18	.01

b. $P(Y = 0) = 153/190$

$P(Y = 1) = 36/190$

$P(Y = 2) = 1/190$

The answer in part b. is different from part a. because in part b. the probability of picking a defective part on the second draw depends upon the result of the first draw.

c. $\mu = 0.2$ defects, $\sigma_x^2 = .18$

d. $\mu = 0.2$ defects, $\sigma_y^2 = .1705$

4.24 "One and one" $E(X) = 1.3125$

"Two-shot foul" $E(X) = 1.50$

The "two-shot foul" has a higher expected value.

4.26 $\mu = 3.29$ $\sigma = 1.1515$

4.28 a. $\mu = 1.82$, $\sigma = 1.0137$

b. Cost: $\mu = \$2,730$, $\sigma = \$1,520.559$

4.30 $\mu_x = .5$

$\sigma_x^2 = .25$

4.32 $P(x = 7) = .06181$, $P(x < 6) = .7805$

4.34 $P(x = 12) = .1873$, $P(x < 6) = .000269$

4.36 a. $P(x \geq 1) = .7627$

b. $P(x \geq 3) = .1035$

4.38 .4233

4.40 a. .0312

b. .5

c. .6875

d. 2.5 wins
e. 3 wins

4.42   a. .4370   b. mean = 2.8 points, standard deviation = 1.908 points   c. .7

4.44   a. $E(X) = 64$, $\sigma_x = 7.871$
      b. $E(Z) = \$640$, $\sigma_z = \$78.71$

4.46   a. $E(X) = 483.6$, $\sigma_x = 10.3146$
      b. $E(Z) = \$967.20$, $\sigma_z = \$20.6292$

4.48   The acceptance rules have the following probabilities:
   (i)   Rule 1: $P(X = 0) = (.8)^{10} = .1074$
  (ii)   Rule 2: $P(X \le 1) = (.8)^{20} + 20(.2)(.8)^{19} = .0692$

The second acceptance rule will have the smaller probability of accepting a shipment containing 20% defectives.

4.50   .210376

4.52   .151769

4.54   .1999

4.56   .3808

4.58   .2619

4.60   .1254

4.62   .8705

4.64   .4232

4.66   .7898

4.68   .0884

4.70   .9380

4.72   Two models are possible—the poisson distribution is appropriate when the warehouse is serviced by many thousands of independent truckers where the mean number of 'successes' is relatively small. However, under the assumption of a small fleet of 10 trucks with a probability of any truck arriving during a given hour is .1, then the binomial distribution is the more appropriate model. Both models yield similar, although not identical, probabilities.

Cumulative Distribution Function
Poisson with mean = 1

x	P(X <= x)
0	0.36788
1	0.73576
2	0.91970
3	0.98101
4	0.99634
5	0.99941
6	0.99992
7	0.99999
8	1.00000
9	1.00000
10	1.00000

Cumulative Distribution Function

Binomial with n = 10 and p = 0.1

x	P(X <= x)
0	0.34868
1	0.73610
2	0.92981
3	0.98720
4	0.99837
5	0.99985
6	0.99999
7	1.00000
8	1.00000
9	1.00000
10	1.00000

4.74 a.

Y	X 1	2	P(y)
0	0.2	0.25	0.45
1	0.3	0.25	0.55
P(x)	0.5	0.5	1

b. $Cov(X, Y) = -.025$, $\rho = -.1005$

4.76 a. Compute marginal probability distributions for X and Y.

Y	X 1	2	P(y)
0	0.3	0.2	0.5
1	0.25	0.25	0.5
P(x)	0.55	0.45	1

b. $Cov(X, Y) = .025$, $\rho = .1005$
c. $\mu_W = 3.4$, $\sigma^2_W = 9.75$

4.78 a.

Y	X 1	2	P(y)
0	0.25	0.25	0.5
1	0.25	0.25	0.5
P(x)	0.5	0.5	1

b. $Cov(X, Y) = 0.0$, $\rho = 0.0$
c. $\mu_W = 2.0$, $\sigma^2_W = .50$

4.80 a.

Y	X 1	2	P(y)
0	0	0.6	0.6
1	0.4	0	0.4
P(x)	0.4	0.6	1

b. $Cov(X, Y) = -0.24$, $\rho = -1.00$
c. $\mu_W = 1.6$, $\sigma^2_W = .48$

4.82 a. $Px(0) = .22$ $Px(1) = .26$ $Px(2) = .43$ $Px(3) = .09$ $\mu_x = 1.39$
       b. $Py(0) = .23$ $Py(1) = .21$ $Py(2) = .30$ $Py(3) = .26$ $\mu_y = 1.59$

c. $P_{Y|X}(0|3) = .1111$ $\quad$ $P_{Y|X}(1|3) = .1111$
$\quad$ $P_{Y|X}(2|3) = .3333$ $\quad$ $P_{Y|X}(3|3) = .4444$
d. $Cov(X, Y) = .3399$
e. No, because $Cov(X,Y) \neq 0$

4.84 a. $Py(0) = .12$ $\quad$ $Py(1) = .24$ $\quad$ $Py(2) = .23$ $\quad$ $Py(3) = .23$ $\quad$ $Py(4) = .18$
b. $P_{Y|X}(y|3) = 1/26; 3/26; 6/26; 8/26; 8/26$
c. No, because $Px,y(3,4) = .08 \neq .0468 = Px(3)Py(4)$

4.86 a.

Y/X	0	1	Total
0	.704	.168	.872
1	.096	.032	.128
Total	.80	.20	1.00

b. $P_{Y|X}(y|0) = .88; .12$
c. $Px(0) = .80$ $\quad$ $Px(1) = .20$ $\quad$ $Py(0) = .872$ $\quad$ $Py(1) = .128$
d. $Cov(X, Y) = .0064$
The covariance indicates that there is a positive association between X and Y, professors are more likely to be away from the office on Friday than during the other days.

4.88 Number of total complaints (food complaints + service complaints) has a mean of (1.36 + 1.64) = 3.00. If the two types of complaints are independent, then the variance of total complaints is equal to the sum of the variance of the two types of complaints because the covariance would be zero. (.8104 + .7904) = 1.6008. The standard deviation will be the square root of the variance = 1.26523.

If the number of food and service complaints are not independent of each other, then the covariance would no longer be zero. The mean would remain the same; however, the standard deviation would change. The variance of the sum of the two types of complaints becomes the variance of one plus the variance of the other plus two times the covariance.

4.90 a. No, not necessarily. There is a probability distribution associated with the rates of return in the mutual fund and not all rates of return will equal the expected value.
b. Which fund to invest in will depend not only on the expected value of the return but also on the riskiness of each fund and how risk averse the client is.

4.92 a. 2.21
b. 1.3513
c. Mean salary = \$913. Standard deviation of salary = \$405.39
d. To earn a salary of \$1,000 or more, the salesperson must sell at least three cars. $P(X \geq 3) = .16 + .12 + .07 = .35$

4.94 a. Positive covariance: Consumption expenditures and disposable income
b. Negative covariance: Price of cars and the number of cars sold
c. Zero covariance: Dow Jones stock market average and rainfall in Brazil

4.96 a. .17
b. $\mu_x = 2.59, \mu_y = 1.1$
c. $Cov(X,Y) = .191$. This implies that there is a positive relationship between the number of years in school and the number of visits to a museum in the last year.

4.98 a. .3369 $\qquad\qquad$ b. .5931
c. $\mu = 44$. The proportion is .55. $\sigma = 4.4497$. The proportion is .05562.

4.100 To evaluate the effectiveness of the analyst's ability, find the probability that x is greater than or equal to 3 at random. $P(x \geq 3) = .16683$

4.102 a. $P(0) = .09072$ $\qquad\qquad$ b. $P(x > 3) = .2213$

4.104 $P(x = 0) = .0907$. Let Y be the number of stalls for both lines. Find the $P(Y \geq 1) = .99177$

4.106 The mean of the trade balance is $10,000. The variance of the trade balance is $17,000.

Chapter 5

5.2 0.45

5.4 0.35

5.6 a.

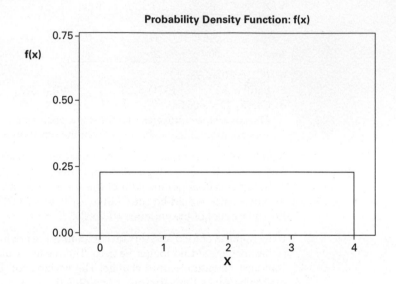

b.

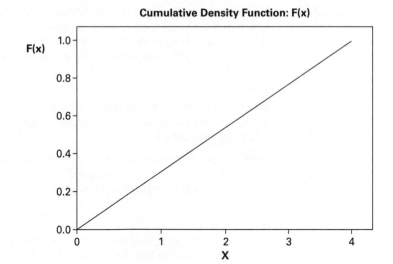

c. .25
d. .25

5.8 a. .2   b. $.4 < P(X < 400) < .6$

5.10 $\mu_W = 900$, $\sigma^2{}_W = 360$

5.12 $\mu_W = 4{,}000$, $\sigma^2_W = 8{,}100$

5.14 $\mu_Y = \$26.4$ million, $\sigma_Y = \$1$ million

5.16 $\mu_Y = \$54{,}000$, $\sigma_Y = \$14{,}400$

5.18   a. .52   b. −.67   c. .84   d. −.25

5.20   a. .9772   b. .3674   c. = .0062   d. 92.8   e. $X = 70$ and 90

5.22   a. .6554   b. .6554
       c. The graph should show the property of symmetry—the area in the tails equidistant from the mean will be equal.
       d. .6006
       e. The area under the normal curve is equal to .8 for an infinite number of ranges—merely start at a point that is marginally higher. The shortest range will be the one that is centered on the z of zero. The z that corresponds to an area of .8 centered on the mean is a Z of ±1.28. This yields an interval of the mean plus and minus $64: [$316, $444].

5.24   a. .2266   b. .2266   c. .5468
       d. (i) The graph should show the property of symmetry—the area in the tails equidistant from the mean will be equal.
       e. (ii) The answers to a, b, c sum to one because the events cover the entire area under the normal curve, which by definition, must sum to 1.

5.26   a. .2148   b. .1587   c. .3692
       d. The answer to a. will be larger because 10 grams is closer to the mean than is 15 grams. Thus, there would be a greater area remaining less than 10 grams than will be the area above 15 grams.

5.28   .0668

5.30 $\mu = 15.265$, $\sigma^2 = 14.317$

5.32   For Investment A, the probability of a return higher than 10%

$$P(Z > \frac{10 - 10.4}{1.2}) = P(Z > -.33) = F_Z(.33) = .6293$$

       For Investment B, the probability of a return higher than 10%

$$P(Z > \frac{10 - 11.0}{4}) = P(Z > -.25) = F_Z(.28) = .5987$$

       Therefore, Investment A is a better choice.

5.34   a. 98.8   b. 183.6   c. .9487

5.36   a. .3721   b. 522.4   c. 400 – 439   d. 520 – 559   e. .2922

5.38   .4990

5.40   a. .0054   b. .0002   c. .9892
       d. $X = 1573.741 \approx 1{,}574$ successes
       e. $X = 1616.46 \approx 1616$ successes

5.42   a. .0000   b. .0005   c. .9990
       d. $P = 38.971\%$ e. $P = 41.642\%$

5.44   a. .0475   b. .3372

5.46   .0207

5.48   .2877

5.50 .864665

5.52 .2019

5.54 .4866

5.56 .3012

5.58 a. $P(X > 3) = 1 - [1 - e^{-(3/\mu)}] = e^{-3\lambda}$ since $\lambda = 1 / \mu$

b. $P(X > 6) = 1 - [1 - e^{-(6/\mu)}] = e^{-(6/\mu)} = e^{-6\lambda}$

c. $P(X > 6 \,|\, X > 3) = P(X > 6)/P(X > 3) = e^{-6\lambda} / e^{-3\lambda}] = e^{-3\lambda}$
    The probability of an occurrence within a specified time in the future is not related to how much time has passed since the most recent occurrence.

5.60 a. .1889   b. .4866   c. .2279

5.62 $\mu_W = 1,300$, $\sigma^2_W = 4,900$

5.64 $\mu_W = 1,700$, $\sigma^2_W = 4,900$

5.66 $\mu_x = 28,000$, $\sigma_x = 12,000$

5.68 $\mu_Y = 162,000$

      $\sigma_Y = 18,027.76$

5.70 The calculation of the mean is correct, but the standard deviations of two random variables cannot be summed. To get the correct standard deviation, add the variances together and then take the square root. The standard deviation: $\sigma = \sqrt{5(16)^2} = 35.7771$.

5.72 a. $\mu_W = 2,850$, $\sigma^2_W = 992,500$
      b. $\mu_W = 2,850$, $\sigma^2_W = 332,500$

5.74 a. $\mu_W = 100$, $\sigma^2_W = 256.90465$
      b. .3483

5.76 a. $\mu_W = -5$, $\sigma^2_W = 21.79449$
      b. .4090

5.78 a.

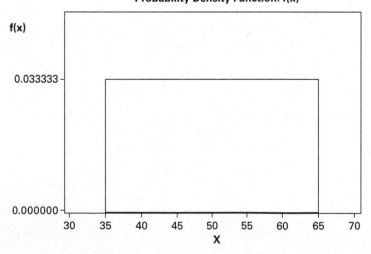

Probability Density Function: f(x)

b. Cumulative density function

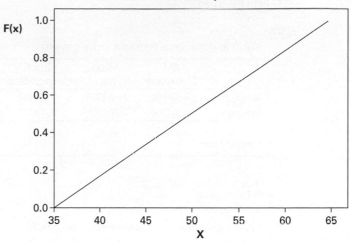

Cumulative Density Function: F(x)

c. 10/30
d. 50

5.80 a. $\mu_Y = 3{,}360$ b. $\sigma_Y = 80$

5.82 Given that the variance of both predicted earnings and forecast error are both positive and given that the variance of actual earnings is equal to the sum of the variances of predicted earnings and forecast error, then the variance of predicted earnings must be less than the variance of actual earnings.

5.84 a. .2119   b. .3759   c. 3.24   d. .7190   e. .3789

5.86 a. .3085
      b. .6826
      c. $X_i = 149.35$
      d. .9916
      e. 0.0417
      f. $90 - 109$
      g. $130 - 149$

5.88 .0436

5.90 $P(Z < 6.45) \approx 1.0000$

5.92 P(fewer than 10 calls in 12-hour period) = .0699
      P(more than 17 calls in 12-hour period) = .2511

5.94 a. .0475
      b. 236.95 (237 listeners)

5.96 .975

5.98 a. $\mu_W = 200$, $\sigma^2_W = 3{,}204.919$
      b. Option 1: $\sigma^2_1 = 3{,}813.744$, Option 2: $\sigma^2_2 = 2{,}665.66$
      To reduce the variance of the porfolio, select Option 2.

5.100 a. .1020   b. .2764

5.102 Mean for portfolio = 22.05
Variance for portfolio = 24.68
The narrowest interval that contains 95% of the distribution of portfolio value is (12.31, 31.79).

5.104

Mean and variance for stock price growth

	3M Company	Alcoa Inc.	Intel Corporation	Potlatch Corp.	General Motors	Sea Containers
Mean	0.001992	0.004389	–0.000082	0.007449	–0.014355	–0.146323
Variance	0.002704	0.005060	0.006727	0.006674	0.014518	0.176663

Covariance

	3M Company	Alcoa Inc.	Intel Corporation	Potlatch Corp.	General Motors
3M Company					
Alcoa Inc.	0.00153782				
Intel Corporation	0.00163165	0.00184360			
Potlatch Corp	0.00012217	0.00197600	0.00144736		
General Motors	–0.00005101	0.00103371	–0.00006588	0.00246545	
Sea Containers	0.00075015	0.00706908	–0.00131221	–0.00151704	0.01077420

Mean for portfolio = –0.0245
Variance for portfolio = 0.0074

5.106

Mean and variance for stock price growth

	AB Volvo	Pentair, Inc.	Reliant Energy, Inc.	TCF Financial Corporation	3M Company	Restoration Hardware, Inc.
Mean	0.019592	0.007641	0.019031	–0.004087	0.001992	–0.013406
Variance	0.004805	0.006227	0.012686	0.004001	0.002704	0.027618

Covariance

	AB Volvo	Pentair, Inc.	Reliant Energy, Inc.	TCF Financial Corporation	3M Company
AB Volvo					
Pentair, Inc.	0.00074848				
Reliant Energy, Inc.	0.00228027	0.00105381			
TCF Financial Corporation	–0.00001514	–0.00021080	–0.00041228		
3M Company	0.00099279	0.00087718	0.00031032	0.00072435	
Restoration Hardware, Inc.	0.00117969	0.00169410	0.00055922	–0.00041072	0.00204408

Mean for 1st portfolio = 0.00513
Variance for 1st portfolio = 0.00225

Mean for 2nd portfolio = 0.01232
Variance for 2nd portfolio = 0.00278

The 2nd portfolio has a higher mean and a higher variance. Recall that risk is directly related to variance. Since the 2nd portfolio has a significantly larger mean and only a slightly larger variance, it would be the better choice.

Chapter 6

6.2 a.   b.

Probability Density Function
```
Binomial with n = 2 and p = 0.5
x   p( X = x )
0      0.25
1      0.50
2      0.25
```

Probability Density Function
```
Binomial with n = 4 and p = 0.5
x   p( X = x )
0      0.0625
1      0.2500
2      0.3750
3      0.2500
4      0.0625
```

c.

Probability Density Function
```
Binomial with n = 10 and p = 0.5
x    P( X = x )
 0    0.000977
 1    0.009766
 2    0.043945
 3    0.117188
 4    0.205078
 5    0.246094
 6    0.205078
 7    0.117188
 8    0.043945
 9    0.009766
10    0.000977
```

6.4 The response should note that there will be errors in taking a census of the entire population as well as errors in taking a sample. Improved accuracy can be achieved via sampling methods versus taking a complete census (see reference to Hogan, 90). By using
sample information, we can make valid inferences about the entire population without
the time and expense involved in taking a census.

6.6 a. $\mu_{\bar{x}} = \mu = 100$, $\sigma_{\bar{x}}^2 = 30$
     b. .0505
     c. .7337
     d. .8997

6.8 a. $\mu_{\bar{x}} = \mu = 400$, $\sigma_{\bar{x}}^2 = 45.7143$
     b. .0384
     c. .7016
     d. .0516

6.10 a. $E(\overline{X}) = \mu_{\bar{x}} = 1{,}200$
     b. $\sigma_{\bar{x}}^2 = 17{,}778$
     c. $\sigma_{\bar{x}} = 133.33$
     d. .1292

6.12 a. .9772   b. .5763   c. .3108   d. $214,000 to $216,000
     e. The results were still valid because of the central limit theorem with the sample size
        being larger than 30.

6.14 a. $\sigma_{\bar{x}} = 5.5$ b. .9909   c. .8980   d. .4329
     e. Higher, higher, lower. The graph will show that the standard error of the sample
        means will decrease with an increased sample size.

6.16 a. $\sigma_{\bar{x}} = 4$ b. .1056   c. .1587   d. .4532

6.18   a. Difference = .2632
      b. Difference = $-.2048$
      c. Difference = $\pm.2304$

6.20   a. n = 68   b. smaller   c. larger

6.22   a. N = 20, correction factor $= \dfrac{0}{19}$

          N = 40, correction factor $= \dfrac{20}{39}$

          N = 100, correction factor $= \dfrac{80}{99}$

          N = 1,000, correction factor $= \dfrac{980}{999}$

          N = 10,000, correction factor $= \dfrac{9,980}{9,999}$

      b. When the population size (N) equals the sample size (n), then there is no variation away from the population mean and the standard error will be zero. As the sample size becomes relatively small compared to the population size, the correction factor tends towards 1 and the correction factor becomes less significant in the calculation of the standard error.
      c. The correction factor tends toward a value of 1 and becomes progressively less important as a modifying factor when the sample size decreases relative to the population size.

6.24   a. .2546   b. .0951   c. = .0086

6.26   a. .1539   b. .0122   c. .8339

6.28   a. .1112   b. .0071   c. .8372

6.30   a. .424   b. .00244   c. .0494   d. .0618

6.32   a. .20   b. .000889   c. .0298   d. .0465

6.34   .7372

6.36   a. .0351   b. .9222   c. .4314   d. Higher, higher

6.38   The largest value for σ_p is when p = .5. In this case, $\sigma_p = \sqrt{\dfrac{(.5)(.5)}{100}} = .05$

6.40   a. .0395
      b. Difference = .0506
      c. Difference = .065
      d. Difference = .0409

6.42   a. .0057

6.44   a. $\sigma_{\hat{p}} = 0.0447$
      b. $P(\hat{p} < 0.33) = 0.0582$
      c. $P(0.38 < \hat{p} < 0.46) = 0.5825$

6.46 $P(Z > 4.61) \approx .0000$

6.48   a. .1587
      b. $s^2 < 57.702$
      c. $s^2 > 151.879$

6.50 Between .01 and .025 (.0201 exactly)

6.52 a. Just greater than .1 (.1187 exactly)
      b. Between .01 and .025 (.0118 exactly)

6.54 a. Between .025 and .05 (.0428 exactly)
      b. Less than .005 (.0004 exactly)

6.56

Descriptive Statistics: C1, C2, C3, C4, C5, C6, C7, C8, ...

Variable	Mean	Variance
C1	4.500	3.667
C2	4.75	4.92
C3	5.00	6.67
C4	4.75	4.92
C5	5.00	6.67
C6	5.25	7.58
C7	5.25	4.92
C8	5.50	6.33
C9	5.75	6.92
C10	5.75	6.92
C11	5.750	1.583
C12	6.000	2.667
C13	6.250	2.917
C14	6.250	2.917
C15	6.750	0.917

$$\bar{x} = \frac{70.518}{15} = 4.7012 \quad E(s^2) = \frac{15(3.91667)}{(14)} = 4.1964$$

which is not equal to $\sigma^2 = \frac{47}{12} = 3.91667$

6.58 a. 163.11%
      b. The probability is .95 that the sample variance is between 30% and 211.33% of the population variance.
      c. The interval in part b. will be smaller.

6.60 a. 41.55%
      b. 50.73%
      c. The probability is .95 that the sample variance is between 34.727% and 199.27% of the population variance.

6.62 Less than .90 (.5438 exactly)

6.64 a. 15 possible samples
      b. (41, 39), (41, 35), (41, 35), (41, 33), (41, 38), (39, 35), (39, 35), (39, 33), (39, 38), (35, 35), (35, 33), (35, 38), (35, 33), (35, 38), (33, 38)
      c. $\frac{2}{15}$ for 34 and 36.5

      $\frac{1}{15}$ for all others

d.. $34P_{\overline{X}}(34) = 34\dfrac{2}{15} = 4.5333$ $37P_{\overline{X}}(37) = 37\dfrac{3}{15} = 7.4$

$35P_{\overline{X}}(35) = \dfrac{35}{15} = 2.3333$ $38P_{\overline{X}}(38) = 38\dfrac{2}{15} = 5.0667$

$35.5P_{\overline{X}}(35.5) = \dfrac{35.5}{15} = 2.3667$ $38.5P_{\overline{X}}(38.5) = \dfrac{38.5}{15} = 2.5667$

$36P_{\overline{X}}(36) = \dfrac{36}{15} = 2.4$ $39.5P_{\overline{X}}(39.5) = \dfrac{39.5}{15} = 2.6333$

$36.5P_{\overline{X}}(36.5) = 36.5\dfrac{2}{15} = 4.8667$ $40P_{\overline{X}}(40) = \dfrac{40}{15} = 2.6667$

The mean of the sampling distribution of the sample mean is $\Sigma \overline{x}P_{\overline{x}}(\overline{x}) = 36.8333$.

which is exactly equal to the population mean: $\dfrac{1}{N}\Sigma x_i = 36.8333$. This is the result expected from the Central Limit Theorem.

6.66 a. .0668   b. .7745   c. 445.6   d. 394.4
e. $s_x = 123.1868$ f. $s_x = 75.966$ g. Smaller

6.68 a. .0228   b. .9544   c. $X_i = 13.3825$
d. $s_x = 8.1414$ e. Smaller

6.70 Let $n = N$, then $\overline{X} = \mu_x$:

$$E\left[\sum_{i-1}^{N}(X_i - \overline{X})^2\right] = n\sigma_x^2 - n\dfrac{\sigma_x^2}{n}\dfrac{N-n}{N-1} = n\sigma_x^2 - \dfrac{N-n}{N-1}\sigma_x^2 =$$

$$\dfrac{\sigma_x^2}{N-1}(nN - n - N + n) = \dfrac{N\sigma_x^2}{N-1}(n-1)$$

Therefore, $E\left[\dfrac{1}{n-1}\sum(X_i - \overline{X})^2\right] = \dfrac{1}{n-1}E\left[\sum(X_i - \overline{X})^2\right] = \dfrac{N\sigma_x^2}{N-1}$

6.72 a. $P(\hat{p} < 0.7) = 0.0262$ b. $P(\hat{p} < 0.7) = 0.2709$ c. $P(\hat{p} < 38,000) = 0.2709$
d. 0.5987

6.74 .005

6.76 .6826

6.78 a. .3739   b. .4397   c. Difference $= \pm.0322$

6.80 a. More than .99 (.9979 exactly)
b. Between .9 and .95 (.9354 exactly)

6.82 a. $\overline{X} = 708.03, s = 8.106, \sigma_{\overline{X}} = 3.625$
b. $P(\overline{X} < 685) = 0.0000$
c. $P(\overline{X} > 720) = 0.0029$

6.84 a. $\overline{X} = 1135.178, s^2 = 11.3382, \sigma_{\overline{X}}^2 = 1.8898$
b. $P(1,120 < \overline{X} < 1,150) = 1.000$

Chapter 7

7.2   a. There appears to be no evidence of non-normality, as shown by the normal probability plot shown below.

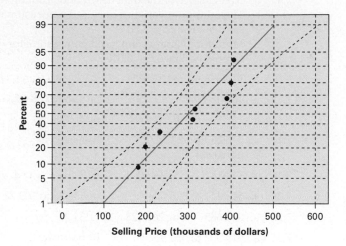

     b. 301.375 thousand dollars
     c. 1046.64
     d. 0.375

7.4   a. Unbiased point estimator of the population mean is the sample mean: $\bar{x} = 24.42$
     b. The unbiased point estimator of the population variance: $s^2 = 85.72$
     c. Unbiased point estimator of the variance of the sample mean: $Var(\overline{X}) = 7.1433$
     d. Unbiased estimator of the population proportion: $\hat{p} = .25$
     e. Unbiased estimator of the variance of the sample proportion: $Var(\hat{p}) = .015625$

7.6   a. $E(\overline{X}) = \dfrac{1}{2}E(X_1) + \dfrac{1}{2}E(X_2) = \dfrac{\mu}{2} + \dfrac{\mu}{2} = \mu$

$$E(Y) = \dfrac{1}{4}E(X_1) + \dfrac{3}{4}E(X_2) = \dfrac{\mu}{4} + \dfrac{3\mu}{4} = \mu$$

$$E(Z) = \dfrac{1}{3}E(X_1) + \dfrac{2}{3}E(X_2) = \dfrac{\mu}{3} + \dfrac{2\mu}{3} = \mu$$

     b. $Var(\overline{X}) = \dfrac{\sigma^2}{n} = \dfrac{1}{4}Var(X_1) + \dfrac{1}{4}Var(X_2) = \dfrac{\sigma^2}{4}$

$$Var(Y) = \dfrac{1}{16}Var(X_1) + \dfrac{9}{16}Var(X_2) = \dfrac{5\sigma^2}{8}$$

$$Var(Z) = \dfrac{1}{9}Var(X_1) + \dfrac{4}{9}Var(X_2) = \dfrac{5\sigma^2}{9}$$

$\overline{X}$ is most efficient since $Var(\overline{X}) < Var(Y)$ and $Var(\overline{X}) < Var(Z)$

c. Relative efficiency between Y and $\overline{X}$: $\dfrac{Var(Y)}{Var(\overline{X})} = 2.5$

Relative efficiency between Z and $\overline{X}$: $\dfrac{Var(Z)}{Var(\overline{X})} = 2.222$

7.8   a. No evidence of the data distribution coming from a non-normal population.
      b. The minimum variance unbiased point estimator of the population mean is the sample mean: $\overline{x} = 3.8079$.
      c. Minimum variance unbiased point estimator of the population variance is the sample variance $s^2 = 0.0105$.

7.10   a. 3.495   b. 23.552

7.12   a. 40.2 to 59.8   b. 81.56 to 88.44   c. 506.2652 to 513.73478

7.14   a. 1.75   b. .63246   c. 2.2136

7.16   a. 3.9926 up to 4.1474   b. narrower
       c. narrower   d. wider

7.18   a. 13.9182   b. 19.007   c. 3.493   d. 7.5407

7.20   a. 541.424 to 578.576   b. 156.28 to 163.72   c. 49.9474 to 66.0526

7.22   a. 83.9685   b. 24.1428   c. 34.22

7.24   a. 519.379 to 522.517   b. narrower

7.26   5.9152

7.28 $41,104.28 up to $44,375.72

7.30   a. .02898   b. .03761   c. .010897

7.32   a. .079055 to .120945   b. 0.0 to .031696   c. 0.4555 to 0.5445

7.34   .5846 up to .8260

7.36   95% confidence interval: .2026 up to .2974

7.38   84.14%

7.40   .1079 up to .2173

7.42   a. 9.8332   b. 34.9218   c. 126.9138

7.44   a. $4.21496 < \sigma^2 < 56.25879$
       b. $3.59066 < \sigma^2 < 82.6446$

7.46   15.3713 up to 78.1027

7.48   66.6444 up to 212.0784
       Assume that the population is normally distributed.

7.50   a. .4062 up to 2.3077

7.52   a. (139.85, 144.15)   b. (230.78, 234.02)   c. (57.77, 60.83)

7.54   a. (0.1882, 0.3118)   b. (0.4849, 0.7497)

7.56   a. (8.2262, 11.1738)
       b. (1466.6390, 2199.9610)

7.58   a. (5.4904, 9.0696)   b. (767.3696, 1,052.6304)

7.60 $95,849.2706 < N\mu < 113,135.9294$

7.62   .4884 up to .6316

7.64   128.688 < Np < 196.812 or between 129 and 197 students intend to take the final.

7.66   It is recommended that he stock 157 gallons.

7.68   129.27 up to 143.17

7.70   a. The minimum variance unbiased point estimator of the population mean is 3.375.
       The unbiased point estimate of the variance is .4993.
       b. .375

7.72   64.24%

7.74   a. 2.064   b. 5.257

7.76   a. 1.729   b. 46.78 or approximately 47 passengers

7.78   a. (3.05620, 3.19980)   b. 0.368162 up to 0.53184   c. 0.30977 up to 0.47023

7.80   a. 28.56856% up to 35.4314% b. 24.0644% up to 31.9356%

7.82   96.76%

7.84   42.0134 up to 43.18664

7.86   a. 442.9139 up to 541.7501   b. 454.8175 up to 529.9025
       c. The 90% interval is narrower.

Chapter 8

8.2   a. .79772   b. −2.59766 to −1.00234   c. 2.07737

8.4 $27.0649 < \mu_x - \mu_y < 47.5351$

8.6   32.0067 up to 47.9933

8.8   a. 24   b. 11   c. 19

8.10   a. $v \approx 24$ b. $v \approx 11$ c. $v \approx 19$ d. $v \approx 11$

8.12   5.4831 up to 14.5169

8.14   5.0579 up to 9.3421

8.16   −.00591 up to .061907

8.18   a. .083367   b. .063062   c. .056126

8.20   .0971 up to .3625

8.22   −0.3001 to −0.0627

8.24   −.0314 up to .0816

8.26   a. 1068   b. 385
       c. Keeping the confidence level constant, fewer observations are needed if the margin
       of error is increased.

8.28   a. 423   b. 601   c. 543

8.30   752

8.32   a. 345   b. 357   c. 385
       d. The required sample size for part (b) is larger than that for part (a), and the required
       sample size for part (c) is larger than that for parts (a) and (b). This shows that the
       required sample size increases as N increases.

8.34   262

8.36   217

8.38   25.4893 to 54.5107

8.40   a. −60.21056 to −19.7894   b. −60.669 to −19.331

8.42   −6.2971 to 2.8971

8.44   −0.04136 to 0.14295

8.46 6.055 up to 13.945. Assume both populations are distributed normally with equal variances and a 90% confidence level. Since both endpoints of the confidence interval are positive, this provides evidence that the new machine provides a larger mean filling weight than the old.

8.48 -1.18066 to 10.18066

8.50 .23915 up to .36085

8.52 178

Chapter 9

9.2 H_0: No change in interest rates is warranted.
H_1: Reduce interest rates to stimulate the economy.

9.4 a. European perspective:
H_0: Genetically modified food stuffs are not safe.
H_1: They are safe.
b. U.S. farmer perspective:
H_0: Genetically modified food stuffs are safe.
H_1: They are not safe.

9.6 a. Reject H_0 if $\bar{x} > \bar{x}_c = \mu_0 + z_\alpha \sigma / \sqrt{n} = 108.225$
b. Reject H_0 if $\bar{x} > \bar{x}_c = \mu_0 + z_\alpha \sigma / \sqrt{n} = 110.28125$
c. Reject H_0 if $\bar{x} > \bar{x}_c = \mu_0 + z_\alpha \sigma / \sqrt{n} = 106.1998$
d. Reject H_0 if $\bar{x} > \bar{x}_c = \mu_0 + z_\alpha \sigma / \sqrt{n} = 107.26994$

9.8 The critical value $\bar{x}_c$ is farther away from the hypothesized value the smaller the sample size n. This is due to the increase in the standard error with a smaller sample size.
The critical value $\bar{x}_c$ is farther away from the hypothesized value the larger the population variance. This is due to the increased standard error with a larger population variance.

9.10 a. .0004   b. .0475   c. .0062   d. .020

9.12 $H_0 : \mu \geq 50; H_1 : \mu < 50$; reject H_0 if $Z_{.10} < -1.28$
$$Z = \frac{48.2 - 50}{3/\sqrt{9}} = -1.8,$$ therefore, reject H_0 at the 10% level.

9.14 a. Reject if $t = \dfrac{\bar{x} - \mu_0}{s/\sqrt{n}} > t_{n-1,\alpha/2}$, $t = 2.00$. Since 2.00 is greater than the critical value of 1.711, there is sufficient evidence to reject the null hypothesis.
b. Reject if $t = \dfrac{\bar{x} - \mu_0}{s/\sqrt{n}} > t_{n-1,\alpha/2}$, $t = 2.00$. Since 2.00 is greater than the critical value of 1.711, there is sufficient evidence to reject the null hypothesis.
c. Reject if $t = \dfrac{\bar{x} - \mu_0}{s/\sqrt{n}} < -t_{n-1,\alpha/2}$, $t = -2.50$. Since -2.50 is less than the critical value of -1.711, there is sufficient evidence to reject the null hypothesis.
d. Reject if $t = \dfrac{\bar{x} - \mu_0}{s/\sqrt{n}} < -t_{n-1,\alpha/2}$, $t = -2.22$. Since -2.22 is less than the critical value of -1.711, there is sufficient evidence to reject the null hypothesis.

9.16 $H_0 : \mu \geq 3; H_1 : \mu < 3$;
$$Z = \frac{2.4 - 3}{1.8/\sqrt{100}} = -3.33,$$ p-value $= .0004$, therefore, reject H_0 at significance levels
less than .04%; $\alpha = .04$

9.18 $H_0 : \mu = 0; H_1 : \mu \neq 0;$

$Z = \dfrac{.078 - 0}{.201/\sqrt{76}} = 3.38$, p-value = .0008, therefore, reject H_0 at significance levels less

than .08%; $\alpha = .08$

9.20 $H_0 : \mu = 0; H_1 : \mu < 0;$

$Z = \dfrac{-2.91 - 0}{11.33/\sqrt{170}} = -3.35$, p-value = .0004, therefore, reject H_0 at any common level

of alpha.

9.22 a. No, the 95% confidence level provides for 2.5% of the area in either tail. This does not correspond to a one-tailed hypothesis test with an alpha of 5%, which has 5% of the area in one of the tails.
   b. Yes.

9.24 $H_0 : \mu = 20; H_1 : \mu \neq 20;$ reject H_0 if $|t_{8, .05/2}| > 2.306$

$t = \dfrac{20.3556 - 20}{.6126/\sqrt{9}} = 1.741$, therefore, do not reject H_0 at the 5% level.

9.26 The population values must be assumed to be normally distributed.
   $H_0 : \mu \geq 50; H_1 : \mu < 50;$ reject H_0 if $t_{19, .05} < -1.729$

$t = \dfrac{41.3 - 50}{12.2/\sqrt{20}} = -3.189$, therefore, reject H_0 at the 5% level.

9.28 a. .2907   b. .30427   c. .28256   d. .2771

9.30 $H_0 : p \leq .25; H_1 : p > .25;$
   $z = 1.79$, p-value = .0367, therefore, reject H_0 at alpha greater than 3.67%.

9.32 $H_0 : p = .5; H_1 : p \neq 5;$
   $z = -1.26$, p-value = .2076. The probability of finding a random sample with a sample proportion this far or further from .5 if the null hypothesis is really true is .2076.

9.34 $H_0 : p = .5; H_1 : p > .5;$
   $z = .85$, p-value = .1977, therefore, reject H_0 at alpha levels in excess of 19.77%.

9.36 $H_0 : p \geq .75; H_1 : p < 75;$
   $z = -1.87$, p-value = .0307, therefore, reject H_0 at alpha levels in excess of 3.07%.

9.38 a. .8349   b. .0233   c. .6876   d. .8349   e. .0694

9.40 a. H_0 is rejected when $\dfrac{\overline{X} - 3}{4/\sqrt{64}} > 1.645$ or when $\overline{X} > 3.082$. Since the sample mean is

   3.07%, which is less than the critical value, the decision is to not reject the null hypothesis.
   b. $\beta = .3594$. The power of the test = $1 - \beta = .6406$

9.42 H_0 is rejected when $\dfrac{p - .5}{\sqrt{.25/802}} < -1.28$ or when p < .477

   The power of the test = $1 - \beta = .9382$

9.44 a. H_0 is rejected when $-1.645 > \dfrac{p - .5}{\sqrt{.25/199}} > 1.645$ or when .442 > p > .558. Since the

   sample proportion is .5226, which is within the critical values, the decision is do not reject the null hypothesis.
   b. $\beta = .1131$

9.46 a. $\alpha = P(Z > 1.33) = .0918$
   b. $\alpha = P(Z > 2.67) = .0038$. Note that the larger sample size results in a smaller standard error of the mean.

c. $\beta = .0668$

d. i) lower, ii) higher

9.48 Reject H_0 at the 10% level.

9.50 Reject H_0 at the 5% level.

9.52 Do not reject H_0 at the 10% level.

9.54 The p-value indicates the likelihood of getting the sample result at least as far away from the hypothesized value as the one that was found, assuming that the distribution is really centered on the null hypothesis. The smaller the p-value, the stronger the evidence against the null hypothesis.

9.56 a. False   b. True   c. True   d. False
e. False   f. True   g. False

9.58 a. $\alpha = P(Z < -2) = .0228$ b. $\beta = P(Z > 3) = .0014$
c. i) smaller   ii) smaller   d. i) smaller   ii) larger

9.60 $H_0 : p = .5; H_1 : p \neq .5;$
$z = -.39$, p-value $= .6966$, therefore, reject H_0 at levels in excess of 69.66%.

9.62 $H_0 : p \leq .25; H_1 : p > .25;$ reject H_0 if $z_{.05} > 1.645$
$z = 2.356$, therefore, reject H_0 at the 5% level.

9.64 Cost Model where W = Total Cost: $W = 1,000 + 5X$
$\mu_W = 1,000 + 5(400) = 3,000$

$\sigma_W^2 = (5)^2(625) = 15,625, \sigma_W = 125, \sigma_{\overline{W}} = \dfrac{125}{\sqrt{25}} = 25$

$H_0 : W \leq 3,000; H_1 : W > 3,000;$

Using the test statistic criteria: $(3,050 - 3,000)/25 = 2.00$ which yields a p-value of .0228, therefore, reject H_0 at the .05 level.

Using the sample statistic criteria: $\overline{X}_{crit} = 3,000 + (25)(1.645) = 3041.1, \overline{X}_{calc} = 3,050,$ since $\overline{X}_{crit} = 3,050 > \overline{X}_{crit} = 3041.1$, therefore, reject H_0 at the .05 level.

9.66 Assume that the population of matched differences are normally distributed.
$H_0 : \mu_x - \mu_y = 0; H_1 : \mu_x - \mu_y \neq 0;$
$t = 1.961$, therefore, reject H_0 at the 10% level since $1.96 > 1.796 = t_{(11, .05)}$

9.68 $H_0 : \mu \leq 40, H_1 : \mu > 40; \overline{X} = 49.73 > 42.86$ reject H_0

One-Sample T: Salmon Weight
```
Test of mu = 40 vs mu > 40

Variable              N      Mean      StDev    SE Mean
Salmon Weigh         39     49.73      10.60       1.70

Variable         95.0% Lower Bound          T      P
Salmon Weigh                  46.86       5.73  0.000
```

Reject the null and accept the alternative that the mean weight is significantly greater than 40

$\overline{X}_{crit} = H_0 + t_{crit}(S_{\overline{x}}) = 42.8662$

Population mean for $\beta = .50$ (power $= .50$): $t_{crit} = 0.0$: 42.8662

Population mean for $\beta = .25$ (power $= .75$): $t_{crit} = .681$: 44.0239

Population mean for $\beta = .10$ (power $= .90$): $t_{crit} = 1.28$: 45.0422

Population mean for $\beta = .05$ (power $= .95$): $t_{crit} = 1.645$: 45.6627

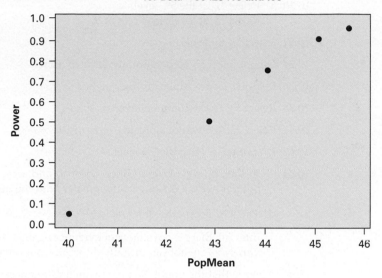

Power Curve
for Beta = 50 .25 .10 and .05

Power

PopMean

9.70   a. Assume that the population is normally distributed. Do not reject H_0 at the 5% level.
      b. Assume that the population is normally distributed. Reject H_0 at the 5% level.

Chapter 10

10.2   a. $t = -1.50$, p-value $= .073$, do not reject H_0 at alpha of .05.
      b. $t = -1.00$, p-value $= .164$, do not reject H_0 at alpha of .05.
      c. $t = -2.00$, p-value $= .028$
      d. $t = -.75$, p-value $= .230$

10.4 $t = 2.239$, p-value $= .0301$, reject H_0 at levels in excess of 3%.

10.6   a. No   b. Yes   c. No   d. No

10.8 $z = 7.334$, reject H_0 at all common levels of alpha.

10.10 $z = -1.0207$, p-value $= .3078$, reject H_0 at levels of alpha in excess of 30.78%.

10.12 $t = 1.108$, do not reject H_0 at the 10% alpha level since $1.108 < 1.645 = t_{(119,.05)}$

10.14   a. $z = -2.65$, p-value $= .004$, reject H_0 at all common levels of alpha.
       b. $z = -1.36$, p-value $= .0869$, reject H_0 at .10 level, but do not reject at the .05 level of alpha.
       c. $z = -2.32$, p-value $= .0102$, reject H_0 at the .05 level, but do not reject at the .01 level
          of alpha.
       d. $z = -3.25$, p-value $= .0006$, reject H_0 at all common levels of alpha.
       e. $z = -1.01$, p-value $= .1562$, do not reject H_0 at any common level of alpha.

10.16 $z = -6.97$, reject H_0 at all common levels of alpha.

10.18 $z = 2.465$, reject H_0 at the 5% level.

10.20 $z = .926$, do not reject H_0 at the 5% level.

10.22   a. $F = 2.451$, reject H_0 at the 1% level since $2.451 > 2.11 \approx F_{(44,40,.01)}$
       b. $F = 1.88$, reject H_0 at the 5% level since $1.88 > 1.69 \approx F_{(43,44,.05)}$
       c. $F = 2.627$, reject H_0 at the 1% level since $2.627 > 2.11 \approx F_{(47,40,.01)}$
       d. $F = 1.90$, reject H_0 at the 5% level since $1.90 > 1.79 \approx F_{(24,38,.05)}$

10.24   Reject H_0 if $F_{(3,6,.05)} > 4.76$, $F = 7.095$, reject H_0 at the 5% level.

10.26 $F = 1.57$, do not reject H_0 at the 10% level since $1.57 < 3.18 \approx F_{(9,9,.05)}$

10.28 No. The probability of rejecting the null hypothesis given that it is true is 5%.

10.30 a. Reject H_0 at the 5% level.
b. Reject H_0 at levels in excess of 5%.

10.32 Reject H_0 at levels in excess of 1%.

10.34 Do not reject H_0 at any common level of alpha.

10.36 Reject H_0 at any alpha of .10 or higher.

10.38 Reject H_0 at any common level of alpha.

10.40 Reject H_0 at levels of alpha in excess of 10.75%.

10.42 Do not reject H_0 at the 5% level.

10.44 a. At the .05 level of significance, reject H_0 and accept the alternative that the mean output per hectare is significantly greater with the new procedure.

b. The 95% acceptance interval is $\dfrac{1}{2.20} \leq \dfrac{s_2^2}{s_1^2} \leq 2.20$. Because F is within the acceptance interval, there is not sufficient evidence against the null hypothesis that the sample variances are not significantly different from each other.

10.46 Assume that the population of matched differences are normally distributed. Reject H_0 at the 10%, but not the 5% level.

10.48 a. $H_0 : \mu_x - \mu_y = 0$; $H_1 : \mu_x - \mu_y > 0$;

Results for: Ole.MTW

Two-Sample T-Test and CI: Olesales, Carlsale
```
Two-sample T for Olesales vs Carlsale
             N      Mean     StDev   SE Mean
Olesales   156      3791      5364       429
Carlsale   156      2412      4249       340


Difference = mu Olesales - mu Carlsale
Estimate for difference:  1379
95% lower bound for difference: 475
T-Test of difference = 0 (vs >): T-Value = 2.52  P-Value = 0.006  DF =
310
Both use Pooled StDev =   4839
```

Reject H_0 at the .01 level of significance.
b. $H_0 : \mu_x - \mu_y = 0$; $H_1 : \mu_x - \mu_y \neq 0$;

Two-Sample T-Test and CI: Oleprice, Carlpric
```
Two-sample T for Oleprice vs Carlpric
N        Mean     StDev   SE Mean
Oleprice  156     0.819     0.139     0.011
Carlpric  156     0.819     0.120    0.0096


Difference = mu Oleprice - mu Carlpric
Estimate for difference:  -0.0007
95% CI for difference: (-0.0297, 0.0283)
T-Test of difference = 0 (vs not =): T-Value = -0.05  P-Value =
0.962  DF = 310
Both use Pooled StDev = 0.130
```

Do not reject H_0 at any common level of significance. Note that the 95% confidence interval contains 0, therefore, no evidence of a difference.

Chapter 11

11.2 a.

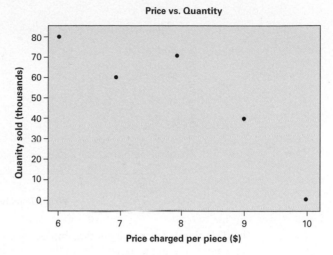

Price vs. Quantity

b. Compute the covariance = –45
c. $b_1 = -18.0$. For a one dollar increase in the price per piece of plywood, the quantity sold of plywood is estimated to decrease by 18 thousand pieces.
d. $b_0 = 194.00$
e. 68 thousand pieces sold

11.4 a.

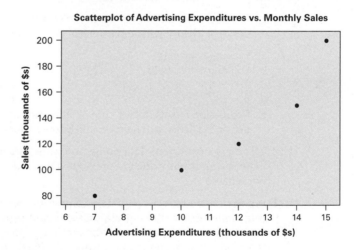

Scatterplot of Advertising Expenditures vs. Monthly Sales

b. It appears that advertising has a positive effect on sales. Note that correlation does not imply causation. Other factors could have been changing at the same time that advertising changed. For example, prices of competitive goods could have been changing or tastes and preferences of consumers, or the number of buyers in the market.
c. $b_1 = 13.5922$, $b_0 = -27.669$

11.6   a.

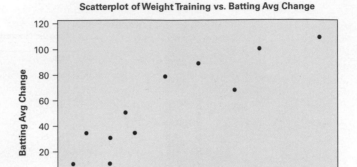

Scatterplot of Weight Training vs. Batting Avg Change

The data shows a positive relationship between the average number of hours spent in the weight training program versus the increment to their batting average. It appears that the weight training program has been effective, although correlation does not necessarily imply causation.

b. Regression equation $= \hat{Y} = -14.4 + 5.47\,X$

11.8   a. Y changes by +36
b. Y changes by –48
c. $\hat{y} = 194$
d. $\hat{y} = 326$
e. Regression results do not "prove" that increased values of X "causes" increased values of Y. Theory will help establish conclusions of causation.

11.10   a. Y changes by +105
b. Y changes by –147
c. $\hat{y} = 394$
d. $\hat{y} = 667$
e. Regression results do not "prove" that increased values of X "causes" increased values of Y. Theory will help establish conclusions of causation.

11.12   There are insufficient data points to create an accurate regression equation. The estimate is significantly outside previous data values so any estimate would be faulty and not reliable.

11.14   A population regression equation consists of the true regression coefficients $\beta_i's$ and the true model error ε_i. By contrast, the estimated regression model consists of the estimated regression coefficients $b_i's$ and the residual term e_i. The population regression equation is a model that purports to measure the actual value of Y as a function of X, while the sample regression equation is an estimate of the predicted value of the dependent variable Y as a function of X.

11.16   The constant represents an adjustment for the estimated model and not the number sold when the price is zero.

11.18   a. $b_1 = 1.80$ $b_0 = 10$ $\hat{y}_i = 10 + 1.80x_i$
b. $b_1 = 1.30$ $b_0 = 132$ $\hat{y}_i = 132 + 1.30x_i$
c. $b_1 = .975$ $b_0 = 80.5$ $\hat{y}_i = 80.5 + .975x_i$
d. $b_1 = .30$ $b_0 = 47$ $\hat{y}_i = 47 + .30x_i$
e. $b_1 = .525$ $b_0 = 152.75$ $\hat{y}_i = 152.75 + .525x_i$

11.20 a. $b_1 = 1.0737$, $b_0 = -.2336$, $\hat{y}_i = -.2336 + 1.0737x_i$

b. For a one unit increase in the rate of return of the S&P 500 index, we estimate that the rate of return of the corporation's stock will increase by 1.07%.

c. When the percentage rate of return of the S&P 500 index is zero, we estimate that the corporation's rate of return will be $-.2336\%$.

11.22 a. $b_1 = .5143$, $b_0 = 2.8854$, $\hat{y} = 2.8854 + .5143x$

b. For a one unit increase in the average cost of a meal, we would estimte that the number of bottles sold would increase by .5148%.

c. Yes. 2.8854 bottles are estimated to be sold, regardless of the price paid for a meal.

11.24 a. $\hat{y} = 1.89 + 0.0896x$

b. 0.0896%. For a one percent pre-November 13 gain, we would estimate that there would be a loss of .0896% on November 13.

11.26 a. SSR = 50,000. SSE = 50,000. $s_e^2 = 1,000$, $R^2 = 0.50$

b. SSR = 63,000. SSE = 27,000. $s_e^2 = 540$, $R^2 = 0.70$

c. SSR = 192. SSE = 48. $s_e^2 = .96$, $R^2 = 0.80$

d. SSR = 60,000. SSE = 140,000. $s_e^2 = 1,944.444$, $R^2 = 0.30$

e. SSR = 54,000. SSE = 6,000. $s_e^2 = 157.8947$, $R^2 = 0.90$

11.28 a. $R^2 = \dfrac{\sum(\hat{y}_i - \bar{y})^2}{\sum(y_i - \bar{y})^2} = \dfrac{\sum[(b_1(x_i - \bar{x}))]^2}{\sum(y_i - \bar{y})^2} = b_1^2\dfrac{\sum(x_i - \bar{x})^2}{\sum(y_i - y)^2}$

b. $R^2 = b_1^2\dfrac{\sum(x_i - \bar{x})^2}{\sum(y_i - \bar{y})^2} = b_1\dfrac{\sum(x_i - \bar{x})(y_i - \bar{y})}{\sum(y_i - \bar{y})^2} = \dfrac{[\sum(x_i - \bar{x})(y_i - \bar{y})]^2}{\sum(x_i - x)^2\sum(y_i - y)^2} = r^2$

c. $b_1 b_1^* = \dfrac{\sum(x_i - \bar{x})(y_i - \bar{y})}{\sum(x_i - \bar{x})^2}\dfrac{\sum(x_i - \bar{x})(y_i - \bar{y})}{\sum(y_i - \bar{y})^2} = r^2$

11.30 a. $R^2 = .1653$. Using the computer, we find that r = $-.4066$, $r^2 = .1653 = R^2$.

11.32 a.

Regression Analysis: Change in Mean a versus Change in Absent
```
The regression equation is
Change in Mean absence illness = 0.0449 - 0.224 Change in Absentee Rate
Predictor                   Coef    SE Coef     T      P
Constant                 0.04485   0.06347   0.71  0.498
Change in Absentee Rate -0.22426   0.05506  -4.07  0.003
S = 0.207325   R-Sq = 64.8%   R-Sq(adj) = 60.9%
```

b. $SST = \sum y^2 - n\bar{y}^2 = 1.1 - 25(0.0)^2 = 1.1$

$\qquad SSR = \sum(\hat{y}_i - \bar{y})^2 = .713$

$SSE = \sum e_i^2 = .387$

$SST = 1.1 = .713 + .387 = SSR + SSE$

c. $R^2 = SSR/SST = .713/1.1 = .648$, 64.8% of the variation in the dependent variable mean employee absence rate due to own illness can be explained by the variation in the change in absentee rate.

11.34 $R^2 = r^2 = .0121$. 1.21% of the variation in the dependent variable annual raises can be explained by the variation in teaching evaluations.

11.36 a. F = 8.857. $F_{\alpha,1,n-2} = 4.170$, therefore, at the .05 level, reject H_0.

b. F = 43.165. $F_{\alpha,1,n-2} = 4.00$, therefore, at the .05 level, reject H_0.

c. F = 20.902. $F_{\alpha,1,n-2} = 4.281$, therefore, at the .05 level, reject H_0.

11.38 a. $b_1 = .5391$, $b_0 = 3.2958$, $\hat{y}_i = 3.2958 + .5391x_i$

b. 2406 up to .8376

11.40 a. $s_e^2 = 144.4686$

   b. $s_b^2 = 1.8991$

   c. -5.0673 up to .9991

   d. $t = -1.476$, therefore, do not reject H_0 at the 10% level since $t = -1.476 > -1.796 = -t_{11,.05}$

11.42 95% Prediction Interval: (56.467, 97.533)
    95% Confidence Interval: (71.371, 82.629)

11.44 95% Prediction Interval: (150.331, 165.669)
    95% Confidence Interval: (155.351, 160.649)

11.46 a. $t = -7.303$, therefore, reject H_0 at the 1% level since $t = -7.303 > -2.807 = -t_{23,.005}$.

   b. $y_{n+1} = 12.6 - 1.2(4) = 7.8$, 90% interval: (4.4798, 11.1203)

11.48 a. $t = 7.689$, therefore, reject H_0 at the 1% level since $t = 7.689 > 2.878 = t_{18,.005}$.

   b. $t = .5278$, therefore, do not reject H_0 at the 20% level since $t = .5278 < 1.33 = t_{18,.10}$.

11.50 $t = 5.1817$, therefore, reject H_0 at the 1% level since $t = 5.1817 > 2.807 = t_{23,.005}$.

11.52 $t = 2.969$, therefore, reject H_0 at the 1% level since $t = 2.969 > 2.947 = t_{15,.005}$.

11.54 $t = -10.251$, therefore, reject H_0 at the .5% level since $t = -10.251 < -3.707 = t_{6,.005}$.

11.56 The 90% confidence interval for prediction of the actual value: (-11.5212 up to 33.337)
    The 90% confidence interval for prediction of the expected value: (4.8197 up to 16.9961)

   The distinction between the two lies in the uncertainty about the expected or mean value as compared to the uncertainty about a single specific value. Both are centered on the same value; however, the uncertainty surrounding a single specific value will be larger as compared to the expected or mean value, because the variation of both the expected value and the individual value about the expected value is included.

11.58 The 90% confidence interval for prediction of the expected value: (.2591 up to .14211)
    95% confidence interval for the prediction of the expected value: (.1362 up to 1.544)

11.60 a. .97802   b. .97802   c. .88247   d. .90615

11.62 .7759

11.64 Reject H_0 at the 2.5% level.

11.66 a. −0.407
    b. Do not reject H_0 at the 10% level.

11.68 Sample correlation = 0.0575
    Do not reject H_0 at the 20% level.

11.70 The Senior Housing return has a beta of 1.369 with a coefficient Student's $t = 3.87$ and an overall R-squared of 20.5%. This means the nondiversifiable risk response for Senior Housing is significantly above the overall market. This firm's return is more responsive to the market.

11.72 The Seagate return has a beta of 1.810 with a coefficient Student's $t = 2.98$ and an overall R-squared of 13.2%. The nondiversifiable risk response for Seagate is substantially above the overall market. For the 60-month period the average monthly return for Seagate was –0.03%, with the average variance equal to 0.0156.

   The Microsoft return has a beta of 0.967 with a coefficient Student's $t = 3.31$ and an overall R-squared of 15.9%. The nondiversifiable risk response for Microsoft is slightly below the overall market. For the 60-month period the average monthly return for Microsoft was 0.00%, with the average variance equal to 0.0006.

The Tata return has a beta of 2.796 with a coefficient Student's $t = 4.14$ and an overall R-squared of 22.8%. The nondiversifiable risk response for Tata is extremely above the overall market. For the 60-month period the average monthly return for Tata was 2.23%, with the average variance equal to 0.0216.

The Tata stock has the most risk and the most return. Microsoft is the least risky but has a low return. If the market is trending upward Tata is the recommended stock. If the market is volatile or trending downward Microsoft is the recommended stock.

11.74 Note that the computed values for the Minitab regression output are exactly the same for all four data sets, but the scatter plots indicate very different patterns of the data and hence different models:
The model of $Y_1 = f(X_1)$ is a good fit for a linear model.
The model of $Y_2 = f(X_2)$ is a non-linear model.
The model of $Y_3 = f(X_3)$ has a significant outlier at the largest value of X1
The model of $Y_4 = f(X_4)$ has only two values of the independent variable.

11.76 Two random variables are positively correlated if low values of one are associated with low values of the other and high values of one are associated with high values of the other:
a. Total consumption expenditures are positively correlated with disposable income.
b. Price of a good or service is negatively related with the quantity sold.
c. The price of peanut butter and the sales of wrist watches are uncorrelated.

11.78 $t = 2.844$, therefore, reject H_0 at the .5% level since $t = 2.844 > 2.660 \approx t_{51,.005}$.

11.80 $t = 2.452$, therefore, reject H_0 at the 1% level since $t = 2.452 > 2.39 \approx t_{60,.01}$.

11.82 To show this, let $x = \bar{x}$ for the regression of y on x, $y = b_0 + b_1 x$
$\hat{y} = b_0 + b_1\bar{x} = \bar{y} - b_1\bar{x} + b_1\bar{x} = \bar{y}$

11.84 a. For a one unit change in the inflation rate, we estimate that the actual spot rate will change by .7916 units.
b. $R^2 = 9.7\%$. 9.7% of the variation in the actual spot rate can be explained by the variations in the spot rate predicted by the inflation rate.
c. $t = 2.8692$, therefore, reject H_0 at the .5% level since $t = 2.8692 > 2.66 = t_{77,.005}$.
d. $t = -.7553$, therefore, do not reject H_0 at any common level of alpha.

11.86 a. For each unit increase in the diagnostic statistics test, we estimate that the final student score at the end of the course will increase by .2875 points.
b. 11.58% of the variation in the final student score can be explained by the variation in the diagnostic statistics test.
c. The two methods are (1) the test of the significance of the population regression slope coefficient (β) and (2) the test of the significance of the population correlation coefficient (ρ).
(1) $H_0 : \beta = 0, H_1 : \beta > 0$
$t = 6.2965$. Therefore, reject H_0 at any common level of alpha.
(2) $H_0 : \rho = 0, H_1 : \rho > 0, r = .3403, t = 6.3098$. Therefore, reject H_0 at any common level of alpha.

11.88 a. $R^2 = 23.88\%$ of the variation of the dependent variable can be explained by the variability of the independent variable x.
b. $t = 2.6863$, therefore, reject H_0 at the 5% level since $t = 2.6863 > 2.069 = t_{23,.025}$.
c. (.2987 up to 2.3013)

11.90 If a linear regression was estimated the slope would be negative and indicate that increased fertilizer reduces yield, which is silly.

11.92 a. The graph with vehicle weight as the independent variable shows a slight positive relationship to crash deaths. The simple regression $R^2 = 5.9\%$. Percent imported cars has a slight negative relationship with a simple regression $R^2 = 8.1\%$. Deaths versus light trucks is a much stronger positive association with a simple regression $R^2 = 52.7\%$. And car age has a weak negative association with a simple regression $R^2 = 17.8\%$. All graphs show an unusual data point of an outlier of .55 crash deaths at the 49th observation of the data set. This data point is much higher than expected given the levels of the independent variables.

b.

Regression Analysis: deaths versus vehwt

```
The regression equation is
deaths = -0.346+0.000147 vehwt
Predictor         Coef     SE Coef     T      P
Constant       -0.3458      0.3022  -1.14  0.258
vehwt       0.00014697 0.00008528   1.72  0.091

S = 0.0786123 R-Sq = 5.9% R-Sq(adj) = 3.9%
```

Regression Analysis: deaths versus impcars

```
The regression equation is
deaths = 0.224-0.00478 impcars
Predictor        Coef  SE Coef     T      P
Constant      0.22371  0.02662  8.40  0.000
impcars     -0.004776  0.002351 -2.03  0.048

S = 0.0777183 R-Sq = 8.1% R-Sq(adj) = 6.1%
```

Regression Analysis: deaths versus lghttrks

```
The regression equation is
deaths = 0.0137 + 0.00974 lghttrks
Predictor       Coef  SE Coef     T      P
Constant     0.01375  0.02359  0.58  0.563
lghttrks    0.009742  0.001346  7.24  0.000

S = 0.0557321 R-Sq = 52.7% R-Sq(adj) = 51.7%
```

Regression Analysis: deaths versus carage

```
The regression equation is
deaths = 5.26 - 0.0723 carage
Predictor       Coef  SE Coef     T      P
Constant       5.263    1.594  3.30  0.002
carage      -0.07234  0.02266 -3.19  0.003

S = 0.0734818 R-Sq = 17.8% R-Sq(adj) = 16.1%
```

c. Independent variables are ranked based on the R^2 of the simple regression.

Variable	R-Sq	Rank
Light trucks	52.7%	1
Car age	17.8%	2
Imported cars	8.1%	3
Vehicle weight	5.9%	4

Crash deaths are positively related to both weight and percent of light trucks. Deaths are negatively related to percent import cars and the age of the vehicle. Light trucks has the strongest linear association followed by age and then vehicle weight.

11.94 a. The scatter plots show market value is positively related to the size of house. Outliers include several houses with a much higher than expected valuation based on their size. Market value is negatively related to tax rate where unusual patterns include homes with the highest market valuation but among the lowest tax rates.

b.

Regression Analysis: hseval versus sizehse

```
The regression equation is
hseval = -40.1 + 11.2 sizehse

Predictor          Coef   SE Coef       T       P
Constant         -40.15     10.11   -3.97   0.000
sizehse          11.169     1.844    6.06   0.000

S = 4.188     R-Sq = 29.4%     R-Sq(adj)  =  28.6%
```

Regression Analysis: hseval versus taxrate

```
The regression equation is
hseval = 26.6 -208 taxrate

Predictor          Coef   SE Coef        T       P
Constant         26.650     1.521    17.52   0.000
taxrate         -207.60     53.27    -3.90   0.000

S = 4.603     R-Sq = 14.7%    R-Sq(adj)  =  13.7%
```

Size of house is a stronger predictor than is the taxrate.
c. Whether tax rates are lowered or not does not have as large an impact as does the size of the house on the evaluation.

11.96 a.

Regression Analysis for Prime Rate

```
The regression equation is
Residential = 224 + 7.79 Prime Rate

Predictor          Coef   SE Coef        T       P
Constant        223.59     18.42    12.14   0.000
Prime Ra          7.786     2.340     3.33   0.001

S = 122.1     R-Sq = 4.5%     R-Sq(adj) = 4.1%
```

Regression Analysis for Federal Rate

```
The regression equation is
Residential = 264 + 2.01 Federal Funds Rate

Predictor          Coef   SE Coef        T       P
Constant        264.34     14.32    10.46   0.000
taxrate           2.014     2.287     1.23   0.220

S = 124.6     R-Sq = 0.6%     R-Sq(adj) = 0.2%
```

The $r^2 = 0.045$ for the regression with the prime rate is higher than the $r^2 = 0.006$ for the regression with the federal rate, so the regression with the prime rate explains more of the variation with the model. Also, the coefficient for the federal rate could statistically be equal to zero, i.e. the P-value is greater than 0.05.
b. Prime rate: (3.19, 12.41), Federal rate: (−1.68, 7.33)
c. Prime rate 239.16, Federal rate 269.97
d. Prime rate: (210.91, 267.41), Federal rate: (248.57, 291.37)

Chapter 12

12.2 a. $\hat{y} = 174$ b. $\hat{y} = 181$ c. $\hat{y} = 311$ d. $\hat{y} = 188$

12.4 a. $\hat{y}$ increases by 8   b. $\hat{y}$ increases by 8   c. $\hat{y}$ increases by 24

12.6 a. $b_1 = .661$: All else equal, an increase in the plane's top speed by one mph will increase the expected number of hours in the design effort by an estimated .661 million or 661 thousand worker-hours.

   b. $b_2 = .065$: All else equal, an increase in the plane's weight by one ton will increase the expected number of hours in the design effort by an estimated .065 million or 65 thousand worker-hours.

   c. $b_3 = -.018$: All else equal, an increase in the percentage of parts in common with other models will result in a decrease in the expected number of hours in the design effort by an estimated .018 million or 18 thousand worker-hours.

12.8 a. $b_1 = .052$: All else equal, an increase of one hundred dollars in weekly income results in an estimated .052 quarts per week increase in milk consumption. $b_2 = 1.14$: All else equal, an increase in family size by one person will result in an estimated increase in milk consumption by 1.14 quarts per week.

   b. The intercept term b_0 of $-.025$ is the estimated milk consumption of quarts of milk per week given that the family's weekly income is 0 dollars and there are 0 members in the family. This is likely extrapolating beyond the observed data series and is not a useful interpretation.

12.10 a. $b_1 = 2.000$, $b_2 = 3.200$ b. $b_1 = -.667$, $b_2 = 1.067$
   c. $b_1 = .083$, $b_2 = .271$ d. $b_1 = .9375$, $b_2 = -.4375$

12.12 a.

```
The regression equation is
salesmw2 = - 647363 + 19895 priclec2 + 2.35 numcust2
```

All else equal, for every one unit increase in the price of electricity, we estimate that sales will increase by 19895 mwh.

All else equal, for every additional residential customer who uses electricity in the heating of their home, we estimate that sales will increase by 2.353 mwh.

   b.

```
The regression equation is
salesmw2 = - 410202 + 2.20 numcust2
```

An additional residential customer is estimated to add 2.2027 mwh to electricity sales.
   The two models have roughly equivalent explanatory power; therefore, adding price as a variable does not add a significant amount of explanatory power to the model. There appears to be a high correlation between the independent variables, which can have an influence on the estimated coefficients. Regression coefficient estimates are conditional on the other predictor variables in the model.

   c.

```
The regression equation is
salesmw2 = 2312260 - 165275 priclec2 + 56.1 degrday2
```

All else equal, an increase in the price of electricity will reduce electricity sales by 165,275 mwh.
   All else equal, an increase in the degree days (departure from normal weather) by one unit will increase electricity sales by 56.06 mwh.
   Note that the coefficient on the price variable is now negative, as expected, and it is significantly different from zero (p-value = .000).

   d.

```
The regression equation is
salesmw2 = 293949 + 326 Yd872 + 58.4 degrday2
```

All else equal, an increase in personal disposable income by one unit will increase electricity sales by 325.85 mwh.

All else equal, an increase in degree days by one unit will increase electricity sales by 58.36 mwh.

12.14 a.

```
The regression equation is
horspwr = 23.5 + 0.0154 weight + 0.157 displace
```

All else equal, a 100 pound increase in the weight of the car is associated with a 1.54 increase in horsepower of the auto.

All else equal, a 10 cubic inch increase in the displacement of the engine is associated with a 1.57 increase in the horsepower of the auto.

b.

```
The regression equation is
horspwr = 16.7 + 0.0163 weight + 0.105 displace + 2.57 cylinder
```

All else equal, a 100 pound increase in the weight of the car is associated with a 1.63 increase in horsepower of the auto.

All else equal, a 10 cubic inch increase in the displacement of the engine is associated with a 1.05 increase in the horsepower of the auto.

All else equal, one additional cylinder in the engine is associated with a 2.57 increase in the horsepower of the auto.

Note that adding the independent variable number of cylinders has not added to the explanatory power of the model. R square has increased marginally. Engine displacement is no longer significant at the .05 level (p-value of .074) and the estimated regression slope coefficient on the number of cylinders is not significantly different from zero. This is due to the strong correlation that exists between cubic inches of engine displacement and the number of cylinders.

c.

```
The regression equation is
horspwr = 93.6 + 0.00203 weight + 0.165 displace - 1.24 milpgal
```

All else equal, a 100 pound increase in the weight of the car is associated with a .203 increase in horsepower of the auto.

All else equal, a 10 cubic inch increase in the displacement of the engine is associated with a 1.6475 increase in the horsepower of the auto.

All else equal, an increase in the fuel mileage of the vehicle by 1 mile per gallon is associated with a reduction in horsepower of 1.2392.

Note that the negative coefficient on fuel mileage indicates the trade-off that is expected between horsepower and fuel mileage. The displacement variable is significantly positive, as expected; however, the weight variable is no longer significant. Again, one would expect high correlation among the independent variables.

d.

```
The regression equation is
horspwr = 98.1 - 0.00032 weight + 0.175 displace - 1.32 milpgal + 0.000138 price
```

All else equal, a 100 pound increase in the weight of the car is associated with a .032 increase in horsepower of the auto.

All else equal, a 10 cubic inch increase in the displacement of the engine is associated with a 1.75 increase in the horsepower of the auto.

All else equal, an increase in the fuel mileage of the vehicle by 1 mile per gallon is associated with a reduction in horsepower of 1.32.

All else equal, an increase in the price by \$100 is associated with a .0138 increase in the horsepower of the auto.

    e. Explanatory power has marginally increased from the first model to the last. The estimated coefficient on price is not significantly different from zero. Displacement and fuel mileage have the expected signs. The coefficient on weight has the wrong sign; however, it is not significantly different from zero (p-value of .953).

12.16 a. $s_e^2 = 86.207$, $s_e = 9.2848$,
      b. SST = 9,500
      c. $R^2 = .7368$, $\bar{R}^2 = .7187$

12.18 a. $s_e^2 = 75.0$, $s_e = 8.660$
      b. SST = 95,000
      c. $R^2 = .8421$, $\bar{R}^2 = .7822$

12.20 a. $R^2 = .5441$, therefore, 54.41% of the variability in milk consumption can be explained by the variations in weekly income and family size.
      b. $\bar{R}^2 = .5103$
      c. $R = .7376$. This is the sample correlation between observed and predicted values of milk consumption.

12.22 a.

```
The regression equation is
Y profit = 1.55 - 0.000120 X2   offices
```

      b.

```
The regression equation is
X1 revenue = - 0.078 + 0.000543 X2 offices
```

      c.

```
The regression equation is
Y profit = 1.33 - 0.169 X1 revenue
```

      d.

```
The regression equation is
X2  offices = 957 + 163 1X1 revenue
```

12.24 a. 95% CI for x_1: .4698 up to 13.1302
          95% CI for x_2: $-.6554$ up to 14.554
          95% CI for $x_3 = -7.2 \pm 2.042$ (3.2); -13.7344 up to $-.6656$
      b. For x_1: $t = 2.194$ $t_{30,.05/.01} = 1.697, 2.457$. Reject H_0 at the 5% level but not at the 1% level.
          For x_2: $t = -1.865$ $t_{30,.05/.01} = 1.697, 2.457$. Reject H_0 at the 5% level but not at the 1% level.
          For x_3: $t = -2.25$ $t_{30,.05/.01} = 1.697, 2.457$. Do not reject H_0 at the 5% level nor at the 1% level.

12.26 a. 95% CI for x_1: 3.4510 up to 32.149
          95% CI for x_2: -0.788 up to 54.588
          95% CI for x_3: -16.88 up to -1.52
      b. For x_1: $t = 2.507$ $t_{35,.05/.01} \approx 1.697, 2.457$. Reject H_0 at the 5% level and at the 1% level.
          For x_2: $t = 1.964$ $t_{35,.05/.01} \approx 1.697, 2.457$. Reject H_0 at the 5% level but not at the 1% level.
          For x_3: $t = -2.421$ $t_{35,.05/.01} \approx 1.697, 2.457$. Reject H_0 at the 5% level but not at the 1% level.

12.28 a. $t = 2.26$. $t_{27,.025/.01} = 2.052, 2.473$, therefore, reject H_0 at the 2.5% level but not at the 1% level.

  b. 90% CI: .5439 up to 1.7361
  95% CI: .4218 up to 1.8582
  99% CI: .1701 up to 2.1099

12.30 a. $t = -.428$, $t_{16,.10} = -1.337$, therefore, do not reject H_0 at the 20% level.

  b. $F = 13.057$, $F_{3,16,.01} = 5.29$, therefore, reject H_0 at the 1% level.

12.32 a. All else being equal, an extra \$1 in mean per capita personal income leads to an expected extra \$.04 of net revenue per capita from the lottery.

  b. 95% CI: .2359 up to 1.5185

  c. $t = -1.383$, $t_{24,.10/.05} = -1.318, -1.711$, therefore, reject H_0 at the 10% level but not at the 5% level.

12.34 a. 95% CI: .1805 up to .2195

  b. $t = -1.19$, $t_{16,.10} = -1.337$, therefore, do not reject H_0 at the 10% level.

12.36 a. 99% CI: .0173 up to .0817

  b. $t = .617$, $t_{30,.10} = 1.31$, therefore, do not reject H_0 at the 20% level.

  c. $t = 2.108$, $t_{30,.025/.01} = 2.042, 2.457$, therefore, reject H_0 at the 5% level but not at the 2% level.

12.38 a. $F = 81.955$, $F_{3,23,.01} = 4.76$, therefore, reject H_0 at the 1% level.

  b. Analysis of Variance table

Sources of Variation	Sum of Squares	Degress of Freedom	Mean Squares	F-Ratio
Regressor	3.549	3	1.183	81.955
Error	.332	23	.014435	
Total	3.881	26		

12.40 a. $F = 16.113$, $F_{2,27,.01} = 5.49$, therefore, reject H_0 at the 1% level.

  b.

Sources of Variation	Sum of Squares	Degrees of Freedom	Mean Squares	F-Ratio
Regressor	88.2	2	44.10	16.113
Error	73.9	27	2.737	
Total	162.1	29		

12.42 a. $F = 6.2449$, $F_{4,24,.01} = 4.22$, therefore, reject H_0 at the 1% level.

12.44 a. $F = 217$, $F_{2,16,.01} = 6.23$, therefore, reject H_0 at the 1% level.

12.46 $$\frac{(SSE^* - SSE)k_1}{SSE/(n - k - 1)} = \frac{n - k - 1}{k_1} \frac{(SSE^* - SSE)/SST}{SSE/SST}$$

$$= \frac{n - k - 1}{k_1} \frac{1 - R^{2*} - (1 - R^2)}{1 - R^2}$$

$$= \frac{n - k - 1}{k_1} \frac{R^2 - R^{2*}}{1 - R^2}$$

12.48 a. $$\bar{R}^2 = 1 - \frac{SSE/(n - k - 1)}{SSE/(n - 1)} = 1 - \frac{n - 1}{n - k - 1}(1 - R^2)$$

$$= \frac{n - 1}{n - k - 1}R^2 - \frac{k}{n - k - 1} = \frac{(n - 1)R^2 - k}{n - k - 1}$$

  b. Since $\bar{R}^2 = \dfrac{(n - 1)R^2 - k}{n - k - 1}$, then $R^2 = \dfrac{(n - k - 1)\bar{R}^2 + k}{n - 1}$

c. $\dfrac{SSR/k}{SSE/(n-k-1)} = \dfrac{n-k-1}{k} \dfrac{SSR/SST}{SSE/SST}$

$$= \dfrac{n-k-1}{k} \dfrac{R^2}{1-R^2} = \dfrac{n-k-1}{k} \dfrac{[(n-k-1)\overline{R}^2 + k]/(n-1)}{[n-1-(n-k-1)\overline{R}^2 - k]/(n-1)}$$

$$= \dfrac{n-k-1}{k} \dfrac{(n-k-1)\overline{R}^2 + k}{(n-k-1)(1-\overline{R}^2)} = \dfrac{n-k-1}{k} \dfrac{\overline{R}^2 + k}{(1-\overline{R}^2)}$$

12.50 $\hat{Y} = 10.638$ pounds

12.52 $\hat{Y} = 2.216$ million worker-hours

12.54 Compute values of y_i when $x_i = 1, 2, 4, 6, 8, 10$

x_i	1	2	4	6	8	10
$y_i = 4x^{1.5}$	4	11.3137	32	58.7878	90.5097	126.4611
$y_i = 1 + 2x_i + 2x_i^2$	5	13	41	85	145	221

12.56 Compute values of y_i when $x_i = 1, 2, 4, 6, 8, 10$

x_i	1	2	4	6	8	10
$y_i = 4x^{1.5}$	4	11.3137	32	58.7878	90.5097	126.4611
$y_i = 1 + 2x_i + 1.7x_i^2$	4.7	11.8	36.2	74.2	125.8	191

12.58 There are many possible answers. Relationships that can be approximated by a non-linear quadratic model include many supply functions, production functions and cost functions including average cost versus the number of units produced.

12.60 a. All else equal, 1% increase in annual consumption expenditures will be associated with a 1.1556% increase in expenditures on vacation travel.

All else equal, a 1% increase in the size of the household will be associated with a .4408% decrease in expenditures on vacation travel.

b. 16.8% of the variation in vacation travel expenditures can be explained by the variations in the log of total consumption expenditures and log of the number of members in the household.

c. 1.049 up to 1.2626

d. $t = -8.996$, therefore, reject H_0 at the 1% level.

12.62 a. All else equal, a 1% increase in the price of beef will be associated with a decrease of .529% in the tons of beef consumed annually in the U.S.

b. All else equal, a 1% increase in the price of pork will be associated with an increase of .217% in the tons of beef consumed annually in the U.S.

c. $t = 2.552$, $t_{25,.01} = 2.485$, therefore, reject H_0 at the 1% level.

d. $F = 13.466$, $F_{4,25,.01} = 4.18$, therefore, reject H_0 at the 1% level.

e. If an important independent variable has been omitted, there may be specification bias. The regression coefficients produced for the misspecified model would be misleading.

12.64 a. Coefficients for exponential models can be estimated by taking the logarithm of both sides of the multiple regression model to obtain an equation that is linear in the logarithms of the variables.

$$\log(Y) = \log(\beta_0) + \beta_1 \log(X_1) + \beta_2 \log(X_2) + \beta_3 \log(X_3) + \beta_4(\log(X)_4 + \log(\varepsilon)$$

Substituting in the restrictions on the coefficients: $\beta_1 + \beta_2 = 1$, $\beta_2 = 1 - \beta_1$, $\beta_3 + \beta_4 = 1$, $\beta_4 = 1 - \beta_3 \log(Y) = \log(\beta_0) + \beta_1 \log(X_1) + [1 - \beta_1] \log(X_2) + \beta_3 \log(X_3) + [1 - \beta_3](\log(X_4) + \log(\varepsilon)$

Simplify algebraically and estimate the coefficients. The coefficient β_2 can be found by subtracting β_1 from 1.0. Likewise the coefficient β_4 can be found by subtracting β_3 from 1.0.

b. Constant elasticity for Y versus X_4 is the regression slope coefficient on the X_4 term of the logarithm model.

12.66

Results for: GermanImports.xls
Regression Analysis: LogYt versus LogX1t, LogX2t

```
The regression equation is
LogYt = -4.07 + 1.36 LogX1t + 0.101 LogX2t
Predictor       Coef     SE Coef        T       P     VIF
Constant     -4.0709      0.3100   -13.13   0.000
LogX1t        1.35935     0.03005    45.23   0.000    4.9
LogX2t        0.10094     0.05715     1.77   0.088    4.9

S = 0.04758      R-Sq = 99.7%    R-Sq(adj) = 99.7%
```

12.68 a. $\hat{y} = 5.78 + 4.87x_1$ b. $\hat{y} = 1.15 + 9.51x_1$ c. $\hat{y} = 13.67 + 8.98x_1$

12.70 a. All else being equal, expected selling price is higher by $3,219 if condo has a fireplace.
b. All else being equal, expected selling price is higher by $2,005 if condo has brick siding.
c. 95% CI: $1,362.88 up to $5,075.12
d. $t = 2.611$, $t_{809,.005} = 2.576$, therefore, reject H_0 at the .5% level.

12.72 35.6% of the variation in overall performance in law school can be explained by the variation in undergraduate GPA, scores on the LSATs, and whether the student's letter of recommendation is unusually strong. The overall model is significant since we can reject the null hypothesis that the model has no explanatory power in favor of the alternative hypothesis that the model has significant explanatory power. The individual regression coefficients that are significantly different than zero include the scores on the LSAT and whether the student's letters of recommendation was unusually strong. The coefficient on undergraduate GPA was not found to be significant at the 5% level.

12.74 a. All else equal, the average rating of a course is 6.21 units higher if a visiting lecturer is brought in than if otherwise.
b. $t = 1.73$, $t_{20,.05} = 1.725$, therefore, reject H_0 at the 5% level.
c. 56.9% of the variation in the average course rating can be explained by the variation in the percentage of time spent in group discussions, the dollars spent on preparing the course materials, the dollars spent on food and drinks, and whether a guest lecturer is brought in. $F = 6.6$, $F_{4,20,.01} = 4.43$, therefore, reject H_0 at the 1% level.
d. .0819 up to .9581

12.76

Results for: Student Performance.xls
Regression Analysis: Y versus X1, X2, X3, X4, X5

```
The regression equation is
Y = 2.00 + 0.0099 X1 + 0.0763 X2 - 0.137 X3 + 0.064 X4 + 0.138 X5
Predictor       Coef     SE Coef       T       P     VIF
Constant       1.997       1.273    1.57   0.132
X1           0.00990     0.01654    0.60   0.556    1.3
X2           0.07629     0.05654    1.35   0.192    1.2
X3          -0.13652     0.06922   -1.97   0.062    1.1
X4           0.0636      0.2606     0.24   0.810    1.4
X5           0.13794     0.07521    1.83   0.081    1.1

S = 0.5416      R-Sq = 26.5%    R-Sq(adj) =   9.0%
```

The model is not significant (p-value of the F-test = .229). The model only explains 26.5% of the variation in GPA with the hours spent studying, hours spent preparing for tests, hours spent in bars, whether or not students take notes or mark highlights when reading, and the average number of credit hours taken per semester. The only independent variables that are marginally significant (10% level but not the 5% level) include number of hours spent in bars and the average number of credit hours. The other independent variables are not significant at common levels of alpha.

12.78 a. A large correlation among the independent variables will lead to a high variance for the estimated slope coefficients and will tend to have a small Student's t statistic. Use the rule of thumb $|r| > \dfrac{2}{\sqrt{n}}$ to determine if the correlation is 'large.'

b. No correlation exists among the independent variables. No effect on the estimated slope coefficients.

c. A large correlation among the independent variables will lead to a high variance for the estimated slope coefficients and will tend to have a small Student's t statistic.

d. Use the rule of thumb $|r| > \dfrac{2}{\sqrt{n}}$ to determine if the correlation is 'large.'

12.80 Correlation between the independent variable and the dependent variable is not necessarily evidence of a small Student's t statistic. A high correlation among the *independent* variables could result in a very small Student's t statistic as the correlation creates a high variance.

12.82–12.84 Reports can be written by following the extended Case Study on the data file **Cotton**—see Section 12.9.

12.86

Regression Analysis: y_FemaleLFPR versus x1_income, x2_yrsedu, ...

```
The regression equation is
y_FemaleLFPR = 0.2 + 0.000406 x1_income + 4.84 x2_yrsedu - 1.55 x3_femaleun
Predictor        Coef     SE Coef        T          P       VIF
Constant         0.16       34.91     0.00      0.996
x1_incom    0.0004060   0.0001736     2.34      0.024       1.2
x2_yrsed        4.842       2.813     1.72      0.092       1.5
x3_femal      -1.5543      0.3399    -4.57      0.000       1.3

S = 3.048      R-Sq = 54.3%  R-Sq(adj) = 51.4%
```

12.88

Regression Analysis: y_manufgrowt versus x1_aggrowth, x2_exportgro, ...

```
The regression equation is
y_manufgrowth = 2.15 + 0.493 x1_aggrowth + 0.270 x2_exportgrowth
              - 0.117 x3_inflation
Predictor         Coef      SE Coef          T         P      VIF
Constant        2.1505       0.9695       2.22     0.032
x1_aggro        0.4934       0.2020       2.44     0.019      1.0
x2_expor       0.26991      0.06494       4.16     0.000      1.0
x3_infla      -0.11709      0.05204      -2.25     0.030      1.0

S = 3.624      R-Sq = 39.3%  R-Sq(adj) = 35.1%
```

12.90 The analysis of variance table identifies how the total variability of the dependent variable (SST) is split up between the portion of variability that is explained by the regression model (SSR) and the part that is unexplained (SSE). The Coefficient of Determination (R^2) is derived as the ratio of SSR to SST. The analysis of variance table also computes the F statistic for the test of the significance of the overall regression—whether all of the slope coefficients are jointly equal to zero. The associated p-value is also generally reported in this table.

12.92 If one model contains more explanatory variables, then SST remains the same for both models but SSR will be higher for the model with more explanatory variables. Since SST = $SSR_1 + SSE_1$ which is equivalent to $SSR_2 + SSE_2$ and given that $SSR_2 > SSR_1$, then $SSE_1 > SSE_2$. Hence, the coefficient of determination will be higher with a greater number of explanatory variables and the coefficient of determination must be interpreted in conjunction with whether or not the regression slope coefficients on the explanatory variables are significantly different from zero.

12.94 $\sum e_i = \sum (y_i - a - b_1 x_{1i} - b_2 x_{2i})$

$\sum e_i = \sum (y_i - \bar{y} + b_1 \bar{x}_{1i} + b_2 \bar{x}_{2i} - b_1 x_{1i} - b_2 x_{2i})$

$\sum e_i = n\bar{y} - n\bar{y} + nb_1 \bar{x}_1 + nb_2 \bar{x}_2 - nb_1 \bar{x}_1 - nb_2 \bar{x}_2$

$\sum e_i = 0$

12.96 a. All else equal, an increase of one question results in a decrease of 1.834 in expected percentage of responses received. All else equal, an increase in one word in length of the questionnaire results in a decrease of .016 in expected percentage of responses received.
   b. 63.7% of the variability in the percentage of responses received can be explained by the variability in the number of questions asked and the number of words.
   c. $F = 23.69$, $F_{2,27,.01} = 5.49$, therefore, reject H_0 at the 1% level.
   d. -3.5938 up to $-.0752$
   e. $t = -1.78$, $t_{27,.05/.025} = -1.703$, -2.052. Therefore, reject H_0 at the 5% level but not at the 2.5% level.

12.98

Regression Analysis: y_rating versus x1_expgrade, x2_Numstudents

```
The regression equation is
y_rating = -0.200 + 1.41 x1_expgrade - 0.0158 x2_Numstudents
Predictor        Coef       SE Coef        T        P      VIF
Constant        -0.2001      0.6968     -0.29    0.777
x1_expgr         1.4117      0.1780      7.93    0.000     1.5
x2_Numst        -0.015791    0.003783   -4.17    0.001     1.5

S = 0.1866        R-Sq = 91.5%   R-Sq(adj) = 90.5%
```

12.100 a. All else equal, each extra point in the student's expected score leads to an expected increase of .469 in the actual score.
   b. 2.4752 up to 4.26276
   c. $t = 2.096$, $t_{103,.025} = 1.96$, therefore, reject H_0 at the 5% level.
   d. 68.6% of the variation in the exam scores is explained by their linear dependence on the student's expected score, hours per week spent working on the course, and the student's grade point average.
   e. $F = 75.008$, $F_{3,103,.01} = 3.95$. Reject H_0 at any common levels of alpha.
   f. $R = .82825$
   g. $\hat{Y} = 75.812$

12.102 a. 110.0795 up to 850.0005
   b. 803.4152 up to 1897.1848
   c. $t = -4.9299$, $t_{2669,.005} = 2.576$, therefore, reject H_0 at the .5% level.
   d. $t = 6.5142$, $t_{2669,.005} = 2.576$, therefore, reject H_0 at the .5% level.

e. 52.39% of the variability in minutes played can be explained by the variability in all 9 variables.

f. $R = .7238$

12.104 A report can be written by following the Case Study and testing the significance of the model. See Section 12.9.

12.106 The correlation matrix indicates that several of the independent variables are likely to be significant; however, high correlation between the independent variables is also a likely result. The regression model with all independent variables is as follows:

Regression Analysis: Salary versus age, Experien, ...
```
The regression equation is
Salary = 23725 - 40.3 age + 357 Experien + 263 yrs_asoc + 493 yrs_full
              - 954 Sex_1Fem + 3427 Market + 1188 C8
Predictor        Coef     SE Coef        T         P      VIF
Constant        23725        1524    15.57     0.000
age            -40.29       44.98     -0.90     0.372      4.7
Experien       356.83       63.48      5.62     0.000     10.0
yrs_asoc       262.50       75.11      3.49     0.001      4.0
yrs_full       492.91       59.27      8.32     0.000      2.6
Sex_1Fem       -954.1       487.3     -1.96     0.052      1.3
Market        3427.2        754.1      4.54     0.000      1.1
C8            1188.4        597.5      1.99     0.049      1.1


S = 2332 R-Sq = 88.2%  R-Sq(adj) = 87.6%
```

Since age is insignificant and has the smallest t-statistics, it is removed from the model.

Removing age as an independent variable, the conditional F test for age is

$F_{x_2} = .80$. Which is well below any common critical value of F. Thus, age is removed from the model. The remaining independent variables are all significant at the .05 level of significance and hence, the equation with age removed is the final regression model. Residual analysis to determine if the assumption of linearity holds true follows:

The residual plot for experience shows a relatively strong quadratic relationship between experience and salary. Therefore, a new variable, taking into account the quadratic relationship is generated and added to the model. None of the other residual plots shows strong evidence of non-linearity. The model with the squared term for experience was added to the independent variables. The squared term for experience is statistically significant; however, the Sex_1Fem is no longer significant at the .05 level and hence is removed from the model:

Regression Analysis: Salary versus Experien, ExperSquared, ...
```
The regression equation is
Salary = 18538 + 888 Experien - 16.3 ExperSquared + 237 yrs_asoc
              + 624 yrs_full + 3982 Market + 1145 C8
Predictor        Coef     SE Coef        T         P      VIF
Constant      18537.8       543.6     34.10     0.000
Experien       887.85       72.32     12.28     0.000     20.4
ExperSqu       -16.275      1.718     -9.48     0.000     16.0
yrs_asoc       236.89       59.11      4.01     0.000      3.9
yrs_full       624.49       48.41     12.90     0.000      2.8
Market        3981.8        602.9      6.60     0.000      1.1
C8            1145.4        466.3      2.46     0.015      1.0

S = 1857       R-Sq = 92.5%    R-Sq(adj) = 92.2%
```

This is the final model with all of the independent variables being conditionally significant, including the quadratic transformation of Experience. This would indicate that a non-linear relationship exists between experience and salary.

12.108 a. The correlation matrix indicates that crash deaths are positively related to vehicle weight and percentage of light trucks and negatively related to percent imported cars and car age. Light trucks will have the strongest linear association of any independent variable followed by car age. High correlation is likely to exist between the independent variables due to the strong correlation between impcars and vehicle weight.

b.

Regression Analysis: deaths versus vehwt, impcars, lghttrks, carage

```
The regression equation is
deaths = 2.60 + 0.000064 vehwt  - 0.00121 impcars + 0.00833 lghttrks
         - 0.0395 carage
Predictor         Coef      SE Coef          T          P        VIF
Constant         2.597        1.247       2.08      0.043
vehwt        0.0000643    0.0001908       0.34      0.738       10.9
impcars      -0.001213     0.005249      -0.23      0.818       10.6
lghttrks      0.008332     0.001397       5.96      0.000        1.2
carage       -0.03946      0.01916       -2.06      0.045        1.4

S = 0.05334      R-Sq = 59.5%      R-Sq(adj) = 55.8%
```

Light trucks is a significant positive variable. Since impcars has the smallest t-statistic, it is removed from the model. Also, remove vehicle weight using the same argument which results in the following final model:

Regression Analysis: deaths versus lghttrks, carage

```
The regression equation is
deaths = 2.51 + 0.00883 lghttrks - 0.0352 carage
Predictor         Coef      SE Coef          T          P        VIF
Constant         2.506        1.249       2.01      0.051
lghttrks      0.008835     0.001382       6.39      0.000        1.1
carage       -0.03522      0.01765       -2.00      0.052        1.1

S = 0.05404      R-Sq = 56.5%      R-Sq(adj) = 54.6%
```

The model has light trucks and car age as the significant variables. Note that car age is marginally significant (p-value of .052) and hence could also be dropped from the model.

c. The regression modeling indicates that the percentage of light trucks is conditionally significant in all of the models and hence is an important predictor in the model. Car age and imported cars are marginally significant predictors when only light trucks is included in the model.

12.110 a. The correlation matrix shows that high correlation between the independent variables is not likely to be a problem in this model since none of the correlations among the independent variables are relatively high.

The range for applying the regression model (variable means +/− 2 standard errors):

Hseval	11.11 to 30.94
Sizehse	5.0 to 5.96
Taxhse	32.35 to 227.91
Comper	.034 to .286
Incom72	2727 to 3995
Totexp	1488848 +/− 2(1265564) = not a good approximation

b. Regression models

Regression Analysis: hseval versus sizehse, Taxhse, ...

```
The regression equation is
hseval = - 31.1 + 9.10 sizehse - 0.00058 Taxhse - 22.2 Comper
         + 0.00120 incom72 + 0.000001 totexp
Predictor         Coef      SE Coef        T         P       VIF
Constant        -31.07        10.09     -3.08     0.003
sizehse           9.105        1.927      4.72     0.000       1.3
Taxhse        -0.000584     0.008910     -0.07     0.948       1.2
Comper          -22.197        7.108     -3.12     0.002       1.3
incom72         0.001200     0.001566      0.77     0.445       1.5
totexp       0.00000125   0.00000038      3.28     0.002       1.5


S = 3.785        R-Sq = 45.0%     R-Sq(adj) = 41.7%
```

Regression Analysis: hseval versus sizehse, Comper, totexp

```
The regression equation is
hseval = - 29.9 + 9.61 sizehse - 23.5 Comper + 0.000001 totexp
Predictor         Coef      SE Coef        T         P       VIF
Constant        -29.875        9.791     -3.05     0.003
sizehse           9.613        1.724      5.58     0.000       1.1
Comper          -23.482        6.801     -3.45     0.001       1.2
totexp       0.00000138   0.00000033      4.22     0.000       1.1


S = 3.754        R-Sq = 44.6%     R-Sq(adj) = 42.6%
```

This is the final regression model. All of the independent variables are conditionally significant. Both the size of house and total government expenditures enhances market value of homes while the percent of commercial property tends to reduce market values of homes.

c. In the final regression model, the tax variable was not found to be conditionally significant and hence it is difficult to support the developer's claim.

12.112 a.

Regression Analysis: Res. Invest. versus GDP, Prime Rate, Money Supply, Govt. Spending

```
The regression equation is
Res. Invest. = 50.3 + 0.0789 GDP - 5.90 Prime Rate - 0.0340
Money Supply - 0.0792 Govt. Spending

Predictor         Coef       StDev         T         P
Constant         50.29       15.25      3.30     0.001
GDP           0.078923    0.007394     10.67     0.000
Prime Ra       -5.9020      0.7707     -7.66     0.000
Money Su     -0.033979    0.007378     -4.61     0.000
Govt. Sp      -0.07918     0.03009     -2.63     0.009

S = 31.90        R-Sq = 93.6%     R-Sq(adj) = 93.5%

Analysis of Variance

Source            DF          SS          MS         F         P
Regression         4     3418627      854657    839.93     0.000
Residual Error   231      235050        1018
Total            235     3653676
```

This will be the final model with prime rate as the interest rate variable since all of the independent variables are conditionally significant.

Regression Analysis Res. Invest. versus GDP, Federal Funds Rate, Money Supply, Govt. Spending

```
The regression equation is
Res. Invest. = 45.1 - 4.23 Federal Funds Rate + 0.0740 GDP
             - 0.0295 Money Supply - 0.0766 Govt. Spending

Predictor        Coef        StDev           T        P
Constant        45.07        16.90        2.67    0.008
Federal        -4.2287       0.7815       -5.41    0.000
GDP            0.073987     0.007793       9.49    0.000
Money Su      -0.029509     0.008067      -3.66    0.000
Govt. Sp      -0.07662       0.03195      -2.40    0.017

S = 33.65      R-Sq = 92.8%     R-Sq(adj) = 92.7%

Analysis of Variance

Source             DF          SS          MS          F        P
Regression          4     3392102      848025     748.90    0.000
Residual Error    231      261575        1132
Total             235     3653676
```

The model with the federal funds rate as the interest rate variable is also the final model with all of the independent variables conditionally significant.

b. For the prime interest rate regression equation, the 95% confidence interval for the interest rate conditional slope coefficient is (–7.420, –4.384). For the federal funds interest rate regression equation, the 95% confidence interval for the interest rate conditional slope coefficient is (–5.768, –2.689).

12.114 a. First run: The correlation matrix indicates several independent variables that should provide good explanatory power in the regression model. We would expect that age, years at associate professor and years at full professor are likely to be conditionally significant:

Regression Analysis: Salary versus age, yrs_asoc, …
```
The regression equation is
Salary = 21107 + 105 age + 532 yrs_asoc + 690 yrs_full
       - 1312 Sex_1Fem + 2854 Market + 1101 C8
Predictor        Coef      SE Coef           T          P      VIF
Constant        21107         1599       13.20      0.000
age            104.59        40.62        2.58      0.011      3.1
yrs_asoc       532.27        63.66        8.36      0.000      2.4
yrs_full       689.93        52.66       13.10      0.000      1.7
Sex_1Fem      -1311.8        532.3       -2.46      0.015      1.3
Market         2853.9        823.3        3.47      0.001      1.0
C8             1101.0        658.1        1.67      0.097      1.1

S = 2569        R-Sq = 85.6%     R-Sq(adj) = 85.0%
```

Then, dropping the C8 variable yields the final model:

Regression Analysis: Salary versus age, yrs_asoc, ...

```
The regression equation is
Salary = 21887 + 90.0 age + 539 yrs_asoc + 697 yrs_full
         - 1397 Sex_1Fem + 2662 Market
```

Predictor	Coef	SE Coef	T	P	VIF
Constant	21887	1539	14.22	0.000	
age	90.02	39.92	2.26	0.026	3.0
yrs_asoc	539.48	63.91	8.44	0.000	2.4
yrs_full	697.35	52.80	13.21	0.000	1.7
Sex_1Fem	-1397.2	533.2	-2.62	0.010	1.2
Market	2662.3	820.3	3.25	0.001	1.0

```
S = 2585       R-Sq = 85.3%     R-Sq(adj) = 84.8%
```

Analysis of Variance

Source	DF	SS	MS	F	P
Regression	5	5585766862	1117153372	167.14	0.000
Residual Error	144	962459821	6683749		
Total	149	6548226683			

This is the final model. All of the independent variables are conditionally significant and the model explains a sizeable portion of the variability in salary.

b. To test the hypothesis that the rate of change in female salaries as a function of age is less than the rate of change in male salaries as a function of age, the dummy variable Sex_1Fem is used to see if the slope coefficient for age (X_1) is different for males and females. The following model is used:

$$Y = \beta_0 + (\beta_1 + \beta_6 X_4)X_1 + \beta_2 X_2 + \beta_3 X_3 + \beta_4 X_4 + \beta_5 X_5$$
$$= \beta_0 + \beta_1 X_1 + \beta_6 X_4 X_1 + \beta_2 X_2 + \beta_3 X_3 + \beta_4 X_4 + \beta_5 X_5$$

Create the variable $X_4 X_1$ and then test for conditional significance in the regression model. If it proves to be a significant predictor of salaries then there is strong evidence to conclude that the rate of change in female salaries as a function of age is different than for males:

Regression Analysis: Salary versus age, femage, ...

```
The regression equation is
Salary = 22082 + 85.1 age + 11.7 femage + 543 yrs_asoc
         + 701 yrs_full - 1878 Sex_1Fem + 2673 Market
```

Predictor	Coef	SE Coef	T	P	VIF
Constant	22082	1877	11.77	0.000	
age	85.07	48.36	1.76	0.081	4.4
femage	11.66	63.89	0.18	0.855	32.2
yrs_asoc	542.85	66.73	8.13	0.000	2.6
yrs_full	701.35	57.35	12.23	0.000	2.0
Sex_1Fem	-1878	2687	-0.70	0.486	31.5
Market	2672.8	825.1	3.24	0.001	1.0

```
S = 2594       R-Sq = 85.3%     R-Sq(adj) = 84.7%
```

The regression shows that the newly created variable of femage is not conditionally significant. Thus, we cannot conclude that the rate of change in female salaries as a function of age differs from that of male salaries.

12.116 a. There exists a positive relationship between EconGPA and all of the independent variables, which is expected. Note that there is a high correlation between the composite ACT score and the individual components, which is again, as expected. Thus, high correlation between the independent variables is likely to be a serious concern in this regression model.

Regression Analysis: EconGPA versus sex, Acteng, ...

```
The regression equation is
EconGPA = - 0.050 + 0.261 sex + 0.0099 Acteng + 0.0064 ACTmath
             + 0.0270 ACTss + 0.0419 ACTcomp + 0.00898 HSPct
71 cases used 41 cases contain missing values
```

Predictor	Coef	SE Coef	T	P	VIF
Constant	-0.0504	0.6554	-0.08	0.939	
sex	0.2611	0.1607	1.62	0.109	1.5
Acteng	0.00991	0.02986	0.33	0.741	2.5
ACTmath	0.00643	0.03041	0.21	0.833	4.3
ACTss	0.02696	0.02794	0.96	0.338	4.7
ACTcomp	0.04188	0.07200	0.58	0.563	12.8
HSPct	0.008978	0.005716	1.57	0.121	1.4

```
S = 0.4971      R-Sq = 34.1%      R-Sq(adj) = 27.9%
```

As expected, multicollinearity is affecting the results. A strategy of dropping the variable with the lowest t-statistic with each successive model causes the dropping of the following variables (in order): (1) ACTmath, (2) ACTeng, (3) ACTss, (4) HSPct. The two variables that remain are the final model of gender and ACTcomp:

Regression Analysis: EconGPA versus sex, ACTcomp

```
The regression equation is
EconGPA = 0.322 + 0.335 sex + 0.0978 ACTcomp
73 cases used 39 cases contain missing values
```

Predictor	Coef	SE Coef	T	P	VIF
Constant	0.3216	0.5201	0.62	0.538	
sex	0.3350	0.1279	2.62	0.011	1.0
ACTcomp	0.09782	0.01989	4.92	0.000	1.0

```
S = 0.4931      R-Sq = 29.4%      R-Sq(adj) = 27.3%
```

Both independent variables are conditionally significant.

  b. The model could be used in college admission decisions by creating a predicted GPA in economics based on sex and ACT comp scores. This predicted GPA could then be used with other factors in deciding admission. Note that this model predicts that females will outperform males with equal test scores. Using this model as the only source of information may lead to charges of unequal treatment.

Chapter 13

13.2 $Y_i = \beta_0 + \beta_1 X_{1i} + \beta_2 X_{2i} + \beta_3 X_{3i} + \beta_4 X_{4i} + \beta_5 X_{5i} + \varepsilon_i$ where Y_i = wages, X_1 = years of experience, $X_2 = 1$ for Germany, 0 otherwise, $X_3 = 1$ for Great Britain, 0 otherwise, $X_4 = 1$ for Japan, 0 otherwise, $X_5 = 1$ for Turkey, 0 otherwise. The excluded category consists of wages in the United States.

13.4 a. For any observation, the values of the dummy variables sum to one. Since the equation has an intercept term, there is perfect multicollinearity and the existence of the "dummy variable trap."

b. β_3 measures the expected difference between demand in the first and fourth quarters, all else equal. β_4 measures the expected difference between demand in the second and fourth quarters, all else equal. β_5 measures the expected difference between demand in the third and fourth quarters, all else equal.

13.6 $Y_i = \beta_0 + \beta_1 X_{1i} + \beta_2 X_{2i} + \beta_3 X_{3i} + \beta_4 X_{4i} + \beta_5 X_{5i} + \varepsilon_i$

where Y_i = per capita cereal sales
X_1 = cereal price
X_2 = price of competing cereals
X_3 = mean per capita income
X_4 = % college graduates
X_5 = mean annual temperature
X_6 = mean annual rainfall
X_7 = 1 for cities east of the Mississippi, 0 otherwise
X_8 = 1 for high per capita income, 0 otherwise
X_9 = 1 for intermediate per capita income, 0 otherwise
X_{10} = 1 for northwest, 0 otherwise
X_{11} = 1 for southwest, 0 otherwise
X_{12} = 1 for northeast, 0 otherwise
X_{13} = $X_1 X_7$—interaction term between price and cities east of the Mississippi

The model specification includes continuous independent variables, dichotomous indicator variables, and slope dummy variables. While the functional form can be linear, non-linearity could be introduced based on an initial analysis of the scatterplots of the relationships. High correlation among the independent variables could also be detected, for example, per capita income and % college graduates may very well be collinear. Several iterations of the model could be conducted to find the optimal combinations of variables.

13.8 Define the following variables for the experiment:

Y = worker compensation
X_1 = years of experience
X_2 = job classification level: 1. Apprentice, 2 Professional, 3. Master
X_3 = individual ability
X_4 = gender: 1. male, 2. female
X_5 = race: 1. White, 2. Black, 3. Latino

Two different dependent variables can be developed from the salary data. Base compensation will be one analysis that can be conducted. The incremental salaries can also be analyzed. Dummy variables are required to analyze the impact of job classifications on salary. Discrimination can be measured by the size of the dummy variable on gender and on race. For each dummy variable, (k-1) categories are required to avoid the 'dummy variable trap.'

13.10 a. $\dfrac{\beta_j}{(1 - \gamma)} = 3.03$

b. $\dfrac{\beta_j}{(1 - \gamma)} = 3.289$

c. $\dfrac{\beta_j}{(1 - \gamma)} = 5.556$

d. $\dfrac{\beta_j}{(1 - \gamma)} = 6.515$

13.12

Regression Analysis: Y Retail Sales versus X Income, Ylag1

```
The regression equation is
Y  Retail Sales = 1752 + 0.367 X  Income + 0.053 Ylag1
21 cases used 1 cases contain missing values

Predictor           Coef       SE Coef          T         P
Constant          1751.6         500.0       3.50     0.003
X  Incom         0.36734       0.08054       4.56     0.000
Ylag1             0.0533        0.2035       0.26     0.796


S = 153.4        R-Sq = 91.7%      R-Sq(adj) = 90.7%
```

$t = .2619$; $t_{18,.10} = 1.33$, therefore, do not reject H_0 at the 20% level.

13.14

Regression Analysis: Y_%stocks versus X_Return, Y_lag%stocks

```
The regression equation is
Y_%stocks = 1.65 + 0.228 X_Return + 0.950 Y_lag%stocks
24 cases used 1 cases contain missing values

Predictor           Coef       SE Coef          T         P
Constant           1.646         2.414       0.68     0.503
X_Return         0.22776       0.03015       7.55     0.000
Y_lag%st         0.94999       0.04306      22.06     0.000

S = 2.351        R-Sq = 95.9%      R-Sq(adj) = 95.5%
```

13.16

Regression Analysis: Y_Birth versus X_1stmarriage, Y_lagBirth

```
The regression equation is
Y_Birth = 21262 + 0.485 X_1stmarriage + 0.192 Y_lagBirth

19 cases used 1 cases contain missing values
Predictor           Coef       SE Coef          T         P
Constant           21262          5720       3.72     0.002
X_1stmar          0.4854        0.1230       3.94     0.001
Y_lagBir          0.1923        0.1898       1.01     0.326


S = 2513         R-Sq = 93.7%      R-Sq(adj) = 93.0%
```

13.18

Regression Analysis: Y_logCons Versus X_LogDI, Y_laglogCons

```
The regression equation is
Y_logCons = 0.405 + 0.373 X_LogDI + 0.558 Y_laglogCons

28 cases used 1 cases contain missing values
Predictor           Coef       SE Coef          T         P
Constant          0.4049        0.1051       3.85     0.001
X_LogDI           0.3734        0.1075       3.47     0.002
Y_laglog          0.5577        0.1243       4.49     0.000


S = 0.03023      R-Sq = 99.6%      R-Sq(adj) = 99.6%

Durbin-Watson statistic = 1.63
```

13.20 a. In the special case where the sample correlations between x_1 and x_2 is zero, the estimate for β_1 will be the same whether or not x_2 is included in the regression equation. In the simple linear regression of y on x_1, the intercept term will embody the influence of x_2 on y, under these special circumstances.

b. $$b_1 = \frac{\sum(x_{2i} - \bar{x}_2)^2 \sum(x_{1i} - \bar{x}_1)(y_{1i} - \bar{y}) - \sum(x_{1i} - \bar{x}_1)(x_{2i} - \bar{x}_2) \sum(x_{2i} - \bar{x}_2)(y_i - \bar{y})}{\sum(x_{1i} - \bar{x}_1)^2 \sum(x_{2i} - \bar{x}_2)^2 - [\sum(x_{1i} - \bar{x}_1)\sum(x_{2i} - \bar{x}_2)]^2}$$

If the sample correlation between x_1 and x_2 is zero, then $\sum(x_{1i} - \bar{x}_1)(x_{2i} - \bar{x}_2) = 0$ and the slope coefficient equation can be simplified. The result is

$$b_1 = \frac{\sum(x_{1i} - \bar{x}_1)(y_{1i} - \bar{y})}{\sum(x_{1i} - \bar{x}_1)^2}$$ which is the estimated slope coefficient for the bivariate

linear regression of y on x_1.

13.22 Initial regression model includes all of the indicated independent variables:

Results for: CITYDAT.XLS

Regression Analysis: hseval Versus Comper, Homper, ...
```
The regression equation is
hseval = - 19.0 - 26.4 Comper - 12.1 Homper - 15.5 Indper
         + 7.22 sizehse + 0.00408 incom72
Predictor         Coef      SE Coef         T         P
Constant        -19.02        13.20     -1.44     0.153
Comper         -26.393         9.890     -2.67     0.009
Homper         -12.123         7.508     -1.61     0.110
Indper         -15.531         8.630     -1.80     0.075
sizehse          7.219         2.138      3.38     0.001
incom72       0.004081      0.001555      2.62     0.010

S = 3.949        R-Sq = 40.1%      R-Sq(adj) = 36.5%
Durbin-Watson statistic = 1.03
```

Initially excluding the insignificant variables Homper and Indper and then excluding median rooms per residence (Sizehse) yields the final model:

Regression Analysis: hseval Versus Comper, incom72
```
The regression equation is
hseval = 4.69 - 20.4 Comper + 0.00585 incom72
Predictor         Coef      SE Coef         T         P
Constant         4.693        5.379      0.87     0.385
Comper         -20.432        7.430     -2.75     0.007
incom72       0.005847      0.001484      3.94     0.000

S = 4.352        R-Sq = 24.7%      R-Sq(adj) = 22.9%
Durbin-Watson statistic = 0.98
```

Note that the coefficient on percent of commercial property for both of the models is negative; however, it is larger in the second model where the median rooms variable is excluded.

13.24 If y is, in fact, strongly influenced by x_2, dropping it from the regression equation could lead to serious specification bias. Instead of dropping the variable, it is preferable to acknowledge that, while the group as a whole is clearly influential, the data does not contain information to allow the disentangling of the separate effects of each of the explanatory variables with some degree of precision.

13.26 a. Graphical check for heteroscedasticity shows no evidence of strong heteroscedasticity.
   b. The auxiliary regression is $e^2 = -63310.41 + 13.75\hat{y}$
   $n = 22$, $R^2 = .06954$, $nR^2 = 1.5299 < 2.71 = \chi^2_{1,1}$ therefore, do not reject H_0 the error terms have constant variance at the 10% level.

13.28 a.

Regression Analysis: y versus X1, X2, X3
```
The regression equation is
y = 0.2 + 0.000406 X1 + 4.84 X2 - 1.55 X3

Predictor        Coef     SE Coef       T       P
Constant         0.16       34.91    0.00   0.996
X1          0.0004060   0.0001736    2.34   0.024
X2              4.842       2.813    1.72   0.092
X3            -1.5543      0.3399   -4.57   0.000

S = 3.04752    R-Sq = 54.3%    R-Sq(adj) = 51.4%
```

b. Graphical check for heteroscedasticity shows no evidence of strong heteroscedasticity.

c. The auxiliary regression is $e^2 = 20.34 - .201\hat{y}$
$n = 50$, $R^2 = .00322$, $nR^2 = .161 < 2.71 = \chi^2_{1,1}$ therefore, do not reject the H_0 that the error terms have constant variance at the 10% level.

13.30 Reject the null hypothesis based on the Durbin-Watson test at both the 5% and 1% levels. Estimate of the autocorrelation coefficient: $r = .75$.

a. Reject the null hypothesis based on the Durbin-Watson test at both the 5% and 1% levels. Estimate of the autocorrelation coefficient: $r = .60$.

b. Reject the null hypothesis based on the Durbin-Watson test at the 5% level. The test is inconclusive at the 1% level. Estimate of the autocorrelation coefficient: $r = .45$.

c. The test is inconclusive at both the 5% level and the 1% level.

d. Do not reject the null hypothesis at either the 5% level or the 1% level. There is insufficient evidence to suggest autocorrelation exists in the residuals.

13.32 a. Do not reject the H_0 that the error terms have constant variance at the 10% level.

b. The Durbin-Watson test gives inconclusive results at both the 5% and 1% levels.

13.34 Do not reject H_0 that the error terms have constant variance at the 10% level.

13.36 Reject H_0 at the 10% level but not at the 5% level.

13.38 a.

Results for: Advertising Retail.xls
Regression Analysis: Retail Sales X(t) versus Advertising Y(t)
```
The regression equation is
Retail Sales X(t) = 2269 + 28.5 Advertising Y(t)

Predictor        Coef      SE Coef           T         P
Constant       2269.5        278.4        8.15     0.000
Advertis       28.504        2.087       13.66     0.000

S = 161.7      R-Sq = 90.3%       R-Sq(adj) = 89.8%
Analysis of Variance
Source           DF           SS          MS         F         P
Regression        1      4874833     4874833    186.52     0.000
Residual Error   20       522728       26136
Total            21      5397561
Durbin-Watson statistic = 1.12
```

b. Reject H_0 at the 5% level, autocorrelation of the residuals exists at the 5% level, test is inconclusive at the 1% level.

c. The fitted regression is

$$y_t - .5597y_{t-1} = 25.6122(1 - .5597) + 1.4482(x_t - .5597x_{t-1})$$

13.40 Do not reject H_0 at the 10% level.

13.42 In the first case, the coefficients of the dummy variables measures the difference between the expected tax revenues (as a percentage of gross national product) in the countries that participate in some form of economic integration versus those that do not. It quantifies the difference between the value of 1 of the dummy variable versus the excluded category.

In the second case, the intercept terms will include the effect of participation by a country in some form of economic integration on tax revenues.

13.44 a. Heteroscedasticity: is defined as when the residuals do not have constant variance at all levels of the dependent variable. It results in parameter estimates that are not efficient and invalidates the confidence interval and hypothesis testing statistics.

b. Autocorrelated errors: Autocorrelation of the residuals is when the error terms are not independent from one another across the order of observation. It results in inefficient parameter estimates and invalidates the confidence interval and hypothesis testing statistics. For models that contain lagged dependent variables, autocorrelated errors will result in inconsistent parameter estimates.

13.46 a. All else equal, the secondary market price of $100 of debt of a country is 9.6 units lower if U.S. bank regulators have mandated write-downs of the country's assets than if otherwise.

b. Reject H_0 at the 1% level.

c. 84% of the variability in the secondary market price of $100 of debt of a country is explained by the variability in each of the independent variables.

d. Any improvement or change in the model characteristics would have to be weighed against the loss of the degrees of freedom from an added independent variable.

13.48 a. All else equal, a one unit increase in the world price of U.S. wheat will yield an estimated decrease of .62 of a unit in the quantity of U.S. wheat exported.

b. Reject H_0 at the .5% level.

c. Reject H_0 at the 1% level.

d. Given that the residuals are autocorrelated, the hypothesis test results of part b. are not valid. The model must be reestimated taking into account the autocorrelated errors.

13.50 a. All else equal, a bank whose head office is in New York will experience a 1.67% higher rate of return than one which is based outside of New York.

b. Reject H_0 at the 5% level.

c. Do not reject H_0 that the error terms have constant variance at the 10% level.

13.52 a. All else equal, an additional room in a dwelling leads to an expected $10.94 increase in the average monthly electrical bill.

b. Do not reject H_0 at the 20% level.

c. An indication of the presence of multicollinearity occurs when, taken as a group, the set of independent variables appears to exert a considerable influence on the dependent variable, but when looked at separately through hypothesis tests, none of the individual regression slope coefficients appear significantly different from zero. So if the F-test of the significance of the overall regression show the model has significant explanatory power and yet none of the individual regression slope coefficients is significant, suspect that multicollinearity exists between the independent variables.

d. If an important independent variable is omitted from the regression model, the least squares estimates will be unreliable due to specification bias.

e. Do not reject the null hypothesis that the error terms have constant variance at the 10% level.

13.54

Regression Analysis: y versus x1, x2
```
The regression equation is
y = - 1.63 + 0.779 x1 + 1.50 x2
Predictor         Coef      SE Coef          T          P
Constant        -1.627        1.130      -1.44      0.166
x1               0.7792       0.1649       4.72      0.000
x2               1.4961       0.1802       8.30      0.000

S = 1.435       R-Sq = 80.2%      R-Sq(adj) = 78.1%
Analysis of Variance
Source             DF            SS          MS          F          P
Regression          2       158.611      79.305      38.50      0.000
Residual Error     19        39.142       2.060
Total              21       197.753

Source          DF       Seq SS
x1               1        16.626
x2               1       141.985
Durbin-Watson statistic = 1.51
```

Test for heteroscedasticity:

$nR^2 = 22(.02215) = .4873 < 2.71 = \chi^2_{1,.1}$, therefore, do not reject H_0 that the error terms have constant variance at the 10% level.

Test for autocorrelation:

$H_0 : \rho = 0,\ H_1 : \rho > 0$

$d = 1.51$, n=22, K = 2

$\alpha = .05$: $d_L = 1.15$ and $d_U = 1.54$

$\alpha = .01$: $d_L = .91$ and $d_U = 1.28$

At the 5% level the Durbin-Watson test is inconclusive. Do not reject H_0 at the 1% level.

13.56 76.6% of the variation in the FDIC examiner work hours can be explained by the variation in total assets of the bank, total number of offices, classified to total loan ratio, management rating and if the examination was conducted jointly with the state.

$$H_0 : \beta_1 = \beta_2 = \cdots = \beta_7 = 0, \quad H_1 : at\ least\ one\ \beta_i \neq 0\ (i = 1, \ldots, >, 7)$$

$$F = \frac{83}{7}\frac{.766}{1 - .766} = 38.814,\ F_{7,83,.01} \approx 2.95,\ \text{therefore, reject } H_0 \text{ at the 1% level.}$$

13.58 a.

```
The regression equation is
Nonresidential = 1282 - 53.0 Prime Rate
Durbin-Watson statistic = 0.05
```

Test for autocorrelation:

$H_0 : \rho = 0,\ H_1 : \rho > 0$, $d = 0.05$, n=114, K = 1, $\alpha = .05$: $d_L = 1.65$ and $d_U = 1.69$

$\alpha = .01$: $d_L = 1.52$ and $d_U = 1.56$, reject H_0 at the 1% level or 5% level.

b.

```
The regression equation is
Nonresidential = - 76.7 + 0.0299 Per capita Income (Lagged) - 0.902
State and local - 0.613 Federal + 0.207 Gross domestic product + 3.94
Prime Rate
Durbin-Watson statistic = 1.59
```

Test for autocorrelation:

$H_0 : \rho = 0$, $H_1 : \rho > 0$, d = 1.59, n=114, K = 5, $\alpha = .05$: $d_L = 1.57$ and $d_U = 1.78$

$\alpha = .01$: $d_L = 1.44$ and $d_U = 1.65$, test is inconclusive at the 1% level and 5% level.

c. The regression with prime rate had a $r^2 = 0.05$ and high autocorrelation. It explained only 5% of the variation. The correction for autocorrelation regression equation using all the predictor variables had a $r^2 = 0.952$ and no autocorrelation. It explained 95.2% of the variation. The second regression model explains the investment much better.

13.60 a. Regression of value added as a function of inputs labor and capital

Regression Analysis: valadded versus labor, capital

```
The regression equation is
valadded = 123 + 2.32 labor + 0.472 capital
Predictor        Coef       SE Coef           T          P
Constant        122.7         170.9        0.72      0.480
labor           2.323         1.033        2.25      0.034
capital        0.4716        0.1123        4.20      0.000

S = 469.9        R-Sq = 96.0%     R-Sq(adj) = 95.6%
Analysis of Variance
Source            DF           SS          MS          F          P
Regression         2    126519178    63259589     286.46     0.000
Residual Error    24      5299991      220833
Total             26    131819169

Source        DF      Seq SS
labor          1   122623731
capital        1     3895447
Durbin-Watson statistic = 2.02
```

b. Plot of residuals vs. labor and capital.

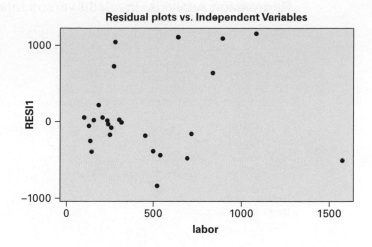

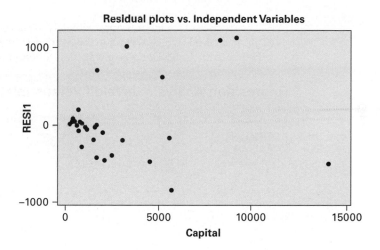

Residual plots indicate possible evidence of increasing variance.

c. Estimate the Cobb-Douglas production function:

Regression Analysis: Invaladd versus Inlabor, Incapital

```
The regression equation is
lnvaladd = 1.29 + 0.596 lnlabor + 0.366 lncapital
```

Predictor	Coef	SE Coef	T	P
Constant	1.2883	0.3225	3.99	0.001
lnlabor	0.5960	0.1293	4.61	0.000
lncapita	0.36638	0.09009	4.07	0.000

```
S = 0.1918     R-Sq = 94.1%     R-Sq(adj) = 93.7%
```

Analysis of Variance

Source	DF	SS	MS	F	P
Regression	2	14.1803	7.0902	192.74	0.000
Residual Error	24	0.8829	0.0368		
Total	26	15.0632			

```
Durbin-Watson statistic = 1.68
```

The coefficient for labor is approximately .60 and the coefficient for capital is roughly .37. Sum is .97, which is close to the restriction implied by the Cobb-Douglas model.
d. Estimate the Cobb-Douglas production function with constant returns to scale.

Regression Analysis: Invaldif versus Inlabdif

```
The regression equation is
lnvaldif = 1.11 + 0.657 lnlabdif
```

Predictor	Coef	SE Coef	T	P
Constant	1.1120	0.1410	7.89	0.000
lnlabdif	0.65723	0.08031	8.18	0.000

```
S = 0.1894     R-Sq = 72.8%     R-Sq(adj) = 71.7%
```

Analysis of Variance

Source	DF	SS	MS	F	P
Regression	1	2.4015	2.4015	66.97	0.000
Residual Error	25	0.8965	0.0359		
Total	26	3.2981			

```
Durbin-Watson statistic = 1.67
```

The coefficient for labor in the Cobb-Douglas model is, $\beta_1 = .657$ and thus the coefficent for capital is $\beta_2 = .343$. These compare favorably to the unrestricted model where the coefficients were $\beta_1 = .60$ *and* $\beta_2 = .37$.
e. The linear model from part a. and the log transformed model from part b. cannot be compared using R2 because the dependent variables are not the same variable. Therefore, the models can only be compared by computing predicted values in value added units and comparing the implied residuals.

Plot of residuals from the unrestricted exponential model (part b.):

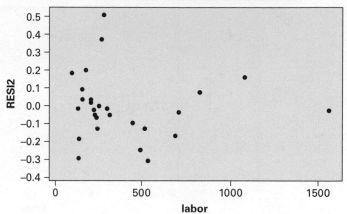

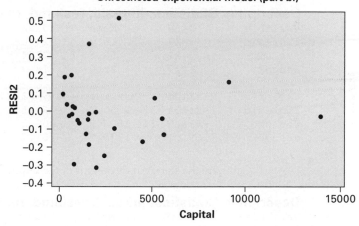

There is no strong evidence that the residuals exhibit strong patterns. However, there are two quite large positive residuals with values around 1,400, which is almost twice that of the next largest positive residuals.

Plot the residuals from the restricted exponential model (part c.):

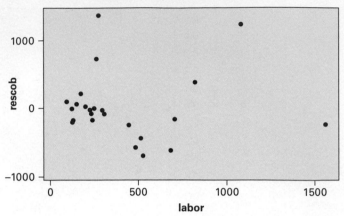

Residual plot vc. independent variable
Restricted exponential model (part c.)

There is no evidence of strong data patterns, may want to check for increasing variance.

Descriptive Statistics: linresid, reslnmd, rescob

Variable	N	Mean	Median	TrMean	StDev	SE Mean
linresid	27	-0.0	-24.0	-12.6	451.5	86.9
reslnmd	27	58.6	-22.4	28.0	486.7	93.7
rescob	27	22.0	-18.7	-3.7	472.4	90.9

Variable	Minimum	Maximum	Q1	Q3
linresid	-841.4	1155.9	-263.6	56.0
reslnmd	-619.5	1503.8	-202.5	90.0
rescob	-691.1	1379.2	-201.7	62.4

Compare the standard deviations of the implied residuals:

Descriptive Statistics: linresid, reslnmd, rescob

Variable	N	Mean	Median	TrMean	StDev	SE Mean
linresid	27	-0.0	-24.0	-12.6	451.5	86.9
reslnmd	27	58.6	-22.4	28.0	486.7	93.7
rescob	27	22.0	-18.7	-3.7	472.4	90.9

Variable	Minimum	Maximum	Q1	Q3
linresid	-841.4	1155.9	-263.6	56.0
reslnmd	-619.5	1503.8	-202.5	90.0
rescob	-691.1	1379.2	-201.7	62.4

Note that both the mean and standard deviation of the implied residuals from the restricted exponential model (part c.) are smaller than from the unrestricted exponential model (part b.)

13.62 a.

```
The regression equation is
Services = - 74.2 + 0.411 Gross domestic product
Durbin-Watson statistic = 0.26
```

Test for autocorrelation:

$H_0 : \rho = 0$, $H_1 : \rho > 0$, d = 0.26, n=113, K = 1, $\alpha = .05 : d_L = 1.65$ and $d_U = 1.69$

$\alpha = .01 : d_L = 1.52$ and $d_U = 1.56$, reject H_0 at the 1% level and 5% level. There is autocorrelation.

b.

```
The regression equation is
Services = 39.4 + 0.288 Gross domestic product + 0.218 Personal
consumption (lagged) - 1.48 Imports of Services - 8.26 Prime Rate
Durbin-Watson statistic = 0.40
```

Test for autocorrelation:

$H_0 : \rho = 0$, $H_1 : \rho > 0$, d = 0.40, n=113, K = 4, $\alpha = .05 : d_L = 1.59$ and $d_U = 1.76$

$\alpha = .01 : d_L = 1.46$ and $d_U = 1.63$, reject H_0 at the 1% level and 5% level. There is still autocorrelation. The new model reduces but does not eliminate autocorrelation.

Chapter 14

14.2 H_0: Mutual fund performance is equally likely to be in the 5 performance quintiles.
H_1: Otherwise

Mutual Funds	Top 20%	2nd 20%	3rd 20%	4th 20%	5th 20%	Total
Observed number	13	20	18	11	13	75
Probability (Ho)	0.2	0.2	0.2	0.2	0.2	1
Expected number	15	15	15	15	15	75
Chi-square calculation	0.266667	1.666667	0.6	1.066667	0.266667	3.8667

$\chi^2 = 3.8667$, $\chi^2_{(4,.1)} = 7.78$. Therefore, do not reject H_0 at the 10% level.

14.4 H_0: Quality of the output conforms to the usual pattern.
H_1: Otherwise

Electronic Component	No Faults	1 Fault	>1 Fault	Total
Observed number	458	30	12	500
Probability (Ho)	0.93	0.05	0.02	1
Expected number	465	25	10	500
Chi-square calculation	0.105376344	1	0.4	1.505376

$\chi^2 = 1.505$, $\chi^2_{(2,.05)} = 5.99$ $\chi^2_{(2,.10)} = 4.61$. Therefore, do not reject H_0 at the 5% or the 10% level.

14.6 H_0: Student opinion of business courses is the same as that for all courses.
H_1: Otherwise

Opinion14-6	Very Useful	Somewhat	Worthless	Total
Observed number	68	18	14	100
Probability (Ho)	0.6	0.2	0.2	1
Expected number	60	20	20	100
Chi-square calculation	1.066666667	0.2	1.8	3.066667

$\chi^2 = 3.067$, $\chi^2_{(2,.10)} = 4.61$. Therefore, do not reject H_0 at the 10% level.

14.8 H_0: Consumer preferences for soft drinks are equally spread across 5 soft drinks.
H_1: Otherwise

Drink14-8	A	B	C	D	E	Total
Observed number	20	25	28	15	27	115
Probability (Ho)	0.2	0.2	0.2	0.2	0.2	1
Expected number	23	23	23	23	23	115
Chi-square calculation	0.391304	0.173913	1.086957	2.782609	0.695652	5.130435

$\chi^2 = 5.130$, $\chi^2_{(4,.10)} = 7.78$. Therefore, do not reject H_0 at the 10% level.

14.10 H_0: Statistics professors preferences for software packages are equally divided across 4 packages.
H_1: Otherwise

Software14-10	M	E	S	P	Total
Observed number	100	80	35	35	250
Probability (Ho)	0.25	0.25	0.25	0.25	1
Expected number	62.5	62.5	62.5	62.5	250
Chi-square calculation	22.5	4.9	12.1	12.1	51.6

$\chi^2 = 51.6$, $\chi^2_{(3,.005)} = 12.84$. Therefore, reject H_0 at the .5% level.

14.12 H_0: Population distribution of arrivals per minute is Poisson.
H_1: Otherwise

Arrivals	0	1	2	3	4+	Total
Observed number	10	26	35	24	5	100
Probability (Ho)	0.1496	0.2842	0.27	0.171	0.1252	1
Expected number	14.96	28.42	27	17.1	12.52	100
Chi-square calculation	1.6445	.2061	2.3704	2.7842	4.5168	11.522

$\chi^2 = 11.52$, $\chi^2_{(3,.01)} = 11.34$ $\chi^2_{(3,.005)} = 12.84$. Therefore, reject H_0 at the 1% level but not at the .5% level.

14.14 H_0: Resistance of electronic components is normally distributed.
H_1: Otherwise
$B = 9.625$. From Table 14.9—Significance points of the Jarque–Bera statistic; 5% point ($n = 100$) is 4.29. Therefore, reject H_0 at the 5% level.

14.16 H_0: Monthly balances for credit card holders of a particular card are normally distributed.
H_1: Otherwise
$B = 6.578$. From Table 14.9—Significance points of the Jarque–Bera statistic; 5% point ($n = 125$) is 4.34. Therefore, reject H_0 at the 5% level.

14.18 a. H_0: No association exists between GPA and major.
H_1: Otherwise
Chi-Sq $= 0.226 + 0.276 + 0.341 + 0.417 + 2.227 + 2.722 = 6.209$
DF $= 2$, p-value $= 0.045$, $\chi^2_{(2,.05)} = 5.99$. Therefore, reject H_0 of no association at the 5% level.

14.20 a.

Age	Method of Learning About Product		
	Friend	Ad	Collective Total
<21	30	20	50
21–35	60	30	90
35+	18	42	60
Row total	108	92	200

b. H_0: No association exists between the method of learning about the product and the age of the respondent.
H_1: Otherwise
Chi-Sq = 0.333 + 0.391 + 2.674 + 3.139 + 6.400 + 7.513 = 20.451
DF = 2, p-value = 0.000, $\chi^2_{(2,.005)}$ = 10.6. Therefore, reject H_0 of no association at the .5% level.

14.22 Reject H_0 at levels of alpha in excess of 1.18%.

14.24 Reject H_0 at levels of alpha in excess of 22.68%.

14.26 Reject H_0 at levels of alpha in excess of .30%.

14.28 Open-ended question. The findings should include statements about the relative size of the firms. The MIPS firms have larger total assets than do non-MIPS comparable firms. This holds true in both the Utilities as well as Industrial industries and for the overall total. Results of interest coverage and long-term debt-to-total-asset ratios varies depending on which test and which type of industry the firms are in. While publicly traded MIPS firms in the utilities industries have significantly higher long-term debt-to-total-asset ratio then do non-MIPS firms, the MIPS firms in the industrials do not.

14.30 Do not reject H_0 at any common level of alpha.

14.32 Reject H_0 at levels in excess of 9.51%.

14.34 Reject H_0 at levels in excess of 2.22%.

14.36 Reject H_0 at levels in excess of .78%.

14.38 Reject H_0 at levels in excess of 69.66%.

14.40 Reject H_0 at levels in excess of 0.03%.

14.42 Reject H_0 at any common level of alpha.

14.44 a. Pearson correlation = 0.183
b. Do not reject H_0 at the .10 level (two-tailed test).
c. An advantage of nonparametric tests is that normality of the variables is not assumed. The asset level variable is highly skewed and not likely to be normal. In addition, the test is less influenced by outliers and hence the extreme values of asset levels would have less weight placed on them.

14.46 Do not reject H_0 at the 10% level.

14.48 Reject H_0 at the .5% level.

14.50 Reject H_0 at the .5% level.

14.52 Reject H_0 at the .5% level.

14.54 Reject H_0 at the .5% level.

14.56 Reject H_0 at the .5% level.

14.58 Reject H_0 at the .5% level.

14.60 Reject H_0 at the .5% level.

14.62 Do not reject H_0 at the 10% level.

14.64 Do not reject H_0 at the 10% level.

14.66 a. There is no evidence of a significant relationship between students' class standing and their opinion on whether a student can easily find books in the college library.
b. The library should test further whether all classes find it "easy" or all classes find it "difficult."

14.68 Reject H_0 at the .5% level, evidence that Becker's conclusions are correct.

14.70 The hypothesis test results in p-value < 0.001. Therefore, the null hypothesis of no association is very clearly rejected, even at the 0.5% level. We conclude that there is an association between candy bar preference and gender.

14.72 Many examples of economic and business data tend to be highly skewed with extreme outliers—e.g., personal income, wealth, sales.

14.74 Reject H_0 at levels of alpha in excess of 58.1%.

14.76 Reject H_0 at levels of alpha in excess of 9.34%.

14.78 Do not reject H_0 at the 20% level.

Chapter 15

15.2 $MSG = \dfrac{879}{3}$, $MSW = \dfrac{798}{16}$, $F = \dfrac{293}{49.875} = 5.87$

$F_{3,16,.05} = 3.24$, $F_{3,16,.01} = 5.29$, therefore, reject H_0 at the 1% level.

15.4 a. $\bar{x}_1 = 62$, $\bar{x}_2 = 53$, $\bar{x}_3 = 52$, SSW = 3608, SSG = 340.9375, SST = 3948.9375
b.

One-way ANOVA: SodaSales versus CanColor

```
Analysis of Variance for SodaSale
Source      DF        SS        MS        F        P
CanColor     2       341       170     0.61    0.556
Error       13      3608       278
Total       15      3949
```

$F_{2,13,.05} = 3.81$, do not reject H_0 at the 5% level.

15.6 a. MINITAB Output Display

One-way Analysis of Variance

```
Analysis of Variance
Source      DF        SS        MS        F        P
Factor       2     354.1     177.1    10.45    0.001
Error       15     254.2      16.9
Total       17     608.3

                                 Individual 95% CIs For Mean
                                 Based on Pooled StDev
Level      N      Mean     StDev    ---------+---------+---------+------
Supplier   6    32.000     3.347                     (------*------)
Supplier   6    24.333     5.007     (------*------)
Supplier   6    34.833     3.817                           (------*-----)
                                     ---------+---------+---------+------
Pooled StDev =    4.116               25.0      30.0      35.0
```

b. Assume $\alpha = 0.05$. Reject H_0 and conclude that the population mean numbers of parts per shipments not conforming to standards are not the same for all three suppliers.
c. Assume $\alpha = 0.05$. $MSD(3) = 3.56$. The Supplier B mean is significantly different from both Supplier A and Supplier C, but the later two are not different.

15.8 a. MINITAB Output Display

One-way Analysis of Variance

```
Analysis of Variance
Source     DF       SS       MS       F       P
Factor      2       89       44    0.28   0.756
Error      18     2813      156
Total      20     2901
                                 Individual 95% CIs For Mean
                                 Based on Pooled StDev
Level      N     Mean    StDev   --+---------+---------+---------+---
Freshman   7    71.71    13.16   (-------------^--------------)
Sophomor   7    75.29    11.19        (--------------*-------------)
Juniors    7    76.57    13.05            (-------------*-------------)
                                 --+---------+---------+---------+---
Pooled StDev =   12.50           63.0      70.0      77.0      84.0
```

b. Assume $\alpha = 0.05$. Fail to reject H_0 and conclude that there is insufficient evidence that the three population mean scores are not equal.

c. Assume $\alpha = 0.05$. $MSD(3) = 9.85$. None of the subgroup means are significantly different from each other.

15.10 a. $\bar{x}_1 = 11.3333$, $\bar{x}_2 = 12.5$, $\bar{x}_3 = 8$

One-way ANOVA: Time versus Rank

```
Analysis of Variance for Time
Source     DF       SS       MS       F       P
Rank        2    51.40    25.70    3.27   0.074
Error      12    94.33     7.86
Total      14   145.73
```

b. $F_{2,12,.05} = 3.89$, do not reject H_0 at the 5% level.

15.12 MINITAB Output Display

One-way Analysis of Variance

```
Analysis of Variance
Source     DF       SS       MS       F       P
Factor      2    48.96    24.48    4.07   0.039
Error      15    90.13     6.01
Total      17   139.09
                                 Individual 95% CIs For Mean
                                 Based on Pooled StDev
Level      N     Mean    StDev   --+---------+---------+---------+---
Confessi   6   10.402    2.268                (--------*-------)
People W   6    7.045    2.182        (-------*--------)
Newsweek   6    6.777    2.850    (-------*--------)
                                 --+---------+---------+---------+---
Pooled StDev =    2.451           5.0       7.5      10.0      12.5
```

Assume $\alpha = 0.05$. Reject H_0 and conclude that the population mean fog indices are not the same for all three magazines. $MSD(3) = 2.12$. The *True Confessions* mean is significantly different from both *People Weekly* and *Newsweek*, but the later two are not different.

15.14 a. $\hat{\mu} = 8.0744$

    b. $\hat{G}_1 = 2.3273$, $\hat{G}_2 = -1.0294$, $\hat{G}_3 = -1.2977$

    c. $\hat{\varepsilon}_{32} = .7483$

15.16 $W = 8.32$, $\chi^2_{(2,.05)} = 5.99$, therefore, reject H_0 at the 5% level.

15.18 $W = 1.18$, $\chi^2_{(2,.10)} = 4.61$, therefore, do not reject H_0 at the 10% level.

Kruskal-Wallis Test: SodaSales versus CanColor

```
Kruskal-Wallis Test on SodaSale
CanColor     N     Median    Ave Rank          Z
1            6      60.00        10.2        1.08
2            5      52.00         7.4       -0.62
3            5      53.00         7.6       -0.51
Overall     16                   8.5
H = 1.18  DF = 2  P = 0.554
H = 1.19  DF = 2  P = 0.553 (adjusted for ties)
```

15.20 $W = 9.3772$, $\chi^2_{(2,.01)} = 9.21$, therefore, reject H_0 at the 1% level.

Kruskal-Wallis Test: Nonconforming versus Supplier

```
Kruskal-Wallis Test on Nonconfo
Supplier     N     Median    Ave Rank          Z
1            6      32.00        10.6        0.61
2            6      24.50         4.3       -2.90
3            6      35.00        13.6        2.29
Overall     18                   9.5
H = 9.38  DF = 2  P = 0.009
H = 9.47  DF = 2  P = 0.009 (adjusted for ties)
```

15.22 $W = .7403$, $\chi^2_{(2,.10)} = 4.61$, therefore, do not reject H_0 at the 10% level.

15.24 $W = 5.2452$, $\chi^2_{(2,.10)} = 4.61$, therefore, reject H_0 at the 10% level.

15.26 a. The null hypothesis tests the equality of the population mean ratings across the classes.

    b. $W = .17$, $\chi^2_{(2,.10)} = 4.61$, therefore, do not reject H_0 at the 10% level.

15.28 Test of H population block means all the same:

$$\frac{MSB}{MSE} = 3.597, F_{5,30,.05} = 2.53, F_{5,30,.01} = 3.70.$$ Reject at the 5% level, do not reject H_0 at the 1% level that the block means differ.

Test of K population group means all the same:

$$\frac{MSG}{MSE} = 4.91, F_{6,30,.05} = 2.42, F_{6,30,.01} = 3.47.$$ Reject H_0 at the 1% level. Evidence suggests the group means differ.

15.30 a.

Two-way ANOVA: earngrowth versus OilCo, Analyst

```
Analysis of Variance for earngrow
Source      DF        SS        MS        F         P
OilCo        4      3.30      0.83      0.31     0.866
Analyst      3     31.35     10.45      3.93     0.036
Error       12     31.90      2.66
Total       19     66.55
```

    b. $F_{4,12,.05} = 3.26 > .31$, therefore, do not reject H_0 at the 5% level.

15.32 a.

Two-way ANOVA: sales versus Quarter, soup

```
Analysis of Variance for sales
Source       DF      SS        MS       F       P
Quarter       3     615.0     205.0    2.10    0.202
Soup          2       6.2       3.1    0.03    0.969
Error         6     586.5      97.7
Total        11    1207.7
```

b. $F_{2,6,.05} = 5.14 > .03$, therefore, do not reject H_0 at the 5% level.

17.34 a.

Two-way ANOVA: Ratings versus Exam, Text

```
Analysis of Variance for Ratings
Source       DF       SS        MS       F       P
Exam          2     0.2022    0.1011    5.20    0.077
Text          2     0.4356    0.2178   11.20    0.023
Error         4     0.0778    0.0194
Total         8     0.7156
```

b. [texts]: $F_{2,4,.05} = 6.94 < 11.20$, therefore, reject H_0 at the 5% level.

c. [exam type]: $F_{2,4,.05} = 6.94 > 5.20$, therefore, do not reject H_0 at the 5% level.

15.36 $\hat{G}_3 = -.1556$
$\hat{B}_1 = .1778$
$\hat{\varepsilon}_{31} = .0556$

15.38 a. Complete the ANOVA table:

Source of Variation	Sum of Squares	df	Mean Square	F Ratio
Fertilizers	135.6	3	45.20	6.0916
Soil types	81.7	5	16.34	2.2022
Error	111.3	15	7.42	
Total	328.6	23		

b. [fertilizers]: $F_{3,15,.01} = 5.42 < 6.0916$, therefore, reject H_0 at the 1% level.

c. [soil types]: $F_{5,15,.05} = 2.90 > 2.2021$, therefore, do not reject H_0 at the 5% level.

15.40 Given, say, ten pairs observations, the F statistic would have 1, 9 degrees of freedom. The test is in the form of a two-tailed test. With alpha = .05, the critical value of F would be 5.12. For a matched–pairs test, the degrees of freedom would be 9, and the area in each tail would be .025. The critical value for t would be 2.262 (which is the square root of the F statistic of 5.12). Therefore, the two tests are equivalent.

15.42 $F \, Ratio: Interaction = \dfrac{MSI}{MSE} = .67$, $F_{20,90,.05} \approx 1.75$, $F_{20,90,.01} \approx 2.20$. Do not reject H_0 at the 5% level. No significant interaction exists between treatment groups A and B. Therefore, go on to test the main effects of each treatment group.

$F \, Ratio: Treatment \, A = \dfrac{MSG_A}{MSE} = 5.73$, $F_{4,80,.05} \approx 2.53$, $F_{4,80,.01} \approx 3.65$. Reject H_0 at the 1% level, there is a significant main effect for group A.

$F \, Ratio: Treatment \, B = \dfrac{MSG_B}{MSE} = 4.00$, $F_{5,80,.05} \approx 2.37$, $F_{5,80,.01} \approx 3.34$. Reject H_0 at the 1% level, there is a significant main effect for group B.

15.44 a. ANOVA table

Source of Variation	Sum of Squares	df	Mean Square	F Ratio
Contestant	364.50	21	17.3571	19.2724
Judges	.81	8	.1013	.1124
Interaction	4.94	168	.0294	.0326
Error	1,069.94	1,188	.9006	
Total	1,440.19	1,385		

H_0: Mean value for all 22 contestants is the same.
H_1: Otherwise
$F_{21,1188,.01} \approx 1.88 < 19.2724$, therefore, reject H_0 at the 1% level.
H_0: Mean value for all 9 judges is the same.
H_1: Otherwise
$F_{8,1188,.05} \approx 1.94 > .1124$, therefore, do not reject H_0 at the 5% level.
H_0: No interaction exists between contestants and judges.
H_1: Otherwise
$F_{168,1188,.05} \approx 1.22 > .0326$, therefore, do not reject H_0 at the 5% level.

15.46 a. ANOVA table

Source of Variation	Sum of Squares	df	Mean Square	F Ratio
Test type	57.5556	2	28.7778	4.7091
Subject	389.0000	3	129.6667	21.2182
Interaction	586.0000	6	97.66667	15.9818
Error	146.6667	24	6.1111	
Total	1,179.2223	35		

b. H_0: No interaction exists between contestants and judges.
H_1: Otherwise
$F_{6,24,.01} = 3.67 < 15.9818$, therefore, reject H_0 at the 1% level.

15.48 a. The implied assumption is that there is no interaction effect between student year and dormitory ratings.

b.

General Linear Model: Ratings versus Dorm, Year

```
Factor      Type  Levels  Values
Dorm        fixed      4  A B C D
Year        fixed      4  1 2 3 4

Analysis of Variance for Ratings_, using Adjusted SS for Tests
Source     DF    Seq SS    Adj SS    Adj MS      F      P
Dorm        3    20.344    20.344     6.781   4.91  0.008
Year        3    10.594    10.594     3.531   2.56  0.078
Error      25    34.531    34.531     1.381
Total      31    65.469
```

Source of Variation	Sum of Squares	df	Mean Square	F Ratio
Dorm	20.344	3	6.781	4.91
Year	10.594	3	3.531	2.56
Error	34.531	25	1.381	
Total	65.469	31		

c. H_0: Mean ratings for all four dormitories is the same.
H_1: Otherwise
$F_{3,25,.01} = 4.68 < 4.91$, therefore, reject H_0 at the 1% level.

d. H_0: Mean ratings for all 4 student years is the same.
   H_1: Otherwise
   $F_{3,25,.05} = 2.99 > 2.56$, therefore, do not reject H_0 at the 5% level.

15.50

Source of Variation	Sum of Squares	df	Mean Square	F Ratio
Color	243.250	2	121.625	11.3140
Region	354.000	3	118.000	10.9767
Interaction	189.750	6	31.625	2.9419
Error	129.000	12	10.750	
Total	916.000	23		

H_0: No interaction exists between region and can color, H_1: Otherwise $F_{6,12,.01} = 4.82 > 2.9419$, therefore, do not reject H_0 at the 1% level.

15.52 One-way ANOVA examines the effect of a single factor (having three or more conditions). Two-way ANOVA recognizes situations in which more than one factor may be significant. Examples of one-way ANOVA includes length of battery life for four different types of cell phones, length of time to get a food order at five different fast-food restaurants, and starting salary for students in four different majors. Two-way ANOVA would include differences in grade point averages for four different majors by gender, weekly sales of an item at a grocery by shelf placement (high, middle, low) and size of sign promoting the product (large, medium, small), strength of concrete by 4 different types of cement and 2 different mixing methods.

15.54

Source of Variation	Sum of Squares	df	Mean Square	F Ratio
Between	5156	2	2,578.000	21.4458
Within	120,802	1,005	120.201	
Total	125,967	1,007		

$F_{2,1005,.01} = 4.61 < 21.4458$, therefore, reject H_0 at the 1% level.

15.56 a.

Source of Variation	Sum of Squares	df	Mean Square	F Ratio
Between	221.3400	3	73.7800	25.6
Within	374.6640	130	2.8820	
Total	596.0040	133		

b. H_0: Mean salaries are the same for managers in all 4 groups.
   H_1: Otherwise
   $F_{3,130,.01} \approx 3.95 < 25.6$, therefore, reject H_0 at the 1% level.

15.58

Source of Variation	Sum of Squares	df	Mean Square	F Ratio
Between	11,438.3028	2	5,719.1514	.7856
Within	109,200.000	15	7,280.000	
Total	120,638.3028	17		

H_0: Mean sales levels are the same for all three periods.
H_1: Otherwise
$F_{2,15,.05} = 3.68 > .7856$, therefore, do not reject H_0 at the 5% level.

15.60 $W = 5.0543$, $\chi^2_{3,.10} = 6.25$, therefore, do not reject H_0 at the 10% level.

15.62 a. $SSW = \sum_{j=1}^{K} \sum_{i=1}^{n_i} (x_{ij} - \bar{x}_i)^2$

$$= \sum_{j=1}^{K} \left[\sum_{i=1}^{n_i} x_{ij}^2 - 2n_i \bar{x}_i^2 + n_i \bar{x}_i^2 \right]$$

$$= \sum_{j=1}^{K} \sum_{i=1}^{n_i} x_{ij}^2 - \sum_{i=1}^{K} n_i \bar{x}_i^2$$

b. $SSG = \sum_{j=1}^{K} n_i (\bar{x}_i - \bar{x})^2$

$$= \sum_{i=1}^{K} n_i \bar{x}_i^2 - 2\bar{x} \sum_{i=1}^{k} n_i \bar{x}_i + n\bar{x}^2$$

$$= \sum_{i=1}^{K} n_i \bar{x}_i^2 - 2n\bar{x}^2 + n\bar{x}^2$$

$$= \sum_{i=1}^{K} n_i \bar{x}_i^2 - n\bar{x}^2$$

c. $SST = \sum_{i=1}^{K} \sum_{j=1}^{n_i} (x_{ij} - \bar{x}_i)^2$

$$= \sum_{i=1}^{K} \left[\sum_{i=1}^{n_i} (x_{ij}^2 - 2\bar{x} \sum_{i=1}^{n_i} x_j + n_i \bar{x}_i^2 \right]$$

$$= \sum_{i=1}^{K} \sum_{i=1}^{n_i} (x_{ij}^2 - 2n_i \overline{xx}_i + n_i x^2)$$

$$= \sum_{i=1}^{K} \sum_{j=1}^{n_i} x_{ij}^2 - n\bar{x}^2$$

15.64

Source of Variation	Sum of Squares	df	Mean Square	F Ratio
Consumers	37,571.5	124	302.996	1.3488
Brands	32,987.3	2	16,493.65	73.4226
Error	55,710.7	248	224.6399	
Total	126,269.5	374		

H_0: Mean perception levels are the same for all three brands.
H_1: Otherwise
$F_{2,248,.01} \approx 4.79 < 73.4226$, therefore, reject H_0 at the 1% level.

15.66

Source of Variation	Sum of Squares	df	Mean Square	F Ratio
Income	.0067	2	.0033	.2000
SAT Score	.8267	2	.4133	24.8000
Error	.0667	4	.0167	
Total	.9000	8		

H_0: Mean GPAs are the same for all three income groups.
H_1: Otherwise
$F_{2,4,.05} = 6.94 > .2000$, therefore, do not reject H_0 at the 5% level.
H_0: Mean GPAs are the same for all three SAT score groups.
H_1: Otherwise
$F_{2,4,.01} = 18.0 < 24.8$, therefore, reject H_0 at the 1% level.

Two-way ANOVA: GPA versus SAT, Income

```
Source    DF       SS        MS       F      P
SAT        2   0.826667  0.413333  24.80  0.006
Income     2   0.006667  0.003333   0.20  0.826
Error      4   0.066667  0.016667
Total      8   0.900000
```

S = 0.1291   R-Sq = 92.59%   R-Sq(adj) = 85.19%

```
                     Individual 95% CIs For Mean Based on
                     Pooled StDev
SAT       Mean      +---------+---------+---------+---------
High      3.36667                        (------*------)
Mod       2.90000   (------*------)
VeryH     3.63333                               (------*------)
                    +---------+---------+---------+---------
                   2.70      3.00      3.30      3.60
```

```
                     Individual 95% CIs For Mean Based on
                     Pooled StDev
Income    Mean      ------+---------+---------+---------+---
High      3.33333        (-------------*-------------)
Low       3.26667   (-------------*-------------)
Mod       3.30000     (-------------*-------------)
                    ------+---------+---------+---------+---
                        3.15      3.30      3.45      3.60
```

15.68 a. $\mu = 3.333$ b. $\hat{G}_2 = 0.0$ c. $\hat{B}_1 = .0667$ d. $\hat{\varepsilon}_{21} = .1333$

15.70 a.

Source of Variation	Sum of Squares	df	Mean Square	F Ratio
Prices	.178	2	.0890	.0944
Countries	4.365	2	2.1825	2.3151
Interaction	1.262	4	.3155	.3347
Error	93.330	99	.9427	
Total	99.135	107		

H_0: Mean quality ratings for all three price levels is the same.
H_1: Otherwise
$F_{2,99,.05} \approx 3.07 > .0944$, therefore, do not reject H_0 at the 5% level.

H_0: Mean quality ratings for all three countries is the same.
H_1: Otherwise
$F_{2,99,.05} \approx 3.07 > 2.3151$, therefore, do not reject H_0 at the 5% level.

H_0: No interaction exists between price and country.
H_1: Otherwise
$F_{4,99,.05} \approx 2.45 > .3347$, therefore, do not reject H_0 at the 5% level.

15.72 a.

Source of Variation	Sum of Squares	df	Mean Square	F Ratio
Income	.0178	2	.0089	.5333
SAT score	2.2011	2	1.1006	66.0333
Interaction	.1022	4	.0256	1.5333
Error	.1500	9	.0167	
Total	2.4711	17		

H_0: Mean GPAs for all three income groups is the same.
H_1: Otherwise
$F_{2,9,.05} = 4.26 > .5333$, therefore, do not reject H_0 at the 5% level.
H_0: Mean GPAs for all three SAT score groups is the same.
H_1: Otherwise
$F_{2,9,.01} = 8.02 < 66.0333$, therefore, reject H_0 at the 1% level.

H_0: No interaction exists between income and SAT score group.

H_1: Otherwise

$F_{4,9,.05} = 3.63 > 1.5333$, therefore, do not reject H_0 at the 5% level.

Chapter 16

16.2   100.0, 122.6, 123.5, 134.5, 142.5, 140.4, 152.2, 161.2, 188.1, 163.4

16.4   a. 100, 102.5, 99.29, 98.21, 100, 99.64, 100, 99.29, 99.29, 100.71, 110.71, 106.07
       b. 101.82, 104.36, 101.09, 100, 101.82, 101.45, 101.82, 101.09, 101.09, 102.55, 112.73, 108

16.6   a. 100, 105.37, 109.6, 112.71, 115.54, 117.23
       b. 100, 104.81, 110.49, 112.14, 115.71, 117.47

16.8   A price index for energy is helpful in that it allows us to say something about price movements over time for a group of commodities, namely, energy prices. A weighted index of prices allows one to compare the cost of a group of products across periods.

16.10 a. $Z = -3.43$ $P(Z < -3.43) = .0003$ b. $Z = -2.57$ $P(Z < -2.57) = .0051$
       c. $Z = 3.43$ $P(Z > 3.43) = .0003$

16.12 $R = 7$; cannot reject H_0 at any common level of significance.

16.14 $R = 9$; cannot reject H_0 at any common level of significance.

16.16 a. $R = 10$; cannot reject H_0 at any common level of significance.
       b. From the time series plot below, strong cyclical behavior is evident.

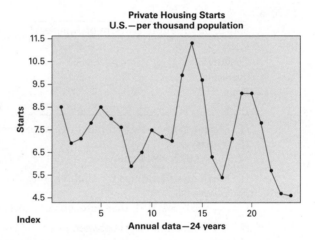

16.18 a. Time series plot of Quarterly sales
       Data patterns evident in the time series plot include strong seasonality and a strong upward trend.

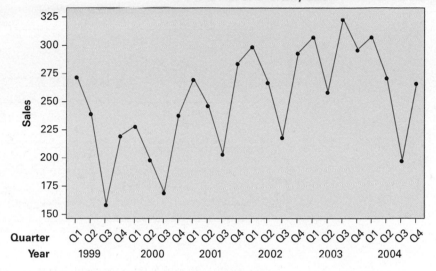

Time Series Plot of Quarterly Sales

b.

Period	4 Period MA	$100\dfrac{X_t}{X_t^*}$	Seas. Factor	Adj. Series
1-1			112.848	241.032
2			99.609	239.938
3	216.500	72.979	79.826	197.930
4	205.875	106.375	107.716	203.312
2-1	202.125	112.802		202.041
2	205.875	96.175		198.777
3	213.500	79.157		211.709
4	224.750	105.895		220.951
3-1	235.000	114.894		239.259
2	245.000	100.408		246.966
3	254.375	79.803		254.302
4	260.625	108.969		263.656
4-1	265.125	112.777		264.958
2	268.125	99.580		268.048
3	270.250	80.666		273.093
4	270.125	108.468		272.011
5-1	270.750	113.389		272.047
2	272.875	94.549		259.013
3	273.250	84.904		290.631
4	274.875	107.685		274.796
6-1	272.125	112.816		272.047
2	264.000	102.652		272.064
3				246.786
4				246.945

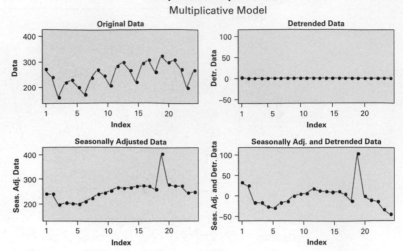

Component Analysis for Sales
Multiplicative Model

The seasonally adjusted data no longer shows the regular quarterly cycle. There is an unusual point in the third quarter of 2003. The value is much higher than expected.

16.20 3-period centered moving average—year-end gold price

Year	3-Point Moving Average
1	*
2	176.000
3	308.667
4	450.333
5	507.667
6	480.000
7	411.333
8	381.000
9	340.667
10	347.333
11	406.667
12	433.667
13	421.667
14	*

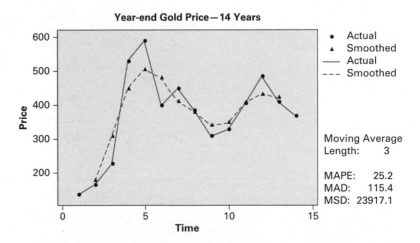

Year-end Gold Price—14 Years

- • Actual
- ▲ Smoothed
- —— Actual
- - - - Smoothed

Moving Average
Length: 3

MAPE: 25.2
MAD: 115.4
MSD: 23917.1

The resulting data shows strong cyclical behavior.

16.22

Year	7ptMA
1	*
2	*
3	*
4	30.4429
5	25.3429
6	23.0000
7	23.4286
8	22.7429
9	21.1286
10	20.6000
11	23.1286
12	28.1000
13	32.0857
14	33.8000
15	35.1571
16	35.7143
17	34.9714
18	31.5143
19	27.4571
20	27.0857
21	34.3286
22	40.5429
23	43.7143
24	48.6000
25	54.4286
26	*
27	*
28	*

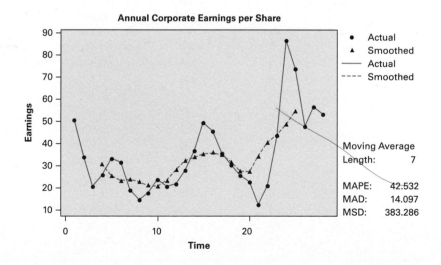

The smoothed data exhibits a cyclical data pattern.

16.24 a.

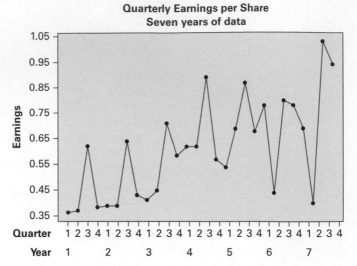

Quarterly Earnings per Share
Seven years of data

The graph shows a strong seasonal component with peaks in the third quarter.

b.

Period	4 Period MA	$100\dfrac{X_t}{X_t^*}$	Seasonal Factor	Adjusted Series
1-1			90.930	.3981
2			86.020	.4301
3	.438	141.902	130.400	.4762
4	.443	86.608	92.649	.4145
2-1	.448	86.830		.4278
2	.456	85.284		.4522
3	.465	137.493		.4900
4	.475	90.761		.4652
3-1	.491	83.643		.4520
2	.520	86.216		.5208
3	.565	126.046		.5460
4	.613	95.347		.6303
4-1	.656	94.458		.6818
2	.677	91.581		.7208
3	.665	133.935		.6833
4	.664	85.843		.6152
5-1	.670	80.582		.5939
2	.681	101.284		.8021
3	.725	120.000		.6672
4	.724	93.955		.7340
6-1	.684	114.077		.8578
2	.688	64.000		.5115
3	.689	116.153		.6135
4	.673	115.985		.8419
7-1	.696	99.102		.7588
2	.745	53.691		.4650
3				.7899
4				1.0146

Component Analysis for Earnings
Multiplicative Model

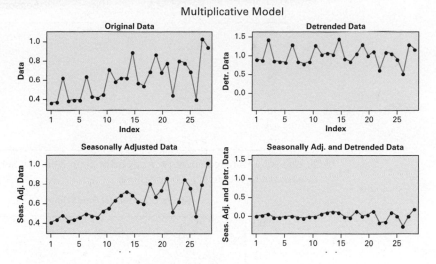

Seasonally adjusted series shows an upward trend in the data with increasing variability.

16.26

Period	4 Period MA	$100\dfrac{X_t}{X_t^*}$	Seasonal Factor	Adjusted Series
1-1			93.701	574.165
2			97.648	634.935
3			119.127	729.476
4			101.932	832.911
5			102.038	928.084
6			97.450	955.365
7	767.750	97.167	99.356	750.834
8	773.750	95.638	100.300	737.789
9	775.000	84.387	87.504	747.395
10	770.333	113.457	113.255	771.707
11	759.667	99.912	98.563	770.069
12	743.000	85.734	89.127	714.721
2-1	730.250	87.094		678.752
2	725.750	91.767		682.043
3	721.458	118.233		716.045
4	712.542	105.678		738.730
5	699.542	112.502		771.280
6	689.458	100.224		709.084
7	684.000	99.415		684.406
8	678.917	102.811		695.915
9	668.208	88.745		677.684
10	651.750	110.625		636.614
11	630.917	95.100		608.751
12	611.417	90.609		621.586
3-1	598.167	98.300		627.526
2	583.625	101.435		606.260
3	570.375	117.467		562.426
4	563.542	96.000		530.748

Period	4 Period MA	$100\dfrac{X_t}{X_t^*}$	Seasonal Factor	Adjusted Series
5	558.250	89.387		489.033
6	551.917	92.586		524.373
7				545.512
8				485.545
9				555.403
10				586.286
11				537.730
12				529.583

16.28 Use smoothing constant of .7 (alpha of .3) in Minitab. Set initial smoothing value at the average of the first '1' observations.

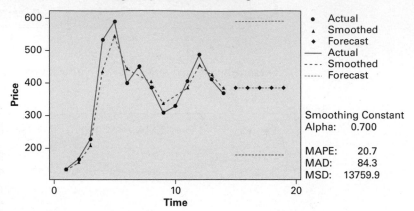

Single Exponential Smoothing

16.30 a. $\alpha = 0.8$:

Year	Smoothed Value
1	50.20
2	37.16
3	23.91
4	25.10
5	31.34
6	31.31
7	21.30
8	15.86
9	17.17
10	22.31
11	20.94
12	21.47
13	26.37
14	34.47
15	46.33
16	45.59
17	37.60
18	31.60
19	26.72
20	23.26
21	14.49
22	19.62

Year	Smoothed Value
23	38.16
24	76.67
25	74.21
26	53.00
27	55.88
28	53.66

$\alpha = 0.6$:

Year	Smoothed Value
1	50.20
2	40.42
3	28.53
4	26.65
5	30.40
6	30.94
7	23.66
8	18.16
9	17.76
10	21.27
11	20.87
12	21.31
13	25.08
14	31.93
15	42.35
16	44.18
17	39.03
18	33.67
19	28.77
20	24.95
21	17.36
22	19.48
23	33.47
24	65.17
25	70.23
26	56.71
27	56.64
28	54.52

$\alpha = 0.4$:

Year	Smoothed Value
1	50.20
2	43.68
3	34.45
4	30.83
5	31.66
6	31.51
7	26.43
8	21.66
9	19.99
10	21.44
11	21.10
12	21.30

Year	Smoothed Value
13	23.82
14	28.89
15	37.06
16	40.39
17	38.48
18	35.13
19	31.28
20	27.73
21	21.56
22	21.29
23	29.90
24	52.46
25	60.91
26	55.63
27	56.02
28	54.85

$\alpha = 0.2$:

Year	Smoothed Value
1	50.20
2	46.94
3	41.67
4	38.42
5	37.31
6	36.11
7	32.65
8	29.02
9	26.72
10	26.09
11	24.99
12	24.32
13	24.97
14	27.28
15	31.68
16	34.43
17	34.66
18	33.75
19	32.10
20	30.16
21	26.59
22	25.45
23	28.92
24	40.40
25	47.04
26	47.17
27	49.06
28	49.86

b. Use the forecast with smoothing constant $\alpha = 0.8$.

16.32 If alpha is 1.0, then the forecast will always be equal to the first observation. $\hat{X}_{t+h} = X_1$

16.34 Using Minitab, the forecasts for the next 5 years are 127.69, 142.91, 158.12, 173.33, and 188.54.

16.36

Winters' Method for FoodPrice

```
Forecasts
Period  Forecast    Lower    Upper
15       125.448  124.599  126.297
16       126.466  125.531  127.402
17       126.967  125.927  128.007
```

16.38 Using Minitab, the forecasts for the next 8 quarters are 247.56, 207.64, 169.99, 197.43, 185.33, 151.95, 121.12, and 136.27. The graph of the data and the forecasts is shown next.

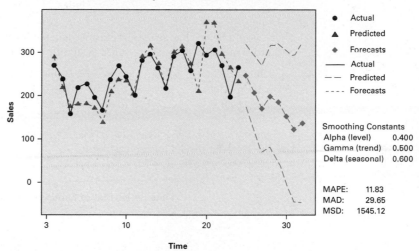

16.40

The first-order autoregressive model is:

$$\hat{y}_t = 87.85 + .169y_{t-1} + a_t$$

$$y_{17} = 87.85 + .169(92) = 103.398$$

$$y_{18} = 87.85 + .169(103.398) = 105.324$$

$$y_{19} = 87.85 + .169(105.324) = 105.650$$

$$y_{20} = 87.85 + .169(105.650) = 105.705$$

16.42

4th order model:
$z - statistic\ for\ \phi_4 = -.218$. Fail to reject H_0 at the 10% level.
3rd order model:
$z - statistic\ for\ \phi_3 = -.909$. Fail to reject H_0 at the 10% level.
2nd order model:
$z - statistic\ for\ \phi_2 = -4.621$. Reject H_0 at the 10% level.
1st order model:
Forecasts from the second order model:
$\hat{y}_{25} = 6.776$, $\hat{y}_{26} = 9.103$, $\hat{y}_{27} = 9.792$, $\hat{y}_{28} = 8.670$, $\hat{y}_{29} = 6.968$

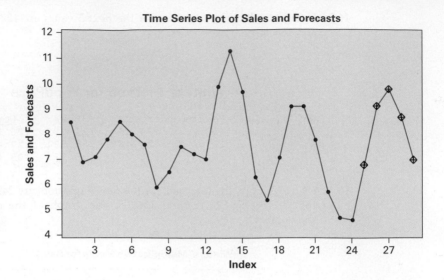

Time Series Plot of Sales and Forecasts

There would be no change if a significance level of 5% were used instead of 10%, the second order model z-statistic of -4.621 is significant at the 10% and 5% level.

16.44 $z - statistic \ for \ \phi_3 = -.303$, Fail to reject H_0 at the 10% level.
2nd order model:
$z - statistic \ for \ \phi_2 = -1.327$, Fail to reject H_0 at the 10% level.
1st order model:
$z - statistic \ for \ \phi_1 = 3.664$, Reject H_0 at the 10% level.
Use the 1st order model for forecasting.
$\hat{y}_{19} = 5.927$, $\hat{y}_{20} = 5.695$, $\hat{y}_{21} = 5.534$, $\hat{y}_{22} = 5.422$

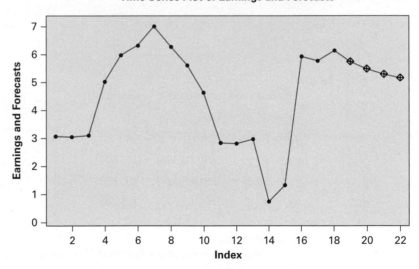

Time Series Plot of Earnings and Forecasts

There would be no change if a significance level of 5% were used instead of 10% the first order model z-statistic of 3.664 is significant at the 10% and 5% level.

16.46 $\hat{X}_{1996} = 202 + 1.1(951) - .48(923) + .17(867) = 952.45$
$\hat{X}_{1997} = 202 + 1.1(952.45) - .48(951) + .17(923) = 950.13$
$\hat{X}_{1998} = 202 + 1.1(950.13) - .48(952.45) + .17(951) = 951.64$

16.48

4th order model:
T-statistic for $\phi_4 = -1.185$. Fail to reject H_0 at the 10% level.
3rd order model:
T-statistic for $\phi_3 = -.846$. Fail to reject H_0 at the 10% level.
2nd order model:
T-statistic for $\phi_2 = -1.490$. Fail to reject H_0 at the 10% level.
1st order model:
T-statistic for $\phi_1 = -3.263$. Reject H_0 at the 10% level.
Use the 1st order model for forecasting.
$\hat{y}_{25} = .070$, $\hat{y}_{26} = -.001$, $\hat{y}_{27} = .041$

16.50 Parts a,b,c:

Period	a. Unweighted	b. Laspeyres Price	c. Laspeyres Quantity
1	100.00	100.00	100.00
2	110.30	109.72	103.78
3	117.43	115.55	100.04
4	127.52	123.47	105.29
5	143.96	137.18	106.00
6	158.22	149.41	105.85

16.52 Forecasts are generated by analyzing each individual component: trend, seasonal, and cyclical. Then, once each component has been analyzed and measured, the information is then incorporated into the forecasting model.

16.54 A seasonally adjusted time series is one that is free from the effects of seasonal influence. Government agencies expend large efforts on seasonal adjustments in order to gain a clearer picture of the underlying data pattern.

16.56 a. $R = 10$; cannot reject H_0 at any common level of alpha.
b.

Strong cyclical behavior as well as a slight downward trend.

c.

Year	Sales	5pt MA
1	853	*
2	693	*
3	715	779.4
4	785	768.2
5	851	781.2
6	797	756.8
7	758	729.8
8	593	709.8
9	650	695.0
10	751	683.8
11	723	763.4
12	702	859.2
13	991	903.4
14	1129	885.0
15	972	852.2
16	631	795.6
17	538	751.2
18	708	739.2
19	907	768.4
20	912	774.6
21	777	727.6
22	569	638.0
23	473	*
24	459	*

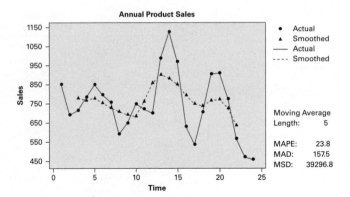

Strong cyclical behavior and a downward trend.

16.58 a.

Moving average
```
Data        PriceIndex
Length      15.0000
NMissing    0

Moving Average
Length: 3

Accuracy Measures
MAPE:  5.6999
MAD:   6.1389
MSD:   84.4352
```

Row	Period	PriceIndex	AVER3	Predict	Error
1	1	79	*	*	*
2	2	87	85.000	*	*
3	3	89	88.667	*	*
4	4	90	89.000	85.000	5.0000
5	5	88	89.000	88.667	-0.6667
6	6	89	90.333	89.000	0.0000
7	7	94	91.667	89.000	5.0000
8	8	92	91.333	90.333	1.6667
9	9	88	92.000	91.667	-3.6667
10	10	96	100.333	91.333	4.6667
11	11	117	109.667	92.000	25.0000
12	12	116	115.667	100.333	15.6667
13	13	114	114.333	109.667	4.3333
14	14	113	112.000	115.667	-2.6667
15	15	109	*	114.333	-5.3333

b.

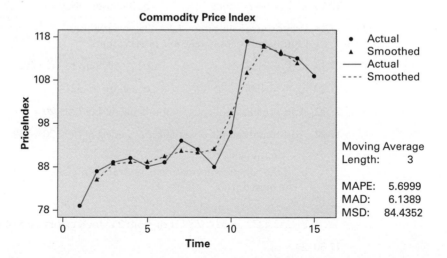

Strong upward trend and cyclical behavior.

16.60 Using Minitab, the forecasts for the next 4 months are 108.27, 105.60, 102.92, and 100.25.

16.62 4th order model:
T-statistic for $\phi_4 = -.216$. Fail to reject H_0 at the 10% level.
3rd order model:
T-statistic for $\phi_3 = .940$. Fail to reject H_0 at the 10% level.
2nd order model:
T-statistic for $\phi_2 = -4.590$. Reject H_0 at the 10% level.
1st order model:
T-statistic for $\phi_2 = 3.40$. Reject H_0 at the 10% level.
Use the 2nd order model for forecasting.
$\hat{y}_{25} = 672.829$, $\hat{y}_{26} = 905.554$, $\hat{y}_{27} = 979.039$

Chapter 17

17.2 a. 40.806 up to 45.794
b. $\bar{x}_{st} = 37.3306$
c. 90% confidence interval: 36.0313 up to 38.6299
95% confidence interval: 35.7825 up to 38.8787

17.4 a. 2.8435 up to 3.3965   b. 3.1431 up to 3.5969
c. 3.0513 up to 3.4166

17.6 a. $N\bar{x}_{st} = 81720$
b. 95% confidence interval: $77{,}542.3153 < N\mu < 85{,}897.6847$

17.8 a. $\hat{p}_{st} = .3467$
b. 90% confidence interval: .2550 up to .4383
95% confidence interval: .2375 up to .4559

17.10 a. 56 observations   b. 68 observations

17.12 a. 55 observations   b. 60 observations

17.14 a. 74 observations   b. 88 observations

17.16 Proportional allocation: take 498 observations.
Optimal allocation: take 471 observations.

17.18 a. $\bar{x}_c = 91.6761$ b. 70.6920 up to 112.6602

17.20 a. $\hat{p}_c = .4507$ b. .38 up to .5214

17.22 Additional sample observations needed is $127 - 20 = 107$.

17.24 Additional sample observations needed is $160 - 30 = 130$.

17.26 a. .559 up to .687
b. If the sample information is not randomly selected, the resulting conclusions may be biased.

17.28 a. .8747 up to 1.2933
b. 242.4279 up to 407.9721 or from 243 total errors up to 408 total errors

17.30 23

17.32 Refer to section 17.1 – Stratified Sampling

Chapter 18

18.2   D is dominated by C. Therefore, D is inadmissible.

18.4   a. D is dominated by C. Hence D is inadmissible and removed from further consideration.

Maximin criterion would select production process C:

Actions	States of Nature			
Prod. Process	Low Demand	Moderate Demand	High Demand	Min Payoff
A	100,000	350,000	900,000	100,000
B	150,000	400,000	700,000	150,000
C	250,000	400,000	600,000	250,000

b. Minimax regret criterion would select production process A:

Actions	Regrets or Opportunity Loss Table			
Prod. Process	Low Demand	Moderate Demand	High Demand	Max Regret
A	150,000	50,000	0	150,000
B	100,000	0	200,000	200,000
C	0	0	300,000	300,000

18.6

Actions	States of Nature			
Prod. Process	Low Demand	Moderate Demand	High Demand	Min Payoff
A	70,000	120,000	200,000	70,000
B	80,000	120,000	180,000	80,000
C	100,000	125,000	160,000	100,000
D*	100,000	120,000	150,000	Inadmissible
E	60,000	115,000	220,000	60,000

*inadmissible

Therefore, production process C would be chosen using the Maximin Criterion.

Actions	Regrets or Opportunity Loss Table			
Prod. Process	Low Demand	Moderate Demand	High Demand	Max Regret
A	30,000	5,000	20,000	30,000
B	20,000	5,000	40,000	40,000
C	0	0	60,000	60,000
D*				Inadmissible
E	40,000	10,000	0	40,000

*inadmissible

Therefore, production process A would be chosen using the Minimax Regret Criterion.

18.8

Action	S1	S2
A1	M_{11}	M_{12}
A2	M_{21}	M_{22}

Then action A1 will be chosen by both the Maximin and the Minimax Regret Criteria if for $M_{11} > M_{21}$ and $M_{12} < M_{22}$ and $(M_{11} - M_{21}) > (M_{22} - M_{12})$

18.10 a.

Actions	Offered Better Position	Not Offered Better Position
Interview	4,500	−500
Don't interview	0	0

b. EMV(Interview) = −250
EMV(Don't Interview) = 0
Therefore, the optimal action: Don't Interview.

18.12 a. EMV(Certificate of Deposit) = 1,200
EMV(Low risk stock fund) = 1,280
EMV(High risk stock fund) = 1,270
Therefore, the optimal action: Low risk stock fund

b. Decision tree:

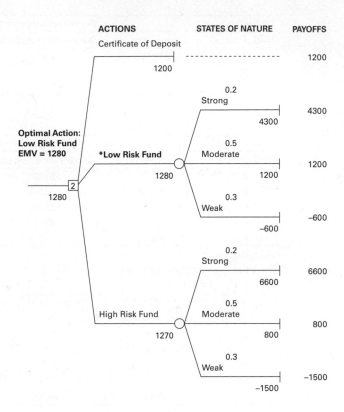

18.14 a. i) false ii) true iii) true
b. No

18.16 a. EMV(New) = 74,000
   EMV(Old) = 58,000
   Therefore, the optimal action: New center
b. Decision tree:

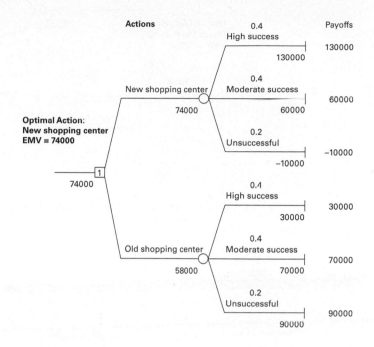

18.18 a. EMV(A) = 660,000 − 550,000p
   EMV(B) = 535,000 − 300,000p
   EMV(C) = 495,000 − 200,000p
   EMV(D) = 460,000 − 150,000p
   EMV(A) > EMV(B) when p < .5
   EMV(A) > EMV(C) when p < .471
   EMV(A) > EMV (D) when p < .5
   For p < .471, the EMV criterion chooses action A, same decision as in 18.13.
   Note that D was "inadmissible."
b. EMV(A) > EMV(B) > EMV(C) > EMV(D) when a > 816,667

18.20 a. EMV(check) = 18,600
   EMV(not check) = 18,400
   Therefore, the optimal action: Check the process.

b. Decision tree:

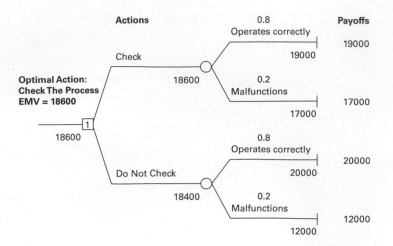

	Actions		0.8 Operates correctly	Payoffs

Check

Optimal Action:
Check The Process
EMV = 18600

18600

19000

19000

0.2
Malfunctions

17000

17000

18600

Do Not Check

18400

0.8
Operates correctly

20000

20000

0.2
Malfunctions

12000

12000

c. EMV(check) = 19,000p + 17,000(1 − p) > 20,000p + 12,000(1 − p) when p < 5/6

18.22 a.

Extra Ordering	6	7	8	9	10
0	0	−10	−20	−30	−40
1	−20	20	10	0	−10
2	−40	0	40	30	20
3	−60	−20	20	60	50
4	−80	−40	0	40	80

b. Per the EMV criterion, the optimal action is to order 2 extra cars:

Extra Orders						
	6	7	8	9	10	EMV
0	0(.1)	−10(.3)	−20(.3)	−30(.2)	−40(.1)	−19
1	−20(.1)	20(.3)	10(.3)	0(.2)	−10(.1)	6
2	−40(.1)	0(.3)	40(.3)	30(.2)	20(.1)	16
3	−60(.1)	−20(.3)	20(.3)	60(.2)	50(.1)	11
4	−80(.1)	−40(.3)	0(.3)	40(.2)	80(.1)	−4

18.24 a. Action A1 is taken if $M_{11}p + M_{12}(1 − p) > M_{21}p + (1 − p)M_{22}$ or $p(M_{11} − M_{21}) >$ $(1 − p)(M_{22} − M_{12})$

b. Action A1 inadmissible implies that A1 will be chosen only if p > 1. In short, for part a. to be true, both payoffs of A1 cannot be less than the corresponding payoffs of A2.

18.26 a. Optimal action per the EMV criterion is action A.

b. $P(L | P) = .5$
$P(M | P) = .4$
$P(H | P) = .1$

c. EMV(A) = 280,000
EMV(B) = 305,000
EMV(C) = 345,000
Therefore, the optimal action: C

d. $P(L | F) = .2903$
$P(M | F) = .5161$
$P(H | F) = .1935$

e. EMV(A) = 383,815, EMV(B) = 385,435, EMV(C) = 395,115
   Therefore, the optimal action: C
f. P(L|G) = .1538
   P(M|G) = .3077
   P(H|G) = .5385
g. EMV(A) = 607,692, EMV(B) = 523,077, EMV(C) = 484,615
   Therefore, the optimal action: A

18.28 a. P(E|P) = .9231, P(not E|P) = .0769
   b. EMV(S) = 50,000, EMV(R) = 114,615. Therefore, optimal action: Retain
   c. P(E|N) = .25, P(not E|N) = .75
   d. EMV(S) = 50,000
      EMV(R) = 23,750
      Therefore, optimal action: Sell

18.30 a. P(2|10%) = .01, P(1|10%) = .18, P(0|10%) = .81
   b. P(2|30%) = .09, P(1|30%) = .42, P(0|30%) = .49
   c. Probability of the states of 10% defective and 30% defective are given:

	# Defective	10% Defect	30% Defect
i	2 defective	.308	.692
ii	1 defective	.632	.368
iii	0 defective	.869	.131

EMV of Actions	Check	Do Not Check
2 defective	17,616*	14,464
1 defective	18,264*	17,056
0 defective	18,737	18,952*

*optimal action given the circumstance

18.32 a. Perfect information is defined as the case where the decision maker is able to gain information to tell with certainty which state will occur.
   b. The optimal action: Low risk stock fund (see Problem 18.12)
      EVPI = .2(6,600 − 4,300) + .5(0) + .3(1,200 − (−600)) = 1,000

18.34 Given that the optimal action is new center
   EVPI = 24,000

18.36 The expected value of sample information is $\sum_{i=1}^{M} P(A_i)V_i$ where $P(A_i) = \sum_{j=1}^{H} P(A_i/s_j)$
   For perfect information, $P(A_i|s_j) = 0$ for $i \neq j$ and $P(A_i|s_j) = 1$ for $i = j$, thus $P(A_i) = P(s_i)$

18.38 EVSI = 23003

18.40 Given that the optimal action retain the patent (see Problem 18.28).
   EVSI = 13,650

18.42 a. EVSI = 34.1   b. EVSI = 55.87   c. The difference = 21.77
   d. None   e. 24.75

18.44 a.

Payoff	−10000	30000	60000	70000	90000	13000
Utility	0	35	60	70	85	100

   b. EU(New) = 64
      EU(Old) = 59
      Therefore, the optimal action: New center

18.46 $94000p - 16000(1-p) = 0 \rightarrow p = 16/110$

Payoff	−160000	0	94000
Utility	0	160/110	100

Slope(-16000,0) = .00009
Slope(0,94000) = .00105
Therefore, the contractor has a preference for risk.

18.48 a. $P(S1) = .3(.6) = .18$, $P(S2) = .42$, $P(S3) = .12$, $P(S4) = .28$
b. $EMV(A1) = 460$, $EMV(A2) = 330$, $EMV(A3) = 0$, $EMV(A4) = 510$
   Therefore, the optimal action: A4
c. Draw the decision tree:

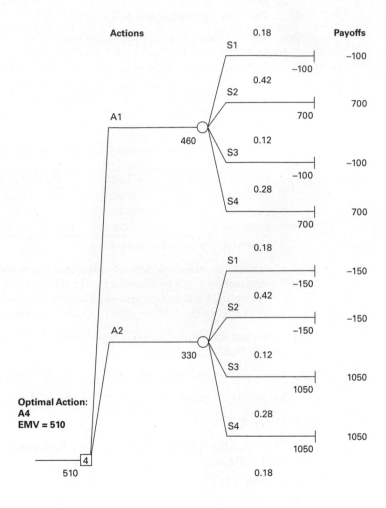

TreePlan (continued for Problem 18.48):

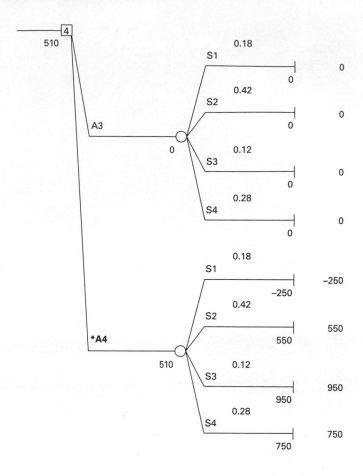

d. EVPI = 204
e. 79

INDEX

Blocking variables, 572–573, 677
Box, George, 744
Box–Jenkins methodology, 745

C

Categorical data analysis
  contingency tables and, 627–631
  goodness-of-fit tests, population parameters unknown, 622–627
  goodness-of-fit tests, specified probabilities, 615–620
  nonparametric tests for independent random samples, 643–647
  nonparametric tests for paired or matched samples, 632–640
  Spearman rank correlation and, 649–650
Categorical variables, 4–5
  graphs to describe, 7–16
Central limit theorem, 252–258
  from linear sum of random variables, 281–282
Central tendency, measures of, 43–52
Change in base period, 710–711
Chebychev's theorem, 59–61
Chi-square distribution, 271–274, 310–311, 313, 384
  F probability distribution and, 411
Chi-square random variable, 616–617
  for contingency tables, 628
Chi-square test
  examples of, 618–619, 630–631
  of variance of a normal distribution, 384–385
Classical probability, 86–87, 90–91
Cluster bar charts, 8, 9, 31–32
Cluster sampling, 3
  estimators for, 763–764
  example of, 765–766
  explanation of, 763
  vs. stratified sampling, 766–767
Cobb–Douglas production function, 530–531
Coefficient estimation, 565–566
Coefficient estimators
  derivation of, 559–560
  least squares, 432–436, 446
  variance, 445–447, 504–505
Coefficient of determination R^2
  adjusted, 501–502

explanation of, 441–442
regression models and, 501
sum of squares decomposition and, 499
Coefficient of multiple correlation, 502
Coefficient of standard errors, 505
Coefficient of variation (CV), 57–58
Collectively exhaustive events, 82
Combinations
  formula for determining number of, 87
  number of, 89–90
Complement rule, 97–98, 105–107
Complements, 82–84
Component bar charts, 8, 9
Composite hypothesis, 358, 364–366
Computer applications. See also Excel; Minitab
  for jointly distributed discrete random variables, 173–174
  of regression coefficient, 435–436
Computer software. See Excel; Minitab
Conditional coefficients, 495
Conditional mean, 173
Conditional probability, 99–101
Conditional probability function, 171
Conditional variance, 173
Confidence interval estimator, 293
Confidence intervals, 287, 293
  based on normal distribution, 294–297
  examples of, 296–297, 303–304, 307–308
  explanation of, 294
  finite populations, 314–319
  for difference between two normal population means, dependent samples, 326–330
  for difference between two normal population means, independent samples, 331–337
  for difference between two population proportions, 338–340
  for mean of normal distribution, population variance known, 293–298
  for mean of normal distribution, population variance unknown, 299–304
  for population mean, 314–317, 751, 764
  for population proportion, 306–308, 755, 764
  for population regression slope, 450–451
  for population total, 314–317, 753
  for predictions, 455–456
  for regression coefficients, 503–507
  for variance of normal distribution, 310–313

forecast, and prediction intervals, 455–456
of two means, dependent samples, 326
of two means, unknown population variances that are assumed to be equal, 333–335
of two means, unknown population variances that are not assumed to be equal, 335–337
reducing margin of error of, 297–298
sample size determination, large populations, 341–345
Student's t distribution and, 300–304
Confidence levels, 294
Consistent estimators, 323
Contingency tables, 28–31
chi-square random variable for, 628
explanation of, 626–627
test of association in, 629–631
Continuous numerical variables, 5
Continuous random variables, 138, 193–197. *See also* Jointly distributed continuous random variables
covariance of, 225–226
expectations for, 198–201
jointly distributed, 225–233
probability density functions and, 194–196
uniform distribution, 196–197
Control charts, 259
Control intervals, 259
Correlation
applications of, 461
coefficient of determination R^2 and, 442–443
coefficient of multiple correlation, 502
hypothesis test for, 461–464
of random variables, 175–176, 226
zero population, 462
Correlation analysis, 460–463
Correlation coefficient analysis, 70–71
Correlation coefficients, 67–68
examples using, 69–72
scatter plots and, 69
Spearman rank, 649–650
Counterfactual argument, 359
Covariance (Cov)
computing using Excel, 71–72
defined, 67–68

example using, 69–70
of random variables, 175, 176–177, 225–226
statistical independence and, 177–178
Criterion of pessimism, 780
Critical value, 360
Cross tables, 28–31
Cross-sectional data, 16
Cumulative distribution function, 193–194, 197
of normal distribution, 203–204
Cumulative frequency distribution, 20
Cumulative line graphs, 22–23
Cumulative mass function, 141
Cumulative probability function, 141–142
Cyclical component, of time series, 718

D

Data
cross-sectional, 16
interval, 6
measurement levels, 5–6
nominal, 5
ordinal, 5–6
presentation errors, 33–37
qualitative, 5
quantitative, 5
ratio, 6
time-series, 16–19
Data files descriptions, 479, 560–562
Data mining, 416
Davies, O. L., 571
Decision (action) nodes, 784, 785
Decision making. *See also* Statistical decision theory
framework for, 775
in uncertain environment, 2–4, 774–777
sampling and, 2–4
Decision rules
expected utility criterion and, 773, 810–812
guidelines for choosing, 390–391
maximin criterion and, 773, 778–780
minimax criterion and, 773, 780–781
Decision trees, 784–788
value of sample information viewed by means of, 800–803
Degrees of freedom, 273, 410–411

more than one observation per cell, 686–693

one observation per cell, 676–684

several observations per cell, 689–693

sum of squares decomposition for, 680–681

Two-way analysis of variance tables, 681, 683

Type I errors, 356–357, 358, 415

Type II errors, 356–357, 358, 377, 415

determining probability of, 378–379

U

Unbiased estimator, 288–289, 290

Uncertainty, decision making under, 2–4, 774–777

Uniform distribution, 196–197, 199–200

Uniform probability distribution, 193

Unions, 81–84, 133–135

Unweighted aggregate index of prices, 706–707

Upper confidence limit, 295

Utility

concept of, 807–810

decision making, 810–812

expected, 810–812

Utility function, 808–810

V

Value of perfect information, 798

Variability

between-groups, 663

interaction as source of, 686

total explained, 560

within-groups, 663

Variables. *See also* Continuous random variables; Discrete random variables; Random variables

bias from excluding significant predictor, 585–587

blocking, 572–573, 677

categorical, 4–5, 7–16

classification of, 4–6

correlation analysis and, 460–463

defined, 4

dependent, 26

dummy, 534–539, 567–571

effect of dropping statistically significant, 546–547

independent, 26

indicator, 534–539

lagged dependent, 580–583

of binomial distribution, 190

of linear functions of a random variable, 189

measures of relationships between, 67–72

numerical, 5, 19–25

relationships between, 422–423

tables and graphs to describe relationships between, 26–33

treatment, 572–573

Variability, measures of, 51–62

Variance, 54–55. *See also* Analysis of variance (ANOVA)

conditional, 173

for grouped data, 64–65

nonuniform, 595

of Bernoulli random variable, 151

of binomial distribution, 154

of continuous random variables, 199–201

of discrete random variables, 144–146, 178, 189

of estimator of population mean, stratified sampling, 758

of linear functions of a random variable, 146–148

of normal distribution, confidence interval estimation for, 310–313

of Poisson probability distribution, 163

sampling distributions of sample, 270–277

Variation, coefficient of, 57–58

Venn diagrams

for addition rule, 98

for complement of event, 83

for intersection of events, 80–81, 133–134

for union of events, 82, 133–134

Verifications, 189–191

Von Neumann, John, 807

W

Wainer, Howard, 33

Waiting line problems, 164–166

Weighted aggregate price index, 707–709

Weighted aggregate quantity index, 709–710

Weighted mean, 62–64

SINGLE PC LICENSE AGREEMENT AND LIMITED WARRANTY

READ THIS LICENSE CAREFULLY BEFORE OPENING THIS PACKAGE. BY OPENING THIS PACKAGE, YOU ARE AGREE-ING TO THE TERMS AND CONDITIONS OF THIS LICENSE. IF YOU DO NOT AGREE, DO NOT OPEN THE PACKAGE. PROMPTLY RETURN THE UNOPENED PACKAGE AND ALL ACCOMPANYING ITEMS TO THE PLACE YOU OBTAINED THEM. *THESE TERMS APPLY TO ALL LICENSED SOFTWARE ON THE DISK EXCEPT THE TERMS FOR USE OF ANY SHAREWARE OR FREEWARE ON THE DISKETTES ARE AS SET FORTH IN THE ELECTRONIC LICENSE LOCATED ON THE DISK.*

1. **GRANT OF LICENSE and OWNERSHIP:** The enclosed computer programs ("Software") are licensed, not sold, to you by Prentice-Hall, Inc. ("We" or the "Company") and in consideration of your purchase or adoption of the accompanying Company text-books and/or other materials, and your agreement to these terms. We reserve any rights not granted to you. You own only the disk(s) but we and/or our licensors own the Software itself. This license allows you to use and display your copy of the Software on a single computer (i.e., with a single CPU) at a single location for academic use only, so long as you comply with the terms of this Agreement. You may make one copy for back up, or transfer your copy to another CPU, provided that the Software is usable on only one computer.

2. **RESTRICTIONS:** You may not transfer or distribute the Software or documentation to anyone else. Except for backup, you may not copy the documentation or the Software. You may not network the Software or otherwise use it on more than one computer orcomputer terminal at the same time. You may not reverse engineer, disassemble, decompile, modify, adapt, translate, or create derivative works based on the Software or the Documentation. You may be held legally responsible for any copying or copyright infringement which is caused by your failure to abide by the terms of these restrictions.

3. **TERMINATION:** This license is effective until terminated. This license will terminate automatically without notice from the Company if you fail to comply with any provisions or limitations of this license. Upon termination, you shall destroy the Documentation and all copies of the Software. All provisions of this Agreement as to limitation and disclaimer of warranties, limita-tion of liability, remedies or damages, and our ownership rights shall survive termination.

4. **DISCLAIMER OF WARRANTY:** THE COMPANY AND ITS LICENSORS MAKE NO WARRANTIES ABOUT THE SOFTWARE, WHICH IS PROVIDED "AS-IS." IF THE DISK IS DEFECTIVE IN MATERIALS OR WORKMANSHIP, YOUR ONLY REMEDY IS TO RETURN IT TO THE COMPANY WITHIN 30 DAYS FOR REPLACEMENT UNLESS THE COMPANY DETERMINES IN GOOD FAITH THAT THE DISK HAS BEEN MISUSED OR IMPROPERLY INSTALLED, REPAIRED, ALTERED OR DAMAGED. THE COMPANY DISCLAIMS ALL WARRANTIES, EXPRESS OR IMPLIED, INCLUDING WITHOUT LIMITATION, THE IMPLIED WARRANTIES OF MERCHANTABILITY AND FITNESS FOR A PARTICULAR PURPOSE. THE COMPANY DOES NOT WAR-RANT, GUARANTEE OR MAKE ANY REPRESENTATION REGARDING THE ACCURACY, RELIABILITY, CURRENTNESS, USE, OR RESULTS OF USE, OF THE SOFTWARE.

5. **LIMITATION OF REMEDIES AND DAMAGES:** IN NO EVENT, SHALL THE COMPANY OR ITS EMPLOYEES, AGENTS, LICENSORS OR CONTRACTORS BE LIABLE FOR ANY INCIDENTAL, INDIRECT, SPECIAL, OR CONSEQUENTIAL DAMAGES ARISING OUT OF OR IN CONNECTION WITH THIS LICENSE OR THE SOFTWARE, INCLUDING, WITHOUT LIMITATION, LOSS OF USE, LOSS OF DATA, LOSS OF INCOME OR PROFIT, OR OTHER LOSSES SUSTAINED AS A RESULT OF INJURY TO ANY PERSON, OR LOSS OF OR DAMAGE TO PROPERTY, OR CLAIMS OF THIRD PARTIES, EVEN IF THE COMPANY OR AN AUTHORIZED REPRESENTATIVE OF THE COMPANY HAS BEEN ADVISED OF THE POSSIBILITY OF SUCH DAMAGES. SOME JURISDICTIONS DO NOT ALLOW THE LIMITATION OF DAMAGES IN CERTAIN CIRCUMSTANCES, SO THE ABOVE LIMITATIONS MAY NOT ALWAYS APPLY.

6. **GENERAL:** THIS AGREEMENT SHALL BE CONSTRUED IN ACCORDANCE WITH THE LAWS OF THE UNITED STATES OF AMERICA AND THE STATE OF NEW YORK, APPLICABLE TO CONTRACTS MADE IN NEW YORK, AND SHALL BENEFIT THE COMPANY, ITS AFFILIATES AND ASSIGNEES. This Agreement is the complete and exclusive statement of the agreement between you and the Company and supersedes all proposals, prior agreements, oral or written, and any other communications between you and the company or any of its representatives relating to the subject matter. If you are a U.S. Government user, this Software is licensed with" restricted rights" as set forth in subparagraphs (a)-(d) of the Commercial Computer-Restricted Rights clause at FAR 52.227-19 or in subparagraphs (c)(1)(ii) of the Rights in Technical Data and Computer Software clause at DFARS 252.227-7013, and similar clauses, as applicable.

Should you have any questions concerning this agreement or if you wish to contact the Company for any reason, please contact in writing:

Multimedia Production
Higher Education Division
Prentice-Hall, Inc.
1 Lake Street
Upper Saddle River NJ 07458